SARADA-TILAKA TANTRAM

SARADA-TILAKA TANTRAM

Text with Introduction
Edited by

ARTHUR AVALON

GYAN

Published by

Gyan Publishing House
5, Ansari Road
Daryaganj, New Delhi-110002
Phone: 011-47034999, 9811692060
E-mail: books@gyanbooks.com

Distribution Network
gyanbooks.com
India, USA, Canada, UK, Australia, France

ISBN : 978-81-212-2412-3 (PB)
First Published, 1933

2nd Impression 2021

Printed at: Gyan Press, Delhi.

Sarada-Tilaka Tantram
Edited by: Arthur Avalon

ŚĀRADĀ-TILAKA TANTRAM

Text with Introduction

Edited By

ARTHUR AVALON

MOTILAL BANARSIDASS
DELHI :: VARANASI :: PATNA

INTRODUCTION.

The text alone of this book was first published by Rasikamohana Chaṭṭopādhyāya, who brought out so many Tantrik works, from Calcutta, in the Bengali year 1285 (A. D. 1880), and it was printed in the Bengali character. Shortly thereafter Pandit Jīvānanda Vidyāsāgara brought out an edition in Devanāgara character. The first edition printed (in Benares) along with the commentary of Rāghavabhaṭṭa was in the Samvat era 1953 (A. D. 1886). This book was also published along with a commentary named Gūḍhārthadīpikā by Mādhavabhaṭṭa in the Samvat era 1941. This latter commentary is older than that of Rāghavabhaṭṭa, for Rāghava in some places cites it and controverts its interpretation. Rāghava says that he wrote his commentary in the Samvat year 1551 (A. D. 1484).

The present edition is published in compliance with the desire of His Highness the late Mahārājādhirāja Rameshwar Singh of Darbhanga, the President of the Āgamānusandhāna-samiti. His knowledge of, and reverence for, the Brahmanik scriptures were very great, and being a great admirer of Rāghava's commentary he felt that a better presentment of the book was desirable. The Benares edition was evidently based on a single manuscript, and suffers in consequence. We have had the advantage of consulting the following manuscripts :—

(1) Manuscript loaned by the Asiatic Society of Bengal through the courtesy of its erudite Secretary Mr. Johan van Manen, C.I.E.

(2) Manuscript loaned by Kumar Sharat Kumāra Roy, M.A., of Dighapatia, Founder and President of the Varendra Research Society, Rajshahi, Bengal.

(3) A summary of Rāghava's commentary presented to us by Rai Īshvarī Prasād of Kālīyasthānā, Patna.

(4) A manuscript belonging to Pandit Amūlya Charaṇa Vidyābhūṣhaṇa, a copy of which was obtained.

(5) A Press Copy of the first eight chapters of the book prepared by the late Pandit Satīsh Chandra Siddhāntabhū*sha*n*a*.

There are several other commentaries on the Shāradā which have not been published. There is one such named Shabdārtha-chintāma*n*i in the Sanskrit College Library, Calcutta, by Premanidhi Pāntha a well-known authority on Tantra Shāstra. His wife Prā*n*amanjarī wrote a commentary on the Tantrarāja an abstruse Tantrik work published as Vols. VIII & XII of the present series.

Nothing much about Lak*sh*ma*n*a Deshikendra the author of the Shāradātilaka is known. At the end of his book he says that his father was Shrīk*rish*n*a*, his grand-father was Āchārya Pa*nd*ita and his great-grand-father was Mahābala. All of them, he says, were men of great piety and erudition and enjoyed great reputation for the same. We are not aware if he wrote any other book. Rāghava places him on a very high pedestal and gives us the further information that Lak*sh*ma*n*a was the disciple of Utpalāchārya and in the line of his Gurus are Utpalāchārya, Somānanda, Vasumat and Shrīka*nth*a. He further says that Lak*sh*ma*n*a was impelled to write the book because of his compassion for men who wanted to know something about all the different forms of worship, but could not do so by reason of the voluminousness of the different Tantras, each of which dealt with a single form of worship, and also because of the abstruse character of the same. These Tantras the majority of men of his time were unable to master, as they were of limited intelligence and short-lived.

Of Rāghava we get the following particulars. His family belonged to Mahārā*sh*t*ra and the name of the village is Janasthāna (Nasik). His grand-father was Rāmeshvara Bha*tt*a and his father P*ri*thvīdhara. Both of them were famed for their great learning. P*ri*thvīdhara migrated to Vārā*n*asī (Benares) and died there. The son was instructed in and became a master of the Vedānta and all other forms of Nyāya, Bha*tt*anaya, Ga*n*ita (Mathematics) in all its forms, Sāhitya (Belles Lettres), Āyurveda, the Kalās (Fine Arts), Kāmashāstra (Science of

Love) and Artha-shāstra (Science of Polity and Political Government). He had a profound knowledge of the Vedas, and was proficient in vocal and instrumental music. The commentary bears ample testimony to the many-sidedness and the encyclopaedic nature of his learning. He is the author, among others, of a commentary on the Līlāvatī and on Kālīdāsa's Shakuntalā. The commentary on the Shāradā gives an adequate idea of not merely the greatness of the spiritual culture of India but shows the great progress that had been made in every sphere of human activity. In expounding the text he has cited passages not from Mantrashāstra alone, but has drawn his materials from mathematical and astronomical works, the Āyurveda, the Vedas and the Upanis*h*ads, the Purā*n*as and the Samhitās, the Shrauta Sūtras and the G*ri*hya Sūtras, the Brāhma*n*as and the Shūlvashāstras, the Darshanas, the Chhandas, the Pancharātras, and a whole host of other authorities named and unnamed.

The Prapanchasāra is one of the books most frequently cited in support of his own interpretations, more so when he differs from that of other people ; and not merely has the text of the Prapanchasāra been utilised for the purpose but in several places Padmapādāchārya's commentary thereon has also been cited as authority. In the majority of instances a text from the Prapanchasāra has been cited as that of the great Āchārya, the expression being always in the honorific plural. Padmapāda's name is also cited in the plural number. This is almost conclusive evidence that the Prapanchasāra is the work of the great monist Shamkarāchārya. There is a tendency among some scholars to cast a doubt about the authorship of the Prapanchasāra. But in the face of the testimony of Rāghavabha*tt*a and other eminent commentatators such as Bhāskararāya, Laks*h*midhara, Nīlaka*nth*a and others, it is hard to agree with them.

Both the Prapanchasāra and the Shāradātilaka contain descriptive accounts of the various aspects of the Brahmanik faith prevalent in India, and in both works the different forms of faith are dealt with in a manner which shows a complete freedom from bias, a characteristic which is peculiarly that of Brahmanik India. That is so because they recognise that all the different forms of faith in the world lead to one goal, as it has been beautifully put by Pu*sh*padanta in his Mahimna-stotra (see Arthur Avalon's 'Greatness of Shiva').

It is perhaps not known that the Guru if he is wise, very seldom, if ever, initiates the disciple into his own form of worship. A disciple is initiated into that form alone for which he is competent. He is not even initiated into the form which was that of his ancestors. It is held that the man who has attained Siddhi in one particular form of worship becomes an adept in every other form and is able to understand fully these other forms. Shamkarāchārya, for instance, was a Vai*shn*ava ; but his soul-stirring hymn to the Devī in the eleventh chapter of the Prapanchasāra would lead any one to believe that he was a Shākta. His hymns to other aspects of the Supreme Brahman such as Shiva and others are just as soulfully worded. It is on this account that one belonging to the Brahmanik faith is enjoined not to speak slightingly of any other Shāstra. We have become accustomed these days to hear of the various forms of worship being in conflict with one another. But in reality there is no conflict. It is only in the early stages of Sādhanā, during, so to say, the period of probation, that the Sādhakas of the different forms of faith devote themselves exclusively to the forms into which they have been severally initiated. Ignorance of this and similar facts has in many instances led to very disastrous and discreditable results on the part of our present-day "scientific" researchers into Indian philosophy and culture generally.

The Shāradātilaka is divided into 25 Chapters, twentyfive being the number of the Sāmkhyan Tattvas. The first chapter, says Rāghava (under verse 87 Chapter XXV), is Prak*ri*ti as it deals with Creation. The twenty-three Chapters which follow demonstrate Prak*ri*ti-Vik*ri*ti, and the last chapter which is devoted to Yoga demonstrates Puru*sh*a which is beyond

Prak*ri*ti and Vik*ri*ti. It may incidentally be noted that the Prapanchasāra as also the Tantrarāja are divided into thirty-six Chapters which is the number of the Shaiva Tattvas.

CHAPTER I.

The first verse of the Shāradā is an adoration of the Supreme Being, Who is named Maha*h*. This Maha*h* may be interpreted to mean the Supreme in either Its Male or Female aspect. This is dealt in detail in Chapters XXIII and XXV. Its body is ever-enduring Bliss. By the fifty letters of the Alphabet which are constantly emanating from that Maha*h*, is this universe of moving and motionless objects, of sound and the meaning thereof, pervaded. Men who are masters of the Vedānta call It Shabda-Brahman which is the inner Chaitanya (stress towards particularized conciousness) which abides in all. The moon adorns Its forehead, and It is the Lord of Speech. The verse as it stands, it will be noted, refers to the Maha*h* (Radiant Energy) in the neuter gender. Rāghava shows how this can be interpreted to apply either to Shiva or Shakti. In doing so, he also shows how the Shiva and the Shakti aspects are intimately connected with one another. The connection is that of A-vinābhāva, i. e., that the one cannot be without the other, like heat and fire, a word and its meaning, and so forth. This Chapter, as has already been stated, deals with Creation. From this, ascending step by step, the Sādhaka reaches to an apprehension of the formless and attributeless Brahman, the first glimpse of which is given in Chapter 23 and which is more fully dealt with in Chapter 25 and of which it is said that any expressions we use with regard to it are merely indicative (Laks*h*aka) and not attributive (Vāchaka). Rāghava discusses how this attributeless Maha*h*, as associated with Shakti, is competent to create.

Verse 2 is an adoration of the consort of the Maha*h* of the first verse. The third verse is an adoration of the Gurus.

Rāghava cites texts which say that the Guru is not to be looked upon as a mortal. He who does so can never attain Siddhi by the repetition of Mantras and worship of Devatās. The reason for this is that the human Guru is but the channel through whom Grace descends, and is the material embodiment of the supreme Shiva or Brahman who is the Guru. Rāghava cites texts from Shruti, Sm*ri*ti and Āgama which show the necessity of a Guru.

In verses 4 and 5 the Author says that he shall in this book give the essential parts of the Tantras which are helpful in the attainment of the fourfold aims of human existence, *viz.*, Dharma, Artha, Kāma and Mok*sh*a. He also speaks of the Creation of the Word and of the Meaning thereof, and of Muni, Chhanda*h*, Devatā and the rules relating to Yantras and Mantras. The word Shāradā is capable of different interpretations. One of these is She who grants the fruit of one's Karma and at the same time destroys the same as Chit-shakti and leads to Liberation. He defines the Muni of a Mantra to mean the sage who discovered the Mantra. Chhanda*h* is that which envelops and thereby protects the Deva who is concealed therein. Devatā is that which is revealed by the Mantra. The Prayoga of a Mantra is the use of it, according to the injunction of the Shāstras, for the attainment of Dharma, Artha, Kāma and Mok*sh*a. He next cites texts from Ār*sh*eya Brāhma*n*a, Kātyāyana Shrauta-sūtra and Yājnavalkya Sm*ri*ti which speak of the absolute necessity for a person practising a Mantra of knowing these. All these however, says Rāghavabha*tt*a, are for those who worship Devatās in their gross form. He then quotes some verses from the Tantrarāja (Chapter 35) which say that one's own Ātmā is the Devatā. It pervades the universe. Nyāsa, Japa, Pūjā, Homa and other rites are useful for the realisation of this. The author next proceeds to describe creation – this has been dealt with by Sir John Woodroffe in his paper 'Creation in the Tantra', which has been reprinted in his book 'Shakti and Shākta'.

Up to verse 13 the author speaks of creative Sound in its Parā state, and this is followed by a description of the workings of Pashyantī and Madhyamā.

Having spoken of Shiva in Its two-fold aspect of Nirguṇa (Attributeless) and Sa-guṇa (Endowed with attributes) and of the manifestation of Shakti, Nāda and Bindu, and of the emanation of Bindu, Nāda and Bīja from the first Bindu, the author proceeds to say that from the second Bindu originated Raudrī and from Nāda originated Jyeshṭhā and from Bīja originated Vāmā and from these three emanated Rudra, Brahmā and Vishṇu. They are respectively Jnāna (wisdom), Ichchhā (will), Kriyā (action) and correspond with Vahni (Fire), Indu (Moon), Arka (Sun). When the first Bindu bursts and divides itself into two, there arises a volume of sound in which the letters of the alphabet are indiscernible. This sound is Shabda-Brahman. Some define Shabda-Brahman to mean mere external spoken sound ; others speak of it as inner sound (Āntara-Shabda). Both these interpretations are erroneous ; for Shabda-Brahman, says Lakshmaṇa, is not something inert (Jaḍa) but is the Chaitanya in all beings, i. e. it is the stress towards articulate sound. This is the Parā stage of Sound. This Shabda-Brahman, it is said in verse 14, assumes the form of Kuṇḍalī and manifests itself in the form of letters in all animate creatures.

In verses 15 and 16 it is said that from Shambhu who is Bindu (Bindvātmā) and one with Kalā (Kalātmā) and co-eval with Kāla (Time) originated Sadāshiva who is the allpervading witness of the world. From Sadāshiva emanated Īsha, from him Rudra, then Vishṇu and then Brahmā. Rāghava says that the eternalness ascribed to Prakṛiti and Kāla is Āpekshaka (consequential).

Purusha alone is by his very nature eternal, for when every thing disappears, Purusha endures. Rāghava cites a text (which also occurs in Kramadīpikā which is a Vaishṇava work) wherein the process of dissolution is described. In verse 17 the author begins to speak of the creation of the Tattvas and says that when there is a change in the unmanifest Prak*ri*ti—the Supreme Substance and the root of all—there emanates therefrom Mahat-tattva which is the aggregate of the three Gu*n*as (Sattva, Rajas and Tamas) and is one with Buddhi, Ahamkāra and Chitta. The Shaivas identify Mahat-tattva with Buddhi-tattva. The Ahamkāra here spoken of is of three kinds, *viz.*, Vaikārika, Taijasa and Bhūtādi. From the first which is Sāttvika emanate the ten Devas, *viz.*, Dik (Space, Ether), Vāta (Air), Arka (Sun), Prachetas (Varu*n*a, Water), the Ashvins (Herbs), Vahni (Fire), Indra (Ruler), Upendra (Vi*sh*n*u*, Protective principle), Mitra (Sun) and Ka (Brahmā, Creative principle). From Taijasa Ahamkāra which is Rājasika emanate besides Manas, the ten organs of sense, namely, five of perception and five of action. And from Bhūtādi Ahamkāra which is Tāmasika originated the five elements, *viz.* Ether, Air, Fire, Water and Earth in the order of the Tanmātras which first originated. From Sound (Shabda-tanmātra) originated Ether ; from Touch (Sparsha-tanmātra), Air ; from Form (Rūpa-tanmātra), Fire ; from Liquidity (Rasa-tanmātra), Water ; and from Smell (Gandha-tanmātra), Earth. The text proceeds to say that Ether is transparent ; Air is black ; Fire, red ; Water, white ; Earth, yellow. The region of Ether is circular, that of Air is hexagonal, of Fire is triangular, of Water is of the form of a half-moon with a lotus therein and that of Earth is square in shape. These have been fully dealt with in the 'Serpent Power' for the English reader. In the Devī-bhāgavata, (Book 3 chapter 4), these have been described in greater detail and in a popular form ; and though there is some difference in minor particulars, a study of that will greatly help in understanding the scheme. The great commentator Nīlaka*nth*a in commenting on the text of the Devī-bhāgavata has cited these verses from the Shāradā.

Verses 25 and 26 say that the regions or Ma*nd*alas of the five Bhūtas contain the letters which belong to the different Bhūtas. It may be noted here that the letters are classified into five classes according to the number of the

Bhūtas. This is described in greater detail in Chapter VI. It is here also stated that the five Bhūtas originate from the five Kalās,—Nivṛitti, Pratishṭhā, Vidyā, Shānti and Shāntyatītā which in their turn have originated from Nāda.

Verse 27 says that this universe of moving and motionless objects is composed of the five Bhūtas. Motionless objects are divided into countless forms such as mountains, trees and the like. Moving objects (V. 28) are of three kinds, *viz.*, (1) Moisture-born (Sveda-ja), (2) Egg-born (Aṇḍa-ja) and (3) Womb-born (Jarāyu-ja). Moisture produces worms and the like, from eggs are born serpents and the like, and from the womb (V. 29) are born human beings and the like.

Then the text goes on describing how out of the union of man and woman conception takes place and explains the cause of the birth of a male, female and hermaphrodite. In verse 31 it is said that some disembodied soul bound by its own actions (Karma) enters into the foetus and animates it.

In this connection Rāghava cites another text which describes the birth of a tree from its seed, the process being somewhat similar to Maithuna Sṛishṭi.

Verses 32 to 38 describe the gradual growth, day after day, month after month, of this foetus ; how from a tiny gelatinous lump it grows into full human shape with all its senses. Rāghava cites among others a text from Adhyātma-viveka which describes this process of growth and says that the Ojo-dhātu (Ojas) comes into the foetus in the eighth month and is then in a constant state of restlessness, now moving into the mother, now returning to the child. This Ojas is of a transparent yellowish red (Shuddham ā-pīta-raktam), and is the immediate cause (Nimitta) of vitality.

In verse 39 the author says that the body born partakes of the nature of Fire and Moon or the Sun and the Moon. The right side is Sun, the left side is Moon. In verse 40, the text speaks of the principal Nāḍis and in Verse 43 it says that the Nāḍis are countless. Verse 44 speaks of the ten airs, *viz.*, Prāṇa, Apāna, Samāna, Vyāna and Udāna ;

also Nāga, Kūrma, K*ri*kara, Devadatta and Dhananjaya. Rāghava says that according to some there are fourteen Vāyus (airs), the names of the other four being Vairambha*n*a, Pradyota, Prak*ri*ta and Sthānamukhya. They function in different ways in the body and are named accordingly. The names of the ten Fires are in the same way given by Rāghava and they are, he says, named differently by different authors.

In verse 47 it is said that the nerves (Snāyu), bones (Asthi) and marrow (Majjā) are derived from the father; and the skin (Tvak), flesh (Māngsa) and blood (Asra) from the mother. Rāghava cites an authority who differs from this view. Verses 48 and 49 describe how the child remains in the womb and its birth.

The text proceeds to say (Vv. 51—57) that thereafter Ku*nd*alinī Shakti who is Chaitanya-rūpā (Consciousness-embodied), all-pervading and lightning-like, who is in all Tattvas and all Devas, subtler than the subtle and is Shabda-Brahman, manifests herself in the child at the time of its birth.

The text then proceeds to describe (Vv. 58-107) how Ku*nd*alinī is in the Mantras, Yantras and every thing else. Verses 108 and 109 say that Ku*nd*alinī who is Shabda-Brahman and all-pervading brings forth Shakti, then Dhvani, therefrom Nāda, Nirodhikā, Ardhendu, Bindu, one from the other. From Bindu comes Parā sound and thereafter Pashyantī, Madhyamā and Vaikharī sounds. Rāghava, in commenting on these, cites texts from the Tantrarāja (Ch. XXVI.) which describe the process by which Parā changes into Pashyantī, Pashyantī into Madhyamā and this last into Vaikharī. He also quotes from the *Ri*gveda (1,164,45) which shows that the three different stages preceding articulate sound are recognised in Shruti also. In verse 112 it is said that Nirodhikā is Fire, Ardhendu (Half-moon) is Moon and Arka (Sun) is the union of the two ; as the letters originated from Bindu, they therefore partake of the nature of Shiva and Shakti, because the Sun is both Shiva and Shakti.

CHAPTER II.

In this chapter the author speaks of the Vaikharī S*rish*t*i*, *i. e.* creation manifest as the spoken word. The letters of the alphabet, it is said (Vv. 1-6), are pushed along the channel of the Sus*h*umnā and articulated with the help of the throat and other vocal organs. Of these articulate letters the vowels are called lunar (Saumya), and the consonants solar (Saura) and the Vyāpakas, letters from Ya (य) to Ks*h*a (क्ष), are fiery (Āgneya). There are 16 vowels, 25 consonants and 10 Vyāpakas. Of the consonants 24 are the 24 Tattvas, the letter M (म) being the Purus*h*a. The first of each couple of vowels is short and the second is long. The four vowels in the middle (*i. e.* 7th, 8th, 9th and 10th) are neuter.

In verse 8 it is said that without the vowels the consonants can not be articulated, It is on this account that the letters are called united Shiva and Shakti (Shiva-Shakti-maya). The vowel which helps the articulation being Shakti (power) and the portion articulated being Shiva. The attention of the reader is drawn to V. 1. of the famous poem by Shamkarā-chārya called the Ānanda-laharī (The Wave of Bliss). In verses 9 and 10 it is said that as the letters of the alphabet have originated from the Bindu from which the five Bhūtas (Elements) have emanated, the letters fall under five heads, and belong to one or other of the five Elements. The commentary says A (अ), Ā (आ), E (ए), Ka (क), Cha (च), *T*a (ट), Ta (त), Pa (प), Ya (य), *Sh*a (ष), are aerial; I (इ), Ī (ई), Ai (ऐ), Kha (ख), Chha (छ), *Th*a (ठ), Tha (थ), Pha (फ), Ra (र), Ks*h*a (क्ष) are igneous, and so forth. The letters are again classified as Lunar, Fiery, Solar ; the 16 vowels are lunar ; the twenty-four consonants (Sparsha) which are to be coupled as Ka-Bha, (क-भ), Kha-Ba (ख-ब) and so forth are solar, and the ten Vyāpaka letters are fiery.

The names of the 38 Kalās of the letters are given in verses 12-16. The Tāra or Pra*n*ava (Omkāra) has fifty Kalās and the names of these are given in verses 17-28.

Verses 29-35 give the fifty names of Rudra which correspond with the fifty letters of the alphabet. Verses 36 to 44 give the names of the Shaktis of the fifty Rudras.

Verses 45 to 56 give the names of the fifty aspects of Vi*shn*u and their respective Shaktis. These also correspond with and are forms of the fifty letters.

Verse 57 says that all Mantras are composed of the Māt*ri*kā letters and Mantras are either masculine, feminine or neuter. Verse 59 says those which end with Hung or Pha*t* are masculine, those ending with Svāhā are feminine and the neuters end with Nama*h*. The text proceeds to say how and when the Mantras awaken, and verses 64 to 110 give an account of the various defects that may be in different Mantras. Verse 111 says that the these defects can be cured by Yoni-mudrā; but, in the case of those who cannot do Yoni-mudrā, the same can be cured by a process described in verses 112-123.

Verses 124-140 of the Chapter contain rules regarding Japa of one's Mantra. There are in this connection injunctions about food, the place where Japa should be done, and the necessity of getting initiated by a good Guru is emphasised. A good Guru is defined (Vv. 141-144) to be a man pure of birth, himself of a pure disposition having his senses controlled. He should know the true meaning of the Āgamas and all Shāstras, and be always doing good to others, as also Japa, Pūjā, Dhyāna, Homa. His mind is always peaceful and he has the power of granting favours. He knows the Vedic teachings, is competent in Yoga and is charming like a Deva. Rāghava has cited a number of authorities and illustrations in amplifying this. The characteristics of a good disciple are also given (Vv. 145-152). He should be of good parentage, of a guileless disposition, be a seeker of the fourfold aims of human existence, read in the Vedas, intelligent, his animal desires completely controlled, always kind towards all animals, possessed of faith in the existence of the next world. He does not associate with the non-believer, is assiduous in his duties, alert in the discharge of his duties towards his parents, not conscious of the pride of birth, wealth and learning in the presence of his Guru, willing to sacrifice his own interests in the discharge of his duties towards the Guru, and ever ready to serve the Guru as a servant.

Verse 153 speaks of the time it usually takes to ascertain the fitness of the disciple. It takes one year in the case of a Brāhma*n*a, two years in the case of a Ks*h*atriya, three in the case of a Vaishya and four for a Shūdra, to ascertain the candidate's competency for initiation.

CHAPTER III.

Speaks of the rites which should be performed before initiation. These are Vāstu-yāga (worship of the Devatās Brahmā and others who keep the Rāks*h*asa (demon) Vāstu down), selection of the site for the erection of a Ma*n*d*a*pa and erection of the same, Homa, the making of the Vedī and directions regarding drawing a Yantra on the Vedī and rites connected therewith. Rāghava has added long notes to what is said by Laks*h*ma*n*a. Great stress is laid on the dimensional accuracy of the Vedī, the Ku*n*d*a* and of everything else used in the different rites which have to be done. The calculations are given in detail.

CHAPTER IV.

Deals with initiation in all its different aspects. The word Dīks*h*ā (initiation) means that which imparts Divya-jnāna (knowledge which illumes) and causes Ks*h*aya (destruction) of evil. Verse 3 speaks of four kinds of Dīks*h*ā, namely, Kriyāvatī, Var*n*amayī, Kalā and Vedha. The first of these, if the occasion demands it, may be an elaborate ritualistic process. It is described in this chapter. The disciple on initiation is instructed to meditate on the oneness of the Mantra, the Devatā and the Guru. When he has realised this he has to advance further and experience the identity of his own Ātmā with these. The commentary gives details regarding bathing and other preliminary rites. The whole of the chapter contains details of ritual which should be performed on the first day. The process by which the mind and body of the disciple is made fit to receive initiation is shortly described. Apart from the importance of the text of the Shāradā and the notes of the commentator for the ritualist, the student of religious psychology will find therein much of interest to him. A careful study will convince any fair-minded critic that these are not meaningless mummery but have a solid and reasonable foundation.

CHAPTER V.

Continues the same subject and begins with injunctions relating to consecration of Fire for the purpose of Homa. Rāghava cites texts which say that when the purificatory rites are being done the Guru meditates on the form of the Brahman adopted for his Sādhanā.

With verse 75 begin the rites to be performed on the second day when Homa is to be done. Verse 77 says that after transferring the Chaitanya of the Shi*sh*ya into himself and uniting it with his own Chaitanya, the Guru should effect a purification of the six Adhvās, namely, Kalā, Tattva, Bhuvana, Var*n*a, Pada and Mantra. The Kalās are Niv*ri*tti, Prati*shth*ā, Vidyā, Shānti and Shāntyatītā named in Chapter I. verse 26. The Tattvas are 36 according to the Shaivas, 32 according to the Vai*shn*avas, 24 according to the Maitras (Sāmkhya). The Shaiva Tattvas are classed under three heads, namely, Pure, Pure-Impure and Impure. The Prak*ri*ti Tattvas are ten. The Tattvas of Tripurā are seven. The names of the five different classes of Tattvas are given in verses 81-89. By Bhuvanādhvā is meant, according to Rāghava, the Etherial, the Aerial, the Igneous, the Aquatic and the Terrestrial regions. The Vāyavīya Samhitā says the Bhuvanas are the different stages of Sādhanā beginning with the Mūlādhāra ending with Unmanī when the mind is merged in the object of adoration. The Var*n*as are the Māt*ri*kā letters. By

Mantrādhvā all the Mantras are meant. Padas are words formed by the combination of the letters. Verses 92-95 describe the process of the purification of the Adhvās. The word Adhvā means a pathway; here, these six are the six paths which lead to Brahman-experience.

Verse 96 says that the Guru first transfers his own Chaitanya into the Shi*sh*ya. This is followed by an account of some further rites. In verse 110 it is said that the Guru should worship his own Devatā who is placed in the body of the Shi*sh*ya and then (V. 111) communicate the Vidyā (Mantra) to the disciple. The Shi*sh*ya then mentally recites the Mantra meditating on the oneness of the Guru, the Mantra and the Devatā and thereafter bows to the Guru lying flat on the ground and placing the feet of the Guru on his head and offers up to the Guru his own body and all he is possessed of. Rāghava here gives a detailed account of all that is done, citing texts from different Shāstras. Other rites connected with Kriyāvatī Dīk*sh*ā end with verse 115.

Verses 116-120 contain rules relating to Var*n*amayī Dīk*sh*ā.

Verses 121 to 126 speak of Kalāvatī and verses 127-139 of Vedhamayī Dīk*sh*ā.

By Vedha Dīk*sh*ā, it is said, the disciple attains the perfection of Shiva immediately on initiation. These three forms of initiation are not for men of average competency. Var*n*a Dīk*sh*ā is for persons who are above the average. Kalāvati is for those of a still higher competency and Vedhamayī is for the highest class of aspirants. In the commentary it is stated that Utpalāchārya the Guru of Lak*sh*ma*n*a was initiated in this way by Somānandāchārya. He gives another instance of initiation in this way, that of Shivasvāmī by Cha*nd*eshvarāchārya. The process is briefly described in verses 127 to 139. This is followed by injunctions relating to Homa after initiation. The commentator cites a text which says that there are, besides the above four, ten other kinds of initiation which go by the generic name of Ā*n*avī.

CHAPTER VI.

Deals with the Devī Mātṛikā or Sarasvatī whose body is composed of the Letters of the Alphabet. The letters taken together form a Mantra of which the *Rishi* is Brahmā, the Chhanda*h* is Gāyatrī and Sarasvatī, the Devatā. It should be noted that whenever a Mantra is mentioned the name of its Muni or *Rishi* is first given, then the Chhanda*h* and then the Devatā.

In the Prapanchsāra (Ch. VII.) also, the Sādhanā of the Devī Sarasvatī is first introduced as she is the Queen of the Letters and Awakener of all knowledge (Bodha-dīpikā).

Verse 4 gives the Dhyāna of Sarasvatī. Her body is composed of the said letters and on her forehead is a fragment of the Moon. Her breasts are large and high. She is carrying in each of her (four) hands (1) the gesture of Jnāna-mudrā, (2) a rosary of Rudrāks*h*a, (3) a jar full of nectar and (4) the gesture of Pustaka-mudrā. She is white and has three eyes.

Rāghava here quotes a long passage from the Tantrāntara giving Dhyānas of all the different letters. Verses 5-8 contain rules relating to Nyāsa of the letters and verse 9 speaks of Purashchara*n*a. It is by Purashchara*n*a that the Sādhaka becomes an adept in the Mantra. The Mantra has to be repeated in manner enjoined a specified number of times followed by Homa and other rites. Verse 10 gives the Yantra. This is followed by rules relating to her rituals with the names of her attendant Shaktis and their Dhyānas. These Shaktis are mostly the intellectual powers personified. After ritualistic worship, Nyāsa (verses 28, 29) should be done in three ways, namely, *Srishti* (creative), Sthiti (continuing), and Samhāra (withdrawing). After Sthiti Nyāsa she should be meditated upon along with her consort. The Dhyāna is given in verse 30. After Samhāra Nyāsa she is to be again meditated upon as the Queen of the Letters. The Dhyāna is given in verse 33.

Verses 34-36 contain the rules relating to Nyāsa and worship. She should next be meditated upon in her aspect of Shāradā. The Dhyāna is given in verse 37. Verses 38-40 describe her ritualistic Nyāsa which is amplified in the commentary. Verse 41 gives the Dhyāna of Ardhanārīshvara. Verse 45 gives a Dhyāna of united Vi*sh*n*u and Lak*sh*mī, like Ardhanārīshvara is of Shiva and his consort. Verse 49 gives another Dhyāna of the Devī as the Queen of the Universe. Verse 53 gives a Dhyāna of Lak*sh*mī.

Verse 57 gives a Dhyāna of the Devī as the Mother of All, (Sakalajananī). The Poet Kālīdāsa has a beautiful hymn to this aspect which is not much known.

Verse 61 contains a Dhyāna of the Devī as having eight hands.

Verse 67 contains a Dhyāna of Brahman as the transcedent Tejas, immeasurable, the one root of the Universe, pervading all creation as Sat and Chit, imperishable, a mass of nectar. The five Mantras, the first of which is the Pra*n*ava point towards him. This is the Prapancha-yāga-mūrti.

Verses 68-82 describe Prapancha-yāga which begins with a particular form of Nyāsa. Rāghava here cites a text which gives the names of the *Rishi* and Chhanda*h* of each of the Mātr*i*kā letters. It is partially corrupt and the different manuscripts have not been of any great help.

Verses 84-86 speak of the wonderful properties of Brāhmī (a kind of bitter herb) and how it helps in the perfection of the intellectual powers as also clear enunciation. This vegetable has been spoken of in several other places in this book. The rest of the chapter gives ritualistic rules.

CHAPTER VII.

Verses 2 to 4 give the Bhūtalipi Mantra. It is made up of the five short vowels, the four compound (Sandhi) vowels, the eight Vyāpaka letters, and the twentyfive Sparsha (consonant) letters. These letters are divided into nine groups and arranged in an order described in the text. Verse 5 says that the letters of the Bhūtas (Elements), Ether, Air and others, are in these nine groups, only there is no Earth-letter in the second and in the ninth group there is neither a Water-letter nor an Earth-letter. The verses which follow give the *Rishis* and the Devatās of the nine groups (Vargas). Var*n*eshvarī (Queen of the Letters) is the Devatā of the Mantra. This is another aspect of the Devī Sarasvatī. The letters are looked at in a different way. The Tantra Shāstra attaches great importance to the letters, as all Mantras are made up of the letters.

Verses 9 to 14 describe the Tree of Letters (Lipitaru) under which the Devī is seated. The tree is made up of the letters. Parasamvit is its seed. Bindu and Nāda are its two tap-roots. Its branches which are the Earth-letters are spread in all directions ; its leaves which are the Water-letters cover the three worlds (upper, middle and lower); its sprouts which are the Fire-letters are bright like gems ; the Air-letters are its flowers and illumine its body ; the Ether-letters are its fruits which are the refuge of all creatures. The honey of heavenly nectar from the tree is sprinkling the Devī. The Vedas, the Āgamas and the like add to its height and beauty. It is Shiva and Shakti. The three worlds find shelter under it. The Munis by the help of this get what they desire.

Verse 15 gives the Dhyāna of the Devī. She is like (of the effulgence of) ten million stainless moons. Her breasts are large and high. On Her head is the crescent moon. Her three eyes are half-closed by reason of the libations of nectar of which she has partaken. In each of her four hands she is carrying the gesture of granting boons, a rosary, the gesture of Jnāna and a skull. She is in the pride of youth. Her body is composed of the Letters of the Alphabet. She is the Queen of Speech.

Verses 16 to 52 contain rules relating to ritualistic worship of the Devī in the course of which the names of the attendant Devatās and the articles of worship are enumerated.

Verse 53 describes Viyat Yantra (Yantra of Ether).

Verse 55 describes the Vāyavīya Yantra (Yantra of Air). Verses 57-59 describe the Āgneya Yantra (Yantra of Fire). Verse 60 describes Vāruṇa Yantra (Yantra of Varuṇa : the Deva of Water) and Verse 62 describes Pārthiva Yantra (Yantra of Earth). These descriptions are in each case followed by a statement as to what the Yantras are useful for.

Verse 65 contains the Vāgvādinī Mantra of ten letters. It grants the power of speech. Rāghava here quotes a hymn by Shamkarāchārya which is not traceable in his collected works. Verse 66 gives the names of the *Rishi*, Chhandah and Devatā of the Mantra and directions about Nyāsa.

Verse 67 contains a Dhyāna of the Devī of the Mantra. Verses 68-79 give rules relating to Purashcharaṇa and ritualistic worship. This is the method followed in the case of almost every Mantra right through the book. That is, the Mantra is followed by the names of the *Rishi*, the Chhandah and the Devatā. This again is followed by the Dhyāna of the Devatā and thereafter are given the rules relating to Purashcharaṇa, worship and Prayoga.

Verse 80 gives the Mantra of sixteen letters. Verse 82 gives the Dhyāna of the Devī of the Mantra and Verses 83-86, the rituals.

Verse 87 gives the Mantra of eleven letters, verse 89, the Dhyāna, verses 90-95, rituals.

Verse 96 gives another Mantra of eleven letters, verse 98 the Dhyāna, verses 99-103, rituals. In the course of this the author advises the use of Brāhmīghṛita which is to be prepared in a way somewhat different from that described in the previous chapter. Verse 104 gives another Mantra, verse 106, the Dhyāna and verses 107-112 describe rituals.

Verses 113-123 give rules of conduct of the worshipper of the Sarasvatī. The fruits and vegetables not to be eatern are named. He should not eat anything stale or kept over-night. He should not chew pan (betel leaf) at night. He should not go with a woman during day time nor with one who is in her flowers. He should not look at a naked woman. He should not cast aspersions on a woman. In the mornings he should remain silent and never at any time speak falsehood. He should not study on the 14th, 8th and 1st day of the lunar half month, nor on the day of an eclipse (Solar or Lunar), nor on the last day of the month. When explaining any thing he should be fully awake and not lazy, avoid yawning and not get angry, avoid spitting and touching any limbs below the waist If a man, a snake, a cat, a frog, a mongoose or any other animal passes between him and his auditor he should stop.

CHAPTER VIII.

This chapter begins by saying, 'I shall now speak of the Mantras of Shrī, which grant wealth and good fortune'. Verse 2 gives a Mantra and 3 speaks of the *Rishi*, Chhanda*h* and Devatā and Nyāsa. Verse 4 gives her Dhyāna, which is as follows :—

I adore Shrī. She is seated on a lotus. Her effulgence is like that of gold. She has a lustrous crown on her head. She is raimented in silk which shines over her rounded buttocks. In two of her hands she is holding two lotuses and with the other two is making the gestures of Vara (Boons-granting) and Abhaya (Fear-dispelling). Four elephants resembling the Himālaya mountain are pouring nectar over her out of golden jars held in their uplifted trunks.

The verses which follow (5-7) give the rules relating to Purashchara*n*a of the Mantra and worship. Verses 8-19 give the names and description of her nine Shaktis, the Anga-devatās and so forth. Verses 20-29 speak of the benefit gained by her worship.

Verse 30 gives another Mantra of Shrī. Verse 31 gives the Dhyāna of the Devī of this Mantra. It says : –

I adore the beloved of Hari. She is seated on a lotus. She is lustrous like the ruby. In two of her lotus hands, she holds two lotuses and the other two are held in the gestures of Vara and Abhaya. Four large elephants of the colour of snow are constantly pouring water out of jewelled jars held in their uplifted trunk. She is the heavenly Pārijāta who grants all desires.

Verses 32 and 33 give the rules of Purashcharaṇa whereby Siddhi is attained in the Mantra.

Verses 34-37 give another Mantra and the names of the *Rishi*, the Chhandaḥ and the Devatā as also the rules relating to Nyāsa. Verse 38 gives the Dhyāna of the Devī of this Mantra which is as follows :—

May Kamalā protect and nourish ye! She is seated on a lotus and has a smiling face. In two of her lotus hands she is holding two lotuses and the other two are held in the gestures of Dāna (Vara) and Abhaya. Her body is luminous like lightning. Over her large and high breasts are shining ropes of pearls. By her sidelong glances she is gladdening (her consort) Hari.

Verses 39 44 give rules regarding Purashcharaṇa, articles of worship and so forth.

Verses 45 to 52 give a fourth Mantra, the names of its *Rishi*, Chhandaḥ and so forth. Verse 53 says that after doing Nyāsa, the Sādhaka is to meditate upon a beautiful garden described in detail in verses 53-71. Having meditated upon this garden he should think of a beautiful Pārijāta tree in the middle of it ; and under it on a jewelled throne, he should meditate on Mahālakshmī seated thereon. The Dhyāna, given in verses 74-88, is as follows :—

Meditate on the Supreme Devatā. She is the lustre of the of the rising sun, luminous with the crescent moon on her shining diadem and the garland she is wearing. She is decked with ornament set with gems. She is leaning forward as if with (the weight of) her (heavy) breasts. In two of her hands, she is holding two lotuses. In one of her other hands is held a sheaf of Shāli paddy and in the other, the gem Kaustubha. Her face is illumined by her gracious smile. Her three eyes are like three fullblown lotuses. On her lotus feet are tinkling bells. The girdle round her waist is set with nine kinds of gems. Her stomacher studded with pearls, rubies and beryls is resting on her belly beautiful with its three folds (Trivali). Her navel is beautiful like a whirlpool in the waters of the Jāhnavī (Gangā : the Ganges). Her breasts are adorned with the paste of sandal, camphor and saffron. Ropes of large pearls, like drops from the rain clouds, adorn her. Her vestment is of silk. Her armlets of pure gold are studded with beryls and her wristlets of shining gold are studded with rubies. She is decked with rings set with rubies. Chains and collars of pure gold adorn her. Her neck resembling (in contour) the conchshell is adorned with various beautiful ornaments. Her gem-studded ear-ornaments resemble the rising sun. Her beautiful lips are red like the hibiscus and coral. Her teeth are like the seeds of the pomegranate. Her face is like the stainless fullmoon. Her three beautiful eyes are shaped like the petals of the lotus. Her eyebrows excel in beauty the bow of Kandarpa (Cupid's bow). Her nose vanquishes the beauty of the Tila flower (sesamum). Her forehead puts to shame the beauty of the half-moon and the Tilaka there, is fragrant with the fragrance of musk. Her lotus face is adorned by curls of hair like hungry black bees (round a lotus). Her hair is tied up with the flowers of the Pārijāta. The crown on her head is studded with priceless gems. She is the abode of charm and beauty and the source of all Greatness (Tejas).

Verses 89-118 give the rules relating to Purashchara*n*a of her Mantra, Āsana-mantra, names of the Pārshvadevatās and other details relating to her worship. The verses which follow (Vv. 119-140) speak of the Prayogas of her Mantra. Verses 141-143 give her Yantra.

Verses 144-145 give another Mantra of twentyseven letters. Verses 146-147 give the Nyāsa of the Mantra. Verse 148 gives the Dhyāna :—

Meditate always on the supreme beloved of Shārngī (Vi*sh*n*u). She is of the redness of vermillion and is seated on a lotus. She is the gem of the ocean of beauty. She is adorned with a crown, armlets, garlands, ear-ornaments, waist-chains and the like. In one of her lotus-like hands is held the casket of wealth (Vasu-pātra) in the other a looking glass and in the other two, are two lotuses. She is surrounded by her hand-maidens.

Verses 149-159 give rules relating to Purashcharaṇa, the articles to be used in her worship, the names of the attendant Devatās and the fruit to be gained by her worship.

Verse 160 speaks of the wellknown Vedik Shrīsūkta. It is to be noted that when Vedik *Riks* are referred to they are rarely set down in the text. The commentator says that the Shrīsūkta which consists of the fifteen *Riks* of the Bahvṛichas is wellknown and he quotes a long passage from the Tantrāntara which gives the rules relating thereto as also the Shrīyantra.

This, it is hoped, will remove the erroneous impression that the Vedas contain no trace of the worship of the female aspect of the Brahman. Later on other instances of this will be found in this book.

Verse 161 to the end of the chapter lay down rules of conduct for the worshipper of Shrī. It is said here that the Sādhaka who wants Shrī should always be truthful. He should face the west when taking his meals. He should be gentle in his speech, and speak with a smiling countenance, and use scents and flowers. He should always be pure, sleep in a pure bed and with a young woman (Taruṇī) and with no one else. He should never eat when he has had oil rubbed over him. He should never rub turmeric on his face, nor sleep when he is impure in any way. He must not write anything on the ground. He must not eat salt or oil by itself. He must always be clean and avoid unclean food and so forth.

The commentator quotes a passage from the Prapanchasāra (Ch. XII.) which also lays down similar injunctions.

CHAPTER IX.

The second verse gives the Bīja of Bhuvaneshvarī. Verse 3 gives the names of the *Rishi*, the Chhanda*h* and the Devatā of the Mantra. Verses 4-13 speak of Nyāsa. It is said in verse 5, that the object of doing Nyāsa is the attainment of Devatābhāva. This means that the Sādhaka's mind becomes competent to receive things divine. The commentator cites a passage from the Prapanchasāra (Ch. X.), showing Shamkarāchārya's method of dealing with this particular class of Nyāsa.

Verse 14 gives the Dhyāna of Bhuvaneshī. She is the lustre of the rising sun. The moon is on her diadem. Her breasts are high. She has three eyes and a smiling face. With two of her hands she is making the gestures of Vara and Abhaya and in the other two, are held an Angkusha and a Pāsha.

Verse 15 speaks of the Purashchara*n*a of her Mantra and Homa. Verses 16 and 17 describe her Yantra. Her nine Pī*th*a Shaktis, named in verse 18, are Jayā, Vijayā, Ajitā Aparājitā, Nityā, Vilāsinī, Doghdhrī, Aghorā, Mangalā. Verse 19 gives her Pī*th*a-mantra. In describing the mode of worship (Vv. 22-32) it is said, among other things, that the following couples (Mithunas) are to be worshipped, *viz*, Gāyatrī and Brahmā, Sāvitrī and Vi*shn*u, Sarasvatī and Rudra, Kuvera and Mahālak*sh*mī, Madana and Rati, Ga*n*esha (Vighnarāja) and Pu*sht*i, his beloved. Each of these couples is described here. There should also be worshipped (Vv. 33-42) the two Nidhis (Gems) and the Angadevatās, namely, - Ananga-kusumā, Ananga-kusumāturā, Ananga-madanā, Ananga-madanāturā, Bhuvana-pālā, Gagana vegā, Shashirekhā and Gagana-rekhā ; as also her sixteen others Shaktis, *viz.*, Karālī, Vikarālī, Umā, Sarasvatī, Shrī, Durgā, U*sh*ā, Lak*sh*mī, Shruti, Sm*ri*ti, Dh*ri*ti, Shraddhā, Medhā, Mati, Kānti and Āryā. The eight Māt*ri*s, Brahmā*n*i and others should also be worshipped. Her hand-maidens, Anangarūpā and others are also to be worshipped. Verses 43 to 50 describe rites for the attainment of worldly advantages. Verses 51-57 describe five Yantras.

Verse 58 gives a different Mantra. Verse 59 speaks of Nyāsa with the Mantra. Verse 60 gives the Dhyāna of the Devī of the Mantra. In this Dhyāna, the Devī is described as of the colour of vermilion. She has three eyes. On her head is a crown of rubies the brightness of which is enhanced by the lustre of the moon on her forehead. She has a smiling face and large breasts. She has two hands, in one of which she is holding a Chas*h*aka (cup) filled with gems and in the other a red lotus. Her feet are resting on a gem-studded jar. She is benign of aspect and is the mother of all.

Verses 61-62 speak of Purashchara*n*a.

Verse 63 says that by daily taking Brāhmī Gh*ri*ta over which the Mantra has been said, the Sādhaka becomes, in the course of a year, a poet. The commentator describes how this Gh*ri*ta should be made. Āyurveda says that Gh*ri*ta (clarified butter) preserves unimpaired the properties of herbs used in medicine. Verses 64-66 give other Prayogas.

Verse 67 gives another Mantra. Verse 68 gives its Nyāsa. Verse 69 gives the Dhyāna of the Devī of the Mantra :—

She is Shyāmā (colour of gold). The moon is on her forehead. With one hand she is making the gesture of Vara and with another hand she is holding a red lotus. In her third hand is a Chas*h*aka full of gems and with the fourth she is making th the gesure of Abhaya. Ropes of pearls shine over her large breasts. She has got three luminous eyes and is seated on a red lotus. She is the beloved of Hara. She is the adored of the Suras (Devas or seekers of the Brahman). She is eternal.

Verses 70-79 describe her worship.

Verse 80 gives another Mantra, its *Rishi*, Nyāsa and so forth.

Verse 81 gives the Dhyāna of the Devī of the Mantra :—

She is seated on a lotus. Two of her hands are held in

the gestures of Vara and Abhaya and in the other two she is holding an Angkusha and a Pāsha.

Verses 82-90 describe the mode of worship.

Verses 91-94 describe the Ghaṭārgala Yantra.

Verse 95 gives a Mantra of sixteen letters. Verses 96-104 describe how the Yantra is to be used and the benefits gained thereby.

Verses 105-108 describe two other Yantras.

CHAPTER X.

In Verse 1, it is said that the Devī Tvaritā is so called because she grants fruits quickly. The Sanskrit word means "quickly". In support of this, the commentator quotes a verse from the Prapanchasāra (Ch. XIII.) where the Sādhanā of the Devī is described. The second line of verse 1 and verse 2 give the Mantra of 12 letters. Verse 3 gives the names of the Muni, Chhandaḥ and so forth.

Verse 4-6 speak of Nyāsa. Verse 7 gives the Dhyāna :—

I adore the Devī Kairātī who is Shyāmā and whose head is adorned by the tail-feathers of a peacock. She is raimented with leaves and ropes of red Gunjā seeds rest on her large breasts. Eight great serpents adorn her ears, arms, waist and toes. She has three eyes and her hands are uplifted to grant boons and dispel fear.

The commentator says that the serpents Ananta and Kulika, who are Vipras, the colour of fire and each possessed of a thousand hoods, are the ear-ornaments. The serpents Vāsukī and Shangkhapāla who are Kshatriyas, yellow of colour each with 700 hoods, are the ornaments for the upper arm. Takshaka and Mahāpadma two other serpents who are Vaishyas, blue of colour, each with 500 hoods are the girdle. Padma and Karkaṭaka who are Shūdras, white of colour, each with 300 hoods are the toe-ornaments.

Verses 8-19 describe Purashcharaṇa of the Mantra and her worship, give the names of her attendant Devatās and describe how these latter are to be worshipped Verses 20-33 describe Homa with different articles for the attainment of different ends, such as, Shānti (Peace), *R*iddhi (Prosperity) and so forth. Verses 34 to 43 describe five different Yantras and speak of the benefits to be gained thereby.

Verse 44 gives the Trika*nt*akī Mantra as also rules relating to Nyāsa therewith. Verse 45 gives the Dhyāna :—

May the three-eyed Devī dispel all your fears ! She is blue below the navel, red below the neck and her face is white. She has four mouths with fierce fangs on the four sides of her belly and is terrific to behold. In her hands she is holding two lights (Dīpa), a conchshell and a Chakra. In her matted hair is the crescent moon.

In verse 48 is given another Mantra of the Trika*nt*akī. Verse 49 speaks of the Purashchara*n*a of this Mantra and the fruits to be gained thereby.

Verse 50 gives the Mantra of 15 letters of Nityā. Verse 51 gives the Nyāsa of this Mantra and verse 54 describes the place of her abode. She is seated there on a lotus placed on a throne. Her Dhyāna is given in verse 55 :—

Adore Nityā ! She has got the young moon on her forehead. She is red and three-eyed, She is carrying a Pāsha and an Angkusha, the wish-granting creeper and a skull and is playing on the melodious Vī*n*ā.

Verses 56 to 68 give the rules of Purashchara*n*a, worship and other details.

Verse 69 gives a Mantra of 12 letters and Verse 70 gives the rules relating to Nyāsa.

Verse 71 gives the Dhyāna :—

Meditate upon the wife of Shiva. She has got the half-moon on her forehead and is red of colour. Her raiment, ornament and decorations are all red. She has three eyes and is elated with wine. In her hands she is carrying a lotus, a Pāsha (noose), S*ri*n*i* (goad) and a skull filled with wine. She is the adored of the immortals.

Verses 72-76 give rules of Purashchara*n*a and other rites.

Verse 77 gives the Mantra of Vajraprastāri*n*ī. It is of

twelve letters. Verses 78-79 name *Rishi*, Chhanda*h*, Devatā.

Verse 80 gives her Dhyāna :—

We seek refuge in the mother who is seated on a lotus of twelve petals placed on a red boat in an ocean of blood. Her body is red ; on her red forehead is shining the crescent moon. She has three eyes and a smiling face. In her hands she is holding a pomegranate, an arrow, a noose, a goad, the bow of Madana (Deva of Love) and a skull. She is bending forward with the weight of her breasts.

Verses 81-87 give rules relating to rituals.

Verse 88 gives the Mantra of Tripu*t*ā, and the following verse names the *Rishi*, Chhanda*h* and Devatā and gives rules of Nyāsa. Verse 90 says that the Devī should be meditated upon as seated on two lotuses placed one above the other on a beautiful throne placed on the pericarp decorated by a *Shat-ko*n*a* (hexagon). The seat is placed on a jewelled altar under a charming canopy under a Kalpa (wish-granting) tree in the middle of a forest of Pārijāta trees.

Her Dhyāna [V. 91.] is as follows :—

Meditate on the primordial Shakti. She is of the colour of a golden lotus and leaning forward with the weight of her breasts. She is adorned with jewelled toe-rings, girdles, neckchains and the like. She has a jewelled crown on her head and three eyes. In her lotus hands she has a bow, a noose, two lotuses, a goad and flowery arrows.

Verse 92 says that she is surrounded by her handmaidens who have large breasts and are carrying fly-whisks, boxes containing betel leaves and mirrors in their hands. The Devī is looking at her votary with eyes which are raining, as it were, a shower of nectar on him.

The following verses describe the ritual. It is here said that Lak*sh*mī and Vi*sh*n*u*, Gaurī and Hara, Rati and Smara are to be worshipped all round her beginning from the S. E. corner and the two gems Shangkha and Padma are to be worshipped on either side, and the Lokapālas are to be worshipped in their feminine aspects.

Verses 101 and 102 contain the Mantra, composed of thirteen letters, of Devī Ashvārū*dh*ā (Seated on a horse). Verse 104 gives her Dhyāna.

Meditate always on her who is seated on a horse. She is red and beautiful. A digit of the moon is on her forehead. She has three eyes. She is adorned with beautiful garlands and bending forward with the weight of her breasts. With her left hand she is pulling the Sādhyā (woman against whom the rites are directed) who is tied by a noose and is helpless with an access of love and in her right hand is a golden cane.

Verses 105-107 describe Purashchara*n*a and 108 her Yantra.

Verse 109 gives the Mantra of Annapūr*n*ā and 110 her Dhyāna :—

Adore Bhagavatī (Annapurnā) ! She is red and clothed in beautiful raiment. She has the young moon on her forehead and is bending forward with the weight of her breasts. She is looking pleased as she is watching Shiva who with the crescent moon on his head is dancing in front of her. She is the giver of good and removes the pains of Samsāra.

The two verses which follow describe her worship.

Verse 113 contain the Mantra of Padmāvatī. Verse 115 is her Dhyāna. She is seated on a lotus. In her two hands she holds two lotuses. She has three eyes and is red of colour and wearing all kinds of ornaments. Her face is beautiful like a lotus.

Verse 119 gives her Yantra.

Verses 120-123 speak of Ama*th*a Nyāsa.

CHAPTER XI.

Verses 1 and 2 contain the Mantra of Durgā and the two following verses speak of the *Rishi*, Chhanda*h*, Devatā and, so forth. Verse 5 is the Dhyāna:—

May Durgā destroy all the evils which beset ye ! She has three eyes and is seated on a lion. On her forehead is the moon. In her four hands which are of the colour of emerald she is holding a conchshell, a bow, a discus and arrows. She is wearing armlets, garlands, wristlets, girdles and toe-rings with tinkling bells thereto. Her ear-ornaments are set with brilliant gems.

The thirteen verses which follow describe the mode of worship. Verse 19 gives the Yantra.

Verses 21 to 24 contain the Mantra of Mahi*sh*amardinī.

Verse 25 is the Dhyāna :—

She is the colour of emerald. She has a (third) eye on her forehead. She is adorned with gems on her head and ears. She is seated on the head of a buffalo. She is holding a Chakra (discus), a Shangkha (conchshell), a K*ri*pā*n*a (sword), a Khe*t*aka (shield), Bā*n*a (arrows), Kārmuka (bow), Shūla (spear) and Tarjanī Mudrā (threatening gesture) in her hands. The moon is on her head. I adore her.

Verses 26-33 describe Purashchara*n*a and Prayoga.

Verse 34 gives the Mantra of Jaya Durgā.

Verse 37 gives the Dhyāna,—

I adore Jaya Durgā who is worshipped by those who seek Siddhi. She is of the colour of the firmament. Her fierce looks frightens the enemies. On her forehead is the crescent moon. She is seated on a lion. In her hands are a Shangkha, a Chakra, a K*ri*pā*n*a and a Trishikha (trident). She has three eyes. Her Tejas (glory, radiance) pervades the three worlds. All the Devas surround her.

Verses 38-40 contain rules of Purashchara*n*a and Prayoga.

Verse 41 contains Shūlini Durgā Mantra.

Verses 42-45 speak of the *Rishi*, Chhanda*h*, Devatā and so forth.

Verse 46 gives her Dhyāna :—

I meditate on Shūlinī. She is seated on a lion and is of the dark colour of the rainladen cloud. In her (eight) hands are a Shūla, a Bā*n*a, a K*ri*pā*n*a, an Ari (discus), a lotus, a mace, a Bow, a Pāsha. She has three eyes and has the moon on her forehead. She is attended by four hand-maidens who are carrying Khe*t*akas. She is the terror of the enemy army.

Verses 47-62 give rules of Purashcharana and so forth.

Verses 63-65 give Vana-Durgā Mantra. The Devī is also called Vindhya-vāsinī. Four verses which follow give name of *Rishi* and so forth. Verse 70 is her Dhyāna :—

Meditate on her who abides in the Vindhya (Mountains). She is seated on a golden lotus and has three eyes. She is lustrous like lightning and has in two of her hands a Shangkha and a Chakra and the other two are in the attitude of granting boons and dispelling fear. Her face is beautiful as the full moon and on her forehead is the crescent moon. Neckchains, armlets, garlands and earrings adorn her. The Devas hymn her. By her side is Shiva.

Verse 71-75 speak of Purashcharana and rituals.

Verse 76 contains a Dhyāna for the Sādhaka who seeks the protection of the Devī :—

She is like the fire of final dissolution (Kāla-pāvaka) and in her hair is the half-moon. She has an eye on her forehead. She is seated on a fear-inspiring lion. In her (eight) hands are held the Chakra (discus), a Shangkha (conch), a Kripāna (sword), a Khetaka (shield), a Chāpa (bow), a Bāna (arrow), a Karotikā (skull) and a Shūla (trident). She subdued the whole army of the Asuras.

Rāghava quotes other similar Dhyānas from the Prapanchasāra and other texts. Different Prayogas are given (Vv. 76-123).

Verse 123 gives the Rakshākara (protective) Yantra of Vindhya-vāsinī. It is helpful in the attainment of wealth, immunity from evil influences and the like.

CHAPTER XII.

This chapter begins with a prayer to Tripurā.

Verse 3 gives the Mantra of Tripurā. Rāghava cites texts which say that she is so called because she created the three (*viz.*, Brahmā, Vishnu and Rudra) and so preceded them, because the three Kāndas of the Vedas are by her pervaded and also because she is even at the time of Pralaya.

Verse 4 says that the Mantra is composed of three parts.

Verses 5-32 contain the names of the *Rishis* and so forth and a long account of how Nyāsas to be done with the Mantra. This is supplemented by Rāghāva by other texts.

Verse 31 gives the Dhyāna :—

She is of the colour of a thousand rising suns and garmented in red silk. Her face beautiful like a red lotus is lighted by her three eyes. Her breasts are smeared with red sandal. She is wearing a garland of heads. On her head is a crown on which is the moon. She is smiling gently. In each of her hands is held a rosary, a book, the gesture of granting boons and that of dispelling fear.

Verses 32-70 contain an account of the Purashcharana and ritualistic worship and Prayoga.

Verse 71-75 describe three Yantras.

Verse 77 gives the Bālā Mantra. Verses 78 and 79 give the Gāyatrī. Verses 81-94 contain a hymn of praise. The opening verse of which says that as even Brahmā and other great Devas do not know the subtle (Sūkshma) form of the Devī who is the source from which the universe emanated the hymner therefore sings the praise of the gross (Sthūla) form.

Verses 96-99 contain the Mantra of Rājamātanginī which is made up of 88 letters. Verses 100-127 contain directions for Nyāsa and verse 128 contains her Dhyāna :—

She is seated on a gem-studded altar and listening to the pleasing notes of the parrots. One of her feet is resting on a lotus. She is playing on a Vīnā. She is elated with the nectar of which she has partaken. She is slightly dark of hue. On her forehead is the crescent moon. Her shining hair is made into a charming knot. Her raiment is red. She is wearing a garland of waterlilies. On her forehead is shining a Tilaka. She has armlets made of conchshells.

This is followed by rules relating to Purashcharana and ritualistic worship.

Verses 157-166 contain a Hymn of the Devī.

CHAPTER XIII.

This chapter gives an account of the worship of the different aspects of Ganesha. The Prapanchasāra (Ch. XVII.) deals with this.

Verse 2 contains the Bīja of Ganesha which is Gang and verse 3 speaks of the way Nyāsa is to be done therewith.

Verse 4 contains the Dhyāna :—

He is the colour of vermilion, three-eyed and has a large belly. In each of his lotus hands is held a tusk (his own), a noose, a goad and the gesture of granting boons. His face is that of the lord of elephants and at the end of his thick trunk is a beautiful pomegranate. On his forehead is shining the young moon and his cheeks are flooded with the copious flow of Dāna (exudations from an elephant's temple when in rut). His raiment and the unguent on his body are red. Huge serpents are his adornment.

Verses 5-26 describe Purashcharana of the Mantra, the articles to be used in his worship, and give the names of the Pītha-shaktis and attendant Devatās.

Verses 27-28 give the Mantra of twenty-eight letters of Mahāganapati.

Verse 29 says that the *Rishi* of the Mantra is Ganaka, the Chhandah is Nivrit Gāyatrī and verse 30 describes the Nyāsa of the Mantra.

Verses 31-38 say that he is to be meditated upon as seated on a lotus consisting of the letters of the alphabet (Mātrikāmbuja). The Sādhaka should meditate upon an island composed of nine gems, placed in an ocean of sugar-cane juice ; a soft gentle breeze blows over the island and makes the waves wash the shore thereof. The place is a forest of Mandāra, Pārijāta and other Kalpa trees and creepers, and the light from the gems thereon casts a red glow on the ground. The six gladdening seasons are always there. The sun and the moon brighten up the place. In the middle of the island is a Pārijāta tree whereon are the nine gems and beneath it is the great Pī*th*a (altar) on which is the lotus whereon is seated Mahāga*n*apati. His face is that of the great elephant with the moon on it. He is red and has three eyes. He is held in loving embrace by his beloved who is seated in his lap and has a lotus in her hand. In each of his ten hands he is holding a pomegranate, a mace, a bow, a trident, a discus, a lotus, a noose, a red water-lily, a sheaf of paddy and his own tusk. He is holding a jewelled jar in his trunk. By the flapping of his ears, he is driving away the bees attracted to his temples by the fluid exuding therefrom, and he is scattering gems from out of the jar held in his trunk. He is wearing a ruby studded crown and is adorned with gems.

Verses 39-61 give a description of Purashchara*n*a and Prayogas.

Verse 62 gives the Bīja of Bhūmi (The Earth).

Verses 63-65 describe the Yantra of Mahāga*n*apati.

Verses 66-67 give the Mantra of 26 letters of Viriga*n*apati and verse 68 speaks of the Muni, Chhanda*h* and Devatā.

Verse 69 gives directions about Nyāsa and says that Viriga*n*apati is to be meditated upon in a place similar to that described in the Dhyāna of Mahāga*n*apati.

Verse 70 gives the Dhyāna :—He is the colour of vermilion and has the face of an elephant. On his head is the half-moon. He has three eyes. In three of his hands he is holding a noose, a goad and a skull full of wine and his fourth hand is resting on the Yoni of his consort Pu*sh*t*i and at the end of his trunk he has a vessel full of wealth. Pu*sh*t*i is touching his Linga and embracing him with her right hand and in her other hand is held a lotus.

Verses 71-76 contain directions regarding Purashchara*n*a, worship, Homa and the like. There is also given here the fruits gained by such worship.

Verse 77 gives the Mantra of twelve letters of Shakti-ga*n*apati and verse 78, the *Rishi*, Chhanda*h* and Devatā and rules of Nyāsa of the Mantra. Verse 79 gives his Dhyāna :—

We adore him who is of the bright colour of pearl. He has the face of an elephant in rut. He has three eyes and the moon is on his forehead. A jewelled crown is on his head. He has a lotus, a goad and a jar full of gems in each of his three hands and his fourth hand is resting on the Yoni of the Devī seated in his lap. His trunk is resting on the jar of gems. The Devī who is of the colour of the lotus is holding in one hand a lotus whilst with the other she is touching his Linga.

Verses 80-83 give the usual rules of Purashcharana, worship and particulars relating to Prayoga.

Verse 84 gives another Mantra of eleven letters and 85 the *Rishi* and other details. Verse 86 gives the Dhyāna :—

I ever meditate upon the Omnipresent One who is of the colour of red hibiscus. He has the face of an elephant with three eyes and the halfmoon is on his forehead. In each of his four hands he is holding a sugarcane, the gesture of granting boons, a noose and a goad. The tip of his trunk is resting on the Yoni of his Shakti who is embracing him and holding the tip of his Linga with one hand and with the other a lotus. She is the colour of molten gold. He is full of desire.

Verses 87-90 give directions about rituals and the like.

Verses 90 and 91 give the Mantra of Kshipraprasādana Ganesha. It is of ten letters. Kshipraprasādana means 'quickly pleased'. Verse 93 give his Dhyāna :—

May the Elephant-headed One protect ye ! He is red and has three eyes. The young moon is on his forehead and he is wearing a shining garland. In each of his hands is held a noose, a goad, a Kalpalatā and one of his own tusks and he has a pomegranate at the tip of his trunk.

Verses 94-102 give rules of worship, Homa and the like.

Verse 103 says when Tarpana (oblation) is made, he is to be meditated upon as seated on a lotus and beautiful like a mountain of gold, and as coming out of the effulgence of the sun, down rows of silver steps into the water with which the Tarpana is made.

Verses 105-106 give the Mantra of Heramba Ga*n*esha and describe the way Nyāsa is to be done therewith.

His Dhyāna is given in verse 107 :—

I adore Heramba who is of the lustre of the sun. He is seated proudly on a lion. He has five faces each like that of an elephant, and one of them is on top and upward turned. They are of the colour of pearl, gold, blue, Kunda flower (white) and red respectively. The moon is on the forehead of each of these. With two of his hands he is making the gestures of granting boons and dispelling fear and in each of the other eight is held a ball of sweets, his tusk, an axe, a skull, a rosary, a hammer, a goad and a trident.

Verses 108-113 contain directions regarding worship, Homa and the like. Verses 114-119 describe the Yantra to be worn as an amulet and give the Mantra to be written thereon.

Verses 119-120 give the Mantra of Subrahma*n*ya or Kārtikeya. Verse 121 gives his Dhyāna :—

We adore Subrahma*n*ya. He is of the colour of vermilion and his face is beautiful like the moon. Beautiful armlets, garlands and other ornaments adorn him. He is holding in each of his hands a lotus, the gesture of dispelling fear, a cock and the weapon Shakti. He is raimented in red and the unguent on his body is also red. He grants the happiness of heaven to, and destroys the fear of, his votaries.

The eight verses which follow give details of worship.

Verses 131-151 are a hymn in adoration of Ga*n*esha. In it he is, among other attributes, spoken of as one with Omkāra and therefore Shabda Brahman.

CHAPTER XIV.

Verses 1-3 give the Mantra of Soma (Chandra, Moon).

Verse 4 contains the Dhyāna :—

I always adore Soma, the ocean of nectar. He is of the whiteness of camphor and pure crystal. His face is the circle of the full moon and the blue tresses which surround it enhance its beauty. Ropes of pearls which adorn his body uproot darkness. In his two hands are held a waterlily and the gesture of granting boons. The stain on his surface is due to the deer he has in his lap.

Verses 5-27 describe Purashcharana, worship and Prayoga.

Verse 28 gives the Mantra of Sūrya (Sun). The Mantra is of eight letters. Verses 29 to 35 contains rules of Nyāsa and other details and verse 36 gives his Dhyāna :—

I adore the Lord of the Day. He is of the redness of the Bandhūka flower and seated on a red lotus. He has three luminous eyes and a ruby crown on his head. He is holding a lotus in each of two of his hands and with the other two is making the gestures of dispelling fear and granting boons. He is adorned with armlets, garlands and so forth.

Verses 37-57 describe Purashcharana, worship and Prayoga.

Verse 58 gives Prayojana-tilaka Mantra and 59 and 60 Nyāsa. Verse 61 gives the Dhyāna of the Devatā :—

I adore Bhānu (an aspect of Sūrya). He is seated on a red lotus. He is the ocean of endless good and the Lord of the limitless Universe. In two of his hands he is holding two lotuses and the other two are held in the attitudes of dispelling fear and granting boons. He is red and is wearing a ruby crown. He has three eyes.

Verses 62-65 give rules of Purashcharana and rituals.

Verse 66 gives the Bīja of Mārtanda Bhairava. This Bīja is very difficult to pronounce and the commentary says that it is only the Guru who can show the way to do it. If this Bīja is placed between two Vimba Bījas and repeated then it becomes very effective. The verses which follow give rules of Nyāsa. Verse 71 gives the Dhyāna of Mārtanda :—

We adore Mārtanda. He is of the redness of a golden lotus and coral. He has four beautiful faces with three eyes in each. He is holding in each of his lotus-like hands a beautiful Khatvānga, a lotus, a discus, a Shakti, a noose, a goad, a very beautiful rosary and a skull. The left half of his body is that of his beloved. On his head is a jewelled crown and he is wearing a shining garland.

Verses 72 to 79 describe the ritual beginning with Purashcharana.

Verses 80-88 give the Ajapā Mantra (Hamsa*h*) and other particulars. The Devatā of the Mantra is the Lord of Girijā who is the beginning of creation. The reason for giving it here, says Rāghava, is that this Mantra partakes of the nature of Agni and Soma—(Agnī*sh*omātmaka).

Verse 83 gives the Dhyāna :—

May he who is half the Mother and half the Lord, who is the Root of the Universe protect ye ! He is of the colour of the rising sun and like a flash of lightning. In his hands are a noose, the gesture of dispelling fear, the gesture of granting boons and a battle-axe. Celestial ornaments made of nine kinds of gems adorn him. His body is Moon (Soma) and Fire (Agni). He has three eyes. On his forehead is the Moon.

In the Nyāsa of the Mantra (Vv. 84-90) parts of the Hamsavatī *Ri*k of the *Ri*gveda is to be used.

Verse 91 states the benefit gained by the Sādhanā of this Mantra. There is a long passage cited by Rāghava from the Tantrāntara in which a more detailed account of the ritual is given. In this, the way we breathe and how often we do it in the course of twentyfour hours and other details are given.

The identity of the Hangsa*h* Mantra with the Pra*n*ava is recognised among Sādhakas and fully explained by, among others, Shamkarāchārya in the Prapanchasāra (Ch. IV.). This Mantra is called the Root of the Universe as it is the breath of life.

It may incidentally be noted that it is this Hangsa*h* and not a 'Swan' which is the carrier (Vāhana) of Brahmā.

Verses 92-94 give the Mantra of Agni (Fire) and other particulars. Verse 95 gives the Dhyāna :—

I adore red Agni. He has a golden garland resting on his shoulders. He is adorned with red garlands and red sandal paste. The mass of flames shining on his head are like so many matted locks. His raiment is very white. In each of his hands he is carrying a Shakti, a Svastika, a Darbhamu*shti*, a rosary, a sacrifical ladle (Sruk) and spoon (Sruva), the gestures of dispelling fear and granting boons. He has three beautiful eyes.

Verses 96-115 deal with Purashcharana and so forth.

Verses 116 and 117 give the Mantra of Turagāgni (Va*d*avāgni : Horsefire) and 119 gives the Dhyāna :—

He is of the form of a horse and he has come out of a golden Ashvattha tree, and is red like a mass of vermilion. Flames are the hairs on his body. His beauty charms the world. Ornaments of priceless gems adorn his neck. Gems come out of his organs (Indriyas) are spread all over the world.

The rest of the chapter describes the ritual and the different benefits derived therefrom.

CHAPTER XV.

This chapter deals with the worship of Vi*shn*u. Verse 2 gives a Mantra of eight letters. The text (Vv. 10-11) speaks of a Mantra of twelve letters and then proceeds (Vv. 12-21) to speak of Nyāsa and other rites.

Verse 22 contains a Dhyāna of Vi*shn*u :—

I ever adore the Supporter of the Universe. He is lustrous with the lustre of ten million rising suns and in his hands are a conchshell, a mace, a lotus and a discus. On either side of him are beautiful Lak*sh*mī and Vasumatī. He has a crown on his head and is wearing armlets, garlands and ear-ornaments. His raiment is yellow. The Kaustubha gem enhances his lustre and on his breast is the sign of Shrīvatsa.

Shrīvatsa is the curl of white hair on the breast of Vi*shn*u.

Verses 23-36 contain ritualistic rules.

Verse 37 gives another Mantra of twelve letters ; and the three following verses speak of the *Rishi* and so forth as also of Nyāsa. Verse 41 contains the Dhyāna. This is similar to the last, only Vasumatī and Lak*sh*mī are not in this and he is described as of the colour of ten million moons of autumn. This aspect is adored by great Munis.

Verse 47 contains a Mantra of 14 letters. The Dhyāna according to this Mantra is in verse 50 :—

He is of the colour of lightning and the moon. Half his body is Vaiku*ntha* (Vi*shn*u) and the other half is Kamalajā (Lak*sh*mī). This union is due to mutual affection. He is adorned with gem-set ornaments. He is carrying in each of his eight hands the Vidyā-mudrā, a lotus, a mirror, a jar of gems, again a lotus, a mace, a conchshell and a discus.

Vi*shn*u is Vaiku*ntha* as he is beyond (*vi*) all Ku*nthā* or limitation. The name Vi*shn*u again, means he who pervades Creation. The word comes from the root *vish* = to enter.

Verse 53 contains a Mantra of eighteen letters ; after naming the *Rish*i and so forth (Vv. 54-57) the Dhyāna is given in verse 58 :—

We worship him who is of the radiance of pearls and is seated on the moon. Nine different kinds of gems are in his ornaments. His lotus-like face is adorned with locks of hair like black bees. In his lotus hands are held a golden jar filled with pure water and a cup of gold full of curd and rice.

Verses 59-68 describe rituals and Yantra.

Verses 69 and 70 contain a Mantra of Vi*shn*u as Hayagrīva (Horse-headed). This is followed by names of *Rish*i and so forth. Verse 72 is the Dhyāna :—

He is of the lustre of the autumnal moon and adorned with ornaments set with pearls. His head is that of a horse. In two of his hands he is holding a discus and a conchshell and the other two are resting on his knees.

Verses 81 gives the Mantra of Rāma.

Verse 84 gives Dhyāna :—I always adore Rāghava who is of the charming radiance of dark rain clouds. He is seated in the Vīrāsana posture, with one hand in the gesture of Jnāna-mudrā and the other resting on his knee. He is adorned with a crown, armlets and various other ornaments. Sītā who is lustrous like lightning and is holding a lotus in her hand is seated by his side and looking at him.

Verses 85-98 describe rituals and the Dhāra*n*a Yantra or amulet.

Verses 99-100 give the Mālā Mantra of forty-seven letters of Rāma and verse 101 gives the Mantra of ten letters.

Verses 103-105 give the Mantra of Varāha and the two following verses speak of Nyāsa and other details.

Verse 108 gives his Dhyāna. Verses 109-127 describe the rituals and Yantra. Verse 128 gives Varāha Bīja.

The Yantra of Varāha (V. 132), buried in manner enjoined, in a selected spot in a village, town or like place, ensures its stability and prosperity.

Verse 134 gives the Dharā-h*ri*daya (Heart of the Earth) Mantra.

Verse 138 gives the Dhyāna :—We adore Vasudhā (Earth as container of all wealth). She is green. She is seated on a lotus. She is adorned with variegated gems and raiment and is bending forward with the weight of her large breasts. She is holding in her hands two lotuses, a sheaf of fresh Shāli-paddy and a parrot.

The rest of the chapter gives ritual.

CHAPTER XVI.

The chapter begins with the Mantra of Nara-simha (Man-lion). This is one of the aspects of Vi*sh*n*u. The Mantra is Vedik. After naming the *Ri*sh*i* and so forth (3-6) the Dhyāna of Nara-simha is given in verse 7 :—

I ever adore the omnipresent Nara-simha. He is of the lustre of a mountain of rubies. By his effulgence are the Rāk*sh*asas panic-struck. Two of his hands rest on his knees and in the other two are held the Chakra and the Shangkha. He has three eyes. His ornaments are brilliant red. Flames of fire issuing from his fangs and tongue light up his face. His hair is standing on end.

This is the placid (Saumya) Dhyāna. Verse 13 gives the Dhyāna of his fierce (Krūra) aspect. As such Nara-hari (Man-lion) is of the effulgence of ten million rising suns. He

6

is ornamented with a shining crown and neckchains. His fangs make his face fierce. By his long arms tipped with shining nails he is tearing open the king of Asuras. The Sun, the Moon and the Fire are his three eyes. His matted hair shining like lightning frightens. He is belching fire.

The word Asura is ordinarily translated as the equivalent of 'Demon'. Shamkarāchārya (*Vide* Com. Sanat-sujātīya) interprets it also to mean a person who seeks the pleasures of the senses. The king is Hira*n*ya-kashipu who, as the name shows, is the embodiment of pride of wealth.

In verse 14, it is said that for the purpose of Saumya (propitiatory) rites the Saumya Dhyāna is appropriate and in Krūra (cruel) rites, the Krūra Dhyāna. After describing (Vv. 15-31) the ritual and the benefits therefrom, the Pūjā Yantra is described in verse 32 and another Yantra in verse 38.

Verse 39 gives the Bīja (Ks*h*raung) of N*ri*simha.

Verses 40-42 give the Mantra of Jvālā-n*ri*simha.

Verse 45 gives his Dhyāna :—He is terrific like the Fire of Pralaya (final dissolution). He has three eyes. Flames of fire add to his lustre. He has fierce fangs and is a terror to the Rāks*h*asas. His matted locks scattered in all directions make him awful to behold. In each of his hands is held, a conchshell, a discus, a sword and a shield.

Verse 48 gives the Mantra of Laks*h*mī-n*ri*simha and verse 50, his Dhyāna.

In his commentary to verse 54 Rāghava quotes long passages from Agasti-samhitā, Mantra-tantra-prakāsha, Vāyavīya samhitā, Kula-prakāsha-tantra, Vaishampāyana-samhitā and some unnamed authorities giving rules relating to Purashchara*n*a. Here is also cited a text from the Vāyavīya-samhitā describing the three forms of Japa, namely, Uchcha (spoken), Upāngshu (muttered) and Mānasa (mental). The Gītā is cited to say that the rite of Japa is the highest rite and the very self of the Lord.

Verse 64 describes a Yantra of N*ri*simha.

Verse 67 gives the Sudarshana Mantra.

The attention of the reader is drawn to the N*ri*simhatāpanī and the *Shat*chakra Upani*sh*ads.

Verse 75 contains the Dhyāna of Vi*sh*nu as Muraripu or Murāri (Enemy of Mura) :—

He is resplendent like the sun at the time of final dissolution. By his glory and radiance he fills up the three worlds. His eyes are red and hair, tawny. He is the terror of all enemies. His fangs are terrific. He is laughing loudly in derision. In his hands are a discus, a conch-shell, a mace, a lotus, a huge hammer, a bow, a noose and a goad. Thus should the enemy of Mura be pictured in the mind.

Mura is usually said to be the name of a demon. It also means anything which distracts the mind and thereby obstructs the path to Liberation.

Verses 76-131 describe Purashchara*n*a and ritual.

Verses 132-140 describe six Yantras.

CHAPTER XVII.

This chapter begins with the Puru*sh*ottama Mantra and the rites relating thereto. In the Prapanchasāra (Ch. XXIII. 2nd Edition) Shamkarāchārya has dealt with the same subject. It is called the Guptapa*t*ala by Rāghava.

A Christian writer speaks of the Prapanchasāra as a "foul book", alluding possibly, to the description of the ecstacy of the devotees of the Mantra. Regrettable as such remarks undoubtedly are, one should not wonder at it, for writers of this type are not capable of the emotions which the true devotee experiences. They do not, it may be surmised, believe in and appreciate their own Bible. If they did, the Song of Solomon would have taught them to be more circumspect in the language used in dealing with sentiments which are foreign to them.

The Mantra given (Vv. 2-11) is one of two hundred letters. The verses which follow give the usual particulars.

After describing a beautiful garden (Vv. 23-29) ; it is said (V. 30) that the Deva Puru*sh*ottama should be meditated upon there, as united with his consort who is of the colour of a lotus and is holding a lotus in her left hand and embracing him with her right. He is looking smilingly at her. He is holding in each of his hands the conchshell, the noose, the hammer, the bow, the arrow, the sword, the mace and the goad.

Verses 31 to 58 contain ritulistic rules.

Verse 59 gives Shrīkara Mantra of eight letters.

Verses 62-65 show how Nyāsa is to be done with the Vedik *R*ik beginning 'Brāhma*n*o'sya mukham āsīt' in the Puru*sh*a-sūkta and verse 67 gives the Dhyāna :—

He is lustrous as a mountain of gold and in his lotus face has lotus-like eyes. On his chest is the gem, Kaustubha. He is beautiful to look at and is adorned with a crown, armlets and other ornaments. He is seated on the bird-king Garu*d*a. In his four hands he is carrying a conchshell, a discus, a mace and a lotus. He is imperishable.

Verses 68-81 describe rituals.

Verses 82 and 83 give the Gopāla Mantra and this is followed by the Dhyāna of the Deva in verse 89. The Dhyāna is preceded by a description of B*ri*ndābana with the thousands of Gopinis whose faces are like lotuses and who in the excess of their desire are reduced to helplessness.

The description may be compared with that in the Gupta-pa*t*ala of the Prapanchasāra.

Verses 90-102 describe ritual and Gopāla Yantra.

Verse 103 gives the Pi*nd*a Bīja.

The commentator cites, under this verse, long passages containing Dhyānas of the boy K*rishn*a.

Verse 104 gives a Mantra of six letters of K*rishn*a, and verse 105, one of ten letters, verse 106, one of sixteen letters and verses 107-109, one of thirty-two letters.

Verse 110 gives the Kāma-linga Yantra. Verse 111 gives a Mantra of thirty-two letters which is to be inscribed on the Yantra. Verses 112-113 give directions as to how the Yantra is to be drawn with the Mantras therein.

Verses 114-116 describe another Yantra and the Mantra to be inscribed therein.

Verse 117 gives the Mantra of Kāma. It is of one letter. Verse 120 gives the Dhyāna of Kāma and verses 121-143 describe rituals. Verse 144 gives his Yantra. Verse 145 gives his Gāyatrī. Verses 146-147 give the Mālā Mantra of Kāma. It is of forty-eight letters. Verse 148 describes another Yantra of Kāma.

Verses 150-161 contain a hymn to Vi*sh*nu wherein he is adored in all his different incarnations. In this among the ten incarnations Buddha is included. In speaking of the Buddha incarnation, it is here said that for the suppression of the Asuras he assumed the Kaupīna (a bit of rag) as his garb and composed Shāstras which are almost irrefutable (Amogha-kalpa). In the Prapanchasāra, Buddha is not recognised as one of the Avatāras.

CHAPTER XVIII.

In this chapter are given various Mantras of Shiva. The name Shiva is derived from the root, *vash*=to rule. His carrier is V*rish*a which means Dharma. Shiva's rule is based on Dharma. V*rish*a is commonly translated to mean a bull, which it also means.

In verse 2 is given his Mantra of six letters. Verses 3-6 describe Nyāsa.

The commentator cites a verse which says that the six limbs (*Shad*anga) of Shiva are,—All-knowingness, Contentment, Limitless knowledge, Self-dependence, Imperishability and Limitless power.

The text proceeds to give (Vv. 7-12) Golaka Nyāsa.

Verse 13 contains the Dhyāna of Shiva :—

He is lustrous like a mountain of silver with the beautifully shining moon on his forehead. He is adorned with gems and carries in each of his four hands a battle-axe, a deer and the gestures of granting boons and dispelling fear. He is gracious of mien, seated on a lotus, raimented with a tiger-skin and surrounded by all the Devas who are singing his praise. He is the source of the universe. His form is the universe. He dispels all fears. He has five faces with three eyes in each.

This is followed by (Vv. 14-31) rules of Purashcharaṇa and other rites.

Verses 32-33 contain a Mantra of eight letters and rules relating there to.

Verse 34 contains the Dhyāna of Shiva as the Deva of the Mantra :—

He is red like the Bandhūka flower and has three eyes. A digit of the moon is on his forehead. He has a smiling face and in each of his hands is held, a trident, a skull and the gestures of granting boons and dispelling fear. On his left knee is seated his beloved, holding in her left hand a beautiful red lotus and with the other hand embracing him. She is adorned with gem-studded ornaments.

Verses 35-48 contain rules of Purashcharaṇa and other rites.

Verse 49 contains the Prasāda Mantra and this is followed by (Vv. 50-55) rules relating to Nyāsa and so forth.

The commentator here cites the Vedik *Ṛ*iks of Ishāna, Tat-purusha, Aghora, Vāma deva and Sadyo-jāta. Verses 56-84 describe how Nyāsa is to be done with the *Ṛ*iks.

Verse 85 contains the Dhyāna of Sadāshiva :—

He is the Lord whose five faces are, respectively, the colour of pearl, yellow, rain-cloud, mother of pearl and hibiscus flower. He has three eyes in each face. He is of the effulgence of millions of fullmoons. In each of his ten hands he has a trident, a battle-axe, a sword, the thunderbolt, the fire, a great serpent, a bell, a goad, a noose and the gesture of dispelling fear. He is adorned with priceless gems.

This is followed by rules relating to Purashcharaṇa and other rites.

Verse 98 contains the Prasāda Mantra of eight letters.

Verse 100 contains the Dhyāna of the Deva :—

I adore him who is of the colour of vermilion. On his

head is a gem-studded crown and the Moon. On his forehead is shining his third eye. His lotus face is illumined with a smile. The gems and ornaments he is wearing are of celestial excellence. On his left knee is placed the right hand of his beloved who, with the other hand, is holding a red water-lily. One of his hands is on the rounded and high breast of his beloved and with the others he holds the Veda, a battle-axe and the gesture of granting boons.

Verses 101-104 contain rules of Purashcharana and rituals.

Verse 105 contains the Mantra of Shiva as *Mrityunjaya* (Conqueror of Death) and verse 108 his Dhyāna :—

His three eyes are the Moon, the Sun and the Fire. He has a smiling face. He is seated on a lotus and another lotus is above him. He is of the effulgence of the moon. One of his hands is held in the gesture of Jnāna-mudrā, and in each of the others is a noose, a deer and a rosary of Aksha beads. The nectar flowing from the Moon in his matted hair, bathes his body. He is wearing garlands and other gems. His beauty charms the universe. He is the Lord of creatures and the Conqueror of Death.

Verses 109-124 contain rules relating to Purashcharana and so forth. Verse 125 says that, he, the Lord of Umā, should be meditated upon in the heart for the alleviation of all pain. Verses 126-128 contain some more ritualistic rules and verse 129 gives his Yantra.

CHAPTER XIX.

Verses 2 and 3 give the Mantra of Dakshinā-mūrti. This is followed by the usual particulars about the name of the *Rishi* and so forth. Verses 10-18 contain a description of the place where he is, and as his subtle (Sūkshma) form is ineffable, the Dhyāna in verse 19 is of his gross (Sthūla) form :—

I adore him who is like the Mount Kailāsa. On his matted locks is the crescent moon. His gaze is fixed on the tip of his nose. He is three-eyed and is seated in the Vīra posture

(Vīrāsana). He is gracious of mien carrying in three of his hands the Jnāna-mudrā, a battle-axe and a deer and one hand is placed on his thigh. Serpents encircle his waist. He is surrounded by the Munis.

It may be noted that all the Dhyānas given in the book are of the Sthūla forms only for the help of the Sādhaka towards that which words cannot describe.

This is followed by rules relating to Purashcharana and so forth.

Verses 25 and 26 contain directions regarding a method of making of Brāhmīghrita by Sādhakas of this Mantra.

Verses 27, 28 give another Mantra and this is followed by, as usual, the name of the *Rishi* and so forth.

Verse 31 contains the Dhyāna of Dakshinā-mūrti as the Deva of this Mantra :—

I adore him who is three-eyed and is of the colour of crystalline silver. In two of his hands are a rosary of pearls and a jar of nectar, and with the other two he is making the gestures of Vidyā and Jnāna. On his forehead is the Moon. He is adorned with many kinds of ornament. Serpents encircle his waist.

Verses 32-41 deal with Purashcharana and rituals.

Verses 42, 43 contain the Mantra of Shiva as Nīlakantha (Blue-throated) and verse 48 is his Dhyāna :—

He is seated on a lotus. His effulgence is that of ten thousand young suns. On his matted locks is a digit of the moon. He is raimented with tiger-skins and great serpents are his adornment. He is beautiful and has five faces with three eyes in each. In each hand of his is held a rosary, a trident, a skullcup and a skull-mounted staff.

Verses 49-54 describe Purashcharana and other rites.

Verse 55 gives the Chintāmani Mantra Verse 58 contains the Dhyāna which is that of Ardhanārīshvara.

Verses 59-82 describe Purashcharana, rituals and Yantras.

Verse 83 contains the Tumburu Bīja.

Verse 90 gives the Dhyāna :—

He is red and has four faces with three eyes to each. His noses are flat. The crescent moon adorns his head. He is decked with priceless adornment. He is smeared with red unguent and his raiment is red. He is decked with red flowers. In his hands are a skull-mounted staff (Kha*t*vānga), a noose, a goad and a white skull-cup.

Verses 91-108 contain Purashchara*n*a and rituals and 109 the Yantra.

Verses 110, 111 contain Kha*d*ga-rāva*n*a Mantra.

Verse 120 gives the Dhyāna :—He has five faces and ten hands, is red in colour and his raiment is red.

This is followed (Vv. 121-132) by Purashchara*n*a and rituals.

CHAPTER XX.

Verses 2-4 give the Aghorāstra Mantra of 51 letters. Verse 10 gives the Dhyāna of Aghora : —

He is dark like the heavily laden rain-clouds. He has three eyes and terrific fangs. His raiment is red, so also is the unguent on his body. In his hands are a battle-axe, a *D*amaru (small drum), a sword, a shield, a bow, an arrow, a trident and a human skull. Serpents circle round him.

He is to be meditated upon as of different hue for different Prayogas ; such as, black for Abhichāra, white for Mok*sh*a and so on.

Verses 12-21 deal with Purashchara*n*a, rituals and Prayogas.

Verses 22 and 23 describe two Yantras.

Verse 25 gives the Pāshupatāstra Mantra of six letters. Verse 27 gives the Dhyāna of Pashupati.

This as also Aghora are fearsome aspects.

Verses 28-31 deal with Purashchara*n*a and other rites.

Verse 32 contains the Mantra of K*sh*etrapāla and verse 34 the Dhyāna :—

He is dark like a mountain of dark blue collyrium. His hair is of a tawny hue. He is raimented with space.

Serpents are his adornment. His eyes are round and angry. In his hands are a mace and a skull. He has terrific fangs. His body is wonderful. I bow to him.

Verses 35-40 deal with Purashcharana, rituals and Prayogas.

Verses 44-45 contain Āpaduddhāraṇa (rescuing from danger) Mantra of Vaṭuka. It is of 21 letters.

Verse 50 gives the Dhyāna of Vaṭuka in his Sāttvika aspect :—

He is a boy, bright and white like crystal. He has three eyes and his face is cheerful and charming with its curly hair. He is decked with ornaments of great beauty, set with nine kinds of gem. His raiment is white. In his two hands he is holding a trident and a stick.

Verse 52 gives the Rājasa Dhyāna of Vaṭuka :—

He is in colour like the rising sun, three-eyed and is smeared with red unguent and wearing a red garland. He has a smiling face. With two of his hands he is making the gestures of granting boons and dispelling fear and in each of his other two hands is held a skull and a trident. His throat is blue. He is decked with hundreds of rich ornaments. On his head is shining the moon. His raiment is of the redness of the Bandhūka flower.

Verse 53 gives the Tāmasa Dhyāna :—

He is of the colour of a blue mountain. He has a digit of the moon on his head, fear-inspiring fangs and three eyes. He has tawny hair and the points of the compass are his raiment. Serpents adorn him and he is wearing a garland of heads and on his feet are toe-rings set with gems. In his hands he holds a serpent, a bell, a skull, a small drum, a goad, a sword, a noose and the fear-dispelling gesture.

Sāttvika Dhyāna is for those who wish to avoid accidental death, seeks happy long life and Liberation (Moksha). Rājasa Dhyāna is for those who seek Dharma, Artha and Kāma and Tāmasa for such as seek to injure their enemies and counteract evil influences.

Verses 55-131 deal with Purashcharaṇa, and Prayoga.

Verses 132-134 give the Yantra for averting danger.

Verses 135-136 contain the Cha*nd*a Mantra of 3 letters.

Verse 139 gives the Dhyāna of Cha*nd*a :—

He is red, three-eyed, garbed in red and on his head is the Moon. He has in each of his hands a battle-axe, a trident, a rosary of crystals, and a Kama*nd*alu.

Verses 140-148 give rules of Purashchara*n*a, and so forth.

Verses 149-159 is a hymn to Shiva :—

Thou art the form of Earth, Water, Fire, Air, Ether, the Sacrificer, the Moon and the Sun.

Thou art beneficent and abidest in all that is :
Obeisance to Thee !
Thou abidest in the Upani*sh*ads,
Thou art Shruti, Shruti owes her birth to Thee.
Thou art beyond the senses.
Thou art the eternal Maha*h* :
To Thee Obeisance again and again.
Thou art neither gross nor subtle.
Thou art good (Shambhu).
Thou destroyest the ills of this world.
Obeisance to Thee, O Bhava !
Thou art far beyond all polemics.
All-knowing Thou art and grantest the fruits of penance,
And the fourfold aims of human life.
Obeisance to Thee and again obeisance !
Thou hast no beginning, no middle and no end.
Thou dispellest all fear.
Attributeless art Thou and great.
Yogins alone can meditate on Thee :
To Thee obeisance and again obeisance !
Thou art the Universe, and beyond thought.
Thou destroyest the pride of Kāma.
Thou annihilatest Time.
On Thy forehead shines the Moon.
To Thee obeisance again and again !

Thou eatest poison and
Art seated on the constantly moving V*ri*sh*a.
The flowing waters of Gangā holds like a string
Thy matted locks in place :
To Thee obeisance !
Pure Thou art and purifiest,
Thou art the innermost Ātmā of the pure.
Thou art the destroyer of Tripura.
Thou art all and Thy name purifies :
To Thee obeisance !
Thou grantest Enjoyment and Liberation to Thy votaries,
And art to them devoted.
Thou hast no home, no cloth to cover Thyself,
Yet art Thou the Ruler of the Universe :
To Thee obeisance again and again !
Thou art the root of the Three (Brahmā, Vi*sh*n*u, Rudra).
Thou hast three eyes. Obeisance to Thee !
Thou art the Light of the three Lights (Sun, Moon, Fire).
Thou destroyest rebirth :
To Thee obeisance !
The gems in the diadems of Devas and Asuras tint,
With a rosy tint, Thy feet.
Charming and beloved Thou art,
And hast to Thy beloved given half Thine own body :
Obeisance to Thee again and yet again !

CHAPTER XXI.

After having described the rituals of the five classes of worshippers (Panchopāsakas) commonly known as Tāntrikas the author here begins to speak of Vedik Mantras. In this chapter he first speaks of the Gāyatrī Mantra which makes the Sach-chid-ānanda Brahman manifest. The twenty-four letters of the Gāyatrī (V. 1) are the twenty-four Tattvas.

Rāghava cites a long passage from the Prapanchasāra (Ch. XXX) which shows how the Vyāh*ri*tis and the Gāyatrī point towards the Brahman.

Verses 2-8 give the names of the *Rishis* of the Vyāh*ri*tis and of the Gāyatrī, the Chhanda*h*, the Devatās and so forth. The Mantra itself being Vedik has not been given.

Verses 9-14 speak of the different forms of Nyāsa to be done.

Rāghava cites a long passage from the Kalpāntara which shows how each single letter of the Gāyatrī has to be placed when doing Nyāsa.

Verse 15 gives the Dhyāna of the Devī Gāyatrī :—

She has five faces which are of the colour of pearl, coral, gold, and blue and white respectively. Each face has three eyes. Her gem-set crown has the Moon on it. The twenty-four letters of the Mantra compose her body. Two of her hands are held in the gestures of granting boons and dispelling fear and in each of the other hands she holds a goad, a whip, a white skull, a noose, a conchshell, a discus and two lotuses.

Rāghava cites texts which shows the different ways the Devī is to be meditated upon in three different times of the day, namely, morning, midday, evening. The Mahānirvā*n*a-tantra also gives the three Dhyānas. (See Avalon's 'Great Liberation' Ch. V.).

Verses 16-31 give directions about Purashchara*n*a and so forth. Rāghava here gives the fourth part of the Gāyatrī, of which use is made by those who seek Liberation.

Verse 32 speaks of the Tri*sht*up Mantra.

The Mantra is given by Rāghava in his commentary and he says that being a very wellknown Mantra in the *Ri*gveda it has not been given by the author. It is of 44 letters.

Verses 33-38 contain information about *Rishi*, Chhanda*h*, Devatā and so forth and the rules of Nyāsa.

Verse 39 gives the Dhyāna of Durgā as Analātmikā (Fire) :—

She is of the effulgence of streaks of lightning and is seated on a lion. She is terrific of aspect and surrounded by young virgins who are carrying swords and shields. She has three eyes and has the Moon on her forehead She has in each of her hands a discus, a conchshell, a sword, a shield, a bow, an arrow, a trident and the Tarjani-mudrā (Chiding gesture).

Verses 40-56 give rules of Purashcharaṇa, ritualistic worship, Prayoga and information about articles to be used in, and the proper time and place for doing, the rites.

In verse 57 it is said that the previous Mantra becomes, if reversed (Vilomapaṭhita), the Āgneyāstra Mantra.

The Dhyāna of the Devatā of the Mantra it is said (V. 59) has to be learnt frnm the Guru.

With verse 60 begins a description of how Vedik Mantras made up of parts of the Trishṭup Mantra are to be used for gaining worldly advantages, injuring enemies and so forth.

In describing these rites the Mantras of Durgā in her different aspects are given. These forms are Atidurgā Gāṇidurgā, Vishva-durgā, Sindhu-durgā, and Agni-durgā.

Verse 146 gives the Yantra.

CHAPTER XXII.

In verse 2 it is said that the Ati-durgā Mantra is called Dināstra and (V. 3) if it is reversed it is called Kṛityāstra.

Verses 3-88 contain injunctions relating to the different purposes for which these Mantras may be used.

Verses 89-97 give the Lavaṇa Mantra and the name of the *Rishi* and other particulars.

Agni, Rātri, Durgā and Bhadrakālī are the Devatās of the Mantra.

Verses 100, 101 give the Chiṭi Mantra of 24 letters. Verse 102 gives the Dhyāna of Agni, 103 of Rātri, 104 of Durgā and 105, of Bhadrakālī.

Verses 106-164 contain rules relating to Purashcharaṇa worship and the manner the Mantra is to be used for the attainment of the object desired.

CHAPTER XXIII.

This chapter speaks of the Traiyambaka or Anu*sh*t*up Mantra. It is of 32 letters. The Mantra which is Vedik is not given in the text but Rāghava supplies it from the *R*igveda.

Verses 2-8 give the name of the *Rish*i, Chhanda*h* and so forth and direction regarding Nyāsa.

Verse 9 gives the Dhyāna :—

I adore Shiva. He is seated on a lotus of transparent whiteness. He is beautiful like Mount Kailāsa. He has three eyes. On his diadem is the digit of the moon. With two of his hands he is bathing his head with nectar out of two jars held in two other hands. In two of his other hands are held a deer and a rosary. On two hands resting on the body are placed two jars.

Verses 10-33 give rules relating to Purashchara*n*a, worship and the way the Mantra is to be used in Prayoga.

Verse 34 says that the Mantra of 100 letters is made up of the letters of the Mantras of Gāyatrī (24), Tri*sht*up (44) and Anu*sht*up (32).

Verse 37 gives the Dhyāna :—

I adore the great Maha*h* who is Truth and immeasurable, the Source of the words of Shruti, Cause of the Universe, spread over the moving and the motionless, the object of meditation of those Munis who have restrained their senses. He is the Sun, Fire and Moon. The hundred letters of the Mantra form his body. He is the Pra*n*ava, all-spreading Nityānanda (Enduring Bliss) and beyond the three Gu*n*as (Sattva, Rajas, Tamas).

Rāghava interprets this verse with illustrations from Shruti and gives an alternative interpretation whereby the Dhyāna becomes applicable to Ku*nd*alinī Shakti.

This shows the relation of in-separateness (A-vinā-bhāva) between Shiva and Shakti.

Verses 38-51 contain Purashchara*n*a and other particulars.

Verse 52 speaks of the Vāru*n*ī *R*ik.

The *Rik* which is in *Rig*veda is supplied by Rāghava.

Verse 57 gives the Dhyāna of Varu*n*a :—

He is seated on a lotus and is lustrous like the moon. Gracious of aspect he is holding in two of his hands a noose and a goad and with the other two, making the gestures of dispelling fear and granting boons. He is adorned with pearls.

This is followed by (Vv. 58-70) rules of Purashchara*n*a worship and so forth.

In verse 71 the author says "I now speak of the rules of Prā*n*aprati*shth*ā (Life-infusing) Mantra whereby the Mantras previously mentioned become quick with Life."

Verses 72-75 describe the Mantra. This is followed by the name of its *Rish*i and so forth.

Verse 85 gives the Dhyāna of the Devī of the Mantra :—

She is red and is seated on a red boat in a red ocean. She has three eyes. In each of her hands is held a noose, a goad, a bow, an arrow, a trident and a skull.

Verses 86-103 give rules of Purashchara*n*a and so forth.

Verse 104 gives the Yantra.

Verses 105-114 describe different kinds of Mudrā.

Verses 115-120 describe different kinds of rosary and the benefits that are respectively derived therefrom.

Verses 121-135 speak of *Shat*karma, that is, the different rites for attaining the six objects, such as, Shānti (Peace), Stambhana (Paralysing) and so forth.

Some of the technological expressions used in the book are also explained (Vv. 136-145). Rāghava has further illustrated this by citing texts from various authorities.

CHAPTER XXIV.

This chapter (Vv. 1-86) describes thirty-six different kinds of Yantras. They are to be worn for averting evil influences, curing fever, averting the effect of Abhichāra employed by an enemy, controlling a recalcitrant wife and various other purposes.

Verses 87-110 is a hymn to the Devī Ānandamayī (Bliss) who is Shabda Brahman and Cause of the Universe.

The hymn begins by saying "O Mother ! I sing Thy praise so that thereby my words may be purified. Thou art the primordial Mother of all. Thou hast created the bodies of Brahmā, Vi*sh*n*u and Shiva and Thou dost create, maintain and withdraw into Thyself the three worlds." Again the hymn says (V. 91) that though the Devī is the first of all (preceded creation) yet She is in the first flush of Her youth ; though She is the daughter of the rocky Mountain (Himālaya) yet is She soft (kind) ; though She is the Mother of the Vedas, She is not seen by them ; though meditated upon, She is beyond the scope of the mind. It is again said (V. 102) that Shiva not satisfied with looking at and admiring Her with two eyes created in the excess of his adoration a third eye on his forehead the more fully to see the beauty of Her thighs.

CHAPTER XXV.

This chapter deals with Yoga. It begins by saying (Vv. 1—3) that according to Vedānta the union of Jīva and Ātmā is Yoga ; according to the Shaivas, the knowledge of the oneness of Shiva and Ātmā is Yoga ; according to the Uttarāmnāya the realisation of the inseprateness of Shiva and Shakti is Yoga. The dualistic Vai*sh*n*avas and others say that the knowledge of the Purā*n*apuru*sh*a is Yoga.

Purā*n*apuru*sh*a, according to the dualistic Vai*sh*n*ava, is Puru*sh*ottama ; Sānkhya says it is Puru*sh*a ; Naiyāyikas say it is Īshvara.

The first thing, the aspirant for Yoga has to do, is (V.4) to conquer the six enemies, namely, Kāma (Desire for sexual and other enjoyment), Krodha (Urge to injure), Lobha (Thirst for wealth and the like), Moha (Ignorance of the Real, the Tattva), Mada (Pride of birth, wealth, learning and the like), Matsara (Envy).

These can be conquered by (V. 5) the eight limbs

(Angas) of Yoga. These are Yama, Niyama, Āsana, Prā*n*āyāma, Pratyāhāra, Dhāra*n*ā, Dhyāna and Samādhi.

Yama, it is said (V. 7.), consists of Ahimsā (Disinclination to injure), Satya (Avoidance of untruth), Asteya (Disinclination to steal), Brahmacharya (Disinclination for sexual enjoyment), K*ri*pā (Compassion), Ārjava (Guilelessness), Ks*h*amā (Absence of anger towards an aggressor), Dh*ri*ti (Imperturbability), Mitāhāra (Restriction of food to just what is needed for the preservation of the body), Shaucha (External purity leading to purity of disposition).

Rāghava cites texts which explain these more fully. He says that by Ahimsā and Brahmacharya, Kāma is vanquished ; and by K*ri*pā and Ks*h*amā, Krodha. By the practice of Asteya, Satya and Ārjava, Lobha is killed. Mitāhāra and Shaucha destroy Moha. By Ks*h*amā and Ārjava is Mada destroyed. Ahimsā, K*ri*pā, Ārjava and Ks*h*amā destroy Matsara.

Niyama comprises (V. 8.) Tapas (Penance), Santos*h*a (Contentment), Āstikya (Belief in a future life leading to the practice of Dharma), Dāna (Charity according to one's means for discharging debts due to the Devas, Pit*ri*s and Manus*h*yas), Devapūjana (Worship of the Is*ht*a-devatā : Form of the Brahman adopted by the Sādhaka), Siddhānta-shrava*n*a (Listening to the teachings of the Upanis*h*ads and other Shāstras), Hrī (Aversion towards low and wicked pursuits), Mati (Discrimination), Japa (Recitation of Mantra with concentration in manner enjoined by the Guru), and Homa.

Verses 9 to 15 describe the five Āsanas, namely, Padma, Svastika, Vajra, Bhadra and Vīra.

Verses 16-22 describe Prā*n*āyāma and its different stages.

Verses 23 defines Pratyāhāra to be the restraint of the senses from the objects thereof.

Verses 24 and 25 describe Dhāra*n*ā. Shortly it means the restraint of the vital air (Prā*n*a-vāyu) in different part of the Sādhaka's system.

This is fully explained by Rāghava by citing a text from Vashi*shth*a Samhitā.

Dhyāna means (V. 26) meditation on the Sādhaka's own I*sht*a-devatā as the Ātmā, with mind unperturbed and immersed in his own Chaitanya.

Samādhi (V. 27) is the constant realisation of the oneness of the Jīvātmā and the Paramātmā.

After saying (V. 28.) that the length of a man's body is 96 fingers' width of his own fingers and that in the human frame are both Shiva and Shakti or as some say both Fire and Moon or as others say both Semen and Blood, the text proceeds to describe Ku*nd*alinī Yoga.

The Nā*d*īs and Chakras are (Vv. 29 – 32) described as in the *Shat*chakra-nirūpa*n*a (*vide* Arthur Avalon's 'Serpent Power').

In speaking of the Chakras or Ādhāras the author says (V. 33.) that there is a difference of opinion as to the number of the same. Verse 34 speaks of the Nā*d*īs.

Rāghava states that some say that there are twelve Chakras, others that there are sixteen and others again, that they are many. He cites some texts in support of this.

Verses 35-38 say that Ku*nd*alinī abides in the Mūlādhāra and resting on the Hamsa*h* unites with the Paramātmā. Hamsa*h* rests on vital breath (Prā*n*a-vāyu).

Verses 39-47 describe how and when the Sādhaka should sit and begin his practices and how he should proceed. Particular attention is drawn to the necessity for the Yogī to know which of the Bhūtas (Elements) is dominant in his system at the time.

Verses 48, 49 speak of the manifestation in the inner consciousness of the Yogī of the ten kinds of Dvani (Sound).

The different sounds are the same as in the Hamsopani*sh*at cited by Rāghava.

Verses 50-53 speak of the origin of the Pra*n*ava. It is here shown how the Pra*n*ava is immanent in the Ajapā

(Hamsa*h*) Mantra which is both male and female—Ham being male (Pum) and Sa*h*, female (Prak*ri*ti).

Verse 54 describes Pra*n*ava. It is supreme Bliss and ever is. It is Chaitanya or Jnāna and inseparate from Ātmā.

Verses 55-57 speak of the ineffable Ku*t*astha Brahman. He is far beyond the word of the Vedas. From him emanate the Shāstras. He is self-manifest, Bliss itself and Light itself. He is Truth and beyond all arguments, the source of the Vedas, the Cause of the Universe, spread over all that is moving and motionless and without compare. He is the innermost Chaitanya. The Sun, Fire and Moon are his body as He is Light (Prakāsha). He is seen by the Yogīs whose senses are controlled. He is realised by the seven parts of the Pra*n*ava. He is immeasurable. The Upani*sh*ads lead up to Him. He is Samvit all-spreading, unchanging and imperishable. He is the transcendent Tejas the massive nectar of Bliss. [The text has the neuter pronoun].

All that has here been said of the Kū*t*astha or Nirgu*n*a Brahman do not describe but merely point towards him.

For the benefit of those who cannot apprehend and worship the Nirgu*n*a or attributeless Brahman, verses 58-61 speak of the worship of the Brahman in his creative and other aspects as preparatory steps towards it. As such He is Hira*n*ya-garbha, variegated Light, Source of the three (Brahmā, Vi*sh*nu and Shiva), the Seed of the Vedas and other Shāstras, the Chaitanya in the region of the Sun, the Puru*sh*a no bigger than the thumb (Angu*shth*a-mātra Puru*sh*a). He is again described as resting on the Great serpent Ananta (Bhujanga-bhoga) in the ocean of milk. He is united with Kamalā (Lak*sh*mī), dark like collyrium with lotus-like eyes, the bridge between Dharma and Adharma (Dvivara*n*a) and so on. Meditation on the Pra*n*ava as one with the body of Shiva is the highest form of image worship.

The inner meaning of Bhujanga bhoga or Ananta-bhoga is different from what is popularly understood. Bhujanga or

Ananta means the Brahman who is endless. He who enjoys (Bhungkte) this Ananta is Ananta-bhoga. The sense is that the Brahman with attributes emanates from and rests on the attributeless Brahman.

Verses 62, 63 speak first of Sabīja Yoga. It is said that Ku*nd*alinī is Pi*nd*a which means lumped up, A. U. M. and is therefore the Pra*n*ava. She is Shiva (Shivātmā). Hamsa*h*, the inner self (Antarātmā) of all, is her place (Pada). Bindu is the form (Rūpa) of limitless lustre. The union of Shiva and Shakti is beyond form. Sādhakas when they go beyond this world of forms to the apprehension of the Union of Ku*nd*alinī with Shiva attain Sāyujya Mukti. When everything is dissolved in Shiva who ever is, and nothing is desired, it is Nirbīja Yoga. This is Sārūpya Mukti.

Verses 64-79 describe Rāja Yoga which is effected by meditation on Ku*nd*alinī whereby the Ātmā is realised.

Ku*nd*alinī (V. 64), when she wakes up and moves from the Mūlādhāra upward like a flash of lightning along the channel of Sus*h*umnā, pierces the six Chakras as she goes upward and when she reaches the Sahasrāra, she unites with her Lord, Para Shiva. Then she returns to her own abode in the Mūlādhāra.

Verses 65-72 give some attributes indicative of the subtle and transcendent nature of Ku*nd*alinī and a description of her progress to the Sahasrāra and end by saying that though, for the purposes of Sādhanā, she is endowed with attributes she cannot be known by them, she can only be meditated upon (Dhyeyā na vedyā gu*n*ai*h*).

Verses 73-76 contain a hymn to Ku*nd*alinī intended further to stimulate the Sādhaka's earnestness for Yoga. It is said (V. 73) when she goes up shining like lightning the lotuses on her path put on a smiling appearance gladdened by the charm of her presence.

Verses 77-82 contains a Dhyāna of Ku*nd*alinī. In this further details of her progress upward is given.

Verse 77 says that the letters of the alphabet, as also the

Shaktis, *D*ākinī and others, the Devas, Brahmā and others are in the six Chakras. Verse 78 says that when Ku*n*d*a*linī moves up like a streak of lightning, she unites with the three Shivas, Svayambhu in the Mūlādhāra, Vā*n*a in the Anāhata and Itara in the Ājnā Chakra. The three coils of Ku*nd*alinī are the three Gu*n*as,—Sattva, Rajas, Tamas.

In Verse 82 it is said that the Yogī gets the fruit of Yoga when with his senses perfectly controlled and his Dhī (higher unerring mind) absolutely immobile, he places his own Ātmā in the Parashiva who is the void not limited by space and time, the mere Chaitanya and in whom the five Kāra*n*as are dissolved.

The five Kāra*n*as or causes of any action, Rāghava says, are,—Upādāna, Samavāyi, Nimitta, Prayojaka, Sahakāri.

The proofs were in part read by Sj. Haridāsa Mitra, M.A. and partly by Sj. Panchānana Sānkhya-Vyākara*n*atīrtha.

April 1933 A.S.

Note on the first Chapter

by Sj. Jnanendra Lal Majumdar.

"I shall speak the beneficial Sāradatilaka which is the essence of the Tantras, the first cause for the attainment of Dharma, Artha, Kāma and Moksa (religious merit, wealth, desire and liberation)". With this introduction (1. 4), the author, Laksmana, begins the book, a compendium of Tantras extant in his time, and in 25 chapters deals with the theory and practice of Tantrik worship. As the Tantra Shāstra is preeminently a practical Shāstra dealing with Upāsanā or worship of the Deity with rites, Mantras and Yoga, the author has devoted only a small chapter, the first, to the philosophy underlying the practice.

The philosophy of the Tantra.

2. "Eternal Shiva should be known as Nirguna and Saguna. Nirguna is dissociated from Prakriti and Saguna is associated with Prakriti" (1. 6). Thus, in the beginning, there were two ultimate principles, Shiva and Prakriti, the principle of consciousness and the principle of unconsciousness. This looks like Sānkhya dualism, but it is not so. For in Sankhya unconscious Prakriti is the Cause and there is no room for God or Ishvara. Nor is it the dualism of the Yoga system of Patanjali, for therein an individual, enjoying freedom from the troubles of the world, is the Ishvara, and Prakriti is the cause. Here (1. 7), however, "the supreme Ishvara who is rich in the wealth of Sat (Existence)-Chit (Consciousness)-Ananda (Bliss) and associated with Prakriti", is the cause. (Light is a better rendering of Chit than Consciousness, and perhaps Life is a better word for Sat than Existence.) It is, therefore, a form of monism in which Shiva is dissociated from and associated with Prakriti (nirgunah sagunashcha). This Shiva cannot be the ultimate principle of absolute consciousness as conceived in Shankara's monism in which the principle of consciousness or Brahma is the only reality, Prakriti and its products being really unreal, and even Ishvara or creator God vanishes in moksha or ultimate dissolution ("Īshvarasturīyagrāsah"-Nrisimhatāpanī Upanisad). Verse I speaks of one Shiva, and not two Shivas, dissociated from and associated with Prakriti. Hence he cannot be identified with Brahma of Shankara's philosophy who is never associated with Prakriti, the unreality. It cannot also be said that the association of Brahma with Prakriti is the view-point of the ignorant Jīva, for here the author is enunciating the first principle in his system of philosophy and presenting an ideal for attainment

by Tāntrik Sādhakas. At least in the absence of further elucidation by the author himself we cannot be justified in identifying his Saguṇa-Nirguṇa Shiva with the Nirguṇa Brahma of Shankara's philosophy. Moreover, it should be considered that Tantra being preeminently an upāsanā shāstra cannot hold up Nirguṇa Brahma, who is in no way associated with the fiction of creation, as the object of upāsanā. Upāsanā must, somehow, be theistic.

3. The authority for such a view of monism may be found in such texts of Shruti as,—

"te dhyānayogānugatā āpashyan devātmashakting svaguṇairnigūḍhām" (Shvetāshvatara Upaniṣad 1, 3)—Rapt in meditative concentration they saw the self-energy (ātma-shakti) of the Divinity hidden by its potencies (guṇas) ;

"māyāng tu prakṛiting vidyān māyinang tu maheshvaram" (*Ibid* IV, 10) —Māyā should be known as Prakṛiti and the Māyī [the lord of of Māyā) as Maheshvara (great Ishvara) ;

"sa vishvakṛidvishvavidātmayonirjnaḥ kālakāla guṇī sarvavit" (*Ibid* VI, 16)—He is the maker of the universe, the knower of the universe, Himself His own cause, the sentient, the death of Death (or time), the possessor of guṇas (potencies), the cogniser of all.

4. The association of the Divinity with Prakṛiti or Māyā is pithily put forth in the Gītā,—"daivī hyeṣā guṇamayī mama māyā duratyayā" (Bhagavad-Gīta VII, 14)—this Divine Māyā of mine, consisting of guṇas (potencies), is difficult to surpass.

5. Indeed all sects of Upāsakas, the treaders of the path of Bhakti principally, seem to have idealised a form of Divinity in which the Supreme, who is all consciousness, is associated with unconscious creative energy for the purpose of creation which is His sport (līlā), maintaining at the same time His own purity and blissfulness. According to the dualistic Vaiṣṇavas, He is ever saguṇa, possessed of infinite inscrutable potencies, the nirguṇa aspect being only a passive phase in His creative manifestation or emanation. He is the infinite God with infinite expansion out of whom an infinite number of atomic Jīvas have been flung out as pawns in His divine Sport of Love, ever remaining distinct from Him but finding their summum bonum in their service of Him in His kingdom of Heaven. According to the Shāktas He is saguṇa as the Creator and nirguṇa as the Liberator, all Jīvas being, on liberation, merged in the infinitude of His eternal Being. He is both saguṇa and nirguṇa, neither saguṇa nor nirguṇa, beyond all guṇas but still of them. Between Him, the Shiva, and the Jīva, there is only the bar of the bonds of individuality (Jīvahood). The Jīva, when he has thrown off this bondage, becomes Shiva, "Pāshabaddho bhavejjīvaḥ pāshamukto maheshvaraḥ".

6. Saguṇa Shiva, "rich in the wealth of Existence or Being, Consciousness and Bliss", is the Self-sufficient (svatantra, svayampūrṇa) energised conscious Being out of whom creation is evolved. He is both the material and the efficient cause of the creation. The first steps of the evolution are as follows—

Table I (verses 7-16)

Saguna Shiva (energised consciousness)
|
Shakti (conscious energy)
|
Nāda (conscious energy in undifferentiated vibration)
|
Para Bindu
or
Shabda—Brahma (conscious energy in undifferentiated consolidation)

Bindu (differentiated conscious energy = Shiva)	Bīja (differentiated conscious energy = Shakti, the seed of creation)	Nāda (the resultant conscious energy in vibration due to the coalescence of Bindu and Bīja)
Rudra = Ichchhāshakti (volition energy) called Fire, representing Tamas guna.	Visnu = Jnāna Shakti (cognition energy) called Sun, representing Sattva guna.	Brahmā = Kriyā Shakti (action energy) called Moon, representing Rajas guna.

7. This is a creative evolution, without any vikāra or diversifying change, in Saguna Shiva, caused by His will (Ishvara-chodita). In Him, the infinite energised conscious Being, there awakes, first of all, conscious energy, the Shakti or Mahāmāyā who is the Mother of the world and with whom He is one. This Shakti or, rather, Shiva-Shakti, rouses in Herself a cosmic creative vibration, not yet gathered in diversified centres, and is called Nāda This infinite undifferentiated conscious vibratory energy becomes next somewhat consolidated (ghanībhūta), that is, attains a state of imminent differentiation (vyākaranonmukhatā).. This is called Para (supreme) Bindu. He is more significantly called Shabda-Brahma, the universal conscious sound, the cosmic toll in which shape Saguna Shiva, the Parameshvara, rings out the creation as an endless diversity of conscious energy. (It should be remembered that mass and energy are interchangeable according to modern science). In the individual living being it is the Kundalinī energy. Shabda—Brahma is the first creative aspect of the Great God out of which evolve the differentiations of conscious energy in three forms, namely Bindu, the parent of will or volition, Bīja, the parent of perception or cognition, and Nāda, the parent of action which springs out of a combination of cognition and volition. (Cf. Parāsya shaktirvividhaiva shrūyate Svābhāvikī jnānavalakriyā cha. Shvetāshvatara Up. VI. 8). In volition there is the play of desire, born of ignorance. In it, therefore, Tamas, that is, the blinding potency (guna) of Prakriti, pre-

dominates. In cognition there is the light of knowledge. In it Sattva, the revealing or enlightening potency of Prakriti, predominates. And in action Rajas, the active or exciting potency of Prakriti, predominates. They represent Rudra, Visnu and Brahmā, the Destroyer, the Preserver and the Creator, of Hindu theology, the differentiated triple aspect of Parama Shiva or Mahāmāyā or Shabda-Brahma who are one.

8. Out of Para Bindu or Shabda-Brahma evolves the endless diversified creation, with which we are acquainted, from the subtlest conscious energy, Mahat or intelligence, to the grossest energy constituting the physical world which seems to be entirely devoid of consciousness, though we have no right to say that it is really so. The following table (Table II) gives the order :—

Table II (verses 17—26)

Para Bindu or Shabda—Brahma
|
Mahat (intelligence)
|
Ahangkāra (egoism ; I—sense)

- (The 10 senses—5 senses of perception and 5 senses of action—are considered as conscious energies, their consciousness aspects being the presiding deities of their unconscious energy aspects, the sense or nerve powers which are the karanas or instruments of their presiding deities.)
  - The deities presiding over the senses, 10 in number (sāttvika)
  - The senses (indriyas), 10 in number
- The Tanmātras, 5 in number, which are the subtle principles of solidity, fluidity, luminosity, vitality and spatiality.

Akāsha (space)	Shabda Tanmātra (sound or spatiality)
Vāyu (life or vital air)	Sparsha Tanmātra (touch or vitality)
Tejas (fire or light)	Rūpa Tanmātra (form or luminosity)
Apa (the waters, liquid and gaseous fluids)	Rasa Tanmātra (taste or fluidity)
Ksiti (earth)	Gandha Tanmātra (smell or solidity)

The original (verse 18) speaks of 10 presiding deities, but Rāghava Bhaṭṭa, following the Sānkhya classification, explains Ka as referring to both Prajāpati, the deity presiding over the sexual organs, and Moon (Chandra), the deity presiding over mind, thus making the number of deities and of the senses eleven, with mind as the 11th sense. But as the text runs, we should rather include mind in Mahat as a phase of the inner sense (Antaḥkaraṇa, verse 17).

9. From Shabda-Brahma or the conscious cosmic sound, the conscious cosmic energy stirred up to the point of diversifying creative potentiality, evolves Mahat or cosmic intelligence, from the Mahat, Ahangkāra or cosmic feeling as I, one universal ego out of which the diversified world of subjects and objects is to evolve, the samaṣṭi Puruṣa comprehending in Himself the world of subjects and objects.

The fulfilment of the "I"—sense, necessitated by the creative urge, comes from the evolution, out of it, of the subject as the cogniser and actor, the object as the cognised and the instruments of cognition and action. Hence evolve the universal deities presiding over the universal indriyas for the cognition of the universal objects, the sense-gods, the senses and the objects of the senses, all out of the universal Ahangkāra. As regards the objects of the senses, Hindu Philosophy has never recognised any essential differences between them. They are all of the same origin, differing only in the degree of cohesion or consolidation and thus giving rise to different distinctive properties cognised by the different senses. They are all manifestations of energy and in their subtle forms are characters rather than matters with characters and are hence called Tanmātrās or Tanmātras (*tat*-that, *mātra*- only), things in their essential character. The subtlest of the Tanmātras is Shabda (sound), a mere vibration or pulsation of energy. From it evolves, in the grosser scale, Akāsha or space, the seat of all material vibrations. The next of the Tanmātras, evolving out of Shabda, is Sparsha (touch), the character which constitutes the root of all perceptions, for all perceptions are primarily the feelings of touch of the perceiver with the objects perceived. It is the vitality or life-principle underlying all perceptions. Out of it evolves, in the grosser field, Vāyu, or vital airs, which in the material body, constitutes its life.

10. The word Vāyu is generally taken to mean the physical air, probably because the presence of air is generally proved by sparsha or touch only. But it is doubtful whether even the ancients could consider the physical air as a subtler matter than light or heat. Moreover, the Rig Veda speaks of the āpa (the waters, as they are usually but perhaps incorrectly translated) as being both water and air. For, the heavenly bodies, the sun and the moon are said to be moving in currents of āpa, certainly meaning thereby currents of physical air which, they thought, pervaded all space (1). The sun is called apāngnapāt,

(1) Cf. Rigveda I, 23, 17 ; VII, 49, 4 ; VII, 85, 3 ; II, 35, 4 ; VII, 30, 4 where celestial waters are spoken of.

that is, the son of āpa (2). Hence āpa would include all fluids, both liquid and gaseous. From such considerations I have taken Vāyu to mean the vital airs, the life-principle of the senses which function through sparsha or touch. In the Upaniṣads the senses or indriyas are called prāṇas (modes of life), and Vāyu is prāṇa, The indriyas are the shaktis of perception, the prāṇas underlying it, and Vāyu constitutes these shaktis or prāṇas. Again, the Chhāndogya Upaniṣad speaks of the physical world as constituted of tejas, āpa and anna (fire, the waters and food or earth) (3). This tripartite (trivṛit) constitution of the physical world can never be complete without air, for even a barbarian will say that air is a necessary constituent of it. Commentators, therefore, who consider Vāyu to mean air, have been obliged to consider the Chhāndogya statement as incomplete and seek to supplement it by statements from the Bṛihadāraṇyaka and other Upaniṣads which speak of the creation of Akāsha and Vāyu before the creation of Tejas. But the proper view should, I think, be to divide the five—Akāsha, Vāyu, Tejas, Apa and Kṣiti—into two groups, placing Akāsha and Vāyu in one group, and Tejas, Apa and Kṣiti in the other, so that the principles of space and vitality may be separated from the principles of heat, light, fluidity and solidity of which the material world, as we call it, is constituted. And this is what the Chhāndogya Upaniṣad seems to have done.

11. From the Sparsha-Tanmātra evolves the Rūpa Tanmātra, the principle of visibility or luminosity, which gives the visible appearance (rūpa) to objects, and from it evolves, in the grosser scale, heat and light (tejas). The next in order is Rasa-Tanmātra or the principle of fluidity which gives to every object its distinctive rasa or taste and from which evolve all liquids and gases. The last is the Gandha-Tanmātra, the principle of solidity which has the distinctive characteristic of smell, it was supposed, and out of which the solid earth is evolved.

12. These five, Bhūtas (existents) as they are called, are forms of Shakti or energy. The energy in Akāsha (space) is called Shāntyatitā, the Very Quiescent. The energy in Vāyu (vital air) is Shānti, the Quiescent. That in Tejas (heat & light) is Vidyā, the Enlightener. That in Apa (the fluids) is Pratiṣṭhā, the Stay. And that in Kṣiti (Earth) is called Nivṛitti, the Final. All these evolve from Nāda, the conscious energy in vibration which is personified in Brahmā, the Creator or Kriyāshakti (action-energy) who is the resultant of the coalescence of Rudra, the Ichchhā-shakti (volition-energy), and Viṣṇu, the Jnāna-shakti (cognition-energy). See Table I.

13. Here ends the order of universal creative evolution by the will of God. The involution is in the reverse order, says Raghava Bhaṭṭa.

14. "All this world, consisting of moving and non-moving things, is

(2) R. V. II, 35 ; I, 22, 6 : VI, 50, 13 ; VII, 34, 15 ; VII, 9, 3 ; X, 2, 7 ; X, 30, 4.

(3) Chhāndogya Up. VI, 2, 3-4.

composed of the five Bhūtas (existents, Ksiti, Apa, Tejas, Vāyu and Akāsha). Many are the forms into which non-moving things are divided such as rocks, plants and so forth. Moving things, however, are divided into three classes, namely, those which are born out of secretions or heat (svedaja), those which are born out of eggs (a*nd*aja) and those which are born out of the womb (jarāyuja). Man belongs to this last class of jarāyujas (uterines)." (Verses 27-29). It should be noted that things are divided into moving and non-moving things and not into living and non-living things. The Hindus have always known plants to be living although non-moving and have always been averse to classify any objects as absolutely non-living. They have rather the idea that there is life or sensation in every thing, however much obscure or crude it may be. Everything in the universe, they suppose, is made up of a conscious factor and an unconscious factor, the conscious factor manifesting itself as the living subject capable of sensation and the unconscious factor manifesting itself as the object of sensation through sight, touch and so forth. This point has been tersely put by Hindu philosophers as "d*r*ishyatvāt jadatvam", the fact of being unconscious comes from the fact of being an object of perception. Thus such parts of a man as are capable of being seen, heard, touched, tasted or smelt, or becoming in any way objects of perception make up the unconscious factor in him and the part of him which can perceive the sensations of sight and so forth is his conscious factor. And it is the blending of these two, the conscious factor and the unconscious factor, which constitutes life. The world is evolved out of energised consciousness, Sagu*n*a or Sakala Shiva, that is, consciousness in intimate association with Gu*n*a or Prak*r*iti or unconsciousness. Hence no part of it is absolutely devoid of consciousness, as no part of it is absolutely devoid of unconsciousness. And through this intimate association of the two there is life or sensibility everywhere, whether we detect it or not.

15. Into the womb enters a Bindu (drop) which is male, female or neuter and a combination of ovum and sperm, "and then an ātmā controlled by the chain of nescience in consonance with previous karma assumes jīvahood (the state of individualised existence) therein (in the Bindu)" (verse 31). The Bindu is surely not the spirit that inhabits it. But the question is, how did the spirit come to inhabit it? Was the spirit in the sperm or was it in the ovum or was it in neither but came later to the body built in the womb? The Shruti leans to the idea that it was in the sperm (vide Panchagnividyā, the science of Five Fires, in Chhāndogya and B*r*ihadāra*n*yaka Upanisads). But the author here seems to hold the idea that it is after the sperm and the ovum have combined to form a Bindu or drop-like substance, the blastosphere, or cytula (as Hæckel calls it), of physiology, that the spirit comes to reside in it. But what again is this spirit (ātmā) that comes to reside in the Bindu that enters into the womb to develop into the future body of the individual? Is it the ātmā who is consciousness itself and eternal and with whom there is no such thing as being born or dying? Or, is it the jivātmā, the consciousness

of life, that is, the conciousness that illumines the mind or subtle body which re-incarnates from gross body to gross body, thus suffering life and death ? Raghava Bha*tt*a, the commentator, thinks that here the appearance of an eternal ātmā has been spoken of in accordance with the Sānkhya conception of multiplicity of eternal ātmās, and considers such an ātmā "as entering a body as one enters a house". But an eternal ātmā, though one of many such ātmas according to Sānkhya, is infinite and inactive (ni*s*kriya) at the same time. Hence it is almost meaningless to say that such an ātmā enters a body and assumes jīvahood therein, if he was not already a jīva there. More probably what the author here means to say is that the jīvātmā, who was, according to Shruti, sleeping in the sperm in the father's body, awakes, in the mother's womb, to assume the burdens jīvahood in the fertilised egg.

16. In the womb the Bindu is nourished by the food taken by the mother and grows into a body complete with all necessary paraphernalia, and at last the child is born into sunlight. It is the belief of all Hindus, a belief that has come down from the days of the Upani*s*ads, that the jīva in the matured foetus is enlightened about his past karma, sorely grieves for the karma that binds him to the wheel of life and death and makes up his mind to undo this karma by meritorious karma in his present life on earth. But the pain of birth makes him unconscious and brings about a total forgetfulness of all this, The author here also echoes this idea.

17. It has been said before that Para Bindu or Shabda-Brahma, the undiversified infinite conscious energy, out of whom evolves the diversified world of subjects and objects, appears in the individual body as Ku*nd*alinī shakti or conscious spiral energy. She is the concious creative energy, the Mother of all things that constitute the individual, the world of Shabda and Artha in him. Shabda is the vibration which gradually becomes language and ultimately issues out of the vocal organs as articulate sound. An Artha is the conceptual counterpart of a Shabda which has first a mental shape or thought-form and ultimately assumes the form of an object perceptible to any of the senses or the mind.

सूचीपत्रम्

* टीकोक्तविषयाः ।

विषया:	पृष्ठाङ्क:

द्वितीय: पटल:

विषय	पृष्ठाङ्क:

तृतीय: पटल:

चतुर्थः पटलः

पञ्चमः पटलः

षष्ठः पटलः

सप्तमः पटलः

दशम: पटल:

एकादश: पटल:

द्वादशः पटलः

त्रयोदशः पटलः

चतुर्दशः पटलः

षोडशः पटलः

सप्तदशः पटलः

अष्टादशः पटलः

ऊनविंशः पटलः

द्वाविंशः पटलः

पञ्चविंशः पटलः

शारदातिलकम् ।

प्रथमः पटलः ।

नित्यानन्दवपु र्निरन्तरगलत्पञ्चाशदर्णैः क्रमाद्
व्याप्तं येन चराचरात्मकमिदं शब्दार्थरूपं जगत् ।
शब्दब्रह्म यदूचिरे सुकृतिन श्चैतन्यमन्तर्गतं
तद्वोऽव्यादनिशं शशाङ्कसदनं वाचामधीशं महः ॥१

श्रीकण्ठं निजताण्डवप्रवणतामोदाप्तमोदोदयं
पश्यन्त्याः कुतुकाद्भुतप्रियतया सञ्जातभावं मुहुः ।
मन्दान्दोलितदुग्धसिन्धुलहरी लीलालसं लोचन-
प्रान्तालोकनमातनोतु भवतां भूतिं भवान्याः शुभम् ॥

संसेव्यमानमृषिभिः सनकादिमुख्यै
र्योगिन गम्यमविनश्वरमादिभूतम् ।
संसारहृन्निगमसारविचारसारं
शैवं महो मनसि मे मुदमादधातु ॥

भद्राय भवतां भूयाद् भारती भक्तिभाविता ।
स्मृतेरुज्जृम्भते यस्या वाग्विलासोऽतिदुर्लभः ॥
शारदातिलके तन्त्रे गुरूणामुपदेशतः ।
पदार्थादर्शटीकेयं राघवेण विरच्यते ॥
सम्प्रदायागतं किञ्चिद् गणितागमसम्भवम् ।
यदुक्तमत्र तत् सन्तो विचारयितुमर्हथ ॥
पिशुनो दूषकश्चेत् स्यान्न तद्दोषाय दूषणम् ।
दोषावहा हि विकृतिर्न स्वभावो हि दुस्त्यजः ॥

अथेश्वरः सर्व्वा अपि श्रुतीर्भवपाशबद्धानां जन्तूनां स्वर्गाय मुक्तये च समुपदिशति स्म । अन्येषां तु स्मृतिशास्त्रादीनां तन्मूलकत्वेन तदर्थप्रतिपादकत्वेन च प्रामाण्यमिति सुप्रसिद्धतरम् । अस्यास्त्वागमस्मृतेः कथं तन्मूलकत्वम् ।

अन्यच्च तैरेव विशेषेण पर्य्यालोचितैः स्वर्गो वा मुक्तिरपि भविष्यतीति किमनयेति प्राप्ते ब्रूमः। "स ऐक्षत बहु स्यां प्रजायेय" इति। तथा च "यतो वा इमानि भूतानि जायन्ते येन जातानि जीवन्ति यत् प्रयन्त्यभिसंविशन्ति तद्विजिज्ञासस्व" इत्युपक्रम्य "आनन्दाद्ध्येव खल्विमानि भूतानि जायन्ते आनन्देन जातानि जीवन्ति आनन्दं प्रयन्त्यभिसंविशन्ति" इत्यादि। "इदं सर्व्वं यदयमात्मा एव" इत्यन्तेनोपसंहृतम्। अथ—

उपक्रमोपसंहारावभ्यासोऽपूर्व्वताफलम्।
अर्थवादोपपत्ती च लिङ्गं तात्पर्य्यनिर्णये॥

इत्युक्तत्वादुपक्रमोपसंहाराभ्यां स्वलीलारूपानाद्यनिर्वाच्याविद्यासहायसम्पन्नं परमानन्दस्वरूपं नित्यशुद्धबुद्धस्वभावं परब्रह्मैव स्वात्मविवर्त्तरूपं सकलं जगत् ससर्जेति श्रुतिवाक्यप्रतिपादितोऽर्थः। नन्वस्तु जगत्सृष्टिकर्त्तृत्वं ब्रह्मणः अनाद्यविद्याङ्गीकरणं किमर्थम् इति चेन्न। तया विना असङ्गस्य तस्य कारणत्वानुपपत्तेः। तथैममर्थं श्रुत्यागमावपि वदतः। "इन्द्रो मायाभिः पुरुरूप ईयते" इति। "शिवो हि शक्तिरहितः शक्तः कर्त्तुं न किञ्चन" इति। एवं जाते जगति निजकर्म्मपाशबद्धा जन्तवोऽनात्मज्ञा उत्पत्तिमरणप्रवाहपतिता नाशक्नुवन् संसारसिन्धुं तरीतुम्। एवम्भूतान् तानवलोक्य परमकारुणतया किञ्चिदुपाधिविशिष्टः सर्व्वाः श्रुतीः समुपदिशति स्म। तत्र सर्व्वासु श्रुतिषु काण्डत्रयं कर्म्मोपासनाब्रह्मभेदेन। तत्र कर्म्मकाण्डं जैमिनिप्रभृतिभिः सम्यक्तया विवृतम्। इदमुपासनाकाण्डं नारदादिभिः ब्रह्मकाण्डं भगवद्व्यासादिभिरपि। श्रुतिमूलकताऽस्य प्रत्यक्षोपलब्धश्रुतिमूलकता अप्रत्यक्षोपलब्धश्रुतिमूलकता च। रामपूर्व्वोत्तरतापनीय-नृसिंहपूर्व्वोत्तरतापनीय-सौराष्टाक्षर-शैवपञ्चाक्षरात्मिका तु साक्षात्श्रुतिरुपलभ्यत एव। तत्र कर्म्मकाण्डे सर्व्वोऽप्यधिकारी। मुमुक्षोरपि तत्त्वज्ञानपर्य्यन्तं स्वचित्तशुद्ध्यर्थं प्रत्यवायपरिहारार्थञ्च कर्म्मकरणेऽधिकारसम्भवात्। तद्वदुपासनाकाण्डेऽपि। यतः साकारोपासनातः स्वर्गादिबहुफलं भवति क्रमतो मुक्तिश्च। कर्म्मकाण्डात्तु स्वर्गादिकं बहुतरव्ययायासेन भवति। ब्रह्मकाण्डान्मुक्तिरपि आदरनैरन्तर्य्यदीर्घकालाभ्याससाध्यानेकेषु जन्मसु तादृशेषु एव गतेषु भवति। "अनेकजन्मसंसिद्धस्ततो याति परां गतिम्" इति वचनात्। अत एतदुपासनाकाण्डमेवागमशास्त्रात्मकं गरीय इति सिद्धम्। तत्रोत्पलाचार्य्यपूज्यपादशिष्यः श्रीलक्ष्मणाचार्य्यः पुर्व्वतन्त्राणामनेकेषामेकैकमन्त्रविधानकथनप्रवृत्तानामतिविततानां गम्भीराणामिदानीन्तनानामल्पबुद्धीनामल्पायुषामेकस्मिन्

सर्व्वमन्त्रविधानमभीप्सूनां पुंसामशक्त्या दुरवगाहत्वमवावलोक्यातिकृपालुः शारदातिलकं तन्त्रं चिकीर्षुश्चिकीर्षितस्याविघ्नेन समाप्त्यर्थं प्रचयगमनार्थञ्च सकलशिष्टैकवाक्यतयाऽभिमतकर्म्मारम्भसमये तत्समाप्तिकामैर्म्मङ्गलमाचरणीयमिति सदाचारानुमितश्रुतिबोधितपरदेवतानुस्मरणलक्षणं मङ्गलं शिष्यशिक्षार्थमुपनिबध्नन्नाह नित्येति । सन्नसोऽनिशं वोऽव्यादित्यन्वयः । तस्माद् एतावतैव परदेवतानुस्मरणस्य सिद्धौ सत्यामप्यस्य पदस्य यत्किञ्चित् क्रियापेक्षायां विघ्नोपशमनद्वाराऽभिलषितफलवितरणरूपावनक्रियानिर्देशेन देवतासाम्मुख्यं दर्शितम् । तत्र सामान्यकर्म्मसम्बन्धे प्राप्ते क्रियमाणस्य ग्रन्थस्य निर्व्विघ्नं पाठमभिप्रेप्सोः शिष्योपरि कृपां सूचयतो व इति कर्म्मणो निर्देशः । वो युष्मान् शिष्यानित्यर्थः । एषामेवात्र सम्बोधनयोग्यत्वात् सम्बोधनप्रधानत्वाच्च युष्मच्छब्दस्य । यतः शिष्यकृपयैव विदितवेद्य आचार्य्यो ग्रन्थकरणे प्रवृत्तः । तेषां कञ्चित्कालमवने सिद्धे स्वशिष्याणां तच्छिष्याणामपि निर्व्विघ्नं पाठसिद्ध्यसम्भवेन ग्रन्थप्रचारो न भवतीत्युक्तमनिशमिति । तथा च तेषां चिरकालावने सिद्धे स्वशिष्याणां तच्छिष्याणामपि निर्व्विघ्नं पाठसिद्धौ ग्रन्थप्रचारो भविष्यतीत्याशयः । किं तन्नस इत्यपेक्षायामाह नित्यानन्दवपुरिति । नित्यो योऽयमानन्दः स वपुर्य्यस्य एतेन शक्त्यभिन्नपरशिवस्वरूपमुक्तम् । ननु "शक्त्या विना शिवे सूक्ष्मे नाम धाम न विद्यते" इत्युक्तेर्निर्गुणस्याऽसङ्गस्य निराकारस्य तस्य कथमवनक्रियाकर्तृत्वम् इत्याह वासामधीशमिति । अनेन शक्त्युपहितं सदाशिवात्मकं रूपं वागुपदेष्टृत्वेनोक्तम् । ननु वागुपदेष्टृत्वं चतुर्मुखोपाध्युपहितस्यापि वर्त्तते तन्निवृत्त्यर्थमाह शशाङ्कसदनमिति । शशाङ्कस्य चन्द्रस्य सदनं स्थानं चन्द्रकलावतंसमित्यर्थः । शब्दसृष्टेरत्र मुख्यत्वात् मन्त्रमयं तत्स्वरूपं सूचयति । यदाभ्यामः विष्णुस्तेन सङ्कर्षणस्तेन औ एतेन सहिता निशा हकारो यत्रेत्युत्तरपदलोपो बहुव्रीहिस्तेन हाविति सिद्धम् । शशाङ्केत्यादिना बिन्दुरुक्तः । तत्र वागैश्वर्य्यमुपबृंहयन् वक्ष्यमाणां शब्दार्थसृष्टिं सूचयन् व्यापकतामाह येन चराचरात्मकमिदं स्थावरजङ्गमात्मकं शब्दार्थरूपं जगत् क्रमाद् व्याप्तम् । कैः निरन्तरगलत्पञ्चाशदर्णैः निरन्तरमनवरतं गलन्तो व्यक्तीभवन्तः पञ्चाशदर्णा वर्णास्तैः । अत्र समासे वर्णशब्दस्य वावलोपो वक्तव्य इति स्वर्णशब्द इव वलोपे अर्णशब्दो वर्णवाची । केचित्तु नित्येत्याद्यर्णैरित्यन्तमेकमेव पदमित्याहुः । अत्र वर्णानामेकपञ्चाशत्त्वेऽपि सामीप्यसम्बन्धेन लक्षणया पञ्चाशत्त्वमुक्तम् । अन्वयानुपपत्तिवत्तात्पर्य्यानुपपत्तेरपि लक्षणाबीजस्याभ्युपगतत्वात् । अथवा "मकारः पुरुषो यतः" इत्युक्तेः तस्य स्वस्वरूपत्वात्

पञ्चाशदित्युक्तिः। यद्वा च्चकारस्य क-ष संयोगात्मकत्वात् तयोरुपदेशेनैवास्योपदेश इत्यपुनरुक्तं पञ्चाशद्ग्रहणम्। यद्वा विसर्गस्य केवलं शक्तित्वात् पञ्चभूतात्मकत्वाभावात् सर्व्ववर्णोत्पत्तिहेतुत्वाच्च तं त्यक्त्वा तथोक्तिः। तदुक्तं "अमायोऽनन्त्य एव वा" इति। क्वचिद्वाह्येऽपि तावतामेवोपयोगाद्वा तथोक्तिः। यद्वा मूलाधारादि आज्ञापर्य्यन्तं षट्चक्रेषु पञ्चाशद्वर्णानामेव स्थितत्वात् पञ्चाशदित्युक्तिः। अनयोर्व्याख्यानयोः बहिरान्तरभेदेन व्यवस्था ज्ञेया। आन्तरस्य च मुख्यत्वात् शास्त्रे सर्व्वत्र मुख्येन व्यवहार इति ज्ञेयम्। अनेनान्तर्म्मातृका-न्यासोऽपि सूचितः। स चान्त्यपटले कुण्डलीप्रस्तावे स्फुटीभविष्यति। अतएव द्वितीयादिचतुर्विंशतिपटलान्तं यत् प्रपञ्चितं तत् सर्व्वं मातृकाविकार इत्यपि सूचितम्। ननु "सर्व्वव्यापी सदाशिवः" इति वक्ष्यमाणत्वात् तस्य स्वत एव सर्व्वव्यापित्वे कुतः कैरिति कारणापेक्षा इति चेत् सत्यम्। तस्य स्वत एव सर्व्वव्यापित्वं किन्तु अत्र शास्त्रे शब्दसृष्टेः मुख्यत्वद्योतनाय निरन्तरगलत्पञ्चाशद्वर्णैरिति कारणतोक्तिः। किञ्च पूर्व्वमपि यत्किञ्चिच्छक्त्युपाधिविशिष्टत्वे वक्ष्यमाणेऽस्मिन् या वाचामधीशमित्युक्तिः सा अत्रच वर्णानामर्थरूपव्यापकतोक्तिरपि। तत्र शब्द-स्वरूपमभिव्याप्य एव अर्थरूपं व्याप्नोतीति क्रमादित्युक्तिः। तेषां शब्दरूपव्यापकता सम्भवत्येव। अर्थरूपव्यापकता तु सर्व्वस्याप्यर्थस्य शब्दप्रकाश्यत्वनियमात् ज्ञेया। तदुक्तं भगवता भर्त्तृहरिणा।

न सोऽस्ति प्रत्ययो लोके यः शब्दानुगमादृते।
अनुविद्धमिदं ज्ञानं सर्व्वं शब्देन गृह्यते॥ इति।

अथवा येषां मते शब्दार्थयोरभेदस्तन्मतमालम्ब्योक्तम्। तदुक्तं तेनैव

एकस्यैवात्मनो भेदः शब्दार्थावपृथक्स्थितौ। इति।

अतएव मन्त्रदैवतयोरैक्यं मन्त्रशास्त्रे। अतएव पूर्व्वं सदाशिवमन्त्रोद्धारः।

यद्वा शक्तिसम्भिन्नत्वात्तस्य शक्त्यंशत्वेन शब्दरूपव्यापकत्वं शिवांशत्वेन अर्थरूप-व्यापकत्वं ज्ञेयम्। तदुक्तं वायवीयसंहितायाम्

शब्दजातमशेषन्तु धत्ते शङ्करवल्लभा।
अर्थस्वरूपमखिलं धत्ते मुग्धेन्दुशेखरः॥ इति।

एतत्पक्षे तृतीया उपलक्षणत्वेन ज्ञेया। उपलक्षणत्वन्तु तदुत्पन्नत्वात्तेषाम्। शब्दसृष्टिप्राधान्यमेवोपबृंहयन्नाह—सुकृतिनो यदन्तर्गतं चैतन्यं शब्दब्रह्म इत्यूचिरे। सुकृतिनस्तत्त्वज्ञा इत्यर्थः। "चैतन्यं सर्व्वभूतानां शब्दब्रह्मेति

मे मतिः" इति वक्ष्यमाणत्वात् । तस्य सर्व्वव्यापित्वात् तदंशस्यैव सर्व्वजन्तु-चैतन्यरूपत्वात् शुद्धब्रह्मणः शब्दब्रह्मत्वं सम्भवत्येव । किञ्च यस्माद् बिन्दोः शब्दब्रह्मण उत्पत्तिस्तस्मादेव बिन्दोः सदाशिवस्याप्युत्पत्तिरित्यपि सम्भवति । तत्र शब्दसृष्टौ शब्दब्रह्मेत्युक्तिः अर्थसृष्टौ सदाशिव इति परं विशेषः ।

भिद्यमानात् पराद्बिन्दोरव्यक्तात्मा रवोऽभवत् ।
शब्दब्रह्मेति तं प्राहुः सर्व्वागमविशारदाः ॥
अथ बिन्द्वात्मनः शम्भोः कालबन्धोः कलात्मनः ।
अजायत जगत्साक्षी सर्व्वव्यापी सदाशिवः ॥

इति वक्ष्यमाणत्वात् । अथवा हेतु-हेतुमद्भावेन योजना कार्य्या । यतः श्रुतिनः यत् अन्तर्गतं चैतन्यं शब्दब्रह्म इत्यूचिरे अतो येन निरन्तरगलत्पद्माशदर्णैः जगत् व्याप्तमिति ।

ततः प्राप्य कुण्डलीरूपं प्राणिनां देहमध्यगम् ।
वर्णात्मनाऽऽविर्भवति गद्यपद्यादिभेदतः ॥

इति वक्ष्यमाणत्वात् ।

अन्ये त्वन्यथा योजयन्ति । यत् परमशिवस्वरूपं श्रुतिनो वेदान्तिनः तत् शब्देन ब्रह्म इत्यूचिरे । अयमर्थः । अस्माभिः परमशिव इत्युच्यते तैस्तु ब्रह्म इत्युच्यत इति शब्दमात्रेण परं भेदः । वस्तुतस्तु नित्यानन्दादिस्वरूपत्वं तैरि-वास्माभिरपि अङ्गीक्रियत एव । तत् कीदृक् वाचामधीशम् "यस्य निःश्वसितं वेदाः" इत्यादिश्रुतेः वाचामधीशत्वं प्रसिद्धमेव । यतो वाचामधीशमतएव निरन्तरगलत्पञ्चाशदर्णैः येन जगद्व्याप्तमिति यथासम्भवं तत्रापि योजनीयम् । यतो वेदस्य वर्णमयत्वात् ।

यद्वाऽत्र शास्त्रे शब्दसृष्टेरर्थसृष्टेरपि कुण्डलिन्या एवोत्पत्तेस्तस्या एव "कुण्डली परदेवता" इति परदेवतात्वोक्तेस्तदनुसरणमेवोचितमिति महःशब्देन तेजोरूपा कुण्डलिनीत्युच्यते । "आदित्येन्द्वग्नितेजोमदृयथत्तत्मयो विभुः" इत्युक्तेः । सा कीदृशी नित्यानन्दवपुः । असावेवास्यपटले कुण्डलीस्वरूपं वक्ष्यति "नित्यानन्द-मयी गलत्परसुधावर्षैः" इत्यादिना । यया कुण्डल्या शब्दार्थरूपं परा-पश्यन्ती-मध्यमा-वैखरीरूपत्वेन शब्दजनकत्वात् कार्यें कारणोपचारात् शब्दरूपं विषयत्वात् अर्थरूपस्वभावेन चरम् पृथिव्यंशाधिक्यात् कार्यें कारणोपचारात् अचरम् एवम्भूतं गच्छतीति जगद् विनश्वरं शरीरं व्याप्तम् ।

यद्वा यया शब्दार्थरूपं चराचरात्मकं जगद् विश्वं व्याप्तम् । "सर्व्वगा

विश्वरूपिणी दिक्कालाद्यनवच्छिन्ना" इत्यग्रत उक्तेः। कैः निरन्तरगलत्पञ्चाशदर्णैः "पञ्चाशद्वर्णगुम्फिता पञ्चाशद्वर्णमालिकां सूते" इति वक्ष्यमाणत्वात्। सुकृतिनः पुण्यात्मानस्तत्त्वज्ञा इत्यर्थः। यां शब्दब्रह्ममयीमाहुः "सा प्रसूते कुण्डलिनी शब्दब्रह्ममयी विभुः" इति वक्ष्यमाणत्वात्। चैतन्यं चिच्छक्तिस्वरूपा। अयमेव वक्ष्यति "तच्चैतन्यरूपा सा" इति। अन्तर्गतं सुषुम्नान्तर्गतमित्यर्थः। "या मूलाधारदण्डान्तरविवरगता" इत्युक्तेः। शशाङ्कसदनं सहस्रारकमले चन्द्रमण्डलगतत्वात्। वाचामधीशं सर्व्वशब्दोत्पादकत्वात् सर्व्वमन्त्रोत्पादकत्वाच्च। तथायमेव वक्ष्यति "विश्वात्मना प्रबुद्धा सा सूते मन्त्रमयं जगत्" इति। यद्वा वाचामधीशं वाग्देवतारूपेत्यर्थः। "शक्तिः कुण्डलिनीति या निगदिता शब्दसंज्ञा" इत्युक्तेः। यद्वा ग्रन्थारम्भे प्रकृते सरस्वती देवता तस्या एव स्मरणाद् ग्रन्थरूपा स्फूर्त्तिर्भवति। किञ्चात्र ग्रन्थे प्रथमतः सरस्वतीमन्त्राणामेव वक्ष्यमाणत्वात्। तेन सरस्वतीदेवतानुस्मरणमेवोचितमिति। तद्वाचामधीशं महः सारस्वतं तेजः वोऽव्यात्। अथ वाचामधीशमित्यनेन केवलं वाग्भवस्य सरस्वतीमन्त्रत्वमुक्तम्।

एतज्जपपरवशो भुवि वाग्भवाख्यं वाचां सुधारसमुचां लभते स सिद्धिम्।

इत्युक्तेः। तत् कीदृक् शशाङ्कसदनम् अनेन चन्द्रकलावतंसत्वेन ध्यानमुक्तम्। यदाहुः

धृतशशधरखण्डोल्लासिकोटीरचूडा
भवतु सपदि वाचामीश्वरी भूतये वः। इति।

पुनः कीदृक् नित्यं सर्व्वदा आनन्दयतीत्यानन्दं आनन्दजनकं वपुर्यस्य तत्। साधकानां सुधारससहोदरसरसस्सूक्तिसंस्फुरणादाह्लादजनकमित्यर्थः। तथाच सरस्वतीस्तवे आचार्य्याः—क्षौमाम्बरपरीधाने मुक्तामणिविभूषणे मुदावासे। इति। पुनः कीदृक् चैतन्यमन्तर्गतम् अनेन सूक्ष्मा परपर्य्याया पराख्या उक्ता। यदाहुः—

स्वरूपज्योतिरेवाहुः सूक्ष्मा वागनपायिनी। इति।

अन्यत्रापि—सूक्ष्मा कुण्डलिनी मध्ये ज्योतिर्म्मात्रा परा मता। इति।

येन महसा निरन्तरगलत्पञ्चाशदर्णैश्चराचरात्मकं शब्दार्थरूपं जगद् व्याप्तम्। अत्र पञ्चाशदर्णैरित्यनेन वर्णरूपा पश्यन्ती उक्ता। शब्दार्थरूपमित्यनेन पदरूपा मध्यमा उक्ता। यत् सारस्वतं महः सुकृतिनः शब्दब्रह्मेत्यूचिरे। अत्र शब्दब्रह्मशब्देन वेदा उच्यन्ते। तेन वेदात्मकमित्यर्थः।

तदुक्तं वार्त्तिककारपादै ब्रह्माधिकरणे—

शब्दब्रह्मेति यद् वेदशास्त्रं वेदाख्यमुच्यते। इति।

अनेन वाक्यरूपा वैखरी उक्ता। यदाहुः—

ध्वनिर्व्वर्णाः पदं वाक्यमित्यास्पदचतुष्टयम्।
यस्याः सूक्ष्मादिभेदेन वागधीशामुपास्महे॥ इति।

अन्यत्रापि—आदिक्षान्तविलासलालसतया तासां तुरीया तु या
क्रोडीकृत्य जगत्त्रयं विजयते वेदादिविद्यामयी। इति।

अपरे त्वत्र ग्रन्थकृता भैरवीमन्त्रोद्धारः कृत इति वदन्ति। तद् यथा। तत् त्रैपुरं महो वोऽव्यात्। कीदृक् अगलत् अविनश्वरम्। पुनः कीदृक् नित्यानन्दवपुः नित्यः पुरुषः तेन हकारः आनन्दमयीत्वात् आनन्दोत्पादकत्वात् वा आनन्दः शक्तिः तेन सः एतौ वपुः शरीरं यस्य। एतेनैतयोः बीजत्रयेऽपि सम्बन्धमुक्तम्भवति। अन्तः मध्यं मध्यबीजमित्यर्थः। तत् कीदृक् क्रमात् कश्च वश्च मश्च करमाः तान् अत्ति लक्षणया गृह्णातीति क्रमात्। तेन ककारः तदधो लकारः। अत्र रेफेण लकारस्य ग्रहणं व्याकरणपरिभाषया। उक्तञ्च "रेण लोऽपीष्यते ग्रहणं तेन" इति। संहितायामपि—"अतएव महेशानि र-लयोः समता भवेत्।" इति। तदधो मकारः पुरुषः तेन हः। पुनः कीदृक् अन्तर्गतं अन्ते रो रेफः गतः सङ्गतो यत्र तत्। पुनः कीदृक् व्याप्तं विः चतुःसंख्या चतुर्थस्वरः तेनाप्तं गृहीतम्। अत्र ग्रन्थकृतो वाररुचः सङ्केतोऽभिप्रेतः। स द्वितीयपटले स्फुटोभविष्यति। "नजि च शून्यं ज्ञेयम्" इति वाररुचः सङ्केतः। तेन शून्यं तस्य बिन्दुरूपत्वात् बिन्दुरुद्धृतः। एतेन षट्कूटं मध्यबीजमुद्धृतम्। अतएव वक्ष्यते "षट्कूटं त्रिपुरामन्त्रम्" इति। एवं मध्यमं बीजमुक्त्वा प्रथमबीजे हकारसकारयोः पूर्व्वमेवोक्तत्वात् एवम् ऐकारोऽपि योजनीयः। कीदृक् प्रथमं शशाङ्कसदनम् एतेन बिन्दुस्थम्। एवं प्रथमबीजमुद्धृतम्। अन्त्यं कीदृक् शब्दार्थरूपं अत्र शब्दशब्देन शब्दादयो गृह्यन्ते अर्थशब्दो विषयवाची। तेन शब्दादयो विषयास्ते च दशेति दशसंख्या तया औकारः तद्रूपं यत्र तत्तथा। अन्यच्च "अङ्कानां वामतो गतिः" इत्युक्तेः वाररुचेन सङ्केतेन तकारस्य षट्संख्या। "पिण्डान्तैरस्वरैरङ्काः" इत्युक्तेः न्यकारान्तयकारस्य एकाङ्कः। एवं षोडश तेन विसर्गः। एवं तृतीयबीजमुद्धृतम्। तदुक्तं सिद्धेश्वरीमन्त्रे—

हंसा त्रयो दन्त्यसकारयुक्ता वस्वब्धिपंक्तिस्वरसंविभिन्नाः।
अन्त्यो विसर्गी इतरौ सबिन्दू मध्यो विरिञ्चीन्द्रहराग्नियुक्तः॥ इति।

अस्यायमर्थः। वसु अष्टसंख्या। अब्धिश्चतुःसंख्या। पंक्तिर्दशसंख्या। तथाच "पंक्तिर्दशाक्षरच्छन्दो दशसंख्यावली अपि" इत्यमरः। हंसा हकारास्त्रयः।

कीदृशाः दन्त्यसकारयुक्ताः। तथा क्रमाद् वसुक्षितिपंक्तिस्वरैः क्लीवान् विना अष्टम ऐ चतुर्थ ई दशम औ तैर्युक्ताः। ऋकारादि स्वरचतुष्टयं नपुंसकं "स्वराणां मध्यकं यत्तु तच्चतुष्कं नपुंसकम्" इत्युक्तत्वात्। नपुंसकस्वरपरित्यागेन विन्दुविसर्गसहितानां स्वराणामष्टम ऐकारः दशम औकार इति बोध्यम्। विशेषमाह तृतीयो विसर्गयुक्तः इतरौ प्रथमद्वितीयौ सानुस्वरौ। मध्यः पुनः विरिञ्च्यादियुतः विरिञ्चिः कः इन्द्रो लः, हरो हः अग्नौ रेफः एतैर्युतः। इदं षट्कूटं मध्यबीजम्। इयं त्रिबीजा भैरवी।

अथच ऐचेति स्वतन्त्रतया निर्देशात् व्याप्तमित्याप्तशब्दग्रहणात् शब्दार्थरूपमिति रूपशब्दोपादानात् केवलास्त्रयः स्वरा एवास्य मन्त्रस्य चेतनीमन्त्र इति सूचितम्। यदाहुः—

शिवाष्टमं केवलमादिबीजं भगस्य पूर्व्वाष्टमबीजमन्यत्।

परं शिरोऽन्तं गदिता त्रिवर्गी सङ्केतविद्या गुरुवक्त्रगम्या॥ इति।

शिव उकारस्तस्याष्टम ऐकारः। भगम् एकारः तस्य पूर्व्वाष्टमश्चतुर्थः स्वरः। शिरो विन्दुः सोऽन्ते यस्य शिरोऽन्त औकारः।

उक्तबीजानां क्रमेण वाग्भव-कामराज-शाक्तत्वमाह। वाचामधीश मित्यनेनाद्यस्य वाग्भवत्वमुक्तम्। चराचरात्मकं मैथुनसृष्टजगतः कामोत्पन्नत्वात् मध्यमबीजस्य कामराजतोक्ता। सुकृतिनः यदन्त्यबीजं शब्दब्रह्मेत्यूचिरे इत्यनेनान्त्यस्य शाक्तत्वमुक्तम्। "त्रिधामजननी देवी शब्दब्रह्मस्वरूपिणी" इति वक्ष्यमाणत्वात्। यदुक्तं सिद्धेश्वरीमते—

वाग्भवं प्रथमं बीजं कामराजं द्वितीयकम्।

शक्तिबीजं तृतीयन्तु चतुर्व्वर्गफलप्रदम्॥ इति।

अथच—"ॐ तत्सदिति निर्देशो ब्रह्मणस्त्रिविधः स्मृतः" इत्युक्तेः शब्दात्मकं ब्रह्म शब्दब्रह्मेति प्रणवम्। चराचरात्मकं जगद् येनेति मैथुनसृष्टेः कामादुत्पत्तेः कामबीजम्। वाचा नकारः। वृहत्तत्त्वन्यासे नकारेण सह शब्दतत्त्वन्यासात्। मस्व*। धीः शक्तिरूपः। ईशः प्रभुः अनेन विसर्गः। "मायाशक्त्यभिधः सर्गः सर्व्वभूतात्मकः प्रभुः" इत्युक्तेः। एवं नमः शब्दः। एवमस्य मन्त्रस्य ह्लादिनी मन्त्र उक्तः। यदाहुः—

कमलं परिलुप्तमध्यमान्त्यस्वरमीशादियुतं सविन्दुनादम्।

निगमादिनमोऽन्तरे विराजद्भुवि देवीहृदयं प्रदिष्टमेतत्॥ इति।

* मस्वरूपं ग्राह्यमित्यर्थः।

त्रयाणां बीजानां सामान्येन विशेषणमाह अनिशमिति । न विद्यते निशा हकारो यत्र आदाविति शेषः । केशवादिन्यासे निशा हकारः शक्तिः । तेनादौ हकाराभावे सकारस्यादित्वमुक्तम् । तेनादौ सकारः पश्चात् हकारः । यद्वा निरित्यनेनैव आद्यबीजस्यापि बिन्दोरुद्धृतत्वात् अनिशं हकाररहितं शशाङ्कसदनम् शशाङ्कः सकारः सदने स्थाने यस्य । अनेन हकारस्य स्थाने सकारः तदधो ह्रस्वपर्यायातः । उक्तञ्च—

भैरवीयमुदिताऽकुलपूर्व्वा देशिकैर्यदि भवेत् कुलपूर्व्वा ।

सैव शीघ्रफलदा भुवि विद्येत्युच्यते पशुजनेष्वतिगोप्या ॥ इति ।

अनेनास्य मन्त्रत्वं विद्यात्वमप्युक्तम् । यत् पिङ्गलामते—

शक्त्याद्या तु भवेद् विद्या शिवाद्यो मन्त्र उच्यते ।

दीक्षाभिषेकपूजा तु प्राणिनां भुक्तिमुक्तिदा ॥ इति ।

अन्यदपि बीजत्रयसामान्यविशेषणमाह पञ्चाशद्वर्णैरुपलक्षितमित्यर्थः । अनेन सर्व्वस्य मन्त्रस्य मातृकान्तरितत्वेन जप उक्तः । यदाहुः

मन्त्रराजममुं समस्तजगद्विमोहनकारणं

मातृकान्तरितं जपेदनुलोमतोऽपि विलोमतः ॥ इति ।

अथवा अनेन विशेषणेन च हहसैं सहसैं इत्यादि हसकलह्रीँ सहकलह्रीँ इत्यादि अहसौः आहसौः इत्याद्यन्तर्मातृकान्यासोऽपि सूचितः । यदाहुः

क्रमेण षट्चक्रवर्णान् तद्दलेषु प्रविन्यसेत् ।

चक्रद्वयक्रमेणैव देवीकूटांश्च मन्त्रवित् ॥ इति ।

अन्यत्रापि मूलाधारकथनप्रस्तावे

चतुर्व्वज्रपत्रेषु देवीनिरुद्धान् जलेन्द्राग्निवायून् न्यसेत् केवलान् वा ।

सबिन्दूनमन्दप्रभावान् प्रसिद्धान् । इति ।

अथवा पञ्चाशच्छब्देन सामीप्यसम्बन्धेन लक्षणया एकपञ्चाशद्वर्णैरुपलक्षितमित्यनेन बीजत्रयस्यापि दीपिन्युद्धारः सूचितः । तत्र प्रथमबीज-दीपिनी तु व्यञ्जनस्वरैः पृथक्कृतैः सप्तदशवर्णात्मिका । द्वितीयबीजदीपिनी तु पूर्व्ववदेव पञ्चविंशत्यक्षरा । तृतीयबीजदीपिनी पूर्व्ववन्नवाक्षरा । एवमेक-पञ्चाशद्वर्णात्मिका । तत्र द्वितीयतृतीययोः चकारस्य सत्त्वात् तस्य चैकमेव व्यञ्जनं गृहीतम् । मातृकायां पृथगुपदेशात् । यद्ययं व्यञ्जनद्वयात्मैव स्यात् तदा क्षवदस्यापि पृथगुपदेशो न स्यात् । तयोरेव बिन्दुद्वयमस्ति तदपि न पृथग्गणितम् । तादृशस्यैव पञ्चदशस्वरत्वात् । प्रणवेऽपि बिन्दुः प्रणवान्तर्गत

अन्तःस्मितोल्लसितमिन्दुकलावतंस-
मिन्दीवरोदरसहोदरनेत्रशोभि।

एवेति न पृथग्गणित इति सर्व्वमनवद्यम्। अयञ्च दीपिन्युद्धारो ग्रन्थकृताऽत्र सूचितः। मया तु भैरवीपटले स्फुटीकरिष्यते।

अथवा बालामन्त्रोद्धारो ग्रन्थकृतोऽभिप्रेत इति। यतो भैरव्यादीनामपि स एव मूलभूतः। यदाहुः बालामुक्ता—

विद्या मूलोत्पत्तिरिया मयोक्ता ज्ञातव्येयं देशिकैः सिद्धिकामैः। इति।

तद्यथा। वाचामधीशमिति वाग्भवम्। अन्तर्मध्यं मध्यस्थम्। क्रमात् कञ्च वञ्च मा लक्ष्मीः तेन ईकारः। रेण पूर्व्ववत्तस्य ग्रहणम्। निरिति बिन्दुः। एवं मध्यमं बीजम्। शशाङ्कः सकारः सत् औकारः। अकारो नकारश्च शून्यद्वयं तेन विसर्गः। "नेत्रे च शून्यं चेयं तथा स्वरे केवले कथिते" इत्युक्तेः। सच्छब्देन कथमौकार-ग्रहणमिति चेदुच्यते। ॐकारस्य तावत् "ॐ तत्सदिति निर्द्देशो ब्रह्मणस्त्रिविधः स्मृतः" इत्युभयोः ब्रह्मवाचकत्वात् "सदोंकारो निगद्यते" इत्युक्तेश्च सच्छब्द-वाचकता। सोऽत्राकृतपररूप केवल एव विवक्षितः। स च सामीप्यसम्बन्धेन अग्रिमस्य लक्षकः। यद्वा "तस्यैवौकारयोगेन स्यादौकाराक्षरं तथा" इति आचार्य्योक्तेः ओकार एव स्वजन्यस्य औकारस्य लक्षकः। यद्वा शशो रूपमस्मिन् इति मत्वर्थीयोऽच् तेन शशशब्दः तेन सः शशन् गमनशीलः शशो हंसः तेन वा सः। अङ्कशब्देन पिण्डन्यायात् अकारः। यथा "स वामदृक् पवनगुणान्वितः कारः" इत्यत्र करशब्देन ककारः। यथा "हरिहयवद्वत् वनम्" इत्यत्र वनशब्देन वकारः। सच्छब्देन ओकार एव। तस्य पूर्व्वेण सह सन्धौ औकारः। अनाभ्यां विसर्गः। ननु प्रणवस्य सबिन्दुकत्वात् बालान्त्यबीजे ग्रन्थकारो विसर्गमात्रं वक्ष्यति। अत्र च बिन्दुविसर्गावुद्धृताविति विरोध इति चेन्न। बालाया मन्त्रभेदेषु क्वचिद् बिन्दुः क्वचिद् विसर्गः क्वचिद्बिन्दुविसर्गावप्युद्धृतौ। तदपि सूचयितुमत्रेदृश उद्धारः कृतः। यदाहुः सनत्कुमारे—

अष्टमस्य तृतीयन्तु चतुर्द्दशसमन्वितम्।
दण्डकुण्डलभेतद्धि सारस्वतमुदाहृतम्॥ इति।

अन्यत्र तु—दन्तान्तेन युतं तु दण्डिसकलं सम्मोहनाख्यं कुलम्। इति।

अन्यत् पूर्व्ववदिति संक्षेपः। एतच्च व्याख्यानद्वयं गुरुवचननियन्त्रितेन मया कृतमिति चन्तव्यं देशिकेन्द्रैः॥ १॥

हेतुस्त्रिलोकविभवस्य नवेन्दुमौले
रन्तःपुरं दिशतु मङ्गलमादराद् वः ॥२
संसारसिन्धोस्तरणैकहेतून्
दधे गुरून् मूर्ध्नि शिवस्वरूपान् ।
रजांसि येषां पदपङ्कजानां
तीर्थाभिषेकश्रियमावहन्ति ॥३

यदुपहितस्य शिवस्य सृष्टिकर्तृत्वं तामुपस्तौति अन्तरिति । नवेन्दुमौलेरन्तःपुरं वो मङ्गलमादराद् दिशत्विति योजना । अत्रापि वो मङ्गलं दिशतु इत्यनेन शिष्यकृपा सूचिता । यद्यपि तत्त्वतः शैवदर्शने

न शिवेन विना शक्तिर्न शक्तिरहितः शिवः ।
न तत्त्वतस्तयोर्भेदश्चन्द्रचन्द्रिकयोरिव ॥

इति शक्ति-शिवयोरैक्यमेव तथापि द्वितीयेन विना सृष्ट्यनुपपत्तेः लीलागृहीतं रूपं स्त्रीस्वरूपं वर्ण्यते । एतेन मैथुनसृष्टिः सूचिता । तस्या जगत्कारणतामाह त्रिलोकविभवस्य हेतुरिति । चराचरात्मकत्वेन विस्तारो विभवः । कीदृशं अन्तःस्मितोल्लसितं कल्पितमिदं जगद् विलसतीति हास्यकारणम् । ईश्वरे साभिलाषतया वा हासः । एतेनास्या ईश्वरक्षोभकता सूचिता । किञ्च "यत्रानुकूल्यं दम्पत्योस्त्रिवर्गस्तत्र वर्द्धते" इति स्मृतेः दम्पत्यानुकूल्यतो विचित्रजगन्निर्माणं सूचितम् । पुनः कीदृक् इन्दुकलावतंसम् । अत्रावतंसशब्देन मुकुटाभरणमुच्यते । तथा नामलिङ्गानुशासने—"पुंस्युत्तंसावतंसौ द्वौ कर्णपूरेऽपि शेखरे" इति । पुनः कीदृक् । इन्दीवरोदरसहोदरनेत्रशोभि । एतेन सर्व्वातिशायि सौन्दर्य्यं वर्णितम् । यद्वा नवेन्दुमौलेरित्यनेन भुवनेशीमन्त्र उक्तः । विशेषणैस्तदुद्धारः । त्रिलोकविभवस्य हेतुः शिवस्तेन हकारः । अन्तः स्मितं प्रकाशो यस्यासावन्तःस्मितोऽग्निः रेफः तेनोल्लसितं युतम् । इन्दुकलावतंसमिति बिन्दुः । इन्दीवरोदरसहोदरे नेत्रे यस्याः सा लक्ष्मीः तेन दीर्घ ईकारः । यद्वा इन्दीवरोदरस्य सहोदरं सुहृत् यन्नेत्रं चन्द्ररूपं तच्च वाममिति दीर्घ ईकारः तेन शोभि युक्तम् । एवं मिलित्वा भुवनेशीबीजम् ॥ २ ॥

यस्य देवे परा भक्तिर्यथा देवे तथा गुरौ ।
तस्यैते कथिता ह्यर्थाः प्रकाशन्ते महात्मनः ॥

सारं वच्यामि तन्त्राणां शारदातिलकं शुभम् ।
धर्म्मार्थकाममोक्षाणां प्राप्तेः प्रथमकारणम् ॥४

इत्यागमात् परदेवताभक्तिवद् गुरुभक्तेरपि विद्याप्राप्तावन्तरङ्गसाधनत्वावगमात् परदेवतायाः स्मरणानन्तरं गुरुनमस्कारमाह भंसारेति । शिवस्वभावान् गुरून् मूर्ध्नि दधे इत्यन्वयः । शिवस्वभावान् शिवस्वरूपानित्यर्थः । एतेन गुरुध्यानं तत्तद्देवतारूपतया कर्त्तव्यमित्युक्तं भवति । तदुक्तम् —

गुरुं न मर्त्त्यं बुध्येत यदि बुध्येत तस्य तु ।
कदापि च भवेत् सिद्धिर्न मन्त्रैर्देवपूजनैः ॥ इति ।

अन्यत्रापि—तस्मादेवं विदित्वा तु गुरुं देवञ्च नान्यथा ।
त्रिकालप्रणिपातेन ध्यानयोगेन संयजेत् ॥ इति ।

अन्यत्रापि—ललाटे नयनं चान्द्रीं कलामपि च दोर्द्वयम् ।
अन्तर्निधाय वच्यामि गुरुर्मर्त्त्ये महीयते ॥ इति ।

मूर्ध्नि दधे इत्यनेन गुरुध्यानं मूर्द्धनि कर्त्तव्यमित्युक्तं भवति । तदुक्तम्—

प्रातः शिरसि शुक्लेऽब्जे द्विनेत्रं द्विभुजं गुरुम् ।
प्रसन्नवदनं शान्तं स्मरेत्तन्नामपूर्व्वकम् ॥ इति ।

अन्यत्रापि—श्रीमद्गुरुपदाम्भोजं मूर्द्धन्येव सदास्थितम् ।
यः स्मरेत् सात्त्विकैर्भावैः सोऽचिरात् खेचरो भवेत् ॥ इति ।

गुरूनिति बहुवचनं पूजार्थं गुरु-परमगुरु-परापरगुरु-परमेष्ठिगुर्व्वपेक्षया वा । तथाच ग्रन्थकृद्गुरुपङ्क्तिः । "श्रीकण्ठं वसुमन्तं श्रीसोमानन्दमुत्पलाचार्य्यान्" इति । "लक्ष्मणमभिनवगुप्तं वन्दे श्रीक्षेमराजञ्च" इति तच्छिष्याः । कीदृशान् संसारसिन्धोस्तरणैकहेतून् । अनेन विना गुरूपदेशं संसारतरणमशक्यमित्यप्युक्तम् । तथाच श्रुतिः—"आचार्य्यवान् पुरुषो वेद" "स गुरुमेवाभिगच्छेत्" इति ।

आगमश्च—अज्ञानतिमिरान्धस्य ज्ञानाञ्जनशलाकया ।
चक्षुरुन्मीलितं येन तस्मै श्रीगुरवे नमः ॥ इति ।

गुरुप्रणाममाहात्म्यमाह रजांसीति । एतेन पादोपसंग्रहणपूर्व्वकं गुरुनमस्कारः कर्त्तव्य इत्युक्तं भवति ॥३॥

सिद्धार्थं सिद्धसम्बन्धं श्रोतुं श्रोता प्रवर्त्तते ।
शास्त्रादौ तेन वक्तव्यः सम्बन्धः सप्रयोजनः ॥

इत्युक्तेः शिष्यबुद्धानुकूलनार्थं ग्रन्थमाहात्म्यं प्रकाशयन् श्रोतृप्रवृत्तिनिमित्तभूतान्

शब्दार्थसृष्टिर्मुनिभिश्छन्दोभिर्देवतैः सह ।
विधिश्च यन्त्रमन्त्राणां तन्त्रेऽस्मिन्नभिधीयते ॥ ५

विषय-प्रयोजन-सम्बन्धाधिकारिणो दर्शयति सारमित्यादिश्लोकद्वयेन। तन्त्राणां सारं श्रेष्ठं संग्रहरूपञ्च इत्यनेनास्योपादेयताऽतिसंक्षिप्तता चोक्ता। तत्र तन्त्राणामिति वैष्णव-शैव-शाक्त-गाणपत्य-सौराणां यतः सारं अतएव शुभम्। शब्दसंक्षेपेऽप्याकाङ्क्षित सकलार्थप्रतिपादकत्वमेव शुभत्वम्। धर्म्मार्थकामेत्यादि वक्ष्यति। तदुपयिको नामनिर्देशः शारदातिलकमिति। शीर्य्यत इति शारं स्थूलं कर्म्मफलं तद्ददातीति शारदा। तत्त्वकारणत्वेन ब्रह्मविद्याधिरूढ़ा मती द्यति खण्डयतीति वा शारदा चिच्छक्तिः। यद्वा शरः स्वतन्त्रं तस्य भावः शारं स्वातन्त्र्यं तद्ददातीति अनाद्यविद्यां परिछिद्य जीवभावनिरासेन परमैश्वर्य्यप्रदायिका। तदुक्तं गौतमेन तन्त्रव्याकरणे—

शरः स्वतन्त्रं हृदयं स्फुरत्ता परमेशिता।
शारसेत्युदिताः शब्दाः पर्य्यायाः स्वार्थवाचकाः॥ इति।

तस्यास्तिलको भूषणम्। अनेनोत्कृष्टता दर्शिता। तत्रापि भूषणान्तरं न भवति किन्तु तिलकरूपः। तेन यथा मुखे वर्त्तमानस्तिलकः सर्व्वतः प्रथमं दृश्यो भवति तद्वदयमपीत्यभिप्रायः। प्रथमं कारणं मुख्यकारणम्। यथा चास्य मुख्यत्वं तथा ग्रन्थसङ्गतिकथनप्रस्तावेऽस्माभिः पूर्व्वमेव प्रपञ्चितम्। शब्दार्थसृष्ट्यादि विषयः। चतुर्व्वर्गः फलम्। अनयोः प्रतिपाद्य-प्रतिपादकभावः सम्बन्धः। तदर्थी चाधिकारी। अस्य शास्त्रस्य च व्युत्पाद्य-व्युत्पादकभावः सम्बन्धः। शास्त्रविषयस्य फलस्य च साध्यसाधनभावः सम्बन्धः। इत्याद्यन्योऽपि यथायथमूहनीयः। सहेति त्रिभिः सम्बध्यते। मुनिभिः तपोयोगबलेन मन्त्रप्रथमज्ञातृभिः प्रथमाराधकैः। तदुक्तं गौतमेन—

महेश्वरमुखाज्ज्ञात्वा गुरुर्यस्तपसा मनुम्।
संसाधयति शुद्धात्मा पूर्व्वं स ऋषिरीरितः॥ इति।

तथाऽन्यत्र—येन यदृषिणा दृष्टं सिद्धिः प्राप्ता च येन वै।
मन्त्रेण तस्य तत् प्रोक्तमृषेर्भावस्तदार्षकम्॥ इति।

छन्दःशब्दव्युत्पत्तिरुक्ताऽन्यत्र—

छादनाच्छन्द उद्दिष्टं वाससी इव चाकृतेः।
आत्मना च्छादितो देवैर्मृत्योर्भीतैस्तु वै पुरा।

आदित्यै वसुभी रुद्रैस्तेन च्छन्दांसि तानि वै ॥ इति ।

तथाऽन्यत्रापि—मृत्युभीतैः पुरा देवैरात्मनश्छादनाय च ।

छन्दांसि संस्मृतानीह छादितास्तैस्ततोऽमराः ।

छादनाच्छन्द उद्दिष्टं सर्वं छन्दोभिरावृतम् ॥ इति ।

तत्तु गायत्र्यादि प्रसिद्धम् । दैवतं तत्तन्मन्त्रोद्दिष्टम् । यदाहुः—

यस्य यस्य च मन्त्रस्य उद्दिष्टा या तु देवता ।

तदाकारं भवेत्तस्य दैवत्वं देवतोच्यते ॥ इति ।

देवतैरिति विनियोगस्याप्युपलक्षणम् । तत्स्वरूपमुक्तमन्यत्र—

पुराकल्पे समुत्पन्ना मन्त्राः कर्मार्थमेव च ।

अनेन चेदं कर्त्तव्यं विनियोगः स उच्यते ॥ इति ।

अन्यत्रापि—धर्मार्थकाममोक्षेषु शास्त्रमार्गेण योजनम् ।

सिद्धमन्त्रस्य सम्प्रोक्तो विनियोगो विचक्षणैः ॥ इति ।

तज्ज्ञानाभावे दोष उक्तोऽन्यत्र—

दौर्बल्यं याति तन्मन्त्रो विनियोगमजानतः ॥ इति ।

छन्द-ऋषि-देवताज्ञानं मन्त्रसाफल्यार्थमवश्यमपेक्षितम् । तदुक्तं छन्दोगाना-मार्षेयब्राह्मणे—

यो ह वा अविदितार्षेयच्छन्दोदैवतब्राह्मणेन मन्त्रेण याजयति वाध्यापयति वा स्थाणुं वर्च्छति गर्त्तं वा पद्यति प्र वा मीयते पापीयान् भवति यातयामान्यस्य छन्दांसि भवन्ति अथ यो मन्त्रे मन्त्रे वेद सर्व्वमायुरेति श्रेयान् भवति अयातयामा-न्यस्य छन्दांसि भवन्ति तस्मादेतानि मन्त्रे मन्त्रे विद्यादृषीणां संस्थानो भवति संस्थानो भवति ब्रह्मणः स्वर्गे लोके महीयते अवन्न जायते पुनरिति ।

कात्यायनोऽपि—एतान्यविदित्वा योऽधीतेऽनुब्रूते जपति जुहोति यजते याजयति वा तस्य ब्रह्मवीर्य्यं यातयामं भवति अनुविज्ञायैतानि योऽधीते वीर्य्य-वत्तरं यो यथार्थवित् तस्य वीर्य्यवत्तमं भवति जपित्वा हुत्वेष्ट्वा फलं प्राप्नोतीति ।

"यस्तु जानाति तत्त्वेन आर्षं छन्दश्च दैवतम् ।" इत्यादिना आगमेऽपि ।

याज्ञवल्क्योऽपि—आर्षं छन्दश्च दैवत्यं विनियोगस्तथैव च ।

वेदितव्यं प्रयत्नेन ब्राह्मणेन विशेषतः ॥

अविदित्वा तु यः कुर्य्याद्यजनाध्ययनं जपम् ।

होममन्यच्च यत् किञ्चित् तस्य चाल्पं फलं भवेत् ॥ इति ।

विधिरिति । न्यास-जप-पूजा-होम-तर्पणाभिषेकसम्पातपातादिः । चकारः शब्द-

निर्गुणः सगुणश्चेति शिवो ज्ञेयः सनातनः ।
निर्गुणः प्रकृतेरन्यः सगुणः सकलः स्मृतः ॥ ६

अध्यादेः प्रधानाप्रधानस्य समुच्चये। मन्त्रयन्त्राणामित्येकपदोपादानेऽपि मुन्यादीनां यथायोगं सम्बन्धः। तत्र मुनिच्छन्दसी होमतर्पणे च मन्त्र एव। देवतादीनि मन्त्रान्तुभयत्रापि। सम्पातपातस्तु यन्त्रे तदुपलक्षितेषु प्रतिकृतिकुम्भशिलाप्रतिमा-गुलिकातैलघृतादिषु सम्बध्यते। एतानि देवतोपासकस्य स्थूलरूपतयोक्तानि। एषां सूक्ष्मरूपं यथा। यदाहुः—

स्वात्मैव देवता प्रोक्ता मनोज्ञा विश्वविग्रहा।
ध्यानस्तु देवतात्मत्वात् स्वात्मनो देहकल्पना॥
जपस्तन्मयतारूपभावनं सम्यगीरितम्।
पूजा तु चञ्चलत्वेऽपि तन्मयत्वाप्रमत्तता॥
होमो विश्वविकल्पानामात्मन्यस्तमयो मतः।
एषामन्योन्यसम्मेलभावनं तर्पणं स्मृतम्॥
अभिषेकस्तु विद्या स्यादात्मैव स्वाश्रयो महान्।
प्रयोगाः स्युरुपाधीनां हेतोः स्वात्मविमर्शनम्॥
मन्त्र्यास्तु भजनं तासामादिमध्यान्तवर्जनम्।
मोहाज्ञानादिदुःखानामात्मन्यस्तमयो दृढम्॥ इति॥४॥५॥

इष्टिं वक्तुमुपोद्घातमाह निर्गुण इति। सनातनो नित्यः शिवो निर्गुणः सगुणश्च ज्ञेयः। आद्यस्य स्वरूपमाह निरिति। प्रकृतेरन्यः तत्सम्बन्धशून्यः। जडा एवात्र प्राधान्येनोद्देश्यत्वात्। तेन सूक्ष्म इत्यर्थः। अतएवान्यशब्दार्था-भावात् न पञ्चमीयम्। तथा सत्यनुवादे पर्य्यवसानं स्यात्। यदुक्तं प्रयोगसारे—

नित्यः सर्व्वगतः सूक्ष्मः सदानन्दो निरामयः।
विकाररहितः साक्षी शिवो ज्ञेयः सनातनः॥ इति।

नारायणीयेऽपि—निष्क्रियं निर्गुणं शान्तमानन्दमजमव्ययम्।
अजरामरमव्यक्तमज्ञेयमचलं ध्रुवम्॥
ज्ञानात्मकं परं ब्रह्म स्वसंवेद्यं हृदि स्थितम्।
सत्यं बुधैः परं नित्यं निर्म्मलं निष्कलं स्मृतम्॥ इति।

द्वितीयस्य स्वरूपमाह स इति। सगुणः सकलः कला प्रकृतिः तत्सहितः। सांख्यमते सत्त्वरजस्तमसां साम्यावस्था प्रधाना परपर्य्याया प्रकृतिः। अतएव सगुण

सच्चिदानन्दविभवात् सकलात् परमेश्वरात्।
आसीच्छक्तिस्ततो नादो नादाद् बिन्दुसमुद्भवः॥ ७

इत्युक्तिः। वेदान्तनये तु अविद्या। शिवतन्त्रे शक्तिः। उक्तञ्च नारायणीय-प्रयोगसारयोः—

तच्छक्तिभूतः सर्व्वेशो भिन्नो ब्रह्मादिमूर्त्तिभिः।
कर्त्ता भोक्ता च संहर्त्ता सकलः स जगन्मयः॥ इति॥६॥

सृष्टिमाह सदिति। तस्याविद्याशबलितत्वेन जड़त्वे कथं सृष्टिकर्त्तृत्वम् इति शङ्कां वारयति सच्चिदानन्दविभवादिति। अनेनाविद्योपहितत्वेऽपि तस्य न स्वरूपहानिरित्यर्थः। सकलाच्छक्तिरासीदिति योजना। शक्तिसहितादेव पुनः शक्तिः कथमासीदिति चेत् सत्यम्। या अनादिरूपा चैतन्याध्यासेन महाप्रलये सूक्ष्मा स्थिता तस्या गुणवैषम्यानुगुणतया सात्त्विक-राजस-तामसस्रष्टव्यप्रपञ्चकार्य्य-साधने उच्छूनावस्थात्वमेव उपचारादुत्पत्तिः। इयञ्च सदुत्पत्तिवादिसांख्यमत-माश्रित्य ग्रन्थकारस्योक्तिरिति ज्ञेयम्। तदुक्तं प्रयोगसारे—

तस्माद् विनिर्गता नित्या सर्व्वगा विश्वसम्भवा। इति।

वायवीयसंहितायामपि—

शिवेच्छया परा शक्तिः शिवतत्त्वैकतां गता।
ततः परिस्फुरत्यादौ सर्गे तैलं तिलादिव॥ इति।

पञ्चरात्रेऽपि—एवमालोक्य सर्गादौ सच्चिदानन्दरूपिणीम्।
समस्ततत्त्वसङ्घात्म-स्फूर्त्त्यधिष्ठानरूपिणीम्।
व्यक्तां करोति नित्यां तां प्रकृतिं परमः पुमान्॥ इति।

तस्या एव नादबिन्दू सृष्ट्युपयोगावस्थारूपौ। तदुक्तं प्रयोगसारे—

नादात्मना प्रबुद्धा सा निरामयपदोन्मुखी।
शिवोन्मुखी यदा शक्तिः पुंरूपा सा तदा स्मृता॥
सैव सर्गक्षमा तेन। इति।

आचार्य्यास्तु—सा तत्त्वसंज्ञा चिन्मात्रज्योतिषः सन्निधेस्तदा।
विचिकीर्षुर्घनीभूता क्वचिदभ्येति बिन्दुताम्॥ इति।

अन्यत्रापि—अभिव्यक्ता परा शक्तिरविनाभावलक्षणा।
अखण्डपरचिच्छक्तिर्व्याप्ता चिद्रूपिणी विभुः॥

परशक्तिमयः साक्षात् त्रिधाऽसौ भिद्यते पुनः ।
बिन्दुर्नादो बीजमिति तस्य भेदाः समीरिताः ॥ ८

बिन्दुः शिवात्मको बीजं शक्तिर्नादस्तयोर्मिथः ।
समवायः समाख्यातः सर्व्वागमविशारदैः ॥ ९

रौद्री बिन्दोस्ततो नादाज्ज्येष्ठा बीजादजायत ।
वामा ताभ्यः समुत्पन्ना रुद्रब्रह्मरमाधिपाः ॥ १०

समस्ततत्त्वभावेन विवर्त्तेच्छासमन्विता ।
प्रयाति बिन्दुभावञ्च क्रियाप्राधान्यलक्षणम् ॥ इति ।

अतएव वक्ष्यमाणशैवतत्त्वेषु शुद्धानां पञ्चानामेव ग्रहणम् । अत्र यद्यप्यन्यैर्ग्रन्थकृद्भि र्नादावस्था नोक्ता तथापि ग्रन्थकृता तारस्य सप्तात्मकत्वं सूचयितुमेतदुक्तिः कृता । कालं प्रस्तुवद्भिराचार्य्यैः सूचितैव नादावस्था । यदाहुः—"रवात्मन्यथो कालतत्त्वे" इति । भुवनेशीस्तुतावप्याचार्य्याः "नमस्ते रवत्वेन तत्त्वाभिधाने" इति ॥ ७ ॥

इच्छाशक्त्या[सत्त्वा]दिरूपतया बिन्दोस्त्रैविध्यमाह परेति । साक्षात् परशक्तिमयः अतः पश्चात्तदवस्थात्मकत्वमेवोक्तम् । अथवा परः शिवः तन्मयः शक्तिमयः एवमुभयात्मकः । "बिन्दुः शिवात्मकः" इति वक्ष्यमाणत्वात् । असौ त्रिधा भिद्यते । एतौ नादबिन्दू प्रथमोक्तनादबिन्दुभ्यामन्यौ तत्कार्य्यरूपौ ज्ञेयौ । तदुक्तं "स बिन्दुर्भवति त्रिधा" इति ॥ ८ ॥

बिन्द्वादेर्भेदत्रयस्य परम्परास्वरूपमाह बिन्दुरिति । धर्म्मिणावुक्त्वा तत्सम्बन्धो वाच्य इत्यभिप्रायेण व्युत्क्रमः शक्त्युत्पत्त्यनुरोधात् पूर्व्वत्र तथाक्रमः । समवायः सम्बन्धः क्षोभ्यक्षोभकरूपः सृष्टिहेतुः । उक्तेऽर्थे प्रमाणमाह सर्व्वागमविशारदैरिति ॥ ९ ॥

रौद्रीति । ततस्तस्माद् बिन्दो रौद्री यतस्तस्य शिवमयत्वम् अतोऽन्वर्थतापि । नादात् ज्येष्ठा इति मध्योच्चारितत्वे तत्त्वेनान्वर्थत्वं ज्ञेयम् । बीजाद् वामा अजायतेति सम्बन्धः । तस्य शक्तिमयत्वादन्वर्थत्वम् । तदुक्तं प्रयोगसारे—

बिन्दुः शिवात्मकस्तत्र बीजं शक्त्यात्मकं स्मृतम् ।
तयोर्योगे भवेन्नादस्तेभ्यो जातास्त्रिशक्तयः ॥

संज्ञानेच्छाक्रियात्मानो वह्नीन्द्वर्कस्वरूपिणः।
भिद्यमानात् पराद् बिन्दोरव्यक्तात्मा रवोऽभवत्॥ ११

रौद्री बिन्दोः समुद्भूता ज्येष्ठा नादादजायत।
वामा बीजादभूच्छक्तिस्ताभ्यो देवास्त्रयोऽभवन्॥ इति ॥१०॥

संज्ञानेति इति। संज्ञाने इच्छाक्रिये तदात्मानः तेन रुद्रब्रह्मरमाधिपाः क्रमेण इच्छा-शक्ति-क्रियाशक्ति-ज्ञानशक्तिस्वरूपाः। क्वचित् ते ज्ञानेच्छेति पाठः सः असाम्प्रदायिक एव। एते वह्नीन्द्वर्कस्वरूपिणो रुद्रब्रह्मरमाधिपाः शब्दसृष्ट्यन्तर्गताः निरोधिकार्द्धेन्दु-बिन्दुरूपाः शक्तेरेवावस्थाविशेषा ज्ञेयाः। एषामिच्छाक्रियाज्ञानात्मत्वं शक्तित उत्पन्न-त्वात्। वक्ष्यति च—"इच्छाज्ञानक्रियात्माऽसौ" इति। ईश्वरप्रत्यभिज्ञायामपि—

यत इच्छन्ति तज्ज्ञातुं कर्त्तुं वा स्वेच्छया क्रियाः।
अनन्तरं हि तत्कार्य्यज्ञानदर्शनशक्तिता॥
ज्ञानशक्तिस्तदर्थं हि योऽसौ स्थलः समुद्यमः।
सा क्रियाशक्तिरुदिता ततः सर्व्वं जगत् परम्॥ इति।

यतः पुनस्तेषां वक्ष्यमाणत्वात् ततो रुद्रसमुद्भवस्ततो विष्णुस्ततो ब्रह्मा इति। अन्यथा पूर्व्वापरविरोधोऽपि स्यात्। यतो ग्रन्थकृत् तस्यां सूर्य्येन्दुपावकान् "प्रणवस्य त्रिभिर्वर्णैरिति" वक्ष्यति। तत्र प्रणवांशा अकारोकारमकारा ब्रह्मविष्णु-रुद्रात्मकाः। "अकाराद् ब्रह्मणोत्पन्नः" इत्यादेर्वक्ष्यमाणत्वात्। आगमान्तरे च—

ब्रह्मविष्ण्वीश्वरास्तत्तन्मण्डलेषु व्यवस्थिताः। इति।

तेन तत्र सूर्य्यरूपः अकारो ब्रह्मा अत्र च सूर्य्यरूपी विष्णुरिति। अतो वक्ष्यमाण-क्रमोऽयंसृष्ट्यनुसारेणानुसन्धेयः। ग्रन्थकृच्च वक्ष्यति—

शब्दार्थभाविभुवनं सृजतीन्दुरूपा या तद्‌बिभर्त्ति पुनरर्कतनुः स्वशक्त्या।
वह्न्यात्मिका हरति तत् सकलं युगान्ते तां शारदां मनसि जातु न विस्मरामि॥

इति। गोरक्षसंहितायामपि—

इच्छा क्रिया तथा ज्ञानं गौरी ब्राह्मी तु वैष्णवी।
त्रिधा शक्तिः स्थिता यत्र तत्परं ज्योतिरोमिति॥

आचार्य्या अपि—आद्यैस्त्रिभेदे स्तपनान्तिकैर्यत्। इति—

शब्दब्रह्मण उत्पत्तिमाह भिद्यमानादिति। पराद् बिन्दोरित्यनेन शक्त्यवस्था-रूपो यः प्रथमो बिन्दुस्तस्मादव्यक्तात्मा वर्णादिविशेषरहितोऽखण्डो नादमात्र उत्पन्नः॥ ११॥

शब्दब्रह्मेति तं प्राहुः सर्व्वागमविशारदाः ।
शब्दब्रह्मेति शब्दार्थं शब्दमित्यपरे जगुः ॥ १२

न हि तेषां तयोः सिद्धिर्जड़त्वादुभयोरपि ।
चैतन्यं सर्व्वभूतानां शब्दब्रह्मेति मे मतिः ॥ १३

तत्स्वरूपमाह शब्देति। सर्व्वागमविशारदाः सर्व्वश्रुत्यर्थविदः। तदुक्तमाचार्य्यैः—

स एवः श्रुतिसम्पन्नैः शब्दब्रह्मेति कथ्यते। इति।

सृष्ट्यान्मुखपरमशिवप्रथमोल्लासमात्रम् अखण्डोऽव्यक्तो नादबिन्दुमय एव व्यापको ब्रह्मात्मकः शब्दः शब्दब्रह्मेत्यर्थः। उक्तञ्च—

क्रियाशक्तिप्रधानायाः शब्दः शब्दार्थकारणम् ।
प्रकृतेर्विन्दुरूपिण्याः शब्दब्रह्माऽभवत् परम् ॥

अथान्तरस्फोटवादिमतं जातिव्यक्तिस्फोटात्मकं वा बाह्यस्फोटमतञ्च दूषयितुमुपक्रमते शब्देति। एके आचार्य्याः शब्दार्थमान्तरस्फोटं शब्दब्रह्मेत्याहुः। यथाहि—"निरंश एवाभिन्नो नित्यो बोधस्वभावः शब्दार्थमय आन्तरः स्फोटः" इति। अपरे वैयाकरणाः पूर्व्वपूर्व्ववर्णोच्चारणाभिव्यक्तं तत्तत्पदसंस्कारसहायचरमपदग्रहणोद्बुद्धं वाक्यस्फोटलक्षणं शब्दमखण्डैकार्थप्रकाशकं शब्दब्रह्मेति वदन्ति। यदाह "एक एव नित्यो वाक्याभिव्यङ्ग्योऽखण्डो व्यक्तिस्फोटो जातिस्फोटो वा बहीरूपः" इति ॥१२॥

तदुभयमतं दूषयन् स्वमतमाह नहीति। तेषां वादिनां मते तयोः शब्दशब्दार्थयोः सिद्धिः शब्दब्रह्मत्वसिद्धिर्न। उभयोस्तयोर्जड़त्वात्। यदि शब्दार्थः शब्दो वा शब्दब्रह्मेत्युच्यते तदा ब्रह्मपदवाच्यत्वं नोपपद्यते। यतः सच्चिदानन्दरूपो ब्रह्मपदार्थः। तौ च जड़ौ। तदुक्तम्—

अनादिनिधनं ब्रह्म शब्दतत्त्वं यदक्षरम् ।
विवर्त्ततेऽर्थभावेन प्रक्रिया जगतो यतः ॥ इति ।

अन्यत्रापि—शब्दब्रह्मेति शब्दावगम्यमर्थं विदुर्बुधाः ।
स्वतोऽर्थानवबोधत्वात् प्रोक्तो नैतादृशो रवः ॥
स तु सर्व्वत्र संस्यूतो जाते भूताकरे पुनः ।
आविर्भवति देहेषु प्राणिनामर्थविस्तृतः ॥ इति ।

तेन सर्व्वागमविशारदा इत्यनेन सहैकवाक्यतैवास्य। तद्बिन्दुरूपरवस्यैव सर्व्वशरीरेष्वाविर्भूतत्वेन वक्ष्यमाणत्वात्। यदुक्तं प्रयोगसारे—

तत् प्राप्य कुण्डलीरूपं प्राणिनां देहमध्यगम्।
वर्णात्मनाऽविर्भवति गद्यपद्यादिभेदतः॥ १४
अथ बिन्द्वात्मनः शम्भोः कालबन्धोः कलात्मनः।
अजायत जगत्साक्षी सर्व्वव्यापी सदाशिवः॥ १५
सदाशिवाद् भवेदीश स्ततो रुद्रसमुद्भवः।
ततो विष्णुस्ततो ब्रह्मा तेषामेवं समुद्भवः॥ १६

सोऽन्तरात्मा तदा देवी नादात्मा नदते स्वयम्।
यथासंस्थानभेदेन स भूयो वर्णतां गतः।
वायुना प्रेर्य्यमाणोऽसौ पिण्डाद् व्यक्तिं प्रयास्यति॥ इति।

केचित्तु शब्दब्रह्मेति शब्दस्यार्थं शब्दमेवाहुरिति योजनां कृत्वा सर्व्वागमविशारदा इत्येकः पक्षः अपरे बिन्दुरिति द्वितीयः तयोर्दूषणमित्याहुः। तत्र। जड़त्वादिति हेतुः प्रथमपक्षे न सम्भवति आचार्य्यमतविरोधश्चापद्येत। तेन सर्व्वागमविशारदा इत्ययमेवपक्षो ग्रन्थकृदभिमत इति॥ १३॥

एवं परां तां शब्दसृष्टिमुक्त्वा सामान्यतः समापयति तत् प्राप्येति। प्राणिनां देहमध्यगं कुण्डलीरूपं कुण्डलिनीस्वरूपं तच्चैतन्यं गद्यपद्यादिभेदतो वर्णात्मना आविर्भवतीति सम्बन्धः। किं कृत्वा। प्राप्य कण्ठादिकरणानीति शेषः। अतएव वक्ष्यमाणा सृष्टिः कुण्डलिनीत इति ज्ञेयम्॥ १४॥

एवं प्राधान्यद्योतनाय प्रथमोद्दिष्टां परां तां शब्दसृष्टिमुक्त्वा पश्यन्त्यादीनां शरीरसृष्टिव्यतिरेकेण वक्तुमशक्यत्वात् तां वक्तुमर्थसृष्टिमारभते अथेति। कला माया तदात्मनः तत उत्पन्नत्वात्। बिन्दुरपि तस्यैवावस्थान्तरम्। तदात्मन इत्युभयत्र कार्य्ये कारणोपचारात्। तदुक्तम्—

सर्व्वज्ञादिगुणोपेतामभिन्नामात्मनः सदा। इति।

यद्वा कला निवृत्त्याद्या अधिष्ठातृसदाशिवादीनां प्रातिलोम्येनोत्पादिकाः तदात्मनः। कालबन्धोरिति। अनाद्यनन्ते काले सृष्टिरूपकालसहायाच्चादात्मन इत्यर्थः। शम्भोः परमशिवात् सृष्टिस्थितिध्वंसनिग्रहानुग्रहकार्य्यपञ्चककर्त्ता अतएव जगन्निर्म्माणबीजरूपो जगत्साक्षी सदाशिवो जातः। अथच कालबन्धोः अतएव कालात्मन इति हेतु-हेतुमद्भावेन योजना।

"सा तु कालात्मना सम्यक् मयैव ज्ञायते सदा" इति आचार्य्योक्तेः।

अनेन विशेषणद्वयेन प्रकृतेः कालस्य च महाप्रलयेऽप्यवस्थानमुक्तम्। अतएव अनयोरापेक्षिकनित्यता। स्वतो नित्यत्वं पुरुषस्यैव। सर्व्वविनाशस्य पुरुषावधित्वादन्यथाऽनवस्थानादित्यादियुक्तिः द्रष्टव्या। अथ च कालबन्धोरिति बन्धुशब्देन कालस्य निमित्तत्वं सूचितम्। यदाहुः—

लवादिप्रलयान्तोऽयं तमःशक्तिविजृम्भितः।
निमित्तभूतः कालोऽयं भावानां जन्मनाशयोः॥ इति।

अन्यत्रापि—अनादिर्भगवान् कालो नान्तोऽस्य द्विज विद्यते।
अव्युच्छिन्नास्ततस्त्वेते सर्गस्थित्यन्तसंयमाः॥ इति।

कालबन्धोरित्यनेन अपरो लवादिप्रलयान्तः कालोऽपि सूचितः। तेनैव परकालस्योक्तत्वात्। स च—

"नलिनीपत्रसंहत्यां सूक्ष्मसूच्यभिवेधने।
दले दले तु यः कालः स कालो लवसंज्ञकः॥
लवैस्त्रुटिः स्यात् त्रिंशद्भिः" इत्यादिना
"तवायुर्मम निश्वासः कालेनैव प्रचोद्यते।"

इत्यन्तेन ग्रन्थसन्दर्भेणाचार्य्यैः विवेचितः। अस्माभिस्तु ग्रन्थगौरवभयात् नोक्तः। अन्ये त्वेवं व्याचक्षते कालबन्धोः कालात्मनः कस्य लस्य इति प्रत्याहारेण व्यञ्जनानि गृहीतानि। अस्येत्यनेन स्वरा अपि गृहीताः। तदात्मन इति। अन्ये त्वन्यथा व्याचक्षते—कस्य लस्य आत्मा दीर्घेकारः। चतुर्णामात्मनां चतुर्थ इत्युक्तः। कालशब्देनार्कस्तेन मः। यद्वा कालशब्देन महाकालो मकारस्य रुद्रमूर्त्तिर्गृहीता। भीमो भीमसेन इतिवत्। तेन मकारः। एवं मिलित्वा कामबीजमुद्धृतम्। तस्मादित्युक्तं भवति। तस्य जगन्मूलत्वात् शम्भोः

भ्रमन्तं योन्यन्तः स्फुरदरुणबन्धूककुसुम-
प्रभं कामं ध्यायेज्जठरशशभृत्कोटिशिखरम्।

इत्यादिना शरीरे मूलाधारे तेजस्त्रयरूपस्य तस्यैवोक्तत्वात् शक्तिरूपत्वाच्च बिन्द्वात्मन इति। तदुक्तम्—

विश्वं भूतेन्द्रियान्तःकरणमयमिनेन्द्वग्निरूपं समस्तं
वर्णात्मैतत् प्रधाने कलनयनमये बीजरूपे क्रमेण।
नीत्वा तां पुंसि बिन्द्वात्मनि तमपि रवात्मन्यथो कालतत्त्वे
तं वै शक्तौ चिदात्मन्यपि नयतु च तां केवले धाम्नि शान्ते॥ इति।

अन्ये तु शम्भोः हकारात् कलाऽर्द्धेन्दुरात्मा ईकारः बिन्दुः बिन्दुरेव कालोऽग्निः

मूलभूतात् ततोऽव्यक्ताद् विकृतात् परवस्तुनः।
आसीत् किल महत्तत्त्वं गुणान्तःकरणात्मकम् ॥ १७

प्रलये सर्व्वविनाशकत्वात्। एवं मायाबीजमुद्धृतम्। तस्मादित्युक्तम् अस्य जगन्मूलबीजभूतत्वं प्रसिद्धमेव। इदञ्च व्याख्यानमाचार्य्यचरणसम्मतमिति। तदुक्तमाचार्य्यैः—

स्वामिन् प्रसीद विश्वेश के वयं केन भाविताः।
किंमूलाः किंक्रियाः सर्व्वमस्मभ्यं वक्तुमर्हथ।
इति पृष्टः परं ज्योतिरुवाच प्रमिताचरम् ॥

इत्यस्य पद्यस्य व्याख्याने पद्मपादाचार्य्यैर्व्याख्यातम्—सर्व्वेश्वर उपादानादिकं संग्रहेणोक्तवान् इत्याह—इति पृष्ट इति। प्रकर्षेण मीयते ज्ञायते इति प्रमिता प्रकृतिः प्रमिनोति जानातीति प्रमितः पुरुषः प्रमिनोति परिच्छिनत्तीति प्रमितः कालः। तेषां प्रमितानां वाचकमक्षरं तदभिन्नं प्रमिताचरम् परा वाक् सतत्त्वं हकार इत्यर्थः। तस्य बीजबिन्दुनादरूपेण प्रकृत्यादिवाचकत्वं द्रष्टव्यम्। एतेन इत्युत्तरमुवाचेत्यर्थः। संग्रहेणोक्तस्याप्रतिपत्तिमालक्ष्य तदेव विवृणोति—

यूयमक्षरसम्भूताः सृष्टिस्थित्यन्तहेतवः। इति।

न क्षरत्यश्नुते वेति व्युत्पत्त्या "अक्षरात् सम्भवतीह विश्वम्" इत्यादिना। तेषामिति। शब्दसृष्टौ तेषामुद्भव उक्त एव। तेषामेवं समुद्भवः अर्थसृष्टावित्यर्थः ॥१५॥१६॥

एवं प्रकृतायामर्थसृष्टौ तत्त्वसृष्टिं वक्तुमारभते मूलेति। मूलभूतात् सर्व्वसृष्टिमूलरूपादतएव परवस्तुनः अव्यक्ताद् बिन्दुरूपात्। यद्वा शब्दब्रह्मणः विकृतात् सृष्ट्युन्मुखात् महत्तत्त्वं महन्नामपदार्थः आसीत् उत्पन्नः। यस्य शैवमते बुद्धितत्त्वमिति संज्ञा। किंरूपं सत्व-रजस्तमोगुणात्मकम् मनोबुद्ध्यहङ्कारचित्तस्वरूपम्। अन्तःकरणचतुष्टयात्मकता तु तत्कारणत्वेन कार्य्ये कारणोपचारात्। एवं शैवसिद्धान्तविदः। तदुक्तमीशानशिवेन—

बोद्धव्यलक्षणा सैव प्रकृतिः शक्तिजृम्भिता।
बुद्धितत्त्वं भवेदुव्यक्तं सात्त्विकं गुणमाश्रिता।
सैव बुद्धिर्महन्नाम तत्त्वं सांख्ये निगद्यते ॥ इति।

वामकेश्वरेऽपि—

अव्यक्तविग्रहाच्छब्दब्रह्मणः सर्व्वकारणम्।
व्यक्तसत्त्वगुणं व्यक्तं बुद्धितत्त्वमजायत ॥ इति।

अभूत्तस्मादहङ्कारस्त्रिविधः सृष्टिभेदतः ।
वैकारिकादहङ्काराद्देवा वैकारिका दश ॥ १८
दिग्वातार्कप्रचेतोऽश्विवह्नीन्द्रोपेन्द्रमित्रकाः ।
तैजसादिन्द्रियाण्यासंस्तन्मात्राक्रमयोगतः ॥ १९

सांख्यमते तु—सत्त्वरजस्तमसां साम्यावस्थारूपं प्रकृतिः प्रधानापरपर्य्यायमव्यक्तशब्देनोच्यते । तत् परवस्तु सर्व्वमूलभूतम् । गुणन्यूनातिरेकेण विकृतात्तस्मात् महानुत्पन्नः । स कोदृशः । गुणान्तःकरणात्मा । गुणाः शब्दस्पर्शरूपरसगन्धतन्मात्राणि । येषामन्तःकरणचतुष्टयस्यापि कारणरूपः । उपचारादुभयात्मकः । तथा तत्सृष्टिक्रमोऽपि प्रकृतेर्म्महान् महतोऽहङ्कार इति ॥ १७ ॥

अभूदिति । तस्मान्महतस्त्रिविधोऽहङ्कारः सृष्टिभेदतो जातः । वैकारिकस्तैजसो भूतादिश्चेति । तदुक्तम्—

अव्यक्तमेव तु व्यक्तं तन्महन्नामलक्षणम् ।
ततोऽहङ्कारतत्त्वं स्यात् सत्त्वादिगुणभेदकम् ॥
सोऽहङ्कारस्त्रिभेदः स्यात् पृथक् सत्त्वादिभेदतः ।
वैकारः सात्विको नाम तैजसो राजसः स्मृतः ।
भूतादिस्तामसस्तेऽपि पृथक् तत्त्वान्यवासृजन् ॥ इत्यादि ।

तत्तत्कार्य्यं वदन्नेवं वैविध्यमुन्मीलयति वैकारिकादित्यादिना । शक्तिसामरस्यविकृतपरमेश्वरादुत्पन्नत्वात् वैकारिकत्वमस्य । तदुत्पन्नत्वाद् देवानामपि तथात्वम् । सांख्यमतेऽपि गुणोद्रेकविकृतप्रधानोत्पत्तेस्तादृक्त्वम् ॥ १८ ॥

तानेवाह दिगित्यादि । अश्वीत्यश्विनीकुमारौ यद्यप्येतौ द्वौ तथापि सहचारित्वात् सहजातत्वादेकत्वेनोक्तिः । उपेन्द्रो विष्णोरेकामूर्त्तिः । मित्रस्तृतीयः सूर्य्यः । तदुक्तं "मित्रो भानुस्तृतीयकः" इति । को ब्रह्मण एका मूर्त्तिः । चन्द्रोऽपि ज्ञेयः । एते इन्द्रियाधिष्ठातृदेवा इति ज्ञेयम् । यदाहुः—

वैकारिका दिगाद्या ये चन्द्रेणैकादश स्मृताः ।
इन्द्रियाणामधिष्ठातृदेवास्ते परिकोर्त्तिताः ॥ इति ।

तैजसादिति । तैजसादहङ्कारादिन्द्रियाणि कर्म्मेन्द्रियाणि ज्ञानेन्द्रियाणि मनश्च । तदुक्तम्—

यच्चापरं मनस्तत्त्वं ससङ्कल्पविकल्पकम् । तैजसादेव सञ्जातम् । इति ।

भूतादिकादहङ्कारात् पञ्चभूतानि जज्ञिरे ।
शब्दात् पूर्व्वं वियत् स्पर्शाद् वायू रूपाद्धुताशनः ॥ २०
रसादम्भः क्षमा गन्धादिति तेषां समुद्भवः ।
स्वच्छं वियन्मरुत् कृष्णो रक्तोऽग्निर्विशदं पयः ॥ २१

अन्यत्रापि—तैजसतस्तत्र मनो वैकारितो भवन्ति चाक्षाणि ।
भूतादेस्तन्मात्राण्येषां यत् सर्गोऽयमेतस्मात् ॥ इति ।

अक्षाणि अक्षाधिष्ठातृदेवताः । सांख्यमते वैकारिकादहङ्कारात् तैजसाहङ्कार-मिलितात् इन्द्रियाण्यासन्निति । एवं तैजसाहङ्कारसहिताद् भूतादेरपि तन्मात्रोत्पत्तिः । तदुक्तम्—

सात्त्विक एकादशकः प्रवर्त्तते वैकारिकादहङ्कारात् ।
भूतादे स्तन्मात्रः स तामसः तैजसादुभयम् ॥ इति ॥ १९ ॥

भूतेति । भूतादिकादहङ्कारात्तन्मात्राक्रमयोगतः पञ्चभूतानि जज्ञिरे इति सम्बन्धः । कः स्वार्थिकः । तत्रादौ आकाशादीनां कारणभूताः पञ्चतन्मात्रा जाताः । शब्दतन्मात्रा-स्पर्शतन्मात्रा-रूपतन्मात्रा-रसतन्मात्रा-गन्धतन्मात्राः । एताभ्य आकाशवायुतेजोजलपृथिवीरूपाणि पञ्चभूतान्युत्पन्नानि । उक्तञ्च—

शब्दः स्पर्शश्च रूपञ्च रसो गन्धश्च पञ्चमः ।
तन्मात्राण्येव विषया भूतादेरभवन् क्रमात् ॥
ततः समभवद्व्योम शब्दतन्मात्ररूपकम् ।
स्पर्शात्मकस्ततो वायुस्तेजोरूपात्मकं ततः ॥
आपो रसात्मिकास्तस्मात् ताभ्यो गन्धात्मिका मही ।
ततः स्थूलानि भूतानि पञ्च तेभ्यो विराडपि ॥ इति ।

तत्र भूतोत्पत्तिप्रकारमाह शब्दादिति । शब्दतन्मात्रात आकाशः स्पर्शतन्मात्रातो वायुः रूपतन्मात्रातोऽग्निः रसतन्मात्रातो जलम् गन्धतन्मात्रातः पृथिवी । केचित् पूर्व्वपूर्व्वानुविद्धानामेषां कारणत्वमाहुः पूर्व्वशब्दसामर्थ्यात् । तदुक्तम्—

शब्दाद्व्योम स्पर्शतस्तेन वायुस्ताभ्यां रूपादग्निरेभ्यो रसाच्च ।
अम्भांस्येभिर्गन्धतो भूः । इति ।

पञ्चभूतवर्णानुपदिशति स्वच्छमिति । स्वच्छं श्वेतम् । अत्र केषाञ्चिदरूपिद्रव्याणां वर्णकथनम् उपासनार्थं स्वशास्त्रानुरोधेन । तेषां स्वरूपमन्यत्रोक्तम्—

पीता भूमिः पञ्चभूतान्येकैकाधारतो विदुः ।
शब्दस्पर्शरूपरसगन्धा भूतगुणाः स्मृताः ॥ २२
वृत्तं दिवस्तत् षड्बिन्दुलाञ्छितं मातरिश्वनः ।
त्रिकोणं स्वस्तिकोपेतं वह्नेरर्द्धेन्दुसंयुतम् ॥ २३
अम्भोजमम्भसो भूमेश्चतुरस्रं सवज्रकम् ।
तत्तद्भूतसमाभानि मण्डलानि विदुर्बुधाः ॥ २४

खमपि सुषिरचिह्नमीरणः स्याच्चलनपरः परिपाकवान् कृशानुः ।
जलमपि रसवद् घना धरा । इति ।

एतैस्तानि ज्ञायन्ते इत्यर्थः । एकैकाधारत इति । स्वस्वकारणाधारेणेत्यर्थः ।

तदुक्तम्—परस्परानुप्रविष्टैर्महाभूतैश्चतुर्विधैः ।
व्याप्ताकाशे जगत् सर्वं दृश्यं निष्पाद्यतेऽखिलम् ॥ इति ।

अन्यत्रापि—व्योम्नि मरुदत्र दहनस्तत्रापस्तासु संस्थिता पृथ्वी । इति ।

भूतगुणाः तत्तद्विशेषगुणा इति नैयायिकाः । यद्वा शब्दो गुणो वियतः ।
शब्दस्पर्शौ वायोः । तौ रूपञ्चाग्नेः । रसेन सह तानि जलस्य । गन्धेन सह
पञ्च पृथिव्या इति सांख्याः । इदमेव स्फोटयितुमेकैकाधारत इत्युक्तिः । उक्तञ्च

ईशानशिवेन—शब्दैकगुण आकाशः शब्दस्पर्शगुणो मरुत् ।
शब्दस्पर्शरूपगुणैस्त्रिगुणं तेज इष्यते ॥
शब्दस्पर्शरूपरसगुणैराप चतुर्गुणाः ।
शब्दस्पर्शरूपरसगन्धैः पञ्चगुणा मही ॥ इति ॥ २०-२२ ॥

भूतमण्डलान्याह वृत्तमिति । दिवः आकाशस्य वृत्तम् । तद्वृत्तमेव
समभागेन वृत्तपरिधिरेखामध्ये षड् बिन्दुलाञ्छितं मातरिश्वनः वायोः । त्रिकोण-
मूर्द्धाग्रम् । "ऊर्द्ध्वं वह्निरधः शक्तिः" इत्युक्तत्वात् ।

अन्यत्रापि—इन्द्रराक्षसवायव्यकोणे स्वाद्वह्निमण्डलम् । इति ।

स्वस्तिकोपेतम् त्रिकोणसम्पातरेखाः सम्बद्धय तत्र स्वस्तिकाकारं कुर्य्यादित्यर्थः ।

तदुक्तम्—हृदि त्रिकोणं निर्गच्छत् स्वस्तिके रक्ततेजसि । इति ।

स्वस्तिकं नाम परस्परसम्बद्धं विदिग्गतचतुर्वक्रं रेखाद्वयम् । वह्नेरिति
पूर्व्वेणान्वेति । अर्द्धेन्दुसंयुतम् अम्भोजमम्भस इति सम्बन्धः । अर्द्धेन्दौ संयुतम्

वर्णैः स्वैरञ्चितान्याहुः स्वस्वनामावृतान्यपि ।
धरादिपञ्चभूतानां निवृत्त्याद्याः कलाः स्मृताः ॥ २५ ॥

अर्द्धेन्दुसंयुतमिति । सप्तमीति योगविभागात् समासः । यद्वा अर्द्धेन्दु अम्भोजं संयुतं उभयं मिलितं अम्भसो मण्डलं तेनार्द्धेन्दुं कृत्वा तदुभयभागे सरोजद्वयं कुर्य्यादिति । यदुक्तमाचार्य्यैः—अब्जोपेतार्द्धेन्दुमद् बिम्बमाप्यम् । इति ।

अन्यत्रापि—अर्द्धचन्द्रं द्रवं सौम्यं शुभ्रमम्भोजसंयुतम् । इति ।

प्रयोगसारेऽपि—अब्जाङ्कोऽर्द्धेन्दुरम्भसः । इति ।

अन्यत्रापि—तेषां क्रमेण शशिबिम्ब समन्तदेव
षड्बिन्दुमद्दहनशस्त्रयुतं त्रिकोणम् ।
अम्भोजयुग्मयशशिखण्ड समानरूपं
वेदास्रकं सदशनन्त्विह मण्डलानि ॥ इति ।

मन्त्रतन्त्रप्रकाशेऽपि—चन्द्रार्द्धमण्डलं वापि श्वेतं पङ्कजयुग्मयुक् । इति ।

स्वायम्भुवे नारसिंहेऽपि—आप्यमर्द्धेन्दुपद्माङ्कितम् । इति ।

यस्तु अष्टदलपद्मं कृत्वा तद्दलाग्रेषु अर्द्धचन्द्राकारान् कुर्य्यात् इति वदति स स भ्रान्त एव । अन्ये तु अर्द्धचन्द्रं कृत्वा तन्मध्ये पद्मं लिखेदिति वदन्ति । तदपि भूतलिपिपटले वक्ष्यमाणत्वात् अत्र न वाच्यम् । सवज्रकं चतुरस्रं भूमेरिति सम्बन्धः । चतुरस्रसम्पातरेखाः सर्व्वत्र अष्टवज्राणि कुर्य्यादिति केचित् । सम्प्रदायविदस्तु चतुरस्ररेखास्वेव अष्टवज्राणि कार्य्याणीति वदन्ति । तदुक्तम्

शौनककल्पे—भूगृहं चतुरस्रं स्यादष्टवज्रविभूषितम् । इति ।

हिरण्यगर्भसंहितायामपि—बाह्ये वज्राष्टभूषितं चतुष्कोणं शुभमथो । इति । आचार्य्यास्तु—"वसुकुलिशगम्" इति । ग्रन्थकारोऽपि—"वज्रेष्वष्टसु" इति ।

अन्योन्याभिमुखतया त्रिवक्रं रेखाद्वयं परस्परसंबद्धं वज्रम् । परस्परसम्बद्धमध्यं रेखाद्वयमिति केचित् । मण्डलध्यानमाह तत्तदिति । अनेन भूम्यादौ मण्डललिखने तत्तद्वर्णरजोभिश्च पूरणमप्युक्तम्भवति ॥ २३ ॥ २४ ॥

वर्णैर्द्वितीये वक्ष्यमाणभूतवर्णैः । स्वस्वनामावृतान्यपीत्यस्याप्ययमर्थः । वक्ष्यमाणभूतलिपियन्त्रेषु यः कर्णिकालिखितो मन्त्रस्तेनावृतानीति । साम्प्रदायिकास्त्वेवं मन्यन्ते । "कलात्मनः" इति पूर्व्वमुक्तेः भूतकारणभूताः बिन्दुतत्त्वनिर्गताः शक्तीः । संहारक्रमेण प्रयोगार्थमाह धरेति । धरादिपञ्चभूतानामुत्पादिका इति शेषः । तदुक्तं वायवीयसंहितायाम्—

निवृत्तिः सप्रतिष्ठा स्याद् विद्या शान्तिरनन्तरम् ।
शान्त्यतीतेति विज्ञेया नाददेहसमुद्भवाः ॥ २६

शक्तिः प्रथमसम्भूता शान्त्यतीतपदोत्तरा ।
शान्त्यतीतपदं शक्तेस्ततः शान्तिपदं क्रमात् ॥
ततो विद्यापदं तस्मात् प्रतिष्ठापदसंग्रहः ।
निवृत्तिपदमुत्पन्नं प्रतिष्ठापदतः परम् ॥
एवमुक्ता समासेन सृष्टिरीश्वरचोदिता ।
आनुलोम्यादथैतेषां प्रातिलोम्येन संहृतिः ॥
अस्मात् पञ्चपदोद्दिष्टान्न सृष्ट्यन्तरमिष्यते ।
कलाभिः पञ्चभिर्व्याप्तं यस्माद् विश्वमिदं जगत् ॥ इति ।

नादेति । नादाद् देहो यस्य स नाददेहो बिन्दुः तत्समुद्भवा इति । यद्वा तासां स्थूलवाचकांशमाह नाददेहसमुद्भवा इति । नादो हकारः नादस्य ध्वनेर्देह उत्पत्तिर्यस्मात् स नाददेहो वायुस्तेन यः । धर्मधर्मिणोरभेदात् देहशब्देनोत्पत्तिरुक्ता । "मारुतस्तूरसि चरन् मन्द्रं जनयति ध्वनिम्" इत्युक्तेर्नादोत्पत्तिहेतुत्वं तस्य । समुद्दीप्यमाना भा दीप्तिर्यस्येति समुद्भोऽग्निस्तेन रः । व स्वरूपम् । तत्र हयरवलानां क्रमेण ग्रहणे कर्त्तव्ये यच्चतुर्णामेव ग्रहणं कृतवान् तेन लकारोऽप्यस्तीति ज्ञेयम् । प्रथमतो नादग्रहणाद् बिन्दुयोगोऽप्येषां ज्ञेयः । एतानि विलोमेन तन्मात्राबीजानि । अथवा नादो हकारस्तस्य देहः स्वरूपं तत्र समुद्भवः स्थितिर्येषां एवम्भूता आईकारादयः आ ई ऊ ऐ औकाराः । एषां सबिन्दुकत्वञ्च ज्ञेयम् । तदुक्तं त्रिकोणोत्तरे—

नादाख्यं यत् परं बीजं सर्व्वभूतेष्ववस्थितम् ।
मूर्त्तिदं परमं दिव्यं सर्व्वसिद्धिप्रदायकम् ।
शान्तं सर्व्वगतं शून्यं मात्रापञ्चकसंस्थितम् ॥ इति ।

केचन क्रमेण एषां ल व र य ह योगमाहुः । तद्यथा—ह्लां ह्वीं ह्रूं ह्यैं हौं । एतानि अपञ्चीकृतभूतबीजानि । अथवा नादो हकारः । शरीरस्य पृथिव्यंशाधिक्याद् देहशब्देन लकारस्तस्य समुद्भवः स्थितिर्यत्र स नाददेहसमुद्भवः । येषु आकारादिषु ते नाददेहसमुद्भवाः । अत्र क्रमेण लवरयह योगमाहुः । तद्यथा—ह्लां ह्वीं ह्रूं ह्रैं ह्लौं । एतानि पञ्चीकृतभूतबीजानि । भूतबीजानामेव तदभिमानिनिवृत्त्यादिबीजत्वं ज्ञेयम् । तदुक्तमाचार्य्यैः "नादकलादिभूता" इति ॥ २५ ॥ २६ ॥

पञ्चभूतात्मकं सर्व्वं चराचरमिदं जगत्।
अचरा बहुधा भिन्ना गिरिवृक्षादिभेदत:॥ २७

एवं भूतान्युक्त्वा जगतस्तदात्मकत्वमाह पञ्चेति। एतेन त्रिवृत्करणपक्ष: पञ्चीकरणपक्षोऽपि सूचित:। तत्र ये तैजसा देवा: तेषामपि शरीरार्द्धो भाग: तैजस: पृथिव्यास्तुर्थांश: चतुर्थांशो जलस्येति त्रिवृत्करणपक्ष:। पञ्चीकरणपक्षे तु पृथिव्यास्त्वारोंऽशा अन्येषामष्टमोऽष्टमोंऽश:। एवमन्यत्रापि। तदुक्तम्—

द्विधा विधाय चैकैकं चतुर्धा प्रथमं पुन:।
स्वस्वेतर द्वितीयांशे योजनात् पञ्च पञ्च ते॥ इति।

अथवा—षडंशास्तेजस: पृथिवीजलवाय्वाकाशानां दशमो दशमोंऽश:। एवं पार्थिवे अस्मदादिशरीरेऽपि षड् भागा: पृथिव्या: अन्येषां दशमो दशमोंऽश:। एवं वरुणादिलोकनिवासिनामाप्यादिशरीराणामपि अवगन्तव्यम्। तदुक्तम्—

पृथिव्यादीनि भूतानि प्रत्येकं विभजेद् द्विधा।
एकैकं भागमादाय पञ्चधा विभजेत् पुन:॥
एकैकभाग मेकैकभूते संवेशयेत् क्रमात्।
तत आकाशभूतस्य स्वभागा: षड् भवन्ति हि॥
वाय्वादिभागाश्चत्वारो वाय्वादिष्वेवमादिशेत्।
पञ्चीकरण मेतत् स्यादित्याहुस्तत्त्ववेदिन:॥ इति।

अन्यत्र विशेष:—

अस्थि मांसं त्वचं स्नायु रोम एव तु पञ्चमम्।
इति पञ्चविधा प्रोक्ता पृथिवी कठिनात्मिका॥
लाला मूत्रं तथा शुक्रं शोणितं मज्ज पञ्चमम्।
अपां पञ्च गुणा एते द्रवरूपा: प्रकीर्त्तिता:॥
क्षुधा तृष्णा भयं निद्रा आलस्यं क्षान्तिरेव च।
उष्णात्मका गुणा एते तेजस: परिकीर्त्तिता:॥
धावनं वल्गनं भुक्तिराकुञ्चनं प्रसारणम्।
एते पञ्च गुणा वायो: क्रियारूपा व्यवस्थिता:॥
रागद्वेषौ तथा लज्जा भयं मोहस्तथैव च।
व्योम्न: पञ्च गुणा एते शून्याख्ये सुषिरात्मनि॥ इति।

चरं जङ्गमम्। अचरं स्थावरम्। चरेषु बहुवक्तव्यत्वात् प्रथमोद्दिष्टं तं विहायाचरा-

चरास्तु त्रिविधा: प्रोक्ता: स्वेदाण्डजजरायुजा: ।
स्वेदजा: क्रिमिकीटाद्या अण्डजा: पन्नगादय: ॥२८

नाह अचरा इति। तत्र ते चरा: स्वेदाण्डजजरायुजा इति वक्ष्यति। तेन शिष्टत्वादेषामौद्भिदत्वमुक्तम्। यदाहु:—

देहश्चतुर्विधो ज्ञेयो जन्तोरुत्पत्तिभेदत: ।
उद्भिज्ज: स्वेदजोऽण्डोऽथ चतुर्थस्तु जरायुज: ।
उद्भिद्य भूमिं निर्गच्छेदौद्भिद: स्थावरस्तु स: ॥ इति ।

एषामुत्पत्तिप्रकारोऽन्यत्रोक्त:—

उद्भिद: स्थावरा ज्ञेयास्तृणगुल्मादिरूपिण: ।
तत्र सिक्ता जलैर्भूमि रन्तरूष्मविपाचिता ॥
वायुना व्यूह्यमाना तु बीजत्वं प्रतिपद्यते ।
तथा चोप्तानि बीजानि संसिक्तान्यम्भसा पुन: ॥
उच्छूनत्वं मृदुत्वञ्च मूलभावं प्रयान्ति च ।
तन्मूलादङ्कुरोत्पत्तिस्तस्मात् पर्णसमुद्भव: ।
पर्णात्मकं तत: काण्डं काण्डाच्च प्रसव: पुन: ॥ इति ॥ २७ ॥

विभागपूर्व्वकं चरानुद्दिशति चरास्त्विति। जनै: प्रत्येकं सम्बन्धं दर्शयन् तद्विशेषानाह स्वेदजा इत्यादिना। क्रमिकीटाद्या इति उभयोरपि दंशकत्वा-दंशकत्वाभ्यां भेद:। आदिशब्देन पतङ्गादीनां ग्रहणम्। यदाहु:—

क्रमिकीटपतङ्गाद्या: स्वेदजा नाम देहिन: । इति ।

तदुत्पत्तिप्रकारोऽन्यत्र दर्शित:—

स्वेदजं स्विद्यमानेभ्यो मूवक्लाक्लर: प्रजायते । इति ।

तेनैषामयोनिजत्वमुक्तम्। यदुक्तं प्रयोगसारे—

किन्त्वत्र स्वेदजा ये तु ज्ञेयास्ते चाप्ययोनिजा: ।
स्थिरा विवायवो भिन्नाश्चत्वारिंशल्लक्षधा ॥ इति ।

पन्नगादय इत्यादिशब्देन पक्षिकच्छपादिग्रहणम्। यदाहु:—

अण्डजा: पक्षिण: सर्व्वे नक्रमत्स्याश्च कच्छपा: । इति ।

तदुत्पत्तिप्रकारोऽपि—

अण्डजो वर्त्तुलीभूताच्छुक्रशोणितसंयुतात् ।
कालेन भिन्नात् पूर्णात्मा निर्गच्छन् प्रक्रमिष्यति ॥ इति ॥ २८ ॥

जरायुजा मनुष्याद्यास्तेषु नृणां निगद्यते ।
उद्भवः पुंस्त्रियोर्योगात् शुक्रशोणितसंयुतात् ॥२९
विन्दुरेको विशेद् गर्भमुभयात्मा क्रमादसौ ।
रजोऽधिके भवेन्नारी भवेद्रेतोऽधिकः पुमान् ।
उभयोः समतायान्तु नपुंसकमिति स्थितिः ॥ ३०

जरायुर्गर्भाशयो जालिकारूपः । मनुष्याद्या इत्यादिशब्देन पश्वादयः । एषां संख्योक्ता प्रयोगसारे—

योनिजाः प्राणिनो भिन्नाश्चतुःषष्टिसहस्रधा । इति ।

तेषु नृणां निगद्यते उद्भव इति सम्बन्धः । यतः सर्व्वशास्त्रस्य मनुष्याधिकारित्वात् । शोणित संयुतादित्यनेन तस्याप्रधानतोक्ता । अतः पुत्रः पितृजात्यादियुक्तः ।

तथाच महाभारते—माता भस्त्रा पितुः पुत्रो येन जातः स एव सः । इति । भस्त्रा वायुधारं चर्म्ममयम् । उभयात्मा शुक्रशोणितात्मा अतएवाग्नीषोमात्मा एको विन्दुर्गर्भं विशेत् । क्रमादसावित्युत्तरेण सम्बध्यते । असौ विन्दुः रजोऽधिकः क्रमान्नारी भवेत् । रेतोऽधिकः क्रमात् पुमान् भवेदिति योजना । अत्राधिक्यमुक्तप्रमाणतो ज्ञेयम् । उक्तप्रमाणसाम्ये नपुंसकोत्पत्तिरित्यपि ज्ञेयम् । यदाहुः—

द्वाविंशती रजोभागाः शुक्रमात्राश्चतुर्दश ।
गर्भसञ्जनने काले पुंस्त्रियोः सम्भवन्ति च ॥
नारी रजोऽधिकेंऽशे स्यान्नरः शुक्राधिकेंऽशके ।
उभयो रुक्तसंख्यायां स्यान्नपुंसकसम्भवः ॥ इति ।

क्रमादित्यनेनैतदुक्तं भवति । स एव विन्दुर्वायुना पृथग् भिन्नः बह्वपत्यतां जनयतीति । यदाहुः वाग्भटे शारीरस्थाने—

शुक्रास्त्रवे पुनः ।
वायुना बहुशो भिन्ने यथास्वं बह्वपत्यता ॥
वियोनिविकृताकारा जायन्ते विकृतैर्मलैः ।
पूर्णषोडशवर्षा स्त्री पूर्णविंशेन संगता ॥
शुद्धे गर्भाशये मार्गे रक्ते शुक्रेऽनिले हृदि ।
वीर्य्यवन्तं सुतं सूते ततो न्यूनाब्दयोः पुनः ॥
रोग्यल्पायुरधन्यो वा गर्भो भवति नैव वा ॥ इति ॥२९॥३०॥

पूर्व्वकर्म्मानुरूपेण मोहपाशेन यन्त्रितः ।
कश्चिदात्मा तदा तस्मिन् जीवभावं प्रपद्यते ॥ ३१

अथ मात्राहृतैरन्नपानाद्यैः पोषितः क्रमात् ।
दिनात् पक्षात् ततो मासाद् वर्द्धते तत्त्वदेहवान् ॥ ३२

तस्मिन् जिन्हौ जीवसञ्चारमाह पूर्व्वेति। पूर्व्वजन्मशतसञ्चितकर्म्मणां मध्ये फलदानोन्मुखं प्रबलमेकं पुण्यपापात्मकं सुखदुःखोभयात्मकफलकं मनुष्यशरीरोपभोगयोग्यं यत् कर्म्म तदनुरूपेण मोहपाशेन अविद्यारूपेण यन्त्रितो बद्धः उत्पद्यते। एतेन नित्यस्यात्मनोऽनुत्पत्तिरुक्ता। गृहमिव देहमात्मा प्रविष्ट इत्यर्थः। कश्चिदिति। "नानात्मानो व्यवस्थातः" इति कणादसूत्रानुसारात्। "पुरुषबहुत्वं सिद्धम्" इति सांख्योक्तेश्च। वेदान्तनये तु—अविद्याकल्पितो भेदोऽङ्गीकर्त्तव्यः। अन्यथा यद्यात्मज्ञानेनाविद्या नष्टा तदा—

ज्ञानाग्निः सर्व्वकर्म्माणि भस्मसात् कुरुतेऽर्जुन ।

इति वचनात् पूर्व्वसञ्चितकर्म्मणां फलदानासामर्थ्यादग्रिमकर्म्मनिर्लेप एव नास्ति।

न लिप्यते कर्म्मभिः स पद्मपत्रमिवाम्भसा ।

इति वचनात् तस्यैकत्वात् मुक्तत्वाच्च अवतार एव न स्यात्। इत्यवतारकारणं मोहपाशेनेत्युक्तम्। तदुक्तमध्यात्मविवेके—

अस्ति ब्रह्म चिदानन्दं स्वयंज्योतिर्निरञ्जनम् ।
सर्व्वशक्ति च सर्व्वज्ञं तदंशा जीवसंज्ञकाः ॥
अनाद्यविद्योपहिता यथाग्नेर्विस्फुलिङ्गकाः ।
दीर्घाद्युपाधिसंभिन्नास्ते कर्म्मभिरनादिभिः ॥
सुखदुःखप्रदैः पुण्यपापरूपैर्नियन्त्रिताः ।
तत्तज्जातियुतं देहमायुर्भोगञ्च कर्म्मजम् ॥
प्रतिजन्म प्रपद्यन्ते । इति ॥ ३१ ॥

अथेति। अत्र प्रकारो योगार्णवे—

आविश्य भुक्तमाहारं स वायुः कुरुते द्विधा ।
संप्रविश्यान्नमध्यस्थं पृथक् किट्टं पृथग् जलम् ॥
अग्नेरूर्द्ध्वं जलं स्थाप्य तदन्नञ्च जलोपरि ।
जलस्याधः स्वयं प्राणः स्थित्वाग्निं धमते शनैः ॥

वायुना व्यूह्यमानोऽग्निरत्युष्णं कुरुते जलम् ।
अन्नं तदुष्णतोयेन समन्तात् पचते पुनः ॥
द्विधा भवति तत् पक्वं पृथक् किट्टं पृथग् रसम् ।
रसेन तेन ता नाडीः प्राणः पूरयते पुनः ॥
प्रतर्पयन्ति सम्पूर्णास्ताश्च देहं समन्ततः ।
मातृ रसवहा नाडी मनुविद्धा पराभिधा ॥
नाभिस्थनाडीगर्भस्थ मालाङ्कतरसावहा । इति ।

दिनादिति । तदुक्तम्—

त्रसरेणुद्वयं जन्तुः चणमात्रेण वर्द्धते ।
नाड़िकामात्रतो यूका युगलञ्च मुहूर्त्ततः ।
यूकानां वेदसंख्यञ्च दिनमात्राद् यवद्वयम् ॥ इति ।

योगार्णवे च— कललं चैकरात्रेण पञ्चरात्रेण वुद्बुदम् ।
शोणितं दशरात्रेण मांसपेशी चतुर्दशे ॥
घनमांसञ्च विंशाहे पिण्डीभावोपलक्षितम् ।
पञ्चविंशति पूर्णाहे पलं सर्व्वाङ्कुरायते ॥
एकमासे तु सम्पूर्णे पञ्चभूतानि धारयेत् ।
मासद्वये तु सम्प्राप्ते शिरोभेदः प्रजायते ॥
मज्जास्थि च त्रिभिर्मासैः केशाङ्गुल्य श्चतुर्थके ।
कर्णाक्षिनासिकानाञ्च रन्ध्रं मासे तु पञ्चमे ॥
आस्यरन्ध्रोदरं षष्ठे पायुरन्ध्रञ्च सप्तमे ।
सर्व्वाङ्गसन्धि सम्पूर्णं मासैरष्टभिरिष्यते ॥ इति ।

अध्यात्मविवेके तु विशेषः—

द्रवत्वं प्रथमे मासे कललाख्यं प्रजायते ।
द्वितीये तु घनः पिण्डः पेशी षड्घनमर्व्वुदम् ॥
पुंस्त्रीनपुंसकानां तु प्रायोऽवस्थाः क्रमादिमाः ।
तृतीये त्वङ्कुराः पञ्च कराङ्घ्रिशिरसो मताः ॥
अङ्गप्रत्यङ्गभागाश्च सूक्ष्माः स्युर्युगपत्तदा ।
विहाय श्मश्रुदन्तादीन् जन्मानन्तरसम्भवान् ॥
एषा प्रकृतिरन्या तु विकृतिः सम्मता सताम् ।
चतुर्थे व्यक्तता तेषां भावानामपि जायते ॥

दोषैर्दूष्यैः सुखं प्राप्तो व्यक्तिं याति निजेन्द्रियैः ।
वातपित्तकफा दोषा दूष्याः स्युः सप्त धातवः ।
त्वगसृङ्मांसमेदोऽस्थिमज्जाशुक्राणि तान् विदुः ॥२२

मातृजञ्चास्य हृदयं विषयानभिकाङ्क्षति ।
अतो मातुर्मनोऽभीष्टं कुर्य्याद् गर्भविवृद्धये ॥
ताञ्च द्विहृदयां नारीमाहुर्दौहृदिनीं बुधाः ।
अदानाद्दोहदानां स्युर्गर्भस्य व्यङ्गतादयः ॥
मातुर्यद्विषयालाभ स्तदार्त्तो जायते सुतः ।
गर्भः स्यादर्थवान् भोगी दौहृदाद् राजदर्शने ॥
अलङ्कारे सुललितो धर्म्मिष्ठस्तापसाश्रमे ।
देवतादर्शने भक्तो हिंस्रो भुजगदर्शने ॥
गोधाशने तु निद्रालु र्बली गोमांसभक्षणे ।
माहिषेण तु रक्ताक्षं लोमशं सूयते सुतम् ॥
प्रबु[बु]द्धं पञ्चमे पिण्ड[त्तं] मांसशोणितपुष्टता ।
षष्ठेऽस्थिस्नायुनखरकेशरोमविविक्तता ॥
बलवर्णौ चोपचितौ सप्तमे त्वङ्गपूर्णता ।
अष्टमे त्वक्स्रुतौ स्यातामोजश्चेतश्च हृद्भवम् ॥
शुद्धमापीतरक्तञ्च निमित्तं जीविते मतम् ।
पुनरम्बां पुनर्गर्भं चञ्चलं तत् प्रधावति ॥
अतो जातोऽष्टमे मासे न जीवत्योजसोज्झितः ॥ इति ।

याज्ञवल्क्योऽपि—पुनर्धात्रीं पुनर्गर्भमोजस्तस्य प्रधावति ।
अष्टमे मास्यतो गर्भो जातः प्राणैर्वियुज्यते ॥ इति ।

एवं यदा ओजो बाले भवेत्तदा माता न जीवतीति ज्ञेयम् । यदा तूभयोर्हृदि तदोजो न स्यात् तदोभयोरपि जीवनं नेति ज्ञेयम् । तत्त्वदेहवान् चतुर्विंशति-तत्त्वात्मकशरीरः । तत्त्वान्यनन्तरमेव वक्ष्यति ॥ २२ ॥

दोषैरिति । सुखं यथा स्यात् तथा दोषैः दूष्यैः प्राप्तः निजेन्द्रियैर्व्यक्तिं याति । अनेनाष्टममासपर्य्यन्तं सूचितम् । दोषादीनेवाह वातेति । तानिति धातून् । एषां पूर्व्वपूर्व्वस्योत्तरोत्तरं प्रति कारणता ज्ञेया । तदुक्तं सुश्रुते—

ज्ञानेन्द्रियाणि श्रोत्रं त्वग् दृग् जिह्वा नासिका विदुः ।
ज्ञानेन्द्रियार्थाः शब्दाद्याः स्मृताः कर्म्मेन्द्रियाण्यपि ॥ ३४

वाक्पाणिपादपायूपस्थसंज्ञान्याहु र्मनीषिणः ।
वचनादानगतयो विसर्गानन्दसंयुताः ॥ ३५

कर्म्मेन्द्रियार्थाः संप्रोक्ता अन्तःकरणमात्मनः ।
मनोबुद्धिरहङ्कारश्चित्तञ्च परिकीर्त्तितम् ॥ ३६

रसासृङ्मांसमेदोऽस्थिमज्जशुक्राणि धातवः ।
भवन्त्यन्योन्यतः सर्व्वे प्रचिताः पित्ततेजसा ॥ इति ।

ननु कथं त्वचोऽसृजं प्रति कारणता इति चेत् सत्यम् । त्वगसृजौ तु रसत उत्पद्येते ।
तदुक्तम्—रसः स नाडीमध्यस्थः शारीरेणोष्मणा भृशम् ।
पच्यते पच्यमानाच्च भवेत् पाकद्वयं पुनः ।
चर्म्माविष्ट्य समन्ताच्च रुधिरञ्च प्रजायते ॥ इति ।
अन्यत्रापि—त्वगसृङ्मांसमेदोऽस्थिमज्जशुक्राणि धातवः ।
सप्त स्युस्तत्र चोक्ता त्वक् रक्तं जाठरवह्निना ॥
पक्वाद्भवेदन्नरसादेवं रक्तादिभिस्तथा ।
स्वस्वकोष्ठाग्निना पक्वै र्जन्यन्ते धातवः क्रमात् ॥ इति ।
नारायणीये तु त्वगित्यादि पठित्वा रसासृगिति पठन्त्येके इत्युक्तम् ॥ ३३ ॥

व्यक्तिं याति निजेन्द्रियैरित्युक्तम् । तानीन्द्रियाणि तत्प्रसङ्गात्तेषां विषयानप्याह ज्ञानेति । अर्थशब्दो विषयवाची उभयत्रापि । शब्दाद्याः शब्दस्पर्शरूपरसगन्धाः । पूर्व्वं भूतगुणेषु उक्तैरत्रादिनोक्तिः इत्यवधेयम् । अन्धु लिङ्गम् । आत्मनः ग्राहकमिति शेषः । तेन मनसो विषय आत्मा इत्युक्तं भवति । अन्तःकरणस्यैव चातुर्व्विध्यमाह मन इत्यादिना । तत्र सङ्कल्पविकल्पात्मकं मनः । सर्व्वभावनिश्चयकारिणी बुद्धिः । ज्ञात्रभिमानयुक्तोऽहङ्कारः । निर्विकल्पकं चित्तम् । इत्येतेषां भेदः । तदुक्तम्—

एषा शक्तिः परा जीवरूपिणी प्रोक्तलक्षणा ।
सङ्कल्पञ्च विकल्पञ्च कुर्व्वाणा तु मनो भवेत् ॥
बुद्धिरूपा तथा सर्व्वभावनिश्चयकारिणी ।
ज्ञात्रस्मीत्यभिमानाढ्या सैवाहङ्कारसंज्ञिता ॥

दशेन्द्रियाणि भूतानि मनसा सह षोड़श।
विकाराः स्युः प्रकृतयः पञ्च भूतान्यहङ्कृतिः॥ ३७
अव्यक्तं महदित्यष्टौ तन्मात्राश्च महानपि।
साहङ्कारा विकृतयः सप्त तत्त्वविदो विदुः॥ ३८

निर्विकल्पात्मिका सैव खलु चित्तस्वरूपिणी।
एवमेकैव बहुधा नर्त्तकीव प्रतीयते॥ इति। ३४-३६॥

एवं पूर्व्वं भूतानि इन्द्रियाण्यप्युक्त्वा तेषां मिलितानां संज्ञान्तराण्यप्याह दशेति श्लोकद्वयेन। अथवा तत्त्वदेहवानित्युक्तं तानि तत्त्वान्याह दशेति। विकारादि-संज्ञास्तत्प्रसङ्गसङ्गत्या उक्ता इति ज्ञेयम्। यद्वा सूचीकटाहन्यायेन दोषाम् दूष्यानुक्त्वा तत्त्वदेहवानित्युद्दिष्टानि तत्त्वानि। तानि कानीत्यपेक्षायामाह ज्ञानेत्यादि। कर्म्मेन्द्रियार्थाः सम्प्रोक्ताः पृथिव्यादय इत्यर्थः। तेन पञ्चभूतानि दशेन्द्रियाणि दशेन्द्रियार्था एवं पञ्चविंशतितत्त्वानि। यदाहुः—

भूतेन्द्रियेन्द्रियार्थैरुद्दिष्टस्तत्त्वपञ्चविंशतिकः। इति।

अथच विसर्गानन्दसंयुता इति भिन्नपदकरणेन पायूपस्थयोः विसर्गस्यैव कार्य्यत्वात् आनन्दरहितत्वेन चतुर्विंशतिरेव तत्त्वमुक्तं भवति। यदाहुः—

व्यानन्दकैश्च तैरपि तत्त्वचतुर्विंशतिस्तथा प्रोक्ता। इति।

मनोबुद्धिरहङ्कारश्चित्तञ्च इत्यनेन वचनादिव्यावर्त्तनेन एतच्चतुष्टययुक्तत्वेन चतुर्विंशतिर्वा तत्त्वानि इत्युक्तं भवति। यदाहुः—

करणोपेतैरेतैस्तत्त्वान्युक्तानि रहितवचनाद्यैः। इति।

सांख्यमतोक्तचतुर्विंशतितत्त्वानि वदन् तेषां कियतामपि तत्प्रसिद्धाः संज्ञा अप्याह दशेति। अनेन दशेन्द्रियाणि पञ्च भूतानि पञ्च तन्मात्राः मनः अहङ्कारः बुद्धिः प्रधानं प्रकृतिरिति चतुर्विंशतितत्त्वानि इत्युक्तम्। ग्रन्थकृदेव पञ्चमे वक्ष्यति—

पञ्च भूतानि तन्मात्रा इन्द्रियाणि मनस्तथा।
गर्व्वो बुद्धिः प्रधानञ्च सैताणीति विदुर्बुधाः॥ इति।

विकाराः स्युरित्येषां नित्यकार्य्यरूपत्वेन विकारता। अष्टौ प्रकृतय इति सम्बन्धः। उत्तरोत्तरं प्रति कारणत्वादेषां प्रकृतित्वम्। अत्र भूतानीति भूतशब्देन तन्मात्रा उच्यन्ते। कारणे कार्य्योपचारात्। भूतानां केवलकार्य्यत्वेन विकारेषूक्तत्वात्। अग्रे तन्मात्रा इति परामर्शाच्च। यदाहुः—

अप्राकृतिकानि सप्त प्रकृतिविकृतिसंज्ञकानि स्युः। इति।

अग्नीषोमात्मको देहो बिन्दुर्यदुभयात्मकः ।

दक्षिणांशः स्मृतः सूर्यो वामभागो निशाकरः ॥ ३९

अव्यक्तं प्रधानापरपर्य्याया प्रकृतिरित्यर्थः । अव्यक्तं महदिति । छन्दोऽनुरोधाद् गोपनार्थं वा व्यत्ययः । साव्यक्तं महदिति वा पाठः । यतोऽत्र संहारक्रमो विवक्षितः ।

यदाहुः—चतुर्विंशतितत्त्वानि प्रकृत्यन्तानि संजगुः । इति ।

अन्यत्र सृष्टिक्रमापेक्षयोक्तम् अव्यक्तम् महदहङ्कृतिभूतानीति । तन्मात्रास्य इति । साहङ्कार इति तन्मात्रविशेषणं तेन व्यत्ययः । चकारेण प्रकृतय इत्यस्य समुच्चयः । तेनैते सप्त प्रकृतिविकृतिशब्दवाच्या इत्यर्थः । उत्तरोत्तरं प्रति पूर्व्वपूर्व्वस्य प्रकृति-भूतत्वात् पूर्व्वपूर्व्वं प्रति उत्तरोत्तरस्य विकृतिभूतत्वादेषां प्रकृतिविकृतित्वम् ।

यदाहुः—मूलप्रकृति रविकृति र्महदाद्याः प्रकृतिविकृतयः सप्त ।

षोड़शकस्तु विकारो न प्रकृतिर्न विकृतिः पुरुषः ॥ इति ।

उपसंहरति तत्त्वविदो विदुरिति । अयमर्थः । ज्ञानेन्द्रियाणीत्यादि एतदन्तं यत्तत्त्वनिरूपणं मया कृतं तत् तत्त्वविदामपि सम्मतमिति । अथ वा तत्त्वविदो विदुरित्यनेन पूर्व्वप्रकारत्रयोक्ततत्त्वानि नास्मत्सम्मतानि । अपितु एतानि प्रकृत्यन्तान्येव चतुर्विंशतितत्त्वानि । पुरुषान्तानि पञ्चविंशतिः । परान्तानि षड् विंशतिः अस्मत्सम्मतानीत्युक्तं भवति । इयं योजना साम्प्रदायिकी । तदुक्तं वायवीयसंहितायाम्—

त्रयोविंशतितत्त्वेभ्यः परा प्रकृतिरुच्यते ।
प्रकृतेस्तु परं प्राहुः पुरुषं पञ्चविंशकम् ॥
तस्य प्रकृतिलीनस्य यः परः स महेश्वरः ।
तदधीनप्रवृत्तित्त्वात् प्रकृतेः पुरुषस्य च ॥ इति ।

केचनान्यथा योजयन्ति । भूतादिकाहङ्कारसृष्टिमुक्त्वा तैजसादिन्द्रियाख्यासम् इत्युद्दिष्टानीन्द्रियाणि तत्प्रसङ्गात्तेषां विषयानप्याह ज्ञानेत्यादि परिकीर्त्तित-मित्यन्तेन । उत्तरव्यवहारशेषतया केषाञ्चिन्मन्त्राणां वर्णतत्त्वन्यासयोगादि-शेषतया च विकारादि दर्शयति दशेत्यादि । तत्त्वविद इदं विदुः । एषां तत्रान्तर्भावात् तत्त्वविद्भिरेताः संज्ञाः कृता इत्यर्थः ॥ ३७ ॥ ३८ ॥

एवं प्रासङ्गिकमुक्त्वा प्रकृतमाह अग्नीति । देहः अग्नीषोमात्मकः । कुत इत्यपेक्षायां हेतुमाह यद् यस्मात् कारणादुभयात्मको बिन्दुः । शुक्लमग्निरूपं रक्तं सोमरूपम् एतदात्मकः ।

नाडीर्दश विदुस्तासु मुख्यास्तिस्रः प्रकीर्त्तिताः ।
इडा वामे तनोर्मध्ये सुषुम्णा पिङ्गला परे ॥ ४०

यदाहुः—कलाषोडशकश्चन्द्रः स्याद् द्वादशकलो रविः ।
कलादशयुतो वह्निः कलाष्टत्रिंशदंशभुक् ॥
सप्त[अष्ट]त्रिंशद् भवन्तीह गर्भाधानस्य हेतवे ।
अग्नीषोमात्मकं तेन गीयते सचराचरम् ॥
कलांशकेन योगेन भूयाद् गर्भस्य सम्भवः ॥ इति ।

एवमप्यग्नीषोमात्मकत्वमित्यर्थः । अग्नीषोमात्मको देहः इत्युक्तम् । तयोः प्रयोगादिविशेषतया देशविशेषे व्यवहाराय स्थितिमाह दक्षिणांश इति । अत्र शास्त्रे दक्षिणभागः क्वचिदग्निशब्देन क्वचित् सूर्यशब्देनापि व्यवह्रियते । "अग्नेयौ दक्षिणो भागः" इत्युक्तेः । वायवीयसंहितायामपि—

द्विधा वै तैजसी वृत्तिः सूर्य्यात्मा चानलात्मिका । इति ॥ ३९ ॥

पूर्व्वोक्तसूर्य्यनिशाकरयोः स्थितिमुपपादयितुं शरीरे नाडीराह नाडीरिति । तासु अनन्तासु दश नाडीः मुख्या विदुरित्यन्वयः । नाड्योऽनन्ताः इति वक्ष्यमाणत्वात् । तासु दशस्वपि तिस्रो मुख्याः प्रकीर्त्तिताः । तासु मुख्या इति पदस्य चावृत्त्या योजना । प्रकीर्त्तिताः इत्यस्योपादानमन्यथा विदुरित्यनेनैव गतार्थत्वात् । उक्तञ्च तत्रायास्तिस्रः । अत्राहस्तिकरणं मुख्यतमाः स्मृताः इति । तासामेव स्थितिमाह इडेति । तनोरिति त्रिषु स्थानेषु सम्बध्यते । वामे इडा वाममुष्कोत्था धनुर्वक्रा सती वामनासापर्य्यन्तं गतेत्यर्थः । तनोर्मध्ये पृष्ठवंशान्तर्गता सुषुम्णा । "या मुण्डाधारदण्डान्तरविवरगता" इत्युक्तेः । परे दक्षिणे दक्षिणमुष्कोत्था धनुर्वक्रा दक्षिणनासापर्य्यन्तं गतेत्यर्थः । यदाहुः—

या वाममुष्कसम्बद्धा सा श्लिषन्ती सुषुम्णया ।
दक्षिणं स्कन्धमाश्रित्य धनुर्वक्रा हृदि स्थिता ॥
वामांशजत्र्वन्तरगा दक्षिणां नासिकामियात् ।
यथा दक्षिणमुष्कोत्था नासाया वामरन्ध्रगा ॥ इति ।

तन्त्रान्तरेऽपि—सुषुम्णाकल्पिता याता मुष्कं दक्षिणमाश्रिता ।
हृद्गता वामभागस्य जत्रुमध्यं समाश्रिता ॥
दक्षिणं नासिकाद्वारं प्राप्नोति गिरिजात्मजे ।
वाममुष्कसमुद्भूता तथाऽन्या सव्यनासिकाम् ॥ इति ।

मध्या तास्वपि नाड़ी स्यादग्नीषोमस्वरूपिणी ॥४१

गान्धारी हस्तिजिह्वा च सुपूषालम्बुषा मता ।

यशस्विनी शङ्खिनी च कुहूः स्युः सप्तनाड्यः ॥४२

अनयोः स्वरूपमुक्तं योगार्णवे—

इड़ा च शङ्खकुन्दाभा तस्याः सव्ये व्यवस्थिता ।

पिङ्गला सितरक्ताभा दक्षिणं पार्श्वमाश्रिता ॥ इति ।

अनेन पिङ्गलेड़योः क्रमेण सूर्य्याचन्द्रमसोः स्थितिरुक्ता भवति ।

"इडायां सञ्चरेच्चन्द्रः पिङ्गलायां दिवाकरः" इत्युक्तेः ॥ ४० ॥

सुषुम्णाया मुख्यत्वं वदन् तत्स्वरूपमाह मध्येति। तास्वपीत्यपिशब्दात् मुख्येत्यनुषज्यते। तासु तिसृषु मध्या सुषुम्णा मुख्या। "सुषुम्णैव च तासु नाड़ी" इत्युक्तेः। सा कीदृशी अग्नीषोमस्वरूपिणी। मुख्यत्वे हेतुत्वेन योज्यम्। यतः पूर्व्वोक्तसोमाग्निरूपयोरिड़ापिङ्गलयोः अत्रैव लयात्। तदुक्तं—"राहोरास्यगतः" इति। अनेनास्या ब्रह्मरन्ध्रपर्य्यन्तं स्थितिरित्यप्युक्तम्। यदाहुः—

तयोः पृष्ठवंशमाश्रित्य मध्ये सुषुम्णा स्थिता ब्रह्मरन्ध्रं तु यावत्। इति ॥४१॥

शिष्टानां सप्तानां नामान्याह गान्धारीति। आसां स्थितिस्वरूपञ्चोक्तम् योगार्णवे—इड़ापृष्ठे तु गान्धारी मयूरगलसन्निभा ।

सव्यपादादिनेत्रान्ता गान्धारी परिकीर्त्तिता ॥

हस्तिजिह्वोत्पलप्रख्या नाड़ी तस्याः पुरःस्थिता ।

सव्यभागस्य मूर्द्धादिपादाङ्गुष्ठान्तमाश्रिता ॥

पूषा तु पिङ्गलापृष्ठे नीलजीमूतसन्निभा ।

याम्यभागस्य नेत्रान्ताद् यावत् पादतलं गता ॥

अलम्बुषा पीतवर्णा कण्ठमध्ये व्यवस्थिता ।

यशस्विनी शङ्खवर्णा पिङ्गलापूर्व्वदेशगा ॥

गान्धार्य्याश्च सरस्वत्या मध्यस्था शङ्खिनी मता ।

सुवर्णवर्णा पादादि कर्णान्ता सव्यभागके ॥

पादाङ्गुष्ठादिमूर्द्धान्तं याम्यभागे कुहूर्मता । इति ।

अन्येस्तु वारणा सरस्वती विश्वोदरा पयस्विनी एता अपि मुख्यत्वेनोक्ताः। यदाहुः—

ताश्च भूरितरास्तासु मुख्याः प्रोक्ताश्चतुर्दश ।

सुषुम्णेड़ापिङ्गला च कुहूरथ सरस्वती ॥

नाड्योऽनन्ताः समुत्पन्नाः सुषुम्णापञ्चपर्व्वसु।
मूलाधारोद्गतप्राण स्ताभिर्व्याप्नोति तत्तनुम्॥ ४३

गान्धारी हस्तिजिह्वा च वारणा च यशस्विनी।
विश्वोदरा शङ्खिनी च ततः पूषा पयस्विनी॥
अलम्बुषा। इति।

अन्यत्रापि—चतुर्दशात्र यद्देहे प्राधाना नाड़यः स्मृताः। इति।
आसां ध्यानं संस्थानञ्च ग्रन्थगौरवभयान्नोक्तम्। मुख्या इत्यनेनैव सूचिताः॥ ४२॥

एवं मुख्या नाड़ीरुक्ता सामान्या आह नाड्य इति। सुषुम्णापञ्चपर्व्वसु अनन्ता नाड्यः समुत्पन्नाः। पञ्चपर्व्वाणि स्वाधिष्ठानमणिपूरकानाहतविशुद्धाज्ञान्तानि। तत्राधोधोग्रन्थिमारभ्योर्द्धोर्द्ध्वग्रन्थिपर्य्यन्तं पर्व्वसमाप्तिः। यद्यपि "ग्रन्थिर्ना पर्व्वपरुषी" इति कोशः "इक्षुपर्व्वावधिः स्मृतः" इति व्यवहारश्च तथाप्यत्र षण्णां ग्रन्थीनां सत्त्वादेवं व्याख्यातम्। आश्वलायनश्रौतसूत्रभाष्यकारेण "पर्व्वण्यंजपेत्" इत्यत्र पर्व्वशब्दस्यैवं व्याकृतत्वात्। एतदभिप्रायेणैव वक्ष्यति "मध्यमाङ्गुलिपर्व्वणि" इति। सुषुम्णायामेतेषु पर्व्वसु इड़ापिङ्गलयो र्योगो भवतीति ज्ञेयम्। अनन्ता इति गणयितुमशक्यत्वादानन्त्यम्। यदाहुः—

पूर्व्वोक्तायाः सुषुम्णाया मध्यस्थायाः सुलोचने।
नाभिहृत्कण्ठदेशस्थ मध्यपर्व्वसमुद्भवाः॥
अधोमुख्यः शिराः काश्चित् काश्चिदूर्द्ध्वमुखास्तथा।
परा स्तिर्य्यग्गतास्तासु तत्र लक्षत्रयाधिकाः॥
नाड्योऽर्द्धलक्षसंख्याताः प्रधानाः समुदीरिताः।
तासु सर्व्वासु बलवान् प्राणो वायुः समन्ततः॥
संस्थितः सर्व्वदा व्याप्तः। इति।

अध्यात्मविवेके तु विशेषः—

अस्थ्नां शरीरे संख्या स्यात् षष्टियुतं शतत्रयम्।
शौखेवास्थिशतान्यत्र धन्वन्तरिरभाषत॥
द्वे शते त्वस्थिसन्धीनां स्यातामत्र दशोत्तरे।
पेशीस्नायुशिरासन्धि सहस्रद्वितयं मतम्॥
नव स्नायुशतानि स्युः पञ्च पेशीशतान्यपि।
अधिका विंशतिः स्त्रीणां स्तनयोर्दिग् भगे दश॥

वायवोऽत्र दश प्रोक्ता वह्नयश्च दश स्मृताः ।

प्राणाद्या मरुतः पञ्च नागः कूर्म्मो धनञ्जयः ॥ ४४

कृकलः स्याद्देवदत्त इति नामभिरीरिताः ।

अग्नयो दोषदूष्येषु संलीना दश देहिनः ॥ ४५

शिराधमनिकानान्तु लक्षाणि नवविंशतिः ।
सार्द्धानि स्युर्नवशती षट्पञ्चाशद्युता तथा ॥ इति ।

तन्नाड़ीनां फलमाह मूलेति । वक्ष्यमाणेभ्यो भिन्नो मुख्यो देहधारक-प्राणाभिधो वायुः । यदाहुः—

राजसः प्राणसंज्ञः स्यान्मुख्यो देहस्य धारकः ।
तद्भेदा दश विख्याता यै व्याप्तं स्याच्छरीरकम् ॥ इति ।

सा चासौ तनुश्च ताम् पूर्व्वोक्तां शरीरम् ॥ ४३ ॥

तद्भेदान् वदन् प्रसङ्गादग्नीनप्याह—वायवोऽत्रेति । तन्नामान्येवाह प्राणाद्या इति । आदिशब्देनापानव्यानोदानसमानाः प्रसिद्धत्वेनादिनोक्ताः । तत्र विशेषो योगार्णवे—इन्द्रनीलप्रतीकाशं प्राणरूपं प्रकीर्त्तितम् ।

आस्यनासिकयो र्मध्ये हृन्मध्ये नाभिमध्यगे ॥
प्राणालय इति प्राहुः पादाङ्गुष्ठेऽपि केचन ।
अपानयत्यपानोऽयमाहारञ्च मलायितम् ॥
शुक्रं मूत्रं तथोत्सर्ग मपानस्तेन मारुतः ।
इन्द्रगोपप्रतीकाशः सन्ध्याजलदसन्निभः ॥
स च मेढ्रे च पायौ च ऊरुवङ्क्षणजानुषु ।
जङ्घोदरे कृकाट्याञ्च नाभिमूले च तिष्ठति ॥
व्यानो व्यानयत्यन्नं सर्व्वव्याधिप्रकोपनः ।
महारजतसुप्रख्यो ह्यानोपादानकारकः ॥
स चाक्षिकर्णयो र्मध्ये कट्यां वै गुल्फयोरपि ।
घ्राणे गले स्फिगुद्देशे तिष्ठत्यत्र निरन्तरम् ॥
स्पन्दयत्यधरं वक्त्रं गात्रनेत्रप्रकोपनः ।
उद्वेजयति मर्म्माणि उदानो नाम मारुतः ॥
विद्युत्पावकवर्णः स्यादुत्थानासनकारकः ।
पादयोर्हस्तयोश्चापि स तु सन्धिषु वर्त्तते ॥

बुभुक्षा च पिपासा च प्राणस्य मनसः स्मृतौ ।
शोकमोहौ शरीरस्य जरामृत्यू षडूर्म्मयः ॥ ४६

पीतं भक्षित माघ्रातं रक्तपित्तकफानिलान् ।
समं नयति गात्राणि समानो नाम मारुतः ॥
गोक्षीरसदृशाकारः सर्व्वदेहे व्यवस्थितः ।
उद्गारे नाग इत्युक्तो नीलजीमूतसन्निभः ॥
उन्मीलने स्थितः कूर्म्मो भिन्नाञ्जनसमप्रभः ।
कृकरस्तु क्षुते चैव जवाकुसुमसन्निभः ॥
विजृम्भने देवदत्तः शुद्धस्फटिकसन्निभः ।
धनञ्जयस्तथा घोषे महारजतवर्णकः ॥
ललाटे चोरसि स्कन्धे हृदि नाभौ त्वगस्थिषु ।
नागाद्या वायवः पञ्च सहैव परिनिष्ठिताः ॥ इति ।

आचार्य्यास्तु—धनञ्जयाख्यो देहेऽस्मिन् कुर्य्यात् बहुविधान् रवान् ।
स तु लौकिकवायुत्वान्मृतञ्च न विमुञ्चति ॥ इति ।

अन्यैस्तु चत्वारो वायवोऽधिका उक्ताः ।

वैरम्भणः स्थानमुख्यः प्रद्योतः प्रकृतस्तथा ।
वैरम्भणादयस्तत्र सर्व्ववायुवशङ्गताः ॥ इति ।

अग्नीनां स्थितिमाह अग्नय इति । तेषां नामान्यन्यत्रोक्तानि—

ते जातवेदसः सर्व्वे कल्माषः कुसुमस्तथा ।
*दहनः शोषणश्चैव तपनश्च महाबलः ॥
पिठरः पतगः स्वर्णः स्वगाधो भ्राज एव च । इति ।

अन्यत्र तु नामान्तराण्युक्तानि—

जृम्भको दीपकश्चैव विभ्रमभ्रमशोभनाः ।
आवसथ्याहवनीयौ च दक्षिणाग्निस्तथैव च ॥
अन्वाहार्य्यो गार्हपत्य इत्येते दश वह्नयः । इति ।

अग्नेरन्यथोक्तानि—भ्राजको रञ्जकश्चैव क्लेदकः स्नेहकस्तथा ।
धारको रन्धकश्चैव द्रावकाख्यश्च सप्तमः ॥
व्यापकः पावकश्चैव श्लेषको दशमः स्मृतः । इति ।

दोषा वातपित्तकफाः । दूष्याः सप्त धातव इति प्रागेवोक्तम् ॥ ४४ ॥ ४५ ॥

स्नाय्वस्थिमज्जा शुक्रात् त्वङ्मांसास्राणि शोणितात् ।
षाट्कौशिकमिदं प्रोक्तं सर्व्वदेहेषु देहिनाम् ॥ ४७

इत्थम्भूतस्तदा गर्भे पूर्व्वजन्मशुभाशुभम् ।
स्मरंस्तिष्ठति दुःखात्मा छन्नदेहो जरायुणा ॥ ४८

कालक्रमेण स शिशुर्मातरं क्लेशयन्नपि ।
सम्पिण्डितशरीरोऽथ जायतेऽयमवाङ्मुखः ॥ ४९

एवं प्राणमुक्त्वा तस्य विशिष्टे अवस्थे वदन् प्रसङ्गात् मनःशरीरयोरप्याह बुभुक्षेति । ऊर्म्मिर्नाम आर्त्त्युत्पादकः अवस्थाविशेषः ॥ ४६ ॥

षडूर्म्मिप्रसङ्गात् षाट्कौशिकं वदन् शुक्रशोणितकार्य्याणि विविच्याचष्टे स्नाय्विति । शुक्रात् पितुः शुक्रात् स्नाय्वादि । शोणितात् मातुः शोणितात् त्वगादि ।

तदुक्तम्—मातृतस्त्रीणि पितृतस्त्रीणि । इति ।

अन्यत्र तु—मृदवः शोणितं मेदो मांसं प्लीहा यकृद् गुदः ।

इत्वामीत्येवमाद्यास्तु भावा मातृभवा मताः ॥

श्मश्रुलोमकचाः स्नायु शिराधमनयो नखाः ।

दशनाः शुक्रमित्यादि स्थिराः पितृसमुद्भवाः ॥ इति ॥ ४७ ॥

गर्भाशये तत्स्थिति प्रकारमाह इत्थम्भूत इति । इत्थम्भूत ऊर्ध्वन्तरितहस्तवद्धश्रोत्रः मातृपृष्ठमाश्रितो मोक्षोपायमभिध्यायन्नित्यर्थः । यदाहुः—

पाण्यन्तरितहस्ताभ्यां श्रोत्ररन्ध्रे पिधाय सः ।

उद्विग्नो गर्भसंवासादास्ते गर्भे भयान्वितः ॥

स्मरन् पूर्व्वानुभूताः स नानायोनीश्च यातनाः ।

मोक्षोपायमभिध्यायन् वर्त्ततेऽभ्यासतत्परः ॥ इति ।

अन्यच्च विशेषः—कृताञ्जलि र्ललाटेऽसौ मातृपृष्ठमभिश्रितः ।

अध्यास्ते सङ्कुचद्गात्रो गर्भे दक्षिणपार्श्वगः ॥

वामपार्श्वाश्रिता नारी क्लीबं मध्याश्रितं मतम् । इति ॥ ४८ ॥

कालक्रमेणेति । कालक्रममाह याज्ञवल्क्यः—"नवमे दशमे वापि" इति ।

अन्यत्रापि—समयः प्रसवस्याथ मासेषु नवमादिषु । इति ।

सम्पिण्डितशरीरः सङ्कुचद्गात्रः अवाङ्मुखः अधोमुखः सन् जायते उत्पद्यते । सूतिमारुतै र्नुन्न इति शेषः । यदाहुः—

क्षणं तिष्ठति निश्चेष्टो भीत्या रोदितुमिच्छति ॥ ५०

ततश्चैतन्यरूपा सा सर्व्वगा विश्वरूपिणी ।
शिवसन्निधिमासाद्य नित्यानन्दगुणोदया ॥ ५१

नवमे दशमे मासि प्रबलैः सूतिमारुतैः ।
निःसार्य्यते वाण इव जन्तुश्छिद्रेण सज्वरः ॥ इति ।

अन्यत्रापि—क्रियतेऽधःशिराः सूतिमारुतैः प्रबलैस्ततः ।
निःसार्य्यते रुजद्गात्रो योनिच्छिद्रेण बालकः ॥ इति ।

क्षणं निश्चेष्ट स्तिष्ठति भूमाविति शेषः ॥ ४८ ॥ ५० ॥

एवं शरीरोत्पत्तिपर्य्यन्तामर्थसृष्टिमुक्ता "तत् प्राप्य" इति सामान्यत उक्तां शब्दसृष्टिं विविच्य वक्तुं भीत्या रोदितुमिच्छति इत्युक्तरोदनस्याप्यव्यक्त-वर्णात्मकत्वात् वर्णोत्पत्तिप्रकारञ्च वदन् सर्व्वमन्त्राणां सामान्यतः कुण्डलीत उत्पत्तिमाह तत इत्यादि । तदुक्तम्—

मूलाधारात् प्रथममुदितो यस्तु भावः पराख्यः
पश्चात् पश्यन्त्यथ हृदयगो बुद्धियुङ् मध्यमाख्यः ।
वक्त्रे वैखर्य्यथ रुरुदिषोरस्य जन्तोः सुषुम्णा-
बद्धस्तस्माद्भवति पवनप्रेरितो वर्णसङ्घः ॥
स्रोतोमार्गस्याविभक्तत्वहेतो स्तत्वार्णानां जायते न प्रकाशः । इति ।

तत्र ततः शरीरोत्पत्त्यनन्तरं चैतन्यरूपा अतएव शब्दब्रह्ममयी सा देवी कुण्डली परदेवता सर्व्वगात्वेण गुणिता अतएव विश्वात्मना सर्व्वात्मना प्रवुद्धा जातप्रबोधा मन्त्रमयं जगत् सूते इति दूरेण सम्बन्धः । तत्र मूलाधारे कुण्डलीभूतसर्पवन्नाडी वर्त्तते । तन्मध्ये वायुवशादस्याः सञ्चरणमेव गुणनम् । तत्र चैतन्यरूपा इति स्वरूपाख्यानम् । सा प्रसिद्धा । सर्व्वगेति सामान्यतो व्याप्तिर्दर्शिता । विश्वरूपिणीति विषयव्याप्तिः । शिवसन्निधिमासाद्य स्थितेति शेषः । अनेन शैवसिद्धान्ते शक्तिशब्दवाच्येयमित्युक्तम् । सन्निधिशब्द औपचारिकः । तन्मते शिवशक्त्योरभेदात् । तदुक्तमभिनवगुप्तपादाचार्य्यैः—

शक्तिश्च शक्तिमद्रूपाद्व्यतिरेकं न वाञ्छति ।
तादात्म्यमनयोर्नित्यं वह्निदाहिकयोरिव ॥ इति ।

यद्वा सम्यङ्निधिः स्वरूपं शिवस्वरूपं प्राप्य इत्यर्थः । वक्ष्यति च—"पिण्डं भवेत् कुण्डलिनी शिवात्मा" इति । गुणानां सत्त्वरजस्तमसां उदयो यस्यां सा ।

दिक्कालाद्यनवच्छिन्ना सर्व्वदेहानुगा शुभा ।
परापरविभागेन परशक्तिरियं स्मृता ॥ ५२

योगिनां हृदयाम्भोजे नृत्यन्ती नित्यमञ्जसा ।
आधारे सर्व्वभूतानां स्फुरन्ती विद्युदाकृतिः ॥ ५३

नित्यानन्दा चासौ गुणोदया च सा। नित्यानन्देत्यनेन कुण्डलिनीस्वरूपमुक्तम्। गुणोदयेत्यनेन सांख्यमते प्रकृतिवाच्येत्युक्तम्। यदाहुः—

प्रधानमिति यामाहु र्या शक्तिरिति कथ्यते। इति ॥ ५१ ॥

इदानीमाध्यात्माधिभूताधिगुणाधिविषयाधिज्योतिषक्रमेण तस्या व्याप्तिमाह दिक्कालेति। सर्व्वदेहानुगेति देहव्याप्तिः। परापरविभागः। काचन परशक्तिः तद्विभागेनापि इयं परशक्तिरेव। यदाहुः—

भूमिरापोऽनलो वायुः खं मनो बुद्धिरेव च।
अहङ्कार इतीयं मे भिन्ना प्रकृतिरष्टधा॥
अपरेयमितस्त्वन्यां प्रकृतिं विद्धि मे पराम्।
जीवभूतां महाबाहो ययेदं धार्य्यते जगत्॥ इति।

यद्वा परः स्थूलः अपरो महास्थूलः महदादिः तद्विभागेन परशक्तिः स्थूला शक्तिः। "स्थूलात् स्थूला" इत्युक्तेः। अनेन महदादिव्याप्तिः। यद्वा सर्व्वदेहानुगेत्यनेन शब्दतोऽर्थतश्च पुंस्त्रीनपुंसकलिङ्गव्याप्तिर्दर्शिता। शब्दतो यथा शिव इत्युच्यते कुण्डलिनीत्युच्यते प्रधानमित्युच्यते। एवम्भूतापि सा स्त्रीत्वेनैव निर्दिश्यते इत्याह परापरेति। परा प्रकृतिः अपरं पुंनपुंसकप्रकृतिः तद्विभागेन तत्त्यागेन इयं परशक्तिः स्मृता। अयमर्थः। यद्यपि लिङ्गत्रयवाच्या तथापि तूर्णमेवाचलभक्तिभारपरिश्रान्त भक्तजनसमस्ताकाङ्क्षाकल्पवल्ली परशक्तिशब्दवाच्येति। अत एव शुभा रमणीया। यदाहुराचार्य्याः—

पुंनपुंसकयोस्तुल्याऽप्यङ्गनासु विशिष्यते। इति।

नित्यक्लिन्नाम्नायेऽपि—

सर्व्वत्रापि स्थिता ह्येषा कामिनीषु विशेषतः।
प्रकाशते ततस्तासामतिक्रान्तिं न कारयेत्॥ इति।

अञ्जसा तत्त्वेन। योगिनां हृदयाम्भोजे नृत्यन्ती नित्यमित्यनेन तैरेव गुरूपदेशेन ज्ञायत इत्यर्थः। "हृत्था दैशिकदेशितैः" इत्युक्तेः। सर्व्वभूतानां

शङ्खावर्त्तक्रमाद् देवी सर्व्वमाहृत्य तिष्ठति ।
कुण्डलीभूतसर्पाणामङ्गश्रियमुपेयुषी ॥ ५४
सर्व्वदेवमयी देवी सर्व्वमन्त्रमयी शिवा ।
सर्व्वतत्त्वमयी साक्षात् सूक्ष्मात् सूक्ष्मतरा विभुः ॥ ५५
त्रिधामजननी देवी शब्दब्रह्मस्वरूपिणी ।
द्विचत्वारिंशद्वर्णात्मा पञ्चाशद्वर्णरूपिणी ॥ ५६
गुणिता सर्व्वगात्रेषु कुण्डली परदेवता ।
विश्वात्मना प्रबुद्धा सा सूते मन्त्रमयं जगत् ॥ ५७

सर्व्वजन्तूनां आधारे मूलाधारचक्रे स्फुरन्तीत्यनेन स्थाननिर्देशः । विद्युदाकृति-रित्यनेन ध्यानमुक्तम् । यदाहुः—

तड़ित्कोटिप्रख्यां स्वरुचिजितकालाननरुचिम् । इति ।

अथवा अनेनानेकशब्दोत्पत्तिहेतुत्वेनानेकविलासवतीत्युक्तम् । शङ्खमध्ये य आवर्त्तः स यथा शब्दमाहृत्य तिष्ठति तद्वदियमपि देवीत्यर्थः । इदमवान्तरवाक्यं भिन्नमेव । शङ्खेति कुण्डलीत्यनयोः हेतुहेतुमद्भावेन योजना । कुण्डलीभूताः कुण्डलाकारतां प्राप्ता ये सर्पास्तेषाम् । केचन कुण्डलीति भिन्नं पदं वर्णयन्ति । भूतानि सर्पाश्च एते यथा कुटिलगतयः तद्वदियमपीत्यर्थ इति । तन्न । कुण्डली परदेवतेत्यनेन पुनरुक्तेः । सर्व्वदेवमयीति देवव्याप्तिः । दिव्यतीति देवी तेजोरूपेत्यर्थः । अनेन तेजोव्याप्तिः । सर्व्वमन्त्रमयीति मन्त्रव्याप्तिः । शिवा शिवरूपेत्यर्थः । यद्वा शिवा कल्याणरूपा । अनेन कल्याणव्याप्तिः । साक्षात् सर्व्वतत्त्वमयीति तत्त्वव्याप्तिः । सूक्ष्मात् सूक्ष्मतरा विभुः इति विरोध-परिहारस्तु सूक्ष्मतरा दुर्ज्ञाना । यद्वा सूक्ष्मात् त्रसरेणोरपि सूक्ष्मतरा अन्तःस्थितत्वात् सूक्ष्मतरा अणुतरा । अनेन अण्वादिव्याप्तिर्दर्शिता । तदुक्तम्—

बालाग्रस्य सहस्रधा विदलितस्यैकेन भागेन या
सूक्ष्मत्वात् सदृशी त्रिलोकजननी । इति ।

विभुः इयत्तया ज्ञातुमशक्या ॥ ५२–५५ ॥

त्रिधामेति सोमसूर्य्याग्निरूपम् । यद्वा त्रिधामेति स्थानत्रयम् । पाताल-भूस्स्वर्गरूपम् । अनेन स्थानव्याप्तिर्दर्शिता । द्विचत्वारिंशद्वर्णात्मेति भूतलिपिमन्त्र-मयी । पञ्चाशद्वर्णरूपिणीति मातृकामयी ॥ ५६ ॥ ५७ ॥

एकधा गुणिता शक्तिः सर्व्वविश्वप्रवर्त्तिनी।
वेदादिबीजं श्रीबीजं शक्तिबीजं मनोभवम्॥ ५८
प्रासादं तुम्बुरं पिण्डं चिन्तारत्नं गणेश्वरम्।
मार्त्तण्डभैरवं दौर्गं नारसिंहवराहजम्॥ ५९
वासुदेवं हयग्रीवं बीजं श्रीपुरुषोत्तमम्।
अन्यान्यपि च बीजानि तदोत्पादयति ध्रुवम्॥ ६०
यदा भवति सा संवित् द्विगुणीकृतविग्रहा।
हंसवर्णौ परात्मानौ शब्दार्थौ वासरक्षपे॥ ६१

एवं सामान्यत उत्पत्तिमुक्त्वा एकद्व्यादिविशेषाकारेण शब्दसृष्टिं वदन् प्रसङ्गादक्षरं तज्जगत्कृच्छब्दसूचितामर्थसृष्टिमप्यभिधातुमुपक्रमते एकधेति। सर्व्वं विश्वं शब्दार्थरूपं तत्प्रवर्त्तिनी तदुत्पादिका शक्तिः। एकधा गुणिता वेदादिबीजमुत्पादयतीति सम्बन्धः। एवमग्रेऽपि बोद्धव्यम्। वेदादिबीजं प्रणवम् अग्रे वक्ष्यति। श्रीबीजम् अष्टमे। शक्तिबीजं नवमे। मनोभवं सप्तदशे। प्रासादम् अष्टादशे। तुम्बुरुमेकोनविंशे। पिण्डमुपान्त्ये। चिन्तारत्नमेकोनविंशे। गणेश्वरं त्रयोदशे। मार्त्तण्डभैरवं चतुर्दशे। दौर्गम् एकादशे। नारसिंहं षोडशे। वाराहं पञ्चदशे। वासुदेवं क्लौं। इदं गोपालबीजत्वेनोद्धृतम्। तद्वासुदेवशब्देनोक्तम्। तत् सप्तदशे। नारदपञ्चरात्रोक्तं वियत्त्वार्णं वासुदेवबीजं वा। हयग्रीवं पञ्चदशे। श्रीपुरुषोत्तममिति श्रीयुक्तपुरुषोत्तममित्युक्तत्वात् शक्तिशक्तिमतोरभेदात् पुरुषोत्तमशक्तिबीजं श्रीपुरुषोत्तमबीजशब्देनोक्तम्। तत् सप्तदशे। अत्र कामबीजमेव पुरुषोत्तमबीजत्वेनोक्तम्।

यदाहुः—धरयालिङ्गितो ब्रह्मा मायाबिन्दुविभूषितः।
पुरुषोत्तमसंज्ञोऽत्र देवो मन्मथविग्रहः॥ इति।

अन्यान्यपीति चन्द्रबीजबिम्बबीजादीनि॥ ५८-६०॥

हंसवर्णौ चतुर्दशे। परात्मानौ वर्णाविति सम्बध्यते। परमात्मवाचकावित्यर्थः। तौ सोहंरूपावन्त्ये। प्रकृतिपुरुषाविति। यद्यपि पुरुषोऽनादिस्तथापि मायाशबलितत्वेनात्र प्रादुर्भाव उपचारात्। अन्यद्युग्मं यद्जगति अस्याः सकाशादजायतेति सम्बन्धः। तच्च ज्योतिर्मन्त्रादि। त्रैपुरं मन्त्रद्वयं द्वादशे। शक्तिविनायकं त्रयोदशे। यद्यप्यग्रे नवाक्षरयोगाद् द्वादशाक्षरस्तथापि

सृजत्येषा परा देवी तदा प्रकृतिपुरुषौ ।
यद्यदन्यज्जगत्यस्यां युग्मं तत्तदजायत ॥ ६२
त्रिगुणीकृतसर्व्वाङ्गी चिद्रूपा शिवगेहिनी ।
प्रसूते त्रैपुरं मन्त्रं मन्त्रं शक्तिविनायकम् ॥ ६३
पाशाद्यं त्र्यक्षरं मन्त्रं त्रैपुटं चण्डनायकम् ।
सौरं मृत्युञ्जयं शक्तिसम्भवं विनतासुतम् ।
वागीशीत्र्यक्षरं मन्त्रं नीलकण्ठं विषापहम् ॥ ६४
यन्त्रं त्रिगुणितं देव्या लोकत्रयं गुणत्रयम् ।
धामत्रयं सा वेदानां त्रयं वर्णत्रयं शुभम् ॥ ६५
त्रिपुष्करं स्वरान् देवी ब्रह्मादीनां त्रयं त्रयम् ।
वह्नेः कालत्रयं शक्तित्रयं वृत्तित्रयं महत् ।
नाड़ीत्रयं त्रिवर्गं सा यद्यदन्यत् त्रिधा मतम् ॥ ६६

बीजत्रयात्मकत्वं त्रयाणां बीजरूपत्वेन प्राधान्यात्। क्लीँ श्रीँ क्लीँ इति तन्त्रान्तरोक्तो वा। पाशाद्यं नवमे। त्र्यक्षरमिति त्रिकण्टकीद्वयं दशमे। विशेषणविशेष्यभावो वा। त्रैपुटं दशमे। चण्डनायकं चण्डेश्वरं विंशे। सौरं चतुर्दशे। मृत्युञ्जय मष्टादशे। शक्तिसम्भवं मन्त्रद्वयं नवमे। शाक्तं शाम्भवमिति पाठे शाम्भवं तन्त्रान्तरोक्तम् प्रणवमायाबीजप्रासादात्मकम्। विनतासुतं क्षिप ॐ इति तन्त्रान्तरोक्तम्। वागीशीत्र्यक्षरं सप्तमे। वागीशमिति पाठे त्र्यक्षरमिति नवमस्थम् शाक्तमेकम्। विषापहं नीलकण्ठमेकोनविंशे ॥ ६१-६४ ॥

यन्त्रं नवमे। गुणत्रयं धामत्रयं चतुर्थे। यद्यप्यथर्व्ववेदोऽस्ति तथापि होत्र-ध्वर्य्यूद्गातृरूपपदार्थत्रयेण यज्ञनिष्पादनात् वेदत्रयमित्युक्तम्। श्रुतिरपि—"सैषा त्रयी विद्या यज्ञे" इति। वर्णत्रयं प्रणवस्य अकारोकारमकाराः। त्रिपुष्करं तीर्थत्रयम्। तस्य ज्येष्ठमध्यमकनीयस्त्वेन त्रित्वम्। स्वरान् उदात्तानुदात्त-स्वरितान्। देव्यः गायत्रीसरस्वतीसावित्र्यः। ब्रह्मादीनां ब्रह्मविष्णुमहेश्वराणां त्रयं नवमे। देवीति भिन्ने पदे कुण्डलीविशेषणम्। वह्नेस्त्रयं दक्षिणाग्नि-गार्हपत्याहवनीयम्। कालत्रयं अतीतवर्त्तमानभविष्यद्रूपम् प्रातर्मध्याह्न-सायंकालरूपं वा। शक्तित्रयं रौद्रीज्येष्ठावामात्मकम् तदाद्ये। प्रभावोत्साह-

चतुःप्रकारगुणिता शाम्भवी शर्म्मदायिणी।
तदानीं पद्मिनीबन्धोः करोति चतुरक्षरम्॥ ६७
चतुरर्णं महादेव्या देवीतत्त्वचतुष्टयम्।
चतुरः सागरानन्तःकरणानां चतुष्टयम्॥ ६८
सूक्ष्मादींश्चतुरो भावान् विष्णोर्मूर्त्तिचतुष्टयम्।
चतुष्टयं गणेशाना मात्मादीनां चतुष्टयम्॥ ६९
ओजापूकादिकं पीठं धर्म्मादीनां चतुष्टयम्।
द्रमकादीन् गजान् देवी यद्वयदन्यच्चतुष्टयम्॥ ७०
पञ्चधा गुणिता पत्नी शम्भोः सर्व्वार्थदायिनी।
त्रिपुरापञ्चकूटं सा तस्याः पञ्चाक्षरद्वयम्॥ ७१

मन्त्ररूपं वा। वृत्तित्रयं यजनाध्यापनप्रतिग्रहरूपम्। "त्रीणि कर्म्माणि जीविकेति" स्मरणात्। कृषिपाशुपाल्यवाणिज्यं वा वृत्तित्रयम्। महदिति पाठे नाडीत्रयस्य विशेषणत्वेन महदिति योज्यम्। नाड़ीत्रयं इड़ापिङ्गलासुषुम्णारूपमाद्ये। त्रिवर्गं धर्म्मार्थकामाः। "त्रिवर्गो धर्म्मकामार्थैः" इत्युक्तेः। अन्यदिति दोषत्रयादि॥ ६५॥ ६६॥

पद्मिनीबन्धोरिति। तन्त्रान्तरोक्तः प्रणवमायाहंसवर्णात्मकः। महादेव्या महालक्ष्म्या अष्टमे। देवीतत्त्वचतुष्टयम् आत्मतत्त्वं विद्यातत्त्वं शिवतत्त्वं सर्व्वतत्त्वञ्चेति। चतुरः सागरानिति। प्रागादिदिगपेक्षया चतुष्ट्वं वस्तुतस्तस्यैकत्वात्। अन्तःकरणानि मनोबुद्ध्यहङ्कारचित्तरूपाणि॥ ६७॥ ६८॥

सूक्ष्मादीनिति आद्ये। सूक्ष्मा परा। आदिशब्देन पश्यन्तीमध्यमावैखर्य्यः।
तदुक्तम्—वैखरी मध्यमा चैव पश्यन्ती चापि सूक्ष्मया।
व्युत्क्रमेण भवन्त्येताः कुण्डलिन्यादितः क्रमात्॥ इति।
भावान् अवस्थाविशेषान् जाग्रत्स्वप्नसुषुप्तितुरीयान्। विशेषणविशेष्यभावो वा। विष्णुमूर्त्तिरष्टमे। गणेशानामिति त्रयोदशे। आत्मादीनामिति चतुर्थे। पीठमिति ओड्डीयानजालन्धरपूर्णगिरिकामरूपाणि। धर्म्मादीनामिति चतुर्थे। अधर्म्मादीनामप्युपलक्षकम्। धर्म्मार्थादीनां वा तदाद्ये। गजान् इत्यष्टमे। अन्यदिति सिद्धादिमण्डलदीक्षा हेरम्बमन्त्र देवीदूतीबीजादि॥ ६९॥ ७०॥

पञ्चरत्नं महादेव्याः सर्व्वकामफलप्रदम् ।
पञ्चाक्षरं महेशस्य पञ्चवर्णं गरुत्मतः ॥ ७२
सम्मोहनान् पञ्च कामान् वाणान् पञ्च सुरद्रुमान् ।
पञ्च प्राणादिकान् वायून् पञ्च वर्णान् महेशितुः ॥ ७३
मूर्त्तीः पञ्च कलाः पञ्च पञ्च ब्रह्मऋचः क्रमात् ।
सृजत्येषा परा शक्ति र्वेदवेदार्थरूपिणी ॥ ७४
षोढ़ा सा गुणिता देवी धत्ते मन्त्रं षड़क्षरम् ।
षट्कूटं त्रिपुरामन्त्रं गाणपत्यं षड़क्षरम् ॥ ७५

पञ्चधेति । क्रमात् पञ्चकूटादिकम् एषा सृजतीति । क्रमस्तु वक्ष्यमाणः शक्तिश्चन्द्रादिकः । एवमग्रेऽपि षट्क्रमादिति पदानि शब्दसृष्टौ संयोज्य वयस्येवार्थस्तेषां व्याख्येयः । पञ्चकूटमिति । ह स क ल र एते पञ्चवर्णाः एकीकृताः कूटशब्देनोच्यन्ते । तस्याः पञ्चाक्षरद्वयमिति । एकः पञ्चकामैरपरे वाणबीजैरेतानि द्वादशे । तदुक्तं दक्षिणामूर्त्तिसंहितायाम्—

त्रिपुरेशी मन्त्रमध्ये वाणाः प्रोक्ता महेश्वरि ।
तैरेव पञ्चभिर्वाणै र्विद्या पञ्चाक्षरी भवेत् ॥
पूर्व्वोक्तपञ्चकामैस्तु पञ्चकामेश्वरी भवेत् । इति ।

पञ्चरत्नमिति । ग्लुं स्लुं म्लुं प्लुं न्लुं इति मन्त्रपञ्चकं तन्त्रान्तरोक्तम् ।

सिद्धाद्या विजया श्यामा वाराही सुन्दरीत्यपि । इति ।

महेशस्येत्यष्टादशे । गरुत्मत इति चतुर्विंशे । सम्मोहनानिति बहुवचनमाद्यर्थम् सम्मोहनादीन् । कामान् वाणान् द्वादशे । सुरद्रुमान् मन्दारपारिजातसन्तानकल्पद्रुमहरिचन्दनान् । वायून् आद्ये । वर्णान् शकादीन् तृतीये । महेशितुरिति पञ्चिमेण सम्बध्यते । मूर्त्तीरष्टादशे । कला निवृत्त्याद्या आद्ये । ब्रह्मऋच ईशानाद्या अष्टादशे । अन्यदिति ज्ञेयम् । तत्र भूतप्रपञ्चभेदादित्यमूर्त्तिपञ्चगव्यादि धत्ते विधत्ते करोतीत्यर्थः ॥ ७१-७४ ॥

षड़क्षरं राममन्त्रं पञ्चदशे । षट्कूटमिति त्रिपुरार्णवोक्तम् । षट्कूटं मध्यबीजम् । तदुक्तम्—

कान्तान्तवान्ताकुलवान्तवाम नेत्रान्वितं दण्डिकुलं सनादम् ।
षट्कूटमेतत् त्रिपुरार्णवोक्तमत्यन्तगुह्यं स्मर एव साक्षात् ॥ इति ।

षड़क्षरं हिमरुचे र्नारसिंहं षड़क्षरम् ।
ऋतून् वसन्तमुख्यान् षड़ामोदादीन् गणाधिपान् ॥ ७६
कोशानूर्म्मीन् रसान् शक्तीः शाकिन्याद्याः षड़ध्वनः ।
यन्त्रं षड़् गुणितं शक्तेः षड़ाधारानजीजनत् ।
षड़्विधं यज्जगत्यस्मिन् सर्व्वं तत् परमेश्वरी ॥ ७७
सप्तधा गुणिता नित्या शङ्करार्द्धशरीरिणी ।
सप्तार्णं त्रिपुरामन्त्रं सप्तवर्णं विनायकम् ॥ ७८

गाणपत्यं तन्त्रान्तरोक्तं चतुर्थ्यन्तं वक्रतुण्डं वर्म्मान्तम् । षड़क्षरं शैवमष्टादशे । षड़क्षरं कृष्णमन्त्रं सप्तदशे । विशेषणविशेष्यभावो वा । हिमरुचेः षड़क्षरं चतुर्दशे । नारसिंहं षोड़शे । षड़क्षरं पाशुपतास्त्रं विंशे । विशेषणविशेष्य-भावो वा । ऋतूनिति त्रयोविंशे । आमोदादीनिति त्रयोदशे । कोशानूर्म्मीनाद्ये । रसान् मधुरादीन् । शक्तीरामोदादीनां त्रयोदशे । शाकिन्याद्या इति विंशे । शक्तीः शाकिन्याद्या इति विशेषणविशेष्यभावो वा । षड़ध्वनः पञ्चमे । यन्त्रं नवमे । आधारान् पञ्चमे । जगति यत् सर्व्वं षड़्विधं षड़ङ्गसीतामन्त्रषट्-कर्म्मासनादि ॥ ७५–७७ ॥

सप्तार्णमिति । सप्तवर्णं पद्मावतीमन्त्रं दशमे । त्रिपुरामन्त्रमिति मायाबीजा-द्यनुलोमविलोमभैरवीमन्त्रः । सप्तवर्णं शङ्खमन्त्रं सप्तदशे । विनायकं सुब्रह्मण्यं त्रयोदशे । यद्वा सप्तार्णं त्रिपुरामन्त्रं विनायकं सप्तवर्णमिति विशेषणविशेष्य-भावः । व्याहृतीनामिति एकविंशे । सप्तवर्णमिति अङ्कुशमन्त्रं सप्तदशे । सुदर्शनं षोड़शे । विशेषणविशेष्यभावो वा । लोकान् भूरादिकान् । गिरीन् विन्ध्यपारियात्रसह्यऋक्षमलयमहेन्द्रशुक्तिमतः । स्वरान् षड़्जऋषभगान्धार-मध्यमपञ्चमधैवतनिषादान् । धातून् त्वगादीन् आद्ये । मुनीन् वशिष्ठकश्य-पात्रिजमदग्निगौतमविश्वामित्रभरद्वाजान् वैवस्वतमन्वन्तरे अत एव ऋषयः सप्त । द्वीपान् जम्बूप्लक्षशाल्मलीकुशक्रौञ्चशाकपुष्करान् । ग्रहानिति । केपाञ्चिन्मते राहुकेत्वोर्ग्रहत्वाभावात् सप्तैवुक्ताः तान् षष्ठे । तथा च वराहमिहिराचार्य्यैः—

अमृतास्वादविशेषात् छिन्नमपि शिरः किलासुरस्येदम् ।
प्राणैरपरित्यक्तं ग्रहभावं नैवमाप्नोति ॥

इत्यादिना ।

सारकं व्याहृतीनां सा समवर्णं सुदर्शनम् ।
लोकान् गिरीन् स्वरान् धातून् मुनीन् द्वीपान् ग्रहानपि ॥ ७९
समिधः सप्त संख्याता सप्त जिह्वा हविर्भुजः ।
अन्यत् सप्तविधं यद्यत् तदस्याः समजायत ॥ ८०
अष्टधा गुणिता शक्तिः शैवमष्टाक्षरद्वयम् ।
विष्णोः श्रीकरनामानं मन्त्रमष्टाक्षरं परम् ॥ ८१
अष्टाक्षरं हरेः शक्ते रष्टाक्षरयुगं परम् ।
भानोरष्टाक्षरं दौर्गं मष्टार्णं परमात्मनः ॥ ८२

एवमुपरागकारणमुक्तमिदं दिव्यदृग्भिराचार्यैः ।
राहुरकारणमस्मिन्नित्युक्तः शास्त्रसद्भावः ॥
योऽसावसुरो राहु स्तस्य वरो ब्रह्मणा पुरा दत्तः ।
आप्यायनमुपरागे दत्तहुतांशेन ते भवितेति ॥

इत्यादिना च बहुना ग्रन्थसन्दर्भेण राहुकेत्वोः ग्रहता निरस्ता। अपिशब्दाद्‌अजीजनदिति क्रियाऽनुषज्यते। समिध इत्युत्तरपदमुत्तरक्रिययाऽन्वेति। हविर्भुजः समिधः सप्त श्रुत्युक्ताः। तथाच श्रुतिः—

सप्त ते अग्ने समिधः सप्त जिह्वाः सप्त ऋषयः सप्त धाम प्रियाणि। इति।

सप्तवृक्षाणां वा—

अर्कः पलाशः खदिरोऽप्यपामार्गोऽथ पिप्पलः। औदुम्बरः शमी। इति।

तदा हविर्भुज इत्यत्र न सम्बध्यते। सप्तजिह्वास्त्रिविधा अपि पञ्चमे। अन्यदिति प्रकृतिविकृतित्रिपुरातत्त्वगरुडमन्त्रयन्त्रपटलमन्त्रहयवैवस्वतमन्वादि ॥ ७९-८० ॥

शैवं द्वयमप्येकोनविंशे। विष्णोः श्रीकरनामानं परमष्टाक्षरं कृष्णस्य द्वावपि सप्तदशे। हरेरिति पञ्चदशे। शक्तेरिति नवमे युगलमपि। भानोरिति चतुर्दशे। दौर्गद्वयमप्येकादशे। परमात्मन इति षष्ठे। नीलकण्ठस्येति। नीलकण्ठशब्देन क्षेत्रपालमन्त्रो गृहीतः स विंशे। तन्त्रान्तरोक्तो वा "ॐ नीलकण्ठाय स्वाहा" इति। वासुदेवात्मकं मनुं मन्त्रम्। आगमशास्त्रे मनुशब्दो मन्त्रस्य संज्ञा। "ॐ नमो वासुदेवाय" इति तन्त्रान्तरोक्तम्।

कामार्गलं सप्तदशे। तस्य कामार्गलत्वेन प्रसिद्ध्यभावात् तन्त्रान्तरोक्तं कामार्गलम्।

अष्टार्णं नीलकण्ठस्य वासुदेवात्मकं मनुम्।
यन्त्रं कामार्गलं दिव्यं देवीयन्त्रं घटार्गलम्॥ ८३
गन्धाष्टकं शुभं देवीदेवानां हृदयङ्गमम्।
ब्राह्मयाद्या भैरवान् सर्पान् मूर्त्तीराशा वसूनपि॥ ८४
अष्टपीठं महादेव्या अष्टाष्टकसमन्वितम्।
अष्टौ सा प्रकृतीर्विघ्नवक्रतुण्डादिकान् क्रमात्॥ ८५

व्योम ब्रह्मेन्द्रलोकेशवह्निवामाक्षिविन्दुमत्।
कर्णिकायां लिखेत् साध्यं कामिनोश्च दलाष्टके॥
मूलं मासकलापत्रेष्वालिखेत् स्वरभेदितम्।
दन्तपत्रेषु तद्भिन्नवर्णैः सान्तैश्च कादिभिः॥
वेष्टयेन्मन्दिरेणैतत् बहिः शक्त्याङ्कुशेन च।
यन्त्रं घटार्गलेनैतत्तुल्यं कामार्गलं विदुः॥ इति।

दिव्यं यमार्गलमित्यर्थः। "दिव्यं यमार्गलं यन्त्रम्" इत्युक्तेः। इदं चतुर्विंशे। देवी भुवनेशी। "हृल्लेखा शक्तिदेव्याख्या" इत्युक्तेः। तस्या यन्त्रं घटार्गलं नवमे।
गन्धाष्टकं त्रिविधमपि तूर्य्ये। देवो विष्णुः देवः शिवस्य देवौ। देवी च देवौ च देवाः तेषाम्। क्वचिद् दिव्यमिति पाठः। तदा देवानामिति सामान्येन। ब्राह्मयाद्याः षष्ठे। अष्टौ भैरवान् नवमे। सर्पांस्त्रयोविंशे। अष्टमूर्त्तीर्विंशे। आशाः पूर्व्वादिदिशः। वसूनिति—

धरो ध्रुवश्च सोमश्च आपश्चैवानिलोऽनलः।
प्रत्यूषश्च प्रभासश्च अष्टौ ते वसवः स्मृताः॥ इति।

अष्टाष्टकसमन्वितमष्टपीठं चतुःषष्टिविधं यथा—

मायामङ्गलनागवामनमहालक्ष्मीचरित्राभृगु-
च्छायाछत्रहिरण्यहस्तिनमहेन्द्रोड्डीश चम्पापुरम्।
षष्ठक्षीरक मञ्जुनेश्वरपुरैलाश्चन्द्रपूः श्रीगिरिः
कोलाकुब्जक पूर्णपर्व्वत कुरुक्षेत्रैकलिङ्गार्बुदाः॥
काश्मीरैकाम्रकाञ्चीमलयगिरिवरैकारकम्बूतदेवी-
कोट्टाख्यातेशजालन्धरसुरभिमनोषाद्रिकाशीप्रयागाः।

अणिमादिगुणान् नागान् वह्नेर्मूर्त्तीर्यमादिकान् ।
अष्टात्मकं जगत्यस्मिन् सर्व्वं वितनुते यदा ॥ ८६

गुणिता नवधा नित्या सूते मन्त्रं नवात्मकम् ।
नवकं शक्तितत्त्वानां तत्त्वरूपा महेश्वरी ॥ ८७

नवकं पीठशक्तीनां शृङ्गारादीन् रसान् नव ।
माणिक्यादीनि रत्नानि नववर्गयुतानि सा ॥ ८८

नवकं प्राणदूतीनां मण्डलं नवकं शुभम् ।
यद्‌यन्नवात्मकं लोके सर्व्वमस्या उदस्यति ॥ ८९

विस्रोतः कामकोट्टोज्जयिनि समधुरं कोशलाकान्यकुब्जौ-
जानीङ्काराट्टहासाविरज इह ततः कुण्डिनं राजगेहम् ॥
नेपालपुण्ड्रवर्द्धनमालवपरसीर कामरूपकेदाराः
विन्ध्यमहामठगोश्रुति काम्पिल्यश्रीपीठमरुदेशाः ॥ इति ।

प्रकृतीशाये । विघ्नान् वक्रतुण्डांश्च त्रयोदशे । अणिमादीति ।

अणिमा महिमा चैव गरिमा लघिमा तथा ।
ईशित्वञ्च वशित्वञ्च प्राकाम्यं प्राप्तिरेव च ॥ इति ।

नागान् गजान् अष्टमे । वह्नेरिति पञ्चमे । यमादिकान् अन्ये । अन्यदिति श्रीवाणरतिप्रिय धूमावतीमन्त्रादि ॥ ८१-८६ ॥

नवधेति । जगति यावान् नवात्मको नवाक्षरो मन्त्रस्तं सूते । सप्ताङ्गनवार्ण-गोपालमन्त्रादि । सेत्यन्तं पूर्व्वक्रियया उत्तरपद्यमुत्तरक्रियया सम्बध्यते । शक्तितत्त्वानामिति प्रकृतिर्नादो बिन्दुः बिन्दुर्नादो बीजं रौद्री जेष्ठा वामेति नव शक्तितत्त्वानि आद्ये । वक्ष्यमाणानि दश सदाशिवव्यतिरिक्तानि नवेत्यन्ये । पीठशक्तीनामिति तत्तन्मन्त्रेष्वपि तत्र तत्र । शृङ्गारादीन् ।

शृङ्गारवीरकरुणाद्भुतहास्यभयानकाः ।
बीभत्सरौद्रशान्ताश्च नव काव्ये रसाः स्मृताः ॥ इति ।

रत्नानि नव वर्गाश्च वक्ष्ये । प्राणदूतीनामिति त्रयोविंशे । मण्डलं नवनाभं तृतीये । यद्‌यदिति । नवकुण्डनवग्रहकूर्म्मचक्रनवकोष्ठादि ॥ ८७-८९ ॥

दशधा विकृता शम्भोर्भामिनी भवदुःखहा ।
दशाक्षरं गणपतेस्त्वरिताया दशाक्षरम् ॥ ९०
दशाक्षरं सरस्वत्या यक्षिण्याः सा दशाक्षरम् ।
वासुदेवात्मकं मन्त्रमश्वारूढ़ादशाक्षरम् ॥ ९१
त्रिपुरादशकूटं सा त्रिपुराया दशाक्षरम् ।
नाम्ना पद्मावतीमन्त्रं रमामन्त्रं दशाक्षरम् ॥ ९२
दशकं शक्तितत्त्वानां तत्त्वरूपा महेश्वरी ।
नाड़ीनां दशकं विष्णो रवतारान् दश क्रमात् ।
दशकं लोकपालानां यद्यदन्यत् सृजत्यसौ ॥ ९३

गणपतेरिति। क्षिप्रप्रसादनस्य त्रयोदशे। त्वरिताया इति दशमे मायाहीनम्। तदुक्तम्—वर्म्म खे च तदन्त्यः शिवयुक् चरमोऽङ्गना द्यु सार्घ्विलवम्।

अन्त्यः सयोनि रस्त्रान्तिकः सतारो मनुर्दशार्णयुतः॥ इति।

वर्म्मेति। वर्म्म हुं। खे स्वरूपम्। च स्वरूपम्। तदन्त्यः छः शिवयुगेकारयुतः छे। चरमः क्षः। अङ्गना स्त्रीँ। द्यु हकारः सार्घ्विलवं उकारानुस्वारयुतं तेन हुं। अन्त्यः क्षः सयोनिरेयुतः क्षे। अस्त्रं फट् तदन्तः। सतारः प्रणवयुक् आदौ। इति त्वरितादशाक्षरोद्धारः। नारायणीयेऽपि—

भुवनेशो भूतदण्डौ कलान्तान्त्यं सयोनिकम्।
तत्पञ्चमं तदन्तं सरुद्रं सामन्तान्तालयम्॥
वामाख्या दीर्घमाद्यञ्च कोपतत्त्वं हरान्तयुक्।
एतत् फड़न्तं तारादि मन्त्रं विद्याद्दशाक्षरम्॥ इति।

भुवनेति। भुवनेशो हः भूतं उः दण्डोऽनुस्वारः तेन हुं। कलाः स्वराः तदन्तः कः तदन्त्यः खः सयोनिकम् एकारयुतं तेन खे। तत्पञ्चमं च तदन्तं छः। सरुद्रम् एकारयुतं तेन छे। सामन्तान्तः विसर्गान्तः। आलयं क्षकारः। वामाख्या स्त्रीँ। आद्यं हुं तद्दीर्घं हूं। कोपतत्त्वं क्षः। हरेण एकारेण अन्ते युक् क्षे। एतत् फड़न्तं प्रणवादिकं दशवर्णम्। सरस्वत्या इति सप्तमे। यक्षिण्या इति तन्त्रान्तरोक्तं "श्रीँ श्रीँ यक्षिणि हं हं हं स्वाहा" इति। वासुदेवात्मकमिति गोपालं सप्तदशे। अश्वारूढ़ेति बीजत्रयं मुक्त्वा दशमे।

एकादशक्रमात् संविद् गुणिता सा जगन्मयी ।
रुद्रैकादशनीमाद्यशक्तेरेकादशाक्षरम् ॥
एकादशाक्षरं वाग्भ्या रुद्रानेकादश क्रमात् ॥ ८४

तन्त्रान्तरे दशाक्षर्या एव उद्धृतत्वात् । तदुक्तम्—

आद्य स्त्रयोदशो दण्डी ततस्त्वेकादशः परम् ।
अष्टमस्य तृतीयं स्यादाद्यतार्त्तीयसंयुतम् ॥
षष्ठाद्यं सप्तमस्यापि द्वितीयं षष्ठपञ्चमम् ।
आद्यैकादशसंयुक्तं पश्चात् सप्तम पञ्चमम् ॥
तत्तूर्य्येण युतं पश्चात् सप्तमस्य द्वितीयकम् ।
आद्यतार्त्तीयसंयुक्तं द्विठः प्रोक्ता दशाक्षरी ॥ इति ।

दशकूटमिति मध्यबीजस्य षट्कूटत्वमाद्यन्तबीजयोः क्रमेण कूटद्वयम् । कूटद्वयमिति मिलित्वा दशकूटं त्रिपुराया इति तन्त्रान्तरोक्तम् "ऐँ स्ह्रैं स्ह्रीं स्ह्रौं त्रिपुरायै नमः" इति । पद्मावतीमन्त्रं तन्त्रान्तरोक्तम् "ॐ ह्रैं पद्मे पद्मावति स्वाहा" इति । रमामन्त्रमष्टमे । राममन्त्रमितिपाठे पञ्चदशे । शक्तितत्त्वानामिति पञ्चमे । नाडीनामित्याद्ये । अवतारानिति सप्तदशे । लोकपालानामिति तूर्य्ये । अन्यदिति अग्निमन्त्रसंस्कार जयदुर्गामन्त्रादि ॥ ८०-८३ ॥

रुद्रैकादशनीमिति ।

षड्ङ्गरुद्रैकावृत्ती रुद्राध्यायस्य तादृशः ।
एकादश तु रुद्रस्य रुद्रैकादशनी त्विति ॥

षड्ङ्गरुद्रस्तु—"यज्जाग्रतः षट्" "सहस्रशीर्षा द्वाविंशतिः" ततः "आशुःशिशानो" "विभ्राट्" इत्यनुवाकद्वयम् शतम् । सहस्रशीर्षेति षोड़शभिर्द्वितीयम् । षड्भि स्तृतीयम् । शतमिति । शतरुद्रीयेणाख्यम् । शतरुद्रस्तु—

षट्षष्टि र्नीलसूक्तञ्च पुनः षोड़शऋग्जपः ।
एष ते ह्रे नमस्ते द्वे नतं विद्वयमेव च ॥
मीदुष्टमचतुष्कञ्च एतत्तु शतरुद्रीयम् । इति ।

आद्यशक्तेः सरस्वत्या एकादशाक्षरं सप्तमे । यद्वा आद्यशक्तेः नित्यक्लिन्नाया-स्तन्त्रान्तरोक्तम् । "क्लीँ नित्यक्लिन्ने मदद्रवे स्वाहा" इति । आद्या इति पाठे देवीविशेषणम् । वाग्भ्या अयमपि सप्तमे । रुद्रानिति—

समुच्चरति सर्व्वात्मा गुणिता द्वादशक्रमात् ।
नित्यामन्त्रं महेशान्या वासुदेवात्मकं मनुम् ॥ ९५
राशीन् भानून् हरे र्मूर्त्तीर्यन्त्रं सा द्वादशात्मकम् ।
अन्यदेतादृशं सर्व्वं यत् तदस्यामजायत ॥ ९६
चतुर्विंशतितत्त्वा सा यदा भवति शोभना ।
गायत्रीं सवितुः शम्भोः गायत्रीं मदनात्मिकाम् ॥ ९७
गायत्रीं विष्णुगायत्रीं गायत्रीं त्रिपदात्मनः ।
गायत्रीं दक्षिणामूर्त्ते र्गायत्रीं शम्भुयोषितः ॥ ९८

हरश्च बहुरूपश्च त्र्यम्बकश्चापराजितः ।
वृषाकपिश्च शम्भुश्च कपर्दी रैवतस्तथा ॥
मृगव्याधश्च शर्व्वश्च कापालीति शिवा मताः । इति ।

अत्राप्यन्यदिति ज्ञेयम् । तच्च शक्तिविनायकमन्त्रादि ॥ ९४ ॥

समुच्चरतीति क्रिया काकाक्षिगोलकन्यायेन पूर्व्वोत्तरवाक्ययोः सम्बध्यते । अन्वाद्यो निर्व्विघ्ननात् सर्व्वोत्तरवाक्ये अन्यदित्यन्तं सम्बध्यते । इत उत्तरं भिन्नमेव वाक्यम् । नित्यामन्त्रं महेशान्या वज्रप्रस्तारिण्यास्त दशमे । वासुदेवं पञ्चदशे । राशीनष्टमे । भानून् हरेर्मूर्त्तीश्च पञ्चदशे । यन्त्रं नवमे । अन्यदिति खड्गमन्त्रादि । एतादृशमित्यनेनैतदुक्तं भवति । त्रयोदशधा गुणिता वागीश्वर्य्यश्वारूढामन्त्रं विश्वेदेवादिकम् । चतुर्दशधा लक्ष्मीवासुदेव-गोपालमन्त्रभुवनादिकम् । पञ्चदशधा नित्याशूलिनीभक्तितिथ्यादिकम् । षोड़शधा चक्रमन्त्रस्वरकलादिकम् । सप्तदशधा लघुपञ्चमीतारादिविद्यामन्त्रा-दिकम् । अष्टादशधा कृष्णवामनमन्त्रमग्निसंस्कारादिकम् । ऊनविंशतिधा कृष्णधरामन्त्रादिकम् । विंशतिधा हलधरोमामहेश्वरमन्त्रादिकम् । एकविंशतिधा वटुकनाममन्त्रतद्यन्त्रादिकम् । द्वाविंशतिधा कृष्णाद्याधिपतिसुमुखीमन्त्रादिकम् । त्रयोविंशतिधा लघुश्यामा पुरुषोत्तमहृदङ्गमन्त्रादिकं सूते इति ॥ ९५ ॥ ९६ ॥

यद्यपि त्रयोदशविश्वेदेवात्मिका चतुर्दशभुवनात्मिका पञ्चदशतिथ्यात्मिकापि सृष्टेर्भगवत्युत्पादितैव तथापि परार्द्धपर्य्यन्तं तस्याः सत्त्वात् वह्नीनां वसुमयत्वात् प्रधानभूता आह चतुरिति । चतुर्विंशति स्तत्त्वस्वरूपं तद्रूप आत्मा यस्याः सा चतुर्विंशतिधा गुणितेत्यर्थः । सवितुरित्येकविंशे । शम्भोरिति तन्त्रान्तरोक्ता ।

चतुर्विंशतितत्त्वानि तस्यामासन् परात्मनि ॥ ९९

द्वात्रिंशद्वेदगुणिता सर्व्वमन्त्रमयी विभुः ।

सूते मृत्युञ्जयं मन्त्रं नारसिंहं महामनुम् ॥ १००

लवणाख्यं मनुं मन्त्रं वरुणस्य महात्मनः ।

हयग्रीवं मनुं दौर्गं वाराहं वह्निनायकम् ॥ १०१

गणेशितुर्महामन्त्रं मन्त्रमन्नाधिपस्य सा ।

मन्त्रं श्रीदक्षिणामूर्त्तेर्मालामन्त्रं मनोभुवः ॥ १०२

"तत्पुरुषाय विद्महे वाग्विशुद्धाय धीमहि । तन्न: शिव: प्रचोदयात्" इति । मदनात्मिका सप्तदशे । विष्णुगायत्री अपि सप्तदशे । पुरुषोत्तमगायत्री च विष्णुगायत्रीशब्देनोक्ता तन्त्रान्तरोक्ता वा । "नारायणाय विद्महे वासुदेवाय धीमहि । तन्नो विष्णु: प्रचोदयात्" इति । त्रिपदात्मनस्त्रिपुरायाः सा द्वादशे । दक्षिणामूर्त्तेरिति । "दक्षिणामूर्त्तये विद्महे ध्यानस्थाय धीमहि । तन्नो घोर: प्रचोदयात्" इति । शम्भुयोषित इति । "सर्व्वमोहिन्यै विद्महे विश्वजनन्यै धीमहि । तन्न: क्लिन्ने प्रचोदयात्" इति । तत्त्वान्याद्ये । एता गायत्र्यस्तत्त्वान्यप्यस्यामासन्नुत्पन्नानि । अत्राप्यन्यदिति ज्ञेयम् । तन्त्राग्निसमृद्धाग्निदक्षिणामूर्त्तिचिटिमन्त्रवक्रतुण्डदुर्गात्वरिताग्निनृसिंहगरुड़हयग्रीवगायत्र्यादि ॥ ९७-९८ ॥

मृत्युञ्जयं वैदिकं त्रयोविंशे । नारसिंहं षोड़शे । महामनुं मन्त्रराजमिति पूर्व्वविशेषणम् । लवणाख्यं द्वाविंशे । वरुणस्येति श्रुत्युक्तम् । महात्मन इति विशेषणम् तेन महावारुणमित्यर्थ: । हयग्रीवं पञ्चदशे । दौर्गं श्रुत्युक्तम् । "अम्बिके अम्बालिके" इत्यादिकम् । वाराहं पञ्चदशे । वह्निनायकम् अन्ध्युपस्थानमन्त्रं पञ्चमे । गणेशितुर्हरिद्रागणेशस्य "ॐ हुँ गं ग्लौं हरिद्रागणपतये वरवरद सर्व्वजनहृदयं स्तम्भय स्तम्भय स्वाहा" । आथर्व्वणिको वक्रतुण्डस्य वा—

रायस्पोषप्रदाता च निधिदो रत्नदो मतः ।

रक्षोहणो वलाहनो वक्रतुण्डाय हूं नमः ॥

महामन्त्रमित्युक्तः अत्रैव वक्ष्यमाणो महागणपतिमन्त्रो वा । सम्प्रदायेन तस्य द्वात्रिंशदक्षरत्वात् । अन्नाधिपस्य तन्त्रान्तरोक्तः "ॐ ह्रीं अन्नरूप रसचतुष्टयरूप नमो नमः अन्नाधिपतये ममान्नं प्रयच्छ स्वाहा" इति । दक्षिणामूर्त्ते-

त्रिष्टुभं वनवासिन्या अघोराख्यं महामनुम्।
भद्रकालीमनुं लक्ष्म्या मालामन्त्रं यमात्मकम्॥ १०३
मन्त्रं सा देवकीसूनो र्मन्त्रं श्रीपुरुषोत्तमम्।
श्रीगोपालमनुं भूमेर्मनुं तारामनुं क्रमात्॥ १०४
महामन्त्रं महालक्ष्म्या मन्त्रं भूतेश्वरस्य सा।
क्षेत्रपालात्मकं मन्त्रं मन्त्रमापन्निवारणम्।
सूते मातङ्गिनीं विद्यां सिद्धविद्यां शुभोदयाम्॥ १०५

रेकोनविंशे। मालामन्त्रं द्वात्रिंशदक्षरं मनोभुवस्तन्त्रान्तरोक्तम्। त्रिष्टुभमिति तदन्तर्गतोक्तोपचारात् द्वात्रिंशदक्षर उच्यते। तदन्तर्गतसप्तत्रिंशन्त्राणामुक्तत्वात्। तन्मध्ये द्वात्रिंशदक्षराणामपि सत्त्वात्। अघोराख्यं तन्त्रान्तरोक्तम्। अस्यकारोक्तस्यैकपञ्चाशदक्षरत्वात्। यदाह—

नकारस्ततो दन्तसंश्लिष्टकालं भगस्यान्ततो वाथ ते तस्य चान्ते।
ततोऽघोररूपा यकारस्य चान्ते हनद्वन्द्वतोऽथो दहद्वन्द्वतश्च॥
पचाभ्यासमुक्ता तथा भ्रामय स्यात् शिरोऽन्तश्च वर्म्मादिकं फट्पदश्च। इति।

नकारेति। "नमो भगवते अघोररूपाय हन हन दह दह पच पच भ्रामय भ्रामय हुँ फट् स्वाहा"। चतुस्त्रिंशदर्णोऽघोरमन्त्रः अघोरानुष्टुप् अघोराग्न्यनाद्याः। ६।६।८।१०।२।२। षडङ्गम्। भद्रकालीमनुं चतुर्विंशे। महालक्ष्म्या दशमे। सर्व्वतोभद्ररूपं यमात्मकमिति मन्त्रद्वयं चतुर्विंशे। देवकीसूनोरिति सुकोष्ठादिकं सप्तदशे। श्रीपुरुषोत्तममन्त्रं तन्त्रान्तरोक्तम्। "ॐ नमो भगवते वासुदेवाय पुरुषोत्तम आयुर्मे देहि विष्णवे प्रभविष्णवे नमः"। श्रीगोपालमनुं यन्त्राङ्कद्वयमपि सप्तदशे। भूमेर्मनुम्—

उद्धृताऽसि वराहेण कृष्णेन शतबाहुना।
मृत्तिके हर मे पापं यन्मया दुष्कृतं कृतम्॥

इति तन्त्रान्तरोक्तम्। तारामनुं तन्त्रान्तरोक्तम्। "ॐ ह्रीँ ह्रीँ हूं नमस्तारायै महातारायै सकलदुस्तरांस्तारय तारय तर तर स्वाहा" इति। महालक्ष्म्या महामन्त्रं श्रीसूक्तलक्षणम्। भूतेश्वरस्य मन्त्रं तन्त्रान्तरोक्तम्। "ॐ नमो भगवते रुद्राय सर्व्वभूताधिपतये भूतप्रेतपिशाचिनीर्नाशय नाशय" इति। क्षेत्रपालात्मकं तन्त्रान्तरोक्तम्। "एह्येहि विदुषि विमुखि नर्त्तय नर्त्तय विघ्न-

अनेन क्रमयोगेन गुणिता शिववल्लभा ।
षट्त्रिंशतश्च तत्त्वानां शैवानां रचयत्यसौ ॥ १०६
अन्यान् मन्त्रांश्च यन्त्राणि शुभदानि प्रसूयते ।
द्विचत्वारिंशता मूले गुणिता विघ्ननायिका ॥ १०७
सा प्रसूते कुण्डलिनी शब्दब्रह्ममयी विभुः ।
शक्तिं ततो ध्वनिस्तस्मान्नादस्तस्मान्निरोधिका ॥ १०८

महाभैरव क्षेत्रपाल इमं बलिं गृह्ण गृह्ण स्वाहा" इति । आपन्निवारणं तन्त्रान्तरोक्तम् । अत्र एकविंशत्यक्षरस्य वक्ष्यमाणत्वात् । मातङ्गिनीं तन्त्रान्तरोक्ताम् । "ॐ ह्रीं ऐं श्रीं नमो भगवति उच्छिष्टचाण्डालि श्रीमातङ्गेश्वरि सर्व्वजनवशङ्करि स्वाहा" इति । सिद्धविद्यां तन्त्रान्तरोक्ताम् । पूर्व्वोक्ताया एव सिद्धेत्यादि विशेषणद्वयं वा । अन्यदित्यपि ज्ञेयम् । तच्च वैष्णवतत्त्वशैवव्यापकमन्त्रादि ॥ १००-१०५ ॥

अनेनेति । अनेन क्रमयोगेन गुणिता षट्त्रिंशद्वारगुणिता इत्यर्थः । शैवानामिति पञ्चमी ॥ १०६ ॥

अन्यान्मन्त्रानिति । तन्त्रान्तरोक्तोच्छिष्टगणपति पुरुषोत्तमव्यापक मन्त्रादीन् । पूर्व्वो यथा—"ॐ नमो भगवते एकदंष्ट्राय हस्तिमुखाय लम्बोदराय उच्छिष्टमहात्मने क्रों ह्रुं ह्रीं हूं घे घे स्वाहा" इति । तृतीयं सप्तदशी । यन्त्राणीति यन्त्रपटलप्रोक्तकोष्ठात्मकयन्त्राष्टमपटलप्रोक्तमहालक्ष्मीयन्त्रादीनि । अनेन क्रमयोगेनेति सामान्योक्तेर्मन्त्रान् यन्त्राणीति च तयोक्तैरष्टत्रिंशता गुणिता अष्टत्रिंशत्कला मन्त्रास्तद्योजादि । [वन] नवदुर्गापुरुषोत्तमनेत्राङ्गमन्त्रादीन् यन्त्राणि इन्द्रश्यामा वराहनृसिंहयन्त्रादीनि सूते इति सूचितम् ॥

द्विचत्वारिंशतेति । मूले मूलाधारे द्विचत्वारिंशता गुणिता विघ्ननायिका कुण्डलिनी अनेन क्रमेण अकारादिसकारान्तां द्विचत्वारिंशदात्मिकां भूतलिपिमन्त्रात्मिकां वर्णमालिकां सृजतीति सम्बन्धः । १०७ ॥

तमेव क्रममाह शक्तिमिति । सा कुण्डलिनी शक्तिं प्रसूते । [शक्तिर्नाम मूलकारणस्य शब्दस्योन्मुखीकरणावस्थेति गूढार्थदीपिकाकारः] । ततः शक्तेर्ध्वनिः । ततः तस्माद् ध्वनिरित्यादि ज्ञेयम् । अयञ्च क्रमो ग्रन्थकृता सर्व्वशेषे उक्तोऽपि एकाक्षरोत्पत्तावप्यनुसन्धेयः । तत्र सत्त्वप्रविष्टा चिच्छक्तिकाख्या परमाकाशावस्था

ततोऽर्द्धेन्दुस्ततो बिन्दुस्तस्मादासीत् परा ततः ।
पश्यन्ती मध्यमा वाचि वैखरी शब्दजन्मभूः ।
इच्छाज्ञानक्रियात्माऽसौ तेजोरूपा गुणात्मिका ॥ १०९
क्रमेणानेन सृजति कुण्डली वर्णमालिकाम् ।
अकारादिसकारान्तां द्विचत्वारिंशदात्मिकाम् ॥ ११०

सैव सत्त्वप्रविष्टा रजोऽनुविद्धा सती ध्वनिशब्दवाच्या अक्षरावस्था सैव तमोऽनुविद्धा नाद शब्दवाच्या अव्यक्तावस्था सैव तमःप्राचुर्यान्निरोधिकाशब्दवाच्या सैव सत्त्व-प्राचुर्यादर्द्धेन्दु शब्दवाच्या तदुभयसंयोगाद् बिन्दुशब्दवाच्या । यदाहुः—

इच्छाशक्तिबलोत्कृष्टो ज्ञानशक्तिप्रदीपकः ।
पुंरूपिणी च सा शक्तिः क्रियाख्या सृजति प्रभुः ॥ इति ।

असावेव बिन्दुः स्थानान्तरगतः पराद्याख्यो भवति । तस्मादिति बिन्दोः । परा मूले पश्यन्ती स्वाधिष्ठाने मध्यमा हृदये वैखरी मुखे । तदुक्तम्—

सूक्ष्मा कुण्डलिनीमध्ये ज्योतिर्मात्रात्मरूपिणी ।
अश्रोत्रविषया तस्मादुद्गच्छन्त्यूर्ध्वगामिनी ॥
स्वयंप्रकाशा पश्यन्ती सुषुम्णामाश्रिता भवेत् ।
सैव हृत्पङ्कजं प्राप्य मध्यमा नादरूपिणी ॥
ततः संजल्पमात्रा स्यादविभक्तोर्द्ध्वगामिनी ।
सैवोरः कण्ठतालुस्था शिरोघ्राणरदस्थिता ॥
जिह्वामूलोष्ठनिस्यूतसर्ववर्णपरिग्रहा ।
शब्दप्रपञ्चजननी श्रोत्रग्राह्या तु वैखरी ॥ इति ।

कादिमतेऽपि—स्वात्मेच्छाशक्तिघातेन प्राणवायुस्वरूपतः ।
मूलाधारे समुत्पन्नः पराख्यो नाद उत्तमः ॥
स एवोर्द्ध्वं तया नीतः स्वाधिष्ठाने विजृम्भितः ।
पश्यन्त्याख्यामवाप्नोति तथैवोर्द्ध्वं शनैः शनैः ॥
अनाहते बुद्धितत्त्वसमेतो मध्यमाभिधः ।
तथा तयोर्द्ध्वं नुन्नः सन् विशुद्धौ कण्ठदेशतः ॥
वैखर्याख्यस्ततः कण्ठशीर्षताल्वोष्ठदन्तगः ।
जिह्वामूलाग्रपृष्ठस्थ स्तथा नासाग्रतः क्रमात् ॥

पञ्चाशद्वारगुणिता पञ्चाशद्वर्णमालिकाम् ।
सूते तद्वर्णतोऽभिन्ना कला रुद्रादिकान् क्रमात् ॥ १११

कण्ठताल्वोष्ठकण्ठोष्ठादन्तोष्ठद्वयतस्तथा ।
समुत्पन्नान्यक्षराणि क्रमादादिक्षकावधि ॥
आदिक्षान्तरतैत्तेषामक्षरत्वमुदीरितम् ॥ इति ।

तथाच श्रुतिः—

चत्वारि वाक्परिमिता पदानि तानि विदुर्ब्राह्मणा ये मनीषिणः ।
गुहा त्रीणि निहिता नेङ्गयन्ति तुरीयं वाचो मनुष्या वदन्ति ॥ इति ।

अथ वा चिच्छक्तिरेव पराख्या चैतन्याभासविशिष्टतया प्रकाशिका माया निष्पन्दा परा वागित्यर्थः । सस्पन्दावस्थाः पश्यन्त्याद्याः । तत्र सामान्यप्रस्पन्दप्रकाशरूपिणीं बिन्दुतत्त्वात्मिकां मूलाधारादिनाभ्यन्तरव्यक्तिस्थानां पश्यन्तीमाह पश्यन्तीति । ज्ञानात्मकत्वात् पश्यन्तीत्यर्थः । बाह्यान्तःकरणात्मिकां हिरण्यगर्भरूपिणीं नादबिन्दुमयीं नाभ्यादिहृदयान्ताभिव्यक्तिस्थानां विशेषसङ्कल्पादिसतत्त्वां मध्यमामाह मध्यमेति । मध्ये मा बुद्धिर्यस्या इति विग्रहः । विराड्रूपिणीं बीजात्मिकां हृदयाद्यास्यान्ताभिव्यक्तिस्थानां शब्दसामान्यात्मिकां वैखरीमाह वाचीति । विशेषेण खरत्वात् वैखरीत्यर्थः । तद्वर्णत इति । ते च ते वर्णाश्च ततः अभिन्ना याः कलाः ताः सूते । रुद्रादिकान् सूते । आदिशब्देन तच्छक्तयः विष्णवः विष्णुशक्तयः पञ्चाशदोषधयश्च पञ्चाशत् कामाः तच्छक्तयश्च पञ्चाशद्गणेशास्तच्छक्तयः पञ्चाशत्क्षेत्रपालास्तच्छक्तयश्च । अत्र पञ्चाशदोषधयो यथा—

चन्दनकुचन्दनागुरुकर्पूरोशीररोगजलघुसृणाः ।
कक्कोलजातीमांसीमुरचोरग्रन्थिरोचनापत्राः ॥
पिप्पलविल्वगुहाकणतृणकलवङ्गाङ्कुभिवन्दिन्यः ।
औदुम्बरी काश्मरिका खिराब्दरपुष्पिकामयूरशिखाः ॥
ब्रह्माग्निमन्थसिंही कुशाश्चदर्भाश्च कृष्णदरपुष्पी ।
रोहिणदुग्धकबृहती पाटलिचित्रा तुलस्यपामार्गाः ॥
शतमखलता द्विरेफा विष्णुक्रान्तामुसल्यथाञ्जलिनी ।
दूर्वाश्रीदेविसहे तथैव लक्ष्मीसदाभद्रे ॥
आदीनामिति कथिता वर्णानां क्रमवशादथौषधयः ।
गुलिकाकषायभसितप्रभेदतो निखिलसिद्धिदायिन्यः ॥ इति ।

आसामोषधीनां प्रयोजनान्तरमप्युक्तं कादिमते—

यो यो मन्त्रस्तस्य तस्य वर्णौषधिविनिर्म्मिता: ।
तत्तद्वर्णोत्थसंख्याभि र्गुलिका मन्त्रसिद्धिदा ॥
तयाभिषेकस्तद्धारणं तत्खादस्तद्विलेपनम् ।
तत्पूजा च तथा सिद्धिलाभाय स्यान्न चान्यथा ॥ इति ।

पञ्चाशत् कामास्तच्छक्तयश्च यथा—

कामकामदकान्ताश्च कान्तिमान् कामगस्तथा ।
कामाचारश्च कामी च कामुक: कामवर्द्धन: ॥
रामो रमश्च रमणो रतिनाथो रतिप्रिय: ।
रात्रिनाथो रमाकान्तो रममाणो निशाचर: ॥
नन्दको नन्दनश्चैव नन्दी नन्दयिता पुन: ।
पञ्चवाणो रतिसख: पुष्पधन्वा महाधनु: ॥
भ्रामणो भ्रमणश्चैव भ्रममाणो भ्रमोऽपर: ।
भ्रान्तश्च भ्रामकश्चैव भ्रान्ताचारो भ्रमावह: ॥
मोहको मोहनो मोहो मोहवर्द्धन एव च ।
मदनो मन्मथश्चैव मातङ्गो भृङ्गनायक: ॥
गायनो गीतिजश्चैव नर्त्तक: खेलकस्तथा ।
उन्मत्तो मत्तकश्चैव विलासो लोभवर्द्धन: ॥
दाड़िमीकुसुमाभाश्च वामाङ्के शक्तिसंयुता: ।
सौम्या रक्ताम्बरा: सर्व्वे पुष्पवाणेक्षुकार्म्मुके ॥
बिभ्राणा: सर्व्वभूषाढ्या: कामा: पञ्चाशदीरिता: ।
रति: प्रीति: कामिनी च मोहिनी कमलप्रिया ॥
विलासिनी कल्पलता [का] श्यामला च शुचिस्मिता ।
विस्मिताक्षी विशालाक्षी लेलिहाना दिगम्बरा ॥
वामा कुब्जा धरा नित्या कल्याणी मोहिनी तथा ।
मदना च सुरश्रेष्ठा लापिनी मर्दिनी तथा ॥
कलहप्रिया चैकाक्षी सुमुखी नलिनी तथा ।
जपिनी पालिनी चैव शिवा सुग्धा रसा भ्रमा ॥
चारुलोला चञ्चला च दीर्घजिह्वा रतिप्रिया ।
लोलाक्षी श्रृङ्खिणी चैव पाटला मादनी तथा ॥

माला च हंसिनी विश्वतोमुखी नन्दिनी तथा ।
रमणी च तथा कान्तिः कलकण्ठी वृकोदरी ॥
मेघश्यामा मदोन्मत्ता एताः पञ्चाशदीरिताः ।
शक्तयः कुङ्कुमनिभाः सर्व्वाभरणभूषिताः ।
नीलोत्पलकरा ध्येया त्रैलोक्याकर्षणक्षमाः ॥ इति ।

पञ्चाशद्‌गणेशाः सशक्तयश्च यथा—

विघ्नेशो विघ्नराजश्च विनायकशिवोत्तमौ ।
विघ्नकृद् विघ्नहर्त्ता च गणैकद्विरदन्तकाः ॥
गजवक्त्रनिरञ्जनौ कपर्दी दीर्घजिह्वकः ।
शङ्कुकर्णश्च वृषभध्वजश्च गणनायकः ॥
गजेन्द्रः सूर्पकर्णश्च स्यात् त्रिलोचनसंज्ञकः ।
लम्बोदरमहानन्दौ चतुर्मूर्त्तिः सदाशिवः ॥
आमोददुर्मुखौ चैव सुमुखश्च प्रमोदकः ।
एकरदो द्विजिह्वश्च शूरवीरसषण्मुखाः ॥
वरदो वामदेवश्च वक्रतुण्डो द्विरण्डकः ।
सेनानीर्ग्रामणीर्मत्तो विमत्तो मत्तवाहनः ॥
जटी मुण्डी तथा खड्‌गी वरेण्यो वृषकेतनः ।
भक्ष्यप्रियो गणेशश्च मेघनादकसंज्ञकः ॥
व्यापी गणेश्वरः प्रोक्ताः पञ्चाशद् गणपा इमे ।
तरुणारुणसङ्काशा गजवक्त्रास्त्रिलोचनाः ॥
पाशाङ्कुशवराभीतिहस्ताः शक्तिसमन्विताः ।
श्रीर्ह्रीश्च पुष्टिशान्ती च स्वस्तिश्चैव सरस्वती ॥
स्वाहामेधाकान्तिकामिन्यो मोहिन्यपि वै नटी ।
पार्व्वती ज्वालिनी नन्दा सुपाशा कामरूपिणी ॥
उमा तेजोवती सत्या विघ्नेशा विघ्नरूपिणी ।
कामदा मदजिह्वा च भूतिः स्याद्भौतिका सिता ॥
रमा च महिषी प्रोक्ता भञ्जिनी च विकर्णपा ।
भ्रूकुटिः स्यात्तथा लज्जा दीर्घघोणा धनुर्धरा ॥
यामिनी रात्रिसंज्ञा च कामान्धा च शशिप्रभा ।
लोलाक्षी चञ्चला दीप्तिः सुभगा दुर्भगा शिवा ॥

निरोधिका भवेद्वह्निरर्द्धेन्दुः स्यान्निशाकरः ।
अर्कः स्यादुभयोर्योगे विन्द्वात्मा तेजसां निधिः ॥ ११२

जाता वर्णा यतो बिन्दोः शिवशक्तिमयादतः ।
अग्नीषोमात्मकास्ते स्युः शिवशक्तिमयाद्रवेः ।
येन सम्भवमापन्नाः सोमसूर्य्याग्निरूपिणः ॥ ११३

इति शारदातिलके प्रथमः पटलः ।

भर्गा च भगिनी चैव भोगिनी सुभगा मता ।
कालरात्रिः कालिका च पञ्चाशच्छक्तयः स्मृताः ॥
सर्व्वालङ्करणोद्दीप्ताः प्रियाङ्कस्थाः सुलोचनाः ।
रक्तोत्पलकरा ध्येया रक्तमाल्याम्बरारुणाः ॥ इति ।

पञ्चाशत् क्षेत्रपालाः क्षेत्रपालमन्त्रे वक्ष्यन्ते । १०८-१११ ॥

वर्णानामग्नीषोमात्मकत्वं सोमसूर्य्याग्निरूपत्वञ्च अग्रे उपयोगीति तद्विविच्याह निरोधिकेति । निरोधिकाया अग्निरूपत्वात् शिवस्वरूपत्वम् । अर्द्धेन्दोः सोमरूपत्वात् शक्तिस्वरूपत्वम् । येन कारणेन शिवशक्तिमयाद्रवेः सम्भवमापन्नाः । रवेः शिवशक्तिमयत्वम् । अर्कः स्यादुभयो र्योगे इत्युक्तेः । तेन सोमसूर्य्याग्निरूपिणो भवन्ति । कार्य्यकारणयोरभेदात् । ११२-११३ ॥

इति श्रीशारदातिलकटीकायां सत्सम्प्रदायकृतव्याख्यायां
पदार्थादर्शाभिख्यायां प्रथमः पटलः ॥ ॐ ॥

द्वितीयः पटलः ।

ततो व्यक्तिं प्रवक्ष्यामि वर्णानां वदने नृणाम् ।
प्रेरिता मरुता नित्यं सुषुम्णारन्ध्रनिर्गताः ॥ १

कण्ठादिकरणैर्वर्णाः क्रमादाविर्भवन्ति ते ।
एषु स्वराः स्मृताः सौम्याः स्पर्शाः सौराः शुभोदयाः ॥ २

आग्नेया व्यापकाः सर्व्वे सोमसूर्य्याग्निदेवताः ।
स्वराः षोडश विख्याताः स्पर्शास्ते पञ्चविंशतिः ॥ ३

एवमर्थसृष्टिं शब्दसृष्टिञ्च मध्यमान्तामभिधाय उक्तानुवादपूर्व्वकं वैखरीसृष्टिं वक्तुं प्रतिजानीते तत इति । प्रेरिता मरुतेति । मरुता क्रमात् प्रेरिताः पश्यन्तीस्थानं प्रापिताः उत्पत्त्युन्मुखीकृता इति यावत् । अतएव सुषुम्णारन्ध्रनिर्गता वर्णाः कण्ठादिकरणैः क्रमादाविर्भवन्ति इति सम्बन्धः । सुषुम्णारन्ध्राख्यनाहतविशुद्धयोः । एकदोच्चारणाभावात् क्रमादित्युक्तम् । तदुक्तं भगवता भर्त्तृहरिणा—

> आत्मा बुद्ध्या समेत्यार्थान्मनो युङ्क्ते विवक्षया ।
> मनः कायाग्निमाहन्ति स प्रेरयति मारुतम् ।
> मारुतस्तूरसि चरन् मन्द्रं जनयति स्वरम् ॥ इति ।

कण्ठादीत्यादिशब्देन ताल्वादिपरिग्रहः । तदुक्तम्—

> अष्टौ स्थानानि वर्णानामुरःकण्ठशिरस्तथा ।
> जिह्वामूलञ्च दन्ताश्च नासिकौष्ठश्च तालु च ॥ इति ।

यत् सर्व्ववर्णानां सोमसूर्य्याग्निरूपत्वमुक्तं तस्यैवाग्रे प्रयोगार्थम् अष्टत्रिंशत्कलादिव्यवहाराय च व्यवस्थया त्रैविध्यमाह एष्विति । एषु वर्णेषु स्वराः अकारादिविसर्गान्ताः स्पर्शाः ककारादिमकारान्ताः व्यापकाः यकारादिक्षकारान्ताः । शुभोदयाः सर्व्वे एव सोमसूर्य्याग्निदेवताः । तत्र स्वराणामुदयमनन्तरमेव वक्ष्यति । अन्येषामुदयस्तु अन्तिमपटले वक्ष्यमाणभूतोदयेनेति ज्ञेयम् । "भूतकलाभिस्तदुदयः" इति आचार्य्योक्तेः । तदत्रैव भूतवर्णकथनेन सूचयिष्यति "विना स्वरैः" इति वक्ष्यमाणप्रकारेण । स्वरादयः कियन्त इत्यपेक्षायामाह स्वरा इति । विख्याताः विशेषेण ख्याताः स्वतन्त्रा इत्यर्थः । यदाहुः—"तेषु स्वराः स्वतन्त्राः स्युः" इति ॥ १-३ ॥

तत्त्वात्मानः स्मृताः स्पर्शा मकारः पुरुषो यतः ।
व्यापका दश ते कामधनधर्म्मप्रदायिनः ॥ ४

ह्रस्वः स्वरेषु पूर्व्वोक्तः परो दीर्घः क्रमादिमे ।
शिवशक्तिमयास्ते स्युर्बिन्दुसर्गावसानिकाः ॥ ५

विन्दुः पुमान् रविः प्रोक्तः सर्गः शक्तिर्निशाकरः ।
स्वराणां मध्यमं यच्च तच्चतुष्कं नपुंसकम् ॥ ६

तत्त्वात्मान इति । प्रकृत्यादिचतुर्विंशतितत्त्वमया इति स्वरूपकथनम् । ननु तेषां पञ्चविंशतिसंख्यकत्वात् कथं चतुर्विंशतितत्त्वमयत्वमत आह मकारः पुरुषो यत इति । यतः कारणान्मकारः पुरुषः परमात्मा च विश्वरूप इत्यर्थः । भादयः प्रकृतिबुद्ध्यहङ्कारमनांसि तन्मात्राः श्रोत्रवागाकाशादयः इतरा वर्णाः । इदञ्च शक्तितत्त्वादिन्यासेषूपयोगीत्युक्तं द्विद्विवर्णक्रमोक्तद्वादशसूर्य्यकलासु अन्त्यत्याग इत्यपि सूचितम् । एवं ते चतुर्विंशतितत्त्वमयाः । "अन्त्य आत्मा रविः स्मृतः" इत्याचार्य्योक्तेः । अत एव सर्व्वबीजेषु विन्दुरूपमकारयोगात् पुरुषैक्यं तेषामिति मन्तव्यम् । मकारस्य बिन्दुरूपत्वात् "विन्दुः पुमान् रविः प्रोक्तः" इति वक्ष्यमाणत्वाच्च । स्वावयवेषु ककारादिषु अनुगतत्वात् सूर्य्यरूपविन्द्वात्मना मकारेण स्पृश्यमानत्वात् स्पर्शाः अतएव सौराः । यद्वा एवं योजना । मकारः पुरुषः अन्ये स्पर्शास्तत्त्वात्मानः । यत इत्यग्रिमेन सम्बध्यते । यतः यकाराद्दश व्यापकाः । एषां दीर्घदूरेषु वर्त्तमानत्वाद् व्यापकत्वम् । तत्राग्नीनामपि सत्त्वादाग्नेया इत्यपि नृसिंहाख्यकालाग्निरूपचकारान्तत्वेन वा आग्नेया इत्यपि द्रष्टव्यम् । ते कामधनधर्म्मप्रदा इति क्रमेण तयाणां फलम् । अतएवाग्रे "कामदायिन्यः स्वरजाः" इत्यादि वक्ष्यति ॥ ४ ॥

स्वराणामेव पृथग्व्यक्तिं दर्शयन् तेषामष्टमूर्त्तितच्छक्तिवाचकत्वाय अग्रे व्यवहाराय च प्रकारद्वयमाह ह्रस्व इति । एकारौकारयोः दीर्घत्वेऽप्यत्र पारिभाषिकं ह्रस्वत्वम् । इमे ह्रस्वदीर्घाः क्रमात् शिवशक्तिमयाः । ह्रस्वाः अ इ उ ऋ ऌ ए ओ एते शिवमयाः पुंरूपाश्च इत्यर्थः । दीर्घाः आ ई ऊ ॠ ॡ ऐ औ एते शक्तिमयाः स्त्रीरूपाश्च इत्यर्थः । विन्दुसर्गावजपायां पुरुषप्रकृतिरूपौ पृथग्भूतावेताविति विवक्षन्नाह ते स्युः विन्दुसर्गावसानिका इति । ते ह्रस्वाः अन्ते विन्दुयुक्ताः दीर्घा अन्ते विसर्गयुक्ताः । ह्रस्वेषु विन्दुरष्टमो दीर्घेषु विसर्गोऽष्टम इत्यर्थः ॥ ५ ॥

पिङ्गलायां स्थिता ह्रस्वा इडायां सङ्गता परे।
सुषुम्णामध्यगा ज्ञेया श्चत्वारो ये नपुंसकाः॥ ७

अत एवाह बिन्दुः पुमानिति। निशाकर इत्युक्तिरितरस्वराणां तत्कला-रूपतिथ्यात्मकत्वात्। शशिरूपं विसर्जनीयं स्वकीयषोडशसंख्यापूर्त्तिकारणतया। स्वरन्ते कथयन्तीति स्वराः अतएव सौम्याः। अयमेव पक्षो ग्रन्थकृदभिमतः। यतो मातृकाषडङ्गकथनाद्यवसरे अक्लीवक्लवदीर्घान्तर्गतैः षड्वर्गकैः क्रमात् इत्यादि-व्यवहारदर्शनात्। कश्चित्तु स्वरेषु पूर्व्वोक्ताः अ इ उ ऋ ऌ एकमात्रो ह्रस्वः परे आ ई ऊ ॠ ॡ ए ऐ ओ औ विन्दुसर्गावसानिकाः संयोगपरश्च दीर्घं इति मन्यते स केवलं नमस्य एव। नपुंसकमिति नपुंसकत्वं धर्म्मः स एषामस्तीति। अर्शआदित्वादच्॥ ६॥

स्वराणामुदयमाह पिङ्गलायामिति। ह्रस्वाः अ इ उ ए ओ। परे दीर्घाः आ ई ऊ ऐ औ विन्दुसर्गयोः रविर्निशाकर इत्यनेनैवोदयस्योक्तत्वात्। एतत्प्रयोजन-मुक्तं गौतमेन—

षट्स्वरोदयजे कर्म्म प्रथितं मारणादिकम्।
फलदं क्रूरकर्म्माद्य ह्रस्वे दीर्घोदयेऽन्यथा॥ इति।

सुषुम्णेति। तत्र प्रकारः उत्तरभागाद्दक्षिणभागप्रवेशारम्भसमये कञ्चित्काल-मुभयत्र वहति देहवायुः। स दक्षिणायनप्रारम्भसमयः। तदा ऋ ऌ कारात्मकं ह्रस्वद्वन्द्वमुदेति। एवं दक्षिणादुत्तरभागप्रवेशप्रारम्भसमये कञ्चित्कालमुभयत्र वहति देहवायुः। स उत्तरायणसंक्रमकालः। तदा ॠॡ दीर्घद्वन्द्वमुदेति। यत् प्रयोगसारे—

स्वरं सप्तममारभ्य चत्वारो ये नपुंसकाः।
ते सुषुम्णाश्रिते प्राणे प्रोद्यन्त्ययनसंक्रमे॥ इति।

अन्ये त्वन्यथा मन्यन्ते ह्रस्वाः अइ उ ऋ ऌ परे दीर्घाः आ ई ऊ ॠ ॡ इति। तदुक्तं प्रयोगसारे—

दक्षिणस्थो यदा प्राण स्तदा स्याद्दक्षिणायनम्।
पञ्चभूतात्मकास्तत्र ह्रस्वाः पञ्चोदयन्ति ते॥
वामाश्रितो यदा प्राणस्तदा स्यादुत्तरायणम्।
पञ्चभूतास्तदा दीर्घास्तत्रोद्यन्ति पृथक् पृथक्॥ इति।

विना स्वरैस्तु नान्येषां जायते व्यक्तिरञ्जसा ।
शिवशक्तिमयान् प्राहुस्तस्माद् वर्णान् मनीषिणः ॥ ८

अन्यत्रापि—

प्राणे दक्षिणनाड़ीस्थे परा चैव तु रेचिका ।
इन्धिकाख्या च विद्याख्या निवृत्तिश्च यथा क्रमात् ॥
प्रतिष्ठा शान्तिसंज्ञा च दीपिका मोचिका तथा ।
सूक्ष्मा चेति स्वराः प्राणे प्रोद्यन्तीड़ाश्रये प्रिये ॥ इति ।

एषां मते यद्यपि एकारादीनामुदयो नोक्तः स्यात् तथापि तेषां सन्ध्यक्षरत्वात् तदुदयेनैवोदयो ज्ञेयः । पद्मपादाचार्य्यैरप्युक्तम्—"बाह्यवटिकापञ्चकेन आध्यात्मिकमयनम् । उक्तविधिविलम्बस्याप्यनुपपत्तौ श्वासोच्छ्वासानां कालावयवसम्पादनं द्रष्टव्यम् । तत्राहोरात्रात्मकौ वा पक्षात्मकौ वा अयनात्मकौ च इच्छावशेन ज्ञातव्यौ" इति ॥ ७ ॥

व्यञ्जनशब्दव्युत्पत्तिं दर्शयन् तेषामपि शिवशक्तिमयत्वमाह विनेति । स्वरैर्विना अन्येषां ककारादीनां व्यक्तिः अञ्जसा प्राकट्येन न भवति । तस्मात् सर्व्वे वर्णाः शिवशक्तिमयाः । व्यक्तिरञ्जसेति व्युत्पत्तिर्दर्शिता । यदाहुः—"तैर्व्यञ्जनाद् व्यञ्जनं भवेत्" इति । एतदुक्तं भवति । स्वराणां पूर्व्वं शिवशक्तिमयत्वमुक्तम् । हलाञ्च विना स्वरैरुच्चारणस्याशक्यत्वात् स्वरसहितोच्चारणे शिवशक्तिमयत्वमिति । एवं स्वरोदयेनैव तत्प्रधानत्वात् व्यञ्जनानामुदयो ज्ञेयः । उक्तञ्च मन्त्रमुक्तावल्याम्—"तत्प्रधानाश्च मन्त्राः" इति ॥ ८ ॥

[अन्ये त्वन्यथा योजयन्ति सोमसूर्य्याग्निरूपिणः इति यदुक्तं तद्विभजते एष्विति । अत्र सूर्य्यरूपबिन्दोः सर्व्वत्र व्यापकत्वात् शुभोदया इति सौरविशेषणमुक्तम् । ननु यद्ययं विभागस्तदा पूर्व्वोक्तो येनेति हेतुः सर्व्ववर्णसामान्येनोक्तो न घटते इत्याशङ्क्याह सर्व्वे सोमसूर्य्याग्निदेवता इति । ननु तथापि विरोधस्तदवस्थ एवेति चेत् । न । इदन्तु तात्त्विकम् विभागस्तु प्रयोगाद्यर्थं इति ज्ञेयम् । स्वराः स्पर्शा व्यापका इति यदुक्तं ते के कियन्त इत्यपेक्षायामाह स्वरा इत्यादि । विशेषेण ख्याता अनेन स्वरा विंशतिरिकश्चेति शिक्षादौ संख्यान्तरश्रुतिर्या सा निरस्ता । व्यापकेषु क्षवद्वापि संयुक्तस्य ग्रहणं स्यादिति शङ्कां वारयति पञ्चविंशतिरिति ॥ १-३ ॥

तत्त्वदेहवानिति पूर्व्वपटलोक्तो यः पुरुषः तं वदन् [प्रकृत्यादितत्त्वानामि-तदुदयेनैवोदय इति सूचयितुम्] तत्त्वानि आह तत्त्वात्मान इति। दशेत्यनेन मूर्द्धन्यस्य लस्य ग्रहणं सूचयति । कामेति क्रमेण त्रयाणां फलम् ॥ ४ ॥

सर्व्वं सोमसूर्य्याग्निदेवता इति यदुक्तं तदेव विवृणोति ह्रस्व इति । ह्रस्वानां पुरुषरूपत्वादग्निसूर्य्यरूपत्वम् स्वरत्वात् सोमरूपत्वम् । दीर्घाणां स्वरत्वेन सोमत्वं ह्रस्वोत्पन्नत्वात् सूर्य्याग्निरूपत्वम् । शास्त्रान्तरानुसारेण दशानामेवैते संज्ञे स्यातामित्यत आह ते स्युरिति । तेषां प्रकारान्तरेण तद्रूपत्वमाह स्वराणामिति । मध्यगमित्यनेन रेफादुत्पत्तिरेषामुक्ता । यदाहुराचार्य्याः—

ऋकाराद्यास्तु चत्वारो रेफोत्था लपराः स्मृताः । इति ।

एतेन ह्रस्वषट्कं हकारोत्थं दीर्घषट्कम् ईकारोत्थम् । तत्र हकारस्य पुंरूपत्वादर्कत्वम् । ईकारस्य शक्तिरूपत्वात् सोमत्वम् । रेफस्याग्निरूपत्वादग्नि-रूपत्वम् । अत्र यद्यपि हकारस्य ह्रस्वषट्कहेतुत्वमिति विभागो नास्माभिरुच्यते तथापि केवलस्योत्पत्तिहेतुत्वमशक्यमिति तदुभयानुवृत्तिरवश्यमपेक्षणीया । एवमितरयोरप्यनुसन्धेयम् । तेन प्रत्येकं सोमसूर्य्याग्निरूपत्वम् । तदुक्तमीश्वर-प्रत्यभिज्ञायाम्—

यदेकतरनिर्म्माणे कार्य्यं जातु न [तत्त्वेन] जायते ।
तस्मात् सर्व्वपदार्थेषु सामरस्यं व्यवस्थितम् ॥ इति ।

सामरस्यं त्रितयसत्त्वम् ॥ ५ ॥ ६ ॥

प्रकारान्तरेण तदेवाह पिङ्गलायामिति । सुषुम्णायां नपुंसकोदये इडा-पिङ्गलयोरपि तत्रान्तर्भावात् तद्वर्णा अपि तत्रान्तर्भवन्ति । ताभ्यां विना तदुदयाभावात् । अतएवोक्तम् प्राक् "अग्नीषोमस्वरूपिणी" इति ॥ ७ ॥

व्यञ्जनानां प्रत्येकं सोमसूर्य्याग्निरूपत्वं दर्शयति विना स्वरैरिति । "शिवशक्ति-मयाद् रवेः येन सम्भवामापन्ना" इत्युपक्रम्य "सर्व्वं सोमसूर्य्याग्निदेवताः" इत्यादिनोक्तमुपसंहरति शिवेति । तस्मादिति पूर्व्वोक्तहेतुत्रयानुवादः । शिवः सूर्य्याग्निरूपः शक्तिः सोमरूपा । अथवा य एव शिवः सैव शक्तिः । शिवशक्त्यो-रभेदात् भुवनेशीबीजात्मिका इत्यप्युक्तम् । यदाहुराचार्य्याः—

यथा स्वरेभ्यो नान्ये स्युर्वर्णाः षड् वर्गभेदिताः । तथा सवित्रानुस्यूतम् ॥ इति ।

एवं त्रिवृत्करणप्रक्रियां भुवनेशीबीजादुत्पत्तिं च सूचयता तेजस्त्रयतः सृष्टिरुक्ता ॥ ८ ॥]

कारणात् पञ्चभूतानां मुद्भूता मातृका यतः ।
ततो भूतात्मका वर्णाः पञ्च पञ्च विभागतः ॥ ९
वाय्वग्निभूजलाकाशाः पञ्चाशल्लिपयः क्रमात् ।
पञ्च ह्रस्वाः पञ्च दीर्घा बिन्द्वन्ताः सन्धिसम्भवाः ॥ १०

अथ पञ्चीकरणप्रक्रियां प्रणवादुत्पत्तिं च सूचयन् भूतानां पृथक्प्रयोगार्थं पुनर्वर्णविभागमाह कारणादिति । अथवा "स्वस्ववर्णयुतानि" इत्युक्तं ते के वर्णा इत्यपेक्षायामाह कारणादिति । कारणात् शिवशक्तिसमवायात् बिन्दोः । मातृकेति अकारादिक्षकारान्तवर्णसमुदायस्य संज्ञा । यत्प्रयोगसारे—

प्रसिद्धा वर्णमाला सा मातृकेत्युच्यते परा । इति ।

पञ्च पञ्च विभागतः दशविभागतः अथ च पूर्वं क्रमात् पञ्चतोऽपि पञ्चेति वीप्सापि ॥ ९ ॥

तदेव उद्दिष्टं कथयति वाय्विति । वाय्वाकाशयोराद्यन्तत्वेन निर्दिष्टत्वात् व्युत्क्रमोक्तिः । पञ्चीकरणप्रक्रियाया मुख्यत्वद्योतनाय तच्च लृसाक्षराणां तत्तद्भूतत्वा [ततत्वा] त्वभावाय च पञ्चाशदिति । विसर्गानन्तर्भावेन तेन न गौणत्वम् । पञ्च ह्रस्वाः पञ्च दीर्घाः इति प्रसिद्धाः । अत्र सन्धिसम्भवानां पृथगुपादानात् न पारिभाषिकह्रस्वदीर्घग्रहः । बिन्द्वन्ता इति सन्धिसम्भव-विशेषणम् । ते च ए ऐ ओ औ । तेषां यथा सन्धिसम्भवत्वं तथोक्तमाचार्यैः—

अकारेकारयोर्योगादेकारो वर्ण इष्यते ।
तस्यैवैकारयोगेन स्यादैकाराक्षरं तदा ॥
उकारयोगे तस्यैव स्यादोकाराह्वयः स्वरः ।
तस्यैवौकारयोगेन स्यादौकाराह्वयः स्वरः ॥
सन्ध्यक्षराः स्युश्चत्वारो मन्त्राः सर्वार्थसाधकाः । इति ।

ननु कथमत्र विसर्गो न गणितः । उच्यते । मूलाधारात् सञ्जातविवक्षोत्थप्रयत्नप्राणपवनप्रेरितः स्थानान्तरमप्राप्य कण्ठादेव निःसरन् प्रकृत्यात्मकः सर्गोऽत्र भूतेषु न गणितः । अत एवाचार्यैः—"कण्ठात्तु निःसरन् सर्गः" इत्यादिना "नश्वरः सर्ग एव स्यात्" इत्यन्तेन सर्गादेव ककारादीनामुत्पत्तिरुक्ता । कादिमतेऽपि—

प्राणाग्नीलाम्बुखात्मानः पङ्क्तयः पञ्च कीर्त्तिताः ।
मायाशक्त्यभिधः सर्गः सर्वभूतात्मकः प्रभुः ॥
तस्मात् तस्यात्र विन्यासो नैकदेशे शिवात्मनि ॥ इति ।

पञ्चशः कादयः षत्तलसहान्ताः समीरिताः।
सोमसूर्य्याग्निभेदेन मातृकावर्णसम्भवाः॥ ११

कादयः शान्ता इति शेषः। एतेन अ आ ए क च ट त प य षा वायव्याः। एवं इ ई ऐ ख छ ठ थ फ र चा आग्नेयाः। एवं भादीनामपि ज्ञेयम्। तदुक्तमाचार्य्यैः—

> ऊदद्युगदादिलला कोर्णसौचतुर्थार्णकावशौ वारः।
> इष्टैव द्वितीयरचा वह्ने रहन्द योनिकादिवर्षाः।
> मरुतः कपोलविन्दुकपञ्चमवर्णाः शहौ तथा व्योम्नः। इति।

अत्र मन्त्रशोधनप्रकरणे स्वकुलान्यकुललक्षणः शोधनप्रकारो नोक्तः। स सूत्रवर्ण-कथनेन सूचितः। फलन्तु पिङ्गलामतोक्तम्। यथा—

> चत्वारिंशत्तथा पञ्च वर्णसंख्या प्रकीर्त्तिता।
> गणस्तु नवभिर्ज्ञेयः पार्थिवादिषु पञ्चसु॥

अत्र ह्रस्वैरेव दीर्घाणां ग्रहणान्नवभिरित्युक्तिः।

> मन्त्रसाधकयोराद्यो वर्णः स्यात् पार्थिवो यदि।
> तत् कुलं तस्य तत् प्रोक्तमेवमन्येषु लक्षयेत्॥
> पार्थिवे वारुणं मित्रमाग्नेये मारुतं तथा।
> ऐन्द्रवारुणयोः शत्रुर्मारुतः परिकीर्त्तितः॥
> आग्नेये वारुणं शत्रुर्वारुणे तैजसं तथा।
> सर्व्वेषामेव तत्त्वानां सामान्यं व्योमसम्भवम्॥
> परस्परविरुद्धानां वर्णानां यत्र सङ्गतिः।
> स मन्त्रः साधकं हन्ति किंवा नास्य प्रसीदति॥ इति।

तन्त्रान्तरेऽपि—वर्णांशकं वदिष्यामि चतुर्मात्रव्यवस्थितम्।

> स्वकुलं मित्रमध्यस्थे अमित्रञ्च चतुर्थकम्॥
> वायव्याग्नेयवारुणपार्थिवञ्च प्रकीर्त्तितम्।
> उत्तरोत्तरसंसिद्धिसमताव्याधिमृत्यवः॥
> प्राप्नुवन्ति समासाद्य मन्त्रिणोऽत्र निबोधतान्।
> मित्रे सिद्धिः समाख्याता उदासीने न किञ्चन॥
> मृत्युर्व्याधिरमित्रे च स्वकुले सिद्धिरुत्तमा।
> नामादिवर्णं साध्यस्य साधकस्य यथाक्रमम्॥

अष्टत्रिंशत् कला स्तत्तन्मण्डलेषु व्यवस्थिताः ।
अमृता मानदा पूषा तुष्टिः पुष्टी रतिर्धृतिः ॥ १२

ऊर्द्ध्वाधस्थं समालिख्य अंशकञ्च निरूपयेत् ।
वायव्ये तैजसं मित्रमुदासीनन्तु वारुणम् ॥
शत्रुञ्च पार्थिवं विद्यात् स्वकुलं वायवं पुनः ।
तैजसे वारुणं शत्रु रुदासीनन्तु पार्थिवम् ॥
वायव्यं मित्रमाख्यातं स्वकुलं तैजसं पुनः ।
वारुणे पार्थिवं मित्रमुदासीनन्तु वायवम् ॥
तैजसन्तु रिपुं विद्यात् स्वकुलं वारुणं पुनः ।
पार्थिवे वारुणं मित्रं तैजसं शत्रुरीरितम् ॥
उदासीनं वायवन्तु स्वकुलं पार्थिवं पुनः ।
एष वर्णांशको नाम सान्वयस्ते निरूपितः ॥ इति ॥ १० ॥ ११ ॥

अष्टत्रिंशत्कलाद्यर्थं पूर्व्वं विभागः कृतः । ताः कला एवाह सोमेति । अनेन प्रणवस्य त्रिभ्यो भेदेभ्योऽकारोकारमकारेभ्य एव अष्टत्रिंशत् कलोत्पत्तिरुक्ता । तत्र प्रथमाक्षरस्य विसर्गरूपत्वात् सोमत्वम् । उकारस्य विसर्जनीयस्य रेफादुत्पत्ते-रग्न्यात्मकत्वम् । मकारस्य सूर्य्यरूपत्वं प्रसिद्धमेव । ननु प्रथमद्वितीययोः कथं सोमाग्निरूपत्वम् । इति चेदुच्यते । अन्त्यपटले अजपातः प्रणवस्योत्पत्तिं वक्ष्यति । तत्र विलोमीकृता अजपा सोऽहं भवति । सकारहकारलोपे पूर्व्ववत् कृते प्रणवसिद्धिः । तत्र प्रथमो वर्णो विसर्गात्मकः । "सर्गः शक्तिर्निशाकरः" इत्युक्तेः । तस्यैव विसर्गस्य सकारादेशे उत्वे च कृते उकारादेशो भवतीति अग्नित्वम् । यद्वा तस्यां सूर्य्येन्दुपावकात् "प्रणवस्य त्रिभिर्वर्णैः" इति वक्ष्यमाणत्वात् तेषां तथात्वम् । तेनैतदुक्तं भवति । प्रणवस्य त्रिभिर्भेदैः अष्टत्रिंशत्कलोत्पत्तिः पञ्चभेदेभ्यः पञ्चाशत्कलोत्पत्तिः । वायवीयसंहितायान्तु—

लोकवृत्तिप्रवृत्त्यर्थं माकाशमरुदाश्रयात् ।
सञ्चरन्ति त्रयो भूता वह्निसूर्य्येन्दुरूपिणः ॥
तेजो रुद्रात्मकं यत्तु स वह्निस्त्रिगुणः स्मृतः ।
भिन्नास्तमोरजःसत्वै स्तद्गुणा नवधाऽभवन् ॥
वह्नेः कला दश प्रोक्ता विन्दुना सह धर्म्मदाः ।
ब्रह्मात्मको रसो यस्तु स सूर्य्यः स चतुर्गुणः ॥

शशिनी चन्द्रिका कान्तिर्ज्योत्स्ना श्रीः प्रीतिरङ्गदा ।
पूर्णा पूर्णामृता कामदायिन्यः स्वरजाः कलाः ॥ १३
तपिनी तापिनी धूम्रा मरीचिर्ज्वालिनी रुचिः ।
सुषुम्णा भोगदा विश्वा बोधिनी धारिणी क्षमा ॥ १४
कभाद्या वसुदाः सौर्य्यष्ठडान्ता द्वादशेरिताः ।
धूम्रार्च्चिरुष्मा ज्वलिनी ज्वालिनी विस्फुलिङ्गिनी ।
सुश्रीः सुरूपा कपिला हव्यकव्यवहे अपि ॥ १५
यादीनां दशवर्णानां कला धर्म्मप्रदा इमाः ।
अभयेष्टकरा ध्येयाः श्वेतपीतारुणाः क्रमात् ॥ १६

तद्गुणा गुणभेदेन पुनर्द्वादशतां गताः ।
तेन द्वादश विख्याताः सूर्य्यस्य धनदाः कलाः ॥
नहि नादकलेत्येवममूर्त्तत्वात् प्रदर्श्यते ।
या च विष्ण्वात्मिका पृथ्वी सोमोऽसौ गुणपञ्चकः ॥
तेऽपि प्रत्येकभेदेन गुणाः पञ्चदशाऽभवन् ।
ताः कलाः सह बीजेन षोडशेन्दोरनङ्गदाः ॥ इति ।

तत्तन्मण्डलेष्विति सोममण्डलसूर्य्यमण्डलाग्निमण्डलेषु । स्वरजा इत्यनेनामृतादीनां पूजने स्वरमादौ कृत्वा पूजेत्युक्तं भवति । तत्र प्रयोगः । अं अमृतायै नमः इत्यादि ॥ ११-१४ ॥

कभाद्या इति । ककारादनुलोमेन द्वादश ठकारपर्य्यन्तं भकाराद् विलोमेन द्वादश डकारपर्य्यन्तमित्यर्थः । तत्र प्रयोगो यथा—कं भं तपिन्यै नमः । खं बं तापिन्यै नमः इत्यादि । हव्यकव्यवहे इति । हव्यकव्यशब्दयोः द्वन्द्वः ततो वहशब्देन समासः । तेन "द्वन्द्वात् परः श्रूयमाणः शब्दः प्रत्येकमभिसम्बध्यते" इति न्यायात् हव्यवहा कव्यवहा इति शक्तिद्वयम् । यादीनामित्यनेन धूम्रार्च्चिरादीनां यादित्वमुक्तम् । प्रयोगस्तु यं धूम्रार्च्चिषे नमः इत्यादि ॥ १५ ॥

अभयेष्टेति । इष्टो वरः । तत्र दक्षिणहस्ते अभयं वामहस्ते वर इति सम्प्रदायविदः । उक्तञ्च—

ऊर्द्ध्वीकृतो दक्षहस्तः प्रसृतोऽभयमुद्रिका ।
अधोमुखो वामहस्तः प्रसृतो वरमुद्रिका ॥ इति ।

दशमपटलस्थामपि भुवनेशीध्याने—

दक्षेऽङ्कुशाभये प्रोक्ते वामे पाशमभीष्टदम्। इति।

तन्त्रान्तरे सरस्वतीध्याने—

साक्षस्रक्कलशौ इं बाहुयुगलाच्चाधः समुद्राभयं

हस्तं दक्षिणमन्यतः सवरदं यस्याः करे पुस्तकम्॥ इति।

सौत्रामणीतन्त्रे पञ्चमीध्याने—

चक्रं खड्गं मुषलमभयं दक्षिणाभिर्भुजाभिः

शङ्खं खेटं हलमपि वरं बिभ्रती वामदोर्भिः॥ इति।

तन्त्रान्तरे नित्याध्याने—

कपालमभयन्तथा।

दधानां दक्षिणैर्हस्तैः। इत्यादि।

अन्यत्रापि—पाशं पताकां चर्म्माऽपि शार्ङ्गं चापं वरं करैः।

दधानां वामपार्श्वस्थैः सर्व्वाभरणभूषितैः॥

अङ्कुशञ्च ततो दण्डं खड्गं बाणं तथाऽभयम्।

दधानां दक्षिणैर्हस्तैरासीनां पद्मविष्टरे॥ इति।

कादिमतेऽपि—ब्रूहि देव महेशान स्थूलसूक्ष्मस्वरूपयोः।

ध्यानयोः कर्म्मणां सिद्धिं विविधां फलयोगतः॥

तासां तत्तत्करेषूक्तेष्वायुधान्यथ शेषतः।

शृणु वक्ष्ये महेशानि क्रमेण त्वं हि साम्प्रतम्॥

वामदक्षिणयोः स्यातां द्विभुजे तु वराभयौ।

पाशाङ्कुशौ चतुर्बाहौ षड्भुजे चापसायकौ॥

चर्म्मखड्गावष्टभुजे गदाशूले दशोदिते। इति।

अतो यत्र यत्र शक्तिध्याने वराभये तत्र तत्र प्रायोऽभयं दक्षिणे वामे वरमिति ज्ञेयम्। यत्तूत्तरषट्के—

वामेनाभयसंयुक्तां वरदां दक्षिणेन तु। इति।

अन्यत्रापि—पुस्तकञ्चाभयं वामे दक्षिणे चाक्षमालिकाम्।

वरदानरतां देवीम्। इति।

एतत् स्वस्वगुरुसम्प्रदायानुसारेण तत्तद्देवताविशेषे बोद्धव्यमित्यलम्। क्रमादिति। सौम्यकलादीनां श्वेतादयः। अनेन वर्णवस्त्रमाल्यभूषाणां ग्रहणम्। एवमग्रेऽपि ज्ञेयम्॥ १६॥

तारस्य पञ्चभेदेभ्यः पञ्चाशद्वर्णगाः कलाः ॥ १७
सृष्टिर्वृद्धिः स्मृतिर्मेधा कान्तिर्लक्ष्मीर्धृतिः स्थिरा।
स्थितिः सिद्धिरिति प्रोक्ताः कचवर्गकलाः क्रमात् ॥ १८
अकाराद् ब्रह्मणोत्पन्नास्तप्तचामीकरप्रभाः।
एताः करधृताक्षस्रक्पङ्कजद्वयकुण्डिकाः ॥ १९
जरा च पालिनी शान्तिरीश्वरी रतिकामु[मि]के।
वरदाऽऽह्लादिनी प्रीतिर्दीर्घा स्युष्टतवर्गजाः ॥ २०
उकाराद् विष्णुनोत्पन्नास्तमालदलसन्निभाः।
अभीतिदरचक्रेष्टबाहवः परिकीर्त्तिताः ॥ २१
तीक्ष्णा रौद्री भया निद्रा तन्द्री क्षुत् क्रोधिनी क्रिया।
उत्कारी मृत्युरेताः स्युः कथिताः पयवर्गजाः ॥ २२
रुद्रेण मार्णादुत्पन्नाः शरच्चन्द्रनिभप्रभाः।
उद्वहन्त्योऽभयं शूलं कपालं बाहुभिर्वरम् ॥ २३

यदर्थं पञ्चभूतेषु विभाग उक्तास्ताः कला उद्दिशति। यद्वा "तद्वर्णतोऽभिन्नाः कलाः" इति पूर्व्वपटलान्ते उद्दिष्टास्ता निर्दिशति तारस्येति। तारस्य प्रणवस्य पञ्चभेदा इति अकारोकारमकारबिन्दुनादाः। यद्यपि शक्तिशान्ताविति प्रणवस्य षष्ठसप्तमभेदौ तथापि तयोरेषु गणना नास्ति। परत्वात्। तदुक्तम्—

सप्तात्मकस्य तारस्य परौ द्वौ तु परौ यतः।
ततस्तु शक्तिशान्ताख्यौ न पठ्येते परैः सह ॥ इति।

पञ्चाशच्छब्दोऽत्र लाक्षणिकः। कलाः क्रमादुत्पन्ना इति शेषः। काकाक्षिगोलकन्यायेनोभयत्र क्रमादिति सम्बध्यते ॥ १७ ॥

तमेव क्रममाह सृष्टिरित्यादिना इति पञ्चाशदाख्याता इत्यन्तेन। अकारात् प्रणवांशादुत्पन्नाः। तद्वाच्येन ब्रह्मणा चोत्पन्ना इति ज्ञेयम्। वाच्यवाचकयोरभेदात्। तदुक्तमाचार्य्यैः—"अकारप्रभवा ब्रह्मजाताः" इति। एवमग्रेऽपि। अक्षस्रक् अक्षमाला। आयुधध्यानं दक्षाधस्तलाद्वामाधस्तलपर्य्यन्तम्। आह्लादिनीति पदच्छेदः। दरः शङ्खः। शरच्चन्द्रस्य निभा कान्तिः तद्वत् प्रभा यासां ताः। निभशब्दः सदृशवाची वा ॥ १८-२३ ॥

ईश्वरेणोदिता बिन्दोः पीता श्वेताऽरुणाऽसिता ।
अनन्ता च षवर्गस्था जवाकुसुमसन्निभाः ॥ २४
अभयं हरिणं टङ्कं दधाना बाहुभिर्वरम् ।
निवृत्तिः सप्रतिष्ठा स्याद्विद्या शान्तिरनन्तरम् ॥ २५
इन्धिका दीपिका चैव रेचिका मोचिका परा ।
सूक्ष्मा सूक्ष्मामृता ज्ञानामृता चाप्यायिनी तथा ॥ २६
व्यापिनी व्योमरूपा स्युरनन्ता स्वरसंयुताः ।
सदाशिवेन सञ्जाता नादादेताः सितत्विषः ॥ २७
अक्षस्रक्पुस्तकगुणकपालाढ्यकराम्बुजाः ।
न्यासे तु योजयेदादौ षोडश स्वरजाः कलाः ।
इति पञ्चाशदाख्याताः कलाः सर्व्वसमृद्धिदाः ॥ २८
श्रीकण्ठानन्तसूक्ष्माश्च त्रिमूर्त्तिरमरेश्वरः ॥ २९
अर्घीशो भारभूतीशस्तिथीशः स्थाणुको हरः ।
झिण्टीशो भौतिकः सद्योजातश्चानुग्रहेश्वरः ॥ ३०
अक्रूरश्च महासेनः षोडशस्वरमूर्त्तयः ।
पश्चात् क्रोधीशचण्डेशपञ्चान्तकशिवोत्तमाः ॥ ३१

बिन्दुकला आह ईश्वरेणेति । बिन्दोरिति । असितेति पदच्छेदः । हरिणं हरिणमुद्राम् । अन्ये मृगशिशुं मन्यन्ते । टङ्कः परशुः । सप्रतिष्ठेति प्रतिष्ठाकलासहिता । परेति कलानाम । सूक्ष्मामृतेत्येका ज्ञानामृतेत्येका । अनन्तेति षोडशी कला । गुणः शूलम् । कराम्बुजमित्युपमासमासः । आद्ये कार्ध्वयोर्दक्षवामयोरन्ये अक्ष इत्यायुधध्यानम् । वैपरीत्यञ्च केचन इच्छन्ति । शक्तिपूजायामयं क्रम उक्तः । शरीरे न्यासक्रममाह न्यासे त्विति । तु पूर्व्वस्माद् विशेषे । सर्व्वसमृद्धिदा इति न्यासफलम् ॥ २४-२८ ॥

रुद्रादिकानिति पूर्व्वप्रकृतान् रुद्रान् उद्दिशति श्रीकण्ठेति । स्थाणुक इति कः स्वार्थे स्थाणुरिति नाम । एकरुद्रस्य कूर्म्मस्य एकनेत्राख्यस्य चतुराननस्येति द्वन्द्वः । आद्यशब्दस्य न संज्ञायामन्तर्भावः । एवमग्रेऽपि आख्यादेः । छगलण्डद्विर-

अथैकरुद्रकूर्मैकनेत्राह्वचतुराननाः ।
अजेशशर्व्वसोमेशास्तथा लाङ्गलिदारुकौ ॥ ३२
अर्द्धनारीश्वरश्चोमाकान्तश्चाषाढ़िदण्डिनौ ।
स्युरद्रिमीनमेषाख्यलोहिताश्च शिखी तथा ॥ ३३
छगलण्डद्विरण्डेशौ महाकालाख्यवालिनौ ।
भुजङ्गेशपिनाकीशखड्गीशाख्यवकास्तथा ॥ ३४
श्वेतभृग्वीशलकुलिशिवाः सम्बर्त्तकस्ततः ।
एते रुद्राः स्मृता रक्ता धृतशूलकपालकाः ॥ ३५
पूर्णोदरी स्याद् विरजा शाल्मली तदनन्तरम् ।
लोलाक्षी वर्त्तुलाक्षी च दीर्घघोणा समीरिताः ॥ ३६
सुदीर्घमुखिगोमुख्यौ दीर्घजिह्वा तथैव च ।
कुण्डोदर्य्यूर्द्धकेशी च तथा विकृतमुख्यपि ॥ ३७
ज्वालामुखी ततो ज्ञेया पश्चादुल्कामुखी ततः ।
सुश्रीमुखी च विद्यामुख्येताः स्युः स्वरशक्तयः ॥ ३८
महाकालीसरस्वत्यौ सर्व्वसिद्धिसमन्विता ।
गौरी त्रैलोक्यविद्या स्यान्मन्त्रशक्तिस्ततः परम् ॥ ३९

खण्डेशाविति ईशशब्द उभयत्र सम्बध्यते । आयुधध्यानं वामदक्षिणयोः । एवमुत्तरत्रापि । इदं सामान्यम् । वक्ष्यमाणं बन्धूकेत्यादि शक्तिसम्भिन्नत्वे ज्ञेयम् । एवं विष्णुष्वपि । यत्तु क्वचित् "तप्तहेमावदातम्" इति तच्छक्तिशक्तिमतोरभेदे शक्तिप्राधान्यादित्यवधेयम् ॥ २८-३५ ॥

आदिपदवाच्या एतच्छक्तीरुद्दिशति पूर्णोदरीति । विष्णुविष्णुशक्तिष्वपि इदमेवानुसन्धेयम् । सुदीर्घमुखिगोमुख्यौ भद्रकालियोगिन्यौ इत्यत्र "ङ्यापोः संज्ञाच्छन्दसो र्बहुलम्" इति बहुलग्रहणात् पूर्व्वपदस्य ह्रस्वः । प्रयोगे तु दीर्घ एव । सर्व्वसिद्धिसमन्वितेति गौरीविशेषणम् । तेन सर्व्वसिद्धिगौरीति शक्तिनाम । अपेक्षितार्थद्योतनिकाकारादिभिः तथैवोक्तेः । अन्यत्रापि "सर्व्वसिद्धग्रभिधा गौरी" इत्युक्तम् । रुद्राणां श्रीकण्ठादीनां । अङ्कः उत्सङ्गः ॥ ३६-४४ ॥

आत्मशक्तिर्भूतमाता तथा लम्बोदरी मता ।
द्राविणी नागरी भूयः खेचरी चापि मञ्जरी ॥ ४०
रूपिणी वीरिणी पश्चात् काकोदर्यपि पूतना ।
स्याद्भद्रकालियोगिन्यौ शङ्खिनी गर्जिनी तथा ॥ ४१
कालरात्रिश्च कुब्जिन्या कपर्दिन्यपि वज्रिणी ।
जया च सुमुखेश्वर्य्या रेवती माधवी तथा ॥ ४२
वारुणी वायवी प्रोक्ता पश्चाद्रक्षोविदारिणी ।
ततश्च सहजा लक्ष्मीर्व्यापिनी माययाऽन्विता ॥ ४३
एता रुद्राङ्कपीठस्थाः सिन्दूरारुणविग्रहाः ।
रक्तोत्पलकपालाभ्यामलङ्कृतकराम्बुजाः ॥ ४४
केशवनारायणमाधवगोविन्दविष्णवः ।
मधुसूदनसंज्ञोऽन्यः स्यात् त्रिविक्रमवामनौ ॥ ४५
श्रीधरश्च हृषीकेशः पद्मनाभस्ततः परम् ।
दामोदरो वासुदेवः सङ्कर्षण इतीरिताः ॥ ४६
प्रद्युम्नश्चानिरुद्धश्च स्वराणां मूर्त्तयः क्रमात् ।
पश्चाच्चक्री गदी शार्ङ्गी खड्गी शङ्खी हली पुनः ॥ ४७
मुषली शूलिसंज्ञोऽन्यः पाशी स्यादङ्कुशी पुनः ।
मुकुन्दो नन्दजो नन्दी नरो नरकजिद्धरिः ॥ ४८
कृष्णः सत्यः सात्वतः स्यात् शौरी शूरो जनार्दनः ।
भूधरो विश्वमूर्त्तिश्च वैकुण्ठः पुरुषोत्तमः ॥ ४९
बली बलानुजो बालो वृषघ्नश्च वृषः पुनः ।
सिंहो वराहो विमलो नृसिंहो मूर्त्तयो हलाम् ॥ ५०

आदिशब्दसंगृहीतान् केशवाद्यान् तच्छक्तीरप्युद्दिशति केशवेत्यादि । हलामिति व्यञ्जनानां वैयाकरणपरिभाषया । आयुधध्यानं वामदक्षिणयोः । एवमुत्तरत्रापि ।

केशवाद्या इमे श्यामाश्चक्रशङ्खलसत्कराः ।
कीर्त्तिः कान्तिस्तुष्टिपुष्टी धृतिः शान्तिः क्रिया दया ॥ ५१
मेधा सहर्षा श्रद्धा च लज्जा लक्ष्मीः सरस्वती ।
प्रीती रतिरिमाः प्रोक्ताः क्रमेण स्वरशक्तयः ॥ ५२
जया दुर्गा प्रभा सत्या चण्डा वाणी विलासिनी ।
विजया विरजा विश्वा विनदा सुनदा स्मृतिः ॥ ५३
ऋद्धिः समृद्धिः शुद्धिः स्याद् भक्तिर्बुद्धिः स्मृतिः क्षमा ।
रमोमा क्लेदिनी क्लिन्ना वसुदा वसुधाऽपरा ॥ ५४
परा परायणा सूक्ष्मा सन्ध्या प्रज्ञा प्रभा निशा ।
अमोघा विद्युता चेति कीर्त्त्याद्याः सर्वकामदाः ॥ ५५
एताः प्रियतमाङ्केषु निषण्णाः सस्मिताननाः ।
विद्युद्दामसमानाङ्ग्यः पङ्कजाभयबाहवः ॥ ५६
मातृकावर्णभेदेभ्यः सर्वे मन्त्राः प्रजज्ञिरे ।
मन्त्रविद्याविभागेन द्विविधा मन्त्रजातयः ॥ ५७
पुंस्त्रीनपुंसकात्मानो मन्त्राः सर्वे समीरिताः ।
मन्त्राः पुंदेवता ज्ञेया विद्याः स्त्रीदेवताः स्मृताः ॥ ५८

वसुधापरेति अपरा वसुधेत्यन्वयः । परेति कलानाम ॥ ४५-५६ ॥

तत श्चैतन्येत्यारभ्य पञ्चाशद्वर्णरूपिणीत्यन्तेन मातृकास्वरूपमुक्तं कुण्डल्याः । तस्या एव मन्त्रा उत्पन्ना इत्यपि । तत्प्रयोगार्थं मन्त्राणां प्रकारत्रये वक्ष्यमाणे हेतुत्वेनोपन्यस्यति । मातृकेति । यत इति शेषः । पूर्वं शिवशक्तिमयादित्यनेन तदुत्पत्तिरुक्ता । तदेव मन्त्रेष्वपि दर्शयति मन्त्रेति । मातृकेति तत इति योज्यम् । अनेन सोमसूर्यात्मकत्वं सर्वेषामुक्तं भवति । यत् प्रयोगसारे—

द्विधा प्रोक्ताश्च ते मन्त्राः सौम्यसौरविभागतः ।
सौराः पुंदेवता मन्त्रास्ते च मन्त्राः प्रकीर्त्तिताः ॥
सौम्याः स्त्रीदेवतास्तद्वद्विद्यास्ते इति विश्रुताः । इति ।

अनयोरुदयेन सर्वेषामुदयोऽप्युक्तो भवति ॥ ५७ ॥

पुंमन्त्रा हुंफडन्ताः स्युर्द्विठान्ताश्च स्त्रियो मताः।
नपुंसका नमोऽन्ताः स्युरित्युक्ता मनवस्त्रिधा ॥ ५९

शस्तास्ते त्रिविधा मन्त्रा वश्यशान्त्यभिचारके।
अग्नीषोमात्मका मन्त्रा विज्ञेयाः क्रूरसौम्ययोः ॥ ६०

कर्म्मणोर्वह्नितारान्त्यवियत्प्रायाः समीरिताः।
आग्नेया मनवः सौम्या भूयिष्टेन्दुस्मृताक्षराः ॥ ६१

प्रयोगविशेषसिद्धार्थं मन्त्राणां त्रैविध्यमाह पुंस्त्रीति। अत्रापि शिवशक्तिमयत्वात् मध्यमचतुष्कस्य नपुंसकत्वात् स्वराणां त्रैविध्ये तान् विना अन्येषामपि उच्चारणाभावात् तदात्मकत्वेन हेतुत्वं योज्यम्। अत्र सर्व्व इत्युक्तेर्न पारिभाषिकमन्त्रग्रहणम्। एवमुत्तरत्रापि। ननु निष्कलचैतन्याखण्डानन्दवाच्यस्य मन्त्रस्य कथं पुंस्त्वादिकल्पनमिति चेत् सत्यम्। वस्तुतो नास्त्येव। उपासकानामर्थे कल्पनामात्रम्। यदाहुः—

चिन्मयस्याद्वितीयस्य निष्कलस्याशरीरिणः।
उपासकानां कार्य्यार्थं ब्रह्मणो रूपकल्पना॥
रूपस्थानां देवतानां पुंस्त्र्यङ्गादिप्रकल्पना। इति। ५८॥

गार्गग्राभिप्रायेणैषां लक्षणमाह पुमिति। हुँफडन्ता इति सम्प्रदायाद् व्यस्तसमस्ततदन्ताः। द्विठान्ता इति स्वाहान्ताः। ठशब्देन साम्यात् अर्थाद् वा बिन्दुरुच्यते। "ठः शून्ये च बृहद्ध्वनौ" इति कोशात्। शून्यं बिन्दुरूपमेव। तस्य द्वित्वं तेन विसर्गः। स च शक्तिरूप इति। तेन द्विठशब्देनाग्निशक्तिः स्वाहोक्ता। प्रयोगसारे तु—

वषट्फडन्ताः पुंलिङ्गा वौषट्स्वाहान्तगाः स्त्रियः।
नपुंसका हुँनमोऽन्ता इति मन्त्रास्त्रिधा स्मृताः॥
तारेणाप्यनुमीयन्ते मन्त्राः स्वाद्यन्तमध्यतः।
प्रत्यासन्नात्मभावेन यथा पुंस्त्रीनपुंसकाः।
बिन्दुसर्गेन्दुखण्डान्तास्तद्वदेव प्रकीर्त्तिताः॥ इति ॥ ५९ ॥

त्रिविधानां क्रमेण प्रयोजनमाह शस्ता इति। उक्तन्तु नारायणीये—

शेषाः पुमांसः शस्तास्ते वश्योच्चाटे विशेषतः।
क्षुद्रक्रियामयध्वंसे स्त्रियोऽन्यत्र नपुंसकाः॥ इति।

आग्नेयाः संप्रबुध्यन्ते प्राणे चरति दक्षिणे।
भागेऽन्यस्मिन् स्थिते प्राणे सौम्या बोधं प्रयान्ति च॥ ६२
नाड़ीद्वयं गते प्राणे सर्व्वे बोधं प्रयान्ति च।
प्रयच्छन्ति फलं सर्व्वे प्रबुद्धा मन्त्रिणां सदा॥ ६३

पूर्व्वं मातृकायाः कुण्डल्या उत्पत्तेरुक्तत्वात् तस्या अग्नीषोमात्मकत्वात् मन्त्राणामपि तद्दर्शयति अग्नीति। कर्म्मणोरिति पूर्व्ववान्वेति। वह्नी रेफः। तारः ॐकारः। अन्त्यः क्षकारः। वियत् हकारः। प्रायःशब्दो बाहुल्यवाची। "प्रायो भूमन्यद्रुते शनैः" इत्यमरः। आग्नेया इति पूर्व्वेण सम्बध्यते। इन्दुः सः। तत्त्वन्यासे इन्दुमण्डलस्य सकारादित्वेन न्यस्तत्वात्। अमृतं वः। अचैकस्य बाहुल्ये तत्त्वम्। तदुक्तमीशानशिवेन—

तारकाशाद्यन्त्यवाय्यन्तवर्णा आग्नेयाः स्युः सौम्यवर्णास्ततोऽन्ये।
आग्नेयोऽपि स्यात्तु सौम्यो नमोऽन्तः सौम्योऽपि स्यादग्निमन्त्रः फडन्तः।
स्यादाग्नेयैः क्रूरकार्य्यप्रसिद्धिः सौम्यैः सौम्यं कर्म्म कुर्य्याद् यथावत्॥ इति।

नारायणीयेऽपि—तारान्त्याग्निवियत् प्रायो मन्त्र आग्नेय इष्यते।

शिष्टः सौम्यः प्रशस्तौ तौ कर्म्मणोः क्रूरसौम्ययोः॥
आग्नेयमन्त्रः सौम्यः स्यात् प्रायशोऽन्ते नमोऽन्वितः।
सौम्यमन्त्रस्तथाग्नेयः फट्कारेणान्वितोऽन्ततः॥ इति।

पिङ्गलामतेऽपि—रौद्रोऽपि शान्ततामेति शान्तजातिसमन्वितः।

मन्त्रः शान्तोऽपि रौद्रत्वं हुँ फट्पल्लवितो यदि॥ इति।

तत्र विशेषो नारायणीये—

मन्त्रावाग्नेयसौम्याख्यौ ताराद्यन्तौ द्वयोर्जपेत्। इति।

अपेक्षितार्थद्योतनिकायां व्याख्यातम्। एकं नक्षत्रमंशकचतुष्टयं भवति। तत्र आग्नेयानां नक्षत्राणां पूर्व्वांशद्वयमग्रम् इतरत् पुच्छम्। सौम्यानां उत्तरांशकद्वयमग्रमितरत् पुच्छम्। पुच्छकाले प्रयोगो न कार्य्य इति गार्ग्यः। आग्नेयसौम्यनक्षत्राणि अक्षिचक्रे वक्ष्यन्ते। तत्र सूर्य्यनक्षत्राणि अग्निनक्षत्राणि। बोधफलमाह प्रयच्छन्तीति। अन्यथा दोषदर्शनात्। यदुक्तं नारायणीये—

सुप्तः प्रबुध्यमानो वा मन्त्रः सिद्धिं न यच्छति।
स्वापकालो वामवहो जागरो दक्षिणावहः॥
आग्नेयस्य मनोः सौम्यमन्त्रस्यैतद्विपर्य्ययः।

छिन्नादिदुष्टा ये मन्त्रा भाजयन्ति न साधकम् ।
छिन्नो रुद्धः शक्तिहीनः पराङ्मुख उदीरितः ॥ ६४
बधिरो नेत्रहीनश्च कीलितः स्तम्भितस्तथा ।
दग्धस्त्रस्तश्च भीतश्च मलिनश्च तिरस्कृतः ॥ ६५
भेदितश्च सुषुप्तश्च मदोन्मत्तश्च मूर्च्छितः ।
हृतवीर्य्यश्च हीनश्च प्रध्वस्तो बालकः पुनः ॥ ६६
कुमारस्तु युवा प्रौढ़ो वृद्धो निस्त्रिंशकस्तथा ।
निर्बीजः सिद्धिहीनश्च मन्दः कूटस्तथा पुनः ॥ ६७

प्रबोधकालं जानीयादुभयोरुभयोर्वहम् ॥ इति ।

अन्यत्रापि—स्वापकाले तु मन्त्रस्य जपो नार्थफलप्रदः । इति ।

अन्यथान्यथा स्वापकाल उक्तः । यदाहुः—

प्राणायाम[पान]संयोगाच्छिवशक्त्योस्तु मेलनम् ।
प्रबोधकालो विज्ञेयः स्वापकालस्ततः परम् ॥ इति ।

अन्यत्र तु प्रबोधार्थं प्रकारान्तरमुक्तम्—

सम्पुटीकृत्य यत्नेन लान्तानाद्यान् सविन्दुकान् ।
पुनश्च सविसर्गान्तान् सकारं केवलं पठेत् ।
एवं जप्तोपदिष्टश्चेत् प्रबुद्धः शीघ्रसिद्धिदः ॥ इति ।

पुंस्त्रीत्यादिस्वरूपकथनेनैषां विरोधोऽपि सूचितः । यदाहुः—

स्त्रीदेवत्या वैरिणः स्युः पुंदैवत्यस्य भूयसा ।
स्त्रीदैवत्येषु सौम्यानां क्रूराणां स्यात् परस्परम् ॥
तथैव पुंदेवतानाम् । इति ।

पूर्व्ववैपरीत्येनोत्तरस्य सङ्गतिः ॥ ६२-६३ ॥

तत्र शक्तिशिवात्मकमातृकातो मन्त्रोत्पत्तेरुक्तत्वात् तदुत्पत्तिनिमित्ताभाववादिदोषाः तदन्तर्गतच्छिन्नादिदोषसम्बन्धा मन्त्रा विरुद्धफला इत्याह छिन्नेति । छिन्नादिदोषैर्दुष्टाः साधकं न पालयन्तीति सर्व्वेषां सामान्यफलम् । वक्ष्यमाणं कचित्तत्तद्विशेषफलं ज्ञेयम् । आदिशब्दार्थमाह छिन्नेति । तथा पुनरित्यनेन कूट एव निरंशसूचक इत्याह । सोऽतिवृद्ध इति निःस्नेहविशेषणम् तेन निःस्नेहानन्तरमतिवृद्धस्ततः पीड़ित इति ॥ ६४-७० ॥

निरंशः सत्त्वहीनश्च ऐकारो बीजहीनकः ।
धूमितालिङ्गितौ स्यातां मोहितश्च क्षुधातुरः ॥ ६८
अतिदृप्तोऽङ्गहीनश्च अतिक्रुद्धः समीरितः ।
अतिक्रूरश्च सव्रीडः शान्तमानस एव च ॥ ६९
स्थानभ्रष्टश्च विकलः सोऽतिवृद्धः प्रकीर्त्तितः ।
निःस्नेहः पीड़ितश्चापि वक्ष्याम्येषाञ्च लक्षणम् ॥ ७०
मनोर्यस्यादिमध्यान्तेष्वानिलं बीजमुच्यते ।
संयुक्तं वा वियुक्तं वा स्वराक्रान्तं त्रिधा पुनः ।
चतुर्धा पञ्चधा वा स्युः स मन्त्रश्छिन्नसंज्ञकः ॥ ७१

मनोरिति । आनिलं यं । आदिमध्यान्तेष्विति समुच्चयः । संयुक्तं वा अक्षरान्तरयुक्तं वियुक्तं वा केवलं वा इत्येकैकं द्विर्द्विः सम्बध्यते । विशिष्टमनिलं वा विशिष्टं बीजं वा यस्य स छिन्नसंज्ञक इति अन्वयः । बीजं शक्तिबीजम् । स्वराक्रान्तं दीर्घस्वराक्रान्तम् । आ ई ऊ ऐ औ एतत्स्वरयुक्तमिति सम्प्रदायविदः । बीजशब्देन मायाबीजं कथमिति चेदुक्तं शैवे—

मायाबीजस्य नामानि मालिनी शिववल्लभे ।
वातावर्त्तिः कला वाणी बीजं शक्तिश्च कुण्डली ॥ इति ।

तदुक्तं पिङ्गलामते—

आदिमध्यावसानेषु यस्य मन्त्रस्य दृश्यते ।
चतुर्धा पञ्चधा द्वेधमेकवीरं स्वरान्वितम् ।
वायुबीजमसौ मन्त्रश्छेदितः परिकीर्त्तितः ॥ इति ।

तत्रैव चाथ मन्त्रांशकबीजविवरणमित्युपक्रम्य व्याख्यातम् । वायुबीजं यकारः । एकवीरो क्षः । स्वराक्रान्तो दीर्घस्वरयुक्तः । यथाक्रमं क्षां क्षीं क्षूं क्षैं क्षौं उदाहरणञ्च तत्रैव प्रदर्शितम् । "अघोरेभ्योऽथ क्षां घोरेभ्यो क्षीं घोरतरेभ्यः क्षूं सर्व्वतः सर्व्वशर्व्वेभ्यो क्षैं नमस्तेऽस्तु रुद्ररूपेभ्यो क्षौं" इति । मन्त्रमुक्तावल्याञ्च—"एकवीरं वा स्वराक्रान्तं विशेषतः" इति । ग्रन्थान्तरे तु—"अर्द्धग्रहो मनुश्छिन्नः" इत्युक्तम् । अर्द्धं ग्रहः क्वचि श्लोके वा मध्ये विच्छिन्नः ।

अन्यत्र तु—"आदिमध्यान्तबीजानां लोपैश्छिन्नाः" इति ॥ ७१ ॥

आदिमध्यावसानेषु भूबीजद्वन्द्वलाञ्छितः ।
रुद्धमन्त्रः स विज्ञेयो भुक्तिमुक्तिविवर्जितः ॥ ७२

मायात्रितत्त्वश्रीबीजरावहीनस्तु यो मनुः ।
शक्तिहीनः स कथितो यस्य मध्ये न विद्यते ॥ ७३

कामबीजं मुखे माया शिरस्यङ्कुशमेव वा ।
असौ पराङ्मुखः प्रोक्तो हकारो बिन्दुसंयुतः ॥ ७४

आद्यन्तमध्येष्विन्दुर्वा न भवेद् बधिरः स्मृतः ॥ ७५

आदीत्येषां समुच्चयः । भूबीजं लं । द्वन्द्वेति प्रत्येकम् । भुक्तिरैहिकं फलम् । तदुक्तं पिङ्गलामते—

आदौ द्विधा त्रिधा मध्ये पुनश्चान्ते द्विधा भवेत् ।
इन्द्रबीजमसौ मन्त्रो रुद्ध इत्यभिधीयते ॥ इति ।

अन्यत्र च—द्विधा पूर्वं त्रिधा मध्ये द्विधान्ते च पुनः प्रिये ।
वज्रयुक्तस्तु यो मन्त्रः स निरुद्धः प्रकीर्त्तितः ॥ इति ।

वज्रं लकारः । उभयत्र त्रिधेति शेषः । चकारेणोभयत्र समुच्चयोऽपि दर्शितः । एतेन केचन भूबीजशब्देन ग्लोमिति वदन्ति तदपि परास्तम् । ग्रन्थान्तरे त्वन्यः प्रकारः—"रुद्धो निःसन्धिकः स्मृतः" इति । स्वरसन्धिर्व्यञ्जनसन्धिर्व्याकरणोक्तो यत्र नास्ति स निःसन्धिकः । तन्त्रान्तरे—"रुद्धाः परिवारसमन्विताः" इति ॥ ७२ ॥

मायेति । माया भुवनेशीबीजम् । त्रितत्त्वं हूँकारः प्रणवो वा । रावः फ्रेंकारः । एषां न समुच्चयः । यदुक्तम्—

मायाबीजं यत्र नास्ति त्रितत्त्वं रावमेव वा ।
श्रीगृहं वापि मन्त्रोऽसौ शक्तिहीनः प्रकीर्त्तितः ॥ इति ।

पिङ्गलामतेऽपि—मायाबीजं त्रितत्त्वं वा श्रीगृहं यत्र नास्ति चेत् ।
शक्तिहीन इति ख्यातः सामर्थ्यं हन्ति मन्त्रिणः ॥ इति ।

अथ मन्त्रांशकबीजविवरणमित्युपक्रम्य त्रितत्त्वं हूँ श्रीगृहं श्रीमिति तत्रैव व्याख्यातम् ।

यस्येति । मुखे आदौ । शिरसि अन्ते । अङ्कुशं क्रोंकारः । वाशब्दः समुच्चये । क्वचिदेव चेति पाठः । तदुक्तं पिङ्गलामते—

कामबीजं न यन्मध्ये मायादावस्तिमोऽङ्कुशः । पराङ्मुख इति प्रोक्तः । इति ।

पञ्चवर्णो मनुर्यः स्याद् रेफार्केन्दुविवर्जितः।
नेत्रहीनः स विज्ञेयो दुःखशोकामयप्रदः॥ ७६

आदिमध्यावसानेषु हंसप्रासादवाग्भवाः।
हकारोबिन्दुमान् जीवो गावं वापि चतुष्कलम्।
माया नमामि च पदं नास्ति यस्मिन् स कीलितः॥ ७७

मन्त्रमुक्तावल्यामपि—

यस्य कामकलाबीजं मध्यस्थाने न विद्यते।
आदौ मायाङ्कुशश्चान्ते विज्ञेयोऽसौ पराङ्मुखः॥ इति।

हकार इति। इन्दुः सः। विन्दुसंयुत इत्यत्रापि सम्बध्यते। आद्यन्तमध्येष्विति न समुच्चयः। तदुक्तम्—

शून्यं विन्दुसमायुक्तं आद्यन्ते वाथ मध्यतः।
न भवेज्जीवबीजं वा यस्यासौ वधिरः स्मृतः॥ इति।

एतेन केचिदिन्दुशब्देन ठकाराख्यमाचक्षते। तदपि परास्तम्॥ ७३-७५॥

पञ्चेति। अर्को हकारः। वैष्णवब्रह्मत्वन्यासेऽर्कमण्डलतत्त्वस्य हकारादित्वेन न्यस्तत्वात्। हकारस्य पुंरूपत्वाद् वा अर्कत्वम्। इन्दुः सकारः। पञ्चेत्यादि उभयं दोषबीजम्। दुःखशोकामयप्रद इति क्रमेण फलम्। यतोऽग्निसूर्यचन्द्राणां नेत्रत्रयात्मकत्वात् एकद्विहानतः काणतापि ज्ञेया। तदुक्तं पिङ्गलामते—

पञ्चाक्षरस्तु यो मन्त्रो वह्निचन्द्रार्कवर्जितः।
नेत्रहीन इति ज्ञेयो दुःखशोकामयावहः॥ इति।

अथ मन्त्रांशकबीजविवरणमित्युपक्रम्य चन्द्रः सः अर्को हः इति तत्रैव व्याख्यातम्॥ ७६॥

आदौति। एषां समुच्चयः हंसआदीनां न समुच्चयः। गावं वा इत्युक्तत्वात्। ग्रन्थान्तरेपि—"हंसं मायात्मकं वापि" इति। हंसः स्वरूपम्। प्रासादबीजं ह्रौं। वाग्भवम् ऐँ। हकारोबिन्दुमान्। जीवः सः। गावः फ्रें। चतुष्कलो हूँ। माया शक्तिबीजम् नमामीति पदञ्च यत्र नास्ति स कीलित इति। अत्र हकारोविन्दुमानित्येकं पदम्। जीव इत्येकम्। तत्र जीवः कीदृशः हकारश्च अकारश्च उकारश्च विन्दुश्च तद्वान्। तेन स्ह्रौं इति सिद्धम्। अत्र अकार उकार बिन्दुरित्यनेन ॐकारः। यथा "अउमाः स्युः" इत्यत्र। तथा च पिङ्गलामते—

एकं मध्ये द्वयं मूर्ध्नि यस्मिन्नस्त्रपुरन्दरौ ।
विद्येते स तु मन्त्रः स्यात् स्तम्भितः सिद्धिरोधकः ॥ ७८

वह्निवायुसमायुक्तो यस्य मन्त्रस्य मूर्द्धनि ।
सप्तधा दृश्यते तं तु दग्धं मन्येत मन्त्रवित् ॥ ७९

नवमस्वरसंयुक्तो जीवाकृष्टः सबिन्दुकः ।
यस्यात्मा दृश्यते नैव किंवा गवचतुष्कलः ॥
प्रासादो वाग्भवो हंसो माया वा यत्र दृश्यते ।
आदिमध्यान्तदेशेषु कीलितं तं प्रचक्षते ॥ इति ।

अथ मन्त्रांशकबीजविवरणमित्युपक्रम्य तत्रैव व्याख्यातम्—नवमस्वर ओकारः । आत्मा हः । गवः फूं । चतुष्कलः हूँ । तन्त्रान्तरे तु—"हंसमायात्मकं वापि" इति पठित्वा क्रोमिति व्याख्यातम् । अन्ये हंसो मायेति पिङ्गलावाक्येऽप्ययमेवार्थ इत्याहुः । अन्यत्र तु—"अन्तरन्तेन बीजेन व्याप्तः कीलित उच्यते ।" इति । ग्रन्थान्तरे—"कीलितो बीजवर्जितः" इति ॥ ७७ ॥

एकमिति । मूर्ध्नि अन्ते । अस्त्रं फट्कारः । पुरन्दरो लः । मध्ये एकः फट्कारो लकारो वा । अन्ते फट्कारद्वयं लकारद्वयं वा । केचन मध्ये फट्कारः अन्ते लद्वयमिति व्याचक्षते । तदसत् । ग्रन्थान्तरविरोधात् । तथा च पिङ्गलामते—

मन्त्रमध्ये द्विधा शान्ते शक्रबीजं भवेद् यदि ।
स्तम्भितं तं वदन्तीयं मन्त्रं मन्त्रविदो बुधाः ॥ इति ।

ग्रन्थान्तरे च—द्विधा त्रिधाऽष्टधा षोढा मन्त्रान्ते यत्र दृश्यते ।
मन्त्रास्त्रं स्तम्भितो मन्त्रः सः शम्भुना प्रकीर्त्तितः ॥

इति ग्रन्थद्वयविरोधात् । "न विद्येते स मन्त्रः" इति प्रामादिकः पाठः । "विद्येते स तु मन्त्रः स्यात्" इति तु साम्प्रदायिकः पाठः । अन्यत्र तु—

स्तम्भितोऽसौ क्रियायां यो नियुक्तो नापि युज्जति । इति ॥ ७८ ॥

वह्निरिति । वह्नी रेफः वायुर्यकारः तेन समवेतः अध ऊर्द्ध्वं वा । मूर्द्धनि आदौ । तदुक्तं पिङ्गलामते—

आदिस्थैः सप्तभिर्बीजैर्मारुतैः पावकाक्षरम् ।
दीपितं यत्र तं मन्त्रमाद्यो दग्धं प्रचक्षते ॥ इति ।

ग्रन्थान्तरे प्रकारान्तरेणोक्तः—"षट्कर्णाङ्कगतो दग्धः" इति ।

अन्यत्र तु—"अग्निबीजाधिका दग्धाः" इति ॥ ७९ ॥

अस्त्रं द्वाभ्यां त्रिभिः षड्भिरष्टाभिर्दृश्यतेऽक्षरैः ।
त्रस्तः सोऽभिहितो यस्य मुखे न प्रणवः स्थितः ।
शिवो वा शक्तिरथवा भीताख्यः स प्रकीर्त्तितः ॥ ८०
आदिमध्यावसानेषु भवेन्मार्गचतुष्टयम् ।
यस्य मन्त्रः स मलिनो मन्त्रवित् तं विवर्जयेत् ॥ ८१

अस्त्रमिति । द्वाभ्यामक्षराभ्यां त्रिभिः षड्भिरष्टभिरक्षरैर्वा यस्य अस्त्र फट्कारो दृश्यते । पिङ्गलामते भीतमन्त्रायमुक्तः ।

आदिमध्यान्तदेशेषु यदि मन्त्रोऽस्त्रसंयुतः । भीत इत्युच्यते तन्त्रे । इति । अन्ये तु "त्रस्तः सोऽभिहितो मन्त्रः" इति पाठमपठन् । तन्त्रान्तरे "त्रासिताः सिद्धिभीषिताः" इति ।

यस्येति । मुखे आदौ । शिवः हः शक्तिः स इति साम्प्रदायिकाः । केचन शिवशब्देन विन्दु शक्तिशब्देन विसर्गमाहुः । तदयुक्तम् । मन्त्रादौ केवलविन्दोः केवलविसर्गस्य वा असत्त्वात् । अक्षरान्तरयुक्तौ ग्राह्य इति चेत् । तद्वरं साम्प्रदायिकार्थानुसरणमेव । ग्रन्थकृदग्रे वक्ष्यति—

हंसौ तौ पुंप्रकृत्याख्यौ हं पुमान् प्रकृतिस्तु सः । इति ।

अयमेव दोषो नामान्तरेणोक्तः पिङ्गलामते—

शिवः शक्तिस्तथौंकारो यस्यादौ नास्ति तं मनुम् ।
वदन्ति मातृकाहीनं हीनसिद्धिप्रदायकम् ॥ इति ।

अथ मन्त्रांशकबीजविवरणमित्युपक्रम्य तत्रैव व्याख्यातं शिवो हं शक्तिः स इति ॥ ८० ॥

आदीति । एषां समुच्चयः । मार्गचतुष्टयमित्यपि समुच्चयः । तेन स्थानत्रये मिलित्वा मार्गचतुष्टयमपेक्षितम् । तदुक्तं पिङ्गलामते—

आदिमध्यान्तदेशेषु चतुर्धा यत्र दृश्यते ।
मकारो मलिनं विद्यात् तं मन्त्रं मन्त्रवित् त्यजेत् ॥ इति ।

अन्यत्र तु— आदौ मध्येऽथ हृदये त्रिधा वै यस्य दृश्यते ।
मन्त्रो मकार ईशेन मलिनः स समीरितः ॥ इति ।

मतान्तरत्वाद्भेदः । हृदयशब्दोऽन्तवाची । अन्यत्र तु "मलैस्त्रिभिः सहजागन्तुकमायाख्यैर्मलिनाः" इति ॥ ८१ ॥

यस्य मध्ये दकारोऽथ क्रोधो वा मूर्द्धनि द्विधा ।
अस्त्रं तिष्ठति मन्त्रः स तिरस्कृत उदाहृतः ॥ ८२
भ्योद्वयं हृदये शीर्षे वषडस्त्रञ्च च मध्यतः ।
यस्यासौ भेदितो मन्त्रस्त्याज्यः सिद्धिषु सूरिभिः ॥ ८३
त्रिवर्णो हंसहीनो यः सुषुप्तः स उदाहृतः ॥ ८४

यस्येति । क्रोधो हुँ बीजं मध्ये दकारक्रोधयोर्विकल्पः । मूर्द्धनि अन्ते । द्विधा अस्त्रमिति सम्बन्धः । मध्यान्तयोः समुच्चयः । तदुक्तं पिङ्गलामते—

दकारः क्रोधबीजं वा यस्य मध्ये व्यवस्थितम् ।
फड् द्वयञ्च स्थितं प्रान्ते यस्यागोः स तिरस्कृतः ॥ इति ।

अन्यत्रापि—यस्य मध्ये दकारस्तु क्रोधबीजं हृदि स्थितम् ।
द्विधा चान्ते च फट्कारः स्याद् यस्य स तिरस्कृतः ॥ इति ।

तन्त्रान्तरे "पराभूतास्तिरस्कृताः" इति ॥ ८२ ॥

भ्योद्वयं प्रमुखे शीर्षे वषड़स्त्रञ्च मध्यत इति । शीर्षे अन्ते वषट् । अस्त्रं फ्रः मध्यतः । यन्मन्त्रमुक्तावल्याम्—

अस्त्रवर्णद्वयं मध्ये वषड़न्ते तथैव च ।
यस्य मन्त्रस्य भिन्नोऽसौ विज्ञेयः सिद्धिवर्जितः ॥ इति ।

पिङ्गलामतेऽपि—अस्त्रवर्णद्वयं मध्ये वषड़न्ते तथादितः ।
अउमाः स्युरसौ मन्त्रो भेदितः परिकीर्त्तितः ॥ इति ।

अथ मन्त्रांशकबीजविवरणमित्युपक्रम्य तत्रैव व्याख्यातम् । अस्त्रं फ्रः । अउमाः ॐकारः । केचन "भ्योद्वयं हृदये शीर्षे वषड़ावू च मध्यतः" इति पठन्ति । अन्ये च "वषट् वौषट् च मध्यतः" इति पठन्ति ।

अन्यत्र—"भिन्नतां नीता भेदिताः" इति ॥ ८३ ॥

त्रिवर्ण इति । त्रिवर्णत्वं हंसहीनत्वमेकस्यैव । तदुक्तं पिङ्गलामते—

वर्णत्रयं भवेद् यत्र हंसहीनं स शम्भुना ।
सुषुप्त इति सिद्धान्ते प्रोक्तोऽभीष्टफलापहः ॥ इति ।

मन्त्रमुक्तावल्यामपि—

वर्णत्रयात्मको मन्त्रो यस्तु हंसविवर्जितः ।
प्रसुप्तः स तु विज्ञेयः सर्व्वसिद्धिफलापहः ॥ इति ।

मन्त्रो वाऽप्यथवा विद्या सप्ताधिकदशाक्षरः ।
फट्कारपञ्चकादिर्यो मदोन्मत्त उदीरितः ॥ ८५
तद्वदस्त्रं स्थितं मध्ये यस्य मन्त्रः स मूर्च्छितः ।
विरामस्थानगं यस्य हतवीर्य्यः स कथ्यते ॥ ८६
आदौ मध्ये तथा मूर्द्ध्नि चतुरस्त्रयुतो मनुः ।
ज्ञातव्यो हीन इत्येष यः स्यादष्टादशाक्षरः ॥ ८७

"अज्ञातदीपकः सुप्तः" इत्येके । अन्यत्र तु—"मायया हतसामर्थ्याः सुप्ताः" इति । अन्यत्र तु—"सुप्तः स्यादासनं विना" इति ॥ ८४ ॥

मन्त्र इति । सप्ताधिकानि अष्टौ दश च अक्षराणि यत्र सः । एवमष्टादशाक्षरः । फट्काराणां पञ्चकमादौ यस्मिन्निति बहुव्रीहिः । तदुक्तम्—

विद्या वा यदि वा मन्त्रो यद्यष्टादशवर्णकः ।
पञ्चफट्कारपूर्व्वः स्यान्मदोन्मत्तः स उच्यते ॥ इति ।

पिङ्गलामतेऽपि—विद्या वा मन्त्रराजो वा यः स्यात् सप्तदशाधिकः ।
फट्काराः पञ्च पूर्व्वश्चेदुन्मत्तः स प्रकीर्त्तितः ॥ इति ।

अत्रापि विशेषणद्वयविशिष्टत्वे दोषः । तद्वदिति पञ्चवारम् । ग्रन्थान्तरे प्रकारान्तरम्—"सम्मूर्च्छिताः पुनर्विचेतन्याः" इति ।

विरामेति । यस्यास्त्रमिति सम्बध्यते । यस्यान्ते अस्त्रमित्यर्थः । "विरामगोऽस्त्रो यो मन्त्रः" इति पाठः क्वचित् । तदुक्तं पिङ्गलामते—

अस्त्रमन्त्रो भवेद् यस्य मध्ये प्रान्ते च शम्भुना ।
हतवीर्य्य इति ख्यातः स मन्त्रो नैव सिद्धिदः ॥ इति ।

अन्यत्रापि—विरामस्थानगं यस्य हतवीर्य्यः स उच्यते । इति । केचन पञ्चधा इत्यप्यनुवर्त्तयन्ति । तदेतद्विरुद्धम् । अन्ये तु "सामर्थ्यवर्जितो हीनवीर्य्यः" इत्याहुः । अन्यत्र तु "निर्वीर्य्यसाधिकाक्षरः" इति ॥ ८५ ॥ ८६ ॥

आदाविति समुच्चयः । चतुर्धास्त्रमित्यपि । स्थानत्रये मिलित्वा अस्त्रचतुष्टयम् । तन्त्रान्तरे तु भीतनाम्ना अयमुक्तः ।

आदावन्ते तथा मध्ये चतुर्धाऽस्त्रेण संयुतम् ।
अष्टादशाक्षरं मन्त्रं भीतं तं भैरवोऽब्रवीत् ॥ इति ।

अष्टादशाक्षरत्वे विशेषः । अत्रापि "यः स्यादष्टादशाक्षरः" इति चरणः काकाक्षि-

एकोनविंशत्यर्णो वा यो मन्त्रस्तारसंयुतः ।
हृल्लेखाङ्कुशबीजाढ्यस्तं प्रध्वस्तं प्रचक्षते ॥ ८८
सप्तवर्णो मनुर्बालः कुमारोऽष्टाक्षरस्तु यः ।
षोडशार्णो युवा प्रौढश्चत्वारिंशल्लिपिर्मनुः ॥ ८९
त्रिंशदर्णश्चतुःषष्टिवर्णो मन्त्रः शताक्षरः ।
चतुःशताक्षरश्चापि वृद्ध इत्यभिधीयते ॥ ९०

गोलकन्यायेनोभयत्र सम्बध्यते इति वा। क्वचित् "ज्ञातव्यो भीत इत्येषः" इति पाठः। अन्यान्तरे तु प्रकारान्तरम्। "अथ वर्जिताः सुसिद्ध सिद्ध साध्याख्यैरंशैर्हीनाः" इति। अन्यत्र तु "हीनो दुष्टादयाशो यः" इति।

यः स्यादिति। तारः प्रणवः। केचन तारं प्रे इति वदन्ति। तदयुक्तम्। ग्रन्थान्तरविरोधात्। यच्चक्तमुक्तावल्याम्—

एकोनविंशत्यर्णो यो यो मन्त्रः प्रणवान्वितः।
महामायाङ्कुशैर्युक्तस्तं प्रध्वस्तं प्रचक्षते॥ इति।

पिङ्गलामतेऽपि— यदि सोऽष्टादशाक्षरः।
विंशत्येकोनवर्णो वा मायोङ्काराङ्कुशान्वितः।
प्रध्वस्त इत्यसौ मन्त्रः शम्भुदेवेन कीर्त्तितः॥ इति।

केचनैतत् परिहाराय "यो मन्त्रः प्रणवान्वितः" इति पाठं पठन्ति। हृल्लेखा माया। तदुक्तं भुवनेशीपारिजाते—

मायाबीजमिदं प्रोक्तं भुवनत्रयमक्षरम्।
हृल्लेखेयञ्च योगेशी भुवनेशी च योगिनी॥ इति॥ ८७॥ ८८॥

सप्तवर्ण इति। चत्वारिंशल्लिपिश्चत्वारिंशदक्षरः। तदुक्तम्—

सप्ताक्षरो भवेद् बालः कुमारश्चाष्टवर्णकः।
चत्वारिंशाक्षरः प्रौढस्तरुणः षोडशाक्षरः॥ इति।

अन्यत्र—"बालो लघुफलात्मकः" इति। ग्रन्थान्तरे तु—"अष्टढा बालकाः कार्ये" इति। अन्यत्र—

गुरोरप्यविधानेन प्राप्तो यौवनगर्व्वितः। इति।

ग्रन्थान्तरे तु "तरुणा अतिदर्पिताः" इति। अन्यत्र तु "प्रौढाः प्रमोत्कटाः" इति॥ ८९॥

नवाक्षरो ध्रुवयुतो मनुर्निस्त्रिंश ईरितः ।

यस्यावसाने हृदयं शिरोमन्त्रश्च मध्यतः ॥ ८१

शिखा वर्म्म च न स्यातां वौषट् फट्कार एव च ।

शिवशक्त्यर्णहीनो वा स निर्वीज इति स्मृतः ॥ ८२

एषु स्थानेषु फट्कारः षोढा यस्मिन् प्रदृश्यते ।

स मन्त्रः सिद्धिहीनः स्यान्मन्दः पङ्क्त्यक्षरो मनुः ॥ ८३

त्रिंशदिति। चतुःशताक्षरः चतुरधिकशताक्षरः मध्यपदलोपी । केचित् चतुःशताक्षर इति चत्वारि शतानि अक्षराणि यस्य इति व्याचक्षते । तन्न । ग्रन्थान्तरविरोधात् ।

त्रिंशदर्णं शतार्णं वा चतुःशताक्षरस्तथा ।

चतुरूर्द्ध्वशतं वापि वृद्ध इत्यभिधीयते ॥ इति ।

पिङ्गलामतेऽपि—त्रिंशद् यत्र शतार्द्धं वा चतुःषष्टिशतं चतुः ।

शतानि सन्ति वर्णानां स मन्त्रो वृद्धसंज्ञकः ॥ इति ।

असावेवाग्रे वक्ष्यति अतिवृद्धलक्षणे—

चतुःशतान्यथारभ्य यावद्वर्णसहस्रकम् । इति ।

तेन च विरोधः स्यात् । ग्रन्थान्तरे च । "छिद्रकर्म्मैव कुर्व्वन्ति वृद्धा स्ते" इति । ८० ॥

नवेति । ध्रुव ॐकारः । नवाक्षरत्वं ध्रुवयुक्तत्वमेकस्यैव । निस्त्रिंशो घातुक इत्यर्थः । पिङ्गलामते—नवाक्षरस्तु निस्त्रिंशो ध्रुवयुक्तोऽपमृत्युदः । इति ।

यस्येति । हृदयमन्त्रः नमः । शिरोमन्त्रः स्वाहा । शिखा वषट् । वर्म्म हुँ । शिवो हं । शक्त्यर्णः स इति । विकल्पद्वयमध्य एव । अत्र "संस्याताम्" इति प्रामादिकः पाठः । "न स्याताम्" इति साम्प्रदायिकः । तदुक्तम्—

हृच्छिरोऽन्ते शिखा वर्म्म मध्ये नेत्रास्त्रकेऽथवा ।

शिवशक्त्यात्मकौ वर्णौ न स्तो यस्य स मन्त्रराट् ।

निर्बीज इति सम्प्रोक्तः सर्व्वकर्मसु गर्हितः ॥ इति ।

तन्त्रान्तरे तु—निर्बीजस्तु समाख्यात आदावोङ्कारवर्जितः । इति ॥८१॥८२॥

एष्विति निर्बीजलक्षणे तन्त्रान्तरोक्तादिग्रहणसूचनार्थम् । तदाह एष्विति । आदिमध्यावसानेषु एषां समुच्चयः । षोढ़ेत्यत्रापि स्थानत्रये मिलित्वा षट् ।

मन्द इति । पङ्क्त्यक्षरो दशाक्षरः । तदुक्तम्—"दशाक्षरो भवेन्मन्दः" इति । तन्त्रान्तरे—"प्रभाहीना मन्दाः" इति ॥ ८३ ॥

कूट एकाक्षरो मन्त्रः स एवोक्तो निरंशकः ।
द्विवर्णः सत्त्वहीनः स्याच्चतुर्वर्णस्तु कीकरः ॥ ८४
षड़क्षरो बीजहीनस्त्वर्द्धसप्ताक्षरो मनुः ।
सार्द्धद्वादशवर्णो वा धूमितः स तु निन्दितः ॥ ८५
सार्द्धबीजत्रयस्तद्वदेकविंशतिवर्णकः ।
विंशत्यर्णस्त्रिंशदर्णो यः स्यादालिङ्गितस्तु सः ॥ ८६
द्वाविंशदक्षरो मन्त्रो मोहितः परिकीर्त्तितः ।
चतुर्विंशतिवर्णो यः सप्तविंशतिवर्णकः ॥ ८७
क्षुधार्त्तः स तु विज्ञेयश्चतुर्विंशतिवर्णकः ।
एकादशाक्षरो वापि पञ्चविंशतिवर्णकः ॥ ८८
त्रयोविंशतिवर्णो वा मन्त्रो दृप्त उदाहृतः ॥ ८९

कूट इति। तदुक्तम्—"कूट एकाक्षरोऽथवा निरंशः स भवेन्मन्त्रः" इति।
द्विवर्ण इति। तदुक्तम्—"द्व्यक्षरः सत्त्ववर्जितः" इति।

अन्यत्र तु—"सत्त्ववर्जिता स्तमसोत्कटाः" इति।

चतुर्वर्ण इति चतुर्बीजः।

पिङ्गलामते विशेषः—

ध्रुवहीनश्चतुर्बीजैः षड्भिर्वा कीकरो मतः। इति ॥ ८४ ॥

षडक्षर इति। अन्यत्र—"बीजवर्जिता ॐकाररहिताः" इति।
सार्द्धेति। अत्रार्द्धसप्ताक्षरत्वम् अर्द्धद्वादशवर्णत्वञ्च अन्ते व्यञ्जनसत्त्वाद् ज्ञेयम्।

सार्द्धबीजत्रयस्तद्वदिति। बीजं वर्णः। तद्वद्धूमित इत्यर्थः। तदुक्तम्—

अर्द्धसप्ताक्षरो मन्त्रः सार्द्धद्वादशवर्णकः।
धूमितः स समाख्यातः सार्द्धवर्णत्रयोऽथवा॥ इति।

त्रिंशदर्णस्य ध्रुवत्वमालिङ्गितत्वञ्च तथैव।

दृप्त इति। उद्देशावसरे अतिदृप्तस्योद्दिष्टत्वात् लक्षणावसरे दृप्तलक्षणं कथं क्रियते इति न मन्तव्यम्। सत्यप्युपसर्गेऽप्यर्थाभेदात्। तदुक्तम्—

धात्वर्थं बाधते कश्चित् कश्चित्तमनुवर्त्तते।
तमेव विशिनष्ट्यन्योऽनर्थकोऽन्यः प्रयुज्यते॥ इति।

षड्विंशत्यक्षरो मन्त्रः षट्त्रिंशद्वर्णकस्तथा ।
त्रिंशदेकोनवर्णो वाऽप्यङ्गहीनोऽभिधीयते ॥ १००
अष्टाविंशत्यक्षरो वा एकत्रिंशदथापि वा ।
अतिक्रुद्धः स कथितो निन्दितः सर्व्वकर्म्मसु ॥ १०१
त्रिंशदक्षरको मन्त्रस्त्रयस्त्रिंशदथापि वा ।
अतिक्रूरः स कथितो निन्दितः सर्व्वकर्म्मसु ॥ १०२
चत्वारिंशतमारभ्य त्रिषष्टिर्यावदापतेत् ।
तावत्संख्या निगदिता मन्त्राः सव्रीड़संज्ञकाः ॥ १०३
पञ्चषष्ट्यक्षरा ये स्युर्मन्त्रास्ते शान्तमानसाः ।
एकोनशतपर्य्यन्तं पञ्चषष्ट्यक्षरादितः ॥ १०४
ये मन्त्रास्ते निगदिताः स्थानभ्रष्टाह्वया बुधैः ।
त्रयोदशाक्षरा ये स्युर्मन्त्राः पञ्चदशाक्षराः ॥ १०५
विकला स्तेऽभिधीयन्ते शतं सार्द्धं शतन्तु वा ।
शतद्वयं द्विनवतिरेकहीनाथवापि सा ॥ १०६

मन्त्रमुक्तावल्यां तथोक्तम्—

चतुर्विंशाक्षरं वाथ मन्त्रमेकादशाक्षरम् ।
शतार्द्धार्द्धं त्रयोविंश मतिदृप्तन्तु तं विदुः ॥ इति ॥ ८५-८८ ॥

षड्विंशतीति । त्रिंशतः एक ऊनो येषु पश्चाद् वहुव्रीहिः । अङ्गहीनो मन्त्रमुक्तावल्याम्—"अष्टत्रिंशदक्षरः" इति चतुर्थोऽप्युक्तः ॥ १००-१०२ ॥

चत्वारिंशतमिति । चत्वारिंशदक्षरमारभ्य एकैकाक्षरवृद्ध्या चतुर्विंशतिप्रकारः सव्रीड़ः । मन्त्रमुक्तावल्याम्—"चतुःषष्ट्यक्षरं यावत्" इति ॥ १०३ ॥

एकोनेति । पञ्चषष्ट्यक्षर आदिर्यस्येत्येतद्गुणसंविज्ञानो वहुव्रीहिः । इतः पञ्चषष्ट्यक्षरादितिवा छेदः । तस्य पूर्व्वं शान्तमानसतोक्ता । मन्त्रमुक्तावल्यामपि—

पञ्चषष्ट्यक्षरा ये च यावदेकोनकं शतम् । इति ।

तेन स्थानभ्रष्ट एकैकाक्षरवृद्ध्या चतुस्त्रिंशत्प्रकारः ॥ १०४ ॥ १०५ ॥

शतमिति । शतद्वयं द्विनवतिरित्येकः सार्द्धशतद्वयं द्विनवतिरेकहीना

शतत्रयं वा यत्संख्या निःस्नेहास्ते मनीषिताः ।
चतुःशतान्यथारभ्य यावद्वर्णसहस्रकम् ॥ १०७
अतिवृद्धः प्रयोगेषु परित्याज्याः सदा बुधैः ।
सहस्रार्णाधिका मन्त्रा दण्डका पीड़िताह्वयाः ॥ १०८
द्विसहस्राक्षरा मन्त्रा खण्डशः शतधा कृताः ।
ज्ञातव्याः स्तोत्ररूपास्ते मन्त्रा एते यथा स्थिताः ॥ १०९
तथा विद्याश्च बोद्धव्या मन्त्रिभिः काम्यकर्मसु ।
दोषानिमानविज्ञाय यो मन्त्रं भजते जड़ः ।
सिद्धिर्न जायते तस्य कल्पकोटिशतैरपि ॥ ११०

तेनैकाधिका नवतिः शतत्रयञ्च । एवं पञ्च पञ्च प्रकाराः ।
पिङ्गलामते तु—

एकद्वित्रिशतैर्वर्णैर्युक्ता निःस्नेहसंज्ञकाः । इति

त्रिप्रकार एव । मन्त्रमुक्तावल्यां पक्षोऽप्युक्तः "त्रिशतं लेकवर्जितम्" इति । केचन शतद्वयमित्येकः प्रकारः । द्विनवति रित्यन्यः । सा एकहीना एकाधिक नवति रित्यपरः प्रकार इत्यूचुः । तन्न । षट्षष्टिप्रभृतीनां एकोनशत पर्यन्तं स्थान-भ्रष्टाक्षयत्वस्योक्तत्वात् । त्रिंशद्वर्षवत् एकस्यैव दोषद्वयदुष्टत्वं भविष्यतीति चेत् तन्न । तत्र शतादारभ्याधिकस्यैव शतत्रय पर्यन्तमुक्तत्वात् । यत्संख्येति सर्वत्र सम्बध्यते । येषां मन्त्राणां संख्या शताधिकास्ते निःस्नेहा इति सम्बन्धः ।

योगेषु प्रयोगेषु ये दण्डकास्ते स्तोत्ररूपास्ते पीड़िताह्वया ज्ञातव्या इति सम्बन्धः ॥ १०६-१०८ ॥

ननु मन्त्राणामेवैते दोषा उक्ता विद्यास्तु निर्दोषा इति आशङ्क्य आह मन्त्रा एते इति । यथा मन्त्रा एते स्थिताः सदोषाः तथा मन्त्रिभिर्विद्या अपि बोद्धव्याः । तदुक्तम्—यथा मन्त्रा स्तथा विद्या भेदभिन्नाः परस्परम् ।

ज्ञातव्या देशिकेन्द्रेण नानातन्त्रेषु भाषिताः ॥ इति ।

काम्यकर्मस्वित्यनेन मुक्त्यर्थं मन्त्रजपे एतद्दोषाभावाद्दशसंस्कारा अपि न कर्त्तव्याः । एतच्चोपलक्षणं । तेन वक्ष्यमाणलक्षणं शोधनादिकं मुक्त्यर्थं न कर्त्तव्यमिति ॥ ११० ॥

इत्यादिदोषदुष्टांस्तान् मन्त्रानात्मनि योजयेत् ।
शोधयेद्दूर्द्धपवनो बद्ध्वा योनिमुद्रया ॥ १११

इत्यादीत्यादिशब्दात् कीलितविपक्षस्थदारितमूकनग्नभुजङ्गमशून्यहतादयोदोषा ज्ञेयाः । तल्लक्षणानि यथा—

"कीलिताः कर्णलक्षदिकुड्यमन्त्रा अभिन्नेण योजिता अपि" ॥ इति ।

"विपक्षस्था रिपोः पक्षमाश्रिताः" इति ।

"आदिमध्यावसानेषु ध्रुवो यस्य न विद्यते ।

स दारित इति ख्यातः तन्त्रेऽस्मिन् कृत्तिवाससा ॥" इति ।

"स्वारं विना भवेन्मूकः" । "पल्लवेन विना मन्त्रो नग्नः संपरिकीर्त्तितः ।" इति ।

"ऋष्यदैवतच्छन्दोभिः परित्यक्तो भुजङ्गमः ।" इति ।

"यस्य जापं शृणोत्यन्यः स मन्त्रः शून्य उच्यते ।" "शिखाहीनो हतः प्रोक्तः" इति ।

शोधनप्रकारमाह मन्त्रानात्मनीति । आत्मैं आत्मादनन्यदेवेति या भावना सा आत्मनि योजना । क्वचिन्मन्त्रान् स्वात्मनि योजयेदिति पाठः ।

प्रकारान्तरेण शोधनमाह शोधयेदिति । वक्ष्यमाणलक्षणां योनिमुद्रां बद्ध्वा मूलाधारोत्पन्नान् मन्त्रवर्णान् ब्रह्मरन्ध्रपर्य्यन्तं गतागतानि कुर्व्वतो ध्यात्वा वायुधारणं कृत्वा सहस्रं जपेदिति शोधनप्रकारमाहुः ।

तदुक्तम्—"योनिं बद्ध्वा बीजं जिह्वादियुग्मेन चोर्ध्वनीं प्राप्य तत्र सहस्रं मन्त्रं जपेत् स मन्त्रः प्रबुद्धः स्यात्" इति । योनिमुद्रालक्षणं यथा—

पार्ष्णिभागात् सुसंपीड्य योनिमार्गं तथा गुदम् ।

अपानमूर्द्ध्वमाकर्षेन्मूलबन्धो निगद्यते ॥

गुदमेढ्रान्तरं योनिस्तामाकुञ्च्य प्रबन्धयेत् ।

युवा भवति वृद्धोऽपि सततं मूलबन्धनात् ॥ इति ।

योनिस्थानमुद्रणात् योनिमुद्रात्वमस्याः । तदाहुः—

सेयं मयोक्ता खलु योनिमुद्रा बन्धस्य देवैरपि दुर्लभोऽस्याः ।
अनेन बन्धेन न साध्यते यन्नास्त्येव तत् साधकपुङ्गवस्य ॥
छिन्ना रुद्धाः कीलिताः स्तम्भिता ये सुप्ता मत्ता मूर्च्छिता हीनवीर्य्याः ।
दग्धास्त्रस्ताः शत्रुपक्षे स्थिता ये बाला वृद्धा गर्व्विता यौवनेन ॥
ये निर्बीजा ये च सत्त्वेन हीना खण्डीभूताश्चाङ्गमन्त्रैर्विहीनाः ।
एते मुद्राबन्धनेनैव योन्या मन्त्राः सर्व्वे वीर्य्यवन्तो भवन्ति ॥ इति ॥ १११ ॥

मन्त्राणां दशसंस्काराः कथ्यन्ते सिद्धिदायिनः।

जननं जीवनं पश्चात् ताड़नं बोधनन्तथा ॥ ११२

अथाभिषेको विमलीकरणाप्यायने पुनः।

तर्पणं दीपनं गुप्तिर्दशैता मन्त्रसंस्क्रियाः ॥ ११३

मन्त्राणां मातृकामध्यादुद्धारो जननं स्मृतम् ॥ ११४

प्रणवान्तरितान् कृत्वा मन्त्रवर्णान् जपेत् सुधीः।

एतज्जीवनमित्याहुर्मन्त्रतन्त्रविशारदाः ॥ ११५

एवं न ये योगिनो योनिमुद्रानभिज्ञाः पवनधारणाशक्ताश्च तान् प्रति दशसंस्कारैः शोधनमाह मन्त्राणामिति। पिङ्गलामतेऽपि—

इत्यादिदोषसंयुक्ता विज्ञेया मन्त्रिणाणवः।
तस्मात् तद्दोषनाशाय क्रमः कोऽपि निगद्यते ॥
जननं जीवनं बोधस्ताड़नं निर्मलीकृतिः।
आप्यायनाभिषेकौ च क्रियाङ्गैः सप्तभिर्ध्रुवम् ॥
शोधिताः सकला मन्त्रा भवन्ति किल कामदाः। इति।

मन्त्रतन्त्रप्रकाशेऽपि—अथास्मै प्रवदेन्मन्त्रं संस्कृतं सुमुहूर्त्तके।
सप्तैते मन्त्रसंस्कारा दुर्लभा भुवि मानवैः ॥
जननं जीवनञ्चेत्यादिना।

अत्र तर्पणदीपनगोपनलक्षणास्त्रयः संस्काराः सामान्यतः प्रसिद्धा इति तान् विहाय सप्तेत्युक्तिरिति ज्ञेयम् ॥ ११२ ॥ ११३ ॥

मन्त्राणामिति। मातृकामध्यादित्यनेनैतदुक्तं भवति। शुभे पीठादौ कुङ्कुमरोचनादिना मातृकाञ्च विलिख्य देयमन्त्रस्यैकैकमक्षरं मातृकातः उद्धरणीयमिति।

तदुक्तम्—वर्णाब्जञ्च संलिख्य समुद्धरेन्मन्त्रजन्मैतत्। इति ॥ ११४ ॥

प्रणवेति। तत्र प्रणवान्तरितत्वमेवम् ॐरां ॐरा ॐमा ॐय ॐन ॐमः। सुधीरित्यनेन शतावृत्त्येत्युक्तम्। तदुक्तम्—

प्रणवसहितांस्तु मन्त्रजवर्णान् प्रजपेच्छतावृत्त्या। एतज्जीवनमुक्तम्। इति। मन्त्रतन्त्रविशारदाः इत्यनेनान्येऽस्य बीजनमिति नाम आहुरित्युक्तं भवति। यत् पिङ्गलामते—प्रणवो बीजमित्युक्तं बीजान्ते तं नियोजयेत्।
अक्षरान्तरितं कृत्वा मन्त्रोऽसौ बीजितो मतः ॥ इति ॥ ११५ ॥

मन्त्रवर्णान् समालिख्य ताडयेच्चन्दनाम्भसा ।
प्रत्येकं वायुना मन्त्री ताड़नं तदुदाहृतम् ॥ ११६
विलिख्य मन्त्रं तं मन्त्री प्रसूनैः करवीरजैः ।
तन्मन्त्राक्षरसंख्यातैर्हन्याद्यान्तेन बोधनम् ॥ ११७
स्वतन्त्रोक्तविधानेन मन्त्री मन्त्रार्णसंख्यया ।
अश्वत्थपल्लवैर्मन्त्रमभिषिञ्चेद् विशुद्धये ॥ ११८
सञ्चिन्त्य मनसा मन्त्रं ज्योतिर्मन्त्रेण निर्दहेत् ।
मन्त्रे मलत्रयं मन्त्री विमलीकरणं त्विदम् ॥ ११९

मन्त्रेति । मन्त्रीत्यनेन भूर्ज्जे कुङ्कुमगोरोचनादिना मन्त्रवर्णान् विलिखेदित्युक्तम् । वायुना यमिति बीजेन । प्रत्येकं शतवारं ताड़येत् । तदुक्तम्—

भूर्ज्जे मन्त्राक्षराणि संलिख्य शतमप्येकैकं चन्दनाम्बुना ।
वायुबीजेन ताड़येत् एतत्ताड़नमुक्तम् ॥ इति ॥ ११६ ॥

विलिख्येति । मन्त्रीत्यनेन भूर्ज्जे कुङ्कुमरोचनादिना लेखनमित्युक्तम् । करवीरजैरिति रक्तकरवीरजपुष्पैः । यान्तेन रमिति बीजेन । तदुक्तम्—

एतस्मिन् विलिखित मन्त्रवर्णसंख्याकरक्तकरवीरैः ।
एतद्बोधनमुक्तं यद्धन्याद्वह्निबीजेन ॥ इति ॥ ११७ ॥

स्वतन्त्रेति । स्वतन्त्रोक्तविधानेन । शैवमन्त्रे शिवतन्त्रानुसारात् शक्तिमन्त्रे शक्तितन्त्रानुसारात् विष्णुमन्त्रे वैष्णवतन्त्रानुसारात् इति ज्ञेयम् । पूर्ववद् भूर्ज्जे मन्त्रवर्णान् विलिख्याऽभिषिञ्चेदिति । मन्त्रीत्यनेन अमुष्य मन्त्रस्यामुकमक्षरमभिषिञ्चामि नमः इति प्रयोग उक्तः । तदुक्तम्—

निजतन्त्रेरितमार्गादभिषिञ्चेत् पिप्पलप्रवालेन ।
भूर्ज्जे विलिखितमन्त्रं शतमष्टौ चाभिषेकोऽयम् ॥ इति ।

पिङ्गलामते विशेषः—

मालतीकलिकाभिस्तु न्यस्यार्णं[र्णं] कर्णिकोपरि ।
अश्वत्थपल्लवैः शुद्धैस्तन्मन्त्राक्षरसम्मितैः ।
अभिषेकं प्रकुर्व्वीत स्वतन्त्रे विहितं यथा ॥ इति ।

मालतीकलिकाभिर्मन्त्राक्षराणि विलिख्याभिषेकं कुर्य्यात् ॥ ११८ ॥

सञ्चिन्त्येति । ज्योतिर्मन्त्रेण वक्ष्यमाणेन । मन्त्रीत्यनेन मूलाधारात्

तारं व्योमाग्निमनुयुग् दण्डी ज्योतिर्मनुर्मतः ।
कुशोदकेन जप्तेन प्रत्यर्णं प्रोक्षणं मनोः ॥ १२०
तेन मन्त्रेण विधिवदेतदाप्यायनं मतम् ।
मन्त्रेण वारिणा मन्त्रे तर्पणं तर्पणं स्मृतम् ॥ १२१
तारमायारमायोगे मनोर्दीपनमुच्यते ।
जप्यमानस्य मन्त्रस्य गोपनन्त्वप्रकाशनम् ॥ १२२

कुण्डलिनीमुत्थाप्य तद्द्वारा [तद्वह्निना] दोषदाह इत्युक्तम् । मलत्रयं सहजमागन्तुकं मायीयमिति । पिङ्गलामतेऽप्युक्तम्—

सहजागन्तुमायाख्यं ज्योतीरूपेण निर्दहेत् ।
मन्त्रे मलत्रयं मन्त्री ततोऽसौ निर्मलो भवेत् ॥ इति ॥ ११९ ॥

ज्योतिर्मन्त्रमाह तारमिति । तारः प्रणवः । व्योम हकारः । अग्नी रेफः । मनुः औ । एतद्युग् दण्डी अनुस्वारयुक्त इति मन्त्रविशेषणम् । "दण्डि" इति पाठे व्योमविशेषणम् । तदुक्तं निघण्टुमातृकायाम्—

असङ्गूरेशको दण्डी बिन्दुकः कामगुह्यकः ।
कम्बुः प्राचीनयोनिश्च क्षोभ्यदुःखप्रलम्बकः ॥ इति ।

एवमग्रेऽपि दण्डशब्दवाच्यत्वं बिन्दोर्ज्ञेयम् । कुशेति । अनेनाष्टोत्तरशतमिति । लेखनं पूर्व्ववदेव । तेनेत्युभयत्र सम्बध्यते । तदुक्तं पिङ्गलामते—

अष्टोत्तरशतालब्धं विप्रुषं कुशवारिणा ।
आप्यायितो भवेन्मन्त्रः प्रत्यर्णं प्रोक्षितो यदि ॥ इति ।

विधिवदिति प्रत्यर्णं सम्यक् । केचन तेन मन्त्रेणेति ज्योतिर्मन्त्रेण इति व्याचक्षते । तदसत् । ग्रन्थान्तरविरोधात् । तदुक्तम्—

आप्यायनं स्वजलैः प्रत्यर्णं कुशपयोभिः स्यात् । इति ।

तेन मूलमन्त्रेणेत्यर्थः । तत्र प्रकारः । देवमन्त्रमुच्चार्य अमुं मन्त्रं तर्पयामि नमः इति जलेन तर्पणं कुर्यादिति । इदमेव मन्त्रतर्पणमित्यर्थः । तदुक्तम्—

तर्पयामि पदं योज्यं मन्त्रान्ते त्विष्ट[ष्वेषु]नामसु । द्वितीयान्तेषु तु पुनः । इति ।

अन्यत्रापि सर्व्वत्र तर्पणेऽयमेव प्रकारो द्रष्टव्यः । इदमप्यष्टोत्तरं शतम् ॥ १२० ॥ १२१ ॥

तारेति । तारः प्रणवः ॐ । माया शक्तिः । रमा श्रीँ ।

संस्कारा दश संप्रोक्ताः सर्वतन्[स]न्त्रेषु गोपिताः ।
यान् कृत्वा सम्प्रदायेन मन्त्री वाञ्छितमश्नुते ॥ १२३

स्वतारराशिकोष्ठानामनुकूलं भजेन्मनुम् ।
प्रापलोभाल्पटुः प्राज्यं कद्रुस्याद्रि रुकः करम् ॥ १२४

लोकलोपपटुः प्राप खलौ द्यो भेषु भेदिताः ।
वर्णाः क्रमात् स्वरान्त्यौ तु रेवत्यंशगतौ स[त]दा ॥ १२५

मन्त्रस्यान्ते भवेन्नामयोगः प्रोच्चाटने मतः ।

इति योगलक्षणस्योक्तत्वादत्र मन्त्र एव नामस्थानीयः । तेन "इमानि बीजान्यादौ कृत्वा मन्त्रं जपेत् समवारम्" इत्याचार्याः । सम्प्रदायेनेति । सम्प्रदायः प्रति संस्कारं मयोक्तोऽनुसन्धेयः ॥ १२२ ॥ १२३ ॥

अथ निर्गुणोपासनाङ्गभूतसगुणोपासनायां प्रवृत्तस्य अवान्तरविचारं दर्शयति स्वतारेति । स्वं नाम तस्य तारा नक्षत्रम् । एवमन्यत्रेऽपि—

दुष्टर्क्षराशिभूतारिवर्णप्रचुरमन्त्रकम् ।
सम्यक् परीक्ष्य तं यत्नाद्वर्जयेन्मतिमान्नरः ॥

इत्युक्तेः तत्र ताराभैत्रीज्ञानाय अक्षरेषु नक्षत्राणि कथयति प्रापेति । अत्र सन्थकारस्य वररुचः सङ्केतोऽभिप्रेतः । स यथा—

कटपयवर्गभवैरिह पिण्डान्त्यैरक्षरैरङ्काः ।
नञि च शून्यं ज्ञेयं तथा स्वरे केवले कथिते ॥ इति ।

अत्र कटौ नववर्णौ पाद्यः पञ्चार्णः योऽष्टार्णो ह्रान्तः । पिण्डं संयुक्ताक्षरम् । तत्रान्त्ये-नाङ्कः । प्रा २ प १ लो ३ भा ४ ल्प १ टु १ प्रा २ ज्यं १ क २ द्रु २ स्या १ द्रि २ रु २ कः २ क १ रं २ लो ३ क १ लो ३ प १ प १ टु १ प्रा २ प १ ख २ लौ ३ द्यो १ । एवमुक्ताङ्कसाध्यक्षरेषु अश्विन्यादयो ज्ञेयाः । भेषु नक्षत्रेषु क्रमाद् वर्णा भेदिताः विभागेन दर्शिता इत्यर्थः । तदेत्युत्तरत्र सम्बध्यते । अत्र षकारखकारयो-र्नागरलिपौ समानत्वात् भ्रान्तिकृतो षकारपाठः । तेन ख इति एकाङ्कः संगृहीतः । स्वरान्त्यौ अं अः रेवत्यंशगतौ । अतो रेवत्यां अं अः ल इत्यक्षरत्रयम् । रेवत्यंश-गताविति पदेनैवोक्तेरङ्केषु न संगृहीतम् । यया वक्ष्यमाणे राश्यक्षरकथने वालं गौरं क्षुरमिति । रेफेण कन्यायामक्षरद्वयमेवोक्तम् । अन्येषां कन्यायां शादय इति पदेनैवोक्तेः । तद्वदत्रापीत्यवधेयम । उत्तरभाद्रपदनक्षत्रे लकारेणाङ्कत्रयं गृहीतम् ।

जन्मसम्पद्विपत् क्षेमः प्रत्यरिः साधको वधः।
मित्रं परममित्रञ्च जन्मादीनि पुनः पुनः॥ १२६

तेन वसहाक्षराणि। तत्र षकारस्य चकारांशत्वात् चकारोऽपि तेनैव गृहीतः। तेनाद्याक्षरचतुष्कम्। तदुक्तमाचार्य्यैः—

ततः क्षकारः सञ्जातो नृसिंहस्तस्य देवता।
स पुनः षसहैः सार्द्धं पञ्चप्रोष्ठपदं गतः॥ इति।

ईशानशिवेऽपि—प्रियलवकटरम्या श्री प्रिया गन्धिरन्या
खगकुलकटकल्लो पालवालेतिसंख्यान्। इति।

नारायणीये तु—राव्येत्यादि षड्विंशतिभेषु वर्णानुक्त्वा अन्त्यसावन्त्यभे उक्तौ। तत्र केचित्तु ल्वाविति पठित्वा व्याख्यान्ति लकारेणाङ्कत्रयं वकारेणाङ्कचतुष्टयमिति। तदसत्। सङ्केतविरोधात्। सङ्केते हि पिण्डान्त्यैरक्षरैरङ्का इत्युक्तम्। एतदभिप्रायेणैव द्विवचनकल्पनम्। तदपि भ्रमेणैव। यतः सङ्केताक्षरेषु साधुत्वार्थं प्रथमैकवचनमेव युक्तम्। न तु संयोगं कृत्वा द्विवचनम्। तथा क्वाप्यदर्शनात्। अतएवायं पाठोऽपेक्षितार्थद्योतनिकादिभिष्टीकाभिरुपेक्षितः। अपरे बवाविति पठित्वा वदन्ति—पवर्गीयबकारेणाङ्कत्रयम् उत्तरेणान्तस्थीयवकारेणाङ्कचतुष्टयमिति। तदपि प्रपञ्चसारेशानादिग्रन्थविरुद्धम्। ततोऽयमेव पाठो नारायणीयेऽपि। परन्तु व्याख्यातुस्तत्र भ्रमः। प्रथमोऽन्तस्थो वकारस्तेन चतुःसंख्या द्वितीयः पवर्गी तेन त्रिसंख्येति सर्व्वं समञ्जसम्। देवदेवेशोकारेण तु प्रपञ्चसारादिविरोधपरिहारार्थं फुल्ला इति पठित्वा तत्र प्रथमलकारेणाङ्कत्रयम् उत्तरलकारेणाङ्कत्रयं गृहीतमिति व्याख्यातम्। तदपि सङ्केतविरुद्धम्। सङ्केते पिण्डेनाङ्कद्वयस्याग्रहीतत्वात्। एतेन अ आ अश्विनी। इ भरणी। ई उ ऊ कृत्तिका। इत्यादि ज्ञेयम्॥ १२४॥ १२५॥

स्वनामाद्यक्षरादित इति वक्ष्यमाणमत्रापि योजनीयम्। तेनायमन्वयः तदा वर्णभेदे स्वनामाद्यक्षरादितः जन्मादीनि पुनः पुनः प्रादक्षिण्येन मन्त्राद्यक्षरावधि गणयेदिति शेषः। तेन यस्मिन्नक्षत्रे साधकनामाद्यक्षरं तदारभ्य मन्त्राद्यक्षरनक्षत्रं यावत् प्रादक्षिण्येन गणनं कृत्वा फलं विचारयेत् इत्यर्थः। तदुक्तम्—

प्रादक्षिण्येन गणयेत् साधकाख्याक्षरात् सुधीः। इति।

अन्यत्रापि—एकादिनवपर्य्यन्तं स्वाख्याद्यर्णप्रपूर्व्वकम्।
यावन्मन्त्राक्षरं धिष्ण्यं फलं तावद् विचारयेत्॥ इति।

अन्यत्रापि—एवं विभक्तवर्णेषु नक्षत्राणि प्रकल्प्य च॥
आरभ्य जन्मनक्षत्रं मन्त्रतारावसानकम्।

इदं तु राशिनामप्रसिद्धनाम्नोरैक्ये ज्ञेयम् ।

विभज्य नवशो राभ विशिखाचलमन्त्रका: ।
वर्ज्याः शिष्टाः समिष्टार्थसिद्धिदाः स्युर्जपादिभिः । इति ।

आद्यतृतीय पञ्चमसप्तमान् वर्जयित्वा शेषं शुभम् । तदुक्तम्—"त्यक्त्वा विपच्चादिमसप्ततारा:" इति । अन्यत्रापि—

रसाष्टनव भद्राणि युगयुग्मगतान्यपि ।
इतराणि न भद्राणि ज्ञातव्यं तन्त्रकोविदैः ॥ इति ।

केचनाद्यमपि शुभमिच्छन्ति । तदुक्तम्—

विपद् वधः प्रत्यरिश्च परित्याज्या मणीषिभिः । इति ।

इदन्त्वाद्यजन्मविषयम् । अत्र तारामैत्रीविचारे योनिमैत्री गणमैत्री चावश्यं विचारणीया । यतस्तयोरपि नक्षत्रात्मकत्वात् । स्वकुलान्यकुलविचारोऽपि ।

पिङ्गलामते—तथैकगणनक्षत्रं स्वकुलं ह्यकुलं परम् । इत्युक्तः ।

तथा मन्त्रमुक्तावल्यामपि स्वकुलान्यकुलविभागकथने तथैकगणनक्षत्रमपि स्वकुलमित्युक्तम् । तत्र योनिमैत्री यथा—

अश्वेभाज फणिद्वयं श्वयुगभुङ्मेषौतवो मूषिक-
स्त्वाखुर्गौः क्रमश्च स्ततोऽपि महिषो व्याघ्रः पुनः सैरिभः ।
व्याघ्रैणौ मृगमण्डलौ कपिरघो बभ्रुद्वयं वानरः
सिंहाश्वौ मृगराट् पशुश्च करटी योनिस्तु भानामियम् ॥ इति ।

अत्राभिजिदपि गृहीत इति कृत्वा अष्टाविंशतिः । अश्व१ हस्ती२ मेषः३ सर्पः ४।५ श्वा ६ मार्जारः ७ मेषः ८ मर्जार ९ मूषिकः १०।११ गौः १२ महिषी १३ व्याघ्रः १४ महिषी १५ व्याघ्रः १६ मृगः १७।१८ श्वा १९वानरः २० नकुलः २१।२२ वानरः २३ सिंहः २४ अश्वः २५ सिंहः २६ गौः २७ हस्ती २८ ।

विरोधस्तु—गोव्याघ्रं गजसिंहमश्वमहिषं श्वैणञ्च बभ्रूरगं
वैरं वानरमेषकं च सुमहत् तद्वद्विडालोन्दुरम् । इति ।
जन्मनक्षत्रयोन्या वै मारणानि यथातथम् ।
कृतानि न चिरेणैव सिद्धिदानि महेश्वरि ॥ इति ।

कार्य्यान्तरोपयोगिताऽप्यस्योक्ताऽन्यत्र । गणमैत्री यथा । तच्च मनुष्यादिगणनक्षत्राणि एकविंशे वक्ष्यति । फलन्तु यथा—वध्यघातकता मता ।

मनुष्यराक्षसानान्तु विरोधो देवरक्षसाम् ।
प्रीति र्देवमनुष्याणां स्वेन स्वेनापि साम्यता ॥ इति ॥ १२६ ॥

वालं गौरं खुरं शोणं शमी शोभेति राशिषु ।
क्रमेण भेदिता वर्णाः कन्यायां शादयः स्मृताः ॥ १२७
लग्नं धनं भ्रातृबन्धुपुत्रशत्रुकलत्रकाः ।
मरणं धर्म्मकर्म्मायव्यया द्वादशराशयः ॥ १२८
चतुरस्रे लिखेद्वर्णांश्चतुःकोष्ठसमन्विते ।
अकारादिक्षकारान्तान् स्वनामाद्यक्षरादितः ॥ १२९

अथाक्षरेषु राशिविभागमाह वालमिति । वा ४ लं ३ गौ ३ रं २ खु २ रं २ शो ५ णं ५ श ५ मी ५ शो ५ भा ४ इति राशिषु वर्णा भेदिताः विभागेनोक्ताः । कन्यायां स्वरान्त्यौ वर्त्तेते शादयश्च स्थिताः । अत्रादिशब्देन शषसहला गृह्यन्ते । क्षकारस्य मीने प्रवेशः ।

यदाहुराचार्य्याः—अमः शवर्गलेभ्यश्च सञ्जाता कन्यका मता । इति ।

तथा—चतुर्भिर्यादिभिः सार्द्धं स्यात् क्षकारस्तु मीनगः । इति ।

अनेन अ आ इ ई मेषः इत्यादि ज्ञेयम् ॥ १२७ ॥

द्वादशराशय इति फलफलिनोरैक्योपचारात् । अत्र प्रकारः । साधकनामाद्यक्षरं यत्र राशौ तं राशिमारभ्य मन्त्राद्यक्षरं यत्र राशौ तत्पर्य्यन्तं गणनीयम् । षष्ठाष्टमद्वादशस्थानानि निन्द्यानि । तदुक्तम्—

साध्याख्याक्षरराश्यन्तं गणयेत् साधकाक्षरात् ।
नैधनारिव्ययाधीना ये वर्णास्ते न शोभनाः ॥ इति ।

यत्तु—एकपञ्चनव बान्धवाः स्मृता युग्मषष्ठदशमास्तु सेवकाः ।
पोषकास्त्रिमुनिरुद्रसम्मिता द्वादशाष्टचतुरस्तु घातकाः ॥

इति वचनं तद्राशिफलप्रकरणपठितं चेत् तदा स्वजन्मराशिमारभ्य मन्त्रराशिपर्य्यन्तं गणनीयमिति भिन्न एव प्रकारः । तदुक्तम्—

राश्यर्णादिकमन्त्राणां सराशिर्जन्मराशितः ।
विचार्य्य मनुराश्यन्तं रिपुहीनं मनुं जपेत् ॥ इति ।

यदि राशिप्रकरणपठितं न भवति तदा वक्ष्यमाणअकडमचक्रफलत्वेन व्याख्येयमिति रहस्यम् ॥ १२८ ॥

सिद्धादिमन्त्रशोधन प्रकारमाह चतुरस्र इति । मन्त्री मन्त्रशास्त्रसम्प्रदायाभिज्ञः । कुर्य्यात् सिद्धादिभिः पुनः सिद्धादीन् इति वक्ष्यमाणत्वात् षोडशकोष्ठोद्धारः

सिद्धादीन् कल्पयेन्मन्त्री कुर्य्यात् सिद्धादिभिः पुनः ।
सिद्धादीन् सिद्धिदः सिद्धो जपात् साध्यो हुतादिभिः ।
सुसिद्धः प्राप्तिमात्रेण साधकं भक्षयेदरिः ॥ १२०

सूचितः । तत्र प्रागपरोऽन्तर्दक्षिणायताः पञ्च रेखाः कुर्य्यात् । तदा षोडशकोष्ठानि सम्पद्यन्ते । तत्र वर्णान् लिखेत् । एकैकान्तरितमिति शेषः । लेखनप्रकारस्तु प्रथमचतुष्कप्रथमे प्रथमम् । प्रादक्षिण्येन द्वितीयप्रथमे द्वितीयम् । प्रादक्षिण्येन तृतीयप्रथमे तृतीयम् । चतुर्थप्रथमे चतुर्थम् । एवं प्रादक्षिण्येन प्रथमद्वितीये पञ्चमम् । द्वितीयद्वितीये षष्ठम् । तृतीयद्वितीये सप्तमम् । चतुर्थद्वितीयेऽष्टमम् । एवं प्रादक्षिण्येन प्रथमतृतीये नवमम् । द्वितीयतृतीये दशमम् । तृतीयतृतीये एकादशम् । चतुर्थतृतीये द्वादशम् । एवं प्रथमचतुर्थे त्रयोदशम् । द्वितीयचतुर्थे चतुर्दशम् । तृतीयचतुर्थे पञ्चदशम् । चतुर्थचतुर्थे षोडशं न्यसेत् । एवं स्वरलिखनं कृत्वा तेनैव क्रमेण कादिवर्णानपि लिखेत् । तदुक्तं कादिमते—

प्रथमप्रथमे त्वाद्यं द्वितीयप्रथमे तथा ।
द्वितीयमन्त्यतश्चान्यत् तथान्यदपि कल्पयेत् ।
तत्तत्कोष्ठेषु विलिखेत् तत्तत्क्रममन्वयम् ॥ इति ।

तन्त्रान्तरे च—कोष्ठचतुष्कचतुष्टयपूर्वाद्येषु लिखतु चतुरोऽन्तः ।
आग्नेयेषु तथैव नैर्ऋत्येष्वेवमानिलेषु पुनः ॥
कादीन् वर्णान् कोष्ठेषु च तेष्वेवमेव लिखतु सुधीः ।
आरभ्य तु चतुर्थान् नैर्ऋत्येषु समापयेन्मतिमान् ॥
यस्य च नामाद्यर्णं यत्र चतुष्के तदादि तस्यैव ।
तस्माच्चतुश्चतुष्कं विज्ञेयं क्रमश एव सिद्धादि ॥
सिद्धादिषु च चतुर्ष्वप्येवं सिद्धादि तेषु विज्ञेयम् ॥ इति ।

अस्य प्रयोजनमाह स्वनामेति । स्वनामाद्यक्षरकोष्ठमारभ्य मन्त्राद्यक्षरकोष्ठं यावदिति शेषः । सिद्धादीनित्यादि । मन्त्रार्थफलकथनावसरे स्वयमेव प्रकटयिष्यति । कल्पयेदिति । एवं यत्र चतुष्के स्वनामाद्यक्षरं तत् सिद्धचतुष्कम् । ततः प्रादक्षिण्येन साध्यादिचतुष्कत्रयमिति । मन्त्री कुर्य्यात् सिद्धादिभिः पुनः सिद्धादीन् इति । यत्र चतुष्ककोष्ठे स्वनामाद्यक्षरं तत् सिद्धसिद्धकोष्ठम् । ततस्तस्मिन्नेव चतुष्के प्रादक्षिण्येन कोष्ठत्रये सिद्धसाध्य-सिद्धसुसिद्ध-सिद्धारीनिति कल्पयेत् । अस्मिन्नेव चतुष्के यदि मन्त्राद्यक्षरमपि स्यात् तदा अनयैव गणनया

सिद्धार्णा बान्धवाः प्रोक्ताः साध्यास्ते सेवकाः स्मृताः ।
सुसिद्धाः पोषका ज्ञेयाः शत्रवो घातका मताः ॥ १३१

सिद्धम् । यद्यस्मिन् चतुष्के स्वनामाद्यक्षरं प्रादक्षिण्येन द्वितीयचतुष्के मन्त्राद्यक्षरं तदा पूर्व्वचतुष्के यस्मिन् कोष्ठे नामाद्यक्षरम् अत्र द्वितीयचतुष्केपि तदेव कोष्ठमारभ्य प्रादक्षिण्येन साध्यसिद्ध-साध्यसाध्य-साध्यसुसिद्ध-साध्यारीन् इति कल्पयेत् । यदि पुनः स्वनामाद्यक्षरचतुष्कात् प्रादक्षिण्येन तृतीयचतुष्के मन्त्राद्यक्षरं तदा पूर्व्ववत् तत् कोष्ठादेव प्रादक्षिण्येन सुसिद्धसिद्धसुसिद्धसाध्यसुसिद्धसुसिद्ध-सुसिद्धारीन् इति कल्पयेत् । यदि पुनः स्वनामाद्यक्षरचतुष्कात् प्रादक्षिण्येन चतुर्थचतुष्के मन्त्राद्यक्षरं तदा पूर्व्ववत् तत् कोष्ठादेव प्रादक्षिण्येन अरिसिद्ध-अरिसाध्य-अरिसुसिद्ध-अर्य्यरीन् इति कल्पयेत् । नन्वत्र द्वितीयादि चतुष्के तमेव कोष्ठमारभ्य गणनमित्यत्र किं नियामकमिति चेत् उच्यते । प्रकृतिक्रम एव नियामकः । स च पञ्चमाध्याये प्रथमचरणे ।

प्रमाणां हि पदार्थानां विकृतौ क्रमचिन्तनम् ।
ते च सक्रमका एव प्राप्यन्ते नोदकादिषु ।
नैराकाङ्क्ष्यात् क्रमस्तेषां न भूयोऽन्यः प्रकल्पते । इत्यादिनोक्तम् ।

तत्र किं नाम ग्राह्यमित्यपेक्षायां पिङ्गलामते—

प्रसिद्धं यद्भवेन्नाम किंवास्य जन्मनाम च ।
यतीनां पुष्पपातेन गुरुणा यत् कृतं भवेत् ।
नाम्नस्तस्यैव वर्णानि विभक्तानि च कारयेत् ॥ इति ।

अन्यत्रापि—लोके प्रसिद्धनामाद्य माता पिता तथा कृतम् । इति ।

अन्यत्रापि—सुप्तो जागर्त्ति येनासौ दूरस्थश्च प्रभाषते ।
वदत्यन्यमनस्कोऽपि तन्नाम ग्राह्यमत्र तु ॥ इति ।

अन्यत्रापि—माता पिता कृतं नाम शोधनीयं प्रयत्नतः । इति ।

अन्ये त्वत्र जन्मनामेव ग्राह्यमित्यूचुः । तदुक्तम्—

जन्मर्क्षाक्षरतो वीक्ष्यं तत्र मन्त्रादिमाक्षरम् ।
चतुर्भिः कोष्ठकैस्त्वेक इति कोष्ठचतुष्टयम् ॥
पुनः कोष्ठककोष्ठेषु सव्यतो जन्मभाक्षरात् ।
सिद्धसाध्यसुसिद्धारि क्रमाज्ज्ञेयं विचक्षणैः ॥ इति ।

जन्मनि जन्मकाले यद्दक्षमश्विन्यादि तेषामक्षराणि "चुचेचोला अश्विनी प्रोक्ता"

इत्यादीनि तस्मात् तदारभ्य तेन जन्मनामाद्याक्षरमारभ्येत्यर्थ:। एवं जन्मभाक्षरादि-त्वत्रापि ज्ञेयम्। अयञ्च जन्मनामप्रसिद्धनाम्नो: विकल्पो ज्ञेय:। किंवास्येत्युक्त:। सिद्धिद इति जपात् सिद्ध:। हुतादिभि: साध्य: सिद्धिद:। प्राप्तिमात्रेण सुसिद्ध: सिद्धिद इति सम्बन्ध:। आदिशब्देन तर्पणादि। सिद्धसिद्धादिफलम् पिङ्गलामतोक्तं यथा—

यथोक्तात् सिद्धसिद्धस्तु तत्साध्यो द्विगुणाज्जपात्।
जपार्द्धात् तत्सुसिद्धस्तु तदरिर्बान्धवापह:॥
द्विघ्नाज्जपात् साध्यसिद्धस्तत्साध्यस्तु निरर्थक:।
तत्सुसिद्ध: सार्द्धजपात् तदरिर्गोत्रजापह:॥
सुसिद्धसिद्धोऽर्द्धजपात् तत्साध्यो द्विगुणाज्जपात्।
तत्सुसिद्धो ग्रहादेव तदरिर्ज्ञातिजातिहा॥
अरिसिद्ध: सुतं हन्यादरिसाध्यस्तु कन्यकाम्।
तत्सुसिद्धस्तु पत्नीघ्नस्तदरि: साधकापह:॥ इति।

पिङ्गलामते प्रत्यक्षरं सिद्धादिगणनोक्ता।

मातापितृकृतं नाम यच्चाप्यभिजनै: कृतम्।
विश्लिष्य तस्य वै वर्णान् स्वरवर्णविभेदत:॥
तथैव मन्त्रबीजानि तत: शोधनमारभेत्।
बिन्दुद्विबिन्दुकोपध्मानीय जिह्वाङ्घ्रिसम्भवान्॥
संहतोच्चारणप्राप्त मधिकाक्षरमेव च।
अपभ्रंशाक्षरं लक्षौ त्यक्त्वा षण्ढचतुष्टयम्॥
मन्त्राक्षरै: सहैकैकं नामवर्णान् विशोधयेत्।
व्यञ्जनैर्व्यञ्जनान्येव स्वरै: सार्द्धं स्वरांस्तथा॥
आद्यमाद्येन संशोध्य द्वितीयेन द्वितीयकम्।
मन्त्रे वाऽप्यथवा नाम्नि वर्णा: स्युर्विषमा यदा॥
तदा मन्त्रं समारभ्य समं यावत् प्रयोजयेत्।
आद्यन्तयो: सिद्धवर्णौ मन्त्रे यस्मिन् वरानने॥
अचिरेणैव कालेन स भवेत् सर्व्वसिद्धिद:।
साध्यान्तादियुतो यस्तु सोऽतिकृच्छ्रेण सिध्यति॥
आदावन्ते सुसिद्धस्तु सर्व्वकामविभूतिद:।
आदावन्ते रिपुर्यस्य भवेत् त्याज्य: स मन्त्रक:॥

आदौ सिद्धोऽन्त्यसाध्यो यो द्विगुणेन स सिध्यति ।
आदौ सिद्धः सुसिद्धान्त्यो यथोक्तात् सिध्यते जपात् ॥
आदौ सिद्धोऽन्त्यशत्रुर्यः स त्याज्यो मन्त्रवित्तमैः ।
साध्यादिश्चैव सिद्धान्त्यः त्रिगुणात् सिध्यते जपात् ॥
आदौ साध्यः सुसिद्धान्त्यः प्रोक्तमार्गेण सिध्यति ।
आदौ साध्योऽन्त्यशत्रुर्यस्तं यत्नात् परिवर्जयेत् ॥
सुसिद्धादिस्तु सिद्धान्त्यो यथोक्तादेव सिध्यति ।
सुसिद्धादिस्तु साध्यान्त्यश्चतुर्गुणमपेक्षते ॥
सुसिद्धादिश्चान्त्यशत्रुर्योऽधमः परिकीर्त्तितः ।
आद्यारिस्त्वन्त्यसिद्धादिः सोऽपि त्याज्योऽखिलकर्म्मणि ॥
आदौ मध्ये तथा चान्ते सिद्धः शुभफलप्रदः ।
सर्व्वसाध्य उदासीनः प्रोक्तस्तन्त्रे स्वयम्भुवा ॥
स्थानत्रितयसुसिद्धः सर्व्वानर्थांश्च साधयत्येव ।
स्थानत्रितयगतारिर्मन्त्रो मृत्युर्न सन्देहः ॥
सिद्धादिः साध्ययुग्मान्तो व्यर्थ इत्युच्यते बुधैः ।
सिद्धादिर्द्विसुसिद्धान्तः सर्व्वकार्य्यार्थसाधकः ॥
सिद्धादिररियुग्मान्तो नाशकः सम्प्रकीर्त्तितः ।
शत्रुर्भवति यदादौ मध्ये सिद्धस्तदन्तके साध्यः ॥
कष्टेन कार्य्यसिद्धिस्तस्य फलं स्वल्पमेव भवेत् ।
अन्ते यदि भवति रिपुः प्रथमे मध्ये च भवति साध्ययुगम् ॥
कार्य्यं विलम्बितं स्यात् प्रणश्यति क्षिप्रमेवान्ते ।
आद्यन्तयोर्यदा साध्यो मध्ये सिद्धः प्रजायते ॥
आद्यन्तयोर्यदा सिद्धो मध्ये साध्यः प्रजायते ।
तावुभौ साध्यसिद्धौ हि जपाधिक्येन सिध्यतः ॥
अरिसम्पुटितः सिद्धः सुसिद्धोऽपि तथा भवेत् ।
सर्व्वनाशकरो ज्ञेयः साधकस्य न संशयः ॥
सिद्धान्तरितसाध्यस्तु सुसिद्धान्तरितोऽथवा ।
शीघ्रं सिध्यति मन्त्रोऽयमीशानः स्वयमब्रवीत् ॥
सिद्धान्तरितशत्रुस्तु सुसिद्धेनापि चेद्भवेत् ।
नासौ रिपुर्भवेन्मन्त्रः किन्तु कष्टेन सिध्यति ॥

साध्यात्करितसिद्धस्तु सुसिद्धोऽपि तथा यदि ।
सिद्धत्यतीवकष्टेन साधकस्य न चान्यथा ॥
रिपुणाऽन्तरितः सिद्धः सुसिद्धोऽपि तथा यदि ।
ईदृशं लक्षणं दृष्ट्वा दूरतः परिवर्जयेत् ॥
रिपुणा दूषितो[न्तरितो] मन्त्रो नैव देयः कदाचन ॥ इति ।

नारायणीयेऽपि—दुष्टार्णप्रचुरो मन्त्रो यः स्यात् स विनिन्दितः । इति ।

अपेक्षितार्थद्योतनिकायां व्याख्यातम् । तत्र पूर्ववन्मातृकाक्षराणि संलिख्य तत्समीपे मन्त्रं नाम च लिखित्वा प्रथमाक्षरेण प्रथमाक्षरं शोधयित्वा पुनर्द्वितीयाक्षरेण द्वितीयाक्षरं शोधयित्वा नामपरिसमाप्तौ पुनर्नाम लिखित्वा यावन्मन्त्रपरिसमाप्तिस्तावच्छोधयित्वा यस्मिन् मन्त्रे दुष्टार्णाः साध्यानां वैरिणश्च इतरेभ्यो बहवो भवन्ति तदा तन्मन्त्रं वर्जयेदित्यर्थः । अत्र केषाञ्चिद्वर्णानां शोधनं नास्तीत्याहुः ।

नमः प्रणवसंयोगाद्बन्धाक्षराणि च ।
वर्जयित्वैव गणनं कर्त्तव्यञ्च सुरेश्वरि ॥ इति ।

तत्त्वसागरवादिना तत्रैव प्रकारान्तरेण सिद्धादिकल्पनमुक्तम् ।

द्वादशारेऽथवा चक्रे कूटवर्णविवर्जितान् ।
आदिक्षान्तान् लिखेद्वर्णान् पूर्वतो यावदीश्वरम् ॥
अङ्कानेकादिभान्यस्तान् लिखेत् पूर्वादितः क्रमात् ।
सिद्धः साध्यः सुसिद्धोऽरि चतुर्द्धाश्च स्फुटोभवेत् ॥
नवैकपञ्चके सिद्धः साध्यः षड्दशयुग्मके ।
त्रिसप्तैकादशे मित्रं वेदाष्टद्वादशे रिपुः ॥
अथवाऽन्यप्रकारेण वच्मि मन्त्रांशकं मनाक् ।
अकारादिहकारान्तं मातृकाक्षरसञ्चयम् ॥
एकैकार्णक्रमान् न्यस्य चतुःकोष्ठेषु मन्त्रवित् ।
सिद्धं साध्यं सुसिद्धञ्च वैरिणं गणयेत् क्रमात् ॥
यत्र यत्र भवन्त्यर्णा नाममन्त्रसमुद्भवाः ।
सिद्धसाध्यादिभेदेन वर्णांस्तैर्मन्त्रमादिशेत् ॥
अथवा मन्त्रनाम्नोस्तु[मार्ण]ञ्चरे राशौ चतुर्हृते ।
सिद्धः साध्यः सुसिद्धोऽरिर्नैक एकादितो भवेत् ॥ इति ।

मन्त्राकपिलपञ्चरात्रे तु—

त्रिविधः कीर्त्तितो मन्त्रः सिद्धः साध्यः सुसिद्धकः ।

अल्पाक्षरो भवेत् सिद्धः साध्यो मालार्द्धमालकौ ।
अत ऊर्द्ध्वं सुसिद्धः स कविस्वे चातिनिन्दितः ॥ इति ।

अन्योऽपि विशेषः—

शुचिराराधयेन्मन्त्रं दृष्टादृष्टफलप्रदम् ।
सकलं निष्कलं सूक्ष्मं तथा सकलनिष्कलम् ॥
कलाभिन्नं कलातीतं षोढ़ा मन्त्रं शिवोऽब्रवीत् ।
सकलं ब्रह्मरन्ध्रस्थं तदधो विद्धि निष्कलम् ॥
मानसं सूक्ष्मनामानं हृत्स्थं सकलनिष्कलम् ।
बिन्दुस्थितं कलाभिन्नं कलातीतं तदूर्द्ध्वतः ।
कला कुण्डलिनी सैव नादशक्तिः शिवोदिता ॥ इति ।

एषु षट्सु स्थानेषु चिन्तितो मन्त्रः स्थानस्थः फलप्रदो नान्यथा । यदुक्तम् मालिनीविजये—स्थानस्था वरदा मन्त्रा ध्यानस्थाश्च फलप्रदाः ।
ध्यानस्थानविनिर्मुक्ताः सुसिद्धा अपि वैरिणः ॥ इति ।

यद्यज्ञानादरिमन्त्रग्रहणं स्यात् तदा तत्त्यागप्रकार उच्यते—

अथारिमन्त्रसंत्यागविधिः सम्यक् प्रकाश्यते ।
शुचिः समाहितो भूत्वा प्रारभेत् प्रवरे दिने ॥
अशेषदुःखनाशाय देशिकः प्रवरं विधिम् ।
तत्रादौ रम्यभवने कुम्भं दीक्षाविधिक्रमात् ॥
मण्डले स्थापयेद् विद्वान् पूरयेत् तं जलैः शुभैः ।
विलोममन्त्रपाठेन तत्रावाह्य तु देवताम् ॥
सकलीकृत्य सम्पूज्याऽऽवरणानि प्रपूजयेत् ।
एवं सावरणामिष्ट्वा मन्त्री मन्त्रस्य देवताम् ॥
हुत्वा विलोममन्त्रेण सर्पिषा गोरपि द्विजः ।
अष्टोत्तरसहस्रं वा तथैवाष्ट शतं सुधीः ॥
ब्रह्मार्पणेन मनुना तत्रान्ते तर्पयेत् प्रभुम् ।
ततो यथावद् दुग्धान्नै देवताभ्यो बलिं हरेत् ॥
विदिक्षु दिक्षु च तथा वक्ष्यमाणैर्मनूत्तमैः ।
आयाहीन्द्र सुराधीश शतमन्यो शचीपते ॥
नमस्तुभ्यं गृहाणेमं पुष्पधूपादिकं बलिम् ।
आयाहि तेजसां नाथ हव्यवाह वरप्रद ॥

गृहाण पुष्पधूपादि बलिमेनं सुपूजितम् ।
प्रेतराज समायाहि भिन्नाञ्जनसमद्युते ॥
बलिं दत्तं गृहीत्वेमं सुप्रीतो वरदो भव ।
नमस्ते रक्षसां नाथ निर्ऋते त्वमिहागतः ॥
गृहाण बलिपूजादि मया भक्त्या निवेदितम् ।
एहि पश्चिमदिक्पाल जल[लोक]नाथ नमोऽस्तु ते ॥
भक्त्या निवेदितां पूजां गृहीत्वा प्रीतिमाप्नुहि ।
प्रभञ्जन प्राणपते त्वमेहि सपरिच्छदः ॥
मया प्रयुक्तं विधिवत् गृहाण बलिमादरात् ।
कुवेरतारकाधीशावागच्छेतां सुरोत्तमौ ॥
पुष्पधूपादिभिः प्रीतौ भवेतां वरदौ मम ।
ईश त्वमेव भगवन् सर्व्वविद्याश्रय प्रभो ॥
पूजितः पुष्पधूपाद्यैः प्रीतो भव विभूतये ।
आयाहि सर्व्वलोकानां नाथ ब्रह्मन् समर्चनम् ॥
गृहाण सर्व्वविघ्नान् मे निवर्त्तय नमोऽस्तु ते ।
आगच्छ वरदाऽव्यक्त विष्णो विश्वस्य नायक ॥
पूजितः परया भक्त्या भव त्वं सुखदो मम ।
ततः सपरिवाराञ्च पूजयेन्मन्त्रदेवताम् ॥
मन्त्रेण विपरीतेन पुष्पदीपोपचारकैः ।
ततस्तु प्रार्थयेद् विद्वान् पूजितां मन्त्रदेवताम् ॥
आनुकूल्यमनालोच्य मया तरलबुद्धिना ।
यदुपात्तं पूजितञ्च प्रभो मन्त्रस्वरूपकम् ॥
तेन मे मनसः क्षोभमशेषं विनिवर्त्तय ।
पापं प्रतिहतञ्चास्तु भूयाच्छ्रेयः सनातनम् ॥
तनोतु मम कल्याणं पावनी[भाविनी]भक्तिरेव ते ।
इति संप्रार्थ्य मन्त्रेशीं मन्त्रं पत्रे विलोमतः ॥
लिखित्वाऽमलकर्पूरचन्दनेन समर्चयेत् ।
कलसोपरि संस्थाप्य भक्त्या परमया सुतः ॥
तत्पत्रं मतिमान् पश्चाद् बद्ध्वा निजशिरस्यथ ।
स्नायात् पूजितकुम्भस्थतोयैर्मन्त्रमयैः शुभैः ॥

पुनश्चान्येन तोयेन कुम्भमापूर्य्य संयतः ।
तन्मध्ये मन्त्रपत्रञ्च निक्षिप्याथ प्रपूजयेत् ॥
तं कुम्भं निम्नगातीरे शुद्धे वाऽन्यजलाशये ।
निक्षिपेदथ विप्रांश्च यथाशक्त्या प्रभोजयेत् ॥
इत्थं कृतविधानस्य रिपुमन्त्रोऽथवा ऋणः ।
नश्यत्येव न सन्देहः कलासिद्धिप्रदायकता ।
जायतेऽतीवसम्पन्नो वर्द्धते तत्कुलं क्रमात् ॥ इति ।

अथ मन्त्रमुक्तावल्युक्त ऋणधनशोधनप्रकारो लिख्यते ।

इन्द्र १४ र्क्ष २७ नेत्र २ रवि १२ पञ्चदश १५ र्तु ६ वेद ४
वङ्गा ६ युधा ८ ष्ट ८ नवभि ९ र्गुणितांश्च साध्यान् ।
दिग् १० भू १ गिरि ७ श्रुति ४ गजाः ८ त्रि ३ मुनी ७ षु ५ वेद४
षड् ६ वह्नि ३ भिश्च गुणितानथ साधकार्णान् ॥
नामाक्षरादकठवाद्गज ८ भक्तशेषं
ज्ञात्वोभयोरधिकशेषमृणं धनं स्यात् ।
मन्त्रो ऋणी शुभफलोऽप्यशुभो धनी च
तुल्यो यदा समफलः कथितो मुनीन्द्रैः ॥ इति ।

तत्र प्रकारः । साध्यस्य मन्त्रस्य साधकस्य शिष्यस्य नामाक्षराणि स्वरव्यञ्जनरूपेण पृथक्कृत्वा स्थापयेत् । ततो आद्यकाया अ-क-ठ-वात्मकम् एकादशैकादशाक्षरं वर्गचतुष्टयं कृत्वा मन्त्राक्षराणि स्वरव्यञ्जनरूपेण पृथक्कृतानि इन्द्रादिभिरङ्कैर्गुणयेत् । साधकनामाक्षराणि स्वरव्यञ्जनरूपेण पृथक्कृतानि दिगादिभिरङ्कैर्गुणयेत् । तत्र गुणनप्रकारः । यस्मिन् स्थाने यो वर्णः तं वर्णं तेनाङ्केन गुणयेत् । तत्स्थानस्थिताङ्कं गुणयेदित्यर्थः । तद्यथा । प्रथमकोष्ठस्थो वर्णोऽकारस्तं चतुर्दशभिः गुणयेत् तत्रैकश्चतुर्दशगुणितश्चतुर्दशैव । तथा द्वितीयकोष्ठस्थो वर्णः इकारस्तं सप्तविंशत्या गुणयेत् । तेन द्वाभ्यां सप्तविंशतिः गुणिता चतुःपञ्चाशत् । एवं तृतीयस्थानस्थो वर्णः उकारो द्विगुणितः षट् भवति । एवं साधकनामाक्षराण्यपि दिगादिभिः गुणयेत् । साधकनाम-मन्त्राक्षरेषु आ ई ऊ ॠ ॡ एषामङ्काः लघुस्वराणामेवाङ्का ज्ञेयाः । ततः सर्वोऽप्यङ्क एकीकृतः अष्टभिः विभाज्यः । यो राशिरधिकः स ऋणी अधमर्णः । ऊनो राशिर्धनी उत्तमर्णः । तत्र मन्त्रश्चेदधमर्णस्तदा ग्राह्यः । न चेन्न ग्राह्यः । अथ कादिमतोक्त ऋणधनशोधनप्रकारो यथा—

नामाद्यक्षरमारभ्य यावन्मन्त्रादिवर्णकम् ।
त्रिधा कृत्वा स्वरैर्भिन्द्यात् तदन्यद् विपरीतकम् ॥ इति ।

अस्यार्थः । साधकनाम्नो यदाद्यक्षरं तत आरभ्य मन्त्राद्यक्षरपर्य्यन्तं मातृकाक्रमेण गणयित्वा तमङ्कं त्रिगुणितं कृत्वा स्वरैः सप्तभिर्हरेत् इति । अयं साधकराशिः । एवं मन्त्राद्यक्षरमारभ्य साधकनामाद्यक्षरपर्य्यन्तं मातृकाक्रमेण गणयित्वा तमङ्कं त्रिगुणितं कृत्वा सप्तभिर्हरेत् इति मन्त्रराशिः । अन्यत् पूर्व्ववत् । तन्त्रान्तरोक्तो वा ऋणधनशोधनप्रकारो यथा —

साध्यनाम द्विगुणितं साधकेन समन्वितम् ।
अष्टभिश्च हरेच्छेषं तदन्यद् विपरीतकम् ॥ इति ।

अस्यार्थः । मन्त्राक्षराणि स्वरव्यञ्जनरूपेण पृथक्कृतानि द्विगुणयेत् । साधकनामाक्षराण्यपि स्वरव्यञ्जनरूपेण पृथक्कृतानि तेषु संयोजयेत् । ततोऽष्टभिर्हरेत् । अयं मन्त्रराशिः । एवं साधकनामाक्षराणि स्वरव्यञ्जनरूपेण पृथक्कृतानि द्विगुणितानि स्वरव्यञ्जनरूपेण पृथक्कृतमन्त्राक्षरैः संयोजितान्यष्टभिर्हरेत् । एवं साधकराशिः । अन्यत् पूर्व्ववत् । एवमुक्तेष्वन्यतमेनावश्यं ऋणधनशोधनं मन्त्रेषु कर्त्तव्यम् । तत्र कथं मन्त्राणां ऋणित्वं तदुक्तं कादिमते—

पूर्व्वजन्मकृताभ्यासात् पापादस्याफलाप्तिकृत् ।
पापे नष्टे फलावाप्तिः काले देहक्षयादृणी ॥
मन्त्रः सम्प्राप्तिमात्रेण प्राक्तनः[प्राक्‌पुतः] सिद्धये भवेत् ।
सिद्धमन्त्राद् गुरो लब्धमन्त्रो यः सिद्धिभाङ् नरः ॥
लक्ष्मीमदादनादृत्य[वान् स सदा पूज्यः]मन्त्रभोगमवाप्तवान् ।
स मन्त्रोऽस्य ऋणी ज्ञेयो भजनं तस्य पूर्व्वगम् ।
तस्मादृणविशुद्धिस्तु कार्य्या सर्व्वैस्तु सर्व्वतः । इति ।

ग्रन्थान्तरे मन्त्रशोधने प्रकारान्तरमुक्तम्—

षड्दलं चक्रमालिख्य प्रागादिषु दलेषु तु ।
अकारादिवर्णानेकैकं लिखेन्निःषष्टकूटकान् ॥
स्वनामाद्यक्षरं यत्र तदारभ्य विचारयेत् ।
उदिते सम्पदुद्दिष्टा द्वितीये सम्पदां चयः ॥
तृतीये तु धनं [धृतिं] विद्यात् चतुर्थे बन्धुविग्रहः ।
पञ्चमे संशयात्मा स्यात् षष्ठः सर्व्वविनाशकः ॥ इति ।

अत्र सर्व्वत्र सिद्धादिशोधनापवादो ग्रन्थान्तरोक्तः ।

पिण्डे तारे खप्नलब्धे षड्णे प्रासादार्कत्रैपुरे नारसिंहे ।
माला मायामातृवाराह कामाख्ये नो दोषः स्वप्नप्रवेदेषु रत्ने ॥ इति ।

मालामन्त्रस्वरूपमुक्तं महाकपिलपञ्चरात्रे—

बहुवर्णास्तु ये मन्त्रा मालामन्त्रास्तु ते स्मृताः ।
दशाधिकाक्षरा माला पञ्चाधिकार्द्धमालिका ॥
न माला पञ्चपर्य्यन्ता वृद्धास्थविरबालकाः ।
वार्द्धके सिद्धिदा माला अर्द्धमाला तु यौवने ॥
बाल्ये पञ्चाक्षराधस्तु मन्त्रः सिद्धिप्रदायकः ॥ इति ।

प्रयोगसारे तु—नवाक्षरान्ता ये मन्त्रा बीजमन्त्राः प्रकीर्त्तिताः ।
पुनर्विंशति वर्णान्ता मन्त्रा मन्त्रास्तथोदिताः ॥
ततोऽधिकाक्षरा मन्त्रा मालामन्त्राः प्रकीर्त्तिताः ।
बाल्ये प्रसिद्धिदा बीजमन्त्रा मन्त्राश्च यौवने ॥
मालामन्त्राश्च वार्द्धक्ये विशेषेण प्रसिद्धिदाः । इति ।

नारायणीयेऽपि—

विंशत्यर्णाधिका मन्त्रा मालामन्त्रा इति स्मृताः ।
दशाक्षराधिका मन्त्रास्तदर्व्वाग् बीजसंज्ञिताः ॥
वार्द्धके सिद्धिदा मालामन्त्रा मन्त्रास्तु यौवने ।
पञ्चाक्षराधिका बाल्ये सिद्धिदाः सर्व्वदाऽपरे ॥ इति ।

अपेक्षितार्थद्योतनिकायामुक्तम् "उक्तावस्थाव्यतिरिक्तावस्थासु बीजमन्त्रमालामन्त्रसिद्धर्थं द्विगुणं जपेत्" इति । तथा—

हंसस्याष्टाक्षरस्यापि तथा पञ्चाक्षरस्य तु ।
एकद्वित्र्यादिबीजस्य सिद्धादीन् नैव शोधयेत् ॥

तथा—एकत्रिपञ्चसप्तार्णनवरुद्रषडर्णके ।
द्वात्रिंशत्यक्षरे मन्त्रे नांशकं परिगण्यते ॥
गारुड़ादिषु सौरेषु वैष्णवे बौद्धजैनयोः ।
महाकूटेषु मन्त्रेषु नैव सिद्धादिशोधनम् ॥
चत्वारिंशाक्षरस्योर्द्ध मेकैकाक्षरवृद्धितः ।
त्रिषष्टिबीजपर्य्यन्तं मन्त्रोऽनेक[नैक]फलप्रदः ॥ इति ।

तथाच—आम्नासिद्धास्तु ये मन्त्रा योगिनीनां प्रसादतः ।
लब्धा ये केऽपि ते मन्त्राः सर्व्वकामफलप्रदाः ॥ इति ।

दीपस्थानं समाश्रित्य कृतं कर्म्म फलप्रदम् ॥ १३२

एतद्व्यतिरिक्तेष्वावश्यकं शोधनम् । यदुक्तम्—

मन्त्रो वा यदि वा विद्या स्तवो वा स्तुतिरेव वा ।
अर्थवन्धुशरीरस्य नाशको भवति क्षणात् ॥
तस्मात् सर्व्वप्रयत्नेन दुष्टं सर्व्वत्र वर्जयेत् ।
न केवलन्तु मन्त्राणां विशेषेण तु देहिनाम् ।
परस्परं समीक्ष्यः स्यात् सम्बन्धो नान्यथा भवेत् ॥ इति ।

यस्तु सिद्धादिभिर्मन्त्रो न मिलति तत्र प्रकारान्तरमुक्तम् । यदाहुः—

एषु दोषेषु सर्व्वत्र मायां कामसथापि वा ।
क्षिप्त्वा चादौ श्रियं दद्यात् तद्दूषणविमुक्तये ॥ इति ।

तथा—तारसम्पुटितो वापि दुष्टमन्त्रोऽपि सिद्ध्यति ।
यस्य यत्र भवेद्भक्तिः सोऽपि मन्त्रोऽस्य सिद्ध्यति ॥ इति ।

तथा भुवनेशीपारिजाते—

मायाबीजसमायुक्तः क्षिप्रं सिद्धिप्रदो भवेत् ।
पिण्डस्तु केवलो मन्त्रो मायाबीजोज्झितः ।
मायाबीजाद्भवेत् प्राणो बीजं चैतन्यबोधवत् ॥ इति ।

तथा—अनुलोमविलोमस्थ क्रमया वर्णमालया ।
प्रत्येकवर्णयुङ्मन्त्रा जप्ताः स्युः क्षिप्रसिद्धिदाः ।
वैरिमन्त्रा अपि नृणामन्ये मन्त्राश्च किं पुनः ॥ इति ।

अग्रे व्यवहाराय सिद्धाद्यक्षराणां संज्ञान्तराण्याह सिद्धार्णा इति ॥ १२८-१३१ ॥

फलस्य पूर्व्वमुक्तत्वात् मन्त्रजपस्थानमाह दीपेति । दीपशब्दार्थोऽन्यत्रोक्तः—

दीप्यते पुरुषो यत्र दीपस्थानं तदुच्यते । इति ।

तथा—दीपौघं सम्प्रवक्ष्यामि यदुक्तं ब्रह्मयामले ।
प्रासादग्रामगेहाद्या ज्ञेया येन शुभाशुभाः ॥
ककारादिक्षकारान्ता वर्णाः स्युर्दीपसंज्ञकाः ।
स्वराः षोडशपीठाख्या ज्ञातव्या मन्त्रिणां वरैः ॥ इति ।

तथा—पीठसंज्ञा स्वराणाञ्च दीपाः स्युर्व्यञ्जनानि हि ।
स्थानं दीपाक्षरं यस्मिन् कोष्ठे तिष्ठति तद्भवेत् ॥
दीपस्थानं तदेतत् स्यात् कूर्म्मचक्रे न संशयः ॥ इति ।

चतुरस्रां भुवं भित्त्वा कोष्ठानां नवकं लिखेत् ।
पूर्व्वकोष्ठादि विलिखेत् सप्तवर्गाननुक्रमात् ॥ १३३
लक्ष्मीशे मध्यकोष्ठे स्वरान् युग्मक्रमाल्लिखेत् ।
दिक्षु पूर्व्वादितो यत्र क्षेत्राख्याद्यक्षरस्थितम् ॥ १३४

तस्य दीपस्थानमिति। कर्म्म जपादिकम्। अतएव वक्ष्यति "मन्त्राणां सिद्धिसाधनम्" इति ॥ १३२ ॥

दीपस्थानज्ञानार्थं कूर्म्मचक्रमाह चतुरिति। तत्र द्वे रेखे पूर्व्वापरायते द्वे दक्षिणोत्तरायते चतुरस्रमध्ये कुर्य्यात्। तदा नवकोष्ठानि सम्पद्यन्ते। तेषु नवसु कोष्ठेषु नव क्षेत्रपालाः पूज्याः। यदुक्तम्—

क्षेत्रपाला नवैतेषु दीपेशा नवकोष्ठके।
अमृतो वृषभः शैलराजो वासुकिरर्थकृत् ॥
शक्तिकृत्[पूः] पद्मयोनिश्च महाशङ्खश्च ते नव।
छायाछत्रगणोपेतान् मध्यात् पूर्व्वादितो यजेत् ॥ इति।

पूर्व्वकोष्ठादि पूर्व्वदिक्कोष्ठमारभ्य इत्यर्थः। सप्तवर्गानिति कचटतपयशान्। अनुक्रमाद् विलिखेत् इति उत्तरान्तम्। अत्र यथासम्भवं मध्यत आरभ्य प्रतिकोष्ठम्। यदुक्तम्—

पूर्व्वकोष्ठे कवर्गस्य पञ्चकं मध्यतः क्रमात्।
मध्यतोऽन्यत्र चाग्नेये चवर्गञ्चैवमेव हि ॥ इति ॥१३३॥

मध्यकोष्ठे स्वरान् युग्मक्रमाल्लिखेदिति। तत्र लेखनप्रकार उक्तोऽन्यत्र—

मध्यकोष्ठे पुरोभागे अकारद्वयमालिखेत्।
आग्नेय्यामिद्वयं विन्यात् याम्ये उद्वयमालिखेत् ॥
नैर्ऋत्ये ऋद्वयं विन्याद्वारुणे लृद्वयन्तथा।
वायव्यामेद्वयं विन्यात् सौम्यामोद्वयमिष्यते ॥
ईशे चान्त्ययुगं विन्यादेवं न्यस्य विचारयेत्। इति।

अयं लेखनक्रमः क्रमेणानेन विभजेत् इति वक्ष्यमाणेन सूचित एव।

क्षेत्राख्येति। अत्र क्षेत्रशब्दो ग्रामादीनामुपलक्षकः।

यदुक्तम्—पीठं क्षेत्रं पुरञ्चापि नगरं ग्राममेव च। इति।

तल्लक्षणमन्यत्रोक्तम्—

कादिनान्तं भवेत् क्षेत्रं ग्रामः स्यात् पादिमान्तकः।

मुखं तत् तस्य जानीयाद्धस्तावुभयतः स्थितौ ।
कोष्ठे कुक्षी उभे पादौ द्वे शिष्टं पुच्छमीरितम् ।
क्रमेणानेन विभजेन्मध्यस्थमपि भागतः ॥ १३५
मुखस्थो लभते सिद्धिं करस्थः स्वल्पजीवनः ।
उदासीनः कुक्षिसंस्थः पादस्थो दुःखमाप्नुयात् ॥ १३६
पुच्छस्थः पीड्यते मन्त्री बन्धनोच्चाटनादिभिः ।
कूर्म्मचक्रमिदं प्रोक्तं मन्त्राणां सिद्धिसाधनम् ॥ १३७

यादिषान्तं पुरं सम्यक् प्रोक्तं देशिकसत्तमैः ।
सहान्तं नगरं प्रोक्तमेतत् क्षेत्रस्य लक्षणम् ॥ इति ।

पीठलक्षणन्तु प्रागुक्तम्—"स्वराः षोडश पीठाख्याः" इति । क्वचित्तु "वनाद्रि-पत्तनग्राम देवगेहकुदादिषु" इत्यप्युक्तम् । उभयतः स्थिताविति प्रत्येकं हस्त-कुक्षिपादेष्वन्वेति । तेनाद्याद्यमभितोऽग्रिमाग्रिमम् पुच्छं शिष्टम् ॥ १३४॥१३५ ॥

अस्य फलमाह मुखस्थ इति । मन्त्रीत्याक्षिप्यते । तस्य तन्त्रोक्तदीक्षाप्रकारेण स्वीकृतमन्त्र इत्यर्थः । अग्रेऽपि मन्त्रिणाम् इति पदद्वये अयमेवार्थोऽनुसन्धेयः । जीव्यतेऽनेनेति जीवनं भोगः स्वल्पं जीवनं यस्य स स्वल्पजीवनः । तदुक्तम्—

मुखस्थः शुभयुग्ज्ञेयः करस्थः स्वल्पभुक्तिमान् । इत्यादिना ।
तथा—मुखे सर्व्वार्थसिद्धिः स्यात् करयोरल्पसिद्धिकृत् । इत्यादिना ।
तथा—तस्मान्मुखं समाश्रित्य सर्व्वकर्म्म समारभेत् ।
तदलाभे करं वापि कूर्म्मस्यान्यं न संश्रयेत् ॥ इति ।

अत्र विशेषो ग्रन्थान्तरोक्तः—

स्थानसाधकयोर्नाम्नोररित्वं यत्र विद्यते ।
तत्तच्च [तदत्र] शास्त्रतो ज्ञात्वा तत्तत् सम्यक् परित्यजेत् ॥
अरित्वमद्वयस्योक्तं गकारेण परस्परम् ।
रुयुग्मस्य ठ[च]कारेण ठ[च]कारस्यापि तेन च ॥
लृद्वयस्य पकारेण पकारस्यापि लृद्वयम् ।
ओयुग्मस्य षकारेण षकारस्यौयुगेन च ॥
जकारस्य टकारेण झ[ञ]कारस्य खकारतः ।
उकारस्य तकारेण फकारस्य धकारतः ॥

भकारस्य तु रेफेण यकारस्य सकारतः।
अरित्वमेषां वर्णानामन्येषां मित्रभावना॥
कूर्मचक्रे रिपुस्थानं साधको यत्नतस्त्यजेत्॥ इति।

उदाहरणञ्च तत्रैव दर्शितम्—

यथा गर्गस्य वैरि स्यादट्टहासं महत् पुरम्।
गयाऽमरेश्वरस्यैवमकाराद्येषु योजयेत्॥
ऋषभस्य चकाराख्यं स्तूतकस्यापि पञ्चकम्।
ओड्डियानं षण्मुखस्य ओड्रं षड्गुणकस्य च॥
जयन्ती टङ्कनस्यारिः खन्धारं झञ्झभट्टतः।
डकदेवस्य तरणिः[ताराख्यं] धूमाख्यं फञ्जकस्य च॥
भट्टस्य रम्यकं वैरि यज्ञमित्रस्य वै स्तरः।
एवं क्रमेण संशोध्य वैरिस्थानं त्यजेद्बुधः॥ इति।

तथा—तेषामाद्यान्वितं वर्णं पूर्वमार्गेषु योजयेत्।
यदि तद्व्यञ्जनापिण्डं यद्याद्यं पीठवर्जितम्॥
नामाक्षराणि सर्वाणि पीठयुक्तानि वर्जयेत्।
तदादिकानि मार्गेण तद्गृहीत्वा स्वरं त्यजेत्॥
ग्रामनामाक्षरेष्वादिमध्यान्तार्णान् विहाय च।
द्वितीयमक्षरं यत्र कोष्ठे तिष्ठति तन्मुखम्॥ इति।

अन्यत्रापि—तत्तन्नामद्वितीयार्णो यत्र तिष्ठति तन्मुखम्। इति।

इदन्तु स्वरादिनामविषयम्। नामादौ संयोगाक्षरे सति विशेषमाह—

अक्षरत्रितयं यत्र ग्रामनामादिषु क्वचित्।
स्वरो मध्याक्षरारूढो यत्र तिष्ठति तन्मुखम्॥
भवतो यदि वर्णौ द्वौ ग्रामनामादिषु स्फुटम्।
आद्यस्वरः यत्र तिष्ठत्वदो वदनमिष्यते॥ इति।

तथा च—क्षेत्रसाधकमन्त्राणामेकमेवाद्यमक्षरम्।
यदि स्यात् स ध्रुवं मन्त्रः सर्वसिद्धिफलप्रदः॥ इति।

फलविशेषमाहाऽन्यः—

मोक्षार्थी वदने कुर्य्याद्दक्षिणे त्वाभिचारिकम्।
श्रीकामः पश्चिमे मूत्वा उत्तरे शान्तिदो भवेत्॥
ईशाने शत्रुनाशः स्यादाग्नेयः शत्रुदायकः।

पुण्यक्षेत्रं नदीतीरं गुहा पर्व्वतमस्तकम् ।
तीर्थप्रदेशाः सिन्धूनां सङ्गमाः पावनं वनम् ॥ १३८

उद्यानानि विविक्तानि बिल्वमूलं तटं गिरेः ।
देवतायतनं कूलं समुद्रस्य निजं गृहम् ।
साधनेषु प्रशस्यन्ते स्थानान्येतानि मन्त्रिणाम् ॥ १३९

नैर्ऋते शत्रुभीतिः स्याद् वायव्ये तु पलायनम् ॥
कूर्म्मचक्रमविज्ञाय यः कुर्य्याज्जपयज्ञकम् ।
तज्जपस्य फलं नास्ति स चानर्थाय कल्पते ॥ इति ।

कादिमते विशेषः—

संवर्द्धायामविस्तारं कृत्वाऽष्टाभिस्तु शेषतः ।
विज्ञाय वर्गं तेष्वेकमाद्यं नाम्नि प्रकल्पयेत् ॥
वास्तुष्वज्ञातरूपेषु प्रसिद्धं नामतो भवेत् ।
व्यञ्जनं देशकूर्म्मे स्याद् गृहकूर्म्मे स्वरास्तथा ॥ इति ।

॥१३६॥१३७॥

पुरश्चरणजपस्य स्थानानि वदन् कूर्म्मचक्रविषयमाह पुण्येति । नदीतीरं पुण्यनदीतीरम् । सामान्यनदीतीरस्य निषिद्धत्वात् । पावनं वनमिति विशेषणविशेष्यभावः । उद्यानानि विविक्तानि पूतानीत्यर्थापि । "विविक्तौ पूतविजनौ" इति कोषः । स्थानान्येतानीत्यनेन तन्त्रान्तरोक्तमपि सूचितम् । यदाहुः—

प्रत्यङ्मुखशिवस्थाने वृषभादिविवर्जिते ।
अश्वत्थबिल्वतुलसीवने पुष्पान्तरावृते ।
गवां गोष्ठेऽश्वत्थमूले पुण्यक्षेत्रेषु शस्यते ॥ इति ।

वायवीयसंहितायामपि—

सूर्य्यस्याग्नेर्गुरोरिन्दोर्दीपस्य च जलस्य च ।
विप्राणाञ्च गवाञ्चैव सन्निधौ शस्यते जपः ॥
अथवा निवसेत् तत्र यत्र चित्तं प्रसीदति ॥ इति ।

तत्रैव स्थानविशेषे फलविशेषोऽप्युक्तः ।

गृहे जपः समः प्रोक्तो गोष्ठे शतगुणस्तु सः ।
आरामे च तथाऽरण्ये सहस्रगुण उच्यते ॥

भैक्ष्यं हविष्यं शाकानि विहितानि फलं पयः ।

मूलं शक्तुर्यवोत्पन्नो भक्ष्याण्येतानि मन्त्रिणाम् ॥ १४०

अयुतं पर्व्वते पुण्ये नद्यां लक्षगुणस्तु सः ।

कोटिर्देवालये प्राहुरनन्तं शिवसन्निधौ ॥ इति ।

एवं शक्तिविशेषमन्त्रेषु अष्टाष्टकपीठादपि ज्ञेयम् । अन्यत्र—

म्लेच्छदुष्टमृगव्यालशङ्कातङ्कादिवर्जिते ।

एकान्ते वा वने निन्दारहिते भक्तिसंयुते ॥

सुदेशे धार्म्मिके राष्ट्रे सुभिक्षे निरुपद्रवे ।

रम्ये भक्तजनस्थाने निवसेन्न पराश्रये ॥

राजानः सचिवा राजपुरुषाः प्रभवो जनाः ।

चरन्ति येन मार्गेण न वसेत् तत्र तत्त्ववित् ॥

जीर्णदेवालयोद्यानगृहवृक्षतलेषु च ।

नदीकूलाद्रिकुञ्जेषु भूच्छिद्रादिषु नो वसेत् ॥ इति ।

॥ १३८॥१३९ ॥

पुरश्चरणकर्त्तुर्भक्ष्याण्याह भैक्ष्यमिति । एतद्ब्रह्मचारियतिपरम् । भिक्षास्वरूपमुक्तमन्यत्र—

वैदिकाचारयुक्तानां शुचीनां श्रीमतां गृहे ।

सत्कुलस्थानजातानां भिक्षा स्यादग्रजन्मनाम् ॥ इति ।

हविष्यमिति व्रतहविष्यं न तु श्राद्धहविष्यादि । तच्च स्मृत्यन्तरे

हैमन्तिकं सितास्विन्नं धान्यमुद्गयवास्तिलाः ।

कलायकङ्गुनीवारा वास्तुकं हिलमोचिका ॥

षष्टिका कालशाकञ्च मूलकं केमुकेतरत् ।

कन्दं [लोणं] सैन्धवसामुद्रे गव्ये च दधिसर्पिषी ॥

पयोऽनुद्धृतसारञ्च पनसाम्रहरीतकी ।

तिन्तिडी[पिप्पली] जीरकञ्चैव नागरङ्गकमेव च ॥

कदली लवली धात्री फलान्यगुडमैक्षवम् ।

अतैलपक्वं मुनयो हविष्यान्नं प्रचक्षते ॥ इति ।

फलं पयो मूलं विहितमित्यनुषज्यते ॥ १४० ॥

पुरुषार्थसमावाप्त्यै सच्छिष्यो गुरुमाश्रयेत् ।
मातृतः पितृतः शुद्धः शुद्धभावो जितेन्द्रियः ॥ १४१
सर्व्वागमानां सारज्ञः सर्व्वशास्त्रार्थतत्त्ववित् ।
परोपकारनिरतो जपपूजादितत्परः ॥ १४२
अमोघवचनः शान्तो वेदवेदार्थपारगः ।
योगमार्गानुसन्धायी देवताहृदयङ्गमः ॥ १४३

सच्छिष्यो गुरुमाश्रयेदित्युक्तम् ॥ अतो गुरुलक्षणमाह मातृत इत्यादिना । मातृतः पितृतः शुद्धः शुद्धपितृमातृप्रसूत इत्यर्थः । सा च शुद्धिर्लोकप्रसिद्धितः शीलान्वेषणतश्च ज्ञेया । यदुक्तम्—

यदकारि कर्म्म गुप्तं यौवनसमये मदान्ध[न्द्धधि]या मात्रा ।
तत् प्रकटयन्ति तनया विगतनयाः स्वधर्म्ममुत्सृज्य ॥ इति ।

शुद्धभावः शुद्धचित्तवृत्तिरित्यर्थः । अन्यथा खलत्वात् शुश्रूषार्ह एव न स्यात् । जितेन्द्रियः । अजितेन्द्रियस्य देवतापराङ्मुखत्वात् ॥ १४१ ॥

सर्व्वागमानां सारज्ञः । अन्यथा शैवादितत्तत्सम्प्रदायानभिज्ञता स्यात् । सर्व्वशास्त्रार्थतत्त्ववित् । अन्यथा आगमशास्त्रविचारानुपपत्तेः । परोपकारनिरतः । अन्यथा शिष्योपरि कृपैव न स्यात् । तत्कृपां विना मन्त्रोऽपि पराङ्मुखो भवति । जपपूजादितत्परः । आदिशब्देन ध्यानहोमौ । अन्यथा लुप्तसमयाचारस्य देवतासान्निध्याभावात् । तदुक्तं पिङ्गलामते—

नाध्यातोऽनर्चितो मन्त्रः सुसिद्धोऽपि प्रसीदति ।
नाजप्तः सिद्धिदानेच्छुर्नाहुतः फलदो भवेत् ॥
पूजां ध्यानं जपं होमं तस्मात् कर्म्मचतुष्टयम् ।
प्रत्यहं साधकः कुर्य्यात् स्वयञ्चेत् सिद्धिमिच्छति ॥ इति ॥१४२॥

अमोघवचनः अनुग्रहक्षमः । शान्तः । अन्यथा लोकगर्हितत्वाऽसेव्यत्वात् । वेदवेदार्थपारगः । अनेन स्वाचारनिष्ठतोक्ता । यदुक्तम्—

वर्णाश्रमाचारवता पुरुषेण परः पुमान् ।
विष्णुराराध्यते पन्था नान्यस्तत्तोषकारकः ॥ इति ।

अन्यत्रापि—विना स्वधर्म्मं यत्किञ्चित् देवताराधनादिकम् ।
परिभ्रश्येत तद्यस्मात् क्षणात् सैकतहर्म्म्यवत् ॥ इति ।

इत्यादिगुणसम्पन्नो गुरुरागमसम्मतः॥ १४४

योगमार्गानुसन्धायी। अन्यथा दीक्षादिदान एवाशक्तिः स्यात्। देवताहृदयङ्गमः देवतावद्धृदयङ्गमो मनोहरः प्रसन्नाकार इत्यर्थः। यथा देवतादर्शनेन मनसि सन्तोषस्तथा तद्दर्शनेनापि मनसि सन्तोषोत्पादात्। तदुक्तम्—

काय्यानुगतं शीलं शीलानुगतं नृणां भवति चित्तम्।
चित्तानुगतं रूपं रूपानुगता गुणाः प्रायः॥ इति।

यत्र च मनसः सन्तोषस्तत्र फलावश्यम्भावः। तदुक्तम्—"यस्मिन्मनश्चक्षुषोरभिरतिस्तस्मिन्नभ्युदयः" इति। तथाऽभियुक्तकालिदासस्मरणमपि—"मनो हि जन्मान्तरसङ्गतिज्ञम्" इति। आदिशब्दान्महाकपिलपञ्चरात्रोक्तम्—

नातिबालो न वृद्धश्च न खञ्जो न कृशस्तथा।
नाधिकाङ्गो न हीनाङ्गो न खल्वाटो न दन्तुरः॥
कुल[कृत]ज्ञं वाग्मिनं शूरं प्रतिष्ठागमपारगम्।
वास्तुविद्याकृताभ्यासं शल्योद्धारविवेकिनम्।
क्रियानुक्रमवेत्तारं मुद्रातत्त्वविवेकिनम्॥ इति।
शुचिः सुवेशस्तरुणः सर्व्वभूतसमानधीः।
धीमाननुद्धतमतिः कृतज्ञः शिष्यवत्सलः।
श्रद्धावाननसूयश्च गृहस्थो गुरुरुच्यते॥

इत्यादिग्रन्थान्तरोक्तञ्च द्रष्टव्यम्।

आचार्य्यमातुलौ ऋत्विक् पितृव्यः श्वशुरो नृपः। इति षड्गुरवोऽप्येते।

इत्यन्यत्रोक्तेरत्र आगमसम्मतः इति विशेषणम्।

संसारसागरे मग्नान् यस्तारयति देहिनः।
तत्त्वप्लवप्रदानेन स एवेह गुरुः स्मृतः॥ इत्युक्तेः।

प्रतिष्ठासारस्वते तु विशेषः—

आर्य्यावर्त्तोद्भवोऽन्यो वा ककाराष्टकवर्जितः।
शैवसिद्धान्तनिपुणः प्रतिष्ठामन्त्रपारगः॥ इति।

वीरागमे च—कुमारीहिमवन्मध्ये स्वतः कृष्णमृगान्विते।
देशे जातस्तु यो विद्वान् आचार्य्यत्वमथार्हति॥ इति।

योगशिवपद्धतावपि—

मध्यदेशकुरुक्षेत्रनाभोज्जयिनिसम्भवाः।
अन्तर्व्वेदिप्रतिष्ठानादावन्त्याश्च गुरूत्तमाः॥

गौड़देशोद्भवाश्चोला मागधाः केरलास्तथा ।
कोशलाश्च दशार्णाश्च गुरवो मध्यमा मताः ॥
कर्णाटकोङ्कणाकोर[श्चैव] कच्छतीरोद्भवास्तथा ।
कालिङ्गाः कामरूपाश्च काम्बोजाश्चाधमाः स्मृताः ॥ इति ।

देवीमते च—आचार्य्यः शैवशास्त्रज्ञः शिवदेशसमुद्भवः ।
ब्रह्मचारी गृहस्थो वा शिवभक्तिपरायणः ।
यजमानानुकूलश्चेज्ज्ञा देशिक उच्यते ॥ इति ।

हयशीर्षपञ्चरात्रेऽपि—
गृहस्थं ब्रह्मचर्य्यस्थं कक्कारा[पाटा]ष्टकवर्जितम् ।
गुरुं कुर्वीत सततमुपवासव्रते रतम् ॥ इति ।

तथा—सर्व्वत्र व्यतिरिक्तन्तु आत्मानं वेत्ति यो द्विजः ।
सर्व्वलक्षणहीनोऽपि स गुरुर्नात्र संशयः ॥
पञ्चरात्रप्रबुद्धस्तु सिद्धान्तार्थस्य तत्त्ववित् ।
सर्व्वलक्षणहीनोऽपि आचार्य्यः स निगद्यते ॥
यस्य विष्णौ परा भक्तिर्यथा विष्णौ तथा गुरौ ।
स एव देशिको ज्ञेयः सत्यमेतद्ब्रवीमि ते ॥ इति ।

शैवदीक्षायाम् अतीतागमे विशेषः—
जटी मुण्डी शिखी वापि शस्तदेशसमुद्भवः ।
शिवशास्त्रार्थतत्त्वज्ञः श्रुतवृत्तान्वितो द्विजः ॥
शिवमेवाश्रितो नित्यं वाङ्मनःकायकर्म्मभिः ।
आचार्य्यः स समुद्दिष्टः शिवदीक्षादिकर्म्मसु ॥ इति ।

शान्तिके च—अनूचानः प्रसन्नात्मा शिवदीक्षाभिषेचितः ।
शिवागमज्ञो मतिमान् शिवपूजापरायणः ॥
रुद्राक्षमालां बिभ्राणस्त्रिशूलाङ्कितविग्रहः ।
विशुद्धदेशकुलजः शीलाचारसमन्वितः ।
वेदशास्त्रार्थतत्त्वज्ञो ज्ञानवान् गुरुरुच्यते ॥ इति ।

प्रतिष्ठापद्धतावपि—
लिङ्गी वि[ङ्गादि]लक्षणज्ञानी निपुणः कर्म्मसन्ततौ ।
देवताध्यासितत्त्वज्ञः षड्विधाध्वविशारदः ॥
शुभाशुभनिमित्तज्ञस्त्वथवा विस्तरेण किम् ।

शिष्यः कुलीनः शुद्धात्मा पुरुषार्थपरायणः ।
अधीतवेदः कुशलो दूरमुक्तमनोभवः ॥ १४५

हितैषी प्राणिनां नित्यमास्तिकस्त्यक्तनास्तिकः ।
स्वधर्म्मनिरतो भक्त्या पितृमातृहितोद्यतः ॥ १४६

सम्यग्जातिपरिज्ञानं वृत्तन्त्वाद्यास्त्रयो गुणाः ।
यस्यैते स गुरुः श्रेष्ठः सर्व्वकामफलप्रदः ॥ इति ।

यतेरपि गुरुतोक्ता मोहशूरोत्तरे—

चीर्णा[तीर्था]चारव्रती सत्त्वी ज्ञानवान् सुसमाहितः ।
नित्यनिष्ठो यतिः ख्यातो गुरुः स्याद् भौतिकोऽपि च ॥ इति ।

वातुलोत्तरेऽपि—विद्ययाऽभयदातारं लौल्यचापलवर्जितम् ।
एवंविधं गुरुं प्राप्य को न मुच्येत बन्धनात् ॥ इति ।

पौष्करे तु—सर्व्वलक्षणहीनोऽपि ज्ञानवान् गुरुरुच्यते ।
ज्ञानञ्च तत्त्वविज्ञानं षड़ध्वज्ञानसंश्रयम् ॥ इति ॥ १४३॥१४४ ॥

शिष्यलक्षणमाह शिष्य इति । कुलीनः शुद्धमातृपितृजः । अन्यथा कुण्ड-गोलादेरशुचित्वात् सर्व्वदा स्पृष्टव्यत्वाभावात् । शुद्धात्मा अक्रूरचित्तः । क्रूरस्य विद्यानुपदेशात् । यत् श्रुतिः—

विद्या ह वै ब्राह्मणमाजगाम । गोपाय मा शेवधिष्टेऽहमस्मि ।
असूयकायाऽनृजवेऽयताय न मा ब्रूया । वीर्य्यवती तथा स्याम् ॥ इति ।

पुरुषार्थपरायणः । अनेनास्य व्यसनहीनतोक्ता । अन्यथा उपदेशानर्थक्यात् । अधीतवेद इत्यनेनास्य शुद्धतोक्ता । यदुक्तम्—

योऽनधीत्य द्विजो वेदमन्यत्र कुरुते श्रमम् ।
स जीवन्नेव शूद्रत्वमाशु गच्छति सान्वयः ॥ इति ।

कुशलः असुग्धः । मुग्धस्य मन्त्रबोधनाक्षमत्वात् । दूरमुक्तमनोभवः । कामिनः सपापत्वादशुद्धचित्तत्वात् मन्त्राराधनानधिकारः । हितैषी प्राणिनां नित्यम् इति । अन्यथा उपदिष्टमन्त्रात् अभिचारादिकर्म्मरतस्य तस्य पापं गुरुमपि स्पृशेत् । आस्तिकः अस्ति परलोक इति बुद्धिर्यस्य । अन्यथा नास्तिकतायां मन्त्रदेवता-नाराधनात् गुरौ देवताकोपो भवेत् । त्यक्तनास्तिकः नास्तिकसंसर्गत्यागी । अन्यथा संसर्गजो दोषः स्यात् । स्वधर्म्मनिरतः आचारवान् । अनाचारिणोऽनधिकारात् । भक्त्या मातृपितृहितोद्यतो न तु दम्भादिना । असावेवास्य परमो धर्म्म उक्तो

वाङ्मनःकायवसुभिर्गुरुशुश्रूषणे रतः ।
त्यक्ताभिमानो गुरुषु जातिविद्याधनादिभिः ॥ १४७

गुर्व्वाज्ञापालनार्थं हि प्राणव्ययरतोद्यतः ।
विहत्य च स्वकार्य्याणि गुरुकार्य्यरतः सदा ॥ १४८

दासवन्निवसेद् यस्तु गुरौ भक्त्या सदा शिशुः ।
कुर्व्वन्नाज्ञां दिवारात्रौ गुरुभक्तिपरायणः ॥ १४९

व्यासादिभिः । वाङ्मन इत्यादिना अवञ्चकतोक्ता । एतादृश इत्यनेन

युवा विनयताशेषकरणः करुणालयः ।

इत्यादि ग्रन्थान्तरोक्तं द्रष्टव्यम् । यत् प्रयोगसारे—

तत्रापि भक्तियुक्ताय पुत्राय वसुदाय च । इति ।

नारायणीयेऽपि—कुर्व्वन्नाचार्य्यशुश्रूषां मनोवाक्कायकर्म्मभिः ।

शुद्धभावो महोत्साहो बोद्धा शिष्य इति स्मृतः ॥

न तूपदेश्यः पुत्रस्य व्यत्ययो वसुदस्तथा । इति ।

नापर इत्यनेनाऽन्यस्य निषेध उक्तः । तथा चान्यत्र शिष्यदोषानुक्त्वा—

एवमादिगुणैर्युक्तं न शिष्यन्तु परिग्रहेत् ।
गृह्णीयाद् यदि तद्दोषः प्रायो गुरुमपि स्पृशेत् ॥
अमात्यदोषो राजानं पतिं जायाकृतो यथा ।
तथा शिष्यकृतो दोषो गुरुं प्राप्नोत्यसंशयः ॥
स्नेहाद्वा लोभतो वापि यदि गृह्णाति दीक्षया ।
तस्मिन् गुरौ सशिष्ये तु देवताशाप आपतेत् ।
तस्माच्छिष्यं गुरुर्नित्यं परीक्ष्य तु परिग्रहेत् ॥ इति ।

भुवनेशीपारिजातेऽपि—

अशिष्ये कथयेद् यस्तु स महापातकी भवेत् । इति ।

ग्रन्थान्तरे तु विशेषः—

गुरूच्यमाने वचने वदेदित्थं वचस्तदा ।
प्रसीद नाथ देवेति तथेति च कृतादरम् ॥
प्रणम्योपविशेत् पार्श्वे तथा गच्छेदनुज्ञया ।
मुखावलोकी सेवेत कुर्य्यादादिष्टमादरात् ॥

आज्ञाकारी गुरोः शिष्यो मनोवाक्कायकर्म्मभिः ।
यो भवेत् स तदा ग्राह्यो नेतरः शुभकाङ्क्षया ॥ १५०

मन्त्रपूजारहस्यानि यो गोपयति सर्व्वदा ।
त्रिकालं यो नमस्कुर्य्यादागमाचारतत्त्ववित् ॥ १५१

स एव शिष्यः कर्त्तव्यो नेतरः स्वल्पजीवनः ।
एतादृशगुणोपेतः शिष्यो भवति नापरः ॥ १५२

असत्यं न वदेदग्रे न बहु प्रलपेदपि ।
कामं क्रोधं तथा लोभं मानं प्रहसनं स्तुतिम् ॥
चापलानि न जिह्मानि कार्य्याणि[नर्म्माणि] परिदेवनम् ।
ऋणदानं तथाऽऽदानं वस्तूनां क्रयविक्रयम् ।
न कुर्य्याद् गुरुणा सार्द्धं शिष्यो भूष्णुः कदाचन ॥ इति ।

प्रयोगसारेऽपि—गुरुर्माता पिता स्वामी बान्धवाः सुहृदः शिवः ।
इत्याधाय मनो नित्यं भजेत् सर्व्वात्मना गुरुम् ॥
असत्यं न गुरौ ब्रूयाद् गुरुनिन्दां न कारयेत् ।
प्रारब्धां वारयेदन्यैरशक्तस्तत्पदं त्यजेत् ॥
गुरौ यथैव शुश्रूषा गुरुभार्य्यासु ताञ्चरेत् ।
ज्येष्ठांश्च गुरुवत् पश्येत् आत्मवच्च कनीयसः ॥
गुरुणा यद्यदादिष्टमिष्टं वाऽनिष्टमेव वा ।
तदा तदाशु सन्तिष्ठेदकौटिल्येन चेतसा ॥
मनोवाक्कर्म्मभिर्नित्यं पूजयेद् भाविनं गुरुम् । इति ।

देव्यागमेऽपि शिववाक्यम्—
गुरोरग्रे पृथक् पूजामौद्धत्यञ्च विवर्जयेत् ।
दीक्षां व्याख्यां प्रभुत्वादि गुरोरग्रे विवर्जयेत् ॥ इति ।

तत्रैव—आसनं शयनं वस्त्रं भूषणं पादुकां तथा ।
छायां कलत्रमन्यच्च यत्तत्स्पृष्टं तु पूजयेत् ॥ इति ।

अन्यत्रापि—यथा देवे तथा मन्त्रे यथा मन्त्रे तथा गुरौ ।
यथा गुरौ तथा स्वात्मन्येवं भक्तिक्रमः स्मृतः ॥ इति ।

॥ १४५-१५२ ॥

एकाब्देन भवेद् योग्यो ब्राह्मणोऽब्दद्वयान्नृपः ।
वैश्यो वर्षैस्त्रिभिः शूद्रश्चतुर्भिर्वत्सरैर्गुरोः ।
स शुश्रूषुः परिग्राह्यो दीक्षायागव्रतादिषु ॥ १५३ ।

इति शारदातिलके द्वितीयः पटलः ।

शिष्यस्य परीक्षावधिकालमाह एकेति । गुरोर्योग्यो भवेदिति सर्व्वत्र सम्बध्यते । शूद्रश्चतुर्भिरिति । ननु शूद्रस्य दीक्षादौ कथमधिकार इति चेत् । मैवम् । वेदाध्ययनतदुक्त कर्म्मस्वेव स्मृतावनधिकारप्रतिपादनादन्यत्राधिकारात् । अतएव शूद्रप्रकरणे

स्मृतिः— नमस्कारेण मन्त्रेण पञ्चयज्ञान् न हापयेत् । इति ।

मन्त्रास्त्वीश्वरप्रोक्तास्तत्र भगवतैव यथायथमधिकारिता दर्शिता । यथाप्रासाद-मन्त्रप्रकरणे भगवानाह—

स्त्रीशूद्राणामयं मन्त्रो नमोऽन्तस्तु शुभावहः ।
एतज्ज्ञात्वा महासेन चाण्डालानपि दीक्षयेत् ॥ इति ।

पिङ्गलामतेऽपि— चतुर्णां ब्राह्मणादीनां दीक्षां कुर्व्वीत मन्त्रवित् । इति ।

अन्यत्रापि— ब्रह्मक्षत्रविशः शूद्रा अर्चायां शुद्धबुद्धयः ।
गुरुदेवद्विजार्चासु रताः स्युरधिकारिणः ॥ इति ।

तेन साक्षाद्वैदिकेषु मन्त्रेषु रामषड़क्षरसौराष्टाक्षरमन्त्रराजप्रभृतिषु प्रणवादिषु च न तस्याधिकारः । तथा च पद्मपादाचार्य्यैः प्रणवव्याख्याने—

अकारोकारमकारात्मेत्यनेन भेदत्रयेण प्रणवादिमन्त्रेषु त्रैवर्णिका एवाधि-कारिणो न स्त्रीशूद्रा इत्यपि सूचितम् इत्युक्तम् ।

तथा च नृसिंहतापनीये—

सावित्रीं प्रणवं यजुर्लक्ष्मीं स्त्रीशूद्राय नेच्छन्ति । सावित्रीं लक्ष्मीं यजुः प्रणवं यदि जानीयात् स्त्रीशूद्रः स्मृतोऽधो गच्छति । इति ।

महाकपिलपञ्चरात्रे नारायणाष्टाक्षरमधिकृत्योक्तम्—

न वेदः प्रणवं त्यक्त्वा मन्त्रो वेदसमुच्छ्रितः ।
तस्माद् वेदपरो मन्त्रो वेदाङ्गश्चागमः स्मृतः ॥
वश्याकर्षादिकं काम्यं दृष्टादृष्टफलप्रदम् ।
वेदेन साध्यते सर्व्वं ब्रह्मयज्ञादिभिः किल ॥

न वेदेन विना यज्ञा न यज्ञा वेद[मन्त्र]वर्जिताः ।
तस्माद् वेदः परो मन्त्रो न मन्त्रो वेदमुज्झितः ॥
न मन्त्रे चाधिकारोऽस्ति शूद्राणां नियमः परः ।
मन्त्राभावादमन्त्रेण भाषितं सर्व्वकर्म्म हि ॥ इति ।

नारदपञ्चरात्रे नारायणाष्टाक्षरमधिकृत्योक्तम्—

ब्राह्मणक्षत्रियविशां पञ्चरात्रं विधीयते ।
शूद्रादीनां न तत् श्रोत्रपदवीमपि गच्छति ॥ इति ।

तथा श्रवणे त्रपुजतुभ्यां कर्णपूरणं उच्चारणे जिह्वाच्छेदः धारणे शरीरभेदः इति वेदविषये तस्य स्मृतिषु दण्डोपदेशादित्यलम् । अन्यत्र वत्सरमात्रं सामान्यत उक्तम्—

गुरुता शिष्यता वापि तयोर्वत्सरवासतः । इति ।

सारसंग्रहेऽपि—सद्गुरुः संश्रितं शिष्यं वर्षमेकं परीक्षयेत् । इति ।

के चन इदं ब्राह्मणविषयमित्यूचुः । दशपटल्यान्तु—

अब्दं परीक्ष्य चार्द्धं वा अन्यथा न कदाचन । इति ।

प्रयागसारे तु—वर्षेषु त्रिषु विप्रस्य षट्सु वर्षेषु भूभृतः ।
विशो नवसु वर्षेषु परीक्षा तत्र शस्यते ॥
समास्वपि द्वादशसु तेषां ये वृषलादयः । इति ।

सिद्धान्तसारसंग्रहे विशेषः—

यथोक्तां दक्षिणां दद्याद् ब्राह्मणः क्षत्रियस्तथा ।
द्विगुणां वैश्यवर्य्यस्तु त्रिगुणां शूद्रसत्तमः ॥
चतुर्गुणां प्रयच्छेत मन्त्रसिद्धिविधीच्छया । इति ॥ १५२ ॥

इति श्रीशारदातिलकटीकायां सत्सम्प्रदायकृतव्याख्यायां
पदार्थादर्शाभिख्यायां द्वितीयः पटलः ॥ ॐ ॥

तृतीयः पटलः ।

ततो वक्ष्यामि दीक्षाङ्गं वास्तुयागपुरःसरम् ।
कृतेन येन मन्त्रज्ञो दीक्षायाः फलमश्नुते ॥ १ ।

एवं पूर्व्वोक्तरीतिप्रपञ्चितस्वरूपसर्व्वपुरुषार्थप्रदमन्त्रस्य ग्रहणोपायो दीक्षा। तां वक्तुं तदङ्गभूतवास्तुयागादिकं प्रपञ्चयितुं प्रतिजानीते तत इति। "अङ्गापूर्व्व-सहकृतं प्रधानापूर्व्वं फलं साधनक्षमं जनयति" इति भट्टन्यायमाश्रित्याह कृतेनेति। तत्र प्रसङ्गादन्यत् किञ्चिद् दीक्षाङ्गं तन्त्रान्तरोक्तमुच्यते—

असिद्धिर्भूमिसम्प्राप्तिर्मरणं बन्धु[बुद्धि]नाशनम् ।
आयुर्वृद्धिः प्रजानाशः सम्पत्ती रत्नसञ्चयः ॥
शुभ[पुत्र]प्राप्तिः स्थाननाशो मेधार्थश्च वशीकृतिः ।
चैत्रादीनां फलं ज्ञेयं मलमासन्तु वर्जयेत् ॥

अन्यत्र तु आषाढ़स्यापि सम्यक्फलतोक्ता—

वैशाखपूर्व्वजे मासे मन्त्रारम्भः सुदुःसहः[खकृत्] ।
वैशाखे धनदायी च ज्यैष्ठे मृत्युप्रदो भवेत् ॥
आषाढ़े पुत्रलाभाय श्रावणे शुभदो मतः ।
भाद्रे चैव ज्ञानहानिस्तथा सद्भिः प्रकीर्त्तिता ॥
आश्विने सर्व्वसिद्धिश्च कार्त्तिके ज्ञानसिद्धिदः ।
शुभकृन्मार्गशीर्षे स्यात् पौषे दुःखविधायकः ।
माघे मेधाविवृद्धिश्च फाल्गुने सर्व्ववश्यता ॥ इति ।

सिद्धान्तशेखरे तु विशेषः—

शरत्काले च वैशाखे दीक्षा श्रेष्ठफलप्रदा ।
फाल्गुने मार्गशीर्षे च ज्यैष्ठे दीक्षा तु मध्यमा ॥
आषाढ़े श्रावणे माघे कनिष्ठा सद्भिरीरिता ।
निन्दितश्चैत्रमासस्तु पौषो भाद्रपदस्तथा ।
निन्दितेष्वपि मासेषु दीक्षोक्ता ग्रहणे शुभा ॥ इति ।

तत्राषाढ़स्य उत्तमानन्तर्गतत्वान्निषेधः कष्टानन्तर्गतत्वाच्च ग्रहणम्। एवं ज्यैष्ठस्यापि निषेध उत्तमानन्तर्भावादेवेति ज्ञेयम्। तथा च

कालोत्तरे—शरद्वसन्तयोर्योगो दीक्षाकर्म्मविधौ स्मृतः ।

तयोरसम्भवे वर्षां विनाऽन्यत्र प्रशस्यते ॥ इति ।

क्रियाकाण्डशेखरेऽपि—

न विना पर्व्वे दीक्षा स्याद् वर्षासु मधुपौषयोः । इति ।

आषाढ़श्रावणनिषेध उत्तमसध्यमानन्तर्भावात् ।

कारणे—आषाढ़पूर्व्वमासे च आषाढ़े मार्गशीर्षके ।

दीक्षां न कारयेद्धीमानन्यमासे तु कारयेत् ॥ इति ।

मार्गशीर्षनिषेध उत्तमानन्तर्भावादेवेति ज्ञेयम् । अगस्त्यसंहितायाम्—

शुक्लपक्षेऽथ कृष्णे वा दीक्षा सर्व्वशुभावहा । इति ।

कालोत्तरे तु—भूतिकामैः सिते मुक्तिकामैस्तु कृष्णपक्षके । इति विशेषः ।

संहितायाम्—पूर्णिमा पञ्चमी चैव द्वितीया सप्तमी तथा ।

त्रयोदशी च दशमी प्रशस्ता सर्व्वकामदाः ॥ इति ।

अन्यत्र तु—कृष्णाष्टम्यां चतुर्दश्यां पञ्चपर्व्वदिनेऽथवा । इति ।

मन्त्रसारसंग्रहेऽपि—

द्वितीया पञ्चमी वापि षष्ठी वापि विशेषतः ।

द्वादश्यामपि कर्त्तव्यं त्रयोदश्यामथापि वा ॥ इति ।

मन्त्ररत्नावल्यान्तु—

चतुर्थीं नवमीं षष्ठीमष्टमीञ्च चतुर्दशीम् ।

पौर्णमासीं विना शेषा हिता उक्ता मुमुक्षुषु ॥ इति ।

तत्त्वसागरसंहितायान्तु—

तां तां तिथिं समालोच्य तद्भक्तांस्तत्र दीक्षयेत् ।

इन्द्रः । कस्य का तिथिरुद्दिष्टा विशेषाद् वद नारद ।

नारदः । ब्रह्मणः पौर्णमास्युक्ता द्वादशी चक्रधारिणः ।

चतुर्दशी शिवस्योक्ता वाचः प्रोक्ता त्रयोदशी ॥

द्वितीया तु श्रियः प्रोक्ता पार्व्वत्याश्च तृतीयिका ।

चतुर्थी गणनाथस्य भानोः प्रोक्ता तु सप्तमी ।

नित्या मार्गेषु पार्व्वत्या अष्टमी च चतुर्दशी ॥ इति ।

विष्णुदीक्षायां पञ्चरात्रे तु विशेषः—

द्वादश्यां शुक्लपक्षस्य सूर्य्यसंक्रमणे तथा । इति ।

संक्रमा विष्णुपदित्र्यतिरिक्ताः । कालोत्तरे च—

दिनच्छिद्राणि मुक्त्वा च याश्च स्युस्त्रिदिनस्पृशः । इति ।

रत्नावल्यान्तु—आदित्यं मङ्गलं सौरिं त्यक्त्वा वारांस्तु भूतये । इति ।

संहितायाम्—रवौ गुरौ सिते सोमे कर्त्तव्यं बुधशुक्रयोः । इति ।

सिते पक्षे इत्यर्थः ।

अन्यत्र—उत्तरात्रयरोहिण्यो रेवती पुष्यवासवम् ।

धनिष्ठा वायुमित्राश्विपित्र्यं त्वाष्ट्रञ्च नैर्ऋतम् ।

ऐशवैष्णवहस्ताश्च दीक्षायान्तु शुभावहाः ॥ इति ।

वासवं ज्येष्ठा । वायुः स्वाती । मित्रम् अनुराधा । अश्वि अश्विनी । पित्र्यं मघा ।
त्वाष्ट्रं चित्रा । नैर्ऋतं मूला । ऐशम् आर्द्रा । वैष्णवं श्रवणम् ।

संहितायामपि—अश्विनीरोहिणीस्वातीविशाखाहस्तभेषु च ।

ज्येष्ठोत्तरात्रयेष्वेवं कुर्य्यान्मन्त्राभिषेचनम् ॥ इति ।

रत्नावल्याम्—त्रीण्युत्तराणि रोहिण्यः पुष्यकं मृगशीर्षकम् ।

हस्ता स्वातिरनुराधा मघा मूलञ्च रेवती ॥

अभिजित् श्रवणञ्च । इति ।

कापिले च—पौष्णं रोहिण्यथादित्यं श्रवणञ्चाश्विनी तथा ।

सावित्रं त्वाष्ट्रवायव्यमैन्द्रं नैर्ऋतमेव च ॥

तिष्यं त्रिरुत्तरार्द्रा च सौम्यं शिष्यत्रिजन्मभम् ।

नक्षत्राणि प्रशस्तानि दीक्षाकर्म्मणि सुव्रते ॥ इति ।

पौष्णं रेवती । आदित्यं पुनर्व्वसु । सावित्रं हस्ता । सौम्यं मृगः ।

नीलतन्त्रेऽपि—रोहिणी श्रवणार्द्रा च धनिष्ठा उत्तरात्रयम् ।

पुष्यः शतभिषा चैव दीक्षानक्षत्रमुच्यते ॥ इति ।

रत्नावल्यान्तु—प्रतिपत् पूर्व्वाषाढ़ा च पञ्चमी कृत्तिका तथा ।

पूर्व्वभाद्रपदा षष्ठी दशमी रोहिणी तथा ॥

द्वादशी सार्पनक्षत्रमश्लेषा च त्रयोदशी ।

नक्षत्रलुप्ता इत्येते देवानामपि नाशकाः ॥ इति ।

अन्यद् वारादिसंयोगात् तिथिनक्षत्रदुष्टत्वं ज्योतिःशास्त्रादवसेयम् ।

तथा—शुभयोगेषु सर्व्वेषु दीक्षा सर्व्वशुभप्रदा । इति ।

रत्नावल्याम्—योगाश्च प्रीतिरायुष्मान् सौभाग्यः शोभनः शुभः ।

सुकर्म्मा च धृतिर्व्वृद्धिर्ध्रुवः सिद्धिश्च हर्षणः ॥

वरीयांश्च शिवः सिद्धो ब्रह्मा ऐन्द्रश्च षोडश । इति ।

तथा—शुभानि करणान्याहुर्दीक्षायाञ्च विशेषतः ।

शकुन्यादीनि विष्टिञ्च विशेषेण विवर्जयेत् ॥ इति ।

संहितायाम्—पञ्चाङ्गशुद्धिदिवसे स्वोदये तिथिवारयोः ।

गुरुशुक्रोदये शुद्धलग्ने द्वादशशोधिते ॥

प्रवृद्धे बलसंयुक्ते शुक्रे देवगुरौ तथा ।

शुभे विधुसमायोगे शुभवर्गे शुभोदये ।

इत्यादौ सर्व्वमन्त्राणां संग्रहः सर्व्वसौख्यकृत् ॥ इति ।

तथा च ज्योतिःशास्त्रे—

नीचस्थे वक्रसंस्थेऽप्यतिचरणगते बालवृद्धेऽस्तगे वा

सन्न्यासो देवयात्रा व्रतनियमविधिः कर्णवेधश्च दीक्षा ।

मौञ्जीबन्धो गणानां परिणयनविधिर्वास्तुदेवप्रतिष्ठा

वर्ज्याः सद्भिः प्रयत्नात् त्रिदशपतिगुरौ सिंहराशिस्थिते च ॥ इति ।

तथा—चरः सर्व्वे विवर्ज्यः स्यात् स्थिरराशिषु सौख्यदा ।

त्रिषडायगताः पापाः शुभाः[सौम्याः] केन्द्रत्रिकोणगाः ।

दीक्षायान्तु शुभाः प्रोक्ता रन्ध्रस्थाः सर्व्वनाशकाः ॥ इति ।

आय एकादशस्थानम् । केन्द्रेत्यनेन प्रथमचतुर्थसप्तमदशमस्थानानि । त्रिकोणेति पञ्चमनवमस्थाने । रन्ध्रम् अष्टमस्थानम् ।

तथा—शिष्यत्रिजन्मदिवसे संक्रान्तौ विषुवेऽयने ।

अन्येषु पुण्ययोगेषु ग्रहणे चन्द्रसूर्य्ययोः ।

शिष्यानुकूले काले वा देहशुद्धिः शुभावहा ॥ इति ।

मन्त्राकपिलपञ्चरात्रेऽपि—एतन्नचलतिथ्यादौ करणे योगवासरे ।

मन्त्रोपदेशो गुरुणा साधनञ्च शुभावहम् ॥ इति ।

क्रियाकाण्डशेखरेऽपि तिथ्यादिसर्व्वमुक्तोक्तम्—

इत्यादिनिपुणं वीक्ष्य दीक्षां कुर्व्वीत देशिकः ।

मौसुसवीं प्रत्ययं न कालादिनियमः स्मृतः ॥ इति ।

रत्नावल्याञ्च—निन्द्यानि तानि सर्व्वाणि प्रशस्तानि विमुक्तये । इति ।

एतच्च वक्ष्यमाणाग्निचक्रमवलोक्य दिनं कर्त्तव्यमिति ।

अपवादोऽपि—शशिदिनकरयोर्ग्रहणे जन्मनि शिष्यस्य मकरसंक्रान्तौ ।

करुणासमये च गुरोः नक्षत्रादीर्थते न दीक्षायाम् ॥ इति ।

तथा—शिष्यजन्मदिवसेषु संक्रमे पग्रहे शशिदिनेशयोरपि ।

पुण्ययोगयुजि वा शुभे नृणां मन्त्रसिद्धिरभिधीयते परा ॥ इति ।

सिद्धान्तशेखरेऽपि—विषुवेऽप्ययनद्वन्द्वे आषाढ्यां[संक्रान्त्यां] दम[मद]नोत्सवे ।

दीक्षा कार्य्या तु कालेषु पवित्रारोपकर्म्मणि ॥ इति ।

कालोत्तरे च—दीक्षायामभिषेके च तथा मन्त्रपरिग्रहे ।

व्रतग्रहणमोक्षे च द्रव्यारम्भणकर्म्मणि ॥

कार्त्तिक्याञ्चैव वैशाख्यां स्वर्भानोरपि दर्शने ।

चन्द्रसूर्य्योपरागे च षड़शीतिमुखेषु च ॥

ग्रहनक्षत्रयोगेषु विषुवेषूत्सवेषु च ।

अयनेषु च सर्व्वेषु योगः सर्व्वार्थसिद्धिदः ॥ इति ।

रुद्रयामलेऽपि—सत्तीर्थेऽर्कविधुग्रासे तं तु दामनपर्व्वणोः ।

मन्त्रदीक्षां प्रकूर्व्वाणो मासर्क्षादीन् न शोधयेत् ॥ इति ।

अगस्त्यसंहितायाञ्च—सूर्य्यग्रहणकाले तु नान्यदन्वेषितं भवेत् ।

सूर्य्यग्रहणकालेन समोऽन्यो नास्ति कश्चन ॥

तत्र यद्यत्कृतं सर्व्वमनन्तफलदं भवेत् ।

न मासतिथिवारादिशोधनं सूर्य्यपर्व्वणि ॥

ददातीष्टं गृहीतं यत् तस्मिन् काले गुरोर्नृषु ।

सिद्धिर्भवति मन्त्रस्य विनायासेन वेगतः ॥

कर्त्तव्यं सर्व्वयत्नेन मन्त्रसिद्धिमभीप्सुभिः ॥ इति ।

तथान्यत्रापि—पुण्यतीर्थे कुरुक्षेत्रे देवीपीठचतुष्टये ।

प्रयागे श्रीगुरौ काश्यां कालाकालं न शोधयेत् ॥ इति ।

तत्त्वसागरसंहितायाम्—

तिथिं विनापि दीक्षायां विशिष्टावसरं शृणु ।

दुर्लभे सद्गुरूणान्तु सकृत्सङ्ग उपस्थिते ॥

तदनुज्ञा यदा लब्धा स दीक्षावसरो महान् ।

ग्रामे वा यदिवाऽरण्ये क्षेत्रे वा दिवसे निशि ।

आगच्छति गुरुर्दैवाद् यदा दीक्षा तदा भवेत् ॥ इति ।

तथा—यदैवेच्छा तदा दीक्षा गुरोराज्ञानुरूपतः ।

न तिथिर्न व्रतं होमो न स्नानं न जपक्रिया ।

दीक्षायाः कारणं किन्तु स्वेच्छावाप्ते तु सद्गुरौ ॥ इति ॥१॥

राक्षसं वास्तुनामानं हत्वाऽधिष्ठाय तत्तनुम् ।
स्थिताखिलपञ्चाशद्देवास्तेभ्यः पूर्व्वं बलिं हरेत् ॥ २

वास्तुयागोत्पत्तिमाह राक्षसमिति । हत्वेति । यदुक्तम्--

कश्यपस्य गृहिणी तु सिंहिका राहुवास्तुतनयावजीजनत् ।
पूर्व्वजो हरिनिकृत्तकन्धरो दैवतैरवरजो निपातितः ॥ इति ।

महाकपिलपञ्चरात्रेऽपि—

पूर्व्वमासीन्महानुग्रः सर्व्वभूतभयङ्करः ।
सदेवैर्निहतो भूमौ स वास्तुपुरुषः स्मृतः ॥
यावद् भूमिः स्थिरा लोके तावद् वास्त्वसुरः स्थितः ।
संहारे तु लयं याति देवैः सर्व्वग्रहादिभिः ॥
विस्तारोऽस्य समन्ताच्च शतकोटिस्तु योजनः ।
संस्थितोऽसौ धरां व्याप्य प्रोत्तानः कृष्णवर्णकः ॥
जानुकूर्परकौ वास्तोर्वह्निवायुप्रकोष्ठगौ ।
पितृपादपुटश्चायमीशमूर्द्धा हृदञ्जलिः ॥
ऊर्द्ध्वकेशः सुपीनश्च वर्त्तुलाक्षोऽसुराकृतिः ॥ इति ।

अन्यथाधोमुखतोक्ता ।

वास्त्वीशनामा ह्यसुरोऽतिकायो देवैः पुरा दत्तवरोऽभिपूज्यः ।
शेते स भूम्यां प्रविसार्य्य पादौ हस्तौ तथाऽधोवदनः सदैव ॥
ईशानेऽस्य शिरो निवेशितमभूद्वास्तोष्पतेर्मारुते
वह्नौ चापि करद्वयं पदयुगं नक्तञ्चराशास्थितम् । इति ।

वास्तुस्वरूपमाहात्म्ये—

अन्धकासुरसंग्रामे पुरा क्रुद्धस्य शूलिनः ।
अपतत् स्वेदपानीयं ललाटाद् भुवि भीषणम् ॥ इत्यादिना ।

सोमशम्भुना तु व्यवस्थोक्ता—

आकुञ्चितकरं वास्तुमुत्तानमसुराकृतिम् ।
स्मरेत् पूजासु कुड्यादिनिवेशे त्वधराननम् ॥
जानुनी कूर्परासक्ते दिशि वातहुताशयोः ।
पैत्र्यां पादपुटौ रौद्र्यां शिरोऽस्य हृदयेऽञ्जलिः ॥ इति ।

स्थिता इति पुनरुत्थानशङ्कया । तदुक्तं महाकपिलपञ्चरात्रे—

बलिमण्डलमेतेषां यथावदभिधीयते ।
पूर्व्वापरायतं सूत्रं विन्यसेदुक्तमानतः ॥ ३

सर्व्वान् देवांस्तु कार्य्येषु पूजयेद् वास्तुसंस्थितान् ।
तेनाऽसौ वर्त्तते नो चेत् उत्तिष्ठेत्त्रासवाञ्छया ॥ इति ।

तेभ्यः पूर्व्वं बलिं हरेदिति ।

तदुक्तम्—ततश्च तेषां ये पूजाविमुखास्तैः कृतानि तु ।
सुकृतानि समादद्युर्दुष्कृतानि च कुर्व्वते ॥
ततस्तेषामर्चनन्तु प्रत्यब्दं कुर्व्वतां सताम् ।
शुभान्येवात्र जायन्ते नैवाऽशुभकथापि च ॥ इति ।

मयेनाप्युक्तम्—गृहादिकरणे यत्र नार्चितो वास्तुदेवतः ।
तत्र शून्यं भवेत् सर्व्वं रक्षोविघ्नादिभिर्हतम् ॥
तस्माद्वास्त्वर्चनं कार्य्यं सम्यक् सम्पदमीप्सुभिः ॥ इति ।

तथा च—शुभकर्म्मणि दीक्षायां मण्डपकरणे गृहादिविधिषु तथा ।
विहितो वास्तुबलिः स्याद्रक्षोविघ्नोपशान्तिसम्पत्करः ॥ इति ।

महाकपिलपञ्चरात्रेऽपि—भूमेः परिग्रहे पूर्व्वं शिलानां स्थापने तथा ।
जलाधारगृहार्थञ्च यजेद्वास्तुं विशेषतः ॥
अपरेष्वपि कार्य्येषु यागहोमादिकेषु च ।
वास्तुमण्डलकं कुर्य्यात् सूत्रयित्वा समं गुरुः ॥
सुसमं सुखदं वास्तु विषमं न सुखावहम् ।
ब्रह्माद्यदितिपर्य्यन्ताः पञ्चाशत् त्रयसंयुताः ॥
सर्व्वेषां किल वास्तूनां नायकाः परिकीर्त्तिताः ।
असंपूज्य [गृह्य] हि तान् सर्व्वान् प्रासादादीन् न कारयेत् ॥
अनिष्पत्तिर्विनाशः स्यादुभयोर्धर्म्मधर्म्मिणोः । इति ॥ २ ॥

यथावत् साकल्येन मण्डलार्थं चतुःषष्टि कोष्ठोत्पादनमाह पूर्व्वेति । विन्यसेदिति । "अस गतिदीप्त्यादानेषु" इत्यस्मो भौवादिकस्य प्रयोगः । उक्तमानतः । उक्तं वास्तुशास्त्रे यन्मानं तेन मानेन इत्यर्थः । क्वचिद्धस्तमानत इति पाठः । महाकपिलपञ्चरात्रे तु विशेषः—

गृहप्रासादकूपानां मण्डपस्य जलस्य च ।
वास्तुमण्डलकं कार्य्यमष्टहस्तन्तु नापरम् ॥ इति ॥ ३ ॥

तन्मध्यं किञ्चिदालम्ब्य मत्स्यौ द्वौ परितो लिखेत् ।
तयोर्मध्ये स्थितं सूत्रं विन्यसेद् दक्षिणोत्तरम् ॥ ४
द्वाभ्यां द्वाभ्यां तथाऽग्राभ्यां कोणेषु मकरान् लिखेत् ।
मत्स्यमध्ये स्थिताग्राणि तत्र सूत्राणि पातयेत् ॥ ५ ।
चतुरस्रं भवेत्तत्र चतुःकोष्ठसमन्वितम् ।
तत् पुनर्विभजेन्मन्त्री चतुःषष्टिपदं यथा ॥ ६ ।

तन्मध्यमिति । तस्य मध्यं किञ्चिदालम्ब्य मध्यात् किञ्चिदधिकं चिह्नमालम्ब्येत्यर्थः । कुत इत्यपेक्षायां सूत्राग्रादिति शेषः । एवं परित उभयतः उत्तरदक्षिणयोः प्राचीसूत्रस्येति शेषः । मत्स्यौ द्वौ चिह्नद्वयं सम्पादयेत् । तत्र प्रकारः । प्राचीसूत्रप्रागग्रे सूत्रादिं निधाय मध्यचिह्नात् सूत्राग्रं भ्रामयेत् । एवमपराग्रादपि । तत एको मत्स्यः । एवमपरत्रापीति द्वितीयो मत्स्यः । तदुक्तं सिद्धान्तशेखरे—सोमसूत्रप्रसिद्ध्यर्थं सूत्राग्रभ्रमणं ततः ।

प्रागग्रे प्रत्यगग्रे च हस्तं दत्त्वा समाचरेत् ॥
उदग्दक्षिणगो मत्स्यो रेखायां जायते क्रमात् ।
शफरस्य मुखे पुच्छे मध्यचिह्ने प्रसारितम् ॥
समन्तात् सोमसूत्रं स्यात् । इति ॥ ४ ॥

द्वाभ्यामिति । तत्र द्वाभ्यां द्वाभ्याम् अग्राभ्यामेकैको मत्स्यः तथा पूर्व्ववत् । तद्यथा । प्राचीसूत्रार्द्धमितेन प्राचीसूत्राग्रस्थितेन सूत्रेण ईशे आग्नेये चार्द्धचन्द्रं कुर्य्यात् । ततस्तेनैव सूत्रेण उत्तरसूत्राग्रस्थितेन ईशे वायव्ये चार्द्धचन्द्रं कुर्य्यात् । एवमीशे मत्स्य उत्पन्नः । तथा पूर्व्ववत् तत्सूत्रेण पश्चिमाग्रस्थितेन वायव्ये नैर्ऋत्ये चार्द्धचन्द्रं कुर्य्यात् एवं वायव्ये मत्स्य उत्पन्नः । तत्सूत्रेण दक्षिणाग्रस्थितेन नैर्ऋत्ये आग्नेये अर्द्धचन्द्रं कुर्य्यात् । तत उभयत्रापि मत्स्यद्वयं जायते । तदुक्तं सिद्धान्तशेखरे—क्षेत्रार्द्धमानसूत्रेण दिक्षु चिह्नं समालिखेत् ।

दिक्षु चिह्नं समाश्रित्य कोणेष्वङ्कान् समालिखेत् ।
क्षेत्रार्द्धमानसूत्रेण प्रतिलोमानुलोमतः ॥ इति ।

एवं मत्स्यचतुष्के जाते तन्मध्यमाग्रं सूत्रचतुष्कं दद्यादित्याह मत्स्येत्यादि ॥ ५ ॥

चतुरस्रमिति वास्तुशरीरस्य चतुरस्रत्वात् । तदुक्तम्—

चतुरस्राकृतिः कश्चिदसुरः सर्व्वनाशकः । इति ।

ईशानाद्रक्षसो यावद् यावदग्नेः प्रभञ्जनः ।
एवं सूत्रद्वयं दद्यात् कर्णसूत्रं समाहितः ॥ ७

महाकपिलपञ्चरात्रेऽपि—देवैः स वास्तुपुरुषः स्थापितश्चतुरस्रकः । इति ।
आचार्या अपि—चतुरस्रसंस्थितिरसौ । इति ।
प्रयोगसारेऽपि—ज्ञेयः स वास्तुपुरुषश्चतुरस्रसंस्थः । इति ।
चतुष्कोष्ठसमन्वितमिति । चतुरस्रमध्ये अधश्च कोणचतुष्के वहिःकोष्ठचतुष्कमपरं गुरुगणेशदुर्गाक्षेत्रेशपूजनार्थमुक्तम् । तदिति । यथाचतुःषष्टिपदं भवेत् तथा तद् विभजेदित्यन्वयः ॥ ६ ॥

ईशानादिति । प्रभञ्जनो वायुस्तद्दैवत्यः कोणस्तच्छब्दवाच्यः तं यावत् । एवं कर्णसूत्रं कर्णसूत्रसंज्ञकं सूत्रद्वयं दद्यात् । शिल्पशास्त्रे कोणसूत्रस्य कर्णसूत्रमिति संज्ञा । समाहित इति काकाक्षिगोलकन्यायेनोभयत्र सम्बध्यते । तत्र समाहितः सावधानो मन्त्री सम्प्रदायेन मन्त्रशास्त्राभिज्ञः पूर्व्वापरायतं सूत्रं विन्यसेदित्यादि सर्वासु क्रियासु कर्त्तृत्वेनान्वेति । अन्ते उपात्तत्वात् । तत्र चतुःषष्टिकोष्ठोत्पादनप्रकारो यथा—चतुर्षु कोष्ठेषु कोणसूत्रचतुष्टयमन्यद्दद्यात् । तन्मध्योत्पन्नमत्स्येषु पूर्व्वापरायते द्वे सूत्रे दक्षिणोत्तरायते च द्वे सूत्रे पातयेत् । एवं षोडशकोष्ठानि सम्पद्यन्ते । ततः चतुर्षु कोणकोष्ठेषु पुनः कर्णसूत्रचतुष्टयं दद्यात् । तदुत्पन्नमत्स्येषु पूर्व्वापरायते द्वे दक्षिणोत्तरायते द्वे च सूत्रे पातयेत् । एवञ्च कृते मध्यकोष्ठद्वये मत्स्या उत्पन्नाः तेषु मत्स्येषु द्वे सूत्रे प्रागपरायते द्वे दक्षिणोत्तरायते च दद्यात् । एवं चतुःषष्टिकोष्ठानि सम्पद्यन्ते । तत्र ग्रन्थान्तरोक्त-कर्णसूत्रद्वयातिरिक्तकर्णसूत्राणि मार्जयेत् । तत्र ईशानशिवोक्तो विशेषः—

पूज्याश्चतुःषष्टिपदेषु विप्रैरेकोत्तराशीतिपदे नृपाद्यैः । इति ।

हयशीर्षपञ्चरात्रे तु—एकाशीतिपदं वास्तु गृहकर्म्मणि शस्यते ।
चतुःषष्टिपदं वास्तु प्रासादेषु प्रशस्यते ॥ इति ।

सोमशम्भावपि—कुर्य्यात् कोष्ठचतुःषष्टि प्रासादे वास्तुमण्डलम् ।
गृहेऽपि वर्त्तयेद् वास्तुं किन्त्वेकाशीतिकोष्ठकैः ॥ इति ।

महाकपिलपञ्चरात्रे—प्रासादार्थं चतुःषष्टिरेकाशीतिर्गृहे तथा । इति ।

तथाऽन्यत्रापि—एकाशीतिपदं कृत्वा वास्तुञ्चैव गृहादिषु ।
चतुःषष्टिपदो वास्तुः प्रासादे ब्रह्मणा स्मृतः ॥ इत्युक्त्वा
मण्डपान् प्रवरान् वक्ष्ये प्रासादस्यानुरूपतः । इत्युक्तम्

ब्रह्माणं पूजयेदादौ मध्ये कोष्ठचतुष्टये।
दिक्चतुष्कोषु पूर्व्वादि यजेदार्य्यमनन्तरम् ॥ ८

तेनाति दैशिकमरुपे इदं वास्तुमण्डलम् ॥ ७ ॥

ब्रह्माणमिति। समाहित इति आदौ मध्ये कोष्ठचतुष्टये ब्रह्माणं पूजयेदिति सम्बन्धः। कोष्ठचतुष्टये एकाकारेण मार्जिते इत्यर्थः। तत्र पद्मं विलिखेत्। तदुक्तं महाकपिलपञ्चरात्रे—

पञ्चविंशत्पदे मध्ये ब्रह्माणञ्चर्चयेत् कजे। इति।

कादिमतेऽपि—सर्व्वमध्ये यजेत् सम्यक् ब्रह्माणं कमलासनम्।
हेमाभञ्च चतुर्वक्त्रं वेदाध्ययनशालिनम् ॥ इति।

आदाविति सरस्वतीसाहित्यमुक्तम्। समाहित इत्यनेनैतदुक्तं भवति। पूर्व्वं पीठमभ्यर्च्य पश्चात् तत्र ब्रह्माणं पूजयेदिति। तत्र मण्डूकादिपरतत्त्वान्तं सम्पूज्य अणिमादि सर्व्वसिद्ध्यन्ता नव पीठशक्तीः सम्पूज्य। ॐ सर्व्वज्ञानक्रियाव्यक्तकमला-सनाय योगपीठाय नमः इति पीठमन्त्रः। ॐ नमो ब्रह्मणे इति मूलमन्त्रः। प्रजापतिः ऋषिः। पंक्तिश्छन्दः। ब्रह्मा देवता। अक्षरैरङ्गानि। अक्षस्रक्स्रुव[क्]-दण्डकमण्डलुधरो ब्रह्मा ध्येयः। अणिमादीनां ध्यानमुक्तं कुलप्रकाशतन्त्रे—

सिन्धुरस्थाऽणिमा पूज्या पीतवर्णा चतुर्भुजा।
वरवज्रधरा दक्षे वामेऽभयनिधानभृत् ॥
महिमां महिषारूढ़ां पूजयेत् कज्जलप्रभाम्।
दण्डाभयधरां वामे दक्षे शक्त्यक्षमालिनीम् ॥
नक्रस्था लघिमा श्यामा पूजनीया चतुर्भुजा।
नागपाशधरा दक्षे तद्वामेऽभयवारिजे ॥
कनकाद्रिनिभा पूज्या कूर्म्मस्था गरिमा तथा।
गदावरधरा दक्षे वामेऽभयनिधानभृत् ॥
पूज्या प्रेतगता नीलविद्युत्पुञ्जनिभेशिता।
वरखड्गधरा दक्षे वामे साभयकर्त्तृका ॥
पूज्या या वशिता धूम्रा मृगस्था सा चतुर्भुजा।
सारविन्दध्वजा दक्षे वामे वरसरोजिनी ॥
छागलस्थाऽतिरक्ताङ्गी स्यात् पूजायां प्रकामता।
शक्त्यक्षमालिनी दक्षे वामे सवरकुण्डिका ॥

विवस्वन्तं ततो मित्रं महीधरमतः परम् ।
कोणार्द्धकोष्ठद्वन्द्वेषु वज्राद्रिपरितः पुनः ॥ ९
सावित्रं सवितारञ्च शक्रमिन्द्रजयं पुनः ।
रुद्रं रुद्रजयं विद्यानापं चाऽप्यापवत्सकम् ॥ १०

पूजनीया वृषारूढ़ा शशितुहिनसन्निभा ।
सत्ति[शक्ति]शूलवरा दक्षे वामे साभयवारिजा ॥
सर्व्वसिद्धिः पद्मरागप्रभा पूज्या चतुर्भुजा ।
साक्षमालारविन्दा च बीजपूरसरोजिनी ॥ इति ।

दिगिति । दिक्चतुष्केषु पूर्व्वादि यजेत् । प्रादक्षिण्येनेति शेषः । कोष्ठचतुष्टये पदमत्राऽप्यन्वेति । एकाकारेण मार्जिते इत्यर्थः । तेन आर्य्यः पूर्व्वदिशि विवस्वान् दक्षिणदिशि मित्रः पश्चिमदिशि महीधरः उत्तरदिशि पूज्यः । तदुक्तमाचार्य्यैः—

प्राग्याम्यवारुणोदग्दिक्कोष्ठचतुःपदेषु समभियजेत् । इति ॥८॥

कोणेति । कोणे ब्रह्मपदस्य कोणभागे अर्द्धे अधऊर्द्धकोष्ठे । कर्णसूत्रेण भेदितत्वात् । यत्र तदर्द्धकोष्ठं तस्य द्वन्द्वानि तेषु वज्रादि आग्नेयादि उपरि कोष्ठे सावित्रं अधः-कोष्ठे सवितारं यजेत् । परित इति चतुर्दिक्षु । तदुक्तम्—

सोमशम्भुना—मध्ये नवपदो ब्रह्मा शेषास्तु पदिकाः स्मृताः ।
षट्पदास्तु मरीच्याद्या दिक्षु पूर्व्वादिषु क्रमात् ।
अष्टौ कोणाधिपास्तत्र कोणार्द्धेष्वष्टसु स्थिताः ॥ इति ।

अत्र यद्यपि उपर्य्यधो वेतिपदं नास्ति तथापि महाकपिलपञ्चरात्रोक्तवास्तु-शरीरावस्थितिनिरूपणेनोपरिक्रमो लभ्यते । तद् यथा—

मस्तके संस्थितो रुद्रः कर्णयोस्तस्य संस्थितौ ।
पर्ज्जन्यश्चादितिश्चैव मुखे चापः सुसंस्थितः ॥
आपवत्सः स्थितः कण्ठे जयन्तश्च दितिः पुनः ।
स्कन्धयोः पञ्चार्गलाद्या महेन्द्राद्या भुजद्वये ॥
वक्षःस्थौ रुद्रसावित्रौ दासस्तु सविता तथा ।
हस्तौ तु हृन्नतौ तस्य ब्रह्मा नाभौ व्यवस्थितः ॥
पृथ्वीधरो मरीचिश्च स्तनयोः कुक्षिगौ पुनः ।
विवस्वान् मित्रनामा च पादयोः पितरः स्थिताः ॥

तत्कर्णसूत्रोभयतः कोष्ठद्वन्द्वेषु देशिकः ।
शर्वं गुहं चार्य्यमणं जृम्भकं पिलपिच्छकम् ॥ ११

पापाद्याश्चैव पूषाद्याः सप्त सप्तोरुजङ्घके ।
इन्द्रो मेढ्रे स्थितस्तस्य जयो वृषणसंस्थितः ॥ इति ।

रुद्र ईशानः । दासी रुद्रजयः । पृथ्वीधरो महीधरः । मरीचिरार्य्यः । पितरः निर्ऋतिः । पापो रोगः । इन्द्रः शक्रः । इति ज्ञेयम् ।

यदुक्तम्—ईशश्चेशानरुद्रोऽसौ तज्जयो रुद्रदासकः ।
मरीचिरार्य्यकः ख्यातः पिता स्याद्राक्षसाधिपः ॥
पापो रोग इति ख्यातः । इति ।

अन्यत्रापि—धातृवह्नी समाश्रित्य कृत्वा चाधः पदत्रयम् ।
सावित्रमर्चयेत्तत्र पदे वासवसंज्ञके ॥
विधिसावित्रयोर्मध्ये सवितारं पदत्र[द्व]ये ।
आश्रित्य पितृधातारौ कृत्वा चाधः पदत्र[द्व]यम् ॥
यजेदिन्द्रं महाभागं पदे लोकसुसंज्ञके ।
तथा चेन्द्रजयः पूज्यो ब्रह्मशक्रसुमध्यगः ॥
आश्रित्य वायुधातारौ कृत्वा चाधः पदत्रयम् ।
तत्र देवं यजेद्रुद्रं पदे भुवनसंज्ञके ॥
तधिश्चवेधसोर्मध्ये तज्जयञ्च पदत्रये ।
ऐशान्यामापकं कामपदत्रयसुसंस्थितम् ॥
तदापवेधसोर्मध्ये यजेद् वत्सं पदत्रये ॥ इति ।

सोमशम्भावपि—सावित्रे रक्तपुष्पाणि वह्न्यधःकोणकोष्ठके ।
तदधःकोष्ठके दद्यात् सवित्रे च कुशोदकम् ॥
हरिद्रौदनमिन्द्राय रक्षोऽधःकोणकोष्ठके ।
इन्द्रजयाय मिष्टान्नमिन्द्राधस्तान्निवेदयेत् ॥
रुद्राय घृतसिद्धान्नं वायुकोणाधरे पदे ।
तदधो रुद्रजयाय मांसमार्द्रं निवेदयेत् ॥
आपोऽथ शिवकोणाधस्तद्वत्साय च तत्तले । इति ।

अग्रे तत्कर्णसूत्रोभयतः इति कर्णसूत्रस्य प्रयोजनत्वादत्र कोणार्धकोष्ठेत्युक्तम् ॥८॥१०॥

तदिति । दिशत्युपदिशति शिष्येभ्यो मन्त्रानिति देशिको मान्त्रिकः ।

चरकीञ्च विदारीञ्च पूतनामर्चयेत् क्रमात् ।
अर्चयेद् दिक्षु पूर्व्वादि सार्द्धाद्यन्तपदेष्विमान् ॥ १२
अष्टावष्टौ विभागेन देवान् देशिकसत्तमः ।
क्रमादीशानपर्जन्यजयन्ताः शक्रभास्करौ ॥ १३
सत्यो वृषान्तरिक्षौ च दिशि प्राच्यामवस्थिताः ।
अग्निः पूषा च वितथो यमश्च गृहरक्षकः ॥ १४
गन्धर्व्वो भृङ्गराजश्च मृगो दक्षिणदिग्गताः ।
निर्ऋति दौवारिकश्च सुग्रीववरुणौ ततः ॥ १५
पुष्पदन्तासुरौ शे[शो]षरोगौ प्रत्यग्दिशि स्थिताः ।
वायुर्नागश्च मुख्यश्च सोमो भल्लाट एव च ।
अर्गलाख्यो दित्यदिती कुवेरस्य दिशि स्थिताः ॥ १६
उक्तानामपि देवानां पदान्यापूर्व्वपञ्चभिः ।
रजोभिस्तेष्वथैतेभ्यः पायसान्नैर्बलिं हरेत् ॥ १७

सर्व्वत्र क्रमादिति वज्राद्यपरितः इति क्रमोऽनुसन्धेयः। सार्द्धाद्यन्तेति। अर्द्धे च ते आद्यन्ते च अर्द्धाद्यन्ते अर्द्धाद्यन्ताभ्यां सह वर्त्तमानानि यानि पदानि तेषु। इदञ्च कर्णसूत्रेणाऽर्द्धीकृतकोणकोष्ठतो लभ्यते ॥११-१६॥

बलिविधानमाह उक्तानामिति। पञ्चभी रजोभिः सर्व्वतोभद्रमण्डले वक्ष्यमाणैः। तत्र कमलानि वक्ष्यमाणप्रकारेणैव पूरयेत्। तत्र मध्यपद्मं श्वेत-मन्यानि रक्तानि। तदुक्तं दिव्यसारस्वते—

मध्ये पदानां नवकं मार्जयित्वा प्रपूरयेत् ।
सितेन रजसा भूयस्तद्दिक्षु च चतसृषु ॥
षट्कं सम्मार्ज्य रजसा रक्तेन परिपूरयेत् ।
शिष्टानि च पदान्यत्र यथास्थानं प्रकल्पयेत् ॥
विचित्राणि ततो मध्ये ब्रह्माणं संप्रपूजयेत् ॥ इति।

पदसीमारेखाः श्वेताः पदानि च विचित्राणि। वासुदेवानां ध्यानं तन्त्रान्तरोक्तं लिख्यते—उक्तानां सर्व्वदेवानां स्वरूपञ्च निगद्यते।

अक्षमालां स्रुचं[वं] दक्षे वामे दण्डकमण्डलुम् ॥

दधानमष्टनयनं यजेन्मध्येऽम्बुजासनम् ।
सर्व्वे चतुर्भुजा देवा वास्तुदेहे व्यवस्थिताः ॥
कृताञ्जलिपुटाः सर्व्वे खड्गखेटकपाणयः ।
ब्रह्माणं संनिरीक्षन्ते तद्वक्त्राभिमुखाश्च ते ॥
स्वस्वस्थाने स्थिताश्चैव साधारणमुदाहृतम् ।
मरीचिः श्वेतवर्णः स्याद् विवस्वान् रक्त[अभ्र]वर्णकः ॥
शातकुम्भसमो[निभो] मित्रः कृष्णवर्णस्तु भूधरः ।
सविता नीलवर्णाभः सावित्रो धूम्रविग्रहः ॥
इन्द्रश्चारुणवर्णाभः शुक्लश्चेन्द्रजयस्तथा ।
रुद्रः प्रबालसदृशः पीतो रुद्रजयस्तथा ॥
आपो गोक्षीरधवल आपवत्सो जपाद्युतिः ।
ईशानः क्षीरधवलः पर्जन्योऽञ्जनसन्निभः ॥
जयन्तोऽञ्जनसङ्काशो महेन्द्रश्चा[:श्या]मलद्युतिः ।
आदित्यो रक्तवर्णः स्यात् सत्यकश्चित्रवर्णकः ॥
वृषो वन्धूकपुष्पाभः कुन्दाभश्चान्तरिक्षकः ।
उद्यद्दिनकराभोऽग्निः पूषा रक्ताब्जसन्निभः ॥
वितथश्चेन्द्रचापाभो विद्युद्वर्णो गृहक्षतः ।
यमश्चाञ्जनसङ्काशो गन्धर्व्वः पद्मरागवत् ॥
भृङ्गराजश्च भृङ्गाभो मृगो जीमूतसन्निभः ।
निर्ऋतिः पावकाभश्च पीतो दौवारिकः स्मृतः ॥
सुग्रीवो नीलकण्ठाभश्चन्द्राभः पुष्पदन्तकः ।
वरुणः स्फटिकाभाङ्गो भृङ्गाभश्चासुरो मतः ॥
शे[शो]षश्चोत्पलसङ्काशः पापयक्ष्मे[रोगश्चेवे]न्द्रनीलवत् ।
वायुः कृष्णाभवर्णः स्यान्नागः शङ्खेन्दुसन्निभः ॥
मुख्यो मौक्तिकसङ्काशो भल्लाटः श्वेतपद्मवत् ।
सोमः स्फटिकसङ्काशोऽर्गलो रक्तोत्पलद्युतिः ॥
दितिः कुन्देन्दुधवला कपिला चादितिः स्मृता ।
चरकी शङ्खसदृशी विदारी पावकद्युतिः ॥
पूतना हिमसङ्काशा मेघाभा पिलपिच्छिका ।
खङ्गञ्च पानपात्रञ्च छुरिकां कर्त्तरीं तथा ॥

दधाना भीमरूपास्ता राक्षस्यः परिकीर्त्तिताः ।
सितो रक्तश्च पीतश्च कृष्णः स्कन्दादिका ग्रहाः ॥
वज्रं शक्तिश्च खड्गञ्च पाशञ्च विकृताननाः ।
दधाना भीषणाः प्रोक्ता ग्रहाः स्कन्दादिकाश्च ते ॥ इति ।

अष्टादशरेखा नाडीत्वेन तत्तद्देवतात्वेन च ज्ञेयाः ।

तदुक्तम्—लक्ष्मी यशोवती कान्ता सुप्रिया सुकला शिवा ।
सुभगा सुमुखी नन्दा नाड्यः प्राचीमुखोद्गताः ॥
धन्या प्राणा विशाला च स्थिरा भद्रा जया निशा ।
विरजा विभवा चैता नाड्यः सौम्यमुखाः स्मृताः ॥ इति ।

पायसान्नैरिति बहुवचनमाद्यर्थम् । तेन वक्ष्यमाणानि लाजादिद्रव्याणि संगृहीतानि । तत्र प्रतिदैवतं बलिद्रव्यभेदा मन्त्राश्चोक्ताः महाकपिलपञ्चरात्रे—

पायसौदनलाजैश्च युक्तं धूपैः प्रसूनकैः ।
अक्षतं तिलसंयुक्तं माषभक्तादिमण्डितम् ।
गृहाणेमं बलिं ब्रह्मन् वास्तुदोषं प्रणाशय ॥
गन्धादिशर्करापूपं पायसोपरि संस्थितम् ।
आर्य्यकाख्य गृहाणेमं सर्व्वदोषं प्रणाशय ॥
चन्दनाद्यर्चितं नाथ कर्पूरागुरुमण्डितम् ।
विवस्वन् वै गृहाणेमं सर्व्वदोषं प्रणाशय ॥
सगुड़ं पायसं नाथ पुष्पादिसुसमन्वितम् ।
गृहाणेमं बलिं हृद्यं मित्र शान्तिं प्रयच्छ मे ॥
माषौदनं समांसञ्च गन्धादिक्षीरसंयुतम् ।
गृहाणेमं महीभृत् त्वं सर्व्वदोषं प्रणाशय ॥

एवमन्तर्बलिं दत्त्वा सर्व्वेषामन्येषां यद्यप्यर्चा आग्नेयादि तथापि ईशानादि बलिं दद्यात् । वचनानुरोधात् । वचनं यथा—

ईशादिदक्षिणावर्त्तो बलिः सामान्यभाषितः ।
सर्व्वेषां खलु वस्तूनां विशेषः पदनिर्णये ॥ इति ।

अन्यत्र पूजापि ईशाद्ये चोक्ता ।

ईशकोणादिषु सुरान् पूजयेच्च विधानतः । इति ।

अन्यत्रापि—ईशानादिचतुष्कोणसंस्थितान् पूजयेद् बुधः । इति ।

तथा—क्षीरं खण्डसमायुक्तं पुष्पादिभिरलङ्कृतम् ।
गृहाणेमं बलिं ब्रह्मन्नाप शान्तिं प्रयच्छ मे ॥
दध्योदं गुड़संमिश्रं गन्धादिवस्तुमण्डितम् ।
गृहाणेमं बलिं वत्स विघ्नमत्र प्रणाशय ॥
पुष्पादिकुशपानीयं कर्पूरागुरुवासितम् ।
सावित्र वै गृहाणेमं शान्तिमत्र प्रयच्छ मे ॥
पिष्टकं सगुडं नाथ रक्तगन्धादिशोभितम् ।
गृहाणेमं बलिं सूर्य्य विघ्नमत्र प्रणाशय ॥
शीतमन्नं तथा पुष्पं कुङ्कुमादिसमन्वितम् ।
गृहाणेमं बलिं ब्रह्मन् शक्रदेव नमोऽस्तु ते ॥
ओदनं घृतसंयुक्तं वस्त्रगन्धादिमण्डितम् ।
गृहाणेमं बलिं ब्रह्मन्निन्द्रजय नमोऽस्तु ते ॥
पक्वापक्वमिदं मांसं वस्त्रपुष्पादिसंयुतम् ।
गृहाणेमं बलिं ब्रह्मन् रुद्रदेव नमाम्यहम् ॥
हृन्मांसं[समांसं] सघृतं पक्वं गन्धपुष्पादिसंयुतम् ।
गृहाणेमं बलिं रुद्रजय स्वस्ति प्रयच्छ मे ॥
रक्तपुष्पं समांसं वै रक्तवस्त्रादिसंयुतम् ।
विदारि वै गृहाणेमं रक्षोविघ्नं विनाशय ॥
पित्तं रक्तास्थिसंयुक्तं रक्तगन्धादिमण्डितम् ।
गृहाणेमं बलिं पापे[पूतने त्वं] रक्षोविघ्नं प्रणाशय ॥
सघृतं माष[मांस]भक्तञ्च वस्त्रगन्धाद्यलङ्कृतम् ।
बलिं गृहाण शर्व्वेमं रक्षोविघ्नं प्रणाशय ॥
मांसं पुष्पादिसंयुक्तं माषभक्तोपशोभितम् ।
गृहाणेमं बलिं स्कन्द रक्षोविघ्नं प्रणाशय ॥
श्वमांसं[सुरसं] पिष्टकैर्युक्तं पक्वमांसोदकान्वितम् ।
अर्य्यमन् वै गृहाणेमं रक्षोविघ्नं प्रणाशय ॥
रक्तमांसोदनं मत्स्यं गन्धधूपसमन्वितम् ।
जृम्भक त्वं गृहाणेमं रक्षोविघ्नं प्रशामय ॥
छागकर्णान्वितं मांसं वस्त्रगन्धादिसंयुतम् ।
पिलिपिच्छ गृहाणेमं रक्षोविघ्नं प्रणाशय ॥

घृतेन साधितं मांसं वस्त्रगन्धादिसंयुतम् ।
चरकि वै गृहाणेमं रक्षोविघ्नं प्रणाशय ॥
सघृतं चाक्षतांश्च वस्त्रगन्धाद्यलङ्कृतम् ।
गृहाणेमं बलिञ्चोग्र वास्तुदोषापहारकम् ॥
उत्पलं पायसैर्युक्तं वस्त्रादिकसमन्वितम् ।
गृहाणेमं बलिं हृद्यं देव[मिघ]राज नमोऽस्तु ते ॥
पञ्चहस्तं सुपीतञ्च ध्वजं भक्तादिमण्डितम् ।
गृहाणेमं बलिं हृद्यं जिष्णुसुत नमोऽस्तु ते ॥
ओदनं घृतसम्पूर्णं पञ्चरत्नादिमण्डितम् ।
गृहाणेमं बलिं हृद्यं[देव] देवराज नमोऽस्तु ते ॥
रक्तपुष्पयुतं भक्तं रक्तगन्धादिभिर्युतम् ।
गृहाणेमं बलिं हृद्यं भास्कर त्वं नमोऽस्तु ते ॥
वितानं धूम्रवर्णाभं गन्धादिकसुशोभितम् ।
वस्त्रयुक्तं[रक्तपुष्पं] गृहाणेमं बलिं सत्य नमोऽस्तु ते ॥
इदन्तु मांसभक्तं वै वस्त्रगन्धादिपूजितम् ।
गृहाणेमं वृष बलिं वास्तुदोषं प्रणाशय ॥
इदन्तु शाद्वलं मांसं नैवेद्यादिसुसंयुतम् ।
गृहाणेमं बलिं हृद्यं व्योम शान्तिं प्रयच्छ मे ॥
सुवर्णं पिष्टकञ्चाथ वस्त्रगन्धादिभिर्युतम् ।
घृतान्वितं गृहाणेमं सप्तजिह्व नमोऽस्तु ते ॥
क्षीरं लाजसमायुक्तं रक्तपुष्पादिमण्डितम् ।
गृहाणेमं बलिं हृद्यं पूषदेव नमोऽस्तु ते ॥
दधिगन्धादिभिर्युक्तं पीतपुष्पसमन्वितम् ।
बलिं वितथ गृह्णेमं विघ्नमत्र प्रणाशय ॥
भक्तं मधुप्लुतं चैवं रक्तवस्त्रादिमण्डितम् ।
गृहाणेमं बलिं हृद्यं यमदेव नमोऽस्तु ते ॥
पक्वमांसौदनं नवनीतं वस्त्रादिमण्डितम् ।
प्रीतिकरं गृहाणेमं गृहरक्ष नमोऽस्तु ते ॥
नानागन्धसमायुक्तं रक्तपुष्पादिभिर्युतम् ।
बलिं गृहाण गन्धर्व्व सर्व्वदोषं प्रणाशय ॥

इमान्तु शाकुनीं जिह्वां माषभक्तोपरिस्थिताम्।
गृहाणेमं बलिं शङ्कराज शान्तिं प्रयच्छ मे॥
यवं घृततिलोपेतं गन्धपुष्पादिसंयुतम्।
गृहाणेमं बलिं हृद्यं मृगदेव नमोऽस्तु ते॥
शर्करासंयुतं खण्डं वस्त्रगन्धादिमण्डितम्।
प्रीतो बलिं गृहाणेमं रक्षोराज नमोऽस्तु ते॥
चन्दनागुरुकाष्ठञ्च गन्धपुष्पादिभिर्युतम्।
गृहाणेमं बलिं हृद्यं दौवारिक नमोऽस्तु ते॥
इदन्तु पायसं नाथ गन्धपुष्पादिमण्डितम्।
सुग्रीव वै गृहाणेमं बलिं शान्तिं प्रयच्छ मे॥
यवा[शाणि]न्नानि च गोदुग्धं भक्तोपरि सुरोपितम्।
गृहाणेमं बलिं हृद्यं जलराज नमोऽस्तु ते॥
माषभ[यु]क्तं कुशस्तम्बं घृतगन्धादिसंयुतम्।
पुष्पदन्त गृहाणेमं सर्व्वदोषं प्रणाशय॥
मधुना साधितं पिष्टं गन्धाद्यैरुपशोभितम्।
बलिं गृहाणासुरेन्द्र सर्व्वदोषं प्रणाशय॥
घृतञ्चाऽन्नसमायुक्तं कर्पूरादिसुवासितम्।
गृहाणेमं बलिं शेष[शोष] सर्व्वशान्तिं प्रयच्छ मे॥
यवजं तण्डुलं नाथ गन्धपुष्पादिशोभितम्।
गृहाणेमं बलिं रोग सर्व्वदोषं प्रणाशय॥
सघृतं मण्डक[मोदक]ञ्चेदमन्नाद्यैरुपशोभितम्।
गृहाणेमं बलिं हृद्यं मृगवाह नमोऽस्तु ते॥
इदञ्च कृशरं चान्नं पुष्पगन्धादिमण्डितम्।
पातालेश गृहाणेमं विघ्नमल प्रणश्यतु॥
नारिकेलोदकं भक्तं पीतवस्त्रादिसंयुतम्।
गृहाणेमं बलिं मुख्य वास्तुदोषं प्रणाशय॥
पायसं मधुना मिश्रं नानापूजो[पीतपुष्पो]पशोभितम्।
गृहाणेमं बलिं सोम सर्व्वदोषं प्रणाशय॥
ओदनं घृतसंमिश्रं गन्धपुष्पसमन्वितम्।
गृहाणेमं बलिं हृद्यं भल्लाट त्वं नमोऽस्तु ते॥

अयं वास्तुबलिः प्रोक्तः सर्व्वसम्पत्समृद्धिदः ॥ १८

माषान्नञ्च घृताभ्यक्तं पुष्पगन्धादिमण्डितम् ।
गृहाणेमं बलिं हृद्यमर्गलाख्य नमोऽस्तु ते ॥
क्षीरं खण्डसमायुक्तं नानापूजो[पुष्पो]पशोभितम् ।
दैत्यमातर्गृहाणेमं सर्व्वदोषं प्रणाशय ॥
पोलिकां मधुसंयुक्तां गन्धवस्त्रादिसंयुताम् ।
गृहाणेमं बलिं हृद्यं देवमातर्नमोऽस्तु ते ॥
स्वर्गपातालमर्त्येषु ये देवा वास्तुसम्भवाः ।
गृह्णन्त्विमं बलिं हृद्यं तुष्टा यान्तु स्वमन्दिरम् ॥
मातरो भूतवेताला ये चान्ये बलिकाङ्क्षिणः ।
विष्णोः पार्षदा ये च तेऽपि गृह्णन्त्विमं बलिम् ॥
पितृभ्यः क्षेत्रपालेभ्यो बलिं दत्त्वा प्रकामतः ।
अभावादुक्तमार्गस्य कुशपुष्पादिभिर्यजेत् ॥ इति ।

सर्व्वसम्पदित्यनेन दिशां बलिरप्युक्तः । तदुक्तं प्रयोगसारे—

वास्तुशेषे क्रियाभूतः सर्व्वरक्षाविभूतिकृत् ।
भूतप्रीतिप्रदश्चाऽस्मिन् दिशां बलिरुदीर्य्यते ॥
दिक्पालपरिषत्सर्व्वभूतानुद्दिश्य नामभिः ।
पूजा विसर्जनान्तो यः स विज्ञेयो दिशां बलिः ॥
दध्यम्बुरजनीपुष्पलाजशक्तुतिलाक्षता ।
द्रव्येण वितरेद्दिक्षु बलिं दिक्क्रमयोगतः ॥
सुराणां तेजसाञ्चैव प्रेतानां[प्रजानां] रक्षसामपि ।
तथा जलानां प्राणानां नक्षत्राणाञ्च यत् पुनः ॥
विद्यानामधिपानाञ्च तान्यथोक्ता[क्तान्] बलिं हरेत् ।
सवाहनपदं प्रोक्ता परिवाराय शक्तये ॥
तत्पार्षदेभ्यश्च ततः सर्व्वेभ्य इति संयुतम् ।
भूतेभ्यश्च क्रमाद्भूयः प्रादक्षिण्यात् क्षिपेद्बलिम् ॥
द्विषत्पिशाचवेतालरक्षोरक्षाभयार्त्तिहा ।
दिशां बलिर्विशेषेण सर्व्वसम्पत्समृद्धिदः ॥
वास्तौ गेहे प्ररोहे [प्रद्रोहे] भूतद्रोहे गृहप्रवेशे च ।
विततं च शान्तिहोमे दिशां बलिः सिद्धये प्रयोक्तव्यः ॥ इति ।

तत्र यथोपदेशं प्रयोगो लिख्यते। अथ यजमान आचार्य्यं वृणुयात्। तत आचार्य्यो वक्ष्यमाणलक्षणां भूमिं परिगृह्य वक्ष्यमाणमार्गेण तच्छुद्धिं विधाय पञ्चब्रह्मभिः पञ्चगव्यैर्भूमिं सिञ्चेत्। तन्मध्ये कनकशलाकया रत्नेन वा तदभावे रजतफलपुष्पधान्यानामन्यतमेन वा—

शान्ता यशोवती कान्ता विशाला प्राणवाहिनी।
सती च सुमना नन्दा सुभद्रा नवमी मता॥

इति नव रेखाः प्रागपरायताः दक्षिणोपक्रमा उदगपवर्गा विलिख्य—

हिरण्या सुव्रता लक्ष्मीर्विभूतिर्विमला प्रिया।
जया कला विशोका च नवमी संस्मृता बुधैः॥

इति नव रेखा दक्षिणोत्तरायताः पश्चिमोपक्रमाः पूर्व्वसमाप्तिका विलिख्य ततः शुक्लडोरकादिना ताः सम्यक्निर्माय पूर्व्वोक्तप्रकारेण पञ्चरजोभिर्मण्डितं पूर्व्वोक्तकोणकोष्ठचतुष्टयोपेतं विचित्रं मण्डलं रचयेत्। तत्पश्चिमदिशि हस्तमात्रं त्रिमेखलं कुण्डं स्थण्डिलं वा विदध्यात्। ततो बहिःकोणकोष्ठस्थान् गुरुगणेशदुर्गाक्षेत्रपालान् चतुष्पदं नाभिगं ब्रह्माणम् तत्पूर्व्वदिशि चतुष्पदं वामस्तनगमार्य्यकम् इत्यादि अर्द्धपदगामदितिं कर्णगामित्यन्तं पूर्व्वोक्ततत्तत्पद-तदङ्गस्थितान् त्रिपञ्चाशद्देवान् पदार्थानुसमयेन ब्रह्मन् इहागच्छ इह तिष्ठेति सर्व्वानावाह्य प्रणवादिनमोऽन्तेन चतुर्थ्यन्तस्वस्वनाममन्त्रेण पाद्यादिभिरुपचारैः प्रपूजयेत्। ततो मण्डलादीशानकोणे अव्रणमक्षतमूलं बहिर्दध्यक्षतविभूषितं चूताश्वत्थन्यग्रोधोडुम्बरप्लक्षपल्लवसंच्छन्नमुखं वस्त्रयुगान्वितम् अन्तर्निक्षिप्तपञ्चरत्नवि-विधफलं निर्मलजलपूर्णं दृढं कलसम् अक्षतानामुपरि स्थापयेत्। तत इमं मे वरुण इति वरुणगायत्र्या वरुणं कलसे न्यसेत्।

गङ्गाद्याः सरितः सर्व्वाः समुद्राश्च सरांसि च।
आयान्तु यजमानस्य दुरितक्षयकारकाः॥

इत्यनेन तीर्थान्यावाह्य अश्वस्थानगजस्थानवल्मीकनदीसङ्गमह्रदगोकुलरथ्यातः सप्त मृत्तिका आनीय कलसे निक्षिप्य "वं वरुणाय नमः" इति मन्त्रेण तत्र कलसे पञ्चोपचारैः वरुणं पूजयेत्। ततः—

मुरा मांसी वचा कुष्ठं शैलेयं रजनीद्वयम्। शटी चम्पकमुस्तञ्च

इति सर्व्वौषधीश्च प्रक्षिपेत्। ततः कुण्डादिसमीपमेत्य संस्कारादि अग्निमुखान्तं कर्म्म कृत्वा ब्रह्मादित्रिपञ्चाशद्देवेभ्यः अष्टोत्तरसहस्रमष्टोत्तरशतमष्टाविंशतिमष्टौ वा प्रत्येकं यवैर्वा कृष्णतिलैर्वा उदुम्बरतदतिरिक्तक्षीरवृक्षीयपालाशखदिरापामार्ग-

कुशदूर्व्वाणामन्यतमसमिद्भिः वा आहुतीर्जुहुयात्। केचित्तु ब्रह्मण आहुतिशतं अन्येषां दशदशाहुतय इत्याहुः। तत ॐ वास्तोष्पतये नमः अनेन वैदिकैर्वा तल्लिङ्गैः पञ्चमन्त्रैः पञ्च विल्वफलानि विल्वबीजानि वा जुहुयात्। तत उत्तरतन्त्रं समाप्य वौषडन्तेनाऽग्निमन्त्रेण वरुणमन्त्रेण वा पूर्णाहुतिं हुत्वा तन्त्रोक्तद्रव्यैः तत्तन्मन्त्रैश्च त्रिपञ्चाशद्देवताभ्यो बलिं दत्त्वा दिशां बलिञ्च विधाय आचार्य्यः प्रत्यङ्मुखो भूत्वा प्राङ्मुखं साध्यं शान्तिकलसोदकेन—

ॐ सुरास्त्वामभिषिञ्चन्तु ब्रह्मविष्णुमहेश्वराः ।

इत्यादिभिः वशिष्ठसंहितोक्तमन्त्रैः वैदिकैश्च मन्त्रैः मङ्गलाभिषेकं कृत्वा सर्व्वौषधिजलैः स्नापयेत्। तत आचार्य्यः पुनः ब्रह्मादिदेवान् पञ्चोपचारैः सम्पूज्य ततः—

यान्तु देवगणाः सर्व्वे पूजामादाय पार्थिवीम् ।

इष्टकामप्रसिद्ध्यर्थं पुनरागमनाय च ॥

इति पठेत्। ततः शिष्य आचार्य्याय दक्षिणां दद्यात्। तत आचार्य्यो मण्डपस्य पश्चिमभागे स्थण्डिलं कृत्वा तस्मिन् साध्यं संस्थाप्य सुदर्शनेनाऽघोरेण वा तं सकलीकृत्य स्वयमपि तन्मूर्त्तिं भूत्वा रक्तोष्णीषवस्त्रोत्तरीय माल्यचन्दनादिनाऽलङ्कृत्य साध्यस्य दक्षिणे भागे उदङ्मुखः स्थित्वा सौवर्णराजतताम्रादीनामन्यतमं पात्रमादाय तत्र तान् ब्रह्मादिदेवतानिवेदित पिण्डान् यथास्थानं निधाय तत्तद्देवताश्च वास्तुपुरुषेण सार्द्धं तत्रैव संस्थाप्य प्रत्येकं पिण्डेषु घृतदीपं निधाय रक्तपुष्पैरलङ्कृत्य साध्यं सम्प्रोच्य तत्पात्रं कराभ्यामादाय—

भूतानि यानीह वसन्ति तानि बलिं गृहीत्वा विधिवत् प्रयुक्तम् ।

अन्यत्र वासं परिकल्पयन्तु क्षमन्तु तान्यत्र नमोऽस्तु तेभ्यः ॥

इति मन्त्रेण साध्यं नीराज्य अन्यस्मिन् पात्रे आढ़कपरिमितं रक्तोदकं भूतक्रूरञ्च निधाय तत्रापि नव दीपान् निधाय तेन नीराज्य खड्गपाणिः स्वयं खड्गहस्तैरनेकैः परिवृतो दीपिकाशतैश्च परिवृतः पञ्चविधवाद्यघोष स्वस्तिसूक्तसंघुष्ट दिग्भागः चत्वरं महावृक्षमूलं वा तड़ागनदीदेवालयानामन्यतमदेशं गत्वा तत्र स्थण्डिलं गोमयेनोपलिप्य प्राङ्मुखस्तत्तद्देवताः संस्थाप्य पिण्डानपि तत्र तत्र निधाय चतुर्दिक्षु भूतक्रूरेण पूर्व्वोक्तमन्त्रेण बलिदानं कृत्वा रक्तोदकं तत्र निःक्षिप्य प्रदक्षिणं परिक्रम्य प्रक्षालितपाणिपादनयनः पुनः पुनरपश्यन्नेव तत्सर्व्वं परिवारान् अग्रतः प्रस्थाप्य स्वयं ध्याननिष्ठः सन् साध्यं समागत्य तस्य रक्षां कुर्य्यात्। इति मुख्यप्रकारः।

यदाहुः—वास्तूपशमनं कुर्य्यात् समिद्भिर्बलिकर्म्मणा ।

होमस्त्रिमेखले कार्य्यः कुण्डे हस्तप्रमाणके ॥

नक्षत्रराशिवाराणामनुकूले शुभेऽहनि ।

ततो भूमितले शुद्धे तुषाङ्गारविवर्जिते ॥ १९

यवैः कृष्णतिलैस्तद्वत् समिद्भिः क्षीरवृक्षजैः ।
पालाशैः खादिरैर्वाऽपामार्गौडुम्बरसम्भवैः ॥
कुशदूर्वामयैर्वापि मधुसर्पिःसमन्वितैः ।
कार्यस्तु पञ्चभिर्बिल्वैर्बिल्वबीजैरथापि वा ॥
होमान्ते भक्ष्यभोज्यैश्च वास्तुदेशे बलिं हरेत् ।
तत्तद्विशेषनैवेद्यमिदं दद्यात् क्रमेण तु ॥ इत्यादिना ।

अन्यथाऽस्य प्रत्यब्दं कालविशेषे कर्त्तव्यतोक्ता । यदाहुः—

एवं सिंहगते भानौ पूर्णायां प्रतिवत्सरम् ।
स्वगेहे वास्तुपूजाया मण्डले सहुतक्रमात् ॥
एवं विदधतो गेहे नाऽकल्याणं कदाचन ॥
अकाल[आबाल]मरणं व्याधिभूतप्रेतादिकानि च ।
न सर्पपीड़ा नान्योन्यकलहान्यशुभानि च ॥
पुत्रपौत्रधनारोग्यपशुदासीसमृद्धिभाक् ।
अरोगी विजयी ख्यातश्चिरं जीवति तद्गृहे ॥
राजवेश्मसु सर्व्वत्र तथा च महिषीगृहे ।
सचिवामात्य सेनानीभवनेषु पुरे तथा ॥
विदध्यात् प्रतिवर्षन्तु प्रोक्तसिद्धैत्र तु देशिकः ।
न चेदुक्तान्यथारूपफलैः क्लेशोऽनिशं भवेत् ॥ इति ॥ १७ ॥ १८ ॥

मण्डपमाह नक्षत्रेति । ज्योतिःशास्त्रसमुक्तप्रकारेण नक्षत्रराशिवाराणां मध्ये साध्यानुकूलनक्षत्रे साध्यानुकूलराशौ अनुकूलवारे शुभेऽहनि ज्योतिःशास्त्रसमुक्तशुभतिथौ ततो मण्डपं रचयेदिति सम्बन्धः । तथा च राजमार्त्तण्डे—

आदित्यद्वयरोहिणीमृगशिरोहस्ताधनिष्ठोत्तरा-
पुष्याविष्णुमघानुराधपवनैः शुद्धैः सुताराान्वितैः ।
सौम्यानां दिवसेषु पापरहिते योगे विरिक्ते तिथौ
विष्टित्यक्तदिने वदन्ति मुनयो वेश्मादिकार्यं शुभम् ॥ इति ।

भूमितले शुद्धे इति । तत्र भूमिपरीक्षोक्ता महाकपिलपञ्चरात्रे—

तत्र भूमिं परीक्षेत वास्तुज्ञानविशारदः ।
स्फुटिता च सशल्या च वल्मिका रोहिणी तथा ॥
दूरतः परिवर्ज्या भूः कर्त्तुरायुर्धनापहा ।
स्फुटिता मरणं कुर्य्यादूषरा धननाशिनी ॥
सशल्या क्लेशदा नित्यं विषमा शत्रुतो भयम् ।
ईशकोणप्लवा सा च कर्त्तुः श्रीदा सुनिश्चितम् ॥
पूर्व्वप्लवा वृद्धिकरी वरदा[बलदा] तूत्तरप्लवा ।
विद्वेषं मरणं व्याधिं कुर्य्याद् वह्निप्लवा मही ॥
या दक्षिणप्लवा [धर्म्मराजप्लवा] भूमिर्नित्यं मृत्युभयप्रदा ।
गृहक्षयकरी सा च भूमिर्या नैर्ऋतप्लवा ॥
धनहानिकरी पृथ्वी कीर्त्तिता वरुणप्लवा ।
वातप्लवा तथा भूमिर्नित्यमुद्वेगकारिणी ॥
श्वेता तु ब्राह्मणी पृथ्वी रक्ता वै क्षत्रिया स्मृता ।
वैश्या पीता च विज्ञेया कृष्णा शूद्रा प्रकीर्त्तिता ॥
ब्राह्मणी घृतगन्धा स्यात् क्षत्रिया रक्त[रस]गन्धकृत् ।
क्षीरगन्धा भवेद् वैश्या शूद्रा विड्गन्धिनी क्षितिः ॥
मधुरा ब्राह्मणी भूमिः कषाया क्षत्रिया स्मृता ।
वैश्या तिक्ताऽथ विज्ञेया शूद्रा स्यात् कटुका मही ॥
ब्राह्मणी भूः कुशोपेता क्षत्रिया स्यात्कुराकुला ।
कुशकाशाकुला वैश्या शूद्रा सर्व्वतृणाकुला ॥
सिता पीता तथा रक्ता कृष्णवर्णसमन्विता ।
स्थिरोदका दृढ़ा स्निग्धा भूमिः सर्व्वसुखावहा ॥
शीतस्पर्शोष्णकाले च वह्निस्पर्शा हिमागमे ।
वर्षासु चोभयस्पर्शा सा शुभा परिकीर्त्तिता ॥ इति ।

हयशीर्षपञ्चरात्रेपि—सुरभीणां रतिर्यत्र सवत्सानां वृषैः सह ।
सुन्दरीणां रतिर्यत्र पुरुषैः सह सत्तम ॥
काश्मीरचन्दनामोद कर्पूरागुरुगन्धिनी ।
कमलोत्पलगन्धा च जातिचम्पकगन्धिनी ॥
पाटलामल्लिकागन्धा नागकेशरगन्धिनी ।
दधिक्षीराज्यगन्धा च मदिरासवगन्धिनी ॥

सुगन्धिर्व्रीहिगन्धा च शुभगन्धयुता च या।
सर्व्वेषामेव वर्णानां भूमिः साधारणी मता॥ इति।

तथा—ज्ञात्वा भूमिं परीक्षेत पूर्व्वोदक्प्लवनां शुभाम्।
असङ्कटां तथाऽऽकृत्वां तृणैस्तोयपरिप्लुताम्॥
संपूर्य्यमाणे खाते तु तथाऽधिकमृदां शुभाम्।
कुसुमप्रकरस्तद्वत् यस्यामम्लानिमृच्छति॥
न निर्व्वाति तथा दीपस्तोयं शीघ्रं न जीर्य्यति।
श्वेतारुणा पीतकृष्णा विप्रादीनां प्रशस्यते॥
आज्यासृग्गन्धमद्यानां तुल्यगन्धा तु या भवेत्।
मधुरा च कषाया च अम्ला च कटुका च या॥
कुशैः शरैस्तथा काशैर्दूर्व्वाभिर्या च संभृता। इति।

प्रयोगसारेऽपि—वितस्तिमात्रविस्तारं निर्माय विवरं भुवि।
निःक्षिपेत् तां मृदं तस्मिन् तासु शिष्टासु शोभनम्॥
समासु मध्यमं विद्यान्न्यूनास्वधममुच्यते।
परीक्ष्यैवं प्रयत्नेन त्यक्त्वा भूमिं कनीयसीम्॥
अङ्गारतुषकेशास्थिहीनं कृत्वाऽथ भूतलम्। इत्यादिना।

तुषेति। तुषा धान्यत्वचः अङ्गारो निर्वापितमुल्मुकम्। आदिशब्दात् अस्थि-केशपाषाणभस्मादिशल्यं तद्वर्जिते। अन्यथा दोषदर्शनात्। यदुक्तम्—

वाशिष्ठाम्—खन्यमाने यदा कुण्डे पाषाणः प्राप्यते भुवि।
तदाऽपमृत्यवे चास्थिकेशाङ्गारैर्धनक्षयः॥
भस्मनाऽग्निभयं प्रोक्तं तुषैः प्रोक्ता दरिद्रता। इति।

तत्र शल्यज्ञानमादियामलोक्ताहिबलचक्राद् ज्ञेयम्। तद्यथा—

अहिचक्रं प्रवक्ष्यामि यथा सर्व्वज्ञभाषितम्।
द्रव्यं शल्यं तथा शून्यं येन जानन्ति साधकाः॥
ऊर्द्ध्वं रेखाष्टकं लेख्यं तिर्य्यक् पञ्च तथैव च।
अहिचक्रे भवन्त्येवमष्टाविंशतिकोष्ठकाः॥
तत्र पौष्णाश्विनीयाम्य कृत्तिकामघभाग्यभम्।
उत्तराफाल्गुनी लेख्या पङ्क्तौ तत्सप्तकं ध्रुवम्॥
अहिर्बुध्नोऽजपादश्च शतभं ब्राह्मसर्पभम्।
पुष्यं हस्तं समालेख्यं द्वितीयां पङ्क्तिमास्थितम्॥

अभिजिद्विष्णू धनिष्ठा सौम्यं रौद्रं पुनर्व्वसुम् ।
चित्रभञ्च तृतीयायां पङ्क्त्यां धिष्ण्यस्य सप्तकम् ॥
विश्वर्चं तोयभं मूलं ज्येष्ठा मैत्रविशाखभौ ।
स्वाती पङ्क्त्यां चतुर्थ्यान्तु कृत्वा चक्रं विलोकयेत् ॥

रेवत्यश्विनी भरणी कृत्तिका मघापूर्व्वोत्तराः प्रथमपङ्क्तौ । उत्तरभाद्रपदा पूर्व्वभाद्रपदा शतभिषा रोहिणी अश्लेषा पुष्या हस्ता द्वितीयपङ्क्तौ । अभिजित्-श्रवणाधनिष्ठामृगशिरआर्द्रापुनर्व्वसुचित्राः तृतीयपङ्क्तौ । तत उत्तराषाढ़ापूर्व्वाषाढ़ामूलज्येष्ठानुराधाविशाखास्वात्यः चतुर्थपङ्क्तौ ।

एवं प्रजायते चक्रे प्रस्तारः पन्नगाकृतिः ।
द्वारशाखा मघा याम्या द्वारस्था कृत्तिका मता ॥
अश्वीशपूर्व्वाषाढ़ादि त्रिकपञ्चचतुष्टयम् ।
रेवतीपूर्व्वभाद्रेन्दोर्भानि शेषाणि भास्वतः ॥
उदयादिगता नाड्यो भघ्नाः षष्ट्याप्तशेषके ।
दिनेन्दुभुक्तायुक्तोऽसौ भवेत् तत्कालचन्द्रमाः ॥
चन्द्रवत् साधयेत् सूर्य्यं ऋक्षस्थं चेष्टकालिकम् ।
पश्चाद् विलोकयेत् तौ च स्वऋक्षेऽथाऽन्यभे स्थितौ ॥
चन्द्रऋक्षे यदाऽर्केन्दू तदा स्यान्निश्चितो निधिः ।
भानुऋक्षे स्थितौ तौ चेत् तदा शल्यं न चाऽन्यथा ॥
स्वस्वभे द्वितीयं ज्ञेयं नास्ति किञ्चिद् विपर्य्यये ।
भुक्तराश्यंशमानेन भूमानं काम्बिकैः करैः ॥ इति ।

तथाच—चन्द्रस्थाने निधिर्ज्ञेयः सूर्य्यस्थाने तु शल्यकम् । इति ।

इदं चक्रं गुरुमुखाद् ज्ञात्वा शल्योद्धारं कुर्य्यादिति । इदञ्च निवर्त्तनपरिमितभूमौ एकमेव कुर्य्यात् । निवर्त्तनस्वरूपञ्च—

दण्डस्तु दशहस्तः स्यात् त्रिंशद्दण्डैर्निवर्त्तनम् । इति ।

तन्मध्ये वारद्वयं अन्यचक्रं लेखनीयम् । तत ऊर्द्ध्वं नेति सम्प्रदायविदः । अथवा महाकपिलपञ्चरात्रोक्त प्रकारेण शल्योद्धारः कर्त्तव्यः । तद्यथा—

प्रासादारम्भकाले च गृहादौ च विशेषतः ।
शल्योद्धारस्तु कर्त्तव्यो यदीच्छेच्छुभमात्मनः ॥
प्रासादारम्भकाले च यदङ्गं स्पृशते पुमान् ।
वास्तुदेहे दृढं तत्र शल्यं विद्याद्विचक्षणः ॥

कण्डूयति शिर: पुंसि शिर:शल्यं समुद्धरेत्।
शल्यं तत्राऽस्थि[स्ति] विज्ञेयं खन्यमाने करत्रये॥
अग्निदाहश्च रोग[ध]श्च धनहानिश्च जायते।
यत्नेनोत्पाटयेच्छल्यं यदीच्छेद्वृद्धमात्मन:॥
बाहू कण्डूयमाने तु निर्दिशेल्लोहशृङ्खलम्।
हस्तद्वयेन सन्तिष्ठेल्लक्षणं कथितं तव॥
स्वामिनो मरणं विद्याद् विदेशे गमनं तथा।
यत्नेनोत्पाटयेच्छल्यं यदीच्छेत् सिद्धिमात्मन:॥
ऊरू कण्डूयमाने तु कांस्यशल्यं विनिर्दिशेत्।
हस्तेनैकेन सन्तिष्ठेल्लक्षणं कथितं तव॥
असती च भवेद् भार्य्या यशोहानिश्च जायते।
यत्नेनोत्पाटयेच्छल्यं यदीच्छेच्छुभमात्मन:॥
हस्तौ कण्डूयमाने तु कङ्कालञ्च विनिर्दिशेत्।
त्रिहस्तेन च सन्तिष्ठेत् खन्यमाने न चान्यथा॥
अग्निदाहश्च रोगश्च सशल्यं मरणं भवेत्।
यत्नेनोत्पाटयेच्छल्यं यदीच्छेद्वृद्धमात्मन:॥
पृष्ठं कण्डूयमाने तु वाडुशल्यं विनिर्दिशेत्।
हस्तेनैकेन सन्तिष्ठेन्नात्र कार्य्या विचारणा॥
स्वामिनाशो भवेत्तत्र भार्य्या वा जायतेऽसती।
पादौ कण्डूयमाने तु हस्तशल्यं विनिर्दिशेत्॥
सार्द्धहस्तेन सन्तिष्ठेल्लक्षणं गदितं तव।
गोनाशो राजदण्डश्च शस्यहानिश्च जायते॥
यद्नेनोत्पाटयेच्छल्यं यदीच्छेत् सिद्धिमात्मन:।
कुक्षिं कण्डूयमाने तु पाषाणं तत्र निर्दिशेत्॥
हस्तद्वितयमानेन लक्षणं गदितं तव।
भुजङ्गदंशस्तत्र स्यात्तस्माच्छल्यं समुद्धरेत्॥
जानू कण्डूयमाने तु भस्म तत्र विनिर्दिशेत्।
हस्तद्वयेन सन्तिष्ठेल्लक्षणं गदितं तव॥
अग्निदाहो मनस्तापः क्लेशदुःखभयानि च।
करोत्येवंविधं कर्म्म तस्मात् तं वै समुद्धरेत्॥

पुण्याहं वाचयित्वा तु मण्डपं रचयेच्छुभम् ।
पञ्चभिः सप्तभिर्हस्तै र्नवभिर्वा मितान्तरम् ॥ २०

गोशृङ्गं पीतमण्डूकः शङ्कः शुक्तिश्च कच्छपः ।
शम्बुकश्च प्रशस्ताः स्युर्याश्चान्या रत्नजातयः ॥
अङ्गारं वै तुषं केशमस्थिशल्यं विचारयेत् ।
खन्यमाने जलं यावच्छल्यदोषो विनश्यति ॥
दूरनीचस्थितं वारि खनितुं नैव शक्यते ।
पञ्चहस्तं प्रखातव्यं शल्यदोषोपशान्तये ॥
शल्योद्धारं ततः कृत्वा पूरयेत् सुसमं यथा ॥ इति ।

हयशीर्षपञ्चरात्रेऽपि—प्रासादे दोषदं शल्यं भवेद् यावज्जलान्तकम् ।
तस्मात् प्रासादिकी भूमिः शोध्या यावज्जलान्तिका ।
शिलान्तं कर्करान्तं वा यावद् वा शुद्धतां व्रजेत् ॥ इति ॥१८॥

पुण्याहं वाचयित्वेति । पुण्याहवाचनं बह्वृचानां प्रसिद्धतरम् । अथवा अस्य यजमानस्य पुण्याहं भवन्तो ब्रुवन्तु एवं स्वस्ति भवन्तः एवम् ऋद्धिं भवन्तः" इति त्रिः पुण्याहवाचनम् । तदुक्तं बोधायनेन—
"पुण्याहं वाक्यं स्वस्त्यृद्धिमित्योङ्कारपूर्वं त्रिस्त्रिरेकैकामाशिषं वाचयित्वा" इति ।

तत्र पूर्व्वादिदिग्ज्ञान-निश्चयपूर्व्वकमेव मण्डपादि कुर्य्यात् । अन्यथा दोषदर्शनात् ।

तदुक्तम्—यदि कुर्य्याद् यथादृष्टं विपन्नो निरयं व्रजेत् ।
भानोर्गत्या दिशो[दिकं] ज्ञात्वा कूर्य्यात् कर्म्माणि देशिकः ॥ इति ।

अन्यत्रापि—वास्तुवैषम्यतो यत्र सम्यङ्न ज्ञायते ककुप् ।
तत्र शङ्कुं प्रतिष्ठाप्य जानीयाच्छुद्धदिक्स्थितिम् ॥ इति ।

तद्विज्ञानोपायस्तत्रैवोक्तः—
तद्गत्या दिक्परिज्ञानं शृणु वक्ष्ये यथाविधि ।
सुसमे भूतले कृत्वा वृत्तं भ्रमणरूपतः ॥
तन्मध्यबिन्दौ शङ्कुन्तु स्थापयेद् द्वादशाङ्गुलम् ।
अग्रच्छायाद्वयवशाद् वृत्ते पूर्व्वापरद्वये ॥
पूर्व्वापराङ्कयोः कृत्वा चिह्ने तमभितस्तथा ।
समान परिभ्रान्त्या कृत्वा वृत्तद्वयं पुनः ॥

तयोः संश्लेषसंजातमध्यदक्षोत्तरस्थिते ।
सन्धिद्वये च प्राक् प्रत्यक् सूत्रं मध्ये तु विन्यसेत् ॥
सूत्रं दक्षोत्तरं तेषामग्रैः प्रागादि कल्पयेत् ॥ इति ।

क्रियासारेऽपि—ज्ञात्वा भूमिं समां तत्र वृत्तं हस्तमितं समम् ।
द्वादशाङ्गुलमानोच्चं शङ्कुं खादिरनिर्मितम् ॥
अलाभे यज्ञवार्क्षं वा तत्र संस्थापयेत् सुधीः ।
तच्छाया संस्पृशेद् यत्र तन्मध्ये मध्यमं स्मृतम् ॥
तिर्य्यक् प्रसारयेत् सूत्रं मध्यं याम्योत्तरे स्मृते ।
कोणाः स्युरन्ये चत्वारश्चतुःसूत्रप्रसारणात् ॥
एवमाशापरिज्ञानं समाख्यातं यथा स्फुटम् ।
ज्ञात्वैवं मण्डपादीनि कुर्य्यात् सम्यग् विचक्षणः ॥ इति ।

तत्र महाकपिलपञ्चरात्रे तु विशेषः—
विषुवे तु गते सूर्य्ये शङ्कुमानं समाचरेत् ।
खादिरं विन्यसेच्छङ्कुं द्वादशाङ्गुलविस्तृतम् ॥
निश्चलीकृत्य हन्तव्यं गृहीत्वा लोहमुद्गरम् ।
अष्टधा च स्वयं हन्यात् प्रशस्तं क्रमतो लघु ॥
हन्यमाने यदा शङ्कौ हस्तात् पतति मुद्गरः ।
तदा ताड़यितुः शोको जायते दुस्तरो महान् ॥
मौञ्जकौशेयकार्पासं प्राणिवालजमेव वा ।
चतुर्यवपरीणाहं सूत्रं शङ्कौ तु वेष्टयेत् ॥
वेष्ट्यमानं यदा सूत्रं शङ्कुं मुञ्चति तत्क्षणम् ।
पुत्रस्य मरणं विद्याच्छिन्ने वै स्वविनाशनम् ॥
तत्रापि नारसिंहेन होमेनाऽशुभनाशनम् ॥ इति ।

मयेनाऽप्युक्तम्—शङ्कुः सारद्रुमैः प्रोक्तस्तस्यायं चित्रवृत्तकम् ।
सम्यक् ज्ञात्वा दिनादौ तु स्थापयेत् समभूतले ॥
शङ्कुद्विगुणमानेन तन्मध्ये वर्त्तुलं लिखेत् ।
पूर्व्वापराह्णयोश्छाया यदा तन्मण्डलान्तगा ॥
तद्बिन्दुद्वयगं सूत्रं पूर्व्वापरदिगिष्यते ।
बिन्दुद्वयान्तरभ्रान्त शफरद्वयपुच्छगम् ॥
दक्षिणोत्तरगं सूत्रमेवं सूत्रद्वयं न्यसेत् ।

तदग्रात्स्वपरान्तानि सूत्राणि च विनिक्षिपेत्।
सूत्राणि स्थपतिः प्राज्ञः प्रागुत्तरमुखानि च॥ इति।

हयशीर्षपञ्चरात्रेऽपि—भूमिं तोयसमां कृत्वा दर्पणोदरसन्निभाम्।
द्वादशाङ्गुलमानेन तत्र वृत्तन्तु भ्रामयेत्॥
मध्ये तु निश्चलं शङ्कुं स्थाप्य छायां निरीक्षयेत्।
वृत्तरेखा तु या बाह्यशङ्कुच्छाया प्रकल्पिता॥
प्रवेशनिर्गमे तस्यां शङ्कुच्छायां निरूपयेत्।
शङ्कुच्छायाग्रचिह्नाभ्यां प्राक्प्रतीच्योः प्रसाधयेत्॥
प्राक्प्रतीचीगते सूर्य्ये उदग्याम्ये तु साधयेत्।
विषुवे विमलव्योम्नि शङ्कुना साधयेद् दिशम्॥
शरद्वसन्तयोरेवमादित्यात् साधयेद् दिशम्।
प्राचीं वा पुष्यवेधेन चित्रास्वात्यन्तरेण वा॥ इति।

अन्यत्रापि—यथैव पूर्व्वापरदिग्विभागविशेषविज्ञान मिहोपदिष्टम्।
समासतस्तं विषयं विविच्य कार्य्याणि कर्म्माणि यथोपदिष्टम्॥ इति।

शास्त्रे तु प्राचीसाधनं यथा—
कृत्तिका श्रवणः पुष्यश्चित्रास्वात्योर्यदन्तरम्।
एतत् प्राच्या दिशो रूपं युगमात्रोदिते पुरे॥ इति।

त्रिकाण्डमण्डनेऽपि—श्रवणस्योदये प्राची कृत्तिकायास्तथोदये।
चित्रास्वात्यन्तरे प्राची न प्राची चन्द्रसूर्य्ययोः॥ इति।

सूक्ष्मपूर्व्वदिगानयनं त्रैराशिकेन कर्त्तव्यम्। तद्यथा। द्वितीयदिवसेऽपि तथैव शङ्कुं संस्थाप्य पूर्व्वापराह्णयो श्चिह्नं कुर्य्यात्। तत्र पूर्व्वापरदिवसद्वयचिह्न-मध्यभुवं तिलादिना विभजेत्। ततस्त्रैराशिककल्पना षष्टिघटिकाभिरेतदन्तरञ्चे लभ्यते पूर्व्वदिनपूर्व्वापरचिह्नयोरन्तरालघटिकाभिस्तदा कियदिति त्रैराशिकम्। तत्र त्रैराशिकसूत्रं यथा—

आद्यन्तयोस्त्रिराशावभिन्नजातौ प्रमाण मिच्छा च।
फलमन्यजाति मध्ये तदन्त्यगुणमादिना विभजेत्॥ इति।

अनेन प्रकारेण या आगता तिलादिप्रमाणिका अन्तरभूस्ताम् उदगयने उत्तरतो दक्षिणायने दक्षिणतः प्रागग्र एवं वर्द्धयेत्। तत्र रेखां कुर्य्यात्। एषा सूक्ष्मा प्राचीति। मण्डपं रचयेदित्यनेनोत्तममध्यमकनीयोभेदेन त्रिविधोऽपि मण्डप उद्दिष्टो भवति। तत्र मण्डपत्रैविध्यं मन्त्रमुक्तावल्यामुक्तम्—

अथ मण्डपनिर्म्माणं ब्रूमहे ब्रह्मणोदितम् ।
श्रेष्ठमध्यमहीनैस्तु मानैस्तच्च त्रिधा मतम् ॥ इति ।

अनेन मानाधिकोऽथवा न्यूनः इत्यादि क्रियासारोक्तदोषपरिहारः सूचितः ।

त्रिविधस्यापि मण्डपस्य प्रमाणमाह पञ्चभिरिति । तत्र यथाश्रुत व्याख्याने तु पञ्चहस्तविस्तारायामवान् पञ्चविंशतिहस्तक्षेत्रफलः कनीयान् मण्डपः । मध्यमस्तु सप्तहस्तविस्तारायामवान् एकोनपञ्चाशद्धस्तक्षेत्रफलः । उत्तमस्तु नवहस्तायामविस्तारवान् एकोत्तराशीतिकरक्षेत्रफलः । तत्रोक्तमण्डपे तावद्विचार्य्यते । ग्रन्थकृदेवाग्रे नवकुण्डीयपक्षमस्मिन्नेव मण्डपे वक्ष्यति । तेषु च कुण्डेषु वक्ष्यमाणप्रकारेण वेद्याः पादान्तरं त्यक्त्वा एका तिस्रः पञ्च वा मेखलाः कार्य्याः । तदुक्तं पिङ्गलामते—

मेखलैकाऽथवा तिस्रो भूतसंख्याऽथवा प्रिये । इति ।

तन्त्रान्तरेऽपि—मेखलाः पञ्च वा तिस्रो वैका वाऽथ सुरेश्वरि । इति ।

सिद्धान्तशेखरेऽपि—सर्व्वेषामेव कुण्डानामेका वा तिस्र एव वा ।
पञ्च वा मेखलास्ताः स्युः । इति ।

प्रतिष्ठासारसंग्रहेऽपि—"मेखलाः पञ्च वा कार्य्याः" इति । तत्र पञ्चमेखलापक्षे कुण्डानामेव न समावेशः । त्रिमेखलापक्षस्तु ग्रन्थकारोक्तः । तत्पक्षे यथाकथञ्चित् कुण्डानामेव समावेशः । होमकर्त्रादीनां प्रचारस्थलमेव नास्ति अतिसङ्कीर्णत्वात् । किञ्च वैश्वदेवार्थं वक्ष्यमाणस्थण्डिलस्य वेद्यां शयीतेति वक्ष्यमाणशयनस्यापि समावेशो नास्ति । कर्म्मान्तरे होमद्रव्याधिक्ये वा कुण्डाधिक्यं तदापि कुण्डसमावेशो नास्ति । मध्यमाधमयोस्तु का कथा । तत्र पञ्चकुण्डीपक्षस्यापि समावेशायोगात् । ग्रन्थकारेण तत्रापि नवकुण्डीपक्ष उपन्यस्तः । स त्वत्यन्तासङ्गत एव स्यात् । तस्मान्न यथाश्रुतव्याख्यानम् । केचित्तु वक्ष्यमाणं वेद्याख्यं मध्यमन्तरशब्दार्थमाहुः । तन्मते पञ्चदशहस्तविस्तारायामः पञ्चविंशत्यधिकद्विशतकरक्षेत्रफलः कनीयान् मण्डपः । मध्यमस्तु एकविंशतिहस्तविस्तारायामः एकचत्वारिंशदधिकचतुःशतकरक्षेत्रफलः । उत्तमस्तु सप्तविंशतिहस्तायामविस्तारः एकोनत्रिंशदधिकसप्तशतकरक्षेत्रफलः । तदपि सतां न सम्मतम् । यतो ग्रन्थान्तरे एतादृशमानस्यानुक्तत्वात् । मन्त्रमुक्तावल्यादौ परमपि मानम्—

चतुर्विंशतिहस्तं वा हस्तविंशतिकं तथा । इति ।

अन्यत्रापि—विंशहस्तप्रमाणेन मण्डपं कूटमेव च । इति ।
विंशतिहस्तं चतुर्विंशतिहस्तमेव चोक्तम् । तेनास्य शारदीयपद्यस्यैवमर्थो

व्याख्येयः। पञ्चभिः सप्तभिरिति समुच्चितम्। तेन द्वादशहस्तायामविस्तारः स चतुश्चत्वारिंशदधिकशतकरचेत्रफलः कनीयान् मण्डपः। ततः पञ्चभिर्नवभिरित्यन्वेति। तेन चतुर्दशहस्तायामविस्तारः चतुरूनद्विशतहस्तचेत्रफलः मध्यमो मण्डपः। ततश्च सप्तभिर्नवभिरित्यन्वेति। तेन षोडशहस्तायामविस्तारः षट्पञ्चाशदधिकद्विशतकरचेत्रफल उत्तमो मण्डपः। इति त्रिविधोऽपि मण्डप उक्तो भवति। तदुक्तं प्रतिष्ठासारसंग्रहे—

स्वल्पो द्वादशहस्तोऽयं द्विद्विवृद्ध्या ततः क्रमात्। इति।

एतेन चतुर्दशहस्तस्य मध्यमतोक्ता षोडशहस्तस्योत्तमता च। सिद्धान्तशेखरेऽपि—

मण्डपोऽर्ककरोऽपिवा। कर्त्तव्यो मण्डपास्त्वन्ये द्विद्विहस्तप्रवृद्धितः॥ इति।

सोमशम्भुनापि— मण्डपोऽर्ककरोऽथवा।

द्विहस्तोत्तरया वृद्ध्या शेषाः स्युर्मण्डपाः शुभाः॥ इति।

महाकपिलपञ्चरात्रेऽपि—हस्तांश्च द्वादशारभ्य क्रमाद् द्वौ द्वौ प्रवर्धय च। इति।

अन्यत्रापि—गृहस्येशानभागे तु मण्डपं कारयेद् बुधः।

द्वादशैरष्टषड्हस्तैः षोडशैर्वा समन्ततः॥ इति।

क्रियासारेऽपि—अथ द्वादशविस्तारः कनिष्ठो मण्डपः स्मृतः। इति।

पञ्चरात्रेऽपि—तथा षोडशभिर्हस्तैर्मण्डपः स्यादिहोत्तमः। इति।

मन्त्रमुक्तावल्यामपि—

उत्तमं मानमित्याहुर्हस्तषोडशकं तथा। इति।

अयञ्च मण्डपश्चतुरस्रः कर्त्तव्यः। यदुक्तं परिशिष्टे कात्यायनेन—"प्रमाणं चतुरस्रमादेशादन्यत्" इति। सिद्धान्तशेखरेपि—"चतुरस्रं चतुर्द्वारम्" इति। समचतुरस्रता तु वास्तुमण्डलप्रोक्तविधानेन विधातव्या।

अत्र विशेषः सिद्धान्तशेखरे—

स्थलादर्काङ्गुलोच्छ्रायं मण्डपस्थलमीरितम्। इति।

महाकपिलपञ्चरात्रे मण्डपं प्रक्रम्योक्तम्—

उच्छ्रायो हस्तमानं स्यात् सुसमं च सुशोभनम्। इति।

अन्यत्रापि—"चमास्त्रं मण्डपमुन्नतम्" इति। नन्वत्र मण्डपत्रये कनीयसैव फलसिद्धेर्मध्यमोत्तमयोरननुष्ठानमेव स्यादिति चेन्न। फलस्य कर्म्मनिष्पत्तेस्तेषां लोकवत् परिमाणतः फलविशेषः स्यात् इति न्यायेन फलतारतम्यकल्पनाददोषः। तथाहि अग्निहोत्रज्योतिष्टोमयोः स्वर्गः फलत्वेन श्रूयते तत्राद्येनैव तत्सिद्धौ द्वितीये महति कोऽपि न प्रवर्त्तेत इत्याशङ्क्य फले तारतम्यकल्पनमाकरे परिहृतम्।

षोडशस्तम्भसंयुक्तं चत्वारस्तेषु मध्यगाः ।

अष्टहस्तसमुच्छ्रायाः संस्थाप्या द्वादशाऽभितः ॥ २१

अर्थाद्वा कल्पनैकदेशत्वात् इत्यनेन कल्पनाया अपि श्रुत्येकदेशत्वेनोक्तेः । किञ्च वार्त्तिककृता स्थानप्रमाणादप्येतत् सिद्ध्यति इत्युक्तम् ।

कर्म्मणामल्पमहतां फलानाञ्च स्वगोचरे ।

विभागस्थानसामान्यादविशेषेऽपि चोदितः ॥ इति ।

एतस्य व्याख्याव्यवस्था कर्म्मणां स्थानसामान्यादुदिता । यथा—

मध्ये स्वसमुदायस्य फलानामपि सा तथा ।

परिमाणस्य सामान्यादनुक्तेऽपि विशेषतः ॥ इति ।

यत्तु केनचित् "दशरविकरायामावल्पौ मतावथ मध्यमौ रविमनुकरायामौ" इति द्वादशहस्तस्योभयरूपत्वमुक्तम् । तदसत् । स्तम्भादिप्रमाणसङ्करापातात् । [यथाश्रुतव्याख्यानमपि एककुण्डपक्षे पञ्चकुण्डीपक्षे यथासम्भवं योजनीयं नतु ग्रन्थकारोक्तनवकुण्डीपक्षे] ॥ २० ॥

मण्डपे स्तम्भनिवेशनप्रकारमाह षोडशेति । चत्वार इति तेषु स्तम्भेषु मध्ये चत्वारो मध्यगा वेदिकोणेषु स्थाप्याः । तदुक्तम् सिद्धान्तशेखरे—

मध्ये स्तम्भचतुष्कं स्यात्तन्मध्ये वेदिका मता । इति ।

अन्यत्रापि—वेदिकोणेषु विन्यस्येत् स्तम्भान् वेदस्वरूपकान् ।

आग्नेयादिक्रमेणैव । इति ।

तेन बहिर्द्वादशस्तम्भस्थापनमपि आग्नेयादिक्रमेणेति ज्ञेयम् । तदुक्तम्—

स्तम्भोच्छ्राये शिलान्यासे सूत्रयोजनकीलके ।

खननावटसंस्कारे प्रारम्भो वह्निगोचरे ॥ इति ।

ते च अष्टहस्तसमुच्छ्रायाः । स्तम्भोच्चत्वं वदता ग्रन्थकृता षोडशहस्तस्यैवोत्तमत्वमुक्तम् । यत् पञ्चरात्रे—

मण्डपार्द्धोच्छ्रितान् वेदसंख्यांश्चूडान्वितांस्तथा । इति ।

अभित इति । मध्यस्तम्भानभित इत्यर्थः । तदुक्तं क्रियासारे—

भूमिं समस्थलीकृत्य परिच्छिद्य च सूत्रतः ।

स्तम्भान् समञ्च संस्थाप्य । इति ।

पञ्चरात्रेऽपि— स्तम्भद्वादशकं पुनः ।

बाह्येऽप्युक्तप्रमाणेन तत्र तत्र विभागतः ॥ इति ॥ २१ ॥

पञ्चहस्तप्रमाणास्ते विच्छिद्रा ऋजवः शुभाः ।
तत्पञ्चमांशं निखनेन् मेदिन्यां तत्त्ववित्तमः ॥ २२
नारिकेलदलैर्वंशैश्छादयेत् तत्समन्ततः ।
द्वारेषु तोरणानि स्युः क्रमात् क्षीरमहीरुहाम् ॥ २३

कीदृशाः षोडशस्तम्भाः । निश्छिद्राः छिद्रवर्जिताः । एतेन दृढत्वमुक्तम् । ऋजवः अवक्राः । क्वचिदपि न स्थूला न कृशा अतएव शुभा इत्यर्थः । एवंविधत्वञ्च तेषां सारवृक्षोद्भवत्वं विना न सम्भाव्यते । सारद्रुमोत्थम् इदमप्यर्थादुक्तम् । यत् पञ्चरात्रे—सारदारुभवान् स्तम्भान् दृढान् कुर्य्यादृजून् समान् । इति । क्रियासारे तु विशेषः—यज्ञीयवृक्षो वेणुर्वा क्रमुकः स्तम्भकर्म्मणि ।

अन्ये विशुद्धवृक्षा वा भवेयुर्नान्यभूरुहाः ॥
गृहशल्यः स्वयं शुष्कः कुटिलश्च पुरातनः ।
असौम्यभूमिजनितः संत्याज्यः स्तम्भकर्म्मणि ॥ इति ।

मध्यमाधमयोर्द्वादशस्तम्भप्रमाणं वैराग्यिकेनानेयं । तत्पञ्चमांशमिति । स्तम्भोच्छ्रायं पञ्चधा विभज्य पञ्चमांशं भुवि निखनेदित्यर्थः ॥ २२ ॥

तत्समन्तत इति । तस्य मण्डपस्य समन्ततः सर्व्वत्र द्वारवर्ज्जंम् वंशैर्नारिकेलदलैश्छादयेत् । नारिकेलदलाभावे कटैर्वेष्टयेत् ।
यद् वास्तुशास्त्रे—कटैः सद्भिस्तु संछाद्या विजयाद्याश्च मण्डपाः । इति ।
हयशीर्षपञ्चरात्रे—मण्डपं मण्डयेदार्द्रशाखाभिस्तु समन्ततः । इति ।
यत्तु क्रियासारे—"भित्तिञ्च परितः कृत्वा" इति तत्तु स्थिरप्रतिमादिमण्डपेष्विति ज्ञेयम् । "नियमोऽयं समाख्यातः स्थिरलिङ्गक्रियासु च" इति तत्रैव वक्ष्यमाणत्वात् ।

तोरणस्थापनमाह द्वारेष्विति । ननु द्वाराणामेवानुक्तत्वात् कथं द्वारेष्वित्युक्तिः । सत्यम् । द्वारेष्वित्यनेनैव द्वाराक्षेपः । तत्प्रमाणं तत्स्थानञ्चोक्तं सत्त्वमुक्तावल्याम्—

दिक्षु द्वाराणि चत्वारि विदध्यात् पञ्चमांशतः । इति ।

क्रियासारेऽपि— दिक्षु द्वाराणि मध्यतः ।
तोरणानि च तेष्वेव द्वारेषु स्थापयेद्बुधः ॥ इति ।

पञ्चरात्रे प्रमाणमुक्तम्—कनीयसि स्याद् द्विकरं चतुरङ्गुलिसम्मितः ।
मध्यमोत्तमयोर्द्वारम् । इति ।

स्वनेदिति निखनेत् पञ्चमांशेनैव ।

यद्वास्तुशास्त्रे—पञ्चमांशं न्यसेद्भूमौ सर्व्वसाधारणो विधिः। इति।
सिद्धान्तशेखरे तोरणस्तम्भमधिकृत्योक्तम्—

पञ्चमांशेन वा खातं सर्व्वेषाञ्च शिवोदितम्। इति।

क्रमादिति। पूर्व्वदक्षिणपश्चिमोत्तरदिक्षु। क्षीरमहीरुहामिति वटोडुम्बराश्वत्थप्लक्षाणाम्। "न्यग्रोधोडुराश्वत्थप्लक्षाः क्षीरमहीरुहाः" इति परिभाषणात्।
तदुक्तं सिद्धान्तशेखरे—न्यग्रोधतोरणं पूर्व्वे याम्ये त्वौडुम्बरं मतम्।

पश्चिमेऽश्वत्थसम्भूतमुत्तरे प्लक्षतोरणम्॥

पूर्व्वे वा प्लक्षसम्भूतं न्यग्रोधश्चोत्तरे मतः॥ इति।

क्रियासारेऽपि—प्लक्षोडुम्बरबोधिद्रुवटाः पूर्व्वादितः क्रमात्।

तोरणानि च चत्वारि। इति।

सोमशम्भुरपि—प्लक्षोडुम्बरकाश्वत्थवटजास्तोरणाः क्रमात्।

पूर्व्वादितो विधातव्या यद्वाद्यन्तविपर्य्ययः।

अलाभादेकमेवैषां सर्व्वाशासु निवेशयेत्॥ इति।

मन्त्रमुक्तावल्यामपि—अथाग्निमीलेति मन्त्रेण विन्यसेत् पूर्व्वतोरणम्।

इषेत्वोर्जेत्वा मन्त्रेण दक्षिणं तोरणं न्यसेत्॥

अग्न आयाहि मन्त्रेण पश्चिमस्य निवेशनम्।

शन्नो देवीति मन्त्रेण दद्यादुत्तरतोरणम्॥ इति।

महाकपिलपञ्चरात्रेऽपि—देवास्तोरणरूपेण संस्थिता यज्ञमण्डपे।

विघ्नविध्वंसनार्थाय रक्षार्थञ्चाध्वरस्य च॥

न्यसेन् न्यग्रोधमैन्द्र्यान्तु याम्याञ्चौडुम्बरं तथा।

वारुण्यां पिप्पलञ्चैव कौवेर्य्यां प्लक्षकं न्यसेत्॥

सुशोभनन्तु पूर्व्वस्यां ऋग्वेदादिसमन्वितम्।

इषे त्वोर्जेत्वा मन्त्रेण सुभद्राख्यन्तु दक्षिणे॥

सुकर्म्माख्यन्तु वारुण्यां सामवेदादिकेन तु।

शन्नो देवीति मन्त्रेण सुहोत्रन्तूत्तरे न्यसेत्॥ इति।

यत्तु केनचित् अश्वत्थोडुम्बरजटिवटैरित्येषां पूर्व्वादिनिवेशनमुक्तं तदसम्बद्धम्। लिखितनानावचनविरोधात्। इदञ्च तोरणस्तम्भनिवेशनं मण्डपाद्वहिर्हस्तमानेनेति ज्ञेयम्। तदुक्तम्—

मण्डपद्वारबाह्ये च वेदिमानेन दिक्क्रमात्।

प्लाक्षमौडुम्बराश्वत्थवटोत्थं तोरणं न्यसेत्॥ इति।

स्तम्भोच्छ्रायः स्मृतस्तेषां सप्तहस्तैः पृथक् पृथक्।

दशाङ्गुलप्रमाणेन तत्परीणाह ईरितः॥ २४

तिर्य्यक्फलकमानं स्यात् स्तम्भानामर्द्धमानतः।

शूलानि कल्पयेन्मध्ये तोरणे हस्तमानतः॥ २५

वास्तुशास्त्रे तु—अश्वत्थोडुम्बरप्लक्षवटशाखाकृतानि तु।

मण्डपस्य प्रतिदिशं द्वाराण्येतानि कारयेत्॥ इति।

द्वारेषु क्रियमाणत्वात् तोरणेषु द्वारनिर्देशः। इदन्तु पश्चिमदक्षिणोत्तरपूर्व्वेषु अपसव्येन वा पश्चिमद्वारादिति ज्ञेयम्। अत्र विशेषः सिद्धान्तशेखरे—

एकमेषामलाभे स्यात्तदभावे शमीद्रुमः।

जम्बूखदिरसाराश्च तालो वा तोरणे स्मृताः॥ इति।

क्रियासारे तु—अवक्राः सत्वचः सार्द्रा दण्डाः स्युस्तोरणे शुभाः। इति॥ २३॥

स्तम्भेति। सप्तहस्तैरिति उत्तममण्डपे यतो ग्रन्थकृत् सर्व्वं मानमुत्तमस्यैवाह। पृथक् पृथगिति मध्यमाधमयोर्भिन्नं भिन्नं मानमित्यर्थः। तेन मध्यमे षड्हस्ताः। अधमे पञ्च हस्ताः। तोरणस्तम्भमधिकृत्य वास्तुशास्त्रे—

पञ्चहस्तप्रमाणास्ते विस्तारेण द्विहस्तकाः।

षडङ्गुलानि वर्द्धन्ते सप्तहस्तास्तथोत्तमाः॥ इति।

अत्र विस्तारेणेति तिर्य्यक्फलकमानम्। मध्यमस्य षड्हस्तता अनुक्ताऽपि न्यायाद् गम्यते। तदुक्तं कात्यायनेन—"औचित्यादर्थात् परिमाणम्" इति। तेषां तोरणस्तम्भानां परीणाहो विशालता स च परिध्यानयनेन ज्ञातव्यः। तत्र स्थूलपरिध्यानयनं भास्कराचार्य्येणोक्तम्—

द्वाविंशतिघ्ने विहृतेऽथ शैलैः स्थूलोऽथवा स्याद् व्यवहारयोग्यः। इति।

व्यासः १० द्वाविंशतिघ्नः २२० शैलैः ७ हृतः ३१ लब्धः एतावान् परिधिर्यस्य काष्ठस्य तस्य दशाङ्गुलो विष्कम्भः॥ २४॥

तिर्य्यगिति। उभयस्तम्भमध्ये देहलीरूपेण उपरि यत् तिर्य्यक्फलकं तस्य मानं स्तम्भानां पञ्चहस्तमितानां तोरणस्तम्भानामर्द्धमानतः। तेन सार्द्धहस्तद्वयं प्रमाणमुक्तम्। स्तम्भानामिति बहुवचनं द्वारबहुत्वात् तोरणस्तम्भानामपि बहुत्वमिति योध्यम्। अनेन कनिष्ठमण्डपे पञ्चहस्ततोरणस्तम्भत्वमपि सूचितम्। इदं तिर्य्यक्फलकमानम् उत्तमस्यैव। अन्ययोः षट्षड्ङ्गुलन्यूनता ज्ञेया। वास्तुशास्त्रे तथोक्तेः। शूलानीति बहुवचनं चतुःसंख्यापरम्। तोरण इत्येकवचनं जातौ। तेन

प्रतितोरणमेकमेकं शूलं कार्य्यम् । तच्च हस्तप्रमाणम् । तत्राङ्गुलत्रयं निवेशः षड्भागः परीणाहः । एतच्च मण्डपत्रये समानम् । तच्च शूलस्वरूपं मध्यकीलः तीक्ष्णाग्रः ऋजुः तमभितो द्वौ तीक्ष्णाग्रौ वक्रौ । मध्यकीलदेशगतवक्रभागाविति । तदुक्तं क्रियासारे—तोरणं घटयित्वैवमूर्द्धे शूलत्रयं न्यसेत् ।

शूलं हस्तायतं तेषाम् । इति ।

पिङ्गलामतेऽपि—शूलेन चिह्निताः कार्य्या द्वारशाखाः स्वमस्तके ।

ऋजु वै मध्यशूलं स्यात् किञ्चिद्वक्रन्तु पक्षयोः ॥

उभयं तत् समाख्यातं अङ्गुलं रोपयेत् तदा । इति ।

यदा तु तोरणे इत्येकवचनं विवक्षितं तदा शूलानीति बहुवचनं कपिञ्जलाधिकरणन्यायेन त्रित्वे पर्य्यवस्यति । हस्तमानत इति त्रयाणां मिलित्वा मानम् । तदुक्तं क्रियासारे—तोरणं घटयित्वैवं मूर्द्ध्नि शूलत्रयं न्यसेत् ।

शूले नवाङ्गुलं दैर्घ्यं तुरीयांशेन विस्तृतिः ।

शेषाणां द्व्यङ्गुला वृद्धिः वेशश्चाऽङ्गुलत्रयान्वितः ॥ इति ।

तेन कनिष्ठे द्व्यङ्गुलप्रवेशः । मन्त्रमुक्तावल्यामपि—

अग्रयोर्मध्यभागे च पट्टिकायां त्रिशूलकान् । इति ।

एतानि तत्काष्ठमयान्येव शैव एव कर्त्तव्यानि इति ज्ञेयम् । वैष्णवे तु विशेषः ।

वास्तुशास्त्रे—मस्तके द्वादशांशेन शङ्खचक्रगदाम्बुजम् ।

प्रागादिक्रमयोगेन न्यसेत् तेषां स्वदारुजम् ॥ इति ।

एषां स्वदारुजत्वोक्तेः शैवे एतत्स्थानीयानां शूलानां न्यायादेव स्वदारुजत्वं प्राप्तम् । तत्र द्वादशांशः तोरणस्तम्भानामेव । पूर्व्ववाक्यशेषे "सप्तहस्तास्तथोत्तमाः" इति तेषामेव प्रकृतत्वात् तेन चतुर्दशद्वादशाङ्गुलानि क्रमेणोत्तमादिषु शाखादीनां मानानि । विस्तारस्तु स्वतुर्य्यांशेनैव । यत्तु केनचित् फलकद्वादशांशेन चतुरङ्गुलादिमानमुक्तम् । तदसत् । तस्याऽप्रकृतत्वात् । शूलमानस्य नवाङ्गुलोक्तेश्च । एषां निवेशनमपि पूर्व्ववज् ज्ञेयम् । ततः प्रतितोरणम् एकैकः कलसः स्थाप्यः प्रतिद्वारपार्श्वे द्वौ द्वौ प्रतिकोणश्चैकैकः । तदुक्तम्—

गन्धपुष्पाम्बरोपेतान् कुम्भांस्तेषु विनिक्षिपेत् ।

ध्रुवं धरां वाक्पतिञ्च विघ्नेशं तेषु पूजयेत् ॥

मण्डपस्य तु कोणस्थकलसेषु क्रमादमी ।

अमृतो दुर्जयश्चैव सिद्धार्थो मङ्गलस्तथा ॥

पूज्या द्वारस्थकुम्भेषु शक्राद्यास्तन्मनूत्तमैः । इति ।

दिक्षु ध्वजान्निबध्नीयाल्लोकपालसमप्रभान्।
वितानदर्भमालाद्यैरलङ्कुर्व्वीत मण्डपम्॥ २६

अन्यत्रापि—मण्डपे कलसौ द्वौ द्वौ द्वारि द्वारि निवेशयेत्।
गालितोदकसम्पूर्णावाम्रपल्लवशोभितौ॥ इति॥ २५॥

दिक्षु ध्वजानिति। ध्वजस्वरूपं प्रतिष्ठासारसंग्रहे—
पीतरक्तादिवर्णाश्च पञ्चहस्ता ध्वजाः स्मृताः।
द्विपञ्चहस्तैर्दण्डैस्ते वंशजैः संयुता मताः॥ इति।

द्विपञ्चहस्तैर्दशहस्तैः। अन्यत्रापि—
पञ्चहस्ता ध्वजाः कार्य्या वैकल्ये तु द्विहस्तकाः।
दण्डश्च दशहस्तः स्यादष्टदिक्षु च तान् न्यसेत्॥ इति।

क्रियासारे तु विशेषः—
ध्वजानां लक्षणं सम्यगुच्यते तु यथातथम्।
मण्डपस्य बहिर्दण्डे र्दशहस्तायतैः सह॥
पूर्व्वाद्यष्टहरित्स्वष्टौ ध्वजान् संस्थापयेत् क्रमात्।
तेषां हस्तद्वयं व्यासो मध्यः स्वकरसम्मितः॥
व्यासार्द्धं शिखरं पुच्छं हस्तत्रितयमानकम्।
मत्स्याभं शिखरं पुच्छशिखरन्तु त्रिकोणकम्॥
तयोर्मध्ये चतुष्कोणं ध्वजानेवं प्रकल्पयेत्।
मातङ्गवस्त्रमहिषं सिंहमत्स्यैणवाजिनः॥
वृषभञ्च यथान्यायं ध्वजमध्ये क्रमाल्लिखेत्।
अथवा दिग्गजानष्टावैरावतपुरःसरान्॥
ध्वजेषु विलिखेद्रक्तधातुभिश्च स[सु]लक्षणम्।
एवं ध्वजानां कथितं लक्षणन्तु शुभावहम्॥ इति।

ध्वजानामावश्यकत्वमुक्तं हयशीर्षपञ्चरात्रे—
अतः परं प्रवक्ष्यामि ध्वजारोपणमुत्तमम्।
यत् कृत्वा पुरुषः सम्यक् समस्तफलमाप्नुयात्॥
यातुधाना गुह्यकाश्च कुष्माण्डाः खेचरास्तथा।
चिन्तयन्त्यसुरश्रेष्ठा ध्वजहीनं सुरालयम्॥
ध्वजेन रहिते ब्रह्मन् मण्डपे तु वृथा भवेत्।

पूजाहोमादिकं सर्व्वं जपाद्यं यत् कृतं बुधैः ॥
रक्षणेन विना यद्वत् देवं नश्यति चेतिवेषः ।
ध्वजं विना देवगृहं तथा नश्येत सर्व्वथा ॥
विष्णुपारिषदाः क्रूराः कुष्माण्डाद्याश्च ये स्मृताः ।
पूजादिकन्तु गृह्णन्ति देवं दृष्ट्वा न रक्षितम् ॥
दृष्ट्वा ध्वजांस्तु देवस्य मण्डपे ज्वलनप्रभान् ।
नश्यन्ति सर्व्वे ते चार्करश्मिक्षिप्तं तमो यथा ॥ इति ।

लोकपालसमप्रभानिति । लोकपालवर्णाश्चतुर्थे वक्ष्यन्ते । पताका निवेशनमप्युक्तम्—

सारसंग्रहे—प्रतिकुण्डं पताकास्तु प्रोक्ताः शास्त्रार्थकोविदैः ।
सप्तहस्ताः पताकाः स्युः सप्तमांशेन विस्तृताः ॥
लोकपालानुवर्णेन नवमी तुहिन[तु हीन]प्रभा । इति ।

सिद्धान्तशेखरेऽपि—पताकाध्वजसंयुक्तम् । इति ।

सोमशम्भुरपि—सप्तहस्ताः पताकाः स्युर्विंशत्यङ्गुलविस्तृताः ।
दशहस्ताः पताकानां दण्डाः पञ्चांशवेष्टिताः ।
पताका आयुधाङ्काश्च पुष्पगन्धसमन्विताः । इति ।

मण्डपालङ्कारमाह वितानेति । वितानश्चन्द्रातपः । दर्भमाला रज्जुग्रथिता दर्भाः । आदिशब्देन दुकूलेन स्तम्भवेष्टनं चूतपल्लवमालाबन्धनमित्यादि ज्ञातव्यम् । तदुक्तं सिद्धान्तशेखरे—चूतपल्लवमालाढ्यं वितानैरुपशोभितम् ।
विचित्रवस्त्रसंछन्नं तुलास्तम्भविभूषितम् ॥
सफलैः कदलीस्तम्भैः क्रमुकैर्नारिकेलजैः ।
फलैर्नानाविधैर्भोज्यैर्दर्पणैश्चामरैरपि ॥
भूषितं मण्डपं कुर्य्याद् रत्नपुष्पसमुज्ज्वलम् । इति ।

हयशीर्षपञ्चरात्रेऽपि—
दर्पणैश्चामरैर्घण्टैः स्तम्भान् वस्त्रैर्विभूषयेत् ।
कलशैर्घटिकाभिश्च साधारैः कर्करैस्तथा ॥ इति ।

मण्डपान्यथाभावे दोष उक्तः क्रियासारे—
अनुक्तसाधनैः क्लृप्तो यदि वा कुटिलाकृतिः ।
मानाधिकोऽथवा न्यूनो मण्डपः कर्त्तृनाशनः ॥
आख्यातसाधनैः क्लृप्तः शोभनः सममानकः ।
मनोज्ञो मण्डपो योऽसौ कर्म्मकर्त्तुः शुभावहः ॥ इति ॥ २६ ॥

तत्त्रिभागमिते क्षेत्रेऽरत्निमात्रसमन्विताम् ।
चतुरस्त्रां ततो वेदीं मण्डलाय प्रकल्पयेत् ॥ २७

वेदिनिर्माणमाह तदिति । तस्य मण्डपमध्यसूत्रस्य यस्त्रिभागः तृतीयभागः तन्मिते क्षेत्रे । अन्यथा क्षेत्रफलस्य तृतीयांशग्रहणे यत्किञ्चिदेव स्यात् ।

तदुक्तम्—ततो मण्डपसूत्रन्तु त्रिगुणं परिकल्पयेत् ।
पूर्व्वादिषु क्रमात् तस्य मध्यभागेन वेदिका ॥ इति ।

फलतश्च नवमभागेन वेदिका भवति । तदुक्तं सिद्धान्तशेखरे—
नवांशं मण्डपं कृत्वा मध्यांशे वेदिका मता । इति ।

अरत्निमात्रसमुन्नतां हस्तमात्रसमुन्नतां चतुरस्त्रां वेदिं मण्डपमध्ये मण्डलाय वक्ष्यमाणसर्व्वतोभद्रमण्डलाय कल्पयेत् । मण्डपकथने तदुक्तम्—

चतुर्द्वारयुक्तं ततस्तस्य मध्ये बुधस्त्रिभागैकभागेन वेदीम् ।
अरत्निप्रमाणोन्नतां दर्पणाभ्रनिभां मनोहारिणीं चापि कुर्य्यात् ॥ इति ।

बहुभिर्ग्रन्थकारैररत्निशब्दो हस्तेऽपि प्रयुक्तः । यथा कादिमते अङ्गुललक्षणमुक्त्वा—
तैश्चतुर्भिर्भवेन्मुष्टि र्वितस्तिस्तैस्त्रिभिर्गुणैः ।
अरत्निस्तद्द्वयेन स्यात्करः तद्द्वयतः शिवे ॥ इति ।

कात्यायनेनापि शुल्वे बहुषु स्थलेषु अरत्निशब्दो हस्ते प्रयुक्तः । अन्त्यमुक्तावल्यामपि अयुतहोमार्थं द्विहस्तकुण्डकथने "दशाङ्गुलाधिकाऽरत्निः" इत्युक्तम् । तत्रैव लक्षहोमे च चतुर्हस्तोक्तौ "चतुर्विंशत्यङ्गुलाधिकाऽरत्निः" इति । तेनात्राऽप्यरत्निशब्दो हस्तमात्रे व्याख्यातः । तदुक्तं वशिष्ठसंहितायाम्—
हस्तोन्नताश्च विस्तीर्णा चतुर्हस्तैः समन्ततः । इति ।

मन्त्रमुक्तावल्यामपि—इष्टकाभिर्मृदा वाऽपि वेदी दर्पणसन्निभा ।
राजहस्तोच्छ्रया कार्य्या विदुषा सिद्धिमिच्छता ॥ इति ।

राजहस्तो मध्यमाङ्गुल्यन्तः । पञ्चरात्रेऽपि—
वेदी मण्डपस्य त्रिभागतः । चतुर्थांशोच्छ्रितिस्तस्याः । इति ।

क्रियासारेऽपि—त्रिभागं मण्डपं कृत्वा मध्यभागस्तु वेदिका ।
हस्तमानं तदुत्सेधं चतुरस्त्रं समं यथा ॥
पक्वाभिर्वाऽप्यपक्वाभिरिष्टकाभिर्दृढं यथा ।
कर्त्तव्या वेदिका श्रेष्ठा तदभावे मृदाऽपि वा ॥
अवक्रपार्श्वा सुस्निग्धा दर्पणोदरसन्निभा । इति ।

प्रागेव दीक्षादिवसात् सप्तभिर्विधिवद्दिनैः ।
सर्व्वमङ्गलसम्पत्त्यै विदध्यादङ्कुरार्पणम् ॥ २८

उत्सेध औच्चत्यम् । सिद्धान्तशेखरे तु विशेषः—

वेदी चतुर्विधा तत्र चतुरस्रा च पद्मिनी ।
श्रीधरी सर्व्वतोभद्रा दीक्षासु स्थापनादिषु ॥
चतुरस्रा चतुष्कोणा वेदी सर्व्वफलप्रदा ।
तड़ागादिप्रतिष्ठायां पद्मिनी पद्मसन्निभा ॥
राज्ञां स्यात् सर्व्वतोभद्रा चतुर्भद्राऽभिषेचने ।
विवाहे श्रीधरी वेदी विंशत्यस्रसमन्विता ।
दर्पणोदरसङ्काशा निम्नोन्नतविवर्जिता ॥ इति ।

वेदिकाया अन्यथाभावे दोष उक्तः क्रियासारे—

वक्रपार्श्वा छिन्नमध्या परुषा हृतशोभना ।
मानहीनाधिका या सा कर्त्तुः कर्म्मविनाशिनी ॥ इति ।

वायवीयसंहितायां तु मण्डपाद्युक्तम्—

कृत्वा पूर्व्वोदितं सर्व्वं विना वा मण्डपादिकम् ।
मण्डलं पूर्व्ववत् कृत्वा स्थण्डिलञ्च विशेषतः ॥ इति ॥ २७ ॥

अङ्कुरार्पणकर्म्माह प्रागेवेति । दीक्षादिवसात् प्राक् सप्तभिर्दिनैरेतेन दीक्षादिनमष्टमं यथा भवति तथा कर्त्तव्यमित्युक्तम् । विधिवदित्यनेन नवभिः पञ्चभिस्त्रिभिः सद्यो वेत्युक्तम् । तदुक्तं सिद्धान्तशेखरे—

प्रतिष्ठायाञ्च दीक्षायां स्था[स्ना]पने चोत्सवे तथा ।
सम्प्रोक्षणे च शान्त्यर्थं विवाहे मौञ्जिबन्धने ॥
सर्व्वमङ्गलकार्य्येषु कारयेदङ्कुरार्पणम् ।
प्रतिष्ठादिवसात् पूर्व्वं नवमे सप्तमे दिने ।
पञ्चमे वा तृतीये वा सद्यो वा चाऽङ्कुरार्पणम् ॥ इति ।

महाकपिलपञ्चरात्रेऽपि—पुण्याहघोषणं कृत्वा ब्राह्मणैः सह देशिकः ।
मङ्गलाङ्कुरयज्ञञ्च कुर्य्यात्तत्रैव चाहनि ॥
सप्तमान्नवमाद्वाऽपि प्रागेव यज्ञकर्म्मणः ॥ इति ।

अन्यत्रापि—उत्सवेषु विविधेष्वपि दीक्षास्थापनादिषु पवित्रविधौ च ।
मङ्गलाङ्कुरविरोपणपूर्व्वं मङ्गलं भवति कर्म्मकृतस्ततः ॥

मण्डपस्योत्तरे भागे शालां पूर्व्वापरायताम्।
गूढ़ां कुर्य्यात् ततस्तस्यां मण्डलं रचयेत् सुधीः॥ २६
पञ्चहस्तप्रमाणानि पञ्च सूत्राणि पातयेत्।
पूर्व्वापरायतान्येषामन्तरं द्वादशाङ्गुलम्॥ ३०
दक्षिणोत्तरसूत्राणि तद्वदेकादशाऽर्पयेत्।
पदानि तत्र जायन्ते चत्वारिंशत् प्रमार्जयेत्॥ ३१

शस्तयोगदिवसात्तु पुरस्तात् सप्तमेऽहनि शुभे नवमे वा।
पञ्चमेऽथ सुदिने सुमुहूर्त्ते मङ्गलाङ्कुरविधिं विदधीत॥ इति।

तत्र पूर्व्वेद्युरुपवासं कृत्वा स्वगृह्योक्तविधिना नान्दीश्राद्धं कृत्वा अङ्कुरार्पणमारभेत्। तदुक्तम्—गुरुर्विशुद्धः प्रागेव शुद्धाहात् सप्तमेऽहनि।

सङ्कल्प्योपोष्य कर्त्तव्यमङ्कुरारोपणं शुभम्॥
कुर्य्यान्नान्दीमुखश्राद्धं पूर्व्वेद्युः स्वस्तिवाचनम्।
स्वगृह्योक्तप्रकारेण तदेतद्विदधीत वै॥ इति।

संहितायामपि—सर्व्वत्राभ्युदयश्राद्धमङ्कुरोत्पादनं तथा।
आदावेव प्रकुर्व्वीत कर्म्मणोऽभ्युदयात्मनः॥ इति॥ २८॥

शालामिति। तत्र—

विंशत्या तु करैर्मानं दशायामेन विस्तृतिः। शालाया उत्तमं मानम्। अत्रैतावत्याः प्रयोजनाभावादेतदर्द्धेन मध्यममानेन शाला कार्य्या। तेन दशहस्तदीर्घा पञ्चहस्तायामा अत्र कर्त्तव्या। तामिवाह पूर्व्वापरायतामिति। दीर्घचतुरस्ररूपां गूढ़ां परितः कटादिपरिवृतां दक्षिणैकद्वारवतीं निवाताञ्च कुर्य्यात्। तदुक्तं प्रयोगसारे—अवागुदक्स्थितां कृत्वा निवातां तां कुटीं दृढ़ाम्। इति। तस्यां वक्ष्यमाणं मण्डलं रचयेत्॥ २८॥

मण्डलमेवाह पञ्चहस्तेति। शालाविस्तारमध्यभागे प्रागपरायतमेकं सूत्रं पञ्चहस्तप्रमाणं दत्त्वा तत्सूत्रस्य दक्षिणोत्तरभागयोः द्वादश द्वादशाङ्गुलान्तरे द्वे द्वे सूत्रे दद्यात्। ततस्तत्पञ्चसूत्रव्यतिभेदीनि एकादशसूत्राणि अर्पयेत्। तद्वदिति द्वादशाङ्गुलान्तराणीत्यर्थः। एवं पञ्चापि हस्ताः संगृहीताः।

तदुक्तं प्रयोगसारे—प्रसार्य्य स्फोटयेत् सूत्रं यथा याम्योत्तरायतम्।
पञ्चहस्तप्रमाणेन द्वे द्वे पार्श्वे च पातयेत्॥

पङ्क्त्यां वीथीश्चतस्रोऽन्तश्चतुष्कोभयपार्श्वयोः ।
वीथ्यौ द्वे च चतुष्कोष्ठत्रयमत्राऽवशिष्यते ॥ ३२
पदानि रञ्जयेत्तानि श्वेतपीतारुणासितैः ।
रजोभिः श्यामलेनाऽथ वीथीरापूरयेत् सुधीः ॥ ३३
पात्राणि विविधान्याहुरङ्कुरार्पणकर्म्मसु ।
पालिकाः पञ्चमुख्यश्च शरावाश्च चतुःक्रमात् ॥ ३४
प्रोक्ताः स्युः सर्व्वतन्त्रज्ञैर्हरिब्रह्मशिवात्मकाः ।
एषामुच्छ्राय उन्नेयः षोड़शद्वादशाष्टभिः ॥ ३५

तद्वत् पूर्व्वोक्तमानेन द्वादशद्वादशाङ्गुले ।
प्राक् प्रत्यक् च समं पश्चात् सूत्राण्येकादश क्रमात् ।
पातयेत् तासु रेखासु पूर्व्वसूत्रान्तरान्तरम् ॥ इति ।

प्रमार्जयेदित्युत्तरत्रान्वेति । पङ्क्त्या चतस्रो वीथीर्मार्जयेत् । बाह्या इत्यर्थः । अन्तरिति वक्ष्यमाणत्वात् । पूर्व्वतश्चतुष्कोष्ठामिकां वीथीम् अष्टकोष्ठां दक्षिणवीथीं पुनश्चतुष्कोष्ठां पश्चिमवीथीम् अष्टकोष्ठामुत्तरवीथीं मार्जयेत् । ततोऽन्तश्चतुष्कस्य मध्यचतुष्कस्य उभयोः पार्श्वयोः पार्श्वद्वये द्वे वीथ्यौ द्विद्विकोष्ठरूपे चात्र मार्जये-दित्यस्यानुषङ्गः । ततः फलितमाहात्रेति । अत्र मण्डले चतुष्कोष्ठत्रयमवशिष्यते इति । तानि शिष्टानि चतुष्कोष्ठत्रयस्थानि पदानि द्वादश । प्रत्येकचतुष्कोष्ठे श्वेतादिभो रजोभी रञ्जयेत् । तत्र श्वेतं वायुपदे । पीतमाग्नेये । अरुणं रक्षःपदे । असितमीशपदे इति सुधीरित्यनेनोक्तम् । तदुक्तमाचार्य्यैः—

पीतारक्तसितासितं प्रतिपदं वज्राादि शर्व्वान्तकम् । इति ।

अथ अनन्तरं श्यामलेन हरितेन वीथीरापूरयेत् ॥ ३०-३३ ॥

अङ्कुरार्पणपात्राण्याह पात्राणीति । स्थूलानि उच्चानि शरावाण्येव पालिका-शब्देनोच्यन्ते । पालिका एव किञ्चिन्नीचाः पञ्चमुखयुक्ताः पञ्चमुख्य उच्यन्ते । शरावाः प्रसिद्धाः । सर्व्वतन्त्रज्ञैरित्यनेन पञ्चदेवतादीक्षादिकर्म्मसु पात्रभेदो नास्तीत्युक्तम् । प्रथमा हरिरूपाः । द्वितीया ब्रह्मरूपाः । तृतीयाः शिवरूपाः । एतेन हरिब्रह्मेशा एषु पात्रेषु पूज्या इत्युक्तं भवति । तदुक्तं सारस्वतमते—

प्रोक्तेषु तेषु पात्रेषु ब्रह्मविष्णुशिवान् यजेत् । इति ।

अङ्गुलैः क्रमशस्तानि शुभान्यावेष्ट्य तन्तुना ।

प्रक्षाल्य देशिकस्तेषु पदेष्वाहितशालिषु ॥ ३६

सगन्धदर्भकूर्च्चेषु पश्चिमादि निवेशयेत् ।

करीषवालुकामृद्भिस्तानि पात्राणि पूरयेत् ॥ ३७

सिद्धान्तशेखरेऽपि—सम्पूजयेच्छरावेषु रुद्रं चन्दनपुष्पकैः ।
पालिकासु तथा विष्णुं ब्रह्माणं घटिकासु च ॥ इति ॥३४॥३५॥

अङ्गुलैः क्रमशः इति पूर्व्वेण सम्बध्यते । महाकपिलपञ्चरात्रे तु विशेषः—

पालिकावक्त्रविस्तारः षोड़शाङ्गुल उच्यते ।
भवेत् कण्ठविलं वा स्यात् तदष्टाङ्गुलविस्तृतम् ॥
पादपीठस्य विस्तारं षड़ङ्गुलमुदाहृतम् ।
चतुरङ्गुल उत्सेधस्तत्स्त्रिशाऽङ्गुलं भवेत् ॥
तत्सन्धेश्च भवेन्नाहं पादपीठार्द्धमेव च ।
भवेत् पञ्चमुखी चैवं घटिका सर्व्वकामदा ॥
चतुरङ्गुलविस्ताराख्याद्दुर्वक्त्राणि पञ्च वै ।
चत्वारि च चतुर्दिक्षु ऊर्द्धमेकं यथाविधि ॥
घटिकायामविस्तारो द्वादशाङ्गुल उच्यते ।
आचार्य्याः कथयन्त्येके षोड़शाङ्गुलमेव वा ॥
द्वादशाङ्गुलविस्तारं शरावस्य मुखं स्मृतम् ।
चतुरङ्गुलविस्तारमधस्तान्मूलमुच्यते ॥ इति ।

अन्यत्रापि—तालमात्रमिह पञ्चमुखी स्याद् व्यासतोच्छ्रयमिता घटिका स्यात् ।
दिक्षु तन्मुखचतुष्टयमेकं मध्यतस्तु समवर्त्तितभागम् ॥
तालविस्तृतमुखन्तु शरावं व्यासतोच्छ्रयगतार्द्धमिताङ्घ्रि ।
दण्डमस्य चतुरङ्गुलनाहं कण्ठमस्य विलवर्जमुदग्रम् ॥
सम्भवे कनकरूप्यताम्रतो मार्त्तिकान्यभिनवान्यथवा स्युः । इति ।

सिद्धान्तशेखरे तु—यथासम्भवमानं वा पालिकादि समाचरेत् । इति ।

तानीति पात्राणि । शुभानीति कृष्णवर्णव्रणादिरहितानि । तन्तुनेति त्रिगुणेन । तत्र पूर्व्वं प्रक्षालनं पश्चात्तन्तुवेष्टनमिति ज्ञेयम् । दर्भकूर्चम् अग्रे वक्ष्यमाणम् । पश्चिमादीति । पश्चिमचतुष्के पालिकाचतुष्टयं मध्यमचतुष्के पञ्चमुखीचतुष्टयं पूर्व्वचतुष्के शरावचतुष्टयं निवेशयेत् । तन्मध्ये आग्नेयादि स्थापनमिति ज्ञेयम् । तदुक्तं

सुधाबीजेन बीजानि दुग्धैः प्रक्षाल्य तत्त्ववित्।
मूलमन्त्राभिजप्तानि पञ्चघोषपुरःसरम्॥ ३८
आशीर्वाग्भिर्द्विजातीनां मङ्गलाचारपूर्व्वकम्।
निर्वपेत्तेषु पात्रेषु देशिको यतमानसः॥ ३९

प्रयोगसारे— तेषु पात्राणि विन्यसेत्।

वह्न्यादीशानपर्य्यन्तं चतुष्कोषु पृथक् पृथक्॥ इति।

करीषेति। करीषं शुष्कगोमयचूर्णम्। एतैरुत्तरोत्तरं सर्व्वाण्येव पात्राणि पूरयेत्। उक्तञ्च हयशीर्षपञ्चरात्रे—पूरयेदुत्तरोत्तरम्। इति।
प्रयोगसारेऽपि—मृद्वालुकाकरीषैश्चोर्द्ध्वतः पात्राणि पूरयेत्। इति।
तत्र विशेषः सिद्धान्तशेखरे—

गन्धादिभिश्च कुद्दालं पूजयित्वा दिनान्तरे।
गीतनृत्यसमायुक्तं गजवाजिसमन्वितम्॥
गुर्व्वादयो रथारूढ़ा गजारूढ़ास्तथा परे।
गत्वा तीरं तड़ागस्य नद्याः पुष्पवनस्य वा॥
तत्र शुद्धं भुवो भागं दर्भैः संमृज्य चास्त्रतः।
अभ्युक्ष्य चार्घ्यतोयेन तत्तन्मन्त्रमनुस्मरन्॥
हृदा भूमिं समावाह्य गन्धपुष्पैः समर्चयेत्।
कुद्दालीमस्त्रमन्त्रेण खात्वा भूमिमथो मृदम्॥
गृहीत्वा वामदेवेन पूरयेत् कांस्यपात्रके।
हृदा मृदश्च संमृज्य वस्त्रेणाच्छाद्य धारयेत्॥
पुरं वा निलयं वापि सर्व्वमङ्गलनिःस्वनैः।
गुरुः प्रदक्षिणं कृत्वा मण्डपं त्वानयेत्ततः॥
एतत्कर्म्म दिवाकाले कुर्य्याद् रात्रौ न बुद्धिमान्। इति॥३६॥३७॥

तेषु बीजावापमाह सुधेति। सुधाबीजेन वमित्यनेन। दुग्धैः गोदुग्धैः प्रक्षाल्येति। महाकपिलपञ्चरात्रे तु विशेषः—

द्वादशाक्षरमन्त्रेण क्षालयित्वा तु वारिणा। इति।

सारस्वतमतेऽपि—बीजानि तानि प्रक्षाल्य जलक्षीरेण च क्रमात्। इति।
एतत् तत्त्ववित् इत्यनेन सूचितम्। मूलेति मूलमन्त्रेण दातव्यमन्त्रेण अभिजप्तानि अष्टोत्तरशतमिति। तदुक्तं महाकपिलपञ्चरात्रे—

शालिश्यामाढ़कीमुद्गतिलनिष्पावसर्षपाः।
कुलत्थकङ्गुमाषाश्च बीजान्यङ्कुरकर्म्मणि॥ ४०
हरिद्राद्भिः समभ्युच्य वस्त्रैराच्छाद्य देशिकः।
बलिविविधपात्राणां दिक्षु पूर्व्वादितो हरेत्॥ ४१

संख्यानुक्तौ शतं साष्टं सहस्रं वा जपादिषु। इति।

पञ्चघोषास्तु पटहढक्कामृदङ्गमुखवाद्यशङ्खाः। मङ्गलाचारेति तत्तद्देशप्रसिद्धा उलूलूध्वन्यादिपूर्व्वकम्। देशिको यतमानस इत्यनेन तानि बीजानि एकीकृत्य रात्रौ मूलमन्त्रेण प्राङ्मुख उदङ्मुखो वा पालिकादिषु निर्वपेदित्युक्तम्। तदुक्तं सिद्धान्तशेखरे—बीजमुख्येन मूलेन प्राङ्मुखो वाप्युदङ्मुखः।
वापयेत् सर्व्वबीजानि पालिकादिष्वनुक्रमात्।
बीजानामधिपः सोमस्तस्माद्रात्रौ तु निर्वपेत्॥ इति।
सारस्वतमतेऽपि—बीजेभ्यो दैवतेभ्यश्च स रात्रौ कान्तिमान् यतः।
तस्माद् गुरुस्तु बीजानि निशायामेव वापयेत्॥ इति॥ ३८॥३९॥

बीजान्याह शालीति। शालयो हैमन्तिकाः। श्यामः श्यामाकः कान्यकुब्जभाषायां सावा इति प्रसिद्धः। आढ़की तूवरी। निष्पावा राजमाषाः। विष्णुपुराणटीकायां श्रीधर्य्यां तथा व्याख्यातत्वात्। "निष्पावान् राजमाषांश्च शुभे दैवे विवर्जयेत्" इति पृथगुक्तेर्न तत्र बाधा। सारस्वतमते प्रत्येकं बीजेषु देवतापूजोक्ता।
स्कन्दं प्रियङ्गौ निष्पावे वायुमग्निं कुलत्थके।
आढ़क्यां निर्ऋतिं सोमं मुद्गे वैवस्वतं तिले॥
प्रजापतिं शालिबीजे[धान्ये] त्वनन्तं सर्षपेऽर्च्चयेत्।
इन्द्रं श्यामे च माषे तु वरुणन्तु नगात्मजे॥ इति।
सिद्धान्तशेखरे तु प्रत्यहं सोमपूजाप्युक्ता।
सोमं सम्पूजयेन्नित्यमधिवासदिनावधि।
अधिवासदिने प्राप्ते सोममुद्वासयेद् गुरुः॥ इति॥ ४०॥

हरिद्रेति। तत्र मन्त्र उक्तः प्रयोगसारे—
त्रियम्बकाय शर्व्वाय शङ्कराय शिवाय च।
सर्व्वलोकप्रधानाय शाश्वताय नमो नमः॥
विकीर्य्याऽनेन मन्त्रेण हरिद्राचूर्णमिश्रितम्।
तोयं प्रवर्षयेत्तेषु सिञ्चेत्तोयैर्दिनं प्रति॥ इति।

प्रणवाद्यैर्नमोऽन्तैश्च रात्रौ रात्रीशनामभिः ।
भूतानि पितरो यक्षा नागा ब्रह्मा शिवो हरिः ॥ ४२

सप्तानामपि रात्रीणां देवताः समुदीरिताः ।
भूतेभ्यः स्युर्लाजतिलहरिद्रादधिसक्तवः ॥ ४३

साज्ञाः पितृभ्यः सतिलास्तण्डुलाः परिकीर्त्तिताः ।
करम्भलाजा यक्षेभ्यो नारिकेलोदकान्विताः ॥ ४४

सक्तुपिष्टञ्च नागेभ्यो ब्रह्मणे पङ्कजाक्षतम् ।
सापूपमन्नं शर्वाय विष्णवे तु गुडौदनम् ॥ ४५

ततो लोकेश्वरेभ्योऽपि वितरेद्दिग्विधवद्बलिम् ।
दीक्षायामभिषेकेषु नववेश्मप्रवेशने ।
उत्सवेषु च सम्पत्त्यै विदध्यादङ्कुरार्पणम् ॥ ४६

इदं देशिक इत्यनेन सूचितम् । वस्त्रैर्नूतनवस्त्रैः बहुवचनं कपिञ्जलाधिकरणन्यायेन त्रित्वे पर्यवस्यति । आच्छाद्येति पात्रचतुष्टयमेकैकेन । रात्रौ बलिं क्षिपेदित्यन्वयः । प्रातः पुनः स्थलमार्जनादिकं कृत्वा द्वितीयरात्र्यादौ बलिदानम् ॥ ४१ ॥

प्रणवाद्यैरिति । तत्र मन्त्रः ॐ भूतेभ्यो नमः [गन्धपुष्पधूपदीपनैवेद्यताम्बूलसहितं बलिं गृह्णन्तु स्वाहा] इति । एवमन्यत्रापि मन्त्रः । महाकपिलपञ्चरात्रे तु विशेषः—ततो गन्धविमिश्रेण सिञ्चेद्वै शुद्धवारिणा ।
त्रिरात्रन्तु यथान्यायं पञ्चरात्रमथापि वा ॥ इति ।
सारस्वरमते तु—प्ररूढ़ान्यङ्कुराण्यन्यो न वीक्षेत कदाचन ।
आचार्य्य एव प्रविशेत्तच्छिष्यो वा तदाज्ञया ॥ इति ।
सिद्धान्तशेखरेऽपि—वस्त्रैराच्छाद्य यत्नेन सुगुप्तानि च कारयेत् । इति ॥ ४२ ॥

सप्तसु रात्रिषु पृथक् पृथक् बलिद्रव्याण्याह भूतेभ्य इति । साज्ञा इत्यन्तं षट् प्रथमरात्रौ । अस्यैव भूतक्रूरेति नाम । तदुक्तम्—"लाजतिलरक्तरजोदधिसक्तन्नानि भूतक्रूराख्यम्" इति । करम्भा दधिसक्तवः । अक्षता अखण्डतण्डुलाः । यदा नवसु रात्रिषु बलिदानं तदा रात्रिद्वये बलिद्रव्यं देवता चोक्ताचार्य्यैः "वैष्णवश्च दौग्धान्नं क्षशरञ्च वैष्णवेयं यदि नवरात्रं क्रमेण बलिरुक्तः" इति ॥ ४३–४५ ॥

तत इति । तत्तद्दिशि पायसादिना बलिर्विधेयः । तत्र नैर्ऋत्यप्रतीच्ययोर्मध्ये

प्राक्प्रोक्ते मण्डपे विद्वान् वेदिकाया बहिस्त्रिधा ॥ ४७

क्षेत्रं विभज्य मध्यांशे पूर्व्वादि परिकल्पयेत्।

अष्टास्वाशासु कुण्डानि रम्याकाराण्यनुक्रमात् ॥ ४८

अनन्तस्य ईशपूर्व्वयोर्मध्ये ब्रह्मणः इति। विधिवदित्यनेन पूर्व्वोक्तो दिशां बलिरत्रापि कर्त्तव्य इति सूचितम्। एषां पात्राणां विनियोगमग्रे वक्ष्यति। अङ्कुरपरीक्षोक्ता सिद्धान्तशेखरे—

यजमानाभिवृद्ध्यर्थं अङ्कुराणि परीक्षयेत्।
सम्यग्गूढं प्ररूढ़ानि कोमलानि सितानि च ॥
धूम्रवर्णान्यपूर्णानि तथा तिर्य्यग्गतानि च।
श्यामलानि च कुब्जानि वर्जयेदशुभानि तु ॥
अवृष्टिं कुरुते कृष्णं धूम्राभं कलहन्तथा।
अपूर्णं जननाशञ्च दुर्भिक्षं श्यामलाङ्कुरम् ॥
तिर्य्यग्गते भवेद् व्याधिः कुब्जे शत्रुभयं तथा।
अशुभे चाङ्कुरे जाते शान्तिहोमं समाचरेत् ॥
मूलमन्त्रेण जुहुयाद् गुरुर्मूर्त्तिधरैः सह।
अघोरास्त्रेण वास्त्रेण शतं वाऽथ सहस्रकम् ॥ इति।

सारस्वतमतेऽपि—प्ररूढ़ैरङ्कुरैः कर्त्तुर्निर्दिशेच्च शुभाशुभम्।
श्यामैः कृष्णैरङ्कुरैरर्थहानिस्तिर्य्यग्रूढैर्व्याधिरान्दोलितैस्तैः।
कुब्जैर्दुःखं दुष्प्ररूढैर्मृतिश्च रोगा भुग्नैः स्थानदेशेष्टहानिः ॥ इति ॥ ४६ ॥

कुण्डस्थानमाह प्रागिति। वेदिकाया बहिः सर्व्वतः क्षेत्रं क्षेत्रमध्यसूत्रं त्रिधा विभज्य तत्तन्मध्यभागे प्रादक्षिण्येन पूर्व्वादि अष्टास्वाशासु रम्याकाराणि कुण्डानि अनुक्रमात् परिकल्पयेदिति सम्बन्धः। विद्वान् पञ्चमेखलादिकमपि जानन्नित्यर्थः। आशासु दिक्षु ईशानान्तास्वित्यर्थः। "पूर्व्वाद्युक्तावधिच्छेदात् क्रम एव विवक्षितः" इति परिभाषणात्। तेन वेद्याः पादमात्रं त्यक्त्वा वक्ष्यमाण-मेखलायोग्यञ्च तत्र स्थानं त्यक्त्वा कुण्डानि कार्य्याणीत्यर्थः सम्पन्नो भवति। तदुक्तं सोमशम्भुना—वेदीपादान्तरं त्यक्त्वा। इति।
सिद्धान्तशेखरेऽपि—त्यक्त्वा वेदिचतुर्भागम्। इति।
नारदीयेऽपि—कुण्डवेद्यन्तरञ्चैव सपादकरसम्मितम्। इति।
अत्र पादशब्दः किञ्चिदधिकोपलक्षकः। तेन मध्यमोत्तममण्डपविषयत्वमस्य।

चतुरस्रं योनिमर्द्धचन्द्रं त्र्यस्रं सुवर्त्तुलम्।

षडस्रं पङ्कजाकारमष्टास्रं तानि नामतः॥ ४९

आचार्य्यकुण्डं मध्ये स्याद् गौरीपतिमहेन्द्रयोः।

हस्तमानमितां भूमिं पूर्व्ववत् परिकल्पयेत्॥ ५०

समन्तात् कुण्डमेतत् स्याच्चतुरस्रं शुभावहम्।

चतुर्विंशत्यङ्गुलाढ्यं हस्तं तन्त्रविदो विदुः॥ ५१

कर्त्तुर्दक्षिणहस्तस्य मध्यमाङ्गुलिपर्व्वणः।

मध्यस्य दीर्घमानेन मानाङ्गुलमुदीरितम्॥ ५२

क्रियासारेऽपि—वेदिकाकुण्डयोर्मध्ये हस्तद्वितयमन्तरम्। इति।
इदं चतुर्विंशति हस्तमण्डपविषयम्। वशिष्ठसंहितायान्तु—

त्रयोदशाङ्गुलं त्यक्त्वा वेदिकायाश्चतुर्दिशम्।
कुण्डानि स्वागमोक्तानि विदध्याद्द्विविधबुधः॥ इति।

अत्र कुण्डानीति समेखलानि॥ ४७॥४८॥

तमेव क्रममाह चतुरस्रमिति। तदुक्तमाम्नायरहस्ये—

नवकुण्डविधाने तु दिक्षु कुण्डाष्टकस्थिते। इति॥ ४९॥

आचार्य्यकुण्डमिति। गौरीपतिमहेन्द्रयोर्मध्ये ईशपूर्व्वदिङ्मध्ये आचार्य्यकुण्डं स्यात्। तदुक्तं तत्रैव—

नवमं कारयेत् कुण्डं पूर्व्वेशानदिगन्तरे। तद्वृत्तं चतुरस्रं वा स्यात्। इति।
तदुक्तं सिद्धान्तशेखरे—पुरन्दरेशयोर्मध्ये वृत्तं वा चतुरस्रकम्।

तदाचार्य्यस्य निर्दिष्टम्। इति।

अन्यत्रापि - मध्ये वृत्तञ्च गौरीपतिसुरपदिशोः पण्डिताः केचिदाहुः। इति।
क्रियासारेऽपि—वृत्तं वा चतुरस्रं स्यान्मध्यस्थानं त्वथेशयोः। इति।

तत्र सर्व्वकुण्डप्रकृतिभूतत्वादादितश्चतुरस्रकुण्डलक्षणमाह हस्तेति। पूर्व्ववदिति वास्तुमण्डलचतुरस्रकरणरीत्या। समन्ताच्चतुर्दिक्षु परिकल्पयेदिति सम्बन्धः। चतुरस्रकुण्डलक्षणे हस्त उक्तः तल्लक्षणनिर्व्वाहार्थम् अङ्गुललक्षणमप्याह चतुरिति। कर्त्तुः संस्कार्य्यस्य शिष्यस्य नत्वाचार्य्यस्य। प्रयोजककर्त्तृत्वेन शिष्येपि कर्त्तृशब्दप्रयोगात्। ननु मुख्यकर्त्तृपदवाच्य आचार्य्य एवात्र किमिति न गृह्यते। इति चेदुच्यते। "दानवाचनान्वारम्भणवरवरणव्रत प्रमाणेषु यजमानं प्रतीयात्" इति

यवानामष्टभिः क्लृप्तं मानाङ्गुलमुदीरितम् ।
चतुरस्रीकृतं क्षेत्रं पञ्चधा विभजेत् सुधीः ॥ ५३

कात्यायनवचनात् । नन्विदं श्रौतं प्रकृतं तान्त्रिकं तत् कथमेकवाक्यत्वमिति चेत् । तन्न । "परोक्तमविरोधि च" इत्युक्तेः । यथा श्रौते सोमयागादौ—

यज्ञोपवीतिना कार्य्यं सदा बद्धशिखेन च ।
शुचिना कर्म कर्त्तव्यम्

इत्याद्यविरुद्धं स्मार्त्तमपि गृह्यते । तद्वदिहापि । अतएवोक्तम् "सर्व्वशाखाप्रत्ययमेकं कर्म्म" इति । तन्त्रविद इत्यनेन तत्तत्तन्त्रोक्तनानाविधाङ्गुललक्षणाभिज्ञा इत्युक्तम् । मध्यमाङ्गुलिपर्व्वण इति । पर्व्वशब्देन मध्यमपर्व्वोच्यते । तन्मध्यस्य दैर्घ्यमानं यत्तदङ्गुलं । अथवा मध्यस्य मध्यमाङ्गुलिपर्व्वणः दैर्घ्यमानं यत्तदङ्गुलमिति सम्बन्धः ॥ ५०-५२ ॥

अग्रे ग्रन्थकृद् यवद्वयक्रमेणैव इत्यादि यवव्यवहारं करिष्यति तत्सिद्ध्यर्थमङ्गुलस्याष्टमो भागो यव इत्याह यवानामिति । मानाङ्गुलमिति तस्यैव संज्ञान्तरम् नत्वङ्गुलस्येदं पृथग्लक्षणम् । वा शब्दादिप्रयोगाभावात् । ग्रन्थान्तरे च—

जालान्तरगते भानौ यत् सूक्ष्मं दृश्यते रजः ।
प्रथमं तत् प्रमाणानां त्रसरेणुं प्रचक्षते ॥
त्रसरेणुस्तु विज्ञेयो ह्यष्टौ ते परमाणवः ।
त्रसरेणव एते स्युरष्टरेणुस्तु संस्मृतः ॥
ते रेणवस्तथा त्वष्टौ बालाग्रं तत् स्मृतं बुधैः ।
बालाग्राण्यष्ट लिख्या तु यूका लिख्याष्टकं स्मृतम् ॥
अष्टौ यूका यवं प्राहुरङ्गुलन्तु यवाष्टकम् ।
रत्निस्त्वङ्गुलपर्व्वाणि विज्ञेयस्त्वेकविंशतिः ॥
चत्वारि विंशतिश्चैव हस्तः स्यादङ्गुलानि तु ॥ इति ।

अङ्गुलद्वयमेकतयैवोक्तम् । त्रैलोक्यसारेऽपि—

कर्त्तुर्मध्याङ्गुलेर्मध्यपर्व्वणोरङ्गुलप्रमा ।
तिर्य्यग्यवोदराण्यष्टावूर्द्ध्वाग्रा व्रीहयस्त्रयः ॥ इति ।

सिद्धान्तशेखरेऽपि मात्राङ्गुलेनैव कुण्डं कर्त्तव्यमित्युक्तम् । तद् यथा—

मात्राङ्गुलेन हस्तः स्यात् कुण्डमाने शिवेरितः ।
मध्यमाङ्गुलिमध्यस्थपर्व्वदैर्घ्येण चोत्तमम् ॥

मात्राङ्गुलेन चानेन मेखलाकण्ठनालयः ।

कर्त्तव्याः कुण्डयोनिश्च । इति ।

अयेनापि—परमाणुक्रमाद् इदं मानाङ्गुलमितीरितम् । इत्यादिना—

यवोऽष्टगुणितोऽङ्गुलम् ।

अङ्गुलन्तु भवेन्मात्रं वितस्तिर्द्वादशाङ्गुलः ॥ इत्यन्तेन ।

हयशीर्षपञ्चरात्रेऽपि—

यवाष्टकैरङ्गुलं स्याच्चतुर्विंशाङ्गुलः करः ।

चतुर्विंशाङ्गुलस्त्वाद्यः स्वाङ्गुष्ठेन तु सम्मितः ॥ इति ।

तत्राङ्गुष्ठरेखामध्यपर्व्वणोरपि समतैव । ननु यद्यपि वाशब्दादिप्रयोगो नास्ति तथापि मात्राङ्गुलमानाङ्गुल शब्दाभ्यामेव विकल्पो भविष्यतीति चेत् । तन्न । तथात्वेऽपि भिन्नतया व्यवहाराभावात् । यत्र तु पञ्चरात्रे पञ्चधाऽङ्गुललक्षणमुक्तं तत्र तु तेषां व्यवस्थाऽप्युक्ता । अत्र तु व्यवस्थाया नोक्तत्वात् पर्य्यायतैव । तत्तु यथा

पञ्चरात्रे—वातायनपथं प्राप्य ये यान्ति रविरश्मयः ।

तेषु सूक्ष्मा विसर्पन्ते रेणवस्त्रसरेणवः ॥

परमाणवस्तेऽष्टौ स्यूरेणवस्तु तदष्टभिः ।

तेऽष्टौ बालाग्रकं तेऽष्टौ लिक्षा यूका तदष्टकम् ॥

तदष्टकं यवास्तेऽष्टावङ्गुलं समुदाहृतम् ।

सा तूत्तमाङ्गुलिः सप्त यवाः सैव तु मध्यमा ॥

षड्यवाः साधमा प्रोक्ता मानाङ्गुलमितीरितम् ।

विन्यस्तैस्तिर्य्यगष्टाभिर्यवैर्मानान्तराङ्गुलम् ॥

शिष्यदक्षिणहस्तस्य मध्यमाङ्गुलिमध्यतः ।

पर्व्वणोरन्तरा दैर्घ्यं मात्राङ्गुलमुदाहृतम् ॥

विनाऽङ्गुष्ठेन शेषाभिर्मुष्टि मङ्गुलिभिः कृतम् ।

चतुर्धा विभजेदेको भागो मुष्ट्यङ्गुलिः स्मृता ॥

यं कश्चित् पुरुषायामं विभज्य दशधा पुनः ।

एकं द्वादशधा भागं कृत्वा तेष्वेकमङ्गुलम् ॥

देहलब्धाङ्गुलं नाम जानीयात् तस्य तत् पुनः ।

उच्छ्रायः प्रतिमायाः स्यान्महामानाङ्गुलाश्रयः ॥

महामानाङ्गुलं यत्तन्मात्राङ्गुलमितीरितम् ।

मानान्तराङ्गुलेनैव प्रतिमाङ्गानि कल्पयेत् ॥

प्रासादादींश्च तेनैव कुर्य्यान्मानान्तरेण वा।
वेदिकापीठशिविकारथादीनां विधिः पुनः॥
मानान्तराङ्गुलेनैव भवेन्नान्येन केनचित्।
यागोपकरणान्यत्र कुर्य्यान्मानाङ्गुलेन वै॥
होमाङ्गानि स्रुवादीनि कुण्डं मुष्ट्यङ्गुलाश्रयम्।
देहलब्धाङ्गुलेनापि कुण्डादीनि प्रकल्पयेत्॥ इति।

बहुषु पुस्तकेषु उभयत्र मानाङ्गुलमित्येव पाठः। एकत्र मानाङ्गुलशब्दः पारिभाषिकः अन्यत्र मानेन प्रमाणेनाऽङ्गुलमिति यौगिको व्याख्येयः॥

चतुरस्रकुण्डक्षेत्रफलं तत्त्वत्रीनोक्तम्। तस्याङ्गुलात्मकत्वात् तदग्राणि चतुर्भुजात्मकत्वात् इत्यधुनोच्यते। तत्तु लीलावत्यां भास्कराचार्य्यैः—

समश्रुतौ तुल्यचतुर्भुजे च तथायते तद्भुजकोटिघातः। इति।

त्रिशत्यां श्रीधराचार्य्योऽपि—

समलम्बकचतुरस्रे त्र्यस्त्रिक्षेत्रे च जायते करणम्।
भूवदनसमासार्द्धं मध्यमलम्बेन संगुणयेत्॥

इत्यनेन प्रकारेण चतुर्विंशतिश्चतुर्विंशत्या गुणिता पञ्चशतानि षट्सप्तत्यधिकानि अङ्गुलानि क्षेत्रफलम्। एतदेव क्षेत्रफलमष्टस्वपि कुण्डेषु ज्ञेयम्। अतः सर्व्वेषामेव कुण्डानामिदमेव प्रकृतिभूतम्। तन्त्रान्तरेऽप्यस्यैव प्रकृतितोक्ता चतुरस्रमुक्त्वा—

तस्मिन्नन्यानि कुण्डानि वदामि तव नामतः। इति।

अन्यत्रापि—क्षेत्रं स्याच्चतुरस्रमत्र जनयेदन्यानि कुण्डान्यपि। इति।

सिद्धान्तशेखरेऽपि—

योन्यादिसर्व्वकुण्डानि चतुरस्राद्भवन्ति हि।
लक्षणं चतुरस्रस्य पूर्व्वं तस्मान्मयोच्यते॥ इत्यादिना
चतुरस्रमिदं प्रोक्तं सर्व्वकुण्डेषु कारणम्॥ इत्यन्तेन।

क्रियासारेऽपि—

चतुष्पदं चतुष्कोणमेतत् क्षेत्राह्वयं भवेत्।
चतुरस्रादिकुण्डानां सर्व्वेषामत्र सम्भवः॥ इति।

चतुरस्रप्रकृतितया योनिकुण्डमाह चतुरस्रीकृतमिति। चतुरस्रीकृतं क्षेत्रं पञ्चधा विभजेत्। तत्र सर्व्वस्य क्षेत्रफलस्य विभागे प्रयोजनाभावाद्भ्यसूत्रस्यैव विभागः कार्य्य इति सुधीरित्यनेनोक्तम्। तत्रायं पञ्चमः अंशः चतुरङ्गुलानि सार्द्धषड्यवाः किञ्चिदूनाः॥ ५२॥

न्यसेत् पुरस्तादेकांशं कोणार्द्धार्द्धप्रमाणतः ।
भ्रमयेत् कोणमानेन तथाऽन्यदपि मन्त्रवित् ।
सूत्रयुग्मं ततो दद्यात् कुण्डं योनिनिभं भवेत् ॥ ५४

एवम्भूतमंशं पुरस्ताद्दक्षिणोदग्गतसूत्रस्योत्तरभागे न्यसेद् वर्द्धयेत् इति मन्त्रविदित्यनेनोक्तम् । ततः कोणार्द्धार्द्धप्रमाणतः कोणमानेन भ्रमयेत् । अत्र कोणशब्देन कोणसूत्रं गृह्यते । तस्यार्द्धं कर्णसूत्रद्वयमध्यसम्पातस्थानम् तदर्द्धम् । अपरकोष्ठयुगले द्वितीयकर्णसूत्रयोगस्थानम् । तत्प्रमाणतः तस्मात्स्थानात् कोणमानेन कोणसंलग्नतया भ्रमयेत् । प्रकारस्तु अपरैककोष्ठकर्णसूत्रद्वयसम्पातस्थाने सूत्रादि संस्थाप्य मध्यतिर्य्यक्सूत्राग्रात् तत्कोणसंलग्नं दक्षिणोदग्गतसूत्रस्य दक्षिणाग्रावधि सूत्राग्रं भ्रमयेत् मन्त्रविदन्यदपि तथा भ्रमयेदित्यर्थः । तत्रापि प्रकारः । द्वितीयापरकोष्ठकर्णसूत्रद्वयसम्पातस्थाने सूत्रादिं संस्थाप्य मध्यग-तिर्य्यग्गतसूत्रस्य द्वितीयाग्रात् तत्कोणसंलग्नं दक्षिणोदग्गतसूत्रस्य दक्षिणाग्रावधि सूत्राग्रं भ्रमयेत् । ततः सूत्रयुग्मं दद्यात् । पार्श्वद्वयस्थवृत्ताग्राभ्यां पुरोवर्द्धित-सूत्राग्रावधि सूत्रद्वयं पातयेत् । एवं योनिनिभमुत्तराभिमुखं कुण्डं भवेत् । तदुक्तं कादिमते—

तन्मध्यपञ्चमांशेन विकाश्य ब्रह्मसूत्रकम् ।
पूर्व्वतः पश्चिमद्वन्द्वकोष्ठयोर्मध्यदेशतः ॥
तत्कोणमानेन तथा भ्रामयेत् पश्चिमाग्रकान् ।
उत्तराग्रावधि तथा दक्षिणाग्रावधि प्रिये ॥
तन्मध्यतिर्य्यक्सूत्राग्र[ताग्र]द्वयावष्टम्भतस्तथा ।
विकाशितब्रह्मसूत्रावधि सूत्रद्वयं क्षिपेत् ॥
योनिकुण्डमिदं भद्रे[भद्रम्] । इति ।

कामिकेऽपि—पञ्चमांशं पुरो न्यस्य मध्ये वेदांशमानतः ।
भ्रमादश्वत्थपत्राभं कुण्डमाग्नेयमीरितम् ॥ इति ।

क्रियासारेऽपि—क्षेत्रे पञ्चांशकं कृत्वा पूर्व्वस्यामेकमंशकम् ।
न्यस्य तन्मध्यसेत् सूत्रे पार्श्वयोर्मध्यमावधि ॥
ततः प्रत्यक्पदद्वन्द्वं भ्रामयेत् तत्तदर्द्धतः ।
पृथक् पृथक् यथा सम्यक् तथा कोणत्रयावधि ॥
एवं कृते स्थिरं कुण्डं भवेदश्वत्थपत्रवत् ॥ इति ।

सिद्धान्तशेखरेऽपि—योन्याख्यमुच्यते कुण्डमाग्नेय्यामुत्तरामुखम् ।

प्रजापतेर्दी[च्यो] प्र[च]तापि च शस्तं तत्रापि पूर्व्ववत् ॥

चतुष्कोष्ठं[ष्णं] समं कुर्य्यादंशं सेत्रस्य पञ्चमम् ।

सोमसूत्रस्य बाह्याये योजयेत् सौम्यभागके ॥

अग्रयोर्गर्भसूत्रस्य न्यसेदंशे च सूत्रकम् ।

सिद्धत्यनेन पत्राग्रं दक्षकोष्ठद्वयस्य तु ॥

मध्यकोष्ठस्य चान्ते च भ्रामयेत्तदभ्रमाद्भवेत् ।

पत्रपृष्ठं सुसंसिद्धं पद्मसम्बन्धपत्रवत् ॥

इतीदं योनिकुण्डं स्यात् । इति ।

अत्र क्षेत्रोपपत्तिरुच्यते । तत्रैकपार्श्वे अर्द्धं वृत्तम् । द्वितीयपार्श्वे अर्द्धं वृत्तम् । एवमेकं वृत्तक्षेत्रम् । वृत्तार्द्धद्वयमध्यस्थमधोमुखं त्रिकोणमेकम् । तदुपर्य्यूर्द्ध्वमुखं त्रिकोणमेकमिति त्रीणि क्षेत्राणि । तत्र त्रयाणामपि पृथक् पृथक् फलमानीयैकीकृतं योनिकुण्डक्षेत्रफलं भवति । तत्र वृत्तक्षेत्रफलं तावदुच्यते ।

व्यासस्य वर्गे भनवाग्नि(३९२७)निघ्ने सूक्ष्मं फलं पञ्चसहस्रभक्ते ।

इति भास्कराचार्य्योक्तप्रकारेण वृत्तक्षेत्रफलानयने श्रीधराचार्य्योक्तिः "त्रिंशत्यां स्थूला" इत्युपेक्षिता । तत्रैकाङ्गुलस्य चतुस्त्रिंशांशेनोनानि सप्तदशाङ्गुलानि व्यासः । तदुपपत्तिरेवं "तत्कृत्योर्योगपदम्" इत्यनेन कर्णप्रमाणमानीय तदर्द्धं व्यासो भवति । इदञ्चाग्रे द्विहस्तकुण्डकरणीकथनप्रस्तावे स्फुटीकरिष्यते । तत्र व्यासस्य न्यासो यथा १६ $\frac{३३}{३४}$ सवर्णितः $\frac{५७७}{३४}$ अस्य यथोक्तकरणेन ज्ञातं क्षेत्रफलं २२६ एको यवस्तस्त्रो यूकास्तिस्त्रो लिख्याः । न्यासांशसवर्णनादिप्रकारस्तु ग्रन्थगौरवभयान्नोक्तः । स तु पाटीगणिते लीलावत्यादौ द्रष्टव्यः । ततोऽधस्त्र्यस्रस्य फलम् ।

"लम्बगुणं भूम्यर्द्धं स्पष्टं त्रिभुजे फलं भवति" इति भास्कराचार्य्योक्तमार्गेण । तत्र भूः २४ अङ्गुलानि लम्बः १२ अङ्गुलानि । ततो भूम्यर्द्धं १२ लम्बः १२ गुणं १४४ । इदं मध्यत्र्यस्रस्य फलम् । तत ऊर्द्ध्वत्र्यस्रस्य फलम् तस्य भूः २४ अङ्गुलानि ग्रन्थकृदुक्तप्रकारेण लम्बः तत्र मध्यसूत्रार्द्धं १२ अङ्गुलानि । ततो वर्द्धितपञ्चमोंऽशः $\frac{२४}{५}$ उभयोः समच्छेदार्थं न्यासः $\frac{१२}{१}$ $\frac{२४}{५}$ समच्छेदौ $\frac{६०}{५}$ $\frac{२४}{५}$ योगः $\frac{८४}{५}$ । ततो यथोक्तकरणेन जातं क्षेत्रफलं २०१ किञ्चिन्न्यूनपञ्चयवाधिकम् । तेन क्षेत्रफलमध्ये सयवद्वयचतुरङ्गुलानि न्यूनानि भवन्ति । उदाहृत कादिमतादिलक्षणेष्वपि इदमेव फलं ज्ञेयम् । तत्र कश्चित् कामिकवचनं ४६८ एतावत् फलमानीय दूषितवानिति

महाभ्रान्त एव। एवं सर्व्वेषामेकवाक्यत्वे सत्यपि च "मानहीने दरिद्रता" इत्यादि "न्यूनाधिकप्रमाणं यद् यजमानविनाशकृत्" इत्यादि दोषापत्तेरिति क्षेत्रफलसाम्यमत्रावश्यमपेक्षितम्। यतो भास्कराचार्य्यश्रीधराचार्य्यप्रोक्तगणितमार्गेण क्षेत्रफलानयनद्वारेणावश्यं कुण्डानि वक्तव्यानि। यत् क्रियासारे—

प्राक्कुण्डे यत् प्रमाणं तदन्येषां क्षेत्रमानकम्। इति।

ग्रन्थकृताऽपि तुल्यक्षेत्रफलानयनार्थमेव समचतुरस्रस्य प्रकृतिता निरूपिता। पञ्चदशशाखोपरि कल्पसूत्रं प्रणीतवतो भगवतः कात्यायनस्यापि परिशिष्टे शुल्वे कुण्डं वक्तुमिच्छोः श्रीधराचार्य्यभास्कराचार्य्यप्रोक्तमार्गेण क्षेत्रफलानयनद्वारैव प्रवृत्तिर्दृश्यते। अतोऽवश्यं क्षेत्रफलसाम्यं वक्तव्यम्। तदाचार्य्येणातिसूक्ष्मगणनायां शिष्यबुद्धिक्लेशो भविष्यतीत्युपेक्षितम्। साम्प्रदायिकास्तदर्थं यवत्रयप्रक्षेपमाहुः एकहस्ते मया क्षेत्रफलसमतार्थं सर्व्वानुगतप्रकारस्तूच्यते।

चतुर्विंशतिधा मध्यसूत्रं भङ्क्त्वा पुरो न्यसेत्।
पञ्चांशांस्त्वेकैकस्य त्रीन् विंशांशान् कोणपादतः॥
वृत्तार्द्धं स्तो मध्यतिर्य्यक्सूत्रान्तञ्च ततोऽर्पयेत्।
पुरोवर्द्धितसूत्रान्तं सूत्रे द्वे स्याद् भगाकृति॥

अनेन प्रकारेण क्षेत्रफलमव्यभिचारीति ज्ञेयम्। अत्र पञ्चाङ्गुलानि त्रयवाणि यूकासार्द्धलिख्याचतुष्टयसहितानि मध्यसूत्रं वर्द्धयेत्। तदा लब्धः १९ $\frac{३}{२०}$ सवर्णितः $\frac{३८३}{२०}$ उक्तक्रमेण जातं क्षेत्रफलं २०५ षड्यवास्तिस्रो यूकाः पञ्च लिख्याः। एवमेकीकृतं सर्व्वं क्षेत्रफलं ५७६। एतत् सूक्ष्ममिति ज्ञेयम्। यत्तु

कादिमते—चतुरस्राभितो या तु त्यक्ता भूः सान्य[ग्र]तः स्थिता।
लभ्यते सर्व्वकुण्डेषु तेन सर्व्वाणि सर्व्वतः।
तत्समान्येव जायन्ते षसवत्त्वङ्गुलात्मना॥ इति।

सिद्धान्तशेखरेऽपि—क्षेत्रस्य चतुरस्रस्य समं सूत्रं चतुर्गुणम्।
योन्यादिसर्व्वकुण्डानां पर्य्यन्तेषु नियोजयेत्॥
चतुरस्रं समं तच्चेच्छुभं योन्यादिकुण्डकम्॥ इति।

तदत्रास्मदुक्तप्रकारेण संवदति।

व्यासे भनन्दाग्नि ३९२७ हृते विभक्ते
खबाणसूर्य्यैः १२५० परिधिः स सूक्ष्मः।

इति प्रकाराद् वृत्तपरिधिः सूक्ष्मः १६०। ३०। स्थूलस्तु ५४ अङ्गुलानि कर्णसूत्र-

चतुरस्रीकृतं क्षेत्रं दशधा विभजेत् पुनः ।
एकांशेकं त्यजेदंशमध ऊर्द्धञ्च तन्त्रवित् ॥ ५५

इयं २१।२१ अङ्गुलानि "तत्कृत्योर्योगपदम्" इत्यनेन प्रकारेण जातम् । मिलित्वा षण्णवत्यङ्गुलात्मता । परन्त्वतिस्थूलमानत्वाद् बहुषु स्थलेषु व्यभिचरतीद-मित्युपेक्षितम् । यतोऽर्द्धचन्द्रे ८८ अङ्गुलानि यवत्रयाधिकानि परिधिः । त्र्यस्रे ८० अङ्गुलानि ३ यवाः २ यूकाः । वृत्ते ८५ अङ्गुलानि किञ्चिदधिकानि । षडस्रे ८८ अङ्गुलानि ४ यवाः ७ यूकाः । अष्टास्रे ८७ अङ्गुलानि ४ यवाः । एवं कुत्रापि न मिलतीति यत्किञ्चिदेतत् ।

केचिच्छारदापद्यमिदमन्यथा व्याख्यातम् । पञ्चमांशेन प्राचीसूत्रं वर्धयेत् । ततः कोणयोः प्रतीचीतिर्य्यक्सूत्रोत्पन्ननैर्ऋत्यवायव्ययोः अर्द्धार्द्धप्रमाणेन एकत्र कोणे पञ्चमांशस्यार्द्धम् अपरत्र कोणेऽपि पञ्चमांशस्यार्द्धं वर्द्धयेत् । कोणमानेन वर्द्धितवायव्यकोणात् प्राचीसूत्रपश्चिमाग्रावधि भ्रमयेत् । तद्वद्वर्द्धितनैर्ऋत्यकोणात् प्राचीसूत्रपश्चिमाग्रावधि भ्रमयेत् । वर्द्धिताभ्यां वायव्यनैर्ऋत्यकोणाभ्यां वर्द्धित-प्राचीसूत्राग्रावधि सूत्रद्वयं दद्यादिति । तदसांप्रदायिकत्वात् एतदर्थप्रतिपादक-शब्दाभावात् लिखित-कादिमतादिविरोधात् स्वकपोलकल्पितम् । सूक्ष्मगणनायां क्षेत्रफलस्याप्याधिक्याद् यत्किञ्चिदेतत् । यदतिगणितज्ञाभिमानिनः आगमज्ञाभि-मानिनश्च लक्षणम् ।

अष्टोनद्विशतांशसूत्रकचतुःकोणे पुरस्ताद्दद-
त्वष्टत्रिंशतमेधयत्वय लवान् श्रोण्योरिमानर्द्धशः ।
अंशात् सूत्रयुगे त्रिकोणमिति तच्छ्रोण्योस्ततोऽर्द्धभ्रमात्
वृत्तार्द्धं बहिरालिखेदिति भवेत् कुण्डोत्तमं योनिवत् ॥ इति ।

चतुरस्रश्रोण्योरपि पश्चिमतिर्य्यक्सूत्रमुभयतः तानष्टत्रिंशदंशान् अर्द्धार्द्धतया वर्द्धयेत् । एकोनविंशतिर्दक्षिणतः एकोनविंशतिरुत्तरत इति यत् तत् स्वकपोल-कल्पितम् । क्रियासार-कादिमत-कामिक-सिद्धान्तशेखरादिविरोधात् । क्षेत्रफलमध्ये च किञ्चिदधिकं क्षेत्रफलमिति [चतुर्दशाङ्गुलानि न्यूनानीति] ज्ञात्वा महद्भिः सन्तोष्टव्यम् । अत्र भ्रामयेदिति लेखकदोषवशात् अपपाठः । मित्वात् "मितां ह्रस्वः" इति ह्रस्वत्वात् भ्रमयेदित्येव पाठः ॥ ५४ ॥

चतुरस्रप्रकृतितया अर्द्धचन्द्रकुण्डमाह चतुरस्रीकृतमिति । क्षेत्रशब्देन पूर्व्ववन्मध्यसूत्रं लक्ष्यते । तद् दशधा विभजेत् । तत्र एकं भागमध उत्तरतः एक-

ज्यासूत्रं पातयेदग्रे तन्मानाद् भ्रमयेत्ततः ।
अर्द्धचन्द्रनिभं कुण्डं रमणीयमिदं भवेत् ॥ ५६

मूर्द्धतो दक्षिणतश्च त्यक्त्वा अग्रे अग्रचिह्ने उत्तरभागे ज्यासूत्रं स्वेच्छाप्रमाणं पातयेत् इति त[म]न्त्रविदित्यनेन सूचितम् । ततस्तन्मानान्मध्ये व्यासमानाद् भ्रामयेत् । तत्र प्रकारः । ज्यासूत्रमध्यसूत्रसन्निपाते सूत्रादिं संस्थाप्य ऊर्द्ध्वभागे यच्चिह्नं कृतं ततो ज्यासूत्रान्तं भ्रामयेत् । तदर्द्धचन्द्रनिभं उत्तराभिमुखं कुण्डं भवेत् ।

तदुक्तं सिद्धान्तशेखरे— अर्द्धचन्द्रमथोच्यते ।
यास्ये तन्मारणे शस्तमुत्तराभिमुखं सदा ॥ इति ।

अत्र क्षेत्रोपपत्तिः । तत्र उभयतो दशांशत्यागेन सर्व्वस्य पञ्चमांशत्यागो भवति । स च ४ अङ्गुलानि ६ यवाः ३ यूकाः १ लिख्याः ४ बालाग्राणि ६ रेणवः ३ त्रसणवः १ परमाणुः । तदायं शिष्टो व्यासः १९ अङ्गुलानि १ यवः ४ यूकाः ६ लिख्याः ३ बालाग्राणि १ रेणुः ४ त्रसरेणवः ७ परमाणवः । तेन पञ्चमांशाधिकैकोनविंशत्यङ्गुलायामः १९ $\frac{१}{५}$ क्षेत्रफलानयनार्थं सवर्णितः $\frac{९६}{५}$ एतद्व्यासेन फलानयने यवार्द्धाधिकमङ्गुलत्रयमधिकं क्षेत्रफलं भवति । तदाचार्य्येणोपेक्षितम् अल्पत्वात् । क्षेत्रफलाव्यभिचारी सर्व्वानुगतप्रकारस्तूच्यते ।

चतुर्विंशतिधा भक्ते सूत्रे व्यासोऽर्द्धचन्द्रके ।
विंशांशत्रयमेकस्य भागा एकोनविंशतिः ।
एतन्मानार्द्धभ्रमेण दलेन्द्वग्रे गुणाङ्कनात् ॥

तदायं व्यासः १९ अङ्गुलानि १ यवः १ यूका ४ लिख्याः ५ बालाग्राणि ३ रेणवः १ त्रसरेणुः ४ परमाणवः । तदा २ अङ्गुले ३ यवाः ३ यूकाः १ लिख्या ५ बालाग्राणि २ रेणू ३ त्रसरेणवः २ परमाणू इममंशमूर्द्धतस्त्यजेत् । एतादृशमेवांशमधस्त्यजेत् । तत्र क्षेत्रफलानयनाय व्यासस्य न्यासः १९ $\frac{३}{२०}$ । तेन एकोनविंशत्यङ्गुलानि एकाङ्गुलस्य विंशतिधा भक्तस्य त्रयो भागाः सवर्णितो यथा $\frac{३८३}{२०}$ तत्र वृत्तफलानयनार्थमयं द्विगुणीकृतः । तत्र छेदस्यैवार्द्धीकरणेन उपरि ततो द्विगुणो भवत्येव तेनायं $\frac{३८३}{२०}$ सम्पूर्णवृत्तव्यासः । ततो "व्यासस्य वर्गे भनवाग्नि" इत्यादिना आनीतं क्षेत्रफलं सर्व्ववृत्तस्य ११५२ एतदर्द्धीकृतम् अर्द्धचन्द्रस्य क्षेत्रफलं ५७६ सूक्ष्मं ज्ञेयम् । अथवा द्विहस्तकुण्डे एतद्व्यासवर्गं द्विगुणीकृत्य तन्मूलमानेयम् । तत्र एव व्यासः । स एवमग्रेऽप्यूह्यम् । यत् कस्यचिदतिगणितज्ञाभिमानिनो लक्षणम् ।

चतुरस्रीकृतं क्षेत्रं चतुर्विंशतिधा भजेत् ।
एकोनविंशत्या त्रिंशद्वादशांशाढ्यया लवैः ॥
प्राच्यन्ताद् विन्यसेत् सूत्रफलं प्रत्यग्धनुःस्थिति ।
तदवश्लेषयेत् प्राच्या तिर्य्यक्सूत्रं ततो भवेत् ॥
कुण्डमर्द्धेन्दुसदृशं प्रत्यग्दृष्टिमनोहरम् ॥ इति ।

अत्रापि सूक्ष्मगणनया अङ्गुलत्रयन्यूनम्। यतस्तेन "व्यासार्द्धत्रय[वर्ग]वर्गात् क्षेत्रफलं दशगुणान्मूलम्" इति श्रीधराचार्य्योक्तेन प्रकारेण जलफलमानीतम्। तच्च स्थूलम्। यतो गणितग्रन्थानामियं शैली यत्स्थूलं सूक्ष्ममपि फलानयनमुच्यते। तत्र भगवता श्रीधराचार्य्येण बृहत्पाट्यां प्रकारद्वयमप्युक्ता तत्संक्षिप्ते त्रिशतीग्रन्थे स्थूला एव प्रकारा लिखिताः। भास्कराचार्य्येण तु लीलावत्यां स्थूला एव सूक्ष्मा अपि प्रकारा उक्ताः। तां बृहत्पाटीञ्चावलोक्य मया सूक्ष्मं फलमिदमानीतम्। तदेव सूक्ष्ममिति मन्यते चेत्तदा मूले अत्यन्तं फलाधिक्यं स्यात्। अन्यच्च अस्योत्तराभिमुखत्वात् प्राच्यन्तात् सूत्रं वर्द्धयेत्। प्रत्यग्धनुःस्थितीत्यत्यन्तमेवासङ्गतम्। स्वग्रन्थे स्वयं योनिलक्षणं वदन्नाह स्म—

मघव-शिखि-कृतान्त-दिक्स्थकुण्डेष्वियमधिमेखलमेव मध्यभागे ।
यमदिशि शशिदिङ्मुखा निवेश्य । इति ।

तेन स्वग्रन्थे पूर्वापरविरोधोऽपि नोपलक्षित इति यत्किञ्चिदेतत्। यत्तु शुल्बे कात्यायनवचनम्—"मण्डलं चतुरस्रं चिकीर्षन् विष्कम्भं पञ्चदशभागान् कृत्वा द्वावुद्धरेच्छेषः करणी" इति। तदपि सम्भवाभिप्रायं न तु सम्यग्गणनाभिप्रायम्। एवमपि चेत् कस्यचिन्महापुरुषस्य मनसि सन्देह उत्पद्यते। तेन प्रत्यक्षं परीक्षा कार्य्या। धातुकाष्ठमृन्मयं वा एकहस्तमितं समं चतुरस्रं पात्रं कारयित्वा तदुक्तमानेन मदुक्तमानेन च एकं हस्तमितं वृत्तं पात्रं कारयित्वा चतुरस्रपात्रं सम्यग् जलेनापूर्य्य तज्जलेनैव वृत्तं पात्रं पूरयेत्। यदैव वृत्तं पात्रं सम्यक् पूर्णतामेति तदेव शुद्धमिति मन्तव्यम्। एतस्यैव यल्लक्षणान्तरम्—

चतुष्कोणक्षेत्रे जिनलवकमध्यस्थितगुणे
विहायाधः सार्द्धद्वयमुपरि तावच्च मतिमान् ।
कलांशेनांशस्योनितमुपरि तिर्य्यक् कुरु गुणं
भ्रमार्द्धं तन्मानादपि शशिदलं कुण्डमिति तु ॥ इति ।

अत्र एकोनविंशत्यङ्गुलानि सार्द्धयवानि व्यासः। तत्र सूक्ष्मगणनायां पञ्चाङ्गुलानि न्यूनानि। तत्कृतस्थूलगणनाप्रकारेणापि सार्द्धमङ्गुलं न्यूनं भवति। यत्तु

चतुर्द्धा भेदिते क्षेत्रे न्यसेदुभयपार्श्वयोः ।
एकैकमंशं तन्मानादग्रतो लाञ्छयेत्ततः ।
सूत्रद्वयं ततः कुर्य्यात् त्र्यस्रं कुण्डमुदाहृतम् ॥ ५७

तेनोक्तं "मण्डलं चतुरस्रम्" इति कात्यायनवचनेन संवाद्यमिति तदयुक्तं संवादाभावात् । सिद्धान्तशेखरे तु—

नवधा भाजिते क्षेत्रे चतुरस्रे समे तदा ।
दक्षिणे चोत्तरे चांशमेकैकन्तु परित्यजेत् ।
सप्तांशमध्यसूत्रेण भ्रमणादर्द्धचन्द्रकम् ॥ इति ।

कामिकेऽपि—चतुरस्रे यवैर्भक्ते त्यक्त्वान्त्याद्यौ तदंशकौ ।
मध्यसप्तांशमानेन कुण्डं खण्डेन्दुवद् भ्रमात् ॥ इति ।

अतोऽत्र अष्टादशाङ्गुलानि एकस्य द्वौ तृतीयांशौ व्यासः । अतोऽल्पत्वं न्यूनं क्षेत्रफलम् ॥ ५५॥५६ ॥

चतुरस्रप्रकृतितया त्र्यस्रकुण्डमाह चतुर्द्धेति । क्षेत्रे चतुरस्रमध्यस्थले चतुर्द्धा भेदिते । उभयपार्श्वयोस्तिर्य्यक्प्रतीचीसूत्रपार्श्वयोरेकैकमंशं वर्द्धयेत् । तन्मानात् चतुर्थांशमानेन अग्रतो लाञ्छयेत् । ततः सूत्रत्रयं दद्यात् । तत्र प्रकारः । तिर्य्यक्प्रतीचीसूत्रपार्श्वयोर्ये लाञ्छने तदवधि प्रतीचीसूत्रं वर्द्धयेदित्येकम् । वर्द्धितनैर्ऋत्यकोणात् मध्यसूत्राग्रदत्तलाञ्छनं यावत् सूत्रं पातयेदिति द्वितीयम् । ततो वर्द्धितवायव्यकोणात् मध्यसूत्राग्रदत्तलाञ्छनं यावत् सूत्रं पातयेदिति तृतीयम् । एवमूर्द्धाग्रं पूर्व्वाभिमुखं त्र्यस्रि कुण्डं भवति । तदुक्तं सिद्धान्तशेखरे—

त्रिकोणं कुण्डमुच्यते ।
नैर्ऋत्ये दर्शितं कुण्डं विद्वेषे पूर्व्ववत् क्रमम् ॥ इति ।

अत्र क्षेत्रोपपत्तिः । भूः २६ लम्बः ३० ततो "लम्बगुणं भूम्यर्द्धम्" इत्यादिना जातं क्षेत्रफलं ५४० । षट्त्रिंशदङ्गुलानि न्यूनानि खर्व्वेष्ट त्र्यस्रम् । यतः षट्त्रिंशद्भुजौ तु "तत्कृत्योर्योगपदं कर्णः" इति प्रकारेणानीतौ पञ्चत्रिंशदात्मकौ । त्र्यस्रकुण्डे तु भुजत्रयसाम्यस्यापेक्षितम् । तदर्थं केचन अन्यथा व्याचक्षते । चतुर्द्धा क्षेत्रे भेदिते एकैकमंशं पार्श्वयोर्वर्द्धयेत् । तन्मानेन वर्द्धितानन्तरं यत् षट्त्रिंशन्मानं तन्मानेनाग्रतो लाञ्छयेत् । तत्र लाञ्छनप्रकारः । वर्द्धितपार्श्वयोः षट्त्रिंशदङ्गुलमितसूत्रस्यादिं निधाय प्राचीसूत्राग्रे लाञ्छयेदिति । ततः पूर्व्ववत् सूत्रत्रयं दद्यादिति । एवं च सति भुजत्रयसाम्यं भवति । उभयपार्श्वे मिलित्वा यवचतुष्टयप्रक्षेपादेक-

हस्तक्षेत्रफलसाम्यं भवतीति बुध इत्यनेन सूचितमिति ते वदन्ति। मया तु समत्रिभुजता अन्यूनानतिरिक्तक्षेत्रफलता च यथा भवति तथा सर्व्वानुगतप्रकार उच्यते ।

चतुर्विंशतिधा भक्ते सूत्रेऽथोभयपार्श्वयोः ।
द्वादशांशांश्चैकस्य भागानेकोनविंशतिम् ।
अर्द्धशो वर्द्धयेत् त्र्यस्रि भवेत् सूत्रत्रयात् समात् ॥

अस्यायमर्थः सम्यक्। षडङ्गुलानि यूकोनयवद्वयाधिकानि एकपार्श्वे वर्द्धयेत्। एवं द्वितीयपार्श्वे । तदा सप्ताङ्गुलानि चत्वारो यवाः षड्यूकाधिकाः प्राक्सूत्रं वर्द्धितं भवति। ततो भूः २६ अङ्गुलानि २ यवाः ६ यूकाः सार्द्धलिख्याद्दयम्। लम्बः २१ अङ्गुलानि ४ यवाः ६ यूकाः। तत्र "लम्बेन निघ्नं कुमुखैक्यखण्डम्" इति प्रकारेण क्षेत्रफलानयनाय लम्बस्य न्यासो यथा $२१\frac{१९}{३२}$ सवर्णितः $\frac{१०११}{३२}$। भूः $२६\frac{९}{१८}$ सवर्णिता $\frac{६९२}{१८}$ मुखं शून्यमत ऐक्यमिदमेव तदर्द्धं छेदस्य द्विगुणत्वात् $\frac{६९२}{३८}$ ततो "लम्बेन निघ्नं कुमुखैक्यखण्डम्" इति कृते छेदेन भक्ते लब्धं क्षेत्रफलं यथा ५७६। अत्र भुजत्रयं सममेव। क्रियासारेऽपि समभुजतोक्ता—

क्षेत्रमष्टांशकं कृत्वा पार्श्वयोरंशकौ बहिः ।
न्यस्त्वा तन्मानसूत्रेण न्यसेत् सूत्रत्रयं समम् ॥ इति ।

क्षेत्रफलमत्रापि व्यभिचरत्येव। यतो २६ लम्बः क्षेत्रफलं ३८०। अतिन्यूनत्वादन्ये एवं व्याचक्षते। पार्श्वयोरंशकाविति एकस्मिन् पार्श्वे अंशद्वयं द्वितीयपार्श्वे अंशद्वयम्। तेन पञ्चदशाङ्गुलानि न्यूनानि क्षेत्रफलमध्ये भवन्ति। द्वितीयमतव्याख्यातशारदापद्यार्थेन संवादश्च भवति। महाकपिलपञ्चरात्रेऽपि समभुजतोक्ता।

द्वात्रिंशदङ्गुलं सूत्रं त्रिधा तत् पातयेद् ध्रुवम् ।
पूर्व्वाग्रं कुण्डकं कृत्वा त्रिकोणं तु प्रकारयेत् ॥ इति ।

अत्रापि क्षेत्रफलं व्यभिचरत्येव। यतः २७ अङ्गुलानि ५ यवाः लम्बः क्षेत्रफलं ४४०। अन्यत्रापि—

प्राग्वैरी १६।८ सार्द्धभागीकृतक्षेत्रतः पार्श्वयोर्न्यस्य भागद्वयं पण्डितः ।
तेन मानेन सूत्रद्वयं विन्यसेत् कुण्डमेतद्भवेद्रुद्रनेत्रात्मकम् ॥ इति ।

इदं लक्षणद्वयं पक्षवतिपरिधिरेखाभिप्रायेण। अग्रे लिखितकादिमतेऽपि समभुजतोक्ता। मयाऽत्र लम्बस्तु गणितापटून् प्रत्युक्तः। गणितज्ञैस्तु

स्वाबाधाभुजकृत्योरन्तरमूलं प्रजायते लम्बः ।

इति लब्धमानीय क्षेत्रफलं सम्पाद्य सन्तोष्टव्यम्। अथवा लब्धं विनैव

सर्व्वदोर्युतिदलं चतुःस्थितं बाहुभिर्विरहितञ्च तद्वतेः।
मूलमस्फुटफलं चतुर्भुजे स्पष्टमेतदुदितं त्रिबाहुके॥

इति प्रकारेणानीय सन्तोष्टव्यम्। मूलशेषाद्यावावानयनार्थं प्रकार उच्यते।

मूलशेषं लवयवसंख्यानिघ्नमथो भजेत्।
द्विघ्नस्यैकेन मूलेन फलं लवयवा मताः॥

अथवा भास्कराचार्य्योक्तं सरणि—

वर्गेण महतेष्टेन वधात् छेदांशयोर्हतात्।
पदं गुणपदक्षुसच्छिन्नं निकटं भवेत्॥

इत्यानेयमासन्नमूलम्। यत् कस्यचिदतिगणितज्ञाभिमानिनः आगमज्ञाभिमानिनश्च लक्षणद्वयम्।

क्षेत्रं त्र्यंशं पुरस्तूर्य्यमधश्चोभयपार्श्वयोः।
वर्द्धयित्वा क्षतैः सूत्रैः कुण्डं त्र्यस्रं त्रिभिर्भवेत्॥ इति।
क्षेत्रस्य मध्यमगुणे जिनभागभक्ते
श्रोण्योः पृथक् शरलवान् परिवर्द्ध्य धीमान्।
अग्रे विनाऽष्टमलवेन दशाथ सूत्रै-
स्त्र्यस्रं त्रिभिर्भवति कुण्डमिह प्रयुक्तैः॥ इति।

अत्र पूर्व्वोक्तलक्षणं किञ्चिन्न्यूनं त्र्यस्रं द्वितीयन्तु महालब्धम्। क्षेत्रफले च एकयवन्यूनता। तेन यत् किञ्चिदेतत्। अत्र क्षेत्रफलसाम्यात् त्र्यस्राकारत्वाच्च त्रिकोणकुण्डतेति चेत् तदा कुण्डस्वरूपमननुगतं स्यात्। यदा ३१ अङ्गुलानि ६ यवाः लब्धः। भूः २६ अङ्गुलानि २ यवौ। अत्रापि क्षेत्रफलं समानमेव। एवं सहस्रधा त्र्यस्रं कुण्डं स्यात्। अतस्त्र्यस्रकुण्डे क्षेत्रफलानयनमेव न प्रमाणम्। समत्रिभुजता चावश्यमपेक्षितेत्यलम्।

अथ शुल्बे कात्यायनः—प्रउगे यावानग्निः सपक्षपुच्छविशेषः तावद् द्विगुणं चतुरस्रं कृत्वा यः पुरस्तात् करणीमध्ये शङ्कुः यौ च श्रोण्योः सोऽग्निः। इति।

अस्यार्थः संक्षिप्त उच्यते। यावतः क्षेत्रस्य त्र्यस्रता कर्त्तुमिष्टा तत्क्षेत्रं द्विगुणितं न्यसेत्। ततः प्रतीचीसूत्रकोणोभयतः सकाशात् मध्यसूत्राग्रावधि सूत्रद्वयं दद्यात् इति। अस्य क्षेत्रफलमङ्गुलद्वयमधिकम्। इदन्तु ऋषिणा शिष्यबुद्धिक्लेशो माभूत् इत्युपेक्षितमिति तद्वृत्तिकारैरेव व्याख्यातम्। इयं लब्धता तु तत्रेष्टकाचितिसम्पादनार्थम्। न तु कुण्डाकारतासम्पादनार्थम्।

नन्विदमेव कल्पद्रुवचनं कुण्डाकारतासम्पादनार्थं प्रमाणमस्तु इति चेत्। तदा शारदातिलककारादिमत-कादिमत-पञ्चरात्र-कामिक-क्रियासार-सिद्धान्तशेखर-आम्नायरहस्य-महाकपिलपञ्चरात्रादिषु अन्येष्वपि बहुषु ग्रन्थेषु मुनिप्रणीतेष्वपि विरोधो दृश्यते। तत्र किं ग्राह्यमिति संशय एव स्यात्। न च वाच्यं कल्पसूत्राणां साक्षादुपलभ्यमानश्रुतिमूलानाम् अनुमितिश्रुतिमूलाभ्यः स्मृतिभ्योऽधिकं प्रामाण्यम्। नानाशाखागतलिङ्गादिकल्पितश्रुत्यर्थोपसंहारोपनिबद्धस्य कल्पस्वरूपत्वात्। प्रयोगशास्त्रमिति चेदित्यस्मिन्नधिकरणे भाष्यकृता कल्पप्रामाण्यस्य व्यवस्थापितत्वात् इति। वार्त्तिककारेणाऽन्यथाधिकरणरचनायाः कृतत्वात्। तथाहि इह कल्पानां प्रामाण्याप्रामाण्यचिन्ता न क्रियते। किं तर्हि कल्पसूत्राण्युदाहृत्य इदं चिन्त्यते। किं तेषां स्वतन्त्राणामेव वेदवत् प्रामाण्यम् उत स्मृतिवत्। श्रुतिपरतन्त्राणामिति तत्र श्रुतिपारतन्त्र्येण स्मृतिवदेव प्रामाण्यं स्थापितम्। किञ्च विरोधाधिकरणे "औडुम्बरीं स्पृष्ट्वोद्गायेत्" इति प्रत्यक्षश्रुतिविरोधात् "औडुम्बरी सर्व्वा वेष्टयितव्या" इति कल्पकृद्वचनं लोभमूलमिति भाष्यकारैः सिद्धान्तितम्। अतः सर्व्वासां स्मृतीनां विरुद्धत्वात् "श्रुतिद्वैधं तु यत्र स्यात् तत्र धर्म्मावुभौ स्मृतौ" इति वचनस्यात्रानवकाशात् अ[स्व]ष्टदोषदुष्टत्वाच्च विकल्पाभावात् सन्देह एव स्थितः। तथा च तत्र विहितस्य कर्म्मणोऽननुष्ठानमेव स्यात्। तस्माद् यत्र समत्रिभुजता तुल्यक्षेत्रफलत्वञ्च भवति तदेव त्रिकोणकुण्डमिति सिद्धान्तः। सर्व्वेषु लक्षणवचनेषु कानिचित् क्षेत्रफलाव्यभिचारीणि कानिचित् समभुजताव्यभिचारीणीति। अतस्तानि त्र्यस्राकारतामात्रसम्पादनफलानीति ज्ञेयम्।

ग्रन्थान्तरे तु—पञ्चभागीकृते क्षेत्रे द्वौ भागौ बाह्यतस्त्यजेत्।
न द्वयोः पार्श्वतस्त्यक्त्वा तस्मान्मध्यं विरच्य च।
कर्णसूत्रद्वयं दद्यात् त्रिकोणं भवति स्फुटम्॥ इति।

अत्र हिनवत्यङ्गुलानि न्यूनानि भुजत्रयसाम्यम्।

सिद्धान्तशेखरेऽपि—चतुरस्रीकृते क्षेत्रे क्षेत्रमष्टांशकं बहिः।
विन्यसेद् गर्भसूत्राग्रे प्रतीचीसूत्रपार्श्वयोः।
सूत्राणां त्रितयं न्यस्येत् त्रिकोणं कुण्डमीरितम्॥ इति।

अत्र च सप्तत्यधिकशताङ्गुलानि न्यूनानि विषमभुजता च।

तस्यैव षष्ठमंशन्तु पार्श्वयोः प्रविकाशयेत्।
प्रत्येकं पश्चिमं सूत्रं तन्मानेनाथ सूत्रयोः॥

अष्टादशांशे क्षेत्रे च न्यसेदेकं बहिर्बुधः।
भ्रमयेत्तेन मानेन वृत्तं कुण्डमनुत्तमम् ॥ ५८

विन्यासाद् ब्रह्मसूत्रान्तात् तदग्रावधिलक्ष्मनात् ॥ इति कादिमते षट्त्रिंशदधिकशताङ्गुलानि न्यूनानि समभुजताऽस्ति। अश्ववतिपरिधि-रेखाभिप्रायं चेदं लक्षणम्।

"त्रिभागवृद्धितो मत्स्यैस्त्रिभिर्निशाचरं भवेत्" इति कामिकेऽपि। तत्र चतुर्वर्गचिन्तामणिकारैः स्थानत्रये भागत्रयवृद्धिरिति व्याख्यातम्। तन्मते चतुःषष्ट्यङ्गुलान्यधिकानि। अन्यैस्तु अग्रे त्र्यंशवृद्धिः उभयपार्श्वे अर्द्धार्द्धतया एकांशवृद्धिरिति व्याख्यातम्। तन्मते चतुःषष्ट्यङ्गुलानि न्यूनानि। उभयमतेऽपि विषमभुजतैवेत्यलम् ॥ ५७ ॥

चतुरस्रप्रकृतितया वृत्तं कुण्डमाह अष्टादशेति। क्षेत्रे पूर्ववच्चतुरस्रमध्यसूत्रे अष्टादशांशेऽष्टादशधा विभक्ते एकमंशं बहिः कस्मिन्नपि सूत्रे वर्द्धयेत्। तेन मानेन मध्यात् तन्मानेन वर्द्धितमानेन भ्रमयेत् तदा वृत्तं पूर्व्वाभिमुखं कुण्डम्। न विद्यते उत्तमं यस्मादित्यनुत्तमम्।

अत्र क्षेत्रोपपत्तिः। तत्राष्टादशांशः १ अङ्गुलं २ यवौ ५ युकाः। तत्र वृत्ते कृते व्यासे एतद्द्विगुणं २ अङ्गुले ५ यवाः २ यूके एतावद्वर्द्धते तदा २६ अङ्गुलानि एकाङ्गुलस्य द्वौ तृतीयांशौ। अयं व्यासः २६$\frac{२}{३}$ सवर्णितः $\frac{८०}{३}$। अथवा अन्यक्षुद्रुक्तप्रकारेणैव न्यासः। तत्र द्वौ अष्टदशांशौ तेन एको नवमांशः तस्य समच्छेदार्थं न्यासः $\frac{२४}{१}$ $\frac{२४}{९}$ समच्छेदौ $\frac{२१६}{९}$ $\frac{२४}{९}$ योगः $\frac{२४०}{९}$ त्रिभिरपवर्त्तितः स एवाङ्कः। ततो "व्यासस्य वर्ग" इत्यादिप्रकारेण लब्धं क्षेत्रफलं पञ्चशती अष्टाधिकानि पञ्चाशद् अङ्गुलानि। तेनाष्टादशाङ्गुलं क्षेत्रं न्यूनं भवति। तेन क्षेत्रफलाव्यभिचारी सर्व्वानुगतप्रकारस्तूच्यते—

वृत्तकुण्डे मध्यसूत्रं चतुर्विंशतिधा भजेत्।
एकांशपञ्चविंशांशसहितं सार्द्धमंशकम्।
बहिर्न्यस्य भ्रमान्मध्याद् वृत्तं कुण्डमितीरितम् ॥

अत्र सार्द्धांशमेकमङ्गुलं चत्वारो यवाः एकस्य पञ्चविंशांशाः २ यूके ४ लिख्या अर्द्ध-सहिताः। वृत्ते कृते एतद्द्विगुणं ३ अङ्गुलानि ० यवाः ५ युकाः १ लिख्या। तेन सर्व्वस्य व्यासस्य न्यासः २७$\frac{२}{२५}$ अयं सवर्णितः $\frac{६७७}{२५}$ "व्यासस्य वर्गे भनवाग्नि"

इत्यादिना लब्धं क्षेत्रफलं ५७६ । इदं सूक्ष्मगणनया क्षेत्रफलम् ।
शुल्बे तु कात्यायनः—

चतुरस्रं मण्डलं चिकीर्षन् मध्यादंशे निपात्य पार्श्वतः परिलिख्य तत्र यदतिरिक्तं भवति तस्य तृतीयेन सह मण्डलं परिलिखेत् स समाधिः । इति ।

अत्रांशशब्देन कोणः । तत्कर्णसूत्रार्द्धं १७ अङ्गुलानि यूकाद्वयोनानि । तच्च मध्यसूत्रात् पञ्चाङ्गुलानि यूकाद्वयन्यूनानि । अधिकं तस्य तृतीयोंऽशोऽङ्गुलमेकम् एकाङ्गुलस्य द्वौ तृतीयांशौ तेन १३ अङ्गुलानि एकस्य द्वौ तृतीयांशौ व्यासार्द्धम् । अयं द्विगुणितो व्यासः २७$\frac{1}{3}$ सवर्णितो यथा $\frac{82}{3}$ । अस्य क्षेत्रफले दशाङ्गुलानि वर्द्धन्ते । यत्तु गणितज्ञाभिमानिनो लक्षणं षोडशधा कृतमध्यमसूत्रक्षेत्रपुरः परिवर्द्धितभागे । एकैक एव ततोऽन्तरचिह्नान् मण्डलकुण्डमिह भ्रमणात् स्यात् इति । अत्र सप्तविंशत्यङ्गुलानि व्यासः । तस्य क्षेत्रफलं ५७२ अङ्गुलानि । अत्र चत्वार्यङ्गुलानि न्यूनानि भवन्ति इति न तदपि सम्यक् । कामिके तु—

कर्णार्द्धाष्टांशसंन्यासाद् वृत्तं कुण्डमिहोदितम् । इति ।

पुरस्तात् सम्यक् न्यासः संन्यासः । अत्र साष्टमांशचतुर्दशाङ्गुलानि व्यासार्द्धमिति महान् व्यभिचारः । ग्रन्थान्तरे तु—

चतुरस्रं पुरा कृत्वा कुण्डक्षेत्रप्रमाणतः ।
नवभागं पुरा कृत्वा चैकभागं बहिर्न्यसेत ॥
तस्मान्मध्यं गृहीत्वैवं भ्रमात्तद्वर्तुलं भवेत् ॥ इति ।

अत्रैकस्य तृतीयांशसहितानि एकोनत्रिंशदङ्गुलानि व्यासः । तेन महत्तरमन्तरम् । केचन एकं भागं बहिर्न्यसेदर्द्धीकृतयेति शेषः । तदा मूलपद्येन सहैकवाक्यता भवति इति वदन्ति । सिद्धान्तशेखरे तु—

चतुरस्रे सुसंसिद्धे तद्बाह्ये भागमष्टमम् ।
क्षेत्रस्य विन्यसेद्दिक्षु मध्यात्सम्मानसूत्रतः ।
भ्रमणभ्रामणेनैवं वृत्तं कुण्डमुदीरितम् ॥ इति ।

अत्र त्रिंशदङ्गुलानि व्यासः तेन महत्तममन्तरम् । अतः सिद्धान्तशेखरवचनं कैश्चिदन्यथा व्याख्यायते । क्षेत्रस्याष्टमं भागं बाह्ये दिक्षु विन्यसेदर्द्धीकृतयेति शेषः । तेनोभयपार्श्वे मिलित्वा अष्टमो भागो भवति । तदा व्यासः २७ क्षेत्रफलं चतुरङ्गुलं न्यूनम् । सूक्ष्मगणनयेति ज्ञातव्यम् । स्थूलगणनायामङ्गीक्रियमाणायां लिखितकात्यायनवचनेन महदन्तरमेव स्यादित्यलम् ॥ ५८ ॥

अष्टधा विभजेत् क्षेत्रं मध्यसूत्रस्य पार्श्वयोः ।
भागं न्यसेदेकमेकं भागेनाऽनेन मध्यतः ॥ ५९
कुर्य्यात् पार्श्वद्वये मत्स्यचतुष्कं तन्त्रवित्तमः ।
सूत्रषट्कं ततो दद्यात् षडस्रं कुण्डमुत्तमम् ॥ ६०

चतुरस्रप्रकृतितया षडस्रं कुण्डमाह अष्टधेति । क्षेत्रं चतुरस्रमध्यसूत्रम् अष्टधा विभजेत् । मध्यसूत्रस्येत्यत्र मध्यसूत्रपदेन दक्षिणोदग्गतसूत्रं गृह्यते । पार्श्वयोरिति वचनात् । अन्यथा मध्य अर्द्धमित्येव ब्रूयात् । तस्य पार्श्वयोर्दक्षिणोत्तराग्रयोः एकमेकं भागं न्यसेद् बहिर्वर्द्धयेत् । ततोऽनेन मानेन वर्द्धितमानेन वर्द्धितचिह्नेन मध्यतो मध्याच्च पार्श्वयुगे वर्द्धितदक्षिणोदग्गतसूत्रमध्यस्य दक्षिणपार्श्वे वामपार्श्वे च पूर्व्वापरभागयोः मत्स्यचतुष्कं कुर्य्यात् । तन्त्रवित्तम इत्यनेन सम्प्रदायेनैवायमर्थो ज्ञेय इत्युक्तम् । तत्र मत्स्योत्पादनप्रकारः । क्षेत्रमध्यादुत्तरकृतचिह्नपरिमितसूत्रस्यादिं क्षेत्रमध्ये निधाय पूर्व्वैशानयोरन्तराले वृत्तार्द्धं कृत्वा तत्र उत्तरकृतचिह्ने तत्सूत्रादिं निधाय तदर्द्धवृत्तभेदि वृत्तार्द्धं कुर्य्यात् । एवं पूर्व्वैशानयोर्दिशोरन्तराले मत्स्यसिद्धिः । एवमेव क्षेत्रमध्याद्दक्षिणकृतचिह्नाच्च पूर्व्वाग्नेयदिशोरन्तराले मत्स्यं कुर्य्यात् । एवमेव क्रमेण पश्चिमवायव्ययोरन्तराले पश्चिमनैर्ऋत्ययोरन्तराले च मत्स्यद्वयं कुर्य्यात् । तत उत्तरचिह्नात् पूर्व्वैशानान्तरालमत्स्यं यावत् एकं सूत्रं पश्चिमवायव्यान्तरालमत्स्यं यावद् द्वितीयं सूत्रं दद्यात् । ततो दक्षिणचिह्नात् पूर्व्वाग्नेयान्तरालमत्स्यं यावत् एकं सूत्रं पश्चिमनैर्ऋत्यान्तरालमत्स्यं यावद् द्वितीयं सूत्रं दद्यात् । एवं सूत्रचतुष्टयदानम् । ततः पूर्व्वमत्स्ययोर्मिथ एकं तद्वत् पश्चिममत्स्ययोर्मिथ एकं सूत्रं दद्यात् । एवं षट्सूत्रसम्पातेन पूर्व्वाभिमुखं षडस्रं कुण्डं भवति । तदुक्तं

क्रियासारे—क्षेत्रं वस्वंशकं कृत्वा बहिः पार्श्वद्वयेऽंशकौ ।
न्यस्त्वाऽनेन प्रमाणेन मध्यात्तुल्यं यथा न्यसेत् ॥
कोणान्यन्यानि चत्वारि पार्श्वयोश्च द्वयं द्वयम् ।
षट्सूत्राणि न्यसेत्तेषु तत् स्यात् षट्कोणकुण्डकम् ॥ इति ।

सिद्धान्तशेखरेऽपि—चतुरस्रे समे सिद्धे क्षेत्रमष्टांशकं बहिः ।
अग्रयोर्गर्भसूत्रस्य योजयेत्तत्प्रदेशतः ॥
गर्भमध्यप्रमाणेन सूत्रेण भ्रमयन्भ्रकम् ।
गर्भमध्ये बहिर्भागे विश्वस्य भ्रमणाङ्कयेत् ॥

उत्तरे दक्षिणे बाह्ये मत्स्ययोर्द्वितयं ततः।
मीने बाह्यांशके मीने मीनयुग्मे ततः क्रमात्।
सूत्रषट्कं न्यसेत् तत्तु कुण्डं षट्कोणमीरितम्॥ इति।

अत्र गर्भसूत्रस्येति दक्षिणोदग्गतसूत्रस्य उत्तरे दक्षिणे इति वर्द्धितदक्षिणोदग्गतसूत्रमध्यस्य उत्तरपार्श्वे दक्षिणपार्श्वे इत्यर्थः।

अत्र क्षेत्रोपपत्तिः। विषमचतुरस्रद्वयं कल्पयेत्। तत एकस्य भूः ३० अङ्गुलानि मुखं १५ लम्बः १३। ततः "लम्बेन निघ्नं कुमुखैक्यखण्डम्" इत्यनेन प्रकारेण लब्धं क्षेत्रफलं २९२ यवचतुष्टयाधिकम्। एवं द्वितीयचतुरस्रस्यापि २९२ यवचतुष्टयाधिकम्। एकत्र मिलितं ५८५। एवं नवाङ्गुलान्यधिकानि भवन्ति। षड्भुजसमता भवत्येव। अत्र "स्वाबाधाभुजकृत्योरन्तरमूलं प्रजायते लम्बः" इत्यनेन लम्बमानसाधनं ज्ञेयम्। यद्वा क्षेत्रत्रयं कल्पयेत्। मध्ये आयतचतुरस्रं पार्श्वयोस्त्र्यस्रद्वयम्। तत्रायतचतुरस्रस्य फलं ३९०। एकस्य त्र्यस्रस्य फलं ९७ यवचतुष्टयाधिकम्। एवं द्वितीयस्यापि। मिलित्वा क्षेत्रफलं ५८५। एवं विषमचतुरस्रचतुष्टयं परिकल्प्य १४६ यवद्वयम् एतावदेकैकस्य फलमानीय सन्तोष्टव्यम्। यद्वा त्र्यस्रषट्कं परिकल्प्य एकैकस्य ९७ यवचतुष्टयाधिकं फलमानीय संवाद्यम्। एवमन्यप्रकारेणापि फलसंवाद ऊहनीयः। अन्ये त्वन्यथा वर्णयन्ति। क्षेत्रचतुरस्रमध्यसूत्रमष्टधा विभजेत्। मध्यसूत्रस्य प्राचीसूत्रस्य पार्श्वयोरध ऊर्द्ध्वञ्च एकं भागं न्यसेत्। मध्यसूत्रस्य दक्षिणोदग्गतस्य च पार्श्वयोरधः ऊर्द्ध्वमेकं भागं न्यसेत्। ततो मध्यतोऽनेन मानेन पार्श्वयुगे मत्स्यचतुष्कं कुर्य्यात्। तत्र मत्स्यकरणप्रकारः। पूर्व्वापरायतसूत्रचिह्नद्वयस्य दक्षिणोत्तरतस्तेन मानेन मत्स्यद्वयं कुर्य्यात्। तत्र चतुरस्रपूर्व्वपरिधिरेखया दक्षिणोत्तरया प्राचीसूत्रस्य यत्र सम्पातः तत उपर्य्यधश्च त्र्यङ्गुलेन तां परिधिरेखामङ्कयित्वा पूर्व्वतः कृतचिह्नदक्षिणभागे अर्द्धवृत्तं कृत्वा परिधिरेखागतदक्षिणचिह्नात् तद्वत्रत्निभेदि अर्द्धवृत्तं कुर्य्यात्। एवं दक्षिणभागे मत्स्यसिद्धिः। एवमुत्तरभागेऽपि। एवमुक्तप्रकारेण चतुरस्रपश्चिमपरिधिरेखायामपि अङ्कद्वयं कृत्वा पश्चिमदिशि कृतचिह्नस्य दक्षिणोत्तरभागयोर्मत्स्यद्वयं कुर्य्यात्। ततो वर्द्धितदक्षिणचिह्नात् पूर्व्वदक्षिणभागमत्स्यं यावदेकं सूत्रं पश्चिमदिग्दक्षिणभागमत्स्यं यावद् द्वितीयं सूत्रं दद्यात्। एवं वर्द्धितोत्तरचिह्नात् पूर्व्वदिगुत्तरभागमत्स्यं यावदेकं सूत्रं पश्चिमदिगुत्तरभागमत्स्यं यावद् द्वितीयं सूत्रम्। एवं सूत्रचतुष्टयदानम्। ततः पूर्व्वमत्स्ययोर्मिथ एकं सूत्रं पश्चिममत्स्ययोर्मिथ एकं

सूत्रम् । एवं षट्सूत्रस्य सम्पातात् षडस्रं कुण्डमिति । अत्र विषमचतुरस्रद्वयं प्रकल्प्य एकस्य चेत्रफलं २७० । एवं द्वितीयस्यापि । मिलित्वा ५४० । तन्मते मध्यसूत्रस्य पार्श्वयोरित्यस्यावृत्तिर्भवति । किञ्च क्वचिन्मध्यसूत्रशब्देन प्राचीसूत्रं गृह्यते क्वचिद्दक्षिणोदग्गतसूत्रं तदसम्बद्धम् । प्रमाणाभावात् । मध्यत इति पदं व्यर्थमेव स्यात् । मतस्योत्पादनार्थं चतुरस्रपरिधिरेखयोर्यदङ्कनं तदपि स्वकपोलकल्पितम् । चेत्रफलमध्ये षट्त्रिंशदङ्गुलानि न्यूनानि विषमभुजता चेत्य-ज्ञानविजृम्भितम् । यत् त्वस्यैव व्याख्याने प्राचीसूत्रपूर्व्वापरभागयोः कोणपात-मिच्छन्ति तेन मतस्था एव अथ तत्र चेत्रफलसाम्यापादनाय बहवः प्रकाराः सम्भाव्यन्ते । तत्र कश्चित्—

अष्टधा विभजेत् चेत्रं मध्यसूत्रादधोपरि ।
भागं न्यसेदेकमेकं पार्श्वयोस्तु दिगङ्कतः ॥
संम्वर्द्ध्य चेत्रेष्वष्टांशं तत ऊर्द्ध्वाधरौ तिमी ।
चेत्राष्टमांशतः कुर्य्याद् दिक्सूत्रे तावदङ्कतः ॥
संभेद्य चेत्रषष्ठांशं गुणैनैवमुदक् तिमी ।
षट्सूत्रीं पातयेत्तेषु षडस्रकुण्डमुत्तमम् ॥ इति ।

अत्र दक्षिणोदग्गतमध्यसूत्रमष्टाङ्गुलं वर्द्धितं चेत्रफलमन्यूनानतिरिक्तमेव । षड्भुजसाम्यं नास्ति । तथा च—

अष्टोनद्विशतांशकेऽन्तरगुणे चेत्रस्य तिर्य्यक्स्थिता-
न्तः सूत्रोभयतो भ २७ वर्द्धनभवाङ्कोर्द्ध्वाधरे चिह्नयेत् ।
तत्त्वां २५ शेषु भषैः पुरोऽप्यधरतोऽङ्कद्वयं २८ ह्यौ भष-
हन्दा द्विद्विगुणे द्विपार्श्वगुणतस्तिस्यो: षडस्रोरितम् ॥ इति

अत्रापि चेत्रफलमन्यूनानतिरिक्तमेव । षड्भुजसाम्यञ्च नास्ति । अन्यच्च इदं वायव्यकुण्डं तच्च पूर्व्वाग्रम् । अत्र च पूर्व्वपश्चिमयोरेव कोणपाताद् योनिस्थापनान-वकाशात् । "न कुर्य्यात् कुण्डकोणेषु योनिं तां तन्त्रवित्तमः" इति । कोणे योनिस्थापनस्य निषेधात् । कुण्डस्य पूर्व्वाग्रता व्याहन्यते । एतल्लक्षणद्वयकृता च स्वग्रन्थे कुण्डान्युक्तोक्तम्—

प्रागादि कुण्डत्रयमुत्तराग्रं याम्यद्वयोनीतरपञ्चकुण्डी ।
प्रागग्रिका पश्चिमयोनिरत्र । इति योनिलक्षणं वदता चोक्तम्—
मघवशिखिकृतान्तदिक्स्थकुण्डेष्वियमधिमेखलमेव मध्यभागे ।
यमदिशि शशिदिङ्मुखी निवेश्या वरुणदिशीतरकुण्ड ऐन्द्रवक्त्रा ॥ इति ।

तेन खग्रन्थे पूर्व्वापरविरोधोऽपि नोपलक्षित इति यत् किञ्चिदेतत्। तथा च। प्राचीमध्यसूत्रमङ्गुलत्रयं वर्द्धयेत्। ततो वर्द्धितचिह्नात् दक्षिणोत्तरतः चतुरङ्गुलमानेन चतुरस्रपूर्व्वपरिधिरेखाङ्काभ्यां मत्स्यद्वयं कुर्य्यात्। एवं पश्चिमदिश्यपि दक्षिणोदग्गतसूत्रम् अङ्गुलत्रयम् अङ्गुलस्य षष्ठांशसहितं वर्द्धयेत्। एवमपि क्षेत्रफलमन्यूनमेव। इतोऽपि बहवः प्रकाराः सम्भाव्यन्ते। क्षेत्रफल-साम्यापादनाय नतु षड्भुजसाम्यापादनाय। एवं कुण्डस्याननुगतता प्रसज्यते। तेन षडस्रकुण्डे षसामपि भुजानां साम्यं क्षेत्रफलसाम्यम् अवश्यमपेक्षितम्। यतोऽत्र क्रियासारे कादिमते कामिके सिद्धान्तशेखरेऽपि षड्भुजसमताया उक्तत्वात्। तत्र सर्व्वानुगत प्रकारस्तूच्यते—

> षडस्रे मध्यसूत्रन्तु चतुर्विंशतिधा भजेत्।
> तच्चैकैकनवांशोनत्र्यंशैः सम्बर्द्ध्य मध्यतः॥
> भ्रमयेत् तेन सद्वृत्तं तद्व्यासार्द्धेन लाञ्छयेत्।
> षट्सु स्थानेषु षट्सूत्रपातनात् तत् षडस्रकम्॥ इति।

अस्यार्थः। त्रयोऽंशा अङ्गुलत्रयम्। तत् कोदृक्। एकस्य नवमोऽंशः तेनोनम्। तेनायं वृत्तव्यासः २८ अङ्गुलानि ६ यवाः २ यूके किञ्चिदूने। तस्य सवर्णनार्थं व्यासः २९ $\frac{७}{९}$ सवर्णितः $\frac{२६८}{९}$ व्यासार्द्धं $\frac{१३४}{९}$ व्यासचतुर्थांशः $\frac{६७}{९}$ इयमेवाबाधा। ततः "स्वाबाधाभुजकृत्योः" इत्यनेनानीय लम्बः। कुमुखैक्यखण्डे लम्बेन गुणिते छेदेन भक्ते लब्धम् एकविषमचतुरस्रस्य क्षेत्रफलं २८८। एवं द्वितीयस्यापि। मिलित्वा क्षेत्रफलं ५७६। अथवा मध्ये आयतचतुरस्रं पार्श्वयोस्त्र्यस्रद्वयं कल्पयेत्। तत्र व्यासचतुर्थांशः शरः अयमेवोभयत्र्यस्रस्य लम्बः। ततः

> व्यासाच्छरोनाच्छरसंगुणाच्च मूलं द्विनिघ्नं भवतीह जीवा।

इति आनीता ज्या २६ किञ्चिदूना। ततो मध्यायतचतुरस्रस्य "तथायते तद्भुज-कोटिघातः" इत्यनेन पूर्व्ववच्च त्र्यस्रद्वयस्यापि फलमानीय सर्व्वमेकीकृतं क्षेत्रफलं ५७६। एवं विषमचतुरस्रचतुष्टयं त्र्यस्रषट्कं वा कल्पयित्वा फलसंवाद ऊहनीयः। अत्र षसां भुजानामपि साम्यमस्ति। तत्तु—

> खखखाभ्ररसैरङ्कै ६०००० वृत्तव्यासे समाहृते।
> खखखाभ्रार्कै १२०००० संभक्ते लभ्यन्ते क्रमशो भुजाः॥

इति भास्कराचार्य्योक्तपरिपाट्या भुजानयनेन समूह्यम्। यत्तु कादिमते—

> तन्मध्यद्वादशांशेन विकाश्य ब्रह्मसूत्रकम्।
> तेन मानेन च तथा कृत्वा वृत्तमपि स्फुटम्॥

चतुरस्रीकृतं क्षेत्रं विभज्याऽष्टादशांशतः ।

एकं भागं बहिर्न्यस्य भ्रामयेत्तेन वर्त्तुलम् ॥ ६१

वृत्तानि कर्णिकादीनां बहिस्त्रीणि प्रकल्पयेत् ।

पद्मकुण्डमिदं प्रोक्तं विलोचनमनोहरम् ॥ ६२

तद्वृत्ते वृत्तमध्यस्य कुर्य्यादङ्कं च लाञ्छनम् ।

तत्र षट्सूत्रपातेन भवेत् कुण्डं षडस्रकम् ॥ इति ।

अत्र क्षेत्रफलमध्ये पञ्चशतषट्सप्तत्यङ्गुलमध्ये द्विसप्तत्यङ्गुलानि न्यूनानि । भुजसाम्यमस्त्येव ।

षड्भागवृद्धितो मत्स्यैश्चतुर्भिः स्यात् षडस्रकम् । इति

कामिके तु महान् व्यभिचारः । भुजसाम्यमस्त्येव । पश्चवर्तिपरिधिरेखाभिप्रायेणेदं लक्षणम् । यत्तु ततस्तन्मत्स्यचतुष्टयानुसारेण चतुरस्रसम्बन्धि पूर्वपश्चिमपरिधिरेखायां लाञ्छनचतुष्टयं विदध्यादिति चतुर्वर्गचिन्तामणिकारव्याख्यानम् तत्तु क्षेत्रफलानुसारेण कल्पितमिति उपेक्षणीयम् । तादृशशब्दाभावात् भुजसाम्याभावाच्च ॥ ५८ ॥ ६० ॥

चतुरस्रप्रकृतितया पद्मकुण्डमाह चतुरस्रीकृतमिति । इदं वृत्तकुण्डे व्याख्यातम् । तत्र कर्णिकादीनां वृत्तानि त्रीणि बहिः प्रकल्पयेदिति । तत्र कृतवृत्ताद्बहिस्त्रीणि वृत्तानि क्रियन्ते चेत् तदा—

यावान् कुण्डस्य विस्तारः खननं तावदीरितम् ।

इति वचनात् न ज्ञायते कियद्वस्तं कुण्डं स्यादिति नैतद्व्याख्यातम् । किं तर्हि बहिरिति वीप्सा मध्यादिति शेषः । तेन वृत्ते कृते मध्याद्बहिः बहिः कर्णिकादीनां त्रीणि वृत्तानि कुर्य्यादित्यर्थः । तदुक्तं क्रियासारे—

कृत्वैवं पूर्व्ववद्वृत्तं तन्मध्ये वर्त्तुलत्रयम् ।

भ्राम्यैवं पङ्कजाकारं कारयेत् कर्णिकादिभिः ॥ इति ।

तदा यत् कृतं सर्व्वबाह्यवृत्तं तदेव दलाग्रवृत्तं स्यात् । तदा दलाग्रकरणे यत् क्षेत्रं त्यज्यते तेनात्यन्तं क्षेत्रस्य न्यूनता स्यात् । पूर्व्वं वृत्तकुण्डे अष्टादशाङ्गुलन्यूनता दर्शिता । अत्र ततोऽपि न्यूनता स्यात् । तेनैवं कैश्चिद् व्याख्यायते । इदं ग्रन्थकृता यद्वृत्तमुक्तं तत्तु क्षेत्रसंग्रहमात्रं कृतं क्षेत्रसीमावृत्तमित्यर्थः । वक्ष्यमाणपद्मकरणे—पद्मक्षेत्रस्य संत्यज्य द्वादशांशं बहिः सुधीः ।

तन्मध्यं विभजेद् वृत्तैस्त्रिभिः समविभागतः ॥

इत्युक्तत्वात् । अत्र व्यासद्वादशांशः अङ्गुलद्वयं सपादं तत्र यत् सीमावृत्तं तस्याध एकाङ्गुलम् एको यवस्तत्र वृत्तं कुर्य्यात् । तदुपर्य्यपि तेनैव मानेन वृत्तं कुर्य्यात् । तेन मध्ये सीमावृत्तं जातम् । तत्रान्तर्वृत्तस्य चतुर्विंशत्यङ्गुलानि यवत्रयं च व्यासः । तत्र समविभागतस्त्रीणि वृत्तानि कुर्य्यात् । ततो वर्द्धितद्वादशांशेन दलाग्राणि कुर्य्यात् । तत्र बहिर्वृत्तस्य अष्टाविंशत्यङ्गुलानि सप्तयवा व्यासः । तत्रोभयवृत्त-क्षेत्रफलमेकीकृत्यार्द्धमस्य क्षेत्रफलम् । अत्रापि व्यभिचारः । यतोऽधोवृत्तस्य क्षेत्रफलं ४६७ सर्व्वोपरिवृत्तस्य क्षेत्रफलं ६५८ एकीकृतं ११२६ एतदर्द्धं ५६३ तेन त्रयोदशाङ्गुलानि न्यूनानि भवन्ति । वस्तुतस्तु पद्मक्षेत्रस्योत्पादको यः पद्मकरण-प्रकारः स सर्व्वतोभद्रमण्डलादाविव ज्ञेयः । नवकुण्डकरणे तत्र क्षेत्रस्याधिक्यं स्यात् । यत्तु ग्रन्थकारेण "वृत्तानि कर्णिकादीनां बहिस्त्रीणि" इति क्रियासारेऽपि "वर्त्तुलत्रयम्" इति तत्तु पत्रोर्द्ध्वभूवृत्ताभिप्रायेणैवेति ध्येयम् । पत्राग्रे वृत्तमधिकं कुर्य्यात् इति सूचयितुं तेनापि क्षेत्रफलमधिकं किञ्चित् । तेन पद्मकुण्डकरणे एव्वृत्तान्येवेति ज्ञेयम् । तेनात्र तद्वदर्द्धनिशाकरकरणमपि नास्ति । अत्र क्षेत्रफलाव्यभिचारी सर्व्वानुगतप्रकारस्तूच्यते ।

पद्मकुण्डे मध्यसूत्रं चतुर्विंशतिधा भजेत् ।
भ्रमयेत् कर्णिकावृत्तं त्र्यंशवृत्तार्द्धमानतः ॥
षडंशवृत्तार्द्धमानभ्रमितवृत्ते तु केशराः ।
नवांशवृत्तार्द्धमाने वृत्ते स्यात् पत्रमध्यभूः ॥
द्वादशांशात्तु वृत्ताज्ज्ञातं पत्रोर्द्ध्वभूः स्मृता ।
दलाग्राणान्तु वृत्तार्द्धं कृत्वा पञ्चदशांशकैः ॥
न्यूनैः पञ्चभिरेकांशश्चतुष्षष्ट्यंशकैर्भ्रमात् ।
रेखाग्रेभ्यः पत्रसीम्नो दलाग्राणि प्रकल्पयेत् ॥

अत्र मध्ये षडङ्गुलव्यासा कर्णिका । "यावान् कुण्डस्य विस्तारः खननं तावदीरितम्" इति वक्ष्यमाणत्वात् । तेन कर्णिकाखननमपि प्राप्तम् । तत्र कर्णिका किञ्चिदुच्चा रक्षणीया । तदुच्चता यद्यप्यत्र नोक्ता तथापि नाभिकथने एकहस्तस्य नाभिं नेत्रवेदाङ्गुलोपेताम् इति वक्ष्यति । तेन सा चतुरङ्गुलव्यासा द्व्यङ्गुलोत्सेधा । तत्र यदि चतुरङ्गुलव्यासाया द्व्यङ्गुल उत्सेधः तदा षडङ्गु-लव्यासायाः कियानुत्सेध इति त्रैराशिकेनोच्चता आनेया । तत्र त्रैराशिकसूत्रम्—

प्रमाणमिच्छा च समानजाती आद्यन्तयो स्तः फलमन्यजाति ।
मध्ये तदिच्छाहतमाद्यहृत् स्यादिच्छाफलं व्यस्तविधिर्विलोमे ॥ इति ।

तत्र त्रैराशिकस्य न्यासः ४।२।६ ततोऽन्त्येन ६ मध्यस्थं २ गुणितं १२। आदिना ४ भक्तं लब्धोच्चता ३। तदुक्तं कामिके—

उत्सेधन्तु ततः कुर्य्यात् कर्णिकार्द्धांशमानतः। इति।

अतो ग्रन्थकृदग्रे योनिकुण्डे योनिम् अब्जकुण्डे नाभिञ्च वर्जयेत् इति वक्ष्यति। सिद्धान्तशेखरेऽपि—योनौ योनिं न कुर्व्वीत पद्मे पद्मं न कारयेत्। इति।

क्रियासारेऽपि— योन्यामम्बुजकुण्डयोः।

क्रमेण योनिं नाभिञ्च न कुर्व्वीत चतुर्मुख॥ इति।

तस्मात् त्र्यङ्गुलं कर्णिकोच्चतां संस्थाप्याऽन्यत् खननीयम्। केशरस्थानमपि खनित्वा अधोभागे केशराणि स्थापयेत्। दलाग्राकारतया दलमध्यः सर्व्वोऽपि खननीयः। तत्र चतुर्विंशतिव्यासवृत्ताद्बहिर्यद्वृत्तं तस्यार्द्धमेव यथा गृह्यते तथा कुशलतया बाह्यहस्तेन दलाग्राणि रचयेत्। यस्तु हस्तत एव पत्राणां वक्रता सा च पत्र-सीमारेखा। पत्रोर्द्ध्वभूवृत्तसम्पातात् पत्रमध्ये रेखां यावदुभयतो रेखादानात्। इदं पद्मकुण्डम्।

अत्र क्षेत्रोपपत्तिः। चतुर्विंशतिव्यासवृत्ते पूर्व्ववत् फलं ४५२ अङ्गुलानि ३ यवाः ४ यूकाः। बहिर्वृत्तस्य एकाङ्गुलस्य दशभिश्चतुःषष्टंशैरूनत्रिंशदङ्गुल-व्यासस्य क्षेत्रफलं ६९८ अङ्गुलानि ४ यवाः ४ यूकाः। मिलितं ११५२। एतदर्द्धं क्षेत्रफलं ५७६। इदमतिसूक्ष्मं फलम्। तदुक्तं कामिके—

चतुरस्राष्टभागेन कर्णिका स्याद्विभागशः।
तद्बहिस्त्वेकभागेन केशराणि प्रकल्पयेत्॥
तृतीये दलमध्यानि चतुर्थे दलकोटयः।
चतुरस्राद्बहिः कुर्य्याद्दलाग्राण्यपि यत्नतः॥ इति।

अत्र क्षेत्रफलं चतुरङ्गुलमधिकम्। यत्तु अतिगणितज्ञाभिमानिनो लक्षणे—

क्षेत्रेऽन्तश्चतुरस्रके विततिवस्वंशेन वृत्तं कृतं
व्यासार्द्धेन तु कर्णिका पुनरियद्वृद्ध्या क्रमात् केशराः।
तद्वृद्ध्या दलमध्यभूः पुनरियद्वृद्ध्या क्रमेणोर्द्ध्वभूः
क्षेत्रव्यासजिनांशकस्य त्रिशिखैरूनं कलांशैः पुनः॥
तत् सम्बद्ध दलाग्रकाणि रचयेत् क्षेत्रार्द्धमुज्झन् विना
स्यात् त्रिंशन्नवविस्तृतीयमियता छिन्नेन वृत्तं बहिः।
स्वव्यासार्द्धमितोच्चतामिह खनेत् त्यक्त्वान्तरा कर्णिकां
कुर्व्वन् केशरचिह्नमष्टदलकं यद्वा चतुर्भिर्दलैः॥ इति।

पूर्व्वोक्तं विभजेत् क्षेत्रं चतुर्विंशतिभागतः ।
एकं भागं बहिर्न्यस्य चतुरस्रं प्रकल्पयेत् ॥ ६२

अत्र क्षेत्रफले एकादशाङ्गुलानि न्यूनानि भवन्ति ।

तथा—भांशन्तु वृत्तव्यासस्य स्वाष्टांशेनाधिकं बहिः ।

सम्बर्द्ध्य मध्यादिलिखेद् बाह्यवृत्तं द्वितीयकम् ॥
तृतीयं तावतैवान्यत् सीमावृत्तान्तरा लिखेत् ।
अष्टसूत्र्या षोड़शधा तत्क्षेत्रं विभजेत्ततः ॥
पत्रमध्यस्थसूत्रान्ताद् यथा बाह्यकरस्तथा ।
तत्पार्श्वसूत्रान्तरस्थवृत्तं सम्पाततो लिखेत् ॥
वृत्तार्द्धे द्वे दलाग्रार्थमन्तर्वीथ्यां हि यावती ।
त्यक्ता भूः स्याद्बहिर्वीथ्यां तावती त्यज्यते यथा ॥
क्षेत्रत्र्यंशेन मध्ये स्यात् कर्णिका स्वदलोन्नता ।
पत्राग्राणि तदाकारात् खनेदखिलमन्तरम् ॥
एवमष्टदलाब्जाभं जायते कुण्डमुत्तमम् ॥ इति ।

अत्र महान् व्यभिचारः । कामिकेऽपि चतुर्दलताप्युक्ता ।

अवशिष्टदलं वेददलमष्टदलन्तु वा । इति ।

अन्यत्रापि—

दशांशे च विन्यस्य बाह्येऽंशमेकं परिभ्राम्य तेनैव वृत्तं दलानाम् ।
बहिर्मध्यमे कर्णिकां वापि कुर्य्यात् भवेदष्टपत्रं बुधः पद्मकुण्डम् ॥ इति ।

अत्राल्पमन्तरम् । सिद्धान्तशेखरे—

चतुरस्रेऽष्टधा भक्ते कुर्य्याद्वृत्तचतुष्टयम् ।
कर्णिकाकेशरे वृत्ते तृतीये पत्रसञ्चयः ॥
दलाग्राणि चतुर्थे स्युर्वृत्तान्येवं प्रकल्पयेत् ।
कोष्ठयुग्मस्य मध्येऽपि भ्रमयन्तं निधाय च ॥
भ्रमणात् सन्धिमारभ्य पत्राग्रं बाह्यतो भवेत् ।
चतुर्दिक्षु चतुष्पत्रं पद्माभं कुण्डमीरितम् ॥
अथवाऽष्टदलं पद्मं कुर्य्यात्क्वाप्योक्तमार्गतः ॥ इति ।

अत्र तु अत्यन्तं न्यूनं क्षेत्रफलम् ॥ ६१ ॥ ६२ ॥

चतुरस्रप्रकृतितया अष्टास्रं कुण्डमाह पूर्व्वोक्तमिति । पूर्व्वोक्तं क्षेत्रं पूर्व्वोक्त-

अन्तस्थचतुरस्रस्य कोणार्द्धार्द्धप्रमाणतः।
बाह्यस्य चतुरस्रस्य कोणाभ्यां परिलाञ्छयेत् ॥ ६४

दिशं प्रति यथान्यायमष्टसूत्राणि पातयेत्।
अष्टास्रं कुण्डमेतद्धि तन्त्रविद्भिरुदाहृतम् ॥ ६५

चतुरस्रमध्यसूत्रं चतुर्विंशतिभागतो विभजेत्। एकं भागं चतुर्दिक्षु बहिर्न्यस्य षड्विंशत्यङ्गुलायामविस्तारं चतुरस्रान्तरं बहिः कुर्य्यादित्यर्थः। अत्र कोणशब्देन कोणसूत्रम्। अन्तःस्थचतुरस्रस्य यत् कोणसूत्रं यूकाचतुष्टयोनचतुस्त्रिंशदङ्गुलानि। तदर्द्धं यूकाद्वयोनसप्तदशाङ्गुलानि। तदर्द्धं यूकोनसार्द्धाष्टाङ्गुलानि। तत्प्रमाणतः बाह्यस्य चतुरस्रस्य कोणाभ्यां सकाशात् परिलाञ्छयेत्। बाह्यचतुरस्रपरिधिरेखास्वमित्यर्थः। कोणाभ्यामितीशाग्नेयाभ्याम्। एवमाग्नेयनैर्ऋताभ्यामित्यादि। ततो दिशं प्रति अष्टसूत्रसम्पातादष्टास्रं कुण्डम्।

तत्र सूत्रपातनप्रकारः। कोणपार्श्वयोर्ये लाञ्छने तयोर्मिथ एकम् एवं दिक्षु सूत्रचतुष्टयम्। बाह्यचतुरस्ररेखासु लाञ्छनद्वयमध्यसूत्राण्येव। चतुर्दिक् सूत्राणि एवमष्टसूत्राणि। तत्राष्टसूत्राणां सम्भवात् अष्टसूत्राणि पातयेदित्युक्तिः। इदमेव यथान्यायमित्यनेनोक्तम्।

अत्र क्षेत्रोपपत्तिः। तत्र त्रीणि क्षेत्राणि मध्ये आयतचतुरस्रं पार्श्वयोर्विषमचतुरस्रे। तत्रायतस्यैको भुजः ८$\frac{१}{६४}$ सवर्णितः $\frac{५७७}{६४}$। द्वितीयो भुजः २६। "तथाऽऽयते तद्भुजकोटिघातः" इति। अनेन लब्धं क्षेत्रफलं २३४ अङ्गुलानि ३ यवाः २ यूके। ततो विषमचतुरस्रद्वयस्य भूः २६ मुखं सवर्णितं $\frac{५७७}{६४}$ तयोर्लम्बः ८$\frac{६३}{१२८}$ सवर्णितः $\frac{१०८७}{१२८}$। "लम्बेन निघ्नं कुमुखैक्यखण्डम्" इति लब्धं क्षेत्रफलम् १४८ अङ्गुलानि ५ यवाः ३ यूकाः। एवं द्वितीयस्यापि। सर्व्वं मिलितं ५३१ अङ्गुलानि ६ यवाः। तेन यवद्वयाधिकचतुश्चत्वारिंशदङ्गुलानि न्यूनानि। अष्टभुजसमता च नास्ति। अन्यूनानतिरिक्त-क्षेत्रफलानयनेनैव कुण्डसिद्धिरिति चेत् तदा अष्टास्राणि अनेकानि कुण्डानि स्युः। तथाहि षड्विंशतिविस्तारायामे बाह्यचतुरस्रे अर्द्धयवसहितसप्ताङ्गुलैः कोणपार्श्वयोः लाञ्छिते सति मध्यायतचतुरस्रस्यैको भुजः २६ अपरो भुजः ११ अङ्गुलानि ७ यवाः। अस्य क्षेत्रफलं ३०८ अङ्गुलानि ४ यवाः। विषमचतुरस्रद्वयस्य भूः २६ मुखं ११ अङ्गुलानि ७ यवाः। लम्बः अर्द्धयवसहितसप्ताङ्गुलानि। अस्य क्षेत्रफलं १२३

अङ्गुलानि ६ यवाः। एवमन्यस्यापि। सर्व्वं मिलित्वा क्षेत्रफलं ५७६। तथा सप्तविंशतिविस्तारायामे बाह्यचतुरस्रे षड्यवाष्टाङ्गुलैः कोणपार्श्वतोऽङ्किते आयतचतुरस्रस्य भुजः २७ अपरः सार्द्धनवाङ्गुलानि तस्य क्षेत्रफलं २५६। विषमचतुरस्रद्वयस्य भूः २७ मुखं सार्द्धनवाङ्गुलानि लम्बोऽष्टाङ्गुलानि षड्यवाः। एकस्य क्षेत्रफलं १६०। एतावदन्यस्यापि। मिलित्वा क्षेत्रफलं ५७६। एवमष्टाविंशत्यायामविस्तारे बाह्यचतुरस्रे सार्द्धयवसहितदशाङ्गुलैः कोणपार्श्वतो लाञ्छिते मध्यायतचतुरस्रस्यैको भुजः २८ अपरः सप्ताङ्गुलानि पञ्चयवाः तत् फलं २१२ विषमचतुरस्रद्वयस्य भूः २८ मुखं सप्ताङ्गुलानि पञ्चयवाः। लम्बो दशाङ्गुलानि सार्द्धौ यवः। अस्य फलं १८१ अङ्गुलानि ४ यवाः। एतावदन्यस्यापि। मिलित्वा क्षेत्रफलं ५७६। एतादृशाः सहस्रशः प्रकाराः सम्भाव्यन्ते। नहि तावन्त्यपि सर्व्वाण्यष्टास्रकुण्डानि। यतः कुण्डस्याननुगतता प्रसज्यते। तेन यत्र तुल्याष्टभुजत्वं तुल्यक्षेत्रफलत्वञ्च तदेवाष्टास्रं कुण्डमिति सम्प्रदायविदः। तस्य सर्व्वानुगत प्रकार सूच्यते।

कुण्डेऽष्टास्रे मध्यसूत्रं चतुर्विंशतिधा भजेत्।
एकसार्द्धाष्टमांशाद्यमंशमेकं बहिर्न्यसेत्॥
चतुर्दिक्ष्वथ तन्मानाच्चतुरस्रान्तरं भवेत्।
षट्चत्वारिंशदेकांश चतुःषष्ट्यंशसंयुतैः॥
सप्तांशैर्लाञ्छयेद्बाह्यचतुरस्रास्त्रिपार्श्वतः।
दिक्ष्वष्टसूत्रसम्पाता दष्टास्रं समबाहुकम्॥

अत्र षड्विंशत्यङ्गुलानि यवत्रयम् एतद्विस्तारायामं बाह्यचतुरस्रम् तत्तु सप्ताङ्गुलानि पञ्चयवाः षड्यूकाः। एतन्मानेन कोणपार्श्वयोर्लाञ्छितम्। तेनात्र मध्यायतचतुरस्रस्यैको भुजः २६ $\frac{3}{8}$ सवर्णितः $\frac{211}{8}$। अपरो भुजः २३ $\frac{7}{16}$ सवर्णितः $\frac{375}{16}$ पूर्व्ववल्लब्धं क्षेत्रफलं २८८। तत ऊर्द्ध्वाधो विषमचतुरस्रद्वयस्य सवर्णिता भूः $\frac{211}{8}$। सवर्णितं मुखं $\frac{175}{16}$। लम्बः ७ $\frac{46}{64}$ सवर्णितः $\frac{494}{64}$ अत्रैकस्य फलं १४४। एतावदपरस्यापि। मिलित्वा क्षेत्रफलं ५७६। एवमत्राष्टानां भुजानां साम्यमाप्नोति। इदमेवाष्टास्रं कुण्डमिति मन्तव्यम्। चतुर्णां भुजानां साम्यं प्रत्यक्षतः सिद्धम्। अन्येषान्तु चतुर्णां "तत्कृत्योर्योगपदं कर्ण" इत्यनेन प्रकारेणानेयम्। तच्छब्देन कोटिभुजौ बहिश्चतुरस्रगौ तत्कर्णौपरिस्थितौ तावत्रैतौ $\frac{494}{64}$। अथवा सुगम प्रकारान्तरमुच्यते।

कुण्डेऽष्टास्रे मध्यसूत्रं चतुर्विंशतिधा भजेत् ।
एकांशद्वयमांशाढ्यं भ्रमद्वया तु वर्त्तुलम् ।
तन्मध्ये दिग्द्वयस्थसूत्रदानादष्टास्रकं समम् ॥

अत्रापि अष्टानामपि भुजानां समता । श्रा तु—

द्विद्विनन्देषुवेदैश्च ४५९२२ वृत्तव्यासे समाहते ।
खखखाभ्रार्क १२०००० संभक्ते लभ्यन्ते क्रमशो भुजा: ॥

इति भास्कराचार्योक्तप्रकारेणानेया । ये तु गणितज्ञस्य लक्षणे—

चतुरस्रे मध्यसूत्रं षष्ठांशेन विवर्द्धयेत् ।
स्वजिनांशाधिकेनाऽथ तावन्मानं बहिर्गतम् ॥
चतुरस्रान्तरं कृत्वा कोणार्द्धेषु लाञ्छयेत् ।
स्थानाष्टके तत: सूत्राण्येकैकं स्यात्तु चिह्नत: ॥
नयेत्तार्त्तीयितार्त्तीयं चिह्नं प्रत्यष्ट बुद्धिमान् ।
तत्सम्पातान्तरं सृष्ट्वा चतुरस्रे तथा उभे ॥
अष्टास्रं दर्शयेत् कुण्डं तुल्यक्षेत्रफलं समम् । इति ।

तथा— क्षेत्रव्यासजिनांशकेषु चतुर: संवर्द्ध्य सार्कं तथा
षट्त्रिंशेन लवेन चैकलवकस्यैतद्द्वितत्या वहेत् ।
वेदास्त्रित्यदुदारदिग्गुणयुतं दिक्कोणमध्ये कृता-
ष्टाङ्केष्वष्टगुणैस्तृतीयमिलितैरष्टास्रिकुण्डं भवेत् ॥ इति ।

एते अपि न साम्प्रदायिके । यत: क्षेत्रफलं यथाकथञ्चित् संवदन्ति । एकलाञ्छनात् तृतीयलाञ्छनपर्य्यन्तं सूत्रपात: क्वचिदप्यनुक्त इति स्वकपोलकल्पितमेतत् । किञ्च एवम्भूते अष्टास्रकुण्डे सति योनिस्थापनस्थानमेव नास्ति। सर्व्वत्र कोणरूपत्वात् कुण्डस्य । ग्रन्थकृदेव वक्ष्यति—

नार्पयेत् कुण्डकोणेषु योनिं तां मन्त्रवित्तम: । इति ।

कामिके तु—क्षेत्राद् द्वादशकं भागं चतुर्दिक्षु तदन्तरे ।
विन्यस्य तत्प्रमाणेन तुर्य्यांशमपरे नयेत् ।
तस्य कर्णप्रमाणेन तद्भुजास्वपि लाञ्छयेत् ॥
तत्राष्टसूत्रसम्पातादष्टास्रं कुण्डमुच्यते । इति ।

अत्र महान् व्यभिचार: । अत्र चतुर्वर्गचिन्तामणिकार: कर्णशब्दस्य कर्णार्द्धमर्थमुक्त्वा कोणयोरानुकूल्यप्रातिकूल्येनाष्टौ लाञ्छनानीति व्याख्याति स्म । तदयुक्तम् । तत्प्रतिपादकवचनाभावात् अतिविषमभुजत्वात् क्षेत्रफलव्यभिचाराच्च ।

अत्र सर्व्वत्र क्षेत्रोत्पत्तिवासनाः ग्रन्थगौरवभयान्न प्रपञ्चिताः। तास्तु मत्कृतायां लीलावतीगणितटीकायां सुबोधिन्यां द्रष्टव्याः।

नोपयोग इह मत्कृते श्रमे केवलागमविदान्तु यद्यपि।

आगमं गणितमप्यवैति यस्तुष्यतु प्रियगुणः स कश्चन॥

अयमुत्तमो नवकुण्डिकागणितपक्षः। एतत्कुण्डकरणाशक्तः सर्व्वाणि कुण्डानि चतुरस्राणि वृत्तानि वा कुर्य्यात्। तदुक्तमाम्नायरहस्ये—

कुण्डानि चतुरस्राणि वृत्तनामाकृतीनि च। इति।

सोमशम्भुनापि—शस्तानि तानि वृत्तानि चतुरस्राणि वा सदा। इति।

अन्यत्रापि—वेदास्राण्येव तानि स्युर्वर्त्तुलान्यथवा क्वचित्। इति।

मध्यमस्तु पञ्चकुण्डीपक्षः। तदुक्तमाम्नायरहस्ये—

नव पञ्चाथवैकं वा कर्त्तव्यं लक्षणान्वितम्। इति।

सोमशम्भुनाऽपि—वेदीपादान्तरं त्यक्त्वा कुण्डानि नव पञ्च वा। इति।

सिद्धान्तशेखरेऽपि—त्यक्त्वा वेदिचतुर्भागं कुण्डानि नव पञ्च वा। इति।

तन्निवेशनमप्याम्नायरहस्य एवोक्तम्—

विधाने पञ्चकुण्डानामैशाने पञ्चमं भवेत्। इति।

ज्ञानरत्नावल्यामपि—दिक्षु वेदास्रवृत्तानि पञ्चममन्त्यैशगोचरम्। इति।

अत्र वृत्तशब्देन वृत्तार्द्धचन्द्रपद्मानि गृह्यन्ते। उक्तचतुरस्रवृत्तविकल्पाभिप्रायेण वा।

सोमशम्भुरपि—कुर्य्यात् कुण्डं क्रमादीशे पञ्चमम्। इति।

नारदीयेऽपि—यत्रोपदिश्यते कुण्डचतुष्कं तत्र कर्म्मणि।

वेदास्रमर्द्धचन्द्रञ्च वृत्तं पद्मनिभं तथा॥

कुर्य्यात् कुण्डानि चत्वारि प्राच्यादिषु विचक्षणः।

पञ्चमं कारयेत् कुण्डमीशदिग्गोचरं द्विज॥ इति।

यत्तु—पञ्चकुण्डी वेन्निवेश्या दिक्ष्वन्त्यशेशपूर्व्वयोः।

इति कस्य चिद्वचनं तदसम्बद्धम्। लिखितग्रन्थविरोधात्। एककुण्डपक्षः कनीयान्। तन्निवेशनमुक्तमाचार्य्यैः—

अथवा दिशि कुण्डमुत्तरस्यां प्रविदध्याच्चतुरस्रमेकमेव। इति।

क्वचित् प्रतीच्यामपि तन्निवेशनमुक्तम्।

भुक्तौ मुक्तौ तथा पुष्टौ जीर्णोद्धारे विशेषतः।

दीक्षाहोमे तथा शान्तौ वृत्तं वरुणदिग्गतम्॥ इति।

सोमशम्भुरपि—एकं वा शिवकाष्ठायां प्रतीच्यां कारयेद्बुधः। इति।

२६

तत्रैककुण्डपक्षे चतुरस्रं वृत्तं वा तत् कार्य्यम् । तदुक्तं क्रियासारे—

चतुरस्रं भवेत् कुण्डं वृत्तं कुण्डमथापि वा ।
स्थिरार्च्चने चरार्च्चायां नित्ये हवनकर्म्मणि ॥ इति ।

पिङ्गलामतेऽपि—कुण्डमेककरं वृत्तं मेखलाकण्ठनाभिमत् ।
नित्यकर्म्मणि दीक्षायां शान्तौ पुष्टौ समं शुभम् ॥ इति ।

एवं हस्तमात्रं कुण्डमुक्तम् । यदुक्तं सिद्धान्तशेखरे—

हस्तमात्राणि सर्व्वाणि दीक्षासु स्थापनादिषु ।
नित्यहोमे च साहस्रे कुर्य्यात् कुण्डानि सर्व्वदा ॥ इति ।

द्विहस्तादिप्रकारस्तूच्यते । एकहस्तक्षेत्रफलं द्विगुणं द्विहस्तस्य त्रिगुणं त्रिहस्तस्य चतुर्गुणं चतुर्हस्तस्येति दशहस्तान्तं ज्ञेयम् । तत्र तन्मूलञ्च तत्तदायामसूत्रञ्च तस्यैव नामान्तराणि करणीमध्यसूत्रादीनि । तत्र भास्कराचार्य्यप्रोक्तसूत्रानुसारेण मूलानयनं ज्ञेयम् । तद्यथा—

त्यक्त्वान्त्याद्विषमात् कृतिं द्विगुणयेन्मूलं समे तद्धृते
त्यक्त्वा लब्धकृतिं तदाद्यविषमाल्लब्धं द्विनिघ्नं न्यसेत् ।
पंक्त्यां पंक्तिहृते समेऽन्त्यविषमात् त्यक्त्वाप्तवर्गं फलं
पंक्त्यां तद्द्विगुणं न्यसेदिति मुहुः पंक्तेर्दलं स्यात् पदम् ॥ इति ।

अस्यार्थो ग्रन्थगौरवभयान्नोक्तः । स तु मत्कृतायां लीलावतीटीकायां सुबोधिन्यां सोदाहरणो द्रष्टव्यः । अथवा एकहस्तस्य यत् कोणसूत्रं तदेव द्विहस्तकुण्डायामसूत्रम् । एवं द्विहस्तकोणसूत्रं चतुर्हस्तकुण्डस्यायामसूत्रं त्रिहस्तकुण्डकर्णसूत्रं षट्हस्तस्य । चतुर्हस्तकर्णसूत्रम् अष्टहस्तस्य । पञ्चहस्तकर्णसूत्रं दशहस्तस्येति ज्ञेयम् । अथ गणितापटून् प्रति दशहस्तान्तं करण्यो लिख्यन्ते ।

एकसप्तदशांशोनचतुस्त्रिंशद् द्विहस्तके ।

एतेन ३३ अङ्गुलानि ७ यवाः ४ यूकाः २ लिख्ये इयती द्विहस्तकरणी ।

एकाष्टाविंशतिशतात् चिसप्तत्याऽथ संयुताः ।
एकचत्वारिंशदङ्गुलयस्तु स्युस्त्रिहस्तके ॥

एतेन ४१ अङ्गुलानि ४ यवाः ४ यूकाः ४ लिख्याः इयती त्रिहस्तकरणी ।

अष्टचत्वारिंशता स्याच्चतुर्हस्ते करण्यथ ।
तृतीयांशन्यूनचतुःपञ्चाशत् पञ्चहस्तके ॥

एतेन ५३ अङ्गुलानि ५ यवाः २ यूके ४ लिख्याः इयती पञ्चहस्तकरणी ।

चतुरेकोनविंशोना ऊनषष्टिस्तदुत्तरे ।

यावान् कुण्डस्य विस्तारः खननं तावदीरितम् ॥ ६६

एतेन ५८ अङ्गुलानि ६ यवाः ३ यूकाः ४ लिक्षाः इयती षड्ढस्तकरणी ।

सप्तहस्ते त्र्यर्द्धयुता त्रिषष्टिः करणी मता ।

अष्टहस्ते त्र्यष्टषष्टिर्युग्मसप्तदशोनिता ॥

एतेन ६७ अङ्गुलानि ७ यवाः ७ यूकाः ४ लिक्षाः इयती अष्टहस्तकरणी ।

द्वासप्तत्यङ्गुला कार्य्या करणी नवहस्तके ।

द्वाभ्यामेकोनविंशाभ्यामूना षट्सप्ततिर्दिशि ॥

एतेन ७५ अङ्गुलानि ७ यवाः १ यूका २ लिक्षे इयती दशहस्तकरणी ।

कलेष्टचतुरस्रन्तु स्याद्योन्याद्युक्तमार्गतः ।

एवं दशान्तं कुण्डानां करण्युक्ता मया स्फुटा ॥ ६३-६५ ॥

अथ कुण्डे खातमाह यावानिति । कुण्डस्य यावान् विस्तारो मध्यसूत्रं तावत्प्रमाणः खातः कार्य्य इत्यर्थः । हस्तमात्राणि सर्व्वाणि कुण्डान्युक्ता

कादिमते—प्रोक्तानां सर्व्वकुण्डानामरत्निः खातमानकम् । इति ।

अरत्निहस्तयोः पर्य्यायता तेनैवोक्ता यथा तथा पूर्व्वमेव दर्शितम् । अन्यत्रापि—

यावन्मानं कुण्डविस्तार उक्तस्तावत् खातस्यापि मानं प्रदिष्टम् । इति ।

आचार्य्याश्च—विंशत्रिश्चतुरधिकाभिरङ्गुलीभिः

सूत्रेणाप्यथ परिसूत्र्य भूमिभागम् ।

ताभिश्च प्रखनतु तावतीभिः । इति ।

वायवीयसंहितायामपि—कुण्डं विस्तारवन्निम्नम् । इति ।

दिव्यसारस्वतेऽपि—चतुरस्रं चतुःकोष्ठं सूत्रैः कृत्वा यथा पुरा ।

हस्तमानेन तन्मध्ये तावन्निम्नायतं खनेत् ॥ इति ।

गणेश्वरविमर्शिन्यामपि—

चतुर्विंशाङ्गुलायामं तावत् खातसमन्वितम् । इति ।

अन्ये तु मेखलया सह खातमाहुः । तदुक्तं मोहशूरोत्तरे—

हस्तमात्रं खनेत्तिर्य्यगूर्द्ध्वं मेखलया सह । इति ।

प्रतिष्ठासारसंग्रहेऽपि—पञ्चत्रिमेखलोच्छ्रायं ज्ञात्वा शेषमधः खनेत् ॥ इति ।

विश्वकर्म्माप्याह—व्यासात् खातः करः प्रोक्तो निम्नं तिथ्यङ्गुलेन तु ।

उन्नता वा नवाङ्गुलैः । इति ।

स एव वक्ष्यति । प्रथमेऽपि—

कुण्डं जिनाङ्गुलैस्तिर्य्यगूर्द्ध्वं मेखलया सह । इति ।

सिद्धान्तशेखरेऽपि—खातं कुण्डप्रमाणं स्यादूर्ध्वं मेखलया सह । इति ।
एतत्पक्षद्वयमध्ये प्रथमपक्ष एव युक्तियुक्तो भाति । यतः—

कुण्डस्वरूपं जानीयात् परमं प्रकृतेर्वपुः । इत्यादिना

मेखलानामङ्गत्वाभिधानात् । तासां भूषणरूपत्वात् तया सह खातो नोपपद्यते । भूषकत्वे कदाचिदकर्त्तव्यतापि स्यादिति चेन्न ।

शृङ्गाररहितं यच्च यजमानविनाशकृत् ।

इत्युक्तेर्भूषणस्याप्यावश्यकत्वात् । अथ "मरणं छिन्नमेखले" इति । तथा "कुण्डं जर्जरखमेखलम्" इति । तथा "मानेनाधिकमेखले व्याधयः संप्रवर्द्धन्ते" इत्यादिना च तदैकल्ये दोषस्योक्तत्वादङ्गत्वमिति चेत् । अस्तु नामाङ्गत्वं तथापि तया सह खातोऽनुपपन्नः । प्रधाने कार्य्यसंप्रत्ययस्य न्याय्यत्वात् । किञ्च खातेन विना कुण्डस्वरूपप्राप्त्यसम्भवादेव दृष्टद्वारासन्निपत्योपकारकाङ्गस्य तस्यादृष्टद्वारा आरादुपकारकाङ्ग मेखलया सह सिद्धिरप्ययुक्ता । उक्तञ्च योगिनीहृदये—

खातं कुण्डायतिस्तुल्यमङ्गत्वं तस्य कीर्त्तितम् ।
सन्निपत्योपकारेण मेखलादेर्विशिष्यते ॥ इति ॥

न च व्रीहीणां प्रोक्षणादिवत् खाताङ्गत्वं मेखलानामिति वाच्यम् । "कुण्डानां मेखलास्तिस्रः" इत्यादिना कुण्डाङ्गत्वेनैव विधानात् । किञ्च प्रधाने कार्य्यसंप्रत्ययश्चेत् नाङ्गीक्रियते तदा द्विहस्तादिकुण्डेष्वपि क्षेत्रद्वैगुण्यं न प्राप्येत । तत्रापि एकहस्तादिखातघनहस्तफलस्य यद् द्वैगुण्यादिकं तन्मूलप्रमाणात् तत्करणी स्यात् । तत्रानिष्टं तव मते च खातस्याननुगतता प्रसज्यते । त्रिमेखलापक्षे अन्यः खातः । पञ्चमेखलापक्षे अन्यः । द्वादशाङ्गुलमेखलापक्षे अन्य इति । अन्यच्च—"निम्नं तिथ्यङ्गुलेन तु उन्नताद्या नवाङ्गुलैः" इति विश्वकर्म्मवचनम् । प्रतिष्ठासारसंग्रहेऽपि—

पञ्चत्रिमेखलोच्छ्रायं ज्ञात्वा शेषमधः खनेत् । इति ।

विशेषवाक्यद्वयैकवाक्यतया "ऊर्द्ध्वं मेखलया सह" इत्यन्यानि सामान्यवचनानि व्याख्येयान्यवश्यम् । "आग्नेयं चतुर्द्धा करोति" इति विशेषविधिविषये । "पुरोडाशं चतुर्द्धा करोति" इति सामान्यविधिवत् । "सामान्यविधिरस्पष्टः संक्रियेत विशेषतः" इति वार्त्तिककृदुक्तेः । तेनानिच्छतापि त्वया एकमेखलकुण्डे मेखलया विना खातोऽङ्गीकर्त्तव्यः । मेखलया सह विधायकाभावात् । अतो मेखलया विनैव खात इति सिद्धान्तः । मेखलया सह खातवचनानि चतुरस्रैकहस्तादिकुण्डेषु । पञ्चाशदादिहोमविधाने खाताधिक्यस्य प्रयोजनाभावात्

कुण्डानां यादृशं रूपं मेखलानाञ्च तादृशम् ॥ ९७

कुण्डानां मेखलास्तिस्रो मुष्टिमात्रे तु ताः क्रमात् ।

उत्सेधायामतो ज्ञेया द्व्येकाद्व्यङ्गुलसम्मिताः ॥ ९८

तद्विषयाणि इति ज्ञेयम् ।

श्रुतिद्वैधन्तु यत्र स्यात्तत्र धर्म्मावुभौ स्मृतौ ।

स्मृतिद्वैधे तु विषयः कल्पनीयः पृथक् पृथक् ॥　इत्युक्तेः ।

एतदभिप्रायेणैव प्रयोगसारे उक्तम्—

कारयेन्मेखलास्तिस्रश्चतुस्त्रिद्व्यङ्गुलाः क्रमात् ।

अथवा मेखलामेकां कुर्य्यात् संक्षेपकर्म्मसु ॥　इति

यत्तु तेनैवोक्तम् अत्र पक्षे बहुवचनसम्मते बहूनामनुग्रहो न्याय्य इति तदपि न सम्यक् । अस्मन्मत एव बहूक्तसत्त्वात् स एव पक्षो ग्राह्यः । उक्तञ्च जैमिनिना—

विप्रतिषिद्धधर्म्मसमवाये भूयसां स्यात् सधर्म्मत्वम् । इति ।

तत्र प्रथमपक्षे अस्य घनहस्तफलं १३८२४ अपरपक्षे १४७२४ ॥ ९९ ॥

अथ मेखला आह कुण्डानामिति । कुण्डानां चतुरस्रयोन्यादीनां यादृशं रूपं चतुरस्रत्वादि मेखलानां तादृशं रूपम् । चतुरस्रे चतुरस्ररूपा मेखला योनौ योनिरूपा मेखला कार्य्येत्यर्थः । एतेन मेखलाः कुण्डाकाराः कार्य्याः । मेखलानां स्वरूपे चतुरस्रत्वहानिर्नास्तीत्युक्तम् । तिस्र इति मध्यमः पक्षः । पञ्चमेखलापक्ष उत्तमः । एकमेखलापक्षः कनीयानिति । यदा तु ग्रन्थकारोक्तत्रिमेखलापक्ष एव उत्तमः पक्षः । तदा द्विमेखलापक्षो मध्यमः । एकमेखलापक्षः कनीयानिति ।

यद्वायवीयसंहितायाम्—

मेखलानां त्रयं वापि द्वयमेकमथापि वा । इति ।

क्रियासारेऽपि—नाभियोनिसमायुक्तं कुण्डं श्रेष्ठं त्रिमेखलम् ।

कुण्डं द्विमेखलं मध्यं नीचं स्यादेकमेखलम् ॥　इति ।

अन्यत्रापि—तिस्रः कुण्डे मेखला मेखले द्वे यद्वा विद्वानेकिकां मेखलां वा । इति ।

सोमशर्म्मा तु—त्रिमेखलं द्विजे कुण्डं क्षत्रियस्य द्विमेखलम् ।

मेखलैका तु वैश्यस्य । इति ।

तत्र सर्व्वकुण्डप्रकृतिभूतैकहस्तकुण्डमुपक्रम्य वेदाग्निनयनाङ्गुलाः इत्युक्तत्वात् सर्व्वत्र करणीषष्ठाष्टद्वादशांशैः क्रमान्मेखलाः स्युरिति गम्यते । "प्रकृतिवद्विकृतिः कार्य्या" इति भाट्टन्यायात् । तदुक्तं सोमशम्भुना—

अरत्निमात्रे कुण्डे स्युस्त्रिद्वेकाङ्गुलात्मिकाः ।
एकहस्तमिते कुण्डे वेदाग्निनयनाङ्गुलाः ॥ ६८

कुण्डानां यश्चतुर्विंशो भागः सोऽङ्गुलसंज्ञकः ।
विभज्यानेन कर्त्तव्या मेखलाकण्ठनाभयः ॥ इति ।

महाकपिलपञ्चरात्रे तु स्पष्टमेव—
कुण्डषड्भागिका त्वाद्या द्वितीयाऽष्टांशका स्मृता ।
तृतीया द्वादशांशा स्यात् । इति ॥

योगिनीहृदयेऽपि—मेखलाः शृणु मे देवि हस्तादिषु विशेषतः ।
षट्नागार्कांशसम्भागैर्मिताः स्युर्गोपिताः शुभाः ॥ इति ।

यत्तु मुष्ट्यादिकुण्डे द्विहस्तादावपि ग्रन्थकृदुक्तं तत् स्थूलमानेनेति ज्ञेयम् । मुष्टिमात्रे त्विति । उत्सेधायामत इति । एकहस्तपर्य्यन्तं सर्व्वत्रान्वेति । तत्रोक्ताङ्गुलमानेन एकविंशत्यङ्गुलं मुष्टिमात्रं कुण्डं मुष्टिरत्न्योः पर्य्यायत्वात् । तत्र मुष्टिकुण्डे सार्द्धत्र्यङ्गुलाऽऽद्या । सपञ्चयवद्व्यङ्गुला मध्या । पादोनद्व्यङ्गुला तृतीया । अरत्निमात्रं कुण्डमुक्ताङ्गुलमानेन सार्द्धद्वाविंशत्यङ्गुलम् । "अरत्निः सकनिष्ठः स षोड़शांशत्रियुक्करः" इत्युक्तेः । तत्र पादोनचतुरङ्गुलाऽऽद्या । ससार्द्धषड्यवद्व्यङ्गुला मध्या । यवोनद्व्यङ्गुला तृतीया ।

अत्र मेखलाकरणप्रकारः । एकहस्ते द्व्यङ्गुलोत्सेधा नवाङ्गुलविस्तृता कण्ठात् प्रभृति आद्या मेखला कार्य्या । तदुपरि द्वितीया त्र्यङ्गुलोत्सेधा सप्ताङ्गुलविस्तृता । तदुपरि चतुरङ्गुलोत्सेधा चतुरङ्गुलविस्तृता । एवं फलतो वेदाग्निनयनाङ्गुलत्वं भवत्येव । उक्तञ्च—

या या तु मेखला पूर्व्वा सा सा भूमिरुदाहृता । इति ।

तेन प्रथमा अन्तर्नवाङ्गुलोच्चा चतुरङ्गुलविस्तारा बहिश्चतुरङ्गुलोच्चा । द्वितीया अन्तः पञ्चाङ्गुलोच्चा त्र्यङ्गुलविस्तारा बहिस्त्र्यङ्गुलोच्चा । तृतीया तु उभयत्र द्व्यङ्गुलोच्चा द्व्यङ्गुलविस्तारा ।

तदुक्तं मोहशूरोत्तरे—"कोण ४ राम ३ यमा२ङ्गुलैः" इति कोणाश्चत्वारः ।

अन्यत्रापि—चतुस्त्रिद्व्यङ्गुला यद्वा तिस्रः सर्व्वत्र शोभना । इति ।

विश्वकर्म्माप्याह—उन्नताद्या नवाङ्गुलैः । इति ।

क्रियासारेऽपि—प्रधानमेखलोत्सेधमुक्तमत्र नवाङ्गुलम् ।
तद्बाह्यमेखलोत्सेधं पञ्चाङ्गुलमिति स्मृतम् ॥

तदुबाह्यमेखलोत्सेधमङ्गुलद्वितयं क्रमात् ।
चतुस्त्रिद्व्यङ्गुलो व्यासो मेखलात्रितयान्वितः ॥ इति ।

लक्षणसंग्रहेऽपि—प्रथमा द्व्यङ्गुलायामा उन्नता सा नवाङ्गुलैः ।
मध्या तु त्र्यङ्गुला बाह्ये तृतीया तु यमाङ्गुलैः ॥ इति ।

सिद्धान्तशेखरेऽपि—

चतुर्विंशतिमो भागः कुण्डानामङ्गुलं स्मृतम् । इति ।

पुनरप्यङ्गुलपरिभाषां कृत्वा

चतुर्भिश्च त्रिभिर्द्वाभ्यामूर्द्ध्वा मध्या त्वधोगता ।
तिस्रः प्रोक्ताः क्रमादेवं विस्तारादुच्छ्रयादपि ॥ इति ।

एतेन प्रथमा चतुरङ्गुला तदुपरि त्र्यङ्गुला तदुपरि द्व्यङ्गुलेति । बहिश्च-तुरङ्गुला तदन्तर्मध्यमा त्र्यङ्गुला द्व्यङ्गुला कण्ठलग्नेति च व्याख्यानद्वयं निरस्तम् । यत्तु कस्यचिल्लक्षणं—

व्यासे चतुर्विंशतिधा विभाजिते तिस्रश्चतुस्त्र्योक्षणभागविस्तृताः ।
समन्ततः कण्ठबहिस्तु मेखला नवर्त्तुरामांशकतुङ्गता मता ॥ इति ।

अत्र द्वितीयतृतीययोः षड्भागत्रिभागत उच्चतोक्ता । तदसम्बद्धम् । लिखितबहु-ग्रन्थविरोधात् एतत्प्रतिपादकवचनाभावाच्च । "विस्तारतुल्योन्नतयश्च कैश्चिदुक्ता इमाः" इति यत्तेनैवोक्तं तदप्यज्ञानविजृम्भितम् । लिखिततत्तत्प्रतिपादकवचनार्था नवबोधात् । यच्च "कोणरामयमाङ्गुलैः" इत्यादीनां वचनानां विस्तारमात्रे पर्य्यवसानं कृतं सोऽप्यबोध एव । यदाचार्य्यैस्तु—

सत्त्वपूर्व्विकगुणान्विताः क्रमात् द्वादशाष्टचतुरङ्गुलोच्छ्रिताः ।
सर्व्वतोऽङ्गुलचतुष्कविस्तृता मेखलाः सकलसिद्धिदा मताः ॥ इति ।

तन्मतानुसारिभिरन्यैरपि सर्व्वेषां मेखलामानं "वितस्त्यष्टतदर्द्धकैः" इत्युक्तम् । तत्तु साक्षात् "सकलसिद्धिदा मता" इत्युक्तत्वात् फलविशेषता ज्ञेया । तत्रापि कण्ठाद्बहिः प्रथममेखला द्वादशाङ्गुलविस्तारा चतुरङ्गुलोच्चा । तदुपरि द्वितीयाऽष्टाङ्गुल-विस्तृता चतुरङ्गुलोच्चा । तदुपरि चतुरङ्गुलोच्चा चतुरङ्गुलविस्तारेति ज्ञेयम् । एवं कुण्डभागे द्वादशाङ्गुलोच्चत्वं भवति । तदुक्तं वशिष्ठसंहितायाम्—

प्रथमा मेखला तत्र द्वादशाङ्गुलविस्तृता ।
चतुर्भिरङ्गुलैस्तस्याश्चोन्नतिश्च समन्ततः ॥
तस्याश्चोपरि वप्रः स्याच्चतुरङ्गुलमुन्नतः ।
अष्टाभिरङ्गुलैः सम्यक् विस्तीर्णस्तु समन्ततः ॥

मेखलानां भवेदन्तः परितो नेमिरङ्गुलात् ।
एकहस्तस्य कुण्डस्य वर्द्धयेत् तत् क्रमात् सुधीः ।
दशहस्तान्तमन्येषां अर्द्धाङ्गुलवशात् पृथक् ॥ ७०

तस्योपरि पुनः कार्यो वप्रः सोऽपि तृतीयकः ।
चतुरङ्गुलविस्तीर्णस्तथोन्नतश्च तथाविधः ॥ इति ।

पञ्चमेखलापक्षे तन्मानमुक्तं लक्षणसंग्रहे—

मेखलाः पञ्च वा कार्य्याः षट्पञ्चाब्धित्रिपक्षकैः । इति ।

सिद्धान्तशेखरेऽपि—षड्बाणाब्धिवह्निनेत्रमिताः स्युः पञ्च मेखलाः । इति ।

द्विमेखलापक्षे तल्लक्षणमुक्तं तन्त्रान्तरे—

षष्ठांशेनाष्टमांशेन मेखलाद्वितयं मतम् । इति ।

एकमेखलापक्षेऽपि—षट्चतुर्द्व्यङ्गुलायामविस्तारोन्नतिशालिनी ।
इति योनिलक्षणं वदता ग्रन्थकृता सूचित एव । तन्मानमुक्तं पिङ्गलामते—

एका षडङ्गुलोत्सेधविस्तारा मेखला मता । इति ।

महाकपिलपञ्चरात्रेऽपि—मेखलैकाऽथवा स्मृता सा चतुर्थांशविस्तारा । इति ।
प्रयोगेऽपि—कण्ठाङ्गुलाद् बहिः कार्य्या मेखलैका षडङ्गुला । इति ।
सिद्धान्तशेखरेऽपि—कुण्डानां मेखलां कुर्य्यादेकाञ्चेत् षड्भिरङ्गुलैः । इति ।
सोमशम्भुरपि—अङ्गुलैः षड्भिरेका च । इति ।
अन्यत्रापि—षडंशविस्तृतोन्नतायवैकिकैव मेखला । इति ।
कामिके तु विशेषः— स्यात्तद्वेदस्तुभागतः ।

मेखलापृथुतोच्छ्रायः कुण्डाकारा तु मेखला ॥
सर्व्वेषान्तु प्रकर्त्तव्या मेखलैकाऽत्र लाघवात् ॥ इति ॥ ६७-६९ ॥

कण्ठमानमाह मेखलानामिति । मेखलानामन्तः परितः सर्व्वतः अङ्गुलादङ्गुलमानात् नेमिरेकहस्तस्य कुण्डस्य भवेदिति सम्बन्धः । अङ्गुलादङ्गुलं व्याप्येत्यर्थः । ल्यब्लोपे पञ्चमी । क्वचिदङ्गुलेति पाठः । तदा सामानाधिकरण्येन योजनीयम् । एतेन कुण्डव्यासचतुर्विंशांशो नेमिरित्युक्तं भवति । द्विहस्तादावपि तत्कर्णव्यासचतुर्विंशांश एव नेमिः । यदर्द्धाङ्गुलवशाद्दशहस्तान्तमन्येषां क्रमात्तां वर्द्धयेदित्युक्तम् । तत्तु तद्द्विहस्ताभिप्रायेण । द्विहस्ते च एकमङ्गुलं यवत्रयं द्वे यूके चतस्रो लिख्याः पञ्च रेणवः चत्वारस्त्रसरेणवः इति । तदुक्तं महाकपिलपञ्चरात्रे—

चतुर्विंशतिभागेन कण्ठो वै परिकीर्त्तितः । इति ।

कुण्डे द्विहस्ते ता ज्ञेया रसवेदगुणाङ्गुलाः ।
चतुर्हस्तेषु कुण्डेषु वसुतर्कयुगाङ्गुलाः ॥ ७१

तेन रत्निमाते सप्तयवः कण्ठः अरत्निमाते सार्द्धसप्तयवः । तदुक्तं मन्त्रमुक्तावल्याम्—

कण्ठोऽष्टयवैर्हस्तमानेषु कुण्डेषु अरत्निमितेषु च सार्द्धसप्तभिर्यवैः रत्निमितेषु च सप्तभिर्यवैः । इति ।

कामिके त्वन्यथोक्तम्—वेदाकांशेन तस्योष्ठः । इति ।

सोमशम्भुरपि—बहिरेकाङ्गुलः कण्ठो द्व्यङ्गुलः क्वचिदागमे । इति ।

साम्प्रदायिकास्तु प्रथमपक्षमेव मन्यन्ते बहुतन्त्रसम्मतेः । तदुक्तम् एकहस्तमुपक्रम्य—

खाताद्वाह्योऽङ्गुलः कण्ठस्तद्वाह्ये मेखलाः क्रमात् । इति ।

पिङ्गलामतेऽपि—खातादेकाङ्गुलं त्याज्यं मेखलानां स्थितिर्भवेत् । इति ।

अन्यत्रापि—कण्ठोऽङ्गुलाद्बहिः कार्य्यः । इति ।

सिद्धान्तशेखरेऽपि—कुण्डे हस्तमिते कण्ठं कुर्य्यादेकाङ्गुलं ततः । इति ।

कालोत्तरे च—खाताद्बाह्योऽङ्गुलः कण्ठः सर्व्वकुण्डेष्वयं विधिः ।

चतुर्विंशतिमं भागमङ्गुलं परिकल्पयेत् ॥ इति ।

तट्टीकाकारैर्व्याख्यातम्—यवोऽष्टगुणितोऽङ्गुलमित्यादिना प्रसिद्धेनैव हस्ताङ्गुलव्यवहारेण होमानुसारात् कुण्डमुक्तम् । इयन्तु खातादिमानकथनार्थं परिभाषा क्रियते । चिकीर्षितकुण्डक्षेत्रं चतुर्विंशतिधा विभज्य यावांश्चतुर्विंशतिमो भागस्तावत्परिमाणमङ्गुलं परिकल्पयेदिति । अतएव सर्व्वकुण्डेष्वयं विधिरित्युक्तम् ।

अन्यत्रापि—कण्ठोऽष्टयवमात्रः स्यात् कुण्डे तु करमात्रके । इति ।

अन्यत्रापि—कुण्डस्यैककरस्य बाह्यपरितो नेमिर्भवेदङ्गुलम् । इति । ॥ ७० ॥

द्विहस्तादिकुण्डानां विस्तारायामं सूचयन् मेखला आह कुण्ड इति । अत्र सर्व्वत्र षष्ठाष्टमद्वादशांशैः पूर्व्वोक्तवन्मेखलाः कार्य्याः । विस्तारोत्सेधतो ज्ञेया इति वक्ष्यमाणं पूर्व्ववत् सर्व्वत्र सम्बध्यते । रसवेदगुणाङ्गुला इति । अत्र मन्त्रमाचार्य्यैरुपेक्षितं शिष्यबुद्धिपरीक्षार्थं शिष्याणामूहापोहबुद्धिर्यथा स्यादिति । तत्र षडङ्गुलानि पञ्च यवाः द्वे यूके तृतीयं प्रथमा । चतुरङ्गुलानि द्वौ यवौ मध्या । द्वे अङ्गुले षड् यवाः पञ्च यूकाः अन्त्या । अत्र यद्यपि त्रिपञ्चसप्तनवहस्तानां मेखला नोक्तास्तथापि अग्रे

एकहस्तमितं कुण्डमेकलक्षे विधीयते ।
लक्षाणां दशकं यावत्तावद्धस्तेन वर्द्धयेत् ॥

कुण्डे रसकरे ताः स्युर्दशाष्टत्र्यङ्गुलान्विताः ।
वसुहस्तमिते कुण्डे भानुपङ्क्त्यष्टकाङ्गुलाः ॥ ७२
दशहस्तमिते कुण्डे मनुभानुदशाङ्गुलाः ।
विस्तारोत्सेधतो ज्ञेया मेखलाः सर्व्वतो बुधैः ॥ ७३
होतुरग्रे योनिरासामुपर्य्यश्वत्थपत्रवत् ॥ ७४

इति त्रिहस्तादीनां विनियोग उक्तः । अतस्तन्मेखलामानमपि पूर्व्ववत् षष्ठाष्टम-द्वादशांशो ज्ञेयः । तत्र त्रिहस्ते षड्ङ्गुलानि सप्त यवाः तिस्रो यूकाः तिस्रो लिख्याः आद्या । पञ्चाङ्गुलानि एको यवः चतस्रो यूकाः चतस्रो लिख्याः अर्द्धसहिताः मध्या । त्रीण्यङ्गुलानि त्रयो यवाः पञ्च यूकाः षड्लिख्यास्त्र्यंशोनाः अन्त्या । चतुर्हस्त इति । वसवोऽष्टौ तर्काः षट् युगानि चत्वारि । अत्र षष्ठाष्टम-द्वादशांशता ग्रन्थकृतैव प्रकटीकृता । एवं पञ्चहस्तादावपि ज्ञेयम् ॥ ७१-७३ ॥

योनिमाह होतुरिति । आसां मेखलानामुपरि मध्यभागे होतुरग्रे अश्वत्थपत्रवद् योनिः कार्य्या । तदुक्तं सोमशम्भुना—

तासामुपरि योनिः स्यान्मध्येऽश्वत्थपत्राभवत् । इति ।

इयञ्च पूर्व्वोक्तयोनिः कुण्डाकारा कार्य्या । होतुरग्रे इत्यनेनैतदुक्तं भवति । वेदी यथा पृष्ठभागे न पतति होतुश्च प्राङ्मुखता उदङ्मुखता वा भवति तथा । केषाञ्चित् पश्चिममेखलोपरि केषाञ्चिद्दक्षिणमेखलोपरि योनिः स्यादनीयेति । तदुक्तम्

स्वायम्भुवे—प्रागग्नियाम्यकुण्डानां प्रोक्ता योनिरुदङ्मुखा ।

पूर्व्वा मुखाः स्मृताः शेषा यथाशोभं व्यवस्थिताः ॥ इति ।

त्रैलोक्यसारेऽपि—दक्षिणस्था पूर्व्वयाम्ये जलस्था पश्चिमोत्तरे ।

नवमस्यापि कुण्डस्य योनिर्दक्षजलस्थिता ॥ इति ।

[अत्र पूर्व्वशब्देनाग्नेयी जलस्थेति नैर्ऋते वायव्ये उत्तरेशाने (?) ।]

सिद्धान्तशेखरेऽपि—इन्द्राग्नियमदिक्कुण्डयोनिः सौम्यमुखी स्मृता ।

योनिः पूर्व्वामुखान्येषु पूर्व्वशान्युत्तरा स्मृता ॥ इति ।

क्रियासारेऽपि—होमकृत्पुरतः स्थाप्या दक्षिणे पश्चिमेऽपि वा । इति ।

सोमशम्भुरपि—पूर्व्वाग्नियाम्यकुण्डानां योनिः स्यादुत्तरानना ।

पूर्व्वानना तु शेषाणां ऐशान्येऽन्यतरा तयोः ॥ इति ।

अतैशान्य इति एकदेशेन नवमं कुण्डं गृहीतम् । एतेन पूर्व्वाग्नेयदक्षिणकुण्डानि नवमञ्च कुण्डमुत्तराग्रम् अन्यानि पञ्चकुण्डानि प्रागग्राणीति ॥ ७४ ॥

मुष्ट्यरत्न्येकहस्तानां कुण्डानां योनिरीरिता ।

षट्चतुर्द्व्यङ्गुलायामविस्तारोन्नतिशालिनी ॥ ७५

तस्याः प्रमाणमाह मुष्टीति । एकहस्तप्रकृतिकत्वात् सर्व्वकुण्डानां चतुःषड्द्वादशांशैरायामविस्तारोन्नतियुक्ता सर्व्वत्र योनिः कार्य्या । तदुक्तं

तन्त्रान्तरे—तूर्य्यषष्ठद्वादशांशैर्योनिः कुण्डायतेर्भवेत् ।

आयता विस्तृता तुङ्गा जिनांशेन तदग्रकम् ॥ इति ।

क्रियासारे—तत्षडङ्गुलमायामं विस्तारं चतुरङ्गुलम् । इति ।

इदन्तु एकमेखलापचे । अन्ये त्वन्यथा वर्णयन्ति । षट्चतुर्द्व्यङ्गुलायामेति षड्द्व्यङ्गुलायामा द्वादशाङ्गुलदैर्घ्या षड्द्व्यङ्गुलविस्तारेति । अष्टाङ्गुलविस्तारा द्व्यङ्गुलोच्छ्रितिरिति । तदुक्तं

स्वायम्भुवे—मेखलामध्यतो योनिः कुण्डार्द्धतंत्रशविस्तृता । इति ।

सिद्धान्तशेखरेऽपि—दीर्घार्कपर्व्वभिर्योनिर्विस्तारेणाऽष्टकाङ्गुला ।

उन्नतिर्द्व्यङ्गुलेनास्याः । इति ।

प्रयोगसारेऽपि—त्रिभागां मध्यतो योनिमायामे द्वादशाङ्गुलाम् ।

द्वादशांशोच्छ्रितां कुर्य्यात् किञ्चित् कुम्भनिवेशिनीम् ॥ इति ।

क्वचिदेकाङ्गुलोऽप्युच्छ्राय उक्तः ।

यन्नारदीये—कुण्डत्र्यंशेन विस्तारो योनिरुच्छ्रायतोऽङ्गुला ।

कुण्डार्द्धेन तु दीर्घा स्यात् । इति ।

त्रैलोक्यसारेऽपि—दैर्घ्यात् सूर्य्याङ्गुला योनिस्त्र्यंशोना विस्तरेण तु ।

एकाङ्गुलोच्छ्रिता सा तु । इति ।

पिङ्गलामतेऽपि—विस्तारोऽष्टाङ्गुलो योनिरुच्छ्रायोऽङ्गुलसम्मितः । इति ।

अन्यत्रापि—"उत्सेधमङ्गुलम्" इति । तेन द्व्यङ्गुलोच्छ्रायैकाङ्गुलोच्छ्राययोर्विकल्पः । अष्टाङ्गुलो विस्तारस्त्वादिभागे । अग्रे सङ्कुचितत्वात् अश्वत्थपत्रवदित्युक्तेः योनिमध्ये किञ्चिन् निम्नं कार्य्यम् । तदुक्तं त्रैलोक्यसारे "मध्ये त्वाज्यधृतिस्तथा" इति । साम्प्रदायिका अपि एतादृशीमेव योनिं मन्यन्ते । अन्ये तु षट्चतुर्द्व्यङ्गुलेति समुच्छ्रितमायामादिषु सम्बध्नते तेन द्वादशाङ्गुलविस्तारा द्वादशाङ्गुलदीर्घा द्वादशाङ्गुलोच्छ्राया योनिः कार्य्येत्याहुः । तदुक्तं पञ्चरात्रे—

अर्काङ्गुलोच्छ्रयां योनिं विदध्यात्तावदायताम् । इति ।

अन्यत्रापि—द्वादशस्वरूपत्वाद् योनिः स्याद् द्वादशाङ्गुला ।

उत्सेधायामतस्तुल्या । इति ।

एकाङ्गुलन्तु योन्यग्रं कुर्य्यादीषदधोमुखम् ।
एकैकाङ्गुलतो योनिं कुण्डेष्वन्येषु वर्द्धयेत् ।
यवद्वयक्रमेणैव योन्यग्रमपि वर्द्धयेत् ॥ ७६

एतत्पत्त्रद्वयमपि यथा स्वगुरुसम्प्रदायमूहनीयम् । इदन्तूक्तप्रमाणं त्रिमेखलापक्षे । यदा द्वादशाङ्गुलमेखलापक्षस्तन्मते योनिरुक्ता ।

प्रयोगसारे—सात्त्विकी मेखला पूर्व्वा विस्तृत्या द्वादशाङ्गुला ।
द्वितीया राजसी प्रोक्ता मेखलाऽष्टाङ्गुलैस्ततः ॥
तृतीया मेखला ख्याता तामसी चतुरङ्गुला ।
पृथग्विस्तारमेतासु चतुरङ्गुलमानतः ॥
स्थितां प्रतीच्यामायामे सम्यक् पञ्चदशाङ्गुलाम् ।
द्विपञ्चाङ्गुलविस्तारां षट्चतुर्द्व्यङ्गुलां क्रमात् ॥
व्यक्ताश्वत्थदलाकारां निम्नां कुण्डे निवेशिताम् ।
त्रयोदशाङ्गुलोत्सेधां योनिं कुण्डस्य कारयेत् ॥ इति ।

प्रतीच्यामिति एककुण्डपक्षानुसारेणेति ज्ञेयम् ॥ ७५ ॥

एकाङ्गुलमिति । एतेन चतुर्विंशांशेन सर्व्वत्र योन्यग्रमपि ईषदधोमुखं कुण्डप्रविष्टं कुर्य्यादित्युक्तम् । तदुक्तं नारदीये—"कुण्डोष्ठो बोधिपल्लवत्" इति । ओष्ठो योन्यग्रं कुण्डप्रविष्टाग्रेत्यर्थः ।

त्रैलोक्यसारेऽपि— प्रविष्टाभ्यन्तरे तथा ।
कुम्भद्वयसमायुक्ता चाश्वत्थदलवन्मता ॥ इति ।

वायवीयसंहितायामपि—
मेखला मध्यतः कुर्य्यात् पश्चिमे दक्षिणेऽपि वा ।
शोभनामग्रतः किञ्चिन्निम्नामुन्नमूलिकां शनैः ॥
अग्रेण कुण्डाभिमुखीं किञ्चिदुत्सृष्टमेखलाम् । इति ।

अत्र ग्रन्थगौरवभयाद्दशहस्तकुण्डान्तं प्रत्येकं योनितदग्रादीनां मानं नोक्तम् । तथापि किञ्चिदुच्यते—आयामः सा[र्धा]ङ्घ्रिविस्तृत्या षष्ठां[सत्र्य]शेनाग्र विस्तृतिः ।
विस्तारार्द्धोदुन्नतिः स्यादुन्नत्यर्द्धोत्तदग्रकम् ॥
एकैकाङ्गुलतो योनिं कुण्डेष्वन्येषु वर्द्धयेत् ।
यवद्वयक्रमेणैव योन्यग्रमपि वर्द्धयेत् ॥

इति तु गणितापटून् प्रति स्थलमानेनोक्तम् । नतु सम्यग्गणनाभिप्रायमिति ॥७६॥

स्थलादारभ्य नालं स्याद् योन्या मध्ये सरन्ध्रकम् ।
नार्पयेत् कुण्डकोणेषु योनिं तां तत्त्ववित्तमः ॥ ७७

कुण्डानां कल्पयेदन्तर्नाभिमम्बुजसन्निभाम् ।
तत्तत्कुण्डानुरूपं वा मानमस्य निगद्यते ॥ ७८

मुष्ट्यरत्न्येकहस्तानां नाभिरुत्सेधतारतः ।
द्वित्रिवेदाङ्गुलोपेता कुण्डेष्वन्येषु वर्द्धयेत् ॥ ७९

यवद्वयक्रमेणैव नाभिं पृथगुदारधीः ।
योनिकुण्डे योनिमब्जकुण्डे नाभिं विवर्जयेत् ॥ ८०

नाभिक्षेत्रं त्रिधा भित्त्वा मध्ये कुर्व्वीत कर्णिकाम् ।
बहिरंशद्वयेनाष्टौ पत्राणि परिकल्पयेत् ॥ ८१

नालमाह स्थलादिति । स्थलादारभ्य योन्या नालं स्यात् । स्थलादारभ्येत्यनेन आद्यमेखलालग्नं नालं कर्त्तव्यमित्युक्तम् । तेन चतुरङ्गुलोत्सेधविस्तारां बाह्यमेखलासन्दष्टां वेदिं कृत्वा तदुपरि नालं स्थापयेदित्यर्थः । कथम् मध्ये सरन्ध्रकं यथा भवति तथा मध्ये मध्यमेखलोपरि परिधिपरिस्तरणार्थं रन्ध्रं विधाय अन्यो मध्यभागः पूरणीय इत्यर्थः । तदुक्तं पञ्चरात्रे—

स्थलादारभ्य योनिः स्याद्बाह्यमेखलया समा । इति ।

यस्तु मध्ये सरन्ध्रकमिति नालविशेषणमित्यवदत् स भ्रान्त एव । यतः सरन्ध्रस्यैव नालशब्दवाच्यत्वात् । तस्य सरन्ध्रकथने तस्यादृष्टार्थापत्तेश्च । न च नालाग्राभ्यां परिध्यादिस्थापनमिति वाच्यम् । दृष्टेनादृष्टबाधायोगात् । परिधिपरिस्तरणस्थलाभावाच्च । प्रयोगसारे तु—योन्याः पश्चिमतो नालमायामे चतुरङ्गुलम् ।

त्रिद्व्येकाङ्गुलविस्तारं क्रमान्मूलनाग्रमिष्यते ॥ इति ॥ ७७ ॥

नाभिमाह कुण्डानामिति । कुण्डानामन्तर्नाभिं कल्पयेत् । कुण्डाकारं पद्माकारं वा नाभिं कृत्वा खातमध्ये स्थापयेदित्यर्थः । "आतपे क्षत्रिये नाभिः प्राण्यङ्गेऽपि द्वयोः" इति नाभिशब्दपुंलिङ्गोऽप्यस्ति । उत्सेधतारतः उच्चत्वविस्ताराभ्याम् । अत्रापि प्राग्वदेकहस्तस्य सर्व्वकुण्डप्रकृतिभूतत्वात् कुण्डविस्तारषष्ठांशेन विस्तृता तदर्द्धोच्चा इत्युक्तं भवति । अम्बुजसादृश्यमेवाह नाभिरिति । कुर्व्वीतेति मन्त्रिणेति शेषः । उक्तञ्च नारायणीये—

पार्श्वे यागभुवः खाते कुण्डे सनाभिमेखला । इति ॥ ७८-८१ ॥

मुष्टिमात्रमितं कुण्डं शतार्द्धे संप्रचक्षते ।
शतहोमेऽरत्निमात्रं हस्तमात्रं सहस्रके ॥ ८२

द्विहस्तमयुते लक्षे चतुर्हस्तमुदीरितम् ।
दशलक्षे तु षड्ढस्तं कोट्यामष्टकरं स्मृतम् ॥ ८३

एकहस्तमितं कुण्डमेकलक्षे विधीयते ।
लक्षाणां दशकं यावत्तावद्धस्तेन वर्द्धयेत् ।
दशहस्तमितं कुण्डं कोटिहोमे विधीयते ॥ ८४

सर्व्वसिद्धिकरं कुण्डं चतुरस्रमुदाहृतम् ।
पुत्रप्रदं योनिकुण्डमर्द्धेन्द्वाभं शुभप्रदम् ॥ ८५

उक्तमुष्ट्यादिकुण्डानां विनियोगमाह मुष्टीत्यादि कोट्यामष्टकरमित्यन्तेन । शतहोमे अरत्निमात्रम् इति छेदः । तदुक्तम्—

मुष्टिमानं शतार्द्धे तु शते चारत्निमात्रकम् । इति ।

संहितायान्तु—कुण्डञ्च कोटिहोमेऽपि तदर्द्धेऽपि कराष्टकम् । इति ॥ ८२ ॥ ८३ ॥

पक्षान्तरमाह एकेति । इदन्तु पुष्पाज्याद्यल्पद्रव्यविषयम् एककर्त्तृकहोमपरं वा पञ्चकरपर्य्यन्तम् । तदूर्द्ध्वन्तु बहुद्रव्यविषयमनेककर्त्तृकविषयं वा ज्ञेयम् । कोट्यामष्टकरमित्यनेन विकल्पो दशहस्तमित्यस्य । सिद्धान्तशेखरे तु विशेषः—

लक्षार्द्धे त्रिकरं कुण्डं लक्षहोमे चतुष्करम् ।
कुण्डं पञ्चकरं प्रोक्तं दशलक्षाहुतौ क्रमात् ॥
षड्ढस्तं लक्षविंशत्यां कोट्यर्द्धे सप्तहस्तकम् । इति ।

अन्यत्रापि—केचिद्धस्तं लक्षहोमे द्विहस्तं लक्षद्वन्द्वे वह्निहस्तं त्रिलक्षे ।
होमे कुण्डं वेदलक्षेऽब्धिहस्तं प्राहुर्दीक्षां पञ्चकं पञ्चलक्षे ॥
रसहस्तं रसलक्षे सप्तकरं सप्तलक्षे स्यात् ।
वसुलक्षे वसुहस्तं नवलक्षे नवकरं कुण्डम् ॥
दशलक्षे दशहस्तं दशकरमेवेह कोटिहोमेऽपि ।
दशहस्तात्र हि कुण्डं परमस्ति महीतलेऽमुष्मिन् ॥ इति ॥ ८४ ॥

अथ कुण्डानां फलविशेषानाह सर्व्वेति । छेदः उच्छेदः उच्चाटनमिति यावत् । अयञ्च फलविशेषः पूर्व्वोक्ततत्तद्दिशि कुण्डकरण एव ज्ञेयः । तदुक्तम्

शत्रुक्षयकरं त्र्यस्रं वर्त्तुलं शान्तिकर्म्मणि ।
छेदमारणयोः कुण्डं षडस्रं पद्मसन्निभम् ॥ ८६

वृष्टिदं रोगशमनं कुण्डमष्टास्रमीरितम् ।
विप्राणां चतुरस्रं स्याद्राज्ञां वर्त्तुलमिष्यते ॥ ८७

वैश्यानामर्द्धचन्द्राभं शूद्राणां त्र्यस्रमीरितम् ।
चतुरस्रन्तु सर्व्वेषां केचिदिच्छन्ति तान्त्रिकाः ।
कुण्डरूपन्तु जानीयात् परमं प्रकृतेर्वपुः ॥ ८८

प्राच्यां शिरः समाख्यातं बाहू दक्षिणसौम्ययोः ।
उदरं कुण्डमित्युक्तं योनिः पादौ तु पश्चिमे ॥ ८९

कामिके—ऐन्द्र्यां स्तम्भे चतुष्कोणमग्नौ भगे भगाकृति ।
चन्द्रार्द्धं मारणे याम्ये द्वेषे निर्ऋतिकोणकम् ॥
वारुण्यां शान्तिके वृत्तं षडस्रमुच्चाटनेऽनिले ।
उदीच्यां पौष्टिके पद्मं रौद्र्यामष्टास्रि मुक्तिदम् ॥ इति ।

पिङ्गलामतेऽपि—कुण्डं कुशेशयाकारं उत्तरे वश्यकर्म्मणि ।
षडस्रमुच्चाटने वायावर्द्धेन्दु मारणे यमे ॥
वेदास्रं स्तम्भने प्राच्यामाकर्षेऽग्नौ भगाकृति ।
वारुण्यां शान्तिके वृत्तमीशे त्वष्टास्रि मुक्तिदम् ॥ इति ।

सिद्धान्तशेखरेऽपि—योन्याख्यमुच्यते कुण्डमाग्नेय्यामुत्तरामुखम् ।
प्रजावृद्धौ च तापि स्यादर्द्धचन्द्रमथोच्यते ॥
याम्ये तन्मारणे शस्तमुत्तराभिमुखं सदा ।
नैर्ऋते त्र्यस्रिकुण्डं स्याद् विद्वेषे पूर्व्ववक्त्रकम् ॥
वृत्तं कुण्डमतो वच्मि वारुण्यां शान्तिके हितम् ।
षडस्रमुच्यते कुण्डं वायावुच्चाटने पटु ॥
पद्मकुण्डमथो वच्मि सौम्ये तत् पुष्टिवर्द्धनम् ।
वच्मि कुण्डमथाष्टास्रमीशाने सर्व्वकामदम् ॥ इति ।

अत्र दीक्षाङ्गतया क्रियमाणयाऽष्टकुण्ड्या संयोगपृथक्त्वन्यायेन तत्तत्कुण्डोक्त-फलसिद्धिरपि ज्ञेया ।

क्रियासारेऽपि—पूर्व्वोक्तलक्षणैर्युक्तं कुण्डं तालप्रमाणकम् ।
उक्तं चरार्च्चने चैव न स्थिरे तु चतुर्मुख ॥
कुण्डमत्रोक्तमार्गेण निर्म्मायाऽथ सलक्षणम् ।
क्षत्रियोऽपि समृद्धो वा शूद्रस्ताम्रेण बन्धयेत् ॥
तदलाभे त्विष्टकाभिः संबद्धा सुदृढं यथा ।
पूर्व्वोदितप्रकारेण मृत्स्नया लेपयेत्तथा ॥
ताम्रेण लक्षणोपेतं कुर्य्यान्मृत्तिकयाऽपि वा ।
एतत् कुण्डं चरार्चायां शस्तं स्यान्न स्थिरार्च्चने ॥

अत्र च पूर्व्ववाक्यैकवाक्यतया तालप्रमाणत्वं ज्ञेयम् ।

अम्लेन ताम्रकं कुण्डं मृन्मयं गोमयाम्भसा ।
सौधञ्च सुधया सम्यक् शोधयेदमरर्षभ ॥
मृन्मयानान्तु कुण्डानां परितः सन्धिभिः सह ।
रक्तमृच्छालिपिष्टाभ्यां भूषयेद्दृक्प्रियं यथा ॥ इति ।

अत्रोक्त कुण्डानां न्यूनत्वे आधिक्ये अन्यथाभावे वा दोषमाह

विश्वकर्म्मा—खाताधिके भवेद्रोगी हीने धेनुधनक्षयः ।
वक्रकुण्डे तु सन्तापो मरणं छिन्नमेखले ॥
मेखलारहिते शोकोऽभ्यधिके वित्तसंक्षयः ।
भार्य्याविनाशनं कुण्डं प्रोक्तं योन्या विना कृतम् ॥
अपत्यध्वंसनं प्रोक्तं कुण्डं यत् कण्ठवर्जितम् ॥ इति ।

आगमान्तरेऽपि—मानाधिके भवेन्मृत्युर्मानहीने दरिद्रता । इत्यादि ।

क्रियासारेऽपि—न्यूनाधिकप्रमाणं यत् कुण्डं जर्जरमेखलम् ।
शृङ्गाररहितं यच्च यजमानविनाशकृत् ॥ इति ।

वशिष्ठसंहितायामपि—अनेकदोषदं कुण्डमत्र न्यूनाधिकं यदि ।
तस्मात् सम्यक् परीक्ष्येदं कर्त्तव्यं शुभमिच्छता ॥ इति ।

सिद्धान्तशेखरेऽपि—मानहीने महाव्याधिरधिके शत्रुवर्द्धनम् ।
योनिहीने त्वपस्मारो वाग्दण्डः कण्ठवर्जिते ॥ इति ।

जयद्रथयामलेऽपि—सूत्राधिके सुहृद्द्वेषो मानहीने दरिद्रता ।
वाग्रोधः कण्ठहीने स्यादसिद्धिर्न्यूनखातके ॥
अधिके चासुरो भोगो मानेनाधिकमेखले ।
व्याधयः संप्रवर्द्धन्ते विभागे स्यादपस्मृतिः ॥

नित्यं नैमित्तिकं काम्यं स्थण्डिले वा समाचरेत् ।
हस्तमात्रेण तत् कुर्य्यात् वालुकाभिः सुशोभनम् ॥ ९०
अङ्गुलोत्सेधसंयुक्तं चतुरस्रं समन्ततः ।
एवं प्रोक्तानि कुण्डानि कथ्यते स्रुक्स्रुवौ ततः ॥ ९१

उच्चाटः स्फुटिते छिद्रमङ्कुले वाच्यता भवेत् ॥ इति ।

अस्यापि क्रियासारे आवश्यकतोक्ता—

दिग्देशकुण्डनिर्मुक्तो योऽनलो लौकिको हि सः ।
तस्माद्दिग्देशकुण्डानि संग्राह्याण्युक्तलक्षणैः ॥
कुण्डमेवंविधं न स्यात् स्थण्डिलं वा समाश्रयेत् । इति ।

कुण्डं खातरूपं योनिः पश्चिमतः इति नित्याभिप्रायेण एककुण्डाभिप्रायेण च ग्रन्थकृदुक्तिः ॥ ८५-८८ ॥

कुण्डानुकल्पमाह नित्यमिति । अङ्गुलोत्सेधसंयुक्तम् । अङ्गुलं पूर्व्वोक्तलक्षणम् । यद्वा अङ्गुलानां हस्तशाखानां चतसृणां य उत्सेधस्तद्युक्तम् ।

यदाहुः स्थण्डिलं रत्निमात्रायामं चाङ्गुष्ठपर्व्वोन्नतमपि सुसमं निर्मितं वालुकाभिश्चतुष्कोणं द्व्यङ्गुलोत्सेधमेके बुधा हस्तविस्तारयुक्तं तदाहुः इति । इदमल्पहोमविषयमिति ज्ञेयम् ।

तदुक्तं वशिष्ठसंहितायाम्—इषुमात्रं स्थण्डिलं वा संक्षिप्ते होमकर्म्मणि । इति ।

क्रियासारे तु स्थण्डिले देशविशेषोऽप्युक्तः—

होमोऽष्टदिक्षु प्राक्प्लक्षः[पुच्छः] प्रागुदक्प्रवणोऽथवा ।
उदक्प्लक्षः[पुच्छः] प्रदेशो वा स्थण्डिलस्य स्थलं स्मृतम् ॥ इति ।

पिङ्गलामते तु विशेषः—

होमे प्रशस्यते कुण्डं स्थण्डिलं वा हसन्तिका । इति ।

वायवीयसंहितायामपि—

अथाग्निकार्य्यं वक्ष्यामि कुण्डे वा स्थण्डिलेऽपि वा ।
वेद्यां वाऽथायसे पात्रे मृन्मये वा नवे शुभे ॥ इति ।
स्थण्डिलं वालुकाभिर्वा रक्तमृद्रजसापि वा । इति क्रियासारे विशेषः ।

होमे अग्निचक्रमपि विलोकनीयम् । तदुक्तमन्यत्र—

नवकोष्ठं समालिख्याऽथेशनिर्ऋतयोः क्रमात् ।
वारीन्द्रेन्द्रे वायुवक्रयोर्दक्षिणोत्तरयोर्न्यसेत् ॥

प्रकल्पयेत् स्रुचं यागे वक्ष्यमाणेन वर्त्मना ।
श्रीपर्णी शिंशपाक्षीरशाखिष्वेकतमं[मयं] गुरुः ॥ ८२
गृहीत्वा विभजेद्धस्तमात्रं षट्त्रिंशता पुनः ।
विंशत्यंशैर्भवेद्दण्डो वेदी तैरष्टभिर्भवेत् ॥ ८३
एकांशेन मितः कण्ठः सप्तभागमितं मुखम् ।
वेदीत्र्यंशेन विस्तारः कण्ठस्य परिकीर्त्तितः ॥ ८४
अग्रं कण्ठसमानं स्यान्मुखे मार्गं प्रकल्पयेत् ।
कनिष्ठाङ्गुलिमानेन सर्पिषो निर्गमाय च ॥ ८५

सूर्य्यादीन् मध्यकोष्ठे तु केतुं न्यस्य फलं दिशेत् ।
आदित्ये च भवेच्छोको बुधे धनसमागमः ॥
शुक्रस्थानेऽर्थलाभः स्यात् शनिर्हानिकरो भवेत् ।
चन्द्रे लाभं विजानीयाद् भौमे च वधबन्धनम् ॥
गुरुः स्यादर्थलाभाय राहुर्हानिकरो मतः ।
केतुना मृत्युमाप्नोति ह्यग्निचक्रे सदैव हि ॥
त्रयं त्रयञ्च गणयेत् सूर्य्यर्क्षाद्दिनभावधि ।
नित्ये नैमित्तिके दुर्गाहोमादौ न विचारयेत् ॥ इति ।

उक्तमुपसंहरन् वक्ष्यमाणमवतारयति एवमिति । स्थण्डिलस्यापि कुण्डानुकल्पत्वेनोक्तत्वात् कुण्डानामिवोपसंहारः कृत इति ज्ञेयम् ॥ ८० ॥ ८१ ॥

स्रुचो लक्षणमाह प्रकल्पयेदिति । श्रीपर्णी काश्मरी । क्षीरशाखिनो न्यग्रोधादयः । तदुक्तं प्रयोगसारे—न्यग्रोधोडुम्बराश्वत्थप्लक्षाः क्षीरमहीरुहाः । इति । वेदित्र्यंशेनेति पादोनत्र्यंशैः कण्ठान्तस्थो विष्कम्भ इत्यर्थः । स च तत्परिध्यानयनेन ज्ञेयः ॥ ८२-८४ ॥

अग्रमिति । अग्रं मुखं कण्ठसमानं वेदीतृतीयांशविस्तारम् । सर्व्वेषां दैर्घ्यस्योक्तत्वात् । सर्पिषो निर्गमायेत्युक्तेः मार्गमिति कण्ठवेदीपरिधिभेदिनम् । तदुक्तं मन्त्रमुक्तावल्याम्—कण्ठाधः कारयेन्मार्गं विद्वानाज्यस्य निर्गमे ।
वेधञ्च मुखतः कुर्य्यात्तप्तलोहशलाकया ॥ इति ।
वशिष्ठसंहितायामपि—
सुषिरं कण्ठदेशे स्याद् विशेद् यावत् कनीयसा । इति ॥ ८५ ॥

वेदिमध्ये विधातव्या भागेनैकेन कर्णिका ।
विदधीत बहिस्तस्या एकांशेनाऽभितोऽवटम् ॥ ८६
तस्य खात त्रिभिर्भागै वृत्तमर्द्धांशतो भवेत् ।
अंशेनैकेन परितो दलानि परिकल्पयेत् ।
मेखला मुखवेद्योः स्यात् परितोऽर्द्धांशमानतः ॥ ८७
दण्डमूलाग्रयोः कुम्भौ गुणवेदाङ्गुलैः क्रमात् ।
गण्डीयुगं यमांशैः स्याद्दण्डस्यानाह ईरितः ॥ ८८
षड्भिरंशैः पृष्ठभागो वेद्याः कूर्म्माकृतिर्भवेत् ।
हंसस्य वा हस्तिनो वा पोत्रिणो वा मुखं लिखेत् ।
मुखस्य पृष्ठभागेऽस्याः सम्प्रोक्तं लक्षणं स्रुचः ॥ ८९

उद्दिष्टवेद्या रचनप्रकारमाह वेदीति । कर्णिका तु खातमध्ये उच्चा रचणीया । तस्या कर्णिकाया बहिः अभितः सर्व्वतः । तेनांशद्वयं संगृहीतम् । अवटो गर्त्तः । त्रिभिर्भागैरङ्गुलद्वयेनेत्यर्थः । बहिरित्यवटस्य परित इति वृत्तं परितः तेनांशद्वयं संगृहीतम् । मुखवेद्योः परितः अर्द्धांशमानतो मेखला स्यादित्यन्वयः । तेनार्द्धांशेन मुखेऽपि मेखला कार्य्या । सा च वृत्ताकारा भवति । तत्र एकेन कर्णिका द्वाभ्यामवटः एकेन वृत्तम् अंशद्वयेन दलानि एकांशेन मेखला । अर्धादर्द्धभागेन परितः समचतुरस्र सीमाघटना कार्य्या । तदुक्तं मन्त्रमुक्तावल्याम्—

अर्द्धाङ्गुला भवेच्छोभा समा वा चित्रितापि वा । इति ।

अत्राङ्गुलशब्दोऽंशवाची । एवमष्टापि भागा उपयुक्ताः । सीम्नः कोणेषु वच्यादिचित्रं कार्य्यमुपदेशात् ॥ ८६ ॥ ८७ ॥

दण्डेति । अत्रांशप्रकरणात् अङ्गुलशब्दोऽंशवाची । तेन मूले त्र्यंशेन मूलभागमुखः अग्रे तु चतुरंशेन वेदिलग्नमुखः कार्य्यः । क्रमादित्यग्रेऽप्यन्वेति । तत्र मूलकुम्भलग्ना दंशा अन्यत्र लग्नापि दंशा गण्डी कङ्कणाकारा कार्य्या । युगशब्दस्य "युगं युग्मे कृतादिषु" इति कोशात् वाच्ये द्वित्वार्थे सम्भवति । लक्षणाङ्गीकरणे प्रमाणाभावात् । तदुक्तं सोमशम्भुना—

मूले चाग्रे च दण्डस्य गण्डी कङ्कणवद्भवेत् । इति ।

एतेनैकादशांशा जाताः । मध्ये नवांशमितो धारणार्थं दण्डोऽवशिष्यते ।

स्रुचश्चतुर्विंशतिभिर्भागैरारचयेत् स्रुवम् ।
द्वाविंशत्या दण्डमानमंशैरेतस्य कीर्त्तितम् ॥ १००
चतुर्भिरंशैरानाहः कर्षाज्यग्राहि तच्छिरः ।
अंशद्वयेन निखनेत् पङ्के मृगपदाकृति ॥ १०१
दण्डमूलाग्रयोर्गण्डी भवेत् कङ्कणभूषिता ।
स्रुवस्य विधिराख्यातः कीर्त्त्यन्ते मण्डलान्यथ ॥ १०२

तदुक्तं महाकपिल पञ्चरात्रे—रसाङ्गुले [द्वे] भवेद्दण्डः । इति ।
अत्र यद्यङ्गुलशब्देनाङ्गुलानि गृह्येरन् तदा सार्द्धास्त्रयोऽंशा दण्डेऽवशिष्यन्ते । ततो धारणार्थमवकाश एव न स्यात् । दण्डस्यानाहो विशालता षड्भिरंशैः कार्य्यः । वेद्याः पृष्ठभागः कूर्म्माकृतिरिति पृथगेव । ये तु दण्डस्यानाहो दैर्घ्यमीरितमिति पृथग् योजयन्ति षड्भिरंशैर्वेद्याः पृष्ठभागः कूर्म्माकृतिरिति च योजयन्ति ते भ्रान्ता एव । आनाहशब्दस्य दैर्घ्यवाचित्वाभावात् दैर्घ्यस्य च प्रागुक्तत्वात् । तदुक्तं मन्त्रमुक्तावल्याम्—

षडङ्गुलपरीणाहो दण्डमध्य उदाहृतः । इति ।

कूर्म्माकृतिरित्यत्र षड्भिरंशैरित्यस्यानर्थक्याच्च अस्याः स्रुचो स्रुवस्य पृष्ठभागे हंसादेर्मुखं लिखेदिति सम्बन्धः । पौत्रिणो वराहस्य ॥ ९८ ॥ ९९ ॥

स्रुवलक्षणमाह स्रुच इति । चतुर्भिरंशैरानाहो विस्तारः । एतस्येति सम्बन्धः । यन्मन्त्रमुक्तावल्याम् "दण्डो वेदाङ्गुलैर्भवेत्" इति । कर्षेति । कर्षलक्षणन्तु—

माषो दशगुञ्जः स्यात् षोडशमाषो निगद्यते कर्षः । इति ।

अंशद्वयेन तच्छिरः कुर्य्यात् । तत् कर्षाज्यग्राहि यथा स्यात् एवं पङ्के मृगपदाकृति खनेदिति सम्बन्धः । कङ्कणभूषिता इत्युक्तेर्गण्डीशब्दोऽत्र घटपर्य्यायः । तदुक्तं मन्त्रमुक्तावल्याम्—मूलाग्रयोः कारयेद् द्वौ कुम्भौ चातिमनोहरौ । इति ।
तौ च विशेषानभिधानात् प्राग्वत् कार्य्यौ । कङ्कणमपि प्राग्वत् कार्य्यम् । अन्यत्र विशेषः—तदलाभे पलाशस्य पर्णाभ्यां हूयते हविः । इति ।
अत्र पर्णाभ्यामिति मध्यमपर्णाभ्यामिति ज्ञेयम् । "मध्यमेन पर्णेन जुहोति" इति श्रुतेः । वायवीयसंहितायामपि—

स्रुक्स्रुवौ तैजसौ ग्राह्यौ न कांस्यायससीसकौ ।
यज्ञदारुमयौ वापि ताम्त्रिकैः [स्मार्त्तैर्वा] शिल्पिसम्मतौ ॥

चतुरस्रे चतुःकोष्ठे कर्णसूत्रसमन्विते।
चतुर्ष्वपि च कोष्ठेषु कोणसूत्रचतुष्टयम्॥ १०३
मध्ये मध्ये यथा मत्स्या भवेयुः पातयेत्तथा।
पूर्व्वापरायते द्वे द्वे मन्त्री याम्योत्तरायते॥ १०४
पातयेत्तेषु मत्स्येषु समं सूत्रचतुष्टयम्।
पूर्व्ववत् कोणकोष्ठेषु कर्णसूत्राणि पातयेत्॥ १०५
तदुद्भूतेषु मत्स्येषु दद्यात् सूत्रचतुष्टयम्।
ततः कोष्ठेषु मत्स्याः स्युस्तेषु सूत्राणि पातयेत्॥ १०६
यावच्छतद्वयं मन्त्री षट्पञ्चाशत् पदान्यपि।
तावत्तेनैव विधिना तत्र सूत्राणि पातयेत्॥ १०७

पर्णैर्वा ब्रह्मवृक्षादेरच्छिद्रे मध्य उत्थिते। इति।
अन्यत्र तु—पलाशपर्णाभावे तु पर्णैर्वा पिप्पलोद्भवैः। इति।
संहितायामपि—पलाशपत्रे निश्छिद्रे कथिते स्रुक्स्रुवौ मुने।
विदध्याद्वाऽश्वत्थपत्रे संक्षिप्ते होमकर्म्मणि॥ इति॥ १००-१०२॥

अथ वेदिकायां सर्व्वतोभद्रादिमण्डलरचनामाह चतुरस्र इति। वास्तुमण्डलोक्तप्रकारेण कर्णसूत्रद्वयसहितं चतुष्कोष्ठयुक्तं चतुरस्रं कुर्य्यादित्यर्थः॥

श्लोकद्वयेन षोड़शकोष्ठोत्पादनप्रकारमाह चतुर्ष्विति। चतुर्षु कोष्ठेषु कोणसूत्रचतुष्कं तथा दद्याद् यथा मध्ये मध्ये मत्स्या भवेयुः। मन्त्री तेषु मत्स्येषु द्वे प्रागपरायते द्वे याम्योत्तरायते इदं समं सूत्रचतुष्टयं पातयेदिति सम्बन्धः। एवं षोड़शकोष्ठीसम्पत्ता भवति॥

चतुःषष्टिकोष्ठोत्पादनप्रकारं सार्द्धपद्येनाह पूर्व्ववदिति। इदं त्रिषु स्थानेष्वन्वेति। तत्र प्रकारः। कोणगतचतुःकोष्ठेषु पूर्व्ववत् कर्णसूत्रचतुष्कं दत्त्वा तदुत्पन्नमत्स्यचतुष्केषु पूर्व्ववत् द्वे प्रागग्रे द्वे उदगग्रे सूत्रे इदं सूत्रचतुष्टयं दद्यात्। एतत् सूत्रचतुष्कपातोत्पन्नान्तरालकोष्ठमत्स्यचतुष्के पुनः द्वे प्रागग्रे द्वे उदगग्रे सूत्रे दद्यात्। एवं चतुःषष्टिकोष्ठानि सम्पद्यन्ते॥ १०३-१०६॥

तेनैव विधिना इत्यस्यायमर्थः। कोणकोष्ठचतुष्के पूर्व्ववत् कर्णसूत्रचतुष्टयं दत्त्वा तदुत्पन्नमत्स्यचतुष्के द्वे प्रागग्रे द्वे उदगग्रे सूत्रे दद्यात्। तत एतत्सूत्र-

षट्त्रिंशता पदैर्मध्ये लिखेत् पद्मं स[सु]लक्षणम् ।
बहिःपङ्क्त्या भवेत् पीठं पङ्क्तियुग्मेन वीथिका ॥ १०८
द्वारशोभोपशोभास्रान् शिष्टाभ्यां परिकल्पयेत् ।
शास्त्रोक्तविधिना मन्त्री ततः पद्मं समालिखेत् ॥ १०९
पद्मक्षेत्रस्य सन्त्यज्य द्वादशांशं बहिः सुधीः ।
तन्मध्यं विभजेद् वृत्तैस्त्रिभिः समविभागतः ॥ ११०
आद्यं स्यात् कर्णिकास्थानं केशराणां द्वितीयकम् ।
तृतीयं तत्र[पद्म]पत्राणामुक्तांशेन दलाग्रकम् ॥ १११
बाह्यवृत्तान्तरालस्य मानं यद् विधिना सुधीः ।
निधाय केशराग्रेषु परितोऽर्द्धनिशाकरान् ॥ ११२

चतुष्कपातोत्पन्नान्तरालकोष्ठमत्स्येषु षट् प्रागग्राणि षडुदगग्राणि सूत्राणि दद्यात् । एवं द्वे शते षट्पञ्चाशत् कोष्ठानि सम्पद्यन्ते ॥ १०७ ॥

कोष्ठानां विनियोगमाह षट्त्रिंशतेति । पद्मलिखनप्रकारमनन्तरमेव वक्ष्यति । बहिरिति त्रिषु स्थानेष्वन्वेति । बहिःपङ्क्त्या परितः अष्टाविंशतिकोष्ठात्मिकया वक्ष्यमाणरीत्या पीठं कुर्य्यात् । तद्बहिः पङ्क्तियुग्मेन परितः अशीतिकोष्ठात्मकेन वक्ष्यमाणरीत्या वीथिकां कुर्य्यात् । तद्बहिः परितः शिष्टाभ्यां पङ्क्तिभ्यां द्वादशोत्तरशतकोष्ठाभ्यां द्वाराणि शोभा उपशोभा अस्रान् कोणान् वक्ष्यमाणरीत्या कुर्य्यात् ॥ १०८ ॥ १०९ ॥

पद्मकरणप्रकारमाह पद्मेति । तत्र षट्त्रिंशत्पदात्मकं पद्मक्षेत्रं तद्दिक्सूत्रद्वयेन कर्णसूत्रद्वयेन चाष्टधा भेदितं वर्त्तते । तान्येव सूत्राणि पत्रमध्यसूत्राणि । तत्र प्रकारः । पद्मक्षेत्रायामं द्वादशधा विभज्य एकांशं सर्व्वतो बहिस्त्यजेत् । ततो दशभागान् षोढा विभज्य मध्ये सूत्रादिं संस्थाप्य अंशद्वयेनैकं वृत्तं तदुपर्य्यंशद्वयेनापरं तदुपर्य्यंशद्वयेनान्यदिति वृत्तत्रयं कुर्य्यात् । आद्यमित्याद्युक्तिस्तु वक्ष्यमाणाङ्गावरणादीनां स्थानसूचनायेत्यवधेयम् । मुक्तांशेनेति द्वादशांशेन तत्र वृत्तमग्रे वक्ष्यति ॥ ११० ॥ १११ ॥

बाह्येति । बाह्यं यत् पत्रवृत्तं तस्य यदन्तरालं तस्य मानेन सुधीः केशराग्रेषु केशरवृत्ताग्रे निधाय सूत्रादिमिति शेषः । विधिना परित उभयतः पद्ममध्य-

लिखित्वा सन्धिसंस्थानि तत्र सूत्राणि पातयेत् ॥ ११३

दलाग्राणाञ्च यन्मानं तन्मानं वृत्तमालिखेत् ।

तदन्तराले तन्मध्यसूत्रस्योभयतः सुधीः ।

आलिखेद्बाह्यहस्तेन दलाग्राणि समन्ततः ॥ ११४

सूत्राणामिति शेषः । अर्द्धनिशाकरान् लिखित्वा सन्धिसंस्थानि अर्द्धनिशाकरसन्धिसंस्थानि चत्वारि सूत्राणि तत्र पातयेदिति सम्बन्धः । मानं यद्विधिनेति पाठे बाह्यवृत्तान्तरालस्य यन्मानं तेन विधिना तेन मानेनेत्यर्थः । तत्रायं विधिः । तत्र वृत्तान्तरालमितसूत्रं केशरवृत्तदिक्सूत्रसम्पाते संस्थाप्य तद्दिक्सूत्रोभयतः पत्रवृत्तस्पर्शिकेशरवृत्तलग्नान्तद्वयम् अर्द्धचन्द्रं लिखेत् । एवं चतुर्षु दिक्सूत्रेषु चतुर्षु कोणसूत्रेषु च कृते अष्टार्द्धचन्द्रा जायन्ते । एतच्च केशराग्रेष्विति बहुवचनादेव लभ्यते । यतोऽष्टपत्रमध्ये अष्टौ केशरस्थानानि ततोऽष्टदलसिद्धिरिति । ततोऽर्द्धचन्द्रयोः परस्परसम्पातरूपाष्टसन्धिषु सम्मुखीनयोर्द्वयोर्द्वयोरेकैकं सूत्रं दद्यात् । एवमष्टपत्राणामपि अष्टौ सीमारेखा उत्पद्यन्ते । सन्ध्यधोवर्त्ति सीमारेखोभयतः स्थितोऽर्द्धनिशाकरांशो मार्जनीयः । तदुक्तं—

दलप्रसिद्ध्यै दलमध्यसन्धौ निधाय सूत्रन्तु दलान्तरालम् ।

दलान्तरालोभयसङ्गमोत्थैः शशाङ्कखण्डैस्तु दलं प्रसिद्ध्येत् ॥ इति ।

अन्यत्रापि—उत्पादितस्य दिक्सूत्रे संस्थाप्यान्यद्दिगन्त्यं तु ।

प्रसार्य कोणसूत्रे द्वे वृत्तदिक्मत्स्यमानतः ॥

निधाय केशराग्रेषु दलसन्धींस्तु लाञ्छयेत् ।

पातयित्वा तु सूत्राणि तत्र पत्राष्टकं लिखेत् ॥ इति ॥११२-११३॥

चतुर्थं वृत्तमाह दलेति । दलाग्राणां यन्मानं बहिः त्यक्त्वा द्वादशांशरूपं तन्मानं चतुर्थं वृत्तं कुर्यात् । दलाग्रकरणप्रकारमाह तदिति । तदन्तराले कृतदलाग्रवृत्तान्तराले तन्मध्यसूत्रस्य पत्रमध्यसूत्रस्योभयतः बाह्यहस्तेन समन्ततो दिक्षु विदिक्ष्वपि दलाग्राणि सुधीरालिखेदिति सम्बन्धः । तत्र प्रकारः । चतुर्थवृत्तान्तराले पत्रमध्यसूत्रस्योभयतः सन्धिसूत्रस्याग्रे सूत्रादिं निधाय मध्यवृत्ततः दलाग्रवृत्त पत्रमध्यसूत्रसम्पातपर्य्यन्तं सूत्रद्वयं दद्यात् । तत्र सूत्रप्रान्त एकः पत्रस्पर्शी द्वितीयो दलाग्रमध्यसूत्रसम्पातस्पर्शी । सूत्रद्वयाग्रभागश्च परस्पराभिमुखो यथा स्यादित्येतदर्थं बाह्यहस्तेनेत्युक्तम् । ततः कर्णिकावृत्तं त्यक्त्वा बाह्यस्त्रीणि वृत्तानि पद्मपत्रमध्यरेखाश्च सर्व्वं सम्यक् मार्जयेत् यथाऽष्टदलं पद्मं दृष्टिमनोहरं दृश्यते । ११४ ॥

दलमूलेषु युगशः केशराणि प्रकल्पयेत् ।
एतत् साधारणं प्रोक्तं पङ्कजं तन्त्रवेदिभिः ॥ ११५
पदानि त्रीणि पादार्थं पीठकोणेषु मार्जयेत् ।
अवशिष्टैः पदैर्विद्वान् गात्राणि परिकल्पयेत् ॥ ११६
पदानि वीथिसंस्थानि मार्जयेत् पङ्क्त्यभेदतः ।
दिक्षु द्वाराणि रचयेद् द्विचतुःकोष्ठकैस्ततः ॥ ११७
पदैस्त्रिभिरथैकेन शोभाः स्युर्द्वारपार्श्वयोः ।
उपशोभाः स्युरेकेन त्रिभिः कोष्ठैरनन्तरम् ।
अवशिष्टैः पदैः षड्भिः कोणानां स्याच्चतुष्टयम् ॥ ११८

केशरप्रकारमाह दलेति । कर्णिकावृत्तस्पर्शी सन्धिगतपत्रसीमासूत्रान्तराले पत्रमध्यसूत्रस्योभयतः एकैकस्मिन् पत्रे द्वौ द्वौ केशरौ कर्णिकावृत्तलग्नमूलौ केशरवृत्तलग्नाग्रौ अग्रे किञ्चित् स्थूलौ परस्परसम्मुखौ कुर्यात् । उपसंहरति एतदिति । यत्र कुत्रापि पङ्कजं कुर्यादिति वक्ष्यति । तत्रायं प्रकारो ज्ञेयः ॥ ११५ ॥

पीठं कुर्यादिति यदुक्तं तत्प्रकारमाह पदानीति । पीठार्थं स्थापितपङ्क्तौ एकैकं कोणकोष्ठं तदुभयपार्श्ववर्त्ति कोष्ठद्वयञ्च एवं च त्रीणि कोष्ठानि पादार्थं मार्जयेत् । अवशिष्टैश्चतुर्भिः पदैः पीठगात्राणि कल्पयेत् । वीथ्यर्थं स्थापितपङ्क्तिद्वयस्यैकाकारेण मार्जनं कार्य्यम् ।

द्वाराण्याह दिक्ष्विति । द्वारार्थं परितः स्थापितपङ्क्तिद्वयमध्ये चतुर्दिक्षु द्वारचतुष्टयार्थम् आन्तरपङ्क्तिस्थं मध्यसूत्रोभयपार्श्ववर्त्ति कोष्ठद्वयं तथा बाह्यपङ्क्तिस्थं मध्यसूत्रपार्श्ववर्त्ति कोष्ठचतुष्टयं द्वारार्थं मार्जयेत् । एवं चत्वारि द्वाराणि स्युः ॥ ११६ ॥ ११७ ॥

शोभा आह पदैरिति । अन्तः पङ्क्तिस्थानि द्वारपार्श्वद्वयगतानि त्रीणि त्रीणि कोष्ठानि बाह्यपङ्क्तिस्थं द्वारपार्श्वद्वयगमेकैकं कोष्ठं मार्जयेत् । एवमष्टौ शोभाः स्युः । उपशोभा इति । अन्तः पङ्क्तिस्थम् उभयतः शोभालग्नमेकैकं कोष्ठं त्रीणि त्रीणि बाह्यपङ्क्तिकोष्ठानि मार्जयेत् । एवमष्टावुपशोभाः स्युः । अवशिष्टैरिति । उभयत उपशोभालग्नान्यन्तःपङ्क्तिस्थानि त्रीणि कोष्ठानि बाह्यपङ्क्तिस्थानि च त्रीणि कोष्ठानि मार्जयेत् । एवं चत्वारः कोणाः स्युः ॥ ११८ ॥

रञ्जयेत् पञ्चभिर्वर्णैर्मण्डलं तन्मनोहरम् ।
पीतं हरिद्राचूर्णं स्यात् सितं तण्डुलसम्भवम् ॥ ११९
कुसुम्भचूर्णमरुणं कृष्णं दग्धपुलाकजम् ।
बिल्वादिपत्रजं श्याममित्युक्तं वर्णपञ्चकम् ॥ १२०
अङ्गुलोत्सेधविस्ताराः सीमारेखाः सिताः शुभाः ।
कर्णिकां पीतवर्णेन केशराण्यरुणेन च ॥ १२१
शुक्लवर्णेन पत्राणि तत्सन्धिं श्यामलेन च ।
रजसा रञ्जयेन्मन्त्री यद्वा पीतैव कर्णिका ॥ १२२
केशराः पीतरक्ताः स्युररुणानि दलान्यपि ।
सन्धयः कृष्ण[शुक्ल]वर्णाः स्युः पीतेनाऽप्यसितेन वा ॥ १२३

मण्डलरञ्जनार्थं पञ्चवर्णानाह रञ्जयेदिति । कुसुम्भेति । अन्यतारुणान्तरमुक्तम् ।

तथा दोषारजः चारसंयुक्तं रक्तमुच्यते । इति ।

पुलाकजं तुच्छधान्यजम् । "पुलाकस्तुच्छधान्यं स्यात्" इति त्रिकाण्डे । तत्प्रक्रिया यथा । तुच्छधान्यस्यार्द्रदाहावसरे दुग्धादिना सिक्त्वा ततो वस्त्रगालितं चूर्णं कुर्यात् । आदिशब्देनाऽन्यहरितपत्रादि । तदुक्तं प्रयोगसारे—

श्यामं श्यामच्छदोद्भूतं रजः प्रोक्तं स्वकर्मसु । इति ।

श्यामशब्देनात्र हरिद्वर्णो गृह्यते । महाकपिलपञ्चरात्रे तु अस्यावश्यकतोक्ता—

पीतं क्षितिस्तु विज्ञेया शुक्लमापः प्रकीर्तिताः ।
तेजो वै रक्तवर्णं स्याच्छ्यामं वायुः प्रकीर्त्तितः ॥
आकाशं कृष्णवर्णञ्च पञ्चमन्तु महामुने ।
सितेऽधिदेवता रुद्रो रक्ते ब्रह्माऽधिदेवता ॥
पीतेऽधिदेवता विष्णुः कृष्णे चैवाऽच्युतः स्मृतः ।
श्यामेऽधिदेवता नागः समाख्यातो मयाऽनघ ॥
शुक्लं ग्रहाय दोहन्ति रक्तं क्रूरगणोद्भवम् ।
कृष्णं सर्व्वासुरोत्साहं नीलं वैनायकीन्तथा ॥
पैशाचीं राक्षसीञ्चैव निहन्ति हरितं रजः ।
तस्माद्धोमेऽभिषेके च यागे चैव विशेषतः ।
वर्त्तयेन्मण्डलं तैस्तु देवसन्तुष्टिकारकम् ॥ इति ।

रञ्जयेत् पीठगर्भाणि पादाः स्युररुणप्रभाः।
गात्राणि तस्य शुक्लानि वीथीषु च चतसृषु ॥ १२४
आलिखेत् कल्पलतिका दलपुष्पफलान्विताः।
वर्णैर्नानाविधैश्चित्रैः सर्व्वदृष्टिमनोहराः ॥ १२५
द्वाराणि श्वेतवर्णानि शोभा रक्ताः समीरिताः।
उपशोभाः पीतवर्णाः कोणान्यसितभानि च ॥ १२६
तिस्रो रेखा बहिः कुर्य्यात् सितरक्तासिताः क्रमात्।
मण्डलं सर्व्वतोभद्रमेतत् साधारणं स्मृतम् ॥ १२७
चतुरस्रां भुवं भित्त्वा दिग्भ्यो द्वादशधा सुधीः।
पातयेत्तच्च सूत्राणि कोष्ठानां दृश्यते शतम् ॥ १२८

तन्त्रान्तरे तु विशेषः—

शक्तास्तु वाञ्छेद् यदि सिद्धिमुग्रां तद्वर्णरत्नैरिह मण्डलानि।
आभूषयेन्मौक्तिक पुष्परागमाणिक्यनीलैर्हरितैश्च रत्नैः॥ इति।

सीमारेखा इति सर्व्वाः। पूर्व्वं श्वेतकमलमुक्त्वा रक्तकमलमाह यद्वेति। विष्णुशाक्तशैवदोचादौ तु व्यवस्थितविकल्पो ज्ञेयः। पीतैर्वेति द्वितीयपक्षेऽपि। पक्षान्तरं समाप्य प्रकृतमाह पीतैर्नेति। स्वेच्छया विकल्पोऽयम्। पीठगर्भाणीति कमलक्षेत्रकोणान्। अत्र गर्भं एषामस्तीति गर्भं कोणस्थानम्। अर्शादित्वादच्। ततो नपुंसकता। तस्येति पीठस्य कल्पलतिकालेखनमुपदेशतो ज्ञेयम् ॥ ११८-१२६ ॥

बहिरिति सर्व्वबाह्यकृतसीमारेखाया बाह्ये इत्यर्थः। वशिष्ठसंहितायान्तु विशेषः।

पीतं पूर्व्वे सितं देयं पश्चिमेऽप्युत्तरे तथा।
रक्तन्तु दक्षिणे कृष्णं पाटलं वह्निसंस्थितम् ॥
नैऋर्त्ये नीलवर्णन्तु वायव्ये धूम्रवर्णकम्।
ईशे गौरं विनिर्दिष्टमष्टपत्रेष्वयं क्रमः॥ इति ॥ १२७ ॥

मण्डलान्तरमाह चतुरस्रामिति। अत्र मत्स्योत्पादनप्रकारासम्भवात् दिग्भ्यो द्वादशधेत्युक्तिः। तत्र चतुर्दिक्षु द्वादशधा भूमिं विभज्य तत्र सूत्राणि पातयेदिति। तत्र प्रकारः। पूर्व्ववत् षोड़शकोष्ठानि कृत्वा तेष्वेकं कोष्ठं समांशेन

चतुश्चत्वारिंशदाढ्यं पश्चात् षट्त्रिंशताऽम्बुजम् ।
कोष्ठैः प्रकल्पयेत् पीठं पङ्क्त्यां नैवात्र वीथिका: ॥ १२९
द्वारशोभे यथापूर्व्वमुपशोभा न दृश्यते ।
अवशिष्टैः पदैः कुर्य्यात् षड्भिः कोणानि तत्त्ववित् ।
विदध्यात् पूर्व्ववच्छेषमेवं वा मण्डलं शुभम् ॥ १३०
चतुरस्रे चतुःषष्टिपदान्यारचयेत् सुधीः ।
पदैश्चतुर्भिः पद्मं स्यान्मध्ये तत्परितः पुनः ॥ १३१
वीथीश्चतस्रः कुर्व्वीत मण्डलान्तावसानिकाः ।
दिग्गतेषु चतुष्केषु पङ्कजानि समालिखेत् ॥ १३२
विदिग्गतचतुष्काणि भित्त्वा षोड़शधा सुधीः ।
मार्जयेत् स्वस्तिकाकारं श्वेतपीतारुणासितैः ॥ १३३

त्रिधा विभज्य तच्चिह्नद्वये प्रागग्रं सूत्रद्वयं दद्यात् । एतत्सूत्रद्वयसम्पातोत्पन्न-प्रतिकोष्ठमत्स्यद्वन्द्वेषु द्वे द्वे उदगग्रे सूत्रे एवमुदगग्रामष्टसूत्रीं पातयेत् । ततस्तत्-सूत्रसम्पातोत्पन्नकोष्ठमत्स्यद्वन्द्वेषु प्रागग्रे द्वे द्वे एवं प्रागग्रां षट्सूत्रीं दद्यात् । एवमेकशतचतुश्चत्वारिंशत् कोष्ठानि जायन्ते । कोष्ठैरिति पूर्व्ववान्वेति । अम्बुजमुक्तप्रकारेणैव । पङ्क्त्यां पीठं पूर्व्ववदेव । अवशिष्टैरिति । तत्रैकं पद-मन्तःपङ्क्तिस्थं पञ्चकोष्ठानि बाह्यपङ्क्तिस्थानि । एवं षड्भिरित्यर्थः । शेषमिति रञ्जनबाह्यरेखात्रयकरणादि ॥ १२८-१३० ॥

नवनाभमण्डलमाह चतुरस्र इति । तत्र पूर्व्ववत् चतुःषष्टिकोष्ठानि कृत्वा तत्र मध्यचतुष्के पूर्व्ववत् पद्मम् । ततश्चतुर्दिक्षु अष्टाष्टकोष्ठिकाश्चतस्रो वीथीः कुर्य्यात् । एवमष्टदिक्षु चतुःकोष्ठाष्टकमवशिष्यते । तद्भित्वा षोड़शधेति पूर्व्ववदेव मार्जये-दिति । मार्जनप्रकारस्तु षोड़शधेति कोष्ठेषु मध्यचतुष्कस्यैकैकं कोष्ठं परस्परविरुद्धै-कैकदिशि सम्मार्ज्य तत्संलग्नबाह्यवीथ्याः कोणकोष्ठादिकोष्ठत्रयं तद्दिक्स्थमेव मार्जयेत् । एवमुपशोभाकारवच्चत्वारि चत्वारि कोष्ठानि मार्जितानि स्वस्तिका-काराणि सम्पद्यन्ते । केचित्त्वन्यथा मार्जनमाहुः । मध्यचतुष्कस्य पूर्व्वदिग्गत-कोष्ठद्वयं पूर्व्वदिशि सम्मार्ज्य तल्लग्नं बाह्यवीथीस्थं दक्षिणदिक्पर्य्यन्तं कोष्ठद्वयं मार्जयेत् । एवं दक्षिणदिग्गतकोष्ठद्वयं दक्षिणदिशि सम्मार्ज्य तल्लग्नं बाह्य-

रजोभिः पूरयेत्तानि स्वस्तिकानि शिवादितः।
प्राक् प्रोक्तेनैव मार्गेण शेषमन्यत् समापयेत्।
नवनाभमिदं प्रोक्तं मण्डलं सर्व्वसिद्धिदम्॥ १३४

पञ्चाब्जं मण्डलं प्रोक्तमेतत् स्वस्तिकवर्जितम्।
दीक्षायां देवपूजार्थं मण्डलानां चतुष्टयम्।
सर्व्वतन्त्रानुसारेण प्रोक्तं सर्व्वसमृद्धिदम्॥ १३५

इति श्रीशारदातिलके तृतीयः पटलः॥

वीथीस्थं पश्चिमदिक्पर्य्यन्तं कोष्ठद्वयं मार्जयेत्। एवं पश्चिमकोष्ठद्वयं पश्चिमदिशि सम्मार्ज्य तन्नग्नं बाह्यवीथीस्थम् उत्तरान्तं कोष्ठद्वयं मार्जयेत्। तत उत्तरस्थं कोष्ठद्वयं उत्तरदिशि सम्मार्ज्य तन्नग्नं बाह्यवीथीस्थं पूर्व्वदिक् पर्य्यन्तं कोष्ठद्वयं मार्जयेत्। पक्षद्वयमपि साम्प्रदायिकमेव। शिवादित ईशानादि वायव्यान्तम्। शेषमिति पद्मरञ्जनादि वीथीषु कल्पलतिकालिखनं रेखात्रयञ्च॥ १३१-१३४॥

स्वस्तिकवर्जितमिति स्वस्तिकचतुष्कं मार्जयेदित्यर्थः। चतुष्टयमिति। एषां विषय उक्तः प्रयोगसारे नवनाभमुक्त्वा—

कलशानां नवानान्तु प्रोक्तमेतत् परं पदम्।
तथा प्राक् प्रस्तुते स्थाने पद्मं सङ्कल्प्य पूर्व्ववत्॥
वीथीस्तद्वच्च संयोज्य चतुष्टयचतुष्टये।
स्वस्तिकान्यालिखेद्दिक्षु कोणकोष्ठानि मार्जयेत्॥
पञ्चानां कलशानाञ्च पदं स्यादेतदुत्तमम्।
चतुरस्रोदितस्थाने तथा पद्मं समालिखेत्॥
कलशस्यैकदेव[तदेक]स्य प्रोक्तं साधारणं पदम्। इति॥ १३५॥

इति शारदातिलकटीकायां सत्सम्प्रदायकृतव्याख्यायां पदार्थादर्शाभिख्यायां राघवभट्टकृतायां तृतीयः पटलः॥ ॐ॥

चतुर्थः पटलः ।

अथ दीक्षां प्रवक्ष्यामि मन्त्राणां हितकाम्यया ।
विना यया न लभ्येत सर्व्वमन्त्रफलं यतः ॥ १

मन्त्रो यः साधयेदेकं जपहोमार्चनादिभिः ।
क्रियाभिर्भूरिभिस्तस्य सिद्ध्यन्त्यन्येऽल्पसाधनात् ॥
सम्यक्सिद्धैकमन्त्रस्य नाऽसाध्यमिह किञ्चन ।
बहुमन्त्रवतः पुंसः का कथा हरिरेव सः ॥

इत्यादिना महाकपिलपञ्चरात्रनारायणीययोः ।

अन्यत्रापि—पुस्तकाल्लिखितो मन्त्रो येन सुन्दरि जप्यते ।
न तस्य जायते सिद्धिर्हानिरेव पदे पदे ॥ इति ।

तथाऽन्यत्रापि—द्विजानामनुपेतानां स्वकर्म्माध्ययनादिषु ।
यथाऽधिकारो नास्तीह स्याच्चोपनयनादनु ॥
तथाऽत्राऽदीक्षितानाञ्च मन्त्रदेवार्चनादिषु ।
नाधिकारोऽस्त्यतः कुर्य्यादात्मानं शिवसंस्कृतम् ॥ इति ।

नारायणीये च—यदृच्छया श्रुतं मन्त्रं छलेनाप्यछलेन वा ।
पत्रेक्षितं वा गाथावत् तज्जपेद् यद्यनर्थकृत् ॥ इति ।

तत्रैव—प्रविश्य विधिवद्दीक्षामभिषेकावसानिकाम् ।
श्रुत्वा तन्त्रं गुरोर्लब्धं साधयेद्दीक्षितं मनुम् ॥ इति ।

अन्यत्रापि—गुरुमुख्याः क्रियाः सर्व्वा भुक्तिमुक्तिफलप्रदाः ।
तस्मात् सेव्यो गुरुर्नित्यं मुक्त्यर्थं सुसमाहितैः ।
गुर्व्वनुक्ताः क्रियाः सर्व्वा निष्फलाः स्युर्यतो ध्रुवम् ॥ इति ।

अन्यत्रापि—जपो देवार्चनविधिः कार्य्यो दीक्षान्वितैर्नरैः ।
नास्ति पापं यतस्तेषां सूतकं वा यतात्मनाम् ॥

इत्यादिना दीक्षागृहीतमन्त्रफलस्योक्तत्वात् तां विना अविधिप्राप्तेभ्यस्तेभ्यः फलं न सिद्ध्यतीति अवश्यवक्तव्यदीक्षां वक्तुं प्रतिजानीते अथेति । अथ मण्डलकथनानन्तरं मन्त्राणां दीक्षां प्रवक्ष्यामि । हितकाम्यया पूर्व्वप्रकृतशिष्याणामिति शेषः । यद्वा वैदिकजनानामिति शेषः । अयमेव साम्प्रदायिकः पाठः । एतेन

सर्व्वसामान्यरूपा मन्त्रदीक्षोच्यते इत्युक्तम् । तदुक्तमीशानशिवेन—

सा तु मन्त्र-शिव-शक्ति-विष्णुभेदाच्चतुर्विधा ।
सामान्यभूता खलु मान्त्रिकी स्याद् दीक्षा स्मृता मन्त्रगणेषु तद्वत् ।
वर्णेषु चापि द्विज पूर्व्वकेषु स्याच्छैवशाक्तेष्वपि वैष्णवेषु ॥ इति ।

प्रयोगसारेऽपि—मन्त्रमार्गानुसारेण साक्षात्कृत्वेष्टदेवताम् ।
गुरुर्बोधयेच्छिष्यं मन्त्रदीक्षेति सोच्यते ॥ इति ।

षडन्वयमहारत्नेऽपि—

त्रिविधा सा भवेद् दीक्षा प्रथमा त्वाणवी परा ।
शाक्तेयी शाम्भवी चान्या सद्योमुक्तिविधायिनी ॥
मन्त्रार्चनासनस्थान ध्यानोपायादिभिः कृता ।
दीक्षा सा त्वाणवी प्रोक्ता यथाशास्त्रोक्तरूपिणी ॥
सिद्धौ स्वशक्तिमालोक्य तया केवलया शिशोः ।
निरुपायं कृता दीक्षा शाक्तेयी परिकीर्त्तिता ॥
अभिसन्धिं विना चार्य्यशिष्ययोरुभयोरपि ।
देशिकानुग्रहेणैव शिवताव्यक्तिकारिणी ॥
सेयन्तु शाम्भवी दीक्षा शिवावेशनकारिणी ॥ इति ।

अतएव ग्रन्थकृद् भैरवीपटले वक्ष्यति "दीक्षां प्राप्य" इति । तत्र शक्तिदीक्षां प्राप्येत्यर्थः । तथा द्वादशाक्षरे "दीक्षितो विजितेन्द्रियः" इति । तत्र वैष्णव-मार्गेण दीक्षित इत्यर्थः । तथा शैवपञ्चाक्षरेऽपि "दीक्षितः शैववर्त्मना" इति । तत्र शक्तिविष्णुशिवदीक्षास्तत्तन्त्रे ज्ञेयाः । मन्त्रिणामिति पाठे मन्त्रिणां हितकाम्यया दीक्षां प्रवक्ष्यामि । उत्तरार्द्धे सर्व्वमन्त्रफलमिति मन्त्रशब्दस्यो-च्चारितत्वात् अत्र मन्त्राणामिति सम्बद्ध्यते इति वदन्ति । परन्तु मुख्यमन्त्रपदस्यैव सम्बन्धाभावात् यदपि मन्त्रपदं तदपि वृत्तिगर्भितमिति न समञ्जसः पाठः । आचार्य्या अपि—

अथ प्रवक्ष्ये विधिवन्मनूनां दीक्षाविधानं जगतो हिताय । इति ।

वायवीयसंहितायाम्—

शाम्भवी चैव शाक्ती च मान्त्री चैव शिवागमे ।
दीक्षोपदिश्यते त्रेधा शिवेन परमात्मना ॥
गुरोरालोकमात्रेण स्पर्शात् सम्भाषणादपि ।
सद्यः संज्ञा भवेज्जन्तोर्दीक्षा सा शाम्भवी मता ॥

दिव्यं ज्ञानं यतो दद्यात् कुर्य्यात् पापस्य संक्षयः।
तस्माद् दीक्षेति संप्रोक्ता देशिकैस्तत्त्ववेदिभिः॥ २

शाक्ती ज्ञानवती दीक्षा शिष्यदेहं प्रविश्य तु।
गुरुणा योगमार्गेण क्रियते ज्ञानचक्षुषा॥
मान्त्री क्रियावती दीक्षा कुण्ड[म्भ]मण्डलपूर्व्विका। इति।

यतो यस्मात् कारणात्। यया दीक्षया विना। सर्व्वे च ते मन्त्राश्च तेषां यत् फलं तन्न लभ्यते न प्राप्यते। एतेनैतदुक्तम्। यः कश्चन मन्त्रो दीक्षयैव शिष्येण गुरुभ्यो ग्राह्यः। अन्यस्य फलदायकत्वनियमाभावात्। किञ्च शिवादिदीक्षया तत्तन्मन्त्राणामेव फलदायकत्वम् अनया तु सर्व्वमन्त्राणाम्। अयञ्च सर्व्वेञ्च तन्मन्त्रफलमिति फलविशेषणत्वेनापि व्याख्येयम्। तेनोपदेशादिमात्रेण सकलं फलं न प्राप्यते। अनया तु सर्व्वमपीत्यर्थः। उपदेशस्यापि तन्त्रान्तरे विहितत्वादिति। मन्त्रशब्दव्युत्पत्तिरुक्ता पिङ्गलामते—

मननं विश्वविज्ञानं त्राणं संसारबन्धनात्।
यतः करोति संसिद्धो मन्त्र इत्युच्यते ततः॥ इति।

रुद्रयामले च—मननात् त्राणनाच्चैव मद्रूपस्यावबोधनात्।
मन्त्र इत्युच्यते सम्यक् मदधिष्ठानतः प्रिये॥ इति।

अन्यत्रापि—गुप्तोपदेशतो मन्त्रो मननात् त्राणनादपि। इति॥ १॥

दीक्षाशब्दव्युत्पत्तिमाह ज्ञानमिति। दद्यात्-क्षयमित्यनयोराद्यवर्णमादायेयं निरुक्तिः। "अप्यक्षरसाम्यान्निर्ब्रूयात्" इति यास्कोक्तेः। तदुक्तं—

ददाति यस्मादिह दिव्यभावं मायामले कर्म्म च संक्षिणोति।
फलं चतुर्वर्गभवञ्च यस्मात्तस्मात्तु दीक्षेत्यभिधानमस्याः॥ इति।

प्रयोगसारेऽपि—दीयते ज्ञानसद्भावः क्षीयते पापसञ्चयः।
तेन दीक्षेति सा ज्ञेया पाशच्छेदाह्वया क्रिया॥ इति।

अत्र दीक्षायामेव तन्त्रेण नित्यपूजाया अपि वक्ष्यमाणत्वात् देशिकैरित्यनेन सूचितम्। स्नानात् पूर्व्वं नित्यकृत्यं किञ्चिदुच्यते। ब्राह्मे मुहूर्त्ते उत्थाय स्मृत्युक्तविधानेन शौचादिकं देहशुद्धिञ्च विधाय रात्रिवासः परित्यज्य वासोऽन्तरं परिधाय मन्त्रस्नानं कृत्वा देवगृहमागत्य सम्मार्जनोपलेपनादिकं कृत्वा देवस्य निर्माल्यमपसार्य्य पूर्व्वदिनावशिष्टपत्रादिनाऽभ्यर्च्य नमस्कुर्य्यात्। अन्यथा दोषदर्शनात्।

यदाहुः—तृषाक्रान्तः पशुर्बद्धः कन्यका च रजस्वला ।
देवता च सनिर्माल्या हन्ति पुण्यं पुराकृतम् ॥ इति ।

तदुक्तं मन्त्रतन्त्रप्रकाशे—

स्मृत्युक्तेन विधानेन सम्यक् शौचं विधाय च ।
प्रक्षाल्य पादावाचम्य कृत्वा न्यासं यतात्मवान् ॥
प्रविश्य देवतास्थानं निर्माल्यमपकृष्य च ।
दद्यात् पुष्पाञ्जलिं विद्वानर्घ्यपाद्ये तथैव च ॥
मुखप्रक्षालनं दद्याद् दद्याद्वै दन्तधावनम् ।
दद्यादाचमनीयञ्च दद्याद्वासोऽमलं शुभम् ॥ इति ।

ततो यथोक्तासने उपविश्य गुरून् मूर्द्धनि ध्यायेत् ।

प्रातःशिरसि शुक्लेऽब्जे द्विनेत्रं द्विभुजं गुरुम् ।
प्रसन्नवदनं शान्तं स्मरेत्तन्नामपूर्व्वकम् ॥
अहं देवो न चान्योऽस्मि ब्रह्मैवाऽहं न शोकभाक् ।
सच्चिदानन्दरूपोऽहं नित्यमुक्तस्वभाववान् ॥

इति गुरुदेवतात्मनामैक्यं भावयित्वा प्रार्थयेत्—

त्रैलोक्यचैतन्यमयादिदेव श्रीनाथ विष्णो भवदाज्ञयैव ।
प्रातः समुत्थाय तव प्रियार्थं संसारयात्रामनुवर्त्तयिष्ये ॥
जानामि धर्म्मं न च मे प्रवृत्तिर्जानाम्यधर्म्मं न च मे निवृत्तिः ।
केनापि देवेन हृदि स्थितेन यथा नियुक्तोऽस्मि तथा करोमि ॥ इति ।

अत्र श्रीनाथ विष्णो इति शिवादावूहः कार्य्यः । चण्डीश शम्भो इत्यादि ततो देवतागुणनामादि कीर्त्तयन् स्नानार्थं नद्यादौ गच्छेत् । स्नात्वेति स्नानादिकोपदेशोऽनुक्रमकथनाय ।

यतश्च—अशुचिवस्त्रमस्नातमनलङ्कारं पुरुषं देवता नाऽधितिष्ठन्ति । इति ।

अनेन मज्जनस्नानाशक्तः स्नानान्तरमपि कुर्य्यादित्युक्तं भवति । यदाहुः—

भूत्वा वा गोरजोभिर्भवति विपदि तत् केवलैर्वाऽपि मन्त्रैः । इति ।

अथच विधिवत् स्नात्वा पूर्व्वाह्णिकीः क्रियाः कृत्वा इति मन्त्रस्नानं अघ्यसन्ध्यां मन्त्रतर्पणञ्च कर्त्तव्यमिति सूचितम् ।

अथ स्नानं प्रवक्ष्यामि सर्व्वपापहरं शुभम् ।
यत् कृत्वा साधकः सम्यक् सर्व्वकर्म्मार्हको भवेत् ॥

इत्यादिना महाकपिलपञ्चरात्रे ।

चतुर्विधा सा सन्दिष्टा क्रियावत्यादिभेदतः।
क्रियावती वर्णमयी कलात्मा वेधमय्यपि॥ ३

वशिष्ठसंहितायामपि—कृत्वादौ वैदिकं स्नानं ततस्तान्त्रिकमाचरेत्।
इत्यादिना च मन्त्रस्नानादिविधिरुक्तः। तत्र मन्त्रस्नानं द्विविधम् आन्तरं बाह्यञ्च।
तत्र वैष्णवस्नानमान्तरमुक्तं वशिष्ठसंहितायाम्—

अनन्तादित्यसङ्काशं वासुदेवं चतुर्भुजम्।
शङ्खचक्रगदापद्ममुकुटं वनमालिनम्॥
तत्पादोदकजां धारां निपतन्तीं स्वमूर्द्धनि।
चिन्तयेद् ब्रह्मरन्ध्रेण प्रविशन्तीं स्वकां तनुम्॥
तया संक्षालयेत् सर्व्वमन्तर्द्देह[मितद्देह]गतं मलम्।
तत्क्षणाद्विरजा मन्त्री जायते स्फटिकोपमः॥
इदं स्नानं वरं मन्त्रात् सहस्रम[स्नाद]धिकं स्मृतम्। इति।

शाक्तमाभ्यन्तरं स्नानमुक्तं श्रीपञ्चमीमते—

स्नानप्रकारो द्विविधो बाह्याभ्यन्तरभेदतः।
आन्तरं स्नानमत्यन्तरहस्यमपि सादरात्॥
कथयामि भवध्वस्त्यै चतुर्वर्गाप्तयेऽपि च।
संवित्त्रयमनुस्मृत्य चरणत्रयमध्यतः॥
स्रवन्तं सच्चिदानन्दप्रवाहं भावगोचरम्।
विमुक्तिसाधनं पुंसां स्मरणादेव योगिनाम्॥
तेनाप्लावितमात्मानं भावयेद्भवशान्तये।
एवमाभ्यन्तरं स्नानम्। इति।

शैवागमे आभ्यन्तरं स्नानमुक्तं—

मनसा मूलमन्त्रेण प्राणायामपुरःसरम्।
कुर्व्वीत मानसं स्नानं सर्व्वत्र विहितञ्च तत्॥ इति।

बाह्यप्रकारस्तूच्यते। स्वशाखोक्तविधिना स्नात्वा प्राणायामपुरःसरमङ्गे षडङ्गानि विन्यस्य—

ब्रह्माण्डोदरतीर्थानि करैः स्पृष्टानि ते रवे।
तेन सत्येन मे देव तीर्थं देहि दिवाकर॥
गङ्गे च यमुने चैव गोदावरि सरस्वति।
नर्मदे सिन्धु कावेरि जलेऽस्मिन् सन्निधिं कुरु॥

ताः क्रमेणैव कथ्यन्ते तन्त्रेऽस्मिन् सम्पदावहाः ॥ ४

आवाहयामि त्वां देवि स्नानार्थमिह सुन्दरि ।
एहि गङ्गे नमस्तुभ्यं सर्व्वतीर्थसमन्विते ॥

इति मन्त्रैरङ्कुशमुद्रयाऽऽदित्यमण्डलात्तीर्थमाकृष्य आवाह्य वमिति अम्भसि नियोज्य सोमसूर्य्याग्निमण्डलानि तत्र सञ्चिन्त्य वं इत्यमृतबीजेन द्वादशधाऽभिमन्त्र्य कवचेनावगुण्ठ्य अस्त्रेण संरक्ष्य मूलमन्त्रेणैकादशवारमभिमन्त्र्य

ॐ आधारः सर्व्वरूप[भूत]स्य विष्णोरतुल्यतेजसः ।
तद्रूपाश्च ततो जाता आपस्ताः प्रणमाम्यहम् ॥

इत्युपस्थाय निमज्जेत् ।

अनेनोपस्थाय तीर्थं निमज्जेच्चिन्तयन् हरिम् ।

इति मन्त्रतन्त्रप्रकाशोक्तेः । तत्र मूलमन्त्रं देवताकृतिञ्च सञ्चिन्त्य उन्मज्ज्य मूलमन्त्रेण सप्तकृत्वो द्वादशकृत्वो वा शङ्खमुद्रया कलशमुद्रया वा आत्मानमभिषिच्य—

सिसृक्षोर्निखिलं विश्वं मुहुः शुक्रं प्रजायते ।
मातरः सर्व्वभूतानामापो देव्यः पुनन्तु माम् ॥
तार-वाक्श्रीबीजेन पुटितत्वेनमुच्चरेत् ।
अलक्ष्मीं मलरूपां याः सर्व्वभूतेषु संस्थिताम् ।
क्षालयन्ति निजस्पर्शादापो नित्यं पुनन्तु माम् ॥

इति मन्त्राभ्याञ्चाभिषिच्य—

यन्मे केशेषु दौर्भाग्यं सीमन्ते यच्च मूर्द्धनि ।
ललाटे कर्णयोरक्ष्णोरापस्तद् घ्नन्तु वो नमः ॥
आयुरारोग्यमैश्वर्य्यमरिपक्षक्षयं सुखम् ।
सन्तोषः क्षान्तिरास्तिक्यं विद्या भवतु वो नमः ॥

इत्यभिषिञ्चेत् । इति बाह्यं मन्त्रस्नानम् ।

अभिषिञ्चेदथात्मानं वारुणैर्मूलविद्यया ।

इति मन्त्रतन्त्रप्रकाशे उक्तेः । तदुक्तम्—

विहितावश्यकः शौचमाचामं दन्तधावनम् ।
मुखप्रक्षालनादीनि कृत्वा स्नानं समाचरेत् ॥
कुम्भमुद्रा[मन्त्रा]ङ्कुशमुद्राभ्यां तीर्थमाकृष्य मण्डलात् ।
आवाह्याऽम्भसि संयोज्य सोमसूर्य्याग्निमण्डलम् ॥

सञ्चिन्त्य मन्त्री तन्मध्ये निमज्जेत् सुसमाहितः ।
मूलमन्त्रं समावर्त्त्य मनसोल्लिख्य चाकृतिम् ॥
उत्थायाऽऽचम्य तत्पश्चात् षडङ्गन्याससंयुतः ।
आत्मानं मूलमन्त्रेण मुद्रया कलशाख्यया ॥
समकृत्वोऽभिषिच्याऽथ मनुना मन्त्रितैर्जलैः । इति ।

वशिष्ठसंहितायामपि—

विन्यस्याङ्गे षडङ्गानि प्राणायामपुरःसरम् ।
श्रीसूर्य्यमण्डलात्तीर्थमाकृष्याऽङ्कुशमुद्रया ॥
वमित्यनेन चाप्लाव्य कवचेनावगुण्ठयेत् ।
संरक्ष्यास्त्रेण मूलेन मन्त्रयेद्रुद्र[द्रस]संख्यया ॥
निमज्ज्य तस्मिन् श्रीदेवं ध्यायेच्छक्त्या जपन्मनुम् ।
उन्मज्ज्य कुम्भमुद्राञ्च बद्ध्वा स्नायाद् द्विषट् ततः ॥
शालग्रामशिलातोयं तुलसीगन्धमिश्रितम् ।
कृत्वा शङ्खे भ्रामयंस्त्रिः प्रक्षिपेन्निजमूर्द्धनि ॥
शालग्रामशिलातोयमपीत्वा यस्तु मस्तके ।
प्रक्षेपणं प्रकुर्व्वीत ब्रह्महा स निगद्यते ॥
विष्णुपादोदकात् पूर्व्वं विप्रपादोदकं पिबेत् ।
विरुद्धमाचरन्मोहादात्महा स निगद्यते ॥
पृथिव्यां यानि तीर्थानि तानि तीर्थानि सागरे ।
ससागराणि तीर्थानि पादे विप्रस्य दक्षिणे ॥
ततः संक्षेपतो देवान् मनुष्यांस्तर्पयेत् पितॄन् ।
पीड़यित्वाम्बरं चोरू प्रक्षाल्याचम्य यत्नतः ॥
धारयेद्वाससी शुद्धे परिधानोत्तरीयके ।
अच्छिन्ने सुदृशे शुक्ले आचमेत् पीठसंस्थितः ॥
ऊर्द्ध्वपुण्ड्रं त्रिपुण्ड्रं वा कृत्वा सन्ध्यां समाचरेत् ॥ इति ।

अङ्कुश-कुम्भ-शङ्खमुद्रालक्षणानि यथा—

दक्षमुष्टिगृहीतस्य वाममुष्टेस्तु मध्यमाम् ।
प्रसार्य्य तर्ज्जन्याकुञ्चेत् सेयमङ्कुशमुद्रिका ॥
दक्षाङ्गुष्ठे पराङ्गुष्ठं क्षिप्त्वा हस्तद्वयेन तु ।
सावकाशामेकांमुष्टिं कुर्य्यात् कुम्भस्य मुद्रिका ॥

वामाङ्गुष्ठन्तु संगृह्य दक्षिणेन तु मुष्टिना ।
कृत्वोत्तानं तथा मुष्टिमङ्गुष्ठन्तु प्रसारयेत् ॥
वामाङ्गुल्यस्तथा श्लिष्टाः संयुक्ताः सुप्रसारिताः ।
दक्षिणाङ्गुष्ठसंस्पृष्टा मुद्रा शङ्खस्य चोदिता ॥

तत्र वैष्णवतिलके विशेषः—

ललाटे तु गदा कार्या मूर्द्ध्नि चापं शरन्तथा ।
नन्दकञ्चैव हृन्मध्ये शङ्खं चक्रं भुजद्वये ॥
शङ्खचक्राङ्कितो विप्रः श्मशाने म्रियते यदि ।
प्रयागे या गतिः प्रोक्ता सा गतिस्तस्य नारद ॥ इति ।

शैवैस्तूर्द्ध्वपुण्ड्रधारणानन्तरमेव भस्मना त्रिपुण्ड्रधारणमपि कार्य्यम् । यतो द्विजाना-मूर्द्ध्वपुण्ड्रस्यावश्यकत्वम् । तदुक्तं ब्रह्माण्डपुराणे—

ऊर्द्ध्वपुण्ड्रमृजुं सौम्यं ललाटे यस्य दृश्यते ।
स चाण्डालोऽपि शुद्धात्मा पूज्य एव न संशयः ॥
अशुचिश्चाप्यनाचारो मनसा पापमाचरन् ।
शुचिरेव भवेन्नित्यमूर्द्ध्वपुण्ड्राङ्कितो नरः ॥
मत्प्रियार्थं शुभार्थं वा रक्षार्थं चतुरानन ।
मद्भक्तो धारयेन्नित्यमूर्द्ध्वपुण्ड्रमतन्द्रितः ॥ इति ।

तत्र त्रिपुण्ड्रधारणविधानं यथा—

भस्माग्निहोत्रसम्भूतमानयेत्कोचितं बुधः ।
यद्वा धरामसंस्पृष्टं सद्योनानीय गोमयम् ॥
वामेन पात्रे संशोष्य[योज्य] अघोरेण विनिर्द्दहेत् ।
तत्पुरुषेण समुद्धृत्येशानेन विशोधयेत् ॥
इत्थन्तु संस्कृतं भस्म अग्निरित्यादिमन्त्रतः ।
विमृज्याङ्गानि संस्पृश्य पुनरादाय मन्त्रतः ॥
तद्रुद्राद्रि[स्मादब्रह्मे]ति यजुषा मन्त्रयेद् रुद्रसंख्यया ।
प्रणवाद्यैश्चतुर्थ्यन्तैर्नामभिश्शंकरैः ॥
पञ्चवर्णाक्षराद्यैश्च भालांसोदरहृत्सु च ।
त्रिपुण्ड्रधारणं कुर्य्यान्मूर्द्ध्नि पञ्चाक्षरेण च ॥
त्रिपुण्ड्रं धारयन्मन्त्री साक्षाच्छिव इवापरः ॥ इति ।

मन्त्रस्तु । "अग्निरिति भस्म वायुरिति भस्म जलमिति भस्म स्थलमिति भस्म व्योमेति

भस्म सर्व्वं ह वा इदं भस्म मन एतानि चक्षूंषि भस्मानि तस्माद्व्रतमेतत् पाशुपतं यद्भस्मनाङ्गानि संस्पृशेत् । तस्मात् ब्रह्म तदेतत् पाशुपतं पशुपाशविमोक्षाय" । यजुषा पञ्चाक्षरेणेत्यर्थः ।

प्रकारान्तरेण वा—

ललाटे ब्रह्मा[ह्म] विज्ञेयो[यं] हृदये हव्यवाहनः ।
नाभौ स्कन्दो गले पूषा रुद्रो दक्षिणबाहुके ॥
आदित्यो बाहुमध्ये च शशी च मणिबन्धके ।
वामदेवो वामबाहौ बाहुमध्ये प्रभञ्जनः ॥
मणिबन्धे च वसवः पृष्ठदेशे हरः स्मृतः ।
शम्भुः ककुदि संप्रोक्तः परमात्मा शिरः स्मृतः ॥ इति ।

वायवीयसंहितायाममन्त्रकमेव त्रिपुण्ड्रधारणमुक्तम् ।

पुनर्न्यस्तकरो मन्त्री त्रिपुण्ड्रं भस्मना लिखेत् । इति ।

भस्मग्रहणमपि तत्रैवोक्तम् ।

शिवाग्नेर्भस्म संग्राह्यमग्निहोत्रोद्भवन्तु वा ।
वैवाह्याग्न्युद्भवं वापि पक्वं शुचि सुगन्धि च ॥
कपिलायाः शकृच्छस्तं गृहीतं गगने पतत् ।
न क्लिन्नं नाति कठिनं न दुर्गन्धि न चोषितम् ॥
उपर्य्यधः परित्यज्य गृह्णीयात् पतितं यदि ।
पिण्डीकृत्य शिवाग्नौ तु तत् क्षिपेन्मूलमन्त्रतः ॥
अपक्वमतिपक्वञ्च सन्त्यज्य भसितं सितम् ।
आदाय वाससाऽऽलोड्य भस्माधारे विनिक्षिपेत् ॥
भस्मसंग्रहणं कुर्य्याद् देवेऽनुद्वासिते सति ।
उद्वासने कृते यस्माच्चण्डभस्म प्रजायते ॥ इति ।

ततः स्वशाखोक्तसन्ध्यां कृत्वा मन्त्रसन्ध्यां कुर्य्यात् । तद्यथा । प्राणायामत्रयं कृत्वा तीर्थजलं दक्षहस्ते गृहीत्वा मूलमन्त्रेण त्रिः संजप्य तेन मूलेन त्रिराचम्य पुनस्तीर्थजलं दक्षहस्तेन सव्यहस्ते निधाय मूलेन त्रिधाऽभिमन्त्र्य तद्गलितोदकबिन्दुभिः सप्तधा मूलेनात्मानं सम्मार्ज्य अवशिष्टं जलं दक्षहस्ते गृहीत्वा नासिकासमीपं नीत्वा इड़या देहान्तराकृष्य क्षालितैः पापसञ्चयैः कृष्णवर्णं तदुदकं दक्षनाड्या विरेचितं ध्यात्वा पुरःकल्पितवज्रशिलायामस्त्रमन्त्रेण प्रक्षिपेत् । इदमघमर्षणम् । पुनरञ्जलिना जलमादाय सूर्य्यमण्डलस्थाय देवायाऽर्घ्यं कल्पयामीति तत्तद्गायत्र्या मूलेन वा

देशिको विधिवत् स्नात्वा कृत्वा पौर्व्वाह्निकीः क्रियाः ।
यायादलङ्कृतो मौनी यागार्थं यागमण्डपम् ॥ ५

त्रिरर्घ्यं दत्त्वा सूर्य्यमण्डलस्थं देवं ध्यायन् मूलमन्त्रेणोपस्थाय तत्तन्त्रगायत्रीं मूलमन्त्रं वाऽष्टाविंशतिवारं जपेत् । ततो मूलमन्त्रमुच्चार्य्य देवं तर्पयामीति अष्टाविंशतिवारं तर्पयित्वा सूर्य्यमण्डले देवतां सञ्चिन्त्य सूर्य्यायार्घ्यं दत्त्वा संहारमुद्रया तीर्थं विसृज्य सूर्य्यादिकं नमस्कृत्य देवतास्तुतिं पठन् यागमण्डपं गच्छेदिति । तदुक्तं मन्त्रतन्त्रप्रकाशे—

कृत्वा सन्ध्यां जपन् स्तोत्रं यायाद्वै यागमन्दिरम् । इति ।

तथा—उक्तेनैव विधानेन कृत्वा स्नानन्तु तान्त्रिकम् ।
वैदिकीं तान्त्रिकीं सन्ध्यां कृत्वा तर्पणमेव च ॥
जपन् स्तोत्राणि नामानि यायाद्देवनिकेतनम् । इति ।

मौनीत्यनेनान्यजनसम्भाषणनिषेधः । संहारमुद्रालक्षणं यथा—

अधोमुखे वामहस्ते ऊर्द्ध्वास्यं दक्षहस्तकम् ।
क्षिप्त्वाऽङ्गुलीरङ्गुलिभिः संयोज्य परिवर्त्तयेत् ॥
प्रोक्ता संहारमुद्रेयमर्पणे तु प्रशस्यते । इति ।

तदुक्तं महाकपिलपञ्चरात्रे—

उपविश्य शुचौ देशे प्राणायामत्रयं क्रमात् ।
परतत्त्वेन कृत्वा वै देहे कुर्व्वीत मार्जनम् ॥
नासामाश्रित्य तोयेन ततस्तेनाऽघमर्षणम् ।
समस्तेन समुद्दिष्टं अर्घ्यं पापहरं शुभम् ॥
उपस्थानं ततः कुर्य्यात् पश्चात्तत्त्वेन मन्त्रवित् ।
स्मृत्वा ज्योतिर्मयं विष्णुं मण्डलस्थं महात्मकम् ॥
जपं पश्चात् प्रकुर्व्वीत मूलमन्त्रेण साधकः ।
गायत्र्या वाऽथ वैष्णव्या प्रणवाद्यन्तकाद्द्वयम् ॥
उपविश्य शुचौ देशे ततस्तर्पणमाचरेत् ।
विष्ण्वाद्या देवतास्तत्र पितॄंश्च मनुजानथ ॥
तर्पयेत्तान् प्रयत्नेन ततस्तीर्थं समापयेत् ।
मूलमन्त्रं जपन् गच्छेद् यावत् प्राप्नोति वै गृहम् ॥
प्राप्य हस्तौ च पादौ च प्रक्षाल्याचम्य यत्नतः ।
यागमण्डपमासाद्य विशेत् कृत्वा प्रदक्षिणम् ॥ इति ।

अन्यत्रापि—

पुनराचम्य विन्यस्य षड‌ङ्गमपि पूर्व्ववत् ।
वामहस्ते जलं गृह्य गलितोदकबिन्दुभिः ॥
सप्तधा प्रोक्षणं कृत्वा मूर्द्ध्नि मन्त्रं समुच्चरन् ।
अवशिष्टोदकं दक्षहस्ते संगृह्य बुद्धिमान् ॥
इड़याऽऽकृष्य देहान्तः चालितैः पापसञ्चयैः ।
कृष्णवर्णं तदुदकं दक्षनाड्या विरेचितम् ॥
दक्षहस्तेऽथ तन्मन्त्री पापरूपं विचिन्त्य च ।
पुरतो वज्रपाषाणे प्रक्षिपेदस्त्रमन्त्रतः ॥
दिनेशायोत्क्षिपेत् तिष्ठन् वारिणा चाऽञ्जलित्रयम् ।
अष्टोत्तरशतावृत्त्या गायत्रीं प्रजपेत् सुधीः ॥
रविमण्डलगं देवं प्रणिपत्य क्षमापयेत् ।
संहारमुद्रया तीर्थमुद्वास्याचम्य वाग्यतः ॥
एवं सन्ध्यां समाप्याथ न्यासकर्म्म समारभेत् ॥ इति ।

शैवागमे तु—ततः शिवात्मकैर्मन्त्रैः कृत्वा तीर्थं शिवात्मकम् ।
मार्जनं संहितामन्त्रैस्तत्तोयेन समाचरेत् ॥
वामपाणिपतत्तोययोजनं सव्यपाणिना ।
उत्तमाङ्गे क्रमान्मन्त्रैर्मार्जनं समुदाहृतम् ॥
नीत्वा तदुपनासाग्रं दक्षपाणिपुटे स्थितम् ।
बोधरूपं सितं तोयं वामयाकृष्य कुम्भयेत् ॥
तत्पापं कज्जलाभासं पिङ्गया रेच्य वर्त्मना[विष्टिना] ।
क्षिपेद् वज्रशिलायां यत्तद्भवेदघमर्षणम् ॥
स्वाहान्तशिवमन्त्रेण कुशपुष्पाक्षतान्वितम् ।
शिवायाऽर्घ्याञ्जलिं दत्त्वा गायत्रीं शक्तितो जपेत् ॥
समाचम्य विधानेन त्वाञ्जलेनाऽर्घ्यमुद्धरेत् ।
रक्तपुष्पादितोयेन मूलमन्त्रेण भानवे ॥ इति ।

वायवीयसंहितायामपि—

आचरेद् ब्रह्मयज्ञान्तं कृत्वा देवादितर्पणम् ।
मण्डलस्थं महादेवं ध्यात्वाऽभ्यर्च्य यथाविधि ।
दद्यादर्घ्यं ततस्तस्मै शिवायादित्यरूपिणे ॥ इति ।

आचम्य विधिना तत्र सामान्यार्घ्यं विधाय च ॥
द्वारमस्त्राम्बुभिः प्रोक्ष्य द्वारपूजां समाचरेत् । ६

शिवसंहितायान्तु—

व्योमव्यापीति यो मन्त्रः पञ्चब्रह्माणि यानि च ।
ये मन्त्राः शिवगायत्र्या रुद्रश्चेति यथाक्रमम् ॥
सर्व्वपापापहा प्रोक्ता विधेयं शिवसंहिता । इति ।
आमीमूमायतो व्योमव्यापिने च प्रकीर्त्तयेत् ।
प्रणवाद्यन्तरुद्धोऽयं व्योमव्यापी प्रकीर्त्तितः ॥ इति ।

अयं सामान्यविधिः । मन्त्रविशेषे आचमनादौ मन्त्रविशेषास्तत्तत्कल्पोक्ता अनुसन्धेयाः । इयञ्च सन्ध्या त्रिकालं कार्य्या । यदगस्त्यसंहितायाम्—

रामाख्यानं गुरुं ध्यात्वा रामसन्ध्यामथाचरेत् । सायं प्रातश्च मध्याह्ने । इति ।
शैवागमेऽपि—प्रातर्मध्याह्नसायाह्ने सन्ध्यां कुर्य्याच्च मन्त्रवित् । इति ॥ २-५ ॥

आचम्येति । तत्र यागमण्डपवाह्यदेशे । महाकपिलपञ्चरात्रे तथोक्तेः । विधिनेति स्मृत्युक्तविधिना वैष्णवादिविधिना च । यदाहुः—

प्राङ्मुखो वोदङ्मुखः सूपवीतो बद्ध्वा चूडां जानुमध्यस्थबाहुः ।
तोयं वीक्षन् सूपविष्टोऽथ मौनी स्यादप्रह्वस्त्वेकधीराचमिष्यन् ॥
अदुष्टरसगन्धाद्यैरकीटाफेणवुद्बुदैः ।
अनुष्णैरम्बुभिः शुद्धैराचामेदपि वीक्षितैः ॥
हृत्कण्ठास्यगताः पुनन्ति विबु[वि]धानापो द्विजातीन् क्रमात्
त्रिः पीता वृषल-स्त्रियावपि सकृत् कुण्डानुलोमादिकान् ।
आचम्य त्रिरपस्त्रिवेदपुरुषाः प्रीणन्ति निर्म्मार्ष्टि यत्
द्विः साथर्व्वं षडङ्गयज्ञपुरुषाः प्रीताः स्युरङ्गुष्ठतः ॥
प्रीणात्यर्कमनामिकानयनयोः स्पर्शात् तथाऽङ्गुष्ठयुक्
साङ्गुष्ठा त्वथ तर्ज्जनी सममिता घ्राणद्वये मारुतम् ।
अङ्गुष्ठेन कनिष्ठिका श्रवणयोराशाश्च नाभेर्वसून्
आत्मानन्तु हृदंसयोर्गिरमुखीन् मूर्ध्नः समस्ताङ्गुलैः ॥ इति ।

यद्वा वैष्णवाचमनं यथा—

केशवाद्यैस्त्रिभिः पीत्वा द्वाभ्यां प्रक्षालयेत् करौ ।
द्वाभ्यामोष्ठौ तु संमृज्येत् द्वाभ्यां मृज्यान्मुखन्तथा ॥

ऊर्द्धोडुम्बरके विघ्नं महालक्ष्मीं सरस्वतीम् ।
ततो दक्षिणशाखायां विघ्नं क्षेत्रेशमन्यतः ॥ ७

एकेन हस्तं प्रक्षाल्य पादावपि तथैकतः ।
संप्रोक्ष्यैकेन मूर्द्धानं ततः सङ्कर्षणादिभिः ॥
आस्यनासाक्षिकर्णांश्च नाभ्युरः कं भुजौ स्पृशेत् ।
एवमाचमनं कृत्वा साक्षान्नारायणो भवेत् ॥
केशवाद्याः पुरा प्रोक्ता वक्ष्ये सङ्कर्षणादिकान् ।
सङ्कर्षणो वासुदेवः प्रद्युम्नश्चानिरुद्धकः ॥
पुरुषोत्तमाधोक्षजनृसिंहाश्च तथाऽच्युतः ।
जनार्दनोपेन्द्रहरिविष्णवो द्वादशैव ते ॥ इति ।

आत्मसाचमनं पिङ्गलामते—

आचम्य चात्मतत्त्वाद्यैः प्रणवाद्यैः स्वधान्तिमैः ।
मन्त्रैस्त्रेधा ततो वक्त्रं नासाक्षिश्रोत्रनाभिहृत् ॥
मस्तकांसान् स्पृशेदुक्तं हृदा श्रोत्राभिवन्दनम् ।
आत्मविद्याशिवास्तत्त्वाः प्रणवो वाग्भवं मतम् ॥ इति ।

शैवागमे तु—संवीक्ष्य त्रिः पिबेदम्बु ब्रह्मतीर्थेन शम्बरैः ।
स्वधान्तैरात्मतत्त्वाद्यैरात्मविद्याशिवात्मकम् ।
क्रमात् तत्त्वत्रयं विद्यात् क्रां क्रीं क्रूं शम्बराः क्रमात् ॥ इति ।

सामान्यार्घ्यं विधाय चेति बहिरेव । सामान्यार्घ्य उक्तो मन्त्रमुक्तावल्याम्—

पात्रमस्त्रेण संशोध्य हृन्मन्त्रेणाभिपूरयेत् ।
तीर्थमावाह्य गन्धादीन् निःक्षिपेत् प्रणवेन तु ।
धेनुमुद्रां दर्शयेच्च सामान्यार्घ उदाहृतः ॥ इति ।

अत्र प्रणवशब्देन यथायथं पञ्चप्रणवानामपि ग्रहणं ज्ञेयम् । तत्र प्रकारः । साधारं पात्रं द्वाराभिमुखं संस्थाप्य ॐ क्षः द्वारार्घ्यं साधयामीति कृत्वा । पात्रमस्त्रेति श्लोकोक्तक्रमोऽनुसन्धेयः । द्वारमिति । अस्त्रमन्त्रमुच्चार्य सामान्यार्घ्यजलेन द्वारं प्रोक्षयेत् । सामान्यास्त्रा[र्घ्या]द्यग्रे वक्ष्यति । अत्र सर्वत्राग्रेऽपि अस्त्रादिप्रस्तुतदेयमन्त्रान्ते अस्त्राय फट् इति सामान्यास्त्रं योजयेत् । एवं सर्वाङ्गमन्त्रेषु । केचनास्त्रादिषु फट्काराद्याः केवलजातीरेवाहुः ॥ ६ ॥

द्वारपूजामेवाह ऊर्द्धेति । द्वारशाखोपरितनतिर्य्यक्काष्ठमूर्द्धोडुम्बरकं देहल्या-

तयोः पार्श्वगते गङ्गायमुने पुष्पवारिभिः ।
देहल्यामर्चयेदस्त्रं प्रतिद्वारमिति क्रमात् ॥ ८

मुदुम्बरशाखाभिधेया प्रवर्त्तते। साऽप्यूर्द्ध्वस्थदेहली चेति सामान्यात्तत्र लक्षणयो-डुम्बरशब्दप्रयोगः। तत्र मध्ये महालक्ष्मीमिति द्वारश्रियम्। पुष्पवारिभिः अर्घ्यजलपुष्पैः प्रपूजयेदिति सम्बन्धः। तदुक्तं—"ऊर्द्ध्वे द्वारश्रियं चेष्ट्वा" इति। अन्यत्रापि—द्वारोपरि नमो द्वारश्रियै तद्दक्षवामयोः। विघ्नं सरस्वतीञ्च। इति। तत ऊर्द्ध्वस्थकोणद्वये दक्षिणादि विघ्नं सरस्वतीं च पूजयेत्। दक्षिणशाखायामिति दक्षिणशाखाधः। अत्र केचन दुर्गापूजामाहुः। अन्यत इति वामशाखाधः। क्षेत्रेशमिति सम्बन्धः। तदुक्तं—

कोणेषु विघ्नं दुर्गाञ्च वाणीं क्षेत्रेशमर्चयेत्। इति।

तयोरिति विघ्नक्षेत्रेशयोः। पार्श्वगते गङ्गायमुने इत्यनेन पूर्ववत् द्वारादिपूजा सूचिता। सैव क्रमादित्यनेनाग्रे उक्ता। वारि सामान्यार्घ्यजलम्। तारसबिन्दुस्वनामाद्यक्षरा-दिङेऽन्त-स्वनामनमोऽन्विता एतेषां मन्त्राः। ॐ द्वां द्वारश्रियै नमः इत्यादिप्रयोगः। तदुक्तं डामरे—ॐकारबिन्दुमध्यस्थं नामधेयाद्यमक्षरम्।

देवतानां स्वबीजं तत् पूजायामृद्धिसिद्धिदम् ॥ इति।

ग्रन्थकृदपि वक्ष्यति "स्वनामाद्यक्षरादिकाः" इति। एतच्च यत्र बीजं नोक्तं तद्विषयं ज्ञेयम्। देहल्यामिति ॐ ह्रः अस्त्राय फट् नमः इत्यस्त्रपूजा। पुष्प-वारिभिरित्येव। तदुक्तं—

हकाररेफौ च विसर्गवन्तावस्त्राय फट्कारवचस्तदन्ते।
उक्त्वान्तरे सर्षपमक्षतान् वा पुष्पाणि मुक्त्वेदय चात्र विद्वान् ॥ इति।

अन्ये तु वास्तुपुरुषपूजामत्रेच्छन्ति। तदुक्तं—

पूज्यो वास्तुपुमांस्तत्र तत्र द्वाः पीठमध्यतः। इति।

एषां ध्यानं तत्तत्प्रकरणे ज्ञेयम्। अतएवात्र महालक्ष्मीपदप्रयोगः। प्रतिद्वार-मित्यनेनैतदुक्तम्भवति। यदाहुः—

द्वारस्य शोभनस्याथ शाखयोर्दक्षवामयोः।
धात्रे विधात्रे गङ्गायै यमुनायै च पूर्वतः ॥
ॐ भद्राय सुभद्राय गोदां कृष्णाञ्च दक्षिणे।
चण्डाय च प्रचण्डाय रेवां तापीञ्च पश्चिमे ॥
ॐ शङ्खपद्मनिधये वाणीं वेणीं तथोत्तरे ॥ इति।

अनन्तरं देशिकेन्द्रो दिव्यदृष्ट्यवलोकनात् ।
दिव्यानुत्सारयेद् विघ्नानस्त्राद्भिश्चान्तरीक्षगान् ॥ ८

सोमशम्भुरपि—स्वनामभिश्चतुर्थ्यन्तैः स्रवन्तीनां द्वयं द्वयम् । इति ।

अन्यत्र तु—भद्रं सुभद्रं गङ्गाञ्च यमुनां द्वारशाखयोः ।
चतुर्थ्यन्तं नमोऽन्तञ्च प्राग्द्वारे सम्प्रपूजयेत् ॥
बलप्रबलचिच्छक्तिमायाशक्तिस्तथैव च ।
चतुर्थ्यन्तं नमोऽन्तञ्च दक्षिणद्वारि पूजयेत् ॥
चण्डं प्रचण्डं गौरीञ्च श्रियञ्च द्वारशाखयोः ।
चतुर्थ्यन्तं नमोऽन्तञ्च पश्चिमे सम्प्रपूजयेत् ॥
जयञ्च विजयञ्चैव शङ्खपद्मनिधी तथा ।
चतुर्थ्यन्तं नमोऽन्तञ्च उत्तरे सम्प्रपूजयेत् ॥ इति ।

केचन वक्ष्यमाणद्वारपालपूजामपि नित्यमाहुः । एतत्सर्वं नित्यपूजायामपि समानं ज्ञेयम् । यदाहुः—

विधेयमेतत् सर्वत्र स्थापितेषु विशेषतः । इति ।

दीक्षायान्तु विशेषस्तन्त्रान्तरोक्तः ।

वैष्णवादिप्रभेदेन द्वारपालान् समर्चयेत् ।
प्रतिद्वारं पार्श्वयोस्तु द्वौ द्वावष्टाविति क्रमात् ॥
नन्दः सुनन्दश्चण्डाख्यः प्रचण्डो बलनामकः ।
प्रबलो भद्रनामा च सुभद्रो वैष्णवा मताः ॥
अथ नन्दिमहाकालौ गणेशवृषभौ पुनः ।
ततो भृङ्गिरिटिः स्कन्दः पार्वतीशश्च सप्तमः ॥
चण्डेश्वरोऽष्टमः शैवा द्वारपालाः क्रमादमी ।
वक्रतुण्डैकदंष्ट्रौ च महोदरगजाननौ ॥
लम्बोदराख्यविकटौ विघ्नराजश्च सप्तमः ।
धूम्रराजोऽष्टमो ज्ञेयो गाणपत्या इति क्रमात् ॥
ब्राह्म्याद्या मातरः प्रोक्ताः शाक्तेया द्वारपालकाः ॥ इति ।

अन्ये तु गोपालरामचन्द्रद्वारपालानन्यानाहुः—

चण्डप्रचण्डौ प्राग् धातृविधातारौ च दक्षिणे ।
जयश्च विजयः पश्चाद् बलः प्रबल उत्तरे ॥ इति ॥ ७ ॥ ८ ॥

अयष्चानन्तरमित्यनेन सूचितः । देशिकेन्द्र इत्यनेन सदाशिवमात्मानं

पार्ष्णिघातैस्त्रिभिर्भौमानिति विघ्नान्निवारयेत् ॥ १०
किञ्चित् स्पृशन् वामशाखां देहलीं लङ्घयेद् गुरुः ।
अङ्गं सङ्कोचयन्नन्तः प्रविशेद्दक्षिणाङ्‌घ्रिणा ॥ ११
नैर्ऋत्यां दिशि वास्त्वीशान् ब्रह्माणञ्च समर्चयेत् ।
पञ्चगव्यार्घ्यतोयाभ्यां प्रोक्षयेद् यागमण्डपम् ॥ १२

विचिन्त्येत्युक्तम् । सदाशिवरूपस्वदृष्ट्यवलोकनमेव दिव्यदृष्ट्यवलोकनम् । अद्भिरिति सामान्यार्घ्यजलैः ॥ ९ ॥

पार्ष्णिघातैरिति । तत्रायं मन्त्रः—

अपसर्पन्तु ते भूता ये भूता भूमिसंस्थिताः ।
ये भूता विघ्नकर्त्तारस्ते नश्यन्तु शिवाज्ञया ॥
अपक्रमन्तु भूतानि पिशाचाः सर्व्वतो दिशम् ।
सर्व्वेषामविरोधेन ब्रह्मकर्म्म समारभे ॥ इति ।

वशिष्ठसंहितायामपसर्पन्त्वित्यादि पठित्वोक्तम् ।

पार्ष्णिघातत्रयं कृत्वा मन्त्रेणानेन मन्त्रवित् ।
भूतसङ्घान् समुत्सार्य्य संविशेदासने बुधः ॥ इति ।

सोमशम्भौ तु—दद्यात् पार्ष्णिस्त्रिभिर्घातैर्भूमिष्ठांस्त्रिविधानपि । इति ।

इत्येवं प्रकारेण विघ्नान् त्रिविधानपीति ॥ १० ॥

अङ्गमिति वामाङ्गम् । सङ्कोचयन्निति निःसरद्विघ्नावकाशदानाय ।

तदुक्तं—उत्सारितानां विघ्नानां दद्यद्वर्त्म तु वामतः । इति ।

अन्यत्रापि—निर्गच्छतां विघ्नकृतामथैषां वामाङ्गसङ्कोचनचेष्टितेन ।
प्रदाय मार्गम् । इति ।

तथान्यत्रापि—वामतः निःसार्य्य विघ्नसङ्घञ्च । इति ।

अन्तः स्पृशन्नित्यादित्रयं दृष्टार्थं देहल्यामपि देवस्य पूजितत्वात् । वास्त्वीशमिति तत्तत्क्षेत्रस्य क्षेत्रपालम् । ते च मया क्षेत्रपालमन्त्रे वक्ष्यन्ते । दिव्यदृष्ट्येत्यादिब्रह्मार्चनान्तं नित्यपूजायामपि समानम् । पञ्चगव्येति । पञ्चगव्यप्रकारमेकविंशे वक्ष्यति । अर्घ्यतोयं सामान्यार्घ्यजलम् । प्रोक्षयेदिति देयमन्त्रेण । तदुक्तम्—नारायणीये—गव्येन प्रोक्षयेद्दीक्षाख्यानं मन्त्रेण शोधितम् । इति ॥ ११ ॥ १२ ॥

चतुष्पथान्तं तच्छुद्धिं विदध्याद् वीक्षणादिना।
वीक्षणं मूलमन्त्रेण शरेण प्रोक्षणं मतम्॥ १३
तेनैव ताडनं दर्भैर्वर्मणाऽभ्युक्षणं मतम्।
चन्दनागुरुकर्पूरैर्धूपयेदन्तरं सुधीः॥ १४
विकिरान् विकिरेत् तत्र सप्तजप्तांश्छराणुना।
लाजाचन्दनसिद्धार्थभस्मदूर्वाङ्कुराक्षताः॥ १५
विकिरा इति सन्दिष्टाः सर्व्वविघ्नौघनाशनाः।
अस्त्रजप्तेन दर्भाणां मुष्टिना मार्जयेच्च तान्॥ १६
ईशस्य दिशि वर्द्धन्या आसनाय प्रकल्पयेत्।
पुण्याहं वाचयित्वा तु ब्राह्मणान् परितोष्य च॥ १७

चतुष्पथान्तमिति पूर्व्वेण सम्बध्यते। तत्र मण्डपाद्बहिः आतोरणस्तम्भ-हस्तमात्रा व्यवहारभूश्चतुष्पथशब्दवाच्या। वीक्षणादिभिश्चतुर्भिस्तच्छुद्धिं मण्डपशुद्धिं कुर्य्यात्। अत्रापि चतुष्पथान्तमित्यन्वेति। वीक्षणादीनेवाह वीक्षणमिति। मूल-मन्त्रेणेति देयमन्त्रेण। शरेणेत्यस्त्रमन्त्रेण। वर्म्मणेति कवचमन्त्रेण। प्रोक्षणाभ्युक्षण-स्वरूपमग्रे वक्तव्यम्। ते च सामान्यार्घ्यजलेनैव। अन्तरमिति मण्डपमध्यम्। सुधीरित्यग्रिमेण सम्बध्यते। अनेन च सोमशम्भूक्तो विशेषः सूचितः।

तत्रेति मण्डपमध्ये। शराणुनेत्यस्त्रमन्त्रेण। अणुशब्दो मन्त्रपर्य्याय आगमशास्त्रे। सिद्धार्था गौरसर्षपाः। भस्म गोमयभस्म। सर्व्वविघ्नौघनाशना इति ध्यानम्।

अस्त्रजप्तेनेति सप्तेत्यनुषज्यते। मार्जयेच्चेति चकारेण विकिरानित्यनुषज्यते। तानित्युत्तरेण सम्बध्यते। सोमशम्भौ तु विशेषः—

विकिरान् शुद्धलाजान् वा सप्तशस्त्राभिमन्त्रितान्।
अस्त्राम्बुप्रोक्षितानेतान् कवचेनावगुण्ठितान्॥
नाना प्रहरणाकारान् विघ्नौघविनिवारकान्।
दर्भाणां तालमानेन कृतान् षट्त्रिंशता दलैः।
सप्तजप्तान् शिवास्त्रेण मुष्टिं तेन तु मार्जयेत् [बोधासिमुक्तमम्]॥

इति। विकिरणमार्जने देयमन्त्रेण॥ १३॥ १६॥

ईशस्येति। सनालं पात्रं वर्द्धनी तस्या आसनाय। ईशस्य दिशीति ऐशान्याम्। तान् विकिरान् प्रकल्पयेत् स्थापयेदिति सम्बन्धः। पुण्याहमिति। पुण्याह-

उक्तेषु मण्डलेष्वेकं वेदिकायां समालिखेत् ।
विशेन्मृद्वासने मन्त्री प्राङ्मुखो वाप्युदङ्मुखः ॥ १८
बद्धपद्मासनो मौनी समाहितजितेन्द्रियः ।
स्थापयेद्दक्षिणे भागे पूजाद्रव्याणि देशिकः ॥ १९

वाचनं तृतीयपटलोक्तम् । एकमिति मण्डलम् । एतावद्दीक्षायामेव । विशेदित्युपविशेत् । मृद्वासन इति अनुद्वेगाय इति दृष्टार्थम् । उद्वेगे सति तत्रैव मनो याति नतु जपपूजादौ । मन्त्रीत्यनेनैतदुक्तम् । अनन्तासनाय नमः । विमलासनाय नमः । पद्मासनाय नमः इति जप्तान् कुशानासने दत्त्वा आसनं सम्पूज्य । आसनमन्त्रस्य मेरुपृष्ठ ऋषिः सुतलं छन्दः कूर्म्मो देवता आसनोपवेशने विनियोगः ।

ॐ पृथ्वि त्वया धृता लोका देवि त्वं विष्णुना धृता ।
त्वञ्च धारय मां नित्यं[देवि] पवित्रं कुरु चासनम् ॥

इति आसनमन्त्रेणोपविशेदिति । तदुक्तम्—

तदासनस्यर्षि मुशन्ति कूर्म्मं छन्दस्तथा स्यात् सुतलं सुधीशः ।
प्रोक्ता तु पृथ्वी किल देवताऽस्य जपादिकर्म्मण्युपयोग उक्तः ॥ इति ।

तत्रासनानि तन्त्रान्तरोक्तानि—

कौशेयं वाऽथ चैलं वा चार्म्मं तौलमयापि वा ।
वेत्रजं तालपत्रं वा काम्बलं दार्भमासनम् ॥
वंशाश्म-दारु-धरणी-तृण-पल्लवनिर्मितम् ।
वर्जयेदासनं मन्त्री दारिद्र्य-व्याधि-दुःखदम् ॥
धर्म्मार्थकाममोक्षाप्त्यैश्चैलाजिनकुशोत्तरे ॥ इति ।

दार्व्वासनेऽन्यत्र विशेष उक्तः—

यतीनामासनं श्लक्ष्णं कूर्म्माकारन्तु कारयेत् ।
अन्येषान्तु चतुष्पादं चतुरस्रन्तु कारयेत् ॥
गोशलक्ष्म्रयं भिन्नं तथा पालाशपिप्पलम् ।
लोहविद्धं सदैवार्कं वर्जयेदासनं बुधः ॥
दानमाचमनं होमं भोजनं देवतार्चनम् ।
प्रौढ़पादो न कुर्व्वीत स्वाध्यायञ्चैव तर्पणम् ॥
आसनारूढ़पादस्तु जानुनोर्वाऽथ जङ्घयोः ।
कृतावसक्थिको यस्तु प्रौढ़पादः स उच्यते ॥ इति ॥ १७ ॥ १८ ॥

बद्धपद्मासन इति । पद्मासनमन्त्ये वक्ष्यति । "अङ्गुष्ठौ च निबध्नीया-

सुवासिताम्बुसम्पूर्णं सव्ये कुम्भं सुशोभनम् ।
प्रक्षालनाय करयोः पश्चात् पात्रं निवेशयेत् ॥ २०

घृतप्रज्ज्वालितान् दीपान् स्थापयेत् परितः शुभान् ।
दर्पणं चामरं छत्रं तालवृन्तं मनोहरम् ॥ २१

मङ्गलाङ्कुरपात्राणि स्थापयेद्दिक्षु देशिकः ।
कृताञ्जलिपुटो भूत्वा वामदक्षिणपार्श्वयोः ॥ २२

नत्वा गुरून् गणेशानं भूतशुद्धिं समाचरेत् ।
करशुद्धिं समासाद्य पश्चात्तालत्रयं ततः ॥ २३

हस्ताभ्याम्" इत्ययं भागो योग एवोपयुक्तः सोऽत्र नास्ति। तन्त्रान्तरे पद्मासन-लक्षणस्य तथैवोक्तत्वात् ।

सव्यं पादमुपादाय दक्षिणोपरि विन्यसेत् ।
तथैव दक्षिणं सव्यस्योपरिष्टान्निधापयेत् ॥
विष्टभ्य कट्योः पार्ष्णी तु नासाग्रन्यस्तलोचनः ।
पद्मासनं भवेदेतत् सर्व्वेषामपि पूजितम् ॥

पद्मासन इत्युपलक्षणम् । यदाहुः—

पद्म-स्वस्तिक-वीरादिष्वेकासनसमाश्रितः ।
जपार्चनादिकं कुर्य्यादन्यथा निष्फलं भवेत् ॥ इति ।

मौनमित्यनेन रागप्राप्तसम्भाषणनिषेधः । तदुक्तम्—

सभ्यैरपि न भाषेत जपहोमार्चनादिषु । इति ।

समाहितः सावधानश्चासौ जितेन्द्रियश्चेति विशेषणसमासः । पूजाद्रव्याणि पुष्पादीनि । देशिक इत्युत्तरेण सम्बध्यते । अनेनार्घ्यपाद्याचमनमधुपर्काचमन-पात्राण्यपि सव्ये स्थापयेदित्युक्तम् ॥ १८ ॥

सुवासितमिति कर्पूरादिना । मनोहरमिति दर्पणादीनां चतुर्णामपि विशेषणम् । दर्पणं स्थापयेदित्यादिरन्वयः । विशेदित्यादि । एतदन्तं नित्य-पूजायामपि समानम् । मङ्गलानि मङ्गलरूपाणि यानि अङ्कुरपात्राणि उक्तरीत्या उप्तबीजानि तानि दिक्षु स्थापयेत् । देशिक इत्यनेनैतदुक्तं भवति । उक्तक्रमेण पूर्व्वादिदिशि एवं त्रिरावृत्त्येति । तेषामिदमेव प्रतिपत्तिकर्म्म इदं दीक्षायामेव । कृताञ्जलिपुटो भूत्वा वामदक्षिणपार्श्वयोः गुरूं गणेशानं नत्वेति

अस्त्रमन्त्रेण दिग्बन्धमपि देशिकः ।

तेन सञ्जनितं तेजो रक्षां कुर्य्यात् समन्ततः ॥ २४

सम्बन्धः । तत्र प्रयोगः । ॐ गं गुरुभ्यो नमः । ॐ गं गणपतये नमः ।
तदुक्तमाचार्य्यैः—

गुर्व्वाद्यास्तारादिका याग[वेऽङ्क]मन्त्रा लोकेशान्तास्ते चतुर्थीनमोऽन्ताः ।

पूजायां स्युर्वह्निकार्य्ये द्विठान्ताः । इति ।

अत्र वह्निकार्य्ये द्विठान्ता इत्युक्तेः वक्ष्यमाणाग्निजिह्वादीनामपि संग्रहः । तदनन्तरं लोकेशमन्त्रैर्होमविधानात् । गुरूनिति बहुत्वया गुरुपरमगुरुपरापरगुरुपरमेष्ठि-गुरवो गृह्यन्ते । यदाहुः—

तत आदित आरभ्य नमेद् गुरुपरम्पराम् । इति ।

तत इमां ऋचं पठेत् । "ॐनमो महद्भ्यो नमोऽर्भकेभ्यो नमो युवभ्यो नम आशिनेभ्यः । यजाम देवान् यदि शक्नुवाम मा ज्यायसः शं समावृक्षि[चक्ष] देवाः" इति ।

करशुद्धिमिति । अत्र करशुद्ध्यादिषु त्रिषु अस्त्रमन्त्रेणेति सम्बध्यते । तत्र करशुद्धिर्नामाऽङ्गुष्ठादिष्वङ्गुलिषु उभयकरान्तः उभयकरयाग्रयोरुभयकरपार्श्वद्वये अस्त्रमन्त्रस्य व्यापकत्वेन न्यासः । तदुक्तम्—

व्याप्यव्यापकयोर्हस्तयोरस्त्रमन्त्रयोर्बाह्ये पार्श्वे । इति ॥ २०-२३ ॥

दिग्बन्धमिति । नाराचमुष्ट्युद्धृततर्ज्जन्या दशदिशि अस्त्रमन्त्रन्यासः ।

तदुक्तं प्रयोगसारे—आच्छाद्य दिक्षु तर्ज्जन्या ज्येष्ठाग्रस्खलिताग्रया । इति ।

अन्यत्रापि—अङ्गुष्ठमग्रं यदि मध्यमाग्रं स्पृशेत् स्युरन्याङ्गुलयस्तत्लग्नाः ।

तदा भवेत् भूतनिषूदनस्य नाराचनाम्नोऽस्त्रवरस्य मुद्रा ॥ इति ।

अन्यत्र विशेषः—प्रणवहृदोरवसाने सचतुर्थि सुदर्शनं तथाऽस्त्रपदम् ।

उक्त्वा फडन्तमनुना कल्पयेच्च दशहरितः ॥ इति ।

देशिक इत्यनेन सुदर्शनमन्त्रेण वक्ष्यमाणाग्निप्राकारमन्त्रेणापि अग्निप्राकारं कुर्य्यादिति सूचितम् । अग्निप्राकारमुद्रोक्ता प्रयोगसारे—

त्रिशूलाग्रौ करौ कृत्वा व्यत्यस्तावभितो नयेत् ।

अस्त्रमुद्रेयमाख्याता वह्निप्रकारलक्षणा ।

परद्रोहोपशमनो नागाशनिभयापहा ॥ इति ।

तदुक्तं—ततोऽस्त्रमन्त्रेण विशोध्य पाणित्रितालदिग्बन्धहुताशशालाम् । इति ।
एषां फलमाह तेनेति ॥ २४ ॥

सुषुम्णावर्त्मनात्मानं परमात्मनि योजयेत् ।
योगयुक्तेन विधिना चिन्मन्त्रेण समाहितः ॥ २५

कारणे सर्व्वभूतानां तत्त्वान्यपि च चिन्तयेत् ।
बीजभावेन लीनानि व्युत्क्रमात् परमात्मनि ॥ २६

सुषुम्णेति । समाहितः सुषुम्णावर्त्मना कुण्डलिन्या आत्मानं योगयुक्तेन विधिना चिन्मन्त्रेण परमात्मनि योजयेदिति सम्बन्धः । तत्रात्मानं जीवात्मानं हृदयकमलस्थितमित्यर्थः । यदाहुः—

हृदम्बुजे ब्रह्मकन्दसम्भूते ज्ञाननालके ।
आराग्रमात्रो जीवस्तु चिन्तनीयो मनीषिभिः ॥ इति ।

योगयुक्तेन विधिना इत्यस्यायमर्थः । गुरूपदिष्टमार्गेण हुँकारेण कुण्डलिनीमुत्थाप्य तां हृदयकमलगतां विभाव्य ततो जीवं मुखे गृहीत्वा सहस्रारगतां विभावयेत् । अत एव समाहित इत्युक्तिः । चिन्मन्त्रेण वक्ष्यमाणात्ममन्त्रेण ।

यदाहुः—नेतव्यो हंसमन्त्रेण द्वादशान्ते सितः परः । इति ।

अन्यत्रापि—जीवं स्वाङ्के स्वनाड्या स्वनिलयत उदनीय तं हंसेन । इति ।

अन्यत्रापि—संयोज्य जीवमथ दुर्गममध्यनाडीमार्गेण पुष्करनिविष्टशिवे सुसूक्ष्मे ।
हंसेन । इति ।

परमात्मनि सहस्रारकर्णिकागते इत्यर्थः । २५ ॥

कारण इति । सर्व्वभूतानां कारणे परमात्मनि बीजभावेन व्युत्क्रमात् लीनानि तत्त्वानि पृथिव्यादीनि चिन्तयेदित्यन्वयः । तत्र सृष्ट्यपेक्षया व्युत्क्रमः । सर्व्वत्र कार्य्यस्य कारणे लयो दृष्टः । अत एव प्रथमपटले सृष्ट्युक्तिः । विना सृष्टिं कार्य्यकारणाज्ञानात् । अतएव सर्व्वभूतानां कारण इति विशेषणोक्तिः । अपिशब्दाद्वर्णानपि ।

यदुक्तम्—सङ्कल्पैरवं ततो न्यासस्थानाद् वर्णांश्च संहरेत् ।

तत्क्रमश्च तन्त्रे —

प्रतिलोमेन चलयो लकारेऽस्य हकारके ।
हकारस्य सकारेऽथ सकारस्य षकारके ॥
क्रमेणाऽकारपर्य्यन्तं लयमुत्पाद्य यत्नतः ।
अकारं ब्रह्मरन्ध्रे च सहस्रारे नियोजयेत् ॥ इति ।

चकारः पूर्व्वसमुच्चये । २६ ॥

ततः संशोषयेद् देहं वायुबीजेन वायुना ।
वह्निबीजेन तेनैव संहरेत् सकलां तनुम् ॥ २७
विश्लेषयेत् तदा दोषानमृतेनामृताम्भसा ।
आप्लाव्याप्लावयेद् देहमापादतलमस्तकम् ॥ २८

तत इति । वायुबीजेन यकारेण । वायुना तदुत्थेनेत्यर्थः । अनेन पूरक उक्तः । वह्निबीजेन रेफेण । तेनैवेत्यग्निबीजोत्थाग्निना सकलां स्वकलुषरूपपापपुरुषसहितां तनुं निर्दहेत् । पापपुरुषध्यानं यथा—

ब्रह्महत्याशिरस्कञ्च स्वर्णस्तेयभुजद्वयम् ।
सुरापानहृदा युक्तं गुरुतल्पकटिद्वयम् ॥
तत्संयोगिपदद्वन्द्वमङ्गप्रत्यङ्गपातकम् ।
उपपातकरोमाणं रक्तश्मश्रुविलोचनम् ॥
खड्गचर्मधरं पापमङ्गुष्ठपरिमाणकम् ।
अधोमुखं कृष्णवर्णं दक्षकुक्षौ विचिन्तयेत् ॥ इति ।

अनेन कुम्भक उक्तः । तदा दाहे जाते दोषान् दोषस्वरूपपापपुरुषभस्म विश्लेषयेदित्यनेन रेचक उक्तः । तत्र भस्मविश्लेषोऽपि वायुबीजेनेति ज्ञेयम् । यदाहुराचार्याः—पूर्व्वविधिना मुञ्चेत् । इति ।
नागभट्टोऽपि—सास्यादिनाथमरुताऽपनयन्नशेषं तद्भस्मराशिम् । इति ।
गणेश्वरविमर्शिन्यामपि—तद्भस्मकूटमखिलं वायुबीजोत्थवायुना । विकीर्य्य । इति ।
अन्यत्रापि—तदुद्यद्वसुवपुरनलप्लुष्टदेहोऽनिलेन तद्भस्मोत्क्षिप्य । इति ।

अत्रस्थानत्रये षोडशचतुःषष्टिद्वात्रिंशत्संख्याक्रमेणेति केचित् । अन्ये द्वादशपञ्चाशत् पञ्चविंशतिसंख्येत्यूचुः । तदुक्तं संहितायाम्—

मरुदग्निसुधाबीजैः पञ्चाशन्मात्रमात्रकम् । इति ।

आचार्य्याश्च—अथवा शोषणदहनप्लावनभेदेन शोधिते देहे ।
पञ्चाशद्भिर्मात्राभेदैर्विधिवत् समानये[यमे]त् प्राणान् ॥
पञ्चाशदात्मकोऽपि च कलाप्रभेदेन तार उद्दिष्टः ।
तावन्मात्रायमनात् कलाश्च विधृता भवन्ति तत्त्वविदा ॥ इति ।

केचित्तु स्थानत्रयेऽपि प्रत्येकं त्रिविधं प्राणायाममपीच्छन्ति । अमृतेनामृतबीजेन वं इत्यनेन । अमृताम्भसा तदुत्थेनामृतेन आपादतलमस्तकं देहमाप्लाव्याप्लावयेदिति सम्बन्धः ॥ २७ ॥ २८ ॥

आत्मलीनानि तत्त्वानि स्वस्थानं प्रापयेत्तदा।
आत्मानं हृदयाम्भोजमानयेत् परमात्मनः॥ २९

स्वस्थानमिति सृष्टिक्रमेण प्रथमपटलोक्तरीत्या। तदेत्यनेन अकारादिक्षान्तान् वर्णान् अपि सृष्टिक्रमेण स्वस्थानं प्रापयेदित्युक्तम्। तदुक्तं—

अमुतः सकलार्णमयीं लपरजपान्निपात्य रचयेच्च तया।

सकलं वपुरमृतीवव्रष्टिमिति। इत्यारचय्य वपुरर्णशतार्द्धकेनेति।

परमात्मनः सकाशात् हंसदेवस्य मनुना आत्मानं हृदयाम्भोजमानयेदिति सम्बन्धः। हंसस्य जीवस्य देवः परमात्मा उपास्यत्वात्। तेन मन्त्रेण सोऽहम् इत्यनेन। यद्वा परमात्मनः मनुना इति सम्बध्यते इति पूर्वं परमात्मनि योजयेदित्युक्तम् तत इत्यर्थाल्लभ्यते। हंसदेवस्य इत्यग्रिमेण सह सम्बध्यते। तदुक्तं वशिष्ठसंहितायाम्—

सोहंमन्त्रेण तामाद्यां[मखीं] नादान्ते सिद्धभाविताम्।
ध्यात्वैवं ब्रह्मरन्ध्राच्च हृदि जीवकलां न्यसेत्॥ इति।

गणेश्वरविमर्शिन्यामपि—सोहंवियाऽऽत्मचैतन्यं समानीय चिदम्बरात्। इति।

तत्र गुरूपदेशतः प्रकारो लिख्यते। श्रीदेवपूजाद्यधिकारसिद्धये भूतशुद्ध्यादिकं करिष्ये इति सङ्कल्प्य मूलाधारादुत्थितां विद्युत्सहस्रप्रभाभास्वरां बिसतन्तुरूपां सुषुम्णामार्गेण हृदयकमलमागतां कुण्डलिनीं विभाव्य हृदयकमलाज्जीवं प्रदीपकलिकाकारं गृहीत्वा द्वादशान्ताम्बुजं सहस्रदलं गतां विभाव्य तत्र जीवात्मानं हंसमन्त्रेण परमात्मनि योजयेत्। ततः पादादिजानुपर्य्यन्तं चतुरस्रं पीतं पृथिवीमण्डलं तत्र पादगमनक्रियागन्तव्यगन्धघ्राणपृथिवीब्रह्मनिवृत्तिसमानवायून् संस्मृत्य ॐ ह्रां ब्रह्मणे पृथिव्यधिपतये निवृत्तिकलात्मने हुं फट् स्वाहा इत्यमुं मन्त्रमुच्चार्य्य तान् सर्व्वान् कुण्डलिनीद्वारा अप्सु प्रविलापयामीत्यपां स्थाने संहरेत्। जान्वादिनाभिपर्य्यन्तं शुक्लमर्द्धचन्द्राकारं जलमण्डलं तत्र हस्तादानादातव्यरसरसनाजलविष्णुप्रतिष्ठोदानान् स्मृत्वा ॐ ह्रीं विष्णवे जलाधिपतये प्रतिष्ठाकलात्मने हुं फट् स्वाहा इत्यमुं मन्त्रमुच्चार्य्य तान् सर्व्वान् कुण्डलिनीद्वारा अग्नौ प्रविलापयामीत्यग्निस्थाने संहरेत्। नाभ्यादिहृदयपर्य्यन्तं त्रिकोणं वह्निमण्डलं रक्तवर्णं तत्र पायुविसर्गविसर्जनीयरूपचक्षुस्तेजोरुद्रविद्याव्यानान् संस्मृत्य ॐ ह्रूं रुद्राय तेजोऽधिपतये विद्याकलात्मने हुं फट् स्वाहा इत्यमुं मन्त्रमुच्चार्य्य तान् सर्व्वान् कुण्डलिनीद्वारा वायौ प्रविलापयामीति वायुस्थाने संहरेत्। ततो हृदादिभ्रूपर्य्यन्तं कृष्णं वर्त्तुलं षड्बिन्दुलाञ्छितं

वायुमण्डलं तत्रोपस्थानन्दतद्विषयस्पर्शस्प्रष्टव्यवायीश्वरशान्त्यपानान् संस्मृत्य ॐ क्षैं ईशानाय वायुधिपतये शान्तिकलात्मने हुं फट् स्वाहा इत्यमुं मन्त्रमुच्चार्य्य तान् सर्व्वान् कुण्डलिनीद्वारा आकाशे प्रविलापयामीत्याकाशस्थाने संहरेत्। ततो भ्रूमध्याद् ब्रह्मरन्ध्रपर्यन्तं स्वच्छं वर्त्तुलम् आकाशमण्डलं तत्र वाग्वदनवक्तव्य-शब्दश्रोत्राकाश सदाशिवशान्त्यतीताप्राणान् संस्मृत्य ॐ क्षौं सदाशिवाकाशाधिपतये शान्त्यतीताकलात्मने हुं फट् स्वाहा इत्यमुं मन्त्रमुच्चार्य्य तान् सर्व्वान् अहङ्कारे प्रविलापयामीत्यहङ्कारे प्रविलाप्य तमहङ्कारं महत्तत्त्वे प्रविलाप्य महत्तत्त्वं मातृकासंज्ञकशब्दब्रह्मस्वरूपायां हृल्लेखार्थभूतायां प्रकृतौ प्रविलापयामीति प्रविलाप्य तां तथाविधां नित्यबुद्धशुद्धस्वभावे स्वप्रकाशे सत्यज्ञानानन्तानन्दलक्षणे परमकारणे परब्रह्मणि प्रविलापयामीति प्रविलापयेत्। तदुक्तं मन्त्रतन्त्रप्रकाशे—

गन्धादि घ्राणसंयुक्तां पृथिवीमप्सु संहरेत्।
रसादि जिह्वया सार्द्धं जलमग्नौ विलापयेत्॥
रूपादि चक्षुषा सार्द्धमग्निं वायौ विलापयेत्।
समीरमम्बरे विद्वान् स्पर्शादि त्वक्समन्वितम्॥
अहङ्कारे हरेद् व्योम सशब्दं तं महत्यपि।
महच्च सर्व्वशक्तीनामव्यक्ते कारणे परे॥
सच्चिदानन्दरूपं यत् वैष्णवं परमं पदम्।
पृथिव्यादिक्रमात् सर्व्वं तत्र लीनं विचिन्तयेत्॥ इति।

ततः शरीरस्थाऽन्तर्यामी ऋषिः सत्यं देवता प्रकृतिपुरुषं छन्दः सशरीरपापपुरुषस्य शोधने विनियोगः इत्युक्त्वा दक्षकुक्षिस्थं शुक्लरूपं पापपुरुषं विचिन्त्य यमिति वायुबीजस्य किष्किन्ध ऋषिः वायुर्देवता जगती छन्दः सशरीरपापपुरुषशोधने विनियोगः इत्युक्त्वा नाभिमूले च षड्बिन्दुमण्डले यं विचिन्तयेत्।

तद्वायुबीजं धूम्रञ्च चञ्चलध्वजसंयुतम्।
धूँ धूँ शब्दयुतं सर्व्वशोधनन्त्वीशदैवतम्॥

इति ध्यात्वा पूरकप्रयोगेन षोड़शवारं द्वादशवारं वा बीजमावर्त्त्य बीजोत्थवायुना सशरीरं पापपुरुषं शोषितं विभावयेत्। ततो रमित्यग्निबीजस्य कश्यप ऋषि-रग्निर्देवता त्रिष्टुप् छन्दः तद्दाहे विनियोगः इत्युक्त्वा

चिन्तयेद्हृदये रक्तं त्रिकोणं वह्निमण्डलम्।
विद्याकलायुतं रुद्रदैवतञ्च रमीरितम्॥

इति ध्यात्वा कुम्भकप्रयोगेन चतुःषष्टिवारं पञ्चाशद्वारं वा बीजमावर्त्तयेत्।

तद्बीजोत्थाग्निना तद् भस्मीभूतं विभावयेत्। ततो रेचकेन द्वात्रिंशन्मात्रया पञ्चविंशतिमात्रया वा पूर्वोक्तरूपं वायुबीजमावर्त्त्य पापपुरुषभस्म रेचयेत्। ततो वमिति वरुणबीजस्य हिरण्यगर्भ ऋषिर्हंसो देवता त्रिष्टुप् छन्दः आवने विनियोगः इत्युक्त्वा

वारुणं मण्डलं मूर्द्धि शुभ्रं चन्द्रार्द्धसन्निभम्।
सितपङ्कजयुग्मस्थं वं स्याद् वरुणदैवतम्॥

इति ध्यात्वा तद्बीजमुतामृतेन तच्छरीरभस्म पिण्डीभूतं विभावयेत्। ततो लमिति पृथिवीबीजस्य ब्रह्मा ऋषिरिन्द्रो देवता गायत्री छन्दः कठिनीकरणे विनियोगः इत्युक्त्वा

आधारमण्डले पृथ्वीमण्डलं वज्रलाञ्छितम्।
चतुष्कोणञ्च कठिनं पीतवर्णेन्द्रदैवतम्।
लं बीजेन समायुक्तं ध्यायेन्मनसि पूर्ववत्॥

इति ध्यात्वा तद्बीजोत्थकाठिन्येन तनुं दृढां भावयेत्। ततो हमित्याकाशबीजस्य ब्रह्मा ऋषिराकाशं देवता पंक्तिश्छन्दः व्यूहने विनियोगः इत्युक्त्वा

आकाशमण्डलं वृत्तं द्वादशान्ते हमुज्ज्वलम्।
शान्त्यतीताकलायुक्तं चिन्त्यमाकाशदैवतम्॥

इति ध्यात्वा तदुत्थेनाकाशेनावकाशं भावयेत्। तदुक्तम्—

ग्लौमिति पृथ्वीबीजेन तस्य सहनतां नयेत्।
ॐ हं वमिति बीजेनाऽवयवीकरणं भवेत्॥ इति।

एवं स्वशरीरं विचिन्त्य परमात्मनः सकाशात् सृष्टिक्रमेण तत्त्वानि स्वस्वस्थानं प्रापयेदिति। ततः परमात्मनः सकाशाज्जीवं सोऽहं मन्त्रेण हृत्पद्ममानयेदिति संक्षेपः। इयञ्च भूतशुद्धिरावश्यकीया।

भूत[पञ्च]शुद्धिविहीनेन कृता पूजाऽभिचारवत्[जपादिकम्]।
विपरीतं फलं दद्यादभक्त्या चार्चनं तथा॥
निर्ऋतिर्विधिहीनानां फलं हन्ति हि कर्मणाम्।
निशाचराधिपत्यञ्च कुरुते शङ्कराज्ञया॥

इति शैवागम उक्तः।

अन्यत्रापि—शरीराकारभूतानां भूतानां यद् विशोधनम्।
अव्ययब्रह्मसम्पर्काद् भूतशुद्धिरियं मता॥
भूतशुद्धिं विना कर्म जपहोमार्चनादिकम्।

मनुना हंसदेवस्य कुर्य्यान्न्यासादिकं ततः ।

ऋषिच्छन्दोदेवतानि न्यसेत् मन्त्रस्य मन्त्रवित् ॥ ३०

भवेत्तन्निष्फलं सर्व्वं प्रकारेणाप्यनुष्ठितम् ॥ इति ।

वक्ष्यमाणप्राणप्रतिष्ठामन्त्रेण एतदनन्तरं स्वप्राणप्रतिष्ठाऽवश्यं कार्त्तव्या । सम्प्रदायाद् गुरूपदेशाच्च । अत्र विशेषो वशिष्ठसंहितायाम्—

हृदि हस्तं सन्निधाय प्राणस्थापनमाचरेत् ।
ततो जन्मादिकद्वाष्टक्रिया संस्कारसिद्धये ।
षोड़शप्रणवावृत्तो: कृत्वा शक्तिं परां स्मरेत् ॥ इति ॥ २८ ॥

अनन्तरकर्त्तव्यमाह हंसदेवस्येति । ततो मूलमन्त्रेण यथाविधि प्राणायामत्रयं विधाय हंसदेवस्य न्यासादिकं कुर्य्यादिति सम्बन्धः । तत्र यथाविधीत्यस्यायमर्थः । यदा अजपान्यासस्तदा अजपया यदा प्रणवन्यासस्तदा प्रणवेन यदा बहिर्मातृकान्यासस्तदा मातृकया । एवं यदा भुवनेशीन्यासस्तदा तया यदा मूलमन्त्रस्य न्यासस्तदा जप्यमानमन्त्रेणेति । तत्र मातृकाप्राणायामे विशेषः । यदाहुः—

इड़या पूरयेत् प्राणं स्वरैः स्पर्शैश्च कुम्भयेत् ।
रेचयेद् यादिकैर्वर्णैस्ततः पिङ्गलया पुनः ॥
तथैव पूरणं वायोः कुम्भनं रेचनं पुनः ।
इड़या स्यात्ततो द्वाभ्यां पूरणादित्रयं पुनः ॥
प्राणायामत्रयं कृत्वा पश्चाद् व्यापकमाचरेत् ।
अकाराद्यैः क्षान्तवर्णैरापादतलमस्तकम् ॥ इति ।

जप्यमानमन्त्रे तु मन्त्रमुख्यैकेन बीजेन प्राणायामः कार्य्यः । सर्व्वेण वा । तत्रैकेन चेत् कुम्भके चतुःषष्ट्यावृत्तिः अष्टाक्षरैश्चेद् द्वात्रिंशद्वारम् इत्यादि ज्ञेयम् । यदाहुः—

अष्टाविंशतिवारमिष्टफलदं मन्त्रं दशार्णं जप-
न्नायच्छेत् पवनं सुशंसितमिति त्वष्टादशार्णेन चेत् ।
अभ्यस्यन्मुनिवार[न्नविचार] मन्यमनुभिर्वर्णानुरूपं जपन्
कुर्य्याद्रेचकपूर्व्वकर्म्मनिपुणः प्राणप्रयोगं नरः ॥ इति ।

न्यासो यथा । अजपाया आद्यं मूले परं शिरसि । तथा दक्षवामभागयोः । तत्रायं प्रयोगः । हं पुरुषात्मने नमः स: प्रकृत्यात्मने नमः । हंसः प्रकृतिपुरुषात्मने नमः । इति व्यापकम् । तद्रूपेणान्तर्मातृकान्यासोऽपि । आदिशब्दात् पूजापूर्व्वदिनजप-

आत्मनो मूर्ध्नि वदने हृदये च यथाक्रमात्।
विधाय मूलमन्त्रेण प्राणायामं यथाविधि ॥ ३१
विदध्यान्मातृकान्यासं मन्त्रन्यासमनन्तरम्।
अङ्गुष्ठादिष्वङ्गुलीषु न्यसेदङ्गैः सजातिभिः ॥ ३२

निवेदनं तद्दिनजपसङ्कल्पश्च। एतदनन्तरं हंसमन्त्रोत्पन्नत्वात् प्रणवस्य न्यासः। सोऽपि ॐ अं ब्रह्मणे नमः ॐ आं विष्णवे नमः इत्यादि मातृकास्थानेषु न्यसेत्। नामानि तु अन्यपटले प्रणवोत्पत्तौ मया वक्ष्यन्ते। तज्जन्यचतुर्नवतिकला न्यासोऽपि सूचितः। तन्न्यासस्थानं यथा—

मूलाधारत्रिकोणेषु विन्यसेदग्निजाः कलाः।
हृत्पङ्कजदलेष्वर्ककला द्वादशसंख्यकाः॥
मूर्द्धिषोड़शपत्राणां मध्ये सोमभवाः कलाः।
नादजास्तु स्वरस्थाने बिन्दुजाः पञ्चवक्त्रके॥
पूर्व्वदक्षिणसौम्येषु पश्चिमोर्द्ध्वमुखेषु च।
हृद्गलांसेषु नाभौ च सोदरे पृष्ठवक्षसोः॥
उरोजयोर्न्यसेच्चापि कला मात्क्षरसम्भवाः।
पादे गुह्ये सोरुजानुजङ्घास्फिक्षु उकारजाः॥
पादहस्ततलघ्राणकेषु बाह्वोश्च पाद[र्श्व]योः।
न्यसेदकारजा गुमकलाः पञ्च प्रविन्यसेत्॥
कास्यहृद्गुह्यपादेषु। इति।

उक्तवक्ष्यमाणानां सामान्यतः ऋष्यादिन्यासमाह ऋषीति। अत एव मन्त्रस्येति सामान्यग्रहणम्। अत्र देवताया अपि प्राप्तत्वादात्मन इत्युक्तिः। तेनाऽजपान्यासे अजपायाः प्रणवन्यासे प्रणवस्य बहिर्मातृकान्यासे मातृकाया भुवनेशीन्यासे तस्या मूलमन्त्रन्यासे जप्यमानस्य मन्त्रस्येति। मन्त्रविद् यथाक्रमाद् इत्यनेन बीजशक्तीनामपि न्यास उक्तः। सदक्षिणवामकोश[कोण]योरित्येके। गुह्यपादयोरित्यन्ये। स्तनयोरित्यपरे। ऋष्यादिन्यासस्यावश्यकतोक्ताऽन्यत्र—

ऋषिच्छन्दोदेवतानां विन्यासेन विना यदा।
जप्यते साधितोऽप्येष तस्य तुच्छफलं भवेत्। इति॥ ३०॥३१॥

बहिर्मातृकान्यासमाह विदध्यादिति। मातृकान्यासं वक्ष्यमाणं प्रपञ्चयागान्तमित्यर्थः। अनन्तरं मन्त्रन्यासं भुवनेशीन्यासं विदध्यादिति सम्बन्धः। यदाहुः—

अस्त्रं तत्तलयोर्न्यस्य कुर्य्यात्तालत्रयादिकम् ।
दिग्बन्धनेव बध्नीयाच्छोटिकाभिः समाहितः ॥ ३३

प्रणवो मातृकादेवी ह्रल्लेखेत्यक्षरत्रयम् ।
दीपनं सर्व्वमन्त्राणामित्याह भगवान् शिवः ॥ इति ।

वायवीयसंहितायाम्—

हंसन्यासस्तु तत्राद्यः प्रणवन्यास एव च ।
तृतीयो मातृकान्यासो ब्रह्मन्यासस्ततः परम् ॥
पञ्चमः कथ्यते सद्भिर्न्यासः पञ्चाक्षरात्मकः ।
एतेष्वेकमनेकं वा कुर्य्यात् पूजादिकर्म्मसु ॥ इति ।

उक्तावक्ष्यमाणानां करन्यासमाह अनन्तरम् अङ्गुष्ठेति। अनन्तरमित्यनेन मूलमन्त्रेण करशुद्धिः कर्त्तव्येत्युक्तम्। अतएव लक्ष्मीपटले वक्ष्यति "हस्तौ संशोध्य मन्त्रेण" इति। तदुक्तम्—

व्याप्यव्याप्योर्हस्तयोर्मन्त्रमन्तर्बाह्ये पार्श्वे तारुद्रं बुधेन। इति।

अङ्गैस्तत्तत्कल्पोक्ताङ्गमन्त्रैः। तत्र हृन्मन्त्रमुच्चार्य्य अङ्गुष्ठाभ्यां नम इत्यादि प्रयोगः। तदुक्तमाचार्य्यैः—

अङ्गुलीषु क्रमादङ्गैरङ्गुष्ठादिषु विन्यसेत्। इति।

सजातिभिरित्यग्रिमेण सम्बध्यते। तत्तलयोरिति तच्छब्देन प्रकृतत्वादङ्गुलय उच्यन्ते। ताभिः करौ लक्ष्यते। तलशब्देनान्तर्बाह्यमपितलंगृह्यते। तेनास्त्रमन्त्रमुच्चार्य्य करतलपृष्ठाभ्यां नम इति अस्त्रमन्त्रप्रयोगः। तदुक्तम्—

अङ्गुष्ठाभ्यां नमो क्रां क्रीं तर्जनीभ्यां नमस्ततः।
मध्यमाभ्यां नमो क्रूं क्रैं अनामिकाभ्यां नमस्ततः ॥
ॐ क्रौं कनिष्ठिकाभ्यां च नमो क्रस्तलपृष्ठयोः। इति।

कुर्य्यात्तालत्रयादिकमिति अङ्गास्त्रविनियोगः। तस्य स्वरूपमुक्तमन्यत्र—

प्रसारिततलाभ्यान्तु तालत्रयमुदीरयेत्। इति।

तालत्रयादिकमित्यादिशब्दोक्तं विशदयति दिग्ब इति। तेनैवेत्यस्त्रमन्त्रेण। छोटिका नाराचमुद्रारूपा।

अङ्गुष्ठतर्ज्जन्यग्राभ्यां स्फोटो नाराचमुद्रिका।

इति तल्लक्षणात्। समाहित इत्यग्रिमेण सम्बध्यते। तत्रैवं सम्बन्धः। ततः समाहितः सुबीजातिभिः अङ्गमन्त्रान् हृदादिषु च विन्यसेदिति। चकारोऽङ्गु-

ष्ठादिष्विति पूर्व्वोक्तसमुच्चयार्थः। तत इति वक्ष्यमाणतत्तत्कल्पोक्ततत्तन्मन्त्रन्यासानन्तरमित्यर्थः। यदाहुः—

आदावृष्यादिविन्यासः करशुद्धिस्ततः परम्।
अङ्गुलिव्यापकन्यासौ हृदादिन्यास एव च॥
तालत्रयञ्च दिग्बन्धः। इति।

अन्यत्रापि—करन्यासं पुरा कृत्वा देहन्यासमतः परम्।
अङ्गन्यासं न्यसेत् पश्चादेष साधारणो विधिः॥ इति।

आचार्य्या अपि षडङ्गन्यासात्परमुक्ता—

जपारम्भे मनूनां हि सामान्येयं प्रकल्पना। इति।

समाहितः सुधीरित्यनेन षडङ्गमुद्राः सूचिताः। तदुक्तमागमान्तरे—

प्रसारिततलेनैव पाणिना हृदयं शिरः।
प्रोक्ता शिखा तथा सम्यगधोऽङ्गुष्ठेन मुष्टिना॥
तथाविधाभ्यां पाणिभ्यां वर्म्मस्कन्धादिनाभिगम्।
तर्ज्जनीमध्यमानामाः प्रोक्ता नेत्रत्रये क्रमात्॥
यदा नेत्रद्वये प्रोक्ते तदा तर्ज्जनीमध्यमे॥ इति।

अत्र प्रसारिततलेनेत्यत्र अङ्गुष्ठवर्ज्जमङ्गुलीचतुष्टयेनेत्यर्थः। तदुक्तम्—

अङ्गुष्ठवर्ज्जमङ्गुल्यस्ततस्तो हृदि मूर्द्धनि।
शिखायां मुष्टिरेव स्यादङ्गुष्ठकृतनालिका॥
सर्व्वाङ्गुलय आनाभेः पाण्योः कवचबन्धनम्॥ इति।

शक्तिषड़ङ्गमुद्रास्तन्त्रान्तरे—

हृदयं मध्यमानामातर्ज्जनीभिः स्मृतं शिरः।
मध्यमातर्ज्जनीभ्यां स्यादङ्गुष्ठेन शिखा स्मृता॥
दशभिः कवचं प्रोक्तं तिसृभिर्नेत्रमीरितम्।
प्रोक्ताङ्गुलीभ्यामस्त्रं स्यादङ्गक्लृप्तिरियं मता॥ इति।

शैवषड़ङ्गमुद्राः शैवागमे—

कृतमुष्टिपदौ[पुटौ] हस्तौ कृत्वाऽङ्गुष्ठौ हृदि न्यसेत्।
हृन्मुद्रेयं समाख्याता शिरोमुद्रा प्रकीर्त्त्यते॥
ललाटाग्रे समाधाय कृतमुष्टिपुटौ करौ।
कुर्य्यादूर्द्ध्वप्रसक्ताग्रौ तर्ज्जन्यौ ज्येष्ठबाह्यतः॥
करौ शिखायां संयोज्य कृतमुष्टिपुटाकृती।

हृदयादिषु विन्यस्येदङ्गमन्त्रांस्ततः सुधीः ।
हृदयाय नमः पूर्वं शिरसे वह्निवल्लभा ॥ ३४
शिखायै वषडित्युक्तं कवचाय हुमीरितम् ।
नेत्रत्रयाय वौषट् स्यादस्त्राय फडिति क्रमात् ॥ ३५
षड़ङ्गमन्त्रानित्युक्तान् षड़ङ्गेषु नियोजयेत् ।
पञ्चाङ्गानि मनोर्यस्य तत्र नेत्रमनुं त्यजेत् ॥ ३६
अङ्गहीनस्य मन्त्रस्य स्वेनैवाङ्गानि कल्पयेत् ।
तत्तत्कल्पोक्तविधिना न्यासानन्यान् समाचरेत् ॥ ३७

ज्येष्ठाऽधःप्रसक्ताग्री कनिष्ठाऽवुद्धृतस्तथा ॥
कुर्य्यात् सेयं शिखामुद्रा सर्व्वोपद्रवनाशिनी ।
कृत्वाऽङ्गुष्ठौ प्रसक्ताग्रौ तर्जन्यौ च त्रिकोणवत् ॥
मूर्द्ध्नि पश्चान्मुखं कृत्वा नयेदुभयपार्श्वतः ।
करौ हृदन्त मुद्रेयं कवचस्याऽभयप्रदा ॥
कृत्वा नेत्रोन्मुखं हस्तं सक्ताङ्गुष्ठकनिष्ठिकम् ।
प्रसार्य्य मध्यमां किञ्चिन्नमवेदितराङ्गुली: ॥
नेत्रमुद्रेयमुद्दिष्टा रक्षोभूतार्त्तिभञ्जिनी ।
परस्परतलद्वन्द्वं पुनरास्फोटयेद् भ्रमम् ॥ इति ॥ ३२ ॥ ३३ ॥

जातिभिरित्युक्तास्ताः का इत्यपेक्षायामाह हृदयेति । पूर्वं प्रथमो मन्त्रः शिरसे एतदनन्तरं वह्निवल्लभा स्वाहेति उच्चरेदित्यर्थः । नेत्रत्रयायेत्युपलक्षणम् । तेन द्विनेत्रे विष्णवादौ नेत्राभ्यां वौषडिति प्रयोगः । षड़ङ्गमन्त्रान् तत्तत्कल्पोक्तानित्येवं प्रकारेणोक्तान् जातिमन्त्रांश्च मिलित्वा षड़ङ्गेषु हृदयादिषु उक्तमुद्राभिर्नियोजयेन्न्यसेदित्यर्थः ॥ ३४॥३५॥३६ ॥

अङ्गेति । अङ्गहीनत्वं नाम नारायणाष्टाक्षरादिवन्मन्त्रोद्धाराभावः । स्वेनैवेत्यावृत्त्या छेदेन वा । एतेनाङ्गानामावश्यकत्वमुक्तम् । यदाहुः—

पूजाजपार्चनाहोमाः सिद्धमन्त्रकृता अपि ।
अङ्गविन्यासविधुरा न दास्यन्ति फलान्यमी ॥ इति ।

गौतमेन षड़ङ्गकरणप्रयोजनमप्युक्तम्—

इज्यमानो हृदात्माऽयं हृदये स्याच्चिदात्मकः ।

कल्पयेदात्मनो देहे पीठं धर्म्मादिभिः क्रमात् ।

अंसोरुयुग्मयोर्विद्वान् प्रादक्षिण्येन देशिकः ॥ ३८

क्रियते तत्परत्वन्तु[परात्मा च] हृन्मन्त्रेण ततः परम् ॥

सर्व्वज्ञादिगुणोपेतैे[युक्ते] संविद्रूपे परात्मनि ।

क्रियते विषयाहारः शिरोमन्त्रेण धीमता ॥

हृच्छिरोरूपचिद्धाममयता[नियता] भावना दृढ़ा ।

क्रियते निजदेवस्य शिखामन्त्रेण सादरम् ॥

मन्त्रात्मकस्य देवस्य मन्त्रवाच्येन[व्याप्तेन] तेजसा ।

सर्व्वतो वर्म्ममन्त्रेण क्रियते न्याससंभृतिः ॥

यद्ददाति परं ज्ञानं संविद्रूपे परात्मनि ।

हृदयादिमयं तेजः स्यादेतन्नेत्रसंज्ञकम् ॥

आध्यात्मिकादिरूपं यत् साधकस्य विनाशयेत् ।

अविद्याजातमस्त्रं तत् परं धाम समीरितम् ॥ इति ।

पूर्व्वं तत इति मन्त्रन्यासानन्तरमिति व्याख्यातम् । तत्र को मन्त्रन्यास इत्यपेक्षायामाह तत्तदिति । न्यासान् मन्त्रन्यासान् । एषामप्यावश्यकतोक्ताऽन्यत्र—

न्यासं विना जपं प्राहुरासुरं विफलं बुधाः ।

न्यासात्तदात्मको भूत्वा देवो भूत्वा तु तं यजेत् ॥ इति ।

कुलप्रकाशतन्त्रेऽपि—

आगमोक्तेन मार्गेण न्यासान् नित्यं करोति यः ।

देवताभावमाप्नोति मन्त्रसिद्धिः प्रजायते ॥

अकृत्वा न्यासजातं यो [जालानि] मूढ़ात्मा प्रभजेन्मनून् ।

सर्व्वविघ्नैश्च बाध्येत व्याघ्रैर्मृगशिशुर्यथा ॥

यो न्यासकवचच्छन्नो मन्त्रं जपति तं प्रिये ।

विघ्ना दृष्ट्वा पलायन्ते सिंहं दृष्ट्वा यथा गजाः ॥ इति ।

वायवीयसंहितायामपि—

नाशिवः शिवमभ्यस्येन्नाशिवः शिवमर्चयेत् ।

नाशिवस्तु शिवं ध्यायेन्नाशिवः शिवमाप्नुयात् ॥ इति ।

ग्रन्थकृदपि—मन्त्राक्षराणि विन्यस्येद्देवताभावसिद्धये । इति ।

एतेन यत्र मन्त्रे अक्षरन्यासो वाचनिको नोक्तस्तत्रापि कर्त्तव्य इत्युक्तम् ॥ ३७ ॥

आत्मयागार्थं देहे पीठकल्पनामाह कल्पयेदिति । आत्मनो देहे न्यस्तैर्धर्म्मादिभिः

धर्म्मं ज्ञानञ्च वैराग्यमैश्वर्य्यं न्यस्यतु क्रमात् ।
मुखपार्श्वनाभिपार्श्वेऽधर्म्मादींश्च प्रकल्पयेत् ॥ ३९

धर्म्मादयः स्मृताः पादाः पीठगात्राणि चापरे ।
अनन्तं हृदये पद्ममस्मिन् सूर्य्येन्दुपावकान् ॥ ४०

पीठं कल्पयेदित्यर्थः । अत्र क्रमादित्यनेनैतदुक्तं भवति । मण्डूकाय नम इत्याधारे । कालाग्निरुद्राय नमः इति स्वाधिष्ठाने । कूर्म्माय नम इति नाभौ । ततो हृदि आधारशक्त्यादिन्यासं कृत्वा पश्चाद्धर्म्मादिन्यास इति । यदाहुः—

न्यसेदाधारशक्तिप्रकृतिकमठशेषक्ष्माचीरसिन्धून्
श्वेतद्वीपञ्च रत्नोज्ज्वलसहित महामण्डपं कल्पवृक्षम् ।
हृद्देशे । इति ।

अंसेति । प्रादक्षिण्येन दक्षिणावर्त्तक्रमेण । विद्वान् देशिकः इत्यनेन दक्षिणांसमारभ्य दक्षोरुपर्य्यन्तं न्यास इत्युक्तम् । अयं पक्षः साम्प्रदायिकः । तदुक्तमीशानशिवेन—आधाराख्यां यजेच्छक्तिं हृदयेऽंसे च दक्षिणे ।

धर्म्मं ज्ञानञ्च सव्यांसे ऊर्व्वोर्वामान्ययोरपि ॥
वैराग्यसंज्ञमैश्वर्य्यम् । इति ।

क्रमादित्युत्तरेण सम्बध्यते ॥

मुखेति । अत्रापि प्रादक्षिण्येनेत्यनुषञ्जनीयम् । क्रमादित्यनेनैतदुक्तम् । मुखं ततो वामपार्श्वं ततो नाभिस्ततो दक्षिणपार्श्वम् । तदुक्तम्—

मुखे च वामपार्श्वे च नाभौ दक्षिणपार्श्वके ।
अधर्म्मञ्चाप्यथाज्ञानमवैराग्यमनैश्वरम् ॥ इति ।

ईशानशिवेनाप्युक्तम्—

अधर्म्मं वदने ततः ।
अज्ञानं सव्यपार्श्वे च नाभौ पार्श्वे च दक्षिणे ॥
अवैराग्यमनैश्वर्य्यम् । इति ।

यत्त्वाचार्य्यवचनम्—"आनननाभिमूलपार्श्वद्वयैः" इति तदपि तट्टीकाकारैराननपार्श्वं नाभिमूलपार्श्वैरित्येव व्याख्यातम् । अधर्म्मादीन् तानेव नञ्पूर्व्वानित्यर्थः ॥

अपर इति अधर्म्मादयः । अस्मिन्नित्यनन्ते । पद्ममिति वक्ष्यमाणलक्षणम् । एतेन पूतेन(?) पूर्व्वपूर्व्वस्योत्तरोत्तरं प्रत्याधारतोक्ता । अस्मिन् पद्मे सूर्य्येन्दुपावकामिति योज्यम् ॥ ३८ ॥ ३९ ॥ ४० ॥

एषु स्वस्वकला न्यसेन्नामाद्यक्षरपूर्व्विकाः।
सत्त्वादींस्त्रीन् गुणान् न्यस्येत्तथैवात्र गुरूत्तमः॥ ४१
आत्मानमन्तरात्मानं परमात्मानमेव तु।
ज्ञानात्मानं प्रविन्यस्य न्यसेत् पीठमनुं ततः॥ ४२
एवं देहमये पीठे चिन्तयेदिष्टदेवताम्।
मुद्राः प्रदर्श्य विधिवदर्घ्यस्थापनमाचरेत्॥ ४३

एष्विति त्रिषु मण्डलेषु। नामादौ यदक्षरं कभादि आदि यादि तत्पूर्व्विकाः। तत्र क्रमः। सूर्य्यमण्डलं विन्यस्य तत्र तत्कलाः ततः सोममण्डलं तत्र तत्कलाः ततो वह्निमण्डलं तत्र तत्कलाः न्यसेदिति। तथैवेति पूर्व्वपूर्व्वस्योपरि। नामाद्यक्षरपूर्व्विकानिति पदमेवाऽत्रानुवर्त्तते। तेन नाम्नो यदाद्यक्षरं तत्पूर्व्विकान् न्यसेदिति। अत्र गुरूत्तम इत्युत्तरेण सम्बध्यते। ततः ॐ सं सत्त्वाय नमः इत्यादिप्रयोगः। तदुक्तम्—"आद्यक्षरैः सत्त्वरजस्तमांसि" इति। एतच्च दिक्प्रदर्शनमात्रम्। पूर्व्वं सर्व्वत्र तथोक्तेः। अत्र परमात्मनि तुशब्दो व्यतिरेके। तेनायमर्थः। आत्मादित्रयेऽप्याद्यक्षरमेव बीजम्। ज्ञानात्मनि तु मायाबीजमिति गुरूत्तमपदेनोक्तम्।

न्यसेत् पीठमनुं ततः इत्यनेनैतदुक्तं भवति। मां मायातत्त्वाय नमः कं कलातत्त्वाय नमः विं विद्यातत्त्वाय नमः पं परतत्त्वाय नमः। हृत्पद्मा‍ग्राद्यष्टदलमूलेषु मध्ये च पीठशक्तिनवकं न्यसेदिति। तदुक्तम्—

मायातत्त्वं कलातत्त्वं विद्यातत्त्वं परं तथा।
विन्यस्य पीठशक्तीश्च ततः पीठमनुं न्यसेत्॥ इति।

अन्यत्रापि— अथाष्टदिक्षु परितो मध्ये च शक्तीर्नव।
न्यस्त्वा पीठमहामनुं च विधिवत्तत्कर्णिकामध्यगम्॥ इति ॥४१॥४२॥

मुद्रा इति। तत्तद्विशेषमुद्राश्च तत्तत्कल्पोक्तास्तत्तत्पटले मया वक्ष्यन्ते। विधिवदित्यनेनैतदनन्तरं मानसीं पूजां कृत्वा देवमभ्यर्थयेदित्युक्तम्। तत्राभ्यर्थनमन्त्रः— ॐ स्वागतं देवदेवेश सन्निधीभव केशव।
गृहाण मानसीं पूजां यथार्थपरिभाविताम्॥ इति।

अत्र केशवेत्यत्र तत्तद्देवतानाम्नामूहः कार्य्यः। तदुक्तम्—

इति ध्यात्वात्मानं पटुविशदधीर्नन्दतनयं
पुरोवुद्ध्यैवार्घ्यप्रभृतिभिरनिन्द्योपहृतिभिः।
यजेत्। इति।

शङ्खमस्त्राम्बुना प्रोक्ष्य वामतो वह्निमण्डले ।

साधारं स्थापयेद् विद्वान् विन्दुस्रुतसुधामयैः ॥ ४४

तोयैः सुगन्धिपुष्पाद्यैः पूरयेत्तं यथाविधि ।

आधारं पावकं शङ्खं सूर्य्यं तोयं सुधामयम् ॥ ४५

अन्यत्रापि—ध्यात्वा देवं प्रदर्श्याऽथ मुद्रा अपि विधानतः ।

पूजाञ्च मानसीं कुर्य्यात्ततोऽर्घ्यस्थापनञ्चरेत् ॥ इति ॥ ४३ ॥

अर्घ्यस्थापनमाचरेदित्युक्तम् । तद्विधिमाह शङ्खमिति । वामतो वामभागे स्वाग्रत इति ज्ञेयम् । यदुक्तम्—"आत्मनः पुरतः शङ्खम्" इति । वह्निमण्डले अर्घ्याग्रे त्रिकोणे साधारं शङ्खमित्यन्वयः । विद्वानित्यनेनात्र वह्निमण्डल इत्युपलक्षणम् इत्युक्तम् । तेन त्रिकोणषट्कोणवृत्तचतुरस्ररूपे शङ्खमुद्रावष्टब्धे पूजितषडङ्गे इति ज्ञेयम् । तदुक्तम्—

अग्रे त्रिकोणमालिख्य षट्कोणञ्च ततो बहिः ।

वर्त्तुलं चतुरस्रञ्च मध्ये मायां विलिख्य च ।

शङ्खमुद्रां प्रदर्श्याऽथ कोणदिक्ष्वङ्गपूजनम् ॥ इति ।

अन्यत्रापि—त्रिकोणषट्कोणवृत्तचतुरस्राणि कारयेत् ।

शङ्खमुद्रामवष्टभ्य षडङ्गानि प्रपूजयेत् ॥ इति ।

बिन्दुर्भ्रूमध्यम् । केचन ब्रह्मरन्ध्रमिति वदन्ति । तत्र चन्द्रमण्डलस्य सत्त्वादिति । बिन्दुस्रुतसुधामयैरिति जलध्यानम् । यत् सोमशम्भौ—

बिन्दुप्रसूत पीयूषरूपतोयाक्षतादिना ।

सदापूर्य्य षडङ्गेन पूजयित्वाऽभिमन्त्रयेत् ॥ इति ।

पूरयेत्तं यथाविधीत्यनेनैतदुक्तम् । बिन्द्वन्तां प्रतिलोममातृकां विलोममूलमन्त्रञ्च जपन्निति । तदुक्तम्—

पूरयेद्विमलपाथसा सुधीरक्षरैः प्रतिगतैः शिरोऽन्तकैः । इति ।

आधारमिति । आधारं पावकमण्डलत्वेन शङ्खं सूर्य्यमण्डलत्वेन तोयमिन्दुमण्डलत्वेन । तेषु मण्डलेषु तत्तत्कला अपि स्मरेत् । केचन पूजयन्त्यपि । तत्र प्रयोगः । स्ववामाग्रतः चतुरस्रवृत्तषट्कोणत्रिकोणमण्डलं कृत्वा शङ्खमुद्रयाऽवष्टभ्य पुष्पाक्षतैः पूजाक्रमेण षडङ्गानि सम्पूज्य आधारमस्त्रमन्त्रेण प्रक्षाल्य मं वह्निमण्डलाय दशकलात्मने अमुकार्घ्यपात्रासनाय नमः इति आधारं प्रतिष्ठाप्य पूर्व्वादग्नेर्दशकलाः पूजयेत् । ततः शङ्खमन्त्रेण [पुरुषोत्तमपटलोक्तशङ्खमन्त्रेण] शङ्खं

स्मरेदब्ज्यार्कचन्द्राणां कलास्तास्वनुक्रमात् ।
मूलमन्त्रं जपेत् स्पृष्ट्वा न्यसेत्तस्याङ्गमन्त्रवित् ॥ ४६

छन्दमन्त्रेणाभिसम्पूज्य हस्ताभ्यां छादयन्नपः ।
जपेद्विद्यां यथान्यायं देशिको देवताधिया ॥ ४७

अस्त्रमन्त्रेण संरक्ष्य कवचेनावगुण्ठ्य च ।
धेनुमुद्रां समापाद्य रोधयेत्तत् स्वमुद्रया ॥ ४८

प्रक्षाल्य अं सूर्य्यमण्डलाय द्वादशकलात्मने अमुकार्घ्यपात्राय नमः इति पात्रमाधारे निधाय प्रादक्षिण्येन द्वादशस्थानेषु सूर्य्यस्य द्वादश कलाः सम्पूज्य विलोममातृकां विलोममूलमन्त्रञ्च जपन् शुद्धोदकेन शङ्खमापूर्य्य उं सोममण्डलाय षोड़शकलात्मने अमुकार्घ्यामृताय नमः इति सम्पूज्य सोमस्य षोड़शकलास्तत्र प्रादक्षिण्येन पूजयेदिति । ततस्तत्र "गङ्गे च" इति मन्त्रेण सूर्य्यमण्डलादङ्कुशमुद्रया तीर्थमावाह्य स्वहृत्कमलाद्देवमप्यावाहयेत् । देशिको देवताधियेति वक्ष्यमाणत्वात् । तदुक्तम्—

तत्र तीर्थमनुनाभिवाहयेत् तीर्थमुष्णरुचिमण्डलात् पुनः ।
स्वीयहृत्कमलतो हरिं तथा । इति ।

अङ्कुशमुद्रालक्षणं स्नानप्रसङ्गे उक्तम् । यद्वेयमङ्कुशमुद्रा । यदाहुः—

ऋजुमध्या मध्यपर्व्वाक्रान्ता तर्जन्यधोमुखी ।
विज्ञेयाऽङ्कुशमुद्रेयं कुञ्चिता मध्यपर्व्वतः ॥ इति ।

स्पृष्ट्वेति । अप इति सम्बध्यते । न्यसेदिति अप्स्विति सम्बध्यते । तस्येति मूलमन्त्रस्य । अङ्गमन्त्रविदित्यनेन वक्ष्यमाणदिक्क्रमपूजनेनैव न्यास इत्युक्तम् ।

अभिसम्पूज्येति अप इति सम्बन्धः । हस्ताभ्यां छादयन्निति देशिक इत्यनेन मत्स्यमुद्रयेत्युक्तम् । तल्लक्षणन्तु—

अधोमुखावुभौ हस्तौ स्वस्योपरि च संस्थितौ ।
पार्श्वद्वयगताङ्गुष्ठौ मत्स्यमुद्रेयमीरिता ॥

अत्र मूलमन्त्रविद्याशब्दाभ्यामिवमादिविधौ पुंस्त्रीदेवताकत्वमविवक्षितमित्युक्तम् । अन्यथैकग्रहणे इतरग्रहणं न स्यात् । यथान्यायमिति सप्तकृत्वोऽष्टकृत्वो वा । इयं संख्या[व्यवस्था] पूर्व्वमपि ज्ञेया । तदुक्तम्—

संस्पृशन् जपतु मन्त्रमष्टशः । इति ॥ ४४ ॥ ४५ ॥ ४६ ॥ ४७ ॥

संरक्ष्येति । तदिति सम्बन्धः । तच्च संरक्षणं छोटिकाभिरिति ज्ञेयम् । अवगुण्ठेत्यत्रापि तदिति सम्बध्यते । तच्चावगुण्ठनमुद्रया । समापाद्येत्य-

दक्षिणे प्रोक्षणीपात्रमाधायाऽद्भिः प्रपूरयेत् ।
किञ्चिदर्घ्याम्बु संगृह्य प्रोक्षण्यम्भसि योजयेत् ॥ ४९

मूलबीजेन । स्वमुद्रयेति सन्निरोधिन्या । अवगुण्ठनधेनुसन्निरोधनमुद्रास्त्रयोविंशि वक्ष्यन्ते । ततः शङ्खोपरि शङ्खमुषलचक्रमहामुद्रायोनिमुद्राः प्रदर्शयेत् ।

यदाहुः—चिन्मयं चिन्तयेत्तीर्थमानीयाऽङ्कुशमुद्रया ।
ब्रह्माण्डोदरतीर्थेभ्यो धेनुमुद्रां प्रदर्श्य च ॥
शङ्खमुद्रां चक्रमुद्रां मुषलाख्याञ्च दर्शयेत् ।
परमीकृत्य यत्नेन गुह्याख्याञ्चैव दर्शयेत् ॥ इति ।

कृष्णमन्त्रे गालिनीप्रदर्शनं राममन्त्रे गरुडमुद्राप्रदर्शनम् इत्यादिविशेषोऽनुसन्धेयः । शङ्खमुद्रालक्षणमुक्तं प्राक् । अन्यासां लक्षणानि तु—

मुष्टिं कृत्वा तु हस्ताभ्यां वामस्योपरि दक्षिणम् ।
कुर्य्यान्मुषलमुद्रेयं सर्व्वविघ्नप्रणाशिनी ॥
मिथः कनिष्ठिके बद्ध्वा तर्जनीभ्यामनामिके ।
अनामिकोर्द्ध्वगाश्लिष्ट दीर्घमध्यमयोरधः ।
अङ्गुष्ठाग्रद्वयं न्यस्येद् योनिमुद्रेयमीरिता ॥ इति ।
विपर्य्यस्ते तले कृत्वा वामदक्षिणहस्तयोः ।
अङ्गुष्ठौ ग्रथयेच्चैव कनिष्ठानामिकान्तरे ।
चक्रमुद्रेयमुद्दिष्टा सर्व्वसिद्धिकरी शुभा ॥ इति ।

महामुद्रालक्षणं त्रयोविंशे वक्ष्यते ।

कनिष्ठाङ्गुष्ठकौ सक्तौ करयोरितरेतरम् ।
तर्जनीमध्यमानामाः संहता भुग्नवर्जिताः[सज्जिताः] ।
मुद्रैषा गालिनी प्रोक्ता शङ्खस्योपरि चालिता ॥ इति ।
हस्तावभिमुखौ कृत्वा रचयित्वा कनिष्ठिके ।
मिथस्तर्जनिके श्लिष्टे श्लिष्टावङ्गुष्ठकौ तथा ॥
मध्यमानामिके द्वे तु द्वौ पक्षाविति कुञ्चयेत् ।
एषा गरुडमुद्रा स्यादशेषविषनाशिनी ॥ इति ॥ ४८ ॥

दक्षिण इति । पात्रं ताम्रादिजं । यदाहुः—

रत्नं रौक्मं रौप्यमब्जं ताम्रं मृत्कांस्यपैत्तलम् ।
पात्रं पालाशमुत्कृष्टान्यमम्भः स्थापनार्चने ।
सर्व्वोत्कृष्टौ ताम्रशङ्खावर्घ्यायाऽब्जोऽतिशस्यते ॥ इति ॥ ४९ ॥

अर्घ्यस्योत्तरतः कार्य्यं पाद्यं साचमनीयकम्।
आत्मानं यागवस्तूनि मण्डलं प्रोक्षयेद् गुरुः॥ ५०
प्रोक्षणीपात्रतोयेन मनुनाऽन्यान्यपि क्रमात्।
न्यासक्रमेण देहे स्वे धर्म्मादीन् पूजयेत्ततः॥ ५१

अर्घ्यस्येत्यर्घ्यपात्रस्य। शक्तौ सत्यां एतानि भिन्नानि। अशक्तौ एकेनैव सर्व्वम्। यदाहुः—एकस्मिन्नथवा पात्रे पाद्यार्घ्यादीनि कल्पयेत्। इति। मनुनेति मूलमन्त्रेण प्रोक्षयेदिति सम्बन्धः। इदञ्च सामान्यविधानम्। अन्यत्र तु मन्त्रविशेषे प्रोक्षणमन्त्र उक्तः। तत्र तेनैव प्रोक्षणमिति ज्ञेयम्। गुरुरित्यनेनेदं प्रोक्षणं त्रिरित्युक्तं भवति। यदाहुः—

प्रोक्षयेन्निजतनुं ततोऽमुना त्रिः करेण मनुनाऽखिलं तथा।
साधनं कुसुमचन्दनादिकम्। इति।

अन्यान्यपि यागवस्तूनि पूजाद्रव्याणि क्रमात् प्रोक्षयेदिति सम्बन्धः॥

आन्तरं यागमाह न्यासेति। तदुक्तम्—

द्विविधं स्यान्नृसमनोर्बाह्यान्तरमुपासनम्।
न्यासेनाद्यान्तरं प्रोक्तमन्येषामुभयं तथा॥ इति।

वायवीयसंहितायामपि—

आदावाभ्यन्तरं यागमग्निकार्य्यावसानकम्।
विधाय मानवः पश्चाद् बहिर्यागं समाचरेत्॥ इति।

तथा संहितायां शम्भुवाक्यमपि—

न गृही ज्ञानमात्रेण परत्रेह च मङ्गलम्।
प्राप्नोति चन्द्रवदने दानहोमादिभिर्विना॥
गृहस्थो यदि जुहुयान्न दद्यादपि नेश्वरि।
पूजयेद् विधिना नैव कः कुर्य्यादेतदन्वहम्॥
न ब्रह्मचारिणो दातुमधिकारोऽस्ति भामिनि।
गुरुभ्योऽपि च सर्व्वेभ्यः को वा दास्यत्यपेक्षितम्॥
नाऽरण्यवासिनां शक्तिर्न ते सन्ति कलौ युगे।
परिव्राड् ज्ञानमात्रेण दानहोमादिभिर्विना॥
सर्व्वदुःखपिशाचेभ्यो मुक्तो भवति नान्यथा।
परिव्राडविरक्तश्च विरक्तश्च गृही तथा॥

पुष्पाद्यैः पीठमन्वन्तं तस्मिंश्च परदेवताम्।
पञ्चकृत्वः पुनः कुर्य्यात् पुष्पाञ्जलिमनन्यधीः॥ ५२
उत्तमाङ्गहृदाधारपादसर्व्वाङ्गके क्रमात्।
विना निवेद्यं गन्धाद्यैरुपचारैः समर्चयेत्॥ ५३
गुरूपदिष्टविधिना शेषमन्यत् समापयेत्।
सर्व्वमेतत् प्रयुञ्जीत प्रोक्षणीस्थेन वारिणा॥ ५४

कुम्भीपाके निमज्जेते द्वावुभौ कमलानने।
पुरुषाः स्त्रियो गृहस्थाश्च मङ्गलैर्मङ्गलार्थिनः॥
पूजोपकरणैः कुर्य्युर्दद्युर्दानानि चार्हणाम्।
वानप्रस्थाश्च यतयो यद्येवं कुर्युरन्वहम्॥
संसारान्न निवर्त्तन्ते विध्यतिक्रमदोषतः।
आरूढयतिता ह्येते भवेयुर्दुःखभाजनम्॥ इति।

अत्र न्यासक्रमेणेत्यनेनैतदुक्तं भवति। मण्डूककालाग्निरुद्रकूर्म्मान् आधार-स्वाधिष्ठाननाभिदेशेषु तत आधारशक्त्यादीन् हृदि पश्चाद्धर्म्मादीनष्टौ यथास्थानं सम्पूज्य पुनर्हृदि शेषादिपरतत्त्वान्ता पूजा। तदुक्तं रामपूर्व्वतापनीये—

मायाविद्ये ये कलापरे तत्त्वे सम्पूजयेद्विमलादीश्च शक्तीः। इति॥५०॥५१॥

पुष्पस्याद्यं गन्धः। बहुवचनमाद्यर्थं तेन गन्धाद्यैरित्यर्थः। एतादृशयुक्तिस्तु आदिशब्देन पुष्पमात्रग्रहणार्था। यद्वा पुष्पाणि च आद्यो गन्धश्च पुष्पाद्यैः। उपचारेषु गन्धानन्तरं पुष्पस्योद्दिष्टत्वात्। पीठमन्वन्तमिति। पीठशक्ति पीठमन्त्र-पर्य्यन्तमित्यर्थः। तस्मिन्निति एवम्भूते देहमये पीठे परदेवतां गन्धाद्यैरुपचारैः समर्चयेदित्यग्रिमेण सम्बन्धः। आद्येन पुष्पम्। तत्र विशेषमाह पञ्चेति।

अनन्यधीरित्यनेन त्रिंशो वा इत्युक्तम्। तदुक्तमाचार्य्यैः—

कुर्य्यात् पुष्पाञ्जलिमपि निजदेहे पञ्चशोऽथवापि त्रिंशः। इति।

विना निवेद्यमिति। अस्यायमभिप्रायः। आसनादिदीपान्तानुपचारान् प्रदर्श्य बाह्ये नैवेद्यं न देयम्। ततो गुरूपदिष्टविधिना कुण्डलिनीमुत्थाप्य द्वादशान्तं नीत्वा तत्रत्यशिवेन समागमय्य तदुत्थामृतधारया देवं प्रीणयेदिति॥ ५२॥५३॥

गुरूपदिष्टेति। अन्यत् शेषं मानसौ धूपदीपौ मन्त्रजपः जपनिवेदनं ब्रह्मार्पणं क्षमापनादि विसर्जनवर्जम्। यदाहुः—

विसृज्य तोयं प्रोक्षण्याः पूरयेत्तां यथा पुरा।
ततस्तन्मण्डलं मन्त्री गन्धाद्यैः साधु पूजयेत् ॥ ५५
शालिभिः कर्णिकामध्यमापूर्य्योपरि तण्डुलैः।
अलङ्कृत्य पुनस्तेषु दर्भानास्तीर्य्य तत्त्ववित् ॥ ५६

ध्यात्वा यजेच्चन्दनाद्यैर्मानसैर्धूपदीपकैः।
भोजनावसरे किञ्चिज्जपं कृत्वा निवेदयेत् ॥ इति।

अशक्तं प्रत्याह सर्व्वमिति। नत्वा गुरूनित्यादि एतदन्तं नित्यपूजायामपि समानम्। विशेषस्त्वयं नित्यपूजायाम्। एतच्छङ्खजलमेव वर्द्धन्यां निक्षिपेदिति। ततः प्राणायामत्रयं कृत्वा अष्टोत्तरसहस्रं नित्यजपं कृत्वा पुनः प्राणायामत्रयञ्च कुर्य्यात्। किञ्चन "क्षिपतु वर्द्धनीजले" इति पुरतो जपस्य परतोऽपि "विहित-मथ तत्त्रयं बुधैः" इति चोक्तेः। तदुक्तं मन्त्रतन्त्रप्रकाशे—

अष्टोत्तरसहस्रन्तु कृत्वाऽन्तर्यागमादरात्।
जपेत् प्रतिदिनं यस्तु नित्य एष जपः स्मृतः ॥
अयने विषुवे चैव ग्रहणे चन्द्रसूर्य्ययोः।
द्वादश्यां पूर्णिमायाञ्च तेषु नैमित्तिको जपः ॥
नित्यात् त्रिगुणितः सोऽथ पूजा चैव हरेस्तथा ॥ इति।

आन्तरं यागमुक्त्वा बहिर्यागमाह तत इति। ततस्तदनन्तरं मन्त्री साधु शोभनत्वेन सर्व्वतोभद्रत्वमुक्तम्। तन्मण्डलं वेदिमध्यलिखितं सर्व्वतोभद्रमण्डलं गन्धाद्यैः पूजयेदिति सम्बन्धः। आदिशब्देन पुष्पम्। मन्त्रीत्यनेन श्रीसर्व्वतोभद्र-मण्डलाय नमः इति पूजामन्त्रः सूचित इति ज्ञेयम् ॥ ५४ ॥ ५५ ॥

शालिभिरिति। उपरि शाल्युपरि तण्डुलैरलङ्कृत्य तण्डुलान् तत्र निक्षिप्ये-त्यर्थः। पुनरनन्तरम्। तेषु तण्डुलेषु। तत् प्रमाणमन्यत्रोक्तम्—

शालींस्तु कर्णिकायाञ्च निक्षिप्याढकसम्मितान्।
तण्डुलांश्च तदष्टांशान् कूर्च्चञ्चोपरि विन्यसेत् ॥ इति।

आढकलक्षणन्तु—"कुडवश्चतुःपलः स्यात्। प्रस्थः कुडवैश्चतुर्भिः स्यात्। प्रस्थैश्चतुर्भि-राढकः।" इति। तदष्टांशानिति कुडवद्वयमितान्। शास्त्रोक्ततोलकाष्टकं पलम्। सप्तविंशतिसाग्रदर्भपत्रमयं वेण्याकारेण ग्रथितं विष्टरापरपर्य्यायं कूर्च्चम्। तदुक्तं डामरे—सप्तविंशतिदर्भाणां वेण्यग्रे ग्रन्थिभूषितम्।
विष्टरे सर्व्वयज्ञेषु लक्षणं परिकीर्त्तितम् ॥ इति

कूर्चमक्षतसंयुक्तं न्यसेत्तेषामथोपरि।
आधारशक्तिमारभ्य पीठं मन्त्रमयं यजेत्॥ ५७

अधः कूर्मशिलारूढां शरच्चन्द्रनिभप्रभाम्।
आधारशक्तिं प्रयजेत् पङ्कजद्वयधारिणीम्॥ ५८

भूर्ध्नि तस्याः समारूढं कूर्मं नीलाभमर्चयेत्।
ऊर्द्ध्वं ब्रह्मशिलासीनमनन्तं कुन्दसन्निभम्॥ ५९

अत्र आत्मादितत्त्वत्रयेण देवं सम्पूज्य बाह्यपूजामारभेदिति सम्प्रदायविदः।

आधारशक्तीति। अत्र प्रथमं गुरुगणपतिपूजनं कुर्य्यात्। तदुक्तम्—
वायव्याद्यादीशपर्य्यन्तमर्चापीठस्योदम्भौरवी पङ्क्तिरादौ।
पूज्योऽथ्याप्याग्निकेयः कराग्रैः पाशं दण्डं मृग्यभीती दधानः॥ इति।

अन्यत्रापि—पीठस्योत्तरे भागे गुरुपङ्क्तिं पूजयेच्च मन्त्रवित्।
यावद् गिरीशकोणं वायोः कोणं समारभ्य॥
अथ गुरुपरमगुरू द्वौ परमेष्टिगुरुं तथाऽभ्यर्च्य।
परमाचार्य्यगुरुश्चादिसिद्धिगुरुमथार्चयेत् स्वगुरुम्॥ इति।

अत्र परमाचार्य्यगुर्वनन्तरं परापरगुरुः परमसिद्धिगुरुरपि ज्ञेयः। तेषां ध्यानं मन्त्रतन्त्रप्रकाशे उक्तम्—
श्वेताम्बरधरा गौरा गुरवः पुस्तकान्विताः।
व्याख्यानमुद्रया युक्ता ध्यायन्तो वा हरिं निजम्।
ध्यातव्याः पूजनादौ च तद्ध्यानाज् ज्ञानवान् भवेत्॥ इति।

शाक्तादौ तु विशेषस्तन्त्रान्तरे—
ते रक्तमाल्याम्बरगन्धभूषाः स्वलङ्कृताः पङ्कजविष्टरस्थाः।
सर्व्वे च सालम्बनयोगनिष्ठाः प्राप्ताखिलैश्वर्य्यगुणाष्टकार्थाः॥ इति।

तत्र श्रीगुरुभ्यो नमः इत्यादि प्रयोगः।
देवं गुरुं गुरुस्थानं क्षेत्रं क्षेत्राधिदेवताः।
सिद्धं सिद्धाधिकारांश्च श्रीपूर्व्वं समुदीरयेत्॥

इत्युक्तेः अर्चयेदित्युक्तम्॥ ५६॥ ५७॥

तदेवाह अध इति। अनेनैतदुक्तं भवति। कर्णिकायां महाकायं रक्तं मण्डूकं मण्डूकाय नमः इति यजेत्। तदूर्द्ध्वं दशभुजं पञ्चवक्त्रं रक्तान्धादक्षिण-वामपार्श्वं कालाग्निरुद्रं कालाग्निरुद्राय नम इति। तदुपरि महाकायं कूर्मं

यजेच्चक्रधरं मूर्ध्नि धारयन्तं वसुन्धराम्।

तमालश्यामलां तत्र नीलेन्दीवरधारिणीम् ॥ ६०

अभ्यर्चयेद्वसुमतीं स्फुरत्सागरमेखलाम्।

तस्यां रत्नमयं द्वीपं तस्मिंश्च मणिमण्डपम् ॥ ६१

यजेत् कल्पतरूंस्तस्मिन् साधकाभीष्टसिद्धिदान्।

अधस्तात् पूजयेत्तेषां वेदिकां मण्डपोज्ज्वलाम् ॥ ६२

पश्चादभ्यर्चयेत्तस्यां पीठं धर्म्मादिभिः पुनः।

रक्तश्यामहरिद्रेन्द्रनीलाभान् पादरूपिणः ॥ ६३

कूर्म्माय नम इति। तदुक्तं शौनककल्पे—

मण्डूकादि पृथिव्यादि कर्णिकायां यजेत् क्रमात्। इति।

नारसिंहकल्पेऽपि—पद्मेऽष्टपत्रे मण्डूकं परतत्त्वान्तमर्च्चयेत्। इति।

कूर्म्मशिलेति। कूर्म्माकारा शिला कूर्म्मशिला तामारूढाम्। पूर्व्वं पूजितः कूर्म्म एव कूर्म्मशिलेति ज्ञेयम्। वक्ष्यमाणस्तु कूर्म्मस्तद्भिन्न एव। तदुक्तं तापनीये—"शक्तिं चाधाराख्यकां कूर्म्मनागौ" इति। शरच्चन्द्रस्येत्यस्यार्थः पूर्व्ववज् ज्ञेयः। ब्रह्मशिलेति मूलप्रतिमाधस्तन शिलायाः संज्ञा। तदुक्तं वायवीयसंहितायाम्—

शोधितां चन्दनालिप्तां श्वभ्रे ब्रह्मशिलां क्षिपेत्।

रत्न[तत्त्व]न्यासं ततः कृत्वा नवभिः शक्तिनामभिः ॥

हरितालादि धातूंश्च बीजं गन्धौषधीरपि।

शिवशास्त्रोक्तविधिना क्षिपेद्ब्रह्मशिलोपरि ॥ इत्यादिना

"लिङ्गं ब्रह्मशिलोपरि। प्रागुदक्प्लवनं किञ्चित्" इत्यन्तेन।

अनन्तमिति। "नाभ्यूर्द्ध्वं नराकृतिमधस्त्वह्याकृतिमेककुण्डलं सहस्रफणाम्" इति तत् स्वरूपम्। अन्यत्र तद्ध्यानमुक्तम्—

द्वात्रिंशद्भिः खलु तत्त्वैर्धराद्यैर्विद्यान्तैः स्वैर्महितं विष्णुतेजः।

आनन्त्यं तत्कथितं ह्यासनं स्यात् पीठाकारः स तु नागोऽह्यनन्तः ॥ इति।

अन्यत्रापि—तत्त्वैर्धरादिविद्यान्तैर्द्वात्रिंशत्संख्यकैरिह।

पीठाकारोऽह्यनन्तः स्यादनन्तासनमीरितम् ॥ इति ॥

नीलेन्दीवरे धारयतीति समासः। वक्ष्यति "इन्दीवरे द्वे" इति।

स्फुरत्सागरमेखलामित्यनेन पृथिव्यनन्तरं सागराय नम इति समुद्रः पूज्य इत्यर्थः।

वृषकेशरिभूतेभरूपान् धर्म्मादिकान् यजेत् ।
गात्रेषु पूजयेत्तांस्तु नञ्पूर्व्वानुक्तलक्षणान् ॥ ६४

आग्नेयादिषु कोणेषु दिक्षु चाथाम्बुजं यजेत् ।
आनन्दकन्दं प्रथमं संविन्नालमनन्तरम् ॥ ६५

तत्र सरस्वतीमन्त्रे विद्याब्धिः लक्ष्मीविष्णुमन्त्रे क्षीराब्धिः गणेशमन्त्रे इक्षुरसः समुद्रः। अन्यत्रामृतसमुद्र इत्यादि ज्ञेयम्। तस्यां विशिष्टायाम् ॥ ५८—६३ ॥

वृषेति। केशरी सिंहः। भूतो देवयोनिः। तत्स्वरूपमुक्तमन्यत्र—

रक्तवस्त्रधराः कृष्णा नखदंष्ट्राः सुदंष्ट्रिकाः।
कर्त्रीखट्वाङ्गहस्ताश्च राक्षसा घोररूपिणः॥
भूतास्तथैव दीनास्याः। इति।

इभो हस्ती। नञ्पूर्व्वान् अधर्म्माज्ञानावैराग्यानैश्वर्य्यान्। उक्तलक्षणानिति रक्तादिवर्णान् वृषभादिरूपान्। उक्तञ्च—

धर्म्मं रक्तं वृषरूपञ्च सिंहं ज्ञानं श्यामं दुष्टभूतञ्च पीतम्।
वैराग्यं स्याद् गजरूपासिताङ्गमैश्वर्य्यञ्च क्रमतः पीठपादाः॥
पीठस्येशा स्युरधर्म्मादयो ये ये चत्वारस्ते क्षुदिताकाररम्याः। इति ॥६४॥

आग्नेयादिष्विति। आदिशब्देन निर्ऋतिवायूीशकोणानां ग्रहणम्। दिक्षु प्रागदक्षिणपश्चिमोत्तरासु। चः समुच्चये। "आशाश्चतस्रो लभ्यन्ते दिक्शब्देन वृषादयः" इति परिभाषणात्। वायवीयसंहितायामपि—

अधर्म्मादींश्च पूर्व्वादीनुत्तरान्तानमनुक्रमात्। इति।

इह देवतापुरोभागस्य पूर्व्वत्वमित्याचार्य्याः। तथा चागमे—

देवसाधकयोरन्तः पूर्व्वा सा दिगिहोच्यते। इति।

अन्यत्रापि—देवाग्रे स्वस्य चाप्यग्रे प्राची प्रोक्ता तु देशिकैः।
प्राच्येव प्राची चोद्दिष्टा मुक्त्वा तु देवतार्चनम्॥ इति।

तन्त्रान्तरेऽपि—यत्रैव भानुस्तु वियत्युदेति प्राचीति तां वेदविदो वदन्ति।
तथा परा पूजकपूज्ययोश्च सदागमज्ञाः प्रवदन्ति तान्तु॥ इति।

अन्यत्रापि द्वारपूजावसरे—

देवस्य मुखमारभ्य दिशं प्राचीं प्रकल्पयेत्।
तदादिपरिवाराणामङ्गाद्यावरणस्थितिः॥ इति।

अत्र युक्तिरपि। देहे पीठदेवतान्यासावसरे मुखे अधर्म्मन्यास उक्तः। स चाग्रभागः।

सर्व्वतत्त्वात्मकं पद्ममभ्यर्च्य तदनन्तरम् ।
मन्त्री प्रकृतिपत्राणि विकारमयकेसरान् ॥ ६६

पञ्चाशद्बीजवर्णाढ्यां कर्णिकां पूजयेत्ततः ।
कलाभिः पूजयेत् सार्द्धं तस्यां सूर्य्येन्दुपावकान् ॥ ६७

महागणपतिपूजावसरे ग्रन्थकृदपि त्रिकोणस्याग्रे पूर्व्वादिचतुर्दिक्षु समर्चयेदित्युक्त्वा अग्रस्थबिल्वतरुञ्चाधः इत्युक्तवान् । तथा रामपूजायां द्वितीयावरणे "हनूमन्तं ससुग्रीवम्" इत्युक्त्वा पुनराह "वाचयन्तं हनूमन्तमग्रतो धृतपुस्तकम् ।" इति । अन्यच्च उत्तराभिमुखत्वेनापि पूजा विहिता । कल्पान्तरे च प्रतीच्यादिमुखत्वेन च । तत्र वाधर्म्मादिपूजनम् अङ्गादिपूजनं च कदाचित् क्रमान्तरेण स्यात् । अन्यदा क्रमेण स्यादित्यादि विरुद्धम् । तन्त्रान्तरे च—

होतुः पूर्व्वं पूर्व्वभागं प्रदिष्टं सव्यं भागं दक्षिणन्त्वागमज्ञैः ।
दद्यं विद्यादुत्तरं भागमग्रं प्रज्ञावद्भिः पश्चिमं भागमुक्तम् ॥ इति ।

नृसिंहकल्पे च—

अथावरणपूजायां पुरः प्राचीं प्रकल्पयेत् ।
तदादिपरिवाराणां प्रादक्षिण्येन पूजनम् ॥ इति ।

नारायणीयेऽपि—शक्तीरग्रादिपत्रेषु लक्ष्म्याद्या धृतचामराः । इति ।
अत एव पीठशक्त्यादिपूजने अग्रदलादीति व्याख्यास्यते । तेनोदङ्मुखपूजादावपि स्वाग्रभागस्य पूर्व्वत्वमाकल्प्य धर्म्मादिपूजनमङ्गादिपूजनमिति ज्ञेयम् । तेन यन्त्रादावपि दलेष्वक्षरलेखने अग्रदलात् प्रभृति लेखनीयमिति ज्ञेयम् । इयं दिक् चरार्चायाम् । अथाम्बुजं यजेदिति वक्ष्यमाणक्रमेण । अत्राम्बुजात् पूर्व्वमनन्ताय नमः इत्यनन्तं पूजयेदित्यथशब्देनोक्तम् ।

तदुक्तम्—हृद्यथ शेषमम्बुजम् । इति ।
शरीरे न्यासावसरे ग्रन्थकृदप्युक्तवान्-"अनन्तं हृदये पद्ममस्मिन् ।" इति ॥६५॥६६॥

कलाभिरिति । तत्र द्वादशकलात्मकसूर्य्यमण्डलाय षोडशकलात्मकचन्द्रमण्डलाय दशकलात्मकवह्निमण्डलाय इति केचन कलाभिः सार्द्धमित्यस्यार्थं व्याचक्षते । अन्ये त्वन्यथा वर्णयन्ति । द्वादशकलादित्वमनुक्तमपि लभ्यते । तेन सूर्य्यमण्डलं सम्पूज्य तत्र द्वादशकलाः ततः सोममण्डलं तत्षोडशकलाः ततः अग्निमण्डलं तद्दशकलाः पूजयेदिति । अयं साम्प्रदायिकः पन्थाः । तस्यामिति

प्रणवस्य त्रिभिर्वर्णैरथ सत्त्वादिकान् गुणान् ।
आत्मानमन्तरात्मानं परमात्मानमर्चयेत् ॥ ६८

ज्ञानात्मानञ्च विधिवत् पीठमन्त्रावसानकम् ।
पीठशक्तीः केसरेषु मध्ये च सवराभयाः ॥ ६९

कर्णिकायाम् । प्रणवस्य त्रिभिर्वर्णैरकारोकारमकारैः । कलाभिः सार्द्धं सूर्य्येन्दुपावकान् पूजयेदिति सम्बन्धः । तदुक्तम्—"सूर्य्येन्दुवह्नीन् प्रणवांशयुक्तान्" इति । एतेन तत्तन्मण्डलाधिष्ठातृदेवता ब्रह्मविष्णीशास्तत्तन्मण्डले पूजनीया इति सूचितम् ।

यदाहुः—सौरे बिम्बे चतुरास्यः किरीटी हंसे सौधं कलशं चाक्षमालाम् ।
ब्रह्मा बिभ्रद्वरदञ्चाभयाख्यं हस्तैर्ध्येयः सितवस्त्रश्चतुर्भिः ॥
सौम्ये बिम्बे गरुड़े मेघनीलश्चक्रं शङ्खं सगदाब्जं दधानः ।
हारी माली कटकी सत्किरीटी विष्णुः पीतं वसनं कौस्तुभञ्च ॥
अग्नेर्बिम्बे वृषभे चन्द्रमौलिः श्वेतो रुद्रो दशबाहुस्त्रिनेत्रः ।
टङ्कणाग्नित्रिशिखाह्युत्कपाल मुद्राक्षस्रग्वरदाभीतिपाणिः ॥ इति ।

अन्यत्रापि—ब्रह्मविष्णीश्वरास्त्वर्च्याः क्रमाद्वै मण्डलत्रये । इति ।

अथ सत्त्वादिकानिति । शुक्लरक्तकृष्णरूपान् । तदुक्तम्—

सितरक्तासिताः प्रोक्ता गुणाः पीठोपरि स्थिताः । इति ।

विधिवदित्यनेनैतदुक्तं भवति । एतदनन्तरं मायाकलाविद्यापरतत्त्वानि सम्पूजयेदिति ।

आत्मादि परतत्त्वान्तमिष्ट्वा शक्तीः प्रपूजयेत् । इत्युक्तेः ।

वैहायसीमन्त्रप्रकाशेऽपि—

सत्त्वं रजः शार्व्वरमंशकञ्च बिम्बानि चार्केन्दुहुताशनानाम् ।
सम्पूजयेदात्मचतुष्टयान्ते विद्यादिकं तत्त्वचतुष्टयञ्च ॥ इति ।

वायवीयसंहितायामपि—

त्रिमण्डलोपर्य्यात्मादितत्त्वत्रितयमासनम् । इति ।

पीठमन्त्रावसानकमित्यनेनाक्षिप्तानां पीठशक्तीनां पूजास्थानमाह पीठेति । केसरेषु पूजितपद्मकेसरेषु । तत्र अग्रदलाद्यष्टसु प्रादक्षिण्येन मध्ये च पीठशक्तिपूजां कृत्वा पीठमन्त्रपूजनमित्यर्थः ।

असत्येनाविशेषोक्तौ क्रमः सर्व्वत्र गृह्यते । इति परिभाषणात् ।

अत एव देहे पीठदेवतान्यासावसरे पीठशक्तिन्यास उक्तो मया । पीठशक्तयः

हेमादिरचितं कुम्भमस्त्राद्भिः क्षालितान्तरम् ।
चन्दनागुरुकर्पूरधूपितं शोभनाकृतिम् ॥ ७०
आवेष्टिताङ्गं नीरन्ध्रं तन्तुना त्रिगुणात्मना ।
अर्चितं गन्धपुष्पाद्यैः कूर्चाक्षतसमन्वितम् ॥ ७१

पीठमन्त्राश्च तत्तन्मन्त्रे वक्ष्यन्ते । सवराभया इति ध्यानम् । आसां वर्णा अप्युक्ता आचार्य्यैः—

श्वेता कृष्णा रक्ता पीता श्यामाऽनलोपमा शुक्ला ।
अञ्जनजपासमाने तेजोरूपाश्च शक्तयः प्रोक्ताः ॥ इति ।

मण्डूकादि एतदन्तं नित्यपूजायामपि समानम् ॥ ६७॥६८॥६९ ॥

एवं पूजिते पीठे कुम्भस्थापनमाह हेमादीति । आदिशब्देन राजतताम्रमृन्मयाः शक्त्यनुसारेण ज्ञेयाः । कुम्भं कलशम् । तदुक्तं महाकपिलपञ्चरात्रे—

सौवर्णं कलशं रम्यं रौप्यं ताम्रमथापि वा ।
निर्दोषं मृन्मयं वापि चन्दनेन विलेपितम् ॥ इति ।

अन्यत्रापि—सौवर्णं राजतं वापि मार्त्तिकं वा यथोदितम् ।
क्षालयेदस्त्रमन्त्रेण कुम्भं सम्यक् सुरेश्वरि ॥ इति ।

अन्यत्र कलशशब्दव्युत्पत्तिः प्रमाणञ्चोक्तम्—

कलां कलां गृहीत्वा वै देवानां विश्वकर्म्मणा ।
निर्म्मितोऽयं सुरैर्यस्मात् कलशस्तेन उच्यते ॥
पञ्चाशदङ्गुलव्यास उत्सेधः षोड़शाङ्गुलः ।
कलशानां प्रमाणन्तु मुखमष्टाङ्गुलं भवेत् ॥ इति ।

पद्मपादाचार्य्यैस्तु कलाः शेरते इति व्युतपत्तिः कृता । अस्त्राद्भिः अस्त्रमन्त्रजप्तोदकैः । त्रिगुणात्मना त्रिगुणेन सत्त्वादिगुणरूपेण च तन्तुना आवेष्टिताङ्गम् । तेन कण्ठे सूत्रवेष्टनं कुर्व्वन्ति । नीरन्ध्रमिति कुम्भविशेषणम् । तदुक्तं वायवीयसंहितायाम्—

सौवर्णं राजतं वापि ताम्रं मृन्मयमेव वा ।
गन्धपुष्पाक्षताकीर्णं कुशदूर्व्वाङ्कुरार्चितम् ।
सितसूत्रावृतं कण्ठे नववस्त्रयुगावृतम् ॥ इति ।

केचित्तु नीरन्ध्रं यथा स्यात्तथा तन्तुना आवेष्टिताङ्गमिति योजयन्ति । तन्मते सर्व्वोऽपि घटः तन्तुवेष्टितो भवति । तदाताङ्गशब्दवैयर्थ्यं स्यात् । अन्यत्र विशेषः—

नवरत्नोदरं मन्त्री स्थापयेत्तारमुच्चरन्।
ऐक्यं सङ्कल्प्य कुम्भस्य पीठस्य च विधानवित्॥ ७२
क्षीरद्रुमकषायेण पञ्चभङ्गभवेन वा।
तीर्थोदकैर्वा कर्पूरगन्धपुष्पसुवासितैः॥ ७३
आत्माभेदेन विधिवन्मातृकां प्रतिलोमतः।
जपन्मूलमनुं तद्वत् पूरयेद् देवताधिया। ७४
शङ्खे क्वाथाम्बुसम्पूर्णे गन्धाष्टकमभीष्टदम्।
विलोड्य पूजयेत्तस्मिन्नावाह्य सकलाः कलाः॥ ७५

कन्याकर्त्तितसूत्रेण त्रिगुणेन च कर्म्मणा।
गुणत्रयात्मकेनैव वेष्टयेदभितः समम्॥ इति।

आदिशब्देन धूपः॥ ७०॥ ७१॥

नवरत्नोदरमिति। नवरत्नानि षष्ठे वक्ष्यन्ते। एवम्भूतं कुम्भं तारमुच्चरन् स्थापयेदित्यन्वयः। अत्र तारशब्देन यथार्हं तत्तन्मन्त्रेषु पञ्चप्रणवानामपि ग्रहणमिति ज्ञेयम्। मन्त्रीत्यनेन सुलभमन्त्रोच्चारोऽप्युक्तः। विधानविदित्यनेन विनापि पञ्चाशदौषधिक्वाथैः तत्कुम्भ सान्निध्योपपादनक्षम इत्युक्तम्॥ ७२॥

क्षीरेति। क्षीरद्रुमकषायेण अश्वत्थोदुम्बरप्लक्षवटवल्कलकषायेण इत्यर्थः। आयुर्वेदोक्तरीत्या चतुर्थांशावशेषः कषायो ग्राह्यः। विधिवदिति सबिन्दुकम्। तद्वदिति विलोमेन। आत्माभेदेन देवताधिया पूरयेदिति सम्बन्धः। आत्मदेवताजलानामैक्यं भावयन्नित्यर्थः॥ ७३॥ ७४॥

शङ्ख इति स्थापितशङ्खादन्यस्मिन्। तत्र शङ्खस्थापनान्तं कर्म्म पूर्व्ववत् कार्य्यम्। क्वाथाम्बुनेति कलशपूरणावशिष्टेन सम्पूर्णे इति। समूलेन हृदयेन गन्धाष्टकं विलोड्य इति पिष्टगन्धाष्टकम्। तदुक्तम्—

अष्टमूर्त्त्यात्मकं पिष्टमष्टगन्धं विलोड्य च। इति।

अभीष्टदमित्यनेन गन्धद्वारा मित्यस्य जप उक्तः। पूजयेदिति शिरसा धेनुमुद्रां प्रदर्श्येति ज्ञेयम्। सकलाः चतुर्नवति। द्वादशात्मन इति सूर्य्यस्य। पञ्चादित्यनेनैतदुक्तम्। अकारजकलानन्तरं हंस इति। उकारजानन्तरं प्रतद्विष्णुरिति। मकारजानन्तरं त्र्यम्बकमिति। बिन्दुजानन्तरं तत्पदादिकम्। नादजानन्तरं विष्णुर्योनिमिति ऋचं पठेत्। पञ्चाशत् एकपञ्चाशत्कलाः तारपञ्चभेदोत्पन्नाः।

दश वक्त्रे: कलाः पूर्व्वं ब्राह्म्या चान्द्रशात्मनः ।
कलाः षोड़श सौमस्य पश्चात् पञ्चाशतं कलाः ॥ ७६

जपित्वा प्रतिलोमेन मूलमन्त्रञ्च मन्त्रवित् ।
समाहितेन मनसा ध्यायन्मन्त्रस्य देवताम् ॥ ७७

प्राणप्रतिष्ठां कुर्व्वीत तत्र तत्र विचक्षणः ।
कलात्मकं शङ्खसंस्थं द्रव्यं कुम्भे विनिक्षिपेत् । ७८

अत्राष्टत्रिंशत्कलाः तत एकपञ्चाशत्कलाः पश्चात् पञ्च गुप्तकलाश्च शङ्खजले पूजनीयाः । ताश्च इच्छाज्ञानाक्रियाचिदात्मानन्दात्मिकाः । एवञ्चाष्टत्रिंशत्कलाः पञ्चाशत्कला एकाधिकाः पञ्च गुप्तकलाश्चेति चतुर्नवतिदेवतात्मकत्वम् । यदाहुराचार्य्याः—

प्रथमं प्रकृतेर्हंसः प्रतद्विष्णुरनन्तरम् ।
त्रियम्बकस्तृतीयः स्याच्चतुर्थस्तत्पदादिकः ॥
विष्णुर्योनिमितीत्यादि पञ्चमः कल्पिता मनुः ।
चतुर्नवतिमन्त्रात्मदेवमा[ता]वाह्य पूज्यताम् ॥
अत्र याः पञ्च संप्रोक्ता ऋचस्तास्तस्य पञ्चभिः ।
कलाप्रभेदैश्च मिथो युज्यन्ते ताः पृथक् पृथक् ॥ इति ।

अन्यत्रापि—चतुर्नवति संख्याश्च समावाह्य कलाः क्रमात् । इति ।

समाहितेनेति । मन्त्रस्य देवतां समाहितेन मनसा ध्यायन् प्रतिलोमेन मूलमन्त्रं जपित्वा तामेवावाह्य पूजयेदिति सम्बन्धः । इदं चकारान्मन्त्रवित्पदाच्च लभ्यते ।

यदाहुः—मूलमन्त्रं समुच्चार्य्य देवमावाह्य मन्त्रवित् ।
अभ्यर्च्य शङ्खसलिलं दिव्यकुम्भे विनिक्षिपेत् ॥ इति ।

समाहितेन मनसेति प्रसङ्गसङ्गत्याऽत्रोक्तं परं सर्व्वत्र ध्याने इदं विशेषणं ज्ञेयम् । अन्यथा ध्यानस्यैव कर्त्तुमशक्यत्वात् ॥७५॥७६॥७७॥

प्राणेति । प्रतिष्ठाशब्दव्युत्पत्तिरुक्ता महाकपिलपञ्चरात्रे—

प्रतिष्ठाशब्दसंसिद्धिः प्रतिपूर्व्वात्तु तिष्ठतेः ।
बह्वर्थत्वान्निपातानां संस्कारादौ प्रतेः स्थितिः ॥
अर्थस्तदयमेतस्य गीयते शाब्दिकैर्जनैः ।
विशेषसन्निधिर्या तु क्रियते व्यापकस्य हि ॥
सम्मूर्त्तौ भावना मन्त्रैः प्रतिष्ठा साऽभिधीयते । इति ।

गन्धाष्टकं तत् विविधं शक्तिविष्णुशिवात्मकम् ।
चन्दनागुरुकर्पूरचोरकुङ्कुमरोचना: ॥ ७८

तत्र प्रयोग: । धूम्रार्चिरागता भवेत्यावाहन्याद्यष्टमुद्रा: प्रदर्श्य यं धूम्रार्चिषे नम इति सम्पूज्य प्राणप्रतिष्ठामन्त्रे अमुष्यपदस्थाने षष्ठ्यन्तं धूम्रार्चि:पदं प्रक्षिप्य प्राणप्रतिष्ठां कूर्य्यात् । एवं सर्व्वास्वपि कलासु । अथवा दशानामप्यग्निकलानाम् एकदैवावाहनादि कृत्वा प्रत्येकं पूजां कृत्वा प्राणप्रतिष्ठामन्त्रे अमुष्यपदस्थाने सर्व्वासां षष्ठ्यन्तं नामोच्चार्य्य प्राणप्रतिष्ठां कुर्य्यात् । कलाध्यानं द्वितीय-पटलोक्तमनुसन्धेयम् । तत्र तत्रेत्यस्यायमर्थ: । प्रथमं दशवह्निकलानां ततो द्वादशसूर्य्यकलानां तत: षोड़शसोमकलानां ततो दशाकारजानां तद्दचस्ततो दशोकारजानां तद्दचस्ततो दश मकारजानां तद्दचस्तत: पञ्चानां बिन्दुजानां तद्दचस्तत: षोड़शनादकलानां तद्दचस्तत: पञ्चगुणकलानाम् । विचक्षण इत्यनेन सर्व्वत्र त्रि: प्राणप्रतिष्ठामन्त्रं जपेदित्युक्तम् । अन्ये तु प्रतिलोमेनेति सर्व्वत्र योजयन्ति । तत्तु आभिचारिकाभिषेकविषयम् । तदा प्रथमं नादकलास्ताद्दक् ततो बिन्दुकलास्ताद्दक् ततो मकारकलास्ताद्दक् तत उकारकलास्ताद्दक् ततोऽकारकलास्ताद्दक् तत: सोमसूर्य्याग्नीनाम् । यदाहु:—

स्थण्डिलाधारगं शङ्खं पूरयित्वा तदम्बुना ।
अष्टमूर्त्यात्मकं पिष्टमष्टगन्धं विलोड्य च ॥
कलानादक्रमेणैव स्वस्वनामसमायुता: ।
हृल्लेखाङ्गानि विन्यस्य प्रत्येकं ता: प्रयोजयेत् ॥
अत्र नादकलान्ते च विष्णुर्योन्यादिकां कलाम् ।
सर्व्वासां व्यापिनीं व्याप्तां सम्यगावाह्य पूजयेत् ॥
स्पृष्ट्वा सुस्थापनमनुं दक्षिणेनैव पाणिना ।
युक्तनादकलानाम्नेत्यादिना योजयेत् त्रिश: ॥
बिन्द्वादितारभेदानां कला: सौम्या दिनेशितु: ।
अग्नेरपि समावाह्य तथैवाभियजेत् क्रमात् ॥ इति ।

विनिक्षिपेदिति मूलमन्त्रेणेति शेष: । तदुक्तम्—

पुनस्तोयं कलात्मकम् ।
उच्चारयेन्मूलमन्त्रं कलशे सन्निधापयेत् ॥ इति ।

अन्यत्रापि—कलशे तत् क्षिपेन्मूलमन्त्रमुच्चार्य्य मन्त्रवित् । इति ॥ ७८ ॥

गन्धाष्टकं विलोड्य इति यदुक्तम् तदाह गन्धाष्टकमिति । शक्तिविष्णुशिवात्म-

जटामांसीकपियुताः शक्तेर्गन्धाष्टकं विदुः ।
चन्दनागुरुह्रीवेरकुष्ठकुङ्कुमसेव्यकाः ॥ ८०

जटामांसीमुरमिति विष्णोर्गन्धाष्टकं विदुः ।
चन्दनागुरुकर्पूरतमालजलकुङ्कुमम् ।
कुशीतकुष्ठसंयुक्तं शैवं गन्धाष्टकं स्मृतम् ॥ ८१

पाशादित्र्यक्षरात्मान्ते स्यादमुष्यपदन्ततः ।
क्रमात् प्राणा इह प्राणास्तथा जीव इह स्थितः ॥ ८२

कमिति तदात्मकतोक्त्या अत्यन्तप्रियत्वं सूचितम् । चोर इति भटिऊर इति कान्यकुब्जभाषायाम् । रोचना गोरोचना । कपि गन्धिवनेति प्रसिद्धम् । ह्रीवेरो वालकम् । कुष्ठं कूठ इति प्रसिद्धम् । सेव्यकमुशीरम् । जटामांसीमुरमिति समाहारद्वन्द्वैकत्वेन नपुंसकत्वम् । मुरा स्वनाम्ना प्रसिद्धा । तमालं पत्रजम् । जलं वालकम् । कुशीतं रक्तचन्दनम् । एतानि समभागानि ग्राह्याणि । गणपतिसंहितायां गणेशगन्धाष्टकमप्युक्तम्—

> स्वरूपं चन्दनं चोरं रोचनागुरुमेव च ।
> मदं मृगद्वयोद्भूतं कस्तूरीचन्द्रसंयुतम् ।
> अष्टगन्धं विनिर्दिष्टं गणेशस्य महाविभोः ॥ इति ॥७९॥८०॥८१॥

प्राणप्रतिष्ठां कुर्व्वीतेत्युक्तमतस्तन्मन्त्रमाह पाशादीति । पाशादित्र्यक्षरो नवमे वक्ष्यते । आत्मा जीवमन्त्रः । अत्र पाशादित्र्यक्षर आदौ आत्ममन्त्रः अन्ते इत्यनेन यं रं लं वं शं षं सं ह्रौं इत्येतान्यष्टबीजानि त्रयोविंशे वक्ष्यमाणानि संगृहीतानि इति सम्प्रदायविदः । अत्र पाशाद्यात्मान्तानां प्रत्यमुष्यपदम् आवृत्तिरपि ज्ञेया । त्रयोविंशे तथा वक्ष्यमाणत्वात् । अमुष्यपदस्यायमर्थः । साध्यदेवतायन्त्रादेः षष्ठ्यन्तं नामपदं प्रयोक्तव्यमिति । तथा च "इममुमुष्य पुत्रममुष्याः पुत्रमस्यै विश एष वः कुरवो राजा" इत्यस्याः श्रुतेः प्रयोगकथने कल्प[श्रौत]सूत्रे कात्यायनः "असावित्यपनोदे" इति । तद्भाष्यञ्च अपनोदः अदःपदमपनोद्य नाम प्रयोक्तव्यमित्यर्थं इति । नारायणीयेऽपि—

> अमुकपदं यद्रूपं यत्र मन्त्रेषु दृश्यते ।
> साध्याभिधानं तद्रूपं तत्र स्थाने नियोजयेत् ॥ इति ।

गट्टीकायामपेक्षितार्थद्योतनिकायामेवमुक्तम् । एतच्च पुरुषोत्तममन्त्रव्यतिरिक्तस्थानेऽवगन्तव्यम् । तत्रामुकशब्दे दुरितपदस्यालक्ष्मीपदस्य वा प्रयोगादिति ।

अमुष्य सर्व्वेन्द्रियाणि भूयोऽमुष्यपदं भवेत् ।
वाङ्मनोनयनश्रोत्रघ्राणप्राणपदान्यथ ॥ ८३
पश्चादिहागत्य सुखं चिरं तिष्ठन्तु ठद्वयम् ।
अयं प्राणमनुः प्रोक्तः सर्व्वजीवप्रदायकः ॥ ८४

तथेति अमुष्यपदं वदेदित्यर्थः । वाङ्मनोनयनमिति नयनपदपर्य्यायस्य चक्षुःपदस्योपलक्षकम् । केवलं छन्दोनुरोधात्तथोपदेशः । तथा च त्रयोविंशे असावेव "सर्व्वेन्द्रियाण्यमुष्यान्ते वाङ्मनश्चक्षुरन्ततः" इति । मन्त्रविदामप्युपदेशे चक्षुःपदमेवोपदिष्टमुपलभ्यते सम्प्रदायविदाम् । तथा चाचार्य्यवचनं दीक्षापटले—

तद्वद्वाङ्मनसी उदीर्य्य तदनुप्राणा इहायायान्त्विति ।

तट्टीकाकाराः पद्मपदाचार्य्या व्याख्यातवन्तः "वाङ्मनसो ग्रहणं चक्षुःश्रोत्रघ्राणप्राणानामुपलक्षणार्थमिति" । तथा प्राणप्रतिष्ठापटले आचार्य्याः—

तद्वद्वाङ्मनसं दृशं श्रुतिमथो घ्राणञ्च सप्राणकम् । इति ।

अत्रापि टीकाकारैर्व्याख्यातम् "दृक्पदेन चक्षुःपदं गृह्यते" इति । एवञ्चेन्न स्यात् क्वचिन्नयनपदं क्वचिच्चक्षुःपदं क्वचिद्दृक्पदं तद्वत् क्वचिल्लोचनपदमपि स्यात् । तच्चायुक्तम् । नहि पर्य्यायेणोच्चारितो मन्त्रः स मन्त्रो भवति अन्यथा मन्त्रोद्धारश्लोका एव मन्त्रा भवेयुः । तस्मान्नयनपदं चक्षुःपदोपलक्षकमिति स्थितम् । घ्राणप्राणपदानीति । अत्र मन्त्रे प्राणा इति बहुवचनान्तता ज्ञेया । वागादीनां बहूनां पदानां द्वन्द्वसमासात् । त्रयोविंशे वक्ष्यति "वाचं श्रोत्रघ्राणपदे प्राणाः" इति । ठद्वयं स्वाहा ।

नन्वत्र मन्त्रे यदमुष्यस्थाने साध्य देवतायन्त्रादेर्नामपदप्रयोगः तस्य कथं मन्त्रत्वमिति चेत् । मीमांसाधिकरणसिद्धान्तसिद्धमिति ब्रूमः । तथाहि द्वितीयेऽध्याये भावार्थचरणे "अनाम्नातेष्वमन्त्रत्वमाम्नातेषु हि विभागः स्यात्" इत्यत्राधिकरणे ऊहप्रवरनामधेयानां मन्त्रत्वममन्त्रत्वं वेति संशय्य तेषाममन्त्रत्वं सिद्धान्तितम् । तत्प्रसङ्गेनेदमपि विचारितं यदूहप्रवरनामधेयानां प्रक्षेपे सर्व्वस्यैवामन्त्रत्वम् उत प्रक्षिप्तस्यैवेति । तत्र प्रक्षिप्तस्यैवामन्त्रत्वं सिद्धान्तितम् । तत्प्रसङ्गानुप्रसङ्गेनेदमपि चिन्तितम् । यत्र मन्त्रे "इममसुष्य पुत्रममुष्याः पुत्रमस्यै विश एष वो राजा" इत्यादौ यत् सर्व्वनामस्थाने राजादिशब्दप्रयोगः तस्यामन्त्रत्वमुत मन्त्रत्वमिति । तत्राम्नातस्य सर्व्वनाम्नो राजादिपदप्रयोगे प्रामाण्यसमर्पकत्वमात्रमिति । ऊहादिवदमन्त्रत्वमिति पूर्व्वः पक्षः । सिद्धान्तस्तु ।

पश्चादश्वत्थपनसचूतकोमलपल्लवैः।
इन्द्रवल्लीसमायुक्तैः सुरद्रुमधिया गुरुः।
कुम्भवक्त्रे पिधायाऽस्मिंश्चषकं सफलीकृतम्॥ ८५
संस्थापयेत् फलधिया विधिवत् कल्पशाखिनाम्।
ततः कुम्भं निर्मलेन क्षौमयुग्मेन वेष्टयेत्॥ ८६
मूलेन मूर्त्तिमिष्ट्वाऽस्मिंस्तस्यां कल्पशाखिनाम्।
आवाह्य पूजयेत्तस्यां लक्ष्मीं मन्त्रस्य देवताम्॥ ८७

भवेदेवं यथाम्नातस्य सर्व्वनाम्नो राजादिपदप्रयोगे प्रासाङ्गसमर्पकत्वं स्यात्। किन्तु सर्व्वनाम्नां तत्स्थाने शब्दान्तरसमर्पकत्वमेव। तथाहि। ऊहे तु "अग्नये त्वाजुष्टं निर्व्वपामि" इति प्रकृतौ श्रुतौ च मन्त्रः। विकृतौ तु सूर्य्यदेवताके चरौ न्यायात् सूर्य्यायेति पदमूह्यते इति। भवतु तस्यामन्त्रत्वम्। एवं प्रवरशब्देनाम्नितदेवलशाण्डिल्यप्रवराभिधायिपदकीर्त्तनम् नामधेयशब्देन च यजमानाभिधायि विष्णुशर्म्मादि नामकीर्त्तनमभिमतम्। तेषाञ्च वेदे अनाम्नानात् "प्रवरनामधेयानि कीर्त्तयेत्" इति वाक्येन च मन्त्रप्रयोज्य विशेषरूपेणाम्नानाभावान्न मन्त्रत्वम्। सर्व्वनाम्नामाम्नानन्तु राजादिविशेषनाम्नाम् आनन्त्यात् आम्नातुमशक्यत्वात् राजादिविशेषार्थप्रतिपादनार्थम्। नचास्य स्वतस्तत्प्रतिपादनसामर्थ्यमस्तीति। स्वयं प्रयोगानर्हं सत् विशेषशब्दानेव प्रयोगार्हानुपलक्षयति। यथा तस्यापत्यमित्यादौ। अतोविवक्षितस्वरूपराजाद्यर्थविशेषविषयानेव शब्दान् मन्त्रवाक्यनिवेशिनो दर्शयति। इत्येतदर्थमेव सर्व्वनामपदं दृष्टार्थेनाऽध्ययनविधिनाऽध्यापितमिति निश्चीयते। तस्माद्राजादिनाम्नामप्याम्नातप्रायत्वान्मन्त्रत्वमेवेति ॥८२॥८३॥८४॥

इन्द्रवल्लीति इन्द्रवारुणी लताविशेषः। चषकं कलशजातीयं शरावादि। विधिवदित्यनेन मूलमन्त्रोच्चारणमुक्तम्। क्षौममित्यतसीमयम्। तदभावे पट्टवस्त्रादि। अन्यत्र एकवस्त्रवेष्टनमप्युक्तम्।

अतिसूक्ष्मतरेणैव विशुद्धेन नवेन च।
मायातत्त्वस्वरूपेण वेष्टयेद्वाससा घटम्॥ इति ॥ ८५ ॥ ८६ ॥

मन्त्रस्य देवतामित्येकमन्त्रदीक्षायाम्।

पञ्चायतनदीक्षापक्षे पञ्चकलशान् संस्थाप्य तत्तत्कलशे तत्तद्देवतामावाहयेदिति मन्त्रीत्यनेनोक्तम्।

तदुक्तमाचार्य्यैः—प्रोक्तेनैवं कलशविधिनैकेन वानेकंकुम्भैः । इति ।

पञ्चायतनदीक्षायां देवतास्थापनक्रम उक्तो ज्ञानमालायाम्—

यदा तु शङ्करं मध्ये ऐशान्यां श्रीपतिं यजेत् ।
आग्नेय्याञ्च तथा हंसं नैर्ऋत्यां पार्व्वतीसुतम् ॥
वायव्याञ्च सदा पूज्या भवानी भक्तवत्सला ।
यदा तु मध्ये गोविन्दमैशान्यां शङ्करं यजेत् ॥
आग्नेय्यां गणनाथञ्च नैर्ऋत्यां तपनन्तथा ।
वायव्यामम्बिकाञ्चैव यजेन्मन्त्री समाहितः ॥
सहस्रांशुं यदा मध्ये ऐशान्यां पार्व्वतीपतिम् ।
आग्नेय्यामेकदन्तञ्च नैर्ऋत्यामच्युतं यजेत् ॥
वायव्यां पूजयेद् देवीं भोगमोक्षैकभूमिकाम् ।
भवानीन्तु यदा मध्ये ऐशान्यां माधवं यजेत् ॥
आग्नेय्यां पार्व्वतीनाथं नैर्ऋत्यां गणनायकम् ।
प्रद्योतनन्तु वायव्यामाचार्य्यस्तु प्रपूजयेत् ॥
हेरम्बन्तु यदा मध्ये ऐशान्यामच्युतं यजेत् ।
आग्नेय्यां पञ्चवक्त्रन्तु नैर्ऋत्यां जगदम्बिकाम् ॥
वायव्यां द्युमणिञ्चैव यजेन्मन्त्री ह्यतन्द्रितः ।
स्वस्थानवर्जिता देवाः शोकदुःखभयप्रदाः ।
तन्मण्डलस्थितो राजा साधकश्च विनश्यति ॥ इति ।

अन्यत्रापि—शम्भौ मध्यगते हरीनहरभूदेव्यो हरौ शङ्करे-
भास्येनागसुता रवौ हरगणेशाजाम्बिकाः स्थापिताः ।
देव्यां विष्णुहरैकदन्तरवयो लम्बोदरेऽजेश्वरा-
र्य्येनाः शङ्करभागतोऽतिशुभदा व्यस्तास्तु ते हानिदाः ॥ इति ।

पठिता अपि—"शं ना रग दे मध्यावा शं गरभेशत: सूशं ग नादे दे ना शं गर ग नाशं भसू विदिक् पूज्याः" इति ।

अन्यत्राग्नेयादिक्रमेण स्थापनमुक्तम् ।

सूर्य्यैकदन्ताच्युतशक्तिरुद्रा विघ्नेश्वरेशाद्रिसुतार्ककृष्णाः ।
श्रीनाथविघ्नेशभगाम्बिकेशा चण्डीश हेरम्बपतङ्गकृष्णाः ॥
श्रीशम्भुसूर्य्याखुरथाम्बकृष्णाः प्रदक्षिणं मध्यविदिक्षु पूज्याः ।
स्वस्थानगाः सर्व्वमनोरथानेव अर्थं विनिघ्नन्ति परत्र संस्थाः ॥ इति ।

अन्यत्रापि—मध्येऽभ्यर्च्य हरिं गणेनगजाशक्नी गणं मध्यतः

शम्भ्वार्य्यारविविष्णवो रविमथो विघ्नाजशक्तीश्वराः।

मध्ये शक्तिमथेशविघ्नरवयो विष्णुश्च मध्ये हरं

सूर्य्येभास्यशिवाच्युता हि विहिता आग्नेयकोणादिमाः॥ इति।

अत्रोभयत्र स्थापनक्रमे फलतः साम्यमेव। पूजा तु गणपतिमारभ्य। यत्र गणपतेर्मुख्यत्वं तत्र सूर्य्यमारभ्येति ज्ञेयम्। यदाहुः—

मुख्ये पुष्पाञ्जलिं दत्त्वा गणेशाद्यर्चनं भवेत्।

गणेश एव मुख्यश्चेत् तत्र सूर्य्यक्रमाद्भवेत्॥ इति।

एतद्व्याख्यानमुभयथा कुर्व्वन्ति। पुष्पाञ्जलिमिति मुख्ये प्रथमतः पुष्पाञ्जलिमात्रं कृत्वा पश्चाद् गणेशाद्यर्चनं कृत्वा मुख्यपूजेति। अपरे तु। पुष्पाञ्जलिशब्देन पूजासमाप्तौ यः पुष्पाञ्जलिः स संगृहीतः। तेन मुख्यदेवपूजानन्तरं गणेशाद्यर्चनमिति। एतच्च स्वस्वगुरुसम्प्रदायानुसारेण ज्ञेयम्। अयमेव देवतास्थापनक्रमो नित्यपूजायामपि समानः। तत्र नित्यपूजा शालग्रामे मणौ यन्त्रे वा पाषाणादिप्रतिमायां वा कार्य्या। तदुक्तं ज्ञानमालायाम्—

गिरिजारतसौख्याय जाता विघ्नपराः सुराः।

तच्छ्रुत्वा चरितं देव्या शापो दत्तोऽतिदारुणः॥

पार्व्वतीशापसंयुक्ता देवा अश्मत्वमागताः।

विष्णुना शङ्करेणापि तथाऽन्यैः सुरसत्तमैः॥

संस्तुता वरदा जाता पाषाणत्वेऽपि भो सुराः।

स्वस्थाने पूजयिष्यन्ति पुरुषार्थचतुष्टयम्॥

दातुं समर्था मद्वाक्यादेष एव वरोऽर्पितः।

तस्मात् पूजा विधातव्या पाषाणप्रतिमासु च॥ इति।

हयशीर्षपञ्चरात्रे—मृन्मयी दारुघटिता लोहजा रत्नजा तथा।

शैलजा गन्धजा चैव कौसुमी सप्तधा स्मृता॥

कौसुमी गन्धजा चैव मृन्मयी प्रतिमा हिता।

तत्कालपूजिताश्चैताः सर्व्वकामफलप्रदाः॥ इति।

महाकपिलपञ्चरात्रेऽपि—

शैलजा लोहजा वापि रत्नजा वाथ दारुजा।

मृन्मयी चेति पञ्चैताः प्रतिमाः परिकीर्त्तिताः॥

सर्व्वेषामेव देवानां महानीला यशःप्रदा।

दारुजा कामदा प्रोक्ता सौवर्णी भुक्तिमुक्तिदा ॥
राजती स्वर्गफलदा ताम्री त्वायुर्विवर्धिनी ।
कांस्या बह्वापदं हन्ति रैतिकी शत्रुनाशिनी ॥
सर्व्वभोगप्रदा शैली स्फाटिकी दौस्थिकारिका ।
महाभोगप्रदा ख्याता मृन्मयी खलु शोभना ॥
मानाङ्गुलप्रमाणेन दशपञ्चाङ्गुलात्मिका ।
गृहे तु प्रतिमा पूज्या नाधिका हि प्रशस्यते ॥ इति ।

अन्यत्रापि—अङ्गुष्ठपर्व्वादारभ्य वितस्तिर्यावदेव तु ।
गृहे तु प्रतिमा कार्य्या नाधिका शस्यते बुधैः ॥ इति ।

यत्तु—सौम्या तु हस्तमात्रा वसुदा हस्तद्वयोच्छ्रिता प्रतिमा ।
क्षेमसुभिक्षाय भवेत् त्रिचतुर्हस्तप्रमाणोच्चा ॥ इति ।

तत् स्थापितप्रतिमाविषयं ज्ञेयम् । मृण्मय्यां तत्रैव विशेष उक्तः—
मृण्मयीं प्रतिमां वक्ष्ये यथावत्तां निबोध मे ।
पक्वापक्वा द्विधा प्रोक्ता मृण्मयी प्रतिमा क्रमात् ॥
सर्व्वे लोका न शंसन्ति प्रतिमां दग्धमृन्मयीम् ।
अपक्वा प्रतिमा शस्ता सैव कार्य्या विचक्षणैः ॥
तुषया नैव कर्त्तव्या नाश्मचूर्णैः कदाचन ।
मृदैव मृन्मयीं कुर्य्याद् यथावदनुपूर्व्वशः ॥
ब्राह्मणस्य सिता मृद्वै क्षत्रियस्यारुणा स्मृता ।
विशां पीता भवेन्मृद्वै कृष्णा शूद्रस्य कीर्त्तिता ॥ इति ।

अन्यच्च विशेषः—नृपभयमत्यङ्गायां हीनाङ्गायामकल्यता कर्त्तुः ।
शातोदर्य्यां क्षुद्भयमर्थविनाशः कृशाङ्गायाम् ॥
मरणन्तु सक्षतायां शस्त्रनिपातेन निर्दिशेत् कर्त्तुः ।
वामे विनता पत्नीं दक्षिणविनता हिनस्त्यायुः ॥
अन्धत्वमूर्द्धदृष्टी करोति चिन्तामधोमुखी दृष्टिः ।
सर्व्वप्रतिमास्वेवं शुभाशुभं भास्करोक्तमवगच्छेत् ॥ इति ।

अन्यत्रापि—नाधिकाङ्गी न हीनाङ्गी कर्त्तव्या देवता क्वचित् ।
अधिका शिल्पिनं हन्यात् कृशा चैवार्थनाशिनी ॥
कृशोदरी तु दुर्भिक्षं निर्मांसा धननाशिनी ।
वक्रनासा तु दुःखाय सङ्क्षिप्ताङ्गी भयङ्करी ॥

चिपिटा दुःखशोकाय प्रवक्रा नेत्रनाशिनी ।
दुःखदा हीनवक्त्रा तु पाणिपादकृशा तथा ॥
हीनाङ्गा हीनजङ्घा च भ्रमोन्मादकरी नृप ।
शुष्कवक्त्रा च राजानं कटिहीना च मारयेत् ॥
पाणिपादविहीनायां जायते मरको महान् ।
जङ्घाहीना च या मूर्त्तिः शत्रुकल्याणकारिणी ॥
पुत्रमित्रविनाशाय हीना वक्षःस्थलेन या ।
सम्पूर्णावयवा या तु आयुर्लक्ष्मीप्रदा सदा ॥
एवं लक्षणमासाद्य कर्त्तव्या मूर्त्तिरुत्तमा ॥ इति ।

अन्यत्र विशेषः—

खण्डिते स्फुटिते भ्रष्टे दग्धे मानविवर्जिते ।
यागहीनेऽथवोच्छिन्ने पतिते दुष्टभूमिषु ॥
अन्यमन्त्रार्चिते चैव पतितस्पर्शदूषिते ।
दशस्वेतेषु नो चक्रुः सन्निधानं दिवौकसः ॥
इति सर्व्वगतो विष्णुः परिभाषां चकार ह ॥ इति ।

अन्यत्र—खण्डितां स्फुटितां जीर्णामवलीढाञ्च वह्निना ।
प्रतिमां वर्जयेद् यत्नाद् भग्नां स्वाङ्गलक्षणाच्युताम् ॥
निक्षिपेद्दारुजामग्नौ तथाऽन्यामप्सु निक्षिपेत् ॥ इति ।

तथा—एकाहपूजाविहतौ कुर्य्याद् द्विगुणमर्चनम् ।
त्रिरात्रे तु महापूजां संप्रोक्षणमतःपरम् ॥
मासादूर्द्ध्वमनेकाहं पूजा यदि विहन्यते ।
प्रतिष्ठेत्यपरे केचित् केचित् संप्रोक्षणक्रमः ॥

संप्रोक्षणलक्षणं यथा तत्रैव—

संप्रोक्षणन्तु देवस्य देवशुद्धाख्य पूर्व्ववत् ।
पञ्च पञ्च क्रमेणैव स्नापयित्वा मृदम्भसा ॥
गवां रसैश्च संस्नाप्य दर्भतोयैर्विशोध्य च ।
प्रोक्षयेत् प्रोक्षणीतोयैर्मूलेनाष्टोत्तरं शतम् ॥
सपुष्पं सकुशं पाणिं न्यस्य देवस्य मस्तके ।
पञ्चवारं जपेन्मूलमष्टोत्तरशतोत्तरम् ॥
ततो मूलेन मूर्द्धादि पीठान्तं संस्पृशेदपि ।

तत्त्वन्यासं लिपिन्यासं मन्त्रन्यासञ्च विन्यसेत् ॥
प्राणप्रतिष्ठामन्त्रेण प्रतिष्ठापनमाचरेत् ।
पूजाञ्च महतीं कुर्य्यात् स्वतन्त्रोक्तां यथाविधि ॥
यागहीनादिषु प्रायः संप्रोक्षणविधिः स्मृतः ॥ इति ।

अन्यत्रापि—शालग्रामे मणौ यन्त्रे मण्डले प्रतिमासु वा ।
नित्यपूजा हरेः कार्य्या न तु केवलभूतले ॥ इति ।

रामपूर्व्वतापनीयेऽपि—

सोभयस्याऽस्य देवस्य विग्रहो यन्त्रकल्पना ।
विना यन्त्रेण चेत् पूजा देवता न प्रसीदति ॥ इति ।

संहितायामपि—

यन्त्रं मन्त्रमयं प्राहुर्देवता मन्त्ररूपिणी ।
यन्त्रेणाऽपूजितो देवः सहसा न प्रसीदति ॥

तथा—सर्व्वेषामपि मन्त्राणां यन्त्रे पूजा प्रशस्यते । इति ।

ईशानशिवेनाप्युक्तम्—

शक्तिं निजैक्येन तथैव चक्रे चित्रे पटे वा यजनं न भूमौ ।
मोहादसौ स्थण्डिलगां यजेच्चेद् भ्रश्येत् त्रिवर्गादिति मन्त्रसिद्धाः ॥ इति ।

शिवपूजा तु शिवमूर्त्तौ शिवलिङ्गे स्थिरे चले वा कार्य्या । तत्र चले पाषाणादिलिङ्गे यत् पञ्चसूत्रादिलक्षणमुक्तं तदवश्यं द्रष्टव्यम् । रत्नलिङ्गादौ तु तल्लक्षणाभावेऽपि न दोषः । तदुक्तं हयशीर्षपञ्चरात्रे—

न कुर्य्याल्लक्षणोद्धारं रत्नजानां चलात्मनाम् ।
सु[स्व]प्रभा लक्षणन्त्वेषां स्वर्णजानामपि द्विज ॥
तस्मान्न लक्षणोद्धारं कुर्य्यात् पाषाणलिङ्गवत् ।
अचलानां तैजसानां क्वचिदिष्येत लक्षणम् ॥
लक्षणं कल्पनीयन्तु स्थाप्यलिङ्गे यथाविधि ।
चललिङ्गे कुशा[ऽङ्गुला]ग्रेण लक्षणं कल्पयेद् गुरुः ॥
मनसा चिन्तयेद्वापि लक्षणं लिङ्गसंस्थितम् ॥ इति ।

सोमशम्भुनाऽपि—

रत्नजे लक्षणोद्धारो न लौहे न सरिद्भवे ।
लिङ्गेषु च न लौहेषु न दृष्टं क्वचिदागमे ॥
स्वरूपं लक्षणं तेषां प्रभा रत्नेषु निर्मला । इति ।

मूलमन्त्रं समुच्चार्य्य सुषुम्णावर्त्मना सुधीः ।
आनीय तेजः स्वस्थानान्नासिकारन्ध्रनिर्गतम् ॥ ८८
करस्थमातृकाम्भोजे चैतन्यं पुष्पसञ्चये ।
संयोज्य ब्रह्मरन्ध्रेण मूर्त्तावावाहयेत् सुधीः ॥ ८९

अन्यत्र तु विशेषः—

गृहे लिङ्गद्वयं नार्च्यं गणेशद्वयमेव च ।
शक्तित्रयं तथा शङ्खं मत्स्यादिदशकाङ्कितम् ॥
द्वौ शङ्खौ नार्चयेच्चैव शालग्रामशिलाद्वयम् ।
द्वे चक्रे द्वारकायास्तु तथा सूर्य्यद्वयं बुधः ॥
एतेषामर्च्चनान्नित्यमुद्वेगं प्राप्नुयाद् गृही । इति ॥ ८७ ॥

आवाह्य पूजयेदित्युक्तम् । तत्रावाहनप्रकारमाह मूलेति । स्वस्थानाद् हृदयकमलात् । अन्ये सूर्य्यमण्डलादित्याहुः । तदुक्तं वैहायसीमन्त्रकोषे—

अथार्कतो वा हृदयारविन्दादावाहयेन्नन्दसुतं सुवेशम् । इति ।

अन्यत्रापि—आवाहयेन्महादेवीं हृदयाम्बुजगह्वरात् ।
सूर्य्यमण्डलतो वापि स्वीयाद्वा द्वादशान्ततः ॥ इति ।

ब्रह्मरन्ध्रेणेति ब्रह्मरन्ध्रद्वारा । करस्थमातृकाम्भोजे पुष्पसञ्चये इति व्यधिकरणसप्तम्यौ । सुधीः मूलमन्त्रमुच्चार्य्य स्वस्थानात्तेजः सुषुम्णावर्त्मना आनीय ब्रह्मरन्ध्रद्वारा नासिकारन्ध्रनिर्गतं तच्चैतन्यं करस्थमातृकाम्भोजे पुष्पसञ्चये संयोज्य मूर्त्तावावाहयेदिति सम्बन्धः । तदुक्तम्—

देवं सुषुम्णामार्गेण आनीय ब्रह्मरन्ध्रकम् ।
वामनासापुटे ध्यात्वा निर्यान्तं स्वाञ्जलिस्थितम् ।
पुष्पमारोप्य तत् पुष्पं प्रतिमादौ निधापयेत् ॥ इति ।

अत्रावाहनमाह्वानम् । तदावाहिन्या । तच्च मूलमन्त्रान्ते आवाहितो भव नमः इति प्रकारेण आगमोक्तश्लोकान्ते वा । यद्वा मूलमन्त्रान्ते आगमश्लोकमुच्चार्य्येति सुधीरित्यनेनोक्तम् । अयमेव मुख्यः प्रकारः । संहितायामपि धूपमन्त्रमुक्त्वा—

एवमित्यन्तु बीजान्ते धूपमन्त्र उदाहृतः । इत्यादिनोक्तम् ।

एवमग्रेऽपि स्थापनादिषूह्यम् । श्लोकस्तु—

आत्मसंस्थमजं शुद्धं त्वामहं परमेश्वर ।
अरण्यामिव हव्याशं मूर्त्तावावाहयाम्यहम् ॥

संस्थापनं सन्निधानं सन्निरोधमनन्तरम् ।
सकलीकरणं पश्चाद् विदध्याद्वगुण्ठनम् ॥ ९०
अमृतीकरणं कृत्वा कुर्व्वीत परमीकृतिम् ।
क्रमादेतानि कुर्व्वीत स्वमुद्राभिः समाहितः ॥ ९१

इदमावाहनादि शालग्रामादौ न कार्य्यम् । यदाहुः—

शालग्रामे स्थावरे वाऽऽवाहनं न विसर्जनम् ।
शालग्रामशिलादौ यन्नित्यं सन्निहितो हरिः ॥ इति ।

अन्यत्रापि—उद्वासावाहने न स्तः स्थिरायामुद्धवार्चने ।
अस्थिरायां विकल्पः स्यात् स्थण्डिले तु भवेद् द्वयम् ॥
शालग्रामार्चने नैव ह्यावाहनविसर्जने । इति ।

अत्र पञ्चायतनपक्षे प्रत्येकं देवतानामावाहनं ततः प्रत्येकं देवतानां स्थापनमिति पदार्थानुसमयो वा उतावाहनादि नैवेद्यान्तम् एकत्र समाप्य पश्चादेवमन्यत्रेति काण्डानुसमय इति संशये अत्र काण्डानुसमय इति सिद्धान्तः । यतः—

मुख्ये पुष्पाञ्जलिं दत्त्वा गणेशाद्यर्चनं भवेत् । इत्युक्तम् ।

तत्रार्चनशब्दः पूजावाचकः सा चाऽऽवाहनादिर्नैवेद्यान्ता । इदञ्च पञ्चमाध्याये द्वितीयचरणे "वचनात्तु परिव्यागान्तम्" इत्यधिकरणे सिद्धान्तितम् ॥ ८८ ॥ ८९ ॥

सुधीः संस्थापनं विदध्यादिति सम्बन्धः । संस्थापनं स्थापनम् । तत् स्थापिन्या । श्लोकस्तु—

तवेयं महिमामूर्त्तिस्तस्यां त्वां सर्व्वगं प्रभो[विभो] ।
भक्तिस्नेहसमाकृष्टं दीपवत् स्थापयाम्यहम् ॥ इति ।

सुधीरित्यनेनासनोपवेशने कर्त्तव्ये इत्युक्तं भवति । तद् यथा मूलमन्त्रान्ते—

सर्व्वान्तर्यामिणि देव सर्व्वबीजमयं शुभम् ।
स्वात्मस्थाय परं शुद्धमासनं कल्पयाम्यहम् ॥

आसनं रुद्राय नमः । ततो मूलमन्त्रान्ते—

अस्मिन् वरासने देव सुखासीनोऽक्षरात्मक ।
प्रतिष्ठितो भवेश त्वं प्रसीद परमेश्वर ॥

उपविष्टो भव नमः । सन्निधानं नैकट्यावस्थानप्रार्थनम् । तत् सन्निधापिन्या ।
श्लोकस्तु— अनन्या तव देवेश मूर्त्तिशक्तिरियं प्रभो ।
सान्निध्यं कुरु तस्यां त्वं भक्तानुग्रहतत्पर ॥ इति ।

सन्निरोधः सन्निरोधनम् अनन्यचित्तप्रार्थनम् । तत् सन्निरोधिन्या । श्लोकस्तु—

आज्ञया तव देवेश कृपाम्भोधे गुणाम्बुधे ।
आत्मानन्दैकतृप्तं त्वां निरुणध्मि पितर्गुरो ॥ इति ।

सिद्धान्तसागरे आवाहनादीनामन्यथा लक्षणमुक्तम् ।

स्वत एवाभिपूर्णस्य तत्त्वस्येहार्चनादिषु ।
सादरं सम्मुखीभावस्तदावाहनमुच्यते ॥
शिवस्याऽऽवाहितस्यास्य विद्यादेहे तु सन्ततम् ।
स्थिरीकरणमुद्दिष्टं स्थापनं भक्तितोऽर्चने ॥
पूजां प्रयोज्यमानान्तु गृहीत्वाऽनुग्रहादिकम् ।
कर्त्तुं सामर्थ्यमस्येह तत् सान्निध्यं प्रचक्षते ॥
आसमाप्तेस्तु पूजायाः सान्निध्यं हि शिवस्य यत् ।
स सन्निरोध उद्दिष्टो विभोरस्यापि शक्तितः ॥ इत्यादिना ।

अनन्तरमित्यनेन सम्मुखीकरणं प्रार्थनञ्च मुद्राद्वयेनोक्तम् । श्लोकौ तु—

अज्ञानाद् दुर्मनस्त्वाद्वा वैकल्यात् साधनस्य च ।
यदाऽपूर्णं भवेत् कृत्यं तदाऽप्यभिमुखो भव ॥
दृशा पीयूषवर्षिण्या पूरयन् यज्ञविष्टरम् ।
मूर्त्तौवायज्ञसम्पूर्त्तेः स्थिरो भव महेश्वर ॥ इति ।

मुद्रालक्षणं यथा—

मुष्टिद्वयस्थिताङ्गुष्ठौ सम्मुखौ च परस्परम् ।
संश्लिष्टावुच्छ्रितौ कुर्य्यात् सेयं सम्मुखमुद्रिका ॥
प्रसृताङ्गुलिकौ हस्तौ मिथः श्लिष्टौ च सम्मुखौ ।
कुर्य्यात् स्वहृदये सेयं मुद्रा प्रार्थनसंज्ञिका ॥ इति ।

सकलीकरणं पूर्णरूपत्वेनावस्थितिप्रार्थनम् । तच्च देवताङ्गे षडङ्गन्यासात् । अवगुण्ठनम् अयोग्यदृष्ट्यविषयत्वापादनम् । तदवगुण्ठन्या । श्लोकस्तु—

अभक्तवाङ्मनश्चक्षुःश्रोत्रदूरात्मितद्युते ।
स्वतेजःपञ्जरेणाऽऽशु वेष्टितो भव सर्व्वतः ॥ इति ।

अमृतीकरणमानन्दपूर्णतावस्थितित्वम् । तद् धेनुमुद्रया । परमीकरणं सर्व्वापराधसहिष्णुत्वम् । तन्महामुद्रया । स्वमुद्राभिरिति त्रयोविंशे वक्ष्यमाणाभिः । समाहित इत्यनेन मूलमन्त्रपुटितमातृकाक्षराणि देवदेहे विन्यसेदित्युक्तम् । पूजायां वक्ष्यमाणत्वात् ॥ ८०॥८१ ॥

अथोपचारान् कुर्व्वीत मन्त्रवित् स्वागतादिकान् ।
स्वागतं कुशलप्रश्नं निगदेदग्रतो गुरुः ॥ ८२

अथेति । उपचारशब्दार्थो ज्ञानमालायामुक्तः ।

भक्त्या चैते कृता देवे साधकं देवसन्निधिम् ।
चारयन्ति यतस्तस्मादुच्यन्ते ह्युपचारकाः ॥
समीपे चारणाद्वाऽपि फलानां ते तथोदिताः ॥ इति ।

मूले षोड़श उक्ता ज्ञानमालायामन्येऽपि । तद् यथा—

अष्टत्रिंशत्षोड़शार्कदशपञ्चोपचारकाः ।
तान् विभज्य प्रवक्ष्यामि के के ते तैः कृतैश्च किम् ॥
आसनं प्रथमं तेषामावाहनमुपस्थितिः ।
सान्निध्यमाभिमुख्यञ्च स्थिरीकृतिः प्रसाधनम् ॥
अर्घ्यञ्च पाद्याचमने मधुपर्कमुपस्पृशम् ।
स्नानं नीराजनं वस्त्रमाचामं चोपवीतकम् ॥
पुनराचामभूषे च दर्पणालोकनं ततः ।
गन्धपुष्पे धूपदीपौ नैवेद्यञ्च ततः क्रमात् ॥
पानीयं तोयमाचामं हस्तवासस्ततःपरम् ।
ताम्बूलमनुलेपञ्च पुष्पदानं पुनः पुनः ॥
गीतं वाद्यं तथा नृत्यं स्तुतिश्चैव प्रदक्षिणम् ।
पुष्पाञ्जलिनमस्कारावष्टत्रिंशत् समीरिताः ॥ इति ।

मन्त्रतन्त्रप्रकाशेऽपि—

आसनं प्रथमं तेषु ततश्चावाहनं मतम् ।
उपस्थानञ्च सान्निध्यम् । इत्यादिना—
पुष्पाञ्जलिनमस्कारौ विष्णुप्रीत्यै भवन्त्यमी ।
त्रिंशच्चाष्टौ समाख्याता उपचारा मनीषिभिः ॥ इत्यन्तेन ।

षोड़श मूले स्पष्टाः । तथा—

आसनस्वागते वस्त्रभूषे त्यक्त्वा तु द्वादश ।
अर्घ्यपाद्याचमान्येव मधुपर्काचमान्यपि ॥
गन्धादयो नैवेद्यान्ता उपचारा दश क्रमात् ।
गन्धपुष्पे धूपदीपौ नैवेद्यं पञ्च संस्मृताः ॥
सपर्य्या पञ्चधा प्रोक्ता तासामेकां समाचरेत् । इति ।

पाद्यं पादाम्बुजे दद्याद् देवस्य हृदयाणुना।

एतच्छ्यामाकदूर्व्वाब्जविष्णुक्रान्ताभिरीरितम्॥ ८३

सुधामन्त्रेण वदने दद्यादाचमनीयकम्।

जातीलवङ्गकक्कोलैस्तदुक्तं तन्त्रवेदिभिः॥ ८४

प्रयोगसारे षष्ठी अप्युक्ताः।

अर्घ्यं गन्धं ततः पुष्पमक्षतं धूपमेव च।

दीपो नैवेद्यं सप्ताङ्गी सपर्य्येत्यपरे जगुः॥ इति।

स्वागतमिति। कुशलप्रश्नमिति स्वागतमित्यस्यार्थकथनम्।

श्लोकस्तु—यस्य दर्शनमिच्छन्ति देवाः स्वाभीष्टसिद्धये।

तस्मै ते परमेशाय स्वागतं स्वागतञ्च मे॥ इति।

एतदनन्तरं सुस्वागतमपि मूलमन्त्रान्ते। श्लोकस्तु—

कृतार्थोऽनुगृहीतोऽस्मि सफलं जीवितं मम।

आगतो देवदेवेश सुस्वागतमिदं पुनः॥ इति। ८२।

पाद्यमिति। हृदयाणुना नमोमन्त्रेण।

श्लोकस्तु—यद्भक्तिलेशसम्पर्कात् परमानन्दसम्भवः।

तस्मै ते चरणाब्जाय पाद्यं शुद्धाय कल्पये॥ इति।

अत्र नमोमन्त्रमुच्चार्य्य श्लोकमुच्चार्य्य पाद्यं गृहाण नमः इति शङ्खस्थजलमुत्सृजेत्।

एवमग्रेऽपि। यत्र मन्त्रविशेषो नोक्तस्तत्र मूलमन्त्र एव ज्ञेयः।

एतदिति। श्यामाकः श्यामा इति प्रसिद्धः। महाकपिलपञ्चरात्रेऽपि—

दूर्व्वा च विष्णुपत्नी च श्यामाकं पद्ममेव च।

पाद्याङ्गानि च चत्वारि कथितानि समासतः॥ इति॥ ८३॥

सुधामन्त्रेण वमित्यनेन। श्लोकस्तु—

वेदानामपि वेदाय देवानां देवतात्मने।

आचामं कल्पयामीश शुद्धानां शुद्धिहेतवे॥ इति।

जाती जातीफलम्। कक्कोलं कोशफलम् कवाव इति कान्यकुब्जभाषायाम्।

तदुक्तमगस्तिसंहितायाम्—

तथाऽऽचमनपात्रेऽपि दद्याज्जातीफलं मुने।

लवङ्गमपि कक्कोलं शस्तमाचमनीयकम्॥ इति।

महाकपिलपञ्चरात्रे आचमनीयद्रव्याण्यन्यथोक्तानि।

अर्घ्यं दिशेत्ततो मूर्ध्नि शिरोमन्त्रेण देशिकः ।
गन्धपुष्पाक्षतयवकुशाग्रतिलसर्षपैः ॥ ९५
सदूर्वैः सर्वदेवानामेतदर्घ्यमुदीरितम् ।
सुधाणुना ततः कुर्यान्मधुपर्कं मुखाम्बुजे ॥ ९६
आज्यं दधिमधून्मिश्रमेतदुक्तं मनीषिभिः ।
तेनैव मनुना कुर्यादद्भिराचमनीयकम् ॥ ९७

कर्पूरमगुरुं पुष्पं द्रव्याण्याचमनीयकम् । इति ।

अत्रच विशेषः—अर्घ्यं त्रिर्ददाति पाद्यं त्रिर्ददाति आचमनीयं षड् ददाति । इति ।

आगताय तथार्चायां स्नातुमासनगाय च ।
पूजातो गन्तुकामस्य दद्यादर्घ्यं विचक्षणः ॥
आगते स्नानकाले च नैवेद्योपक्रमे तथा ।
पाद्यस्यापि समुद्दिष्टः समयस्त्रिविधो बुधैः । इति ॥ ९४ ॥

शिरोमन्त्रेण स्वाहेत्यनेन । महाकपिलपञ्चरात्रे कुशाग्रस्थाने फलमुक्तम् ।

सिद्धार्थमक्षतञ्चैव दूर्वा च तिलमेव च ।
यवं गन्धं फलं पुष्पमष्टाङ्गन्त्वर्घ्यमुच्यते ॥ इति ।

सर्वदेवानामिति सर्वत्र सम्बध्यते । पाद्याद्युक्तद्रव्याणि सर्वदेवतासु समानानीत्यर्थः ।

श्लोकस्तु—तापत्रयहरं दिव्यं परमानन्दलक्षणम् ।
तापत्रयविनिर्मुक्तं तवार्घ्यं कल्पयाम्यहम् ॥ इति ।

मधुपर्कमिति । श्लोकस्तु—

सर्वकालुष्यहीनाय परिपूर्णसुखात्मक ।
मधुपर्कमिमं देव कल्पयामि प्रसीद मे ॥ इति ।

अत्रार्घ्यादिप्रोक्तद्रव्याभावे केवलतण्डुलानेव निक्षिपेत् । तदुक्तं मन्त्रतन्त्रप्रकाशे—

द्रव्याभावे प्रदातव्याः क्षालितास्तण्डुलाः शुभाः । इति ।

अन्यत्रापि—तण्डुलान् प्रक्षिपेत्तेषु द्रव्यालाभे तु तत्समान् । इति ।

तेनैव मनुना सुधाणुनेत्यर्थः । श्लोकस्तु—

उच्छिष्टोऽप्यशुचिर्वाऽपि यस्य स्मरणमात्रतः ।
शुद्धिमाप्नोति तस्मै ते पुनराचमनीयकम् ॥ इति

मधुपर्कान्ते आचमनमुपलक्षणम् । तेन स्मृत्युक्तनिमित्तेऽप्याचमनं दद्यात् । स्नानान्ते वासोदानान्ते उपवीतदानान्ते नैवेद्यान्ते ।

गन्धाद्भिः कारयेत् स्नानं वाससी परिधापयेत् ।
दद्याद् दिव्योपवीतञ्च हाराद्याभरणैः सह ॥ ९८

तदुक्तं महाकपिलपञ्चरात्रे—

स्नाने वस्त्रे तथा भक्ष्ये दद्यादाचमनीयकम् । इति ।

एवं बह्व्याचमनीयानि । तदुक्तं ज्ञानमालायाम्—

पाद्ये च मधुपर्के च स्नाने वस्त्रोपवीतयोः ।
भोजने चाचमनं देयम् । इति ।

स्नानात् पूर्व्वं महाकपिलपञ्चरात्रे तु विशेषः—

गन्धं तैलमथो दद्याद् देवस्याप्रतिमं ततः । इति ।

श्लोकस्तु—स्नेहं गृहाण स्नेहेन लोकनाथ महाशय ।
सर्व्वलोकेषु शुद्धात्मन् ददामि स्नेहमुत्तमम् ॥ इति ।

तत उद्वर्त्तनम् । महाकपिलपञ्चरात्रे—

रजनी सहदेवी च शिरीषो लक्ष्मणापि च ।
सदाभद्रा कुशाग्राणि उद्वर्त्तनमिहोच्यते ॥ इति ।

अन्यत्रापि—अभ्यङ्गोद्वर्त्तने चापि महास्नानं समाचरेत् । इति । ९५-९७ ॥

गन्धाद्भिरिति । तदुक्तं मन्त्रतन्त्रप्रकाशे—

शुद्धतोयाद् गन्धतोयं श्रेष्ठं शतगुणोत्तरम् ।
गङ्गादितीर्थतोयानां फलं शास्त्रप्रणोदितम् ॥
तत्र तत्राधिगन्तव्यम् । इति ।

तथा—नाहरेन्मलिनं तोयं केशकीटादिदूषितम् ।
मलिनेनापि भाण्डेन व्यङ्गेनाऽशुचिना तथा ॥ इति ।

तत्रैव विशेषः—अक्षता गन्धपुष्पाणि स्नानपात्रे तथा त्रयम् । इति ।

श्लोकस्तु—परमानन्दबोधाब्धिनिमग्ननिजमूर्त्तये ।
साङ्गोपाङ्गमिदं स्नानं कल्पयाम्यहमीश ते ॥ इति ।

एतदनन्तरं शङ्खजलेन देवायाऽभिषेकं कुर्य्यात् । यदाहुः—

शतं सहस्रमयुतं शक्त्या चैवाभिषेचयेत् ।
शङ्खं सम्पूर्य्य तेनैव सपुष्पेण च देवताम् ॥ इति ।

अन्यत्रापि—अ[स्व]शक्त्या गन्धतोयेन संस्नाप्य जगदीश्वरम् । इति ।

अत्र विशेषः—महाभिषेकं सर्व्वत्र शङ्खेनैव प्रकल्पयेत् ।
सर्व्वत्रैव प्रशस्तोऽब्जः शिवसूर्य्यार्चनं विना ॥ इति ।

न्यासक्रमेण मनुना पुटितैर्मातृकाक्षरैः।

अभ्यर्च्य देवीं गन्धाद्यैरङ्गादीन् पूजयेत् ततः॥ ९९

तत्र विशेषस्तु तन्त्रान्तरे—

प्रतिमापटयन्त्राणां नित्यं स्नानं न चाचरेत्।

कारयेत् पर्व्वदिवसे तथा मलनिवारणम्॥ इति।

वाससीति द्विवचनेनोत्तरीयं गृहीतम्। श्लोकौ तु—

मायाचित्रपटाच्छन्न निजगुह्योरुतेजसे।

निरावरणविज्ञान वासस्ते कल्पयाम्यहम्॥

यमाश्रित्य महामाया जगत्सम्मोहिनी सदा।

तस्मै ते परमेशाय कल्पयाम्युत्तरीयकम्॥ इति।

तत्र विशेषो मन्त्रतन्त्रप्रकाशे—

पीतं कौशेयवसनं विष्णोः प्रीत्यै प्रकीर्त्तितम्।

रक्तं शक्त्यर्कविघ्नेषु ईश्वरस्य सितं प्रियम्।

मलहीनं तथाऽच्छिद्रं क्षौमं कार्पासमेव वा॥

तैलादिदूषिताद्रोगः सच्छिद्राद्दाच्युता भवेत्।

जीर्णाद्दरिद्रता कर्त्तुर्मलिनात् कीर्त्तिहीनता॥ इति।

यज्ञोपवीतमिति। श्लोकस्तु—

यस्य शक्तित्रयेणेदं संप्रोतमखिलं जगत्।

यज्ञसूत्राय तस्मै ते यज्ञसूत्रं प्रकल्पये॥ इति।

हाराद्याभरणैरिति। श्लोकस्तु—

स्वभावसुन्दराङ्गाय नानाशक्त्याश्रयाय ते।

भूषणानि विचित्राणि कल्पयाम्यमरार्चित॥ इति। ९८॥

न्यासेति। उपचारात् पूर्व्वं कृतो यो देवदेहे न्यासः तत्क्रमेण मूलमन्त्रपुटितमेकैकमक्षरं कृत्वेत्यर्थः।

वर्णैर्मनुप्रपुटितैः क्रमशः शताद्धै-

र्न्यासक्रमादभियजेत् सकलासु मन्त्री।

गन्धादिभिः प्रथमतो मनुदेवतासु

त्रैलोक्यमोहन इति प्रथितः प्रयोगः॥ इत्याचार्य्योक्तेः।

अभ्यर्च्य देवीमिति। अत्र देवीमित्युपलक्षणं स्वेष्टदेवतामित्यर्थः। क्वचिद्देवमिति पाठः। पुटितलक्षणं त्रयोविंशे वक्ष्यति। ततो गन्धाद्यैरभ्यर्च्य

गन्धैश्चन्दनकर्पूरकालागुरुभिरीरितः।
कमले करवीरे द्वे कुमुदे तुलसीद्वयम्॥ १००
जातीद्वयं केतके द्वे कह्लारं चम्पकोत्पले।
कुन्दमन्दारपुन्नागपाटला नागचम्पकम्॥ १०१
आरग्वधं कर्णिकारं पारन्ती नवमल्लिका।
सौगन्धिकं सकोरण्टं पलाशाशोकमल्लिकाः॥ १०२

पुनरन्तरमङ्गादीनावरणानि चार्चयेत्। इति क्रमविधायकम्। गन्धाद्यैरित्यादि-शब्देन पुष्पम्। अङ्गादीनिति तत्तत्कल्पोक्ताङ्गाद्यत्यादि। अस्यायमाशयः। मुख्यदेवे गन्धपुष्पे दत्त्वा अङ्गादिलोकपालान् सम्पूज्य धूपादि दद्यादिति॥ ९९॥

गन्धाद्यैरित्युक्तं तत्स्वरूपमेवाह गन्ध इत्यादिना। श्लोकस्तु—

परमानन्दसौरभ्यपरिपूर्णदिगन्तर।
गृहाण परमं गन्धं कृपया परमेश्वर॥ इति।

इदं गन्धदानं कनिष्ठिकयेति ज्ञेयम्। यदाहुः—

शङ्खपात्रस्थितं गन्धं सर्व्वैर्दद्यात् कनिष्ठया। इति।

ततो गन्धमुद्रां प्रदर्शयेत्। तल्लक्षणन्तु—

कनिष्ठाङ्गुष्ठसंयुक्ता गन्धमुद्रा प्रकीर्त्तिता। इति।

कमले इति। द्वे इति श्वेतरक्ते। श्लोकस्तु—

तुरीयवनसम्भूतं नानागुणमनोहरम्।
अमन्दसौरभं पुष्पं गृह्यतामिदमुत्तमम्॥ इति।

ततः पुष्पमुद्रां प्रदर्शयेत्।

केतके द्वे इति श्वेतपीते। मन्दारोऽर्कः। पुन्नागो नागकेशरः। आरग्वधो राजवृक्षः घनवदर इति कान्यकुब्जभाषायाम्। पारन्ती लताभेदः। सौगन्धिकं कह्लारभेदः। देशिकैः पूजायामुपदिष्टानीत्यनेनान्येषु पुष्पाध्यायेषु विहितानि ग्राह्याणि तत्तद्देवतानां निषिद्धानि त्याज्यानीत्युक्तं। ज्ञानमालायाम्—

नाक्षतैरर्चयेद् विष्णुं न तुलस्या विनायकम्।
न दूर्व्वया यजेद् दुर्गां बिल्वपत्रैर्दिवाकरम्॥
उन्मत्तमर्कपुष्पञ्च विष्णौ वर्ज्यं सदा बुधैः।
देवीनाथार्कमन्दारावादित्ये तगरं तथा॥
गणेशाय च सूर्य्याय रक्तपुष्पमति प्रियम्।

धुस्तूरं सर्जकं बिल्वमर्जुनं मुनिपुष्प[पत्र]कम् ।
अन्यान्यपि सुगन्धीनि पत्रपुष्पाणि देशिकैः ॥ १०३
उपदिष्टानि पूजायामाददीत विचक्षणः ।
मलिनं भूमिसंस्पृष्टं कृमिकेशादिदूषितम् ॥ १०४

शिवे कुन्दं न[म]दन्तीश्च यूथीं बन्धूककेतके ॥
अर्वा रक्तां त्रिसन्ध्ये द्वे सिन्दूरं कूटजानि च ।
मालतीं कुसुम्भं रक्तां हयारिं बर्बरां त्यजेत् ॥
उग्रगन्धमगन्धञ्च कृमिकेशादिदूषितम् ।
अशुचपात्रपाणस्थवासोभिः कुत्सितात्मभिः ॥
आनीतं नार्पयेच्छम्भोः प्रमादादपि दोषकृत् ।
कलिकाभिस्तथा नेज्यं विना चम्पकपङ्कजैः ॥
शुष्कैर्न पूजयेद्विष्णुं पत्रैः पुष्पैः फलैरपि ।
स्नात्वानीतैः पर्य्युषितैः याचितैः कृष्णवर्णकैः ॥
सायं विकासितैः पुष्पैः स्वयञ्च पतितैर्भूवि ।
वर्जयेद्बृहतीहन्दं काञ्चनारं कुरण्टकम् ॥
सर्व्वपुष्पैः सदा पूजा विहिता विहितैरपि ।
कर्त्तव्या सर्व्वदेवानां भक्तियोगोऽत्र कारणम् ॥
पुष्पं वा यदि वा पत्रं फलं नेष्टमधोमुखम् ।
दुःखदं तत् समाख्यातं यथोत्पन्नं तथाऽर्पणम् ॥
चित्रपूजासु सर्व्वासु न विद्वस्यापि दूषणम् ।
अधोमुखार्पणं नेष्टं पुष्पाञ्जलिविधौ न तत् ॥
लक्षपूजासु सर्व्वासु पुष्पमेकैकमर्पयेत् ।
समुदायेन चेत् पूजा लक्षपुष्पार्पणन्तु तत् ॥ इति ।

मन्त्रतन्त्रप्रकाशेऽपि—

पुष्पं पञ्चविधं प्रोक्तं मुनिभिर्नारदादिभिः ।
परापरोत्तमञ्चैव मध्यमञ्च तथाऽधमम् ॥
सौवर्णन्तु परं प्रोक्तमपरं चित्रवस्त्रजम् ।
वृक्षगुल्मलतापुष्पमुत्तमं परिकीर्त्तितम् ॥
अधमं पत्रतोयादि मध्यमन्तु फलात्मकम् ।

भङ्गस्पृष्टं समाघ्रातं त्यजेत् पर्य्युषितं गुरुः ।
देवस्य मस्तकं कुर्य्यात् कुसुमोपहितं सदा ॥ १०५
पूजाकाले देवताया नोपरि भ्रामयेत् करम् ।
अगुरुशीरगुग्गुलुशर्करामधुचन्दनैः ॥ १०६

उत्सृष्टं न क्रियायोग्यं सदायोग्ये परापरे ॥
पत्रेषु तुलसी श्रेष्ठा बिल्वमामलकं शुभम् ।
मरुको देवकह्लारो विष्णुक्रान्ता तथैव च ॥
अपामार्गोऽथ गान्धारी पत्री सुरभिसंज्ञिका ।
नागवल्लीदलं दूर्व्वा कुशपत्रं तथा मतम् ॥
पञ्चस्वागस्त्यवृक्षस्य पुष्पं धात्रीदलं तथा ।
फलेऽप्यामलकं श्रेष्ठं वादरं तिन्तिणीभवम् ॥
दाड़िमं मातुलुङ्गञ्च जम्बीरं पनसोद्भवम् ।
कदली चूतसम्भूतं श्रेष्ठं जम्बूफलन्तथा ॥
यजेदेतैः सदा विष्णुं पत्रैः पुष्पैः फलैस्तथा । इति ।

तथा—दिवसे दिवसोत्फुल्लैः पुष्पैः पूजा तथा निशि ।
पुष्पाभावे प्रवालैर्वा पूजयेच्च न कोरकैः ॥ इति ।
अन्यार्थमाहृतं दुष्टं तथैवान्योपभुक्तकम् । इति ।

गुरुरित्यनेन केषुचित् पर्य्युषितेषु दोषाभाव इत्युक्तम् ।
यत् ज्ञानमालायाम्—

न पर्य्युषितदोषोऽस्ति जलजोत्पलचम्पके ।
तुलस्यगस्त्यवकुले बिल्वगङ्गाजले तथा ॥ इति ।

पश्चिकैतैर्दिनसंख्यया केषाञ्चित् पर्य्युषितदोषाभाव उक्तः ।

बिल्वापामार्गजातीतुलसिशमिशता केतकीभृङ्गदूर्व्वा
मन्दाम्भोजाह्विदर्भा मुनितिलतगरा ब्रह्मकह्लारमल्ली ।
चम्पाश्वारातिकुम्भीमरुवकदमना विश्वतोऽह्नानि च स्युः
त्रिंशत्त्रेयकार्य्यरीशोदधिनिधिवसुभूभूयमा भूय एवम् ॥ इति ।

शता शतपत्रम् । भृङ्गं भृङ्गराजः । मन्दो मन्दारः । आह्वि द्रोणकलशः । ब्रह्म पलाशः । अश्वारातिः करवीरः । एषां यथायोग्यं पत्रपुष्पाणि ग्राह्याणि । ऋतयः षट् । यमो द्वयम् । एवम् एकादशाद्या आह्नवानां दिनसंख्या । भूय

धूपयेदाज्यसंमिश्रैर्नीचैर्देवस्य देशिकः ।
वर्त्त्या कर्पूरगर्भिण्या सर्पिषा तिलजेन वा ॥ १०७

आरोप्य दर्शयेद्दीपानुच्चैः सौरभशालिनः ।
स्वादूपदंशं विमलं पायसं सहशर्करम् ॥ १०८

एवमस्यार्थः । द्वितीयाद्यस्त्वा दर्भादीनामियं दिनसंख्येति । स्मृत्यन्तरेऽपि—

पङ्कजं पञ्चरात्रं स्यात् दशरात्रञ्च बिल्वकम् ।
तुलस्यैकादशाहात्तु पुनः प्रक्षाल्य पूजयेत् ॥ इति

तुलस्यां निर्माल्यदोषोऽपि नास्ति । यदाहुः—

सद्यः पर्य्युषिता वापि निर्माल्या नैव दूष्यति ।
तथान्यैर्न हरेस्तुष्टिस्तुलस्या तुष्यते यथा ॥ इति ॥ १००-१०६ ॥

उद्दिष्टमुक्त्वा प्रकृतमाह धूपयेदिति । वामहस्तेन घण्टामन्त्रेणार्चितां घण्टां वादयन् धूपं दद्यादित्यर्थः । देशिक इत्यनेन घण्टामन्त्रेण तत्पूजनमप्युक्तम् ।

यदाहुः—जयध्वनि ततो मन्त्रमातः स्वाहेत्युदीर्य्य च ।
अभ्यर्च्य वादयन् घण्टाम् । इति ।

शैवागमे तु—धूपभाजनमस्त्रेण प्रोक्ष्याऽभ्यर्च्य हृदाणुना ।
अस्त्रेण पूजितां घण्टां वादयन् गुग्गुलुं दहेत् ॥ इति ।

श्लोकस्तु—वनस्पतिरसोपेतो गन्धाढ्यः सुमनोहरः ।
आघ्रेयः सर्व्वदेवानां धूपोऽयं प्रतिगृह्यताम् ॥ इति ।

तदुक्तम्—घण्टां गन्धाक्षतकुसुमकैरर्चितां वादयानः । इति ।

अन्यत्रापि—ततः समर्पयेद्धूपं घण्टां वाद्य जयस्वनैः । इति ।

अत्र प्रयोगः । धूपपात्रमस्त्रेण प्रोक्ष्य नमोमन्त्रेण पुष्पं दत्त्वा वामया तर्जन्या संस्पृशन् मूलमन्त्रं श्लोकञ्च पठित्वा साङ्गाय सपरिवाराय देवाय धूपं समर्पयामि नमः इति शङ्खजलमुत्सृज्य धूपमुद्रां प्रदर्श्य घण्टामन्त्रेणार्चितां घण्टां वामहस्तेन वादयन् देवतागुणनामयशःस्तुत्यादि कीर्त्तयन् देवं धूपयेत् । उक्तञ्च—

धूपस्थानं समभ्यर्च्य तर्जन्या वामया स्पृशन् ।
सङ्कल्प्यैवं ततः पुष्पाञ्जलिं दत्त्वा यशः पठेत् ॥

बह्वृच परिशिष्टेऽपि—

धूपस्य व्यजनेनैव धूपेनाङ्गविधूपने ।
नीराजनेषु सर्व्वेषु देव[गुण]नामादि कीर्त्तयन् ॥

कदलीफलसंयुक्तं साज्यं मन्त्री निवेदयेत् ।
तत्र तत्र जलं दद्यादुपचारान्तरान्तरा ॥ १०९

जयघोषं प्रकुर्व्वीत कारणञ्चापि कीर्त्तयेत् ।
तथा मङ्गलघोषञ्च जगद्दीजस्य च स्तुतिम् ॥ इति ।

मन्त्रतन्त्रप्रकाशे तु—

न दहेद् दूषितं धूपं कार्पासास्थिशिरोरुहैः । इति ।

एवं दीपदानेऽपि घण्टावादनादि सर्व्वं पूर्व्ववत् कुर्य्यात् । विशेषस्त्वयं उत्सर्गे वाममध्यमया दीपपात्रस्पर्शः । दीपमुद्रादर्शनञ्च । श्लोकस्तु –

सुप्रकाशो महादीपः सर्व्वतस्तिमिरापहः ।
सबाह्याभ्यन्तरंज्योतिर्दीपोऽयं प्रतिगृह्यताम् ॥ इति ।

उक्तञ्च ज्ञानमालायाम् —

सर्व्वनादप्रिया देवा नेकः कर्त्तुञ्च तान् क्षमः ।
सर्व्वनादमयी घण्टा रवात्मा[र्था] सर्व्वनादकृत् ॥ इति ।

नीचैरिति देवतानाभिदेशे उच्चैरिति नेत्रदेशे इत्याचार्य्याः । "इत्याद्यति विशदधीः पादपर्य्यन्तमुच्चैः" इत्युक्तेः । बहुवर्त्तिदीपपक्षे विषमा एव वर्त्तिसंख्या ग्राह्या ।

यदाहुः—आरत्रिकन्तु विषमबहुवर्त्तिसमन्वितम् । इति ।

प्रयोगसारे तु—तैलेन कपिलाज्येन सिक्थकेनापरेण वा ।

स्नेहेन वर्त्तिसंयुक्तं दीपमुच्चैः प्रदर्शयेत् ॥ इति ।

तत्र सर्पिषा चेद्दीपः तदा दक्षिणतः तैलेन चेत्तदा वामत इति सम्प्रदायः । एवञ्च सितावर्त्तिश्चेद्दक्षिणतः रक्ता चेद्वामतो निवेदनमिति ॥ १०७ ॥ १०८ ॥

मन्त्रीत्यनेनैतदुक्तं भवति नैवेद्यम् अस्त्रमन्त्रजप्तजलेन सम्प्रोक्षयेत् ।

शैवागमे तु—ततो मृत्युञ्जयेनैव वौषडन्तेन सप्तधा ।

जप्तैः सदर्भशङ्खस्थैः सिञ्चेत् तत्तोयबिन्दुभिः ॥ इति ।

ततश्चक्रमुद्रयाऽभिरक्ष्य वायुबीजेन द्वादशवाराभिमन्त्रितजलेन हविः सम्प्रोक्ष्य तदुत्थवायुना तद्दोषं संशोष्य[ध्य] दक्षिणकरतलेऽग्निबीजं विचिन्त्य तत्पृष्ठलग्नं वामकरतलं कृत्वा नैवेद्ये प्रदर्श्य तदुत्थाग्निना तद्दोषं दग्ध्वा वामकरतलेऽमृतबीजं विचिन्त्य तत्पृष्ठलग्नं दक्षिणकरतलं कृत्वा नैवेद्ये प्रदर्श्य तदुत्थामृतधारया प्लावितं विभाव्य मूलमन्त्रजप्तजलेन सम्प्रोक्ष्य तदखिलममृतात्मकं ध्यात्वा तत् स्पृष्ट्वा मूलमन्त्रमष्टधा जप्त्वा धेनुमुद्रां प्रदर्श्य जलगन्धपुष्पैरभ्यर्च्य देवतायै पुष्पाञ्जलिं समर्प्य तन्मुखात्तेजो निर्गतमिति ध्यात्वा वामाङ्गुष्ठेन मुख्यं नैवेद्यपात्रं स्पृष्ट्वा

दक्षिणकरेण जलं गृहीत्वा स्वाहान्तं मूलमन्त्रम्

सत्पात्रसिद्धं सुहविर्विविधानेकभक्षणम् ।
निवेदयामि देवाय सानुगाय गृहाण तत् ॥

इति श्लोकञ्च जपित्वा साङ्गाय सपरिवाराय देवाय नैवेद्यं समर्पयामि नमः इति जलमुत्सृज्य नैवेद्यमुद्रां प्रदर्शयेत् । ततः सपुष्पाभ्यां हस्ताभ्यां नैवेद्यपात्रं त्रिः प्रोक्षन्—"निवेदयामि भवते जुषाणेदं हविर्हरे" इति जपेत् ।

तत्र हरे इति पदस्थाने तत्तद्देवतानामोह्यम् । यदाहुः—

प्रक्षोक्षितं तदरिमुद्रिकयाऽभिरक्ष्य वायव्यतोयपरिशोषितमग्निदोष्णा ।
संदह्य वामकरसौधरसाभिपूर्णं मन्त्रामृतीकृत मथाभिमृशन् प्रजप्यात् ॥
मनुमष्टशः सुरभिमुद्रिकया परिपूर्णमर्चयतु गन्धमुख्यैः ।
हरिमर्चयेदथ कृतप्रसराञ्जलि रास्यतोऽस्य विसरेच्च महः ॥
वीतिहोत्रदयितान्तमुच्चरन् मूलमन्त्रमथ निक्षिपेज्जलम् ।
अर्पयेत्तदमृतात्मकं हवि र्दोर्युजा सकुसुमं समुद्धरन् ॥

निवेद्यार्पणमन्त्रोऽयं सर्व्वार्चासु निजाख्यया । इति ।

ततो वामकरेण ग्रासमुद्रां दक्षिणकरेण प्राणादिमुद्राश्च दर्शयन् प्राणाय स्वाहेत्यादि-मन्त्रान् जपेत् । यदाहुः—

ग्रासमुद्रां वामदोष्णा विकचोत्पलसन्निभाम् ।
प्रदर्शयन् दक्षिणेन प्राणादीनाञ्च दर्शयेत् ॥

स्पृशेत् कनिष्ठोपकनिष्ठिके द्वे स्वाङ्गुष्ठमूर्द्धा प्रथमेह मुद्रा ।
तथा परातर्जनिमध्यमे स्यादनामिकामध्यमिके च मध्या ॥
अनामिकातर्जनिमध्यमा स्यात्तद्वच्चतुर्थी सकनिष्ठिकास्ताः ।
स्यात् पञ्चमी तद्वदिहोपदिष्टाः प्राणादिमुद्रा निजमन्त्रयुक्ताः ॥
प्राणापानोदानव्यान समानाः क्रमाच्चतुर्थ्या युक्ताः ।
ताराधारा वध्वा येहाः क्रमशाध्वनस्त एते मनवः ॥ इति

पुष्पादिमुद्रालक्षणानि च—

ज्येष्ठाङ्गुष्ठस्य पुष्पस्य युक्ता धूपस्य तर्जनी ।
दीपस्य मध्यमानामा नैवेद्यस्य प्रकीर्त्तिता ॥
इतराङ्गुलिसंयोगात् पञ्चमुद्राः प्रकीर्त्तिताः ।
मन्त्रादिष्वपि दत्तेषु[भिरेषु] मुद्राश्चेमाः प्रदर्शयेत् ॥
मुद्रया यत् कृतं कर्म्म तदक्षयफलप्रदम् ॥ इति ।

तत्रेति । उपचाराणाम् अन्तरान्तरा पुष्पाञ्जलिं दत्त्वा जलं दत्त्वा स्वहस्तं प्रक्षालयेदिति परमगुरवः । इदानीं तन्त्रान्तरोक्तो विशेषो लिख्यते ।

अनिर्माल्यं सनिर्माल्यमर्चनं द्विविधं स्मृतम् ।
दिव्यैर्मनोभवैर्द्रव्यैर्गन्धपुष्पैः स्रगादिभिः ॥
यदर्चनमनिर्माल्यं दिव्यभोगापवर्गदम् ।
ग्राम्यारण्यादिसम्भूतैर्यागद्रव्यैर्मनोरमैः ॥
भक्त्यैर्यत् क्रियते सम्यक् सनिर्माल्यं तदर्चनम् ।

तत्र तत्त्वसागरसंहितायां निर्माल्यत्वमुक्तम्—

जातमात्राणि पुष्पाणि घ्रातान्येव निसर्गतः ।
पञ्चभिश्च महाभूतैर्भानुना शशिना तथा ॥
प्राणिभिश्च द्विरेफाद्यैः पौष्पैरेव न संशयः ।
अतो निर्माल्यमित्युक्तम् । इति

निर्माल्यञ्चेत् अनेन फलं कथमित्याशङ्क्य तत्रैवोक्तम्—

ज्ञातपुष्पात् फलं सिध्येदल्पं नो मानसाद् यथा ।
तस्मादपरिहार्यत्वादन्यथा चानुपायतः ॥
अल्पबुद्धित्वतो नॄणां बाह्यपुष्पैर्भवेत् क्रिया । इति ।

तथा—पुनस्त्रिधा मता पूजा उत्तमाधममध्यमा ।
अधिकारिनिमित्ताभ्यां भिद्यते शतधा पुनः ॥
यागोपकरणैः कृत्स्नैः क्रियमाणोत्तमा मता ।
यथालब्धैर्विनिष्पाद्या दृष्टैः पूजा तु मध्यमा ॥
पत्रपुष्पाम्बुनिष्पाद्या पूजा चाधमसंज्ञिता ।
विदिताखिलवेदार्थैर्ब्रह्मर्षिभिरकल्मषैः ॥
क्रियमाणा तु या पूजा सात्त्विकी सा विमुक्तिदा ।
राजर्षिभिस्तपोनिष्ठैर्भगवत्तत्त्ववेदिभिः ॥
या पूजा क्रियते सम्यक् राजसी सा सुखप्रदा ।
स्त्रीबालवृद्धमूर्खाद्यैर्भक्तैश्च[र]क्षुद्रमानसैः ॥
या पूजा क्रियते नित्यं तामसी सा प्रकीर्त्तिता ।
आतुरी सौतकी चैव त्रासी दौर्बोधिकी तथा ॥
साधनाभाविनी चेति पञ्चधा भिद्यते पुनः ।
यदि लङ्घनपर्यन्तो व्याधिरात्मनि दृश्यते ॥

तदा पूजा न कर्त्तव्या स्थण्डिले प्रतिमासु च ।
न स्नानं दन्तकाष्ठं वा कुर्य्याद्धोममथापि वा ॥
रविमण्डलमालोक्य प्रतिमामथवा पुनः ।
मूलमन्त्रं सकृज्जप्त्वा पुष्पं साक्षतमुत्क्षिपेत् ॥
अशक्तो व्याधिभिरत्युग्रैः क्लान्तश्चैवोपवासकैः ।
निजसामयिकैर्वापि स्वकर्त्तव्यं समापयेत् ॥
स्नात्वा[सुस्त्वा] देवमथाग्नींश्च गुरून् विप्रान् प्रपूज्य च ।
एतावत्कालविच्छिन्ना पूजा युष्मत्प्रसादतः ॥
न दोषो मेऽस्त्विति प्रार्थ्य पुनः पूर्व्ववदाचरेत् ।
अथ सूतकिनः पूजां वदाम्यागमचोदिताम् ॥
स्नात्वा नित्यञ्च निर्वर्त्त्य मानस्या क्रियया तु वै ।
बाह्यपूजाक्रमेणैव स्थान[ध्यान]योगेन पूजयेत् ॥
यदि कामी न चेत् कामी नित्यं पूर्व्ववदाचरेत् ।
प्रवासिनो वक्ष्यते पूजा यथैवागमचोदिता ॥
लब्धं वा यदिवाऽलब्धमर्घ्यपात्रादि साधनम् ॥
पूजोदकेन कर्त्तव्या न चेत्तोयञ्च विद्यते ॥
यदि सम्पूजयेद्देवं भावनाकुसुमादिभिः ।
दौर्बोधिकीं प्रवक्ष्यामि पूजामागमचोदिताम् ॥
मूर्खस्त्रीबालवृद्धाद्या दुर्बोधा इति भाविताः ।
रत्नमण्डपधर्म्मादिचतुष्कमुरगोम्बुजम् ॥
मूलमूर्त्तिस्तथाङ्गानि तेषां पूजा विधीयते ।
अन्येषामपि सर्व्वेषां प्रोक्ता संक्षेपकर्म्मणि ॥
सर्व्वोपचारवस्तूनामलाभे भावनैव हि ।
निर्मले[र्मास्ये]नोदकेनाथ पूर्णतेत्याह नारदः । इति ।

पूजाकरणासमर्थं प्रति—

आराधनासमर्थश्चेद्दद्यादर्चनसाधनम् ।
यो दातुं नैव शक्नोति कुर्य्यादर्चनदर्शनम् ॥
नैकञ्च यस्य विद्येत सोऽधो यात्येव नान्यथा ।
यस्तु भक्त्या प्रयत्नेन स्वयं सम्पाद्य चाखिलम् ॥
साधनञ्चाऽर्चयेद्विद्वान् स समग्रफलं लभेत् ।

अङ्गादिलोकपालान्तं यजेदावरणान्यपि ।
केशरेष्वग्निकोणादि हृदयादीनि पूजयेत् ॥ ११०
नेत्रमग्रे दिशास्वस्त्रं ध्यातव्या अङ्गदेवताः ।
तुषारस्फटिकश्यामनीलकृष्णारुणार्चिषः ॥ १११

यो ऽर्चयेद्विधिवद्भक्त्या परानीतैश्च साधनैः ॥
पूजाफलार्द्धमेवाऽस्य न समग्रफलं लभेत् । इति ॥१०८॥

अङ्गादीन् पुनरर्चयेदित्युक्तम् । तचाद्यन्ते सामान्ये इति । तयोर्ध्यानस्थान-प्रयोगान् वक्तुम् आदिशब्दार्थञ्च प्रकटयितुं पुनः संगृह्णाति । तत्स्वरूपमाह अङ्गादीति । पूजावसरस्य प्रागुक्तत्वात् अतएव वक्ष्यति "एवं सम्पूज्य विधिव-द्विदेद्यान्तम्" इति । अङ्गम् अङ्गावृतिरादौ यत्र तत् । लोकपालावृतिरन्ते यत्र तत् । अङ्गादिलोकपालान्तमिति क्रियाविशेषणम् । लोकपालशब्देनैव स्वास्त्रा-वृतिग्रहणं ज्ञेयम् । एतच्च सम्भवाभिप्रायं बहुषु स्थलेषु तथा दर्शनात् न नियमः । अपिशब्दादत्रापि अन्तरान्तरा जलं दद्यादित्यनुषज्यते ।

अङ्गपूजायाः सर्व्वसामान्यम् अर्चनस्थानमाह केशरेष्विति । अग्निकोणादी-त्यादिशब्देन नैर्ऋतवायव्येशानकोणेषु । तदुक्तम्—

वह्न्यादीशान्तमङ्गानि हृदादिकवचान्तिकम् ।
अर्चयेत् पुरतो नेत्रमस्त्रं दिक्षु बहिः पुनः ॥ इति ।

अन्यत्रापि—हुतवहनिर्ऋतिसमीरणशिवदिक्षु हृदादिवर्म्मान्तम् । इति ।
अन्ये तु आग्नेयेशाननैर्ऋतवायव्यकोणेष्विति व्याचक्षते ।

यदाहुः—इष्ट्वा हृदयमाग्नेय्यामैशान्यान्तु शिरो यजेत् ।
नैर्ऋत्यान्तु शिखा पूज्या वायव्यां कवचं यजेत् ॥
अभ्यर्च्य पुरतो नेत्रं दिक्षु शस्त्रमथार्चयेत् । इति ।

अन्यत्रापि—अग्नीशासुरवायव्यमध्यदिक्ष्वङ्गपूजनम् । इति ।
यथागुरूपदेशश्च निर्णयः । अत्राग्नेयादीनि पुरःकल्पितपूर्व्वदिगपेक्षया न तु प्रसिद्धानीति ॥ ११० ॥

नेत्रमग्र इति कर्णिकायां देवस्य पुरतः । शिरःप्रभृतिमन्त्रेषु पूजायां नमोऽन्तता ज्ञेया । होमे तु हृदयादीनां स्वाहान्तता । आद्यद्वितीययो-स्तज्जातियुक्तत्वादेव न तत्प्रयोगः । अधिकरणसिद्धश्चायमर्थः । तथा हि "मन्त्रे स्ववाक्यशेषत्वं गुणोपदेशात् स्यात्" इत्यत्राधिकरणे स्वाहाकारेण वषट्कारेण

वरदाभयधारिण्यः प्रधानतनवः स्त्रियः ।
पश्चादभ्यर्चनीयाः स्युः कल्पोक्तावृतयः क्रमात् ॥ ११२
अन्ते यजेल्लोकपालान् मूलपारिषदान्वितान् ।
हेतिजात्यधिपोपेतान् दिक्षु पूर्व्वादितः क्रमात् ॥ ११३

वा देवेभ्यो हविर्ददातीति सामान्येन विहितया स्वाहाकारान्ततया पृथिव्यै स्वाहा अन्तरिक्षाय स्वाहेत्यादिषु मन्त्रेषु न पुनस्तस्य बाधः । सामिधेनीष्वासदस्त्ववदुप-संहाराभावान्नान्यमन्त्रेषु बाधश्चेति स्थितम् ॥ १११ ॥

प्रधानतनवः स्त्रिय इति पत्नद्वयमिति पद्मपादाचार्य्याः ।

उक्तञ्च — वरदाभयधारिण्यो महिलाकृतयोऽङ्गदेवताः पूज्याः । इति ।

आवरणानीत्युक्तानां स्थानमाह पश्चादिति । पश्चादङ्गावृत्यनन्तरमित्यर्थः । इदमपि प्रायिकम् । तत्पूर्व्वमप्यावृतीनां सत्त्वात् ॥ ११२ ॥

अन्त इति बाह्ये । चतुरस्रे आवरणान्तत्वस्य पूर्व्वमुक्तेः । एतच्च व्याख्यानं वैहायसीमन्त्रकोषे वायवीयसंहितायाञ्च तथा दर्शनात् । सत्सम्प्रदायाच्च । पूर्व्वादितो दिक्षु क्रमाच्च । अन्ते इन्द्रमग्निं इत्यादीन् लोकपालान् यजेदिति सम्बन्धः । तत्र सामान्यत इन्द्राय नम इत्यादि प्रयोगे प्राप्ते विशेषमाह मूलेत्यादिना । अन्ते इत्यत्रापि सम्बध्यते । तेनेदं पदं सर्व्वान्ते देयमेवेत्यर्थः । तच्च प्रयोगलिखने स्फुटीभविष्यति । मूलपारिषदान्वितानित्यस्यायमर्थः । यदा शक्त्यावरणे इन्द्रादि पूजा तदा प्रत्येकं शक्तिपारिषदायेति लोकपालानां वज्रादीनाञ्च विशेषणं ज्ञेयम् । एवं शिवपूजायां प्रत्येकं शिवपारिषदायेति । एवं गणेश-पूजायां प्रत्येकं गणेशपारिषदायेति । एवं सूर्य्यपूजायां प्रत्येकं सूर्य्यपारिषदायेति । एवं विष्णुपूजायां प्रत्येकं विष्णुपारिषदायेति । चरणव्यत्ययो गोपनार्थं कृतः । हेतीत्यत्रापि अन्त इति सम्बध्यते । इन्द्रायेत्यादेरन्त इत्यर्थः । अत्रापि प्रयोगे जात्यधिपानां पूर्व्वमुच्चारणं पश्चाद्धेतीनाम् । मूले तु हेतिशब्दस्याल्पाच्तरत्वात् पूर्व्वनिपातः । हेतयः आयुधानि । जातयः सुरतेजःप्रेतरक्षोजलप्राणनक्षत्रभूत-नागलोकाः । सवाहनान् सपरिवारानित्यपि ज्ञेयम् । वाहनानि तु ऐरावताज-महिषनरमकरमृगाश्ववृषभरथहंसाः । तदुक्तमाचार्य्यैः—

जात्यधिपहेतिवाहनपरिवारान्ताः क्रमेण यष्टव्याः । इति ।

वक्ष्यति च स्वयं नित्यामन्त्रे—

लोकपालान् यजेदन्ते वाहनायुधसंयुतान् । इति ।

इन्द्रमग्निं यमं रक्षो वरुणं पवनं विधुम् ।

ईशानं पन्नगाधीशमथ चाब्जं पितामहम् ॥ ११४

पीतो रक्तो सितो धूम्रः शुक्लो धूम्रः सितावुभौ ।

गौरोऽरुणः क्रमादेते वर्णतः परिकीर्तिताः ॥ ११५

स्वाधिकारानिति ध्येयम् । तदुक्तं वैशायनीयकोशे—

लोकेश्वरान् पार्थिवमण्डले सम्पूज्यान् प्रयतात् सम्यगुपनाथ ।

सदा अर्चयेत्स्वस्वमनुप्रपूर्वैर्यजेत् स स्यात् निजकामसिद्धये ॥ इति ।

स्वस्वबीजाद्यानित्यपि ध्येयम् । बीजानि लं रं मं क्षं वं यं सं हं आं ह्रीं । तदुक्तं

मन्त्रमहार्णवपञ्चरात्रे—

रागुर्लोकान्तरीयन्तु द्वितीयं वह्निलोमतः ।

चतुर्थं कामुलोमेन रागुलोमेन चाष्टमम् ॥

तृतीयं वामुलोमेन वामलोमात् तृतीयकम् ।

चतुर्थं सकलं वर्णं रागुलोमेन संस्थितम् ॥

चतुर्थं कामुलोमेन तृतीयं भविलोमतः ।

स्वरोपान्त्यस्वराभ्यां भेदितं सर्वमेव तत् ॥

आनुपूर्व्येण तद्बीजं सप्तान्तं वामधारिणम् ॥ इति ।

एतानि दीर्घस्वरीति केचित् । अनन्तब्रह्मणोर्मायापाद्यबीजं इति केचित् ।

तदुक्तम्—पूर्वाग्निवरुणाद्यन्तवरुणानिलमेश्वरैः ।

अनन्तबिन्दुसंयुक्तैरन्त्यैः पार्श्वेन मायया ॥ इति ।

तत्र रक्ष इति निर्ऋतिं पवनं वायुं विधुं सोमं पन्नगाधीशम् अनन्तं पितामहं

ब्रह्माणम् । दिक्षु पूर्व्वादिषु क्रमादिति । अत्र प्रसिद्धा एव पूर्व्वादयो ग्राह्याः ।

तदुक्तम्—प्रयजेत् स्वदिक्ष्वमलधीः स्वजातिबीजसंस्थितवाहनविवरसंयुतान् । इति ।

नारायणीये च—इन्द्रादींश्च स्वदिक्षु । इति ।

अन्यत्रापि—इन्द्रादिकान् लोकपालान् स्वस्वदिक्षु समर्चयेत् । इति ।

तत्राष्टदिक्षु अष्ट पूजयितव्याः । निर्ऋतिवरुणयोर्मध्ये अनन्तम् । इन्द्रेशानयोर्मध्ये

ब्रह्माणम् । तदुक्तं वायवीयसंहितायाम्—

विष्णुं नैर्ऋते विधिमैश्वरे ।

अपि: पद्मस्य वक्त्रान्यन्यान्यायुधान्यपि ॥

प्रसिद्धरूपास्त्राद्यास्तु लोकेशानां क्रमाद्यजेत् । इति ।

वज्रं शक्तिं दण्डमसिं पाशमङ्कुशकं गदाम् ।
शूलं चक्रं पद्ममेषामायुधानि क्रमाद्विदुः ॥ ११६
पीतशुक्लसिताकाशविद्युद्रक्तासितासिताः ।
करविन्दपाटलाभा वज्राद्याः परिकीर्त्तिताः ॥ ११७
एवं सम्पूज्य विधिवन्निवेद्यान्तं ततो गुरुः ।
दक्षिणे स्थण्डिलं कृत्वा तत्राऽऽधाय हुताशनम् ॥ ११८
संस्कृत्य विधिवद्विद्वान् वैश्वदेवं समाचरेत् ।
तत्र सम्पूज्य गन्धाद्यैर्देवतामुक्तविग्रहाम् ॥ ११९

अत्र नैर्ऋते ऐश्वरे इति तत्सामीप्यलक्षकमिति ज्ञेयम् । अत्र क्वचिद् ब्रह्माणं पूजयित्वा अनन्तं पूजयेदिति क्रमः । स पौराणिक इति ज्ञेयं न तान्त्रिकः । महाकपिलपञ्चरात्रहयशीर्षपञ्चरात्रप्रपञ्चसारादिबहुतन्त्रविरोधात् । तथा चाचार्याः—

अनन्तब्रह्मपर्य्यन्तैः पञ्चमीन्द्रादिभिर्मता ।
चक्रपद्मान्तिकैः षष्ठी वज्राद्यैः ॥ इति ।

प्रयोगो यथा । ॐ लं इन्द्राय सुराधिपतये सायुधाय सवाहनाय सपरिवाराय सशक्तिकाय विष्णुपारिषदाय नमः इति । एवं ॐ रं अग्नये तेजोऽधिपतये इत्यादि । एषां पूजायां लोकपालमुद्रा दर्शनीया । यदाहुः—

पाणिमूले सुसंलग्ने शाखाः सर्व्वाः प्रसारिताः ।
लोकेशानामियं मुद्रा तेषामर्चासु दर्शयेत् ॥ इति ॥ ११२-११५ ॥

वज्रमिति । असिं खड्गं । आकाशो नीलवर्णः । करविन्दः नीलपुष्पोऽतसीप्रायो वृक्षः । तत्पुष्पवर्ण इत्यर्थः ।

तदुक्तमाचार्य्यैः—करविन्दारुणवर्णाः । इति ।

तत्र प्रयोगो यथा ॐ वज्राय वज्रलाञ्छितमौलये सायुधाय सवाहनाय सपरिवाराय सशक्तिकाय विष्णु पारिषदाय नमः इत्याद्यूह्यम् । तदुक्तमाचार्य्यैः—

अर्च्या बहिर्निजसुलक्षितमौलियुक्ताः
स्वस्वायुधाभयसमुद्यतपाणिपद्माः । इति ।

मूलेन मूर्त्तिं कृप्तेत्यादि निवेद्यान्तमिति नित्यपूजायामपि समानम् । विद्वान् विधिवत् संस्कृत्येत्यनेन वीक्षणादयश्चत्वारः संस्कारा घृतसंस्कारा अग्नेराज्याहुतिक्रमेण गर्भाधानादि संस्काराश्च कर्त्तव्या इत्युक्तं भवति ॥ ११६॥११७॥११८॥११९ ॥

तारव्याहृतिभिर्हुत्वा मूलमन्त्रेण मन्त्रवित् ।
सर्पिष्मता पायसेन पञ्चविंशतिसंख्यया ॥ १२०

हुत्वा व्याहृतिभिर्भूयो गन्धाद्यैः पुनरर्चयेत् ।
तां योजयित्वा पीठस्थमूर्त्तौ वह्निं विसर्जयेत् ॥ १२१

अवशिष्टेन हविषा विकिरेत् परितो बलिम् ।
देवतायाः पार्षदेभ्यो गन्धपुष्पाक्षतान्वितम् ॥ १२२

ततो नैवेद्यमुद्धृत्य शोधयित्वा जलं पुनः ।
पञ्चोपचारैः सम्पूज्य दर्शयेच्छत्रचामरे ॥ १२३

कर्पूरशकलोन्मिश्रं ताम्बूलञ्च निवेदयेत् ।
सहस्रावृत्त्य संजप्य मूलमन्त्रमनन्यधीः ।
तज्जपं सर्व्वसम्पत्त्यै देवतायै समर्पयेत् ॥ १२४

तारव्याहृतिभिरिति । अत्राद्याश्चतस्रः सताव्याहृतिभिः एका समस्तेन । भूयोऽनन्तरं व्याहृतिभिर्हुत्वेति सम्बन्धः । पूर्व्ववदिति शेषम् । पुनरनन्तरं गन्धाद्यैस्तां देवताम् अर्चयेत् । आदिपदेन पुष्पधूपदीपनैवेद्यानि । पीठस्थमूर्त्तौ योजयित्वा तामित्यनुषज्यते ॥ १२०॥१२१॥१२२ ॥

तत एतेनैतदुक्तं भवति । पानार्थं जलं दद्यात् । मूलमन्त्रान्ते

श्लोकस्तु—समस्तदेवदेवेश सर्व्वतृप्तिकरं परम् ।
अखण्डानन्दसम्पूर्णं गृहाण जलमुत्तमम् ॥ इति ।

ततो भोजनशेषोदकञ्च दत्त्वा निर्गततेजो देवमुखे संहृत्य नैवेद्यांशं विश्वक्सेनादिभ्यो दद्यादिति । तदुक्तम्—

मुख्याद्दीशानतः पात्रान्नैवेद्यांशं समुद्धरेत् ।
सर्व्वदेवस्वरूपाय पराय परमेष्ठिने ।
श्रीरामसेनायुक्ताय विश्वक्सेनाय ते नमः ॥
गणेशे वक्रतुण्डाय सूर्य्ये चण्डांशवेऽर्पयेत् ।
शक्तावुच्छिष्टचाण्डाल्यै शिवे चण्डेश्वराय च ॥ इति ।

देवतायाः पार्षदेभ्य इत्यत्रापि पारिषदशब्देनैषामेव ग्रहणम् । सर्व्वसम्पत्त्यै देवतायै इति व्यधिकरणे चतुर्थ्यौ ।

समर्पयेदिति । अत्र नित्यपूजायां ताम्बुलछत्रादर्शचामराणि समर्प्य—

बुद्धिः सुवासना कृष्ण दर्पणं मङ्गलानि च ।
मनोवृत्तिर्विचित्रा ते नृत्यरूपेण कल्पिता ॥
ध्वनयो गीतरूपेण शब्दा वाद्यप्रभेदतः ।
छत्राणि नव पद्मानि कल्पितानि मया प्रभो ॥
सुषुम्णाध्वजरूपेण प्राणाद्याश्चामराश्रया ।
अहङ्कारो गजत्वेन वेगः तूर्णो रथात्मना ॥
इन्द्रियाण्यश्वरूपाणि शब्दादि रथवर्त्मना ।
मनः प्रग्रहरूपेण बुद्धिः सारथिरूपतः ।
सर्वमन्यत्तथा कृतं सर्वोपकरणात्मना ॥

इति श्लोकान् पठित्वा यथाशक्ति मूलमन्त्रं जप्त्वा

गुह्यातिगुह्यगोप्ता त्वं गृहाणास्मत्कृतं जपम् ।
सिद्धिर्भवतु मे देव त्वत्प्रसादात्त्वयि स्थिते ॥

इत्यनेन तं जपं देवतायै निवेदयेत् । तदुक्तं गौतमीये—

मन्त्री श्लोकं पठित्वा तु दक्षहस्तेन साधके ।
मूलाणुनाऽर्घ्यतोयेन देवहस्ते निवेदयेत् ॥ इति ।

ततः पराङ्मुखमर्घ्यं दत्त्वा शङ्खं पूजयेत् । तदुक्तं मन्त्रतन्त्रप्रकाशे—

पूजयेद् गन्धपुष्पाद्यैः शङ्खं च देववद् बुधः । इति ।

अन्यत्रापि—त्रैलोक्ये यानि तीर्थानि वासुदेवस्य चाज्ञया ।
शङ्खे तिष्ठन्ति विप्रेन्द्र तस्माच्छङ्खं सदाऽर्चयेत् ॥

ततः प्रदक्षिणं कुर्यात् । तत्र विशेषस्तन्त्रान्तरे—

एकां चण्ड्यां रवौ सप्त तिस्रो दद्याद् विनायके ।
चतस्रः केशवे दद्यात् शिवस्यार्द्धं प्रदक्षिणम् ॥ इति ।

ततः स्तुत्वा नत्वा नित्यहोमं कुर्यात् । तत्र तन्त्रान्तरे विशेषः—

अग्न्याधानादिकं कार्यं नित्यहोमे न विद्यते । इति ।

ततश्चुलुकोदकेन "इतः पूर्वं प्राणबुद्धिदेहधर्माधिकारतो जाग्रत्स्वप्नसुषुप्त्यवस्थासु मनसा वाचा हस्ताभ्यां पद्भ्यामुदरेण शिश्ना यत् कृतं यदुक्तं यत् स्मृतं तत् सर्वं ब्रह्मार्पणं भवतु स्वाहा । मां मदीयञ्च सकलं हरये समर्पये ॐ तत् सत्" इति ब्रह्मार्पणमन्त्रेणात्मानं समर्प्य स्वहृत्कमले संहारमुद्रया देवमुपसंहरेदिति विशेषः । संहारमुद्रालक्षणमुक्तमेव । प्रसादस्वीकारे तत्तद्देवताभक्तेन तत्तद्देवताप्रसादः स्वीकर्त्तव्य एव । पञ्चदेवतापूजायान्तु विष्णोरेव शालग्रामशिलास्वर्चादन्येषाञ्च ।

ततः शम्भोर्दिशि गुरुर्वेदिकायां पूर्वकल्पिते ॥ १२५

हेमवस्त्रादिसंयुक्तां कर्करीं तोयपूरिताम् ।

संस्थाप्य तस्यां सिंहस्थां खड्गखेटकधारिणीम् ॥ १२६

घोररूपां महिमाख्यां पूजयेदस्त्रदेवताम् ।

शलासनेन सम्पूज्य तामादाय गुरुः पुनः ॥ १२७

रक्षेति लोकपालानां नालमुखेन वारिणा ।

देवानां श्रावयन्नन्तः परिक्रम्य प्रदक्षिणम् ॥ १२८

अस्त्रमन्त्रं समुच्चार्य यथापूर्वं निवेशयेत् ।

अभ्यर्च्य भूयो गन्धाद्यैरस्त्रं तत्र स्थिरासने ॥ १२९

ततश्च संस्कृते वह्नौ गोक्षीरेण चरुं पचेत् ।

अस्त्रेण क्षालिते पात्रे नवे ताम्रमयादिके ॥ १३०

तथा च बह्वृचपरिशिष्टे—

पवित्रं विष्णुनैवेद्यं सुरसिद्धर्षिभिः स्मृतम् ।

अन्यदेवस्य नैवेद्यं भुक्त्वा चान्द्रायणं चरेत् ॥

ग्राह्यं शिवनिर्माल्यं पत्रं पुष्पं फलं जलम् ।

शालग्रामशिलास्पर्शात् सर्वं याति पवित्रताम् ॥ इति ।

अन्यो विशेषस्तन्त्रान्तरे

विक्षेपादस्य शालिश्यामाकपक्षोमार्थेनान्तरा ।

उच्छिष्यति तदा न्यासं षडङ्गं विन्यसेत् पुनः ॥ इति ॥१२३॥१२४॥

शम्भोर्दिशीति ऐशान्याम् । कर्करीं सनालं जलपात्रम् । तस्यां कर्कर्याम् एवम्भूतामस्त्रदेवतां पूजयेदित्यन्वयः । शलासनेन फलुष्किलासनेन । तामिति । गुरुस्तां कर्करीमादाय नालमुखेन वारिणा लोकपालानां रक्षेति देवानां श्रावयन् अन्तर्मण्डपान्तर्वेद्याः परितः प्रदक्षिणं परिक्रम्य यथापूर्वं तां निवेशयेदिति सम्बन्धः । तत्र कर्कर्याम् । स्थिरासने निश्चलासने उपविष्ट इत्यर्थः ॥ १२५-१२८ ॥

तत इति । संस्कृते वह्नाविति आचार्येण स्वकुण्डे संस्कृते । यतोऽग्रिमपटले वक्ष्यमाणाग्निजननकर्म आचार्येण अस्मिन्नेव काले कृतमस्ति तस्यानुवादः संस्कृते वह्नाविति । तदुक्तं प्रयोगसारे—

तण्डुलान् शालिसम्भूतान् मूलमन्त्राभिमन्त्रितान् ।
प्रसृतीनां पञ्चदश क्षिप्त्वा चाऽस्त्रमनुं जपेत् ॥ १३१
प्रक्षाल्य पात्रवदनं पिधाय कवचाणुना ।
प्राङ्मुखो मूलमन्त्रेण देशिकेन्द्रश्चरुं पचेत् ॥ १३२
स्रुवेणाज्येन संस्विन्ने दद्यात्तस्याभिघारणम् ।
मूलेन पश्चात्तत्पात्रं कवचेनाऽवतारयेत् ॥ १३३
अस्त्रजप्ते कुशास्तीर्णे मण्डले विधिवद् गुरुः ।
तं विभज्य त्रिधा भागमेकं देवाय कल्पयेत् ॥ १३४
अन्यमग्नौ प्रजुहुयादपरं देशिकः स्वयम् ।
शिष्येण सार्द्धं भुञ्जीत विहिताचमनस्तदा ॥ १३५

कुण्डमन्त्रेण संप्रोक्ष्य तत्राधाय हुताशनम् ।
सान्वाधानादिकं देवं यथावत् पूजयेत्ततः ॥
कृत्वा तण्डुलनिर्वापं तस्मिन् शौरि पचेच्चरुम् ॥ इति ।

नारायणीयेऽपि—तत्र सम्भृतसम्भारः शिवमिष्ट्वा विधानतः ।
मूलमूर्त्यङ्गविद्याभिस्तण्डुलक्षेपणादिकम् ॥
कृत्वा चरुं पचेत् शौरिं पुनस्तद्वदिभर्जत् त्रिधा ।
निवेद्यैकं परं हुत्वा सशिष्योऽन्यद् भुजेद् गुरुः ॥ इति ॥ १३० ॥

तण्डुलानिति । प्रसृतीनां पञ्चदशभिः परिमितानिति शेषः । तण्डुलान् प्रक्षाल्याऽस्त्रमनुं जपन् क्षिप्त्वा इति सम्बन्धः । प्रसृतिलक्षणमग्रे वक्ष्यते ॥१३१॥१३२॥

स्रुवेणेति । संस्विन्ने चरौ स्रुवेण कृत्वा मूलमन्त्रेण आज्येन तस्याभिघारणं दद्यादिति सम्बन्धः । विधिवद् गुरुरित्यनेन मूलेन कुशेन समविभागः कार्य्य इत्युक्तम् ॥ १३३ ॥ १३४ ॥

अन्येति । अग्नाविति कुण्डाग्नौ देशिकः प्रजुहुयादित्यनेनैतदुक्तम् । "साज्येन चरुणा तथा" इत्यग्निपटले मूलमन्त्रेण पञ्चविंशतिवारमुक्तो होमोऽत्रानुसन्धेयः इति । भुञ्जीतेति । तत्र विशेषः सोमशम्भौ—

चरोस्तृतीयभागन्तु ग्रासत्रितयसम्मितम् ।
अष्टग्रासप्रमाणं वा दर्शनस्पर्शवर्जितम् ॥

आचान्तं शिष्यमानीय सकलीकृत्य देशिकः ।
तालप्रमाणं ऋज्वग्रं क्षीरवृक्षादिसम्भवम् ॥ १३६

दन्तकाष्ठं तदा दद्याच्छिष्याय नियतात्मने ।
दन्तान् विशोध्य स पुनस्तत् प्रक्षाल्य विसर्जयेत् ॥ १३७

पालाशे पुटके मुक्तौ भुक्तौ पिप्पलपत्रजे ।
हृदा सम्भोजयेन्मन्त्री पूतैराचमयेज्जलैः ॥ इति ॥१३५॥

सकलीकृत्येति मन्त्रषडङ्गमस्याङ्गे न्यस्येति । तालेति । प्रहृतपाणेरङ्गुष्ठाग्रान्मध्यमाग्रं यावत्तालः । तदुक्तम्—

अङ्गुष्ठमध्यमाङ्गुल्यौ ये हस्तस्य प्रसारिते ।
तदग्रयोरन्तरालं तालमाहुर्मनीषिणः ॥ इति ।

देशिको दद्यादित्यनेन दानमन्त्र उक्तः । यत् पिङ्गलामते—

माया दण्डिनि ठद्वन्द्वं प्रदद्यादमुना च तत् । इति ।

विसर्जनानन्तरं तत्परीक्षा कर्त्तव्येति विसर्जयेदित्यनेनोक्तम् ।

प्रक्षाल्य निक्षिपेद्भूमौ वामतो वामपाणिना । इति ।

प्रयोगसारे विशेषः । स यथा नारायणीये—

दन्तकाष्ठं हृदा जप्तं क्षीरिवृक्षादिसम्भवम् ।
सम्मार्ज्य दन्तांस्तच्छित्वा प्रक्षाल्यैतद्भुवि क्षिपेत् ॥
दिक्षु पूर्वाद्यधोर्द्ध्वासु तस्याग्रपतनं क्रमात् ।
वृद्धिस्तापो मृतिर्वित्तं क्षयं शान्तिर्गदो धनम् ॥
सुखवृद्धिः परं दुःखं फलान्येतानि शंसति । इति ।

अन्यत्रापि—धीश्रीतापवियोगापमृत्युशुभदुःखताशमैश्वादौ ।
रदधावनाग्रपाते कुफले मूलाहुतिस्तिलैर्दिशति ॥ इति ।

अन्यत्रापि—अथात्र चूतवृक्षस्य द्वादशाङ्गुलमानतः ।
दन्तकाष्ठं प्रदातव्यं तदन्ताग्रविचर्वितम् ॥
ऊर्द्ध्वास्यं क्षेपयेत्तत्र मण्डले पीठमुख्ययेत् ।
पश्चिमोत्तरवह्नीन्द्रे शुभः पातोऽन्यथाऽशुभः ॥
दुर्निमित्तविनाशाय जुहुयाच्छतमस्त्रतः ॥ इति ।

वायवीयसंहितायान्तु—

त्यक्तं तद्दन्तपवनं दृश्यते गुरुणा यदि ।

यथाविधि समाचान्तं शिखाबन्धाभिरक्षितम् ।

शिष्यं सार्द्धममुना वेद्यां दर्भास्तरे गुरुः ।

शयीत तस्यां तां रात्रिमधिवासः समीरितः ॥ १३८

इति श्रीशारदातिलके चतुर्थः पटलः ।

प्रागुदक्पश्चिमेभागे शिवमन्त्राभिवेसरम् ॥

अथास्यासामुखे तस्मिन् गुरुस्तद्दोषशान्तये ।

शतमर्धं तदर्धं वा जुहुयान्मूलमन्त्रतः ॥ इति ॥ १३६॥१३७ ॥

यथाविध्याचान्तं यथाविधि शिखाबन्धाभिरक्षितं विधायेति सम्बन्धः । तत्राचमने विधिः पूर्वं मयोक्त एव । शिखाबन्धे तु यथाविधीत्यनेनैतदुक्तं भवति । मूलमन्त्रस्य सजातिशिखामन्त्रेण अघोरादिमन्त्रेण वा शिखां बध्नीयादिति ।

शयीतेति । गुरुस्तस्यां वेद्याममुना शिष्येण सार्द्धं दर्भास्तरे तां रात्रिं शयीतेति सम्बन्धः । वेद्यामिति सामीप्यमधिकरणार्थम् । तदुक्तं नारायणीये—

पुनस्तं शिष्यमाचान्तं शिखाबन्धाभिरक्षितम् ।

कृत्वा वेद्यां सहात्मेन स्वपेद् दर्भास्तरे गुरुः ॥ इति

गुरुरित्यनेन देवदक्षिणभागे पूर्वशिरसा शिष्यं स्वापयेदित्युक्तम् ।

स्वप्रमाणमथाश्रित्य स्वापयेत् पूर्वमस्तकम् ।

इति पिङ्गलामते उक्तेः ।

सोमशम्भौ तु—ब्रह्मस्थान् दर्भशय्यायां पूर्वशीर्षांश्च दीक्षितान् ।

हृदा सङ्गशय्यायां यतीन् दक्षिणमस्तकान् ॥ इति ।

वायवीयसंहितायान्तु—

देवस्य दक्षिणे भागे शिष्यं तमधिवासयेत् ।

अहतास्तरणास्तीर्णे सदर्भशयने शुचिः ॥

मन्त्रिते च शिवं ध्यायन् प्राक्शिरस्को निशि स्वपेत् ।

शिखाबद्धस्य सूत्रस्य शिखया तच्छिखां गुरुः ॥

आवेष्ट्याहतवस्त्रेण समाच्छाद्य च वर्मणा ।

रेखात्रयञ्च परितो भस्मना तिलसर्षपैः ।

कृत्वाऽस्त्रजप्तैस्तस्याश्च दिगीशानां बलिं हरेत् ॥ इति ।

स्वप्रमाणमस्त्रो वैष्णवेषु मन्त्रतन्त्रप्रकाशे—

ॐ नमः सकललोकाय विष्णवे प्रभविष्णवे ।

विश्वाय विश्वरूपाय स्वप्नाधिपतये नमः ।
स्वप्नमाणवमन्त्रोऽयं कथितो नारदादिभिः ॥ इति ।

शैवव्यवहारे तु पिङ्गलामते—

तारो हिलिद्वयं शूलपाणये ठिठ ईरितः ।
स्वप्नमाणवमन्त्रोऽयं शम्भुना परिकीर्त्तितः ॥ इति ।

तन्त्रान्तरोक्तो विशेषः—

नमोऽजाय त्रिनेत्राय पिङ्गलाय महात्मने ।
वामाय विश्व[विष्णु]रूपाय स्वप्नाधिपतये नमः ॥
स्वप्ने कथय मे तथ्यं सर्व्वकार्येष्वशेषतः ।
क्रियासिद्धिं विधास्यामि त्वत्प्रसादान्महेश्वर ॥

इति मन्त्रेण स्वापकाले देवं संप्रार्थ्य स्वपेत् ।

प्रातश्च स्वप्नपरीक्षा कार्य्या । तदुक्तं पिङ्गलामते—

स्वप्ने शुभाशुभं दृष्टं प्रच्छेत् प्रातः शिशुं गुरुः ।
शुभे शुभं वदेत्तस्य जुहुयादशुभे मतम् ।
अस्त्रेणेति क्रमात् प्रोक्तो विधिः शिष्याधिवासने ॥ इति ।

अन्यत्रापि—क्रूरेऽथवा मध्यमा स्यादहष्टे तूत्तमोत्तमा[मापि च] ॥ इति ।

महाकपिलपञ्चरात्रेऽपि—

गुरुपादार्चनं कृत्वा उपवासी जितेन्द्रियः ।
दर्भशय्यां गतो रात्रौ दृष्ट्वा स्वप्नं निवेदयेत् ॥
कन्यां छत्रं रथं दीपं प्रासादं कमलं नदीम् ।
कुञ्जरं वृषभं माल्यं समुद्रं फणिनं द्रुमम् ॥
पर्व्वतञ्च हयं मेध्यमामांसं सुरासवम् ।
एवमादीनि सर्व्वाणि दृष्ट्वा सिद्धिमवाप्नुयात् ॥
चाण्डालं करभं कारुं गर्त्तं शून्यममङ्गलम् ।
तैलाभ्यक्तं नरं नग्नं शुष्कवृक्षं सकण्ट[नपुंस]कम् ॥
प्रासादमत[नि]लं दृष्ट्वा नरो रोगमवाप्नुयात् ।
दृष्ट्वा दुःस्वप्नकञ्चैव होमात् सिद्धिमवाप्नुयात् ॥ इति ।

अत्रोपवासीति रागतः प्राप्तभोजननिषेधः न तु वचनविहितचरुभोजननिषेधः ।

सम्मतन्त्रप्रकाशेऽपि—अथ प्रातः समुत्थाय स्वप्नं दृष्ट्वा विचारयेत् ।
भद्रे भद्रं विजानीयादभद्रे जुहुयाच्छतम् ॥ इत्यादि ।

नारायणीये तु—स्वप्नान् संवीक्षितान् शिष्यः प्रभाते श्रावयेद् गुरुम् ।

शुभैः सिद्धिः परैर्भक्तिः । इति ।

अधिवासः समीरित इति मन्त्रग्रहणपूर्व्वदिने । पिङ्गलामते तु सद्योऽधि-वासोऽप्युक्तः ।

सद्योऽधिवासमथवा प्रकुर्व्वीत यथाविधि । इति ।

मन्त्रतन्त्रप्रकाशेऽपि—

दिनद्वये नैव कुर्य्याद्दीक्षाकर्म्म विचक्षणः ।
सद्योऽधिवासनं कुर्य्यादेकस्मिन् दिवसे यदि ॥

अधिवासशब्दार्थं उक्तो महाकपिलपञ्चरात्रे—

वसतेरधिपूर्व्वस्य भावे घञ्प्रत्यये कृते
अधिवास इति ह्येव प्रयोगः सिद्धिमेति च ॥
गुर्व्वादिसहितो वासो रात्रौ नियमपूर्व्वकः ।
सोऽस्यार्थो हि निपातानामनेकार्थतया मतः ॥ इति ॥१३८॥

इति श्रीशारदातिलकटीकायां सत्सम्प्रदायकृतव्याख्यायां
पदार्थादर्शाभिख्यायां चतुर्थः पटलः ॥ ॐ ॥

पञ्चमः पटलः ।

ततोऽग्निजननं वक्ष्ये सर्व्वतन्त्रानुसारतः ।
आचार्य्यकुण्डे विधिवत् संस्कृते शास्त्रवर्त्मना ॥ १
अष्टादश स्युः संस्काराः कुण्डानां तन्त्रचोदिताः ।
वीक्षणं मूलमन्त्रेण शरेण प्रोक्षणं मतम् ॥ २
तेनैव ताडनं दर्भैर्वर्म्मणाऽभ्युक्षणं स्मृतम् ।
अस्त्रेण खननोद्धारौ हृन्मन्त्रेण प्रपूरणम् ॥ ३
समीकरणमस्त्रेण सेचनं वर्म्मणा मतम् ।
कुट्टनं हेतिमन्त्रेण वर्म्ममन्त्रेण मार्जनम् ॥ ४
विलेपनं कलारूपकल्पनं तदनन्तरम् ।
त्रिसूत्रीकरणं पश्चाद्धृदयेनाऽर्चनं मतम् ॥ ५

अधिवासदिवस एवास्त्रदेवतापूजानन्तरं आचार्य्यकर्त्तव्यकुण्डसंस्कारादिकमाह तत इति । शास्त्रवर्त्मना विधिवत् । संस्कृते आचार्य्यकुण्डे सर्व्वतन्त्रानुसारतोऽग्नि-जननं वक्ष्य इति सम्बन्धः ॥ १ ॥

तमेव विधिमाह अष्टादशेति । शरेणेत्यस्त्रमन्त्रेण । अत्र सर्व्वत्र अस्त्रादिमन्त्रा देयमन्त्रस्य ज्ञेयाः । वीक्षणं मूलमन्त्रेणेति प्रथमत उक्तेः केचन जातिमन्त्रमेवाहुः । तन्न साम्प्रदायिकम् । प्रोक्षणमित्युत्तानेन हस्ताग्रेण । "उत्तानेन हस्तेन प्रोक्षयेत्" इति स्मरणात् ॥ २ ॥

अभ्युक्षणमिति मुष्टिबन्धेन सर्व्वत्र सेचनम् । उद्धारः खातमृदः पूरणम् अन्यमृदा सेचनमभ्युक्षणमिव । अभेदाल्लवर्णानुवर्त्तनात् कश्चित्तमनुवर्त्तते इत्युक्तेः ॥३॥

हेतिमन्त्रेणेत्यस्त्रमन्त्रेण । वर्म्ममन्त्रेणेत्यग्रिमेषु चतुर्षु सम्बध्यते । तदुक्तं सोमशम्भुना—सम्मार्जनं समालेपं कलारूपप्रकल्पनम् ।

विसूत्रोपरिधानञ्च वर्म्मणाऽभ्यर्चनं हृदा ॥ इति ।

कलारूपकल्पनमिति चन्द्रसूर्य्याग्निकलारूपकल्पनम् । त्रिसूत्रीकरणमिति सूत्र-त्रयवेष्टनम् ॥ ४ ॥ ५ ॥

अस्त्रेण वज्रीकरणं हृन्मन्त्रेण कुशैः शुभैः ।
चतुष्पथं तनुत्रेण तनुयादक्षपाटनम् ॥ ६
यागे कुण्डानि संस्कुर्य्यात् संस्कारैरेभिरीरितैः ।
अथवा तानि संस्कुर्य्याच्चतुर्भिर्वीक्षणादिभिः ॥ ७
तिस्रस्तिस्रो लिखेद्रेखा हृदा प्रागुदगग्रगाः ।
प्रागग्राणां स्मृता देवा मुकुन्देशपुरन्दराः ॥ ८
रेखाणामुदगग्राणां ब्रह्मवैवस्वतेन्दवः ।
अथवा षट्कोणावृतं त्रिकोणं तत्र संलिखेत् ॥ ९
सर्व्वाण्यभ्युक्ष्य तारेण योगपीठमथार्चयेत् ।
वागीश्वरीमृतुस्नातां नीलेन्दीवरसन्निभाम् ॥ १०

वज्रीकरणमिति वज्रवद्दृढ़ीकरणम् । चतुष्पथमिति मध्यात् कुशैश्चतुर्दिक्षु मार्गचतुष्टयकरणम् । तनुत्रेणेति कवचमन्त्रेण । अक्षपाटनमिन्द्रियोत्पाटनम् इत्येके । अन्ये तु अक्षपाटना राक्षसाः न विद्यन्ते अक्षपाटना यस्मिन् तत् । हुंकारेण राक्षसनिवारणं कुर्य्यादित्यर्थः । अन्ये तु साम्प्रदायिकाः अट पट गतौ गतिर्ज्ञानम् आदिक्षान्तानां पाटनं व्याप्तिः । अशक्तान् प्रत्याह अथवेति ॥ ६ ॥ ७ ॥

तिस्र इति । तिस्रस्तिस्रो रेखा लिखेत् । ग्रा इत्यनेनैतदुक्तं भवति । प्रागग्राणाम् उदक्संस्थत्वम् उदगग्राणां पूर्व्वसंस्थत्वमिति । सर्व्वाः प्रादेशमिताः इत्यपि सम्प्रदायात् । तदुक्तं सौतामणितन्त्रे —

प्राचीपूर्व्वमुदक्संस्थं दक्षिणारम्भमालिखेत् ।
उदगग्रं पुरःसंस्थं पश्चिमारम्भमालिखेत् ।
तिस्रस्तिस्रो लिखित्वैवं प्रोक्षयेद्वाग्भवेन च ॥ इति ।

अथवा षट्कोणावृतं त्रिकोणं लिखेत् । अत्र केचित् षट्कोणवृत्तत्रिकोणम् इति पाठमपठन् । तदज्ञानविजृम्भितम् । तथा च आचार्य्याः—

अथवा षट्कोणावृतत्रिकोणके गुरुजनोपदेशेन । इति ।

तथा च यामले—षट्कोणेनावृतं देवि त्रिकोणञ्चात्र संलिखेत् । इति ।
अन्यत्रापि—कृत्वा रेखाश्च मध्यतः । षट्कोणं त्रिकोणञ्च । इति ॥ ८ ॥ ९ ॥

सर्व्वाणीति । एतानि प्रणवेनाऽभ्युक्ष्य योगपीठं वागीशीयोगपीठं मण्डूकादि-

वागीश्वरेण संयुक्तामुपचारैः प्रपूजयेत् ।

सूर्यकान्तादिसम्भूतं यद्वा श्रोत्रियगेहजम् ॥ ११

आनीय वह्निं पात्रेण क्रव्यादांशं परित्यजेत् ।

संस्कुर्यात् तं यथान्यायं देशिको वीक्षणादिभिः ॥ १२

परत्वाक्षं सम्पूज्य नवशक्तीः पीठशक्तीः सम्पूज्य ह्रीं वागीश्वरीयोगपीठाय नम इति योगपीठं पूजयेत् । अत्र सारतन्त्रेण यथाशं तत्सम्बन्धेषु पञ्चप्रणवानामपि ग्रहणं ज्ञेयम् । प्रपूजयेदिति । पीठे ऋतुबीजेन वागीश्वरीं साध्यमन्त्रेण वागीशम् । तदुक्तं गणेश्वरविमर्शिन्याम्—

ऋतुबीजेन वागीशीं वागीशं साध्यमन्त्रतः । इति ।

अन्यत्रापि—साध्यमन्त्रेण तं देवम् इत्यादिना ।

सूर्यकान्तादीत्यादिशब्देन अरणिजन्यः । तदुक्तम्—

जातं मार्तण्डकान्तादुत वह्निमथनैः श्रोत्रियागारजं वा । इति ।

श्रोत्रियगेहजमिति । श्रोत्रियत्वं वेदाध्ययनेन तन्त्रोक्तजुहोतृत्वेन च । तेन आहिताग्नित्वे तात्पर्यम् । तदुक्तं वशिष्ठसंहितायाम्—

प्रमथ्य विधिनैवाग्निमाहिताग्नेर्गृहादपि ।

आनीय चादपीतात् । इति ।

पात्रेणेति कांस्यादिपात्रेण । पात्रान्तरपिहितेन इत्याचार्याः ।

अन्यत्र तु—श्रोत्रियागारजं वापि सूर्यकान्तोद्भवन्तु वा ।

अरणीसम्भवं वापि क्षिप्तं स्वर्णादिभाजने ॥ इति ।

अन्यैरपि—पात्रान्तरेण पिहिते ताम्रपात्रादिके शुभे ।

अग्निप्रणयनं कुर्याच्छरावे तादृशेऽपि च ॥ इति ।

अन्यत्रापि—तैजसे विधिवत् पात्रे वरकनकमये ताम्रपात्रेऽथ वापि

मृत्पात्रे वा पिधायाऽस्त्रादिमुखमतिः । इति ।

यत्तु स्मृतिसारे—शरावे भिन्नपात्रे वा कपाले चोल्मुकेऽपि वा ।

नाग्निप्रणयनं कुर्याद् व्याधिहानिभयावहम् ॥

इति वचनम् तस्य मुख्यपात्रसम्भवे शरावो न ग्राह्य इत्यत्र तात्पर्यम् ।

क्रव्यादांशं परित्यजेदिति । अस्त्रमन्त्रेण नैर्ऋत्य इति ज्ञेयम् ।

तदुक्तम्—अस्त्रेणाऽग्निं समादाय कवचेन पिधाय च ।

क्रव्यादांशन्तु चाऽस्त्रेण नैर्ऋत्ये सन्त्यजेत् प्रिये ॥ इति ।

औदर्य्यबैन्दवाग्निभ्यां भौमस्यैक्यं स्मरन् वसोः ।
योजयेद् वह्निबीजेन चैतन्यं पावके तदा ॥ १३

तारेण मन्त्रितं मन्त्री धेनुमुद्रामृतीकृतम् ।
अस्त्रेण रक्षितं पश्चात्तनुत्रेणाऽवगुण्ठितम् ॥ १४

अर्चितं त्रिः परिभ्राम्य कुण्डस्योपरि देशिकः ।
प्रदक्षिणं तदा तारमन्त्रोच्चारणपूर्व्वकम् ॥ १५

अन्यत्र वह्निबीजेन क्रव्यादांशत्यागः । तदुक्तम्—

वह्निबीजेन मन्त्री

क्रव्यादांशं त्यजेत् तं तदनु च मनुना शोधयेदस्त्रकेन । इति ।

मन्त्रमुक्तावल्यान्तु विशेषः—

आनीयाऽस्त्रेण नैर्ऋत्ये क्रव्यादांशं परित्यजेत् ।

देवांशं मूलमन्त्रेण स्थापयेत् पुरतः सुधीः ॥ इति ।

यथान्यायमित्यनेन प्रोक्षणाभ्युक्षणे तथा कार्य्ये यथा आनीतोऽग्निस्तिष्ठतीत्युक्तम् । वीक्षणादिभिरित्यादिशब्देन संस्कारत्रयम् ॥ १०॥११॥१२ ॥

औदर्य्येति । विन्दुः प्रसिद्धः परमात्मस्वरूपः । तस्याग्नीषोमस्वरूपत्वात् । तद्भवो वह्निर्बैन्दवः । अन्ये बिन्दुः भ्रूमध्यमिति । भौमस्य पार्थिवस्य । वसोरग्नेः ॥ १३ ॥

तारेणेति । पूर्व्ववत्तारशब्दार्थः । अमृतीकृतमित्यमृतबीजेनेत्याचार्य्याः । तदुक्तम्—अमृतीकरणं ततो विदध्याज्जलबीजेन सबिन्दुना कृशानोः । इति । रक्षितमिति दिग्बन्धेन । प्रदक्षिणमिति पूर्व्वेण सम्बध्यते ।

तारमन्त्रोच्चारणेति तारस्य प्रणवस्य मन्त्रस्य मूलमन्त्रस्योच्चारणम् । तदुक्तम्

योनाविमं विन्यसेत् स्वाभिवक्त्रं पश्चादग्निं मूलमन्त्रेण मन्त्री । इति ।

अत्रापि तारशब्दार्थः पूर्व्ववत् । "रं वह्निचैतन्याय नमः" इति पद्मपादाचार्य्याः । अन्ये तु तारशब्देन ह्रँकारं मन्त्रशब्देन वह्निचैतन्याय नमः इत्याहुः । तदुक्तम्—

ह्रँ वह्निपूर्व्वं चैतन्यं चतुर्थ्यन्तं नमोऽन्वितम् ।
मन्त्रमुच्चार्य्य पश्चात्तं वह्निमुत्थाप्य देशिकः ॥
भूमिष्ठजानुको भूत्वा कुण्डस्योर्द्ध्वं प्रदक्षिणम् ।
भ्रामयित्वा त्रिधा तत्र वागीशीगर्भगोचरे ॥
शिवबीजमिति ध्यात्वा निक्षिपेदाशुशुक्षणिम् ॥ इति ।

शिवबीजधियेति । इदं शैवे । शैवतन्त्रे तथोक्तेः । स एव वक्ष्यति च-

आत्मनोऽभिमुखं वह्निं जानुस्पृष्टमहीतलः ।
शिवबीजधिया देव्या योनाविव विनिक्षिपेत् ॥ १६

पश्चाद्देवस्य देव्याश्च दद्यादाचमनादिकम् ।
ज्वालयेन्मनुनाऽनेन तमग्निमथ देशिकः ॥ १७

चित्पिङ्गलं हनदहपचयुग्मान्युदीर्य्य च ।
सर्व्वज्ञाज्ञापय स्वाहा मन्त्रोऽयं प्रागुदीरितः ॥ १८

अग्निं प्रज्वलितं वन्दे जातवेदं हुताशनम् ।
सुवर्णवर्णममलं समिद्धं विश्वतोमुखम् ॥ १९

नाम्नापि शिवाग्निरिति कल्पयेत् । इति ।

नारायणीयेऽपि—शिवाग्निं जनयित्वा । इति ।

अत एव संहितायाम्—

लक्ष्मीमृतुमतीं तत्र प्रभोर्नारायणस्य च ।
ग्राम्यधर्म्मेण सञ्जातमग्निं तत्र विचिन्तयेत् ॥ इति ।

अत एव ग्रन्थकृदपि "वह्नेः पितरौ" इति सामान्यतो वक्ष्यति ।

अग्रे च—जुहुयाद् वैष्णवे वह्नौ । इति ।

जानुभ्यां स्पृष्टं महीतलं येनेति विग्रहः । वायवीयसंहितायान्तु—

वह्निबीजं समुच्चार्य्य त्वादधीताऽग्निमासने ।
योनिमार्गेण वा तद्वदात्मनः सम्मुखेन च ॥ इति ॥ १४॥१५॥१६ ॥

आचमनादिकमित्यादिशब्देन आचमनोत्तरोपचारग्रहणम् । "उपचारैः प्रपूजयेत्" इत्युक्तेः । ज्वालयेदिति । अनेन वक्ष्यमाणेन ।

तत्र विशेषः जुहुधुश्च हुताग्निश्च पाणिशूर्पस्रुवादिभिः ।
न कुर्य्यादग्निधमनं न कुर्य्याद् व्यजनादिना ॥
मुखेनैव धमेदग्निं मुखादेषो ह्यजायत ।
नाग्निं मुखेनेति तु यत् लौकिके योजयेत्तु तत् ॥ इति ॥ १७ ॥

चित्पिङ्गलमिति शब्दकर्म्मणि द्वितीया मन्त्रे तु सम्बुद्ध्यन्तम् । हनेत्यादित्रयाणां युग्मानि । ज्वालयेन्मनुनाऽनेनेति यो मन्त्रः प्रागुदीरितः उद्दिष्टः स मन्त्रोऽयमीरित इत्यर्थः । क्वचित्तु समुदीरित इत्येव पाठः । अत्र अग्निज्वालने ज्वालिनीमुद्रां प्रदर्शयेत् । तल्लक्षणन्तु—

उपतिष्ठेत विधिवन्मनुनाऽनेन पावकम् ।
विन्यसेदात्मनो देहे मन्त्रैर्जिह्वा हविर्भुजः ॥ २०
लिङ्गपायुशिरोनक्त्रघ्राणनेत्रेषु सर्वतः ।
वह्नीरार्घीशसंयुक्ताः सादियान्ताः सबिन्दवः ॥ २१
वर्णा मन्त्राः समुद्दिष्टा जिह्वानां सप्त देशिकैः ।
जिह्वास्तास्त्रिविधाः प्रोक्ता गुणभेदेन कर्मसु ॥ २२
हिरण्या गगना रक्ता कृष्णाऽन्या सुप्रभा मता ।
बहुरूपाऽतिरक्ता च सात्त्विक्यो यागकर्मसु ॥ २३
पद्मरागा सुवर्णान्या तृतीया भद्रलोहिता ।
लोहिताऽनन्तरं श्वेता धूमिनी च करालिका ॥ २४
राजस्यो रसना वह्नेर्विहिताः काम्यकर्मसु ।
विश्वमूर्तिस्फुलिङ्गिन्यौ धूम्रवर्णा मनोजवा ॥ २५

प्रणिबन्धौ समौ कृत्वा करौ तु प्रसृताङ्गुली ।
मध्यमे मिलिते कृत्वा तन्मध्येऽङ्गुष्ठकौ क्षिपेत् ॥
एषं सा परमा मुद्रा ज्वालिनी होमकर्मणि । इति ॥ १८ ॥ १८ ॥

विधिवदित्यनेनैतदुक्तं भवति उत्थाय कृताञ्जलिपुटो भूत्वा मन्त्रं जपेदिति । अनेनाग्निमित्यादिना । सर्वत इति सप्तमं स्थानं सर्वाङ्गे इत्यर्थः । "सर्वाङ्गेषु जिह्वाश्च" इत्याचार्योक्तेः । इदञ्च न्यासस्थानम् । बहुरूपायाः पूजायास्तथात्व माणत्वात् । उक्तञ्च—

सलिङ्गगुदमूर्धास्यनासानेत्रेषु च क्रमात् ।
विन्यसेदतिरिक्तां ताः सर्वाङ्गे बहुरूपिणीम् ॥ इति ।

उद्देशक्रमस्तु बीजोद्धारलोकर्यायेत्यवधेयम् ॥

वह्नीति । वह्नी रेफः इरो यः अर्घीश ऊकारः एतद्युक्ताः । सादियान्ताः सकारादियकारान्ताः । वैपरीत्येन एते वर्णाः सबिन्दवो मन्त्रा भवन्ति ॥२०॥२१॥

जिह्वानामिति त्रिविधानामपि । तत्र प्रयोगः स्रूँ हिरण्यायै नमः लिङ्गे इत्यादि । कात्यायरेतसोऽग्नेः । अधिदेवता चाह अमर्त्येति । अत्र जिह्वानामधिदेवताकथनं तत्तत्स्थानेषु न्यासार्थम् । तेन सुरेभ्यो नम इत्यादि । अन्ये तु

लोहिताख्या करालाख्या काली तामस्य ईरिताः ।
एताः सप्त नियुज्यन्ते क्रूरकर्म्मसु मन्त्रिभिः ॥ २६
स्वस्वनामसमाभाः स्युर्जिह्वाः कल्याणरेतसः ।
अमर्त्य-पितृ-गन्धर्व-यक्ष-नाग-पिशाचकाः ।
राक्षसाः सप्तजिह्वानामीरिता अधिदेवताः ॥ २७
वह्नेरङ्गमनून् न्यस्येत्तनावुक्तेन वर्त्मना ।
सहस्रार्च्चिः स्वस्तिपूर्ण उत्तिष्ठपुरुषः पुनः ॥ २८
धूमव्यापी सप्तजिह्वो धनुर्द्धर इति क्रमात् ।
षडङ्गमनवः प्रोक्ता जातिभिः सह संयुताः ॥ २९

सुराधिपतये हिरण्यायै नमः इत्यादि । किञ्च तत्तद्देवतां जिह्वामध्यस्थां बुद्धा तस्यां तस्यां तत्तद्द्रव्यैः तत्तत्कर्म्मणि क्रियमाणे फलसिद्धिरिति प्रदर्शनार्थम् ।
तथा च आचार्य्याः —

जिह्वासु त्रिदशादीनां तत्तत्कार्य्यसमाश्रये ।
जुहुयाद्वाञ्छितां सिद्धिं दद्युस्ता देवतामयाः ॥ इति ।

गणेश्वरविमर्शिन्यां द्रव्यविशेषोऽप्युक्तः—

एधांसि च हिरण्यायां गगनायां चरुं घृतम् ।
सिद्धार्थं बहुरूपायां रक्तायान्तु यवांस्तथा ॥
कृष्णायान्तु हुनेल्लाजैः सुप्रभायान्तु शक्तुभिः ।
तिलांश्चैवाऽतिरक्तायां कनकायान्तु सर्व्वदा ।
सर्व्वद्रव्याणि जुहुयात् साधकः सर्व्वकर्म्मसु ॥ इति ।

कर्म्माण्यपि तन्त्रान्तरे—

फलन्तु कामभेदेन क्रमादासामुदीर्य्यते ।
वश्याकर्षणयोराद्या गगना स्तम्भने मता ॥
विद्वेषमोहयो रक्ता कृष्णा मारणकर्म्मणि ।
सुप्रभा शान्तिके पुष्टौ सुरक्तोच्चाटने मता ।
एकैव बहुरूपा तु सर्व्वकामफलप्रदा ॥ इति ॥ २२-२७ ॥

वह्नेरिति । तनौ स्वशरीरे । आत्मन इत्यनुषज्यते । एवमग्रेऽपि । उक्तेन पूर्व्वपटलोक्तेन । सहस्रार्च्चिरादीनां चतुर्थ्यन्तत्वं सम्प्रदायात् । प्रयोगस्तु सहस्रार्च्चिषे हृदयाय नम इत्यादि ॥ २८ ॥ २९ ॥

मूर्त्तीरष्टौ तनौ न्यस्येद् देशिको जातवेदसः ।
मूर्द्धांसपार्श्वकट्यन्धु कटिपार्श्वांसके पुनः ॥ २०

प्रदक्षिणवशान् न्यस्येदुच्यन्ते ता यथाक्रमात् ।
जातवेदाः सप्तजिह्वो हव्यवाहनसंज्ञकः ॥ २१

अश्वोदरजसंज्ञोऽन्यः पुनर्वैश्वानराह्वयः ।
कौमारतेजाः स्याद्विश्वमुखो देवमुखः स्मृताः ॥ २२

ताराग्नयेपदाद्याः स्युर्नत्यन्ता वह्निमूर्त्तयः ।
आसनं कल्पयित्वाऽग्नेर्मूर्त्तिं तस्य विचिन्तयेत् ॥ २३

इष्टं शक्तिं स्वस्तिकाभीतिमुच्चैर्दीर्घैर्दोर्भिर्धारयन्तं जवाभम् ।
हेमाकल्पं पद्मसंस्थं त्रिनेत्रं ध्यायेद्वह्निं बद्धमौलिं जटाभिः ॥ २४

परिषिञ्चेत्ततस्तोयैर्विशुद्धैर्मेखलोपरि ।
दर्भैरगर्भैर्मध्यस्थमेखलायां परिस्तरेत् ॥ २५

मूर्त्तीरिति । अंसपार्श्वकटिषु वामेषु । अन्धु गुदम् । केचन लिङ्गमित्याहुः । पश्चात् कटिपार्श्वांसकेषु दक्षिणेषु ॥ २० ॥ २१ ॥ २२ ॥

ताराग्नय इति । तारः प्रणवः अग्नये इति पदं एते आदौ यासां ता इति विग्रहः । नत्यन्ता इति न्यासे पूजायाञ्च । होमे तु स्वाहान्तत्वमित्युक्तम् । आसां नमसा योगाच्चतुर्थ्यन्तत्वम् । प्रयोगस्तु हूँ अग्नये जातवेदसे नमो मूर्द्ध्नीत्यादि ।

आसनं कल्पयित्वेति । तनावित्यनुषज्यते । मण्डूकादिपरतत्त्वान्तं चतुर्दश-पटलोक्तपीठशक्तिपूर्व्वकम् रं अग्न्यासनाय नम इति एषां देहे न्यास आसन-कल्पना ॥ २३ ॥

ध्यानमाह इष्टमिति । इष्टं वरम् । दक्षाधःकरादारभ्याधःकरपर्य्यन्तमिष्टादीनि ध्येयानि । स्वस्तिकयुक्ता अभीतिरिति मध्यपदलोपी समासः । आकल्पो भूषा ॥२४॥

तत इति । अन्तर्यागक्रमेण स्वहृदये वह्निं सम्पूज्येत्यर्थः । परिस्तरेदिति । प्रागुदगग्रतया । तदुक्तं गणेश्वरविमर्शिन्याम्—

पूर्व्वाग्रैरुत्तराग्रैश्च दर्भैरग्निं परिस्तरेत् । इति ।

अन्यत्रापि—अथ दर्भैर्हरिधनददिशाग्रैः परिस्तीर्य्य कुण्डम् । इति ॥ २५ ॥

निक्षिपेद्दिक्षु परिधीन् प्राचीवर्जं गुरूत्तमः ।
गार्दक्रियेण सम्पूज्यास्तेषु ब्रह्मादिमूर्त्तयः ॥ ३६
ध्यातं वह्निं यजेन्मध्ये गन्धाद्यैर्मनुनाऽमुना ।
वैश्वानरजातवेदपदे पश्चादिहावह ॥ ३७
लोहिताक्षपदस्यान्ते सर्व्वकर्म्माणि साधय ।
वह्निजायावधिः प्रोक्तो मन्त्रः पावकवल्लभः ॥ ३८
मध्ये षट्स्वपि कोणेषु जिह्वा ज्वालारुचो यजेत् ।
केशरेष्वङ्गमार्गेण पूजयेदङ्गदेवताः ॥ ३९

गुरूत्तम इत्यनेन एकमेखलादिकुण्डेऽपि परिस्तरणादि कार्य्यमित्युक्तम् । यदाहुः—

एकमेखले कुण्डे निखिलमपि मेखलाधस्तात् परिस्तरेद्द्विमेखले ।
द्वितीयमेखलोपरि त्रिमेखले तदन्तरालमेखलोपरि न्यसेत् ॥ इति ।

प्राचीवर्जं दिक्षु परिधीन् निक्षिपेदित्यन्वयः । परिधयस्तु कात्यायनोक्ताः । परिधीन् परिदधात्यार्द्रान्बाहुमात्रान् पालाशवैकङ्कतकाश्मर्य्यबैल्वान् । इति । स्थण्डिलेऽपि परिस्तरणपरिधिनिक्षेपोऽवश्यकर्त्तव्यः । मध्यस्थमेखलायामित्युक्तत्वात् । स्थण्डिले मेखलानामभावात् परिस्तरणाद्यपि न कार्य्यमिति न मन्तव्यम् । यतस्तदग्निस्थापनाङ्गं न कुण्डाङ्गम् । ग्रन्थकृता तु स्वोक्तत्रिमेखलकुण्डे परिस्तरणादि कर्त्तव्यमित्यपेक्षायां मध्यस्थमेखलायामित्युक्तम् । यदाहुः—

बाह्येऽथ स्थण्डिलं च त्रिपरिधिसहितं प्रागुदग्रास्तदर्भम् । इति ।

अन्यत्रापि—स्थण्डिलके सिकतानां बाह्येऽथ विन्यसेत् परिधीन् । इति ॥ ३६ ॥

मध्ये इति मण्डूकादिपीठमन्त्रान्तमन्त्रैः पूजिते कुण्डमध्ये इत्यर्थः ।
तदुक्तं सौत्रामणितन्त्रे— कुण्डमध्ये विधानवित् ।
पद्मासनान्तमाधारशक्त्यादिमनुभिः क्रमात् ॥
उपर्य्युपरि सम्पूज्य वह्नेरासनमग्रतः ।
पूर्व्वादिदलमूलेषु मध्ये पूज्याः क्रमेण तु ॥ इति ।

अग्निमन्त्रमाह वैश्वानर इति । वह्निजाया स्वाहा ॥ ३७ ॥ ३८ ॥

अङ्गावरणपूजामाह मध्ये इति । अनेन षट्कोणकर्णिकमष्टदलमग्निपीठमुक्तम् । ज्वालारुच इति जिह्वाख्यानम् । तदुक्तं प्रयोगसारे—

जिह्वाः सर्व्वाः परिज्ञेया ज्वालाभासाः स्वरूपतः । इति ।

अपिभिन्नक्रमः । तच्च षट्सु कोणेषु मध्येऽपि जिह्वा यजेदिति सम्बन्धः । तत्र षट्सु कोणेषु ईशादि वायुकोणान्तं यथान्यासं षड्जिह्वाः सम्पूज्य यथान्यस्तां बहुरूपां मध्ये पूजयेदिति सम्प्रदायविदः । तदुक्तं सोमशम्भौ—

रुद्रेन्द्रवह्निमांसाद वरुणानिलगोचरे ।
हिरण्याद्याः स्थिता वह्नेः रसनाः षट् ह्यनुक्रमात् ॥
मध्यतो बहुरूपा तु । इति ।

गणेश्वरविमर्शिन्यामपि—

मध्ये च कोणषट्के च जिह्वाः सम्पूजयेत्ततः ।
हिरण्या तप्तहेमाभा शूलपाणिदिशि स्थिता ॥
वैदूर्यवर्णा गगना प्राच्यां दिशि समाश्रिता ।
तरुणादित्यसङ्काशा रक्ता जिह्वाऽग्निदिक्स्थिता ॥
कृष्णा नीलाब्जसङ्काशा नैर्ऋत्यां दिशि संस्थिता ।
सुप्रभा पद्मरागाभा वारुण्यां दिशि संस्थिता ॥
अतिरक्ता जवाभासा वायव्यां दिशि संस्थिता ।
बहुरूपा यथार्थाभा दक्षिणोत्तरसंस्थिता ॥
एता ज्वाला रुचा पीता वराभययुता अपि । इति ।

अन्यत्रापि—कोणषट्के च मध्ये च जिह्वा अङ्गानि केशरे । इति ।

वायवीयसंहितायामपि—

हिरण्या प्रागुदग्जिह्वा कनका पूर्वतः स्थिता ।
रक्ताग्नेयी नैर्ऋतौ च कृष्णाऽन्या सुप्रभा मता ॥
अतिरक्ता मरुज्जिह्वा स्वनामानुगुणप्रभा ।
त्रिशिखा मध्यमा जिह्वा बहुरूपा समाह्वया ॥
तच्छिखैका दक्षिणतो ज्वलन्ती वामतः परा ।
स्वबीजानन्तरं वाच्या । इति ।

यथाश्रुतपाठक्रमादपरिणः केचन प्रथमां मध्ये ततः शिवकोणादि प्रादक्षिण्येन वायुकोणान्तं यथान्यस्तास्ताः षट् जिह्वाः पूजयेदित्याहुः । तेषामयमभिप्रायः । तत्तत्कर्म्मणि तां तां मध्यस्थामिष्ट्वा ईशादिषु अन्या यजेदिति । तदुक्तम्—

कुण्डस्य मध्ये त्वथ सा प्रशस्ता जिह्वा हिरण्या भुवि कर्म्मणादौ ।
स्तम्भनादिषु मता कनकाख्या द्वेषणादिषु मता खलु रक्ता ॥
मारणे निगदिता भुवि कृष्णा सुप्रभा बुधवरैरथ शान्त्याम् ।

दलेषु पूजयेन्मूर्त्तीः शक्तिस्वस्तिकधारिणीः।
लोकपालांस्ततो दिक्षु पूजयेदुक्तलक्षणान्॥ ४०
पश्चादादाय पाणिभ्यां स्रुक्स्रुवौ तावधोमुखौ।
त्रिः सम्प्रतापयेद्वह्नौ दर्भानादाय देशिकः॥ ४१

उच्चाटनेऽतिरक्ता। इति।
सम्प्रदायविदुक्तं तु दीक्षायामेव बहुरूपायाः सर्व्वकामफलप्रदत्वात्।
उक्तञ्च—सा तनुतं सध्ये शुभानि सदा। इति।
तन्त्रान्तरे तु—अन्ये त्वागमपारगामलधियः प्राहुर्बुधाः सुप्रभां

वृतारेः ककुभि स्थितां पितृपतेः कृष्णां हिरण्यां पुनः।
वारुण्यां बहुरूपिकां पुरभिदो रक्तामुदीच्यां स्थिता-
माग्नेय्यामतिरक्तिकाञ्च कनकां कुण्डस्य मध्ये स्थिताम्॥ इति।

एतदनन्तरमधिदेवतापूजाऽप्येषु स्थानेषु ज्ञेया। उक्तमार्गेणेति पूर्व्वपटलोक्तेन। तत्र पूजाप्रकारः। सहस्रार्चिषे हृदयाय नमः स्वस्तिपूर्णाय शिरसे स्वाहा नमः इत्यादि॥ ३९॥

मूर्त्तीः पूजयेदिति यथान्यस्ताः। एतदन्तरं मातृभैरवाहुतिमपीच्छन्ति पद्मपादाचार्य्याः। क्वचित् "दलाग्रे मातरः पूज्याः सासिताङ्गादिभैरवाः" इत्यधिकः पाठोऽपि। दिक्ष्विति मेखलाश्रितदर्भेष्विति प्रसिद्धपूर्व्वादिदिक्ष्वित्यपि ज्ञेयम्।

यदाहुः—मध्ये च कोणषट्के च जिह्वाभिः केशरेष्वपि।

अङ्गमन्त्रैस्ततो बाह्ये अष्टाभिर्मूर्त्तिभिः क्रमात्॥
मेखलाश्रितदर्भेषु दिक्पतीन् पूर्व्वतः क्रमात्। इति।

उक्तलक्षणान् प्राक्पटलोक्तस्वरूपान्॥ ४०॥

पश्चादित्यनेन सूचितः तन्त्रान्तरोक्तोऽवश्यकर्त्तव्यो विशेषो लिख्यते। स्ववामभागे प्रागग्रान् कुशानास्तीर्य्य तेषामुपरि प्रणीताप्रोक्षणीपात्रे आज्यस्थालीचरुस्थाल्यौ स्रुक्स्रुवौ विसंसितौ कुशमूलकौ पञ्चपलाशसमिधः एवमुक्तान्यन्यान्यपि पात्राणि द्वन्द्वशोऽधोमुखानि निधाय मूलेन पवित्रेण प्रोक्षितानि पात्राणि उत्तानीकृत्य प्रणीतापात्रं जलेनापूर्य्य तत्र तीर्थान्यावाह्य पवित्रमक्षतादि च निक्षिप्योत्पूय उत्तरस्यां दिशि संस्थाप्य तज्जलं किञ्चित् प्रोक्षणीपात्रे निधाय तेन जलेन नमोमन्त्रेण मूलमन्त्रेण वा सर्व्वं हवनीयद्रव्यजातं प्रोक्ष्य "अत्र कर्म्मणि कृताकृतावेक्षकत्वेन त्वं ब्रह्मा भवेति" ब्रह्माणमावाह्याऽभ्यर्च्यासने उपवेशयेदिति। तदुक्तं संहितायाम्—

तदग्रमध्यमूलानि शोधयेत्तैर्यथाक्रमात् ।
गृहीत्वा वामहस्तेन प्रोक्षयेद्दक्षिणेन तौ ॥ ४२

पात्राण्यासाद्य विधिवद् द्वन्द्वशोऽपि मन्त्रवित् ।
तान्यवोक्ष्य पवित्रेण चोत्तानानि विधाय च ॥
पुनः प्रक्षालयेत् पात्रं परिपूर्य शुभाम्बुना ।
दत्त्वाऽक्षतान् पवित्रञ्च तदुत्पूय निधाय तत् ॥
दिश्युत्तरस्यां तत्पात्रं प्रणीतेत्युच्यते बुधैः ।
ततः किञ्चित् प्रणीताम्बु प्रोक्षण्यादाय तज्जलैः ॥
यज्ञसाधनसम्भारं प्रोक्षयेन्मूलमन्त्रतः ।
ततो ब्रह्माणमावाह्याऽभ्यर्चयेन्मूलमन्त्रतः ॥ इति ।

तत्राधोमुखेन हस्तेन सेचनमवोक्षणम् । "अवाङ्मुखेन हस्तेनावोक्षयेत्" इति सूत्रणात् । अन्यत्रापि—

वामे चास्तीर्य दर्भान् बलरिपुहरिदग्रान् तदूर्ध्वं निधाय
पात्राणि द्वन्द्वशोऽधोवदनमथ तथोत्तानवक्त्राणि कृत्वा ।
कुम्भस्थेनाऽभिपूर्य्याम्बुतममय जलैर्मन्त्रपूतैरथैभिः
अभ्युक्ष्योपेतकूर्चैः सकलमपि हृदा सन्न्यगं द्रव्यजातम् ॥

अन्यत्रापि—

स्ववामभागे प्रागग्रान् दर्भानास्तीर्य्य चोपरि ।
यथावित्तानुसारेण सौवर्णादीनि कर्म्मणि ॥
अधोमुखानि पात्राणि द्वन्द्वरूपेण विन्यसेत् ।
उत्तानीकृत्य पात्राणि जलाद्यैः सम्प्रपूरयेत् ॥ इति ।

अन्यत्रापि—

ततो वामभागे परिस्तीर्य्य दर्भान् पुलोमात्मजावल्लभाशागताग्रान् ।
तदूर्ध्वं न्यसेद् द्वन्द्वरूपेण पात्राण्यथाऽधोगतास्यानि सर्व्वाणि धीमान् ॥
अथोत्तानितेष्वेषु पात्रेषु विद्वान् जलैरम्बुमापूर्य्य तीर्थानि तत्र ।
सुसञ्चिन्त्य तैः प्रोक्षयेत् कूर्चदर्भैः हृदा सव्यभागे स्थितं द्रव्यजातम् ॥ इति ।

स्रुक्स्रुवसंस्कारमाह आदायेति । आदानम् ऊर्ध्वमुखयोरेवेति ज्ञेयम् । तावधोमुखौ तापयेदित्युक्तः । पाणिभ्यां दक्षिणवामाभ्यां । शोधयेदिति प्रत्येकम् । यथाक्रमादित्यस्यायमर्थः । दर्भमूलैस्तन्मूलं दर्भमध्यैस्तन्मध्यं दर्भाग्रैस्तदग्रमिति । दक्षिणेन दक्षिणहस्तेन । प्रोक्षयेदिति प्रोक्षण्युदकेन ॥ ४१ ॥ ४२ ॥

पुनः प्रताप्य तौ मन्त्री दर्भानग्नौ विनिक्षिपेत् ।
आत्मनो दक्षिणे भागे स्थापयेत्तौ कुशास्तरे ॥ ४३
आज्यस्थालीमथादाय प्रोक्षयेदस्त्रवारिणा ।
तस्यामाज्यं विनिक्षिप्य संस्कृतं वीक्षणादिभिः ॥ ४४

पुनरित्यनेन पाणिद्वयस्यानधोमुखौ त्रिश इत्युक्तम् । एवं दर्भानग्नौ विनिक्षिपेदिति प्रतिपत्तिकार्यम् । मन्त्रीत्यनेन मूलमध्याग्रेषु क्रमेण इच्छाज्ञानक्रियाशक्तीनां न्यासः । नमोमन्त्रेण स्रुचि शक्तिं स्रुवे शम्भुं विन्यसेदिति ज्ञेयम् । शैवे तु आत्मादितत्त्वत्रयम् । यदाहुः—

गृहीत्वा स्रुक्स्रुवावूर्ध्ववदनाधोमुखौ क्रमात् ।
प्रताप्याग्नौ त्रिधा दर्भमूलमध्याग्रकैः स्पृशेत् ॥
पुनस्त्रिशः प्रताप्याऽधोमुखावग्नौ कुशान् क्षिपेत् ।
मूलमध्याग्रके न्यस्येच्छक्तीरिच्छादिकाः क्रमात् ॥
स्रुचि शक्तिं स्रुवे शम्भुं विन्यसेद्धृदयात्मना । इति ।

शैवागमे तु—गृहीत्वा स्रुक्स्रुवावूर्ध्ववदनाधोमुखौ क्रमात् ।
प्रताप्याऽग्नौ त्रिधा दर्भमूलमध्याग्रकैः स्पृशेत् ॥
कुशभागप्रदेशेषु आत्मविद्याशिवात्मकम् ।
क्रमात्तत्त्वत्रयं न्यस्य हां हीं हूं शंवरैः क्रमात् ॥
स्रुचि शक्तिं स्रुवे शम्भुं विन्यस्य हृदयात्मना ।
त्रिसूत्रवेष्टितग्रीवौ पूजितौ कुसुमादिभिः ॥
कुशानामुपरिष्टात्तौ स्थापयित्वा स्वदक्षिणे । इति ।

एवं स्रुक्स्रुवयोरष्टौ संस्कारा उक्ताः । ताविति स्रुक्स्रुवौ सर्वत्र पुंस्त्वेन पाठक्रम एवानुसन्धेयः ॥ ४३ ॥

आज्यसंस्कारमाह आज्येति । अस्त्रवारिणेति अस्त्रमन्त्रजसेन प्रोक्षणीजलेन । वीक्षणादिभिः संस्कृतमाज्यं तस्याम् आज्यस्थाल्यां विनिक्षिप्येत्यन्वयः । अत्राज्यं गव्यादि ज्ञेयम् । तदुक्तं पिङ्गलामते—

उत्तमं गोघृतं ज्ञेयं मध्यमं माहिषोद्भवम् ।
अधमं छागलीजातं तस्माद् गव्यं प्रशस्यते ॥ इति ।

अत एव ग्रन्थकृत्तत्र तत्र वक्ष्यति गव्येन सर्पिषा इति माहिषोद्भवसंज्ञता इति मेषोद्भवाख्या इति च ॥ ४४ ॥

निरुह्य वायव्येऽङ्गारान् हृदा तेषु निवेशयेत् ।
इदं तापनमुद्दिष्टं देशिकैस्तन्त्रवेदिभिः ॥ ४५
सन्दीप्य दर्भयुगलमाज्ये क्षिप्त्वाऽनले क्षिपेत् ।
गुरुर्हृदयमन्त्रेण पवित्रीकारणन्त्विदम् ॥ ४६
दीप्तेन दर्भयुग्मेन नीराज्याज्यं स वर्मणा ।
अग्नौ विसर्जयेद्दर्भमभिद्योतनमीरितम् ॥ ४७
घृते प्रज्वलितान् दर्भान् प्रदर्श्याऽस्त्राणुना गुरुः ।
जातवेदसि तान् न्यस्येदुद्योतनमिदं मतम् ॥ ४८

निरुह्येति । कुण्डाग्नितः पृथक्कृत्वा हृदा निवेशयेत् इत्याज्यस्थालीमिति शेषः । तन्त्रवेदिभिर्देशिकैरिदं तापनमुद्दिष्टं पश्चाद् दिष्टमुक्तमित्यर्थः । तेन पूर्वं मूलमन्त्रेणाऽभिमन्त्रणं स्वीयब्रह्ममूर्तिभावनमिति संस्कारद्वयं सूचितम् ।

यदाहुः—गव्यमाज्यं समादाय मूलेनैवाऽभिमन्त्रितम् ।
स्वकां ब्रह्ममयीं मूर्त्तिं सञ्चिन्त्याग्नौ प्रतापयेत् ॥ इति ।

शैवागमेऽपि—गव्यमाज्यं समादाय मूलमन्त्राभिमन्त्रितम् ।
स्वकां ब्रह्ममयीं मूर्त्तिं सञ्चिन्त्य च । इति ।

वायवीयसंहितायामपि—
न्यस्य मन्त्रं घृते मुद्रां दर्शयेद् धेनुसंज्ञिताम् । इति ।

एवं संस्कारद्वयं वक्ष्यमाणाश्च षट्संस्काराः । एवं घृतेऽप्यष्टसंस्काराः ।

यदुक्तं पिङ्गलामते—
कुण्डे चाष्टादश ज्ञेयाः संस्काराः शिवशास्त्रतः ।
घृते स्रुचि स्रुवे चाष्टौ । इति ॥ ४५ ॥

सन्दीप्येति । दर्भयुगलं सन्दीप्य हृदयमन्त्रेणाज्ये क्षिप्त्वा अनले क्षिपेदित्यन्वयः । नीराज्य इत्यभितः परिभ्राम्य । स इति गुरुः । वर्मणेति कवचमन्त्रेण । वर्मणा आज्यं स नीराज्य इति सम्बन्धः । दर्भमिति दर्भयुग्मम् । अत्र संस्कारत्रये वक्ष्यमाण संस्कारद्वयेऽपि दर्भाणामग्नौ प्रक्षेपः प्रतिपत्तिकर्म । अतएव मन्त्राभावोपि तत्र ततश्च केनापि कारणेन तद्दर्भनाशे जाते सति अग्निप्रक्षेपरूपं कर्म दर्भाणां न प्रयोजकम् । एतच्चतुर्थाध्याये प्रतिपादितम् । अग्नौ तानिति । एवं स्रुक्स्रुवसंस्कारेऽपि ॥ ४६ ॥ ४७ ॥ ४८ ॥

गृहीत्वा घृतमङ्गारान् प्रत्यूह्याऽग्नौ जलं स्पृशेत् ।
अङ्गुष्ठोपकनिष्ठाभ्यां दर्भौ प्रादेशसम्मितौ ॥ ४९

धृत्वोत्पुनीयादस्त्रेण घृतमुत्पवनन्त्विदम् ।
तद्वद्धृदयमन्त्रेण कुशाभ्यामात्मसम्मुखम् ॥ ५०

घृते संप्लवनं कुर्य्यात् संस्काराः षडुदीरिताः ।
प्रादेशमात्रं सग्रन्थि दर्भयुग्मं घृतान्तरे ॥ ५१

निक्षिप्य भागौ द्वौ कृत्वा पक्षौ शुक्लेतरौ स्मरेत् ।
वामे नाडीमिडां भागे दक्षिणे पिङ्गलां पुनः ।
सुषुम्णां मध्यतो ध्यात्वा कुर्य्याद्धोमं यथाविधि ॥ ५२

स्रुवेण दक्षिणाद्भागादादायाऽऽज्यं हृदा गुरुः ॥ ५३

जुहुयादग्नये स्वाहेत्यग्नेर्दक्षिणलोचने ।
वामतस्तद्वदादाय वामे वह्निविलोचने ॥ ५४

जुहुयादथ सोमाय स्वाहेति हृदयाणुना ।
मध्यादाज्यं समादाय वह्नेर्भालविलोचने ॥ ५५

घृतं गृहीत्वेत्याज्यस्थालीम् उद्वास्येत्यर्थः । प्रत्यूह्य संयोज्येत्यर्थः । स एतदनन्तरं जलस्पर्शं कुर्यात् । अङ्गुष्ठेति । उपकनिष्ठाऽनामा । अङ्गुष्ठोपकनिष्ठाभ्यां हस्तद्वयस्येति शेषः । उत्पुनीयादित्यग्निसम्मुखमिति ज्ञेयम् । उक्तञ्च शैवागमे—प्रादेशमात्रदर्भाभ्यामङ्गुष्ठानामिकाग्रकैः ।

घृताभ्यां सम्मुखं वह्नेरस्त्रेणोत्पवनञ्चरेत् ॥ इति ।

तद्वदिति । हस्तद्वयस्य अङ्गुष्ठानामिकाग्राभ्यां धृत्वेत्यर्थः । अत्रापि संस्कारद्वये कुशयोर्वह्निप्रक्षेपलक्षणं प्रतिपत्तिकर्म्म ज्ञेयम् ।

होमविधिमाह प्रादेशेति । घृतान्तरे घृतमध्ये । शुक्लेतरौ वामे शुक्लपक्षः दक्षे कृष्णपक्षः । ध्यात्वेति तिस्रोऽपि घृत एव ॥ ४९ ॥ ५० ॥ ५१ ॥ ५२ ॥

यथाविधीत्युक्तं विधिमाह स्रुवेणेति । तद्वदिति स्रुवेण हृदयाणुना वामत आदायेति सम्बन्धः । हृदयाणुना मध्यादाज्यं समादायेति सम्बन्धः । हेति सम्पातयेद् भाग इति केचन पठन्ति । तत्र हेतिराहुतिशेषः । ये तु इति

जुहुयादग्नीषोमाभ्यां स्वाहेति हव्यवाहना ।
इन्द्रमन्त्रेण स्रुवेणाज्यं भागादादाय दक्षिणात् ॥ ५६
जुहुयादग्नये स्विष्टिकृते स्वाहेति तन्मुखे ।
हेति सम्पातयेद् भागे स्वाज्यस्याऽन्वाहुतिक्रमात् ॥ ५७
इत्यग्निनेत्रवक्त्राणां कुर्य्यादुद्घाटनं गुरुः ।
सताराभिर्व्याहृतिभिराज्येन जुहुयात् पुनः ॥ ५८
जुहुयादग्निमन्त्रेण त्रिवारं देशिकोत्तमः ।
गर्भाधानादिका वह्नेः क्रिया निर्वर्त्तयेत् क्रमात् ॥ ५९
अष्टाभिराज्याहुतिभिः प्रणवेन पृथक् पृथक् ।
गर्भाधानं पुंसवनं सीमन्तोन्नयनं पुनः ॥ ६०
अनन्तरं जातकर्म्म स्यान्नामकरणं तथा ।
उपनिष्क्रमणं पश्चादन्नप्राशनमीरितम् ॥ ६१

सम्पादयेदिति पठन्ति तन्मते "इति समासो"। स्वाहान्तहोमं विधाय अग्निनेत्रवक्त्राणां कुर्य्यादुद्घाटनं गुरुः। ये तु हेति सम्पातयेदिति पठन्ति तन्मते स्वान्तं होमं विधाय हा इत्यस्यान्ते यस्माद् भागाद् या आज्याहुतिर्गृहीता तस्मिन्नेव भागे तस्य सम्पातं कुर्य्यादिति सम्बन्धः। साम्प्रदायिकास्त्विममेव पाठमिच्छन्ति। अन्वाहुति आहुतिमनु प्रत्याहुति इत्यर्थः। तदुक्तं शैवागमे—

स्रुवेणादाय होमयेत् ।
स्वेत्यग्नौ हेति तद्भागशेषमाज्यं क्षिपेत् क्रमात् ॥ इति ॥५३-५७॥

इत्यग्नीति। तेनाहुतिचतुष्टयेन नेत्रत्रयवक्त्राणामुद्घाटनम्। क्रमेणेत्यर्थः। सताराभिर्व्याहृतिभिरिति व्यस्तसमस्ताभिः। अतएव नारायणीये "पञ्चभिर्मनुभिर्हुनेत्" इति। पुनरनन्तरमिति उत्तरेण सम्बध्यते। अग्निमन्त्रेणेति वैश्वानरेति पूर्व्वोक्तेन। प्रणवेनेति पञ्चापि प्रणवा गृहीताः। देशिकोत्तम इत्यनेन तत्तन्मन्त्रेषु यथास्वं विनियोगो विज्ञेय इत्युक्तम् ॥ ५८ ॥ ५९ ॥

गर्भाधानादिका इत्यादिशब्दसंगृहीतमेवाह गर्भाधानमिति। पुनरनन्तरं जातकर्म्म अनन्तरं तथा नामकरणं स्यादिति सम्बन्धः। अनन्तरमित्यस्यायमर्थः। वक्ष्यमाणं पञ्चसमिद्धोमलक्षणं नालापनयनं कर्म्म कृत्वा सूतकं विशोध्य तथा

चौलोपनयने भूयो महानाम्न्यं महाव्रतम् ।
अथोपनिषदं पश्चाद् गोदानोद्वाहकौ स्मृतिः ॥ ६२

शुभेषु स्युर्विवाहान्ताः क्रियास्ताः क्रूरकर्म्मसु ।
मरणान्ताः समुद्दिष्टा वह्नेरागमवेदिभिः ॥ ६३

ततश्च पितरौ तस्य सम्पूज्यात्मनि योजयेत् ।
समिधः पञ्च जुहुयान्मूलाद्यघृतसंप्लुताः ॥ ६४

ततस्तद्देवतानाम्नाऽग्नेर्नामकरणं कुर्य्यात् । यथा कृष्णाग्निर्नारायणाग्निर्दुर्गाग्निरिति । ततोऽग्नेः पितरावात्मनि संयोज्योपनिष्क्रमणादि संस्कारान् कुर्य्यात् । आदिशब्द-कथनार्थमिदमक्रमेणोक्तिः । तदुक्तं वायवीयसंहितायाम्—

जातं ध्यात्वैवमाकारं जातकर्म्म समाचरेत् ।
नालापनयनं कृत्वा ततः संशोध्य सूतकम् ॥
शिवाग्निरिति नामाऽस्य कृत्वाहुतिपुरःसरम् ।
पित्रोर्विसर्जनं कृत्वा चौलोपनयनादिकम् ॥
अथोद्वाहावसानञ्च कृत्वा संस्कारमस्य तु । इति ।

शैवागमेऽपि—
गर्भाधानादिकाः क्रियाः ।
जातकर्म्मान्तिका वह्नेर्वाग्भवेन पृथक् पृथक् ॥
आज्याहुत्यष्टकैः कृत्वा वागाद्यग्निर्भवेति च ।
नाम कृत्वा ततो वह्नेरन्नप्राशनपूर्व्वकम् ॥
विवाहान्तं वाग्भवेन पूर्व्वोक्ताष्टाहुतिक्रमात् । इति ।

अत्र गोदानानन्तरं समावर्त्तनमनुक्तमपि कर्त्तव्यमित्याचार्य्याः ।
तदुक्तं गणेश्वरविमर्शिन्याम्—

समावर्त्तनमुद्वाहमाधानञ्च ततः परम् । इति ।

अन्यत्रापि—तेनैव समावर्त्तनविवाहयोराहुतीर्जुहुयात् । इति ।

अन्यत्रापि—कुर्व्वीत समावर्त्तनमुद्वाहं तेनैव विधिना । इति ।

केचित्तु तथोपनिषदं स्नानम् इति पठित्वा स्नानं समावर्त्तनमिति व्याख्यान्ति । तन्मते समावर्त्तनानन्तरं गोदानम् । प्रयोगस्तु ॐ अस्याग्नेर्गर्भाधानसंस्कारं करोमि स्वाहा इत्यादि ॥ ६० ॥ ६१ ॥ ६२ ॥ ६३ ॥

तत इति । नामकरणानन्तरं तस्य वह्नेः पितरौ पूर्व्वोक्तौ । समिधः पञ्च जुहुयादिति । नालापनोदाय जातकर्म्मानन्तरमित्यर्थः । तदुक्तं शैवागमे—

मन्त्रैर्जिह्वाङ्गमूर्त्तीनां क्रमादङ्गैर्यथाविधि ।
प्रत्येकं जुहुयादेकामाहुतिं म[ति]न्त्रवित्तमः ॥ ६५

अवदाय स्रुवेणाज्यं चतुः स्रुचि पिधाय ताम् ।
स्रुवेण तिष्ठन्नेवाऽग्नौ देशिको यतमानसः ॥ ६६

जुहुयाद्वह्निमन्त्रेण वौषडन्तेन सम्पदे ।
विघ्नेश्वरस्य मन्त्रेण जुहुयादाहुतीर्दश ॥ ६७

वह्निनामस्त्रमन्त्रेण ततो नालापनुत्तये ।
समिधः पञ्च होतव्याः प्रान्ते मूले घृतप्लुताः ॥ इति ।

वायवीयसंहितायान्तु—

ताः पालाश्यः परा वापि यज्ञीया द्वादशाङ्गुलाः ।
अवक्रा न स्वयं शुष्काः सत्वचो निर्व्रणाः समाः ॥
दशाङ्गुला वा विहिताः कनिष्ठाङ्गुलिसन्निभाः ।
प्रादेशमात्रा वाऽलाभे होतव्याः सकला अपि ॥ इति ॥ ६४ ॥

मन्त्रैरिति न्यासप्रस्तावोक्तैः । क्रमादिति न्यासक्रमात् । यथाविधीत्यनेन होमे स्वाहान्तत्वमुक्तं स्मारयति । प्रयोगस्तु । रूं हिरण्यायै स्वाहेत्यादि । एतदनन्तरं ॐ सुरेभ्यः स्वाहेत्याद्यधिदेवताहोमेऽपि । सहस्रार्चिषे हृदयाय नमः स्वाहेत्यादि । ॐ अग्नये जातवेदसे स्वाहेत्यादि । म[ति]न्त्रवित्तम इत्यनेन लोकपालतदस्त्राहुति-ग्रहणं ज्ञेयम् । तदुक्तं गणेश्वरविमर्शिन्याम्—

जुहुयादङ्गमन्त्राद्यैस्ताराद्यैश्च सकृत् सकृत् ।
तत्तत्स्थानेषु शितधीः स्वाहान्तैश्च यथाक्रमम् ॥ इति ।

प्रयोगसारेऽपि—सर्वे मन्त्राः प्रयोक्तव्याः स्वाहान्ता होमकर्मसु । इति ॥ ६५ ॥

अवदायेति । यतमानसो देशिकः स्रुवेणाज्यं चतुर्वारं स्रुचि निधाय तां स्रुचं स्रुवेण पिधाय तिष्ठन्नेव वौषडन्तेन वह्निमन्त्रेणाऽग्नौ जुहुयादित्यन्वयः । यतमानसो दशिक इत्यनेन समपादत्वं शृङ्गाग्रव्यग्रलोचनादिकत्वमुक्तम् । वौषडन्तेनेति स्वाहापदस्थाने वौषट्पदप्रक्षेप इति । शैवागमे तु विशेषः—

घृतेन स्रुचि पूर्णायां निधायाऽधोमुखं स्रुवम् ।
शृङ्गाग्रे पुष्पमारोप्य पश्चाद्वामेन पाणिना ॥
पुनः सव्येन तौ धृत्वा शङ्खसन्निभमुद्रया ।
समुन्नतोर्द्ध्वकायश्च समपादः समुत्थितः ॥

सामान्यं सर्व्वतन्त्राणामेतदग्निम[मु]खं मतम् ।

ततः पीठं समभ्यर्च्य देवताया हुताशने ॥ ६८

अर्चयेद्वह्निरूपां तां देवतामिष्टदायिनीम् ।

तन्मुखे जुहुयान्मन्त्री पञ्चविंशतिसंख्यया ॥ ६९

आज्येन मूलमन्त्रेण वक्त्रैकीकरणान्विदम् ।

वह्निदेवतयोरैक्यमात्मना सह भावयन् ॥ ७०

मूलमन्त्रेण जुहुयादाज्येनैकादशाहुतीः ।

नाड़ीसन्धानमुद्दिष्टमेतदागमवेदिभिः ॥ ७१

नाभौ तन्मूलमाधाय स्रुङ्गाग्रे व्यस्तलोचनः ।

वामस्तनान्तमानीय तयोर्मूलमतन्द्रितः ॥ इति ।

विघ्नेश्वरस्येति। महागणपतेर्दशधा विभक्तेन पूर्व्वपूर्व्वानुविद्धेनेति ज्ञेयम्। समस्तेनाहुतिचतुष्टयं दद्यादित्यपि। तदुक्तं गणेश्वरविमर्शिन्याम्—

महागणेशमन्त्रेण पूर्व्वपूर्व्वयुतेन च ।

तारादिबीजषट्केषु करणेष्वद्विवर्णकैः ॥

भिन्नेषु दशधा हुत्वा समस्तेन सुरेश्वरि। इति ।

तथा चाचार्य्याः—ताराद्यैर्दशभिर्भेदैः पूर्व्वपूर्व्वसमन्वितैः ।

मनुना गाणपत्येन जुहुयाच्च दशाहुतीः ॥

जुहुयाच्च चतुर्वारं समस्तेनैव तेन तु ॥ इति ।

अन्यत्रापि—महागणेशमन्त्रेण पूर्व्वपूर्व्वयुतेन च ।

भिन्नेन दशधा हुत्वा सामान्येन सुरेश्वरि ॥ इति ॥ ६६ ॥ ६७ ॥

देवताया इति। प्रकृतदेयमन्त्रदेवताया इत्यर्थः। देवतामिति सावरणाम्। वक्त्रैकीकरणमिति। तदुक्तं शैवागमे—

इतीष्टवक्त्रे वक्त्राणामन्तर्भावस्तु चैकता ।

अथवा कुण्डसानत्वं यदीष्टवदने स्मरेत् ॥

अन्तर्भाव्यानि वक्त्राणि तदैकीकरणं मतम् ॥ इति॥६८॥६९॥७०॥

नाड़ीसन्धानमिति। अग्निदेवतात्मनां त्रयाणां नाड्येकीकरणम्। अङ्गमुख्यानामावृतीनामिति प्रकृतदेयमन्त्रदेवताया इत्यर्थः। अत्राप्यङ्गेत्यादि सम्भवाभिप्रायम्। सम्यगित्यनेन यत्राङ्गावृतेराद्यत्वं नास्ति तत्र यथावृत्ति-

जुहुयादङ्गमुख्यानामावृतीनामनुक्रमात् ।
एकैकामाहुतिं सम्यक् सर्पिषा देशिकोत्तमः ॥ ७२
ततोऽन्येष्वपि कुण्डेषु संस्कृतेषु यथाविधि ।
आचार्य्यो विहरेदग्निं पूर्व्वादिषु समाहितः ॥ ७३
ऋत्विजो गन्धपुष्पाद्यैरङ्गाद्यावरणान्विताम् ।
तन्त्रोक्तदेवतामिष्ट्वा पञ्चविंशतिसंख्यया ।
मूलेनाज्येन जुहुयुः साज्येन चरुणा तथा ॥ ७४
प्रातरुत्थाय जुहुयुः पुनराज्यान्वितैस्तिलैः ।
द्रव्यैर्वा कल्पविहितैः सहस्रं साष्टकं पृथक् ॥ ७५

स्तदादीनामाहृतीनामित्युक्तम् । देशिकोत्तम इत्यनेन मूलमन्त्रेण दशाहुतयो होतव्या इत्युक्तम् । यदाहुः—

परिवारस्यैकैकां देव्यास्तु दशाहुतीर्जुहुयात् । इति ॥ ७१ ॥ ७२ ॥

संस्कृतेष्विति । ऋत्विग्भिरिति शेषः । तेन ऋत्विजः स्वे स्वे कुण्डे अष्टादशसंस्कारान् यथाविधि कुर्युः । आचार्य्योऽग्निविहरणं कुर्य्यात् सर्व्वैर्वेत्यर्थः । पूर्व्वादिषु ईशान्ते । समाहित इत्यनेनाविच्छेदेनाग्निविहरणमुक्तम् ॥ ७३ ॥

देवतामिष्टेति । अत्र पूजानन्तरं तत्तद्देवताङ्गावृत्यादीनां पूर्व्ववदेकैकामाहुतिं हुत्वा मूलदेवताया दशाहुतीर्जुहुयुरिति ज्ञेयम् । साज्येन चरुणा तथेति । पूर्व्वपटले यश्चरु कारितस्तस्य भागत्रयं कृतम् । एको भागो देवतायै निवेदितः अन्यमग्नौ प्रजुहुयादित्युक्तम् । तस्यैवायं होमः । तथेति मूलेन पञ्चविंशतिवारम् ॥ ७४ ॥

द्वितीयदिनकृत्यमाह प्रातरिति । जुहुयुरित्याचार्य्याः प्रत्येकमृत्विजश्च । तत्र विशेषो वायवीयसंहितायाम्—

स्रुवेणाज्यं समित् पाण्या स्रुचा शेषं करेण वा ।
तत्र दिव्येन होतव्यं तीर्थेनार्षेण वा तथा ॥ इति ।

पृथक् प्रत्येकमष्टोत्तरसहस्रं तत्र समिद्धेऽग्नौ होतव्यम् । अन्यथा दोषदर्शनात् । तदुक्तं बह्वृचपरिशिष्टे—

अन्धो बुधः सधूमे च जुहुयाद् यो हुताशने ।
यजमानो भवेदन्धः सपुत्र इति च श्रुतिः ॥ इति ।

ततः सुधौतदन्तास्यं स्नातं शिष्यं समाहितम् ।
पाययित्वा पञ्चगव्यं कुण्डस्यान्तिकमानयेत् ॥ ७६

विलोक्य दिव्यदृष्ट्या तं तच्चैतन्यं हृदम्बुजात् ।
गुरुरात्मनि संयोज्य कुर्यादध्वविशोधनम् ॥ ७७

उक्तं कलाध्वा तत्त्वाध्वा भुवनाध्वेति च त्रयम् ।
वर्णाध्वा च पदाध्वा च मन्त्राध्वेत्यपरं त्रयम् ॥ ७८

छन्दोगपरिशिष्टेऽपि —

योऽनर्चिषि जुहोत्यग्नौ व्यङ्गारिणि च मानवः ।
मन्दाग्निरामयावी च दरिद्रश्चोपजायते ॥
तस्मात् समिद्धे होतव्यं नासमिद्धे कथञ्चन ।
आरोग्यमिच्छतायुश्च श्रियमात्यन्तिकीं तथा ॥ इति ।

महाकपिलपञ्चरात्रेऽपि —

अप्रदीप्ते न होतव्यं धूमके नाप्यनिन्धिते ।
प्रदीप्ते लेलिहानेऽग्नौ होतव्यं कर्मसिद्धये ॥ इति ॥ ७५ ॥

होमानन्तरं गुरुकृत्यमाह तत इति । पञ्चगव्यं पाययित्वेति मत्कृपवास्य एव । पञ्चगव्यप्रकारं तु एकविंशे वक्ष्यति । तदुक्तं प्रयोगसारे —

पञ्चगव्यं यथा प्रोक्तं पीत्वाऽऽचान्तं यथाविधि ।
द्वारेण दक्षिणेनाथ यागस्थानं प्रवेशयेत् ॥ इति ।

तच्चैतन्यमिति । तद्धृदो वहन्नाड्या अङ्कुशमुद्रया चैतन्यमाकृष्य स्ववहन्नाडीमार्गेण स्वहृदि संयोजयेदित्यर्थः । तदुक्तम् —

हृदि स्थितं तच्चैतन्यं प्रस्फुरत्तारकाकृति ।
आदाय स्थापयेत् स्वीये हृदयेऽङ्कुशमुद्रया ॥ इति ।

अध्वविशोधनमिति । तदुक्तं अङ्कुन्दयमहार्णवे —

शोधनं नाम तत्त्वानां कारणैकत्वचिन्तनम् ।
वर्णादीनां कलानाञ्च तस्यां विन्दैक्यचिन्तनम् ॥ इति ॥७६॥७७॥

उक्तमिति । इति त्रयम् इति च त्रयम् उक्तं तन्त्रविद्भिरिति शेषः । आद्यास्त्रयोऽर्थरूपाः परे त्रयः शब्दरूपाः । तदुक्तं वायवीयसंहितायाम् —

तत्र शब्दास्त्रयो धातुस्त्रयस्त्वर्थाः समीरिताः । इति ।

निवृत्त्याद्याः कलाः पञ्च कलाध्वेति प्रकीर्त्तितः ।
तत्त्वाध्वा बहुधा भिन्नः शिवाद्यागमभेदतः ॥ ७९
षट्त्रिंशच्छिवतत्त्वानि द्वात्रिंशद्वैष्णवानि तु ।
चतुर्विंशतितत्त्वानि सैवाणि प्रकृतेः पुनः ॥ ८०
उक्तानि दश तत्त्वानि सप्त च त्रिपदात्मनः ।
तत्त्वानि शैवान्युच्यन्ते शिवः शक्तिः सदाशिवः ॥ ८१
ईश्वरो विद्यया सार्द्धं पञ्च शुद्धान्यमूनि हि ।
माया कालश्च नियतिः कला विद्या पुनः स्मृता ॥ ८२
रागः पुरुष एतानि शुद्धाशुद्धानि सप्त च ।
प्रकृतिर्बुद्ध्यहङ्कारो मनो ज्ञानेन्द्रियाण्यथ ॥ ८३
कर्म्मेन्द्रियाणि तन्मात्रा पञ्च भूतानि देशिकाः ।
एतान्याहुरशुद्धानि चतुर्विंशतिरागमे ॥ ८४

अन्यत्रापि—मन्त्राध्वा च पदाध्वा च वर्णाध्वा चेति शब्दतः ।
भुवनाध्वा च तत्त्वाध्वा कलाध्वा चाऽर्थतः क्रमात् ॥ इति ।
अत्र तु संहारक्रमेणोक्तिः मूले तु सृष्टिक्रमेणेति ज्ञेयम् ॥ ७८ ॥
बहुधेति पञ्चधा । सैवाणि सांख्यानि । तदुक्तं वायवीयसंहितायाम्—
पौराणानि च तत्त्वानि त्रिपुरायाश्च कानि चित् ।
सांख्ययोगप्रसिद्धानि तत्त्वान्यपि च कानि चित् ॥
शिवशास्त्रप्रसिद्धानि ततोऽन्यान्यपि क्वतुक्षयः । इति ।
त्रिपदात्मनस्त्रिपुरायाः ॥ ७९ ॥ ८० ॥ ८१ ॥
शुद्धानीति । आणवकार्म्ममायीयमलत्रयरहितत्वात् शुद्धत्वम् । तत्राणवो नाम सदाशिवस्य स्वस्थानवमर्षः । कार्म्मो नाम पुण्यपापवानहमिति प्रतीतिः । मायीयो नाम अहङ्कारादावात्मबुद्धिः । उक्तञ्च वायवीयसंहितायाम्—
शिवः शक्तिस्ततो नादस्तस्माद्विन्दुः सदाशिवः ।
तस्मान्महेश्वरो जातः शुद्धा विद्या महेश्वरात् ॥ इति ॥ ८२ ॥
शुद्धाशुद्धानीति । कारणत्वेन मलत्रयराहित्याच्छुद्धत्वम् कार्य्यरूपत्वेन तद्युक्तत्वादशुद्धत्वम् । तदुक्तं वायवीयसंहितायाम्—

शैवानामिति तत्त्वानां विभागोऽत्र प्रदर्शितः ।
जीवप्राणधियश्चित्तं ज्ञानकर्म्मेन्द्रियाण्यथ ॥ ८५

तन्मात्राः पञ्च भूतानि इत्यग्न्यं तैजसां त्रयम् ।
वासुदेवादयश्चेति तत्त्वान्येतानि शार्ङ्गिणः ॥ ८६

पञ्च भूतानि तन्मात्रा इन्द्रियाणि मनस्तथा ।
गर्व्वो बुद्धिः प्रधानञ्च सैवाणीति विदुर्बुधाः ॥ ८७

निवृत्याद्याः कलाः पञ्च ततो बिन्दुः कला पुनः ।
नादः शक्तिः सदापूर्व्वः शिवश्च प्रकृतेर्विदुः ॥ ८८

आत्मविद्या शिवः पश्चाच्छिवो विद्या स्वयं पुनः ।
सर्व्वतत्त्वञ्च तत्त्वानि प्रोक्तानि लिपदात्मनः ॥ ८९

तत्त्वाध्वा कथितो ह्येष तत्तदागमवेदिभिः ।
ईरितो भुवनाध्वेति भुवनानि मनीषिभिः ॥ ९०

वर्णाध्वेति वदन्त्यर्णानादिक्षान्तान् मनीषिणः
वर्णसङ्घः पदाध्वा स्यान्मन्त्राध्वा मन्त्रराशयः ॥ ९१

सा वाचामीश्वरी शक्तिर्वागीशाख्यस्य शूलिनः ।
या सा वर्णस्वरूपेण मातृकेति विजृम्भते ॥
अथानन्तसमायोगान्मायां कालमवासृजत् ।
नियतिञ्च कलां विद्यां कलातो रागपूरुषौ ॥ इत्यादि ।
षट्त्रिंशत् संख्ययोपेतः शुद्धाशुद्धोभयात्मकः । इत्यन्तेन ॥८३॥८४॥

ज्ञानकर्म्मेन्द्रियाणीति दश । पञ्चेत्युभयत्र सम्बध्यते । तैजसां त्रयमग्नीन्दुसूर्य्याः । वासुदेवादयश्चत्वारोऽष्टमे वक्ष्यन्ते ॥ ८५ ॥ ८६ ॥

इन्द्रियाणि दश । गर्व्वोऽहङ्कारः । बुद्धिर्महत्तत्त्वम् । प्रधानं प्रकृतिः । स्वयमात्मा ॥ ८७ ॥ ८८ ॥ ८९ ॥

स्वकपोलकल्पितत्वशङ्कां वारयति तत्तदागमवेदिभिरिति । भुवनानि आकाशवायुतैजसाप्यपार्थिवभुवनानि पञ्च । वायवीयसंहितायान्तु—

आधाराद्युन्मन्यन्तश्च भुवनाध्वा प्रकीर्त्तितः । इति ।

वर्णसङ्घः सबिन्दुवर्णाः । वायवीयसंहितायान्तु—

क्रमादेतानध्वनः षट् शोधयेद् गुरुसत्तमः।
पदान्धुनाभिहृद्भालमूर्द्धस्वपि शिशोः स्मरेत्॥ ९२
ततः कूर्चेन विधिवत्तं स्पृशेत् जुहुयाद् गुरुः।
आचार्य्यकुण्डे संशुद्धैस्तिलैराज्यपरिप्लुतैः॥ ९३
शोधयाम्यमुमध्वानं स्वाहेति पृथगध्वना।
ताराद्यमाहुतीरष्टौ क्रमात्तान् विलयं नयेत्॥ ९४
शिवे शिवात्तान् संलीनान् जनयेत् सृष्टिमार्गतः॥ ९५

अनेकभेदसम्भिन्नः पदाध्वा पदसंहतिः।
महामन्त्रोपमन्त्राणां वर्त्ततेऽवयवात्मना॥
प्रधानावयवत्वेन सोऽध्वा पञ्चपदात्मकः। इति।

मन्त्रराशय: अकचटतपया: सप्त मन्त्रा:॥ ९०॥ ९१॥

मूर्द्धनि ब्रह्मरन्ध्रे। तत्रायं शोधनप्रकारः। पादे कलाध्वानं स्मृत्वा पदगुह्यहृद्भ्रूशिरःसु स्वबीजादिका: कला विन्यस्य पश्चात् कलाध्वविशोधनम्। एवं तत्त्वाध्वानम् अन्धौ स्मृत्वा विलोमेषु पूर्व्वस्थानेषु तान् विन्यस्य पश्चात् तत्त्वाध्वशोधनम्। एवं भुवनाध्वानं नाभौ स्मृत्वा अनन्तरस्थानेषु स्वबीजाद्यान् विन्यस्य पश्चात् तच्छोधनम्। एवं हृदि वर्णाध्वानं संस्मृत्य शुद्धान् वर्णान् तद्देहे विन्यस्य पश्चाद्वर्णाध्वशोधनम्। एवं भाले पदाध्वानं संस्मृत्य सबिन्दुवर्णान् विन्यस्य तच्छोधनम्। एवं मूर्द्धनि मन्त्राध्वानं संस्मृत्य सप्त मन्त्रान् तत्तत्स्थानेषु व्याप्य पश्चात्तदध्वविशोधनमिति गुरुसत्तम इत्यनेनोक्तम्। विधिवदित्यनेन शिष्य इति ज्ञेयम्। तं गुरुं स्पृशेदिति भिन्नं वाक्यम्। तदुक्तं नारायणीये—

ध्यानेनात्मनि तं शिष्यं संहृत्य प्रलयक्रमात्।
पुनरुत्पाद्य तत्पाणौ दद्याद्दर्भांश्च मन्त्रितान्॥ इति।

केचन तं स्पृशन्निति पठन्ति। तदा विधिवदित्यनेन वामकरस्थेनेति ज्ञेयम्। गुरुरष्टावाहुतीः अध्वना ताराद्यं पृथक् जुहुयादिति सम्बन्धः। शोधयामीति अमुष्येत्यर्थः। संशुद्धैरित्यवकरं दूरीकृत्य प्रक्षाल्य संशोषितैरित्यर्थः। प्रयोगस्तु। ॐ अमुष्य कलाध्वानं शोधयामि स्वाहा इत्यादि॥ ९२॥ ९३॥ ९४॥

शिवे सहस्रारस्थिते इति पूर्व्वेण सम्बध्यते। क्रमादित्यग्रिमम्। पूर्व्वस्मिन्निति शिवपर्य्यन्तम्। शिवात् सृष्टिमार्गतस्तान् जनयेदिति सम्बन्धः। सृष्टिमार्गतः

विलोकयन् दिव्यदृष्ट्या तं शिशुं देशिकोत्तमः ।
आत्मस्थितं तच्चैतन्यं पुनः शिष्ये नियोजयेत् ॥ ९६

स्रुचा पूर्णाहुतिं दत्त्वा मूलमन्त्रेण मन्त्रवित् ।
उद्वास्य देवतां कुम्भे साङ्गां सावरणां गुरुः ॥ ९७

पुनर्व्याहृतिभिर्हुत्वा जिह्वादीनां विभावसोः ।
एकैकामाहुतिं हुत्वा परिषिच्याऽद्भिरात्मनि ॥ ९८

पूर्व्वस्मादग्निमं नियोजयेदिति । यथा आनीतं तथैवेत्यर्थः । अनेन अध्व-विशोधनेन शरीरशुद्धिः कृता भवति । यतः षड़ध्वमयमेव शरीरम् । यदाहुः—

शान्त्यतीतकलामूर्द्धा शान्तिवक्त्रशिरोरुहा ।
निवृत्तिजानुजङ्घाङ्घ्रि र्भुवनाध्वशिरोरुहा ॥
मन्त्राध्वमांसरुधिरा पदवर्णशिरायुता ।
तत्त्वाध्वमज्जमेदोऽस्थिधातुरेतोयुता शिवे ॥ इति । ९५ ॥ ९६ ॥

मूलमन्त्रेणेति । देशिक इत्यनेन वौषडन्तेनेत्युक्तम् । तदुक्तं वायवीयसंहितायाम्—

ततो होमावशिष्टेन घृतेनापूर्य्य वै स्रुचम् ।
निधाय पुष्पं तस्याग्रे स्रुवेणाऽधोमुखेन ताम् ॥
सदर्भेण समाच्छाद्य मूलेनाऽञ्जलिनोत्थितः ।
वौषड़न्तेन जुहुयाद्धारान्तु यवसम्मिताम् ॥
इत्थं पूर्णाहुतिं कृत्वा । इति ।

उद्वास्य अग्नित उद्वासनं कृत्वा कुम्भे आनीय इत्यर्थः । देशिको गुरुरित्यनेन देवतायाः अङ्गावृत्यादीनाम् एकैकामाहुतिं हुत्वा उद्वासनमित्युक्तं भवति । व्याहृतिभिर्व्यस्तसमस्ताभिः ।

साम्प्रदायिकास्तु व्याहृतिशब्देनात महाव्याहृतय उच्यन्ते इत्याहुः । ताश्च । ॐ भूरग्नये च पृथिव्यै च महते च स्वाहा । ॐ भुवो वायवे चान्तरीक्षाय च महते च स्वाहा । ॐ स्वरादित्याय च दिवे च महते च स्वाहा । ॐ भूर्भुवः स्वश्चन्द्रमसे च नक्षत्रेभ्यश्च दिग्भ्यश्च महते च स्वाहा इति ।

उक्तञ्च—पुनः समापयेद्धोमं महाव्याहृतिपूर्व्वकम् । इति ।
विभावसोर्जिह्वादीनाम् इत्यादिशब्देन अधिदेवताङ्गमूर्त्तिलोकपालतदायुधानि । परिषिच्येति पावकमिति सम्बध्यते । अद्भिः प्रोक्षणुदकैरित्यर्थः ॥

पावकं योजयित्वा स्वे परिधीन् सपरिस्तरान् ।
नैमित्तिके दहेन्नग्नौ नित्ये तु न दहेदिमान् ॥ ९९

नेत्रे शिष्यस्य बध्नीयान्नेत्रमन्त्रेण वाससा ।
करे गृहीत्वा तं शिष्यं कुण्डतो मण्डलं नयेत् ॥ १००

तस्याञ्जलिं पुनः पुष्पैः पूरयित्वा यथाविधि ।
कलशे देवताप्रीत्यै क्षेपयेन्मूलमुच्चरन् ॥ १०१

व्यपोह्य तं नेत्रबन्धमासीनं दर्भसंस्तरे ।
आत्मयागक्रमाद्भूयः संहृत्योत्थाप्य देशिकः ॥ १०२

स्वे आत्मनि पावकं योजयित्वेति । तत्र प्रार्थनमन्त्रेण संप्रार्थ्य पश्चादुद्वासनम् । तदुक्तं गणेश्वरविमर्शिन्याम्—

भो भो वह्ने महाशक्ते सर्वकर्मप्रसाधक ।
कर्मान्तरेऽपि सम्प्राप्ते सान्निध्यं कुरु सादरम् ।
इतिमन्त्रेण संप्रार्थ्य वह्निमुद्वासयेदपि ॥ इति ॥ ९७॥९८॥९९ ॥

वाससेति नवेन शुक्लेन ।

तदुक्तं महाकपिलपञ्चरात्रे—नवेन शुक्लवस्त्रेण नेत्रे बद्ध्वा । इति ।

पिङ्गलामते तु विशेषः—

नेत्रवस्त्रेण तन्नेत्रे नेत्रमन्त्रेण बन्धयेत् । इति ।

मन्त्रतन्त्रप्रकाशेऽपि—अथ नेत्रेण तन्नेत्रे बद्ध्वा नेत्रेण देशिकः । इति ।

नारायणीये तु—नेत्राद्यैर्नेत्रं नेत्रेण बन्धयेत् । इति ।

मण्डलं नयेदिति । प्रादक्षिण्येन पश्चिमद्वारमिति शेषः । तदुक्तं नारायणीये—

न्यासं शिष्यतनौ कृत्वा तं प्रदक्षिणमानयेत् ।
पश्चिमद्वारमानीय क्षेपयेत् कुसुमाञ्जलिम् ॥ इति ।

यथाविधि क्षेपयेदित्यनेन विशेषः पिङ्गलामतोक्तः संगृहीतः ।

पुष्पैरञ्जलिमापूर्य योगपीठे प्रदापयेत् ।
पश्चिमोत्तरकद्वन्द्वे पुष्पपातः शुभोऽशुभे ।
अष्टोत्तरशतं शान्त्यै जुहुयादस्त्रमन्त्रतः ॥ इति ॥ १००॥१०१ ॥

आत्मयागक्रमाद्वक्ष्यमाणप्रपञ्चयागक्रमेणेति केचित् । साम्प्रदायिकास्तु आत्मयागः अन्तर्यागः तत्क्रमात् तत्रोक्तभूतशुद्धिक्रमेणेत्यर्थः । तत्र भूतसंहारस्य

तत्तन्मन्त्रोदितान् न्यासान् कुर्य्याद् देहे शिशोस्तदा ।
पञ्चोपचारैः कुम्भस्थां पूजयित्वेष्टदेवताम् ॥ १०३

तस्याः तन्त्रोक्तमार्गेण विदध्यात् सकलीकृतिम् ।
मण्डलेऽलङ्कृते शिष्यमन्यस्मिन्ननुप्रवेशयेत् ॥ १०४

भूतसृष्टेश्चोक्तत्वात् । देहं संहृत्य भूयोऽनन्तरमुत्पाद्येत्यन्वयः । तदुक्तं प्रयोगसारे—

गुणांशेन पृथिव्यादिभूतानि विलयं नयेत् ।
यथावत् पिण्डसंस्थानि संहारक्रमयोगतः ।
ततः सृष्टिक्रमेणैव पिण्डं सम्भावयेत्तदा ॥ इति ।

मन्त्रतन्त्रप्रकाशेऽपि—उपविश्यासने दिव्ये संहरेत्तस्य विग्रहम् ।
गन्धादिघ्राणसंयुक्तां पृथिवीमप्सु संहरेत् ॥ इत्यादिना
उत्पन्नं भावयेत्ततः । इत्यन्तेन ।

अन्यत्रापि—अथाभिषेकमण्डपे सुखोपविष्टमासने ।
गुरुर्विशोधयेदमुं पुरेव शोषणादिभिः ॥ इति ।

नारायणीयेऽपि—शोषादिना सुखासीनं तत्र संशोधयेद् गुरुः । इति ।

अत्र देवताप्रार्थनमाहुराचार्य्याः ।

कारुण्यनिलये देवि सर्व्वसम्पत्तिसंश्रये ।
शरण्यवत्सले मातः कृपामस्मिन् शिशौ कुरु ॥
आणवप्रमुखैः पाशैः पाशितस्य सुरेश्वरि ।
दीनस्याऽस्य दयाधारे कुरु कारुण्यमीश्वरि ॥
ऐहिकामुष्मिकैर्भोगैरपि सम्बर्द्धतामयम् ।
त्व[मद्]भक्तिः सकला चास्मै दीयतां निष्कलाश्रये ॥ इति ॥ १०२॥१०३ ॥

अन्यस्मिन् मण्डल इति । मण्डलाद्बहिरैशान्याम् । तदुक्तं सोमशम्भुना—

यागालयाद्दिशीशस्य रचिते स्नानमण्डपे ।
कुर्य्यात् करद्वयायामां वेदिमष्टाङ्गुलोच्छ्रिताम् ॥
श्रीपर्ण्याद्यासने तत्र विन्यस्यानन्तमासनम् ।
शिष्यं निवेश्य पूर्व्वास्यं सकलीकृत्य पूजयेत् ॥ इति ।

प्रयोगसारे—अथैशान्यां दिशि यथा मन्त्रविन्यस्तविग्रहम् ।
पीठस्थं चतुरस्रायां वेद्यां दर्भाग्रपाणिना ॥
अभिषिञ्चेत् स्वयं शिष्यमात्मतत्त्वानुवर्त्तिनम् ॥ इति ।

नदत्सु पञ्चवाद्येषु सार्द्धं विप्राशिषा गुरुः ।
विधिवत् कुम्भमुद्धृत्य तन्मुखस्थान् सुरद्रुमान् ॥ १०५
शिष्यो: शिरसि विन्यस्य मातृकां मनसा जपन् ।
मूलेन साधितैस्तोयैरभिषिञ्चेत् तमात्मवित् ॥ १०६
पूजितां पुनरादाय वर्द्धनीमस्त्ररूपिणीम् ।
तस्यां सुसाधितैस्तोयैः सिञ्चेद्रक्षार्थमञ्जसा ॥ १०७
अवशिष्टेन तोयेन शिष्यमाचामयेद् गुरुः ।
ततस्तं सकलीकुर्य्याद्देवतात्मानमात्मवित् ॥ १०८
उत्थाय शिष्यो विमले वाससी परिधाय च ।
आचम्य वाग्यतो भूत्वा निषीदेत् सन्निधौ गुरोः ॥ १०९

उपवेशयेदिति भुक्तौ प्राङ्मुखं मुक्तावुदङ्मुखमिति ज्ञेयम् । तदुक्तं सोमशम्भौ—

स्नाने तूदङ्मुखं मुक्तौ पूर्ववक्त्रञ्च भुक्तये । ऊर्द्ध्वकायं समारोप्य । इति ।

अन्यत्रापि—मण्डले त्वीशदिक्कृत्वा मुमुक्षूनुत्तराननान् ।

भुक्तये पूर्ववक्त्रांच शिष्यांस्तत्र निवेशयेत् ॥ इति । १०४

विधिवन्मातृकां मनसा जपन् मूलेनाऽभिषिञ्चेदिति सम्बन्धः । तत्र विधिवदिति विलोमपठितां मूलञ्च तादृग्रूपमिति । तदुक्तमाचार्य्यैः—

यथा पुरा पूरितमत्वरैर्घटं सुधामयैः शिष्यतनौ तथैव तैः ।

प्रपूरयन्मन्त्रिवरोऽभिषेचयेदवामये मङ्क्षु यथेष्टसम्पदाम् ॥ इति ।

अन्यत्रापि—सुमतिरभिषिञ्चेन्नरो मन्त्रजापी । इति ।

अन्यत्रापि— अभिषिचयता यथावत् ।

चाद्यैरान्तैर्वर्णैरपि पूर्णतनुस्त्रिकक्रमन्त्रार्णैः ॥ इति ।

सुसाधितैरित्यनुवादमात्रम् उभयत्रापि । पूजितामित्यप्यनुवादः । अञ्जसा तत्त्वेन । ॥ १०५॥१०६॥१०७ ॥

अवशिष्टेनेति अभिषेकावशिष्टकलशस्थेन । देवतात्मानमभिषेकेन । सन्निधौ समीपे । संक्रान्तामित्यभिषेकेन । देशिकोत्तम इत्यनेनाद्यशब्देन धूपदीपे एव ग्राह्ये इत्युक्तम् । तयोरिति शिष्यदेवतयोः । तत्र इत्यनेन शिष्यमूर्द्धनि हस्तं दत्त्वाऽष्टोत्तरशतं मन्त्रं जपेदिति सूचितम् । तदुक्तं वशिष्ठ-

देवतामात्मनः शिष्ये संक्रान्तां देशिकोत्तमः ।
पूजयेद् गन्धपुष्पाद्यैरैक्यं सम्भावयंस्तयोः ॥ ११०

दद्याद्विद्यां ततस्तस्मै विनीतायाऽम्बुपूर्व्वकम् ।
गुरोर्लब्ध्वा पुनर्विद्यामष्टकृत्वो जपेत् सुधीः ॥ १११

गुरुविद्यादेवतानामैक्यं सम्भावयन् धिया ।
प्रणमेद्दण्डवद्भूमौ गुरुं तं देवतात्मकम् ॥ ११२

संहितायाम्—ततस्तच्छिरसि स्वस्य हस्तं दत्त्वा शतं जपेत् ।
अष्टोत्तरं ततो मन्त्रं दद्यादुदकपूर्व्वकम् ॥ इति ।

अन्यत्रापि—अथ सम्पादयेन्मन्त्रं हस्तं शिरसि धारयन् ।
समोऽस्त्वित्यक्षतं दद्यात् । इति ।

मन्त्रतन्त्रप्रकाशेऽपि—
विश्वात्मा स्वयमाचार्य्यस्तन्मूर्द्ध्नि स्वकरं न्यसेत् । इति ॥१०८॥१०९॥११०॥

दद्यादिति दक्षिणकर्णे त्रिवारं यावत् पाठं वा । तदुक्तम्—
ऋष्यादियुक्तमथ मन्त्रवरं यथावद् ब्रूयात् त्रिशो गुरुरनर्घ्यमवामकर्णे । इति ।

अम्बुपूर्व्वकमिति ब्राह्मणविषयम् । एतदन्तरम्—
आवयोस्तुल्यफलदो भवत्वेवमुदीरयेत् ।
प्रसन्नवदनस्तस्मै शिष्याय मुनिपुङ्गवः ॥
स्वतो ज्योतिर्मयीं विद्यां गच्छन्तीं भावयेद् गुरुः ।
आगतां भावयेच्छिष्यः । इति ॥

वायवीयसंहितायान्तु—
अथ गुर्वाज्ञया शिष्यः शिवाग्निगुरुसन्निधौ ।
भक्त्यैवमभिसन्धाय दीक्षावाक्यमुदीरयेत् ॥
वरं प्राणपरित्यागश्छेदनं शिरसोऽपि वा ।
न त्वनभ्यर्च्य भुञ्जीयां भगवन्तं त्रिलोचनम् ॥ इति ।

विद्यादानान्तरं गुरुरष्टोत्तरसहस्रं मन्त्रं जपेत् । तदुक्तम् "अष्टोत्तरं सहस्रं स्वशक्तिहानानवाप्तये जप्यात्" इति । नारायणीयमहाकपिलपञ्चरात्रयोरपि—
मन्त्रं दत्त्वा सहस्रं वै स्वसिद्ध्यै देशिको जपेत् । इति ॥ १११ ॥

प्रणमेदिति । त्वत्प्रसादादहं देव कृतकृत्योऽस्मि सर्व्वतः ।
मायामृत्युमहापाशाद् विमुक्तोऽस्मि शिवोऽस्मि च ॥

तस्य पादाम्बुजद्वन्द्वं निजमूर्द्धनि योजयेत् ।
शरीरमर्थं प्राणांश्च सर्व्वं तस्मै निवेदयेत् ॥ ११३

इति मन्त्रं पठन्निति ज्ञेयम् । तत्र अष्टाङ्गः पञ्चाङ्गो वा प्रणामः कार्य्य इत्यर्थः ।

यदाहुः—दोर्भ्यां पद्भ्याञ्च जानुभ्यामुरसा शिरसा दृशा ।
मनसा वचसा चेति प्रणामोऽष्टाङ्ग ईरितः ॥
बाहुभ्याञ्च सजानुभ्यां शिरसा वचसा धिया ।
पञ्चाङ्गकः प्रणामः स्यात् सर्व्वत्र प्रवराविमौ ॥ इति ।

अर्थं निवेदयेदित्यनेन गुरवे दक्षिणां कुम्भादिकञ्च दद्यादित्युक्तम् । यदाहुः—
द्रव्यार्द्धं गुरवे दद्याद् दक्षिणां वा तदर्द्धकम् । इति ।

मन्त्रतन्त्रप्रकाशेऽपि—
आचार्य्यादनभिप्राप्तः प्राप्तश्चाऽदत्तदक्षिणः ।
सततं जप्यमानोऽपि मन्त्रः सिद्धिं न गच्छति ॥
सर्व्वस्वं वा तदर्द्धं वा वित्तशाठ्यविवर्जितः ।
गुरवे दक्षिणां दत्त्वा ततो मन्त्रग्रहो मतः ॥ इति ।

वायवीयसंहितायाम्—
सखड्गं गुरवे दद्याद् यागोपकरणैः सह । इति ।

अन्यत्रापि—तां वित्तशाठ्यं परिहृत्य दक्षिणां
दत्त्वा तनुं स्वाञ्च समर्पयेत् सुधीः । इति ।

अन्यत्रापि—कृतकृत्यस्तथा शिष्यः सर्व्वं तस्मै निवेदयेत् ।
यच्च यावच्च तद्भक्त्या गुरोराकृष्टचेतनः ॥
गोभूहिरण्यं विपुलं शय्यावेशादिकं बहु ।
नचेदर्द्धं तदर्द्धं वा तद्दशांशमथापि वा ॥
अक्लेशादन्नवस्त्रादि दद्याद् वित्तानुसारतः ॥ इति ।

तथा—कुम्भादिकञ्च सकलं गुरवे तु समर्प्य च । इति ।

अन्यत्रापि—विभवानुरूपतोऽसौ दातव्या दक्षिणा च निजगुरवे ।
प्राणप्रदानकर्त्रे न च कार्य्यं वित्तशाठ्यममलधिया ॥ इति ।

ततो गुरोः कृत्यं तन्त्रान्तरोक्तं लिख्यते ।
ज्ञानसम्पत्ते सदाचारं नित्यं कार्य्यं तथैव च ।
मन्त्रसिद्धिप्रकारांश्च शिष्यायाऽभिवदेद् गुरुः ॥

इति मन्त्रतन्त्रप्रकाशे । अन्यत्रापि—

अभिवन्द्य ततः शृणोतु सम्यक् समयान् भक्तिभरावनम्रमूर्त्तिः । इति ।

तत्र सदाचार उक्तः प्रयोगसारे—

देवस्थाने गुरुस्थाने श्मशाने वा चतुष्पथे ।
पादुकासनविण्मूत्रमैथुनानि परित्यजेत् ॥
देवं गुरुं गुरुस्थानं क्षेत्रं क्षेत्राधिदेवताः ।
सिद्धं सिद्धाधिकारांश्च श्रीपूर्व्वं समुदीरयेत् ॥
प्रमत्तामन्त्यजां कन्यां पुष्पितां पतितस्तनीम् ।
विरूपां मुक्तकेशीञ्च कामार्त्तांञ्च न निन्दयेत् ॥
कन्यायोनिं पशुक्रीड़ां दिग्वस्त्रां प्रकटस्तनीम् ।
नालोकयेत् परद्रव्यं परदारांश्च वर्जयेत् ॥
धान्यगोगुरुदेवाग्नि विद्याकोशनरान् प्रति ।
नैव प्रसारयेत् पादौ नैतानपि च लङ्घयेत् ॥
आलस्यमदसम्मोहशाठ्यपैशून्यविग्रहान् ।
असूयामात्मसन्मानं परनिन्दाञ्च वर्जयेत् ॥
लिङ्गिनं व्रतिनं विप्रं वेदवेदाङ्गसंहिताः ।
पुराणागमशास्त्राणि कल्पांश्चापि न दूषयेत् ॥
युगं मुषलमश्मानं दाम चुल्लीमुदूखलम् ।
शूर्पसम्मार्जनीदण्डध्वजवैदूर्य्यमायुधम् ॥
कलशं चामरं छत्रं दर्पणं भूषणन्तथा ।
भोगयोग्यानि चान्यानि यागद्रव्याणि यानि च ॥
महास्थानेषु वस्तूनि यानि वा देवतालये ।
दिव्योक्तानि पदार्थानि भूताविष्टानि यानि वै ॥
लङ्घयेन्जातु नैतानि नैतानि च पदा स्पृशेत् ।
या गोष्ठी लोकविद्विष्टा या च स्वैरविसर्पिणी ॥
परहिंसात्मिका या च न तामवतरेत् सदा ।
प्रतिग्रहं न गृह्णीयादात्मभोगविधित्सया ॥
देवतातिथिपूजार्थं यत्नतोऽप्यर्जयेद्धनम् ।
धारयेदार्जवं सत्यं सौशील्यं समतां धृतिम् ॥
क्षान्तिं दयामनायासं दिव्यां शक्तिञ्च सर्व्वदा ।

अत्रोक्तान् यः सदा ह्येतान्नैष्ठिकामुषिकोचितान्॥
आचारानाचरेत् शान्तिं दीक्षितः सोऽधिगच्छति। इति।

तथा—विभीतकार्ककारञ्ज स्नुहीच्छायां न चाश्रयेत्।
स्तम्भदीपमनुष्याणामन्येषां प्राणिनां तथा॥
नखाग्रकेशनिष्ठ्यूत स्नानवस्त्रघटोदकम्।
एतत्स्पर्शं त्यजेद् दूरं खरश्वाजरजस्तथा॥ इति।

मन्त्रतन्त्रप्रकाशे सोमशम्भौ तु—

न निन्देत् कारणं देवं न शास्त्रं तेन निर्मितम्।
न गुरुं साधकञ्चैव लिङ्गच्छायां न लङ्घयेत्॥
नाद्यान्नङ्केश्च निर्माल्यं न दद्याच्छिवदीक्षिते॥ इति।

षड़न्वयमहारत्नेऽपि—

न लङ्घयेद् गुरोराज्ञामुत्तरं न वदेत्तथा।
रात्रौ दिवा च तस्याज्ञां दासवत् परिपालयेत्॥
असत्यमशुभं तद्वद्बहुवादं परित्यजेत्।
अप्रियञ्च तथालस्यं कामक्रोधौ विशेषतः॥
अप्रच्छन्नमुखो ब्रूयाद् गुरोरग्रे कदापि न।
अभिमानं न कुर्व्वीत धनजात्याश्रमादिभिः॥
गुरुद्रव्यं न भोक्तव्यं तेनाऽदत्तं कदाचन।
दत्तं प्रसादवद् ग्राह्यं लोभतो न कदाचन॥
अद्वैतं देवपूजाञ्च गुरोरग्रे परित्यजेत्।
पादुकायोगपट्टादि गुरुचिह्नानि साधनम्॥
न लङ्घयेत् स्पृशेन्नैव पादाभ्यां प्रणमेत् सदा।
पर्य्यङ्कशयनं तद्वत्तथा पादप्रसारणम्॥
अङ्गभङ्गञ्च लीलाञ्च न कुर्य्याद् गुरुसन्निधौ।
गमनागमने कुर्य्यात् प्रणम्य गुरु पादुकाम्॥
विचार्य्य कार्य्यं कुर्व्वीत गुरुकार्य्यं प्रसादवान्।
छायां न लङ्घयेत्तद्वन्न गच्छेत् पुरतो गुरोः॥
पश्चात्पादेन निर्गच्छेत् प्रणम्य च गुरोर्गृहात्।
गुरोरग्रे न कुर्व्वीत प्रभावं शिष्यसंग्रहम्॥
अहङ्कारं न कुर्व्वीत नोल्वणं धारयेद्वपुः।

ततः प्रभृति कुर्व्वीत गुरोः प्रियमनन्यधीः ।
ऋत्विग्भ्यो दक्षिणां दत्त्वा समग्रां प्रीतमानसः ॥ ११४

ब्राह्मणांस्तर्पयेत् पश्चाद्भक्ष्यभोज्यैः सदक्षिणैः ।
एषा क्रियावती दीक्षा प्रोक्ता सर्व्वसमृद्धिदा ॥ ११५

अथ वर्णात्मिकां वक्ष्ये दीक्षामागमवेदिताम् ।
पुंप्रकृत्यात्मका वर्णाः शरीरमपि तादृशम् ॥ ११६

प्रगुरोः सन्निधौ नैव स्वगुरुं प्रणमेद्बुधः ॥
नमस्काराय चोद्युक्तं गुरुर्दृष्ट्वा निवारयेत् । इति ।

तथा—न नियोगं गुरोर्दद्याद् युष्मदा नैव भाषयेत् । इति ॥११२॥११३ ॥

गुरोः प्रियं कुर्व्वीतेत्यनेन गुरुसन्तोषस्य मुख्यत्वमुक्तं भवति । तदुक्तं दशपटल्याम्—शिष्येणापि प्रकर्त्तव्या शुश्रूषा च गुरोः सदा ।
शुश्रूषया विना विद्या न भवेत् सा फलप्रदा ॥
गुरौ तुष्टे शिवस्तुष्टः शिवे तुष्टे जगत्त्रयम् ।
गुरौ रुष्टे महेशानि नाहं त्राता त्वया सह ।
तस्मात् सर्व्वप्रयत्नेन गुरोः कोपं न कारयेत् ॥ इति ।

ऋत्विग्भ्य इति ब्रह्मादिभ्यः । तत्र प्रणीतामार्जनं कृत्वा ब्रह्मणे दक्षिणां दत्त्वा ब्रह्माणमुद्वास्य हुतचरुशेषं प्राशयेदिति ज्ञेयम् । तदुक्तं संहितायाम्—
प्रणीतामार्जनं कृत्वा दद्याच्च ब्रह्मदक्षिणाम् ।
स्वस्ववित्तानुसारेण लोभमोहविवर्जितः ॥
ततो ब्रह्माणमुद्वास्य ब्राह्मणान् भोजयेदथ ।
आशीर्वचोभि र्विदुषां मेधमानः सुखी भवेत् ॥
हुतशेषं ततः प्राश्य कुक्कुटाण्डप्रमाणकम् ।
मन्त्रितं मन्त्रगायत्र्या । इति ।

अन्यच्च "त्र्यायुषं यमदग्ने" इति मन्त्रेण भस्म धारयेत् ।
पूर्णपात्रं पूर्य्यतोयैः समस्तकृत्वोऽभिमन्त्रितैः ।
आत्मानमभिषिञ्चेत्तैः सदूर्व्वैस्तुलसीदलैः ॥ इति । ११४॥११५ ॥

क्रमप्राप्तां वर्णात्मिकां दीक्षामाह अथेति । तत्तदिति । देशिकोत्तमः तच्चैतन्यं शिष्यचैतन्यं परमात्मनि संयोज्य देवताभावात् स्वस्य देवतात्वात् अतएव आत्मा-सितत्वात् । स्वस्याज्ञया विधिना प्रतिलोमेन वर्णस्थानोभयप्रातिलोम्येन तत्तत्-

यतस्तस्मात्तनौ न्यस्येद् वर्णान् शिष्यस्य देशिकः ।
तत्तत्स्थानयुतान् वर्णान् प्रतिलोमेन संहरेत् ॥ ११७
स्वाज्ञया देवताभावाद् विधिना देशिकोत्तमः ।
तदा विलीनतत्त्वोऽयं शिष्यो दिव्यतनुर्भवेत् ॥ ११८
परमात्मनि संयोज्य तच्चैतन्यं गुरूत्तमः ।
तस्मादुत्पाद्य तान् वर्णान् न्यस्येच्छिष्यतनौ पुनः ॥ ११९
सृष्टिक्रमेण विधिवच्चैतन्यञ्च नियोजयेत् ।
जायते देवताभावः परानन्दमयः शिशोः ॥ १२०

स्थानयुतान् वर्णान् संहरेत् । अग्रिमं स्थानं वर्णं पूर्व्वस्मिन् स्थाने वर्णे च संहरेदित्यर्थः । गुरूत्तम इत्युत्तरेण सम्बध्यते । तस्मात् परमात्मनः । विधिवदिति पूर्व्वस्मात् स्थानाद् वर्णादग्रिमं स्थानं वर्णञ्च । चैतन्यञ्चेति चकारेण शिष्यतनावित्यनुषज्यते । तदुक्तमाचार्य्यैः—

अग्नीन्दुयोगविकृता लिपयो हि सृष्टास्ताभिर्विलोमपठिताभिरिदं शरीरम् ।
भूतात्मकं त्वगसृगादियुतं समस्तं संव्यापयेन्निशितधीर्विधिना यथावत् ॥

अन्त्यावुभस्त्वमून् वादिषु मलिपिषु तांस्तांश्चतुर्वर्गवर्णै-
ष्वेतानस्यप्यदस्त्वहृति तदपि परेषु स्वरेषु क्रमेण ।
संहृत्य स्थानयुक्तं च्यपितसकलदेहो ललाटस्थितान्तः
प्राप्तिव्याप्तद्विसप्ताधिकभुवनतलो यातु मज्ञावमेव ॥
मूलाधारात् स्फुरिततड़िदाभाप्रभा सूक्ष्मरूपो-
ऽप्युत्क्रान्त्यामस्तकमणुतरा तेजसां मूलभूता ।
सौषुम्नाध्वा चरणनिपुणा सा सविन्नानुविद्धा
ध्याता सद्योऽमृतमथ रवेः स्रावयेत् सार्द्धसोमात् ॥
शिरसि निपतिता या बिन्दुधारा सुधाया
भवति लिपिमयी सा ताभिरङ्गं सुखाद्यम् ।
विरचयतु समस्तं पातितात्मस्य तेज-
स्यनल इव घृतस्योद्दीपयेदात्मतेजः ॥

संहृत्य चोत्पाद्य शरीरमेवं तेजोमयं व्याप्तसमस्तलोकम् ।
सञ्चिन्त्य मन्त्रात्मकमात्मरूपं तच्छिष्यमात्मन्यपि सन्दधीत ॥ इति ॥११६-१२०॥

एषा वर्णमयी दीक्षा प्रोक्ता सम्वित्प्रदायिनी ।
ततः कलावती दीक्षा यथावदभिधीयते ॥ १२१
निवृत्त्याद्याः कलाः पञ्च भूतानां शक्तयो यतः ।
तस्माद् भूतमये देहे ध्यात्वा ता वेधयेच्छिशोः ॥ १२२
निवृत्तिर्जानुपर्य्यन्तं तलादारभ्य संस्थिता ।
जानुनोर्नाभिपर्य्यन्तं प्रतिष्ठा व्याप्य तिष्ठति ॥ १२३
नाभेः कण्ठावधि व्याप्ता विद्या शान्तिस्ततः परम् ।
कण्ठाल्ललाटपर्य्यन्तं व्याप्ता तस्माच्छिखावधि ॥ १२४
शान्त्यतीता कला ज्ञेया कलाव्याप्तिरितीरिता ।
संहारक्रमयोगेन स्थानात् स्थानान्तरे गुरुः ॥ १२५
संयोज्य वेधयेद् विद्वानाज्ञया ताः शिवा[वो]वधि ।
इयं प्रोक्ता कला दीक्षा दिव्यभावप्रदायिनी ॥ १२६
ततो वेधमयीं वक्ष्ये दीक्षां संसारमोचनीम् ।
ध्यायेच्छिष्यतनोर्मध्ये मूलाधारे चतुर्दले ॥ १२७
त्रिकोणमध्ये विमले तेजस्त्रयविजृम्भिते ।
वलयत्रयसंयुक्तां तड़ित्कोटिसमप्रभाम् ॥ १२८

कलावतीदीक्षाक्रममाह तत इति । ध्यात्वेत्यत्र यद् ध्यानमुद्दिष्टं तन्निवृत्तिरित्यादि ईरितेत्यन्तेनोक्तम् । तलात् पादतलात् । जानुनोर्नाभेः कण्ठात् तस्माल्ललाटादारभ्येति सम्बन्धः । स्थानात् स्थानान्तरे ताः संयोज्य संहारक्रमयोगेन शिशोर्देहे वेधयेदिति सम्बन्धः । संहारः पूर्व्ववदेव स्वस्वकारणे । शिवावधि शिवपर्य्यन्तम् । शिवात् सृष्टिमार्गेणोत्पत्तिरनुक्तापि पूर्व्ववदेवाऽनुसन्धेया । १२१—१२६ ॥

वेधमयीं दीक्षामाह तत इति । तनोर्मध्ये मूलाधारे त्रिकोणमध्ये व्यधिकरणः सप्तम्यः । शिष्यतनोर्मध्ये चतुर्दले मूलाधारे त्रिकोणमध्ये एवम्भूतां शक्तिं ध्यायेदिति सम्बन्धः । कीदृशीं शक्तिं वलयत्रयसंयुक्ताम् । अत्र यद्यपि अनेकपरिमितानि वलयानि तथापि वेदत्रयादेः प्रधानतमस्त्रष्टेर्वलयत्रयादुत्पत्तेस्तदुक्तिः । पुनः कीदृशीम् । षट्चक्रं भित्त्वा मध्यमार्गेण सुषुम्नामार्गेण परशिवावधि

शिवशक्तिमयीं देवीं चैतन्यमात्रविग्रहाम्।
सूक्ष्मां सूक्ष्मतरां शक्तिं भित्त्वा षट्चक्रमञ्जसा ॥ १२९
गच्छन्तीं मध्यमार्गेण दिव्यां परशिवावधि।
वादिसान्तदलस्थार्णान् संहरेत् कमलासने ॥ १३०
तं षट्पत्रमये पद्मे वादिलान्ताक्षरान्विते।
स्वाधिष्ठाने समायोज्य वेधयेदाज्ञया गुरुः ॥ १३१
तान् वर्णान् संहरेद् विष्णौ तं पुनर्नाभिपङ्कजे।
दशपत्रे डादिफान्तवर्णाढ्ये योजयेद् गुरुः ॥ १३२
तान् वर्णान् संहरेद् रुद्रे तं पुनर्हृदयाम्बुजे।
कादिठान्तार्कवर्णाढ्ये योजयित्वेश्वरे गुरुः ॥ १३३
तान् वर्णान् संहरेदस्मिंस्तं भूयः कण्ठपङ्कजे।
स्वराढ्यषोडशदले योजयित्वा स्वरान् पुनः ॥ १३४
सदाशिवे तान् संहृत्य तं पुनर्भ्रूसरोरुहे।
द्विपत्रे हक्षलसिते योजयित्वा ततो गुरुः ॥ १३५
तद्वर्णौ संहरेद् बिन्दौ कलायां तं नियोजयेत्।
तां नादेऽनन्तरं नादं नादान्ते योजयेद् गुरुः ॥ १३६

गच्छन्तीम्। षट्चक्राणि तु मूलाधारस्वाधिष्ठानमणिपूरकानाहतविशुद्धाज्ञाख्यानि। कमलासने ब्रह्मणि आधाराधिष्ठातृदेवतायाम्। एवं विष्णवादयः स्वाधिष्ठानाद्यधिष्ठातृदेवाः ज्ञेयाः। तं ब्रह्माणम्। तान् वर्णान् बादिलान्तान्। तं विष्णुं नाभिपङ्कजे मणिपूरके योजयेत्। ततो वेधयेदित्यनुषङ्गः। तान् वर्णान् डादिफान्तान्। तं रुद्रम्। अर्कपत्राढ्ये द्वादशपत्राढ्ये। हृदयाम्बुजे अनाहते योजयित्वा वेधयेदित्यनुषङ्गः। गुरुस्तान् वर्णान् कादिठान्तान् ईश्वरे संहरेदित्यन्वयः। भूयोऽनन्तरमीश्वरमस्मिन् कण्ठपङ्कजे विशुद्धौ योजयित्वा वेधयेदित्यनुषङ्गः। तान् स्वरान् सदाशिवे संहृत्येत्यन्वयः। तं सदाशिवं भ्रूसरोरुहे आज्ञायां योजयित्वा वेधयेदित्यनुषङ्गः। अग्रे नियोजयेदित्यादेर्वेधयेदित्यर्थः। तद्वर्णौ हक्षौ। बिन्दौ शिवे। बिन्दुः शिवात्मकः इत्युक्तेः। तं शिवम्। कलादीनि भ्रूमध्याद्-

तमुन्मन्यां समायोज्य विधु[षा]वक्त्रान्तरे च ताम् ।
तां पुनर्गुरुवक्त्रे तु योजयेद् देशिकोत्तमः ॥ १३७
सहैवमात्मना शक्तिं वेधयेत् परमेश्वरे ।
गुर्वाज्ञया छिन्नपाशस्तदा शिष्यः पतेद्भुवि ॥ १३८
सञ्जातदिव्यबोधोऽसौ सर्व्वं विन्दति तत्क्षणात् ।
साक्षात् शिवो भवत्येष नात्र कार्य्या विचारणा ॥ १३९
एषा वेधमयी दीक्षा सर्व्वसम्वित्प्रदायिनी ।
क्रमाच्चतुर्विधा दीक्षा तन्त्रेऽस्मिन् सम्यगीरिता ॥ १४०

पर्य्युपरि एतानि षट्चक्राणि । अत एव सहस्रारस्य द्वादशान्तता । एवं पूर्व्वोक्तक्रमेण आत्मना शिष्यजीवात्मना शक्तिं कुण्डलिनीं परमेश्वरे शिवे वेधयेदिति सम्बन्धः । शक्तिं विना वेधस्य कर्त्तुमशक्यत्वात् । अत एवादौ मूलाधारे शक्तिं ध्यायेदित्युक्तिः । ततश्च स्वाधिष्ठानादावपि शक्त्या एव वेध इति ज्ञेयम् । छिन्नपाशः पाशत्रयविमुक्त इत्यर्थः । यत् प्रयोगसारे—

पाशस्तु सत्सु चासत्सु कर्म्मस्वास्था समीरिता ।
त्रिविधः स तु विज्ञेयः पाशो बन्धैकसाधनः ॥
प्रथमः सहजः पाशस्तथा चागन्तुकः परः ।
प्रासंगि[संसर्गि]कस्तृतीयः स्यादिति पाशत्रयं स्मृतम् ॥ इति ।

यथा ग्रन्थकृत्परमगुरुसोमानन्दाचार्य्यकृतवेधेन ग्रन्थकृद्गुरव उत्पलाचार्य्या शिवात्मानो जाताः । ग्रन्थकृद्गुरुपङ्क्तिस्तु तृतीयश्लोकव्याख्याने दर्शिता । तथा चण्डेश्वराचार्य्यकृतवेधेन शिवस्वामी शिवात्मा जातः । तथा श्रीकण्ठाचार्य्या ऊचुः—

कालज्ञानं तथा कालवञ्चनान्यतनौ तथा ।
प्रवेशो वेध इत्यादि प्रसन्ने लभ्यते शिवे ॥ इति ।

उपसंहरति क्रमादिति । षडन्वयमहारत्ने इयमाणवी दीक्षा दशविधा इत्युक्तम् ।

तद्यथा—आणवी बहुधा दीक्षा शाक्तेयी शाम्भवी पुनः ।
एकधैवेति विद्वद्भिः पठ्यते शास्त्रकोविदैः ॥
आणवी बहुधेत्युक्ता तद्भेदमधुनोच्यते ।
स्मार्त्ती मानसिकी यौगी चाक्षुषी स्पार्शनी तथा ॥
वाचिकी मान्त्रिकी हौत्री शास्त्री चेत्याभिषेचिकी ।

विदीर्थ्य गुरुः स्मृत्वा शिष्यं पाशत्रयं क्रमात् ॥
विश्लिष्य लयभोगाङ्गविधानेन परे शिवे ।
सम्यग् योजनरूपेषा स्मार्त्ती दीक्षेति कथ्यते ॥
स्वसन्निधौ समासीनमालोक्य मनसा शुचिम् ।
मलत्रयादुपायैर्या मोचिका सा तु मानसी ॥
योगोक्तक्रमतो योगी शिष्यदेहं प्रविश्य तु ।
गृहीत्वा तस्य चात्मानं स्वात्मना योजनात्मिका ॥
योगदीक्षेति सा प्रोक्ता मलत्रयविनाशिनी ।
शिवोऽहमिति निश्चित्य वीक्षणं करुणार्द्रया ॥
दृशा सा चाक्षुषी दीक्षा सर्व्वपापप्रणाशिनी ।
स्वयं परशिवो भूत्वा निःसन्दिग्धमना गुरुः ॥
शिवहस्तेन शिष्यस्य समन्त्रं मूर्द्ध्नि संस्पृशेत् ।
स्पर्शदीक्षेति सा प्रोक्ता शिवाभिव्यक्तिकारिणी ॥

[**शिवहस्तलक्षणं सोमशम्भौ—**

गन्धैर्मण्डलकं स्वीये विदध्याद् दक्षिणे करे ।
विधिनाचाऽर्चयेद् देवमित्थं स्याच्छिवहस्तकम् ॥ इति ।]

गुरुवक्त्रं निजवक्त्रं विभाव्य गुरुरादरात् ।
गुरुवक्त्रप्रयोगेन दिव्यमन्त्रादिकं शिशौ ॥
मुद्रान्यासादिभिः सार्द्धं दद्यात् सेयं हि वाचिकी ।
दीक्षा परा तथा मन्त्रन्याससंयुक्तविग्रहः ॥
स्वयं मन्त्रतनुर्भूत्वा सक्रमं मन्त्रमादरात् ।
दद्याच्छिष्याय सा दीक्षा मान्त्री मलविघातिनी ॥
कुण्डे वा स्थण्डिले वापि निक्षिप्याऽग्निं विधानतः ।
लयभोगक्रमेणैव प्रत्यध्वानं यथाक्रमम् ॥
मन्त्रवर्णकलातत्त्वपदविष्टपमेव च ।
शुद्ध्यर्थं होमरूपेषा हौत्री दीक्षा समीरिता ॥
योग्यशिष्याय भक्ताय शुश्रूषार्चापराय च ।
सार्द्धं शास्त्रपदा त्वया शास्त्री दीक्षेति सोच्यते ॥
शिवञ्च शिवपत्नीञ्च कुम्भे सम्पूज्य सादरम् ।
शिवकुम्भाभिषेकात् सा दीक्षा स्यादाभिषेचिकी ॥ १२७—१४० ॥

अथाऽत्र होमद्रव्याणां प्रमाणमभिधीयते ।
कर्षमात्रं घृतं होमे शुक्तिमात्रं पयः स्मृतम् ॥ १४१
उक्तानि पञ्च गव्यानि तत्समानि मनीषिभिः ।
तत्समं मधु दुग्धान्नमक्षमात्रमुदाहृतम् ॥ १४२
दधि प्रसृतिमात्रं स्याल्लाजाः स्युर्मुष्टिसम्मिताः ।
पृथुकास्तत्प्रमाणाः स्युः शक्तवोऽपि तथोदिताः ॥ १४३
गुडं पलार्द्धमात्रं स्याच्छर्कराऽपि तथा मता ।
ग्रासार्द्धं चरुमानं स्यादिक्षुः पर्व्वावधिर्मतः ॥ १४४
एकैकं पत्रपुष्पाणि तथाऽपूपानि कल्पयेत् ।
कदलीफलनारङ्गफलान्येकैकशो विदुः ॥ १४५
मातुलङ्गं चतुःखण्डं पनसं दशधा कृतम् ।
अष्टधा नारिकेलानि खण्डितानि विदुर्बुधाः ॥ १४६

कर्षमात्रमिति । कर्षलक्षणं प्रागुक्तम् । तैलस्याप्येतदेव प्रमाणमिति ज्ञेयम् । शुक्तिमात्रमिति । कर्षद्वयं शुक्तिः । अक्षमात्रं कर्षमात्रम् । प्रसृतिमात्रं पलद्वयमात्रम् । मुष्टिसम्मिताः पलसम्मिताः । पृथुकाश्चिपिटकाः । पलार्द्धमानं कर्षद्वयम् । ग्रासार्द्धं अशीतिरक्तिकामानम् । तदुक्तम्—

गुञ्जाभिर्दशभिर्माषः शाणो माषचतुष्टयम् ।
द्वौ शाणौ धटकः कालो बदरं द्रङ्क्षणश्च यः ॥
तौ द्वौ पाणितलं कर्षः सुवर्णं कवलग्रहः ।
पिचुर्विडालपदकं तिन्दुकोऽक्षश्च तद्द्वयम् ॥
शुक्तिरष्टमिका ते द्वे पलं बिल्वं चतुर्थिका ।
मुष्टिराम्रं प्रकुञ्चोथ द्वे पले प्रसृतिस्तथा । इति ।

मातुलङ्गं बीजपूरम् । उर्व्वारुकं कर्कटी । समिध इति । तत्र विशेषः—

विशीर्णा द्विदला ह्रस्वा वक्रा स्थूला कृशा द्विधा ।
कृमिदष्टाश्च दीर्घाश्च निस्त्वचः परिवर्जिताः ॥
विशीर्णाऽऽयुःक्षयं कुर्य्याद् द्विदला व्याधिसम्भवम् ।
ह्रस्वायां मृत्युमाप्नोति वक्रा विघ्नकरी तथा ॥

त्रिधा कृतं फलं बिल्वं कपित्थं खण्डितं त्रिधा।
उर्व्वारुकफलं होमे चोदितं खण्डितं त्रिधा॥ १४७
फलान्यन्यानि खण्डानि समिधः स्युर्दशाङ्गुलाः।
दूर्व्वात्रयं समुद्दिष्टं गुड़ूची चतुरङ्गुला॥ १४८
व्रीहयो मुष्टिमात्राः स्युर्मुद्गमाषा यवा अपि।
तण्डुलाः स्युस्तदर्द्धांशाः कोद्रवा मुष्टिसम्मिताः॥ १४९
गोधूमरक्तकलमा विहिता मुष्टिमानतः।
तिलास्तुलुकमात्राः स्युः सर्षपास्तत्प्रमाणकाः॥ १५०
शुक्तिप्रमाणं लवणं मरीचान्येकविंशतिः।
पुरं वदरमानं स्याद्रामठं तत्समं स्मृतम्॥ १५१
चन्दनागुरुकर्पूर कस्तूरीकुङ्कुमानि च।
तिन्तिड़ीबीजमानानि समुद्दिष्टानि देशिकैः॥ १५२

स्थूलाभिर्हरते लक्ष्मीं कृशायां याजकक्षयः।
द्विधायां नेत्ररोगाः स्युः कीटदष्टाऽर्थनाशिनी॥
द्वेषं प्रकुर्व्वते दीर्घा प्राणघ्नी निस्त्वचः स्मृताः।
सक्षीरा नाधिकान्यूनाः समिधः सर्व्वकामदाः।
आर्द्रत्वचं समच्छेदां तर्जन्यङ्गुलिवर्त्तुलाम्॥
ईदृशीं होमयेत् प्राज्ञः प्राप्नोति विपुलां श्रियम्।
श्रौते स्मार्त्ते च तन्त्रोक्ते समिधः परिकीर्त्तिताः॥ इति।

विशेषान्तरं प्रयोगसारे—

श्लेष्मातकपिशाचतरू त्यक्त्वाऽन्येभ्यः समाहरेत् समिधः। इति।

मुष्टिमात्राः पलसम्मिताः। तदर्द्धांशाः कर्षद्वयमिताः। तुलुकमात्राः कर्षमात्राः। पाणितलशब्देन चुलुकग्रहणात्। शुक्तिः कर्षद्वयम्। पुरं गुग्गुलुः। वदरमानमशीतिगुञ्जामितम्। रामठं हिङ्गुः। शैवागमे तु—

खण्डत्रयन्तु मूलानां सूक्ष्माणि पञ्च होमयेत्।
कन्दानामष्टमं भागं लतानामङ्गुलद्वयम्॥ इति। १४१—१५२

वैश्वानरं स्थितं ध्यायेत् समिद्धोमेषु देशिकः ।
शयानमाज्यहोमेषु निषण्णं शेषवस्तुषु ॥ १५३

आस्यान्तर्जुहुयादग्नेर्विपश्चित् सर्व्वकर्म्मसु ।
सधूमोऽग्निः शिरो ज्ञेयं निर्धूमश्चक्षुरेव हि ॥ १५४

ज्वलत्कृशो भवेत् कर्णः काष्ठमग्नेर्नसस्तथा ।
प्रज्वलोऽग्निस्तथा जिह्वा एतदेवाऽग्निलक्षणम् ॥ १५५

कर्णहोमे भवेद् व्याधिर्नेत्रेऽन्धत्वमुदीरितम् ।
नासिकायां मनःपीड़ा मस्तके धनसंक्षयः ॥ १५६

स्वर्णसिन्दूरबालार्ककुङ्कुमक्षौद्रसन्निभः ।
सुवर्णरेतसो वर्णः शोभनः परिकीर्त्तितः ॥ १५७

स्थितमुत्थितम् । आस्यान्तरिति । आस्यादीनां लक्षणमुक्तमन्यत्र—

सधूमोऽग्निः शिरो ज्ञेयो निर्धूमश्चक्षुरेव च ।
ज्वलत्कृशो भवेत् कर्णः काष्ठमग्नेश्च नासिका ॥
अग्निर्लीलायते यत्र शुद्धस्फटिकसन्निभः ।
तन्मुखं तत्र विज्ञेयं चतुरङ्गुलमानतः ॥ इति ।

शुकप्रोक्ते वनदुर्गाकल्पे तु—

सर्व्वकार्य्यप्रसिद्ध्यर्थं जिह्वायां तत्र होमयेत् ।
चक्षुःकर्णादिकं ज्ञात्वा होमयेद् देशिकोत्तमः ॥
अग्निकर्णे हुतं यत्तु कुर्य्याच्चेद् व्याधितो भयम् ।
नासिकायां महद्दुःखं चक्षुषोर्नाशनं भवेत् ॥
केशे दारिद्र्यदं प्रोक्तं तस्माज्जिह्वासु होमयेत् ।
यत्र काष्ठं तत्र श्रोत्रे यत्र धूमस्तु नासिके ॥
यत्राऽल्पज्वलनं नेत्रे यत्र भस्म तु तच्छिरः ।
यत्रैव ज्वलितो वह्निस्तत्र जिह्वा प्रकीर्त्तिता ॥ इति ।

विपश्चिदित्यनेनैतदुक्तम् । शत्रुनाशकहोमे एतदङ्गेषु हवनात् तत्तदङ्गक्षयो भवति ।

यदाहुः—वह्नेः शिरसि नासायां श्रोत्रे चक्षुषि वा तथा ।
जुहुयाच्चेत् तदा क्षिप्रं तदङ्गानि विनाशयेत् ॥ इति । १५३—१५६

क्षौद्रं मधु । स्वर्णकुङ्कुमक्षौद्रसन्निभो वर्णः शोभन इति । आकृष्टाविति ज्ञेयम् ।

भेरीवारिदहस्तीन्द्रध्वनिर्वह्नेः शुभावहः ।
नागचम्पकपुन्नागपाटलायूथिकानिभः ॥ १५८
पद्मेन्दीवरकह्लारसर्पिर्गुग्गुलुसन्निभः ।
पावकस्य शुभो गन्ध इत्युक्तं तन्त्रवेदिभिः ॥ १५९
प्रदक्षिणास्त्यक्तकम्पाश्छत्राभाः शिखिनः शिखाः ।
शुभदा यजमानस्य राज्यस्यापि विशेषतः ॥ १६०
कुन्देन्दुधवलो धूमो वह्नेः प्रोक्तः शुभावहः ।
कृष्णः कृष्णगतेर्वर्णो यजमानं विनाशयेत् ॥ १६१

यदाहुः श्रीमतङ्गपारमेश्वरे—

दिव्यानामप्यदिव्यानामाकृष्टाविष्यते सदा ।
ध्मातचामीकरप्रख्यो हरितालनिभश्च यः ॥
हरिद्राकुनटीवर्णो रोचनाभश्च शस्यते ॥ इति ।

सिन्दूरबालार्क इति जयार्थ इति ज्ञेयम् ।

पद्मरागद्युतिः श्रेष्ठो लाक्षारससमोऽपि वा ।
बालार्कवर्णो हुतभुग् जयार्थं शस्यते बुधैः ॥

इति तत्रोक्तेः । अन्यकर्मणि तु तत्रैव—

इन्द्रगोपकसङ्काशः शोणिताभोऽथ पावकः ।
शक्रचापनिभः शस्तः कुङ्कुमाम्बुनिभस्तथा ॥
रक्तानां पुष्पजातीनां तुल्यो वर्णः प्रशस्यते ॥ इति ॥ १५७ ॥

भेरीत्याद्युपलक्षणम् ।

जीमूतवल्लकीशङ्खमृदङ्गध्वनितुल्यकः ।
शब्दोऽग्नेः सिद्धये होतुरतोऽन्योऽसिद्धिदः स्मृतः ॥ इति ।

नागेत्याद्युपलक्षकम् । "सुगन्धद्रव्यगन्धोऽग्निर्घृतगन्धश्च शोभनः" इत्युक्तेः ।

पद्मगन्ध आयुषे इन्दीवरादिगन्धः सौभाग्ये । तदुक्तम्—

नीलोत्पलसमो गन्धः सौभाग्ये शस्यतेऽञ्जसा ।
आयुषे पद्मगन्धः स्याद् बिल्वगन्धश्च सुव्रते ॥ इति ।

विशेषोऽपि—उग्रगन्धोऽभिचारेऽत्र प्रशस्तः सर्वदाऽनलः । इति ॥ १५८॥१५९ ॥

छत्राभा इत्युपलक्षणम् । "छत्राकारभुजः श्रेष्ठो ध्वजचामरसन्निभः" इत्युक्तेः ॥

श्वेतो राष्ट्रं निहन्त्याशु वायसस्वरसन्निभः ।
खरस्वरसमो वह्नेः ध्वनिः सर्व्वविनाशकृत् ॥ १६२
पूतिगन्धो हुतभुजो होतुर्दुःखप्रदो भवेत् ।
छिन्नावर्त्ता शिखा कुर्य्यान्मृत्युं धनपरिच्चयम् ॥ १६३
शुकपत्त्रनिभो धूमः पारावतसमप्रभः ।
हानिं तुरगजातीनां गवाञ्च कुरुतेऽचिरात् ॥ १६४

कृष्णो यजमानं श्वेतो राष्ट्रं निहन्तीति । यत्र कर्म्मणि रक्तपीतादिवर्णो विहितस्तत्रेति ज्ञेयम् । न तु सामान्यतः । यदाहुः—

ज्ञात्वा कर्म्मानुरूपां तां तस्य तस्याऽनुकूलताम् ।
कर्म्मणः सततं ग्राह्यस्त्याज्यो वा तद्विलोमतः ॥ इति ।

विशेषस्तत्रैव—मारणोच्चाटनोत्सादकर्म्मस्वस्मिन् सुशोभनः ।
कृष्णानां पुष्पजातीनां वर्णो वह्नेरिहेष्यते ॥
शङ्खस्फटिककुन्देन्दुवर्णेभ्योऽपि सितः शुभः ।
शान्तिके पौष्टिके वापि विहितः सर्व्वदाऽनलः ॥ इति ।

त्याज्यं कृष्णत्वमपि तेनैवोक्तम्—
षट्पदाञ्जननिस्त्रिंशतुल्यो वर्णो न सिद्धिदः । इति ।

अन्योऽपि विशेषः—
मार्जाराक्षिनिभोऽग्राह्यः शुकपिच्छाभ एव च ।
मयूरकण्ठसदृशश्चित्रपारावतप्रभः ॥ इति ॥ १६०॥१६१॥१६२ ॥

पूतिगन्धो दुर्गन्धः । मृत्युमित्यादि यथाक्रमम् । एवंविध इत्यनेनैतदुक्तं भवति ।

वृषकुञ्जरयानेन तुल्योऽग्निः पुष्टिदः सदा ।
विमानानां वितानानां प्रासादानाञ्च यो भवेत् ॥
आकारेणाऽथ हंसानां मयूराणाञ्च शस्यते ।
सिंहाकृतिः सदा वह्निः सद्यः सिद्धिकरः स्मृतः ॥
शेषाणां दंष्ट्रिणां रूपं न शस्तं होमकर्म्मणि ।
खरोष्ट्रमहिषादीनां रूपमत्र न सिद्धये ॥
स्निग्धः प्रदक्षिणावर्त्तः सुशब्दश्चापि यो भवेत् ।
वेद्यः सोऽर्थप्रसिद्ध्यर्थमन्यथा विघ्नकारकः ॥

एवंविधेषु दोषेषु प्रायश्चित्ताय देशिकः ।
मूलेनाज्येन जुहुयात् पञ्चविंशतिमाहुतीः ॥ १६५

इति श्रीशारदातिलके पञ्चमः पटलः ।

रूक्षश्चटचटाशब्द अपसव्यगतिः सदा ।
उल्लिखेद् वसुधां यश्च यश्चाधःशिख एव च ।
नेष्यतेऽसौ मुनिश्रेष्ठ शास्त्रेऽस्मिन् पारमेश्वरे ॥ इति ।

पञ्चविंशतिमिति । दोषद्वयदर्शने दोषत्रयदर्शने वा प्रतिनिमित्तं नैमित्तिकमावर्त्तते इति न्यायात् तावत्कृत्वः पञ्चविंशतिराहुतयो होतव्या इति । ॥ १६३॥१६४॥१६५ ॥

इति श्रीशारदातिलकटीकायां सत्सम्प्रदायकृतव्याख्यायां
पदार्थादर्शाभिख्यायां पञ्चमः पटलः ॥ ॐ ॥

षष्ठः पटलः ।

अथ वर्णतनुं वक्ष्ये विश्वबोधविधायिनीम् ।
यस्यामनुपलब्धायां सर्व्वमेतज्जगज्जडम् ॥ १
ऋषिर्ब्रह्मा समुद्दिष्टो गायत्री छन्द ईरितम् ।
सरस्वती समाख्याता देवता देशिकोत्तमैः ॥ २
अक्लीबह्रस्वदीर्घान्तर्गतैः षड्वर्गकैः क्रमात् ।
षडङ्गानि विधेयानि जातियुक्तानि देशिकैः ॥ ३

दीक्षाकथनानन्तरं मन्त्रा वक्तव्या अतस्तेषां प्रकृतिभूतां मातृकां वक्तुं प्रतिजानीते अथेति। वर्णतनुं मातृकाम्। विश्वेषां सर्व्वेषां बोधानां ज्ञानशक्तिप्रसरात्मकानां तदुत्पादकानां वैखरीमध्यमापश्यन्तीपरारूपाणां विधायिनी उन्मीलिनी शक्तिस्तामित्यर्थः ॥ १ ॥

समुद्दिष्ट इत्यनेन विधिपदयोगः। ईरितमित्यनेन देवीपदयोगः। समाख्यातेत्यनेन मातृकापदयोगः। पद्मपादाचार्य्यसम्मतमेतत्। देशिकोत्तमैरित्यनेन बीजशक्ती अपि वक्तव्ये इति सूचितम्। तत्र केचित् हलो बीजानि स्वराः शक्तयः। तदुक्तं दक्षिणामूर्त्तिसंहितायाम्—

हलो बीजानि शक्तयः स्वराश्च परमेश्वरि। इति।

एतएव बीजशक्ती प्रपञ्चयागव्यतिरिक्तभूतलिप्यन्तसर्व्वमातृकामन्त्राणामिति ज्ञेयम्। अन्यत्रान्ये बीजशक्ती उक्ते। यदाहुः—

बीजमस्य स्मृतं घोषः शक्तिर्जीवः प्रकीर्त्तितः। इति।

अन्यत्रान्ये। यदाहुः—

अकारं बिन्दुसहितं बीजमस्य प्रकीर्त्तितम्।
द्विबिन्दुसहितोऽकारः शक्तिरित्यभिधीयते॥ इति।

विनियोगस्तु मातृकामन्त्रजपकाले जपे विनियोग इति। अन्यत्र मन्त्राङ्गत्वेन न्यासेऽनुष्ठीयमानामुकमन्त्राङ्गत्वेन न्यासे विनियोग इति ज्ञेयम् ॥ २ ॥

अक्लीबेति। क्लीबा नपुंसकाः ऋ ॠ ऌ ॡ तद्रहिताः अक्लीबा ये ह्रस्वदीर्घाः अ इ उ ए ओ अं एते ह्रस्वाः परे षट् दीर्घाः तदन्तर्गतैस्तन्मध्यस्थैः। षट् च ते वर्गाश्च

पञ्चाशल्लिपिभिर्विभक्तमुखदोःपन्मध्यवक्षःस्थलां
भास्वन्मौलिनिबद्धचन्द्रशकलामापीनतुङ्गस्तनीम् ।
मुद्रामक्षगुणं सुधाढ्यकलशं विद्याञ्च हस्ताम्बुजै-
र्बिभ्राणां विशदप्रभां त्रिनयनां वाग्देवतामाश्रये ॥ ४

काश्च ते । बहुवचनमाद्यर्थम् । कादयः क च ट त प यास्तैः । क्रमाद्धृदयादि । जाति-युक्तानि हृदयाय नम इत्यादियुक्तानि । प्रयोगस्तु अं कं खं गं घं ङं आं हृदयाय नमः इत्यादि । देशिकैरित्यनेनैतदुक्तं भवति । अत्र नपुंसकचतुष्टयेन करशुद्धिं विधाय "अङ्गुष्ठादिष्वङ्गुलीषु न्यसेदङ्गैः सजातिभिः" इत्युक्तेः अं कं खं गं घं ङं आं अङ्गुष्ठाभ्यां नमः इत्यादि करतलकरपृष्ठान्तं षडङ्गानि विन्यस्य ततो दक्षवाम-करतलयोः तत्पृष्ठयोः करयोः दक्षिणकनिष्ठादिवामाङ्गुष्ठान्तमङ्गुलीषु षोडश स्वरान् विन्यस्य वामतर्जनीमारभ्य दक्षिणतर्जन्यन्तमेकैकस्यां पर्व्वस्वग्रे चतुरश्चतुरो वर्णान् इति क्रमेण कादिसान्तान् विन्यस्य अङ्गुष्ठयोः हलौ सर्व्वाङ्गेषु क्षकारं न्यसेदिति करस्य मातृकान्यासो ज्ञेयः । एवं सर्व्वत्र बोद्धव्यम् ।

यत् प्रयोगसारे—तलतत्पृष्ठतद्व्याप्तग्रा षडादौ विन्यसेत्ततः ।
कनिष्ठाङ्गुलिमारभ्य दक्षिणास्वङ्गुलीषु च ॥
वामाङ्गुष्ठान्तकं न्यस्य ततश्च व्यञ्जनान्यपि ।
वामतर्जनीमारभ्य चतुष्टयचतुष्टयम् ॥
यथाङ्गुलिक्रमेणैव यावद्दक्षिणतर्जनीम् ।
न्यसेदङ्गुष्ठयोः शेषे करन्यासः समीरितः ॥ इति ॥ ३ ॥

पञ्चाशदिति । विभक्तत्वं वक्ष्यमाणन्यासस्थानकथनेनैव स्फुटीभविष्यति । मुद्रा ज्ञानमुद्रा अङ्गुष्ठतर्जनीयोगरूपा पार्श्वाभिमुखी । यदाहुः—

श्लिष्टाग्रेऽङ्गुष्ठतर्जन्यौ प्रसार्य्याऽन्याः प्रयोजयेत् ।
पार्श्वस्याभिमुखी सेयं ज्ञानमुद्रा प्रकीर्त्तिता ॥ इति ।

विद्यां पुस्तकं तन्मुद्रेत्यर्थः ।

वाममुष्टिः स्वाभिमुखी बद्धा पुस्तकमुद्रिका । इति ।

विशदप्रभां शुभ्रवर्णाम् । इदं वस्त्राङ्गरागमाल्यानामुपलक्षकम् । एवमग्रेऽपि सर्व्वत्र वर्णवाचकेषु द्रष्टव्यम् । ऊर्द्ध्वादि आद्ये दक्षिणे परे वामे इत्यायुधध्यानम् । अत्र ध्यानानन्तरमायुधमुद्राः प्रदर्शयेत् । एवमग्रेऽपि सरस्वतीमन्त्रान्तं ज्ञेयम् । प्रत्यक्षरध्यानं तन्त्रान्तरोक्तं यथा—

चामीकरनिभः शूलगदाराजङ्कुजाष्टकः ।
चतुरास्योऽतिकायः स्यादकारः कूर्म्मवाहनः ॥
पाशाङ्कुशकरा श्वेता पद्मसंस्थेभवाहना ।
षष्ठ्यूर्द्ध्वयोजनमिता स्यादा मौक्तिकभूषणा ॥
पीतं कराब्जकुलिशपरशुं वैरिनाशनम् ।
देशकयोजनमानं स्यादिकारं कच्छपस्थितम् ॥
दशयोजनदीर्घाङ्गिनाहाऽसौ हंसवाहना ।
ईः स्यात् पुष्टिप्रदा श्वेता मौक्तिकाढ्या सितानना ॥
गदाङ्कुशकरं काकवाहनं कृष्णभूषणम् ।
योजनद्विसहस्राणां मानमुद्वयमच्चरम् ॥
पाशशक्तिभुजं रक्तं वह्निबिम्बस्थितोष्ट्रगम् ।
उक्तप्रमाणं कालघ्नमृक्त्ववर्णद्वयं भवेत् ॥
चतुरस्राब्जहंसस्थं पुष्परागसमप्रभम् ।
पाशवज्रकरं रौद्रं लृयुग्मं स्यान्निरोधनम् ॥
गदाफलारिपद्माढ्यकरं हारविभूषणम् ।
चक्रवाकस्थितं श्याममेकारं तु महद्भवेत् ॥
नवकुन्दनिभा शूलवज्रबाहा द्विपस्थिता ।
कोटियोजनमाना स्यादैमूर्त्तिः कविताकरी ॥
चिन्मयं सर्व्वगं शान्तं द्विसहस्रकरोज्ज्वलम् ।
पीतं गोवृषसंस्थं स्यादोरूपं श्रीकरात्मकम् ॥
तप्तहेमनिभा पाशचक्रबाहुर्विभूतिदा ।
योजनानां सहस्रेण स्यादौवर्णामितौजसा ॥
नवकुङ्कुमसंच्छायः पद्मस्थो रक्तभूषणः ।
चतुर्भुजः स्यादंवर्णः श्रीकरो रिपुनाशकः ॥
वज्रशूलकरं चुर्द्रं[युद्ध]फलदं खरवाहनम् ।
सहस्रयोजनमितं स्वरान्तं द्विभुजं स्मरेत् ॥
भूबिम्बगजसंस्थः स्यान्नवकुङ्कुमसन्निभः ।
शूलवज्रकरः कार्य्यः सहस्रद्वययोजनः ॥
पाशतोमरहस्तः खो मेषसंस्थो निरोधनः ।
योजनानां सहस्रेण मितः कृष्णो विभीषणः ॥

पाशाङ्कुशकरः पद्मे फणिसंस्थोऽरुणप्रभः ।
गकारः सर्पभूषः स्याच्छतयोजनसंस्थितः ॥
उष्ट्रोलूखलसंस्थः स्याद् गदावज्रकरोऽमितः ।
योजनानां सहस्रेण द्विमुखो घः सितेतरः ॥
कोटियोजनदीर्घाहिनाहं कृष्णं ज्वलत्प्रभम् ।
द्विभुजं काकवाहं स्यात् ङार्णं क्षुद्रफलप्रदम् ॥
युगाग्रपद्मसंस्थः स्याच्चतुर्बाहुः सितप्रभः ।
चः कपर्द्दी सुगन्धाढ्यः कोटियोजनसंस्थितः ॥
सितस्त्वावस्थितः पद्मे चतुर्बाहुश्छवर्णकः ।
जझौ च कोटिमानौ स्तश्चतुर्बाहू सितप्रभौ ॥
योजनानां सहस्रैः स्यात् सम्मितं काकवाहनम् ।
विद्वेषकरणं ञार्णं कृष्णवर्णं भुजद्वयम् ॥
क्रौञ्चस्थो द्विभुजष्टः स्यान्नागनद्धो महाध्वनिः ।
धरापद्मगजेन्द्रस्थष्ठवर्णो द्विकरोज्ज्वलः ॥
लक्षयोजनमानः स्याद् गरनाशकरो विभुः ।
डवर्णोऽप्यष्टबाहुः स्याच्चतुर्वक्त्रः स्वलङ्कृतः ॥
योजनानां सहस्रेण मितः कुवलये स्थितः ।
अग्निबिम्बाजगो ढार्णो दशबाहुर्ज्वलत्प्रभः ॥
सहस्रमानं व्याघ्रस्थं योजनानां हि णं भवेत् ।
षष्टिहायनसंस्थः स्याच्चतुर्बाहुः स्वलङ्कृतः ॥
सहस्रमानो गन्धाढ्यः कुङ्कुमाभश्च ताच्चरः ।
कोटियोजनमानः स्यादष्टबाहुश्चतुर्मुखः ॥
पीतवर्णो वृषारूढस्थवर्णोऽपि भयङ्करः ।
द्विमुखं षड्भुजं कोटिमानं दं महिषस्थितम् ॥
सिंहवाहश्चतुर्बाहुर्धश्चतुर्लक्षसम्मितः ।
द्विभुजं काकवाहं नं तत्सहस्रैर्मितं भवेत् ॥
विंशभुजो दशास्यः पः कोटिमानो वकस्थितः ।
दशकोटिमितः फार्णो योजनानां भुजद्वयः ॥
कण्ठीरवसिताम्भोजे निषण्णश्चञ्चलः सितः ।
षड़ास्यो द्विभुजो बः स्याद्दशकोटिमितोऽरुणः ॥

ललाटमुखवृत्ताक्षिश्रुतिघ्राणेषु गण्डयोः ।
ओष्ठदन्तोत्तमाङ्गास्यदोःपत्सन्ध्यग्रकेषु च ॥ ५
पार्श्वयोः पृष्ठतो नाभौ जठरे हृदयेऽसके ।
ककुद्यंसे च हृत्पूर्वं पाणिपादयुगे तथा ॥ ६
जठराननयोर्न्यस्येन्मातृकार्णान् यथाक्रमात् ।
त्वगसृङ्मांसमेदोऽस्थिमज्जाशुक्रात्मकान् विदुः ॥ ७

नीलोत्पललसद्धंसवाहनः पुष्टिदायकः ।
त्रिहस्तं त्रिमुखं व्याघ्रवाहनं भीषणाकृतिम् ॥
दशलक्षमितं भार्णं धूम्राभं स्यान्महाबलम् ।
चतुर्भुजो मकारः स्यात् सविषोरगसन्निभः ॥
मण्डितो मुण्डमालाभिः शशिखण्डविराजितः ।
व्याघ्रश्चतुर्मुखो[भुजो] धूम्रो यार्णः स्यान्मृगसंस्थितः ॥
त्रिकोणाम्बुजमेषस्थो रार्णो बाहुचतुष्टयः ।
चतुरस्राभदन्तीन्द्र पृष्ठेनोपरि राजिता ॥
चतुर्भुजा लकारस्य मूर्त्तिः स्याद् घुसृणप्रभा ।
अब्धिस्थपद्मनक्रस्थो द्विभुजो वः सितः स्मृतः ॥
करद्वयाब्जगा हेमवर्णा शार्णाकृतिस्तथा ।
सहस्रमानः कृष्णाभो द्विभुजः कार्म्मणोऽथ षः ॥
कोटिमानः सितः सः स्याद्धंसगो[द्वयाङ्गो] द्विभुजान्वितः ।
हार्णः श्वेतस्त्रिबाहुः स्याद् व्याघ्रशीतांशुशेखरः ॥
पाशाभयकरा लार्णमूर्त्तिः श्वेता गजस्थिता ।
भूबिम्बशैलसंस्थः क्षो दशबाहुर्मणिप्रभः ॥
मूर्त्तिभेदा यथाऽर्णानां मयाऽत्र प्रतिपादिताः ॥ इति ॥ ४ ॥

अथ न्यासस्थानान्याह । ललाटे केशान्ते । केशान्ताननवृत्त इत्युक्तेः । मुखवृत्तेत्येकं स्थानम् । दक्षिणावर्त्तेन अक्ष्यादि गण्डान्तं दक्षादि । ओष्ठदन्तयो-रूर्ध्वादि । आस्ये तदन्तः जिह्वायामित्यर्थः । दोःपदोर्दक्षादि । दोःपत्सन्ध्य-ग्राणि च पञ्च शेषयोरङ्गुलिसन्धित्वात् । पार्श्वयोर्दक्षादि । अंसक इति दक्षांसे । ककुदि ग्रीवायाम् । अंस इति वामे । हृत्पूर्वं पाणिपादयुग इति स्थानचतुष्टयम् । जठराननयोरित्यत्रापि हृत्पूर्वमिति सम्बध्यते । तदुक्तं

वा[या]दिहा[सा]न्तान् न्यसेदात्मपरमज्ञानपूर्व्वकान्।
दीक्षितः प्रोक्तमार्गेण न्यसेल्लक्षं समाहितः॥ ८
जपेत् तत्संख्यया विद्वानयुतं मधुराप्लुतैः।
विदधीत तिलैर्होमं मातृकामन्वहं जपेत्॥ ९

मन्त्रमुक्तावल्याम्—हृदंसककुदंसेषु हृदादि करयोर्युगे।
त्वगसृङ्मांसमेदोऽस्थिमज्जाभिर्यादिषान्तगान्॥
हृदादिपादयुग्मे च तदाद्युदरके तथा।
तदादि मूर्द्धनि प्राज्ञो न्यसेत् सादीन् कषान्तगान्॥ इति।

केचनोत्तरांसशब्देन कक्षाद्वयं व्याचक्षते। तेषां मते अंसद्वये वर्णद्वयं ककुद्येकं कक्षाद्वये वर्णद्वयं पार्श्वयोर्युगे एकं पादयोर्युगे एकमिति न्यासः। अयं साम्प्रदायिकः। तदुक्तं दक्षिणामूर्त्तिसंहितायाम्—
हृद्दोर्मूलेषु संन्यस्य तथापरगले न्यसेत्।
कक्षाद्वये हृदारभ्य पाणिपादयुगे तथा।
जठराननयोर्व्यापरा न्यसेदित्यर्णरूपिणीम्॥ इति।

आचार्या अपि—हृद्दोर्मूलापरगलकक्षेषु। इति।

तत्र प्रयोगः—अं नमः केशान्ते। आं नमः मुखवृत्ते इत्यादि।

उक्तञ्च—ओमाद्यन्तो नमोऽन्तो वा सबिन्दुर्बिन्दुवर्जितः।
पञ्चाशदक्षरन्यासः क्रमेणैव विधीयते॥ इति।

यथाक्रमादित्यनेनैतदुक्तं भवति। सौस्थानिकौत्थानिकस्नानभोजनानुष्ठानेषु लिपिर्विन्यस्तव्येति। तत्र सौस्थानिके उक्तप्रकारेण एकपञ्चाशद्वर्णन्यासः। औत्थानिके सप्तवर्गाणां मुखबाहुपादद्वयनाभिहृत्सु व्यापकत्वेन न्यासः। तद्देवताः ब्रह्मसरस्वतीविष्णुश्रीरुद्रोमासर्व्वेश्वराः। स्नाने अकथादिवर्गत्रयस्य मुखमध्यपादेषु न्यासः। एतद्देवताः चन्द्रसूर्य्याग्नयः। भोजनकाले समस्तस्य मस्तकादिपादान्तो न्यासः। देशकालाद्यपेक्षया सर्व्वत्र प्रयोक्तव्या इति। [त्वगसृगित्यादि पूर्व्वकानित्यन्तं श्लोकार्द्धद्वयं केषुचित् पुस्तकेषु नास्ति]। तत्संख्यया लक्षसंख्यया। एकवारं न्यासं कृत्वा एकवारं जपेदित्यर्थः। समाहित इत्यनेन कृतपुरश्चरणधर्म्म इत्युक्तम्।

तदुक्तम्—पञ्चाशद्वर्णमूर्त्तिं तामेवं ध्यात्वा सुविग्रहे।
स्थानेषु क्रमतो न्यस्य पूर्व्वोक्तेषु जपेल्लिपिम्॥
पञ्चाशत्संख्यया नित्यं यावल्लक्षं प्रपूर्य्यते। इति।

व्योमेन्द्वोरसनार्णकर्णिकमचां द्वन्द्वैः स्फुरत्केशरं
पत्रान्तर्गतपञ्चवर्गयशलार्णादित्रिवर्गं क्रमात् ।
आशास्वस्रिषु लान्तलाङ्गलियुजा क्षौणीपुरेणावृतं
पद्मं कल्पितमत्र पूजयतु तां वर्णात्मिकां देवताम् ॥ १०

आधारशक्तिमारभ्य पीठशक्त्यन्तमर्चयेत् ।
मेधा प्रज्ञा प्रभा विद्या धीर्धृतिस्मृतिबुद्धयः ॥ ११
विद्येश्वरीति सम्प्रोक्ता भारत्या नव शक्तयः ।
वर्णाब्जेनासनं दद्यान्मूर्त्तिं मूलेन कल्पयेत् ॥ १२

मधुरात्रैरिति पयोघृतमधुयुतैः । तदुक्तं प्रयोगसारे—

पयोमधुघृतञ्चेति समं त्रिमधुरं स्मृतम् । इति ॥ ५॥६॥७॥८॥९ ॥

व्योमेति । व्योम हः इन्दुः सः औ स्वरूपं रसनार्णो विसर्गः । "व्योमाविः स चतुर्दशस्वरविसर्गान्तस्फुरत्कर्णिकम्" इत्युक्तेः । अचां स्वराणाम् । अत्र केशरेषु स्वरलिखनं पत्रेषु वर्गलिखनञ्च । अग्रपत्रादिकर्णिकाभिमुखत्वेन चेति ज्ञेयम् । आशासु दिक्षु । अस्रिषु कोणेषु । लान्तो वः । लाङ्गली ठः । अनयोः रेखासंलग्नतया लिखनं ज्ञेयम् । तदुक्तं दक्षिणामूर्त्तिसंहितायाम्—

चतुरस्रं ततः कुर्य्यात् सिद्धिदं दिक्षु संलिखेत् ।
ठकाराणां चतुष्कञ्च रेखान्तं बाह्यतस्ततः ॥
वारुणञ्च समालिख्य देवीमावाहयेत् सुधीः । इति ।

अत्र पूजायन्त्रेऽपि अक्षरादिलिखनस्योक्तेः । केषाञ्चिन्मते इदमेव धारणयन्त्रमिति सूचयति । पद्ममिति श्वेतम् । स्मरेत् पद्मं तथा श्वेतम् इत्युक्तेः । तेन श्वेतकमलासना ध्येयेत्यर्थः । १० ॥

अर्चयेदिति चतुर्थोक्तप्रकारेण । तत्र मण्डूककालाग्निरुद्रकूर्म्मशिलाः सम्पूज्य पश्चादाधारशक्त्यादिपूजने पृथिव्यनन्तरं विद्याब्धिं सम्पूज्य अन्ते मायाकलाविद्यापरतत्त्वानि सम्पूज्य पीठशक्तिपूजनमिति सर्व्वत्र क्रमोऽनुसन्धेयः ।
पीठशक्तीराह मेधेति । आसां ध्यानं यथा—

कृताञ्जलिद्वयकरास्तत्तदूर्द्ध्वकरद्वये ।
दधत्यः पुस्तकं कुम्भं श्वेताः सुन्दरमूर्त्तयः ॥ इति ।

पीठमन्त्रमुद्धरति वर्णाब्जेनेति । ह्सौः मातृकायोगपीठाय नमः इति मन्त्रेणासन-

आवाह्य पूजयेत् तस्यां देवीमावरणैः सह।
अङ्गैरावरणं पूर्व्वं द्वितीयं युग्मशः स्वरैः॥ १३
अष्टवर्गैस्तृतीयं स्यात् तच्छक्तिभिरनन्तरम्।
पञ्चमं मातृभिः प्रोक्तं षष्ठं लोकेश्वरैः स्मृतम्॥ १४
लोकपालायुधैः प्रोक्तं वज्राद्यैः सप्तमं ततः।
विधिनाऽनेन वर्णेशीमुपचारैः प्रपूजयेत्॥ १५
व्यापिनी पालिनी पश्चात् पावनी क्लेदिनी तथा।
धारिणी मालिनी भूयो हंसिनी शान्तिनी स्मृता॥ १६
शुभ्राः पत्रेषु सम्पूज्या धृताक्षगुणपुस्तकाः।
ब्राह्मी माहेश्वरी भूयः कौमारी वैष्णवी मता॥ १७
वाराह्यनन्तरेन्द्राणी चामुण्डा सप्तमी मता।
अष्टमी स्यान्महालक्ष्मीः प्रोक्ताः स्युर्विश्वमातरः॥ १८

पूजा। अयं पीठमन्त्रः सर्व्वमातृकामन्त्रसाधारण इति ज्ञेयम्। अन्ये त्वन्यथा व्याचक्षते। वर्णाब्जेन वर्णाब्जकर्णिकाबीजादिना आसनमन्त्रेणेति। तत्र प्रयोगः। ह्सौः सर्व्वशक्तिकमलासनाय नमः। एवमग्रे सरस्वतीमन्त्रेऽपि। पद्मपादाचार्य्यैस्तु ॐ ह्रीं वर्णाब्जाय सरस्वत्यासनाय नमः इति पीठमन्त्रः सूचितः इत्युक्तम्॥११॥१२॥

आवाह्येति। चतुर्थोक्तप्रकारेण। अङ्गैरावरणं कर्णिकामध्ये इति ज्ञेयम्। युग्मशः स्वरैरिति। तत्र प्रयोगः। अं आं नमः। "बीजैः पूजा स्याद् विभक्त्या वियुक्तैः" इत्याचार्य्योक्तेः। एवमष्टवर्गेष्वपि। उक्तञ्च संहितायाम्—

नियोज्य स्वरयुग्मान्ते नमस्कारं पृथक् पृथक्।
तथैव कादिवर्गेषु नमस्कारं पृथक् क्षिपेत्॥ इति।

तच्छक्तिभिरिति वर्गशक्तिभिः पत्रमध्योपरि। अत्र तच्छक्तीनां वर्गरूपमन्त्रादित्वं ज्ञेयम्। तथा स्वयमेव वक्ष्यति—

वर्णमन्त्रयुताः प्रोक्तलक्षणाः सर्व्वसिद्धिदाः। इति।

अनन्तरमिति चतुर्थम्। मातृभिरिति पत्राग्रे। लोकेश्वरैरायुधैश्चेति पश्चाद् बहिर्भूपुरे। [शान्तिनीत्यत्र शङ्खिनीति पाठोऽपि दृश्यते]॥१३॥१४॥१५॥१६॥१७॥१८॥

दण्डं कमण्डलुं पश्चादक्षसूत्रमथाऽभयम्।
बिभ्रती कनकच्छाया ब्राह्मी कृष्णाजिनोज्ज्वला॥ १९
शूलं परश्वधं क्षुद्रदुन्दुभिं नृकरोटिकाम्।
वहन्ती हिमसङ्काशा ध्येया माहेश्वरी शुभा॥ २०
अङ्कुशं दण्डखट्वाङ्गौ पाशञ्च दधती करैः।
बन्धूकपुष्पसङ्काशा कौमारी कामदायिनी॥ २१
चक्रं घण्टां कपालञ्च शङ्खञ्च दधती करैः।
तमालश्यामला ध्येया वैष्णवी विभ्रमोज्ज्वला॥ २२
मुषलं करवालञ्च खेटकं दधती हलम्।
करैश्चतुर्भिर्वाराही ध्येया कालघनच्छविः॥ २३
अङ्कुशं तोमरं विद्युत् कुलिशं बिभ्रती करैः।
इन्द्रनीलनिभेन्द्राणी ध्येया सर्व्वसमृद्धिदा॥ २४
शूलं कृपाणं नृशिरः कपालं दधती करैः।
मुण्डस्रङ्मण्डिता ध्येया चामुण्डा रक्तविग्रहा॥ २५
अक्षस्रजं बीजपूरं कपालं पङ्कजं करैः।
वहन्ती हेमसङ्काशा महालक्ष्मीः समीरिता॥ २६

ब्राह्म्यादीनामायुधध्यानम्। ब्राह्म्याम् आयुधध्यानं वामोर्द्ध्वादि वामाधस्तनं यावत्। माहेश्वर्य्याञ्च दक्षाधूर्द्ध्वयोराद्ये अधस्तनयोरन्त्ये। कौमार्य्यां वामोर्द्ध्वादि दक्षिणोर्द्ध्वपर्य्यन्तम्। वैष्णव्यां दक्षोर्द्ध्वतो वामोर्द्ध्वं यावत्। वाराह्यां दक्षाधस्तनाद् वामाधः पर्य्यन्तम्। इन्द्राण्यां चामुण्डायाञ्च दक्षवामयोरूर्द्ध्वादि। महालक्ष्म्यां दक्षोर्द्ध्वहस्तमारभ्य वामोर्द्ध्वपर्य्यन्तम्। आसां वाहनान्यपि ध्येयानि। तानि तत्तद्देवतानामिति ज्ञेयम्। ब्राह्म्यां हंस इति। तत्र वराह्यां महिषः।

तदुक्तम् —वाराहीञ्च प्रवक्ष्यामि महिषोपरि संस्थिताम्। इति। चामुण्डायां प्रेत इति ज्ञेयम्। वाराही वराहवक्त्रा। चामुण्डा निर्मांसा ध्येया। आसु च कौमारी-वैष्णवी-इन्द्राणी-महालक्ष्म्यो द्विनेत्राः अन्यास्त्रिनेत्राः। आसां बीजानि तन्त्रान्तरोक्तानि। यथा—

पूजयेन्मातृकामित्थं नित्यं साधकसत्तमः ॥ २७

न्यसेत् सर्गान्वितान् सृष्ट्या ध्यात्वा देवीं यथाविधि ।
सर्गबिन्द्वन्तिकान् न्यस्य डार्णाद्यान् स्थितिवर्त्मना ॥ २८

विद्यात् पूर्व्वोदितान् विद्वानृष्यादीनङ्गसंयुतान् ।
ध्यायेद् वर्णेश्वरीमत्र वल्लभेन समन्विताम् ॥ २९

सिन्दूरकान्तिममिताभरणां त्रिनेत्रां
विद्याक्षसूत्रमृगपोतवरं दधानाम् ।
पार्श्वस्थितां भगवतीमपि काञ्चनाङ्गीं
ध्यायेत् कराब्जधृतपुस्तकवर्णमालाम् ॥ ३०

अष्टौ दीर्घाः कादयोऽष्टौ सानन्ता बिन्दुयोगतः ।
इन्द्र आकाशसंयुक्तो बीजान्यासां क्रमाद् विदुः ॥ इति ।

साधकसत्तम इत्यनेन एवम्प्रकारेण साधितां मातृकामन्यमन्त्राङ्गत्वेन विनियुंज्यादित्युक्तं भवति ॥ १८॥२०॥२१॥२२॥२३॥२४॥२५॥२६॥२७ ॥

सृष्टिन्यासमाह न्यसेदिति । यदा सृष्ट्या सृष्टिमार्गेण न्यसेत् तदा सर्गान्वितानिति । यत्तदोरध्याहारेणाऽन्वयः । एवमग्रेऽपि । यथाविधीत्यनेनैतदुक्तं भवति । अत्र सृष्टिमातृका देवता । पूर्व्ववद् विसर्गान्तैर्वर्णैः षडङ्गन्यासः । ऋषिच्छन्दसी ध्यानं पूजादिकमपि सर्व्वं पूर्ववदेव । न्यासस्थानान्यपि पूर्व्वोक्तान्येवेति । प्रयोगस्तु । अः नमः केशान्ते । आः नमः मुखवृत्ते इत्यादि ।

स्थितिन्यासमाह सर्गेति । डार्णाद्यानिति ठपर्य्यन्तानित्यर्थः । सर्गबिन्द्वन्तिकानिति । बिन्दुसर्गान्वितत्वं प्रत्यक्षरमिति ज्ञेयम् । विद्वानित्यनेनैतदुक्तं भवति स्थितिमातृकादेवताषड़ङ्गान्यपि पूर्व्ववदेव सर्गबिन्द्वन्तिकवर्णैः कार्य्याणीति । तत्र प्रयोगः । डंः नमः दक्षिणगुल्फे । ढंः नमः दक्षिणपादाङ्गुलिमूले । इत्यादि क्षान्तं विन्यस्य अंः नमः केशान्ते इत्यादि ठंः नमः दक्षिणजानुनीत्यन्तं न्यसेत् ।

तदुक्तं शैवे—डकारादि ठकारान्तां योजयेत् परदेवताम् । इति ।
अत्र केचित् सृष्टौ अकारादि ठकारपर्य्यन्तं न्यासं कारयन्ति । स्थितौ डकारादि सकार पर्य्यन्तं । तदविचारितरमणीयम् । समस्तमातृकावृत्तेर्न्यासत्वात् । अत्रेति स्थितिन्यासे ॥ २८॥२९ ॥

पार्श्वं वामम् । आयुधध्यानम् ऊर्द्ध्वादि । दक्षे अक्षमालावरौ वामे मृगपोतविद्ये

अभ्यर्चनादिकं सर्व्वं विदध्यात् पूर्व्ववर्त्मना।
बिन्दुयुक्तामिमां न्यस्येत् संहृत्या प्रतिलोमतः॥ ३१
विद्यात् पूर्व्वोदितान् विद्वान् ऋष्यादीनङ्गसंयुतान्।
ध्येया वर्णमये पीठे देवी वाग्वल्लभा शिवा॥ ३२

अक्षस्रजं हरिणपोतमुदग्रटङ्कं
विद्यां करैरविरतं दधतीं त्रिनेत्राम्।
अर्द्धेन्दुमौलिमरुणामरविन्दवासां
वर्णेश्वरीं प्रणमत स्तनभारनम्राम्॥ ३३

न्यासार्च्चनादिकं सर्व्वं कुर्य्यात् पूर्व्वोक्तवर्त्मना।
तारोत्थाभिः कलाभिस्तां न्यसेत् साधकसत्तमः॥ ३४

इति। उक्तञ्च पद्मपादाचार्य्यैः—वराक्षसूत्रमृगपुस्तकधरेतदेवम्। वर्णमाला-मक्षमालामिमं दक्षे विद्या वामे। कराञ्जेति उपमासमासः। इति॥ ३०॥

संहारन्यासमाह बिन्दुयुक्तामिति। प्रतिलोमतः क्षकारादि अकारान्तम्। स्थानानि तु तान्येव। विद्वानित्यनेनैतदुक्तं भवति। संहारमातृकादेवताषडङ्गा-न्यपि पूर्व्ववदेव बिन्द्वन्तैर्वर्णैः कार्य्याणीति। तदुक्तम्—

ततः सबिन्दुके न्यासे ऋषिश्छन्दस्तु पूर्व्ववत्।
संहारशारदादेवी सबिन्द्वर्णैः षडङ्गकम्॥ इति।

प्रयोगस्तु—क्षं नमः हृदादि मुखे लं नमः हृदादि जठरे इत्यादि॥ ३१॥३२॥

अक्षेति। उदग्रस्तीक्ष्णः ऊर्द्ध्वाग्रो वा टङ्कः परशुः। आयुधध्यानं दक्षोर्द्ध्वादि परशुवर्णमाले। परे वामे। उक्तञ्च पद्मपादाचार्य्यैः—अक्षमालाटङ्कमृगपुस्तकधरां ध्यायेत् इति। अरविन्दवासां श्वेताब्जस्थाम्। का नाम सृष्टिः स्थितिः संहृतिर्वेति। अन्तर्गतस्य बहिरवभासः सृष्टिः। शिवेऽवभासः स्थितिः। संस्कारमात्रशेषतया अन्तरवस्थानं विनाशः। यदाहुः—

चिद्रूपस्यात्मनः सर्व्वजगतामीशितुः प्रभोः।
ग्राह्यग्राहकवैचित्र्यप्रकाशः सृष्टिरीश्वरि॥
अत्र स्थितिः स्याज्जगतामवभासः समीरितः।
संस्कारमात्रशेषोऽयं विनाशः संहृतिः शिवे॥ इति।

एवं ध्यानेन न्यासत्रयं कर्त्तव्यमित्यर्थः॥ ३३॥

कलान्यासमाह तारोत्थाभिरिति। प्रणवपञ्चभेदसमुत्पन्नाभिः सृष्ट्यादिभिः

वर्णाद्यास्तारसंयुक्ता न्यस्तव्यास्ता नमोऽन्विताः ।
ऋषिः प्रजापतिश्छन्दो गायत्रं समुदाहृतम् ॥ ३५
कलात्मा वर्णजननी देवता शारदा स्मृता ।
ह्रस्वदीर्घान्तरगतैः षडङ्गं प्रणवैः स्मृतम् ॥ ३६

हस्तैः पद्मं रथाङ्गं गुणमथ हरिणं पुस्तकं वर्णमालां
टङ्कं शुभ्रं कपालं दरममृतलसद्धेमकुम्भं वहन्तीम् ।
मुक्ताविद्युत्पयोदस्फटिकनवजवाबन्धुरैः पञ्चवक्त्रै-
स्त्र्यक्षैर्वक्षोजनम्रां सकलशशिनिभां शारदां तां नमामि ॥ ३७

अर्चयेदुक्तमार्गेण शारदां सर्व्वकामदाम् ।
तार्त्तीयपूर्व्वां तां न्यसेन्नमोऽन्तां रुद्रसंयुताम् ॥ ३८

कलाभिः सह तां मातृकां न्यसेदित्युक्तस्थानेषु । साधकसत्तम इत्यनेन प्रणवत्रयादित्वमप्युक्तं भवति । वर्णाद्या इति अकारादिवर्णाद्याः । एवम्भूतास्तारसंयुक्ताः । अनेनायं क्रमः । प्रथमतः प्रणवः पश्चादकाराक्षरं पश्चात् कलानाम । अत एवाद्यसंयुक्ता शब्दा नमोऽन्विता इति सम्प्रदायात् अन्ते नमसा योगात् चतुर्थ्यन्तत्वम् । न्यसेदित्यनेन नैराकाङ्क्ष्येऽपि पञ्चभेदकलानामादौ न्यासस्थापनायाह न्यस्तव्यास्ता इति । तत्र तु "न्यासे तु योजयेदादौ षोडश स्वरजाः कलाः" इत्युक्तत्वात् प्रथमं नादकलानां निवृत्त्यादीनां न्यासः पश्चादकारोकारबिन्दुजानां सृष्ट्यादीनाम् । प्रयोगस्तु । ॐ अं निवृत्त्यै नमः केशान्ते इत्यादि । कलात्मा वर्णजननी शारदा देवतेति । कलात्मा मातृका देवतेत्यर्थः । ह्रस्वदीर्घान्तरगतैरिति । अक्लीवह्रस्वदीर्घस्वरमध्यगतैरित्यर्थः । अं ॐ आं हृदयाय नमः इत्यादि प्रयोगः ॥ ३४॥३५॥३६ ॥

हस्तैरिति । रथाङ्गं चक्रम् । गुणोऽक्षसूत्रम् । वर्णमालामक्षमालाम् । टङ्कः परशुः । शुभ्रमिति कपालविशेषणम् । दरः शङ्खः । आयुधध्याने दक्षाधस्तनतो वामाधस्तनपर्य्यन्तं पुस्तकाक्षमालयोर्विपर्य्ययः । तदुक्तं पद्मपादाचार्य्यैः—पद्मचक्रगुणमृगाक्षसूत्रपुस्तकटङ्ककपालशङ्खकलशधरा ध्येया इति । मुक्तेति ऊर्द्ध्वादिमुखानां वर्णाः । सकलशशिनिभां शुभ्रवर्णाम् । सर्व्वकामदामिति विनियोगोक्तिः । अतएव पद्मपादाचार्य्याः "सर्व्वत्र सर्व्वं च" इति ॥ ३७ ॥

श्रीकण्ठमातृकामाह तार्त्तीयेति । तार्त्तीयं भैरव्याः तृतीयं वक्ष्यमाणम् । केचन रेफवर्जितं तद्वदन्ति । अयमेव साम्प्रदायिकः पक्षः । यतो मातृकाक्ष-

सधातुप्राणशक्त्यात्मयुक्ता यादिषु ते क्रमात् ।
ऋषिः स्याद्दक्षिणामूर्त्तिर्गायत्रं छन्द ईरितम् ॥ ३९

कर्णिकाबीजमेवं संगृहीतं भवति । भैरवीत्रिंशद्भेदमध्ये एकस्य भेदस्य तार्त्तीयं रेफवर्जितं भवत्येव । ग्रन्थकृदत एव षडङ्गावसरे ह्स्रां षड्दीर्घयुक्तेन इति वक्ष्यति । न्यसेदित्युक्तस्थानेषु । साम्प्रदायिकास्तु प्रणवशक्तिप्रासादपञ्चाक्षरीयोगमाहुः । रुद्रसंयुतामिति सशक्तिकश्रीकण्ठादिसहिताम् । नमोऽन्तामित्यनेन चतुर्थीयोगोऽप्युक्तः । ह्सौं अं श्रीकण्ठेशपूर्णोदरीभ्यां नमः केशान्ते इत्यादि प्रयोगः । अयं साम्प्रदायिकः पक्षः । अत्र ग्रन्थकृता छन्दोऽनुरोधादीशशब्दः क्वचिन्न दत्तः । न्यासावसरे सोऽवश्यं देय इति । केचित्तु पूर्णोदरीसहिताय श्रीकण्ठाय नमः इति वदन्ति । अन्ये तु पूर्णोदर्य्यै श्रीकण्ठाय नमः इत्याहुः । तदुभयमतेऽपि रुद्राणां प्राधान्यमिति ते वदन्ति । पूर्णोदरीश्रीकण्ठाभ्यां नमः इत्यपि केचिदिच्छन्ति । तत्पक्षत्रयमप्यसाम्प्रदायिकम् । सहितशब्दस्याऽनुक्तस्याऽधिकस्य प्रथमपक्षे प्रयोगः । द्वितीयपक्षे उभयत्र चतुर्थ्यनुपपन्ना । एकत्र नमोयोगात् प्राप्यते अन्यत्र प्रापकाभावात् । पक्षत्रये च रुद्रसंयुताम् इत्युक्तत्वात् मातृकाया रुद्रैः सहाऽव्यवधानेन संयोगो न भवति । अतः साम्प्रदायिकः पक्ष एव ज्यायान् । अपेक्षितार्थद्योतनिकाकारस्तु श्रीकण्ठेशाय पूर्णोदर्य्यै नमः इति प्रयोगमाह स्म । तदप्ययुक्तम् । यतो ध्याने अग्नीषोमादिवत् समुच्चितयोरेव देवतात्वं प्रतीयते । अस्मिंश्च प्रयोगे देवतयोः समुच्चितत्वम् । पृथक्चतुर्थीनिर्देशेनेतरेतरनिरपेक्षयोरेव तत्प्रतीतिः । किञ्च । यदग्नये च प्रजापतये च सायं जुहोतीत्यत्र शब्दद्वयकृत परस्परापेक्षयोः प्रत्येकं क्रियान्वयाभावेऽपि देवतासमुच्चयस्येष्टत्वात् । अत्र तु तदभावेन प्रत्येकं नमोऽन्वयात् सुतरां तत्समुच्चया प्रतीतिः । तेन होमादावपि श्रीकण्ठेशपूर्णोदरीभ्यां स्वाहेत्येकैवाहुतिः । एवं केशवादिकामगणेशन्यासेष्वपि द्रष्टव्यम् । यत्तु क्वचित् केशवाय च कीर्त्त्यै चेत्युद्धारः स छन्दोऽनुरोधेनेति ज्ञेयम् ॥ ३८ ॥

सधात्विति । ते रुद्रा यादिषु यकारादिषु दशसु व्यापकेषु । धातवः त्वगसृङ्मांसमेदोऽस्थिमज्जाशुक्राणि प्राणः शक्तिरात्मा च एतद्युक्ताः क्रमात् ज्ञेयाः । अत्र यद्यपि रुद्रपदं समासगर्भितं तथापि सर्व्वनाम्ना परामृश्यते । "सर्व्वनाम्नानुवृत्तिर्वृत्तिच्छन्नस्य" इति वामनसूत्रात् । प्रयोगस्तु । ह्सौः यं त्वगात्मभ्यां वालीशसुमुखीश्वरीभ्यां नमः हृदये इत्यादि । अत्र आत्मशब्दः सम्प्रदायात् प्रयुज्यते । ग्रन्थान्तरे आत्मशब्दस्थाने क्रोधशब्दमुक्त्वा आत्मशब्दः सर्व्वत्र प्रयोक्तव्य इत्युक्तम् ।

अर्द्धनारीश्वरः प्रोक्तो देवता तत्त्ववेदिभिः।
ह्सा षड्दीर्घयुक्तेन कुर्य्यादङ्गानि देशिकः॥ ४०

तथा—यादीन् धातुप्राणशक्तिक्रोधाख्यानात्मने युतान्। इति। अन्यत्रापि—जीवं शक्तिं क्रोधमप्यात्मने तान्। इति। आचार्य्यास्तु—तावपि धातवो याद्याः सप्तसमीरणाश्च सपरश्चः क्रोध इत्यब्धिके। इति। अत्र चकारस्य नरसिंहबीजत्वात् क्रोधशब्दोक्तिः। पद्मपादाचार्य्यैः प्रथमपद्यव्याख्याने विरचितेत्यादिना मातृकास्थानोक्तिराख्यायते। एभिरिति सप्त धातवः क्षकारेण प्राणः शक्तिश्चाभिहिता। कशब्देन सुखार्थेन परमात्मोक्त इति यादिन्यासस्थानानीत्युक्तम्। तन्मतानुसारेणेह मूलकारिण आत्मग्रहणं कृतम्। ननु त्वगादिपरमात्मान्तस्य देवतात्मनो यादिन्यासेनैव साधकशरीरे सन्निधाने सति किमवशिष्टाक्षरन्यासेनेति। देवतावयवविशेषरचनाकल्पनेति ब्रूमः। न च प्रथमं सामान्यकल्पना पुनर्विशेषकल्पनेति नियमोऽस्ति। येन लिपिन्यासस्य चकारादित्वं स्यात्। सर्व्वत्र नित्यमेव सामान्यविशेषरूपं हि देवताशरीरम्। तस्य साधकशरीरे सन्निधिर्न्यासेनोत्पाद्यते। अतः प्रथममकारादिन्यासेन अवयवविशेषसन्निधिस्मरणे न कश्चिद्दोषः। न च संहारक्रमेण मातृकान्यासे प्रथमं सामान्यसंहारः पश्चाद्विशेषसंहार इति क्रमकोपः। उभयोरप्यात्मन्येव संहारात्। न च सामान्यसंहारेणैव संहृतत्वात् विशेषाणां पृथक्संहरणमनर्थकम्। विशेषसंहारक्रमचिन्तायाः कर्त्तव्यत्वात्। षड्दीर्घाः आ ई ऊ ऐ औ अः। तद्युक्तेन ह्सा हकारसकारेण देशिक इत्यनेन मिलितेन इत्युक्तम्। प्रयोगस्तु। ह्सां हृदयाय नम इत्यादि। अन्ये तु ह्सामादिकानि मातृकाङ्गानि एवमिच्छन्ति। साम्प्रदायिकास्तु प्रणवमायालक्ष्मीपञ्चाक्षरीब्रह्माणिमाहेश्वरिकौमारिवैष्णविवाराहीन्द्राणीः स्वबीजाद्याः रक्षयुग्मान्ता अमुकवाहनेप्रमुखरक्षयुग्मान्ता अमुकहस्तेप्रमुखमांरक्षयुग्मान्ता दीर्घत्रयाक्रान्तमायापुटितमातृकाङ्गानि तार्त्तीयञ्च सञ्जीवनि जर्द्धकेशिनि जटिलकेशिनि विश्वरूपिणि ताराचिणि हिः मारय शब्दानुच्चार्य्य हृदयादीन्युच्चारयेत् इति। प्रयोगस्तु। ॐ ह्रीँ श्रीँ नमः शिवाय नमः हँ ब्रह्माणि रक्ष रक्ष हंसवाहने रक्ष रक्ष पद्महस्ते मां रक्ष रक्ष ह्रां ह्रीँ ह्रूँ अं कं खं गं घं ङं आँ ह्रां ह्रीँ ह्रूँ ह्सौः सञ्जीवनि हृदयाय नमः इत्यादि। बीजानि तु माँ कँ क्रौँ हुँ ईँ। आयुधानि पद्मशूलशक्तिचक्रगदावज्राणि। व्यापकमन्त्रस्तु ॐ ह्रीं श्रीं नमः शिवाय हं चामुण्डे रक्ष रक्ष वेतालवाहने रक्ष रक्ष पाशहस्ते मम सर्व्वाङ्गं रक्ष रक्ष ह्रां ह्रीँ ह्रूँ ह्रस्वषट्कं आदिचान्तं दीर्घषट्कमुच्चार्य्य ह्रां ह्रीँ

बन्धूककाञ्चननिभं रुचिराक्षमालां
पाशाङ्कुशौ च वरदं निजबाहुदण्डैः ।
बिभ्राणमिन्दुशकलाभरणं त्रिनेत्र-
मर्द्धाम्बिकेशमनिशं वपुराश्रयामः ॥ ४१

पूर्व्वोक्तेनैव मार्गेण पूजयेत् तं यथाविधि ।
स्मराद्यां मातृकां न्यस्येत् केशवादिनमोऽन्विताम् ॥ ४२

ह्सूँ ह्सौः सर्व्वाङ्गव्यापिनि स्वाहा इति व्यापकं कृत्वा श्रीकण्ठमातृकां न्यसेदिति । अत्रान्ते मुखादौ अष्टव्यापकमन्त्राः सम्प्रदायतो ज्ञेयाः । यत् प्रयोगसारे—

मातरोऽष्टौ समुत्पन्ना वर्णानां नायिकाश्च ताः ।
व्यापिनी पालिनी देवी पावनी क्लेदिनी पुनः ॥
धारिणी मालिनी भूयो हंसिनी शान्तिनी तथा ।
वर्णानां नायकाश्चाष्टौ भैरवाः समुदाहृताः ॥ इति ।

अष्टमो व्यापकन्यासस्तु आदिक्षान्तमुच्चार्य्य संहारभैरवशान्तिनीभ्यां नमः सर्व्वाङ्गे । ॥ ३८।४० ॥

बन्धूकेति । आयुधध्यानं दक्षे अर्द्धादि अङ्कुशाक्षमालेऽपरे वामे ॥ ४१ ॥

यथाविधीत्यनेनैतदुक्तं भवति । स्मराद्यां बालाद्यां वा काममातृकां न्यसेत् । क्लीँ अं कामरतिभ्यां नमः इति केशान्ते इत्यादिप्रयोगः । एतद्ध्यानं यथा—

रक्ताङ्गरागकुसुमाम्बरमात्तभूषं
नीलोत्पलाब्जकरशक्तिसुभूषिताङ्गम् ।
ध्यायेत् प्रसूनशरमिक्षुधनुर्धरञ्च
सद्दाड़िमीकुसुमभासमनङ्गमूर्त्तिम् ॥ इति ।

एवं गणपतिबीजाद्यां षड्बीजाद्यां वा गणपतिमातृकां न्यसेत् । तत्र प्रयोगः गं अं विघ्नेशश्रीभ्यां नमः केशान्ते इत्यादि । ध्यानञ्च—

तारुण्योन्मदचारुलोहितलसत्कान्त्यङ्गरागाम्बरं
सद्रक्तोत्पलहस्तया वनितया वामाङ्कमारूढ़या ।
हस्ताब्जैर्वरमङ्कुशं गुणमभीतिं धारयन्तं शुभं
ध्यायेयं गणपं गजेन्द्रवदनं नेत्रत्रयोद्भासितम् ॥ इति ।

अत्रोभयोरपि व्यापकेषु त्वगादियोगोऽप्यनुसन्धेयः ।

केशवादिमातृकान्यासमाह स्मराद्यामिति कामबीजाद्याम् । साम्प्रदायिकास्तु

सधातुप्राणशक्त्यात्मयुक्ता यादिषु विष्णव: ।
ऋषि: प्रजापति: प्रोक्तो गायत्रं छन्द ईरितम् ॥ ४३
अङ्गलक्ष्मीर्हरि: साक्षाद् देवताऽत्र समीरिता ।
दीर्घयुक्तेन बीजेन षडङ्गानि समाचरेत् ॥ ४४

हस्तैर्बिभ्रत् सरसिजगदाशङ्खचक्राणि विद्यां
पद्मादर्शौ कनककलशं मेघविद्युद्विलासम् ।
वामोत्तुङ्गस्तनभविरलाकल्पमाश्लेषलोभा-
देकीभूतं वपुरवतु व: पुण्डरीकाक्षलक्ष्म्यो: ॥ ४५

त्रिपुटानारायणाष्टाक्षरयोगमिच्छन्ति । अन्ये प्रणवत्रययोगं परे प्रणवत्रयपुटितत्वम् । केचन श्रीबीजयोगमिति । यथासम्प्रदायं व्यवहार: । प्रयोगस्तु क्लीं अं केशवकीर्त्तिभ्यां नम: केशान्ते इत्यादि । केचन केशवाय कीर्त्त्यै नम: इत्यपीच्छन्ति । ॥ ४२ ॥

सधात्विति । यं त्वगात्मने पुरुषोत्तमाय वसुधायै नम: हृदय इत्यादि । दीर्घयुक्तेनेति । दीर्घा: षट् पूर्वोक्ता: तद्युक्तेनादिबीजेन कामबीजेन तेन क्लां क्लीं इत्यादि हृदयादिषु ज्ञेयम् । अन्ये तु क्लामादिकानि मातृकाङ्गान्यवेच्छन्ति । साम्प्रदायिकास्तु मायानारायणाष्टाक्षराजपापरमात्ममन्त्रस्वरपुटितै: कादिवर्णै: देवीपद्मिनीविष्णुपत्नीवरदाकमलरूपाशूलिनीयुक्तै: हृदयादीन्यङ्गानि इति मन्वते । प्रयोगस्तु । ॐ नमो नारायणाय हंस: सोहं अं कं खं गं घं ङं आं ॐ नमो नारायणाय हंस: सोहं देव्यै हृदयाय नम: इत्यादि ॥ ४३॥४४ ॥

हस्तैरिति । मेघेत्यादि वपुर्विशेषणम् । आकल्पो भूषा । आयुधध्यानं दक्षिणाधोहस्तमारभ्य वामाधस्तनं यावत् । तेन पुरुषायुधानि दक्षिणत: स्त्र्यायुधानि वामत इति सिध्यति । पद्मपादाचार्य्याणां सम्मतमेतत् । उक्तञ्च—

विद्यारविन्दमुकुरामृतकुम्भपद्म-
कौमोदकीदरसुदर्शनशोभिहस्तम् । इति ।

अत्र वामोर्द्ध्वादि दक्षोर्द्ध्वान्त: क्रमो ज्ञेय: । अन्यत्र यदस्मिन् न्यासे चतुर्भुजध्यानं तत् केवलविष्णो: न लक्ष्मीसहितस्येति ज्ञेयम् । अयमप्यावश्यक: । यदाहु:—

केशवादिरयं न्यासो न्यासमात्रेण देहिनाम् ।
अच्युतत्वं ददात्येव सत्यं सत्यं न चान्यथा ॥ इति ॥ ४५ ॥

अथाऽर्चनादिकं सर्व्वं प्राग्वन्मन्त्री समाचरेत्।
शक्तिपूर्व्वां तनौ न्यस्येन्मातृकां मन्त्रवित्तमः॥ ४६
ऋषिः शक्तिः स्मृतं छन्दो गायत्रं देवता बुधैः।
सम्प्रोक्ता विश्वजननी सर्व्वसौभाग्यदायिनी॥ ४७
दीर्घार्द्धेन्दुयुजाऽङ्गानि कुर्य्यान्मायात्मना बुधः॥ ४८

उद्यत्कोटिदिवाकरप्रतिभटोत्तुङ्गोरुपीनस्तनी
बद्धार्द्धेन्दुकिरीटहाररसनामञ्जीरसंशोभिता।
बिभ्राणा करपङ्कजैर्जपवटीं पाशाङ्कुशौ पुस्तकं
दिश्याद् वो जगदीश्वरी त्रिनयना पद्मे निषण्णा सुखम्॥ ४९

पुरोदितेन विधिना देवीमन्वहमर्चयेत्।
न्यसेच्छ्रीबीजसम्पन्नां मातृकां विधिना तनौ॥ ५०
ऋषिर्भृगुः स्मृतं छन्दो गायत्रं देवता स्मृता।
समस्तसम्पदामादिर्जगतां नायिका बुधैः॥ ५१
प्राक्प्रस्तुतेन बीजेन कुर्य्यादङ्गानि साधकः॥ ५२

विद्युद्दामसमप्रभां हिमगिरिप्रख्यैश्चतुर्भिर्गजैः
शुण्डादण्डसमुद्धृतामृतघटैरासिच्यमानामिमाम्।

ऋषिः शक्तिरिति वशिष्ठपुत्रः। सर्व्वसौभाग्यदायिनीति विनियोग उक्तः। दीर्घेति। दीर्घाः षड्दीर्घाः अर्द्धेन्दुर्बिन्दुः। एतद्युक्तेन मायात्मना बीजेनेति शेषः। प्रयोगस्तु ह्रां हृदयाय नमः इत्यादि। केचन ह्रामादिकानि मातृकाङ्गान्येवेच्छन्ति। एवमग्रेऽपि॥ ४६॥४७॥४८॥

उद्यदिति। मञ्जीरो नूपुरः। जपवटीमक्षमालाम्। आयुधध्यानं दक्षे अधआदि अङ्कुशाक्षमाले परे वामे। उक्तञ्च पद्मपादाचार्य्यैः—अक्षसूत्राङ्कुशपाश-पुस्तककरा ध्येया इति॥ ४९॥

समस्तसम्पदामादिरिति विनियोगोक्तिः। प्राक्प्रस्तुतेनेति पूर्व्वोक्तेन मार्गेण षड्दीर्घयुक्तेनेत्यर्थः। बीजेन श्रीबीजेनेत्यर्थः। तेन श्रां श्रीमित्यादि षडङ्गम्। एतदादीनि मातृकाङ्गानि वा॥ ५०॥५१॥५२॥

बिभ्राणां करपङ्कजैर्जपवटीं पद्मद्वयं पुस्तकं

भास्वद्रत्नसमुज्ज्वलां कुचनतां ध्यायेज्जगत्स्वामिनीम् ॥ ५३

आराधयेदिमां प्रोक्तवर्त्मना कुसुमादिभिः ।

न्यसेत् स्मराद्यां वपुषि मातृकां मङ्गलप्रदाम् ॥ ५४

ऋषिः सम्मोहनः प्रोक्तश्छन्दो गायत्रमुच्यते ।

देवता मन्त्रिभिः प्रोक्ता समस्तजननी परा ॥ ५५

स्मरेण दीर्घयुक्तेन विदध्यादङ्गकल्पनाम् ॥ ५६

बालार्ककोटिरुचिरां स्फटिकाक्षमालां

कोदण्डमिक्षुजनितं स्मरपञ्चबाणान् ।

विद्याञ्च हस्तकमलैर्दधतीं त्रिनेत्रां

ध्यायेत् समस्तजननीं नवचन्द्रचूडाम् ॥ ५७

अर्चनादिक्रियाः सर्वाः प्रोक्ताः पूर्वविधानतः ।

शक्तिश्रीकामबीजाद्यां देवीं वर्णतनुं भजेत् ॥ ५८

विद्युदिति । आयुधध्यानं दक्षाधस्ताद् वामाधःपर्यन्तम् ॥ ५३ ॥

स्मराद्यामित्यनेन कामश्रीशक्त्यादिकामपि न्यसेदित्युक्तम् । तस्य त एव ऋष्याद्याः । द्विरुक्तैर्बीजैरङ्गानि ।

पञ्चबाणपद्माङ्कुशाक्षमालापुस्तकपाशपद्मधनुर्धराऽरुणा ध्येया । आयुधध्यानं दक्षाधस्तनमारभ्य वामाधस्तन पर्यन्तम् ।

न्यासपूजादिकं पूर्ववदेव । सौकर्य्याय ध्यानश्लोकोऽपि—

सा पञ्चबाणकमलाङ्कुशकाक्षमाला-

विद्यागुणाब्जधनुरष्टकरा त्रिनेत्रा ।

रक्ताऽरुणाम्बरविलेपनभूषणाढ्या

पायात्तु वर्णजननी शशिशेखरा वः ॥

मङ्गलप्रदामिति विनियोगोक्तिः । दीर्घयुक्तेन षड्दीर्घयुक्तेन ॥ ५४॥५५॥५६ ॥

बालेति । विद्यां पुस्तकम् । अक्षमालां पञ्चबाणान् दक्षे अधस्तनादि । वामे पुस्तकचापौ । इत्यायुधध्यानम् । तदुक्तं पद्मपादाचार्य्यैः—अक्षस्रक्शरचापपुस्तकधरा ध्येया इति ॥ ५७॥५८ ॥

ऋषिः पूर्व्वोदितश्छन्दो गायत्रं देवता बुधैः ।
सम्मोहनी समुद्दिष्टा सर्व्वलोकवशङ्करी ॥ ५९
आवर्त्तितैस्त्रिभिर्बीजैः षडङ्गानि प्रकल्पयेत् ॥ ६०

ध्यायेयमक्षवलयेक्षुशरासपाशान्
पद्मद्वयाङ्कुशशरान् वरपुस्तकञ्च ।
आबिभ्रतीं निजकरैररुणां कुचार्त्तां
सम्मोहनीं त्रिनयनां तरुणेन्दुचूडाम् ॥ ६१

यजेदावरणैः सार्द्धमुपचारैः सुशोभनाम् ।
प्रपञ्चयागं वक्ष्यामि सच्चिदानन्दसिद्धिदम् ॥ ६२
वेदादिः शक्तिरजपा परमात्ममहामनुः ।
वह्नेर्जाया च कथिता पञ्चमन्त्राः शुभावहाः ॥ ६३
तारशक्त्यादिकां न्यस्येदजपात्मद्विठान्तिकाम् ।
मातृकामुक्तमार्गेण सृष्ट्या देहे विधानवित् ॥ ६४

पूर्व्वोदित इति । सम्मोहनी सर्व्वलोकवशङ्करीति विनियोगोक्तिः । ५९ ॥

अवर्त्तितैरिति द्विवारम् । प्रथमातिक्रमे कारणाभावात् । एवं षड्बीजानि भवन्ति । क्लीँ हृदयाय नमः इत्यादि प्रयोगः ॥ ६० ॥

ध्यायेयमिति । इक्षुशरासः इक्षुधनुः । आयुधध्यानं दक्षे ऊर्द्धादि अङ्कुश-पद्मशराक्षमालाः । वामे पाशपद्मधनुःपुस्तकानि । तदुक्तं पद्मपादाचार्य्यैः—
अक्षस्रक्पद्मशरपद्माङ्कुशपाशपद्मेक्षुधनुःपुस्तकधराऽरुणा ध्येया इति ॥ ६१ ॥

प्रपञ्चेति । सच्चिदानन्दसिद्धिदमिति विनियोगोक्तिः । वेदादिः प्रणवः । अजपा हंसः । आत्ममहामनुः सोहं । वह्नेर्जाया स्वाहा । प्रणवो बीजं हृल्लेखा शक्तिः । शुभावहा इत्यनेनास्य स्वातन्त्र्यमप्युक्तम् । यदाहुः—

स्वतन्त्रोऽपि यदा सिद्धिं कुर्य्यादष्टाक्षरो मनुः ।
तस्माद् यथावत् प्रजपेद्धीमान् मोक्षपरः पुमान् ॥ इति ।

साम्प्रदायिका वाग्भवहृल्लेखासम्पुटमाहुः । ६२॥६३ ॥

तारशक्त्यादिकामिति । आत्मा परमात्ममन्त्रः । अजपायाः पूर्व्वमुक्तत्वात् । द्विठः स्वाहा । प्रतिवर्णमादौ तारमाये अन्ते त्वजपादयः । ॐ ह्रीं अं हंसः

ऋषिर्ब्रह्मा समुद्दिष्टश्छन्दो गायत्र्यीरितम् ।
समस्तवर्णसंव्याप्तं परं तेजोऽस्य देवता ॥ ६५
स्वाहाद्यैः पञ्चसनुभिः पञ्चाङ्गानि प्रकल्पयेत् ।
अस्त्रं दिक्षु बुधः कुर्य्याद् भूयो हरिहराक्षरैः ॥ ६६
ताराादिपञ्चमनुभिः परिचीयमानं
मानैरगम्यमनिशं जगदेकमूलम् ।
सच्चित्समस्तगमनश्वरमच्युतं तत्
तेजः परं भजत सान्द्रसुधांशु[धाम्बु]राशिम् ॥ ६७

सोऽहं स्वाहा केशान्ते इत्यादि प्रयोगः । संहारस्य वक्ष्यमाणत्वात् अत्र सृष्ट्येत्युक्तिः । विधानविदित्यनेनैतदुक्तं भवति । षडङ्गन्यासपूर्व्वकं सावरणं महागणपतिं ध्यात्वा चतुश्चत्वारिंशद्वारं गणेशबीजं सकृद् गणानां त्वा इत्येवं चतुरावृत्ति महागणपतिमन्त्रं प्रजप्य यथोक्तां शुद्धमातृकां विविन्यस्य अ क च ट त प यादिकानपि सप्त मुखदोःपदुदरहृन्मूर्द्धसु न्यसेदिति ॥ ६४॥६५ ॥

स्वाहाद्यैरिति विपरीतैः । स्वाहा हृदयाय नमः सोऽहं शिरसे स्वाहा इत्यादि प्रयोगः । दिक्ष्विति छोटिकाभिः । भूयोऽनन्तरं षडङ्गादित्यर्थः । हरिहराक्षरैरिति यथा श्रुतैः । तदुक्तम्—

जायाग्नेर्हृदयमथो शिरश्च सोऽहं
हंसात्मा त्वथ च शिखा स्व[मा]यश्च वर्म्म ।
ताराख्यं समुदितमीक्षणं तथास्त्रं
प्रोक्तं स्याद्धरिहरवर्णमङ्गमेव ॥ इति ।

ह्रि क्ष इति केचित् । ६६ ॥

तारादीति । तत् प्रसिद्धं परं तेजः ब्रह्म अनिशं सर्व्वदा भजत । अन्येषां तेजसामेतद्व्याप्यत्वादस्य परत्वम् । सान्द्रसुधांशु धाम्बु]राशिमिति व्यस्तरूपकम् । तेन पुंलिङ्गत्वदोषोऽपि न । अङ्गुल्यः पल्लवान्यासन् इतिवत् । एतेनानन्दमयत्वं ध्वनितम् । अच्युतम् अविकारि । अविनश्वरमविध्वंसि । समस्तगं व्यापकम् । चित् स्वप्रकाशज्ञानरूपम् । सत् सत्तात्मकम् । "सदेवेदं सर्व्वं सदात्" इति "चिदेवेदं सर्व्वं काशते" इति श्रुतेः । जगदेकमूलं तत्परिणामरूपत्वाद् जगतः । मानैरगम्यम् । "यतो वाचो निवर्त्तन्ते" इति श्रुतेः । अत एवास्य एतैः

पञ्चभूतमया वर्णा वर्गशः प्रागुदीरिताः ।
तस्माज्ज्ञानेन्द्रियात्मानः प्रपञ्चं तन्मयं विदुः ॥ ६८

परिचीयमानम् एतेषां जपेन लभ्यमित्यर्थः । तत्र तारस्य पञ्चावयवस्य प्रलीनाशेष-विकृतित्वात् देवीतारावयवानामपि तदवयवैः अभेदानन्दप्रत्ययार्थे पर्यवसायि-त्वात् । अजपामन्त्रयोरपि जीवपरमात्मतादात्म्यत्वात् पञ्चद्विठावयवानामपि सर्व्वत्रानुगतचिदर्थत्वात् । संहितायान्तु—

प्रणवस्थित्कला ज्ञेया मायाव्याप्तिस्वरूपिणी ।
हंसः पदेन देवेशि साक्षादात्मस्वरूपिणी ॥
तत्रत्यबिन्दुत्रितयात् सृष्टिस्थितिलयात्मिका ।
प्रसूता बिन्दुनाद्येन वामेयं ब्रह्मरूपिणी ॥
बिन्दुनाऽथ द्वितीयेन पालयन्ती जगत्त्रयम् ।
ज्येष्ठेयं वैष्णवी माया वाद्या सत्त्वगुणा प्रिये ॥
अन्त्येन बिन्दुना सर्व्वं रसन्ती तमसावृता ।
रौद्री बिन्दुत्रयं देवि प्रसूते चाम्बिका तदा ॥
आत्मानं दर्शयत्येषा हंसाख्या संहृतिर्यदा ।
तदेयं दर्पणाकारा ततो ज्योतिर्म्मयी भवेत् ॥
वर्णाभ्यां वह्निजायायाः परं ज्योतिरिति प्रिये ।
एवं विचारयन् मन्त्री साक्षाद् ब्रह्म भवेत्तु सः ॥ इति ।

अत्र प्रपञ्चयागमूर्त्तेः पूजा नोक्ता सा तन्त्रान्तरोक्ता यथा—

मातृकामन्त्रसम्प्रोक्ते पीठे सल्लिपिपङ्कजे ।
प्रपञ्चयागमूर्त्तिन्तु समावाह्य प्रपूजयेत् ॥
स्वरैराद्यावृतिः प्रोक्ता द्वितीया कादिमूर्त्तिभिः ।
तृतीया तु समुद्दिष्टा भारत्या द्यष्टशक्तिभिः ॥
चतुर्थी मातृभिः सार्द्धमसिताङ्गादिभैरवैः ।
वासवादिदिशां नाथैः पञ्चमी त्वायुधैः परा ॥ इति ॥ ६७ ॥

प्रपञ्चयागं वक्ष्यामीत्युक्तम् । तत्र प्रपञ्च इज्यते हूयते यत्रेति प्रपञ्चयागः । तमेव होमप्रकारं वदन् न्यासान्तरमपि सूचयति पञ्चभूतेति । प्रागिति द्वितीये । ज्ञानेन्द्रियात्मान इत्युपलक्षणम् । तेनाकाशवर्णाः । ज्ञानकर्म्मेन्द्रियात्मानः वायुवर्णाः तदर्थरूपाः अग्निवर्णाः प्राणादिदशवायुरूपा इत्याद्यूह्यम् । तन्मयं पञ्चभूतमयम् । ॥ ६८ ॥

देहोऽपि तादृशस्तस्मिन् न्यस्येद् वर्णान् विलोमतः।
तत्तत्स्थानयुतान् मन्त्री जुहुयात् परतेजसि॥ ६९
एवं वर्णमयं होमं कृत्वा दिव्यतनुर्भवेत्।
न्यस्य मन्त्री यथान्यायं देहे विश्वस्य मातरम्॥ ७०

तादृश इति पञ्चभूतमयः। तत्र वर्णान् न्यस्येदिति। तत्र प्रकारः पृथिव्या दशवर्णान् प्रपञ्चयागवदुच्चार्य्य पादतलादिजानुपर्य्यन्तं विन्यसेत्। एवमाकाशान्तं विन्यसेत्। विलोमत इति। पुनराकाशादिवर्णान् तत्तत्स्थानेषु भूमिपर्य्यन्तं विन्यसेत्। तत्तदिति विपरीतन्यासे ध्यानम्। एवं ध्यानं कृत्वा विपरीतं न्यसेत्॥ ६८॥

पूर्व्वोक्तं प्रपञ्चयागेऽप्यतिदिशति एवमिति। तत्र प्रकारः ॐ क्रौँ चं हंसः सोऽहं स्वाहा इति भान्तं विन्यसेत्। तत्र चकारं तदधिष्ठातृदेवतां तत्तत्स्थानञ्च तदवच्छिन्ने चैतन्ये जुहोमीति ध्यायन्नेव संहारन्यासं कुर्य्यादिति तात्पर्य्यार्थः। अयं साम्प्रदायिकः पक्षः। तदुक्तम्—

आधारोद्यत्कुक्षिविन्दूत्थिताया वक्त्रे सूर्येन्दुं ग्रसन्त्याः प्रियायाः।
चाद्यान्तार्णान् पातयेत् वह्निसोमप्रोतान् मन्त्री मुच्यते रोगजातैः॥ इति।

एवमुक्तसर्व्वविधमातृकान्यासस्य मन्त्रान्तरादौ कर्त्तव्यतामाह न्यस्येति। मन्त्री यथान्यायमित्यनेनैतदुक्तं भवति। सर्व्वान् मातृकान्यासान् कर्त्तुमशक्तः शाक्ते कलामातृकादीन् शैवे श्रीकण्ठमातृकादीन् वैष्णवे केशवमातृकादीन् शुद्धप्रपञ्चयागमातृके सर्व्वत्र न्यसेदिति। तदुक्तम्

जपादौ सर्व्वमन्त्राणां विन्यासेन लिपेर्विना।
कृतं तन्निष्फलं विद्यात् तस्मात् पूर्व्वं लिपिं न्यसेत्॥ इति।

कादिमतेऽपि—मातृकायाः षडङ्गञ्च मातृकान्यासमेव च।
सर्व्वासां प्रथमं कृत्वा पश्चात्तन्त्रोदितं न्यसेत्॥ इति।

आचार्य्याश्च—लिपिन्यासादिकान् साङ्गान्। इति।

नारायणीये च—अङ्गानि च न्यसेत् सर्व्वे मन्त्राः साङ्गास्तु सिद्धिदाः। इति।

अन्यत्रापि—

रुद्रैर्युक्तां केवलां वा मनूनां कर्म्मारम्भे मातृकां विन्यसेद् यः।
मन्त्रान् सद्यः कुर्व्वते तस्य सिद्धिं पापैः सार्द्धं याति नाशं जरा च॥ इति।

अनन्यधीरित्यनेन मातृकापुटितजपेन मन्त्रसिद्धिरुक्ता। तदुक्तम्—

जपेन्मन्त्रान् भजेद्देवान् यजेदग्निमनन्यधीः।
द्रव्यैश्च जुहुयादग्नौ मन्त्रवित् तन्त्रचोदितैः॥ ७१

अश्वत्थोडुम्बरप्लक्षन्यग्रोधसमिधस्तिलाः।
सिद्धार्थपायसाज्यानि द्रव्याण्यष्टौ विदुर्बुधाः॥ ७२

अमीभिर्जुहुयाल्लक्षं तदर्द्धं वा समाहितः।
सर्व्वान् कामानवाप्नोति परां सिद्धिञ्च विन्दति॥ ७३

एभिरर्कसहस्राणि हुत्वा मन्त्री विनाशयेत्।
रिपून् क्षुद्रग्रहान् भूतान् ज्वरान्कोपांश्च पन्नगान्॥ ७४

कुलप्रकाशतन्त्रे—मन्त्री तु प्रजपेन्मन्त्रं मातृकाक्षरसम्पुटम्।
क्रमोत्क्रमात्कृतावृत्त्या मासात् सिद्धो भवेन्नरः॥
मातृकाजपमात्रेण मन्त्राणां कोटिकोटयः।
सुसिद्धाः स्युर्न सन्देहो यस्मात् सर्व्वं तदुद्भवम्॥ इति।

प्रयोगसारेऽपि—मातृकायां तु सिद्धायां सिद्धाः स्युर्मन्त्रजातयः।
सर्व्वे मन्त्रा यतो मग्ना मातृकायामितस्ततः॥ इति॥ ७०॥७१॥

सर्व्वमातृकामन्त्राणां काम्यकर्म्माण्याह द्रव्यैरिति। द्रव्याण्याह अश्वत्थेति। जुहुयाल्लक्षमिति द्वादशसहस्राणि पञ्चशती एकैकेन द्रव्येण। तदर्द्धं वेति। षट्सहस्राणि पञ्चाशदधिका द्विशती एकैकेन द्रव्येण। समाहित इत्यनेन तस्याप्यर्द्धमिति सूचितम्। "मन्त्री तदर्द्धमथवापि तदर्द्धकं यः" इत्युक्तेः। तदा त्रिसहस्री सपादशतमेकैकेन द्रव्येण॥ ७१॥७२॥७३॥

अर्कसहस्राणीति। तदा सार्द्धसहस्रमेकैकेन। मन्त्रीत्यनेनैतदुक्तम्। विद्या-दीनामल्पत्वमहत्त्वे विचार्य्य द्विगुणं चतुर्गुणं वा होमः कार्य्य इति।
उक्तञ्च—द्वादशसहस्रमथवा तद्द्विगुणं तच्चतुर्गुणं वाथ जुहुयात्। इति।
तदा सहस्रत्रयं सहस्रषट्कं वैकैकेन। एवमुत्तरत्रापि। अत्यल्पत्वे एकादिशता-वृत्त्येत्यपि ज्ञेयम्। तदुक्तम्—

एकद्विकत्रिकचतुष्कशताभिवृत्त्या
तां तां समीक्ष्य विकृतिं प्रजुहोतु मन्त्री। इति।

क्षुद्रं नारायणीयोक्तम्—

स्तम्भद्वेषौ तथोन्माद उच्चाटो भ्रममारणे।
व्याधिश्चेति स्मृतं क्षुद्रम्। इति॥ ७४॥

मन्त्राणामयथावृत्तिप्रतिपत्तिसमुद्भवान् ।
विकारान् नाशयेदाशु होमोऽयं समुदीरितः ॥ ७५

एभिस्त्रिमधुरोपेतैर्जुहुयाल्लक्षमानतः ।
अचिरादेव स भवेत् साक्षाद् भूमिपुरन्दरः ॥ ७६

अमीभिः साधको हुत्वा वश्यादीनपि साधयेत् ।
हुत्वा लक्षं तिलैः शुद्धैर्मुच्यते सर्व्वपातकैः ॥ ७७

पायसान्नेन जुहुयान्मन्त्री सर्व्वसमृद्धये ।
पद्मानां लक्षहोमेन महतीं श्रियमाप्नुयात् ॥ ७८

घृतेन जुहुयाल्लक्षं प्राप्नुयात् कीर्त्तिमुत्तमाम् ।
जातीकुसुमहोमेन सर्व्वलोकवशं नयेत् ॥ ७९

संशोधितैस्त्रिमध्वक्तैर्लवणैर्लक्षमानतः ।
जुहुयाद् गुलिकाः कृत्वा वशयेत् सर्व्वमञ्जसा ॥ ८०

प्रयोगान्तरमाह मन्त्राणामिति । अयथावृत्तिर्वर्णानामन्यथोच्चारणम् । अप्रतिपत्तिः अयं मन्त्रः फलदो नेति ज्ञानम् । तदुद्भवान् विकारान् । तत्र अयथावृत्तेर्विकारो वातकुष्ठादिः अप्रतिपत्तेर्विकार उन्माद इति नारसिंहे प्रपञ्चितम् । तेन यथावृत्तिश्च प्रतिपत्तिश्च यथावृत्तिप्रतिपत्ती पश्चाद्नञा सम्बन्धः । होमः समुदीरित इति सहस्रावृत्त्येति ज्ञेयम् । "शमयेदचिरात् सहस्रहुत्या" इत्युक्तेः ॥७५॥

त्रिमधुरोपेतैरिति । एभिरष्टभिः । पयोमधुघृतं त्रिमधुरम् । तदुक्तम्—

आज्यं क्षीरं मधु तथा मधुरत्रयमुच्यते । इति ।

पयःस्थाने शर्करा वा ॥ ७६ ॥

अमीभिरष्टभिः । साधक इत्यनेन लक्षार्द्धमब्दत्रयादर्वागित्युक्तम् । यदाहुः—

लक्षं तदर्द्धकं वा मधुरत्रयसंयुतैर्हुनेदेतैः ।

अब्दत्रयादर्वाक् त्रिभुवनमखिलं वशीकुरुते ।

शुद्धैरिति अवकरं दूरीकृत्य प्रक्षाल्य संशोधितैरित्यर्थः । जुहुयाल्लक्षमिति सम्बध्यते । होमेनेति लक्षमानत इति सम्बध्यते । संशोधितैस्त्यक्तावकरैः लवणैः गुलिकाः कृत्वा इति सम्बन्धः । हुत्वा लक्षमित्यादिका संख्या महति कार्य्ये ।

जुहुयाच्च कार्य्यगुरुतालाघवमभिवीक्ष्य योग्यपरिमाणम् ।

इत्युक्तेः ॥ ७७॥७८॥७९॥८० ॥

लिखित्वा पत्रखण्डेषु मातृकार्णान् पृथक् पृथक् ।
अभ्यर्च्य जुहुयाद् वह्नौ तत्पत्राक्षरमुच्चरन् ॥ ८१
अभिचारहरो होमः सर्व्वरक्षाप्रसिद्धिदः ।
सहस्रहोमे वितरेद् दक्षिणां निष्कमानतः ॥ ८२

लिखित्वेति । पत्रखण्डेषु तालपत्रादिखण्डेषु मातृकार्णान् पृथक् प्रत्येकं लिखित्वा पृथक् प्रत्येकमभ्यर्च्य अग्नौ मातृकापीठमिष्ट्वा तत्पत्रस्थाक्षरमुच्चरन् जुहुयादिति सम्बन्धः ।

तत्र प्रत्यक्षरमृषिच्छन्दोदेवताशक्तिबीजान्युच्चार्य्य ध्यानं कृत्वा तेनैवाक्षरेण गन्धादि दद्यादित्यर्चनाक्रमः ।

तत्र ऋष्यादि यथा—अर्जुन्यायनमध्ये द्वौ भार्गवस्तौ प्रतिष्ठिका ।

अग्निवेश्यः सुप्रतिष्ठा त्रिषु चाब्धिषु गौतमः ॥
गायत्री च भरद्वाज उष्णिगेकारके परे ।
लोहित्यायनकोऽनुष्टुप् वशिष्ठो बृहती द्वयोः ॥
माण्डव्यो दण्डकस्यापि स्वराणां मुनिछन्दसी ।
मौद्गायनस्य पङ्क्तिः केऽजस्त्रिष्टुप् त्रितये घङोः ॥
योग्यायनस्य जगती गोपाल्यायनको मुनिः ।
छन्दोऽतिजगती चे छेत्रषकः शर्करी ह्यजः ॥
शर्करी काश्यपश्चातिशर्करी झञयोष्टठोः ।
शुनकोष्टिः सौमनस्योऽत्यष्टिर्डे कारणो धृतिः ॥
ढणोर्माण्डव्यातिधृति सांकृत्यायनकः कृतिः ।
त्रिषु कात्यायनस्तु स्यात् प्रकृति र्नपकेषु वै ॥
दाक्षायनाकृति व्याघ्रायणो भे विकृतिर्मता ।
शाण्डिल्यसंकृती मेऽथ काण्डव्यातिकृती यरोः ॥
दाण्डायनोत्कृतो लेऽथ वै जातायनदण्डकौ ।
लाट्यायनो दण्डकः शे बसहे जयदण्डकौ ॥
माण्डव्यदण्डकौ लक्षे कादीनामृषिछन्दसी ।
एवमुक्ता देवताश्च श्रीकण्ठादय ईरिताः ॥
बीजमस्याः शक्तयस्तु पूर्णोदर्य्यादयो मताः ॥ इति ।

ध्यानं पूर्व्वोक्तम् । तदुक्तमनुसन्धेयम् । निष्केति सुवर्णचतुष्कम् ॥ ८१॥८२ ॥

अर्द्धं वा शक्तितो दद्याद् यथोक्तं फलमाप्नुयात् ।
अनया सप्त संजप्तं पिबेत् प्रातर्दिने दिने ॥ ८३
सलिलं स भवेद् वाग्मी लभते कवितां पराम् ।
ब्राह्मीरसे वचाकल्के पयसा विपचेद् घृतम् ॥ ८४

अनयेति। अयमत्र प्रयोगक्रमः। स्वयं देवताविग्रहो भूत्वा लिपिपद्मे जलमादाय वालादशाक्षरी ताः विपरीतदशाक्षरी वाला च एवं वान्तं जप्त्वा त्वाद्यन्तमेवं सबिन्दुकञ्च पुनः सबिन्दुविसर्गम् आदिचान्तञ्च जप्त्वा भ्रूमध्ये अक्षराणां दीपशिखावद्व्याप्तिं ध्यायन् पिबेदिति। वर्णानामास्यान्तरुद्गमनम् आस्यात् धाम्नाद्याकारेण निर्गमनञ्च ध्यायन् पुनर्द्विवारं पिबेदिति ॥ ८३ ॥

सलिलमिति पूर्व्वेण सम्बध्यते। भवेदित्यर्कमासत इति ज्ञेयम्।

अनेडमूकोऽपि कवित्वगर्व्वितः पराञ्च सिद्धिं लभतेऽर्कमासतः। इत्युक्तेः।

ब्राह्मीरस इति। अत्र घृतं जीवद्वत्सैकवर्णगोरेव ग्राह्यम्। दुग्धमपि तादृश्या एव। आयुर्वेदोक्तप्रकारेण च घृतपाकः। तत्र "कल्काच्चतुर्गुणः स्नेहः" इति सामान्यतः स्नेहस्य चतुर्थभागः कल्क उक्तः। अत्र त्वयं स्वरसपाक इति कृत्वा स्नेहाष्टमांशः कल्को ग्राह्यः। तदुक्तम्—

स्नेहः सिध्यति शुद्धाम्बुनिःक्वाथस्वरसैः क्रमात् ।
कल्कस्य योजयेदंशं चतुर्थं षष्ठमष्टमम् ॥ इति ।

अत्र ब्राह्मीरसः स्वरसः। तदुक्तम्—

सम्पिष्टार्द्रं वस्तु वस्त्रगालितं स्वरसं विदुः। इति।

कल्क इति। "कल्को दृषदि पेषितः" इति। तत्रायं क्रमः। प्रस्थद्वयमितं घृतं पलद्वयमितः श्वेतवचाकल्कः। घृताच्चतुर्गुणो ब्राह्मीरसः चतुर्गुणं क्षीरम्।

पञ्चप्रभृति यत्र स्युर्द्रवाणि स्नेहसंविधौ।
तत्र स्नेहसमान्याहुरर्वाक् च स्याच्चतुर्गुणम् ॥

इत्युक्तत्वात्। चतुर्गुणं जलं देयम्। तदुक्तम्—

क्षीरदध्यारनालेषु पाको यत्रेरितः क्वचित्।
चतुर्गुणं जलं तत्र वीर्य्याधानार्थमाचरेत् ॥ इति।

पाकज्ञानञ्च—नाङ्गुलिग्राहिता कल्के न स्नेहेऽग्नौ सशब्दता।
वर्णादिसम्पच्च यदा तदैनं शीघ्रमाहरेत् ॥

तथान्यत्र—स्नेहस्य पाके कल्कस्तु वर्त्तितो वर्त्तिवद्भवेत्।

अयुतं मातृकाजप्तमर्चितश्च विधानतः ।
पिबेत् प्रातः स मेधावी भवेद् वाक्पतिसन्निभः ॥ ८५
ब्राह्मीं सहस्रसंजप्तां वचां वा पयसा पिबेत् ।
स लभेन्महतीं मेधामचिरान्नाऽत्र संशयः ॥ ८६
पूर्व्वोक्तं पङ्कजं कृत्वा कुम्भं संस्थाप्य पूर्व्ववत् ।
क्वाथेन पूरयेन्मन्त्री यथावत् क्षीरशाखिनाम् ॥ ८७
अष्टगन्धं विलोड्याऽस्मिन्नवरत्नसमन्विते ।
आवाह्य पूजयेद् देवीं मातृकाभुक्तमार्गतः ॥ ८८

तथा—घृतस्य फेनोपरमस्तैलस्य च तदुद्भवः ।
लेहस्य तन्तुमत्ताप्सु मज्जनं सरणं न च ॥ इति ।

इदं घृतं पानार्थमिति । अत्र सम एव पाकः । तदुक्तम्—
स्नेहः पक्को भवेत् सिद्धेः पाकः पाने भवेत् समः ।
खरोऽभ्यङ्गे मृदुर्नस्ये सामान्येयं प्रकल्पना ॥ इति ॥ ८४ ॥

विधानत इति । ततो घृतं समुत्तार्य्य शीतलमयुतजप्तं मातृकापीठं घृते विभाव्य मातृकोक्तविधानेन पूजितं पिबेदिति । भवेदिति संवत्सरादिति ज्ञेयम् । "कविर्भवति वत्सरतः" इत्युक्तेः । तन्त्रान्तरे तु विशेषः—

पलं श्वेतवचाचूर्णं कर्षं तुरगगन्धि च ।
कृष्णा हरिद्रा सिन्धूत्थं धात्री रुक्मिश्चमेचजम् ॥
प्रतिनिष्कन्तु संचूर्ण्य घृतप्रस्थे विनिक्षिपेत् ।
ब्राह्मीरसे चतुःप्रस्थे पचेन्मृद्वग्निपाकवित् ॥
ब्राह्मीघृतमिदं प्रोक्तमनयाऽयुतमन्त्रितम् ।
पिबेत् सूर्य्योपरागे तु सर्व्वज्ञत्वमवाप्नुयात् ॥
दिनादौ वा लिहेन्नित्यं पञ्चाशदभिमन्त्रितम् ।
वाग्विलाससमो विन्देत् कविवृन्देषु सम्मतम् ॥ इति ॥ ८५॥८६ ॥

पूर्व्वोक्तमिति । मातृकापूजावसरोक्तम् । पूर्व्ववदिति तुर्य्योक्तरीत्या । क्वाथेन कषायेण । यथावदिति चतुर्थांशावशिष्टेन सबिन्दुकां मातृकां जपन् पूरयेदिति च । क्षीरशाखिनामिति तत्त्वचामित्यर्थः । अष्टगन्धमिति शाक्तम् । नवरत्नानि वक्ष्यन्ते । सहस्रसाधितैः सहस्रसंजप्तैरित्यर्थः । भानुवारे शुभे लग्ने तोयैरभि-

सहस्रसाधितैस्तोयैरभिषिञ्चेत् प्रियं नरम्।
भानुवारे शुभे लग्ने ब्राह्मणानपि भोजयेत्॥ ८९

गुरवे दक्षिणां दद्याद् भक्तियुक्तः स्वशक्तितः।
रत्नाकरं विशेषेण कृत्याद्रोहोपशान्तिदम्॥ ९०

ऐश्वर्य्यजननं पुंसां सर्व्वसौभाग्यसिद्धिदम्।
अभिषेकमिमं प्राहुर्विश्वसम्मोहनप्रदम्॥ ९१

पूर्व्वोक्तमण्डलं कृत्वा मन्त्री नवपदान्वितम्।
मध्यादि स्थापयेत् तेषु पदेषु कलशान् नव॥ ९२

तन्तुभिर्वेष्टितान् शुद्धान् बहिश्चन्दनचर्चितान्।
सुधूपवासितान् मन्त्री दूर्व्वाक्षतसमन्वितान्॥ ९३

आपूर्य्य शुद्धतोयैस्तान् वेष्टयेदंशुकैस्तु तान्।
मुक्तामाणिक्यवैदूर्य्यगोमेदान् वज्रविद्रुमौ॥ ९४

पद्मरागं मरकतं नीलञ्चेति यथाक्रमात्।
उक्तानि नवरत्नानि तेषु कुम्भेषु निक्षिपेत्॥ ९५

विष्णुक्रान्तामिन्द्रवल्लीं देवीं दूर्व्वाञ्च निक्षिपेत्।
स्थापयेत् कुम्भवक्त्रेषु कोमलांश्चूतपल्लवान्॥ ९६

विन्यसेदक्षतोपेतांश्चषकांश्च फलान्वितान्।
मध्ये कुम्भे समाराध्य देवीं मन्त्री वृषादितः॥ ९७

षिञ्चेदिति सम्बन्धः। मासमिति ज्ञेयम्। "तच्चापि मासम्" इत्युक्तेः। नरमिति लिङ्गमविवक्षितम्। "नारी वन्ध्याऽपि नानाविधगुणनिलयं पुत्रवर्य्यं प्रसूते" इत्युक्तेः। सम्बलनं [सम्मोहनं ?] इति वक्ष्यम्॥ ८७॥८८॥८९॥९०॥९१॥

नवपदान्वितमिति नवनाभम्। शुद्धान् व्रणकालिमादिरहितान्। सुधूपवासितानित्यन्तः यथाक्रमात् निक्षिपेदिति मध्यादितः सर्व्वत्र सर्व्वाणि। देवीमिति सहदेवीम्। निक्षिपेदिति सर्व्वत्र सर्व्वाः। वृषा इन्द्रः तदादित इति पूर्व्वादितः। वासवो वृत्रहा वृषा इति कोशः। दिक्षु कुम्भेषु इति व्यधिकरणे सप्तम्यौ। वर्गा अकाराद्याः व्यस्तसमस्ताः त एव मन्त्रास्तद्युतास्तदाद्याः। विद्यां

अर्चयेद् दिक्षु कुम्भेषु व्यापिन्याद्याः पुरोदिताः ।
वर्णमन्त्रयुताः प्रोक्तलक्षणाः सर्व्वसिद्धिदाः ॥ ९८

शर्कराघृतसंयुक्तं पायसञ्च निवेदयेत् ।
स्पृष्ट्वा कुम्भान् कुशैर्विद्यां जपेत् साग्रं शतं शतम् ॥ ९९

अभिषिञ्चेद् विलोमेन साध्यं तं दक्षदक्षिणम् ।
सर्व्वपापक्षयकरं शुभदं शान्तिसिद्धिदम् ॥ १००

कृत्याद्रोहादिशमनं सौभाग्यश्रीजयप्रदम् ।
पुत्रप्रदं च वन्ध्यानामभिषेकमिमं विदुः ॥ १०१

ज्वरार्त्तस्य पुरः स्थित्वा जपेत् साग्रं सहस्रकम् ।
ज्वरो नश्यति तस्याशु क्षुद्रभूतग्रहा अपि ॥ १०२

परतेजसि सञ्चिन्त्य शुभ्रं सुतसुधामयम् ।
विधुं विद्यां जपेद् योगी विषरोगविनाशकृत् ॥ १०३

वलीपलितरोगघ्नः क्षुत्पिपासाप्रणाशनः ।
पुष्टिदः सर्व्वसौभाग्यदायी लक्ष्मीशुभप्रदः ॥ १०४

सोमसूर्य्याग्निरूपाः स्युर्वर्णा लोहत्रयं तथा ।
रौप्यमिन्दुः स्मृतो हेम सूर्य्यस्ताम्रं हुताशनः ॥ १०५

लोहभागाः समुद्दिष्टाः स्वराद्यक्षरसंख्यया ।
तैर्लोहैः कारयेन्मुद्रामसङ्कलितसङ्गताम् ॥ १०६

मातृकाम् । साग्रमष्टोत्तरम् । शतं शतमित्यनेन प्रतिकुम्भम् ॥ ९२—९९ ॥
विलोमेनेति ईशानादि स्थितैर्घटैरित्यर्थः । तदुक्तम्—

प्रयोगसारे—पुनरन्त्यादिमध्यान्तमभिषिञ्चेत् प्रियां स्त्रियम् । इति ।

क्षुद्ररोगग्रहा अपि नश्यन्तीत्यनुषज्यते ॥ १००॥१०१॥१०२ ॥

परतेजसि सहस्रारकमलकर्णिकास्थित परमशिवे । विधुं तत्रत्यमेव ॥ १०३॥१०४ ॥

त्रिशक्तिमुद्रिकामाह सोमेति । लोहत्रयमिति । "सर्व्वञ्च तैजसं लोहम्" इत्युक्तत्वात् रूप्यहेमताम्राणां लोहशब्देनाभिधानम् । तथेति सोमसूर्य्याग्निरूपमित्यर्थः । तदेवाह रौप्यमिन्दुरिति । स्वरादीति । रौप्यं १६ सुवर्णं २५ ताम्रं १० । केचित्तु वर्णानां द्वादशकलात्मकत्वात् सुवर्णभागा द्वादशेति वदन्ति ।

साग्रं सहस्रं संजप्य स्पृष्ट्वा तां जुहुयात् ततः।
तस्यां सम्पातयेन्मन्त्री सर्पिषा पूर्व्वसंख्यया॥ १०७
निक्षिप्य कुम्भे तां मुद्रामभिषिक्तोक्तवर्त्मना।
आवाह्य पूजयेद् देवीमुपचारैः समाहितः॥ १०८
अभिषिच्य विनीताय दद्यात् तां मुद्रिकां गुरुः।
इयं रक्षःक्षुद्ररोगविषज्वरविनाशिनी॥ १०९
व्यालचौरमृगादिभ्यो रक्षां कुर्य्याद् विशेषतः।
युद्धे विजयमाप्नोति धारयन्मनुजेश्वरः॥ ११०
विभजेन्मातृकां मन्त्री नव वर्गान् यथाक्रमात्।
अष्टावष्टौ स्वराः स्पर्शाः पञ्चशो व्यापका अपि॥ १११
नववर्गाः समुत्पन्ना नववर्गेश्वरा ग्रहाः।
अर्केन्दुरक्तज्ञगुरुभृगुमन्दाहिकेतवः॥ ११२

अयमेव पक्षः साम्प्रदायिकः। शैवागमेऽपि —

ताम्रतारसुवर्णानामर्कषोडशखेन्दुभिः। इति।

अत्र व्युत्क्रमेण संख्येति व्याख्यातम्। असङ्कलितेति। असङ्कलिताममिलितां पश्चात् सङ्गतां मिलिताम्। तत्र प्रकारः। तत्तद्भागमितस्य लोहत्रयस्य मुद्रिकात्रयं कृत्वा पश्चात् संयोजयेदिति। साग्रमिति अष्टाधिकम्। संजप्य मातृकामिति शेषः। ततो मन्त्री पूर्व्वसंख्यया अष्टोत्तरसहस्रमिति। सर्पिषा जुहुयादिति सम्बन्धः। तस्यां सम्पातयेदिति। सम्पातो नाम स्रुवस्थाहुतिशेषाज्यस्य प्रत्याहुति मुद्रिकायां पातः॥ १०५॥१०६॥१०७॥

अभिषिक्तोक्तेति। एककलशप्रोक्तेन। आवाह्येति कुम्भे। अभिषिच्येति साध्यम्। व्यालः सर्पः। मृगो व्याघ्रः॥ १०८॥१०९॥११०॥

नवरत्नमुद्रिकामाह विभजेदिति। मन्त्रोत्थेन नवग्रहन्यासोऽपि सूचितः। तत्र प्रकारः। स्वरानुक्त्वा सोममण्डलाय नमः इति मूर्द्धादिगलपर्य्यन्तम् कादिमान्तमुच्चार्य्य सूर्य्यमण्डलाय नमः इति गलादि हृदयान्तम् याद्यानुक्त्वा वह्निमण्डलाय नमः इति हृदयादिपादान्तं व्यापकं न्यसेदिति मण्डलत्रयन्यासः। आदिठान्तमुक्त्वा सोममण्डलाय नमः इति मूर्द्धादि हृदयान्तं डादि सान्तमुक्त्वा

माणिक्यं मौक्तिकं चारु विद्रुमं गारुडं पुनः।
पुष्परागं लसद्वज्रं नीलं गोमेदकं शुभम्॥ ११३

वैदूर्य्यं नव रत्नानि मुद्रां तैः कल्पयेच्छुभाम्।
जपहोमादिकं सर्व्वं कुर्य्यात् पूर्व्वोक्तवर्त्मना॥ ११४

यो मुद्रां धारयेदेनां तस्य स्युर्वशगा ग्रहाः।
वर्द्धते तस्य सौभाग्यं लक्ष्मीरव्याहता भवेत्॥ ११५

कृत्या द्रोहा विनश्यन्ति नश्यन्ति सकलापदः।
रक्षोभूतपिशाचाद्या नेक्षन्ते तं भयाकुलाः॥ ११६

उपर्य्युपरि वर्द्धन्ते धनरत्नादिसम्पदः।
मुद्रिकायाः प्रसादेन राजलक्ष्मीः स्थिरा सदा॥ ११७

तार्त्तीयोज्ज्वलकर्णिकं स्वरयुगैराविर्भवत्केसरं
वर्गोल्लासिवसुच्छदं वसुमतीगेहेन संवेष्टितम्।

अग्निमण्डलाय नमः इति हृदादिपादान्तं न्यसेदित्यग्नीषोमन्यासः। आदिक्षान्तमुक्ता हंसः पुरुषात्मने नमः इति व्यापकत्वेन न्यसेदिति हंसन्यासः। एते न्यासा यथाक्रमादितिपदेन सूचिताः। ततः अं आं इं ईं उं ऊं ऋं ॠं सूर्य्याय भगवते नमः इत्यादिक्रमेण केतवन्तं विन्यस्य पुनः प्रथमोक्तन्यासत्रयं वैपरीत्येन कुर्य्यादिति ग्रहन्यासः। तत्र शेषाष्टस्वरैः सोमः कवर्गेणाऽङ्गारकः चवर्गेण बुधः टवर्गेण बृहस्पतिः तवर्गेण शुक्रः पवर्गेण शनैश्चरः यवर्गेण राहुः षवर्गेण केतुः। अयमत्र न्यासक्रमः। स्थानानि तु मूलाधारलिङ्गनाभिहृदयगललम्बिकाभ्रूमध्यललाटब्रह्मरन्ध्राणीति। व्यापका यकाराद्याः। अपीत्यपिशब्दात् पञ्चशः इत्यत्राप्यन्वेति।

ग्रहक्रममाह अर्केति। रक्तो मङ्गलः। ज्ञो बुधः। मन्दः शनैश्चरः। अहिः राहुः॥ १११॥ ११२॥

चार्व्वित्यनेनातिलोहितप्रवालस्य ग्रहणमुक्तम्। लसदित्यनेन षट्कोणवज्रस्यैव ग्रहणमुक्तम्। पूर्व्वोक्तवर्त्मनेति पूर्व्वमुद्रोक्तप्रकारेण॥ ११३—११७॥

धारणयन्त्रमाह तार्त्तीयेति। तार्त्तीयं पूर्व्वोक्तं कर्णिकाबीजम्। ताराधीश्वरः ठकारः। आकारसाम्यात्। गौड़लिपौ तादृक्स्वरूपस्य लिखितत्वात्। वारिवर्णो वकारः। ताभ्यां विलसन्तौ यौ दिक्कोणौ ताभ्यां संशोभितम्। तेनात्र पूर्व्वयन्त्रादयमेव विशेषः। उक्तं कादिमते "ठं वं भूदिग्विदिक्षु च" इति।

ताराधीश्वरवारिवर्णविलसद्दिक्कोणसंशोभितं
यन्त्रं वर्णतनोः परं निगदितं सर्व्वामयघ्नं परम् ॥ ११८

इति श्रीशारदातिलके षष्ठः पटलः ॥

आचार्य्यैः पूर्व्वोक्तं पूजायन्त्रमेव धारणयन्त्रमुक्तम् । इदमपि पद्यं केचित् तदनुसारेण व्याख्यायते । विलसन्तौ यौ दिक्कोणौ ताभ्यां संशोभितम् । तेन विदिक् विकोण इति जातम् । ततो विदिक्षु ठकारः । विकोणशब्देन दिश उच्यन्ते । ततो दिक्षु वकार इत्यर्थः । तदुक्तमाचार्य्यैः—

क्ष्माबिम्बेन च सप्तमार्णवयुजाश्वाशासु संवेष्टितं
वर्णाब्जं शिरसि स्मृतं विषगदप्रध्वंसि मृत्युञ्जयम् । इति ।

इति श्रीशारदातिलकटीकायां सत्सम्प्रदायकृतव्याख्यायां
पदार्थादर्शाभिख्यायां षष्ठः पटलः ॥ ॐ ॥

सप्तमः पटलः ।

अथ भूतलिपिं वक्ष्ये सुगोप्यामतिदुर्लभाम् ।
यां प्राप्य शम्भोर्मुनयः सर्व्वान् कामान् प्रपेदिरे ॥ १

पञ्च ह्रस्वाः सन्धिवर्णा व्योमेराग्निजलं धरा ।
अन्त्यमाद्यं द्वितीयञ्च चतुर्थं मध्यमं क्रमात् ॥ २

पञ्चवर्गाक्षराणि स्युर्वान्तं श्वेतेन्दुभिः सह ।
एषा भूतलिपिः प्रोक्ता द्विचत्वारिंशदक्षरैः ॥ ३

आयस्वराणां वर्गाणां पञ्चमाः प्राणसंयुताः ।
वर्गाद्या इति विज्ञेया नव वर्गाः स्मृता अमी ॥ ४

व्योमेराग्निजलक्षोणीवर्गवर्णान् पृथग् विदुः ।
द्वितीयवर्गे भून्नं स्यान्नवमे न जलं धरा ॥ ५

अथ मातृकाविशेषं भूतलिपिमन्त्रमाह अथेति। शम्भोः सकाशाद् यां प्राप्येत्यन्वयः। सर्व्वान् कामानित्यनेन विनियोग उक्तः ॥ १ ॥

मन्त्रमुद्धरति पञ्चेति। पञ्च ह्रस्वाः अ इ उ ऋ ऌ प्रथमो वर्गः। सन्धिवर्णाः ए ऐ ओ औ द्वितीयो वर्गः। व्योम हः। ईरो यः। अग्नो रः। जलं वः। धरा लः। अयं तृतीयः। पञ्चवर्गाक्षराणां क्रममाह अन्त्यमिति। अन्त्यं ङः आद्यं कः द्वितीयं खः चतुर्थं घः मध्यमं गः। अयं क्रमोऽग्रेऽपि चतुर्षु। एवं वर्गाष्टकम्। वान्तं शः। श्वेतः षः। श्रीकण्ठादिपाठात् इन्दुः सः। अयं नवमः ॥ २॥३ ॥

नववर्गाद्यक्षराण्याह आयस्वराणां इति। अश्च ए च अस्वराणश्चेति द्वन्द्वः। तत्र अ ए इत्यनयोः वृद्धिरेचीति वृद्धौ कृतायां ऐ। ततो अमित्यस्मिन् परतः एचोऽयायवावः इति आयित्कृते आयस्वराणं इति सिध्यति। अस्वराणो हः। वर्गाणां अकचटतपानाम् ॥ ४ ॥

वर्गवर्णानां भूतात्मकतामाह व्योमेति। पृथक् प्रत्येकं नववर्गाणां प्रथमादयो वर्णा व्योमादिरूपा इत्यर्थः। क्वचिन्नव वर्णान् पृथग्विदुरिति पाठः। तत्र नवेति

विरिञ्चिविष्णुरुद्रार्कप्रजापतिदिगीश्वराः ।
क्रियादिशक्तिसहिताः क्रमात् स्युर्वर्गदेवताः ॥ ६

ऋषिः स्याद्दक्षिणामूर्त्तिर्गायत्रं छन्द ईरितम् ।
देवता कथिता सद्भिः साक्षाद् वर्णेश्वरी परा ॥ ७

हादिषड्वर्गकैः कुर्य्यात् षडङ्गानि सजातिभिः ।
ध्यायेल्लिपितरोर्मूले देवीं तन्मयपङ्कजे ॥ ८

वदन्ति सुधियो वृक्षं नित्यं वर्णमयं शुभम् ।
परसम्विन्महाबीजं बिन्दुनादमहाशिफम् ॥ ९

पृथिव्यक्षरशाखाभिः सर्व्वाशासु विजृम्भितम् ।
सलिलाक्षरपत्रैः स्वैः संछादितजगत्त्रयम् ॥ १०

वह्निवर्णाङ्कुरैर्दीप्तं रत्नैरिव सुरद्रुमम् ।
मरुद्वर्णलसत्पुष्पैर्द्योतयन्तं वपुःश्रियम् ॥ ११

आकाशार्णफलैर्नम्रं सर्व्वभूताश्रयं परम् ।
परामृताख्यमधुभिः सिञ्चन्तं परमेश्वरीम् ॥ १२

वीप्सा ज्ञेया । पृथक् प्रत्येकं व्योमवाय्वादिरूपान् नव वर्णान् विदुरिति योजना । तत्रान्त्योपान्त्ययोः सप्ताष्टाक्षरात्मकत्वात् कथं नववर्णत्वमित्याह प्रथमपाठे प्रत्येकवर्गवर्णानां पञ्चभूतात्मकत्वमुक्तं तद्द्वितीयनवमयोर्न घटत इत्यत आह द्वितीयेति । उभयत्रोभयसम्भवाभिप्रायमिति भावः । द्वितीयवर्गस्य चतुरक्षरात्मकत्वात् ख्वात्मकमक्षरं नास्ति । नवमस्य त्रिवर्णात्मकत्वादुभयोरभावः ॥ ५ ॥

नववर्गदेवता आह विरिञ्चीति । दिगीश्वरा इन्द्रयमवरुणसोमाः । सर्व्वे कीदृशाः । क्रियादिशक्तिसहिताः विरागत्तक्रियाज्ञानेच्छाशक्तिभिरुपेताः । केचित्तु दिगीश्वर इत्येकः क्रियाशक्त्यादयस्तिस्र इति नव देवता इच्छन्ति ॥ ६॥७ ॥

हादीति । तृतीयवर्गेण हृदयम् । एवमन्यैरष्टमान्त्यैरन्यानि । हं यं रं वं लं हृदयाय नम इत्यादि प्रयोगः । ध्यायेदिति । तन्मयपङ्कजे वर्णाब्जे ॥ ८ ॥

लिपितरोरित्युक्तं तत्स्वरूपमाह नित्यमिति । वैयाकरणभाट्टमते वर्णानां नित्यत्वात् । परसम्वित् कुण्डलिनी । परब्रह्मेति कश्चित् । शिफा मूलम् । नित्यमित्युक्तं चेत् तस्य कथं बीजादुत्पत्तिः । अभिव्यञ्जकत्वेन बीजवदुपचर्य्यते ।

वेदागमादिभिः क्लृप्तं समुन्नतिमनोहरम् ।
शिवशक्तिमयं साक्षाच्छायाश्रितजगत्त्रयम् ॥ १३
एनमाश्रित्य मुनयः सर्व्वान् कामानवाप्नुयुः ॥ १४
अङ्कोन्मुक्तशशाङ्ककोटिसदृशीमापीनतुङ्गस्तनीं
चन्द्रार्द्धाङ्कितमस्तकां मधुमदादालोलनेत्रत्रयाम् ।
बिभ्राणामनिशं वरं जपवटीं विद्यां कपालं करै-
राद्यां यौवनगर्व्विंतां लिपितनुं वागीश्वरीमाश्रये ॥ १५
आधारदेशेऽधिष्ठाने नाभौ हृदि गले पुनः ।
बिन्दौ नादे ततः शक्त्यां शिवे देशिकसत्तमः ॥ १६
नवाधारेषु विन्यस्य स्वरान् नव यथाविधि ।
हादिवर्णौस्तनौ न्यसेन्मुखे ऊर्द्धादितः सुधीः ॥ १७
ऊर्द्धमाहेन्द्रयाम्योदक्पश्चिमेषु समाहितः ।
दोःपत्सु पञ्चवर्गाणां वर्णान् देशिकसत्तमः ॥ १८

स्वैरित्यनेन द्वितीयोक्तभूतवर्णनिरासः । इदं पृथिव्यादिष्वपि योज्यम् । वेदागमेति । एतद्रूपेण दृक्षस्योच्चत्वमित्यर्थः ॥ ८॥१०॥११॥१२॥१३॥१४ ॥

ध्यायेदित्युक्तं तत् ध्यानमाह अङ्क इति । अङ्कः कलङ्कः तेन उन्मुक्तस्त्यक्तः । आयुधध्यानं वामाद्यधस्तनयोराद्ये तदूर्द्धयोरन्ये । अन्ये तूर्द्धादि दक्षे आद्ये परे वामे इत्याहुः ॥ १५ ॥

आधारेति । आधारदेशे गुदमेढ्रान्तराले । अधिष्ठाने लिङ्गे । बिन्दौ भ्रूमध्ये । नादे केशान्ते । शक्त्यां तदूर्द्धदेशे । शिवे द्वादशान्ते । नवाधारेषु आधाराद्युक्तनवचक्रेषु । यथाविधीत्यनेन तत्तदाधारभावनां कृत्वेत्युक्तं भवति । अत एव आधारेत्याद्युक्तापि पुनर्नवाधारेष्वित्युक्तिः । आधारभावना अन्त्यपटले वक्ष्यते । देशिकसत्तम इत्यनेन वर्णानां सबिन्दुकत्वमुक्तम् ॥ १६॥१७ ॥

ऊर्द्धादित इति यदुक्तं तदेव विवृणोति ऊर्द्धेति । स्वस्यैव पञ्चमुखकल्पनया न्यास इति सुधीरित्यनेनोक्तम् । समाहित इत्यनेन वर्णानां सबिन्दुत्वमुक्तम् । दोःपदिति । देशिकसत्तमः अग्रमूलोपमूलाग्रमध्यदेशक्रमेण दोःपत्सु जठरादि-पृष्ठान्तेषु पञ्चवर्गाणां वर्णान् न्यसेदित्युत्तरेण सम्बन्धः । मूलञ्च अग्रञ्च

अग्रमूलोपमूलाग्रमध्यदेशक्रमेण तु ।
जठरे पार्श्वयुगले नाभौ पृष्ठे समाहितः ॥ १९
गुह्यहृद्भ्रूबिले न्यस्येत् शादिवर्णत्रयं क्रमात् ।
सृष्ट्यां सर्गावसाना स्यात् स्थितौ वह्निमरुत्पथः ॥ २०
वियद्भूमिक्रमान्न्यस्येद् बिन्दुसर्गावसानिकाम् ।
संहृतौ प्रतिलोमेन विन्यसेद्बिन्दुभूषिताम् ॥ २१
आगमोक्तेन मार्गेण दीक्षितः साधकोत्तमः ।
लक्षं न्यस्येज्जपेत्तावदयुतं जुहुयात् तिलैः ॥ २२
पूजयेदन्वहं देवीं पीठे प्रागीरिते सुधीः ।
वर्णाब्जेनासनं दद्यान्मूर्त्तिं मूलेन कल्पयेत् ॥ २३

मूलाग्रे तयोः समीपमुपमूलाग्रम्। अग्रञ्च मूलञ्च उपमूलाग्रञ्च मध्यदेशश्चेति विग्रहः। अग्रमङ्गुल्यन्तः। मूलमंसोरुमूलम्। उपमूलं कूर्परजानुनी। उपाग्रं करपादाङ्गुलिप्रथमसन्धिः। मध्यदेशो मध्यसन्धिः मणिबन्धगुल्फे। समाहित इत्यनेन समाधानपरतया स्थानविपर्ययाभावद्रष्टेत्युक्तम्। देशिकसत्तम इत्यनेन वर्णानां सबिन्दुकत्वमुक्तम्। भ्रूबिले भ्रूमध्ये। क्रमादिति स्वरादिषु सर्व्वत्र सम्बध्यते। अत्र एतन्मन्त्रोक्तक्रमादित्यर्थः। सृष्टाविति। सर्गावसाना भूतलिपिरिति शेषः।

स्थितौ बिन्दुसर्गावसानिकां तां क्रमान्न्यसेदिति सम्बन्धः। कः क्रम इत्यपेक्षायामाह वह्नीति। तत्र वह्न्यादीनामेकैकं वर्णं विन्यस्य पुनस्तेनैव क्रमेण न्यसेत्। तत्रायं क्रमः। उं: इं: ऋं: अं: लृं: ओं: ऐं: औं: एं: इत्यादि। आगमोक्तेन कुलप्रकाशतन्त्रप्रोक्तेन। दीक्षितस्तावदिति लक्षं। तत्र एको न्यासः एका आवृत्तिश्चेति क्रम इति साधकोत्तम इत्यनेनोक्तम् ॥ १८॥१९॥२०॥२१॥२२ ॥

पूजयेदिति। अत्र कश्चित् प्रागीरिते पीठे इत्युक्तेरष्टपत्र एव षोड़शशक्तीनां द्विरावृत्त्या द्वात्रिंशन्मितानां चतुरावृत्त्या चतुःषष्टिमितानामष्टावृत्त्या पूजनम् अन्यथा पीठे प्रागीरिते इति व्याहन्येतेत्युवाच। तदसाम्प्रदायिकम्। तेषां मते अष्टावृतित्वं व्याहन्येत। आवृत्तिर्नाम सर्व्वत आवरणत्वेन पूजनम्। तदेकधा अष्टशक्तिपूजनेनैव जातम्। तदतिरिक्तद्वितीयावृत्तिश्चेत् पूज्यते आवृत्त्यन्तरमेव भवति। न तु तस्यास्तत्रान्तर्भावः। मन्त्रान्तरेषु न च दृष्टपूर्व्वम्। साम्प्रदायिकपक्षे तु पीठे प्रागीरिते इत्यस्यायमर्थः। प्रागुक्तपीठशक्तिपीठमन्त्रानत्रापि पूजयेदिति।

देवीं सम्पूजयेत् तस्यामङ्गाद्यावरणैः सह ।
आदावङ्गावृतिः पश्चादम्बिकाद्याभिरीरिता ॥ २४
द्वितीया मातृभिः प्रोक्ता तृतीया ह्यष्टशक्तिभिः ।
चतुर्थी पञ्चमी प्रोक्ता द्वात्रिंशच्छक्तिभिः पुनः ॥ २५
चतुःषष्ट्या स्मृता षष्ठी शक्तिभिर्लोकनायकैः ।
सप्तमी पुनरेतेषामस्त्रैः स्यादष्टमावृतिः ॥ २६
एवं पूज्या जगद्धात्री श्रीभूतलिपिदेवता ।
स्थानेषूक्तेषु विधिवदभ्यर्च्याऽङ्गानि पूजयेत् ॥ २७
अम्बिकावाग्भवी दुर्गा श्रीशक्ति श्चोक्तलक्षणाः ।
ब्राह्म्याद्याः पूर्व्ववत् पूज्याः कराली विकराल्युमा ॥ २८
सरस्वतीश्रीदुर्गोषा लक्ष्मीश्रुत्यौ स्मृतिर्धृतिः ।
श्रद्धा मेधा मतिः कान्तिराय्या षोड़श शक्तयः ॥ २९

इदं सर्व्वत्रानुसन्धेयम् । तथा च ग्रन्थकृन्महागणपतिपूजावसरे वक्ष्यति प्रागुक्ते पूजयेत् पीठे इति । तत्र यदि पूर्व्वोक्तमेकाक्षरगणपति निर्दिष्टम् अष्टदलमात्रपीठं गृह्यते तदा या षट्कोणादिषु पूजा वक्ष्यते साऽनुपपन्ना स्यात् । ध्याने च त्रिकोण-षट्कोणमातृकाम्बुजं यत् पीठमुक्तं तदप्यसङ्गतं स्यात् । यद्युच्येत प्रागुक्ते पीठे इति ध्यानोक्त इत्यर्थ इति तदा पीठशक्तिपीठमन्त्रपूजाप्रापकवचनाभावात् तत्पूजा न स्यादेवेत्यलम् । तेनात्राऽष्टदलं षोड़शदलं भूपुरं चतुर्द्वारञ्च कृत्वा तत्र प्रागुक्ताः पीठशक्तीः सम्पूज्य वर्णाब्जेनासनं दत्त्वा मूर्त्तिं मूलेन सङ्कल्प्य तत्र देवीमभ्यर्च्य केसरेषु यथापूर्व्वमङ्गानि चाभ्यर्च्य तदुपरि दिग्दलेषु चतस्रोऽम्बिकाद्याः तदग्रे ब्राह्म्याद्याः षोड़शदलादिषु कराल्याद्याः पूजयेदिति । वर्णाब्जेनेति । ह्सौः वर्णाब्जाय भूतलिपियोगपीठाय नमः इति प्रयोगः । तस्यां मूर्त्तौ ।

अङ्गादीत्यादिशब्दं विवृणोति आदावित्यादि । अङ्गावृतेः पूजास्थानमाह स्थानेष्विति । उक्तेषु तुर्य्योक्तेषु । विधिवदित्युक्त्या ध्यानानि । अम्बिकाद्येत्यादि-शब्दं विवृणोति पूजयेदिति । आसां ध्यानं स्वस्वप्रकरणेऽनुसन्धेयम् । मातृपूजा-ध्यानमाह उक्तेति । उक्तलक्षणाः प्राक्पटलोक्तध्यानाः । पूर्व्ववदिति पूर्व्वोक्त-स्थानेषु ॥ २३॥२४॥२५॥२६॥२७॥२८ ॥

ह्यष्टशक्त्यादिशब्दान् विवृणोति करालीति । पूज्या इति षोड़श दलेषु ।

खड्गखेटकधारिण्यः श्यामाः पूज्याः स्वलङ्कृताः ।
विद्याह्रीपुष्टयः प्रज्ञा सिनीवाली कुहूः पुनः ॥ ३०
रुद्रा वीर्य्या प्रभा नन्दा स्यात् पोषा ऋद्धिदा शुभा ।
कालरात्रिर्महारात्रिर्भद्रकाली कपर्दिनी ॥ ३१
विकृतिर्दण्डिमुण्डिन्यौ सेन्दुखण्डा शिखण्डिनी ।
निशुम्भशुम्भमथिनी महिषासुरमर्दिनी ॥ ३२
इन्द्राणी चैव रुद्राणी शङ्कराईशरीरिणी ।
नारी नारायणी चैव त्रिशूलिन्यपि पालिनी ॥ ३३
अम्बिका ह्लादिनी चैव द्वात्रिंशच्छक्तयः स्मृताः ।
चक्रहस्ताः पिशाचास्याः सम्पूज्याश्चारुभूषणाः ॥ ३४
पिङ्गलाक्षी विडालाक्षी समृद्धि र्वृद्धिरेव च ।
श्रद्धा स्वाहा स्वधाभिख्या मायासंज्ञा वसुन्धरा ॥ ३५
त्रिलोकधात्री सावित्री गायत्री त्रिदशेश्वरी ।
सुरूपा बहुरूपा च स्कन्दमाताऽच्युतप्रिया ॥ ३६

रुद्रा वीर्य्येति पाठः। तेन रुद्रा सप्तमी वीर्य्या अष्टमी। प्रभा नवमी। नन्दा दशमी। शुभेति विशेषणं न शक्तिनाम।

तदुक्तं संहितायाम्—रुद्रा वीर्य्या प्रभा नन्दा पोषिणी ऋद्धिदा तथा। इति। दण्डिमुण्डिन्याविति। दण्डिनी मुण्डिनी इति शक्तिद्वयम्। "विकृतिर्दण्डिनी चैव" इत्युक्तेः। निशुम्भशुम्भमथनीत्येका। सम्पूज्या इति षोडशपत्राग्रतत्सन्धिषु।

तदुक्तं संहितायाम्—पूर्वादिक्रमतः पूज्या दलाग्रेषु च सन्धिषु। इति। ॥ २८॥३०॥३१॥३२॥३३॥३४॥

स्वधेति अभिख्या यस्याः मायेति संज्ञा यस्याः सा इति विग्रहः।

तथा चाचार्य्याः—मायाभिख्या वसुन्धरा। इति।

अन्यत्रापि—श्रद्धा स्वाहा स्वधाख्या च मातृका च वसुन्धरा। इति। स्थितिः संहृतिरेव च इत्यत्र संस्थितिः स्थितिरेव च इति क्वचित् पाठः। अयमेव साम्प्रदायिकः। परेति शक्तिनाम। सुरेत्येका असुरविमर्दिनीत्यपरा।

तदुक्तम्—सप्तममुख्यथ सुरा तथाऽसुरविमर्दिनी। इति।

विमला चामला पश्चादरुणी पुनरारुणी ।
प्रकृतिर्विकृतिः सृष्टिः स्थितिः संहृतिरेव च ॥ ३७
सन्ध्या माता सती हंसी मर्दिका रञ्जिका परा ।
देवमाता भगवती देवकी कमलासना ॥ ३८
त्रिमुखी सप्तमुख्यन्या सुराऽसुरविमर्दिनी ।
लम्बोष्ठी चोर्द्ध्वकेशी च बहुशीर्षा वृकोदरी ॥ ३९
रथरेखाह्वया पश्चाच्छशिरेखा तथाऽपरा ।
गगनवेगा पवनवेगा च तदनन्तरम् ॥ ४०
ततो भुवनपालाख्या ततः स्यान्मदनातुरा ।
अनङ्गाऽनङ्गमदना तथैवाऽनङ्गमेखला ॥ ४१
अनङ्गकुसुमा विश्वरूपाऽसुरभयङ्करी ।
अक्षोभ्यासत्यवादिन्यौ वज्ररूपा शुचिव्रता ॥ ४२
वरदाख्या च वागीशा चतुःषष्टिः समीरिताः ।
चापबाणधराः सर्व्वा ज्वालाजिह्वा महाप्रभाः ॥ ४३
दंष्ट्रिण्यश्चोर्द्ध्वकेश्यस्ता युद्धोपक्रान्तमानसाः ।
सर्व्वाभरणसन्दीप्ताः पूजनीयाः प्रयत्नतः ॥ ४४
लोकेशाः पूर्व्ववत् पूज्यास्तद्वद्वज्रादिकान्यपि ।
इत्थं यः पूजयेन्मन्त्री श्रीभूतलिपिदेवताम् ॥ ४५

तथा अपरेति शक्तिनाम । तदनन्तरं पवनवेगेति सम्बन्धः । असुरभयङ्करीति पदच्छेदः । अक्षोभ्या च सत्यवादिनी च इति विग्रहः । पूजनीयाः प्रयत्नत इति चतुरस्रान्तरयादि प्रादक्षिण्येन ।

तदुक्तं संहितायाम्—एताः शक्तीश्च पूजयेत् । प्रादक्षिण्यक्रमेणैव । इति ।

॥ ३५॥३६॥३७॥३८॥३९॥४०॥४१॥४२॥४३॥४४ ॥

पूर्व्ववदिति तुर्य्योक्तवत् । तदुक्तं संहितायाम्—

तद्वहिर्लोकपालांश्च भूबिम्बे पूजयेत् प्रिये । इति ।

तद्वदिति चतुर्थोक्तवत् ॥ ४५ ॥

श्रीवाख्यो: स भवेद् भूमिर्देवैरप्यभिवन्द्यते ।
कमलैरयुतं हुत्वा राजानं वशमानयेत् ॥ ४६
उत्पलैर्जुहुयात् तद्वन्महालक्ष्मीः प्रजायते ।
पलाशकुसुमैर्हुत्वा वत्सरेण कविर्भवेत् ॥ ४७
राजीलवणहोमेन वनितां वशमानयेत् ।
मातृकोक्तानि कर्म्माणि कुर्य्यादन्यापि साधकः ॥ ४८
भूतलिप्या पुटीकृत्य यो मन्त्रं भजते नरः ।
क्रमोत्क्रमाच्छतावृत्त्या तस्य सिद्धो भवेन्मनुः ॥ ४९
सुषुप्तभुजगाकारां कुण्डलीं मध्यवर्त्मना ।
सङ्गमय्य परं स्थानं प्राणवित् तां परामृतैः ॥ ५०
प्लावयेन्मूर्द्ध्नि मूलान्तं योगोऽयं सर्व्वसिद्धिदः ।
अनया न्यस्तदेहस्तु तेजसा भास्करो भवेत् ॥ ५१
यन्त्रक्रिया विशेषांस्तु ज्ञात्वा कर्म्माणि साधयेत् ॥ ५२

बिन्द्वाढ्यं गगनं तदेव शिवयुक् ज्ञानी चतुर्थ्या युतो
नत्यन्तो मनुरेष मध्यविहितः साध्यस्य वर्ण्णैश्चरैः ।

तद्वदित्ययुतम् । उत्तरप्रयोगद्वयेऽपीयमेव संख्या ॥ ४६॥४७॥४८ ॥

मन्त्रान्तरस्यापि अनयैव सिद्धिमाह भूतेति । क्रमोत्क्रमात् पुटीकृत्येत्यन्वयः । सिद्धो भवेन्मनुरिति । स मन्त्रस्तस्य सिद्ध्यतीत्यर्थः । मासमात्रेणेति ज्ञेयम् । तदुक्तम् कुलप्रकाशतन्त्रे—मासमात्रं जपेन्मन्त्रं भूतलिप्यर्णसंपुटम् ।

क्रमोत्क्रमात् सहस्रं तु तस्य सिद्धो भवेन्मनुः ॥ इति ।

यद्वा साध्यारिस्थानपतितः सिद्धस्थान गतमन्त्रफलं ददातीत्यर्थः । ४९ ॥

मध्यवर्त्मनेति सुषुम्णामध्यमार्गेणेत्यर्थः । मूर्द्ध्नि परं स्थानं सङ्गमय्येति । षट्चक्रभेदक्रमेण परं स्थानं द्वादशान्तं शिवस्थं प्रापय्य । प्राणविदित्यनेन योगीत्युक्तम् । मूलान्तं मूलाधारपर्य्यन्तम् । परामृतैः प्लावयेदिति सम्बन्धः । अस्यान्यमन्त्राङ्गत्वमाह अनयेति ॥५०॥५१॥५२ ॥

वियद्यन्त्रमाह बिन्द्विति । गगनं हः बिन्द्वाढ्यं हं । तदेव सबिन्दुकं गगनं । शिव एकारस्तद्युक् तेन हें । अत्रैकादश रुद्रा इति शिवशब्देन एकादशसंख्या

पत्रेष्वक्षरशो हकारपुटितांस्तद्भूतवर्णान् लिखे-
च्छिष्टञ्चान्त्यदले विलिख्य मतिमान् वृत्तेन संवेष्टयेत् ॥ ५३

वियद्‌यन्त्रमिदं प्रोक्तं लाक्षाचन्दननिर्मितम् ।
रोहिण्यामुदये राहोर्विषघ्नं सर्व्वशान्तिदम् ॥ ५४

लक्षिता । तथा चैकादशस्वरस्तेन एकारः शिवशब्दवाच्यः । ज्ञानीशब्दश्चतुर्थ्या युतः चतुर्थ्येकवचनेन युतस्तेन ज्ञानिने । नत्यन्तो नमोऽन्त एष मनुर्मन्त्रः मध्यविहितः कर्णिकायां लेख्य इत्यर्थः । साध्यस्य विषादिग्रस्तदेवदत्तादेः बन्धवरैः "सिद्धार्णा बान्धवा प्रोक्ताः" इत्युक्तः सिद्धकोष्ठाक्षरैः सह पत्रेषु तद्भूतवर्णान् एतत्पटलोक्तव्योमभूतवर्णान् अक्षरशः प्रत्यक्षरं हकारपुटितान् लिखेत् । अन्त्यं नवमं अन्त्यदले तेन अष्टमदले व्योमभूतवर्णद्वयं प्रत्येकं हकारपुटितं लिखेत् । मतिमानित्यनेन सर्व्वाण्यक्षराणि सबिन्दुकानीत्युक्तम् । सर्व्वाक्षराणि सबिन्दुकानि इति सम्प्रदायविदः । देवदत्तस्य विषं हर हरेति क्रिया मध्ये लेख्या ॥ ५३ ॥

लाक्षा अलक्तकः । रोहिण्यामुदये राहोरिति । अत्र तात्कालिक नक्षत्रमुहूर्त्ते तत्तद्भूतग्रहोदये तत्तद्यन्त्रं लेखनीयम् । तत्र दिवसे नवमं रोहिणीमुहूर्त्तं रात्रावप्यष्टमं रोहिणीमुहूर्त्तम् । तत्र राहोरुदये । वायुभूतोदये राहोरुदयो भवति । यतः प्रतिराशौ पञ्चभूतोदयस्य नियतत्वात् नवग्रहोदयोऽप्यस्त्येव ।

यदुक्तम्—प्राणाग्नीलाम्बुखात्मानः पवनाः स्युर्यथाक्रमम् ।
गुरुराहू भृगुकुजौ बुधार्कौ चन्द्रसूर्य्यजौ ॥
क्रमाच्चतुर्षु भूतेषु व्योम सर्व्वात्मकं भवेत् । इति ।

अन्यत्रापि—गुरुराहू च वायव्ये चरतोऽग्नौ भृगुः कुजः ।
भूम्यां बुधरवी ज्ञेयौ जले चन्द्रशनैश्चरौ ॥
आकाशं सग्रहं विद्यादेवं सर्व्वेषु राशिषु ।
षष्ट्युत्तरैस्त्रिशतैः श्वासैरेका तु नाड़िका ॥
पञ्चभिर्नाड़िकाभिस्तु राशिरेकः प्रकीर्त्तितः ।
दिनं मेषादिमीनान्तैरेकं द्वादशराशिभिः ॥
राशिष्वेतेषु भूतेषु विज्ञातव्या ग्रहोदयाः ।
एकैकस्मिन् भवन्त्यत्र राशौ भूतानि पञ्च च ॥
वायुर्वह्निस्तथा भूमिरापः खमिति पञ्चमम् ।
एकैकस्मिन् पञ्चसूक्ष्माण्युदयन्ति हि तेषु च ॥

यौ द्वौ साक्ष्यधरेन्दुखण्डशिरसौ स्यातां क्रमात् ङेयुतं
कोपेशं नमसाऽन्वितं विरचयेन्मध्ये दलेष्वष्टसु ।
वायव्यान् यपुटान् विलिख्य विधिना शिष्टार्णमन्त्ये दले
यन्त्रं वायुगृहेण वेष्टितमिदं स्यात्तालपत्रे स्थितम् ॥ ५५

सर्वेषामेव राशीनां वायव्याद्या तु नाडिका ।
द्वितीया नाडिकाऽऽग्नेयी तृतीया पार्थिवी मता ॥
चतुर्थी वारुणी ज्ञेया व्योमाख्या पञ्चमी स्मृता ।
पूर्वोदयास्तु सर्वत्र सौम्याः पापास्त्वनन्तराः ॥
राहुः कुजो रविः सौरिरेते दक्षिणतः शुभाः ।
गुरुर्भृगुर्बुधश्चन्द्रः सव्ये सौम्याः शुभावहाः ॥
एवं राशिषु भूतेषु ग्रहोदय उदीरितः । इति ।

भूतोदयमन्यपटले वक्ष्यति ।

नक्षत्रमुहूर्त्तान्युक्तानि ज्योतिःशास्त्रे—

आर्द्राऽश्लेषाऽनुराधा च मघा चैव धनिष्ठिका ।
पूर्वाषाढ़ोत्तराषाढ़े अभिजिद्रोहिणी तथा ॥
ज्येष्ठा विशाखा मूलञ्च नक्षत्रं शततारका ।
उत्तरा पूर्वफल्गुन्यौ दिने पञ्चदश क्षणाः ॥
रात्रावार्द्रा तथा चाष्टौ पूर्वभाद्रपदादयः ।
पुनर्वसुत्रयः पुष्यः श्रुतिस्तिस्रः करादिकाः ॥

श्रुतिः श्रवणा । करादिका हस्तादिकाः । तिस्रः हस्ताचित्रास्वात्यः । एवमग्रेऽपि ज्ञेयम् । अन्ये तु यदा रोहिणीनक्षत्रे राहुर्भवति तदा कर्त्तव्यमित्याहुः ॥ ५४ ॥

वायव्यं यन्त्रमाह यौ द्वाविति । अक्षि इकारः । "असव्यमविशेषोक्तौ" इति परिभाषणात् । अधर एकारः । इन्दुखण्डो बिन्दुः । अक्षि च अधरश्च अक्ष्यधरौ एताभ्यां सह वर्त्तमानौ साक्ष्यधरौ तौ च ताविन्दुखण्डशिरसौ चेति विग्रहः । क्रमादित्यस्ति तेन यिं यें इति । कोपेशं ङेयुतं कोपेशाय । नमसान्वितं नमोयुक्तमिमं मन्त्रं मध्ये कर्णिकायां रचयेल्लिखेत् । वायव्यान् एतत्पटलोक्त-वायुभूतवर्णान् विधिना यपुटान् अक्षरश इत्यर्थः । बिन्द्वन्तानित्यपि । वायुगृहेण "वृत्तं दिवस्तत् षड्बिन्दुलाञ्छितं मातरिश्वनः" इत्युक्तेः षड्बिन्दुलाञ्छितेन वृत्तेन वेष्टयेत् । अत्रापि पूर्ववत् कर्म्म लिखनीयम् ॥ ५५ ॥

स्वात्यां मन्दोदये यन्त्रं वायव्ये निखनेद्रिपोः।
द्वार्य्युच्चाटनकृत् तस्य मृतिर्वा भवति ध्रुवम्॥ ५६

वह्नेर्बीजयुगं क्रमाच्छ्रवणसद्यार्द्धेन्दुयुक् स्यात् स्वरौ
रौः फट्हृन्मनुरेष मध्यविहितः पत्रेषु वज्राङ्कवान्।
वर्णान् वह्निनिरोधितान् प्रविलिखेत् साध्याक्षरैः पोषकै-
रन्यस्त्राऽन्यदले कृशानुपुरगं भूर्जोदरे कल्पितम्॥ ५७

शुभवारर्क्षसंयोगे लाक्षाकुङ्कुमनिर्मितम्।
रक्षाकृत् सर्व्वभूतानां यन्त्रमाग्नेय मीरितम्॥ ५८

घातकाक्षरमिश्रं तत् कृत्तिकायां कुजोदये।
चिताङ्गारेण तद्वस्त्रे लिखितं नाशयेद्रिपुम्॥ ५९

नासार्द्धेन्दुसदम्बु तन्मनुयुतं सार्द्धेन्दुर्ङेन्तो विधु-
र्विध्वन्ते तु भुवे नमो निगदितो मध्ये मनुर्वारुणान्।

स्वात्यां मन्दोदये इति। स्वातीनक्षत्रमुहूर्त्ते यदा मन्दस्य शनैश्चरस्य उदयः जलभूतोदय इत्यर्थः। रिपोर्द्वारि वायव्यं यन्त्रं निखनेदित्यन्वयः। ५६॥

आग्नेयमाह वह्नेरिति। श्रवण उ सद्य ओ अर्द्धेन्दुर्बिन्दुः। क्रमादेतद्युक्तं वह्नेर्बीजयुगं रेफद्वयं तेन रुं रों इति। अन्यत् स्वरूपम् हृन्नमःपदम्। एष मनुर्मन्त्रः मध्यविहितः कर्णिकास्थः। वह्निनिरोधितान् रेफपुटितान् प्रत्यक्षरमिति ज्ञेयम्। अत्र रोध एकाक्षरत्वात् सम्पुटे पर्य्यवस्यति। साध्याक्षरैः पोषकैः साध्यस्य पोषकाक्षरैः "सुसिद्धाः पोषका ज्ञेयाः" इत्युक्तेः सुसिद्धकोष्ठाक्षरैरित्यर्थः। कृशानुपुरगं सस्वस्तिकत्रिकोणमध्यगं घातकाक्षरमिश्रं पोषकाक्षरस्थानमित्यर्थः॥ ५७॥

"वैरिणो घातका मताः" इत्युक्तेः अरिकोष्ठाक्षराणि घातकाक्षराणि। कृत्तिकायां कृत्तिकानक्षत्रमुहूर्त्ते कुजोदये मङ्गलोदये वह्निभूतोदये इत्यर्थः। तद्वस्त्रे चितावस्त्रे। नाशयेदिति गृहादिनिखातम्॥ ५८॥५९॥

वारुणयन्त्रमाह नासेति। नासा ऋः अर्द्धेन्दुर्बिन्दुस्तद्युक्तं अम्बु वः तेन वृँ। तदम्बु वः मनुरौ तद्युतं सार्द्धेन्दुः सबिन्दुः तेन वौं। अत्र मनुशब्देन चतुर्दश मनव इति चतुर्दशसंख्या लक्षिता। तया चतुर्दशस्वरः तेन औकारो मनुशब्दवाच्यः। ङेन्तो विधुर्विधवे। विध्वन्ते विधुशब्दान्ते भुवे तेन विधुभुवे

वर्णान् पत्रपुटेषु वारुणपुटान् साध्यस्य बध्नूचरे
राशिस्थाप्यपुरेण वेष्टितमिदं यन्त्रं भवेद् वारुणम् ॥ ६०

भूर्जपत्रे लिखेदेतत् रक्तचन्दनवारिणा ।
वरुणर्क्षोदये काव्ये यन्त्रं वश्यादिकृद्भवेत् ॥ ६१

गण्डो बिन्दुविभूषितो वसुमती स्यात्तादृशी गण्डयो-
र्मध्यस्थौ तु जगौ लुके नतिरिमं मन्त्रं लिखेन्मध्यतः ।
लान्तान् लार्णपुटीकृतान् वसुमतीवर्णान् दलेष्वालिखेत्
सेवावर्णयुतान् यथाविधि भुवो गेहेन संवेष्टयेत् ॥ ६२

ज्येष्ठायामुदिते सौम्ये हृदि गैरिकनिर्मितम् ।
पार्थिवयन्त्रमचिरात् सर्वत्र स्तम्भकृद्भवेत् ॥ ६३

गुह्याद् गुह्यतरां नित्यां श्रीभूतलिपिदेवताम् ।
यः सेवते शुभैः पुत्रैर्धनधान्यैश्च पूर्य्यते ॥ ६४

नमः इति । अयं मनुर्मन्त्रः मध्ये कर्णिकायां निगदित उक्तः लेख्यत्वेनोक्त इत्यर्थः । वारुणपुटान् वकाराक्षरपुटितान् प्रत्यक्षरं सबिन्दुकान् । आप्यपुरेण पार्श्वद्वयपङ्कजद्वयसहितार्द्धेन्दुना ॥ ६० ॥

वारुणर्क्षं शतभिषा तन्मुहूर्त्ते काव्ये शुक्रे उदिते वह्निभूतोदये इत्यर्थः । वश्यादीत्यादिशब्दात् आकर्षणमोहनादि ॥ ॥६१ ॥

पार्थिवयन्त्रमाह गण्ड इति । बिन्दुभूषितो गण्डः ग्लं । वसुमती लकारः तादृशी बिन्दुमती तेन लं । गण्डयोः वर्णयोः मध्यस्थौ जगौ वर्णौ । तत्र गण्डयो-रिति । अत्र प्रथमं गकारमात्रम् उत्तरत्र परसवर्णयुक् ण्डकारः तेन गजगण्ड इति सिद्धम् । लुके स्वरूपम् । नतिर्नमः । इमं मन्त्रं मध्यतः कर्णिकायां लिखेत् । अत्रैकाक्षरन्यूनत्वाल्लान्तानीत्युक्तम् । तेनाष्टमे दले सबिन्दुलकारत्रयं लेख्य-मित्यर्थः । लार्णपुटीकृतान् प्रत्यक्षरम् । सेवावर्णयुतान् "साध्यास्ते सेवकाः स्मृताः" इत्युक्तेः साध्यस्य साध्यकोष्ठाक्षरैरित्यर्थः । यथाविधीति सबिन्दुका-नित्यर्थः ॥ ६२ ॥

ज्येष्ठायां ज्येष्ठानक्षत्रमुहूर्त्ते सौम्ये बुधे उदिते भूमेरुदये इत्यर्थः । हृदि हृत्-पात्रे । सर्वत्र स्तम्भकृदिति वाय्वग्निजलशुक्रखड्गधारासेनादिस्तम्भनं ज्ञेयम् । तत्र शुक्रादौ धारणं सेनादौ निखननमिति यथायथं सुधीभिर्बोध्यम् ॥ ६३॥६४ ॥

अद्रिर्वरुणसंरुद्धो वदवाग्वादिनि ठद्वयम् ।
वागीश्वर्या दशार्णोऽयं मन्त्रो वाग्विभवप्रदः ॥ ६५

एवं मातृकामन्त्रानुक्त्वा तद्भेदभूतान् सरस्वतीमन्त्रान् वक्तुकामो दशाक्षरं वाग्वादिनीमन्त्रमुद्धरति अद्रिरिति। अद्रिर्दकारः वरुणेन वकारेण संरुद्धः सम्पुटितः तेन वदव इति जातम्। वदवाग्वादिनि स्वरूपम्। ठद्वयं स्वाहा। वाग्विभवो प्रकर्षेण ददातीति वाग्विभवप्रद इति। अनेनास्य विनियोगं दर्शयता बहवो भेदाः सूचिताः। तदुक्तं सारस्वतमते—

तारमायासम्पुटोऽयं महासारस्वतप्रदः। इति।

वाग्बीजमायाद्य आचार्यस्तुतावुद्धृतः।

वाग्बीजं भुवनेश्वरीं वदवदेत्युक्त्वाथ वाग्वादिनि
स्वाहा वर्णविशीर्णपातकभरां ध्यायामि नित्यां गिरम्। इति।

वाग्बीजमायापुटित इति केचित्। मायाद्य इत्यन्ये। तन्त्रान्तरे केवलवाग्भवाद्योऽप्युद्धृतः। अत्रैव शिवशक्तियोग इति केचित्। अपरे वैपरीत्यमपीच्छन्ति। प्रयोगसारे बालादिरप्युद्धृतः। पञ्चप्रणवपुटित एक आदौ मध्ये स्वाहादौ च बालाबीजयुतोऽपरः। वाग्भवपुटितसम्बोधनः परः। बालातार्तीयपुटितसम्बोधनोऽन्यः। कामबीजपुटितसम्बोधनः पञ्चमः। स्वाहादौ बालायुतः षष्ठः। एवमस्या अन्येऽपि भूयांसो भेदास्ते ग्रन्थगौरवभयान्नोक्ताः। स्वस्वगुरुसम्प्रदायात् ज्ञेयाः। तदुक्तमाचार्यैः स्तवे—

आद्यन्त पञ्चप्रणवप्रभिन्नविद्येश्वरि प्रोज्ज्वलशूलहस्ते।
भक्तद्विषां कार्मणयन्त्रविद्याः प्रत्यङ्गिरे त्वं जय संहरन्ति ॥
वीप्सावसाने समसायकेन युक्तां तदादावपि वाग्भवेन।
सम्बोधनान्ते समनुद्विचन्द्रैर्विद्योत्तमां देवि तवानतोऽस्मि ॥
मध्ये स्थितं वाग्भवबीजयोर्वा त्वन्नामसारस्वतसम्पुटं वा।
जात्यापि मूकस्य हठात् कवित्वं वागीशि तन्नौमि यदातनोति ॥
कामेश्वरीसम्पुटिताय नित्यं नारीनराणामपि मोहकाय।
कस्मैचिदस्मै सततं नमोऽस्तु त्वन्नामदेवाय गिरामधीशे ॥
यद्बालया पल्लवितं जडानां त्वन्नामरत्नं रसनाविराजि।
उद्दामकाव्यप्रकरप्रभाभिरुल्लासतेऽस्मै नतिमातनोमि ॥ इति।

अन्ये सम्बोधनान्ते वागीश्वरीति सम्बुद्धिमधिकामाहुः। एषां ध्यानविशेषा गुरुमुखात् ज्ञेयाः। ६५ ॥

ऋषिः कण्वो विराट् छन्दो देवता वाक् समीरिता।
शिरःश्रवणहृङ्नासावदनाम्बुगुदेष्विमान्।
न्यस्याऽर्णान् प्राग्वदङ्गानि मातृकोक्तानि कल्पयेत्॥ ६६

ऋषिरिति। धिषणो वा ऋषिः ज्ञेयः। तदुक्तमीशानशिवेन—

ऋषिस्तु धिषणो मतस्त्वथ परे च कण्वं विदुः। इति।

वागिति बीजं स्वाहेति शक्तिः। ब्रह्म बीजं माया शक्तिः। जीवो बीजं बुद्धिः शक्तिः। उदानो बीजं कुण्डलिनी शक्तिः। इदं सूक्ष्मं बीजादित्रयं सर्व्वमन्त्रेषु ज्ञेयम्। तदुक्तं प्रयोगसारे—

ईश्वरो जगतां बीजं शक्तिर्गुणमयी त्वजा।
परमात्मा तथा बुद्धिर्वायुः कुण्डलिनीति च॥
चतुर्विधे बीजशक्ती सामान्यं त्रितयं त्विदम्। इति।

मन्त्रतन्त्रप्रकाशेऽपि—

चतुर्विधे बीजशक्ती सर्व्वमन्त्रेषु चिन्तयेत्।
त्रितयं तत्र सामान्यं तदिदानीं निरूप्यते॥
ईश्वरो जगतां बीजमाद्यं ब्रह्म तदुच्यते।
तस्य माया समाख्याता शक्तिर्गुणमयी तु या॥
स एव भगवान् देवो बुद्धिसाक्षी द्वितीयकम्।
बीजमत्र समाख्यातं बुद्धिः शक्तिरुदाहृता।
उदानश्चित्समायुक्तस्तृतीयं बीजमुच्यते।
शक्तिः कुण्डलिनी तत्र सामान्यं त्रितयन्त्विदम्॥
ज्ञातव्यं सर्व्वमन्त्रेषु बीजशक्ती ततो निजे॥ इति।

अर्णानिति लिङ्गम्। प्राग्वदिति चतुर्थोक्तप्रकारेण। जातियुक्तानि। अं कं खं गं घं ङं आं हृदयाय नमः इत्यादि। सम्प्रदायविदस्तु अन्यथाऽङ्गानि मन्यन्ते। ॐ क्रां वद ऋग्वेद हृत्। ॐ क्रीं वद यजुर्वेद शिरः। ॐ क्रूं वाक् सामवेद शिखा। ॐ क्रैं वादिनि अथर्व्ववेद वर्म्म। ॐ क्रौं स्वाहा षडङ्ग नेत्रम्। ॐ क्रः समस्तमन्त्रसुखार्थं पुराणन्यायमीमांसाधर्म्मशास्त्रेतिहासकल्पगाथानाराशंसीरिति अस्त्रम्। तदुक्तं सारस्वतमते—

यमनेत्रधरा वह्नियुगलार्घेर्मनोः क्रमात्।
क्रामाद्यैश्चैव वेदाद्यैरङ्गैरङ्गानि कल्पयेत्॥ इति।

पद्मपादाचार्य्यास्तु मातृकाङ्गान्ते वदहृदयाय नम इत्याद्यूचुः॥ ६६॥

तरुणशकलमिन्दोर्बिभ्रती शुभ्रकान्तिः

कुचभरनमिताङ्गी सन्निषण्णा सिताब्जे।

निजकरकमलोद्यल्लेखनीपुस्तकश्रीः

सकलविभवसिद्ध्यै पातु वाग्देवता नः॥ ६७

दशलक्षं जपेन्मन्त्रं दशांशं जुहुयात्ततः।

पुण्डरीकैः पयोभ्यक्तैस्तिलैर्वा मधुराप्लुतैः॥ ६८

मातृकोदीरिते पीठे वागीशीमर्चयेत् सुधीः।

वर्णाब्जेनासनं दद्यान्मूर्त्तिं मूलेन कल्पयेत्॥ ६९

आदावङ्गानि सम्पूज्य पश्चाच्छक्तीरिमा यजेत्।

योगा सत्या च विमला ज्ञाना बुद्धिः स्मृतिः पुनः॥ ७०

मेधा प्रज्ञा च पत्रेषु मुद्रापुस्तकधारिणीः।

दलाग्रेषु समभ्यर्च्या ब्राह्म्याद्यास्ता यथाविधि॥ ७१

लोकपाला बहिः पूज्यास्तेषामस्त्राणि तद्बहिः।

एवं सम्पूजयेन्मन्त्री जपहोमादितत्परः॥ ७२

ब्रह्मचर्य्यरतः शुद्धः शुद्धदन्तनखादिकः।

संस्मरन् सर्व्ववनिताः सततं देवताधिया॥ ७३

तरुणेति। तरुणशकलं बालखण्डम्। करकमलेत्युपमितसमासः। दक्षे लेखनी वामे पुस्तकमित्यायुधध्यानम्॥ ६७॥

सुधीरित्यनेनावाहनादिश्लोकेषु स्त्रीलिङ्गयोग उक्तः। पीठमन्त्रमुद्धरति वर्णाब्जेनेति। ह्सौः वाग्वादिनीयोगपीठाय नम इति प्रयोगः॥ ६८॥६९॥

पश्चाच्छक्तीरिति। पश्चादिति चतुर्थावरणे। तेनादावङ्गावृतिः कर्णिकायाम्। द्वितीया स्वरद्वन्द्वाष्टकेन। तृतीयाऽष्टवर्गैः। चतुर्थी योगादिशक्तिभिः। दक्षिणादित इति यावत्। तासां ध्यानमुक्तमीशानशिवेन—

सपुस्तकजपस्रजो विमलहारमत्युज्ज्वलाः

शशाङ्कसदृशप्रभाः प्रतिदलस्थिताः शक्तयः।

चतुर्थवृतिगा यजेत् कथितदक्षिणाशादिकाः॥ इति।

कवित्वं लभते धीमान् मासैर्द्वादशभिर्ध्रुवम् ।
पीत्वा तन्मन्त्रितं तोयं सहस्रं प्रत्यहं जपेत् ॥ ७४

महाकविर्भवेन्मन्त्री वत्सरेण न संशयः ।
उरोमात्रे जले स्थित्वा ध्यायन्मार्त्तण्डमण्डले ॥ ७५

स्थितां देवीं प्रतिदिनं त्रिसहस्रं जपेन्मनुम् ।
लभते मण्डलात् सिद्धिं वाचामप्रतिमां भुवि ॥ ७६

पलाशबिल्वकुसुमैर्जुहुयान्मधुरोक्षितैः ।
समिद्भिर्वा तदुत्थाभिर्यशः प्राप्नोति वाक्पतेः ॥ ७७

होमोऽयं सर्व्वसौभाग्यलक्ष्मीवश्यप्रदो भवेत् ।
राजवृक्षसमुद्भूतैः प्रसूनैर्मधुराप्लुतैः ॥ ७८

तत्समिद्भिश्च जुहुयात् कवित्वमतुलं लभेत् ।
एवं दशाक्षरी प्रोक्ता सिद्धये वाचमिच्छताम् ॥ ७९

हृदयान्ते भगवति वदशब्दयुगं ततः ।
वाग्देवि वह्निजायान्तं वाग्भवाद्यं समुद्धरेत् ॥ ८०

आचार्य्यास्तु—मातृकोक्तविधिनाऽक्षराम्बुजे । इति ।
यथाविधीति पूर्व्वपटलोक्तध्यानाः । बहिश्चतुरस्रे ॥ ७०॥७१॥७२॥७३ ॥

धीमान् तन्मन्त्रितं तोयं पीत्वा द्वादशभिर्मासैः ध्रुवं कवित्वं लभते इत्यन्वयः । धीमानित्यनेन सप्तवाराभिमन्त्रणं हस्तेन पिधानं सप्तवारं पानञ्च सूचितम् । पाने पूर्व्वोक्तध्यानमनुसन्धेयम् ।

मण्डलादित्येकोनपञ्चाशद्दिवसैरित्यर्थः । सर्व्वसौभाग्यलक्ष्मीवश्यप्रद इति । अत्र सौभाग्यवश्ययोर्बालादित्वं लक्ष्म्यै श्रीबीजादित्वम् एवं पापविमुक्तौ नृसिंह-बीजादित्वमपि ज्ञेयम् इति पद्मपादाचार्य्याः ।

राजवृक्षः श्योनाकः । कल्पाद् यन्त्रमुच्यते—

वाग्बीजगर्भनरसालिख पंक्तियन्त्रपत्रेषु मन्त्रलिपयो लिपिभिः परीतम् ।
आदित्यकाववििभिरिष्टफलप्रदं तद्यन्त्रं भवेत् करधृतं कविताकरञ्च ॥ इति ।

॥ ७४॥७५॥७६॥७७॥७८॥७९ ॥

मन्त्रान्तरमुद्धरति हृदयेति । हृदयान्ते नमोऽन्ते । भगवति स्वरूपम् ।

मनुं षोड़शवर्णाढ्यं वागैश्वर्य्यफलप्रदम् ।
मनोः षड्भिः पदैः कुर्य्यात् षड़ङ्गानि सजातिभिः ॥ ८१

शुभ्रां स्वच्छविलेपमाल्यवसनां शीतांशुखण्डोज्ज्वलां
व्याख्यामक्षगुणं सुधाढ्यकलशं विद्याञ्च हस्ताम्बुजैः ।
बिभ्राणां कमलासनां कुचनतां वाग्देवतां सुस्मितां
वन्दे वाग्विभवप्रदां त्रिनयनां सौभाग्यसम्पत्करीम् ॥ ८२

हविष्याशी जपेत् सम्यक् वसुलक्षमनन्यधीः ।
दशांशं जुहुयादन्ते तिलैराज्यपरिप्लुतैः ॥ ८३
मातृकोक्ते यजेत् पीठे देवीं प्रागीरितक्रमात् ।
पिबेत्तन्मन्त्रितं तोयं प्रातःकाले दिने दिने ॥ ८४
विद्वान् वत्सरतो मन्त्री भवेन्नास्ति विचारणा ।
अभिषिञ्चेज्जलैर्जप्तैरात्मानं स्नानकर्म्मणि ॥ ८५

अत्र नमःशब्दविसर्गस्य रोरुत्वे गुणे च ओकार इति ज्ञेयम् । वदशब्दयुगं वद वद । वाग्देवि स्वरूपम् इति । वदेति शेषः । कीदृक् मनुः । वह्निजाया स्वाहा अन्ते यस्य वाग्भवं वाग्बीजं एतदाद्यं यस्य । अत्र हसयोगोऽपीति केचित् । वैपरीत्यमित्यन्ये । वागैश्वर्य्य फलप्रदमित्यनेन विनियोगं वदता ऋषिबीजादित्वमपि सूचितम् । अत्र बीजशक्ती पूर्व्वोक्ते ज्ञेये । ऋष्यादिकमपि पूर्व्वोक्तमेव । षड्भिः पदैरिति बीजमाद्यं पदं वदवदेति तुर्य्यम् । अन्ये तु वदवदेति पदद्वयम् प्रतिपदमादौ वाग्बीजयोगमाहुः ॥ ८०॥८१ ॥

शुभ्रामिति । व्याख्या व्याख्यानमुद्रा । तल्लक्षणं यथा—

श्लिष्टाग्रेऽङ्गुष्ठतर्जन्यौ प्रसार्य्याऽन्याः प्रदर्शयेत् ।
प्रयोज्याऽभिमुखं सैषा मुद्रा व्याख्यानसंज्ञिता ॥ इति ।

अक्षगुणम् अक्षमालाम् । विद्यां पुस्तकम् । दक्षोर्द्ध्वतो वामोर्द्ध्वपर्य्यन्तम् आयुधध्यानम् । कमलासनामिति श्वेतकमलस्थाम् ॥ ८२ ॥

सम्यगिति वक्ष्यमाणः पुरश्चरणनियम उक्तः । वसुलक्षमष्टलक्षम् । अनन्यधीर्मन्त्रार्थदत्तमनाः ।

तदुक्तम्—जपतु मन्त्रमनन्यसंस्मृतिर्यथाविधि । इति ।

तर्पयेत्तां जलैः शुद्धैरतिमेधामवाप्नुयात् ।
पुष्पगन्धादिकं सर्व्वं तज्जप्तं धारयेत् सुधीः ।
सभायां पूज्यते सद्भिर्वादे च विजयी भवेत् ॥ ८६

तारो मायाऽधरो बिन्दुः शक्तिस्तारं सरस्वती ।
ङेऽन्ता नत्यन्तिको मन्त्रः प्रोक्त एकादशाक्षरः ॥ ८७

ब्रह्मरन्ध्रे भ्रुवोर्मध्ये नवरन्ध्रेषु च क्रमात्
मन्त्रवर्णान् न्यसेन्मन्त्री वाग्भवेनाऽङ्गकल्पना ॥ ८८

वाणीं पूर्णनिशाकरोज्ज्वलमुखीं कर्पूरकुन्दप्रभां
चन्द्रार्द्धाङ्कितमस्तकां निजकरैः संबिभ्रतीमादरात् ।
वीणामक्षगुणं सुधाढ्यकलशं विद्याञ्च तुङ्गस्तनीं
दिव्यैराभरणैर्विभूषिततनुं हंसाधिरूढ़ां भजे ॥ ८९

जपेद् द्वादशलक्षाणि तत्सहस्रं सिताम्बुजैः ।
नागचम्पकपुष्पैर्वा जुहुयात् साधकोत्तमः ॥ ९०

प्रागोरितेति दशाचार्य्योक्तमार्गेण । पिबेदिति पूर्व्वोक्तमनुसन्धेयम् । पुष्पगन्धादि-कमित्यत्र कामादित्वं ज्ञेयम् । तज्जप्तमिति सप्तवारम् । अभिषिञ्चेदित्यादि अवाप्नुयादित्यन्तमेकः प्रयोगः ॥ ८३॥८४॥८५॥८६ ॥

हंसवागीश्वरीमन्त्रमुद्धरति तार इति । तारः प्रणवः । माया भुवनेशी-बीजम् । अधर ऐ बिन्दुश्च तेन वाग्भवम् । सरस्वती ङेन्ता सरस्वत्यै । नत्यन्तिको नमोऽन्तः । अत्र वाग्भवे ह्सयोग माहुः । केचित् परे सह योगमिच्छन्ति । वाग्भवं बीजं माया शक्तिः । अन्ये प्रणवं बीजमाहुः । ऋषिः पूर्व्वोक्तः । त्रिष्टुप् छन्दः । हंसवागीश्वरी देवता । नवरन्ध्रेषु कर्णनेत्रनासाद्वयमुखलिङ्गगुदेषु । मन्त्री क्रमादित्यनेनोक्तम् । वाग्भवेनेति तारमायासम्पुटेनेति परमगुरवः । अन्ये तु वाग्भवाद्येन षड़् दीर्घयुक्त मायाबीजेनेत्याहुः ॥ ८७॥८८ ॥

वाणीमिति । क्वचिन्मुद्रामिति पाठः । यदा विद्यामिति पाठः तदा आयुध-ध्यानं पूर्व्ववत् । द्वितीयपाठे दक्षोर्द्धादि अक्षस्रक्-मुद्रे अन्यत्रान्ये ॥ ८९ ॥

साधकोत्तम इत्यनेन जपाव्यवधानेन नियमस्थ एव होमं कुर्य्यादित्युक्तम् । वर्णाब्जेनेति ह्सौः हंस वागीश्वरीयोगपीठाय नम इति प्रयोगः ॥ ९० ॥

मातृकोक्ते यजेत् पीठे वक्ष्यमाणक्रमेण ताम् ।
वर्णाब्जेनासनं कुर्य्यान्मूर्त्तिं मूलेन कल्पयेत् ॥ ८१
देव्या दक्षिणतः पूज्या संस्कृता वाङ्मयी ततः ।
प्राकृता वामतः पूज्या वाङ्मयी सर्व्वसिद्धिदा ॥ ८२
इष्ट्वा पूर्व्ववदङ्गानि प्रज्ञाद्याः पूजयेत्ततः ।
प्रज्ञा मेधा श्रुतिः शक्तिः स्मृतिर्वागीश्वरी मतिः ॥ ८३
स्वस्तिश्चेति समाख्याता ब्राह्म्याद्यास्तदनन्तरम् ।
लोकेशानर्च्चयेद् भूयस्तदस्त्राणि च तद्बहिः ॥ ८४
इति सम्पूजयेद्देवीं साक्षाद्वाग्वल्लभो भवेत् ।
दशाक्षरीसमुक्तानि कर्म्माण्यत्रापि साधयेत् ।
पूजनं पूर्व्ववत् कुर्य्यादत्रापि साधकोत्तमः ॥ ८५
वाचस्पतेऽमृते भूयः प्लुवः प्लुरिति कीर्त्तयेत् ।
वागाद्यो मुनिभिः प्रोक्तो रुद्रसंख्याक्षरो मनुः ॥ ८६
कुर्य्यादङ्गानि विधिवद्वागाद्यैः पञ्चभिः पदैः ।
मातृकां विन्यसेत् पूर्व्वं पूर्व्ववत्तां यथाविधि ॥ ८७

पूज्या संस्कृतेति । एतयोर्ध्यानमुक्तं सारस्वतमते—

दक्षिणे संस्कृता पूज्या योगमुद्राकरद्वया ।
सततं निःसरच्छब्दवदनाऽन्या च वामतः ॥ इति ॥ ८१॥८२ ॥

पूर्व्ववदिति तुर्य्योक्तरीत्या केसरेषु । वाग्वल्लभ इत्यनेन विनियोग उक्तः । ॥ ८३॥८४॥८५ ॥

मन्त्रान्तरमुद्धरति वाचेति । वागाद्यो वाग्भवाद्यः । एकादशाक्षर इत्युक्तेः अमृते परे पूर्व्वेण सन्धिः न मन्त्रे । तदुक्तं नारायणीये—

वाक्कूर्म्मः पार्श्वयुक् शुक्रं ति केशान्ते मृते प्लुवः ।
प्लुरन्ता दशवर्णेयं विद्या मुख्या सरस्वती ॥ इति ।

ऐं बीजं प्लुः शक्तिः । पूर्व्वोक्तमृष्यादिकं कुर्य्यादिति । अत्र वाग्भवेन द्वत् मन्त्रैश्चतुर्भिः पदैश्चत्वार्य्यङ्गानि । विधिवदिति । अनेन समस्तेनास्त्रमित्युक्तं भवति ।

आसीना कमले करैर्जपवटीं पद्मद्वयं पुस्तकं
बिभ्राणा तरुणेन्दुबद्धमुकुटा मुक्तेन्दुकुन्दप्रभा ।
भालोन्मीलितलोचना कुचभराक्रान्ता भवद्भूतये
भूयाद् वागधिदेवता मुनिगणैरासेव्यमानाऽनिशम् ॥ ९८

रुद्रलक्षं जपेन्मन्त्रं दशांशं जुहुयाद् घृतैः ।
मातृकाकल्पिते पीठे पूजयेत्तां यथा पुरा ॥ ९९
पलाशकुसुमैर्हुत्वा परां सिद्धिमवाप्नुयात् ।
कदम्बकुसुमैस्तद्वत् फलैः श्रीवृक्षसम्भवैः ॥ १००
अचिराच्छ्रियमाप्नोति वाचां कुन्दसमुद्भवैः ।
नन्द्यावर्त्तप्रसूनैर्वा हुत्वा वाग्वल्लभो भवेत् ॥ १०१
ब्राह्मीरसे वचाकल्के कपिलाज्यं पचेज्जपन् ।
पिबेद्दिनादौ तन्नित्यं सर्व्वशास्त्रार्थविद्भवेत् ॥ १०२

ननु पञ्चभिः पदैः कुर्य्यादङ्गानि इत्युक्तेरत्र पञ्चाङ्गमेवास्तीति केचित् । नैतत् सारम् । यतः कुर्य्यादाङ्गानीति विधिना षडङ्गमेव प्राप्तम् । तत्कथनाकाङ्क्षायां पञ्चभिः पदैरित्युक्तिः । वागाद्यैरिति क्रमार्थम् । पदैरित्येतावत्युच्यमानेऽत्र षट् तानि कथमिति सन्देह एव स्यात् । तत्र गोपनेन व्यस्तसमस्तं बोधयितुं विधिवदित्युक्तिः पञ्चभिरित्यनेन प्रधानबाधायोगाच्च । किञ्च यत्र तथैवेष्टं तत्र तथैव विधास्यति । मन्त्रस्य पञ्चाङ्गमिति कल्पयेदित्यादिना ॥ ८६॥८७ ॥

कमले इति सिते । दक्षाधस्ताद्वामाधः पर्य्यन्तमायुधध्यानम् ॥ ९८ ॥

रुद्रलक्षमेकादशलक्षम् । यथा पुरेत्येकादशाचर्य्युक्तमार्गेण । तद्वदिति वाक्सिद्धिमाप्नुयादित्यर्थः । अचिराद् वाचां श्रियं वाक्सम्पदं प्राप्नोतीति सम्बन्धः । नन्द्यावर्त्तो गन्धतगरः । वेति कुन्दसमुद्भवैरित्यनेन विकल्पः ॥ ९९॥१००॥१०१ ॥

ब्राह्मीरस इति । अत्रापि स्वरसपाक इति कृत्वा घृतस्याष्टमांशः स्वकल्कः घृत चतुर्गुणो ब्राह्मीरसः । अन्यत् पूर्व्ववत् । वचाकल्प इति क्वचित् पाठः । जपन् पचेदिति सम्बन्धः । अनया विद्यया जप्तं सप्तवासरमिति शेषः । नित्यं दिनादौ पिबेदिति त्रिवर्षं पञ्चवर्षं वा । अनया विद्ययेत्यादि सर्व्वं ब्राह्मीपक्षेऽपि योजनीयम् । सर्व्वेत्यादि मेधावीत्यादि उभयमुभयस्य फलं समयप्रमाणभेदेन । तदुक्तं

अनया विद्यया जप्तं ब्राह्मीपत्रं प्रभक्षयेत् ।
न विस्मरति मेधावी श्रुतान् वेदागमान् पुनः ।
बहुना किमियं विद्या जपतां कामदो मणिः ॥ १०३
तोयस्थं शयनं विष्णोः सकेवलचतुर्मुखः ।
बिन्द्वर्धीशयुतो वह्निर्बिन्दुसद्योऽम्बुसान् भृगुः ॥ १०४
उक्तानि त्रीणि बीजानि सद्भिः सारस्वतार्थिनाम् ।
अङ्गानि कल्पयेद् बीजैर्द्विरुक्तैर्जातिसंयुतैः ॥ १०५

नारायणीये—

ब्राह्मीरसस्य कपिलाज्ययुतं प्रभाते जप्तं तया पिबति यश्चुलुकं त्रिवर्षम् ।
एकोदितं स खलु धारयति त्रिरुक्तं पञ्चाब्दतो मुखभ्रष्टं न तु विस्मरेत्तत् ॥
तत्पञ्चवादनमपि स्मृतमेवम् । इति ।

कामदो मणिरिति । अनेनैतत् सूचितम् ।

एतज्जप्तं सुवीरजमपास्यति नेत्ररोगम् । इति ।
सूत्राशी त्रिधिलक्षं जप्त्वा योऽङ्कोलसर्पिषा जुहुयात् ।
अष्टसहस्रं वेत्ति स भूतं भव्यं भविष्यञ्च । इत्यादिकम् ॥१०२॥१०३॥

मन्त्रान्तरमुद्धरति तोयस्थमिति । विष्णोः शयनमनन्त आकारः । तोयस्थं वकारस्थं तेन वा । चतुर्मुखः ककारः सकेवलः स्वररहितः तेन वाक् । अयमेव मन्त्रांश इति केचित् । तदुक्तं नारायणीये—

खड्गीशो यः प्रांशुकः सान्तवेधाः कर्णान्तस्थो यः सदण्डो भुजङ्गः ।
साम्बो दन्तो बिन्दुमान् यो भृगुः स्युर्वागीश्वर्यास्त्रीणि बीजान्यमूनि ॥ इति ॥
तद्योकाकारेण वागिति मन्त्रांश उक्तः । अन्ये तु चतुर्मुखः कः सकेवलः बिन्दुमान् तेन कां । एवं सबिन्दुकस्य बीजत्वमुपपद्यत इति ते वदन्ति ।

सम्प्रदायविदस्तु पूर्वोद्धृतं यत् वाक्पदं तल्लक्षितं वाग्भवबीजमित्याहुः । एवं बीजत्वमप्युपपन्नं सारस्वतञ्च भवति । अन्ये तु प्रकारान्तरेण वाग्भवबीजोद्धारं कुर्वन्ति । विष्णोस्तोयस्थं शयनम् आकारः कशब्देन शिरस्तेन अकारः इ इति स्वरूपम् । कश्च इश्चेति समासे के इति पदम् । कीदृक् शयनं सके केसहितं वलनं वलः संमेलनं तस्मिन् जाते चतुर्मुखः कः तेन शिरः । ततो बिन्दुरिति । अर्धीश ऊ वह्नी रेफः सद्य ओकारः अम्बु वकारः भृगुः सकारः । सारस्वतार्थिनामित्यनेन विनियोग उक्तः । आद्यं बीजं अन्त्यं शक्तिः पूर्वोक्तमृष्यादिकम् । १०५ ॥

मुक्ताहारावदातां शिरसि शशिकलालङ्कृतां बाहुभिः स्वै-
र्व्याख्यां वर्णाक्षमालां मणिमयकलशं पुस्तकञ्चोद्वहन्तीम् ।
आपीनोत्तुङ्गवक्षोरुहभरविनमन्मध्यदेशामधीशां
वाचामीडे चिराय त्रिभुवननमितां पुण्डरीके निषण्णाम् ॥ १०६

त्रिलक्षं प्रजपेन्मन्त्रं जुहुयात्तद्दशांशतः ।
पायसेनाज्यसिक्तेन संस्कृते हव्यवाहने ॥ १०७
वागीशीं पूजयेत् पीठे विधिना मातृकोदिते ।
प्राक्प्रस्तुतेन मार्गेण प्रत्यहं साधकोत्तमः ॥ १०८
व्याघातकुसुमैर्हुत्वा वाक्सिद्धिमतुलां लभेत् ।
जातिपुष्पैः सिताम्भोजैः सिक्तैश्चन्दनवारिणा ॥ १०९
नन्द्यावर्त्तैः शुभैः कुन्दैर्हुत्वा वाक्सिद्धिमाप्नुयात् ।
जपन् बीजत्रयं मन्त्री सभायां जयमाप्नुयात् ॥ ११०
सितां वचां वा ब्राह्मीं वा जप्तां खादेद्दिने दिने ।
मेधां काममवाप्नोति साधको नात्र संशयः ॥ १११
एवमुक्तेषु मन्त्रेषु दीक्षितो यतमानसः ।
एवं यो भजते भक्त्या स भवेद्भुक्तिमुक्तिभाक् ॥ ११२
सुसितैर्गन्धकुसुमैः पूजा सारस्वते विधौ ।
दूर्वा बीजाङ्कुरं पुष्पं राजवृक्षसमुद्भवम् ॥ ११३

मुक्तेति । व्याख्या व्याख्यानमुद्रा पूर्वोक्ता । दक्षोर्द्धतो वामोर्द्धपर्य्यन्तमायुध-ध्यानम् । १०६ ॥

विधिनेति वक्ष्यमाण श्वेतगन्धपुष्पादिना । प्राक्प्रस्तुतेनेति एकादशाध्यायोक्त-मार्गेणेत्यर्थः । साधकोत्तमः सरस्वत्युपासकसमयस्थ इत्यर्थः । व्याघातो राजवृक्षः "आरग्वधो दीर्घफलो व्याघातश्चतुरङ्गुलः" इति कोषः । नन्द्यावर्त्तैर्गन्धतगरैः । शुभैः सुगन्धिभिरिति कुन्दविशेषणम् । काममत्यर्थम् । दीक्षित इति ग्रन्थकृदुक्तप्रकारेणेत्यर्थः ॥ १०७॥१०८॥१०९॥११०॥१११॥११२ ॥

सारस्वतसमयानाह सुसितैरिति । बीजाङ्कुरं यवाङ्कुरम् । सिन्धुवारो निर्गुण्डी ।

उत्पलानि प्रशस्तानि सिन्धुवाराङ्कुराणि च ।
भजन् सरस्वतीं नित्यमेतानि परिवर्जयेत् ॥ ११४
आघ्रातं गृञ्जनं बिल्वं करञ्जं लशुनन्तथा ।
तैलं पलाण्डुं पिण्याकं शाङ्गाष्टमपि भोजने ॥ ११५
सर्व्वं पर्य्युषितं त्याज्यं सदा सारस्वतार्थिना ।
नाचरेन्निशि ताम्बूलं स्त्रियं गच्छेद्दिवा न च ॥ ११६
न सन्ध्ययोः स्वपेज्जातु नाशुचिः किञ्चिदुच्चरेत् ।
प्रदोषेषु भवेन्मौनी दिग्वस्त्रां न विलोकयेत् ॥ ११७
न पुष्पितां स्त्रियं गच्छेन्न निन्देद्वामलोचनाम् ।
न मृषा वचनं ब्रूयान्नाक्रामेत् पुस्तकं सुधीः ॥ ११८
अक्षराढ्यानि पत्राणि नोपेक्षेत न लङ्घयेत् ।
चतुर्दश्यष्टमीपर्व्वप्रतिपद्ग्रहणेषु च ॥ ११९
संक्रमेषु च सर्व्वेषु विद्यां नैव पठेद् बुधः ।
व्याख्याने सन्त्यजेन्निद्रामालस्यं जृम्भनं पुनः ॥ १२०
क्रोधं निष्ठीवनं तद्वन्नीचाङ्गस्पर्शनन्तथा ।
मनुष्यसर्पमार्जारमण्डूकनकुलादयः ॥ १२१

एतानि वक्ष्यमाणानि भोजने परिवर्जयेदिति सम्बन्धः । आघ्रातं अवार इति कान्यकुब्जभाषायाम् । गृञ्जनं गाजर इति प्रसिद्धम् । कलञ्जं कृष्णबीजः फलविशेषः कलिङ्गड़ इति गुर्जरभाषायां खर्बुजा इति गौड़भाषायाम् । रोड इति कान्यकुब्जभाषायाम् । तैलं प्रत्यक्षं व्यञ्जनाद्यसम्पृक्तम् । शाङ्गाष्टं सिंघाड़ इति कान्यकुब्जभाषायाम् । साङ्गुष्ठमित्यपपाठः साङ्गुष्ठभोजनस्य विहितत्वात् । यदाहुः—

दानं प्रतिग्रहो होमो भोजनं बलिरेव च ।
साङ्गुष्ठेन सदा कार्य्यमसुरेभ्योऽन्यथा भवेत् ॥ इति ।

सर्व्वं पर्य्युषितं घृतपक्वमपि । नाचरेन्निशि ताम्बूलमित्यस्यायमर्थः । रात्रौ मुखे ताम्बूलं कृत्वा न शयनं कार्य्यमित्यर्थः । स्मृतिरपि—"ताम्बूलं वदनात् त्यजेत्" इति । दिग्वस्त्रां नग्नां स्वीयामपि ॥ ११३॥११४॥११५॥११६॥११७॥११८॥११९॥१२० ॥

अन्तरा यदि गच्छेयुस्तदा व्याख्यां परित्यजेत् ।
निशासु दीपभ्रंशे च सद्यः पाठं परित्यजेत् ॥ १२२

ज्ञात्वा दोषानिमान् सम्यक् भक्त्या यो भारतीं भजेत् ।
वाचां सिद्धिमवाप्नोति वाचस्पतिरिवापरः ॥ १२३

॥ श्रीँ ह्रीँ ॥

इति श्रीशारदातिलके सप्तमः पटलः ॥

शौचाङ्गानि नाभ्यधोवर्त्तीनि । आदिशब्दात् पत्त्रादयः ॥ १२१॥१२२॥१२३ ॥

इति श्रीशारदातिलकटीकायां सत्सम्प्रदायकृतव्याख्यायां
पदार्थादर्शाभिख्यायां सप्तमः पटलः ॥ ॐ ॥

अष्टमः पटलः ।

अथ वक्ष्ये श्रियो मन्त्रान् श्रीसौभाग्यफलप्रदान् ।
यस्याः कटाक्षमात्रेण त्रैलोक्यमभिवर्द्धते ॥ १

वान्तं वह्निसमारूढं वामनेत्रेन्दुसंयुतम् ।
बीजमेतच्छ्रियः प्रोक्तं चिन्तामणिरिवापरः ॥ २

ऋषिर्भृगुर्निवृच्छन्दो देवता श्रीः समीरिता ।
षड्दीर्घयुक्तबीजेन कुर्य्यादङ्गानि षट् क्रमात् ॥ ३

अथ प्रकारपञ्चके केन चित् प्रकारेण मन्त्राणां वक्तव्यत्वे प्राप्तेऽत्र शक्तिमन्त्राणां प्रकृतत्वात् शक्तिमन्त्रादित्वेन वक्तुमिच्छन् ब्रह्मशक्तिवाचकान् सरस्वतीमन्त्रान् उक्त्वा विष्णुशक्तिवाचकान् लक्ष्मीमन्त्रान् वक्तुमुपक्रमते अथेति । श्रीसौभाग्येति विनियोगोक्तिः । त्रैलोक्यमिति लक्षणया त्रैलोक्यनिवासिजना उच्यन्ते ।
यदु विष्णुपुराणम्—स श्लाघ्यः स गुणी धन्यः स कुलीनः स बुद्धिमान् ।
स शूरः स च विक्रान्तो यस्त्वया देवि वीक्षितः ॥ इति । १ ॥

मन्त्रमुद्धरति वान्तमिति । वान्तं शः वह्नी रेफ वामनेत्रं ईकारः इन्दुर्बिन्दुः । चिन्तामणिरित्यनेनैतदुक्तं भवति प्रणवादित्वं शक्त्यादित्वं वा वागादित्वं वा कामादित्वं वा तत्तद्योगे तत्तद्देवतानामुपसर्जनत्वञ्च । यथा प्रणवादित्वे परमात्मस्वरूपिणी श्रीर्देवता एवं शक्त्यादित्वे शक्तिस्वरूपिणी श्रीर्देवता इत्यादि । शकारो बीजम् ईकारः शक्तिः । षड्दीर्घेति क्लीबरहितैः । नेत्राभ्यां वौषडिति पञ्चमाङ्गे प्रयोगः । तेन यत्र यत्र नेत्रद्वयं तत्र तत्रायं प्रयोगो ज्ञेयः । तन्त्रान्तरे पञ्चाङ्गान्युक्तानि । महाश्रियै महाविद्युत्प्रभे स्वाहा हृत् । श्रियै विजयै स्वाहा शिरः । गौरि महाबले बन्ध बन्ध स्वाहा शिखा । धृतिः स्वाहा वर्म्म । महाकायै पद्महस्ते हुँ फट् अस्त्रम् इति । कल्पान्तरे तु श्रियै स्वाहा हृत् । श्रीँ फट् शिरः । श्रीँ नमः शिखा । श्रियै प्रसीद नमः वर्म्म । श्रीँ फट् अस्त्रम् । इति पञ्चाङ्गम् । उक्तञ्च नारायणीये—अस्याङ्गानि द्विधोक्तानि तयोरेकं समाश्रयेत् । इति । क्रमादित्यनेन शक्त्यादियोगे दीर्घप्रयोगः प्रणवादित्वे तद्योग इति सूचितम् ॥२॥३॥

कान्त्या काञ्चनसन्निभां हिमगिरिप्रख्यैश्चतुर्भिर्गजै-
र्हस्तोत्क्षिप्तहिरण्मयामृतघटैरासिच्यमानां श्रियम्।
बिभ्राणां वरमब्जयुग्ममभयं हस्तैः किरीटोज्ज्वलां
क्षौमाबद्धनितम्बबिम्बलसितां वन्देऽरविन्दस्थिताम्॥ ४

भानुलक्षं जपेन्मन्त्री दीक्षितो विजितेन्द्रियः।
श्रियमभ्यर्चयेन्नित्यं सुगन्धिकुसुमादिभिः॥ ५
तत्सहस्रं प्रजुहुयात् कमलैर्मधुरोक्षितैः।
जपान्ते जुहुयान्मन्त्री तिलैर्वा मधुराप्लुतैः॥ ६
बिल्वैः फलैर्वा जुहुयात् त्रिभिर्वा साधकोत्तमः।
अत्र सम्यग् यजेत् पीठं नवशक्तिसमन्वितम्॥ ७
विभूतिरुन्नतिः कान्तिः सृष्टिः कीर्त्तिश्च सन्नतिः।
पुष्टिरुत्कृष्टिर्ऋद्धिश्च संप्रोक्ता नव शक्तयः॥ ८

कान्त्येति। हिमगिरीति उच्चत्वं श्वेत्यञ्च। अरविन्देति श्वेतम्। इदं सर्व्वं श्रीमन्त्रे ज्ञेयम्। वामाधस्तात् दक्षाधस्तनपर्य्यन्तम् आयुधध्यानम्। तदुक्तं नारायणीये—चतुर्भुजां सुवर्णाभां सपद्मोर्द्ध्वभुजद्वयाम्।
दक्षिणाभयहस्तां तां वामहस्तवरप्रदाम्। इति।

अत्र ध्यानानन्तरं लक्ष्मीमुद्रा दर्शनीया।
चक्रमुद्रां तथा बद्ध्वा मध्यमे द्वे प्रसार्य्य च।
कनिष्ठिके तथानीय तदग्रेऽङ्गुष्ठकौ क्षिपेत्।
लक्ष्मीमुद्रा परा ह्येषा सर्व्वसम्पत्प्रदायिका॥ इति।

इयञ्च सर्व्वलक्ष्मीमन्त्रसाधारणीति ज्ञेयम्॥ ४॥

भानुलक्षं द्वादशलक्षम्। मन्त्रीत्यनेन नारायणाष्टाक्षरस्य शेषतया दशांशजप उक्तः। अतएव वक्ष्यति विष्णुभक्तो दृढ़व्रतः इति। जपान्त इत्यनेन जपाव्यवधाने तन्नियमत्वेन होमः कार्य्य इत्युक्तं भवति। त्रिभिर्वेति समुच्चितचतुर्थः पक्षः। तत्राप्येकैकेन द्रव्येण सहस्रचतुष्कं होतव्यम्। अथवा त्रिभिः साधकोत्तमो जुहुयात् इत्यनेन कमलवासिनीमहालक्ष्मीश्रीसूक्तैः सकृत् सकृत् हुत्वा पश्चान्मूलेन होतव्यमित्युक्तम् भवति। साधकोत्तम इति काकाक्षिगोलकन्यायेन उभयत्र

मन्त्रावाह्य यजेद्देवीं परिवारैः समन्विताम् ।
बीजाद्यमासनं दत्त्वा मूर्त्तिं मूलेन कल्पयेत् ॥ ९
यजेत् पूर्व्ववदङ्गानि दिग्दलेष्वर्चयेत्ततः ।
वासुदेवं सङ्कर्षणं प्रद्युम्नमनिरुद्धकम् ॥ १०
हिमपीततमालेन्द्रनीलाभान् पीतवाससः ।
शङ्खचक्रगदापद्मधारिणस्तान् चतुर्भुजान् ॥ ११
विदिग्गतेषु पत्रेषु दमकादीन् यजेद् गजान् ।
दमकं सलिलञ्चैव गुग्गुलुञ्च कुरुण्टकम् ॥ १२

लक्ष्यते। साधकोत्तमोऽत्र सम्यगित्यनेनैतत् सूचितं भवति। श्रीपूजायां मण्डूकादि परतत्त्वान्तं चतुर्थपटलोक्तरीत्या अभ्यर्च्य श्रीबीजाद्या नव पीठशक्तयः प्रागादिदिक्षु मध्ये च पूज्याः ॥ ५॥६॥७॥८ ॥

अत्रेत्यष्टपत्रे श्रीबीजकर्णिके ।
तदुक्तमाचार्य्यैः—रुचिराष्टपत्रमथ वारिरुहम् । इति ।
पद्मपादाचार्य्यैर्व्याख्यातं श्रीबीजयोगः कर्णिकायां रुचिरत्वम् इति ।
संहितायामपि—अष्टपत्रं लिखेद् यन्त्रं बहिर्भूबिम्बभूषितम् ।
मध्ये बीजं विनिक्षिप्य । इति ।

पीठमन्त्रमुद्धरति बीजाद्यमिति। श्रीँ सर्व्वशक्तिकमलासनाय नमः इति पीठमन्त्रः सर्व्वश्रीमन्त्रसाधारण इति ज्ञेयम् । पद्मपादाचार्य्यैस्तु श्रीँ श्रीदेव्यासनाय नमः श्रीँ श्रीदेवीमूर्त्तये नमः इति पीठमूर्त्तिमन्त्रावुक्तौ। अत्र पद्मं श्वेतं ध्येयम् । तदुक्तं प्रयोगसारे—

सङ्कल्प्याम्भोरुहं शुभ्रं कर्णिकायां यजेच्छ्रियम् । इति । ९ ॥

पूर्व्ववदिति चतुर्थपटलोक्तरीत्या केसरेषु। वासुदेवादीनामायुधध्यानं नारायणमन्त्रे वक्ष्यमाणमनुसन्धेयम् ॥ १०॥११ ॥

विदिग्गतेष्विति वास्तवदिगपेक्षया। यत्तु नारायणीये—
आग्नेयादिषु पत्रेषु गुग्गुलुश्च कुरुण्टकः ।
दमकः सलिलश्चेति हस्तिनो रजतप्रभाः ॥
हेमकुम्भधरा ध्येयाः । इति
तत्र प्रसिद्धाग्नेयदिशमङ्गीकृत्येत्यवधेयम् ॥ १२ ॥

यजेच्छङ्खनिधिं देव्या दक्षिणे दयितान्विताम् ।
मुक्तामाणिक्यसङ्काशौ किञ्चित्स्मितमुखाम्बुजौ ॥ १३
अन्योन्यालिङ्गनपरौ शङ्खपङ्कजधारिणौ ।
विगलद्रत्नवर्षाभ्यां शङ्खाभ्यां मूर्ध्नि लाञ्छितौ ॥ १४
तुन्दिलं कम्बुकनिधिं वसुधारां घनस्तनीम् ।
वामतः पङ्कजनिधिं प्रियया सहितं यजेत् ॥ १५
सिन्दूराभौ भुजाश्लिष्टौ रक्तपद्मोत्पलान्वितौ ।
निःसरद्रत्नधाराभ्यां पद्माभ्यां मूर्ध्नि लाञ्छितौ ॥ १६
तुन्दिलं पङ्कजनिधिं तन्वीं वसुमतीमपि ।
दलाग्रेषु यजेदेता बलाक्याद्याः समन्ततः ॥ १७
बलाकी विमला चैव कमला वनमालिका ।
विभीषिका मालिका च शाङ्करी वसुमालिका ॥ १८
पङ्कजद्वयधारिण्यो मुक्ताहारसमप्रभाः ।
लोकेशानर्चयेदन्ते वज्राद्यस्त्राणि तद्बहिः ॥ १९

देव्या दक्षिणे वामत इति कर्णिकायाः । मुक्तामाणिक्येति क्रमेण शङ्खनिधि-वसुधारयोः वर्णौ । शङ्खपङ्कजधारिणावित्युभयमुभयत्र । एवमग्रेऽपि । आयुध-ध्यानमेषां दद्यादि । कम्बुकनिधिं शङ्खनिधिम् । वसुधारामिति शङ्खनिधि-शक्तिनाम । घनस्तनीमित्यन्तं पूर्वं ध्यानम् । पङ्कजनिधिं पद्मनिधिम् । वसुमती-मिति पङ्कजनिधिशक्तिनाम । अपिशब्दाद्यं घनस्तनीमित्यपि । एतदन्तं द्वितीयावरणमूर्तीः चतुष्कनिधियुगैरपरैरित्युक्तं ॥ १३॥१४॥१५॥१६॥१७ ॥

बलाकीति । आसां ध्यानं नारायणीये—

बलाकीं वामनां श्यामां श्वेतपङ्कजधारिणीम् ।
अर्द्धबाहुद्वयां ध्यायेत् श्रीदूतीं द्वारि पूर्व्वतः ॥
अर्द्धोक्तेन हस्तेन रक्तपङ्कजधारिणीम् ।
श्वेताङ्गीं दक्षिणे द्वारि चिन्तयेद्वनमालिकाम् ॥
हरितां दोर्द्वयेनोर्द्धमुद्वहन्तीं सिताम्बुजम् ।
ध्यायेद् विभीषिकां भक्त्या श्रीदूतीं द्वारि पश्चिमे ॥

इत्थं यो भजते देवीं विधिना साधकोत्तमः ।
धनधान्यसमृद्धिः स्याच्छ्रियमाप्नोत्यनिन्दिताम् ॥ २०
नाभिप्रमाणे सलिले स्थित्वा मन्त्रमिमं जपेत् ।
त्रिलक्षं प्रयतो मन्त्री देवीं ध्यात्वाऽर्कमण्डले ॥ २१
स भवेदल्पकालेन रमाया वसतिः स्थिरा ।
विष्णुगेहस्थबिल्वस्य मूलमास्थाय मन्त्रवित् ॥ २२
त्रिलक्षं प्रजपेन्मन्त्रं वाञ्छितं लभते धनम् ।
अशोकवह्नौ जुहुयात्तण्डुलैराज्यलोडितैः ॥ २३
वशयत्यचिरादेव त्रैलोक्यमपि मन्त्रवित् ।
जुहुयात्तण्डुलैः शुद्धैरर्काग्नौ नियुतं वशी ॥ २४
राज्यश्रियमवाप्नोति राजपुत्रो महौजसाम् ।
जुहुयात् खादिरे वह्नौ तण्डुलैर्मधुरोक्षितैः ॥ २५

तथाऽक्षमालाष्टग् ज्ञेया चोड्डाभाऽन्यत्र शाङ्करी । इति ।

प्रयोगसारे—विमला कमला चाथ मालिका वनमालिका ।
कोष्ठे विदिक्षु सम्पूज्या दूतीरेताः । इति ।

अत्र तु कमलावनमालिकयोर्व्यत्यासः कल्पान्तरत्वेन समाधेयः ॥ १८॥१९ ॥

विधिना साधकोत्तम इत्यनेनावाहनादि श्लोकेषु पञ्चाङ्गयोग उक्तः ॥ २० ॥

प्रयतो मन्त्रीत्यनेन श्रीँ रक्तगर्भायै नमः इति मन्त्रस्य शतांशेन जपः सूचितः । ध्यात्वाऽर्कमण्डलेत्यत्राऽभयवरदाभ्यां निधिपात्ररत्नकुम्भधराभ्यां रक्ता ध्येयेति ज्ञेयम् ।

तदुक्तम्—स्तनमात्रे जले तिष्ठन् रविमण्डलपीठगाम् ।
नवयावकसङ्काशां श्रियं माणिक्यभूषणाम् ॥
निधिपात्रमहारत्नपूर्णकुम्भकरद्वयाम् ।
त्रिलक्षजापी मनुजो न चिरात् स्याद्धनेश्वरः ॥ इति ॥२१॥२२॥२३॥

अशोकवह्नाविति अशोककाष्ठसमिद्धेऽग्नावित्यर्थः । जुहुयादिति नियुतमिति सम्बध्यते । मन्त्रविदित्यनेनात्र प्रयोगे कामादित्वं सूचितम् । शुद्धैरित्यव-वरं दूरीकृत्य प्रक्षाल्य शोधितैरित्यर्थः । आज्यलोडितैरित्यत्रापि योज्यम् । अर्काग्नावर्ककाष्ठसमिद्धेऽग्नावित्यर्थः । नियुतं लक्षम् ।

राजा वश्यो भवेच्छीघ्रं महालक्ष्मीश्च वर्द्धते ।
बिल्वच्छायामधिवसन् बिल्वमिश्रहविष्यभुक् ॥ २६
संवत्सरद्वयं हुत्वा तत्फलैरथवाऽम्बुजैः ।
साधकेन्द्रो महालक्ष्मीं चक्षुषा पश्यति ध्रुवम् ॥ २७
हविषा घृतसिक्तेन पायसेन ससर्पिषा ।
हुत्वा श्रियमवाप्नोति नियुतं मन्त्रवित्तमः ॥ २८
मधुराक्ताकणाम्भोजैर्जुहुयाल्लक्षमादरात् ।
न मुञ्चति रमा तस्य वंशमाभूतसंप्लवम् ॥ २९
वाग्भवं वनिता विष्णोर्माया मकरकेतनः ।
चतुर्बीजात्मको मन्त्रश्चतुर्वर्गफलप्रदः ।
अङ्गानि कुर्य्यात् दीर्घाढ्यरमाबीजेन मन्त्रवित् ॥ ३०

तथा च श्रुतिः—एका दश च शतञ्च सहस्रञ्चायुतञ्च नियुतञ्च प्रयुतञ्चार्बुदञ्च न्यर्बुदञ्च समुद्रश्च मध्यञ्चान्तश्च परार्द्धश्च । इति ।

त्रिकाण्डेऽपि—कोट्याः शतादिसंख्यान्या वा लक्षानियुतञ्च तत् । इति । जुहुयाल्लक्षमिति सम्बध्यते । खादिर इति तत्काष्ठाग्नावित्यर्थः । शीघ्रमित्यनेनात्रापि कामयोगः सूचितः । हुत्वेत्यष्टोत्तरसहस्रम् । तत्फलैः बैल्वैः । अम्बुजैरिति तदभावे । हविषेति चरुणा ॥ २३॥२४॥२५॥२६॥२७॥२८ ॥

मधुरेति । तत्र ध्यानविशेषस्तन्त्रान्तरे—

दधतीं मातुलिङ्गञ्च निक्षिपातं सरोरुहे ।
रक्तां सुरतरोर्मूले संस्थितां शोभनां श्रियम् ॥
अलङ्कृतां महारत्नैर्ध्यात्वा रक्ताम्बरान्विताम् ।
जुहोति लक्षं स्वाद्वक्तैः सरोजैरिन्दिरालये ॥ इति ।

आभूतसंप्लवमाकल्पम् ॥ २९ ॥

मन्त्रान्तरमुद्धरति वाग्भवमिति । विष्णोर्वनिता श्रीबीजम् । मकरकेतनः कामबीजम् । चतुर्वर्गफलावह इत्यनेन विनियोगं वदतैतदुक्तं भवति । धर्मार्थं वाग्भवादित्वं अर्थार्थं लक्ष्मीबीजादित्वं कामार्थं कामबीजादित्वं मोक्षार्थं मायाबीजादित्वमिति । पूर्व्वोक्ता ऋष्याद्याः । द्वितीयं बीजं तृतीयं शक्तिः ।

अङ्गानीति । दीर्घाढ्यं षड्दीर्घयुतं यद्रमाबीजं तेनेत्यर्थः ॥ ३० ॥

माणिक्यप्रतिमप्रभां हिमनिभैस्तुङ्गैश्चतुर्भिर्गजै-
र्हस्ताग्राहितरत्नकुम्भसलिलैरासिच्यमानां सदा ।
हस्ताब्जैर्वरदानमम्बुजयुगाभीतीर्दधानां हरेः
कान्तां काङ्क्षितपारिजातलतिकां वन्दे सरोजासनाम् ॥ ३१

भानुलक्षं हविष्याशी जपेदन्ते सरोरुहैः ।
जुहुयादरुणैः फुल्लैस्तत्सहस्रं जितेन्द्रियः ॥ ३२
रमायाः कल्पिते पीठे तद्विधानेन पूजयेत् ।
कुर्य्यात् प्रयोगांस्तत्रस्थान् मनुना तेन साधकः ॥ ३३
निधिभिः सेव्यते नित्यं मूर्त्तिमद्भिरुपस्थितैः ।
दीर्घा यादिर्विसर्गान्तो ब्रह्मा भानुर्वसुन्धरा ॥ ३४
वान्ते सिन्धे प्रिया वह्नेर्मनुः प्रोक्तो दशाक्षरः ।
ऋषिर्दक्षो विराट् छन्दो देवता श्रीः समीरिता ॥ ३५
देव्यै हृदयमाख्यातं पद्मिन्यै शिर ईरितम् ।
विष्णुपत्न्यै शिखा प्रोक्ता वरदायै तनुच्छदम् ॥ ३६
अस्त्रं कमलरूपायै नमोऽन्ताः प्रणवादिकाः ।
अङ्गमन्त्राः समुद्दिष्टा ध्यायेद्देवीमनन्यधीः ॥ ३७

हस्ताब्जैरिति उपमितसमासः । वरदानमित्येकम् । आयुधध्यानं पूर्व्ववत् ॥३१॥

मन्त्रान्तरमाह दीर्घेति । प्रणवोत्थकलासु दीर्घा नकारः । यादिः मः । विसर्गान्तः सविसर्ग इति मकारविशेषणम् । ब्रह्मा कः । भानुः मकारः । अत्र आत्मा रविः स्मृतः इत्युक्तेः । यद्वा महाकालो मकारमूर्त्तिः महाकालशब्दवाच्यं विषं च । तद्दक्षिणनासापुटगतम् । तेनादित्यो मः । तदुक्तम्—

रविः पिङ्गलायां चरत्येष तस्माद्विषं दक्षिणे भाग उक्तं मुनीन्द्रैः । इति । तेन यत् क्वचिदपि विषशब्देन मकारो गृह्यते तदपि व्याख्यातम् । वसुन्धरा लः । वा स्वरूपम् । सिन्धे स्वरूपम् । वह्नेः प्रिया स्वाहा । अत्रापि मन्त्रे प्रणवशक्ति-वाक्कामादित्वमिति पद्मपादाचार्य्याः । पूर्व्ववत्तत्तद्देवतानामुपसर्ज्जनत्वञ्च । श्रीँ बीजं स्वाहा शक्तिः ॥ ३२॥३३॥३४॥३५ ॥

पञ्चाङ्गमन्त्रानाह देव्यै इति । ॐ देव्यै नमः हृदयाय नमः इत्यादि प्रयोगः ।

आसीना सरसीरुहे स्मितमुखी हस्ताम्बुजैर्बिभ्रती
दानं पद्मयुगाभये च वपुषा सौदामिनीसन्निभा ।
मुक्ताहारविराजमानपृथुलोत्तुङ्गस्तनोद्भासिनी
पायाद्वः कमला कटाक्षविभवैरानन्दयन्ती हरिम् ॥ ३८

दशलक्षं जपेन्मन्त्रं मन्त्रविद्विजितेन्द्रियः ।
दशांशं जुहुयान्मन्त्री मधुराक्तैः सरोरुहैः ॥ ३९
श्रीपीठे पूजयेद्देवीमङ्गानि प्रथमं यजेत् ।
बलाकाद्यास्ततः पूज्या लोकेशास्त्वावृती अपि ॥ ४०
इति सम्पूजयेद्देवीं सम्पदामालयो भवेत् ।
समुद्रगायां सरिति कण्ठमात्रजले स्थितः ॥ ४१
त्रिलक्षं प्रजपेन्मन्त्री साक्षाद् वैश्रवणो भवेत् ।
आराध्योत्तरनक्षत्रे देवीं स्रक्चन्दनादिभिः ॥ ४२
नन्द्यावर्त्तभवैः पुष्पैः सहस्रं जुहुयात्ततः ।
पौर्णमास्यां फलैर्बिल्वैर्जुहुयान्मधुराप्लुतैः ॥ ४३
पञ्चम्यां विशदाम्भोजैः शुक्रवारे सुगन्धिभिः ।
अन्यैर्वा विशदैः पुष्पैः प्रतिमासं विशालधीः ।
स भवेदब्दमात्रेण सर्व्वदा सम्पदां निधिः ॥ ४४

पद्माङ्कत्वादेवाभावः ॥ ३६॥३७ ॥

आसीनेति । दानं वरम् । आयुधध्यानं तु पूर्व्ववत् । ३८ ॥

मन्त्रविदित्यनेन नारायणाष्टाक्षरस्य शेषतया दशांशं जपः । शतांशेन रत्नगर्भामन्त्रजपोऽपि सूचितः । मधुरं त्रिमधुरम् । सम्पदामित्यनेन विनियोगोक्तिः । समुद्रगायां साक्षादिति शेषः । वैश्रवणः कुबेरः ॥ ३९॥४०॥४१॥४२ ॥

आराध्येत्यादि सम्पदां निधिरित्येकः प्रयोगः । उत्तरानक्षत्र इति उत्तरात्रयमपि ज्ञेयम् । आराध्येति सहस्रमिति च सर्व्वत्र सम्बध्यते । मधुराप्लुतैस्त्रिमधुराद्रैरिति । अन्यैर्वेति वाशब्दः समुच्चये । एकत्रोभयसन्निपाते पृथगुभयहोमो न तन्त्रं भिन्नद्रव्यत्वात् भिन्ननिमित्तत्वाच्च ॥ ४२॥४३॥४४ ॥

वाग्भवं शम्भुवनिता रमा मकरकेतनः ।
तार्त्तीयश्च जगत् पार्श्वो वह्निबीजसमुज्ज्वलः ॥ ४५
अर्घीशाढ्यो भृगुस्त्यै इत्यन्त्रोऽयं द्वादशाक्षरः ।
महालक्ष्म्याः समुद्दिष्टस्ताराद्यः सर्व्वसिद्धिदः ॥ ४६
ऋषिर्ब्रह्मा समुद्दिष्टश्छन्दो गायत्रमीरितम् ।
देवता जगतामादिर्महालक्ष्मीः समीरिता ॥ ४७
हस्तौ संशोध्य मन्त्रेण तारादिहृदयान्तिकम् ।
बीजानां पञ्चकं न्यस्येदङ्गुलीषु यथाक्रमम् ॥ ४८
मन्त्रशेषं न्यसेन्मन्त्री तलयोरुभयोरपि ।
मूर्द्धादि चरणं यावन्मन्त्रेण व्यापकं न्यसेत् ॥ ४९
मूर्द्धास्यवक्षोगुह्याङ्घ्रौ पञ्च बीजानि विन्यसेत्
शेषान् न्यसेत् सप्त वर्णान् हृदये सप्तधातुषु ॥ ५०
अङ्गानि पञ्चभिर्बीजैरस्त्रं शिष्टाक्षरैर्भवेत् ।
ज्ञानैश्वर्य्यादिभिर्युक्तैश्चतुर्थ्यन्तैः सजातिभिः ॥ ५१

मन्त्रान्तरमुद्धरति वाग्भवमिति । शम्भुवनिता मायाबीजम् । तार्त्तीयं बालाया भैरव्या वा । केचिद्रेफहीनं भैरव्या इति वदन्ति । अयमेव साम्प्रदायिकः पक्षः । जगत् स्वरूपम् । पार्श्वः पकारः । वह्निबीजसमुज्ज्वलः रेफयुक्तः तेन प्र । अर्घीशः ऊ तेनाढ्यो भृगुः सकारः तेन सू । त्यै स्वरूपम् । इत्यमः । ताराद्यः प्रणवाद्यः त्रयोदशाक्षर इति शेषः । सर्व्वसिद्धिद इत्यनेन विनियोग उक्तः । प्रणवो बीजं तार्त्तीयं शक्तिः ॥ ४५॥४६॥४७ ॥

हस्तभावनामाह हस्तौ संशोध्येति । हस्तयोर्मूलमन्त्रं व्यापकत्वेन विन्यसेदित्यर्थः । मन्त्रेणेति मूलमन्त्रेण । तारादिहृदयान्तिकमिति मन्त्रशेषस्यापि विशेषणम् । यथाक्रममङ्गुलीष्विति अङ्गुष्ठाद्यासु ।

मूर्द्धादीत्यत्रापि न्यासे तारादिहृदयान्तिकमिति सम्बध्यते । अङ्गानीत्यत्रापि । ज्ञानैश्वर्य्यादिभिर्युक्तैरिति व्यधिकरणे तृतीये । चतुर्थ्यन्तैः ज्ञानैश्वर्य्यादिभिर्युक्तैरिति बीजैः । शिष्टाक्षरैरित्युभयविशेषणम् । अङ्गानीति नेत्रान्तानि । ऐं ज्ञानाय हृदयाय नमः । श्रीं ऐश्वर्य्याय शिरसे स्वाहा । इत्यादि प्रयोगः । के चन

ज्ञानमैश्वर्य्यशक्ती च बलवीर्य्ये सतेजसी।
ज्ञानैश्वर्य्यादयः प्रोक्ताः षट् क्रमादङ्गदेवताः॥ ५२

एवं न्यस्तशरीरोऽसौ स्मरेदुद्यानमुत्तमम्।
चम्पकाशोकपुन्नागपाटलैरुपशोभितम्॥ ५३

लवङ्गमाधवीबिल्वदेवदारुनमेरुभिः।
मन्दारपारिजाताद्यैः कल्पवृक्षैः सुपुष्पितैः॥ ५४

चन्दनैः कर्णिकारैश्च मातुलिङ्गैश्च वञ्जुलैः।
दाड़िमीलकुचाङ्कोलैः पूगैः कुरवकैरपि॥ ५५

कदलीकुन्दमन्दारनारिकेलैरलङ्कृतम्।
अन्यैः सुगन्धिपुष्पाढ्यैर्वृक्षसङ्घैश्च मण्डितम्॥ ५६

मालतीमल्लिकाजाती केतकीशतपत्रकैः।
पारन्तीतुलसीनन्द्यावर्त्तैर्दमनकैरपि॥ ५७

सर्व्वर्त्तुकुसुमोपेतैर्नमल्लिकुपशोभितम्।
मन्दमारुतसम्भिन्नकुसुमामोदिदिङ्मुखम्॥ ५८

तस्य मध्ये सदोत्फुल्लैः कुमुदोत्पलपङ्कजैः।
सौगन्धिकैश्च कह्लारैर्नवैः कुवलयैरपि॥ ५९

हंससारसकारण्डभ्रमरैश्चक्रनामभिः।
अन्यैः कलकलारावैर्विहगैरुपशोभिते॥ ६०

महासरसि तन्मध्ये पुलिनेऽतिमनोहरे।
परितः पारिजाताढ्यं मण्डपं मणिकुट्टिमम्॥ ६१

सम्प्रदायादात्मनेशब्दमप्याहुः। तन्मते ऐँ ज्ञानात्मने हृदयाय नमः इत्यादि प्रयोगः॥ ४८॥५९॥५०॥५१॥५२॥

नमेरु रुद्राक्षः। तस्य मध्ये महासरसि। तन्मध्ये पुलिने मनसा मण्डपं सञ्चिन्त्य तन्मध्ये पारिजातं भावयेदित्युत्तरेण सम्बन्धः।

॥ ५३॥५४॥५५॥५६॥५७॥५८॥५९॥६०॥६१॥

उद्यदादित्यसङ्काशं भास्वरं भूमिभीतलम् ।
चतुर्द्वारसमायुक्तं हैमप्राकारशोभितम् ॥ ६२
रत्नोपक्लृप्तिसंशोभिकपाटाष्टकसंयुतम् ।
नवरत्नसमाक्लृप्ततुङ्गगोपुरतोरणम् ॥ ६३
हेमदण्डसमालम्बिध्वजावलिपरिष्कृतम् ।
नवरत्नसमाबद्धस्तम्भराजिविराजितम् ॥ ६४
सहस्रदीपसंयुक्तदीपदण्डविराजितम् ।
तप्तहाटकसंक्लृप्तवातायनमनोहरम् ॥ ६५
नानावर्णांशुकोद्भवसुवर्णशतकोटिभिः ।
किङ्किणीमालिकायुक्तपताकाभिरलङ्कृतम् ॥ ६६
जातरूपमयैरत्नविचित्रैरतिविस्तृतैः ।
माणिक्यवज्रवैदूर्य्यस्वर्णमालावलीयुतैः ॥ ६७
अन्तरान्तरसम्बद्धरत्नैर्दृष्टिमनोहरैः ।
विचित्रैस्त्रिवर्णैश्च वितानैरुपशोभितम् ॥ ६८
सर्व्वरत्नसमायुक्तं हेमकुट्टिममुज्ज्वलम् ।
केतकीमालतीजातीचम्पकोत्पलकेसरैः ॥ ६९
मल्लिकातुलसीजातीनन्द्यावर्त्तकदम्बकैः ।
एतैरन्यैश्च कुसुमैरलङ्कृतमहीतलम् ॥ ७०
अम्बुकाश्मीरकस्तूरीमृगनाभितमालकैः ।
चन्दनागुरुकर्पूरैरामोदितदिगन्तरम् ॥ ७१
एवं सञ्चिन्त्य मनसा मण्डपं सुमनोहरम् ।
तन्मध्ये भावयेन्मन्त्री पारिजातं मनोहरम् ॥ ७२

नानावर्णांशुकेनेति पताकाविशेषणम् । जातरूपमयैरित्यादि वितानैरित्यस्य विशेषणम् । तथा च पृथिव्यनन्तरं चोरसिन्धुं द्वीपम् उद्यानं महासरः पुलिनं मण्डपं पारिजातं रत्नसिंहासनं सम्पूजयेत् । शेषं समानम् । कुट्टिममिति ।

तस्याधस्तात् स्मरेन्मन्त्री रत्नसिंहासनं महत्।
तस्मिन् सञ्चिन्तयेद्देवीं महालक्ष्मीं मनोरमाम् ॥ ७३

बालार्कद्युतिमिन्दुखण्डविलसत्कोटीरहारोज्ज्वलां
रत्नाकल्पविभूषितां कुचनतां शालेः करैर्मञ्जरीम्।
पद्मं कौस्तुभरत्नमप्यविरतं सम्बिभ्रतीं सुस्मितां
फुल्लाम्भोजविलोचनत्रययुतां ध्यायेत् परां देवताम् ॥ ७४

शिञ्जन्मञ्जीरसंशोभिपदाम्भोजविराजिताम्।
नवरत्नगणाकीर्णकाञ्चीदामविभूषिताम् ॥ ७५

मुक्तामाणिक्यवैदूर्य्यसम्बद्धोदरबन्धनाम्।
विभ्राजमानां मध्येन वलित्रितयशोभिना ॥ ७६

जाह्नवीसरिदावर्त्तशोभिनाभिविभूषिताम्।
पाटीरपङ्ककर्पूरकुङ्कुमालङ्कृतस्तनीम् ॥ ७७

वारिवाहविनिर्मुक्तमुक्तादामगरीयसीम्।
वहन्तीमुत्तरासङ्गं दुकूलपरिकल्पितम् ॥ ७८

तप्तकाञ्चनसन्नद्धवैदूर्य्याङ्गदभूषणाम्।
पद्मरागस्फुरत्स्वर्णकङ्कणाढ्यकराम्बुजाम् ॥ ७९

माणिक्यशकलाबद्धमुद्रिकाभिरलङ्कृताम्।
तप्तहाटकसत्कॢप्तमालाग्रैवेयशोभिताम् ॥ ८०

विचित्रविविधाकल्पां कम्बुसङ्काशकन्धराम्।
उद्यद्दिनकराकारमणिताटङ्कमण्डिताम् ॥ ८१

"कुट्टिमोऽस्त्री निबद्धा भूः" इति कोषः। अम्बु सुगन्धिद्रव्यम्। कुमकुमा इति कान्यकुब्जभाषायाम्। कस्तूरीमृगस्य नाभिरिति विग्रहः। एवं सञ्चिन्त्य मनसा मण्डपमिति पूर्व्वं मण्डपमित्युक्तं तस्यैवानुवादः। तन्मध्ये इत्यस्य विशेषणैर्व्यवहितत्वेन सम्बन्धस्य बुद्धिस्थत्वात् ॥ ६२—७३ ॥

कोटीरो मुकुटः। आयुधध्यानन्तु पूर्व्ववत्। ७४ ॥

पाटीरं चन्दनं। ग्रैवेयं कण्ठभूषा। कम्बुः शङ्खः ॥ ७५—८१ ॥

रत्नाङ्कितलसत्स्वर्णकर्णपूरोपशोभिताम् ।
जवाविद्रुमसत्ताबल्यललिताधरपल्लवाम् ॥ ८२

दाडिमीफलबीजाभदन्तपङ्क्तिविराजिताम् ।
कलङ्कार्श्यनिर्मुक्तशरच्चन्द्रनिभाननाम् ॥ ८३

पुण्डरीकदलाकारनयनत्रयसुन्दरीम् ।
भ्रूलताजितकन्दर्पकार्मुकविभ्रमाम् ॥ ८४

विकसत्तिलपुष्पश्रीविजयोद्यतनासिकाम् ।
ललाटकान्तिविभवविजितार्द्धसुधाकराम् ॥ ८५

सान्द्रसौरभसम्पन्नकस्तूरीतिलकाङ्किताम् ।
मत्तालिमालाविलसदलकाढ्यमुखाम्बुजाम् ॥ ८६

पारिजातप्रसूनश्रीवाहिधम्मिल्लबन्धनाम् ।
अनर्घ्यरत्नघटितमुकुटाङ्कितमस्तकाम् ॥ ८७

सर्व्वलावण्यवसतिं भवनं विभ्रमश्रियः ।
तेजसां जन्मभूमिं तां महालक्ष्मीं मनोहराम् ॥ ८८

एवं सञ्चिन्तयन् देवीं हविष्याशी जितेन्द्रियः ।
भानुलक्षं जपेन्मन्त्रं दशांशं जुहुयाद् घृतैः ॥ ८९

जुहुयाच्छ्रीफलैः पद्मैः प्रत्येकमयुतं ततः ।
तर्पयेत् सलिलैः शुद्धैः सुगन्धैरयुतद्वयम् ॥ ९०

श्रीबीजस्योदिते पीठे महालक्ष्मीं प्रपूजयेत् ।
श्रीबीजेनासनं दद्यान्मूर्त्तिं मूलेन कल्पयेत् ॥ ९१

पूजयेद्दक्षिणे पार्श्वे देव्याः शङ्करनन्दनम् ।
अन्यतः पुष्पधन्वानं पुष्पाञ्जलिकरं यजेत् ॥ ९२

मत्तालिमालेव विलसन्तः ये अलका इति विग्रहः ॥ ८२—८८ ॥

घृतैरेव दशांशं होमः । अयुतद्वयहोमस्त्वधिकः । पीठे अष्टदलद्वादशदल-चतुरस्रचतुर्द्वाररूपे । शङ्करनन्दनं गणेशं स्कान्दमित्यपरे । पुष्पाञ्जलिकरमित्युभय-

अङ्गानि पूर्व्वमुक्तेषु स्थानेषु विधिवद् यजेत् ।
उमाद्याः पत्रमध्यस्थाः शक्तीरष्टौ यजेत् क्रमात् ॥ ९३

यथोमा श्रीसरस्वत्यौ दुर्गा धरणिसंयुता ।
गायत्री देव्युषा चैव पद्महस्ताः सुभूषणाः ॥ ९४

जह्नुसूर्य्यसुते पूज्ये पादप्रक्षालनोद्यते ।
शङ्खपद्मनिधी पूज्यौ पार्श्वयोर्धृतचामरौ ॥ ९५

धृतातपत्रं वरुणं पूजयेत् पश्चिमे ततः ।
सम्पूज्य राशीन् परितो यजेदथ नव ग्रहान् ॥ ९६

पूजयेद् दिग्गजान् दिक्षु चतुर्दन्तविभूषितान् ।
ऐरावतः पुण्डरीको वामनः कुमुदोऽञ्जनः ॥ ९७

पुष्पदन्तः सार्व्वभौमः सुप्रतीकश्च ते क्रमात् ।
अभ्यर्चयेदथेन्द्रादीन् तदस्त्राण्यपि तद्बहिः ॥ ९८

आगमोक्तेन विधिना सुगन्धैः सुमनोहरैः ।
पूजयेद् गन्धपुष्पाद्यैर्देवीमन्वहमादरात् ॥ ९९

दूर्व्वाभिराज्यसिक्ताभिर्जुहुयादायुषे नरः ।
दशरात्रं समिद्धेऽग्नावष्टोत्तरसहस्रकम् ॥ १००

ध्यानम् ॥ ८९॥९०॥९१॥९२ ॥

पूर्व्वमुक्तेषु तुर्य्योक्तेषु । विधिवदिति शिरआद्यङ्गेषु नमोयोग उक्तः । अथवा यथान्यासमात्मनेपदसहितानीत्युक्तम् । पद्मे हस्तयोर्यस्याः सा पद्महस्ता । पश्चादष्टानां पद्महस्ताशब्दानामेकशेषे बहुवचनं ज्ञेयम् । जह्नु इत्यारभ्य पश्चिम इत्यन्तं तृतीयावरणम् । सम्पूज्येति द्वादशदले । राशीनिति । तद्वर्णा आचार्य्यैरुक्ताः—

चापनीरजयुक्कन्याः पीताः स्युरुभयास्त्वमी ।
वणिङ्मकरमेषाश्च कुलीरा रक्तरोचिषः ॥
चरावशिष्टाश्चत्वारः सिताः श्वेताः पृथङ्मताः । इति ।

तत्तन्नामानुरूपं स्वरूपं ज्ञेयम् । इदं चतुर्थावरणम् । अथ परितो यजेत् नव ग्रहानिति । तद्वर्णास्तत्स्वरूपञ्च चन्द्रमन्त्रे वक्ष्यति । दिग्गजानिति श्वेतान् । दिक्ष्विति स्वस्वदिक्षु । अष्टोत्तरसहस्रकमिति इयमपि प्रत्यहम् ॥ ८३-१०१ ॥

गुडूचीराज्यसंसिक्ता जुहुयात् समवासरम् ।
अष्टोत्तरसहस्रं यः स जीवेच्छरदां शतम् ॥ १०१
हुत्वा तिलान् घृताभ्यक्तान् दीर्घमायुरवाप्नुयात् ।
आरभ्याऽर्कदिनं मन्त्री दशवारं दिने दिने ॥ १०२
आज्याक्तार्कसमिद्धोमादारोग्यं लभते ध्रुवम् ।
कण्ठमात्रोदके स्थित्वा ध्यात्वा देवीं दिवाकरे ॥ १०३
ऊर्ध्वबाहुर्दशशतमष्टोत्तरमिमं जपेत् ।
आरोग्यं लभते सद्यो[मर्त्यो] वाञ्छितान्यपि मन्त्रवित् ॥ १०४
शालिभिर्जुह्वतो नित्यमष्टोत्तरसहस्रकम् ।
अचिरादेव महती लक्ष्मीः सञ्जायते ध्रुवम् ॥ १०५
प्रसूनैर्जुहुयान्मन्त्री लक्ष्मीवल्लीसमुद्भवैः ।
नन्द्यावर्त्तसमुत्थैर्वा सिद्धार्थैश्च घृतप्लुतैः ॥ १०६
महतीं श्रियमाप्नोति मान्यते सर्वजन्तुभिः ।
मरीचजीरकोन्मिश्रैर्नारिकेलरजोयुतैः ॥ १०७
सगुडैराज्यसम्पक्तैरपूपैराज्यलोलितैः ।
जुहुयात् पायसाहारो मन्त्रविद्विजितेन्द्रियः ॥ १०८
अष्टोत्तरशतं नित्यं मण्डलाद्धनदो भवेत् ।
हविषा गुडमिश्रेण जुहुयादन्नवान् भवेत् ॥ १०९
जपापुष्पाणि जुहुयादष्टोत्तरसहस्रकम् ।
गृहीत्वा प्रजपेद्भस्म नागवल्लीरसान्वितम् ॥ ११०
तिलकं तनुयात्तेन सर्ववश्यकरं भवेत् ।
ब्रह्मवृक्षसमित्पुष्पैर्ब्राह्मणान् वशयेद्वशी ॥ १११

हुत्वेत्यष्टोत्तरसहस्रम् । इदमुत्तरप्रयोगेऽपि । अर्कदिनमादित्यवासरः । जुहुयादित्यष्टोत्तरं सहस्रम् । लक्ष्मीवल्ली तु ताम्बूलाकारपत्रा रक्तमध्यविन्दुः श्वेतपुष्पा । वाशब्दः समुच्चये । मण्डलादेकोनपञ्चाशद्दिनैः । धनदः कुबेरः ।

जातीपुष्पैश्च राजानं वैश्यान् रक्तोत्पलैः सुधीः ।
शूद्रान्नीलोत्पलैर्हुत्वा वशयेन्मन्त्रवित्तमः ॥ ११२
पुष्पैर्मधूकजैर्हुत्वा वशमानयति स्त्रियः ।
कृत्वा नवपदात्मानं मण्डलं यन्त्रभूषितम् ॥ ११३
अभिषेकं प्रकुर्वीत विधिना सर्व्वसिद्धये ।
कलशान् स्थापयेत्तेषु पदेषु शुभलक्षणान् ॥ ११४
चन्दनालिप्तसर्व्वाङ्गान् दूर्व्वाक्षतसमन्वितान् ।
दुकूलवेष्टितानेतान् पूरयेत्तीर्थवारिणा ॥ ११५
नवरत्नसमायुक्तं कर्षकाञ्चनकल्पितम् ।
मध्यकुम्भे क्षिपेत् पद्मं यन्त्राढ्यं देशिकोत्तमः ॥ ११६
चन्दनोशीरकर्पूरजातीकक्कोलकुङ्कुमम् ।
कुष्ठागुरुतमालैलायुतं संपिष्य भागतः ॥ ११७
विलोड्य सर्व्वकुम्भेषु रत्नान्यपि विनिःक्षिपेत् ।
लक्ष्मीर्दूर्व्वा सदाभद्रा सहदेवी मधुव्रता ॥ ११८
मुषली शङ्खवल्ली च क्रान्तापामार्गपल्लवान् ।
प्रियङ्गुमुद्गगोधूम व्रीहींश्च सतिलान् यवान् ॥ ११९

प्रजपेदित्यष्टोत्तरशतमित्यादि । भस्मेति हुतजवाभस्म । ब्रह्मवृक्षः पलाशः । "ब्रह्म वै पलाशः" इति श्रुतेः ॥ १०२—११२ ॥

अभिषेकमाह कृत्वेति । नवपदात्मानं तृतीयोक्तं नवनाभम् । यन्त्रभूषितं वक्ष्यमाणं यन्त्रं तन्मध्यकर्णिकायां लिखेदित्यर्थः । विधिनेति उद्दिष्ट विधिमाह कलशानित्यादिना । कर्षकाञ्चननिर्मितं षड्शीतिकाधिकशतरक्तिकापरिमितसुवर्ण-निर्मितम् । यन्त्राढ्यं वक्ष्यमाणयन्त्रयुक्तम् । तेन यन्त्रपद्ममित्यर्थः । जाती जातीफलम् । भागत इति समविभागतः । रत्नानि मातृकापटलोक्तानि नव । सर्व्वकुम्भेषु इति । अत्रापिमा सम्बध्यते ॥ ११३—११८ ॥

लक्ष्मीः पूर्व्वोक्तलक्षणा १ दूर्व्वा २ सदाभद्रा भद्रमुस्ता ३ सहदेवी ४ मधुव्रता भृङ्गराजः ५ मुषली मुषलीकन्दः ६ शङ्खवल्ली इन्द्रवारुणी ७ क्रान्ता विष्णुक्रान्ता

शालितण्डुलमाषांश्च प्रक्षाल्यैतेषु निक्षिपेत् ।
धात्रीलकुचबिल्वानां कदलीनारिकेलयोः ॥ १२०
फलान्यपि विनिक्षिप्य पुष्पाण्येतानि निक्षिपेत् ।
पद्मं सौगन्धिकं जातिं मल्लिकां बकुलं तथा ॥ १२१
चम्पकाशोकपुन्नागतुलसीकेतकोद्भवम् ।
पल्लवानि वटाश्वत्थ प्लक्षोडुम्बरशाखिनाम् ॥ १२२
ब्रह्मकूर्चं विनिक्षिप्य चषकैः सफलाक्षतैः ।
पिधाय कुम्भवक्त्राणि क्षौमैराच्छादयेत्ततः ॥ १२३
आवाह्य मध्यकलशे महालक्ष्मीं प्रपूजयेत् ।
यजेदुमाद्याः शिष्टेषु कलशेष्वष्टसु क्रमात् ॥ १२४
गन्धैर्मनोहरैः पुष्पैर्धूपदीपसमन्वितैः ।
निवेद्य भक्ष्यभोज्यानि तान् स्पृष्ट्वा प्रजपेन्मनुम् ॥ १२५
त्रिसहस्रं जपस्यान्ते साध्यमानीय संयतम् ।
संस्थाप्य स्थण्डिले पीठं तस्मिंस्तं विनिवेशयेत् ॥ १२६
रम्यैराभरणैर्वस्त्रैरलङ्कृत्य तमादरात् ।
सुमङ्गलाभिर्नारीभिः क्षिप्तपुष्पाक्षतान्वितम् ॥ १२७
अर्चितानां द्विजातीनामाशीर्वादपुरःसरम् ।
नदत्सु पञ्चवाद्येषु मुहूर्ते शोभने सुधीः ॥ १२८
मध्यस्थं कुम्भमुद्धृत्य महालक्ष्मीमनुं स्मरन् ।
अभिषिञ्चेत् क्रमादन्यैः कलशैरपि देशिकः ॥ १२९
करेणाऽस्य शिरः स्पृष्ट्वा प्रयुञ्जीताशिषं गुरुः ।
भद्रमस्तु शिवञ्चाऽस्तु महालक्ष्मीः प्रसीदतु ॥ १३०

* अपामार्गपत्र ८ एतानि प्रक्षाल्य एतेषु नवकुम्भेषु प्रत्येकं निक्षिपेदित्यर्थविशेषान्वयः । प्रियङ्गुः कङ्गुः । निक्षिपेदिति प्रत्येकम् ॥ ११८॥११९॥१२० ॥

फलान्यपीति पल्लवानीति च सर्व्वकुम्भेषु । ब्रह्मकूर्चं दीक्षापटलोक्तम् । तान्

रक्षन्तु त्वां सदा देवाः सम्पदः सन्तु सर्व्वदा।
अथोत्थायाऽभिषिक्तः सन् वाससी परिधाय च ॥ १३१
यथाविधि समाचम्य दण्डवत् प्रणमेद् गुरुम्।
वस्त्रैराभरणैर्धान्यैर्धनै[र्गन्धै]र्गोमहिष्यादिभिः ॥ १३२
दासीदासैश्च विविधैस्तोषयेद्देवताधिया।
ब्राह्मणान् भोजयेत् पश्चाद्दीनान्धकृपणैः सह ॥ १३३
महान्तमुत्सवं कुर्य्याद्भवने बन्धुभिः सह।
तदा कृतार्थमात्मानं मन्यते मनुजोत्तमः ॥ १३४
अभिषिक्तो नरपतिः परान् विजयतेऽचिरात्।
पट्टेच्छुः पट्टमाप्नोति राजपुत्रो न संशयः ॥ १३५
अभिषिक्ता सती वन्ध्या सूते पुत्रं महामतिम्।
महारोगेषु जातेषु कृत्याद्रोहेषु देशिकः ॥ १३६
भूतेषु दुर्निमित्तादौ विदध्यादभिषेचनम्।
सर्व्वसम्पत्करं पुंसां सर्व्वसौभाग्यसिद्धिदम् ॥ १३७
सर्व्वरोगप्रशमनं सर्व्वामहिनिवारकम्।
गर्भरक्षाकरं स्त्रीणां दीर्घायुर्जनकं परम् ॥ १३८
प्रसूतानामपि स्त्रीणां सूतिकागाररक्षकम्।
प्रणष्टपुष्पगर्भाणां पुष्पगर्भाभिरक्षणम् ॥ १३९
आसन्नमृत्युभीतानां नाशनञ्च महीभृताम्।
अभिषेकमिमं प्राहुरागमार्थविशारदाः ॥ १४०

वेदादिस्थितसाध्यनाम युगशः श्रीशक्तिमाराच्चितं
किञ्जल्केषु दिनेशपत्रविलसन्मन्त्राक्षरं तद्बहिः।

सृष्टेति क्रमादिना युगपत्। सुमङ्गलाभिः चिरण्टीभिरित्यर्थः। आशिषमेवाह भद्रमस्त्विति ॥ १२०—१४० ॥

यन्त्रमाह वेदादीति। पद्मं पद्मरूपं यन्त्रं लिखेदिति सम्बन्धः। किं विशिष्टम्।

पद्मं व्यञ्जनकेसरं स्वरलसत्पत्राष्टयुग्मं धरा-
विम्बाभ्यां वषडन्तया त्वरितया यन्त्रं लिखेद्‌ वेष्टितम् ॥ १४१
भूपुरद्वयकोणेषु हस्रौ लेख्यौ पुनः पुनः।
महालक्ष्मीयन्त्रमिदं सर्व्वैश्वर्य्यफलप्रदम् ॥ १४२
सर्व्वदुःखप्रशमनं सर्व्वापद्विनिवारणम्।
बहुना किमिहोक्तेन परमस्मान्न विद्यते ॥ १४३
शम्भुपत्नी श्रिया रुद्धा कमौ भगवती मही।
ब्रह्मादित्यौ धरा दीर्घा लः चादिर्भगवान् भकत् ॥ १४४
प्रसीदयुगलं भूयः श्रीरुद्धा भुवनेश्वरी।
महालक्ष्मि नमोऽन्तः स्यात् प्रणवादिरयं मनुः ॥ १४५

वेदादिः प्रणवः तदन्तः साध्यनाम साध्यसाधककर्म्मनाम यत्र तत् कर्णिकाया-मिति ज्ञेयम्। किञ्जल्केष्विति वक्ष्यमाणत्वात्। पुनः कीदृक्। किञ्जल्केषु केसरस्थानेषु युगशो द्विशः श्रीशक्तिमारान्वितम्। आद्ये किञ्जल्के श्रीशक्ती परे मारश्रियौ तत्परे शक्तिमारौ इति क्रमेणेति सम्प्रदायविदः। तेन बीज-त्रयस्याष्टावृत्तयः। पुनः कीदृक्। दिनेशपत्रेषु द्वादशपत्रेषु विलसन्ति मन्त्राक्षराणि यत्र। पुनः किं विशिष्टम्। तद्बहिः व्यञ्जनकेसरम् व्यञ्जनानि ककारादीनि केसरेषु यत्र तत्। केसराणां द्वित्वात् व्यञ्जनद्वयमेकैकस्मिन् केसरस्थाने लेखनीयमित्यर्थः। पुनः कीदृक् स्वरैर्लसद् युक्तं पत्राष्टयुग्मं षोड़शपत्रं यस्मिन् तत्। धराविम्बाभ्यां परस्परव्यतिभिन्नाभ्यां वेष्टितम्। त्वरितया सहेति सम्बन्धः। इदञ्चोपरिष्टात् प्रभृति। तेन त्वरितया संवेष्ट्य पश्चाद् भूगृहाभ्यां वेष्टयेत्। अत्र परस्परव्यतिभिन्नत्वम् अर्थलभ्यम्। यदुपर्य्युपरि चतुरस्रकरणे एकेनैव चतुरस्रेण साक्षाद् यन्त्रवेष्टनम्। अन्येन तु चतुरस्रस्यैव वेष्टनं न मन्त्रस्य। परम्परया यन्त्रवेष्टनत्वमिति चेन्न। व्यतिभिन्नत्वे तु उभयोरपि साक्षादेव यन्त्रवेष्टितत्वसम्भवात्। कीदृश्या त्वरितया। वषडन्तया तत्र फट्-कारस्थाने वषट्कार इति साम्प्रदायिकाः। अन्ये तु वषट्कारमधिकमाहुः। हस्रावित्यष्टधाहत्तौ ॥ १४१॥१४२॥१४३ ॥

मन्त्रान्तरमाह शम्भ्विति। शम्भुपत्नी मायाबीजम्। श्रिया रुद्धा श्रीबीज-पुटिता। एकाक्षरत्वाद्रोधः सम्पुटे पर्य्यवस्यति। कमौ ककारमकारौ।

सप्तविंशत्यक्षराढ्यः प्रोक्तः सर्व्वसमृद्धिदः।
कमले हृदयं प्रोक्तं शिरः स्यात् कमलालये॥ १४६
शिखा प्रसीद तेनैव कवचं चतुरक्षरैः।
अस्त्रमेतैः पदैः कुर्य्यात् त्रिबीजपुटितैः पृथक्॥ १४७

सिन्दूरारुणकान्तिमब्जवसतिं सौन्दर्य्यवारां निधिं
कोटीराङ्गदहारकुण्डलकटीसूत्रादिभिर्भूषिताम्।
हस्ताब्जैर्वसुपत्रमब्जयुगलादर्शौं वहन्तीं परा-
मावीतां परिचारिकाभिरनिशं ध्यायेत् प्रियां शार्ङ्गिणः॥ १४८

लक्षं जपेत् फलैर्बिल्वैर्जुहुयान्मधुरोक्षितैः।
दशांशं संस्कृते वह्नौ प्राक्प्रोक्तेनैव वर्त्मना॥ १४९
श्रीबीजोक्ते यजेत् पीठे वक्ष्यमाणक्रमेण ताम्।
अङ्गावृत्तेर्बहिः पूज्या मूर्त्तयः श्रीधरादयः॥ १५०

भग एकारस्तद्युक्ता मही लः तेन ले। नागरलिपौ एकारस्य भगरूपत्वात् भगशब्दवाच्यता। ब्रह्मादित्यौ ककारमकारौ। धरा लकारः। दीर्घा दीर्घयुक्ता तत्र प्रथमातिक्रमे कारणाभावादाकारयुक्ता तेन ला। चादिलः मूर्द्धन्य इत्यर्थः। मरुत् यकारः। भगवानिकारयुक्तः तेन ये ति। महालक्ष्मीति स्वरूपम्। इदं पदं के चन चतुर्थ्यन्तमपीच्छन्ति। एभिस्तु यकारस्य कीलकत्वात् न तथोद्धृतम्। अन्ये तु दिक्शब्दादौ भेदमुद्धृत्याष्टाविंशतिवर्णमाहुः। सर्व्वसमृद्धिद इति विनियोगोक्तिः। श्रीँ बीजं माया शक्तिः। कमलवासिनी चास्या ऋष्यादयः। तेनैवेति प्रसीदेत्यनेन। चतुरक्षरैरिति महालक्ष्मिपदेन। त्रिबीज-पुटितैरिति मन्त्रादिस्थप्रणवव्यतिरिक्तत्रिबीजैः। पृथक् प्रत्येकं कुर्य्यादङ्गानीति शेषः। तत्र प्रयोगो यथा। श्रीँ ह्रीँ श्रीँ कमले श्रीँ ह्रीँ श्रीँ हृदयाय नमः इत्यादि॥ १४४॥१४५॥१४६॥१४७॥

आयुधध्यानं दक्षाधस्ताद्वामाधः पर्य्यन्तम्॥ १४८॥

अङ्गावृत्तेर्बहिः केसरेषु। तेन कर्णिकायामङ्गपूजा। अत एव दलमूलेषु सम्पूज्येत्युक्तिः। पत्रमध्येष्विति दिक्पत्रमध्येषु। दमकादिकान् इति विदिक्-पत्रमध्येषु। तदग्रेषु पत्राग्रेषु। ये साधकोत्तमा उपासते इति सम्बन्धः।

श्रीधराख्यं हृषीकेशं वैकुण्ठं विश्वरूपकम्।
वासुदेवं सङ्कर्षणं प्रद्युम्नमनिरुद्धकम्॥ १५१
दलमूलेषु संपूज्य पद्ममध्येषु संयजेत्।
भारतीं पार्व्वतीं चान्द्रीं शचीञ्च दमकादिकान्॥ १५२
दलाग्रेष्वर्च्चयेद् बाणान् महालक्ष्म्याः क्रमादमून्।
अनुरागञ्च संवादं विजयं वल्लभं मदम्॥ १५३
हर्षं बलञ्च तेजश्च लोकनाथाननन्तरम्।
तदायुधानि तद्वाह्ये पूजयेत् साधकोत्तमाः॥ १५४
अनेन विधिना देवीं महालक्ष्मीमुपासते।
ये तेषु निवसेल्लक्ष्मीरस्मरन्ती निजालयम्॥ १५५
उत्पलैर्जुहुयाल्लक्षं चन्दनाक्तसि लोलितैः।
शत्रूणां लभते राज्यं विना युद्धेन पार्थिवः॥ १५६
जपन् राजसभां गच्छेत् सम्भाव्येत तया नरः।
दूर्व्वा देवी महालक्ष्मीर्विष्णुक्रान्ता मधुव्रता॥ १५७
मुशली शक्रवल्ली च सदाभद्राऽञ्जलिप्रिया।
हरिचन्दनकर्पूरचन्दनाङ्कोलरोचनाः॥ १५८
मालूरकेसरी कुष्ठं सर्व्वं पिष्ट्वा निशारसैः।
अष्टोत्तरसहस्रन्तु जपित्वा तिलकक्रियाम्॥ १५९
कुर्व्वतो मन्त्रिणः सर्व्वे वशे तिष्ठन्त्यहर्निशम्।
श्रियो मन्त्रं भजेन्मन्त्री श्रीसूक्तान्यपि संजपेत्॥ १६०

साधकोत्तमा इत्यनेनैतदुक्तं भवति सत्यवादित्वादिलक्ष्म्युपासकसमयनिष्ठा इति।
॥ १४८॥१५०॥१५१॥१५२॥१५३॥१५४॥१५५॥१५६ ॥

तयेति सभया। देवी सहदेवी। मधुव्रता भृङ्गराजः। सदाभद्रा भद्रमुस्ता। अञ्जलिप्रिया अञ्जलिनी। हाताजोड़ीति कान्यकुब्जभाषायाम्। हरिचन्दनं पीतचन्दनम्। मालूरं बिल्वम्। केसरो नागकेसरः। निशा हरिद्रा।

श्रीसूक्तं पञ्चदशर्चं बह्वृचानां प्रसिद्धतरम्। तद्विधानं यथा—

आद्यायाः श्रीर्ऋषिः प्रोक्तस्तत आनन्दकर्दमौ ।
चिक्लीतश्चेन्दिरापुत्रौ मुनयः संप्रकीर्त्तिताः ॥
चतुर्दशानां छन्दः स्यादनुष्टुप् तिसृणां पुनः ।
चतुर्थ्यां बृहती पञ्चषष्ठयोस्त्रिष्टुबीरिता ॥
सप्तमादिषु चाष्टानामनुष्टुप् परिकीर्त्तितम् ।
प्रस्तारपङ्क्तिरन्त्याया अम्बी देवी प्रकीर्त्तिता ॥
आद्यन्ते बीजशक्ती स्तो विनियोगो धनाप्तये ।
मूर्द्धाक्षिकर्णघ्राणेषु मुखग्रीवाकरद्वये ॥
स्तनाभिलिङ्गपायूरुजानुजङ्घापदे न्यसेत् ।
हिरण्मयी च चन्द्रा च रजताद्या स्रजा तथा ॥
सुवर्णाद्या स्रजा चैव हिरण्या चैव पञ्चमी ।
हिरण्यवर्णा एताभिर्न्नमोऽन्ताभिरथाङ्गकम् ॥
रक्ताब्जसंस्थां पद्माक्षीं विचित्रानेकभूषणाम् ।
अरुणाब्जरजःपुञ्जवर्णां सद्गलशेखराम् ॥
अब्जयुग्मं वराभीती धारयन्तीं निजैर्भुजैः ।
देवीं त्रिलोकजननीमेवं ध्यायेत्तु देशिकः ॥
शुक्लप्रतिपदाद्येकादश्यन्तं प्रजपेन्मनुम् ।
अर्कसाहस्रमिध्मैस्तु बिल्वैः पद्मैर्घृतेन च ॥
पायसेन त्रिमध्वक्तैर्दशांशं जुहुयात्ततः ।
पुरोदितेन विधिना श्रीपीठे पूजयेच्छ्रियम् ॥
मूर्त्तिं मूलेन सङ्कल्प्य उपचारांस्तु षोडश ।
मन्त्रैस्तु पञ्चदशभिर्न्यस्तैः कुर्य्यात् समस्तकैः ॥
तत आवरणार्चायां केसरेष्वङ्गपूजनम् ।
पद्मा च पद्मवर्णा च पद्मस्थार्द्रा तुरीयका ॥
तर्पयन्ती च तृप्ता च ज्वलन्ती सप्तमी तथा ।
स्वर्णप्राकाराष्टमी स्यादेताः पत्रेषु संयजेत् ॥
लोकेशानायुधैः सार्द्धमेवं पूजा समीरिता । इति ।

अथ सर्व्वश्रीमन्त्रान्ते तन्त्रान्तरोक्तं श्रीयन्त्रं लिख्यते ।

अथातः सम्प्रवक्ष्यामि श्रियो यन्त्रं शृणु प्रिये ।
सर्व्वसिद्धिप्रदं यन्त्रं सर्व्वसम्मोहनं परम् ॥

तेजस्करं पुष्टिकरं श्रीकरञ्च यशस्करम् ।
अमृतत्वप्रदं नृणां सर्व्वाभीष्टफलप्रदम् ॥
शत्रूणां नाशनञ्चैव मित्राणां वर्द्धनं परम् ।
स्वसेनाह्वरणञ्चैव परसेनापसारणम् ॥
आथर्व्वणादिभिर्मन्त्रैः शत्रुभिः पीड़िते सदा ।
रक्षणं परमन्त्राणां छेदनञ्च महेश्वरि ॥
धारणाच्चायुरारोग्यं श्रीसौभाग्यधनप्रदम् ।
अष्टपत्रं महापद्मं कर्णिकाकेसरैर्युतम् ॥
श्रीबीजं नामसंयुक्तं कर्णिकायां समालिखेत् ।
अयुतं वारुणं बिन्दुभूषितं प्राग्दले लिखेत् ॥

अकारयुतं सबिन्दुकं हल्मात्रं वकारमित्यर्थः । एवञ्च वं इति भवति ।

वैष्णवं बिन्दुसद्बीजं तस्य दक्षिणदिग्दले ।

अं इति भवति ।

नान्तं यान्तसमायुक्तं सबिन्दुं वारुणे दले ।

नान्तः पकारः । यान्तो रेफः । एवञ्च प्रं इति भवति ।

विष्णुं बिन्दुसमायुक्तं सौम्ये वै दिग्दले लिखेत् ।

अं इत्यर्थः ।

जान्तं वह्निसमायुक्तं बिन्दुमद्वह्निदिग्दले ।

जान्तो झकारः । वह्निः रेफः । एवं झ्रं इति भवति ।

वान्तं विष्णुसमायुक्तं बिन्दुमन्नैर्ऋते दले ।

वान्तः शकारः । विष्णुः अकारः । एवं शं इति भवति ।

ब्रह्मणो द्वादशं बीजं पञ्चमस्वरसंयुतम् ।
बिन्दुनादसमायुक्तं विलिखेत् पावने दले ॥

ब्रह्मा कः तस्मात् द्वादशो वर्णः ठकारः । पञ्चम स्वरः उकारः । एवं ठुं इति भवति ।

वर्गाद्यं शान्तसंयुक्तं एकादशसमन्वितम् ।
बिन्दुनादसमायुक्तं न्यसेदीशानदिग्दले ॥

वर्गाद्यः ककारः । शान्तः षः । एकादश एकारः । क्षें इति भवति ।

तद्बाह्ये परितो मन्त्री श्रीबीजं प्रथमावृतौ ।
द्वितीयं कामबीजेन शक्तिबीजं तृतीयके ॥
ततो भूपुरमालिख्य प्राङ्मुखः सुप्रसन्नधीः ।

भूयसीं श्रियमाकाङ्क्षन् सत्यवादी भवेत् सदा ।
प्रत्यगाशामुखोऽश्नीयात् स्मितपूर्व्वं प्रियं वदेत् ॥ १६१

भूषयेद् गन्धपुष्पाद्यैर्वात्मानं नियतः शुचिः ।
शयीत शुभ्रशय्यायां तरुण्या सह नान्यया ॥ १६२

नग्नो नाऽवतरेदम्भस्तैलाभ्यक्तो न भक्षयेत् ।
हरिद्रां न मुखे लिम्पेन्न स्वपेदशुचिः क्वचित् ॥ १६३

न वृथा विलिखेद्भूमिं न बिल्वं द्रोणमम्बुजम् ।
धारयेन्मूर्ध्नि नैवाऽद्यात् लोणं तैलञ्च केवलम् ॥ १६४

मलिनो न भवेज्जातु कुत्सितान्नं न भक्षयेत् ।
द्रोणपङ्कजबिल्वानि पद्भ्यां जातु न लङ्घयेत् ॥ १६५

सहदेवीमिन्द्रवल्लीं श्रीवल्लीं विष्णुवल्लभाम् ।
कन्यां जम्बुं प्रवालञ्च धारयेन्मूर्ध्नि सर्व्वदा ॥ १६६

गुरुं संपूज्य यत्नेन वस्त्रधान्यधनादिभिः ॥
गन्धपुष्पाक्षताद्यैश्च यन्त्रं संपूजयेत् प्रिये ।
सहस्रं च जपं कृत्वा सर्व्वसिद्धिकरं प्रिये ॥
रौप्ये पत्रेऽथ लौहे वा भूर्ज्जे वा लिख्य धारयेत् ॥
श्रीबीजे नाम संलिख्य ठान्तं तद्बाह्यतो लिखेत् ।
बिन्दुयुक्तेन लान्तेन वेष्टयित्वा निरन्तरम् ॥
पुनरष्टदलं पद्मं श्रीँ क्लीँ प्रतिदलं लिखेत् ।
महामायां त्रिकोणाभ्यां वेष्टयित्वा बहिस्ततः ।
इदं धारयतो नित्यं वर्द्धते श्रीर्न संशयः ॥ इति ॥ १५७—१६० ॥

कमलोपासकस्य धर्म्मानाह भूयसीमिति । प्रत्यगाशामुखः पश्चिमास्यः । तरुण्येति । न च वृद्धया । उक्तं च "वृद्धा तु कुरुते ज्वरम्" । पञ्चपञ्चाशद्वर्षोपरि स्त्रीणां वृद्धता । नान्ययेत्यनेन एतदुक्तं भवति । यदाहुः—

दुष्टां कष्टान्ववायां कलहकलुषितां मार्गदुष्टामनिष्टा-
मन्यासक्तामसक्तामतिविपुलकृशाङ्गीमतिह्रस्वदीर्घाम् ।
रोगार्त्तां भोगलोलां प्रतिपुरुषचलां राजकान्तामकान्तां
काकाक्षीमेकचारां रहकुसुमयुतां न स्पृशेदिन्दिरार्थी ॥ इति ॥

इत्याचारपरो नित्यं विष्णुभक्तो दृढव्रतः ।

श्रियमाप्नोति महतीं देवानामपि दुर्लभाम् ॥ १६७

इति श्रीशारदातिलके अष्टमः पटलः ॥ श्रीः ॥

द्रोणं गूमा इति कान्यकुब्जभाषायाम् । श्रीदेवी श्रीलता । विष्णुवल्लभा विष्णुक्रान्ता । कन्या घृतकुमारी ॥ १६१॥१६२॥१६३॥१६४॥१६५॥१६६ ॥

इत्याचारेति । तन्त्रान्तरोक्ताचारग्रहणम् । तदुक्तं नारायणीये—

न जिघ्रेन्नाक्रमेच्चास्य तद्बीजं न च भक्षयेत् ।
न स्यान्मलिष्ठो न छिन्द्यात् बिल्वं भूमौ शयीत न ॥
लवणामलकं वर्ज्यं नागादित्यतिथौ क्रमात् ।
पञ्चम्यामुत्तरे च स्त्री वर्ज्या प्रत्यङ्मुखोऽशने ॥
बिल्वेन मार्जयेत् दन्तान् त्रिसन्ध्यं प्रणमेच्च तान् ।
प्रातर्भक्ष्यास्तिलास्तेन[सेव्या] धात्र्या लक्ष्मीं च भक्षयेत् ॥
धारयेन्मूर्ध्नि तत्पुष्पमुत्तरे मधुरान्नभुक् ।
पायसं बिल्वबीजं च भक्षयेच्छुक्लपर्व्वणि ॥ इति ।

प्रयोगसारेऽपि—

धान्य गो गुरु हुताशनराणां न स्वपेदुपरि नाप्यनुवंशं
नोत्तरापरशिरा न च नग्नो नार्द्रपाणिचरणः श्रियमिच्छन् ।
नाभ्यञ्जयादपि तैलमेव रजनीं नैवानुलिम्पेन्मुखे ॥ इति ॥ १६७ ॥

इति श्रीशारदातिलकटीकायां सत्सम्प्रदायकृतव्याख्यायां पदार्थादर्शाभिख्यायां श्रीमन्त्रनिरूपणं नाम अष्टमः पटलः ॥ ॐ ॥

नवमः पटलः ।

अथ वक्ष्ये जगद्धात्रीमधुना भुवनेश्वरीम् ।
ब्रह्मादयोऽपि यां ज्ञात्वा लेभिरे श्रियमूर्जिताम् ॥ १

नकुलीशोऽग्निमारूढो वामनेत्रार्द्धचन्द्रवान् ।
बीजं तस्या यथाख्यातं सेवितं सिद्धिकाङ्क्षिभिः ॥ २

ऋषिः शक्तिर्भवेच्छन्दो गायत्री देवता मनोः ।
कथिता स्वरसङ्घेन सेविता भुवनेश्वरी ॥ ३

एवं सरस्वतीश्रीमन्त्रानुक्त्वा तदन्तर्गतत्वात् एतदनन्तरं भुवनेशीमन्त्रान् वक्तुमारभते अथेति। यां ज्ञात्वा इत्यनेन अस्याः अपरा नानापि भेदाः सूचिताः। तत्र वाक्पुटितत्वं वाक्श्रीपुटितत्वं श्रीकामपुटितत्वं कामश्रीपुटितत्वं ग्रन्थकार एव वक्ष्यति। एवं कामपुटितत्वं श्रीवाक्पुटितत्वं वाक्कामपुटितत्वं कामवाक्पुटितत्वमिति चत्वारो भेदाः स्वयमूहनीयाः। तदुक्तम्—

कामाद्यन्ता प्रभवति यदा सर्व्वकामेश्वरी सा
साद्यन्तश्रीः सुतधनफला वाक्प्रदा वाग्भवेन ॥
एवं व्यस्तैर्विरचितपुटा कामधुक् सा हि शक्तिः। इति।

अन्यत्रापि—संपुटीकृत्य वा मन्त्रो कामबीजेन सुन्दरि ।
अभ्यसन् नियताहारः त्रैलोक्यं वशमानयेत् ॥ इति।

पद्मपादाचार्य्यैः प्रणवपुटितत्वं श्रीबीजचतुष्टयपुटितत्वमिति भेदद्वयमन्यदप्युक्तम्। श्रियमूर्जितामिति विनियोगसूचनम् ॥ १ ॥

मन्त्रमुद्धरति नकुलीश इति। नकुलीशो हकारः अग्नी रेफः वामनेत्रम् ईकारः अर्द्धचन्द्रो बिन्दुः। एवं मिलित्वा बीजमेकम्। सिद्धिकाङ्क्षिभिः सेवितामित्यनेन अस्य केवलस्यापि सकलपुरुषार्थ साधनता सूचिता। तथा च भुवनेश्वरीपारिजाते—

मत्समः पुरुषो नास्ति त्वत्समा नास्ति चाङ्गना ।
मायाबीजसमो मन्त्रो न भूतो न भविष्यति ॥ इति।

शक्तिरिति वशिष्ठपुत्रः। तदुक्तं संहितायाम् "ऋषिः शक्तिर्वशिष्ठस्य सुतः" इति। हं बीजं ईं शक्तिः। तदुक्तं दशपटल्याम्—

हं बीजम् ईं शक्तिः अस्य इष्टार्थे विनियोजनम्। इति ॥ २॥३ ॥

षड्दीर्घयुक्तबीजेन कुर्य्यादङ्गानि षट् क्रमात् ।
संहारसृष्टिमार्गेण मातृकान्यस्तविग्रहः ॥ ४
मन्त्रन्यासं ततः कुर्य्याद् देवताभावसिद्धये ।
हृल्लेखां मूर्द्ध्नि वदने गगनां हृदयाम्बुजे ॥ ५
रक्तां करालिकां गुह्ये महोच्छुष्मां पदद्वये ।
ऊर्द्ध्वप्राग्दक्षिणोदीच्यपश्चिमेषु मुखेषु च ॥ ६
सद्यादिह्रस्वबीजाढ्या न्यस्तव्याः भूतसप्रभाः ।
अङ्गानि विन्यसेत् पश्चाज्जातियुक्तानि षट् क्रमात् ॥ ७

षड्दीर्घेति। अत्र तु षडङ्गमन्त्रोद्धारमात्रं कृतम्। न्यासं वक्ष्यति न्यासावसरे। संहारसृष्टिमार्गेणेति। अत्राल्पस्वरत्वात् सृष्टिशब्दस्य पूर्व्वनिपातः कर्त्तव्यः। स च न कृतः तेन संहारन्यासं कृत्वा सृष्टिन्यासं कुर्य्यात्। तदुक्तं संहितायाम्—

अकाराद्यर्णपर्य्यन्तां विपरीतक्रमेण तु ।
गुरूपदेशविधिना मातृकां प्रथमं न्यसेत् ॥
संहारमातृकान्यासो ब्रह्मानन्दरसोज्ज्वलः । इति ।

आचार्य्या अपि—संहृत्य चोत्पाद्य शरीरमेवम्। इति।
पदद्वये इति। एकदैव एकहस्तेनेति ज्ञेयम् अन्यथा मन्त्रावृत्तिप्रसङ्गात्।
॥ ४ ॥ ५ ॥ ६ ॥

सद्यादीति। सद्य ओकारस्तदादयः। पञ्चह्रस्वाः अनेन विलोमप्रकारेण नपुंसकव्यतिरिक्ताः पञ्चह्रस्वा गृह्यन्ते। ओ ए उ इ अ सद्यादि ह्रस्वा यस्मिन् एवं भूतं यद्बीजं तदाढ्या इति सम्प्रदायविदः। तेन ह्रों ह्रें ह्रुं ह्रिं ह्रं इति बीजानि भवन्ति। गूढ़ार्थदीपिकाकारस्तु ओ ए ऌ ऋ उ इमान् पञ्चह्रस्वान् उक्तवान्। तन्न। सर्व्वत्राग्रेऽपि सम्प्रदायानुसारेण सद्यादिग्रहणे नपुंसकव्यतिरिक्तानामेव ग्रहणात्। यत् तु केचन स्वरमात्रं बीजत्वेनाहुः तदपि न। बीजशब्दोपादानवैयर्थ्यात्। उक्तञ्च दशपटल्याम्—

सद्योष्ठश्रुतिनेत्राद्यैर्विद्यां संभेद्य मन्त्रवित् ।
हृल्लेखादीन् प्रविन्यस्येत् ॥ इति ।

भूतसप्रभा इति। पृथिव्यादिक्रमेणेत्यर्थः। तेन हृल्लेखा पीता गगना विशदा रक्ता रक्ता महोच्छुष्मा कृष्णा करालिका स्वच्छेति। अङ्गानीति। पूर्व्वोक्तैः

ब्रह्माणं विन्यसेद्भाले गायत्र्या सह संयुतम्।
सावित्र्या संयुतं विष्णुं कपोले दक्षिणे न्यसेत्॥ ८
वागीश्वर्य्या समायुक्तं वामगण्डे महेश्वरम्।
श्रिया धनपतिं न्यस्येद् वामकर्णाग्रके पुनः॥ ६
रत्या स्मरं मुखे न्यस्य पुष्ट्या गणपतिं न्यसेत्।
सव्यकर्णोपरि निधी कर्णगण्डान्तरालयोः॥ १०
न्यस्तव्यौ वदने मूलं भूयश्चैतांस्तनौ न्यसेत्।
कण्ठमूले स्तनद्वन्द्वे वामांसे हृदयाम्बुजे॥ ११
सव्यांसे पार्श्वयुगले नाभिदेशे च देशिकः।
भालांसपार्श्वजठरे पार्श्वांसापरके हृदि॥ १२

स्वजातिभिरङ्गमन्त्रैरित्यर्थः। अतएव पश्चादिति। तदुक्तमाचार्य्यैः—

हृल्लेखाख्यां गगनां रक्तां च करालिकां महोच्छुष्माम्।
मूर्द्धनि वदने हृदये गुह्ये पादयोर्न्यस्येत्तदङ्गैश्च॥ इति॥ ७॥

योनिन्यासमाह ब्रह्माणमिति। तत्र ह्रां ह्रीं ह्रूं इति गायत्र्यादीनां बीजानि। ह्रं ह्रिं ह्रुं इति ब्रह्मादीनाम्। अन्येषां स्वस्वबीजानि। निध्योराद्यक्षरं बीजमिति ज्ञेयम्। तत्र प्रयोगः। ह्रां गायत्रीसहिताय ह्रं ब्रह्मणे नम इत्यादि। शक्तिनामादित्वं पूजायां स्फुटीभविष्यति। वामकर्णाग्रके वामकर्णोपरि। शाखे वृक्षवत् व्यवहारात्। सव्यकर्णोपरि दक्षकर्णोपरि। वामस्य पूर्व्वमुक्तेः। निधी शङ्खपद्मौ तत्स्वरूपौ सशक्तिकौ। कर्णगण्डान्तरालयोरिति दक्षवामयोः। मूलं मूलमन्त्रम्। वदन इति तदेकदेशचिबुकं लक्ष्यते। एतानिति ब्रह्मादीन् मूलान्तान्। अयमेव साम्प्रदायिकः पाठः। केचन एतां तनौ न्यसेदिति पठन्ति। तन्मते एतां भुवनेशीं कण्ठादिषु नवसु स्थानेषु न्यसेत्। स्तनद्वन्द्वे दक्षवामे। सव्यांसे दक्षिणांसे। यद्यपि "वामं शरीरे सव्यं स्यात्" इति कोषः। तथाप्यत्र सव्यशब्देन दक्षिण एव गृह्यते। वामस्य पूर्व्वं पृथगुक्तेः। तथा च शैवागमे "विन्यसेत् सव्यवामयोः" इति बहुषु स्थलेषु व्यवहारः। "सव्यं दक्षिणवामयोः" इति कोषान्तरं च। पार्श्वयुगले दक्षवामे। देशिक इत्यनेन सबीजत्वमुक्तम्। भालांसेति मातृकान्यासस्थानम्। अंसपार्श्वे वामगते। पार्श्वांसौ दक्षिणौ। अपरकं ककुत्। यद्यप्यपरगलशब्देन ककुदुच्यते तथाप्यत्र भीमो भीमसेन

ब्रह्माण्याद्यास्ततो न्यस्या विधिना प्रोक्तलक्षणाः।
मूलेन व्यापकं देहे न्यस्य देवीं विचिन्तयेत् ॥ १३

उद्यद्दिनद्युतिमिन्दुकिरीटां तुङ्गकुचां नयनत्रययुक्ताम्।
स्मेरमुखीं वरदाङ्कुशपाशाभीतिकरां प्रभजेत् भुवनेशीम् ॥ १४

प्रजपेन्मन्त्रविन्मन्त्रं द्वात्रिंशल्लक्षमानतः।
त्रिस्वादुयुक्तैर्जुहुयादष्टद्रव्यैर्दशांशतः ॥ १५

इतिवत् प्रयोगः। तदुक्तमाचार्य्यैः

अलिकांसपार्श्वकुक्षिषु पार्श्वांसापरगलहृत्सु च क्रमशः।
ब्रह्माण्याद्या विधिवत् न्यस्तव्या मातरोऽष्ट मन्त्रितमैः ॥

विधिनेति स्वबीजाद्याः। प्रोक्तलक्षणा मातृकापटलोक्तध्यानाः। व्यापकमिति कराभ्यां मस्तकाद्यापादाङ्गुष्ठम् ॥ ८ ॥ ९ ॥ १० ॥ ११ ॥ १२ ॥ १३ ॥

ध्यानमाह उद्यदिति। इनः सूर्यः। रक्तपद्मस्थाम् इत्यपि। आयुधध्यानं वामाधोहस्ते वरं दक्षिणोर्द्धे अङ्कुशम्। वामोर्द्धे पाशं दक्षाधोऽभयमिति सम्प्रदायविदः। तदुक्तं महासम्मोहने--

दक्षिणे चाङ्कुशं दद्यादु वामे पाशं प्रदापयेत्।
वरदं वामतो दद्यादभयं दक्षिणे करे ॥ इति ॥ १४ ॥

प्रजपेदिति मन्त्रार्थानुसन्धानपूर्व्वकम् हरिहरात्मकप्रकृतिपुरुषाकारेण अवस्थिताया आद्यशक्तेः प्रतिपादकोऽयं मन्त्रः। अतएव भुवनेशीति नाम।

तदुक्तम्—हरित्वाच्च हरत्वाच्च पुंप्रकृत्योस्तु युक्तयोः।
श्लिष्टोच्चारितमेवेदं शब्दं तद्रूपमीरितम् ॥ इति।

संहितायान्तु—व्योमबीजे महेशानि कैलासादि प्रतिष्ठितम्।
वह्निबीजात् सुवर्णादि निष्पन्नं बहुधा प्रिये ॥
तेनायं वर्त्तते लोके भूमण्डल समास्थितः।
तुर्य्यस्वरेण पाताले शेषरूपेण धार्य्यते ॥
महाभूमण्डलं तस्मात् पातालस्यापि नायिका।
अतएव महेशानी भुवनाधीश्वरी प्रिये ॥
हकारे व्योम तुर्य्येण स्वरेणाऽनिलसम्भवः
विकारे सति रेफेण साक्षाद् वह्निस्वरूपिणी ॥
वह्नेर्वीर्य्यं वसु ह्येवं तस्माद् रेफो वसुन्धरा।

दद्यादर्घ्यं दिनेशाय तत्र सञ्चिन्त्य पार्व्वतीम्।
पद्ममष्टदलं बाह्ये वृत्तं षोड़शभिर्द्दलैः॥ १६

विलिखेत् कर्णिकामध्ये षट्कोणमतिसुन्दरम्।
ततः संपूजयेत् पीठं नवशक्तिसमन्वितम्॥ १७

जयाख्या विजया पश्चादजिता चाऽपराजिता।
नित्या विलासिनी दोग्ध्री अघोरा मङ्गला नव॥ १८

अतएव महेशानि रलयोः समता भवेत्॥
बिन्दुचक्रामृताद् देवी प्लावयन्ती जगत्त्रयम्।
द्रवरूपा भवेत् तस्मात् द्रवन्ती चार्द्दमालया॥
अतएव महेशानी भुवनेशीति कथ्यते। इति।

मन्त्रविदित्यनेन हसकलयोगः। मोक्षार्थं प्रणवयोगोऽपि सूचितः। यद्वा तन्त्रान्तरोक्तं पुरश्चरणम्। यथा—

एकलिङ्गे शिवागारे दक्षिणां मूर्त्तिमाश्रितः।
बद्धपद्मासनो भस्मस्नायी च कुशविष्टरः॥
कृष्णाष्टमीं समारभ्य यावत् स्यात् तच्चतुर्द्दशी।
नित्यमिष्ट्वा शिवं शक्तिं जपेन्मन्त्रं सहस्रकम्॥
दधिक्षौद्रघृताभ्यक्ता व्याघातसमिधो हुनेत्।
ततः साग्रं सहस्रं च ध्यायेत् सर्व्वेश्वरीमुमाम्॥ इति।

त्रिःस्वादुयुक्तैः त्रिमधुरोपेतैः।
तदुक्तं प्रयोगसारे—पयोमधुघृतं चेति समं त्रिमधुरं स्मृतम्। इति।

अन्ये पयःस्थाने शर्करामाहुः—

जपाद्दशांशं जुहुयादथाष्टद्रव्यैर्गुड़क्षौद्रघृतावसिक्तैः। इति।
तट्टीकाकारैः गुड़ः शर्करेति व्याख्यातम्। अष्टद्रव्यैरिति मातृकापटलोक्तैः॥ १५॥

दद्यादिति मूलेन। तत्रेति सूर्य्यमण्डले। इयं सौरी शक्तिरिति कृत्वा अत्रार्घ्यदानप्राधान्यादत्रोक्तिः। परन्तु सर्व्वमन्त्रेषु तत्तन्मन्त्रदेवतां सूर्य्यमण्डले संचिन्त्य सूर्य्यमण्डले सूर्य्यायार्घ्यः कर्त्तव्य इति ज्ञेयम्। तच्चया सन्ध्याकथनावसरे उक्तम्। अत्र ध्यानानन्तरम् आयुधपुस्तकज्ञानयोनिबीजमुद्राः प्रदर्शयेत्।

यदाहुः—एवं शक्तिं परां ध्यात्वा सम्यक् मुद्राः प्रदर्शयेत्।
पाशाङ्कुशाभयाभीष्टपुस्तकज्ञानयोनयः॥ इति।

तत्र पाशमुद्रालक्षणं यथा—

वाममुष्टिस्थतर्जन्या दक्षमुष्टिस्थतर्जनीम् ।
संयोज्याऽङ्गुष्ठकाग्राभ्यां तर्ज्जन्यग्रे स्वके क्षिपेत् ।
एषा पाशस्य मुद्रेति विद्वद्भिः परिकीर्त्तिता ॥ इति ।

शेषमुद्रालक्षणानि मया पूर्व्वमुक्तानि । वीजमुद्रा गुरुमुखादवगन्तव्या । अत्र स्वपूजासाधनप्रोक्षणमन्त्रोऽयं ज्ञेयः ।

प्रणवो वाग्भवो माया स्त्रीबीजं परमामृतम् ।
रूपे भगवति प्रोक्ता चन्द्रमण्डलवासिनि ॥
चन्द्रामृतेन पुरयद्वितयं द्रव्यमित्यपि ।
इदं पवित्रयद्वन्द्वं श्रीमायावाक्द्विठस्ततः ॥
तेनामृतेन सम्प्रोक्षेदात्मानं साधनानि च । इति ।

पूजायन्त्रमाह पद्ममिति । षट्कोणमिति ऊर्द्ध्वाधोऽग्रत्रिकोणे परस्परभेदिते । अतिसुन्दरमित्यनेन यथा समं भवति तथा कर्त्तव्यमित्युक्तं भवति । तत्र त्रिकोणादीनां समत्वे प्रकार उच्यते—

छित्वा वृत्तप्रागगुणाङ्घ्रिं तिर्य्यगन्यौ तु पार्श्वयोः ।
त्र्यराः षट् त्वन्यतोऽप्येवं द्वादशारा उदीच्यपि ॥ इति ।

समं प्राचीसूत्रं कृत्वा तन्मध्यमालम्ब्य यथेप्सितं वृत्तं कृत्वा तत्र प्राचीसूत्रं चतुर्धा विभजेत् । एकस्मादग्रात् तुर्य्यांशं सन्त्यज्य एकं तिर्य्यक्सूत्रं पातयेत् । पार्श्वयोः सूत्रद्वयदानात् त्र्यस्रम् । एवमन्यतोऽपि कृते षडस्रम् । एवम् उदग्दक्षिणतः कृते द्वादशास्रमित्यर्थः । वृत्तप्रमाणमाचार्य्यैरुक्तम्—

षडङ्गुलप्रमाणेन वर्त्तुलं कर्त्तरालिखेत् ।
षडङ्गुलावकाशेन तद्बहिश्च प्रवर्त्तयेत् ॥
वर्त्तुलं तावता भूयस्तद्बहिश्च तृतीयकम् ।
मध्यवर्त्तुलमध्ये तु हृल्लेखाबीजमालिखेत् ॥
द्वितीय वर्त्तुलाश्लिष्टमीषत्श्लिष्टषडस्रकम् ।
पुटितं मण्डलं वज्रैरस्रग्रात् मध्यवर्त्तुलम् ॥
इन्द्राग्निरक्षोवरुण वाय्वीशान्तास्त्रकं लिखेत् । इति ।

अत्रोपरिवृत्तद्वयमपि षट्कोणसमत्वानयनार्थेव इति ज्ञेयम् । एतदुपरि चतुरस्रञ्च ज्ञेयम् । अन्यशक्तिमन्त्रपूजायन्त्रे तथोक्तेः । चतुर्द्वारमित्यपि । तस्य साधारणत्वात् अत्र नोक्तिः । तत इति नित्यजपानन्तरमित्यर्थः । अन्तर्यागानन्तरं

बीजाद्यमासनं दत्त्वा मूर्त्तिं तेनैव कल्पयेत् ।
तस्यां संपूजयेद्देवीमावाह्यावरणैः सह ॥ १९
मध्यप्रागयाम्यसौम्येषु पश्चिमेषु यथाक्रमम् ।
हृल्लेखाद्याः समभ्यर्च्याः पञ्चभूतसमप्रभाः ॥ २०
वरपाशाङ्कुशाभीतिधारिण्यो मितभूषणाः ।
स्थानेषु पूर्व्वमुक्तेषु पूजयेदङ्गदेवताः ॥ २१
षट्कोणेषु यजेन्मन्त्री पश्चान्मिथुनदेवताः ।
इन्द्रकोणे लसद्दण्डकुण्डिकाक्षगुणाभयाम् ॥ २२

तस्य कृतत्वात् ॥ १६ ॥ १७ ॥ १८ ॥

पीठमन्त्रमुद्धरति बीजाद्यमिति । तत्र प्रयोगः । मूलबीजमुच्चार्य्य सर्व्वशक्ति-कमलासनाय नमः इति । तदुक्तम्—

सर्व्वशक्तिपदं प्रोच्य ङेऽन्तं च कमलासनम् ।
नम इत्यासनं पूज्य तत्तद्बीजादिकं शिवे ॥ इति ।

अयं पीठमन्त्रः सर्व्वभुवनेशीमन्त्रसाधारण इति ज्ञेयम् । अस्याः पद्मं रक्तं ध्येयम् । तदुक्तं प्रयोगसारे—

रक्ताम्भोजं समाधाय रत्नसिंहासनोपरि । तत्रावाह्य हृदा देवीम् । इति । तेनैवेति । मध्यादि एता यथाक्रमं समभ्यर्च्या इत्यन्वयः । आदिशब्दार्थमाह प्रागिति । हृल्लेखाद्या इति यथान्यस्ताः । आसामायुधध्यानं देवीवत् ।

पूर्व्वमुक्तेषु चतुर्थपटलोक्तेषु आग्नेयादिषु । तानि आग्नेयादीनि कर्णिकान्तःस्थानि इति ज्ञेयम् । अङ्गानि केसरेषु इति यद्वक्ष्यमाणं ग्रन्थकृता सामान्योक्तस्य अनुवादः कृतः अयमाशयः । अङ्गानि केसरेष्विति अन्यत्र । इह तु कर्णिकायामेव पूजेति ।

तदुक्तमाचार्य्यैः—हृल्लेखाद्यास्तदनु च पूर्व्ववदङ्गानि पूजनीयानि । इति ।

केचित्तु उभयत्र षडङ्गन्यासस्थलद्वयेऽप्यङ्गपूजनम् इत्याहुः । तच्च प्रपञ्च-सारादिविरुद्धम् ॥ १९॥२०॥२१ ॥

अथ पूजाप्रकारः । प्रथममूर्द्धाग्रत्रिकोणकोणेषु प्रादक्षिण्येन पश्चादीशानान्तां पूजामभिदधदधराग्रत्रिकोणकोणेषु प्रादक्षिण्येन पूजामाह षट्कोणेष्विति । अतएवेत्युक्तिः । वामोर्द्ध्वादि आद्ये दक्षोर्द्ध्वादि अपरे इत्यायुधध्यानम् ।

गायत्रीं पूजयेन्मन्त्री ब्रह्माणमपि तादृशम् ।
रक्ष:कोणे शङ्खचक्रगदापङ्कजधारिणीम् ॥ २३
सावित्रीं पीतवसनां यजेद्विष्णुञ्च तादृशम् ।
वायुकोणे परश्वक्षमालाभयवरान्विताम् ॥ २४
यजेत् सरस्वतीमित्थं रुद्रं तादृशलक्षणम् ।
वह्निकोणे यजेद्रत्नकुम्भं मणिकरण्डकम् ॥ २५
कराभ्यां बिभ्रतं पीतं तुन्दिलं धननायकम् ।
आलिङ्ग्य सव्यहस्तेन वामेनाम्बुजधारिणीम् ॥ २६
धनदाङ्कसमारूढां महालक्ष्मीं प्रपूजयेत् ।
वारुणे मदनं बाणपाशाङ्कुशशरासनम् ॥ २७
धारयन्तं जवारक्तं पूजयेद्रत्नभूषणम् ।
सव्येन पतिमाश्लिष्य वामेनोत्पलधारिणीम् ॥ २८
पाणिना रमणाङ्कस्थां रतिं सम्यक् समर्चयेत् ।
ऐशाने पूजयेत् सम्यग्विघ्नराजं प्रियान्वितम् ॥ २९
सृणिपाशधरं कान्तावराङ्गस्पृक्कराङ्गुलिम् ।
माध्वीपूर्णकपालाढ्य विघ्नराज दिगम्बरम् ॥ ३०
पुष्करे विगलद्रत्नस्फुरच्चषकधारिणम् ।
सिन्दूरसदृशाकारामुद्दाममदविभ्रमाम् ॥ ३१
धृतरक्तोत्पलामन्यपाणिना तु ध्वजस्पृशम् ।
आश्लिष्टकान्तामरुणां पुष्टिमर्चेद्दिगम्बराम् ॥ ३२

गायत्र्यां दक्षवामयोरूर्द्ध्वयोः आद्ये अधस्थयोः परे इति। सावित्र्यां वामोर्द्ध्वात् वामाधस्तनं यावत्। सरस्वत्यां रत्नकुम्भो वामेऽन्यो दक्षिणे। धननायके दक्षिणाधस्तात् वामाधःपर्य्यन्तम्। मदने वामदक्षयोः ऊर्द्ध्वयोः अङ्कुशपाशौ। कान्तावराङ्गस्पृगिति अधोवामेन। माध्वीत्यादि दक्षिणाध इति विघ्नराजे। पुष्करं करिहस्ताग्रे। उद्दामेत्यादि शक्तिध्यानम्। धृतरक्तोत्पलमिति दक्षिणेन। अन्येनेति वामेन ॥ २२-३२ ॥

कर्णिकायां निधी पूज्यौ षट्कोणस्थाऽथ पार्श्वयोः।
अङ्गानि केसरेष्वेताः पश्चात् पत्रेषु पूजयेत्॥ ३३
अनङ्गकुसुमा पश्चादनङ्गकुसुमातुरा।
अनङ्गमदना तद्वदनङ्गमदनातुरा॥ ३४
भुवनपाला गगनवेगा चैव ततः परम्।
शशिरेखाऽथ गगनरेखा चेत्यष्ट शक्तयः॥ ३५
पाशाङ्कुशवराभीतिधारिण्योऽरुणविग्रहाः।
ततः षोडशपत्रेषु करालो विकरालयुमा॥ ३६
सरस्वती श्रीर्दुर्गोषा लक्ष्मीश्रुत्यौ स्मृतिर्धृतिः।
श्रद्धा मेधा मतिः कान्तिरार्य्या षोडश शक्तयः॥ ३७
खड्गखेटकधारिण्यः श्यामाः पूज्याश्च मातरः।
पश्चाद् बहिः समभ्यर्च्याः शक्तयः परिचारिकाः॥ ३८
प्रथमाऽनङ्गरूपा स्यादनङ्गमदना ततः।
मदनातुरा भुवनवेगा भुवनपालिका॥ ३९
स्यात् सर्वशिशिरानङ्गवेदनाङ्गमेखला।
चषकं तालवृन्तञ्च ताम्बूलं छत्रमुज्ज्वलम्॥ ४०

कर्णिकायामिति पद्मकर्णिकायाम्। निधी इति यथान्यस्तौ। एता इति अनन्तरं वक्ष्यमाणाः अनङ्गकुसुमाद्याः। आसां ध्यानं देवीवत् ज्ञेयम्। खेटकम् फरी इति कान्यकुब्जभाषायाम्। श्यामा इत्यन्तं पूर्व्वशक्तिध्यानम्। पूज्याश्चेति चकारो भिन्नक्रमः। मातर इत्येतदनन्तरं द्रष्टव्याः। मातरश्चेति चकारात् वक्ष्यमाणशक्तयश्च। तेन मातरो यथान्यस्ताः पश्चाद्बहिः पूज्याः। पश्चाद्बहिः परिचारिका अपि अष्टदिक्षु। एता द्विभुजा वामहस्ते रक्तोत्पलं परहस्ते चषकादि। तदुक्तं प्रयोगसारे

रक्ता रक्तोज्ज्वलाकल्पा रक्तान्तायतलोचनाः।
रक्तोत्पलकरा ध्येयाः सुन्दराः परिचारिकाः॥

अत्र सर्व्वत्र तर्पणादीनामन्येषामप्यङ्गानां सत्त्वात् यत् ध्यानपूजाजपहोमानेवाह

चामरे चांशुकं पुष्पं बिभ्राणा करपङ्कजैः ।
सर्व्वाभरणसन्दीप्तान् लोकपालान् बहिर्यजेत् ॥ ४१
वज्रादीन्यपि तद्बाह्ये देवीमित्थं प्रपूजयेत् ।
पूज्यते सकलैर्देवैः किं पुनर्मनुजोत्तमैः ॥ ४२
मन्त्री त्रिमधुरोपेतैर्हुत्वाऽश्वत्थसमिद्वरैः ।
ब्राह्मणान् वशयेच्छीघ्रं पार्थिवान् पद्महोमतः ॥ ४३
पलाशपुष्पैस्तत्पत्नीर्मन्त्रिणां कुमुदैरपि ।
पञ्चविंशतिसङ्ख्यैर्जलैः स्नानं दिने दिने ॥ ४४

तेनैषां नित्यकर्त्तव्यत्वं सूचितम् । तदुक्तं पिङ्गलामते—

नाध्यातो नार्चितो मन्त्रः सुसिद्धोऽपि प्रसीदति ।
नाजप्तः सिद्धिदाने च्छुर्नाहुतः फलदो भवेत् ॥
पूजां ध्यानं जपं होमं तस्मात् कर्म्मचतुष्टयम् ।
प्रत्यहं साधकः कुर्य्यात् स्वयञ्चेत् सिद्धिमिच्छति ॥
जपश्रान्तः शिवं ध्यायेत् ध्यानश्रान्तः पुनर्जपेत् ।
जपध्यानसमायुक्तः शीघ्रं सिध्यति मन्त्रवित् ॥ इति ।

षट्कोणेषु यजेत् मन्त्री इत्यत एतदन्तं मन्त्रीति कर्तृपदमनुवर्त्तते । तेन चैतदन्तं समयाचारत्वेनैव सूचितम् । यदाहुः—

योगिशो सिद्धिमन्विच्छन् सद्व्रतानि समाचरेत् ।
नाऽद्यादनर्चयन् देवीं नेन स्नान्मलिनाकृतिः ॥
नाऽसत्यं प्रवदेत् किञ्चिन्नोपेयाद्विधवां क्वचित् ।
धारयेत् सर्व्वतो रम्यं रत्नालङ्कारमन्वहम् ॥
कन्यां रक्तदिने रक्तां यजेद्देवीमनुस्मरन् ।
अशुद्धो विचरेन्नैव विविक्ते शयने स्वपेत् ॥
न निन्दयेत् स्त्रियं जातु विशेषेण तु कन्यकाम् ॥ इति ।

देवीमित्थं प्रपूजयेत् इत्यनेन एतदुक्तं भवति । आवरणेषु षोडशशक्त्यनन्तरं द्वात्रिंशच्छक्तयस्तदनन्तरं चतुःषष्टिशक्तयोऽर्च्या इति । ताश्च भूतलिपिमन्त्रे उक्ता ज्ञेयाः । तत्फलमेवाह पूज्यते सकलैर्देवैरिति । किं पुनः मनुजोत्तमै-रित्यनेन एतदुक्तं भवति । स्तोक्तं मध्ये यदनङ्गकुसुमाद्यष्टशक्त्यावरणं तदन्तस्य

आत्मानमभिषिञ्चेद् यः सर्वसौभाग्यवान् भवेत्।
पञ्चविंशतिसञ्जप्तं जलं प्रातः पिबेन्नरः॥ ४५
अवाप्य महतीं प्रज्ञां कवीनामग्रणीर्भवेत्।
कर्पूरागुरुसंयुक्तं कुङ्कुमं साधु साधितम्॥ ४६
गृहीत्वा तिलकं कुर्य्याद्राजवश्यमनुत्तमम्।
शालिपिष्टमयीं कृत्वा पुत्तलीं मधुरान्विताम्॥ ४७
जप्तां प्रतिष्ठितप्राणां भक्षयेद्रविवासरे।
वशं नयति राजानं नारीं वा नरमेव वा॥ ४८
कण्ठमात्रोदके स्थित्वा वीक्ष्य तोयगतं रविम्।
त्रिसहस्रं जपेन्मन्त्रमिष्टां कन्यां लभेन्नरः।
अन्नं तन्मन्त्रितं मन्त्री भुञ्जीत श्रीप्रसिद्धये॥ ४९
लिखित्वा भस्मना मायांससाध्यां फलकादिषु।
तत्काले दर्शयेदन्तं सुखं सूयेत गर्भिणी॥ ५०

फलम्। मनुजेति। ततो यत् षोड़शशक्त्यावरणं तदेतस्य फलम् तदुक्तमेिति। तदुक्तं महासम्मोहने—

चतुर्भिर्वा त्रिभिर्वापि द्वयेनैकेन वा पुनः।
सर्व्वैरावरणैरेवं भोगार्थी विस्तरं यजेत्॥ . इति।

तथा गर्भावरणं शाक्तानां मध्ये तेषां प्रपूजनमिति तत्रैव। तेनास्याः सप्तावरणादारभ्य एकादशावरणान्ता पूजेति सूचितम्। एवं पञ्चावरणा षड़ावरणापि इत्यपि मन्त्री इत्यनेनैतदुक्तं भवति—

सिद्धः प्रसिद्धस्तेजस्वी त्यागी योगी जितेन्द्रियः।
सर्व्वज्ञः सुभगः श्रीमान् निराधिः प्रियदर्शनः॥
चौरादिव्यालवेताल गुह्यकासुरदानवैः।
न भयं जायते तस्य सिद्धमन्त्रस्य देहिनः॥
ग्रामे वा नगरे वाऽपि सभायां राजसन्निधौ।
प्रसिद्धः पूज्यते सद्भिर्लभते वाञ्छितं हितम्॥ इति।

शक्त्यन्तःस्थितसाध्यकर्म्म भवने वह्नेर्वृतं शक्तिभि-
र्बाह्ये कोणगते युतं हरिहरैर्वर्णैः कपोलार्पितैः ।
पश्चात्तैः पुनरौंयुतैर्लिपिभिरप्यावीतमिष्टार्थदं
यन्त्रं भूपुरमध्यगं त्रिगुणितं सौभाग्यसम्पत्प्रदम् ॥ ५१

मन्त्री शीघ्रमित्यनेन अयुतहोम इत्युक्तम् । यत् प्रयोगसारे—

वश्यायाऽश्वत्थराजीवतिलक्षीरैर्यथाक्रमात् ।
जुहुयाद् ब्राह्मणादीनां तथैवाऽयुतसंख्यया ॥ इति ।

साधुसाधितमित्यष्टोत्तरसहस्रं जप्तम् । पुत्तलीमिति द्वादशाङ्गुलायामाम् । भवयेदिति दक्षिणपादाङ्गुष्ठादिवामपादाङ्गुष्ठान्तम् । स्त्रियान्तु वैपरीत्यम् । भस्मनेति गोमयभस्मना । चतुरस्र इति ज्ञेयम् ।

पुत्तलभावनायां पलाशभस्म इत्यपेक्षितार्थद्योतनिकायाम् । तदुक्तं नारायणीये—भस्मना लिखितां साध्यां हृल्लेखां शक्रवेश्मनि । इति ॥ ३२-५० ॥

त्रिगुणितं यन्त्रमाह शक्त्यन्तरिति । एवंभूतं त्रिगुणितं यन्त्रं सौभाग्यसम्पत्प्रदमित्यन्वयः । कीदृक् तत् । वह्निभवने ऊर्द्ध्वाग्रे त्रिकोणे । शक्त्यन्तः शक्तिबीजमध्यस्थितम् । साध्येति साधकोपलक्षकम् । साध्यसाधककर्म्माणि यत्र तत् । तत्र प्रयोगः । देवदत्तस्य यज्ञदत्तं वशं कुरु कुरु इति । तदुक्तं रामपूर्व्वतापनीये—लिखेत् साध्यं द्वितीयान्तं षष्ठ्यन्तं साधकं तथा ।
कुरुद्वयञ्च तत्पार्श्वे । इति ।

तत्र बीजरेफभागे साध्यनाम । चतुर्थस्वरभागे साधकनाम । तयोर्मध्ये साधकांशे कर्म्म लिखेत् । तदुक्तं संहितायाम्—

तच्छक्तिरेफभागे तु साध्यनामाक्षरं लिखेत् ।
तुरीयस्वरभागे तु साधकस्य वशं कुरु ।
साध्यस्योपरि संस्पृष्टं विलिखेत् सर्व्वसिद्धये ॥ इति

आचार्य्याश्च—मध्यवर्त्तुलसंस्थाया हृल्लेखायाः कपोलयोः ।
अधरे साध्यनामार्णं साधकस्योत्तरे लिखेत् ॥
अन्तराग्निश्रियोः कर्म्म साधकांशे समालिखेत् । इति ।

अनेनावश्यं वृत्तान्तः शक्तिं लिखेदित्यप्युक्तम् । अन्यत्रापि "ठकारवेष्टितां कृत्वा" इति । बाह्ये त्रिकोणाग्रभागेषु । शक्तिभिरिति बहुवचनं कपिञ्जलाधिकरणन्यायेन त्रित्वे पर्य्यवस्यति । तेन त्रिभिः शक्तिबीजैः वृतम् । आवरणं च गरुडद्वय-

बीजान्तःस्थितसाध्यनाम शरशो मायावमामन्मथै-
र्वीतं वह्निपुरद्वये रसपुटेष्वाख्याढ्यबीजत्रयम् ।
सात्मानात्मकमौशिखं हरिहरैरावद्धगण्डं बहिः
षड्बीजैरनुबद्धसन्धिलिपिभिर्वीतं ग्रहाभ्यां भुवः ॥ ५२

लिखित हरिहरवर्णबहिर्भागे ।

तदुक्तम्—कोणाग्रेषु परां लिखेत् । इति ।

आचार्य्याश्च—शक्त्या विःसाध्यमिन्द्रानिलनिर्ऋतिगबीजानुविद्धं पुरेऽग्नेः । इति ।

अत्रावरणमित्थम् । एकैकस्य रेफाग्रेण तत्तद्बीजं प्रदक्षिणीकृत्य अन्य-स्याधो नीत्वा तदौकाराग्रं बध्नीयादिति । तदुक्तं

संहितायाम्—स्थानत्रयेऽपि बन्धस्तु कथ्यते सिद्धिदायकः ।
तद्बीजत्रयरेफाग्रं प्रादक्षिण्येन वेष्टयेत् ॥
अधस्तत्त्रितयं चाऽस्य मायाग्रेण च वेष्टयेत् ।
अन्योन्यकलनारम्यः शक्तिबन्ध उदाहृतः ॥ इति ।

कोणगतेषु तत्त्रिकोणान्तःकोणेषु ईं लिखेत् ।

तदुक्तम्—त्रिकोणस्यान्तरालेषु वामनेत्रं सबिन्दुकम् । इति ।

कपोलार्पितैर्हरिहरैर्वर्णैरुपलक्षितम् । कपोलयोः त्रिकोणकोणपार्श्वयोः हरि-रित्येकत्र हर इत्यपरत्र च । केचन ह्रि ह्र इत्याहुः । तन्न । मानाभावात् ।

तथा च संहितायाम्—प्रत्येककोणपार्श्वेषु हर्य्यर्णौ च हराक्षरौ । इति ।

पश्चात् तदनन्तरं तैः हरिहरैः ईंयुतैः । तेन हरि ईं हर ईं इत्यक्षरैरावीतम् ।

तदुक्तं संहितायाम्—पुनरेतद्द्वयोर्मध्ये तुर्य्यं चैव सबिन्दुकम् ।
इत्यर्णैर्वेष्टयेद्वाह्ये वृत्तं कुर्य्याद्वहिस्ततः ॥ इति

गौरीतन्त्रेऽपि—हरिबीजं हरानादीन् चान्तवर्णांश्च वाह्यतः । इति ।

आचार्य्याश्च—मध्ये समायैस्तैः । इति ।

पद्मपादाचार्य्यास्तु प्रत्येकमीं योगमाहुः । हरि ईं हर ईं इति ।

लिपिभिः अकारादि क्षकारान्तैः । अपिशब्दः पूर्व्वसमुच्चये । आवीतं वेष्टितम् । भूपुरमध्यगं तद्बहिः भूपुरं लिखेदित्यर्थः । आचार्य्यैस्तु इदमेवाष्टदलयुक्तं पूजायन्त्रमुक्तम् ॥ ५१ ॥

षड्गुणितं यन्त्रमाह बीजान्तरिति । इदं षड्गुणितं यन्त्रं लिखेदिति सम्बन्धः । कीदृक् यन्त्रम् । वह्निपुरद्वये परस्परव्यतिभिन्ने त्रिकोणद्वये ।

तत्रैवम् उक्तपरिमाणं वृत्तं कृत्वा प्राक्प्रत्यक्सूत्रमास्फाल्य तदग्रयो: सूत्रमवष्टभ्य वृत्तार्द्धपरिमाणेन सूत्रेण मत्स्यद्वयं कुर्य्यात्। एवं कृते मत्स्यचतुष्कं निष्पद्यते। पूर्व्वमत्स्यद्वये पश्चिममत्स्यद्वये च दक्षिणोत्तरगं सूत्रद्वयमास्फाल्य प्राक्सूत्रस्य प्रागग्रे सूत्रादिं निधाय पश्चिममत्स्यद्वयोदरयो: तिर्य्यक्सूत्रद्वयमास्फालयेत्। पुन: प्राक्सूत्रस्य पश्चिमाग्रे सूत्रादिं निधाय पूर्व्वदिङ्मत्स्यद्वयोदरयो: तिर्य्यक्-सूत्रद्वयमास्फालयेत्। प्राक्सूत्रं वृत्तं च मार्जयेत्। एवं कृते संपुटितं वह्निपुरद्वयं जायते। तत्र बीजं शक्तिबीजं तदन्त:स्थितं साध्यनाम यत्र तत् तथा। साध्यसाधककर्म्मनामलिखनं तु पूर्व्ववदेव।

शरश: पञ्चधा। तत्र षट्कोणाभ्यन्तरे एवं पञ्चभिर्मायाबीजै: एकं वेष्टनम्। तदन्तराले एवं पञ्चभि: श्रीबीजै: द्वितीयं वेष्टनम्। तदन्तराले एवं पञ्चभि: कामबीजै: तृतीयं वेष्टनम्। एवं पञ्चदशबीजैरेकं वेष्टनं पर्य्यवसन्नं भवति।

तदुक्तं पद्मपादाचार्य्यै:—तत्र मायाबीजेन पञ्चधा वृत्तेनैकावृति:। पुनस्तदन्तराले एव श्रीबीजेन। तथैव तदन्तराले मारबीजेन। इति।

तदुक्तम्—पुटितं वह्निमालिख्य मध्ये शक्तिं नियोजयेत्।
ठकारवेष्टितं कृत्वा बहि: शक्तिं तु पञ्चधा॥
विलिख्य तद्वहिस्तद्वत् श्रीबीजं कामराजकम्। इति।

आचार्य्या अपि—हरमाया: पञ्चकृत्व: स्युर्बहिर्गर्भवर्त्तुलम्।
तद्वहि: शरमायाश्च कलमायाश्च तद्वहि:॥ इति।

अतोऽत्र वृत्तान्तरे च शक्तिबीजं मायाबीजं विलिख्य पश्चाद् बीजत्रयवेष्टनम्। रसपुटेषु षट्सु कोणेषु। आख्याख्यबीजत्रयम्। अत्र आख्याशब्देन साध्यसाधककर्म्मनामानि उच्यन्ते। बीजत्रयं पूर्व्वप्रकृतं शक्तिश्रीमान्मथम्। तदुक्तम्—

वह्ने: कोणत्रये श्रीमत्पश्चीये त्रितयं लिखेत्।
शक्तिश्रीकामबीजानां सदगडं साधकार्णवत्॥ इति।

लिखेदिति द्विरावृत्त्या। सा च सात्मानात्मकशब्दादेव लभ्यते। तत्र सात्मकं सबिन्दु अनात्मकं पर्य्युदासेन सविसर्गम्। तत्र एवं लेखनक्रम:। ईकारगते तु ऊर्द्ध्वभागकोणत्रये साधकनामवन्ति सबिन्दूनि त्रीणि बीजानि लिखेत्। तत: प्रादक्षिण्येन रेफगते अधोभागकोणत्रये साध्यनामकर्म्मवन्ति सविसर्गाणि लिखेत्। तदुक्तम्—

वह्न्यो: कोणेषु षट्सु च।
ऊर्द्ध्वभागे सबिन्दूनि त्रीणि बीजानि संलिखेत्॥

चिन्तामणिनृसिंहाभ्यां लसत्कोणमिदं लिखेत्।
यन्त्रं षड्गुणितं दिव्यं वहतां सर्व्वसिद्धिदम्॥ ५३

साधकाख्यायुतान्येवमधोभागेषु तान्यपि।
सविसर्गाणि साध्याख्या कर्म्मवन्ति च संलिखेत्॥ इति।

ईं शिखं कोणान्तरप्रदेशे ईम् इति लिखेत्। हरिहरैराबद्धगरुडम्। गरुडशब्देन षट्कोणकोणपार्श्वद्वयमुच्यते। तेन पूर्व्ववत् हरिहरान् वर्णान् लिखेत्। बहिः षट्कोणाग्रेषु षड्भिः मायाबीजैरनुबद्धसन्धिः। तत्र बद्धसन्धीत्येतावताऽपि अर्थप्राप्तौ यदनुबद्धसन्धीति वदति। तेन एकान्तरितसन्धिबन्धो विवक्षितो ग्रन्थकृतः। तदाहुराचार्य्याः—

एकैकान्तरितास्तासु संबध्युरितरेतरम्।
शिखाभिरान्तराभिस्तु बाह्याबाह्याभिरान्तराः॥ इति।

संहितायामपि—पूर्व्ववच्छक्तिबन्धस्तु कार्य्योऽत्रैकान्तरत्वतः। इति। अन्यत्रापि मन्त्रमुक्तावल्यादौ एकैकान्तरितबद्धसन्धित्वमेव उक्तम्। युक्तिश्चात्र एकान्तरितबन्धे स्वस्वत्रिकोणगबीजबन्धो भवति। तत्र प्रकारः। स्वस्वरेफेण तत्तद्बीजं प्रदक्षिणीकृत्य अन्यस्याधो नीत्वा एकान्तरित बीजस्य ईकाराग्रेण बध्नीयात्। सम्प्रदायविदश्चैवं मन्यन्ते। अन्ये तु सन्धौ बीजलिखनमाहुः।

तदुक्तम्—षट्सु कोणान्तरालेषु हृल्लेखाषट्कमालिखेत्। इति। इदमुत्तरयन्त्रेऽपि। लिपिभिरिति सामान्योक्तेः। क्रमेण व्युत्क्रमेण च वेष्टनम्। यदाहुराचार्य्याः—वर्णाः क्रमगताः शुभाः तद्बहिः प्रतिलोमाश्च। इति। संहितायामपि—अनुलोमेन तद्वृत्तमध्ये पञ्चाशदक्षरा।
तद्वृत्तबाह्यतस्तद्वत् विलोमेन च मातृका॥ इति।
भुवो गृहाभ्यां परस्परभेदित दिग्विदिक्कोणाभ्यां वेष्टयेत्।
तदुक्तमाचार्य्यैः—ततो विदर्भितं भूमिमण्डलद्वयमालिखेत्। इति॥

चिन्तामणिनृसिंहाभ्यामिति ईशानादिलेखनक्रमः। तेन दिक्कोणे नृसिंहबीजं विदिक्कोणे चिन्तामणिबीजं शेवम्।

तदुक्तम्—महादिक्स्थनृसिंहार्णं चिन्तारत्नाश्रितात्मकम्। इति। विशेषश्चायमुक्तो दक्षिणामूर्त्तिसंहितायाम्—

ततः कोणेषु सन्धिषु विलिख्य शूलान्। इति।
आचार्य्याश्च—बहिः षोडशशूलाङ्कम्। इति॥ ५२॥ ५३॥

बीजं व्याहृतिभिर्वृतं ग्रहयुगद्वन्द्वे वसोः कोणगं
दौर्गं बीजमनन्तरं लिपियुगैराबद्धगण्डं लिखेत् ।
गायत्र्या रविशक्तिबद्धविवरं त्रिष्टुब्वृतं तत्ततो
वीतं मातृकया धरापुरयुगे सत्सिंहचिन्तामणिम् ॥ ५४

अथ द्वादशगुणितं यन्त्रमाह बीजमिति । वसोरग्नेः ग्रहयुगं षट्कोणम् । तद्द्वन्द्वे द्वादशकोणे । क्वचित् गुहमुखद्वन्द्व इति पाठः । तत्र गुहः स्कन्दः तस्य मुखानि षट् तद्द्वन्द्वे द्वादशकोणे । तत्र पूर्व्वोक्तप्रकारेण षट्कोणे कृते तत्रोत्पन्नयोः मत्स्ययोः दक्षिणोदग्गतं सूत्रमास्फाल्य तदग्रयोः सूत्रमवष्टभ्य वृत्तार्द्धपरिमाणेन सूत्रेण मत्स्यचतुष्टयं कुर्य्यात् । तत्र दक्षमत्स्यद्वये उत्तर-मत्स्यद्वये च पूर्व्वप्रत्यग्गतं सूत्रद्वयम् आस्फाल्य दक्षोत्तरसूत्रस्याग्रे सूत्रादिं निधाय उत्तरमत्स्योदरयोः तिर्य्यक्सूत्रद्वयमास्फालयेत् । पुनर्दक्षोत्तरसूत्रस्य द्वितीयाग्रे सूत्रादिं निधाय दक्षमत्स्यद्वयोदरयोः तिर्य्यक्सूत्रद्वयमास्फालयेत् । दक्षोत्तरसूत्रं मार्जयेत् । एवं द्वादशकोणे कृते बीजं शक्तिबीजं साध्यसाधक-कर्मसहितं पूर्व्ववदालिख्य सप्तव्याहृतिभिर्विलोमाभिरावीतं कुर्य्यात् ।
यत् संहितायाम्—वेष्टयेत् प्रतिलोमतः सप्तव्याहृतिभिर्मन्त्री । इति ।
आचार्य्याश्च—शक्तिं प्रवेष्टयेच्च प्रतिलोमव्याहृतिभिरन्तःस्थाम् । इति ।
पद्मपादाचार्य्यैः व्याख्यातम्—सप्तव्याहृतिभिरिति ।

कोणगमिति । द्वादशसु कोणेषु दुरिति दुर्गाबीजमालिख्य अन्तरे कोणाग्रभागे ईं इति लिखेत् ।
तदुक्तं संहितायाम्—दुरात्मकं द्वादशारे सबिन्दुं तुर्य्यमेव च । इति ।
तदुक्तमाचार्य्यैः—कोणान्तर्दुं बीजकम् । इति ।

तथा—रविकोणेषु दुरन्तां मायां विलिखेदथात्र बिन्दुमतीम् । इति ।
नारायणीये च—अद्रिस्तद्बीजं शिवशक्तिवान् । इति ।
अपेक्षितार्थद्योतनिकायाम् ऋष्यादिकमुक्तम् । काश्यपः ऋषिः गायत्री छन्दः दुर्गा देवता । अष्टपत्रे कमले दूर्व्वाश्यामां त्रिनेत्रां शूलबाणखड्गचक्रशङ्खखेटकधनुः-कपालानि दक्षिणाधःक्रमेण धारयन्तीं ध्यायेत् । लक्षं जपेत् । जपदशांशं तिलैर्होमः । पूजादिकं वनदुर्गावत् ज्ञेयम् । गायत्र्याः प्रसिद्धायाः लिपियुग्मै-रक्षरयुगैः आबद्धगण्डं प्रत्येकं कोणपार्श्वयोर्विलोमतः गायत्र्यक्षरस्य द्वितयं द्वितयं लिखेदित्यर्थः । त्रियमिति पृथक्करणेन चतुर्विंशतिरक्षराणि । "इयादि

यन्त्रं दिनेशगुणितं प्रोक्तं रक्षाप्रसिद्धिदम् ।
सर्वसौभाग्यजननं सर्वशत्रुनिवारणम् ॥ ५५

लिखेत् सरोजं रसपत्रयुक्तं मध्ये दलेष्वप्यभिलिख्य मायाम् ।
स्वरावृतं यन्त्रमिदं वधूनां पुत्रप्रदं भूमिगृहान्तरस्थम् ॥ ५६

षट्कोणमध्ये प्रविलिख्य शक्तिं कोणेषु तामेव विलिख्य भूयः ।
ससाध्यगर्भं वसुधापुरस्थं यन्त्रं भवेद्वश्यकरं नराणाम् ॥ ५७

पुरणे" इति पिङ्गलसूत्रात् ।

यत् संहितायाम्—छन्दशो विलिखेद्वर्णान् गायत्र्यास्तु विलोमतः । इति ।
आचार्य्या अपि—गायत्रीं प्रतिलोमतः प्रविलिखेदस्रैः कपोलम् । इति ।
गायत्रीं द्वाविंशे वक्ष्यति । रविशक्तिभिः कोणाग्रबहिःस्थापित द्वादशशक्तिबीजैः क्षत्रविवरम् । अत्रापि पूर्व्ववत् एकान्तरितत्वेन बन्धनम् ।
यत् संहितायाम्—पूर्व्ववच्छक्तिबन्धन्तु कुर्य्याद् द्वादशधा प्रिये ।
एकैकान्तरितं रम्यम् । इति ।
आचार्य्याश्च—एकैकान्तरितास्ताः परस्परं शक्तयश्च सम्बध्युः । इति ।
त्रिष्टुब्वृतं त्रिष्टुभा जातवेदस इति प्रतिलोमेन वेष्टितम् ।
तदुक्तम्—तद्बहिःकोणपार्श्वेषु विलोमाग्नेय सन्मनुम् । इति ।
त्रिष्टुभं द्वाविंशे वक्ष्यति । मातृकया अकारादिक्षान्तया विलोमया च वीतम् ।
तदुक्तं संहितायाम्—अनुलोमां विलोमाञ्च मातृकां वेष्टयेद्बहिः । इति ।
आचार्य्या अपि—वर्णान् प्रानु [प्रति] गतांश्च । इति ।
पूर्व्ववत् परस्परव्यतिभेदिधरापुरयुग्मं लिखेत् । सत्सिंहचिन्तामणिमिति पूर्व्वादितेन दिक्कोणे नृसिंहबीजं विदिक्कोणे शैवं चिन्तामणिबीजम् । इदं दिनेशगुणितं द्वादशगुणितम् । अस्य पूर्व्वयन्त्रापेक्षया फलादिद्वैगुण्यं ज्ञेयम् ॥५४॥५५॥

यन्त्रान्तरमाह लिखेदिति । रसपत्राणि षट्पत्राणि तद्युक्तम् । मायामिति ससाध्याम् सप्तसु स्थानेषु । स्वरावृतम् अकारादिविसर्गपर्य्यन्तैः स्वैरावृतम् । नारायणीये तु अत्र चतुरस्रं नोक्तम्—
मध्ये षट्पत्रपद्मस्य लिखेद्देवीं दलेषु च ।
स्वरावृतमिदं यन्त्रं धारयेत् पुत्रकामिनी ॥ इति ॥ ५६

यन्त्रान्तरमाह षड़िति । ससाध्यगर्भमिति सप्तसु स्थानेषु इति ॥ ५७ ॥

वाग्भवं शम्भुवनिता रमाबीजत्रयात्मकम्।
मन्त्रं समुद्धरेन्मन्त्री त्रिवर्गफलसाधनम्॥ ५८

षड्दीर्घभाजा मध्येन वाग्भवाद्येन कल्पयेत्।
षडङ्गानि मनोरस्य जातियुक्तानि मन्त्रवित्।
कुर्य्यात् पूर्व्वोदितान्न्यासान् तथैवात्रापि साधकः॥ ५९

सिन्दूरारुणविग्रहां त्रिनयनां माणिक्यमौलिस्फुर-
त्तारानायकशेखरां स्मितमुखीमापीनवक्षोरुहाम्।
पाणिभ्यां मणिरत्नपूर्णचषकं रक्तोत्पलं बिभ्रतीं
सौम्यां रत्नघटस्थसव्यचरणां ध्यायेत् परामम्बिकाम्॥ ६०

रविलक्षं जपेन्मन्त्रं पायसैर्मधुरप्लुतैः।
दशांशं जुहुयान्मन्त्री पीठे प्रागीरिते यजेत्॥ ६१

देवीं प्रागुक्तमार्गेण गन्धाद्यैरतिशोभनैः।
हुत्वा पलाशकुसुमैर्वाक्श्रियं महतीं लभेत्॥ ६२

ब्राह्मीघृतं पिबेज्जप्तं कवित्वं वत्सराद्भवेत्।
सिद्धार्थान् लवणोपेतान् हुत्वा मन्त्री वशं नयेत्॥ ६३

मन्त्रान्तरमुद्धरति वाग्भवमिति। वाग्भवं द्वादशस्वरः सबिन्दुः। शम्भुवनिता शक्तिबीजम्। त्रिवर्गेति विनियोगोक्तिः। आद्यं बीजं मध्यं शक्तिः। ऋषि-च्छन्दसी पूर्व्वोक्ते। अतएव पाशादिमन्त्रे ऋष्याद्याः पूर्व्वमुक्ता इति। प्रत्याहार-क्रमेणोक्तम्॥ ५८॥

षड्दीर्घेति। ऐँ ह्रां हृत् ऐँ ह्रीं शिरः इत्यादि प्रयोगः। मन्त्र-विदित्युत्तरेण सम्बध्यते॥ ५९॥

ध्यानमाह सिन्दूरेति। मौलिर्मुकुटः। शेखरः शिरोभूषणम्। रत्नपूर्णो घटः रत्नघटः। रक्तपद्मस्थामित्यपि॥ ६०॥

रविलक्षं द्वादशलक्षम्। प्रागीरिते भुवनेशीप्रोक्ते। गन्धाद्यैरिति चतुर्थ्यौक्तैः। अतिशोभनैरिति। आवरणाङ्गदेवताभ्यो विविक्तोक्तैरित्यर्थः॥६१॥६२॥

ब्राह्मीघृतमिति। अत्र घृताच्चतुर्गुणे ब्राह्मीरसे घृतं पचेत्।

नरनारीनरपतान्नात्र कार्य्या विचारणा ।
चतुरङ्गुलजैः पुष्पैश्चन्दनाम्भःसमुक्षितैः ॥ ६४
हुत्वा वशीकरोत्याशु त्रैलोक्यमपि साधकः ।
जुहुयादरुणाम्भोजैरयुतं मधुराप्लुतैः ॥ ६५
राज्यश्रियमवाप्नोति सतिलैस्तण्डुलैस्तथा ।
प्रागुक्तान्यपि कर्म्माणि मन्त्रेणानेन साधयेत् ॥ ६६
वाग्बीजपुटिता माया विद्येयं त्र्यक्षरी मता ।
मध्येन दीर्घयुक्तेन वाक्पुटेन प्रकल्पयेत् ॥ ६७
अङ्गानि जातियुक्तानि क्रमेण मनुवित्तमः ।
यथा पुरा समुद्दिष्टान्न्यासान् कुर्वीत मन्त्रवित् ॥ ६८
श्यामाङ्गीं शशिशेखरां निजकरैर्दानं च रक्तोत्पलं
रत्नाढ्यं चषकं परं भयहरं संबिभ्रतीं शाश्वतीम् ।
मुक्ताहारलसत्पयोधरनतां नेत्रत्रयोल्लासिनीं
वन्देऽहं सुरपूजितां हरवधूं रक्तारविन्दस्थिताम् ॥ ६९
तत्त्वलक्षं जपेन्मन्त्रं जुहुयात्तद्दशांशतः ।
पलाशपुष्पैः स्वाद्वक्तैः पुष्पैर्वा राजवृक्षजैः ॥ ७०

उक्तं च—स्वकल्कोऽपि भवेत् स्नेहो यः साध्यः केवले द्रवे । इति । अन्यत् मातृकापटलोक्तमनुसन्धेयम् । सिद्धार्था गौरसर्षपाः । चतुरङ्गुलो राजवृक्षः ॥ ६३॥६४॥६५॥६६ ॥

मन्त्रान्तरमाह वागिति । बीजशक्ती ऋषिश्छन्दश्च पूर्ववत् । मध्येनेति मायाबीजेन । दीर्घयुक्तेन षड्दीर्घयुक्तेन । प्रयोगस्तु । ऐं ह्रां ऐं हृत् ऐं ह्रीं ऐं शिरः इत्यादि । मन्त्रविदित्यनेन हृल्लेखादि बीजादौ वाक्पुटत्वम् उक्तम् । मूलमिति इमं मन्त्रम् ॥ ६७ ॥ ६८ ॥

ध्यानमाह श्यामाङ्गीमित्यादि । दानं वरः । भयहरम् अभयम् । परम् उत्कृष्टं चषकविशेषणम् । रक्तपद्मस्थामिति । आयुधध्यानं पूर्ववत् ॥ ६९ ॥

तत्त्वलक्षं चतुर्विंशतिलक्षम् । स्वाद्वक्तैः त्रिमधुराप्लुतैः ॥ ७० ॥

हृल्लेखाविहिते पीठे पूजयेत् परमेश्वरीम् ।
मध्यादि पूजयेत् मन्त्री हृल्लेखाद्याः पुरोदिताः ॥ ७१

मिथुनानि यजेन्मन्त्री षट्कोणेषु यथा पुरा ।
अङ्गपूजा केसरेषु पूज्याः पत्रेषु मातरः ॥ ७२

भैरवाङ्कसमारूढाः स्मेरवक्त्रा मदालसाः ।
असिताङ्गो रुरुश्चण्डः क्रोध उन्मत्तसंज्ञकः ॥ ७३

कपाली भीषणः पश्चात् संहारी चाऽष्टभैरवाः ।
शूलं कपालं प्रेतञ्च बिभ्राणाः क्षुद्रदुन्दुभिम् ॥ ७४

गजत्वगम्बरा भीमाः कुटिलालकशोभिताः ।
दीर्घाद्या मातरः प्रोक्ता ह्रस्वाद्या भैरवाः स्मृताः ॥ ७५

पूज्याः षोड़शपत्रेषु कराल्याद्याः पुरोदिताः ।
तद्बाह्येऽनङ्गरूपाद्याः लोकेशास्त्राणि तद्बहिः ॥ ७६

एवमाराधयेद् देवीं शास्त्रोक्तेनैव वर्त्मना ।
वशं नयति राजानं वनिताश्च मदालसाः ॥ ७७

मनुनाज्येन जुहुयाल्लभते वसु वाञ्छितम् ।
सुगन्धैः कुसुमैर्हुत्वा श्रियमाप्नोति वाञ्छिताम् ॥ ७८

मन्त्रेणाऽनेन संजप्तमश्नीयादन्नमन्वहम् ।
भवेदरोगी नियतं दीर्घमायुरवाप्नुयात् ॥ ७९

हृल्लेखाविहिते भुवनेशीप्रोक्ते । तदुक्तं भुवनेशीपारिजाते—

मायाबीजमिदं प्रोक्तं भुवनत्रयमक्षरम् ।
हृल्लेखयञ्च योगेशी । इति ।

पुरोदिता इति स्वस्वबीजसंयुक्ताः । यथापुरेति स्वस्वगन्धादिकानि सव्यानानि ॥ ७१ ॥ ७२ ॥

भैरवाङ्केत्यादिना ध्यानविशेषः उक्तः । अन्यत् मातृकापटलोक्तमनुसन्धेयम् । क्षुद्रदुन्दुभिः डमरुः । भैरवायुधध्यानं तु दक्षोर्द्धादि दक्षाधःपर्य्यन्तम् । दीर्घा आकाराद्या अष्टौ तदाद्या मातरः अष्टौ यथाक्रमम् । अन्यत् ब्राह्मादिकं

अनन्तो बिन्दुसंयुक्तो माया ब्रह्माऽग्नितारवान् ।
पाशादित्र्यक्षरो मन्त्रः सर्व्ववश्यफलप्रदः ।
ऋष्याद्याः पूर्व्वमुक्ताः स्युर्बीजेनाङ्गक्रिया मता ॥ ८०

वराङ्कुशौ पाशमभीतिविद्यां करैर्वहन्तीं कमलासनस्थाम् ।
बालार्ककोटिप्रतिमां त्रिनेत्रां भजेऽहमाद्यां भुवनेश्वरीं ताम् ॥ ८१

हविष्यभुग्जपेन्मन्त्रं तत्त्वलक्षं जितेन्द्रियः ।
तत्सहस्रं प्रजुहुयाज्जपान्ते मन्त्रवित्तमः ॥ ८२
दधिक्षौद्रघृताक्ताभिः समिद्भिः क्षीरभूरुहाम् ।
तत्संख्यया तिलैः शुद्धैः जलाक्तैर्जुहुयात्ततः ॥ ८३

पूर्व्वोक्तमनुसन्धेयम् । एवं कृत्वाद्या इत्यत्रापि । अत्र अ इ उ ऋ लृ ए ओ अं इति पारिभाषिकह्रस्वग्रहणम् । प्रयोगस्तु । अं असिताङ्गभैरवाङ्कस्थायै आं चां ब्राह्म्यै नमः इत्यादि ॥ ७३ ॥ ७४ ॥ ७५ ॥ ७६ ॥ ७७ ॥ ७८ ॥ ७९ ॥

मन्त्रान्तरमाह अनन्त इति । अनन्त आकारः । बिन्दुसंयुक्तस्तेन आं । ब्रह्मा ककारः । अग्निः रेफः । तारः प्रणवः । ताभ्यां युक्तस्तेन क्रों । प्रथमबीजस्य पाश इति नाम । अन्त्यस्य अङ्कुश इति । यदाहुराचार्य्याः—

बिन्द्वन्तिका प्रतिष्ठा सन्दिष्टा पाशबीजमिति मुनिभिः ।
निजभूर्दहनाप्यायिनिशशधरखण्डान्वितोऽङ्कुशो भवति ॥ इति ॥

अतएव पाशादि त्र्यक्षरो मन्त्र इति । सर्व्ववश्येति विनियोगोक्तिः । बीजशक्ती पूर्व्ववत् । बीजेनेति मायाबीजेन । षड्दीर्घयुक्तेन पाशाङ्कुशपुटितेनेति परमगुरवः । प्रयोगस्तु आं क्रां क्रों हृदयाय नमः इत्यादि । पाशाङ्कुशपुटितबीजाद्यानां हृल्लेखाद्यानां न्यासोऽपि कर्त्तव्यः ॥ ८० ॥

ध्यानमाह वरेति । अभीतिमुद्रामभयम् । कमलासनस्थां रक्तकमलासनस्थाम् । आयुधध्यानम् पूर्व्ववत् ॥ ८१ ॥

तत्त्वलक्षं चतुर्विंशतिलक्षम् । तदुक्तमाचार्य्यैः—

जपेच्चतुर्विंशतिलक्षमेवं सुयन्त्रितो मन्त्रवरं यथावत् । इति ।

हविष्यभुक् जितेन्द्रिय इति पुरश्चरणधर्म्माणाम् उपलक्षणम् । तत्सहस्रं चतुर्विंशतिसहस्रम् । प्रत्येकं षट्सहस्रमित्याह । क्वचित् षट्सहस्रमित्येव पाठः । तदुक्तमाचार्य्यैः—

पयोद्रुमाणाञ्च समित्सहस्रषट्कं दधिक्षौद्रघृतावसिक्तम् । इति ।

हृल्लेखाविहिते पीठे नवशक्तिसमन्विते।
अर्चयेत् परमेशानीं वक्ष्यमाणक्रमेण ताम्॥ ८४
हृल्लेखाद्या यजेदादौ कर्णिकायां यथाविधि।
अङ्गानि केसरेषु स्युः पत्रस्था मातरः क्रमात्॥ ८५
इन्द्रादयः पुनः पूज्यास्तेषामस्त्राणि तद्बहिः।
एवं संपूजयेद् देवीं साक्षाद्वैश्रवणो भवेत्॥ ८६
पूज्यते सकलैर्लोकैस्तेजसा भास्करोपमः।
अनेनाऽधिष्ठितं गेहं निशि दीपशिखाकुलम्॥ ८७
दृश्यते प्राणिभिः सर्वैर्मन्त्रस्याऽस्य प्रभावतः।
सर्षपैर्लोणसंमिश्रैराज्याक्तैर्जुहुयान्निशि॥ ८८
राजानं वशयेत् सद्यस्तत्पत्नीमपि साधकः।
अन्नवानन्नहोमेन श्रीमान् पद्महुताद्भवेत्॥ ८९
राजवृक्षसमुद्भूतैः पुष्पैर्हुत्वा कविर्भवेत्।
अरोगी तिलहोमेन घृतेनायुरवाप्नुयात्।
प्राक्प्रोक्तान्यपि कर्माणि साधयेत् साधकोत्तमः॥ ९०

जपान्ते इति जपाव्यवधानेन नियमश्च एवेत्यर्थः। मन्त्रवित्तम इत्यनेन होमे स्वाहान्तता सूचिता। क्षौद्रं मधु क्षीरभूरुहामिति। अश्वत्थोदुम्बर प्लक्षवटानां प्रत्येकं षटसहस्रं होम इति। तत्संख्यया चतुर्विंशति संख्यया॥ ८२॥ ८३॥

हृल्लेखाविहिते भुवनेशीप्रोक्ते। तत्पीठशक्तयोऽत्रापि पूज्या इत्यर्थः। नवशक्तिसमन्विते इत्यनेन पीठमन्त्रस्य अन्यत्वम्। तेन पीठमन्त्रे बीजत्रययोग इत्युक्तम्। अत्र षट्कोणकर्णिकम् अष्टदलं पद्मं पीठम्। षोड़शदलं नास्ति। तत्र पूजाया अनुक्तत्वात्। यथाविधीति बीजद्वयपुटित बीजाद्या इत्युक्तम्। मातर इति भैरवाङ्कस्थाः। पूज्यत इति कर्मप्रत्ययेन देवानुग्रह उक्तः। साक्षात् वैश्रवणः कुबेरोपमः। वशयेदिति। तत्र जपप्रकार उक्तः तन्त्रान्तरे—

क्रीँकाराद्यां तयोर्नाम श्रां क्रों च विनियोजयेत्। इति॥ ८४॥

८५॥ ८६॥ ८७॥ ८८॥ ८९॥ ९०॥

आलिख्याऽष्टदिगर्गलान्युदरगं पाशादिकं त्र्यक्षरं
कोष्ठेष्वङ्गमनून् परेषु विलिखेदष्टार्णं मन्त्रद्वयम् ।
अच्पूर्व्वापरषट्कयुग्लयवरान् व्योमासनानर्गले-
ष्वालिख्येन्द्रजलाधिपादिगुणशः पङ्क्तिद्वयं तत्परम् ॥ ९१

घटार्गलं यन्त्रमाह आलिख्येति । अत्राष्टानाम् अर्गलानां साम्येन आनयन-प्रकार उच्यते—कर्णार्द्धमित्या मध्ये द्विसूत्राङ्कास्तत् द्वये द्वये ।

चतुरस्रान्तरे सूत्रैः परिध्येधनमिच्छया ॥

वास्तुमण्डलोक्तरीत्या एकं चतुरस्रं प्रागुत्तरसूत्रोपेतं कृत्वा तत्र कोणसूत्रार्द्धमानेन चतुर्दिक्षु मध्यात् प्रागुदक्सूत्रे अङ्कयेत् । द्वयोर्द्वयोरङ्कयोः सूत्रदानात् दिग्गतकोणं पूर्व्वव्यतिभेदि चतुरस्रान्तरं जायते । ततः अष्टपरिधीनाम् इच्छया वर्द्धनं कृत्वा अर्गलाकारं कुर्य्यात् । सर्व्वत्र दिक्कर्णगुणाः मार्ज्याः । एवम् अष्टौ दिगर्गलानि आलिख्य मध्ये वृत्तं कृत्वा तत्र पाशादित्र्यक्षरमालिख्य चतुरस्रद्वयान्तःसन्धिषु वृत्तं कृत्वा तदष्टकोष्ठेषु पूजाप्रकारेण आग्नेयादि विदिक्कोष्ठेषु हृच्छिरःशिखा-कवचान्यालिख्य मध्ये अग्रभागे नेत्रं दिक्कोष्ठेषु अस्त्रमालिखेत् ।

तदुक्तम्—अष्टकोणेषु विलिखेत् षडङ्गानि यथाक्रमम् ।

अग्नीशासुरवायव्यकोणेषु मनुवित्तमः ॥

कवचास्त्राणि संलिख्य मध्ये नेत्रं लिखेद्बुधः ।

चतुर्दिगन्तकोणेषु चतुर्धास्त्रं लिखेत् प्रिये ॥ इति ।

तदुपर्य्यष्टकोष्ठेषु पाशाद्यष्टाक्षरम् अथादि लिखित्वा पुनश्च बाह्यसन्धिषु वृत्तं कृत्वा तदुत्पन्नेषु अष्टसु कोष्ठेषु कामिन्यष्टाक्षरम् आलिख्य वर्द्धिताष्टपरिधिसन्धिषु वृत्तात् बहिः वृत्तं कृत्वा तदुत्पन्नेषु षोड़शकोष्ठेषु अष्टयुगार्णं शाक्तं षोड़शाक्षरं विलिखेत् इत्यनेन पूर्व्वेणान्वय इत्यपि केचन । अन्ये चतुरस्रद्वयान्तर्बहिःसन्धिषु वृत्तद्वयम् कारयित्वा वर्द्धिताष्टपरिधिसन्धिवृत्ताद्बहिः वृत्तं कारयन्ति । तत्र कोष्ठेषु अष्टयुगार्णं विलिखेत् इत्याहुः । अन्ये तु चतुरस्रबाह्यसन्धीनामुपरि वृत्तमेकं वर्द्धिताष्टपरिधिसन्धिषु च द्वितीयं वृत्तं कारयन्ति । तत्पक्षत्रयमपि असङ्गतम् । श्रौतस्य क्रमस्य बाधितत्वात् । कर्णिकावृत्तलग्नाधोमुखत्रिकोणाकाराष्ट-कोष्ठानां शून्यत्वाच्च । किञ्च पूर्व्वपक्षे वृत्तत्रयकल्पनमन्यपक्षयोर्वृत्तद्वयकल्पनं च अप्रामाणिकम् । यावता विना न निर्व्वाहस्तावदेव कल्पनमर्हति नाधिकम् । अत एकमेव वृत्तं कल्पनीयम् । उपरिवृत्तस्य तु पद्मकर्णिकात्वेन सर्व्वै-रेवाङ्गीकरणात् । अतो वक्ष्यमाणसाम्प्रदायिकार्थानुसरणमेव श्रेयः ।

कोष्ठेष्वष्टयुगार्णमात्मसहितां युग्मस्वरान्तर्गतां
मायां केसरगां दलेषु विलिखेन्मूलं त्रिपङ्क्तिक्रमात्।
त्रिःपाशाङ्कुशवेष्टितञ्च लिपिभिर्वीतं क्रमादुत्क्रमात्
पद्मस्थेन घटेन पङ्कजमुखेनावेष्टितं तद्बहिः॥ ९२

तत्परम् अच्पूर्व्वेत्यालिख्य कोष्ठेषु अष्टयुगार्णमालिख्य केसरगां मायां विलिखेदिति सम्बन्धः। अचां स्वराणां नपुंसकस्वरव्यतिरिक्तानाम्। नपुंसकव्यतिरिक्तत्वं पूर्व्वापर षट्कशब्देन प्राप्यते। पूर्व्वषट्कं अ आ इ ई उ ऊ अपरषट्कं ए ऐ ओ औ अं अः। एतद्युक्तान् लयवरान् व्योम्नः आसना स्थितिर्येषु ते व्योमासनास्तानिति बहुव्रीहिः कार्य्यः। "स्यादास्था त्वासना स्थितिः" इति कोषः। अर्गलेषु इन्द्रजलाधिपादि पूर्व्वपश्चिमादि गुणशः अक्षरत्रितयक्रमेण पङ्क्तिद्वयं लिखेत्। इमानि सर्व्वाणि सबिन्दूनि। तत्र लेखनप्रकारः। पूर्व्वार्गलायां मर्द्दितरेखासन्निहितवृत्तमारभ्योत्तरतः ह्लं ह्लां ह्लिं इत्यर्गलान्तमालिख्य पुनर्दक्षिणतोऽर्गलाग्रमारभ्य ह्लीं ह्लुं ह्लूं इति वृत्तान्तमालिखेत्। एवं प्रादक्षिण्यं भवति। तदुक्तं संहितायाम्— शक्रेरजलवह्न्याख्यं बिन्दुव्योमान्वितं कुरु।

तद्बीजं स्वरसंयुक्तं ऋ ॠ ऌ ॡ विवर्जितम्॥
एवं द्वादशधा तत्र चतुर्धा कुरु सुन्दरि।
वृत्तादिवसुकोणान्तं लिखेद् वृत्तान्तकं प्रिये॥
आद्यं त्रिकं पूर्व्वमुख्यं लिखेदुत्तरतः प्रिये।
द्वितीयं पूर्व्वमुख्यं तु लिखेत् दक्षिणतः सुधीः॥ इति।

पश्चिमार्गलायां दक्षिणतो वृत्तमारभ्य ह्लें ह्लैं ह्लों इत्यर्गलान्तमालिख्य पुनरुत्तरतो ऽर्गलाग्रमारभ्य ह्लौं ह्लं ह्लः इति वृत्तान्तमालिखेत्। तदुक्तम्—

तृतीयं पश्चिमे भागे तथा दक्षिणतो लिखेत्।
चतुर्थमार्गले तद्वत् पश्चिमे तूत्तरान्ततः॥ इति।

एवमाग्नेयार्गलायां पूर्व्वतः पूर्व्ववत् ह्रं ह्रां ह्रिं इत्यालिख्य पश्चिमतः पूर्व्ववत् ह्रीं ह्रुं ह्रूं इति लिखेत्। तदुक्तम्—

भुवं त्यक्त्वाऽर्कबीजानां तत्र वायुं नियोजयेत्।
अग्न्यर्गलायां त्रितयमाद्यं पूर्व्वत आलिखेत्॥
तथा पश्चिमतोऽप्यन्यत् त्रिकं संविलिखेत् प्रिये। इति।

एवं वाय्वर्गलायां पश्चिमतः पूर्व्ववत् ह्रें ह्रैं ह्रों इत्यालिख्य पूर्व्वतः पूर्व्ववत् ह्रौं ह्रं ह्रः इति लिखेत्। तदुक्तम्—

मारुतार्गलकं तद्वत् लिखेत् पश्चिमतस्त्रिकम् । पूर्व्वतोऽपि च देवेशि । इति । एवं याम्यार्गलायां पूर्व्वतः पूर्व्ववत् ह्रं ह्रां ह्रिं इत्यालिख्य पश्चिमतः पूर्व्ववत् ह्रीं ह्रुं ह्रूं इति लिखेत् । तदुक्तम्—

वायुं हित्वाऽर्कबीजानां वरुणं तत्र निक्षिपेत् ।
याम्ये त्रिकं पूर्व्वतस्तु द्वितीयं पश्चिमान्तगम् ॥ इति ।

एवमुत्तरार्गलायां पश्चिमतः पूर्व्ववत् ह्रें ह्रैं ह्रों इत्यालिख्य पूर्व्ववत् पूर्व्वतः ह्रौं ह्रं ह्रः इति लिखेत् । तदुक्तम्—

अथोत्तरार्गलायां तु त्रिकं पश्चिमतो लिखेत् । चतुर्थं पूर्व्वतो देवि । इति । एवं कन्या[नैर्ऋत्या]र्गलायां दक्षिणतः पूर्व्ववत् क्रं क्रां क्रिं इत्यालिख्य उत्तरतः पूर्व्ववत् क्रीं क्रुं क्रूं इति लिखेत् । तदुक्तम्—

नीरं हित्वाऽर्कबीजानां रेफं तत्र विनिक्षिपेत् ।
लिखेद्रक्षोऽर्गलायां तु त्रिकमाद्यं त्रिकं परम् ॥
दक्षिणोत्तरतो मन्त्री । इति ।

एवं शैवार्गलायाम् उत्तरतः पूर्व्ववत् क्रें क्रैं क्रों इत्यालिख्य दक्षिणतः पूर्व्ववत् क्रौं क्रं क्रः इति लिखेत् । तदुक्तम्—

क्रमाच्छैवार्गले पुनः ।
आदावुत्तरतो देवि पश्चाद्दक्षिणमार्गतः ॥ इति ।

पद्मपादाचार्य्यास्तु—चतुरस्रद्वयात्मकमष्टकोणं लिखित्वा कोणाष्टगतमृजुरेखाद्वयम् ऋजु प्रसारयेत् । यथा रेखाद्वयं मध्ये परस्परलग्नं क्षुद्रदुन्दुभ्याकारं भवति तथा प्रसार्य्य दुन्दुभिमध्योभयभागयोः वृत्तद्वयं विधाय बहिर्वृत्तस्य अष्टदुन्दुभ्यग्ररेखाद्वयादारभ्य अर्गलसमाग्राण्यष्टदलानि विरच्य वृत्तत्रयाद्बहिरब्जपुटितं घटं रचयेदिति यन्त्रशरीरस्य निर्म्माणप्रकारः ।

चतुरस्रसम्बन्धादष्टकोष्ठेषु अङ्गानि तदनन्तरकोष्ठेषु पाशाद्यष्टाक्षरं तदनन्तरकोष्ठेषु कामिन्याद्यष्टाक्षरम् अर्गलेषु अच्पूर्व्वेति तदन्तरालकोष्ठद्वयेषु दुन्दुभ्याकारेषु षोडशाक्षरं लिखेदिति । मन्त्रलेखनस्य एवं श्रौतक्रमोऽपि अनुष्ठितो भवति । अयञ्च पक्षः साम्प्रदायिकः । तदुक्तं दक्षिणामूर्त्तिसंहितायाम्—

ततो भूबिम्बयुगलं संपुटीकृत्य योजयेत् ।
अष्टकोणं यथा देवि जायते दृङ्मनोहरम् ॥
अष्टदिक्षु तदग्राभ्यां रेखे आक्रम्य मान्त्रिकः ।
रेखाभ्यामर्गलाकारं विदध्याद्देवि सुन्दरम् ॥

घटार्गलमिदं यन्त्रं मन्त्रिणां प्राभृतं मतम् ।

एकेनैव तु मानेन रचयेदर्गलाष्टकम् ।
वृत्तं तदग्रे चन्द्रस्य बिम्बवद् रचयेद्बुधः ॥
पुनरन्यः समाकृष्य पूर्ववृत्तमनुत्तमम् ।
विलिख्य साधकेन्द्रस्तु वसुकोष्ठयुगं क्रमात् ॥
व्यक्तं यथा भवेद्देवि कोणानां च वसुद्वयम् ।
अर्गलानि च रम्याणि यथा सम्यग् भवन्ति हि ॥ इति ।

ततस्तदुपरि अष्टदलपद्मपत्रेषु केसरगां मायाम् । चतुर्थस्वरो मायाशब्दवाच्यः । तथा च त्रिषट्कमातृकायाम्—

ईस्त्रिमूर्तिर्वामनेत्रं शेखरः कौटिलस्तथा ।
वाग्मी शुद्धस्य जिह्वाख्यो मायाविष्णुः प्रकाशितः ॥ इति ।

आत्मा आत्ममन्त्रो हंसः इति ताभ्यां सहिताम् उभयपार्श्वे युताम् अकाराद्या-कारद्यन्तगतां लिखेत् । तेनायमर्थः । प्रतिकेसरम् अं हंसः ईं हंसः आं इति सप्ताक्षराणि लिखेत् । तदुक्तम्—

हंसः पदं वामनेत्रं बिन्दिन्दुपरिभूषितम् ।
पुनर्हंसः पदं चैतत् पद्माणां मनुमालिखेत् ॥
स्वरद्वन्द्वोदरगतं सप्तार्णं चाष्टधा भवेत् । इति ।

आचार्य्याश्च—पद्मस्य केसरेषु च युगस्वरान्वितां तथा मायाम् । इति ।
पद्मपादाचार्य्यास्तु अं हं ईं सः आं एवमादयः केसरेषु लेख्या इत्याहुः । दलेषु त्रिपङ्क्तिक्रमात् मूलं लिखेत् । तत्र पङ्क्तिद्वयं तिर्य्यक् विलिख्य तदुपरि एकां पङ्क्तिं लिखेदिति सम्प्रदायविदः । अन्ये तु अधोऽधः पङ्क्ति-त्रयलेखनं वदन्ति । त्रिरिति । तत्रैका पाशाङ्कुशाभ्यां द्वितीया क्रमलिपिभिः तृतीया व्युत्क्रमलिपिभिरित्यर्थः । तदुक्तम्—

पाशाङ्कुशाभ्यां तद्बाह्ये वृत्ताकारेण वेष्टयेत् ।
अनुलोमप्रकारेण मातृकावेष्टनं प्रिये ॥
तथैव प्रतिलोमेन मातृकावेष्टनं लिखेत् । इति ।

आचार्य्याश्च—पाशाङ्कुशबीजाभ्यां प्रवेष्टयेद् बाह्यतश्च नलिनस्य ।
अनुलोमविलोमगतैः प्रवेष्टयेदक्षरैश्च तद्बाह्ये ॥ इति ।

पद्मस्थेन तूर्द्धमुखाब्जकर्णिकास्थेन घटेन पङ्कजमुखेन अधोमुखपङ्कजवदनेन वीतम् । प्राभृतमुपपदारूपम् ॥ ८१॥८२॥८३ ॥

पाशश्रीशक्तिकन्दर्पकामशक्तीन्दिराङ्कुशाः ॥ ९३

प्रथमोऽष्टाक्षरो मन्त्रस्ततः कामिनि रञ्जिनि ।

स्वाहान्तोऽष्टाक्षरः सद्भिरपरः कीर्त्तितो मनुः ॥ ९४

अष्टार्णमन्त्रमाह पाशेति। पाशः आं कन्दर्पः कामबीजम् इन्दिरा श्रीबीजम् अङ्कुशः क्रों। अयमपि स्वतन्त्रो मन्त्रः। अस्य ऋष्यादिकं यथा—

ऋष्याद्या अजगायत्रयशक्तयः समुदीरिताः ।
षड्दीर्घमायया ऽङ्गानि सर्व्वैरष्टाङ्गमिष्यते ॥
आनन्दरूपिणीं देवीं पाशाङ्कुशधनुःशरान् ।
बिभ्रतीं दोर्भिररुणां कुचार्त्तां हृदि भावयेत् ॥
अष्टलक्षं जपेत् साज्यैर्दशांशं जुहुयात्तिलैः ।
शाक्ते पीठे यजेद्देवीं द्वन्द्वलेखाद्याभिरङ्गकैः ॥
मातृभिर्लोकनाथैश्च वज्राद्यैः पञ्चमावृतिः ।
स्त्रीवश्याकर्षणादौ तु विनियोग उदाहृतः ॥ इति ।

द्वितीयमष्टाक्षरमुद्धरति तत इति। अयमपि स्वतन्त्रो मन्त्रः। अस्यर्ष्यादिकं
यथा—ऋषिः सम्मोहनश्छन्दो निवृत् प्रोक्तोऽस्य देवता ।
सर्व्वसम्मोहिनी चाङ्गं द्विरावृत्तपदैर्भवेत् ॥
श्यामाङ्गीं वल्लकीं दोर्भ्यां वादयन्तीं सुभूषणाम् ।
चन्द्रावतंसां विविधगानैर्मोहयन्तीं जगत् ॥
पूर्व्वमेवायुतद्वन्द्वं दशांशं जुहुयात्ततः ।
मधूकजैस्त्रिमध्वक्तैः सर्व्वं मोहयते जगत् ॥
पूजा मातङ्गिनीपीठे रत्याद्यास्तु त्रिकोणके ।
पञ्चकोणे पञ्चबाणाः केसरेष्वङ्गपूजनम् ॥
अनङ्गकुसुमाद्यास्तु पत्रेष्वग्रे च मातरः ।
लोकपालैश्च वज्राद्यैः सप्तावृत्तिरियं मता ॥

नारायणीये तु—लाक्षया लिखितं वामहस्तेऽष्टदलपङ्कजे ।
वश्यं स्यादर्पितं मन्त्रं पूर्व्ववत् क्रिययाऽपि च ॥
भूर्जे लिखित्वा चाष्टारे धारयेद् वाञ्छवश्यकृत् ।
मन्त्रं विविक्तकुड्यादाविमं संलिख्य साधकः ।
पश्यन्नेव जपेन्मौनी तूर्णमायाति काङ्क्षिता ॥ इति ॥ ९३॥९४ ॥

ह्रीँ गौरि रुद्रदयिते योगेश्वरि सवर्म्म फट् ।

द्विठान्तः षोड़शार्णोऽयं मन्त्रः सद्भिरुदीरितः ॥ ८५

षोड़शाक्षरमन्त्रमुद्धरति ह्रीमिति । वर्म्म हुं । अयमपि स्वतन्त्रो मन्त्रः । अस्य ऋष्यादिकं यथा—

ऋषिस्त्वजः समुद्दिष्टश्छन्दोऽनुष्टुप् च देवता ।
गौरीचण्डकात्यायनी वश्यसम्पत्प्रदायिका ॥
षड्दीर्घमायया कुर्य्यात् षडङ्गानि मनोरथ ।
हेमाभां बिभ्रतीं दोर्भिर्दर्पणाञ्जन साधने ॥
पाशाङ्कुशौ सर्व्वभूषां तां गौरीं सर्व्वदा भजे ।
एकलक्षं जपेन्मन्त्रं तद्दशांशं हुनेत् घृतैः ॥
धर्म्मादिकल्पिते पीठे पीठशक्तीरिमा यजेत् ।
प्रभा ज्ञाना च वाग्वागीश्वरी स्यात् ज्वालिनी परा ॥
वामा ज्येष्ठा च रौद्री च गुह्यशक्तिश्च ता नव ।
क्रमस्त्वयलीववर्जस्वराद्या भृगुणाऽन्विताः ॥
गौं गौरि मूर्त्तये ह्रच पीठमन्त्रश्च कल्पिते ।
एवं पीठे यजेद्देवीं चन्दनाद्यैर्मनोहरैः ॥
सुभगायै च विद्महे ङेऽन्ते स्यात् काममालि च ।
न्यै स्यात् धीमहि तन्नो च गौरी स्यात्तत् प्रचोदयात् ॥
गायत्र्या त्वनया सर्व्वानुपचारान् प्रकल्पयेत् ।
अङ्गानि पूर्व्वमभ्यर्च्य सुभगाद्यास्ततो यजेत् ॥
भृगुः शाम्बुः सद्वितुर्य्यषष्टार्कैन्दुस्तदादिकाः ।
सुभगा ललिता चान्या कामिनी काममालिनी ॥
दिक्ष्वन्यत्राऽप्यायुधानि लोकपालैस्तदायुधैः ।
वामाख्या नाम निशया वामोरौ विलिखेत् निशि ॥
आच्छादयन् वामदोष्णा तन्मनाः प्रजपेन्मनुम् ।
शतं सहस्रं लोलाक्षीमानयेत् काममोहिताम् ॥ इति ।

नारायणीये तु नृवश्ये दक्षिणं विदुरिति विशेषः ।
एतन्मन्त्रेण संजप्तं गन्धपुष्पजलादि च ।
दत्तं संसेवितं सर्व्वजनतावश्यकारकम् ॥
चण्डकात्यायनी विद्या त्रिषु लोकेषु दुर्लभा ॥ इति ॥ ८५ ॥

लिखित्वा भूर्जपत्रादौ यन्त्रमेतद् यथाविधि।
धारयन् वामबाहौ वा कण्ठे वा निजमूर्द्धनि॥ ९६
वशयेत् सकलान् मर्त्यान् विशेषेण महीपतीन्।
नीलपट्टे विलिख्यैतद् गुटिकां कृत्य तत् पुनः॥ ९७
साध्यप्रतिकृतेः सिक्थनिर्मिताया हृदि न्यसेत्।
पात्रे त्रिमधुरापूर्णे निःक्षिप्यैनां विधानतः॥ ९८
संपूज्य गन्धपुष्पाद्यैर्बलिं निःक्षिप्य रात्रिषु।
मूलमन्त्रं जपेन्मन्त्री नित्यमष्टसहस्रकम्॥ ९९
सप्ताहाद्वाञ्छितां नारीमाकर्षेत् स्मरविह्वलाम्।
भूर्जपत्रे विलिख्यैतद् गुटिकां कृत्य तत् पुनः॥ १००
लाक्षया ताम्ररजतकाञ्चनैर्वेष्टयेत् क्रमात्।
तत्कुम्भे न्यस्य संपूज्य यथावद्भुवनेश्वरीम्॥ १०१
संस्पृश्य तं जपेन्मन्त्रं दिवाकरसहस्रकम्।
अभिषिच्य प्रियं साध्यं बध्नीयाद् यन्त्रमाशिखम्॥ १०२

यथाविधि लिखित्वा इत्यनेन पुष्यार्कादौ कृतोपवासादिरित्युक्तम्। पुष्यार्कस्य अष्टमे भागे इत्युक्तेः। नीलपट्टे विलिख्यैतदिति अनामारक्तादिभिः। तदुक्तम्—लिखेदनामारक्तेन लातेन्द्रियमलैः सह। इति। सिक्थं मधूच्छिष्टम्। विधानतः सम्पूज्येति इस्तमाचखातां रक्तैर्गन्धादिभिरित्यर्थः। उक्तञ्च नारायणीये—काञ्जिकाधो निधायैनां रक्तपुष्पैः समर्चयेत्। इति। बलिमिति पायसादिना। ब्रह्मचर्येणैव निक्षिप्येति दत्त्वा। मूलमन्त्रं त्र्यर्णं। आकर्षेदिति प्रकारान्तरेण वा। तदुक्तं नारायणीये—

तापयेत् पुत्तलीं चाग्नौ यथा सा न प्रलीयते इति॥ ९६-१००॥

ताम्रेति पूर्वोक्तप्रमाणैः। यथावदिति ब्रह्मचर्य्यक्रममार्गेण। तं कुम्भम्। मन्त्रमिति कर्णिकास्थम्। दिवाकरेति द्वादश। भित्तौ विलिख्येति गैरिकया।

तदुक्तम्—गैरिकया लिखेद् यन्त्रं गृहभित्तौ वरानने।
ग्रहाणां चैव सर्व्वेषां द्विषतां चैव नाशनम्॥
विलिख्य पूज्यते तत्र सर्व्वे मूढाः सुमोहिताः।
भवन्ति वशगास्तस्य न पुनर्यान्ति विक्रियाम्॥

कान्तिपुष्टिधनारोग्ययशांसि लभते नरः ।
भित्तौ विलिख्य तन्मन्त्रं पूजयेन्नित्यमादरात् ॥ १०३
भूतप्रेतपिशाचास्तं न वीक्षितुमपि क्षमाः ।
तद्विलिख्य शिरस्त्राणे साधितं धारयन् भटः ।
युद्धे रिपून् बहून् हत्वा जयमाप्नोति पार्थवत् ॥ १०४

वज्राङ्किते वह्निपुरद्वये तां पाशाङ्कुशाद्यामुदरस्थसाध्याम् ।
मध्येऽथ कोणेषु च बाह्यवृत्ते पुनः पुनस्तत् विलिखेत् समन्तात् ॥
भूर्जे लिखितमेतत् स्यात् सर्व्ववश्यकरं नृणाम् ।
आरोग्यैश्वर्य्यजननं युद्धेषु विजयप्रदम् ॥ १०५॥१०६

भूर्जे सरोजे स्वरकेसराढ्ये वर्गाष्टपत्रे वसुधापुरस्थे ।
पाशाङ्कुशाभ्यां गुणशः प्रबद्धां मायां लिखेन्मध्यगतां ससाध्याम् ॥
सर्व्वोत्तममिदं यन्त्रं धारितं कुरुते नृणाम् ।
आरोग्यैश्वर्य्यसौभाग्यविजयादीननारतम् ॥ १०७॥१०८

इति श्रीशारदातिलके नवमः पटलः ।

शत्रवो दुर्जया दुष्टाः सर्व्वे ते तस्य किङ्कराः ।
न तस्य जायते दुष्टो हिंसको न च बाधकः ॥
ग्रहयक्षपिशाचाश्च भूतवेतालदंष्ट्रिणः । इति ॥ १०१-१०४ ॥

यन्त्रान्तरमाह वज्रेति । वह्निपुरद्वये परस्परव्यतिभिन्ने षट्कोणे । वज्राङ्किते स्वस्तिकस्थाने । वह्निपुरद्वये मध्ये इति अधिकरणे सप्तम्यौ । तां मायाम् । तदिति त्र्यक्षरम् ॥ १०५ ॥ १०६ ॥

यन्त्रान्तरमाह भूर्जे इति । पाशाङ्कुशाभ्यां प्रबद्धां मायां गुणशः त्रिशो लिखेदिति सम्बन्धः । प्रबद्धां निबद्धाम् । यदा लिखेदित्येव पाठः तदा लिखेत् सरोजं स्वरकेसराढ्यं वर्गाष्टपत्रं वसुधापुरस्थम् इति पठनीयम् । अन्ये लिखेदित्येव पठित्वा लिखेत् यन्त्रम् इति शेषः । तत् कीदृक् इत्यपेक्षायां सरोजे मायां लिखेदिति वदन्ति ॥ १०७ ॥ १०८ ॥

इति श्रीशारदातिलकटीकायां सत्सम्प्रदायकृतव्याख्यायां
पदार्थादर्शाभिख्यायां नवमः पटलः ॥ ॐ ॥

दशमः पटलः ।

ततोऽभिधास्ये त्वरितां त्वरितं फलदायिनीम् ।
तारो मायावर्म्मबीजऋद्धिरीशस्वरान्विता ॥ १
कूर्म्मस्तदन्त्यो भगवान् चः स्त्री दीर्घतनुच्छदम् ।
संवर्त्तो भगवान्माया फडन्तो द्वादशाक्षरः ॥ २
मुनिरर्जुन आख्यातो विराट्छन्दः समीरितम् ।
त्वरिता देवता प्रोक्ता पुरुषार्थफलप्रदा ॥ ३

एवं भुवनेश्वरीमन्त्रानुक्त्वा अत्र पाशादिमन्त्रस्य नित्यामन्त्रत्वात् तत्प्रसङ्गादन्यान् त्वरितानित्यादिमन्त्रान् वक्तुमुपक्रमते तत इति। त्वरितफलदायिनीमिति त्वरिताशब्दव्युत्पत्तिर्दर्शिता। तदुक्तम्—

भक्तियुतानां त्वरया सिद्धिकरी चेति मन्त्रिणां सततम् ।
देव्यास्त्वरिताख्या स्यात् त्वरितं क्ष्वेलग्रहादिहरणतया ॥ इति ।

मन्त्रमुद्धरति तार इति। तारः प्रणवः माया शक्तिबीजं वर्म्मबीजं हुं। ऋद्धिः कलान्यासे खः ईशस्वर एकादशस्वरः एतेनान्विता तेन खे। कूर्म्मश्चकारः तदन्त्यः छः भग एकारस्तद्वान् भगवान् एकारयुक्तस्तेन छे। चःस्त्री स्वरूपम्। अत्र क्षकारः सविसर्गो ज्ञेयः। सामन्तमालयमित्युक्तेः। दीर्घतनुच्छदं हूं। संवर्त्तः क्षः भगवानेकारयुक्तः तेन क्षे। अस्याश्च देव्याः शापोऽस्तीति प्रसिद्धिः। तेन केचन क्षे इति वर्णं कीलकं मन्यन्ते। तदर्थं च क्षेकारं पूर्वमुच्चार्य्याऽन्ते ह्रंकारमुच्चारयति। दक्षिणामूर्त्तिसंहितायां तु—कवचं स्त्रीमिमे बीजे कीलके तु प्रकीर्त्तिते। इति।

केचन पूर्व्वं ह्रंकारं पश्चात् क्षेकारमिति महती आचार्य्याणां विप्रतिपत्तिः। तत्र यथा वृक्षादीनां क्वचिद् ग्रन्थयो भवन्ति तथैव मन्त्राणामपि स्वभावादेव कीलाख्या ग्रन्थयो भवन्ति। तेन कालविलम्बासिध्यादयो दोषा भवन्ति। स च अक्षरविशेषगत एव जायते। तत्र केषु चिन्मन्त्रेषु तदक्षरमुद्धृत्य शास्त्रीयेण केन चिदक्षरेण परिपूर्य्य जपं कुर्वन्ति केषु चित्तदनुद्धृत्यैवाऽक्षरान्तरप्रक्षेपेण जपं कुर्वन्ति। केषुचित् कीलाख्यो विद्यमानोऽपि दोषावहो न। यथा वृक्षादिषु विद्यमाना अपि ग्रन्थयः केषुचिदेव दोषावहाः केषुचित्तु गुणायैव भवन्ति।

यथा—चन्दनस्य त्रयः श्रेष्ठा ग्रन्थिकर्पटकोटराः। इति।

मायाविवर्जितान् वर्णान्मूर्ध्नि भाले गले हृदि।
नाभिगुह्योरुयुग्मेषु जानुजङ्घापदेषु च॥ ४
विन्यस्य व्यापकं कुर्यात्समस्तेनैव साधकः।
कूर्म्माद्यैः सप्तभिर्वर्णैः पूर्व्वपूर्व्वविवर्जितैः॥ ५
द्वाभ्यां द्वाभ्यां षडङ्गानि कल्पयेत्साधकोत्तमः॥ ६

यदाहुः—दुष्टोऽस्थः कीलको ज्ञातः सिद्धेस्तु प्रतिबन्धकः।
अदुष्टः कीलको ज्ञातः स्यात् सुसिद्धिप्रदायकः॥ इति॥
तत्र तु तत्कीलकदोषापहाराय मायाद्वयसहितो मन्त्र उद्धृतः। तदुक्तमाचार्य्यैः—
ताराग्तेऽस्यादावपि मायाबीजं प्रयोजयेत् मन्त्री।
तेन हि काङ्क्षितसिद्धिः भूयादचिरेण मन्त्रविदाम्॥ इति॥
नारायणीयेऽपि—फट्ताराद्यं तयोर्द्व्या युक्तं तत् सर्व्वसिद्धिदम्। इति।
प्रणवो बीजं माया शक्तिः। हुं बीजमिति पद्मपादाचार्य्याः। पुरुषार्थेति विनियोगोक्तिः॥ १॥२॥३॥

अक्षरन्यासमाह मायेति। अनेन दशवर्णानामेव न्यासः। तत्र ऊरु-युग्मादिस्थानद्वयेऽपि एकैकाक्षरन्यासः। पदेष्विति पादयोः। साधक इत्यनेन व्यापके मायासहितोच्चारणमुक्तम्।

षडङ्गमाह कूर्म्माद्यैरिति। कूर्म्मसकारस्तस्याद्यः खे। बहुवचनम् आद्यर्थं तेन खेप्रभृतिभिः सप्तभिर्वर्णैः अत्र कूर्म्माद्यैः सप्तभिर्वर्णैरिति। प्रधानेन पूर्वक्रियान्वये प्रकाराकाङ्क्षायामरुणाधिक न्यायेन द्वाभ्यां द्वाभ्यामित्यस्य पार्ष्णिकोन्वयः। तेन खे च इति हृत्। च के शिरः के सः शिखेत्यादि।
तदुक्तं नारायणीये दशाक्षरं मन्त्रमुद्धृत्य—
नवमान्तं तृतीयादिपदस्यावर्णसप्तकम्।
तेनाङ्गानि द्विवर्णानि कर्त्तव्यान्युपदेशतः॥ इति।
केचित्तु कूर्म्मसकारः स आद्यो येषां तैः सप्तभिर्वर्णैरिति व्याचक्षते। तन्मते मायाविवर्जितानिति पदमनुवृत्य पश्चाद्विभक्तिविपरिणामेन विवर्जितैरिति मत्वा प्रकृते योजनीयं तेन चकारादिफडन्तैः षडङ्गम्।
तदुक्तं कादिमते दशाक्षरं मन्त्रमुद्धृत्य—
विद्या चतुर्थवर्णादि सप्तभिरक्षरैस्तथा।
कुर्यादङ्गानि युग्मार्णैः षट्क्रमेण कराङ्गयोः॥ इति।

श्यामां बर्हिकलापशेखरयुतामाबद्धपर्णांशुकां
गुञ्जाहारलसत्पयोधरभरामष्टाहिपान् बिभ्रतीम् ।
ताटङ्काङ्गदमेखलागुणरणन्मञ्जीरतां प्रापितान्
कैरातीं वरदाभयोद्यतकरां देवीं त्रिनेत्रां भजे ॥ ७

संहितायां च—च छे युग्मं हृच्छिरस्तत् छेचो युग्मं शिखा ततः ।
घः स्त्रीयुगं च कवचं स्त्रो हुमाद्ययुगं तथा ॥
ह्रं चे नेत्रे तु विन्यस्य ठे फडस्त्रं प्रकीर्त्तितम् ॥ इति ।

एतत्पक्षद्वयमपि स्वस्वगुरुसम्प्रदायानुसारेण बोद्धव्यम् । साधकोत्तम इत्यनेन स्त्रीमिति कुण्डलिनीबीजस्य षड्दीर्घयुक्तमायाबीजस्य च अङ्गमन्त्रेषु योगः सूचितः । अतएव नारायणीये उपदेशत इत्युक्तिः ॥ ४ ॥ ५ ॥ ६ ॥

ध्यानमाह श्यामामिति । कलापो बर्हः । इदं वलयादीनामुपलक्षकम् । तदुक्तं नारायणीये—

मायूरवलया पिञ्छमौलिः किसलयांशुका ।
सिंहासनस्था मायूरछत्रा बर्हिध्वजान्विता ॥ इति ।

ताटङ्कादीन् प्रापितानष्टाहिपान् सर्पेन्द्रान् बिभ्रतीम् । तत्रानन्तकुलिकौ ताटङ्कतां गतौ वासुकीशङ्खपालौ अङ्गदतां गतौ तक्षकमहापद्मौ मेखलतां गतौ कर्कोटकपद्मनागौ नूपुरतां गतौ ध्येयौ ।

तदुक्तं नारायणीये—विप्राहिकुण्डला राजनागकेयूरसंयुता ।
वैश्यनागकटीबन्धा वृषलनाग नूपुरा ॥ इति ।

एषां ध्यानमुक्तम्—

अनन्तकुलिकौ विप्रौ वह्निवर्णावुदाहृतौ ।
प्रत्येकं तु सहस्रेण फणानां समलङ्कृतौ ॥
वासुकिः शङ्खपालश्च क्षत्रियौ पीतवर्णकौ ।
प्रत्येकं तु फणासप्तशतसंख्याविराजितौ ॥
तक्षकश्च महापद्मो वैश्यावेतावहो स्मृतौ ।
नीलवर्णौ फणापञ्चशततुङ्गोत्तमाङ्गकौ ॥
पद्मकर्कोटकौ शूद्रौ फणात्रिशतकौ सितौ ॥ इति ।

आयुधध्यानं वामदक्षिणयोरिति सम्प्रदायविदः ॥ ७ ॥

लक्षं संजप्य मन्त्रज्ञो मनुमेनं जितेन्द्रियः।
दशांशं जुहुयाद्बिल्वैर्मधुराक्तैः समिद्वरैः॥ ८

हृल्लेखाकल्पिते पीठे नवशक्तिसमन्विते।
पूजयेत् त्वरितां देवीं वक्ष्यमाणविधानतः॥ ९

संवर्तको बिन्दुयुतः कवचं सकलं वियत्।
वज्रदेह पुरुद्वन्द्वमाभाष्य हिंगुलुद्वयम्॥ १०

गर्जयुग्मं वियत्सेन्दु वर्म्मान्त्यो दीर्घबिन्दुमान्।
पञ्चाननाय हृदयं पीठमन्त्रः प्रकीर्त्तितः॥ ११

दद्यादासनमेतेन मूर्त्तिं मूलेन कल्पयेत्।
अङ्गैः प्रणीतां गायत्रीं केसरेष्वर्चयेत् क्रमात्॥ १२

मन्त्रज्ञ इत्यनेन ॐ क्रीं नमो नित्ये स्वाहेति मन्त्रस्य दशांशजपः। शिवपञ्चाक्षरस्य किङ्करमन्त्रस्य ॐ क्रीं नमो भगवते शबराय महाकिरातरूपाय कङ्कालधराय हूं फट् स्वाहेत्यस्य च शतांशजपः॥ ८॥

हृल्लेखाकल्पिते भुवनेशीप्रोक्ते। तत्पीठशक्त्योऽत्रापि पूज्या इत्यर्थः। नवशक्तिसमन्वित इत्यनेन पीठमन्त्रस्याऽन्यत्वं सूचयति। अत्र पीठमष्टदलमेव। षोड़शदलपूज्यदेवतानामनुक्तत्वात्। तदुक्तं संहितायाम्—

अष्टपत्रं लिखेत्पद्मं बहिर्भूबिम्बमालिखेत्।
प्रत्येकं वसुपत्रेषु कवचं चाष्टधा लिखेत्॥
मध्ये तु भुवनेशानीं वेष्टयेन्मातृकां बहिः।
सर्वरक्षाकरं नाम चक्रमेतदुदाहृतम्॥
अत्रावाह्य पुनर्देवीमुपचारैः समर्चयेत्। इति।

आचार्य्याश्च—अष्टहरिविधृतसिंहासने सामावाह्य सरसिजे देवीम्। इति॥ ९॥

आसनमन्त्रमुद्धरति संवर्त्तक इति। बिन्दुयुतः संवर्त्तकः क्षं कवचं हुं। सकलं सबिन्दु कलाशब्देनार्द्धेन्दुः तेन बिन्दुवाचकत्वम्। वियत् हं वज्रदेहपुरुपुरु स्वरूपम्। हिमाभाष्येति सम्बन्धः। सेन्दु सबिन्दु वियत् हं। वर्म्म हुं अन्त्यः क्षः दीर्घ आकारः बिन्दुः तद्वान् तेन क्षां। हृदयं नमः॥

आवरणपूजामाह अङ्गैरिति। क्रमादित्यत्रादिषट्सु केसरेषु षड़ङ्गानि सम्पूज्य कौबेरेशानयोः प्रणीतां गायत्रीं च पूजयेत् इति सम्प्रदायविदः।

दलेषु पूजयेदेताः श्रीबीजाद्याः सुभूषिताः ।
हुङ्कारीं खेचरीं चण्डां छेदनीं क्षेपणीं स्त्रियम् ॥ १३
हूङ्कारीं क्षेमकारीं च लोकेशायुधभूषणाः ।
फट्कारीमग्रतो बाह्ये कोदण्डशरधारिणीम् ॥ १४
द्वारस्य पार्श्वयोः पूज्ये हैमवेत्रकराम्बुजे ।
जयाख्या विजयाख्या च किङ्कराय पदं ततः ॥ १५
रक्षरक्षपदस्यान्ते त्वरिताज्ञा स्थिरो भव ।
वर्म्मास्त्रान्तेन मनुना किङ्करं तद्वहिर्यजेत् ॥ १६

तदुक्तमाचार्य्यैः—अङ्गैः सह प्रणीतां गायत्रीं पूजयेद्दिशां क्रमतः । इति । पद्मपादाचार्य्यैरप्येवमेव व्याख्यातम् ।

अन्यत्रापि—अष्टसिंहासने पूज्या दले पूर्व्वादिके क्रमात् ।
अङ्गप्रणीतां गायत्रीम् । इति ।

त्रोतलामतेऽपि—यजेत्तत्राष्टपत्रेषु पूर्वाशाद्यङ्गदेवताः ।
सौम्ये प्रणीतामैशे च गायत्रीमभिपूजयेत् ॥ इति ।

मन्त्रदेवप्रकाशिकाकारादीनामिदमेव सम्मतम् ॥ १०॥११॥१२ ॥

दलेष्विति । एता वक्ष्यमाणा मन्त्रार्णशक्तयः सुभुषिता इत्यस्य व्याख्यानम् । लोकेशेति । भूषणशब्दो वर्णवाहनोपलक्षणः । तेनेन्द्रादीनामिव तासां वर्णायुधभूषणवाहनानीत्यर्थः । उक्तं च त्रोतलामते—

इन्द्रादिलोकपालानां वर्णवाहायुधैः समाः । इति

श्रयत इति देव्याः । केचनात्र लोकपालतदायुधपूजां न कारयन्ति शक्तीनामेव तद्रूपत्वादिति । अन्ये योषिद्रूपान् पूजयन्ति । तदुक्तं त्रोतलामते—

योषिद्भूतान् दिशां नाथान् तद्बाह्यावरणे यजेत् । इति ।

अन्ये तु दलाग्रेषु भैरवाङ्कस्था मातरः पूज्या इत्याहुः । उक्तं च त्रोतलामते—

तद्बाह्ये भैरवानष्टौ पीठमातृसमन्वितान् इति ॥ १३॥१४ ॥

द्वारस्य पार्श्वयोः द्वारबाह्यपार्श्वयोः । द्वारबाह्ये स्थिते इत्युक्तेः । एते अपि द्विभुजे देवतासमानवर्ण्णे च । उक्तं च शक्ती तत्सदृशे इति ।

किङ्करमन्त्रमुद्धरति किङ्करायेति । वर्म्म हुं । अस्त्रं फट् । किङ्करो नाम देव्याः प्रेष्यभूतो भूतविशेषः । सोऽपि द्विभुज एव । तद्बहिर्द्वारबहिर्भागे । बर्बरमूर्द्धजमुद्धुषितकेशं कुटिलकेशमिति यावत् ।

लगुडं बिभ्रतं कृष्णां कृष्णाम्बरमूर्द्धजम् ।
आरण्यैरक्षणैः पुष्पैरतिमुक्तैः सुगन्धिभिः ॥ १७

पूजयेद् धूपदीपाद्यैर्नृत्यगीतैर्मनोरमैः ।
एवं सिद्धमनुर्मन्त्री नारीनरनरेश्वरैः ॥ १८

मान्यते वत्सरादर्वाक् लक्ष्म्या जितधनेश्वरः ।
योनिकुण्डं प्रकल्प्यात्र कुर्य्याद्धोमं निजेच्छया ॥ १९

मल्लिकाकुसुमैर्हुत्वा वशयेदखिलं जगत् ।
कृत्याद्रोहादिशमनं पलाशकुसुमैर्हुतिम् ॥ २०

इक्षुखण्डैः शुभैर्हुत्वा महतीमृद्धिमाप्नुयात् ।
दीर्घमायुरवाप्नोति दूर्व्वाहोमेन साधकः ॥ २१

धान्यैः प्रक्षालितैर्हुत्वा श्रियमिष्टां समाप्नुयात् ।
यवैर्धान्यसमृद्धिः स्याद्धोधूमैरिष्टसिद्धयः ॥ २२

शीतलातन्त्रे विशेषः—प्रेतासनगतं द्वारबाह्यदेशेऽतिभीषणम् । इति ।

त्वरितामन्त्रजापी त्वरितागायत्रीं जपेत् । यदाहुः—

त्वरितादेविशब्दान्ते विद्महे वर्णमुच्चरेत् ।
विद्यां धीमहि च प्रोक्ता तन्नो देवी प्रचोदयात् ॥
गायत्री त्वरितायास्तु जपात् सान्निध्यकारिणी । इति ।

निजेच्छयेति । अनेनैतदुक्तम् । वक्ष्यमाणप्रयोगेषु कार्य्यगौरवलाघवात् सहस्रं वक्ष्यमाणायुतसंख्या त्रियुता वा होमस्य । जपस्यापि तावतीति ।

तदुक्तम्—हुतसंख्या साहस्री त्रियुता वाथाऽयुतान्तिकी भवति ।
यावत्संख्यो होमस्तावज्जप्यश्च मन्त्रिणा मन्त्रः ॥ इति ।

अन्यत्रापि—हुतसंख्या च साहस्री सहस्रत्रियुतावधि ।
लाघवं गौरवं कार्य्यं विचार्य्य निपुणश्चरेत् ॥ इति ।

एतद्धोमदशांशेन पञ्चाक्षरकिङ्कराभ्यामपि होमः सर्व्वप्रयोगेष्विति ज्ञेयम् ॥

वशयेदित्यत्र कामादित्वम् । कृत्याद्रोहादीत्यत्र नृसिंहादित्वम् । महती-मृद्धिमिति श्र्यादित्वम् । दीर्घमायुरवाप्नोतीति मृत्युञ्जयादित्वम् । साधक इत्यनेन त्रिःकृतपुरश्चर्य्य इत्युक्तम् ॥ १५ ॥ १६ ॥ १७ ॥ १८ ॥ १९ ॥ २० ॥ २१ ॥

प्रक्षालितैरिति तिलान्तानां विशेषणम् । श्रियमिष्टामिति श्रीयोगोऽपि ।

तण्डुलैरच्चया सिद्धिः स्याद् वृद्धिर्महती तिलैः ।
मन्त्री नीलोत्पलैर्हुत्वा नृपपत्नीं वशं नयेत् ॥ २३
प्रबुद्धैः पङ्कजैर्हुत्वा वशं नयति मेदिनीम् ।
अशोकैः पुत्रमाप्नोति मधूकैरिष्टमाप्नुयात् ॥ २४
फलैर्जम्बुभवैर्हुत्वा लभते धनमीप्सितम् ।
पुष्पैः पाटलिसम्भूतैरिष्टामाप्नोति सुन्दरीम् ॥ २५
पुष्पैर्बकुलसम्भूतैः कीर्त्तिः स्यादनपायिनी ।
दीर्घमायुर्लभेद्दाम्रैस्सम्पकैः काञ्चनं लभेत् ॥ २६
कुर्व्वीत सर्षपैर्होमं शत्रोर्नाशकरं सुधीः ।
पत्रैर्बकुलजैर्हुत्वा शीघ्रमुत्सादयेदरीन् ॥ २७
शाल्मलीपत्रहोमेन सपत्नान् नाशयेद् ध्रुवम् ।
कोद्रवैः कण्डनैस्तद्वन्निम्बैर्विद्वेषयेन्मिथः ॥ २८
माषहोमेन मूकः स्यादुन्मत्तोऽक्षैर्भवेदरिः ।
अयुतं होमसंख्या स्याज्जपस्तावान् प्रकीर्त्तितः ॥ २९
स्नानं तन्मन्त्रितैस्तोयैः सर्व्वव्याधिहरं स्मृतम् ।
तज्जप्तं चुलुकं तोयं मुखे क्षिप्तं विषापहम् ॥ ३०

पुत्रमाप्नोतीति कामयोगः । मेदिनीमिति मेदिनीस्था लोका लच्यन्ते । बहुत्वं व्यंग्यम् । इष्टां सुन्दरीमिति बालायोगः ॥ २२ ॥ २३ ॥ २४ ॥ २५ ॥

कीर्त्तिः स्यादित्यजपायोगो ज्ञेयः । अनपायिनी अविनश्वरा । लभेरात्मनेपदित्वात् कथं लभेदिति । लभत इति लभः पचाद्यच् लभ इवाचरेदिति । आचारे नाम धातोः क्विप् । सनाद्यन्ता इति धातुत्वम् । ततः परस्मैपदमिति समाधिः । क्वचिद्भवेदित्येव पाठः । आम्रैरिति । अत्र पुष्पैरित्यनुषज्यते । उत्सादयेदिति वायुबीजादित्वम् । सपत्नान् शत्रून् । कण्डनैस्तुषकणैः । तद्वन्नाशयेदित्यर्थः । निम्बैः निम्बफलैः । अक्षैर्बिभीतकफलैः । विषापहमिति गरुडबीजयोगः । मन्त्रविदित्यनेन नृसिंहबीजयोगः । त्रिलोहीति । साधु साधिता एतन्मन्त्रजप्ता कृतसम्पाता च । अत्रापेक्षितार्थद्योतनिका-

आर्त्ताय भेषजं दद्यान्मन्त्रेणाऽनेन मन्त्रवित् ।
स भवेद् व्याधिनिर्मुक्तो मन्त्रस्याऽस्य प्रभावतः ॥ ३१

त्रिलोहीमुद्रिकाऽनेन मनुना साधु साधिता ।
कृत्याद्रोहादिशमनी सर्व्वव्याधिविनाशिनी ॥ ३२

सर्व्वसम्पत्प्रदा नित्यं सर्व्ववश्यकरी मता ।
यद्यद्वाञ्छति मन्त्रज्ञस्तत्तदेतेन साध्यते ॥ ३३

मध्ये सरोजे दशपत्रयुक्ते मायां लिखेद्वाञ्छितसाध्यगर्भाम् ।
तारादिवर्णान् दश मन्त्रसंस्थान् षट्कोणबीजं वसुधापुरस्थम् ॥ ३४

कृत्याद्रोहादिशमनं व्यालचौरभयापहम् ।
विधृतं त्वरितायन्त्रं विशेषाद्विजयप्रदम् ॥ ३५

तारे हुं विलिखेत्सरोजकुहरे साध्याभिधानान्वितं
मन्त्रार्णान् वसुसंख्यकान् वसुदलेष्वालिख्य तद्वाह्यतः ।
शक्त्या त्रिःपरिवेष्टितं घटगतं पद्मस्थमब्जाननं
यन्त्रं वश्यकरं ग्रहादिभयहृल्लक्ष्मीप्रदं कीर्त्तिदम् ॥ ३६

कोष्ठानां शतमेकविंशतियुतं कृत्वा भुवं मध्यतः
साध्याढ्यं त्वरितां शिवादि विलिखेन्मायां विना मन्त्रवित् ।

कारेण लोहानां प्रत्येकं समभागा उक्ताः । यद्यद्वाञ्छति मन्त्रज्ञ इत्यनेन प्रणवयोगे मुक्तिकरी वाग्योगे धर्म्मज्ञानकरी शक्तियोगे सर्व्वकरीति सूचितम् ॥ २६-३३ ॥

यन्त्रमाह मध्य इति । मध्ये सरोजे इति व्यधिकरणे सप्तम्यौ । वाञ्छितं वश्यादि साध्यस्य तद्गर्भाम् । तारादीनिति । मायाव्यतिरिक्तान् । विशेषाद्विजयप्रदमित्यनेन मायायां दुर्गाबीजे साध्यलेखनमिति सूचितम् ॥ ३४ ॥ ३५ ॥

यन्त्रान्तरमाह तार इति । सरोजकुहरे अष्टदलकर्णिकायाम् । मन्त्रार्णानिति मायाद्वयतारवर्णरहितान् । तेषामन्यत्र विनियोगात् । अब्जाननमिति । घटमुखमेव तद्रूपत्वेन यन्त्रे उपचरितम् । कीर्त्तिदमिति । अजपायां साध्यनामेति ज्ञेयम् ॥ ३६ ॥

यन्त्रान्तरमाह कोष्ठानामिति । दक्षिणोदक्पूर्वापरायतद्वादशद्वादशरेखाभिः शतमेकविंशतियुतं कोष्ठानि जायन्ते । मध्यत इति सप्तम्यर्थे तसिः । तत्र

रेखाग्रेषु लसत्त्रिशूलमत् सकृत् संजप्य सम्पातितं
यन्त्रं क्ष्वेडमहाभिचारशमनं वश्यावहं श्रीप्रदम् ॥ ३७

शिवादि ईशानादि प्रदक्षिणक्रमेण द्वादशावृत्ति मन्त्रं लिखेत् । अत्र क्ष्वेडशमने गरुडबीजे साध्यलिखनम् । महाभिचारशमने नृसिंहबीजे । वश्ये कामबीजे श्रिये श्रीबीजे सर्वार्थे शक्तावित्यादि ज्ञेयम् । साम्प्रदायिकास्त्वन्यथा व्याचक्षते । ध्रुवं मध्यतः शिवादि विलिखेत् । अत्र पञ्चम्यर्थे तसिः । आदिशब्देन आग्नेयनैर्ऋत-वायव्यानि । तेनायमर्थः । मध्ये प्रणवं विलिख्य तत ईशगतपञ्चसु कोणकोष्ठेषु पञ्चप्रणवान् लिखेत् । एवमाग्नेयादिषु पञ्चसु कोणकोष्ठेष्वपि । मायां विना साध्याढ्यं यथा स्यात्तथा त्वरितां मन्त्रविद्विलिखेदिति । अत्र मन्त्रविच्छब्देन लेखनक्रमः सूचितः । साध्याढ्यमित्यनेन ध्रुवे प्रति कोष्ठं चैकैकवर्णक्रमेण साध्यलिखनम् । मध्यध्रुवे च सर्वकर्मसाध्यलिखनमित्यर्थः । अत्राक्षरलेखन-क्रमः । तत्रेशानतारपञ्चके आद्यस्य प्रणवस्य पूर्वदिग्गतपदचतुष्के हुमादिकेऽन्त्य-वर्णचतुष्कं विलिख्य तद्दक्षिणकोष्ठे क्षः आलिख्य ततूपश्चात् पदचतुष्के शेषं वर्णचतुष्कं मध्यप्रणवान्तं लिखेदित्येकावृत्तिः । ततो द्वितीयतारस्य पूर्वपदत्रये हुं खे चेति विलिख्य पूर्वलिखितानुवाचनेन द्वितीया । एवं तृतीयतारपूर्वपदद्वये हुं खे विलिख्य पूर्वलिखितोपजीवनेन तृतीया । एवं चतुर्थतारपूर्वपदे हुमालिख्य पूर्वलिखितोपन्यासेन चतुर्थी । पुनः पञ्चमं प्रणवमारभ्य पूर्वलिखितवाचनेनैव पञ्चम्यावृत्तिः । एवमेव प्रणवपञ्चकमारभ्य पूर्वपदावृत्ति-पञ्चकम् । एवमेकस्मिन् कोणे दशावृत्तयः । एवमाग्नेयादिकोणत्रयेऽपि । तथाचा-चार्यवचने "अनुविलिखेद्वा" इति छेदं कृत्वा वाशब्दः समुच्चये दशावृत्ति लिखेदिति व्याख्यातम् । नारायणीये च—

भूर्जे सकारकपुटे जवशूलदीप्ते
कोणेषु तारमुदरे निहितस्य नाम्नः ।
फट् स्याद्दिशासु च यथा लिखिता तथैषा
मालार्णयुक् प्रति पुटं हरति ग्रहार्त्तिम् ॥ इति

कारकेति १२१ जवेति ४८ । अन्यत् स्पष्टम् । तन्त्रान्तरोक्तं यन्त्रान्तरं—

रेखाः पूर्वापरा द्वादशगिरिशमिता दक्षिणोदक् च कृत्वा
साध्यं मध्यस्थकोष्ठेष्वप्यसुरपतिदिक्कोष्ठकेषु ध्रुवः स्यात् ।
पश्चात्तेष्वस्त्रमन्त्या मनुभवलिपयः शेषकोष्ठेषु लेख्या
बाधन्ते यन्त्रयुक्तं न नरमथ सुराः किं पुनर्मानवौघाः ॥ इति ॥३७॥

एकाशीतिपदेषु टान्तविवरे साध्यं लिखेन्मध्यतः
पश्चात् पङ्क्तिषु दिग्गतासु लिपिशो जूंसः शिखान्तं लिखेत् ।
शिष्टेष्वीशनिशाचरादि विलिखेल्लक्ष्मीमनुं पङ्क्तिशः
शस्त्राविर्वषडन्तया त्वरितया वीतं चतुर्दिक्ष्वपि ॥ ३८

लान्तैः प्रवीतं कमलासनेन घटेन वीतं कमलासनेन ।
संसाधितं चक्रमनुग्रहाख्यं दध्याद्यथावत्कनकादिबद्धम् ॥ ३९

क्रत्यापमृत्युरोगादीन् क्ष्वेडभूतमहाग्रहान् ।
जीवेद्वर्षशतं पुत्रैः पौत्रैर्लक्ष्म्या च नन्दति ॥ ४०

यन्त्रान्तरमाह एकेति। दश पूर्व्वापरायता दश दक्षिणोत्तरायता रेखा विलिखेत्। एवम् एकाशीतिकोष्ठानि जायन्ते। तत्र मध्यकोष्ठे टान्तं ठं विलिख्य तन्मध्ये साध्यं विलिखेत्। साध्यमित्युपलक्षणं साधकादीनामपि। दिग्गतासु पङ्क्तिष्विति। मध्यकोष्ठात्पूर्व्वापरदक्षिणोत्तरचतुःकोष्ठात्मकचतुःपङ्क्तिषु। जूंसः स्वरूपम्। शिखान्तं वषडन्तं तेन जूंसः वषट् इति लिपिशः एकैकाक्षरक्रमेण लिखेत्। लक्ष्मीमनुं वक्ष्यमाणं श्रीमित्यादिकम्। शस्त्रं फट् तस्मिन्नाविर्भवत् यत् वषट् तदन्ते यस्याः सा तया त्वरितया त्वरितामन्त्रेण चतुर्दिक्षु दिशि दिशि एकैकावृत्त्या वेष्टयेत्। तदुक्तम्—

दिक्दिक्संख्यामन्त्रपदादिर्वषडन्ताम्। इति।

अन्यत्रापि—वषडन्ता बहिः श्रीन्ना दिक्षु ठं कलशं वह्निः। इति।
अत्र केचन अन्यथा व्याचक्षते। अस्त्रं च आविर्भवदधिकं वषट् यत्रेति। तेन फट्कारं समुच्चार्य्य वषट्कारमुच्चारयेदिति। तदयुक्तं तन्त्रान्तरविरोधात्।
तदुक्तम्—त्वरिता वषडन्ता स्यात् फट्कारपरिवर्जिता। इति।
अत्र वेष्टने अग्रे च मायासहितो मन्त्रः ॥ ३८ ॥

लान्तैर्वकारैः। प्रकर्षेण वीतमिति मालाकारेणेत्यर्थः।
तदुक्तमाचार्य्यैः—मेदोमालावेष्टितबिम्बम्। इति।
दध्यात् धारयेत्। यथावदित्युक्तप्रमाणेन। कनकादीत्यादिशब्देन रजतताम्रे ॥३८॥
तन्त्रान्तरेऽस्य फलमुक्तम्—

यमेन तु धृतं यन्त्रं ब्रह्मणा विष्णुना पुरा।
बुधेन भैरवेणापि हेरम्बेन गुहेन च ॥
सर्व्वे ते वशमायान्ति विद्यायाश्च प्रसादतः।

श्री सा माया यामा सा श्री सानो याज्ञेज्ञेया नोसा।
माया लीला लाली यामा याज्ञे लाली लीला ज्ञेया॥ ४१
लिखेच्चतुःषष्टिपदेषु विद्वानीशादि कन्यादि रमामनुं तम्।
बाह्ये यथावत् त्वरिताभिवीतं लान्तैश्च वीतं वरकाञ्चनस्थम्॥ ४२
देशे पुरे वा नगरे गृहे वा विनिःक्षिपेच्चक्रमिदं यथावत्।
तत्र ध्रुवं गोमहिषाभिवृद्धिः सम्यक् प्रजाशस्यसमृद्धयः स्युः॥ ४३

कवचं भगवांश्चण्डो मेरुः सर्गसमन्वितः।
त्रिकण्टकी समाख्याता विद्या वर्णत्रयात्मिका।
द्विरुक्तैर्मन्त्रवर्णैः स्यादङ्गक्लृप्तिरितीरिता॥ ४४

नीला नाभेरधस्तादरुणरुचिरधः कण्ठदेशात्सिताऽऽस्या-
द्वक्त्रैर्दंष्ट्राकरालैरुदरपरिगतैर्भीषणाङ्गी चतुर्भिः।

त्रिलोके यानि दुःखानि कृत्रिमाकृत्रिमाण्यपि॥
क्षीयन्ते तान्यसन्देहो विद्याराज्ञीप्रभावतः।

कुड्ये समे खटिकया भवने लिखित्वा संपूजयेत्परमनुग्रहचक्रमेतत्।
सर्वो नरो भवति तत्र कुटुम्बवर्गः सर्वात्मना वशयतीह मनुष्यलोकम्॥ इति॥४०॥

यन्त्रान्तरमाह लिखेदिति। प्रागपरदक्षिणोत्तरायता नव रेखा विलिख्य चतुःषष्टिपदं कुर्यात्। कन्यादि नैर्ऋत्यादि। रमामनुं श्रीसेत्यादि। यथावदिति वषड्क्तया चतुर्दिक्ष्वपि। अत्र मध्यगतचतुर्षु कोष्ठेषु ठकारमालिख्य तन्मध्ये साध्यसाधककर्मनामानि लिखेत्। यथावद्विनिक्षिपेदिति। हस्तमात्रप्रमाणे क्षिप्तं पूजितमित्युक्तम्॥ ४१॥ ४२॥ ४३॥

मन्त्रान्तरमाह कवचमिति। कवचं हुं। चण्डः खः भगवानेकारयुक्तः तेन खे। मेरुः क्षः। अत्र अकारादिलान्तानां पञ्चाशद्वर्णानाम् अक्षमालात्वात् मेरुस्थानीयः क्षकारो मेरुशब्दवाच्यः। सर्गसमन्वितो विसर्गयुक्तः। इदमेव पूर्व्वमन्त्रेऽप्ययं सविसर्ग इति द्योतयति। तदुक्तं नारायणीये—

यत्तोतलायाश्च दशाक्षराया बीजं द्वितीयं सतृतीयशस्तम्।
त्रिकण्टकीनाम तदा सुसिध्येत्। इति।

आद्यं बीजं अन्त्यं शक्तिः॥ ४४॥

नीलेति। आस्यात् सितेत्यन्वयः। दंष्ट्राकरालैः उदरपरिगतैः चतुर्भिर्वक्त्रै-

दीप्ती कम्बुरथाङ्गं करसरसिरुहैर्धारयन्ती जटान्तः-
स्फुर्जच्छीतांशुखण्डा भवतु भयहरा देवता वह्निनेत्रा ॥ ४५

विलक्षं प्रजपेदेनमाज्येनाऽन्ते दशांशतः।
हुत्वा प्राक् प्रोक्तमार्गेण पूजयेत्तां त्रिकण्टकीम् ॥ ४६

त्रिशूलमुद्रां पाणिभ्यां बद्धात्मानं त्रिकण्टकीम्।
ध्यायन् स्पृष्ट्वा जपेद् यस्तं सद्यस्तं मुञ्चति ग्रहः ॥ ४७

चेकह्वा स्त्री विवर्णेयं विद्या वश्या त्रिकण्टकी।
मन्त्रार्णैर्वीप्सितैः कुर्य्यादङ्गषट्कं यथा पुरा ॥ ४८

पूर्वोक्तां देवतां ध्यायन् मन्त्रं त्रिनियुतं जपेत्।
दशांशं सर्पिषा हुत्वा वशयेद्वनितां नरान् ॥ ४९

तारो माया वाग्भवान्ते नित्यक्लिन्ने मदद्रवे।
वाङ्माया वह्निजायान्तो मन्त्रः पञ्चदशाक्षरः ॥ ५०

द्वाभ्यां द्वाभ्यां पुनर्द्वाभ्यां द्वाभ्यां पञ्चभिरक्षरैः।
वाचं विना समस्तेनाप्यङ्गषट्कमथाचरेत् ॥ ५१

भीषणाङ्गीति सम्बन्धः। उदरपरिगतैरिति उदरचतुःपार्श्वे। कम्बुः शङ्खः। आयुधध्यानमूर्द्ध्वयोर्दक्षवामयोराद्ये तदधस्तनयोरन्त्य इति ॥ ४५ ॥ ४६ ॥

त्रिशूलमुद्रामिति। सा तु "कनिष्ठाङ्गुष्ठसंयोगात् शेषाणां तु प्रसारणात्" इति। एतन्मन्त्राद्याक्षरद्वयं छे युक्तमन्ते विषहा त्रिकण्टकी ज्ञेया।
तदुक्तं नारायणीये—तस्याः त्रिपञ्चमपुटो विषहा च षष्ठः। इति।
ऋष्यादिसर्व्वं पूर्व्वेण समानं त्रितयस्य ॥ ४७ ॥

मन्त्रान्तरमाह चे इति। वश्येति विनियोगोक्तिः। आद्यं बीजं मध्यं शक्तिः। वीप्सितैर्द्विरुक्तैः। त्रिनियुतं त्रिलक्षम् ॥ ४८ ॥ ४९ ॥

नित्यामन्त्रमाह तार इति। वाग्भवम् ऐँ। अनन्तरवक्ष्यमाणनित्यामन्त्रोक्तकन्दर्पादिकमत्र ज्ञेयम्। प्रणवो बीजं स्वाहा शक्तिः। श्रिये श्रीबीजादित्वं रोगशमनादौ दुर्गाबीजादित्वम्। दुःखदौर्भाग्यशमने कामबीजादित्वम्। जरापमृत्युशमने मृत्युञ्जयादित्वम्। मदद्रवे इत्यतः पूर्वं साध्यनामप्रयोगोऽपि। एवं वक्ष्यमाणमन्त्रयोरपि ज्ञेयम्। वाचं विनेत्युभयत्र सम्बध्यते। तेन त्रयोदशभिरक्षरैरुक्तरीत्या पञ्चाङ्गानि कृत्वा शिष्टसमस्तेनास्त्रमित्यर्थः। अथानन्तर-

द्वीपं त्रिकोणं विपुलं सुरद्रुमममनोहरम् ।
कूजत्कोकिलनादाढ्यं मन्दं मारुतसेवितम् ॥ ५२
भृङ्गपुष्पलताकीर्णमुद्यचन्द्रदिवाकरम् ।
स्मृत्वा सुराब्धिमध्यस्थं तस्मिन्माणिक्यमण्डपे ॥ ५३
रत्नसिंहासने न्यस्ते त्रिकोणोज्ज्वलकर्णिके ।
पद्मे सञ्चिन्तयेद्देवीं साक्षात्त्रैलोक्यमोहिनीम् ॥ ५४

नित्यां भजेद् बालशशाङ्कचूडां पाशाङ्कुशौ कल्पलतां कपालम् ।
हस्तैर्वहन्तीमरुणां त्रिनेत्रामास्फालयन्तीं कलवल्लकीं ताम् ॥ ५५

त्रिलक्षं प्रजपेन्मन्त्रमाज्येन जुहुयात्ततः ।
दशांशं पूजयेत्पीठं चतुःशक्तिसमन्वितम् ॥ ५६
आंपूर्वां द्राविणीं वामां शम्भुकोणे समर्चयेत् ।
आह्लादकारिणीं ज्येष्ठामींकाराद्यां हुताशने ॥ ५७
पूजयेत् क्षोभिणीं रौद्रीमूंकाराद्यां निशाचरे ।
मध्ये[वायौ] यजेद् गुह्यशक्तिं वाग्भवाद्यां विचक्षणः ॥ ५८

मित्यनेन वाग्भवेन पुनरङ्गानि कुर्यात् इति । तदुक्तं नारायणीये—

रात्रिक्रूरांशसंख्यैः स्ववर्णैः स्वेन च वाग्विना ।
न्यस्याङ्गषट्कं वाचैव पुनश्चाङ्गानि विन्यसेत् । इति ॥ ५० ॥ ५१ ॥

द्वीपमिति । सुराब्धिमध्यस्थं त्रिकोणं द्वीपं स्मृत्वा तस्मिन् द्वीपे माणिक्यमण्डपे रत्नसिंहासने पद्मे देवीं चिन्तयेदित्यन्वयः । व्यधिकरणे सप्तम्यः उभयत्र । त्रिकोणमित्यधोमुखम् । सुराब्धीत्यनेनैतदुक्तं पृथिव्यनन्तरं सुराब्धिं त्रिकोणं द्वीपं माणिक्यमण्डपं रत्नसिंहासनं पीठन्यासे न्यस्येदिति । शेषं समानम् । इदमग्रिममन्त्रेऽपि ज्ञेयम् । त्रैलोक्यमोहिनीमित्यनेन विनियोगोक्तिः ॥ ५२ ॥ ५३ ॥ ५४ ॥

कलवल्लकीमास्फालयन्तीमित्यनेन षट्करेत्युक्तं भवति । आयुधध्यानं तु पूर्ववत् ॥ ५५ ॥

चतुःशक्तिसमन्वितमिति पीठशक्तयस्तत्र । तत्र द्राविणीमित्यादीनि तु वामाज्येष्ठारौद्रीणां विशेषणानि । अत्र शक्तित्रयमीशादिकोणेषु विन्यस्य तुर्यां मध्ये न्यसेदित्यर्थः । तदुक्तं नारायणीये—

कोणेष्वीशादि मध्ये च तत्र शक्तीर्न्यसेदिमाः । इति ।

मायाद्यमासनं दत्त्वा मूर्त्तिं मूलेन कल्पयेत् ।
तत्र सम्पूजयेद्देवीं वक्ष्यमाणक्रमेण तु ॥ ५९

अङ्गार्चनं केसरेषु दलेष्वेताः समर्चयेत् ।
आद्या नित्या सुभद्राऽन्या मङ्गला नरवीरिणी ॥ ६०

सुभगा दुर्भगा भूयः सप्तमी स्यान्मनोन्मनी ।
अष्टमी रुद्ररूपा च वीणावादनतत्पराः ॥ ६१

रक्ता मनोरमा दूत्यः सुवेषा सन्मन्थराः ।
आद्यान्त्ययुग्मरहिताः स्वराः क्लीबविवर्जिताः ॥ ६२

बिन्द्वन्ता मनवस्तासामनङ्गस्मरमन्मथाः ।
कामो मारश्च पञ्चेषुपाशाङ्कुशधनुर्भृतः ॥ ६३

अपराङ्गनिषङ्गाढ्या रक्ताः पूज्याः सुभूषणाः ।
मान्मथं व्योमसर्गाढ्यं तेषां बीजमुदाहृतम् ॥ ६४

रतिः स्याद्विरतिः प्रीतिर्विप्रीतिर्मतिदुर्मती ।
धृतिश्च विधृतिस्तुष्टिर्वितुष्टिश्च दश स्मृताः ॥ ६५

रक्ता वीणाकरा द्वे द्वे कामानां पार्श्वयोः स्थिताः ।
सर्व्वाभरणसम्पन्नाः पूज्याः स्मेरमुखाम्बुजाः ॥ ६६

मध्ये यजेद् गुह्यशक्तिमिति पाठः । वायाविति पाठो ज्ञानेनोपस्कृतो मन्तव्यः । ॥ ५६ ॥ ५७ ॥ ५८ ॥

मायाद्यमिति । भुवनेशीबीजमुच्चार्य्य सर्व्वशक्तीत्यादिना पीठपूजेत्युक्तम् ॥ ५९ ॥ ६० ॥

आद्येति । नित्या आद्या प्रथमा । आदीति स्वराणामाद्यन्ते द्वे युग्मे क्लीबाश्च तद्रहिता अन्ये अष्टौ बिन्दुयुतास्तासां मन्त्राः ॥ ६० ॥ ६१ ॥ ६२ ॥

अनङ्गेत्यादीनां पञ्चानामष्टदलोपरि परितः पूजा । आयुधध्यानं दक्षाधस्ताद्वामाधःपर्य्यन्तम् ॥ ६३ ॥

अपराङ्गनिषङ्गाढ्याः पृष्ठस्थतूणीराः । मान्मथं कामबीजम् । व्योमसर्गाढ्यं हकारविसर्गयुक्तम् ॥ ६४ ॥

रतिरित्यादि दश शक्तिनामानि ॥ ६५ ॥ ६६ ॥

क्लीबौष्ठद्वयनिर्मुक्तस्वराढ्यश्चतुराननः ।
बिन्दुमान् बीजमेतासां क्रमाल्लोकेश्वरान् बहिः ॥ ६७

एवं संपूजयेद्देवीं देवानामपि दुर्लभाम् ।
परमैश्वर्य्यमाप्नोति प्रार्थ्यते वनिताजनैः ॥ ६८

वाग्भवं मान्मथं बीजं नित्यक्लिन्ने मदो पुनः ।
द्रवे वह्निवधूमन्त्रो द्वादशार्णोऽयमीरितः ॥ ६९

ऋषिः सम्मोहनश्छन्दो निवृन्नित्या च देवता ।
वाचा कृत्वा षडङ्गानि नित्यां ध्यायेन्निजेष्टदाम् ॥ ७०

अर्द्धेन्दुमौलिमरुणाममराभिवन्द्या-
मम्भोजपाशसृणिपूर्णकपालहस्ताम् ।
रक्ताङ्गरागवसनाभरणां त्रिनेत्रां
ध्यायेच्छिवस्य वनितां मदविह्वलाङ्गीम् ॥ ७१

चतुर्लक्षं जपित्वाऽन्ते मधुराक्तैर्मधूकजैः ।
कुसुमैरयुतं हुत्वा तोषयेद् गुरुमात्मनः ॥ ७२

शक्तिपीठे यजेद्देवीं वक्ष्यमाणेन वर्त्मना ।
अङ्गान्यर्चेद्यथापूर्वं ततः शक्तीरिमा यजेत् ॥ ७३

क्लीबेति । क्लीबचतुष्टयम् ओष्ठद्वयम् एऐ । एतन्निर्मुक्ता ये दश स्वराः तदाढ्यः तद्युक्तश्चतुराननः जकारः तेन जं जां जिं जीं जुं जूं जों जौं जं जः इति मन्त्राः । क्रमादिति पूर्व्ववान्वेति । लोकेशास्त्राण्यनुक्तानि अपि पूजनीयानि । चतुर्थपटले सामान्यत उक्तः ॥ ६७ ॥ ६८ ॥

मन्त्रान्तरमाह वागिति । मदो मकारदकारौ । क्लीँ बीजं स्वाहेति शक्तिः । वाचेति वाग्भवेन । षड्दीर्घकामबीजयुक्तेनेति परमगुरवः । निजेष्टदामिति विनियोगोक्तिः ॥ ६९ ॥ ७० ॥

अर्द्धेन्द्विति । सृणिः अङ्कुशः । पूर्णेति सुरापूर्णम् । आयुधध्यानं पूर्व्ववत् ॥ ७१ ॥ ७२ ॥

शक्तिपीठ इति । शक्तिपीठोक्ता नव शक्तयोऽत्र पूज्या इत्यर्थः । यथापूर्व्वमिति तुर्य्योक्तरीत्या । रक्ताम्बुजेक्षणा इत्यत्र रक्ताम्बुजप्रभा इत्यपि ॥ ७३॥७४॥७५॥७६ ॥

नित्या निरञ्जना क्लिन्ना क्लेदिनी मदनातुरा ।
मदद्रवा द्राविणी च द्रविणेत्यष्टशक्तयः ॥ ७४

नीलोत्पलकपालाढ्यकरा रक्ताम्बुजेक्षणाः ।
लोकपालान् यजेदन्त्ये वाहनायुधसंयुतान् ॥ ७५

सिद्धमन्त्रं जपेन्मन्त्री सहस्रं शयनस्थितः ।
यां विचिन्त्य स्त्रियं रात्रौ सा समायाति तत्क्षणात् ॥ ७६

वाङ्मायाऽनन्तरं नित्ये भूयो क्लिन्ने मदद्रवे ।
द्विठान्तो रविसंख्यार्णो मनुर्वश्यप्रदायकः ॥ ७७

अङ्गिराः स्यादृषिस्त्रिष्टुप् छन्दो मुनिभिरीरितम् ।
वज्रप्रस्तारिणी प्रोक्ता देवताऽभीष्टदायिनी ॥ ७८

वज्रप्रस्तारिणीमन्त्रमाह वागिति । वाक् वाग्भवम् । अन्ये एवं योजयन्ति । मायानन्तरं क्लिन्ने भूयः पश्चाद्वाक् । ततो नित्येति अविभक्तिकोऽयं निर्देशः । ततो मदद्रवे । ठः बिन्दु द्विठः बिन्दुद्वयं विसर्गः । सर्गः शक्तिरित्युक्तेः भुवनेशीबीजम् । रविसंख्यार्णः द्वादशाक्षर इत्युक्तेर्वाग्भवान्तरमङ्कुशबीजम् । एतेनैतदुक्तं भवति । प्रथमतो माया ततः क्लिन्ने ततो वाग्भवाङ्कुशौ ततो नित्यमदद्रवे ततो मायाबीजम् । तदुक्तमाचार्य्यैः—

स्मरदीर्घेऽधरकाग्न्यौ दीर्घेत्यक्ष्वेलदद्रलान्तशिवाः ।
अभितः शक्तिनिरुद्धो द्वादशवर्णोऽयमीरितो मन्त्रः ॥ इति ।

नारायणीयेऽपि—क्लिन्ने वागङ्कुशौ नित्यशब्दः कालश्च दद्रवे ।
वक्ष्येशीशक्तिरुद्धैषा । इति ।

अन्ये वाग्भवरहितं मायाद्यमेकादशाक्षरमाहुः ।
तदुक्तं नारायणीये—नतौ साक्षिलचौ क्लिन्ने कालोऽक्षिश्च द्रवे शिरः । इति ।

आचार्य्याश्च—निद्रयोरन्तरा त्वक्लिन्नेमदाः स्युश्च वे शिरः ।
मायादिकस्तथा । इति ।

मन्त्रद्वयमपि साम्प्रदायिकमेव । वक्ष्यमाणविधिः सर्व्वेषां समान एव । प्रथममन्त्रे वाक् बीजं स्वाहा शक्तिः । द्वितीयमन्त्रे वाक् बीजं माया शक्तिः । तृतीये माया बीजं स्वाहा शक्तिः । वश्येति अभीष्टदेति च विनियोगोक्तिः ॥ ७७ ॥ ७८ ॥

वाग्भवेन षडङ्गानि विदध्यान्मन्त्रवित्तमः ।
वज्रप्रस्तारिणीं ध्यायेत् समाहितमना ततः ॥ ७९

रक्ताब्धौ रक्तपोते रविदलकमलाभ्यन्तरे सन्निषण्णां
रक्ताङ्गीं रक्तमौलिस्फुरितशशिकलां स्मेरवक्त्रां त्रिनेत्राम् ।
बीजापूरेषुपाशाङ्कुशमदनधनुःसत्कपालानि हस्तै-
र्बिभ्राणामानताङ्गीं स्तनभरनमितामम्बिकामाश्रयामः ॥ ८०

मन्त्री मन्त्रं जपेल्लक्षं जपान्ते जुहुयात्ततः ।
अयुतं राजवृक्षोत्थैर्घृतसिक्तैः समिद्वरैः ॥ ८१

शक्तिपीठे यजेद्देवीमरुणैः कुसुमादिभिः ।
अङ्गानि केसरेषु स्युरर्चनीया दलेष्विमाः ॥ ८२

हृल्लेखा क्लेदिनी क्लिन्ना क्षोभिणी मदनातुरा ।
निरञ्जना रागवती सप्तमी मदनावती ॥ ८३

वाग्भवेनेति । षड्दीर्घमायायुक्तेनेति परमगुरवः । द्वितीयमन्त्रे तु ।

द्वाभ्यां वा चैकेन द्वाभ्यां द्वाभ्यां तथा पुनर्द्वाभ्याम् ।
मन्त्राक्षरैर्विदध्यादङ्गविधिं जातिसंयुतैर्मन्त्री ॥ इति ।

अस्मिन् पक्षे वाग्भवेन शिर इति शेषः । एवं षडङ्गानीति श्लोकयोजना । मन्त्रवित्तम इत्यनेन तन्त्रान्तरोक्तान्यङ्गानि सूचितानि । आह्लादिनी हृत् क्लिन्ने शिरः क्लेदिनि शिखा नित्ये वर्म मद नेत्रं द्रवेऽस्त्रमिति तानि ॥ ७९ ॥

रक्ताब्धावित्यनेनैतदुक्तं भवति । पृथिव्यनन्तरं रक्तसमुद्रं रक्तपोतं भानुदलाब्जं पीठन्यासे न्यसेदिति । शेषं समानम् । इषुर्बाणः । मदनधनुरिक्षुचापम् । आयुधध्यानं वामोर्ध्वतः पाशचापकपालानि दक्षोर्ध्वतः अङ्कुशशरबीजपूराणि । केचन द्वितीयमन्त्रे बीजपूरस्थाने दाडिममाहुः । स्तनभरस्य भरणमाधिक्यं तस्मादानताङ्गी । आदिशब्देन रक्तगन्धः । स्वयमप्येतादृशवेष एव । तदुक्तम्—

शक्तिपीठे पूज्या देवी कुसुमानुलेपनैररुणैः । स्वयमप्यलङ्कृताङ्गः । इति ।
तृतीयेऽङ्गानि ध्यानं च । तथा वर्णद्वन्द्वैस्त्वाङ्गविधिः स्मृतः । पूर्वोक्तारूपामभयपाशाङ्कुशकपालिनीमिति । समिद्वरैः श्रेष्ठसमिद्भिः ॥ ८० ॥ ८१ ॥ ८२ ॥

आवरणपूजामाह अङ्गानीति । केसरेषु यान्यङ्गानि सामान्यत उक्तानि तानि स्युः । त्रिकोणोपरि कर्णिकायामिति शेषः । ध्यानस्य नारायणीये तथोक्तेः ।

मेखला द्राविणी पश्चाद्वेगवत्यपरा स्मृता ।
कपालोत्पलधारिण्यः शक्तयो रक्तविग्रहाः ॥ ८४

मातरो दिग्विदिक्ष्वर्च्याः पुनः पूज्या दिगीश्वराः ।
भजेन्मन्त्री मनुं नित्यमर्चनादिभिरादरात् ॥ ८५

दारिद्र्यरोगनिर्मुक्तः स जीवेच्छरदां शतम् ।
अस्मिन्मन्त्रे रतो मन्त्री वशयेदखिलं जगत् ॥ ८६

नित्यं मन्त्रैर्बुधः कुर्य्यान्मुखक्षालनमन्वहम् ।
अञ्जनं तिलकं पुष्पं धारयेन्मन्त्रितं सुधीः ॥ ८७

ताम्बूलं मन्त्रितं भक्ष्येन्मन्त्री स स्याज्जगत्प्रियः ।
श्रीमायामदनैः प्रोक्तो मन्त्री बीजत्रयात्मकः ॥ ८८

रक्तसिन्धुचरत्पोतमासपत्राब्जयोनिगा । इति ।

तदुक्तं च—अङ्गैः शक्तिभिराभिराशाधिपैः क्रमात् पूज्या । इति ।

तन्त्रान्तरेऽपि त्रिकोणषट्कोणद्वादशदलं पीठमुक्तम्—

अङ्गानि पूजयेदादौ त्रिकोणस्थास्तु पूजयेत् ।

इच्छाज्ञानक्रियासंज्ञाः षट्कोणेष्वर्चयेत्ततः ॥

डाकिन्याद्याः द्वादशस्तु हृल्लेखाद्याः समर्चयेत् । इति ।

अत्र द्वादश । पुस्तकेषु बिन्दुद्वयस्य रेखात्मकता लेखकदोषवशात् ।
उक्तं च नारायणीये—मेखला द्राविणी वेगवती कामस्य ताः स्मृताः । इति ।
आचार्य्या अपि—सस्मरा द्वादश प्रोक्ताः । इति ।
अत एव शक्तय इत्युक्तिः । अन्यथा ध्यानमात्रमेव वदेत् । तेन शक्तीनामिदं ध्यानम् । स्मरस्तु प्रसिद्धध्यान इति भावः । रक्तविग्रहाः अरुणदेहाः ॥८२॥८३॥८४॥

मातरो दिग्विदिक्ष्विति । द्वादशदलाद्बहिः स्थानमात्रनिर्देशः । तेन पुरोभागादिप्रादक्षिण्येन चतुरस्रान्तरष्टदिक्षु मातृपूजनम् । दिगीश्वरा इति तदस्त्रोपलक्षकम् । तृतीये तु आवरणपूजा अङ्गैः पूर्व्वमन्त्रोक्ताष्टशक्तिभिर्नीकपालैस्तदस्त्रैश्च ।

दीक्षितः प्रजपेल्लक्षं मनुमेनं हुनेत्ततः ।

मधूकपुष्पैः स्वाद्वक्तैरयुतं हविषाऽथवा ॥ इति ॥ ८५॥८६॥८७॥

त्रैपुटमन्त्रमाह श्रीति । सम्मोहन इत्युपलक्षणम् । भृगुशक्तिसम्मोहना क्षपय

ऋषिः सम्मोहनश्छन्दो गायत्री देवता मनोः।
त्रिपुटाख्या ह्रिकान्तैस्तैर्बीजैरङ्गानि षट् क्रमात्॥ ८९

पारिजातवने रम्ये मण्डपे मणिकुट्टिमे।
रत्नसिंहासने सौम्ये पद्मे षट्कोणशोभिते।
अधस्तात् कल्पवृक्षस्य निषण्णां देवतां स्मरेत्॥ ९०

चापं पाशाम्बुजसरसिजान्यङ्कुशं पुष्पबाणान्
बिभ्राणां तां करसरसिजै रत्नमौलिं त्रिनेत्राम्।
हेमाब्जाभां कुचभरनतां रत्नमञ्जीरकाञ्ची-
ग्रैवेयाद्यैर्विलसिततनुं भावयेच्छक्तिमाद्याम्॥ ९१

चामरादर्शताम्बूलकरण्डकसमुद्गकान्।
वहन्तीभिः कुचार्ताभिर्दूतीभिः परिवारिताम्।
करुणामृतवर्षिण्या पश्यन्तीं साधकं दृशा॥ ९२

इति शेषम्। आद्यं बीजं द्वितीयं शक्तिः॥ ८८॥ ८९॥

पारिजातेति। पारिजातवने मण्डपे कल्पवृक्षस्याऽधस्तान्मणिकुट्टिमे रत्नसिंहासने पद्मे निषण्णां देवतां स्मरेदित्यन्वयः। व्यधिकरणः सप्तम्यः। पद्मे चतुःपत्रे अष्टपत्रे च। तत्र षट्कोणकर्णिकायां चतुःपत्रमन्यत् तत्कर्णिकायाम्। उक्तं च नारायणीये—यजेदेनां चतुःपत्रे षट्कोणस्थाम्बुजे च ताम्। इति। अथ चैतदुक्तं भवति। अनन्तरं सुवर्णभूमिं पारिजातवनं रत्नमण्डपं मणिकुट्टिमं रत्नसिंहासनं पूजयेत्। शेषं समानम्।

नवकनकभासुरोर्वीविरचितमणिकुट्टिमे सकल्पतरौ।

इत्याद्याचार्योक्तेः॥ ९०॥

चापमितीक्षुचापम्। आयुधध्यानं वामाधस्तात् दक्षाधःपर्यन्तम्। तदुक्तम् आचार्यैः—ध्यायेद्धृताब्जयुगपाशवराङ्कुशेक्षु-
चापां सपुष्पविशिखां नवहेमवर्णाम्॥ इति॥ ९१॥

ताम्बूलकरण्डकमित्येकम्। समुद्गकः सम्पुटकः गन्धादिस्थापनपात्रम्। दूतीभिरिति द्राविणी सूर्या आदित्या प्रभावतीति चतस्रः। सौम्यादिचतुर्दलस्थाः। एता अपि द्विभुजाः। दक्षिणहस्ते चामरादि वामहस्तेऽभयम्। तदुक्तम्—

निरायुधे करे प्रोक्तो वरः साधारणः सदा। अभयश्च। इति।

भानुलक्षं जपेदेनं मनुं तावत्सहस्रकम् ।
बिल्वारग्वधसम्भूतैर्मधुराक्तैः समिद्वरैः ॥ ९३

जवापुष्पैश्च जुहुयात्तोषयेदमुना गुरुम् ।
हृल्लेखाविहिते पीठे पूजयेत्तां विधानतः ॥ ९४

आग्नेयादिषट्कोणेषु लक्ष्म्याद्याः परिपूजयेत् ।
लक्ष्मीं हेमप्रभां तन्वीं सवराब्जयुगाभयाम् ॥ ९५

चक्रशङ्खगदाम्भोजधरं हेमनिभं हरिम् ।
पाशाङ्कुशाभयाभीष्टधरां गौरीं जवारुणाम् ॥ ९६

मृगटङ्काभयाभीष्टधरं स्वर्णनिभं हरम् ।
नीलोत्पलकरां सौम्यां रतिं काञ्चनसन्निभाम् ॥ ९७

धृतपाशाङ्कुशेष्वासपुष्पेषुमरुणं स्मरम् ।
पूर्ववन्निधियुग्मं तद्यजेदुभयपार्श्वयोः ॥ ९८

बहिरङ्गानि सम्पूज्य पूज्याः पत्रेषु मातरः ।
लोकेशान् वनितारूपानर्चयेत् सौम्यविग्रहान् ॥ ९९

नारायणीये तु कृताञ्जलित्वमुक्तम्—

तद्दूतीश्च कृताञ्जलीः ।

सौम्यादि दृष्टिनीं सूर्यामादित्यां च प्रभावतीम् । इति ॥ ९२ ॥

भानुलक्षं द्वादशलक्षम् । आरग्वधो राजवृक्षः । विधानत इत्यनेन तन्त्रान्तरोक्तं यन्त्रे बीजलिखनं सूचितम् । तदुक्तं संहितायाम्—

षट्कोणं पूर्वमालिख्य मध्ये विद्यां लिखेत् सुधीः ।
वीप्सया तां तु षट्कोणकोणेषु क्रमतो लिखेत् ॥
बाह्ये वसुदलं कुर्य्यादीर्घस्वरविभूषितम् ।
चतुरस्रं चतुर्द्वारभूषितं मण्डलं लिखेत् ॥ इति ।

टङ्कः परशुः । इष्वासो धनुः । आयुधध्यानं स्वस्वप्रकरणेऽनुसन्धेयम् ॥ ९३॥९४ ॥ ॥ ९५॥९६॥९७॥९८ ॥

पूर्ववदिति सशक्तिकध्यानम् । उभयपार्श्वयोः षट्कोणपार्श्वयोः । एतदन्तमावरणम् । बहिरिति । षट्कोणादष्टदलकेसरेषु । सौम्यविग्रहानित्यनेन "उत्तुङ्गयौवनोन्मत्तदेव्याराधनगर्विंतान्" इति तन्त्रान्तरोक्तमुक्तं भवति ॥ ९९ ॥

इत्थं यः पूजयेद्देवीं नित्यं भक्तिसमन्वितः ।
सम्प्राप्य कवितां दिव्यां प्राप्य लक्ष्मीमनन्तराम् ॥ १००
सौभाग्यमतुलं लब्ध्वा विहरेत् सुचिरं भुवि ।
पाशाङ्कुशपुटा शक्तिर्झिण्टीशो गगनं सदृक् ॥ १०१
परमेश्वरिशब्दान्ते द्विठान्तः प्रणवादिकः ।
अश्वारूढामनुः प्रोक्तस्त्रयोदशभिरक्षरैः ॥ १०२
द्वाभ्यामेकेन चैकेन द्वाभ्यां पञ्चभिरक्षरैः ।
द्वाभ्यामङ्गानि षट् कुर्य्यात्ततो देवीं विचिन्तयेत् ॥ १०३

कवितामित्यत्र वाग्भवादित्वम् । प्राप्य लक्ष्मीमिति श्रीबीजादित्वम् । तदुक्तं नारायणीये—श्रीकामशक्तिबीजात्मा श्रीकरो वश्यकृन्मनुः । इति ।

सौभाग्यमिति कामादित्वं मायामध्यत्वम् । मायान्तत्वे तु त्रिपुरामन्त्रात्सर्भावः । एवमुभयशक्त्यादित्वे यशस्करं ज्ञेयम् । यद्बीजादिको मन्त्रस्तदादिकान्यङ्गान्यपि कुर्य्यात् ॥१००॥१०१॥

अश्वारूढामन्त्रमाह पाशेति । पाश आं अङ्कुशः क्रों शक्तिर्मायाबीजं तेन पाशादित्वरत्तरः । त्रयोदशभिरक्षरैरित्युक्तेराद्यन्तयोः पाशाभ्यां पुटितत्वं न स्पृश्यत इति ज्ञेयम् । झिण्टीशः ए गगनं हः सदृगिकारस्तत्सहितं तेन हि । साम्प्रदायिका अस्य एहि पदस्य द्विरुक्तिं वागादित्वं च वदन्ति । अन्ये तु अश्वितः शरतो वाणतः ऋक्पादान् त्रीन् पठित्वा अन्ते द्विठाङ्कुशमायापाशप्रणवा इति ।

"यदद्य कच्चवृत्रहन्नुदगा अभि सूर्य्य । सर्वं तदिंद्र ते व शे" इति ऋक् । अस्य ब्रह्मा ऋषिः विराट् छन्दः प्रणवो बीजं स्वाहा शक्तिः । अन्ये पूर्व्वोक्तामेव दशाक्षरीं मन्यन्ते—

मूर्द्धालिकाक्षिनासास्यवक्त्रकण्ठेषु च क्रमात् ।
हृन्नाभिध्वजमूलाङ्घ्रिष्वक्षराणि प्रविन्यसेत् ॥ इति ।

त्रयोदशाक्षरन्यासो यथा—

मूर्द्धालिकाक्षिकर्णाक्षिनासास्यास्याङ्गुलेषु च ।
हृन्नाभिध्वजमूलाङ्घ्रिष्वक्षराणि प्रविन्यसेत् ॥ इति ।

षड्दीर्घमायया दशाक्षर्य्या षडङ्गम् । अन्योक्तषडङ्गेष्वपि षड्दीर्घमायायोगमाहुः साम्प्रदायिकाः । दशाक्षर्य्या ध्यानम्—

अरुणामरुणाकल्प मरुणाम्बरभूषणाम् ।

रक्ताश्वाधिरूढां शशधरशकलाबद्धमौलिं त्रिनेत्रां
पाशेनाबद्ध्य साध्यां स्मरशरविवशां दक्षिणेनानयन्तीम् ।
हस्तेनाऽन्येन वेत्रं वरकनकमयं धारयन्तीं मनोज्ञां
देवीं ध्यायेदजस्रं कुचभरनमितां दिव्यहाराभिरामाम् ॥ १०४

बाणलक्षं जपेन्मन्त्रमाज्येनाऽन्ते जितेन्द्रियः ।
दशांशं जुहुयाद्देवीं शक्तिपीठे समर्चयेत् ॥ १०५

पाशादित्र्यक्षरोक्तेन विधानेन समाहितः ।
आज्याक्तान्नहुतान्मन्त्री लभते वाञ्छितं फलम् ॥ १०६

लवणैर्मधुसंसिक्तैर्होमेन वशयेन्नृपान् ।
तेनैव विधिना मन्त्री वशयेद्वनितामपि ॥ १०७

चतुर्भुजां त्रिनेत्रां च प्रसन्नवदनां शिवाम् ॥
खड्गं चर्म च यष्टिं च दधानां दक्षवामयोः ।
अधस्ताद्धेमवेत्रं स्यात् पाशस्तस्योर्ध्वतः स्थितः ॥
कण्ठे बद्ध्वाऽथ पाशेन साध्यं वेत्रसमाहतम् ।
बद्धाञ्जलिकरं व्योम्नि भ्रमन्तं पातितं पदे ॥
आकर्षयन्तीं ध्यायेत्ताम् । इति ॥ १०१ ॥ १०२ ॥ १०३ ॥

त्रयोदशाक्षर्या ध्यानमाह रक्तामिति । अश्वेति रक्तोऽश्वः । स्मरशरविवशां साध्यां पाशेनाबध्य कण्ठ इति शेषम् । "कण्ठे बद्ध्वाऽथ पाशेन" इति उक्तेः । अन्येन वामेन हस्तेनानयन्तीम् । पुनः किं विशिष्टाम् । दक्षिणेन वेत्रं धारयन्तीम् ।

तदुक्तम्—अश्वारूढा कराग्रे नवकनकमयीं वेत्रयष्टिं दधाना
हस्तेऽन्येनानयन्ती । इति ॥ १०४ ॥

बाणलक्षं पञ्चलक्षम् । दशाक्षर्यां तु
हविष्याशी जपेद्वर्णलक्षं होमं दशांशतः ।
विदध्यात्तु पलाशैर्वा जवापुष्पैश्च वा प्रिये ।
कुसुम्भकुसुमैर्वाज्यैरन्यैर्वा रक्तपुष्पकैः ॥ इति ।

पूजा तु—पद्मपत्रान्तयुगलं षट्कोणाष्टदलाब्जयुक् ।
चतुरस्रद्वयं द्वारद्वययुक्तमिति प्रिये ॥
चक्रं विधाय तां देवीमावाह्याऽत्र प्रपूजयेत् ।

आलिख्य कोष्ठानि विकारसंख्यान्यन्तश्चतुष्के प्रणवं ससाध्यम् ।
अन्येष्वपि द्वादश मन्त्रवर्णान् लिखेदिदं यन्त्रमशेषवश्यम् ॥ १०८

मायाहृद्भगवत्यन्ते माहेश्वरिपदं वदेत् ।
अन्नपूर्णे ठयुगलं मनुः सप्तदशाक्षरः ।
अङ्गानि मायया कुर्य्यात्ततो देवीं विचिन्तयेत् ॥ १०९

रक्तां विचित्रवसनां नवचन्द्रचूडा-
मन्नप्रदाननिरतां स्तनभारनम्राम् ।
नृत्यन्तमिन्दुशकलाभरणं विलोक्य
हृष्टां भजेद्भगवतीं भवदुःखहन्त्रीम् ॥ ११०

अङ्गैर्बाणैश्च शब्दाद्यैराकर्षण्यन्तिकैः परम् ॥
श्रोत्रादिभिश्च बुद्ध्यन्तैराकर्षण्यन्तिमैः परम् ।
प्राणात्मशक्तिचैतन्यं मनोऽहङ्कारभावकान् ॥
शरीरं चाष्टपत्रेष्वाकर्षणीपदपश्चिमान् ।
ब्राह्म्याद्या लोकपालांश्च तदस्त्राणि च तद्बहिः ॥ इति ।

यन्त्रं च—त्रिकोणषट्कोणवृत्तं यन्त्रं कृत्वा सवृत्तकम् ।
तन्मध्ये विलिखेत् पूर्वं विद्याद्यं च ततः परम् ॥
वर्णत्रयं त्रिकोणेषु षट्कोणेषु षडक्षरान् ।
तद्बाह्यवृत्तवीथ्या तु मातृकां वेष्टयेत् क्रमात् ॥
एवं मध्ये प्रविन्यासाद्दश यन्त्राणि कल्पयेत् ।
जपपूजनसम्पातैर्वश्याकृष्टिवसुश्रियः ।
भूरत्नकीर्त्तिसौभाग्यनिधिकान्तीश्च साधयेत् ॥ इति ॥१०५॥१०७॥

यन्त्रमाह आलिख्येति । विकाराः षोडश । लिखेदिति अश्वादिप्रादक्षिण्येन ॥ १०८ ॥

अन्नपूर्णामन्त्रमाह मायेति । हृन्नमः । अत्र नमःशब्दसकारस्य रोरुत्वे गुणे च उकार इति ज्ञेयम् । ठयुगलं स्वाहा । अत्र सप्तदशाक्षर इत्युक्तेः रि अ इत्यत्र न यणादेशः । केचनास्य प्रणवादित्वमाहुः । ब्रह्मा ऋषिः अनुष्टुप् छन्दः माया बीजं स्वाहा शक्तिः । माययेति षड्दीर्घयुक्तया ॥ १०९ ॥

अन्नप्रदाननिरतामिति विनियोगोक्तिः । इन्दुशकलाभरणं शिवम् ॥ ११० ॥

यथाविधि जपेन्मन्त्रं वसुयुग्मसहस्रकम्।
साज्येनाऽन्नेन जुहुयात् तद्दशांशमनन्तरम्॥ १११
शक्तिपीठे यजेद्देवीमङ्गलोकेश्वरायुधैः।
प्रातरेनं जपेन्मन्त्रं नित्यमष्टोत्तरं शतम्॥ ११२
एतस्याऽन्नसमृद्धिः स्याच्छ्रिया सह महीयसी।
माया पद्मावतिपदं ततः पावकवल्लभा॥ ११३
सप्तार्णो मनुराख्यातः सर्व्ववश्यप्रदायकः।
अङ्गानि मायया कुर्य्यात् ध्यायेत् त्रैलोक्यमोहिनीम्॥ ११४
पद्मासनस्थां करपङ्कजाभ्यां रक्तोत्पले संदधतीं त्रिनेत्राम्।
आबिभ्रतीमाभरणानि रक्तां पद्मावतीं पद्ममुखीं भजामि॥ ११५
पञ्चलक्षं जपेन्मन्त्रं दशांशं जुहुयाद् घृतैः।
शक्तिपीठे यजेद्देवीमङ्गाद्यावरणैः सह॥ ११६
किञ्जल्केष्वङ्गपूजा स्यात् पूज्याः पत्रेषु मातरः।
लोकपाला बहिः पूज्यास्तदस्त्राणि ततो बहिः॥ ११७
इत्थं यो भजते मन्त्रं जपहोमार्चनादिभिः।
सुभगः सर्व्वनारीणां भवेत् काम इवापरः॥ ११८
षड्स्रमध्ये प्रविलिख्य शक्तिं कोणेषु शिष्टानि षडक्षराणि।
तद्बाह्यतो मातृकयाऽभिवीतं पद्मावतीयन्त्रमिदं प्रशस्तम्॥ ११९

यथाविधीति पुरश्चरणोक्तमार्गेण। वसुयुग्मसहस्रं षोड़शसहस्रम्। एतस्य साधकस्य॥ १११॥११२॥११३॥

पद्मावतीमन्त्रमाह मायेति। सर्व्ववश्येति विनियोगोक्तिः। त्रैलोक्यमोहिनीमित्यपि। ब्रह्मा ऋषिः गायत्री छन्दः माया बीजं स्वाहा शक्तिः। अत्रापि माययेति पूर्व्ववत्॥ ११३॥ ११४॥

पद्मावतीध्यानमाह पद्मेति॥ ११५॥

पञ्चलक्षं लक्षद्वयम्॥ ११६॥ ११७॥ ११८॥

यन्त्रमाह षडस्रेति॥ ११९॥

तारं शिरसि विन्यस्य देवीं सञ्चिन्त्य भारतीम् ।
शक्तिबीजं न्यसेद्भाले संस्मृत्य भुवनेश्वरीम् ॥ १२०
अमसौ नेत्रयोर्न्यस्येत् ध्यात्वा सूर्य्यं हुताशनम् ।
मुखवृत्तेन विन्यस्येट्टान्तं चन्द्रमनुस्मरन् ॥ १२१
जिह्वायां विन्यसेद्बीजं रमायास्तां विचिन्तयन् ।
स्वाहार्णौ गण्डयोर्न्यस्येत् तद्गजेन्द्रधिया सुधीः ॥ १२२
अमठं न्यासमाख्यातं कुर्वन् प्रतिदिनं नरः ।
कीर्त्तिश्रीकान्तिमेधानां वल्लभो भवति ध्रुवम् ॥ १२३

इति श्रीशारदातिलके दशमः पटलः ।

अमठन्यासमाह तारमिति। अमसौ अं बिन्दुः अः विसर्गः। मुखवृत्तेन मुखवृत्त इत्यर्थः। क्वचिन्मुखे वृत्तेनेति पाठः। वृत्तेन वृत्तरूपेण मुखे न्यसेदिति। टान्तं ठकारम्। तद्गजेन्द्रधिया लक्ष्मीगजेन्द्रबुद्ध्या। विचिन्त्येत्युक्तेः तत्तत्प्रकरणे तत्तद्ध्यानमनुसन्धेयम्। तत्र तर्जन्यनामिकाकनिष्ठाः समाकुञ्च्य युक्ताभ्यां मध्यमाङ्गुष्ठाभ्यां गजशुण्डाकाराभ्यामयं न्यासः कर्त्तव्य इत्युपदेशः साम्प्रदायिकानाम्। गजेन्द्रध्यानं यथा—

तारकुन्देन्दुधवलौ गलगण्डमदोत्कटौ ।
लसत्पुष्करशोभाढ्यौ स्फुरद्दन्तौ गजौ भजे ॥ इति ।

कीर्त्तिश्रीत्यनेनास्य स्वातन्त्र्यमुक्तम्। तत्र प्रयोगः। ॐ सरस्वत्यै नमः ह्रीं उमायै नमः अं सूर्य्यमण्डलाय अः वह्निमण्डलाय ठं सोममण्डलाय श्रीं श्रियै स्वां दन्तिने। हां दन्तिने। अस्य छन्दऋष्यादिकं यथा। अमठश्री मन्त्रस्य लक्ष्मीनारायण ऋषिः। बृहती छन्दः। अमठश्रीः देवता। ह्रीं बीजं श्रीं शक्तिः। सर्व्ववश्यार्थे विनियोगः। ॐ श्रीं हृत्। श्रीकरि शिरः। धनकरि शिखा। धान्यकरि वर्म्म। ऋद्धिकरि नेत्रम्। पुष्टिकरि अस्त्रम् ॥ १२७ ॥

इति श्रीशारदातिलकटीकायां सत्सम्प्रदायकृतव्याख्यायां पदार्थादर्शाभिख्यायां त्वरितामन्त्रकथनं नाम दशमः पटलः ॥ १० ॥

ततो दुर्गामनुं वक्ष्ये दृष्टादृष्टफलप्रदम् ।
मायाऽन्तिः कर्णबिन्द्वाढ्यो भूयोऽसौ सर्गवान् भवेत् ॥ १
पश्चान्तकः प्रतिष्ठावान् मारुतो भौतिकासनः ।
तारादिर्हृदयान्तोऽयं मन्त्रो वस्वक्षरात्मकः ॥ २
ऋषिश्च नारदश्छन्दो गायत्रं देवता मनोः ।
दुर्गा समीरिता सद्भिर्दुरितापन्निवारिणी ॥ ३
नमस्कारवियुक्तेन मूलमन्त्रेण साधकः ।
क्रमाद्यैः सह कुर्व्वीत षडङ्गानि यथाविधि ॥ ४

एवं नित्यामन्त्रानुक्त्वा द्वादशगुणिते दुर्गाबीजस्योक्तत्वात् दुर्गामन्त्रान् वक्तुमुपक्रमते तत इति । मन्त्रमुद्धरति मायेति । माया शक्तिबीजम् । अन्तिर्दकारः कर्ण उकारः बिन्दुरनुस्वार एतदाढ्य इत्यनेन दुं । भूयोऽसौ दुकारः सर्गवान् विसर्गयुक्तः । अनेन एतादृशमपि बीजमिति सूचितम् । एतदर्थमेव सर्गवानित्युक्तिः । मन्त्रे तु रेफ एव । उपसर्गस्य तादृग्रूपत्वात् । पश्चान्तको गकारः । प्रतिष्ठावानाकारयुक्तः तेन गा इति । मारुतो यकारः । भौतिक ऐकारस्तदासनस्तेन यै । तदुक्तम्—

तारमायास्वबीजानि दुर्गायै हृदयान्तिकः । इति ।

साम्प्रदायिकाः मायाबीजानन्तरं कामबीजमाहुः । दुं बीजं माया शक्तिः । दुरितेत्यादिना विनियोगोक्तिः ॥ १ ॥ २ ॥ ३ ॥

नमस्कारेति । मूलमन्त्रेण नमस्कारवियुक्तेन । क्रमाद्यैः क्रांक्रीमित्याद्यैः सह षडङ्गानि कुर्व्वीतेति सम्बन्धः । प्रयोगस्तु । ॐ ह्रीं दुं दुर्गायै क्रां हृदयाय नमः । ॐ ह्रीं दुं दुर्गायै क्रीं शिरसे स्वाहा इत्यादि ।
तदुक्तम्—तारो माया च दुर्गायै क्रमाद्यन्ताङ्गकल्पना । इति ।
अत्र चकारेण दुर्गाबीजस्य समुच्चय इति तट्टीकाकारैर्व्याख्यातम् । यथाविधीति । शक्तिषडङ्गमुद्रासूचनम् ॥ ४ ॥

सिंहस्था शशिशेखरा मरकतप्रख्यैश्चतुर्भिर्भुजैः
शङ्खं चक्रधनुःशरांश्च दधती नेत्रैस्त्रिभिः शोभिता ।
आमुक्ताङ्गदहारकङ्कणरणत्काञ्चीरणन्नूपुरा
दुर्गा दुर्गतिहारिणी भवतु वो रत्नोल्लसत्कुण्डला ॥ ५

वसुलक्षं जपेन्मन्त्रं तिलैर्मधुरलोलितैः ।
पयोऽन्धसा वा जुहुयात्तत्सहस्रं जितेन्द्रियः ॥ ६

पीठमित्थं यजेत् सम्यक् नवशक्तिसमन्वितम् ।
प्रभा माया जया सूक्ष्मा विशुद्धा नन्दिनी पुनः ॥ ७

सुप्रभा विजया सर्व्वसिद्धिदा नव शक्तयः ।
अज्भिर्क्लृस्वत्रयक्लीबरहितैः पूजयेदिमाः ॥ ८

प्रणवानन्तरं वज्रनखदंष्ट्रायुधाय च ।
महासिंहाय वर्म्मास्त्रं नतिः सिंहमनुर्मतः ॥ ९

सिंहस्थेति । आयुधध्यानं वामाधूर्द्ध्वयोराद्ये अधस्थयोः परे । आमुक्ता धृता अङ्गदादयो यथेति विग्रहः । दुर्गतिः दुष्टा गतिर्दारिद्र्यं च । सर्व्वदुर्गामन्त्रेषु ध्यानानन्तरमियं मुद्रा दर्शनीया—

मुष्टिं बद्ध्वा कराभ्यां तु वामस्योपरि दक्षिणम् ।
कृत्वा शिरसि सम्पूज्या दुर्गामुद्रेयमीरिता ॥ इति ।

आयुधमुद्रादर्शनं च ॥ ५ ॥

वसुलक्षमष्टलक्षम् । पयोऽन्धसा पायसेन । तत्सहस्रमष्टसहस्रम् । इत्थं वक्ष्यमाणप्रकारेण । सर्व्वसिद्धिदेति शक्तिनाम । आसां ध्यानमन्यत्रोक्तम्—

आदिस्वरैर्बिन्दुयुतैरेकाराद्यैः षडक्षरैः ।
एताः सर्व्वा जवापुष्परक्तवर्णाः स्मिताननाः ॥
चापबाणाञ्जलिकराः शुक्लमाल्यानुलेपनाः ।
आक्षत्रयान्ते सम्पूज्या दलमध्येष्वनुक्रमात् ॥ इति ।

अज्भिरिति । क्लृस्वत्रयं ऋ ऌ ॡ क्लीबाश्च । तद्रहितैरज्भिः स्वरैः नवभिरित्यर्थः । प्रयोगस्तु । आं प्रभायै नम इत्यादि ॥ ६ ॥ ७ ॥ ८ ॥

सिंहमन्त्रमाह प्रणवेति । प्रणवानन्तरं प्रणवमुच्चार्य्य । वज्रनखदंष्ट्रायुधायेति सिंहाय इति च स्वरूपम् । वर्म्म हुं अस्त्रं फट् । नतिर्नमःपदम् ॥ ८॥१० ॥

दद्यादासनमेतेन मूर्त्तिं मूलेन कल्पयेत् ।
तस्यां सम्पूजयेन्मूर्तौ देवीमावाह्य मन्त्रवित् ॥ १०

अङ्गावृतिं पुराऽभ्यर्च्य शक्तीः पत्रेषु पूजयेत् ।
जया च विजया कीर्त्तिः प्रीतिः पश्चात् प्रभा पुनः ॥ ११

श्रद्धा मेधा श्रुतिः प्रोक्ता स्वनामाद्यक्षरादिकाः ।
पत्राग्रेष्वर्चयेदष्टावायुधानि यथाक्रमात् ॥ १२

चक्रशङ्खगदाखड्गपाशाङ्कुशशरान् धनुः ।
लोकेश्वरांस्ततो बाह्ये तेषामस्त्राण्यनन्तरम् ॥ १३

इत्थं जपादिभिर्मन्त्री मन्त्रे सिद्धे विधानवित् ।
कुर्य्यात् प्रयोगानेतेन मनुना स्वमनीषितान् ॥ १४

प्रतिष्ठाप्य विधानेन कलशान् नव शोभनान् ।
रत्नहेमादिसंयुक्तान् पदेषु नवसु स्थितान् ॥ १५

मध्यस्थे पूजयेद्देवीमितरेषु जयादिकाः ।
सम्पूज्य गन्धपुष्पाद्यैरभिषिञ्चेन्नराधिपम् ॥ १६

राजा विजयते शत्रून् साधको विजयश्रियम् ।
प्राप्नोति रोगी दीर्घायुः सर्व्वव्याधिविवर्जितः ॥ १७

अभ्यर्च्येति तुर्यीक्तरीत्या । जयेति । आसां ध्यानमुक्तमन्यत्र—

भ्राजन्मरकतप्रख्याः सर्व्वाश्च शशिभूषणाः ।
दधत्यः सायकं हस्तैः शूलकार्मुकतर्जनीः ।
जयाद्याः पूजनीयाः स्युर्जमित्याद्यर्णसंयुताः ॥ इति ॥११॥१२॥१३॥

विधानवित् प्रयोगान् कुर्व्वीतेति । अनेनैतदुक्तं भवति । श्रीबीजादिः श्रिये । मृत्युञ्जयादिः दीर्घायुषि । नृसिंहबीजादिः वैरिजये । सर्व्वपुटितत्वे सर्व्वकामावाप्तिः । कामादित्वे पुत्रावाप्तिरिति । एतद्बीजयोगः शक्त्यनन्तरं ज्ञेयः ॥ १४ ॥

प्रतिष्ठाप्य विधानेनेति मातृकापटलोक्तविधिना । हेमादीत्यादिशब्देन शाक्तं गन्धाष्टकम् । पदेषु नवसु इति नवनाभमण्डलस्येति शेषः । गन्धपुष्पाद्यैरित्याद्यशब्देन धूपदीपनैवेद्यानि । सम्पूज्येत्युपलक्षणम् । तेन सम्पातयुक्ताः जप्ताश्चेति ज्ञेयम् ।

मन्त्र्याऽभिषिक्ता विधिना लभते तनयं वरम्।
मन्त्रेणाऽनेन संजप्तमाज्यं क्षुद्रज्वरापहम्।
गर्भिणीनां विशेषेण जप्तं भस्मादिकं तथा॥ १८

मध्ये तारे बीजमन्तःस्थसाध्यं पत्रेष्वष्टौ मन्त्रवर्णान् विलिख्य।
त्रिष्टुब्वीतं वेष्टितं मातृकार्णैर्यन्त्रं दौर्गं भूपुरस्थं विदध्यात्॥ १९

क्षुद्रभूतमहारोगचौरसर्पनिवारणम्।
विजयश्रीप्रदं पुंसां गर्भिणीनां सुखप्रदम्॥ २०

भान्तं वियत् सनयनं श्वेतो मर्दिनि ठद्वयम्
अष्टाक्षरीयमाख्याता विद्या महिषमर्दिनी॥ २१

महिषहिंसिके हुंफट्हृदयं परिकीर्त्तितम्।
महिषशत्रो शार्ङ्गी हुंफट्शिरोऽङ्गं समुदाहृतम्॥ २२

महिषं भीषयद्वन्द्वं हुंफडन्तः शिखामनुः।
महिषं हनयुग्मान्ते देवि हुंफट्तनुच्छदम्॥ २३

महिषान्ते सूदनि हुंफडन्तमस्त्रमीरितम्।
मन्त्रैरेतैर्जातियुक्तैः पञ्चाङ्गानि प्रकल्पयेत्॥ २४

यदाहुः—कषायसलिलैः कुम्भानभिपूर्य यथाविधि।
त्रिसहस्रं जपेन्मन्त्रं घृतसम्पातसंयुतम्॥
तैस्त्वभिषिक्तः शुद्धात्मा पूर्वेद्युः समुपोषितः।
जयेच्छत्रून् यथाद्राजा प्राप्नोति विजयं श्रियम्॥
रोगी तु ग्रहपीडाभ्यो मुच्यते व्याधिभिस्तथा। इति।

आज्यं भक्षितमिति शेषः। भस्मादिकं छुतमिति शेषः। आदिशब्दाद् गन्धपुष्पादि। तथेति क्षुद्रग्रहापहमित्यर्थः॥ १५॥१६॥१७॥१८॥

यन्त्रमाह मध्य इति। मध्ये तारे इति व्यधिकरणे सप्तम्यौ। मध्ये कर्णिकायाम्। तारे प्रणवे। बीजं दौर्गम्। अन्तःस्थसाध्यं मध्यस्थितसाध्यसाधकनामकर्मसहितं विलिख्येति सम्बन्धः। त्रिष्टुप् जातवेदाः स हाविंशे वक्ष्यते॥ १९॥ २०॥

महिषमर्दिनीमन्त्रमाह भान्तमिति। भान्तं मकारः वियत् हकारः सनयनमिकारसहितस्तेन महि। श्वेतः ष। मर्दिनि स्वरूपम्। ठद्वयं स्वाहा।

गारुडोपलसन्निभां मणिमौलिकुण्डलमण्डितां
नौमि भालविलोचनां महिषोत्तमाङ्गनिषेदुषीम् ।
चक्रशङ्खकृपाणखेटकबाणकार्मुकशूलकान्
तर्जनीमपि बिभ्रतीं निजबाहुभिः शशिशेखराम् ॥ २५
अष्टलक्षं जपेन्मन्त्रं तत्सहस्रं तिलैः शुभैः ।
हुत्वा प्रागीरिते पीठे यजेन्महिषमर्दिनीम् ॥ २६
सम्पूज्याऽङ्गानि पत्रेषु दुर्गाख्यां वरवर्णिनीम् ।
आर्य्याह्वयां तृतीयां च चतुर्थीं कनकप्रभाम् ॥ २७
पञ्चमीं कृत्तिकासञ्ज्ञां षष्ठीमप्यभयप्रदाम् ।
कन्यां सुरूपां प्रभजेन्मन्त्री दीर्घस्वरैः क्रमात् ॥ २८

उक्तं हि नारायणीये—विषं हि मज्जा कालोऽग्निरत्रिनिशो नि ठद्वयम् । इति ।
मं भौजं स्वाहा शक्तिः । अस्य आकमत्सो नाम ऋषिः । प्रकृति छन्दः ।
अन्ये मार्कण्डेयमृषिमाहुः । शिखावर्म्मणो मन्त्रेऽपि महिषशब्दो द्वितीयान्तो ज्ञेयः ॥ २१॥२२॥२३॥२४ ॥

ध्यानमाह गारुडेति । गारुडोपलः गरुडोद्गारमणिः । आयुधानि दक्षवामयोः पूर्व्वयोराद्ये तदधोधस्तयोः परे परे । तर्जनीमिति तर्जनीमुद्राम् ।

तल्लक्षणं यथा—तर्जन्येकाकिनी तूर्द्ध्वा शेषाः संमिलिताश्चधः ।
मुद्रेयं तर्जनी प्रोक्ता वक्तुः श्रोतुस्तु भीतिदा ॥ इति ॥

तदुक्तमीशानसंहितायाम्—

ध्यायेच्छ्यामां महादुर्गां सर्व्वाभरणभूषिताम् ।
जटामुकुटशोभाढ्यां स्फुरच्चन्द्रकलान्विताम् ॥
पीताम्बरधरां देवीं पीनोन्नतकुचद्वयाम् ।
चक्रशङ्खलसद्धस्तां तदधः खड्गखेटकौ ॥
बाणचापौ च तदधः सशूलां तर्जनीमधः । इति ॥ २५ ॥

प्रागीरिते अव्यवहिते दौर्गे पीठे ॥ २६ ॥

सम्पूज्याऽङ्गानीति केसरेष्विति शेषः । पत्रेष्वित्यग्रिमेण सम्बध्यते । दीर्घस्वरैरिति क्लीबद्वयान्यरहितैरिति शेषः । दीर्घशब्देन पारिभाषिकग्रहणम् । तेन आ ई ऊ ए ऐ ओ औ अः एभिरष्टभिरित्यर्थः । नारायणीये पूर्व्वपटले

यजेदग्रेष्वायुधानि चक्रशङ्खासिखेटकान्।
बाणं बाणासनं शूलं कपालं यादिभिः क्रमात्॥ २९
लोकपालाः पुनः पूज्यास्तदस्त्राणि ततः परम्।
वशयेत्तिलहोमेन नरान् नरपतीनपि॥ ३०
सिद्धार्थैर्जुहुयान्मन्त्री रोगान्मुच्येत तत्क्षणात्।
पद्मैर्हुत्वा जयेच्छत्रून् दूर्व्वाभिः शान्तिमाप्नुयात्॥ ३१
पलाशकुसुमैः पुष्टिं धान्यैर्धान्यश्रियं व्रजेत्।
काकपक्षैः कृतो होमो द्वेषं वितनुते नृणाम्॥ ३२
मरीचहोमान्मरणं रिपुराप्नोति सर्व्वथा।
क्षुद्रारिचोरभूताद्यान् ध्यात्वा देवीं विनाशयेत्॥ ३३
तारो दुर्गेयुगं रक्तमन्त्यं ढान्तं सलोचनम्।
द्विठान्ता जयदुर्गेयं विद्या वेद्या दशाक्षरी॥ ३४

अनन्तस्त्वार्घियोन्यादित्युक्त्वा उत्तरपटले आद्यैः स्वरैः क्रमादित्युक्तम्। एतदभिप्रायेणैवापेक्षितार्थद्योतनिकायां व्याख्यातम् आद्यैः आ ई ऊ ए ऐ ओ औ अः इति स्वरैरिति ॥२७॥२८॥

अग्रेषु पत्राग्रेषु। यादिभिरिति हान्तैरित्यर्थः॥ २९॥

वशयेदिति कामबीजादित्वम्। मन्त्रीत्यनेन मृत्युञ्जयादित्वं सूचितम्। जयेदिति स्वबीजादित्वम्। शान्तिमिति नृसिंहादित्वम्। पुष्टिमिति तार्क्षीयादित्वम्। धान्यश्रियमिति श्रीबीजादित्वम्॥ ३०॥३॥१३२॥

मरीचेति। मरीचशब्दो दीर्घमध्योऽप्यस्ति। तथा च शब्दभेदप्रकाशे "मरीचं मरिचं तथा" इति। मरणमिति स्वबीजादित्वम्॥ ३३॥

जयदुर्गामन्त्रमाह तार इति। तारः प्रणवः। दुर्गेयुगं दुर्गे दुर्गे। रक्तं रेफः। अन्त्यं क्षः ढान्तं णः सलोचनम् इकारसहितमित्युभयविशेषणम्। तेन क्षिणि। द्विठान्ता स्वाहान्ता। तदुक्तं नारायणीये—

तारो दुर्गेद्वयं वह्निरन्त्यं ढान्तं सदृक् शिरः। इति।

अपेक्षितार्थद्योतनिकायां व्याख्यातम्। सदृगित्युभयविशेषणम्। तेन क्षिणीति। मार्कण्डेयो मुनिः बृहती छन्दः प्रणवो बीजं स्वाहा शक्तिः॥ ३४॥

तारादि दुर्गे हृदयं दुर्गे शिर उदीरितम्।
दुर्गायै स्याच्छिखा वर्म्म भूतरक्षिणि कीर्त्तितम् ॥ ३५

तारादि दुर्गेक्षितयं रक्षिण्यक्षि समीरितम्।
तारादि दुर्गेयुगलं रक्षिण्यस्त्रं समीरितम् ॥ ३६

कालाभ्राभां कटाक्षैररिकुलभयदां मौलिबद्धेन्दुरेखां
शङ्खं चक्रं कृपाणं त्रिशिखमपि करैरुद्वहन्तीं त्रिनेत्राम्।
सिंहस्कन्धारूढां त्रिभुवनमखिलं तेजसा पूरयन्तीं
ध्यायेद् दुर्गां जयाख्यां त्रिदशपरिवृतां सेवितां सिद्धिकामैः ॥ ३७

बाणलक्षं जपेन्मन्त्रं घृतेन जुहुयात्ततः।
दशांशं संस्कृते वह्नौ ब्राह्मणानपि भोजयेत् ॥ ३८

अष्टाक्षरोदिते पीठे पूजयेत् पूर्व्ववत् सुधीः।
मन्त्रं जपन् विशेद् युद्धे शत्रून् हन्याद्विशेषतः ॥ ३९

प्रजपेद् व्यवहारादौ तत्रापि विजयी भवेत्।
अर्चयेदस्त्रशस्त्राणि जयार्थी विद्ययाऽनया ॥ ४०

तारादीति वर्म्मान्तं सम्बध्यते ॥ ३५॥३६ ॥

कालेति। त्रिशिखं त्रिशूलम्। आयुधध्यानमष्टाक्षरीवत्। सिद्धिकामैरिति विनियोगोक्तिः ॥ ३७ ॥

बाणलक्षं पञ्चलक्षम्। ब्राह्मणानपि भोजयेदित्यनेन पुरश्चरणे ये दश प्रकारास्ते सूचिताः। तदुक्तम्—

जपो होमस्तर्पणं च स्नाभिषेकोऽघमर्षणम्।
सूर्य्यार्घ्यं जलपानं स्यात् प्रणामं देवपूजनम् ॥
ब्राह्मणानां भोजनं च पूर्व्वपूर्व्वदशांशतः। इति

इदं सर्व्वमन्त्रपुरश्चरणे ज्ञेयम्। केचन प्रकारपञ्चकमेवाहुः—

जपो होमस्तर्पणं च पूजा ब्राह्मणभोजनम्। इति।

सर्व्वत्र जपादिभिरित्यादिशब्दार्थोऽयमेव ज्ञेयः। अष्टाक्षरोदिते दुर्गाष्टाक्षरोदिते। सुधीरिति। अनेन अत्रापि प्रयोगे प्रणवानन्तरं स्वबीजादिप्रक्षेप इति ज्ञेयम्। अस्त्रं बाणादि। शस्त्रं खड्गादि ॥ ३८॥३९॥४० ॥

ज्वलज्ज्वलपदस्यान्ते शूलिनीति पदं वदेत् ।
दुष्टग्रहं हुमस्त्रान्ते वह्निजायावधिर्मनुः ॥ ४१
भूतेन्द्रियाक्षरैः प्रोक्तो ग्रहक्षुद्रादिनाशकः ।
ऋषिर्दीर्घतमाः प्रोक्तः ककुप् छन्द उदाहृतम् ॥ ४२
शूलिनी देवता प्रोक्ता समस्तसुरवन्दिता ।
दुर्गे हृद्वरदे शीर्षं विन्ध्यवासिनि तच्छिखा ॥ ४३
असुरान्ते मर्दिनि स्याद् युद्धपूर्व्वप्रिये पुनः ।
त्रासयद्वितयं वर्म्म देवसिद्धसुपूजिते ॥ ४४
नन्दिनि स्याद्रक्षयुगं महायोगेश्वरि क्रमात् ।
शूलिन्याद्या हुंफडन्ताः पञ्चाङ्गमनवः स्मृताः ॥ ४५

शूलिनीदुर्गामन्त्रमाह ज्वलेति । अत्र भूतानि पञ्च । इन्द्रियाणि ज्ञानकर्म्मेन्द्रियाणि दश । तेषां सङ्कलने पञ्चदशसंख्या भवन्ति । न तु "अङ्कानां वामतो गतिः" इति क्रमेण मन्त्राक्षरगणना विधेया । तथा सति पञ्चोत्तरशताक्षरसंख्या भवति । भूतेन्द्रियाक्षरैः पञ्चदशाक्षरैः । हुं बीजं स्वाहा शक्तिः । ग्रहेत्यादि विनियोगोक्तिः । ग्रहाणामष्टादशानाम् । क्षुद्राणां स्तम्भविद्वेषोच्चाटनभ्रममारणव्याधीनाम् । आदिशब्दात् भूतप्रेतडाकिन्यादीनाम् । नाशक इत्यनेन विनियोगं वदता प्रणवशक्तिनृसिंहदुर्गाबीजपुटितत्वं षषडन्तत्वमपि सूचितम् । दुर्गे हृदिति हृन्मन्त्रः । एवं शीर्षेऽपि । तच्छिखेति । तस्य मन्त्रस्य शिखामन्त्र इत्यर्थः । युद्धपूर्व्वप्रिये युद्धप्रिये । देवेत्यादि महायोगेश्वरि पर्य्यन्तम् । अस्त्रमिति शेषः ।

"वर्म्मासुरान्ते मर्दिनि युद्धपूर्व्वप्रिये पुनः । त्रासयद्वितयं चास्त्रम्" ।

इति वा पाठः । पञ्चाङ्गमनवः क्रमात् प्रत्येकं शूलिन्याद्या हुंफडन्ताः स्मृता इति सम्बन्धः । प्रयोगस्तु शूलिनि दुर्गे हुंफट् हृदयाय नम इत्यादि । साम्प्रदायिकास्तु पूर्व्वपूर्व्वानुविद्धत्वमङ्गानां वदन्ति । तेन शूलिनि दुर्गे वरदे हुं फट् शिरसे स्वाहा इत्यादि प्रयोगः । अन्ये तु कामनाविशेषेऽन्यथाऽङ्गान्याहुः ।

दुर्गे हृदयमाख्यातं वरदे तच्छिरः शिखा ।
विन्ध्यवासिनि वर्म्म स्यादसुरान्ते तु मर्दिनि ॥
युद्धप्रिये युतं चास्त्रं त्रासयद्वितयं भवेत् ।
एषामादौ शूलिनीति पदं तारादिकं वदेत् ॥

अध्यारूढां मृगेन्द्रं सजलजलधरश्यामलां हस्तपद्मैः
शूलं बाणं कृपाणमरिजलजगदाचापपाशान् वहन्तीम् ।
चन्द्रोत्तंसां त्रिनेत्रां चतसृभिरभितः खेटकान् बिभ्रतीभिः
कन्याभिः सेव्यमानां प्रतिभटभयदां शूलिनीं भावयामि ॥ ४६

मनुमेनं जपेन्मन्त्री वर्णलक्षं विचक्षणः ।
सर्पिषाऽन्नेन होमस्तु तद्दशांशमितो भवेत् ॥ ४७

प्रागुक्ते पूजयेत् पीठे वक्ष्यमाणेन वर्त्मना ।
विधाय पूजामङ्गानां पूज्याः पत्रेषु शक्तयः ॥ ४८

अवसाने तु सर्वेषां देवसिद्धसुपूजिते ।
नन्दिनि रक्षयुग्मं च महायोगेश्वरीत्यपि ॥
वर्म्मास्त्रबीजे चामूनि ग्रहरक्षाकराणि हि ।
पञ्चाशदावृत्तिन्यासाज्ज्वरस्तीव्रोऽपि नश्यति ॥ इति ।

तत्र प्रयोगः । ॐ शूलिनि दुर्गे देवसिद्धसुपूजिते नन्दिनि रक्षरक्ष महायोगीश्वरि हुं फडित्यादि । एतदभिप्रायेणैवाचार्य्यैः—

वर्म्म चासुरमर्दिन्या युद्धपूर्व्वप्रिये तथा । त्रासयद्वितयं चास्त्रम् ।

इति पठित्वा देवेत्यादि पठित्वा

अङ्गकर्म्मैव रक्षाकृत् प्रोक्तं ग्रहनिवारणम् । इति पठितम् ।

अत्रापि मल्लिखितपाठे सर्व्वं समञ्जसम् । क्रमादित्यनेन साम्प्रदायिकानुसारिपुर्व्वपूर्व्वानुविद्धत्वमपि सूचितमेव ॥ ४१॥४२॥४३॥४४॥४५ ॥

अध्यारूढामिति । मृगेन्द्रं सिंहम् । अराणि विद्यन्ते यत्र तत् । अरि चक्रम् । जलजं शङ्खः ।

आचार्य्याश्च—बिभ्राणा शूलबाणास्यरिसदरगदाचापपाशान् कराब्जैः । इति ॥ ग्रन्थकृच्च पूजावसरे "दलाग्रेषु तदस्त्राणि चक्रं शङ्खमसिं पुनः" इति शङ्खपूजामेव वक्ष्यति । चतसृभिरिति । जया विजया भद्रा शूलकात्यायिन्याख्याभिरित्यर्थः । असिनेति सहार्थे तृतीया । तद्योगाभावेऽपि वृद्धो यूनेतिवत् । दक्षिणाधस्ताद्वामाधःपर्य्यन्तमायुधध्यानम् ॥ ४६ ॥

वर्णलक्षं मन्त्रवर्णपरिमितलक्षम् । विचक्षण इति । पुरश्चरणे ये नियमास्तज्ज्ञ इत्यर्थः ॥ ४७ ॥

प्रागुक्ते दुर्गाष्टाक्षरोक्ते । पूजां विधायेति केसरेष्विति शेषः । पत्रेत्वष्टमी । आसां

दुर्गाद्या वरदा विन्ध्यवासिन्यसुरमर्द्दिनी ।
युद्धप्रिया पञ्चमी स्यात् देवसिद्धसुपूजिता ॥ ४९
सप्तमी नन्दिनी प्रोक्ता महायोगेश्वरी परा ।
दलाग्रेषु तदस्त्राणि शङ्खं चक्रमसिं पुनः ॥ ५०
गदेषुचापशूलानि पाशं पश्चाद् दिशाधिपान् ।
इत्थं जपादिभिः सिद्धः कुर्य्यात् कर्म्म निजेप्सितम् ॥ ५१
अष्टोत्तरसहस्रं यस्तिलैस्त्रिमधुराप्लुतैः ।
नित्यं प्रजुहुयात्तस्य शक्तिः स्यादतिमानुषी ॥ ५२
अष्टोत्तरशतं नित्यं सर्पिषा जुहुयान्नरः ।
वाञ्छितं वत्सराद्‌र्वाक् प्राप्नुयान्महतीं श्रियम् ॥ ५३
दूर्व्वाहोमो भवेन्नृणां सर्व्ववाञ्छितसिद्धिदः ।
छुरिकाद्यानि शस्त्राणि जप्तानि मनुनाऽमुना ॥ ५४
सम्पाताज्यविलिप्तानि वितरन्ति जयश्रियम् ।
अश्वत्थार्कसमिद्भिर्वा तिलैर्वा मधुरोक्षितैः ।
होमो वशयति क्षिप्रमीप्सितान्मन्त्रिणो नरान् ॥ ५५

ध्यानमुक्तमन्यत्र—अम्बुदाभा धनुर्बाणकरा दुर्गादिका यजेत् । इति ।

त्रिमधुराप्लुतैः पयोमधुघृतप्लुतैः । पयःस्थाने शर्करेति केचित् । शक्तिः स्यादतिमानुषीति वत्सरादर्वागिति ज्ञेयम् ।

तदुक्तम्—अप्रतिहताऽस्य शक्तिर्भूयात् प्रागेव वत्सरतः । इति ॥ ४८॥४९॥५० ॥ ॥ ५१॥५२॥५३ ॥

दूर्व्वाहोम इति । अष्टोत्तरशतमिति ज्ञेयम् ।

तदुक्तम्—दूर्व्वया त्रिकयुजेप्सितं लभेत् सम्यगष्टशतसंख्यया हुतात् । इति ।

छुरिकाद्यानीत्यादिशब्देन कृपाणनखराद्यानि ग्राह्याणि । सम्पाताज्यविलिप्तानि पश्चादमुना मनुना जप्तानीति सम्बन्धः । सम्पातार्थं होमः पञ्चसहस्रः । जप्तानीति । दशसाहस्रम् । तदुक्तम्—

खड्गे तीक्ष्णे समावाह्य गन्धाद्यैरभिपूज्य ताम् ।
आज्येन जुहुयात्पञ्चसहस्रं प्रोक्तमार्गतः ॥

उद्यद्दायुधहस्तां तां देवीं कालघनप्रभाम् ।
ध्यात्वात्मानं जपेन्मन्त्रं स्पृष्टार्त्तं मुञ्चति ग्रहः ॥ ५६
सर्पाखुवृश्चिकादीनां विषमाशु विनाशयेत् ।
मनुनाऽनेन विधिवन्मन्त्रविद्देवताधिया ॥ ५७

सम्पाताज्यविलिप्तोऽसौ प्रजप्तो मनुनाऽमुना ।
पंक्तिसंख्यासहस्रेण शक्तो मन्त्रविशेषवित् ॥
तत्खड्गहस्तो योद्धा स्याद्रिपुसेनाविमर्दकः । इति ।

अत्र खड्ग इत्यायुधोपलक्षणम् । "क्षुरिकाक्रपाणनखराः" इत्याचार्य्योक्तेः । अश्वत्थेति । होमसंख्या द्वादशसहस्रं ज्ञेया । तदुक्तम्—

आर्कैर्मन्त्री त्रिमधुरयुतैरर्कसाहस्रमिध्मै-
राश्वत्थैर्वा त्वतिविशदचेतास्तिलैर्वा जुहोतु । इति ॥

क्षिप्रमित्यनेनैतदुक्तं भवति । रक्तवर्णां पाशाङ्कुशधनुर्बाणधरां देवीं ध्यात्वा पाशेन साध्यस्य बन्धः अङ्कुशेनाकर्षणमिति चिन्तयेत् । मन्त्रिण इति षष्ठी । नरानिति लिङ्गमविवक्षितम् ॥ ५४॥५५ ॥

उद्यदिति । एवम्भूतदेवीरूपमात्मानं ध्यात्वा आर्त्तं स्पृष्ट्वा मन्त्रं जपेदिति सम्बन्धः । मुञ्चति ग्रह इति । आविश्य सन्त्याजित इति शेषः । आविश्य क्षणमित्युक्तेः । ग्रह इति वचनमविवक्षितम् । तेनाष्टादश ग्रहा इत्यर्थः । आवेशनप्रकारस्तु—सम्प्रोक्तलक्षणैः सम्यग्विज्ञायाऽष्टादश ग्रहान् ।

ग्रस्तभूर्ध्नि विचिन्त्यैतान् द्विभुजान् स्रस्तलोचनान् ॥
ज्वालामयैर्मन्त्रजापी पातयेच्चुलुकोदकैः ।
आविष्टं क्षणमात्रेण त्याजयेदखिलान् ग्रहान् । इति ॥

सन्त्याजनप्रकारस्तु । आत्मरोगिणोर्मध्ये उक्तरूपां दुर्गां ध्यात्वा कनिष्ठादित्रयम् अङ्गुष्ठेनाऽवष्टभ्य दृढमुष्टिं कृत्वा तर्जनीं दक्षिणकर्णपार्श्वे प्रसार्य्य अतिद्रुतं चक्रवद् भ्रामयेदित्यनया चक्रमुद्रया मोचयेदिति । तदुक्तम्—

अन्तराथ पुनरात्मरोगिणोरम्बिकामपि निजायुधाकुलाम् ।
संविचिन्त्य जपतोऽरिमुद्रया विद्रवन्त्यवशविग्रहा ग्रहाः ॥ इति ।

सर्पेति । आदिशब्देन श्वादीनां ग्रहणम् । मन्त्रविद्विधिवद्देवताधिया आत्मन इति शेषः ।

विधिवदनेन मनुना विषं विनाशयेदिति सम्बन्धः । विधिवद्देवताबुद्धिस्तु

मन्त्रेणानेन सञ्जप्तान् बाणानादाय साधकः ।
विमुञ्चेत् प्रतिसेनायां सा द्रुतं विद्रुता भवेत् ॥ ५८

शूलपाशधरां देवीं ध्यात्वात्मानमनाकुलः ।
प्रविशेद् युद्धदेशं यो जित्वा याति स निर्व्रणः ॥ ५९

जुहुयात्तिलसिद्धार्थैर्लक्षमेकं यथाविधि ।
नामयुक्तं जपन्मन्त्रं यस्याऽसौ मृत्युमेष्यति ॥ ६०

ध्यानविशेषेण । तदुक्तम्—

अहिमूषिकवृश्चिकादिजं वा बहुपात्कुक्कुरलूतिकोद्भवं वा ।
विषमाशु विनाशयेन्नराणां प्रतिपत्त्यैव च विन्ध्यवासिनी सा ॥ इति ।

ध्यानविशेषस्त्वन्यत्रोक्तः—

शरच्छशाङ्कसङ्काशां स्मितवक्त्राम्बुजोज्ज्वलाम् ।
चक्रशङ्खसुधाकुम्भयुग्महस्ताम्बुजां शुभाम् ॥
मुग्धञ्च विषमेतेन सिञ्चन्तीं सितभूषणाम् ।
अमृतार्द्रामिमां दुर्गां ध्यायन् हन्याद्विषं नरः ॥ ५६॥५७॥ इति ।

सञ्जप्तान् बाणानिति । बाणाग्रे तां देवीं ध्यात्वेति ज्ञेयम् । तदुक्तम्—
आधाय बाणे निशिते च देवीं क्षेमङ्करीं मन्त्रमिमं जपित्वा । इति ॥ ५८ ॥

प्रविशेदिति । मन्त्रं जपन्निति शेषः । तदुक्तम्—

आत्मानमार्य्यां प्रतिपद्य शूलपाशान्वितां वैरिबलं प्रविश्य ।
मन्त्रं जपन्नाशु परायुधानि गृह्णाति मुष्णाति च बोधमेषाम् ॥ इति ।

निर्व्रणत्वं होमजननेनायुधग्रहणादिति ज्ञेयम् ।

तन्त्रान्तरे तु—श्यामवर्णा महाकाया ज्वलदग्निविलोचना ।
पाशं डमरुकं शूलं चूर्णं मोहनसंज्ञितम् ॥
हस्तैश्चतुर्भिर्बिभ्राणा नागेन्द्रैः समलङ्कृता ।
अतिदीर्घैर्महाकेशैराकीर्णैः परितश्चमूम् ॥
आच्छादयन्ती कृष्णाभैरट्टहासपरायणा ।
ध्याता दुर्गाऽचिरेणैव मोहयेच्छत्रुवाहिनीम् ॥ इति ॥ ५९ ॥

यथाविधि नामयुक्तं मन्त्रं जपन् जुहुयादिति सम्बन्धः । यथाविधीति । पल्लवप्रकारेण जपे होमे स्वाहादावित्यर्थः ।

गुटिकां गोमयोत्पन्नां हुत्वाऽष्टशतसंख्यया ।
सप्ताहात् कुरुते मन्त्री विद्वेषं स्निग्धयोर्मिथः ॥ ६१

गृहीत्वा गोमयं व्योम्नि त्रिसहस्रं जपेत्ततः ।
गमिष्यतां द्वारदेशे निखातं स्तम्भनं भवेत् ॥ ६२

बहुनोक्तेन किं सर्व्वं साधयेन्मनुनाऽमुना ।
उत्तिष्ठपदमाभाष्य पुरुषि स्यात्पदं ततः ॥ ६३

पितामहः सनेत्रेन्दुः स्वपिषि स्याद्भयं च मे ।
समुपस्थितमुच्चार्य्य यदि शक्यमनन्तरम् ॥ ६४

अशक्यं वा पुनस्तस्मै वदेद्भगवति ततः ।
शमयाऽग्निवधूः सप्तविंशद्वर्णात्मको मनुः ॥ ६५

तदुक्तम्—पल्लवे साध्यनामादौ भवेन्मन्त्रपदक्रमः ।
मारणे चैतदुद्दिष्टम् । इति ।

इदन्तु जपकर्मणि । होमे तु स्वाहापदात् पूर्व्वं नामोच्चारणम् ।

उक्तञ्च गौतमेन—स सर्व्वजनमन्त्रेषु तत्र नामानि योजयेत् ।
होमे स्वाहापदात् पूर्व्वं मन्त्रान्ते जपकर्मणि ॥ इति ।

तदुक्तमाचार्य्यैः—तिलसिद्धार्थैर्जुहुयाल्लक्षं मन्त्री सपत्ननामयुतम् ।
स तु रोगाभिहतात्मा म्रियतेमेति न तत्र सन्देहः ॥ इति ॥ ६० ॥

अष्टशतेत्यष्टोत्तरशतम् । विद्वेषमित्यत्र वियोगमित्यपि ।
द्विष्टौ मिथो वियोगितौ भवतः । इत्युक्तेः ।

ध्यानविशेषोऽन्यत्र—दधती मुशलं शूलं गरकुम्भद्वयं करैः ।
कृष्णा दिगम्बरा ध्येया मूर्त्तिर्विद्वेषकारिणी ॥ इति ।

गोमयमित्यानडुहमित्युपदेशात् । व्योम्नि गोमयं गृहीत्वेति । भूमिस्पृग्गोमयं न ग्राह्यमित्यर्थः । तदुक्तम्—"अस्पृष्टकुङ्गोमयस्त्वन्तरिक्षे" इति ॥ ६१ ॥ ६२ ॥

वनदुर्गामन्त्रमाह उत्तिष्ठेति । ततः पुरुषि पदं स्यादित्यन्वयः । पितामहः ककारः सनेत्रेदुः इकारबिन्दुसहितः । तेन किमिति । भयं च मे इति चकारो न मन्त्रमध्ये । यदि शक्यमशक्यञ्चेति । अमन्त्रमेव स्वरूपम् । भगवतिमिति शब्दकर्मणि द्वितीया मन्त्रे तु सम्बुद्धिः । अत्र वा तन्मे अक्षराणि कीलकानि । ह्रुं दुर्गे इत्यकीलकानि । तदुक्तमीशानसंहितायाम्—

ऋषिरारण्यकश्छन्दोऽप्र[प्य]त्यनुष्टुबुदाहृतम् ।
देवता वनदुर्गा स्यात् सर्व्वदुर्गतिमोचनी ॥ ६६

पादाष्टसन्धिषु गुदलिङ्गाधारोदरेषु च ।
पार्श्वहृत्स्तनकण्ठेषु पुनर्बाह्वष्टसन्धिषु ॥ ६७

मुखनासाकपोलाक्षिकर्णभ्रूमध्यमूर्द्धसु ।
मन्त्राक्षराणि विन्यस्येद्देवताभावसिद्धये ॥ ६८

षड्भिश्चतुर्भिरष्टाभिरष्टाभिः षड्भिरिन्द्रियैः
मन्त्रार्णैरङ्गक्लृप्तिः स्याज्जातियुक्तैर्यथाक्रमम् ॥ ६९

गुणबीजं समुद्धृत्य उत्तिष्ठेति पदं ततः ।
पुरुषेति समुद्धृत्य ब्रह्माणं सूक्ष्मसंयुतम् ॥
सबिन्दुकं समुच्चार्य्य स्वपिषीति पदं वदेत् ।
भयं मे च समाभाष्य तथा च समुपस्थितम् ॥
यदि शक्यमिति प्रोच्य अशक्यं समुदीर्य च ।
वर्म्मबीजं समुद्धृत्य दुर्गे भगवतीति च ॥
शमयेति समुद्धृत्य तथा स्वाहा पदं वदेत् ।
एवमेषा महादेवी निष्कीला सर्व्वसिद्धिदा ॥
गुणान्ते भुवनेशानीं दुर्गाबीजं नियोजयेत् ।
वर्म्मणोऽन्ते स्वकं बीजमुक्त्वा चान्ते विलोमतः ॥
पूर्व्वोक्तबीजत्रितयं योजयेत् क्रौञ्चदारणा ।
तदा प्रदीपिता विद्या निष्कीला सर्व्वसिद्धिदा ॥ इति ।

उकारो बीजं स्वाहा शक्तिः । दुमिति बीजमिति पद्मपादाचार्य्याः । सर्व्वेत्यादि विनियोगोक्तिः ॥ ६३ ॥ ६४ ॥ ६५ ॥ ६६ ॥

अक्षरन्यासमाह पादेति । पादभुजसन्धयः प्रत्येकं चत्वारः । अत्र पार्श्वस्तननासाकपोलाक्षिकर्णानां स्थानद्वन्द्वं ग्राह्यम् । इन्द्रियैः पञ्चभिः । यथाक्रममित्यनेनैतदुक्तं भवति । प्रत्येकं दुर्गायै रक्षरक्षेत्येतदन्तैरङ्गमिति । तदुक्तमीशानसंहितायाम्—

ऋतुवेदाहिवस्वङ्गभूतसंख्याक्षरान्वितैः ।
दुर्गायै रक्षरक्षेति युक्तैरङ्गान्यथाचरेत् ॥ इति ॥६७॥६८॥६९॥

सौवर्णाम्बुजमध्यगां त्रिनयनां सौदामिनीसन्निभां
चक्रं शङ्खवराभयानि दधतीमिन्दोः कलां बिभ्रतीम् ।
ग्रैवेयाङ्गदहारकुण्डलधरामाखण्डलाद्यैः स्तुतां
ध्यायेद्विन्ध्यनिवासिनीं शशिमुखीं पार्श्वस्थपञ्चाननाम् ॥ ७०

एवं ध्यात्वा जपेल्लक्षचतुष्कं तद्दशांशतः ।
जुहुयाद्धविषा मन्त्री शालिभिः सर्पिषा तिलैः ॥ ७१

प्रागीरिते यजेत् पीठे देवीमङ्गादिभिः सह ।
अङ्गपूजा यथापूर्वं दलमूलेष्विमा यजेत् ॥ ७२

आर्य्या दुर्गा च भद्राख्या भद्रकाली ततोऽम्बिका ।
क्षेमाऽन्या वेदगर्भाख्या क्षेमङ्कर्य्यष्ट शक्तयः ॥ ७३

अस्त्राणि पत्रमध्येषु शङ्खचक्रासिखेटकान् ।
बाणकोदण्डशूलानि कपालान्तानि पूजयेत् ॥ ७४

ब्राह्म्याद्याः स्युर्दलाग्रेषु लोकपालास्ततः परम् ।
सिद्धमन्त्रः प्रयोगेषु देवीमित्थं विचिन्तयेत् ॥ ७५

आयुधध्यानं दक्षाद्यूर्ध्वयोराद्ये तदधस्तनयोरन्त्ये । अन्ये तु दक्षोर्द्ध्वादि दक्षाधस्तनं यावत् ॥ ७० ॥

तद्दशांशत इति अयुतचतुष्टयम् । तत्र चत्वारि द्रव्याणि एकैकेनैकैकेन युतमित्यर्थः । हविषा पायसेन । शालिभिर्हैमन्तिकैः । सर्पिषा घृतेन । तिलैश्चेति चतुर्भिः ॥ ७१ ॥

यथापूर्व्वमिति । आग्नेयादिकोणेषु पुरतो दिक्षु चेति । एतच्च पूजनं कर्णिकान्तः केसरेषु अग्रे शक्तिपूजाया उपदिष्टत्वादिति । अष्ट शक्तय इति । आसां ध्यानमन्यत्रोक्तम्—

आर्य्यादिशक्तयः खेटखड्गचापधनुर्धराः ।
अहिभिर्भूषिताङ्ग्यस्ताः पूजनीया भयानकाः ॥ इति ।

ततः परमिति । वज्रादिपूजोक्ता । प्रयोगेष्विति । बहुवचनाच्छान्त्यादौ नृसिंह-बीजादिपुटितत्वम् । युद्धमारणयोः षोड़शभुजाध्यानम् । साम्बुमेघश्यामत्वं महिषोत्तमाङ्गस्थत्वं च । रक्षायामष्टभुजत्वं दूर्व्वाश्यामलाङ्गत्वं महिषोत्तमाङ्गस्थत्वं च ध्येयमित्युक्तम् ।

कालपावकसन्निभां कलिताईचन्द्रशिरोरुहां
भालनेत्रविभूषणां भयदायिसिंहनिषेदुषीम् ।
चक्रशङ्खकृपाणखेटकचापबाणकरोटिका-
शूलवाहिभुजां भजे विजिताखिलासुरसैनिकाम् ॥ ७६

प्रातःस्नानरतो नित्यमष्टोत्तरसहस्रकम् ।
जपेत्तस्याशु सिद्ध्यन्ति धनधान्यादिसम्पदः ॥ ७७
अनेनैव विधानेन ग्रहक्षुद्ररिपूञ्जयेत् ।
नाभिमात्रोदके स्थित्वा देवीमर्कगतां स्मरन् ।
जपेदष्टोत्तरशतं लभेत महतीं श्रियम् ॥ ७८

तदुक्तमाचार्यैः—

चक्रदरखड्गखेटकशरकार्मुकशूलसंज्ञककपालैः ।
ऋष्टिमुशलकुन्तनन्दकवलयगदाभिन्दिपालशक्त्याख्यैः ॥
उद्यद्विकृतिभुजाढ्या माहिषदर्पे सजलजलदसङ्काशा ।
अरिशङ्खकृपाणखेटबाणान् सधनुःशूलकतर्जनीर्दधाना ॥
भवतां महिषोत्तमाङ्गसंस्था नवदूर्वासदृशी श्रियेऽस्तु दुर्गा ॥ इति ।

अन्यत्रापि—ज्वलदग्निनिभां सिंहस्कन्धारूढां भयावहाम् ।
ध्यायेत् षोडशबाहुं तां सम्यक् वैरिविमर्दने ॥
श्यामलाङ्गीमष्टबाहुं महिषासुरसंस्थिताम् ।
आयुःसिद्ध्यै चिन्तयेत् ताम् । इति ॥ ७२॥७३॥७४॥७५ ॥

कालपावकः प्रलयाग्निः । करोटिका कपालम् । आयुधानि दक्षैरूर्ध्वतः चक्रखड्गशरशूलानि । वामैरूर्ध्वतः शङ्खखेटकधनुःकपालानि ध्येयानि । इदं ध्यानं रक्षार्थमिति ज्ञेयम् ॥ ७६॥७७ ॥

अनेनैवेति । तत्र विधानम् । प्रातःस्नानादिकम् । जपस्त्वयुतम् ।

तदुक्तम्—सौम्ये कर्मफलावाप्त्यै सहस्रं प्रजपेत् मनुम् ।
उच्चाटनादिक्षुद्रेषु विशेषात्तं तथाऽयुतम् ॥ इति ॥

अत्र मन्त्रे भयशब्दात् पूर्वं ग्रहपदादिदानं ज्ञेयम् । ग्रहभयं क्षुद्रभयं रिपुभयम् । एवमग्रेऽपि चौरभयमित्यादि ज्ञेयम् । क्षुद्रशब्दार्थं उक्तो नारायणीये—

स्तम्भो विद्वेषणोच्चाटावुन्मादो भ्रममारणे । व्याधिश्चेति स्मृतं क्षुद्रम् । इति । नाभिमात्रोदक इति नद्यादौ । देवीं स्मरन्निति तन्मन्त्रान्तरोक्तध्यानम् ।

अयुतं वटवृक्षोत्थैः सशृङ्गैरर्चितेऽनले ।
होमं समिद्वरैः कुर्य्याद्नाशयेदापदां कुलम् ॥ ७९

घोराभिचारभूतादीन् शमयेद्विधिनाऽमुना ।
अपामार्गसमिद्भिर्वा तिलैर्वा काननोद्भवैः ॥ ८०

अभीष्टसिद्धौ जुहुयादार्कैर्मन्त्री समिद्वरैः ।
सहस्रमर्कवारादि दिवसान् दश संयतः ॥ ८१

सारान् शुद्धान् समादाय शकलान्मनुनाऽमुना ।
जुहुयादेधिते वह्नौ सप्तरात्रमतन्द्रितः ॥ ८२

साधयेदखिलं शश्वदभीष्टं मन्त्रवित्तमः ।
कुमुदैर्वशयेद्विप्रान् नृपतीन् पद्महोमतः ॥ ८३

तत्पत्नीरुत्पलैः फुल्लैर्वैश्यान् कह्लारहोमतः ।
शूद्रान् लवणहोमेन जातीपुष्पैः सभां पुनः ॥ ८४

व्रीहिभिर्जुहुयान्नित्यं वत्सरात् व्रीहिमान् भवेत् ।
दूर्व्वाहोमेन दीर्घायुर्मधुना रत्नवान् भवेत् ॥ ८५

अन्नैरन्नसमृद्धिः स्यादाज्येन लभते धनम् ।
गोदुग्धेन गवां वृद्धिमाप्नुयान्नाऽत्र संशयः ॥ ८६

यदाहुः—शङ्खारिनिधिपाशेष्टकरां रक्तां स्वलङ्कृताम् ।
भानुबिम्बसरोजस्थां दुर्गामेतां स्फुरत्प्रभाम् ॥
अष्टोत्तरशतं नद्यां नाभिमात्रे जले स्थितः ।
संयतः प्रजपेन् मन्त्रमचिराच्छीघ्रसिद्धये ॥ इति ।

महतीं श्रियमिति । श्रीबीजादित्वमपि ज्ञेयम् ॥ ७८ ॥

अर्चिते अनले सशृङ्गैः साग्रभागैर्वटवृक्षोत्थैः समिद्वरैरयुतं होमं कुर्य्यादिति सम्बन्धः । काननोद्भवैस्तिलैर्जर्त्तिलैः ॥ ७९ ॥ ८० ॥

मन्त्रीति । अनेन सूर्य्यचतुरक्षरादित्वं सूचितम् । सहस्रमिति प्रत्यहम् ॥८१॥

सारानिति खादिरान् । अतन्द्रित इति । त्रिदिनमित्यप्युक्तं भवति ।

तदुक्तम्—शुद्धैः खदिरसारैस्त्रिदिनं वा सप्तरात्रकमपि । इति ।

अखिलमिति सौम्यं क्रूरं च । तत्र विशेषस्तन्त्रान्तरे—

ज्वरे ग्रहे गरे सर्पे तर्जन्या संस्पृशञ्जपेत् ।
स्मृत्वा शूलकरां देवीं तत्क्षणादेव तान् हरेत् ॥ ८७

इर्भितं साध्यनामार्णैः पत्रे मनुमिमं लिखेत् ।
कुलालमृत्कृतायां तत् प्रतिमायां हृदि न्यसेत् ॥ ८८

कृतप्राणप्रतिष्ठां तां पूजितां कुसुमादिभिः ।
निधायाऽग्रे जपेन्मन्त्रमष्टोत्तरसहस्रकम् ॥ ८९

सन्ध्यासु पञ्चमासेन ध्रुवमाप्नोति वाञ्छितम् ।
अभ्यर्च्य देवीमनले तीक्ष्णतैलेन मन्त्रवित् ॥ ९०

हुत्वाऽयुतं निधायाऽग्रे तीक्ष्णांस्त्रिंशच्छरान् पुनः ।
तेषु सम्पातयेद् भूयः स्पृष्ट्वा तान्नियुतं जपेत् ॥ ९१

नवकुम्भनिभां देवीं शूलं डमरुकं भुजैः ।
शरं चापं सौधकुम्भयुगलं दधतीं पराम् ॥
ध्यात्वा दुर्गां महाकायां भीषणास्यां सुभूषिताम् ।
आज्येन जुहुयान्मध्ये सव्ये [मध्ये] पौष्टिककर्म्मणि ॥
यदि क्षुद्रविधौ क्ष्वेलरसपूर्णघटद्वयम् ।
दधतीं चिन्तयेद्देवीं षड्भुजां प्रोक्तलक्षणाम् ॥
विलोममनुना विद्वान् शकलैर्घृतसंयुतैः ।
सारैर्विशुद्धैर्जुहुयात् पश्चिमाशामुखः सुधीः ॥ इति ।

मन्त्रवित्तम इत्यनेनाऽत्रापि सूर्य्यचतुरक्षरादित्वं सूचितम् ॥ ८२-८६ ॥

तर्जन्येति वामया । तान् ज्वरादीन् ॥ ८७ ॥

इर्भितमिति । तत्प्रकारस्त्रयोविंशे वक्ष्यते । पत्र इति भूर्जे । कुलालमृदिति । कुम्भकारस्य पात्रघटनसमये करलग्नमृत्तिका तया कृतायां प्रतिमायां द्वादशाङ्गुलायां हृदि तदिति लिखितमन्त्रं पत्रं न्यसेत् । निधायाऽग्रे इति । पीठादेरुपरि स्वपादतलाधः । सन्ध्यास्विति । पञ्चदशदिनसायंकालसन्ध्यास्वित्यर्थः । वशमायाति वाञ्छित इति क्वचित् पाठः ॥ ८८ ॥ ८९ ॥ ९० ॥

अभ्यर्च्येति । वन्यकुसुमचन्दनैः । तीक्ष्णतैलेनेति कटुतैलेन राजिकातैलेनेति केचित् । हुत्वेति सम्बन्धः । मन्त्रविदित्यनेनैतदुक्तं भवति । स्वस्तिकादौ दुकूलावृतं पीठं संस्थाप्य तत्र शरान्निधाय तेषु देवीमावाह्य सम्पूज्य

वेधयेत् परसेनायां यथानष्टा दिशो दश ।
प्राप्नुयान्नष्टसंज्ञा सा पलायनपरायणा ॥ ९२
जपित्वा सितगुञ्जानां कुडवं कुलिकोदये ।
विकिरेच्छत्रुसेनायां गूढः सञ्चापणादिषु ॥ ९३
ज्वरमारी महारोगैः पीड़िता सैन्यनायकैः ।
परस्परविरोधेन नश्येद् गच्छेन्म्रियेत सा ॥ ९४

ततस्त्रिकोणकुण्डे अग्निमाधाय तत्रापि देवीमभ्यर्च्य जुहुयादिति ।

तदुक्तम्—पीठे स्वस्तिकमध्यस्थे मायाचक्रगतेऽपि वा ।
विधिवत् पूजयेत् सूक्ष्मदुकूलादिसमावृते ॥
निधाय निशितान् स्वर्णपुङ्खांस्त्रिंशच्छिलीमुखान् ।
कात्यायनीं समावाह्य गन्धाद्यैः प्रवरैर्यजेत् ॥
त्रिकोणकुण्डे पूर्वोक्तक्रमोत्पन्नविभावसौ ।
आवाह्य षोड़शभुजां तामिष्ट्वा चन्दनादिभिः ॥
सिद्धार्थतैलं जुहुयात् सहस्रमथवाऽयुतम् ।
नियुतं तत्र लब्धेन सम्पातेन विलेपयेत् ॥
उद्वास्य देवीं तत्रैव हुतसंख्यं जपेदिति ।
रक्तेन तन्तुना पुङ्खसन्धिं वेष्टयेद् घटम् ॥
तेषु विद्धेषु दक्षेण धन्विना वैरिवाहिनी ।
विनष्टसंज्ञा शक्रेण पालिताऽप्यनुधावति ॥ इति ॥

नियुतं लक्षम् ॥

वेधयेदिति । एतादृशं क्रूरकर्म्म प्रतिलोममन्त्रेणेति पद्मपादाचार्य्याः । **स्वबीजाद्येनाऽनुलोमेन वा ॥ ९० ॥ ९१ ॥ ९२ ॥**

कुडवमिति । पलचतुष्टयम् । कुडवं चतुःपलं स्यादित्युक्तेः । **कुलिकोदये विकिरेदिति** । कुलिकस्य कालविशेषस्योदये । तल्लक्षणं ज्योतिषरत्नमालायाम्—

मन्वर्कदिग्वस्वृतुवेदपक्षैर्वारान्मुहूर्त्तैः कुलिका भवन्ति ।
दिवा निरेकैरथ यामिनीषु ते गर्हिताः कर्म्मसु शोभनेषु ॥ इति ।

मनु १४ अर्क १२ दिक् १० वसु ८ ऋतु ६ वेद ४ पक्ष २ ।

सैन्यनायकैः परस्परविरोधेन पीड़ितेत्येव । पूर्व्वहेतोर्नश्येत् भ्रश्येत् । द्वितीयहेतोर्गच्छेदिति निवृत्य गच्छेदित्यर्थः । समुच्चयेन तृतीयम् ॥ ९२॥९३॥९४ ॥

सेनासंस्तम्भने मन्त्री कारस्करसमुद्भवैः ।
पुष्पैः सहस्रं जुहुयात्तत्परैस्तां निवर्त्तयेत् ॥ ९५

अङ्गारवारे कुलिके जप्त्वा भस्म चितोद्भवम् ।
विनिक्षिपेद्रिपोर्मूर्ध्नि विद्विष्टो देशतो व्रजेत् ॥ ९६

मरुन्निपातितैः पत्रैः कारस्करसमुद्भवैः ।
तस्य पादरजोयुक्तैर्होमादुच्चाटयेदरीन् ॥ ९७

कारस्करमयीं कृत्वा प्रतिमामतिशोभनाम् ।
जप्तां प्रतिष्ठितप्राणां छेदयेदङ्कुशः पुनः ॥ ९८

मन्त्रीति पृथिवीबीजादित्वं सूचितम् । ध्यानविशेषश्च—

पीतां पाशगदाशूलसायोमुष्टिलसद्भुजाम् ।
क्रूरास्यां देवतामूर्त्तिं ध्यायेत् स्तम्भनकर्मणि ॥ इति ॥

कारस्कर इति विषतिन्दुकः । कुचिला इति कान्यकुब्जभाषायाम् । तत्पत्रैस्तां निवर्त्तयेदिति । कारस्कारसहस्रपत्रहोमेन सेनानिवर्त्तनं कुर्यादित्यर्थः ॥९५॥

अङ्गारेति भौमे । तत्र च दशमो मुहूर्त्तः कुलिको भवति । तस्मिन् समये रिपोर्मूर्ध्नि भस्म निक्षिपेदिति सम्बन्धः । जप्त्वेत्यष्टोत्तरशतमित्यादि ।

अष्टोत्तरशतं जप्तं यच्छिरसि प्रक्षिपेच्चिताभस्म । इत्युक्तेः ।

विनिक्षिपेदिति । देवीं ध्यायन् । तत्र ध्यानविशेषस्तन्त्रान्तरे—

कृष्णां करालवदनां भुजङ्गैरभिमण्डिताम् ।
मारीचूर्णादिदहनशूलराजद्भुजाकुलाम् ॥
दिगम्बरां महादुर्गां चिन्तयेद् द्वेषणादिषु ।
उत्सादस्तम्भणोच्चाटकृत्येच्छाधावनोद्यताम् ॥ इति ॥

तस्य पादरजोयुक्तैरिति । तस्य वैरिणः पादरजो वामपादरज इति परमगुरवः । उच्चाटयेदिति । वायुबीजादित्वं ज्ञेयम् ॥ ९६॥९७ ॥

प्रतिमामिति षसवत्यङ्गुलायामाम् । यदाहुः—

मारणे दारुरूपां तां द्वादशाङ्गुलसंमिताम् ।
षसवत्यङ्गुलां वापि कुर्यान्मात्राङ्गुलैः क्रमात् ॥
होमार्थं कल्पितायास्तु तस्याः प्रोक्तो विधिः परः ।
वश्याकर्षणयोः प्रोक्तां तां कुर्याद् द्वादशाङ्गुलैः ॥ इति ॥

काकोलूकवसायुक्तामष्टोत्तरसहस्रकम् ।
कृष्णे पक्षे चतुर्दश्यां श्मशाने हव्यवाहने ॥ ९९

जुहुयान्म्रियतेऽरातिरेवमेव दिनत्रयात् ।
उन्मत्तसमिधां होमान्मृताः स्युः शत्रवः क्षणात् ॥ १००

उलूककाकयोः पक्षैः स्ववसारक्तसंयुतैः ।
जुहुयान्निशि कान्तारे शत्रुः कालातिथिर्भवेत् ॥ १०१

जप्तामष्टोत्तरशतावृत्त्या । छेदयेदिति अष्टोत्तरसहस्रम् । अङ्गम इति । दक्षिणाङ्गुष्ठादि वामाङ्गुष्ठान्तम् । श्मशाने हव्यवाहन इति व्यधिकरणे सप्तम्यौ । एवमेवेति ।

तदुक्तम्—द्रुमकुड्यनिपातेन निर्वातेनाऽरिखड्गतः ।
सलिले पावके सर्पदंशाच्चत्तद्विपाद् भटात् ॥
यक्षराक्षसगन्धर्वपिशाचब्रह्मराक्षसैः ।
अन्यैर्वा कारणैः क्षिप्रं नाशमेति रिपुर्ध्रुवम् ॥ इति ।

दिनत्रयादिति । चतुर्दशीत्रयादित्यर्थः । "त्रिचतुर्दशीप्रयोगादर्वाङ्म्रियते रिपुर्न सन्देहः" इत्युक्तेः । मारणे ध्यानविशेषोऽपि तन्त्रान्तरे—
कालमेघनिभां दुर्गां दन्दशूकविभूषणाम् ।
निशितं दधतीं खड्गं निजदक्षिणपाणिना ॥
सव्येन पाणिना साध्यं केशे संगृह्य कर्षतीम् ।
सिंहस्कन्धस्थितां ध्यायेन्मन्त्री मारणकर्मणि ॥ इति ।

अन्योऽपि विशेषः—शान्तिके पौष्टिके चापि वश्ये स्तम्भनकर्मणि ।
जपेत् स्वमन्त्ररक्षायै मन्त्रमष्टोत्तरं शतम् ॥
उच्चाटनोत्सादने च द्वेषणे मोहने भ्रमे ।
मारणे च जपेन्मन्त्री मनुं तद्वत् सहस्रकम् ॥ इति ।

उन्मत्तेऽत्र ध्यानविशेषः ।
शतभक्ताढ्यं चूर्णं कपालं गरपूरितम् ।
दधाना शाबरी दुर्गा ध्येया मादनकर्मणि ॥ इति ।

उन्मत्त इति । धुस्तूरः ॥ ९८ ॥ ९९ ॥ १०० ॥

पक्षैरिति पक्षैः । स्ववसारक्तम् उलूककाकवसारक्तम् । कान्तार इति वने ॥ १०१ ॥

शत्रोः प्रतिकृतिं मन्त्री प्रतिष्ठितसमीरणाम् ।
विशेषणविलिप्ताङ्गीमत्युषणे निक्षिपेज्जले ॥ १०२
ज्वराक्रान्तो भवेच्छीघ्रं दुग्धसेकाच्छमं नयेत् ।
तर्जनीं त्रिशिखं दोर्भ्यां धारयन्तीं भयङ्करीम् ॥ १०३
रक्तां ध्यात्वा रवेर्बिम्बे प्रजपेदयुतं मनुम् ।
मारयेदचिरादेव रिपून् बन्धुसमन्वितान् ॥ १०४
खड्गखेटकरां क्रुद्धां सन्नद्धां भानुमण्डले ।
ध्यात्वा मन्त्रं जपेन्मन्त्री नाशयेदचिरादरीन् ॥ १०५
चापबाणधरां भीमां सिंहस्थां ज्वलनोपमाम् ।
सृजन्तीं बाणनिवहान्धावन्तीं तादृशं रिपुम् ॥ १०६
ध्यात्वा जपेन्मनुमिममयुतं तोयमध्यगः ।
रिपुं च परसेनां च द्रुतमुच्चाटयेद् ध्रुवम् ॥ १०७

शत्रोः प्रतिकृतिमिति । यदि शत्रोर्जन्मनक्षत्रं ज्ञायते तदा तन्नक्षत्रवृक्ष-काष्ठमयीम् । तदज्ञाने कारस्करमयीं द्वादशाङ्गुलाम् । नक्षत्रवृक्षा द्वाविंशे वक्ष्यन्ते । प्रतिष्ठितसमीरणामिति कृतप्राणप्रतिष्ठाम् । उषणमिति मरिचम् । "मरिचं श्यामलं प्रोक्तं वल्लोजं चोषणं स्मृतम्" इति रुद्रः । प्रतीकारमाह दुग्धेति ।

तर्जनीमिति । तर्जनीमुद्रां प्रागुक्ताम् । त्रिशिखमिति त्रिशूलम् । सन्नद्धां कृतसन्नाहाम् । भानुमण्डले ध्यात्वा पूर्ववदयुतं मन्त्रं जपेदिति सम्बन्धः । मन्त्रीति । वेलाकालादिज्ञः ॥१०२॥१०३॥१०४॥१०५॥

तादृशमिति । धावन्तम् । तोयमध्यग इति जान्वधोभागपर्यन्तम् ।

कारस्करमयीं कृत्वेति । उलूककाकयोः पत्रैरिति । तर्जनीं त्रिशिखं दोर्भ्यामिति । खड्गखेटकरां सन्नद्धामिति । द्रुतमुच्चाटयेद्ध्रुवमित्यादि क्रूरकर्म वेलाकालकलातिथिनक्षत्ररिक्तास्तस्य ग्रहचौष्टवर्गप्रातिलोम्यं पातालादियोगांश्च ज्ञात्वा तत्समये कृतं शीघ्रसिद्धिदं भवति । तत्र वेला नाम चन्द्रोदयमारभ्य पञ्चदशघटिकापर्यन्तं समुद्रस्य क्षोभो भवति सा चन्द्रवेला । तदा क्रूरकर्माणि न कुर्यात् । तदनन्तरं पुनः पञ्चदशघटिकापर्यन्तं वेला नास्ति तदा क्रूरकर्म कुर्यात् । पुनस्तदनन्तरं पञ्चदशघटिकापर्यन्तं वेला । पुनस्तावत्कालं सा नास्ति ।

आनित्यकसमिद्धोमान्मुच्यते रोगशोकतः ।
पुष्पैस्तदीयैर्वशयेन्मधुराक्तैर्मतङ्गजान् ॥ १०८

रक्षायै पञ्चगव्येन लिम्पेज्जप्तेन दन्तिनः ।
गव्याज्यतिलसिद्धार्थैरानित्यकसमिद्वरैः ॥ १०९

दुग्धान्नपञ्चगव्याभ्यां तण्डुलेन घृतेन च ।
एतैः पृथक् पृथक् द्रव्यैरष्टोत्तरसहस्रकम् ॥ ११०
जुहुयाद्दिनशो विप्रान् भोजयेन्मधुरादिभिः ।
गुरवे दक्षिणां दद्याद्वस्त्राभरणसंयुताम् ॥ १११

कालस्तु—कुलिकः स्थविरो योगस्तारा वैनाशिकी कुजः ।
अष्टमो राशिरित्याद्यास्ताराः स्युः क्षुद्रकर्मणि ॥ इति ।

कला नाम चन्द्रकला सा शुक्ले वर्द्धते कृष्णे लुप्यति । तदष्टमीमारभ्याऽमावास्यापर्यन्तं कुर्यात् । तिथिरिक्ताः प्रसिद्धाः । नक्षत्ररिक्ता विषनाड्यः ।

अन्यत्र तु—आयुर्दायं रिपोर्ज्ञात्वा लग्नोक्षणानुगुण्यतः ।
तदात्विकग्रहाणां च स्थितिमष्टकवर्गकम् ॥
त्रयाणामानुकूल्येन कुर्यात्तदभिचारकम् ।
अन्यथा क्रूरकर्माणि कुर्वाणं नाशयन्ति हि ॥
तान्येव कर्माणि ततस्तत्त्रयप्रातिकूल्यतः ।
विदध्यादन्यथा शक्त्या नैष्फल्यं चात्मनाशनम् ॥
रिपोरष्टमलग्ने च काले त्वष्टमराशिगे ।
स्थाने कुर्यादनिष्टानि तद्विनाशाय साधकः ॥
पातालयोगे नीचाख्ये विषयोगे च मृत्युजे ।
नाशयोगे च दिनजमृत्यौ क्रकचयोगके ॥
चण्डीशचण्डायुधके महाशूले च काणके ।
रक्तस्थूणे कण्टकाख्ये स्थूणे पञ्चार्कसंज्ञके ॥
कुर्यात्प्रयोगान् प्रत्यर्थिभङ्गाय निधनाय च ।
निग्रहाय निरोध्यैवं कुर्यात् सिद्धिमवाप्नुयात् ॥ इति ।

अष्टमो राशिश्चक्रमन्ते वक्ष्यते । अन्ये योगाः ज्योतिःशास्त्रतो ज्ञेयाः ॥१०६॥१०७॥

आनित्यकमिति । कान्यकुब्जभाषायाम् एरञ्चि इति । गव्याज्यमित्येकम् । एतैरित्यष्टभिर्द्रव्यैः । दिनशः प्रत्यहम् । पृथक् जुहुयादिति । क्रमेण प्रथमदिने

मातङ्गाश्चतुरङ्गाश्च वर्द्धन्ते विधिनाऽमुना ।
सर्व्वव्याधिविनिर्मुक्ताः क्षुद्रपीडाविवर्जिताः ॥ ११२

कारयेद्‌ब्रह्मवृक्षेण शिल्पिनायुधपञ्चकम् ।
शङ्खखङ्गरथाङ्गानि शार्ङ्गं कौमोदकीं क्रमात् ॥ ११३

पञ्चगव्येषु निःक्षिप्य तानि स्पृष्ट्वा मनुं जपेत् ।
सम्यक् पञ्चसहस्राणि तेषु सम्पातयन् पुनः ॥ ११४

तावदाज्येन जुहुयान्मन्त्रैः स्वैः पूजयेत् क्रमात् ।
उद्धृत्य पञ्चगव्येभ्यः पूर्व्ववत् प्रजपेन्मनुम् ॥ ११५

प्रथमद्रव्येण द्वितीये द्वितीयेनेति ज्ञेयम् । दिनश इति विप्रान् भोजयेदित्यत्राप्यन्वेति ॥ १०८ ॥ १०९ ॥ ११० ॥ १११ ॥ ११२ ॥

कारयेदिति । तालप्रमाणम् । ब्रह्मवृक्षेणेति पलाशेन । द्विजभूमिस्थेन सफलेनेति ज्ञेयम् । शिल्पिनेति । निपुणतरेणेतिशेषः । तदुक्तमाचार्य्यैः । साधुशिल्पविदेति । रथाङ्गं चक्रम् । शार्ङ्गं धनुः । कौमोदकीं गदाम् । क्रमादित्यस्यायमर्थः । महान्तं पलाशं दिक्षु अङ्कयित्वा छित्त्वा क्रकचेन पञ्चधा निर्भिद्य मध्यभागेन शङ्खं पूर्व्वादि चतुर्दिग्भागैः खड्गादीनि कारयेदिति । तदुक्तमाचार्य्यैः—

द्विजभूरुहं महान्तं छित्त्वा निर्भिद्य पञ्चधा भूयः ।
आशाक्रमेण पञ्चायुधा विधेयाश्च साधु शिल्पविदा ॥ इति ॥११३॥

पञ्चगव्येषु निक्षिप्येति । पलाशस्यैव पात्रं कृत्वा तन्मध्ये पञ्चगव्यं विनिक्षिप्य तत्र तानि निक्षिप्येत्यर्थः । मनुं मूलमन्त्रम् । पञ्चसहस्राणीति समुदायेन । सम्यगिति प्रत्येकं सहस्रजपः । तेषु आयुधेषु सम्यक् सम्पातयन् तावत् पञ्चसहस्रेण जुहुयात् । सम्यगिति । प्रत्यायुधमेकैकसहस्ररीत्या । मन्त्रैः स्वैरिति सप्तदशभिर्वक्ष्यमाणैः । पूजयेदिति । प्राणप्रतिष्ठापूर्व्वं पात्र एव । क्रमादिति । मध्यस्थशङ्खप्रभृतीत्यर्थः । पूर्व्ववदिति । पुनस्तानि स्पृशन् तावत्संख्यम् । ईशानसंहितायान्तु—

द्विजभूम्यां स्थितं छित्त्वा फलाढ्यं विप्रभूरुहम् ।
मूलाग्रहीनं निर्भिद्य पञ्चधा सर्व्वतः समम् ॥
मध्याद्यंशैः क्रमाच्छङ्खं नन्दकं चक्रमेव च ।
शार्ङ्गं कौमोदकीं तालप्रमाणं परिकल्पयेत् ॥

अवटान् पञ्च निखनेद्दिक्षु मध्यादिषु क्रमात् ।
अवटेष्वेषु पूर्णेषु पञ्चगव्येन साधकः ॥ ११६
आयुधानि प्रजप्तानि पञ्चघोषपुरःसरम् ।
विन्यसेत्तेषु मध्यादि पूजां कुर्य्याद्यथा पुरा ॥ ११७
वालुकाभिः समापूर्य्य मृद्भिः कुर्य्यात्समस्थलम् ।
बलिञ्च विकिरेत्तत्र तेषां मन्त्रैर्यथाक्रमम् ॥ ११८
दिक्पतिभ्यो बलिं दत्त्वा ब्राह्मणान् भोजयेत्ततः ।
दीनान्धकृपणादींश्च तोषयेद्भोजनादिभिः ॥ ११९
गुरवे दक्षिणां दद्यादात्मवित्तानुसारतः ।
यत्रैवं विहिता रक्षा देशे वा नगरे पुरे ॥ १२०
ग्रामे गेहेऽथवा तत्र वर्द्धन्ते सम्पदः सदा ।
अश्मपातादयो दोषा भूतप्रेतादिसंयुताः ॥ १२१
अभिचारकृताः कृत्यारिपुचौराद्युपद्रवाः ।
नेक्ष्यन्ते तां दिशं भीतास्तर्जिता देवताज्ञया ॥ १२२

सपञ्चगव्ये तत्पात्रे निक्षिपेत्तं निधाय च ।
स्वस्तिके सम्यगभ्यर्च्य जपेल्लक्षसहस्रकम् ॥
घृतेन तावद्धुत्वाज्यसम्पातेन यथाविधि ।
आलिप्य तावद्भूयोऽपि जपेन्मन्त्रमिदं सुधीः ॥
खात्वाऽवटान् हस्तमानान् मध्ये पूर्व्वादि दिक्षु च ।
तत्र पीठं समभ्यर्च्य मूलमन्त्रेण विन्यसेत् ॥
तानि शङ्के महादुर्गामावाह्याऽस्मिन् स्थितां यजेत् ।
तत्तदायुधमूर्त्तीश्च दिशाद्युदितलक्षणाः ॥
अस्त्रमन्त्रेण परितः प्राकारं परिकल्पयेत् इति ॥ ११४ ॥ ११५ ॥

अवटानिति । हस्तमात्रान् । साधक इत्यनेन मूलमुच्चरन् विन्यसेदित्युक्तम् । प्रजप्तानीत्यनुवादः । विन्यसेदिति मूलेन । यथापुरेति । स्वस्वमन्त्रैः । यथाक्रममिति मध्यादि ॥ ११६ ॥ ११७ ॥ ११८ ॥ ११९ ॥ १२० ॥ १२१ ॥ १२२ ॥

पद्मं भानुदलान्वितं प्रविलिखेत्तत्कर्णिकायां पुन-
स्तारं शक्तिगबीजसाध्यसहितं तत्केसरेषु क्रमात् ।
मर्दिन्या मनुसंभवान् युगलशो वर्णान् पुनः पत्रगा-
न्मन्त्रार्णान् गुणशो विधाय विलिखेदन्त्यं तदन्त्ये इली ॥ १२३

मातृकावर्णसंवीतं भूपुरद्वयमध्यगम् ।
यन्त्रं विन्ध्यनिवासिन्याः प्रोक्तं सर्व्वसमृद्धिदम् ॥ १२४

रक्षाकरं विशेषेण क्षुद्रभूतादिनाशनम् ।
राज्यदं भ्रष्टराज्यानां वश्यदं वश्यमिच्छताम् ॥ १२५

सुतार्थिनीनां सुतदं रोगिणां रोगशान्तिदम् ।
बहुना किमिहोक्तेन यन्त्रं तत् कामदो मणिः ॥ १२६

इति श्रीशारदातिलके एकादशः पटलः ।

यन्त्रमाह पद्ममिति । भानुदलान्वितं द्वादशदलान्वितं पद्मं लिखेत् । तत्कर्णिकायां शक्तिगं मायाबीजगं यद्बीजं दौर्गं सविसर्गं तत्र यत् साध्यं तेन सहितं तारं लिखेत् । एतेन द्वादशदलपद्मकर्णिकायां प्रणवं विलिख्य तत्र मायाबीजं तत्र दौर्गं बीजं तत्र साध्यं लिखेदित्युक्तं भवति । मर्दिन्या इति महिषमर्दिन्याः । युगलश इत्यनेन महिषमर्दिनीमन्त्रस्यावृत्तित्रयमुक्तम् । मन्त्रार्णान् मूलमन्त्रार्णान् । गुणशस्त्रिस्त्रः । अन्त्यमेकमक्षरमन्त्ये द्वादशे लिखेत् ॥ १२३ ॥ १२४ ॥ १२५ ॥ १२६ ॥

इति श्रीशारदातिलकटीकायां सत्सम्प्रदायकृतव्याख्यायां पदार्थादर्शाभिख्यायामेकादशः पटलः ।

द्वादशः पटलः ।

अज्ञानतिमिरध्वंसि संसारार्णवतारकम् ।
आनन्दबीजमवतादतर्क्यं त्रैपुरं महः ॥ १

अथ वक्ष्ये परां विद्यां त्रिपुरामतिगोपिताम् ।
यां ज्ञात्वा सिद्धिसङ्घानामधिपो जायते नरः ॥ २

वियद्भृगुहुताशस्थो भौतिको बिन्दुशेखरः ।
वियत्तदादि केन्द्राग्निस्थितं वामाक्षिबिन्दुमत् ।
आकाशभृगुवह्निस्थो मनुः सर्गेन्दुखण्डवान् ॥ ३

एवं दुर्गामन्त्रानुक्त्वा मातृकापटले तार्त्तीयस्योद्दिष्टत्वाद्भैरवीमन्त्रं वक्तुमुपक्रमते। अज्ञानेति। त्रिपुराशब्दव्युत्पत्तिरुक्ताऽन्यत्र—

त्रिमूर्त्तिसर्गाच्च पुराभवत्वात् त्रयीमयत्वाच्च पुरैव देव्याः ।
लये त्रिलोक्या अपि पूरणत्वात् प्रायोऽम्बिकायास्त्रिपुरेति नाम ॥ इति ।

सिद्धेश्वरीमते तु—ब्रह्मविष्णुमहेशानैस्त्रिदेवैरर्चिता पुरा ।
त्रिपुरेति तदा नाम कथितं दैवतैः पुरा ॥ इति ।

अतिगोपितामित्यनेनेतदुक्तं भवति। मयाऽपि गुप्तमेव स्वरूपमुद्धृतमिति। अन्यथा विद्यां वक्ष्ये इति प्रतिज्ञाय विद्या वेद्येत्युपसंहारः अथ च मन्त्र उद्धृतः इदमसङ्गतं स्यात्। यतः "शक्त्याद्या तु भवेद्विद्या शिवाद्यो मन्त्र उच्यते" इत्युक्तेः।

तदुक्तम्—एषा सा शाम्भवी विद्या गुप्ता कुलवधूरिव ।
कर्णात्कर्णोपदेशेन सञ्चरत्यवनीतले ॥ इति ।

सिद्धेत्यादि विनियोगोक्तिः ॥१॥२॥

मन्त्रमुद्धरति वियदिति। वियत् हः भृगुः सः हुताशो रेफः। ते तिष्टन्त्यत्र सः सुपि स्थः बाहुलकादधिकरणे कः। भौतिक ऐ बिन्दुरनुस्वारः इत्याद्यं कूटम्। वियत् हः तदादिः सः। कः स्वरूपम्। इन्द्रो लः अग्नी रः। एते स्थिता यत्रेत्याहिताग्न्यादिः। वामाक्षि ई बिन्दुरनुस्वार इति द्वितीयं कूटम्।

आकाशो हः भृगुः सः वह्नी रेफः मनुरौ सर्गो विसर्गः इन्दुखण्डः अनुस्वारः इति तृतीयं कूटम्। आद्यन्तयो रेफः कीलकम्। तदुक्तमाचार्य्यैर्भैरवीस्तवे—

आद्यं तृतीयमनलोर्जितमेव बीजं
कूटं द्वितीयमनलेन विराजमानम् । इति ॥३॥

वाग्भवं प्रथमं बीजं कामबीजं द्वितीयकम् ।
तृतीयं कामराजाख्यं त्रिभिर्बीजैरितीरिता ॥ ४
पञ्चकूटात्मिका विद्या वेद्या त्रिपुरभैरवी ।
ऋषिः स्याद्दक्षिणामूर्तिश्छन्दः पङ्क्तिः समीरितः ॥ ५

एषां प्रत्येकं नामान्याह वाग्भवमिति। पञ्चकूटात्मिकेति। हसकलरेति पञ्चव्यञ्जनसंयोगात् पञ्चकूटात्मकत्वं रेफरहितत्वेन चतुष्कूटत्वं रेफोपरि नादयोगे षट्कूटत्वं ज्ञेयम्। अस्यास्त्रिंशत्प्रस्तारभेदा ग्रन्थगौरवभयान्नोक्ताः। ते तन्त्रान्तरात् द्रष्टव्याः। आद्यं बीजं मध्यं शक्तिः अन्त्यं वा शक्तिः।

व्यस्तबीजध्यानफलमुच्यते सारस्वतमतात्—

नवकुन्दनिभां देवीं मुक्ताजालविभूषणाम् ।
मुद्राकपालविद्याक्षमालाराजन्महाभुजाम् ॥
वाग्भवं यो महेशानि लक्षं जपति संयतः ।
कविता जायते तस्य नानावृत्तार्थशोभना ॥
रक्तां सुरतरोर्मूले विलसन्मणिपीठगाम् ।
सृणिपाशकपालेक्षुमातुलिङ्गधनुःकराम् ॥
रत्नैरलङ्कृतां पुष्पैर्मदाघूर्णितलोचनाम् ।
हेलाविलाससम्पन्नां नवयौवनसुन्दरीम् ॥
देवीं ध्यात्वा जपेल्लक्षं यो बीजं मध्यमं वशी ।
त्रैलोक्यं क्षोभयेदाशु पुरावत् सिद्धिभागसौ ॥
अक्षमालासुधाकुम्भमुद्रापुस्तकधारिणीम् ।
नवकुन्देन्दुसाङ्काशां राजन्मौक्तिकभूषणाम् ॥
शक्तिं संविन्मयीं ध्यात्वा बीजं सारस्वतं वशी ।
यो जपेज्जायते तस्य कविता भुवि सन्तता ॥ इति ॥

तन्त्रान्तरे च—विद्याकामो वाग्भवाख्यं शुक्लवस्त्रानुलेपनः ।
मौक्तिकाभरणो भूमिगृहे जप्यात् त्रिलक्षकम् ॥
गद्यपद्यान्युद्गिरन्तीं स्वं वाणीमिति भावयन् ।
पलाशैरेव जुहुयात् पुष्पैस्त्रिमधुराप्लुतैः ॥
स जायते कविश्रेष्ठः सुन्दरीणां च वल्लभः ।
त्रिलोकी वश्यकामश्चेत् कामराजं द्वितीयकम् ॥

देवता देशिकैरुक्ता देवी त्रिपुरभैरवी ।
नाभेराचरणं न्यस्येद्वाग्भवं मन्त्रवित् पुनः ॥ ६
हृदयान्नाभिपर्य्यन्तं कामबीजं प्रविन्यसेत् ।
शिरसो हृत्प्रदेशान्तं तार्त्तीयं विन्यसेत् ततः ॥ ७
आद्यं द्वितीयं करयोस्तार्त्तीयमुभयोर्न्यसेत् ।
मूर्द्धाधारे हृदि न्यस्येद् भूयो बीजत्रयं क्रमात् ॥ ८

कस्तूरीकुङ्कुमामोदमधुरोऽरुणभूषणः ।
रक्तक्षौमाम्बरधरो जपेन्मन्त्रत्रयं सुधीः ॥
नेत्राञ्चलैर्मदालोलैर्वशे विदधती जगत् ।
अम्बिकेति स्वकं रूपं ध्यायन् हृष्टेन चेतसा ॥
जुहुयान्मालतीपुष्पैः शीतकर्पूरसंप्लुतैः ।
जगन्ति तस्य वश्यानि भवन्ति बहुनाऽत्र किम् ॥

वाग्विलासमधिगन्तुमना यो बीजमन्त्यमपि पुष्करलक्षम् ।
संजपेद्विमलभूषणवस्त्रोऽसौ भवेत् कविवरोऽमितकीर्त्तिः ॥
मालतीमुकुलकैर्दलहृद्यैश्चन्दनाक्तसि घने निमज्जितैः ।
श्रीकरी कुसुमकैर्हुतक्रिया सैव चाशु कविताकरी मता ॥ इति ॥

अत्र चान्यकृताऽतिगुप्ततरत्वाद्बीजत्रयस्य दीपन्युद्धारो न कृतः । तेन च विनेयं विद्या न सिद्धिदा । अतस्तदुद्धारः सिद्धेश्वरीतन्त्राल्लिख्यते—

वागीश्वर्य्यास्तु मन्त्रे हुतवहदयितास्थानगं वाग्भवाख्यं
क्लिन्ने क्लेदिन्यपि स्यादिह तदनु महाक्षोभमित्येव योज्यम् ।
तस्मात् कुर्विंत्यसौ चेन्मनुरयमुदितो रुद्रवर्णस्तदन्त-
स्तारान्मोचं तदन्ते कुरुपदसहितं स्याच्च सम्मोहनाख्यम् ॥
बीजानां दीपनानि स्युरिह हि मनवो यैः सुदीप्तः सदैव
त्रैबीजो मन्त्रराजो भवति जपविधौ सर्व्वसम्पत्तिकारी ।
विद्यानां पारगामी युवतिजनमनःक्षोभकारी विहारी
मन्त्री स्यात् सर्व्वसम्यग्ररतिपतिसदृशो मुक्तबाधश्चिरायुः ॥ इति ॥

चैतन्याद्यादन्युद्धारः प्रथमश्लोकव्याख्यानोक्तोऽनुसन्धेयः । उत्तरषट्के तु—

आदिमेन तु सा लुप्ता मध्यमेन तु कीलिता ।
अन्तिमेन तु सा छिन्ना तेन विद्या न सिध्यति ॥

नवयोन्यात्मकं न्यासं कुर्य्याद्बीजैस्त्रिभिः पुनः।
कर्णयोश्चिबुके भूयः शङ्खयोर्वदने पुनः॥ ९
नेत्रयोर्नसि विन्यस्येदंसयोः पिठरे पुनः।
ततः कूर्परयोः कुक्षौ जानुनोर्ध्वजमूर्द्धनि॥ १०
पादयोर्गुह्यदेशे च पार्श्वयोर्हृदयाम्बुजे।
स्तनयोः कण्ठदेशे च रत्यादिमथ विन्यसेत्॥ ११
मूले रतिं हृदि प्रीतिं भ्रुवोर्मध्ये मनोभवाम्।
बालाबीजैस्त्रिभिर्न्यस्येत् स्थानेष्वेषु विलोमतः॥ १२
अमृतेशीं च योगेशीं विश्वयोनिं क्रमादिमाः।
विलोमबीजैर्विन्यस्येन्मूर्त्तिन्यासमथाचरेत्॥ १३

आदिमादिमनादिं च मध्यं मध्यममध्यमम्।
अन्त्यमन्त्यमनन्त्यं च त्रिपुरा शीघ्रसिद्धिदा॥
आदिमध्ये तु मध्यादावन्त्यमध्ये तु संस्थितौ।
पुरःक्षोभाय जप्तव्यं विधिनाऽनेन साधकैः॥ इति।

अन्यत्र तु—आद्यं बीजं मध्यमे मध्यमादावन्त्यं चान्त्ये योजयित्वा जपेद् यः।
त्रैलोक्यान्तःपातिनो भूतसङ्घा वश्यास्तस्यैश्वर्य्यभाजो भवेयुः॥
आद्यं कृत्वा चावसानेऽन्त्यबीजं मध्ये मध्यं चादिमे साधकेन्द्रः।
कुर्य्यान्नित्यं यो जपेन्मन्त्रमेनं जीवन्मुक्तः सोऽश्नुते दिव्यसिद्धिम्॥ इति।

करयोरिति वामदक्षिणयोः।

तदुक्तम्—हस्ततले च सव्ये दक्षाङ्गये द्वितीये। इति॥ ४॥५॥६॥७॥८॥

नवयोन्यात्मकमिति यदुक्तं तमेवाह कर्णेति। त्रित्रिस्थानैरेकैका योनिः। अत्र वामाङ्गादिन्यास इति केचित्। अत एव पूजायां वामकोण इत्याद्युक्तिः। शङ्खयोरिति। ललाटपार्श्वास्थिप्रदेशयोः। त्रिकाण्डशेषमपि—"शङ्खो निधौ ललाटास्थि"। नसीति नासिकायाम्। पिठरे उदरे। उखाकारत्वात्तस्य। कुक्षावित्यनेन नैकस्याद्योन्याकारतासिद्धये नाभिभागो लक्ष्यः। तदुक्तम्। कौर्पर-योर्नाभिमण्डले न्यसेदिति। क्वचिन्नाभाविति पाठः। ध्वजो लिङ्गम्॥९॥१०॥११॥

रत्यादीति यदुक्तं तदेवाह मूल इति। विलोमतस्त्रिभिर्बालाबीजैः विन्यसेदिति सम्बन्धः। स्थानेष्वेष्विति उत्तरत्र सम्बध्यते। तत्र विलोमत्वं नामेद रतेर्वाग्भवं प्रीतेरन्त्यं मनोभवाया मध्यमिति।

स्वस्वबीजादिकं पूर्व्वं मूर्त्तीशानमनोभवम् ।
न्यसेदङ्गी तत्पुरुषं मकरध्वजसात्मवित् ॥ १४

हृद्यघोरकुमारादिकन्दर्पं तदनन्तरम् ।
गुह्यदेशे प्रविन्यस्येद्वामदेवादिमन्मथम् ॥ १५

सद्योजातं कामदेवं पादयोर्विन्यसेत्ततः ।
ऊर्द्ध्वप्राग्दक्षिणोदीच्यपश्चिमेषु मुखेषु तान् ॥ १६

प्रविन्यसेद्यथापूर्व्वं भृगुर्व्योमाग्निसंस्थितः ।
सद्यादि पञ्चकस्वस्थो बीजमेषां प्रकीर्त्तितम् ॥ १७

षड्दीर्घयुक्तेनाद्येन बीजेनाऽङ्गक्रिया मता ।
पञ्चबाणांस्तनौ न्यस्येन्मन्त्री त्रैलोक्यमोहनान् ॥ १८

द्रामाद्यां द्राविणीं मूर्ध्नि द्रींमाद्यां चोभिणीं पदे ।
क्लीं वशीकरणीं वक्त्रे गुह्ये ब्लूंबीजपूर्व्विकाम् ॥ १९

यदाहुः—कामस्य कामबीजं रतिबीजं वाग्भवं समुद्दिष्टम् ।
सम्मोहनाख्यमन्त्यं प्रीतेर्बीजं तथा प्रोक्तम् ॥ इति ।

एष्विति । पूर्व्वोक्तस्थानेषु विलोमबालाबीजैः सह अमृतेश्याद्या न्यसेदित्यन्वयः । अत्रापि विलोमत्वं पूर्व्ववदेव ॥ १२॥१३ ॥

स्वस्वबीजादिकमिति । मूर्त्तीनां वक्ष्यमाणानि बीजानि मनोभवादीनां क्रमेण वनिताचतुर्थबाणवाग्भवकाममायाबीजानि ज्ञेयानि । उभयत्र आदिशब्दः तत्पूर्व्वत्वमात्रं बोधयति । तेनैकपद्यम् । तान् ईशानमनोभवादीन् । तेनायं प्रयोगः । ह्स्रौं ईशानाय क्लीं मनोभवाय नम इत्यादि ॥ १४ ॥ १५ ॥ १६ ॥

यथापूर्व्वमिति । स्वस्वबीजादिकमिति च यदुक्तं तानि बीजान्युद्धरति भृगुरिति । भृगुः सः व्योम हः अग्नी रेफः ताभ्यां सम्यग्युत इति । ऊर्द्ध्वाधोभागे क्रमेण । सद्यादिपञ्चकस्था विलोमेन औ ए उ इ अ इति ॥ १७ ॥

षडिति । षड्दीर्घयुक्तेन बीजेन मध्यबीजेन । आद्येन बीजेन मन्त्राद्येन । सम्प्रदायात् आम्नायेनेत्यपि ज्ञेयम् । तेनायं प्रयोगः । ह्स्रौः हसकल क्रां क्रीं ह्स्रौं हृत् ५क्रीं क्रीं ह्स्रौं शिरः ५क्रू क्रीं ह्स्रौं शिखा ५ क्रैं क्रीं ह्स्रौं वर्म्म ५क्रौं क्रीं नेत्रं ५क्रः क्रीं ह्स्रौं अस्त्रम् ॥ १८ ॥

द्रामाद्यामिति । अत्र सर्व्वत्राचार्य्येण मस्थाने ङः पठितः । अन्यत्र तु द्रां

आकर्षणीं हृदि पुनः सर्गान्तर्भृगुसंयुतम् ।
सम्मोहनीं क्रमादेवं बाणन्यासोऽयमीरितः ॥ २०

भालभ्रूमध्यवदनलम्बिकाकण्ठहृत्सु च ।
नाभ्यधिष्ठानयोः पञ्च ताराद्याः सुभगादिकाः ॥ २१

न्यस्तव्या विधिना देव्यो सम्बिणा सुभगा भगा ।
भगसर्पिण्यथ परा भगमालिन्यनन्तरम् ॥ २२

अनङ्गाऽनङ्गकुसुमा भूयश्चाऽनङ्गमेखला ।
अनङ्गमदना सर्व्वा मदविभ्रमन्थराः ॥ २३

प्रधानदेवतावर्णभूषणाद्यैरलङ्कृताः ।
अक्षस्रक्पुस्तकाभीतिवरदाव्यकराम्बुजाः ॥ २४

वाक्कामं ब्लूं पुनः स्त्रीं सताराः पञ्चोदितास्त्वमी ।
न्यासं कुर्य्याद्भूषणाख्यं ततः साधकसत्तमः ॥ २५

द्रीं क्लीं ब्लूं स आदिका बाणा इति । तदुक्तं त्रिपुरासारे—

अद्रीशो मुखवृत्तवह्निसहितस्त्वाद्यं सदण्डस्त्रिमू-
र्त्याक्रान्तमनन्तवृत्तमेव खलु तद्बीजं द्वितीयं भवेत् ॥
मुखान्तस्थितं देवराजाधिरूढं सवामेक्षणं वक्त्रपूर्व्वेण युक्तम् ।
भपूर्व्वं सवृत्तारिषष्ठस्वराढ्यपेशं कतुर्य्यं कपूर्व्वेण युक्तम् ॥ इति ।

अद्रीशो दः मुखवृत्तम् आ वह्नी रः सदण्डः सानुस्वारः । इदमाद्यं द्रामिति । तदेव त्रिमूर्त्तिना ईकारेण आक्रान्तमाननवृत्तमाकारो यस्येदृशं द्रीमिति द्वितीयम् । मुखान्तः कः देवराजो लः वामेक्षणम् ई । वक्त्रपूर्व्वम् अनुस्वारः तेन क्लीं इति तृतीयम् । भपूर्व्वं वः वृत्तारिणा लकारेण षष्ठस्वरः ऊकारः तेन युतम् तेन ब्लूमिति बीजं भवति । कं जलं तद्बीजं वकारः तत्तुरीयं सः ककारपूर्व्वो विसर्गः तेन सहितम् एतावता सः इति पञ्चमम् ।

हृदीत्युत्तरत्र सम्बध्यते । सर्गान्तो भृगुः सः । लम्बिकेति । मुखमध्ये स्थानविशेषः । क्वचित्कर्णिकेति पाठः । तदा "कर्णिका कर्णभूषणम्" इति त्रिकाण्डो । विधिनेति । चतुर्थीनमोऽन्तत्वम् । सम्बिणेत्यनेन समुच्चितपूर्व्वा इत्युक्तं भवति ॥ १८ ॥ २० ॥ २१ ॥ २२ ॥ २३ ॥ २४ ॥

तारानेवाह । वागिति वाग्भवम् । कामः कामबीजम् । अन्यत् स्वरूपम् ।

न्यसेच्छिरसि भालभ्रूकर्णाक्षियुगले नसि ।
गण्डयोरोष्ठयोर्दन्तपङ्क्त्योरास्ये न्यसेत् स्वरान् ॥ २६

चिबुकेऽथ गले कण्ठे पार्श्वयोः स्तनयुग्मके ।
दोर्मूलयोः कूर्परयोः पाण्योस्तत्पृष्ठदेशतः ॥ २७

नाभौ गुह्ये पुनश्चोर्वोर्जानुनोर्जङ्घयोस्ततः ।
स्फिचोः पत्तलयोः पश्चाच्चरणाङ्गुष्ठयोर्द्वयोः ॥ २८

कादिरान्तान् न्यसेद्वर्णान् स्थानेष्वेषु समाहितः ।
काञ्च्यां ग्रैवेयके पश्चात् कटके हृदि गुह्यके ॥ २९

कर्णकुण्डलयोर्मौलौ वलयान् पत्रसान् लहौ ।
अष्टाविमान् प्रविन्यस्येदेवं देशिकसत्तमः ।
एवं न्यस्तशरीरोऽसौ ध्यायेत् त्रिपुरभैरवीम् ॥ ३०

उद्यद्भानुसहस्रकान्तिमरुणक्षौमां शिरोमालिनीं
रक्तालिप्तपयोधरां जपवटीं विद्यामभीतिं वरम् ।
हस्ताब्जैर्दधतीं त्रिनेत्रविलसद्वक्त्रारविन्दश्रियं
देवीं बद्धहिमांशुरत्नमुकुटां वन्दे समन्दस्मिताम् ॥ ३१

भूषणाख्यमिति । भूषणरूपैर्वर्णैर्न्यासो भूषणन्यासः । तमेवाह । ततः साधकसत्तमो न्यसेदिति । मातृकावर्णानिति शेषः । साधकसत्तम इत्यनेन सबिन्दुत्वं तत्तत्स्थाने भूषणरूपत्वेन ध्यानं चोक्तम् ॥ २५ ॥

न्यासस्थानान्येवाह शिरसीति । कण्ठस्तन्मणिर्गलस्तदधोभागः । अत्र कर्णादिषु द्विद्वि वर्णन्यासः । भ्रूस्थाने एकम् । पाण्योरेकम् । तत्पृष्ठदेशे एकमिति सम्प्रदायविदः । स्फिक्शब्देनोच्चत्वसाम्याद् गुल्फौ लक्ष्येते । कटके मूर्द्धन्यो लः । हृदि तालव्यः शः कर्णकुण्डलयोर्मूर्द्धन्यदन्त्याविति विवेक इति देशिकसत्तम इत्येतेनोक्तम् ॥ २६॥२७॥२८॥२९॥३० ॥

उद्यदिति । शिरसां मुण्डानां माला यस्यां सा तामिति विग्रहः । रक्तेति रक्तचन्दनम् । आयुधध्यानं दक्षाधऊर्द्ध्वयोराद्ये तदधःस्थयोरन्त्ये । दक्षोर्द्ध्वतः दक्षाधःपर्य्यन्तमिति केचित् । अत्र ध्यानान्तरं बाणबीजपूर्व्वकं पञ्चमुद्रा गुरुवक्त्रगम्या दर्शयेत् ॥ ३१ ॥

दीक्षां प्राप्य जपेन्मन्त्रं तत्त्वलक्षं जितेन्द्रियः ।
पुष्पैर्भानुसहस्राणि जुहुयाद् ब्रह्मवृक्षजैः ॥ ३२
त्रिमध्वक्तैः प्रसूनैर्वा करवीरसमुद्भवैः ।
पद्मं वसुदलोपेतं नवयोन्याढ्यकर्णिकम् ॥ ३३
इच्छादिशक्तिभिर्युक्तं भैरव्याः पीठमर्चयेत् ।
इच्छा ज्ञाना क्रिया पश्चात् कामिनी कामदायिनी ॥ ३४

दीक्षां प्राप्येति । शक्तिदीक्षां प्राप्येत्यर्थः । सा च तन्त्रान्तर सिद्धेश्वरीमतादितो ज्ञेया । तत्त्वभानुशब्दयोः सरूपाणामित्येकशेषः । तत्त्वलक्षं षट्त्रिंशल्लक्षम् । होमस्तु षट्त्रिंशत्सहस्रं पलाशकुसुमैः । इयं चतुःकूटस्य संख्या । त्रिमध्वक्तैः पयोमधुघृतयुक्तैः । केचित् पयःस्थाने शर्करामाहुः । इदमुभयत्र सम्बध्यते । तत्त्वलक्षं चतुर्विंशतिलक्षम् । होमस्तु चतुर्विंशतिसहस्रं करवीरैः । इयं संख्या पञ्चकूटस्य । तत्त्वलक्षं द्वादशलक्षम् । तन्त्रान्तरे द्वादशतत्त्वानामप्युपदिष्टत्वात् । तदुक्तं प्रयोगसारे—

अतो द्वादशतत्त्वानि वदन्त्येके विपश्चितः । इति ।

तत्पक्षे प्रसूनैर्वेति वाशब्दः समुच्चये मिलितोभयैर्द्वादशसहस्रं होमः । इयं च संख्या षट्कूटस्येति ज्ञेयम् । तदुक्तमाचार्यैः—

दीक्षां प्राप्य विशिष्टलक्षणयुजः सत्सम्प्रदायाद् गुरो-
र्लब्ध्वा मन्त्रममुं जपेत् सुनियतस्तत्त्वार्कलक्षावधि ।
स्वाहान्तैश्च नवैः पलाशकुसुमैः सम्यक्समिद्धेऽनले
मन्त्री भानुसहस्रकं प्रतिजुहेदश्वारिसूनैरपि ॥ इति ॥

तत्र तत्त्वानि षट्त्रिंशच्चतुर्विंशतिः अर्कं द्वादश । भान्तीति भानवः षट्त्रिंशत्तत्त्वानि चतुर्विंशतितत्त्वानि द्वादशादित्याश्चेति पद्मपादाचार्यैः व्याख्यातम् । अत्रापि भानुशब्दार्थोऽयमेव ज्ञेयः ॥ ३२॥३३ ॥

पूजायन्त्रमाह पद्ममिति । नवयोन्याढ्यकर्णिकं पद्ममस्याः पूजायन्त्रमिति शेषः । तदुद्धारप्रकार उच्यते—

द्वितीयादिद्विद्विभागे योनी सन्ध्यध्वनाग्निना ।
भित्त्वा ध्वंशगुणान् वृत्तान् बहिः पद्मं समुल्लिखेत् ॥

अस्यार्थः । यथेच्छप्रमाणं वृत्तं कृत्वा तत्प्राक्सूत्रं चतुर्धा विभज्य तत्रैकं भागम् उर्द्ध्वतस्त्यक्त्वा द्वितीयं भागमारभ्य तृतीयभागान्तम् अधराग्रत्र्यस्रं कृत्वा ततो

रती रतिप्रिया नन्दा नवमी स्यान्मनोन्मनी ।
वरदाभयधारिण्यः संप्रोक्ता नव शक्तयः ॥ ३५

वाग्भवं लोहितो रायै श्रीकण्ठः लोहितोऽनलः ।
दीर्घवान् यै परा पश्चादपरायै ह्सौः पुनः ॥ ३६
सदाशिवमहाप्रेतं ङेऽन्तं पद्मासनं नमः ।
अनेन मनुना दद्यादासनं श्रीगुरुक्रमम् ॥ ३७
प्राङ्मध्ययोन्यन्तराले पूजयेत् कल्पयेत् पुनः ।
पञ्चभिः प्रणवैर्मूर्त्तिं तस्यामावाह्य देवताम् ॥ ३८
पूजयेदागमोक्तेन विधानेन समाहितः ।
तारा वाक् शक्तिः कमला ह्सखफ्रें ह्सौः स्मृताः ॥ ३९

मध्यादारभ्य चतुर्थान्तं द्वितीयमधरार्धं तस्त्रं कृत्वा तदुभयसन्धिभेदिप्रथम-भागमारभ्य ऊर्ध्वार्धं तृतीयान्तपर्यन्तं तस्त्रं कुर्यादिति । तदुक्तम्—

वक्षेः पुरद्वितयवासवयोनिमध्यसव्यमवह्निवरुणेश्वसमाश्रिताङ्गि । इति ।

वरदाभयधारिण्य इति स्मरणमात्रम् । चतुर्थपटल एवासां ध्यानस्योक्तत्वात् ॥ ३३ ॥ ३४ ॥ ३५ ॥

पीठमन्त्रमुद्धरति वागिति । वाग्भवं बालाद्यबीजम् । लोहितः पः । रायै स्वरूपम् । श्रीकण्ठः अकारः । अनलो रः दीर्घवानाकारयुक्तः तेन रा इति । यै परा इति स्वरूपम् । अपरायै स्वरूपम् । परा अपरायै इत्यत्र तु सन्धिः । ह्सौः इति पिण्डम् । सदाशिवमहाप्रेतान्तं स्वरूपम् । प्रेतमिति द्वितीया शब्दकर्मणि । ङेऽन्तं चतुर्थ्येकवचनान्तं पद्मासनं तेन पद्मासनाय ॥ ३६॥३७ ॥

प्राङ्मध्ययोन्यन्तराले श्रीगुरुक्रमं पूजयेदिति सम्बन्धः । श्रीगुरुक्रमस्तु त्रिविधः । दिव्यौघः सिद्धौघो मानवौघश्चेति । तत्र परप्रकाशानन्द परमेशानन्द-परमशिवानन्दकामेश्वर्यानन्दमोक्षानन्दकामानन्दामृतानन्दा दिव्यौघः । ईशान-तत्पुरुषाघोरवामसदानन्दाः सिद्धौघः । मानवौघस्तु स्वस्वगुरुसंप्रदायात् ज्ञेयः । पीठस्योत्तरभागे गुरुपङ्क्तिं प्रपूजयेत् इति । सामान्यविधेः अपवादोऽयं प्राङ्मध्ययोन्यन्तराल इति ॥ ३८ ॥

आगमोक्तेनेत्युत्तरषट्कप्रोक्तेन । आगमशब्दव्युत्पत्तिरुक्ता तन्त्रान्तरे—

आगतं शिववक्त्रात्तु गतं तु गिरिजामुखे ।
मतं च वासुदेवस्य तस्मादागम उच्यते ॥ इति ।

वामकोणे यजेद्देव्या रतिमिन्दुसमप्रभाम् ।
रतिं पाशधरां सौम्यां मदविभ्रमविह्वलाम् ॥ ४०
प्रीतिं दक्षिणकोणस्थां तप्तकाञ्चनसन्निभाम् ।
अङ्कुशं प्रणतिं दोर्भ्यां धारयन्तीं समर्चयेत् ॥ ४१
अग्रे मनोभवां रक्तां रक्तपुष्पाद्यलङ्कृताम् ।
इक्षुकार्मुकपुष्पेषून्धारयन्तीं शुचिस्मिताम् ॥ ४२
अङ्गान्यभ्यर्चयेत् पश्चाद्यथापूर्व्वं विधानवित् ।
दिक्ष्वग्रे च निजैर्मन्त्रैः पूजयेद्बाणदेवताः ॥ ४३
हस्ताब्जैर्धृतपुष्पेषुप्रणामा भूतसप्रभाः ।
अष्टयोनिष्वष्ट शक्तीः पूजयेत् सुभगादिकाः ॥ ४४
मातरो भैरवाङ्कस्था मदविभ्रमविह्वलाः ।
अष्टपत्रेषु सम्पूज्या यथावत् कुसुमादिभिः ॥ ४५
लोकपालांस्ततो दिक्षु तेषामस्त्राणि तद्बहिः ।
पूर्व्वजन्मकृतैः पुण्यैस्त्वामेनां परदेवताम् ॥ ४६
यो भजेदुक्तमार्गेण स भवेत् संपदां पदम् ।
एवं सिद्धमनुर्मन्त्री साधयेदिष्टमात्मनः ॥ ४७

अत एव समाहितः सावधान इत्युक्तिः । पञ्चभिः प्रणवैरिति यदुक्तं तानेवाह तारा इति । वाक् वाग्भवम् । शक्तिर्मायाबीजम् । कमला श्रीबीजम् । अन्यत्त्विषुद्वयम् । रतिप्रीत्योर्ध्याने एकहस्तेऽस्त्रं द्वितीये नमस्कारः ॥ ३९॥४०॥४१॥४२ ॥

यथापूर्व्वमिति । आग्नेयादिषु केसरेषु मध्ययोन्यन्तरे चतुर्दिक्षु च । विधानविदित्यनेन मध्ययोनिबाह्यदेश इत्युक्तम् ॥ ४३ ॥

हस्ताब्जैरिति । सव्यहस्ते बाणः अन्यहस्ते नमस्कारः । तदुक्तम्—

द्राविण्याद्याः क्रमशः सर्वाः सर्व्वाभरणशोभिता समदाः ।
सव्यकरकलितबाणाः शेषकरैः कृतनमस्काराः ॥ इति ।

भूतसप्रभा इति । पृथिव्यादिवर्णतुल्यवर्णा इत्यर्थः । सुभगादिका इति यथान्यस्ताः ॥ ४४ ॥

मातरइति । चण्डिकान्ताः । तदुक्तमाचार्य्यैः—

मातृगणं सचण्डिकान्तं दलेष्वपि यजेदसिताङ्गकाद्यैः । इति ।

यथावदित्यनेन दीर्घाद्या मातरो ह्रस्वाद्या भैरवा इत्युक्तम् । सम्पदां पदमित्य-

जुहुयादरुणाम्भोजैरम्बोभिर्मधुराप्लुतैः।
लक्षसंख्यं तदर्द्धं वा प्रत्यहं भोजयेद् द्विजान्॥ ४८

वनिता युवती रम्याः पूजयेद् देवताधिया।
होमान्ते धनधान्याद्यैस्तोषयेद् गुरुमात्मनः॥ ४९

एवं कृते जगद्वश्यो रमाया भवनं भवेत्।
रक्तोत्पलैस्त्रिमध्वक्तैररुणैर्वा हयारिजैः॥ ५०

पुष्पैः पयोऽन्नैः सघृतैर्होमो विप्रं वशं नयेत्।
वाक्सिद्धिं लभते मन्त्री पलाशकुसुमैर्हुतात्॥ ५१

कर्पूरागुरुसंयुक्तं गुग्गुलुं जुहुयात् सुधीः।
ज्ञानं दिव्यमवाप्नोति तेनैव स भवेत् कविः॥ ५२

क्षीराक्तैरमृताखण्डैर्होमः सर्व्वापमृत्युजित्।
दूर्व्वाभिरायुषे होमः क्षीराक्ताभिर्दिनत्रयम्॥ ५३

मेनाख्याः सम्पत्प्रदेत्यपि नामेति सूचितं भवति॥ ४५॥४६॥४७॥४८॥४९॥

जगन्ति वश्यानि यस्येति बहुव्रीहिः। रमाया भवनं भवेदिति। तत्र ध्यानविशेषः—

मातुलिङ्गलिपिपात्रपङ्कजैः शोभमानकरपङ्कजां शिवाम्।
संविचिन्त्य खलु पौष्टिकक्रियां कुर्व्वतो भवति भूतिरञ्जसा॥ इति।

हयारिजैरिति करवीरजैः। सघृतैः पयोन्नैर्वेति तृतीयः पक्षः। वशं नयेदिति। ध्यानविशेषो यथा—

पाशाङ्कुशोद्यतकरामरुणां प्रसन्नां माणिक्यवज्रखचितैरपि भूषिताङ्गीम्।
मूर्त्तिं विचिन्त्य विदधीत पुरोक्तमार्गाद्वश्यक्रियां च नयनाञ्जनकानि मन्त्री॥

इति। भवेत्कविरिति। ध्यानविशेषः संनिरुक्तौ—

सारस्वतमयीं मूर्त्तिमादिमूर्त्तिसमन्विताम्।
यः स्मरेत् द्वादशान्ते स्यात् सोऽचिराद्वाक्पतिर्भवेत्॥ इति।

अमृता गुडूची। अपमृत्युजिदिति। ध्यानविशेषो गौतमेनोक्तः—

कुर्य्याच्छान्तिककर्म्माणि शुक्लवस्त्रां विचिन्त्य ताम्।
वराभयसुधाकुम्भपुस्तकायुधधारिणीम्॥ इति॥५०॥५१॥५२॥५३॥

गिरिकर्णीभवैः पुष्पैर्ब्राह्मणान् वशयेद्धुतात् ।
कह्लारैः पार्थिवान् पुष्पैस्तद्वधूः कर्णिकारजैः ॥ ५४
मल्लिकाकुसुमैर्हुत्वा राजपुत्रान् वशं नयेत् ।
कोरण्टकुसुमैर्वैश्यान् वृषलान् पाटलोद्भवैः ॥ ५५
अनुलोमविलोमान्तःस्थितसाध्याह्वयान्वितम् ।
मन्त्रमुच्चार्य्य जुहुयान्मन्त्री मधुरलोलितैः ॥ ५६
सर्षपैः पटुसंमिश्रैर्वशयेत् पार्थिवान् जपात् ।
अनेनैव विधानेन तत्पत्नीस्तत्सुतानपि ॥ ५७
जातीबिल्वफलैः पुष्पैर्मधुरत्रयलोलितैः ।
नरनारीनरपतीन् होमतो वशयेद्ध्रुवम् ॥ ५८
मालतीवकुलोद्भूतैः पुष्पैश्चन्दनलोलितैः ।
जुहुयात् कवितां मन्त्री लभते वत्सरान्तरे ॥ ५९
मधुरत्रयसंयुक्तैः फलैर्बिल्वसमुद्भवैः ।
जुहुयाद्वशयेल्लोकं श्रियमाप्नोति वाञ्छिताम् ६०
पाटलैः कुमुदैः कुन्दैरुत्पलैर्नागचम्पकैः ।
नन्द्यावर्त्तैर्विकसितैः कृतमालैर्जुहोति यः ॥ ६१
जायते वत्सरादर्वाक् श्रिया विजितपार्थिवः ।
साज्यमन्नं प्रजुहुयाद्भवेदन्नसमृद्धिमान् ॥ ६२
कस्तूरीकुङ्कुमोपेतं कर्पूरं जुहुयाद्वशी ।
कन्दर्पादधिकं सद्यः सौन्दर्य्यमधिगच्छति ॥ ६३
लाजान् प्रजुहुयान्मन्त्री दधिक्षीरमधुप्लुतान् ।
विजित्य रोगानखिलान् स जीवेच्छरदां शतम् ॥ ६४

गिरिकर्णी अपराजिता । पटु लवणम् । नन्द्यावर्त्तैर्गन्धतगरैः । कृतमालै राजवृक्षजैः । पाटलैरित्यादिना विकसितैरिति विशेषणात् पुष्पैरिति लभ्यते ।

पादद्वयं मलयजं पादं कुङ्कुमकेसरम् ।
पादं गोरोचनायाश्च तानि पिष्ट्वा हिमाम्भसा ॥ ६५
विदध्यात्तिलकं भूयो यान् पश्येद् यैर्विलोक्यते ।
यान् स्पृशेत् स्पृश्यते यैर्वा वश्याः स्युस्तस्य तेऽचिरात् ॥ ६६
कर्पूरकपिचोराणि समभागानि कल्पयेत् ।
चतुर्भागा जटामांसी तावती रोचना मता ॥ ६७
कुङ्कुमं सप्तभागं स्याद् दिग्भागं चन्दनं मतम् ।
अगुरुर्नवभागः स्यादिति भागक्रमेण च ॥ ६८
हिमाद्भिः कन्यया पिष्टमेतत् सर्वं सुसाधितम् ।
आदाय तिलकं भाले कुर्य्याद् भूमिपतीन् नरान् ॥ ६९
वनितां मदगर्वाढ्यां मदोन्मत्तान् मतङ्गजान् ।
सिंहव्याघ्रान् महासर्पान् भूतवेतालराक्षसान् ।
दर्शनादेव वशयेत् तिलकं धारयन्नरः ॥ ७०

मध्याद्यं नवयोनिषु प्रविलिखेद्वीजानि वर्णांस्त्रिशो
गायत्र्याः पुनरष्टपत्रविवरेष्वालिख्य लिप्या वृतम् ।
भूबिम्बद्वितयेन मन्मथयुजा कोणेषु संवेष्टितं
यन्त्रं त्रैपुरमीरितं त्रिभुवनप्रक्षोभकं श्रीप्रदम् ॥ ७१

अस्मिन् यन्त्रे समावाह्य सम्यक् सम्पूज्य देवताम् ।
होमेन कृतसम्पातं लाक्षालोहत्रयावृतम् ॥ ७२

हिमाम्भसा नीहारोदकेन ॥ ५४—६६ ॥

कपि रक्तचन्दनम् । चोरं कचूरं शटीति यावत् । दिग्भागं दशभागम् । कन्यया पिष्टमिति । कृष्णचतुर्दशीरात्रौ श्मशाने सम्प्रदायेन पिष्टम् । सुसाधितमिति एतच्चमत्कारजनम् ॥ ६७॥६८॥६९॥७० ॥

यन्त्रमाह मध्येति । प्रविलिखेत् प्रादक्षिण्येन एवं त्रिरावृत्तिर्भवति । गायत्र्यास्त्रिपुरागायत्र्याः । लिप्या मातृकया । भूबिम्बद्वितयेन परस्परव्यतिभिन्नेन । मन्मथबीजं भैरव्या एव ॥ ७१॥७२॥७३ ॥

विधृतं बाहुना यन्त्रं युद्धेषु विजयावहम्।
वादे वाग्विजयं कुर्य्यात् कवित्वं पुष्कलं दिशेत्।
आयुरारोग्यमित्राणि पुत्रान् पौत्रान् विवर्द्धयेत्॥ ७३

कामं षट्कोणमध्ये लिखतु पुनरिमं षट्सु कोणेषु पश्चात्
पत्रेषु द्व्यष्टसंख्येष्वमुमथ पुरतो व्योमबीजेन वीतम्।
क्षौणीबिम्बान्तरस्थं भुजदललिखितं रोचनाकुङ्कुमाभ्यां
प्रोक्तं सौभाग्यसम्पन्निरुपमकविताकीर्त्तिदं यन्त्रमेतत्॥ ७४

वह्नेर्गेहयुगान्तरस्थमदने मायां लिखेद्वाग्भवम्।
षट्कोणेष्वथ सन्धिषु प्रतिलिखेद्धुङ्कारमावेष्टयेत्।
स्त्रींबीजेन समीरितं त्रिभुवनप्रक्षोभकं त्रैपुरं
यन्त्रं पञ्चमनोभवात्मकमिदं सौन्दर्य्यसंपत्करम्॥ ७५

यन्त्रान्तरमाह काममिति। कामं भैरवीमध्यबीजम्। इमं कामम्। द्व्यष्टसंख्येषु षोडशसंख्येषु। अमुं कामम्। व्योमबीजं हं। भुजदलं भूर्जपत्रम्॥ ७४॥

यन्त्रान्तरमाह वह्नेरिति। मदने प्रसिद्धे। वाग्भवं प्रसिद्धम्। सन्धिष्विति। कोणानभितो हृत्तमध्ये। स्त्रींबीजेनेत्येकत्वं विवक्षितम्। सर्वं स्त्रींबीजमध्ये लिखेदित्यर्थः। तदुक्तम्—

मनोभवस्य सकले कुक्षौ तदेतत् क्षिपेत्। इति।

पञ्चमनोभवात्मकमिति। पञ्चभिः कामबीजैर्यन्त्रस्योक्तत्वात्। पञ्चकाममन्त्रा यथा—कपञ्चमं शुचिनयनान्तसंयुतं सवामदृक्पवनगुणान्वितः करः।
रविस्वरो हरिहयविष्णुषष्ठवदनं ततस्तर उपरान्वितो भृगुः॥
तेषां शिरःसु विदधीत बुधोऽर्धचन्द्रा-
नेवं मया निगदिताः खलु पञ्च कामाः॥ इति।

कं जलं तद्बीजं वः तत्पञ्चमो हः। शुचौ रेफः नयनान्त ई तेन मायाबीजम्। वामदृगीकारः पवनात् यकाराद् गुणः तृतीयो लः। तदन्वितः करः ककारस्तेन कामबीजम्। रविस्वरः द्वादशस्वर ऐ। हरिहयो लः विष्णुरकारः तस्मात् षष्ठ ङकारः तद्युक्तं वनं बकारस्तेन ब्लूं। तरस्वरूपम्। उः परो यस्मात्तेन ईं तद्युक्तो भृगुः सकारस्तेन स्त्रीं। सर्वे सार्धचन्द्राः सानुस्वाराः॥ ७५॥

अधरो बिन्दुमानाद्यो ब्रह्मेन्द्रस्थः शशीयुतः ।
द्वितीयं भृगुसर्गाढ्यो मनुस्तार्त्तीयमीरितम् ॥ ७६
एषा बालेति विख्याता त्रैलोक्यवशकारिणी ।
जपपूजादिकं सर्व्वमस्याः पूर्व्ववदाचरेत् ॥ ७७

बालाबीजैस्त्रिभिरित्युद्दिष्टं बालामन्त्रमुद्धरति अधर इति । अधरो बिन्दुमान् ऐं । ब्रह्मा ककारः इन्द्रो लः शशी बिन्दुः ई स्वरूपम् । तेन क्लीं । भृगुः सः सर्गो विसर्गः तेनाढ्यो मनुरौ तेन सौः इति । अन्यत्र सबिन्दुरुक्तः । तदुक्तं सनत्कुमारे—अष्टमस्य तृतीयं तु चतुर्दशसमन्वितम् ।
दण्डकुण्डलमेतद्धि सारस्वतमुदाहृतम् ॥ इति ॥

अस्या विद्यायाः शाप इति त्रिपुरासारे । तदुद्धारो यथा—
देव्या शप्ता येन विद्येयमाद्या पूर्व्वं तेन प्राणहीनाऽभवत् सा ॥
शिवशक्तिबीजमतएव शम्भुना निहितं तयोरुपरि पूर्व्वबीजयोः ।
अकुलं कुलोपरि च मध्यमाधरे दहनं ततः प्रभृति सोर्जिताऽभवत् ॥ इति ।

पूर्व्ववदित्युक्तत्वात् । प्रथमबीजस्य वाग्भवमिति नाम । मध्यस्य कामबीजमिति । तृतीयस्य शक्तिरिति । एतत्प्रसिद्धैव पूर्व्वमग्रेऽपि वाग्भवकामशब्देनोभयोर्व्यवहार इति ज्ञेयम् । अतएवांशतः अत्रोद्धारः । व्यस्ताव्यस्तजपध्यानादि पूर्व्वोक्तमत्राप्यनुसन्धेयम् । अन्त्यं सबिन्दु बीजं मध्यं शक्तिः । तदुक्तम्—
अमुष्य मन्त्रस्य वदान्त्ययुक्तं बीजं सदण्डं नकुलीशपूर्व्वम् ।
शक्तिस्तु साखण्डलकर्णपूर्व्वं सहार्द्धजैर्वा ठकमाननान्तम् ॥ इति ॥

अन्येस्त्वेतन्मध्यमबीजस्य नित्यामन्त्रत्वमप्युक्तम् ।
यदाहुः—नित्या भूत्वा जपेत् कामबीजमिष्टार्थसिद्धये ।
पञ्चकृत्वाद्यबीजेन विन्यसेन्मुखपञ्चके ॥
षड्दीर्घेण षडङ्गानि कृत्वा नित्यां निजेष्टदाम् ।
मदिराम्भोधिमध्यस्थरक्तपङ्कजमध्यगाम् ॥
सुरूपां कुङ्कुमप्रख्यामाकुञ्चितशिरोरुहाम् ।
चतुर्भुजां महादेवीं पाशाङ्कुशधरां शिवाम् ॥
वामेतरकरासक्तकपालापूरितासवाम् ।
वामहस्तसमासक्तकपालासवदायिनीम् ॥
आत्माभेदेन तां ध्यात्वा मन्त्रं लक्षं शनैर्जपेत् ।

मान्मथं त्रिपुरादेवि विद्महे पदमीरयेत् ।
उक्त्वा कामेश्वरि पदं प्रवदेद्धीमही ततः ॥ ७८

तदन्ते प्रवदेद् भूयस्तन्नः क्लिन्ने प्रचोदयात् ।
गायत्र्येषा समाख्याता त्रैपुरी सर्व्वसिद्धिदा ॥ ७९

स्तुत्याऽनया त्वां त्रिपुरे स्तोष्येऽभीष्टफलाप्तये ।
यया व्रजन्ति तां लक्ष्मीं मनुजाः सुरपूजिताम् ॥ ८०

ब्रह्मादयस्तुतिशतैरपि सूक्ष्मरूपां
जानन्ति नैव जगदादिमनादिमूर्त्तिम् ।
तस्माद्वयं कुचनतां नवकुङ्कुमाभां
स्थूलां स्तुमः सकलवाङ्मयमातृभूताम् ॥ ८१

सद्यःसमुद्यतसहस्रदिवाकराभां
विद्याक्षसूत्रवरदाभयचिह्नहस्ताम् ।
नेत्रोत्पलैस्त्रिभिरलङ्कृतपद्मवक्त्रां
त्वां तारहाररुचिरां त्रिपुरे भजामः ॥ ८२

मधूकपुष्पैर्जुहुयाद्दशांशं मन्त्रसिद्धये ॥
नित्यक्लिन्नोक्तमार्गेण पूजां कुर्य्यादतन्द्रितः ।
राजानं राजपत्नीं च वशीकर्त्तुं य इच्छति ॥
स तस्योरः समारुह्य मनसा तन्मयो जपेत् ।
यन्नामसहितं कृत्वा नित्यां विद्यां जपेन्नरः ॥
तामाकर्षयते नित्यं वशीकुर्य्याच्च भूपतिम् ।
अनया मातृकां देवीं ग्रथित्वा नियुतं जपेत् ॥
त्रैलोक्यमखिलं तस्य वशे तिष्ठति दासवत् ।
न्यस्तमध्याङ्गुलीं बद्ध्वा क्षोभिणीं नाम पुष्कलाम् ॥
शय्यागतः स्मरेन्नित्यमिष्टामाकर्षकृज्जपेत् ॥ इति ।

क्षोभिणी मुष्टिः ॥ ७६॥७७ ॥

गायत्रीमुद्धरति मान्मथमिति । प्रसिद्धं मान्मथम् । अन्यत् स्वरूपम् ॥७८॥७९॥

त्रिपुरास्तुतिमारभते स्तुत्येति । यया स्तुत्या ॥ ८०॥८१ ॥

तार उज्ज्वलो यो हारस्तेन रुचिराम् । मुक्ता शुद्धौ च तारः स्यादित्यमरः ॥८२॥

सिन्दूरपुञ्जरुचिरं कुचभारनम्रं
जन्मान्तरेषु कृतपुण्यफलैकगम्यम् ।
अन्योन्यभेदकलहाकुलमानभेदै-
र्जानन्ति किं जडधियस्तव रूपमम्ब ॥ ८३
स्थूलां वदन्ति मुनयः श्रुतयो गृणन्ति
सूक्ष्मां वदन्ति वचसामधिवासमन्ये ।
त्वां मूलमाहुरपरे जगतां भवानि
मन्यामहे वयमपारकृपाम्बुराशिम् ॥ ८४
चन्द्रावतंसकलितां शरदिन्दुशुभ्रां
पञ्चाशदक्षरमयीं हृदि भावयन्ति ।
त्वां पुस्तकं जपवटीमसृताढ्यकुम्भं
व्याख्यां च हस्तकमलैर्दधतीं त्रिनेत्राम् ॥ ८५
शम्भुस्त्वमद्रितनयाकलितार्द्धभागो
विष्णुस्त्वमम्ब कमलापरिबद्धदेहः ।
पद्मोद्भवस्त्वमसि वागधिवासभूमि-
स्तेषां क्रियाश्च जगति त्रिपुरे त्वमेव ॥ ८६
आश्रित्य वाग्भवभवांश्चतुरः परादीन्
भावान् पदेषु विहितार्थसुदीरयन्तीम् ।
कण्ठादिभिश्च करणैः परदेवतां त्वां
संविन्मयीं हृदि कदापि न विस्मरामि ॥ ८७

अन्योन्यं परस्परं यो भेदकलहस्तेनाकुलानि यानि मानानि प्रमाणानि तद्भेदैस्तद्विशेषैः ॥ ८३॥८४॥८५॥८६ ॥

वाग्भवबीजेनाकारसाम्यात् त्रिकोणमाधारमण्डलमुच्यते। तत्र भवान् तदुत्पन्नान्। तत्र यद्यपि परायाः एवोत्पत्तिस्तथापि अन्यासामपि तत्स्थूलरूपत्वात्तथोक्तिः। यद्वा वाग्भवं कुण्डलिनी तद्भवांस्तदुत्पन्नान्।

"शक्तिः कुण्डलिनीति या निगदिता आईमसंज्ञा" इत्युक्तेः।

एवम्भूतांश्चतुरः परादीन् परापश्यन्तीमध्यमावैखरीरूपान् भावान्। पदेषु स्थानेषु आधारनाभिकण्ठमुखेषु क्रमादाश्रित्य कण्ठादिभिः करणैर्विहितार्थ-

आकुंच्य वायुमवजित्य च वैरिषट्क-
मालोक्य निश्चलधिया निजनासिकाग्रम् ।
ध्यायन्ति मूर्ध्नि कलितेन्दुकलावतंसं
त्वद्रूपमम्ब कृतिनस्तरुणार्कबिम्बम् ॥ ८८

त्वं प्राप्य मन्मथरिपोर्वपुरर्द्धभागं
सृष्टिं करोषि जगतामिति वेदवादः ।
सत्यं तदद्रितनये जगदेकमात-
र्नोचेदशेषजगतः स्थितिरेव न स्यात् ॥ ८९

पूजां विधाय कुसुमैः सुरपादपानां
पीठे तवाम्ब कनकाचलगह्वरेषु ।
गायन्ति सिद्धवनिताः सह किन्नरीभि-
रास्वादितासवरसारुणनेत्रपद्माः ॥ ९०

विद्युद्विलासवपुषः श्रियमावहन्तीं
यान्तीं स्ववासभवनाच्छिवराजधानीम् ।
सौषुम्णमार्गकमलानि विकाशयन्तीं
देवीं भजे हृदि परामृतसिक्तगात्रीम् ॥ ९१

आनन्दजन्मभवनं भवनं श्रुतीनां
चैतन्यमात्रतनुमम्ब समाश्रयामि ।
ब्रह्मेशविष्णुभिरभिष्टुतपादपद्मां
सौभाग्यजन्मवसतिं त्रिपुरे यथावत् ॥ ९२

मौक्तिताग्रम् उदीरयन्तीम् ॥ ८७ ॥

वायुं प्राणापानरूपम् । वैरिषट्कं कामक्रोधलोभमोहमदमत्सररूपम् ॥८८॥

मन्मथरिपोः पुरुषस्य ब्रह्मणो वाऽर्द्धभागं सन्निधिम् । तत् सत्यं वेदवादत्वात् । विपक्षे प्रतिकूलं तर्कमाह नोचेदिति । त्वदधिष्ठानाभावादिति भावः ॥ ८९ ॥

स्ववासभवनात् मूलाधारात् । शिवराजधानीं सहस्रदलकमलम् । सुषुम्णायां भवं सौषुम्णं तदेव मार्गं येषां तानि । क्वचित् सौषुम्णसद्मकमलानीति पाठः । कमलान्याधारादीनि सहस्रान्तानि ॥ ९०॥९१ ॥

आनन्दजन्मभवनं श्रुतीनां भवनमिति व्यस्तं रूपकद्वयम् ॥ ९२ ॥

शब्दार्थभावि भुवनं सृजतीन्दुरूपा
या तद्बिभर्ति पुनरर्कतनुः स्वशक्त्या ।
वह्न्यात्मिका हरति तत् सकलं युगान्ते
तां शारदां मनसि जातु न विस्मरामि ॥ ९३

नारायणीति नरकार्णवतारिणीति
गौरीति खेदशमनीति सरस्वतीति ।
ज्ञानप्रदेति नयनत्रयभूषितेति
त्वामद्रिराजतनये विबुधा वदन्ति ॥ ९४

ये स्तुवन्ति जगन्मातः श्लोकैर्द्वादशभिः क्रमात् ।
त्वामनुप्राप्य वाक्सिद्धिं प्राप्नुयुस्ते परां गतिम् ॥ ९५

वाङ्मायाकमलास्तारं नमोऽन्ते भगवत्यथ ।
श्रीमातङ्गीश्वरि वदेत् सर्व्वजनमनोहरि ॥ ९६

सर्व्वादि मुखराज्यन्ते सर्व्वादिमुखरञ्जिनि ।
सर्व्वराजवशं पश्चात् करि सर्व्वपदं वदेत् ॥ ९७

स्त्रीपुरुषवशं ब्रह्मा नेत्रमभ्यासनं पुनः ।
सर्व्वदुष्टमृगवशङ्करि सर्व्वभृगुस्त्रव ॥ ९८

शब्दार्थयोर्भावः सत्ता यत्र तत् । शारं कर्म्मफलं द्यति खण्डयतीति शारदा चिच्छक्तिः ॥ ९३॥९४ ॥

द्वादशभिरिति सद्य इत्यादिभिः विस्मरामीत्यन्तैः । आद्यपद्यद्वयस्य मुखबन्धरूपत्वाच्छेषयोरपि स्वरूपफलनिर्देशात् । अथच द्वादशभिरिति पदेन कोशभेदात् द्युमणिमालानामकः प्रबन्ध उक्तः । तल्लक्षणमुक्तं भामहेन—

अथ द्युमणिमाला स्यात् पद्यैर्द्वादशभिः समैः ।
प्रत्येकं नायकोत्कर्षप्रकाशनपरायणैः ॥
मुखबन्धे श्लोकयुग्मं तथा शेषे द्वयं मतम् ।
कृता द्युमणिमालेयं कीर्त्तिवृद्धिकरी नृणाम् ॥ इति ॥ ९५ ॥

राजमातङ्गिनीमन्त्रमुद्धरति वागिति । वाक् वाग्भवम् माया शक्तिबीजम् । कमला श्रीबीजम् तारः प्रणवः । नमोऽन्ते नम इत्यस्यान्ते । ब्रह्मा कः । नेत्रमिकारः अभ्यासनं तेन रि । भृगुः सः स्त्रव स्वरूपम् । रविर्मकारः

शाङ्करि स्यात् सर्व्वलोकममुकं शिवयुग्भवि: ।
वशमानय जायाग्नेरष्टाशीत्यक्षरो मनु: ॥ ९९

न्यासान्मन्त्री तनौ कुर्य्याद्वक्ष्यमाणान् यथाक्रमम् ।
शिरो ललाटभ्रूमध्ये तालुकण्ठगलोरसि ॥ १००

अनाहते भुजद्वन्द्वे जठरे नाभिमण्डले ।
स्वाधिष्ठाने गुह्यदेशे पादयोर्दक्षिणान्ययो: ॥ १०१

मूलाधारे गुदे न्यस्येत् पदान्यष्टादश क्रमात् ।
गुणैकद्विचतु:षड्भिर्वसुषट्पर्व्वताष्टभि: ॥ १०२

दशपङ्क्त्यष्टवेदाग्निचन्द्रयुग्मगुणाक्षिभि: ।
पदक्लृप्तिरियं प्रोक्ता मन्त्रवर्णैर्यथाक्रमम् ॥ १०३

रत्याद्या मूलहृदयभ्रूमध्येषु विचक्षण: ।
वाक्शक्तिलक्ष्मीबीजाद्या मातङ्ग्यन्ता: प्रविन्यसेत् ॥ १०४

शिरोवदनहृद्गुह्यपादेषु विधिवन् न्यसेत् ।
हृल्लेखां गगनां रक्तां भूयो मन्त्री करालिकाम् ॥ १०५

महोच्छुष्मां स्वनामादिवर्णबीजपुर:सरा: ।
मातङ्ग्यन्ता: षडङ्गानि तत: कुर्व्वीत साधक: ॥ १०६

शिवयुगेकारयुक्त: तेन मे । दक्षिणामूर्त्ति: ऋषि: गायत्रीच्छन्द: माया बीजं स्वाहा शक्ति: ॥ ९६॥९७॥९८॥९९ ॥

कण्ठस्तन्मणिर्गलस्तदधोभाग: । अनाहते हृदये । गुह्यदेशे लिङ्गे । दक्षिणान्ययोरिति सार्व्वत्रिकोऽपि क्रम: क्वचिद्वक्तव्य इत्यत्रोक्त: ॥१००॥१०१॥१०२॥

पदविभागमाह गुणेति । गुणास्त्रय: पर्वता: सप्त पङ्क्तिर्दश वेदाश्चत्वार: अग्नयस्त्रय: चन्द्र एक: अक्षि द्वयम् ॥ १०२ ॥ १०३ ॥

रत्याद्या इत्यादिशब्देन प्रीतिमनोभवे । बीजाद्या इति समुच्चितबीजाद्या इत्युक्तम् । मातङ्ग्यन्ता इति प्रत्येकम् । ऐं ह्रीं श्रीं रत्यै मातङ्ग्यै नम इत्यादि प्रयोग: । एवमग्रेऽपि ॥ १०४ ॥

विधिवदिति । पञ्चमुखेष्वपि न्यसेदित्युक्तम् । स्वनाम्नां ये आदिवर्णा: ते एव बीजानि । तत्पुर:सरा: तदाद्या इति पूर्व्वोक्तबीजापवाद: । मातङ्ग्यन्ता

वर्णैश्चतुर्भिर्विंशत्या हृत् त्रयोदशभि: शिर: ।
शिखाऽष्टादशभि: प्रोक्ता वर्म्म तावद्भिरक्षरै: ॥ १०७

स्यात् त्रयोदशभिर्नेत्रं द्वाभ्यामस्त्रं समीरितम् ।
विभक्तैर्मूलमन्त्रार्णैर्वाग्न्यासमथाचरेत् ॥ १०८

मूर्द्धपादास्यगुह्येषु हृदम्भोजे प्रविन्यसेत् ।
द्राविणीं क्षोभिणीं भूयो वद्धनीं मोहनीं पुन: ॥ १०९

आकर्षणीं स्वनामादिबीजाद्या शुभलक्षणा: ।
मातङ्ग्यन्तास्ततो न्यस्येन्मन्मथान् वदनांसयो: ॥ ११०

पार्श्वकक्ष्योर्नाभिदेशे कटिपार्श्वांसके पुन: ।
बीजत्रयादिकान्मन्त्री मन्मथं मकरध्वजम् ॥ १११

मदनं पुष्पधन्वानं पञ्चमं कुसुमायुधम् ।
षष्ठं कन्दर्पनामानं मनोभवरतिप्रियौ ॥ ११२

मातङ्ग्यन्तास्ततो न्यस्येत् स्थानेष्वेतेषु मन्त्रवित् ।
प्रथमाऽनङ्गकुसुमा भूयोऽन्याऽनङ्गमेखला ॥ ११३

अनङ्गमदना तद्वदनङ्गमदनातुरा ।
अनङ्गमदनवेगा भूयश्चाऽनङ्गसंभवा ॥ ११४

सप्तम्यनङ्गभुवनपालिनी स्यादथाऽष्टमी ।
अनङ्गशशिरेखाऽन्या मातङ्ग्यन्ता: समीरिता: ॥ ११५

इत्यस्य पश्चात्तनेन सम्बन्ध: । तत: साधक: विभक्तैर्मूलमन्त्रार्णै: षडङ्गानि कुर्वीतेति सम्बन्ध: । साधक इत्यनेन ज्ञानैश्वर्यादियोग: सूचित: ।

विभागमाह वर्णैरिति ॥ १०५॥१०६॥१०७॥१०८ ॥

स्वनामेति । स्वनामादौ बीजाद्या: पूर्वोक्तद्रामादिबीजादिका: मातङ्ग्यन्ता न्यसेदिति सम्बन्ध: । शुभलक्षणा इत्यन्वर्थाभिधाना इत्यर्थ: ॥ १०९॥११० ॥

ततो मातङ्ग्यन्तान् मन्मथान् न्यसेदिति सम्बन्ध: । वदनांसयोरिति वामांसादारभ्य न्यास: । बीजत्रयादिकानिति मन्त्राद्यबीजत्रयाद्यान् ॥११०॥१११॥११२॥

समीरिता एता मातङ्ग्यन्ता: । ततो एतेषु पूर्वोक्तस्थानेषु न्यसेदिति सम्बन्ध: । ॥ ११३॥११४॥११५ ॥

विन्यस्तव्यास्तनौ मूलेऽधिष्ठाने मणिपूरके ।
हृत्कण्ठाख्ये भ्रुवोर्मध्ये मस्तके मन्त्रिणा ततः ॥ ११६

आद्ये लक्ष्मीसरस्वत्यौ रतिः प्रीतिश्च कान्तिका ।
शान्तिः पुष्टिस्तथा तुष्टिर्मातङ्गीपदशेखराः ॥ ११७

मूलमन्त्रं प्रविन्यस्येन्निजमूर्द्धनि मन्त्रवित् ।
आधारदेशेऽधिष्ठाने नाभौ पश्चादनाहते ॥ ११८

कण्ठे वक्त्रे भ्रुवोर्मध्ये मस्तके विन्यसेत् क्रमात् ।
ब्राह्म्याद्याः पूर्व्वमुद्दिष्टा मातङ्गीपदपश्चिमाः ॥ ११९

एषु स्थानेषु विन्यस्येदसिताङ्गादिभैरवान् ।
मातङ्ग्यन्तान् न्यसेन्मन्त्री मूलमन्त्रं स्वमूर्द्धनि ॥ १२०

आधारदेशेऽधिष्ठाने नाभौ पश्चादनाहते ।
कण्ठदेशे भ्रुवोर्मध्ये बिन्दौ भूयः कलापदे ॥ १२१

निरोधिकायामर्द्धेन्दौ नादनादान्तयोः पुनः ।
उन्मन्यां विष्णुवक्त्रे च ध्रुवमण्डलके शिवे ॥ १२२

मातङ्ग्यन्ताः प्रविन्यस्येद्वामां ज्येष्ठामतः परम् ।
रौद्रीं प्रशान्तिं श्रद्धाख्यां पुनर्माहेश्वरीमथ ॥ १२३

क्रियाशक्तिं सुलक्ष्मीं च सृष्टिसंज्ञां च मोहिनीम् ।
प्रमथां श्वासिनीं विद्युल्लतां चिच्छक्तिमप्यथ ॥ १२४

मूले मूलाधारे। अधिष्ठाने लिङ्गमूले। मणिपूरके नाभौ। मातङ्गीपदशेखरा मातङ्ग्यन्ता एता मन्त्रिणा तनौ विन्यस्तव्या इति सम्बन्धः। पूर्व्वमिति षष्ठे। मातङ्गीपदं पश्चिममन्तिमं यासां ताः ॥ ११६॥११७॥११८॥११९ ॥

एषु पूर्व्वोक्तस्थानेषु मातङ्ग्यन्तान् असिताङ्गादिभैरवान् नवमोक्तान् विन्यसेदिति सम्बन्धः ॥ १२० ॥

भ्रुवोर्मध्य इत्यारभ्य शिवान्तमूर्द्धोर्द्धादिस्थानानि ज्ञातव्यानि ॥ १२१॥१२२ ॥

मातङ्ग्यन्ता इमाः प्रविन्यसेदिति सम्बन्धः। क्रियाशक्तिमित्येका सृष्टिसंज्ञामित्येका प्रमथामित्येका सुन्दरानन्दामित्येका ॥ १२३॥१२४॥१२५ ॥

ततश्च सुन्दरानन्दां नन्दबुद्धिमिमाः क्रमात् ।
शिरोभालहृदाधारेष्वेता बीजत्रयादिकाः ॥ १२५

मातङ्ग्यन्ताः प्रविन्यस्येद्यथावद्देशिकोत्तमः ।
मातङ्गीं महदाद्यां तां महालक्ष्मीपदादिकाम् ॥ १२६

सिद्धलक्ष्मीपदाद्यां तां मूलमाधारमण्डले ।
न्यस्य तेनैव कुर्व्वीत व्यापकं देशिकोत्तमः ।
एवं न्यस्तशरीरोऽसौ चिन्तयेदात्मदेवताम् ॥ १२७

ध्यायेयं रत्नपीठे शुककलपठितं शृण्वतीं श्यामलाङ्गीं
न्यस्तैकाङ्घ्रिं सरोजे शशिशकलधरां वल्लकीं वादयन्तीम् ।
कह्लाराबद्धमालां नियमितविलसच्चूलिकां रक्तवस्त्रां
मातङ्गीं शङ्खपत्रां मधुमदविवशां चित्रकोद्भासिभालाम् ॥ १२८

अयुतं प्रजपेन्मन्त्री तद्दशांशं मधूकजैः ।
पुष्पैस्त्रिमधुरोपेतैर्जुहुयान्मन्त्रसिद्धये ॥ १२९

त्रिकोणकर्णिकं पद्मम् अष्टपत्रं प्रकल्पयेत् ।
अष्टपत्रावृतं बाह्ये वृत्तं षोडशभिर्दलैः ॥ १३०

चतुरस्रसमायुक्तं कान्त्या दृष्टिमनोहरम् ।
एतस्मिन् पूजयेत् पीठे नव शक्तीः क्रमादिमाः ॥ १३१

एता वक्ष्यमाणाः । यथावद्देशिकोत्तम इत्यनेन बीजत्रयादिकान् मन्त्रीत्यादौ एता बीजत्रयादिका इत्यन्ते मध्ये च मन्त्रविन् मन्त्रिणा मन्त्रविन् मन्त्रीति चोक्तत्वात् मध्ये या देवतास्तासामपि बीजत्रयादित्वं ज्ञेयमित्युक्तम् ।

आदिशब्दार्थमाह मातङ्गीमिति । महदाद्यां तां महामातङ्गीम् । तेनैवेति मूलेन ॥ १२५॥१२६॥१२७ ॥

ध्यायेयमिति । चूलिका केशबन्धः । शङ्खपत्रं शङ्खताटङ्कम् । चित्रकं तिलकम् । तथा च त्रिकाण्डशाम् । "तमालपत्रतिलकचित्रकाणि विशेषकम्" इति । अत्र ध्यानान्तरं वीणायोनिमुद्रे दर्शयेत् ॥ १२८॥१२९ ॥

त्रिकोणकर्णिकमिति योनिकर्णिकम् । पूर्व्ववदिति यथान्यस्ता वामकोणादि । एवमग्रेऽपि यथान्यासमेव पूजा । सा यथापूर्व्वमिति तुर्य्यौक्त-

विभूतिरुन्नतिः कान्तिः सृष्टिः कीर्त्तिश्च सन्नतिः ।
व्युष्टिरुत्कृष्टिरृद्धिश्च मातङ्गीपद्मपश्चिमाः ॥ १३२

सर्व्वान्ते शक्तिकमलासनाय नम इत्यथ ।
वाक्शक्तिलक्ष्मीबीजाद्यो मनुरासनसंज्ञकः ॥ १३३

मूलेन मूर्त्तिं सङ्कल्प्य तस्यामावाह्य देवताम् ।
अर्च्चयेद्विधिनाऽनेन वक्ष्यमाणेन मन्त्रवित् ॥ १३४

रत्याद्यास्त्रिषु कोणेषु पूजयेत् पूर्व्ववत् सुधीः ।
हृल्लेखाद्याः पञ्च पूज्या मध्ये दिक्षु च मन्त्रिणा ॥ १३५

पाशाङ्कुशाभयाभीष्टधारिण्यो भूतसप्रभाः ।
अङ्गानि पूजयेत्पश्चाद्यथापूर्व्वं विधानवित् ॥ १३६

बाणानभ्यर्च्चयेद्दिक्षु पञ्चमं पुरतो यजेत् ।
दलमध्येषु सम्पूज्या अनङ्गकुसुमादयः ॥ १३७

पाशाङ्कुशाभयाभीष्टधारिण्योऽरुणविग्रहाः ।
पत्राग्रेषु पुनः पूज्या लक्ष्म्याद्या वल्लकीकराः ॥ १३८

बहिरष्टदलेष्वर्च्या मन्मथाद्या मदोद्धताः ।
अपराङ्गनिषङ्गाढ्याः पुष्पास्त्रेक्षुधनुर्धराः ॥ १३९

पत्रस्था मातरः पूज्या ब्राह्म्याद्याः प्रोक्तलक्षणाः ।
तदग्रेष्वर्च्चयेद्विद्वानसिताङ्गादिभैरवान् ॥ १४०

पुनः षोडशपत्रेषु पूज्याः षोडश शक्तयः ।
वामाद्याः कलवीणाभिर्गायन्त्यः श्यामविग्रहाः ॥ १४१

चतुरस्रचतुर्दिक्षु चतस्रः पूजयेत् पुनः ।
मातङ्ग्याद्या मदोन्मत्ता वीणाललितमाणयः ॥ १४२

स्थानेषु । विधानविदिति कर्णिकायाम् । दिक्ष्विति दिक्केसरेषु । पुनरनन्तरम् । वल्लकी वीणा ॥ १३०—१३८ ॥

बहिरष्टदलेषु दलमूलेषु । अपराङ्गे पृष्ठभागे । निषङ्गस्तूणीरः तेनाढ्याः । पुष्पास्त्रं पुष्पबाणः । प्रोक्तलक्षणाः षष्ठपटलोक्तध्यानाः ॥ १३८—१४२ ॥

आग्नेयकोणे विघ्नेशं दुर्गां नैऋत्ये यजेत् ।
वायव्ये बटुकं पश्चादैशान्ये क्षेत्रपं यजेत् ॥ १४३
लोकपाला बहिः पूज्या वज्राद्यैरायुधैः सह ।
मन्त्रेऽस्मिन् साधिते मन्त्री साधयेदिष्टमात्मनः ॥ १४४
मल्लिकाजातिपुन्नागैर्होमाद्वाग्मी भवेत् ।
फलैर्बिल्वसमुद्भूतैस्तत्फलैर्वा हुताद्भवेत् ॥ १४५
राजपुत्रस्य राज्याप्तिः पद्मैः श्रियमाप्नुयात् ।
उत्पलैर्वशयेद्विश्वं लक्ष्मीपुष्पैस्तथा नरः ॥ १४६
बन्धूकपुष्पैर्बकुलैर्जवोत्थैः किंशुकोद्भवैः ।
वशाय जुहुयान्मन्त्री मधुना सर्वसिद्धये ॥ १४७
लवणैर्मधुरोपेतैर्हुत्वा कर्षति सुन्दरीम् ।
वंजुलस्य समिद्धोमो वृष्टिं वितनुतेऽचिरात् ॥ १४८
क्षीराक्तैरमृताखण्डैर्होमो नाशयति ज्वरम् ।
दूर्व्वाभिरायुराप्नोति जहत्यैर्वैश्यमाप्नुयात् ॥ १४९
अन्नवानन्नहोमेन तण्डुलैर्धनवान् भवेत् ।
सर्व्वं त्रिमधुरोपेतं होमद्रव्यमुदाहृतम् ॥ १५०
नन्द्यावर्त्तभवैः पुष्पैर्होमो वाक्सिद्धिदायकः ।
निम्बप्रसूनैर्जुहुयादीप्सितां श्रियमश्नुते ।
पलाशकुसुमैर्होमात्तेजस्वी जायते नरः ॥ १५१

आग्नेयकोण इति । इयं पूजा सर्व्वशक्तिमन्त्रसाधारणीति ज्ञेयम् । अत एव सर्व्वशक्तिमन्त्राणामन्ते उक्ता ॥ १४३॥१४४ ॥

मल्लिकेति त्रितये पुष्पैरिति ज्ञेयम् । फलैरित्यग्रे वक्ष्यमाणत्वात् ॥१४५॥१४६॥

बन्धूकपुष्पैरिति । पुष्पपदोपादानात् सान्निध्यात् बकुलादित्रयमपि पुष्पम् कदम्बैरित्यपि पुष्पैः । सर्व्वमिति । अन्यग्रन्थानुरूपं पूर्व्वोक्तमपि
॥ १४७॥१४८॥१४९॥१५०॥१५१ ॥

चन्दनागरुकर्पूररोचनाकुङ्कुमादिभिः ।
वश्याय जुहुयान्मन्त्री वशयेदखिलं जगत् ॥ १५२
एतानि कृत्वा तिलकं कुर्य्याल्लोकप्रियो भवेत् ।
निर्गुण्डीमूलहोमेन निगडान्मुच्यते नरः ॥ १५३
निम्बतैलान्वितैर्लोणैर्होमः शत्रुविनाशनः ।
हरिद्राचूर्णसंमिश्रैर्लवणैः स्तम्भयेत्परान् ॥ १५४
रसवद्भिः फलैः पत्रैः पुष्पैः परिमलान्वितैः ।
हुत्वा सम्यगवाप्नोति साधकः सर्व्वमीप्सितम् ॥ १५५
देवतां जगतामाद्यां मातङ्गीमिष्टदायिनीम् ।
अवाप्तुमिष्टतां वाचं भूषयेद्रत्नमालया ॥ १५६

आराध्य मातश्चरणाम्बुजं ते
ब्रह्मादयो विस्तृतकीर्त्तिमापुः ।
अन्ये परं वाग्विभवं मुनीन्द्राः
परां श्रियं भक्तिभरेण चान्ये ॥ १५७

चन्दनेति यक्षिगन्धाष्टकम् । तेन आदिशब्देन जटामांसीकचूररक्तचन्दनानि । वशयेदिति । अष्टद्रव्यहोमसमुदायफलम् । एतानीति कर्पूरकपित्थौराणि समभागानीति पूर्वमन्त्रप्रयोगोक्तभागक्रमानीत्यर्थः । तिलकमिति । कन्यया क्षिमोदकेन कृष्णचतुर्दश्यां निशि पिष्टेन एतन्मन्त्रजप्तेन कृतम् ॥ १५२॥१५३ ॥

निम्बतैलान्वितैरिति । तत्तैलाकृष्टिप्रकारो यथा—

बीजानि जलपिष्टानि कांस्यपात्रे खरातपे ।
स्थापयेत्तस्य तत्तैलं निःसरत्येव नाऽन्यथा ॥ इति ॥

परान् शत्रून् ॥ १५४॥१५५ ॥

मातङ्गीस्तुतिमारभते देवतामिति । रत्नमालेति प्रबन्धनाम । तद्योगात् स्तुतिनामापि । तल्लक्षणमुक्तं भामहेन—

नेष्टप्रसिद्धनामाङ्कं श्लोकयुग्मं शुभावहम् ।
कुर्य्यादाद्यन्तयोस्तस्य शिखाबन्धं समाधिना ॥
सुभङ्गिः शोभना सा स्यात् रत्नमाला नवाधिका ।
मालायां नवरत्नादौ रचितायामिति क्रमात् ॥

नमामि देवीं नवचन्द्रमौले-
र्मातङ्गिनीं चन्द्रकलावतंसाम् ।
आम्नायवाग्भिः प्रतिपादितार्थं
प्रबोधयन्तीं शुकमादरेण ॥ १५८

विनम्रदेवासुरमौलिरत्नै-
र्नीराजितं ते चरणारविन्दम् ।
भजन्ति ये देवि महीपतीनां
व्रजन्ति ते सम्पदमादरेण ॥ १५९

मातङ्गलीलागमने भवत्याः
शिञ्जानमञ्जीरमिषाद्भजन्ते ।
मातस्त्वदीयं चरणारविन्द-
मकृत्रिमाणां वचसां निगुम्फाः ॥ १६०

पदात्पदं शिञ्जितनूपुराभ्यां
कृतार्थयन्ती पदवीं पदाभ्याम् ।
आस्फालयन्ती कलवल्लकीं तां
मातङ्गिनी मद्धृदयं धिनोतु ॥ १६१

नीलांशुकाबद्धनितम्बबिम्बां
तालीदलेनाऽर्पितकर्णभूषाम् ।
माध्वीमदाघूर्णितनेत्रपद्मां
घनस्तनीं शम्भुवधूं नमामि ॥ १६२

भवन्त्येकादश श्लोकाः पण्डितप्रमुदाकराः ॥ इति ॥ १५६ ॥

नवचन्द्रमौलेर्देवीं पट्टराज्ञीमिति सम्बन्धः ॥ १५७॥१५८॥१५९ ॥

अकृत्रिमाणां वचसां निगुम्फा वेदाः ॥ १६० ॥

पदात्पदं पदेपदे इत्यर्थः । कृतार्थयन्ती स्वगमनेनेति शेषः । धिनोतु प्रीणयतु ॥ १६१॥१६२ ॥

तड़िल्लताकान्तमनर्घ्यभूषं
चिरेण लक्ष्यं नवरोमराज्या ।
स्मरामि भक्त्या जगतामधीशि
वलित्रयाङ्कं तव मध्यबिम्बम् ॥ १६३

नीलोत्पलानां श्रियमाहरन्तीं
कान्त्या कटाक्षैः कमलाकराणाम् ।
कदम्बमालाञ्चितकेशपाशां
मातङ्गकन्यां हृदि भावयामः ॥ १६४

ध्यायेयमारक्तकपोलकान्तं
बिम्बाधरन्यस्तललामरम्यम् ।
आलोलनीलालकमायताक्षं
मन्दस्मितं ते वदनं महेशि ॥ १६५

स्तुत्याऽनया शङ्करधर्म्मपत्नीं
मातङ्गिनीं वागधिदेवतां ताम् ।
स्तुवन्ति ये भक्तियुता मनुष्याः
परां श्रियं नित्यमुपाश्रयन्ति ॥ १६६

इति श्रीशारदातिलके द्वादशः पटलः ।

कदाचिल्लक्ष्यं कदाचिदलक्ष्यमिति तडिल्लताकान्तम् । अनर्घ्यभूषं [अलब्धभूषं] निश्चित्य वपुषोऽकरणात् स्वच्छेत् शरीरस्थितिः कथमित्याह चिरेणामुष्यियं न प्रत्यक्षदृश्यमिति भावः ॥ १६३ ॥

कान्त्या देहकान्त्या नीलोत्पलानां श्रियमाहरन्तीं कटाक्षैः कमलाकराणां श्रियमाहरन्तीमिति सम्बन्धः । मातङ्गकन्यामिति । मातङ्गपुत्रीरूपामित्यर्थः ॥१६४॥

बिम्बाधर एव न्यस्तं ललामं भूषाविशेषः तेन रम्यम् ॥ १६५॥१६६ ॥

इति श्रीशारदातिलकटीकायां सत्सम्प्रदायकृतव्याख्यायां
पदार्थादर्शाभिख्यायां द्वादशः पटलः ।

त्रयोदशः पटलः ।

अथ वक्ष्ये गणपतेर्मन्त्रान् सर्व्वार्थसिद्धिदान् ।
यान् लब्ध्वा मानवा नित्यं साधयन्ति मनोरथान् ॥ १

पञ्चान्तकं शशिधरं बीजं गणपतेर्विदुः ।
गणकः स्यान्मुनिश्छन्दो निचृद्विघ्नोऽस्य देवता ॥ २

षड्दीर्घभाजा बीजेन कुर्य्यादङ्गक्रियां मनोः ॥ ३

"मुख्ये पुष्पाञ्जलिं कृत्वा गणेशाभ्यर्चनं भवेत्" इत्युक्तेः शक्तिमन्त्रानुक्त्वा क्रमप्राप्तान् गणपतिमन्त्रान् वक्तुमुपक्रमते अथेति । सर्व्वार्थसिद्धिदानिति विनियोगोक्तिः ॥१॥

गणपतिबीजमुद्धरति पञ्चान्तकमिति । पञ्चान्तको गकारः शशी बिन्दुस्तद्युतम् तेन गं इति । अथ च शशी विसर्गस्तद्युतः गः इत्यपि भवति । "सर्गः शक्तिर्निशाकरः" इत्युक्तेः । गोपनायैवमुद्धारः । इदं द्वयं उक्तरगाणोक्तम् । पूजाप्रयोगादिकमुभयोः समानम् । केचन औकारयुतमाहुः ।

तदुक्तं प्रयोगसारे—बीजमिन्दुमदौयुक्तं कत्ततीयं तथैव च । इति ।

नारायणीये तु—खान्तं सान्तविषं सबिन्दुसकलं बिन्द्वौयुतं केवलम् ।
पञ्चैतानि पृथक् फलं विदधते बीजानि विघ्नेशितुः ॥ इति ॥

आचार्य्यैस्तु प्रणवादिरुक्तः—

चतुर्थो विलोमेन तारादिर्बिन्दुसंयुतः ।
वैघ्नो मन्त्रो ह्रदन्तोऽर्चाविधौ होमे द्विठान्तकः ॥
गणकः स्यादृषिश्छन्दो निचृद्विघ्नोऽस्य देवता ।
बीजेन दीर्घयुक्तेन दण्डिनाऽङ्गक्रिया मता ॥ इति ॥

गकारो बीजं बिन्दुः शक्तिः । अन्यत्र सर्गः शक्तिः ॥ २ ॥

षडङ्गमाह षडिति । प्रयोगसारे पञ्चाङ्गमप्युक्तम्—

आदौ गणं जयायोक्त्वा स्वाहा हृदयमुच्यते ।
एकदंष्ट्राय सम्भाष्य हुंफड्विद्याच्छिरस्ततः ।
शिखाप्यचलशब्दादिकर्णिनत्यन्ततो नमः ॥
कवचं गजवक्त्राय नमो नम इतीरितम् ।
महोदराय चण्डाय हुंफडित्यस्त्रमिष्यते ॥
एतान्यङ्गानि विन्यस्येत्पञ्चोक्तानि मनीषिभिः ।
सप्तांशुना वा बीजेन षडङ्गान्यपि योजयेत् ॥ इति ॥ ३ ॥

सिन्दूराभं त्रिनेत्रं पृथुतरजठरं हस्तपद्मैर्दधानं
दन्तं पाशाङ्कुशेष्टान्युरुकरविलसद्बीजपूराभिरामम् ।
बालेन्दुद्योतिमौलिं करिपतिवदनं दानपूरार्द्रगण्डं
भोगीन्द्राबद्धभूषं भजत गणपतिं रक्तवस्त्राङ्गरागम् ॥ ४

आयुधध्यानं तु ऊर्ध्वस्थवामदक्षयोरङ्कुशपाशौ । अधःस्थयोः स्वदन्तवरदे ।
सर्वोऽपि गणपतिरेकदन्तो ध्येयः । सदन्तो दक्षिणपार्श्वे । द्वितीयस्य ध्यानं यथा—

ध्यायेत् स्वैक्येन देवं बृहदुदरतनुं तं चतुर्बाहुमेक-
दन्तं पाशाङ्कुशाढ्यं गजमुखमरुणं दन्तभक्ष्ये दधानम् ॥ इति ॥

पुष्करं च दक्षहस्तस्थितभक्ष्योपरि । ओंकारयुक्तबीजे तु ध्यानम्—

रक्ताक्षमालापरशुं च दन्तं भक्ष्यं च दोर्भिः परितो दधानम् ।
हेमाभकान्तिं त्रिदशं गजास्यं लम्बोदरं चैकरदं नमामि ॥ इति ।

अत्रापि पुष्करं पूर्ववज् ज्ञेयम् । इदमेव मायाबीजाद्यं यदा तदा ध्यानम्—

अमृताम्भोधिमध्ये तु वारिजे कुङ्कुमप्रभे ।
ऋतुसंख्यदलोपेते चिन्तयेद्गणनायकम् ॥
पाशाङ्कुशधरं देवं जवाकुसुमसन्निभम् ।
वामपार्श्वगतां देवीमालिङ्गन्तं सुलोचनम् ॥
सुवर्णचषकं शुभ्रं मधुना पूरितं सदा ।
पिबन्तीं वामहस्तेन योगिनीं मदमोहिताम् ॥
रक्तवर्णां महादेवीमालिङ्गन्तीं सुमध्यमाम् ।
बाहुनैकेन विघ्नेशं मत्तं रक्तविलोचनम् ॥
तद्रूपांश्चिन्तयेद्विद्वान् गणान् पूर्वादितः क्रमात् ॥ इति ।

अत्र ध्यानानन्तरमियं गणपतिमुद्रा प्रदर्शनीया—

मुखात्प्रलम्बितं हस्तं कृत्वा संकुचिताङ्गुलिम् ।
मध्या तर्जनिगताग्राङ्गुष्ठं चाधःस्थमध्यमम् ॥
कुर्यान्मुद्रा गणेशस्य प्रोक्तेयं सर्वसिद्धिदा ॥ इति ।

यद्वा—तर्जनीमध्यमासन्धिनिर्गताङ्गुष्ठमुष्टिका ।
अधोमुखी दीर्घरूपा मध्यमा विघ्नमुद्रिका ॥ इति ॥

यद्वा—कुञ्चिताग्रस्य हस्तस्य मूले नासानियोगतः । गणेश्वरी भवेन् मुद्रा । इति ।
इयं सर्वगणपतिमन्त्रसाधारणीति ज्ञेयम् ॥ ४ ॥

वेदलक्षं जपेन्मन्त्रं दशांशं जुहुयात्ततः ।
मोदकैः पृथुकैर्लाजैः सक्तुभिस्त्वेक्षुपर्वभिः ॥ ५
नारिकेलैस्तिलैः शुद्धैः सुपक्वैः कदलीफलैः ।
अष्ट द्रव्याणि विघ्नस्य कथितानि मनीषिभिः ॥ ६
तीव्रादिशक्तिभिर्युक्ते पीठे विघ्नेश्वरं यजेत् ।
तीव्राख्या ज्वालिनी नन्दा भोगदा कामरूपिणी ॥ ७
उग्रा तेजोवती सत्या नवमी विघ्ननाशिनी ।
सर्व्वादिशक्तिकमलासनाय हृदयावधिः ॥ ८
पीठमन्त्रोऽयमेतेन प्रदद्यादासनं विभोः ।
मूलेन मूर्त्तिं सङ्कल्प्य तस्यां विघ्नेश्वरं यजेत् ॥ ९

वेदलक्षं चतुर्लक्षम्। दशांशमिति। तत्र होमोऽष्टभिर्द्रव्यैर्वक्ष्यमाणैः अष्टमष्टमयुतमेकैकेन द्रव्येण होतव्यम्। केचित्तु अष्टद्रव्यमेलनमाहुः। तन्न। आहुतिप्रमाणसन्देहापातात्। मूले च प्रत्येकं पृथक्क्रियान्वयाच्च। विशिष्टस्य द्रव्यान्तरत्वेनाऽष्टद्रव्यहोमकरणासम्भवाच्च। तदुक्तं भट्टाचार्य्यैः—

नैव व्रीहिभिरिष्टं स्याद्यवैर्न च यथाश्रुतैः ।
मिश्रैरिज्येत चेत्। इति।

तथा मिश्राणां विध्यदर्शनादिति च। नन्वेवं त्रिमधुरमेलनमपि न कार्य्यमिति चेत्। नैवम्। "सर्व्वम् त्रिमधुरोपेतं होमद्रव्यमुदाहृतम्" इति वचनात् तन्मेलनस्य पशुपुरोडाशाद्यवदानानाम् उपस्तारप्रत्युपस्ताराज्यमेलनवत् अविरोधात्। तदुक्तं गणेश्वरविमर्शिन्याम्—अष्टद्रव्यैस्त्रिमध्वक्तैर्जुहुयाच्च पृथक् पृथक्। इति। पृथुकैश्चिपिटकैः। शुद्धैरित्यनेनाऽवकरं दूरीकृत्य प्रक्षाल्य शोषितैरित्युक्तम्। एषु मन्त्रेषु गायत्र्या प्रोक्षणादिकं कुर्य्यात्। गायत्री यथा—
एकदंष्ट्राय विद्महे वक्रतुण्डाय धीमहि। तन्नो विघ्नः प्रचोदयात्। इति ॥५॥६॥

तीव्रेति। आसां ध्यानं यथा—

पाशाङ्कुशाञ्जलिकरा नवकुङ्कुमसन्निभाः ।
तीव्राद्याः पूजनीयाः स्युः शक्तयो मणिभूषणाः ॥ इति ॥ ७॥८ ॥

विभोरिति। पीठमन्त्रादौ स्वबीजाद्यत्रमुक्तम्। प्रथमं पूजयेदिति। अत्र प्रथममित्यङ्गाद्यपेक्षया प्राथम्यं यतश्चतुर्थपटले अङ्गादिलोकपालान्तं पूजयेदिति

कर्णिकायां चतुर्दिक्षु प्रथमं पूजयेदिमान् ।
गणाधिपं गणेशानं ततोऽवं गणनायकम् ॥ १०

गणक्रीडं पीतगौररक्तनीलरुचः क्रमात् ।
सर्व्वान्नागेन्द्रभूषाढ्यान् भव्यलक्षितपुष्करान् ॥ ११

यथापूर्व्वं ततोऽभ्यर्च्य केसरेष्वङ्गदेवताः ।
पत्रमध्येषु विधिवद्वक्रतुण्डादिकान् यजेत् ॥ १२

वक्रतुण्डमेकदंष्ट्रं महोदरगजाननौ ।
लम्बोदराख्यं विकटं विघ्नराजमनन्तरम् ॥ १२

धूम्रवर्णं दलाग्रेषु ब्राह्म्याद्याः पूजयेत्ततः ।
लोकपालांस्तदस्त्राणि देवमित्थं समर्च्चयेत् ॥ १३

सिद्धमन्त्रः प्रकुर्वीत प्रयोगान् कल्पचोदितान् ।
तर्पयेत्सलिलैः शुद्धैर्दिनशो गणनायकम् ॥ १४

चतुश्चत्वारिंशदाद्यं चतुःशतमतन्द्रितः ।
प्राप्नुयान्मण्डलादर्वागभीष्टमखिलं नरः ॥ १५

सामान्यत उक्तम् । तदपवादायात्र प्रथममित्युक्तिः । यद्व्याख्यानावसरे अत एव मयोक्तं ग्रन्थकृता इदं वचनं सम्भवाभिप्रायेणोक्तमिति ॥ ९॥१०॥११ ॥

यथापूर्व्वं चतुर्थपटलोक्तरीत्या । विधिवदिति गणपतिबीजादि । इत्थं समर्च्चयेदिति । मन्त्रत्रयस्य पूजा समानैव । तदुक्तमीशानशिवेन—

पद्मान्तकं बिन्दुयुतं सनादं बीजं गणेशस्य वदन्त्यथान्ये ।
अकारविन्द्वन्तमुदीरयन्ति तुल्यस्तयोः स्याद्विधिरेव उक्तः ॥ इति ।

मायाबीजादौ तु षड्दले आमोदादीन् पूजयेदिति विशेषः । तर्पणप्रयोगाश्च सर्व्वमन्त्राणां साधारणा एव । तर्पणे तु सर्व्वेषामयं विशेषः ।

क्रीडन् हैममयोदयाद्रिशिखरे स्थित्वाऽवतीर्णः क्षुधा
सोपानेषु समेत्य रुक्मकलितेष्वन्नादि भक्ष्यं बहु ।
भुक्त्वा प्रीतमना यथा पुरमसौ सम्पूजितो विघ्नराट्
कुर्य्यादित्युषसि स्मृतः स सकलान् कामांस्तथा तर्पितः ॥ इति ॥१२॥१३॥

तर्पयेदिति । गं गणेशं तर्पयामीति प्रयोगः । क्रमाच्चतुःशतमिति ।

नारिकेलैः कृतो होमश्चतुर्थ्यां श्रीप्रदो भवेत् ।
शुक्लपक्षप्रतिपदमारभ्य दिनशः सुधीः ॥ १६
चतुर्थ्यन्तं नारिकेलसक्तुलाजतिलैः क्रमात् ।
चतुःशतं प्रजुहुयाद्वश्याः स्युः सर्वजन्तवः ॥ १७
सतिलैस्तण्डुलैर्होमो लक्ष्मीवश्यप्रदो भवेत् ।
लाजैस्त्रिमधुरोपेतैर्होमैः कन्यां प्रयच्छति ॥ १८
अनेन विधिना कन्या वरमाप्नोति वाञ्छितम् ।
आज्याक्तहविषा होमः साधयेदीप्सितं नृणाम् ॥ १९
दध्ना विलोलितैर्लोणैर्होमो निशि चतुर्दिनम् ।
संवादं कुरुते तद्वश्यं वितनुते सदा ॥ २०
श्वेतार्कभवमूलेन रक्तचन्दनदारुणा ।
कुम्भकेन निम्बेन दन्तिदन्तेन वा कृतम् ॥ २१
विघ्नेश्वरं समभ्यर्च्य शीतांशुग्रहणे जपेत् ।
स्पृष्ट्वा मन्त्री निराहारस्तं शिखायां समुद्वहन् ॥ २२
युद्धेषु व्यवहारादौ विजयश्रियमाप्नुयात् ।
मन्त्रेणाऽनेन संजप्ता रोचना मदसंयुता ॥ २३

प्रतितिथि द्रव्यचतुष्टयेन तावान् होमः ॥ १५॥१६ ॥

वश्या इति । तत्र विशेषः प्रयोगसारनारायणीययोः ।

साध्यं पाशाङ्कुशाभ्यामिह विधिवदुपानीय तस्योपरिस्थो
वश्याकाङ्क्षी जपेत्तं सपदि विधिरयं हन्ति रुष्टस्य रोषम् । इति ॥१७॥

सतिलैरिति । अत्रापि शुक्लप्रतिपदमारभ्य चतुर्थ्यन्तं चतुःशतहोमः ।

लाजैरिति । अत्रापि शुक्लप्रतिपदमारभ्य चतुर्थ्यन्तं चतुःशतहोमः । तत्रैव प्रतिपदमारभ्य सप्तमीपर्यन्तमिति विशेषः । तदुक्तम्—

मधुरत्रयसिक्ताभिर्लाजाभिः सप्तवासरम् । इति ॥ १८ ॥

अनेन विधिनेति । एतादृशेषु स्त्रीणामप्यधिकार इति सूचितम् ॥ १९ ॥

चतुर्दिनमिति । प्रतिपदमारभ्य चतुर्थीपर्यन्तम् । संवादः संवननम् ॥२०॥

जपेदिति । ग्रहणादिमोक्षान्तम् ॥ २१॥२२॥२३ ॥

मदो गजमदः ॥ २३॥२४ ॥

तिलकक्रियया सर्व्वान् वशं नयति मानवान् ।
अनुलोमविलोमस्थबीजे नाम समालिखेत् ॥ २४
नवनीते समभ्यर्च्य सहस्रं प्रजपेन्मनुम् ।
अष्टोत्तरशतं भूयो मूलमन्त्रं प्रजप्य तत् ॥ २५
भक्षयेन्मौनमास्थाय यामिन्यां सप्तवासरम् ।
स वश्यो जायते शीघ्रं साधकस्य न संशयः ॥ २६

अनुलोमेति । बीजयोर्मध्ये साध्यसाधककर्म्मनामानि नवनीते लिखेत् । अनुलोमविलोमेत्यनेन बीजयोः पुटितत्वमात्रमुक्तम् । नवनीत इति नूतने । बीजवेष्टितमित्यपि ज्ञेयम् । तदुक्तमाचार्य्यैः—

नवनीते नवे लिख्यादनुलोमविलोमकम् ।
उदरस्थितसाध्याख्यं तद्बीजं तत्प्रवेष्टितम् । इति ॥

नवनीत इत्युपलक्षणमपूपादेरपि । "कार्य्योऽयं विधिरपूपे च" इति नारायणीये उक्तेः । समभ्यर्च्येति । साध्यगणेशम् । भूयोऽनन्तरम् अष्टोत्तरशतमिति मूलमन्त्रं प्रजप्येत्यत्राऽन्वेति । तन्नवनीतं भक्षयेदिति सम्बन्धः । सप्तवासरमिति । प्रतिपदादि सप्तमीपर्य्यन्तमित्यर्थः । तन्त्रान्तरोक्तं यन्त्रत्रयमुच्यते ।

अष्टारं पद्ममालिख्य कर्णिकोपरि तस्य च ।
गौरीं बिन्दुसमायुक्तां नाम्ना सार्द्धं समालिखेत् ॥
प्रागादिदलमूलेषु मूर्त्तिबीजान्यथालिखेत् ।
कोणपत्रेषु चाग्नीशनिर्ऋत्यनिलसौम्यतः ॥
क्रमादङ्गाद्यवर्णांश्च ततः पत्राग्रकेषु च ।
मातृशक्त्यादिवर्णांश्च ततः पद्मस्य बाह्यतः ॥
स्वदिक्षु लोकपालानामाद्यवर्णानि समालिखेत् ।
बहिः षोडशपत्राढ्यं तत्पत्रेषु स्वरान् लिखेत् ॥
शिष्टं मातृकयाऽऽवेष्ट्य पाशेनैवाऽङ्कुशेन च ।
तस्मिन्नावाह्य देवेशं विघ्नं यन्त्रे समर्चयेत् ॥
क्षौमादिसूत्रे सम्बद्ध गले यो मूर्ध्नि धारयेत् ।
तस्य हस्तगता लक्ष्मीर्वाणी जिह्वागता सदा ॥
मेधा मनोगता कीर्त्तिर्वर्द्धमाना सदा दिशि । इति ।

श्रीशक्तिस्मरभूविघ्नबीजानि प्रथमं वदेत् ।
ङेऽन्तं गणपतिं पश्चाद्वरान्ते वरदं पठेत् ॥ २७
सर्वं सर्वजनं मे वशमानय ठद्वयम् ।
अष्टाविंशत्यक्षरोऽयं ताराद्यो मनुरीरितः ॥ २८

पद्ममित्यष्टदलम् । अष्टारमिति तदुपरि । कर्णिकोपरि कर्णिकामध्ये । गौरी गकारः । मूर्त्तिबीजानीति । चिप्रप्रसादनोक्ताष्टमूर्त्त्याद्यक्षराणि । अङ्गेति पञ्चाङ्गपत्रे पञ्चमं सौम्ये । मातर एव शक्तयस्तासामाद्यर्णान् । स्वदिक्ष्विति स्वस्वदिक्ष्वष्टारे । शिष्टं मातृकया ककारादिकया । तथा—

षट्कोणं प्रविलिख्य तस्य जठरे बिन्द्वाद्यपञ्चान्तकं
नाम्ना भूर्जतरुत्वचि प्रविलिखेद्गोरोचनादूर्वया ।
एकारान्वितकालवर्णमथ युक् दन्तेन गान्तं ततः
शक्राणं शिरसा वहन्नपि विधिवद्वीर्वंश पश्चाद्रसः ॥
माया वायुसखस्य मन्त्रवरमालिख्याऽथ कोणेषु त-
द्बाह्ये पाशमथाङ्कुशं प्रविलिखेद्भूमण्डलं बाह्यतः ।
यन्त्रं गन्धमनोहरैश्च कुसुमैरभ्यर्च्य विघ्नेश्वरं
यो धत्ते शिरसि स्वयं विपुलां लक्ष्मीं लभेत् मानवः ॥ इति ।

मेघोल्काय स्वाहेति मन्त्रः । तथा—

बीजेन रंदहनयुग्मगबीजवीतं
कोणे गमालिख कलावसुकेसरेऽब्जे ।
गायत्रिवर्णदलकेऽप्यथ कादिवीतं
भूबीजयुक्क्षितिगृहेऽखिलदं हि यन्त्रम् ॥ इति ॥ २४॥२५॥२६ ॥

महागणपतिमन्त्रमुद्धरति श्रीति । भूबीजमग्रे वक्ष्यमाणम् । वरदमिति शब्दकर्म्मणि द्वितीया मन्त्रे तु सम्बुद्धिः । सर्व्वजनमिति मन्त्रेऽपि द्वितीयान्तम् । अत्र केचन यकारं कीलकं मन्यमाना गणपतिपदं संबुद्ध्यन्तमाहुः । अन्ये श्रीमहागणपतिपदं संबुद्ध्यन्तं वशंपदद्वित्वमप्याहुः । इदं ग्रन्थकारस्यापि सम्मतमेव । यतो द्वात्रिंशद्भेदगुणितेत्यत्र गणेशितुर्महामन्त्रमित्युक्तत्वात् । अन्ये विघ्नं चतुर्थ्या युतमित्याचार्य्यपद्ये विघ्नशब्दो महागणपतिपदोपलक्षक इत्याहुः । एवमिहापि गणपतिशब्दः । यथागुरूपदेशं च निर्णयः । पद्मपादाचार्य्यैस्तु । "दीक्षितो मन्त्रीत्यनेन चतुर्थीं परित्यज्य संबुद्धिस्वीकारः" इत्युक्तम् । मन्त्रदेव-

गणकः स्यादृषिश्छन्दो गायत्री निचृदन्विता ।
महागणपतिः प्रोक्तो देवता देववन्दिता ॥ २९

षड्बीजस्यस्वबीजेन दीर्घभाजा प्रकल्पयेत् ।
षडङ्गानि मनोरस्य यथाविधि विधानवित् ॥ ३०

नवरत्नमयं द्वीपं स्मरेदिक्षुरसाम्बुधौ ।
तद्वीचिधौतपर्यन्तं मन्दमारुतसेवितम् ॥ ३१

मन्दारपारिजातादि कल्पवृक्षलताकुलम् ।
तदुद्भूतरत्नच्छायाभिररुणीकृतभूतलम् ॥ ३२

उद्यद्दिनकरेन्दुभ्यामुद्भासितदिगन्तरम् ।
तस्य मध्ये पारिजातं नवरत्नमयं स्मरेत् ।

ऋतुभिः सेवितं षड्भिरनिशं प्रीतिवर्द्धनैः ॥ ३३
तस्याऽधस्तान्महापीठे रचिते मातृकाम्बुजे ।
षट्कोणान्तस्त्रिकोणस्थं महागणपतिं स्मरेत् ॥ ३४

प्रकाशिकाकारादिभिरपि संवुद्ध्यन्तस्यैवोद्धृतत्वात्। गं बीजं स्वाहा शक्तिः। तदुक्तम्। षष्ठं बीजं हिठः [बीजान्तजौ] शक्तिरिति ॥ २७॥२८॥२९ ॥

षडङ्गमाह षड्बीजस्येति। यथाविधीति। तत्तज्जातियुतानि शेवषडङ्ग-मुद्राभिरिति च। विधानविदित्यनेनायं प्रयोगः सूचितः। ॐ गां हृत् श्रीं गीं शिरः ह्रीं गूं शिखा क्लीं गैं वर्म ग्लौं गौं नेत्रं गं गः अस्त्रम्। एष पक्षः साम्प्रदायिकः। केचित्तु प्रणवादिबीजपञ्चकमुच्चार्य गामित्यादिप्रयोगेण षडङ्गक्लृप्तिं वदन्ति। अपरे षड्बीजानां प्राक् गामादीन्याहुः ॥ ३० ॥

नवरत्नमयं द्वीपमित्यादेरयमर्थः। पृथिव्यनन्तरमिक्षुसमुद्रं नवरत्नमयं द्वीपं नवरत्नमयं पारिजातमिति न्यसेत्। शेषं समानम्। नवरत्नमयमिति। नवरत्नमय-द्वीपादुत्पत्तेः पारिजातस्यापि नवरत्नमयत्वम्। अन्ये तु माणिक्यमूलं वैडूर्या-ङ्कुरं इन्द्रनीलशाखं प्रवालपल्लवं मरकतच्छदं गोमेदश्रृङ्गं मौक्तिककोरकं वज्रपुष्पं पद्मरागफलमित्याहुः। गणेश्वरविमर्शिन्यामपि—

मणिवज्रप्रवालाख्यफलप्रसवपल्लवैः। इत्यादि ॥ ३१॥३२॥३३ ॥

पीठे रचित इति व्यधिकरणे सप्तम्यौ। षट्कोणान्तः त्रिकोणस्थमिति। अत्राधोमुखं त्रिकोणं ग्राह्यम्। इदं च मातृकापद्मकर्णिकायामिति ज्ञेयम् ॥ ३४ ॥

हस्तीन्द्राननमिन्दुचूडमरुणच्छायं त्रिनेत्रं रसा-
दाश्लिष्टं प्रियया सपद्मकरया स्वाङ्कस्थया सन्ततम् ।
बीजापूरगदाधनुस्त्रिशिखयुक्चक्राब्जपाशोत्पल-
व्रीह्यग्रस्वविषाणरत्नकलशान् हस्तैर्वहन्तं भजे ॥ ३५

गण्डपालीगलद्दानपूरलालसमानसान् ।
द्विरेफान् कर्णतालाभ्यां वारयन्तं मुहुर्मुहुः ॥ ३६

कराग्रधृतमाणिक्यकुम्भवक्त्रविनिःसृतैः ।
रत्नवर्षैः प्रीणयन्तं साधकान्मदविह्वलम् ॥ ३७

माणिक्यमुकुटोपेतं रत्नाभरणभूषितम् ।
ध्यायन्नेवं जपेन्मन्त्री चतुर्लक्षं समाहितः ॥ ३८

हस्तीति । हस्तीन्द्रो गजश्रेष्ठः । सपद्मकरया वामहस्ते पद्मं दक्षेणालिङ्गनम् । धनुरिक्षुधनुः । त्रिशिखं त्रिशूलम् । वामाधस्ताद्दक्षिणाधःपर्यन्तमायुधध्यानम् । कनककलशस्तु शुण्डाग्रे । तदुक्तम्—

वामोर्ध्वादिक्रमेण ।

चक्रप्रासरसालकार्मुकगदासद्बीजपूरद्विज-
व्रीह्यग्रोत्पलपाशपङ्कजकरं शुण्डाग्रजाग्रद्घटम् ॥ इति ॥

महागणपतिस्तवेऽपि वामदक्षयोरूर्ध्वादिक्रमेण ।

चक्राब्जशूलपाशासिचूतपल्लवगुडकलशमञ्जरिकाः
दाडिमरदमणिकुम्भानाबिभ्रतमाश्रये महागणपम् ॥ इति ।

द्राविडास्त्वन्यथा व्याचक्षते । अधोवामदक्षयोराद्ये । तदूर्ध्वयोरपरे । तदूर्ध्वयोर्मध्ये । तदूर्ध्वयोरुपान्त्ये । तदूर्ध्वयोरन्त्ये इति । उक्तं च गणेश्वरविमर्शिन्याम्—

दक्षाधःकरमारभ्य वामाधःस्थकरान्तिकम् ।
गदाशूलाब्जकह्लारविषाणं दक्षिणैः करैः ॥
शाल्यग्रपाशचक्रेक्षुचापसद्बीजपूरकम् ।
वामैर्दधानं मञ्जीरविलसच्चरणाम्बुजम् ॥
लीलया रत्नकलशं पुष्कराग्रे निधाय च । इति ।

अन्ये तु प्रथमध्यान एव बीजपूरव्यत्ययमिच्छन्ति । अन्ये तु तद्रदयोरेव व्यत्यस्तत्वमिच्छन्ति । तेन वामदक्षयो रदबीजपूरौ प्रतिभातः । मन्त्रीति । दशांशं

चतुःसहस्रसंयुक्तं चत्वारिंशत्सहस्रकम्।
दशांशं जुहुयाद् द्रव्यैरष्टाभिर्मोदकादिभिः॥ ३९
तर्पयेदहिनशो नित्यं प्रागुक्तेनैव वर्त्मना।
प्रागुक्ते पूजयेत्पीठे विधिना गणनायकम्॥ ४०
त्रिकोणबाह्ये पूर्व्वादि चतुर्दिक्षु समर्चयेत्।
अश्वत्थबिल्ववृक्षाधः श्रियं श्रीपतिमर्चयेत्॥ ४१
पद्मयुग्मधरा पद्मा शङ्खचक्रधरो हरिः।
दक्षिणे वटवृक्षाधो गौरीं गौरीपतिं यजेत्॥ ४२
पाशाङ्कुशधरा गौरी टङ्कशूलधरो हरः।
पश्चिमे पिप्पलस्याऽधो रतिं रतिपतिं यजेत्॥ ४३
रतिरुत्पलहस्ताढ्या कोदण्डास्त्रधरः स्मरः।
सौम्ये प्रियङ्गुवृक्षाधो महीं पोत्रिणमर्चयेत्॥ ४४
शुकव्रीह्यग्रहस्ता भूर्गदाचक्रधरः पतिः।
देवाग्रे पूजयेल्लक्ष्मीसहितं गणनायकम्॥ ४५
षट्सु कोणेषु सम्पूज्या आमोदाद्याः प्रियान्विताः।
आमोदं सिद्धिसहितमग्रकोणे समर्चयेत्॥ ४६
समृद्ध्या युतमभ्यर्चेत् प्रमोदं वह्निकोणतः।
सुमुखं कान्तिसंयुक्तमीशकोणे समर्चयेत्॥ ४७

पुष्टिमन्त्रजप उक्तः। स गुरुमुखादवगन्तव्यः॥ ३५॥३६॥३७॥३८॥३९॥

प्राक्प्रोक्तेनेति। चतुःशतं चतुश्चत्वारिंशद्वारमित्यर्थः। प्रागुक्ते पीठे इति। पूर्व्वमन्त्रोक्ताः पीठशक्तयः पीठमन्त्रश्चात्रापि ज्ञेया इत्यर्थः। गणनायकं पूजयेदिति त्रिकोण इति शेषः। विधिनेति वक्ष्यमाणेन। यन्त्रं तु ध्यानावसर एवोक्तम्। सावरणमिति शेषः॥ ४०॥

पञ्चमिथुनपूजामाह त्रिकोणेति। टङ्कः परशुः। उत्पलयुक्तौ हस्तौ ताभ्यामाढ्या। अस्त्रं बाणः। पोत्रिणं वराहम्। वह्निकोणतः इति। पुरःकल्पितपूर्व्वदिगपेक्षया यो वह्निकोणस्तत्रेत्यर्थः। एवमीशकोण इत्यत्रापि। एवं पश्चिमनैर्ऋतवायुकोणेष्वपि ज्ञेयम्।

दुर्मुखं मदनावत्या यजेद्दक्षकोणके ।
विघ्नं मदद्रवायुक्तं कोणे नैर्ऋतके यजेत् ॥ ४८
वायव्ये विघ्नकर्त्तारं द्राविण्या सहितं यजेत् ।
पाशाङ्कुशाभयाभीष्टधारिणोऽरुणविग्रहाः ॥ ४९
गण्डभित्तिगलद्दानपूरधौतमुखाम्बुजाः ।
विघ्नास्तत्प्रमदाः सर्व्वा मदाघूर्णितलोचनाः ॥ ५०
एकहस्तधृताम्भोजा इतरालिङ्गितप्रियाः ।
षट्कोणपार्श्वयोः पूज्यौ शङ्खपद्मनिधी क्रमात् ॥ ५१
निजप्रियाभ्यां सहितौ पूर्व्वोदीरितलक्षणौ ।
केसरेष्वङ्गपूजा स्याद् ब्राह्म्याद्याः पत्रमध्यगाः ॥ ५२
बहिर्लोकेश्वराः पूज्या वज्रादीनि ततः परम् ।
इत्थं जपादिभिः सिद्धः प्रयोगान् स्वमनीषितान् ॥ ५३
साधयेदष्टभिर्द्रव्यैरन्यैर्वा कल्पचोदितैः ।
पद्महोमेन भूपालांस्तत्पत्नीरुत्पलैः शुभैः ॥ ५४
मन्त्रिणः कुमुदैः फुल्लैर्विप्रान् पिप्पलसम्भवैः ।
समिद्वरैर्नरपतीनुदुम्बरसमुद्भवैः ॥ ५५
प्लक्षैर्वैश्यान् वटोद्भूतैः शूद्रान्मन्त्री वशं नयेत् ।
मधुना स्वर्णलाभः स्याद्गोदुग्धेन लभेत गाः ॥ ५६
आज्यहोमेन महतीं श्रियमाप्नोति मानवः ।
दध्ना सर्व्वसमृद्धिः स्यादन्नैरन्नपतिर्भवेत् ॥ ५७

तदुक्तमाचार्य्यैः—अथामोदप्रमोदौ सुमुखदुर्मुखौ च तमभितोऽस्त्रियुगे ।
पृष्ठे च दुर्मुखाख्यस्त्वसुमभितो विघ्नविघ्नकर्त्तारौ ॥ इति ।
विघ्ना इति पूर्व्वेण सम्बध्यते । पूर्व्वोदीरितेत्यष्टमपटले । एतदन्तद्वितीयावृत्तिः ।
॥ ४१॥४२॥४३॥४४॥४५॥४६॥४७॥४८॥४९॥५०॥५१॥५२॥५३॥५४ ॥

पद्महोमेन भूपालानित्यादेर्मन्त्री वशं नयेदित्यादिना सम्बन्धः । मन्त्रीत्यनेन सर्व्वपदस्थाने साध्यनामित्युक्तम् । समिद्वरैरिति । अन्येऽपि त्रिषु सम्बध्यते ॥ ५४ ॥
॥ ५५॥५६॥५७ ॥

वृष्टिकामः प्रजुहुयाद् वेतसानां समिद्वरैः ।
कुसुम्भकुसुमैर्हुत्वा वासांसि लभतेऽचिरात् ॥ ५८

प्रत्येकमादौ मूलेन चतुर्वारं प्रतर्पयेत् ।
श्रीशक्तिरतिभूलक्ष्मीः स्वबीजाद्याः प्रियान्विताः ॥ ५९

आमोदादीन् स्वबीजाद्यान् शक्तियुक्तांश्च तर्पयेत् ।
चतुश्चतुः पृथक्मन्त्री शङ्खपद्मनिधी तथा ॥ ६०

वृष्टीति । अत्र स्वबीजानन्तरममृतबीजं ज्ञेयम् ॥ ५८ ॥

चतुरावृत्तितर्पणप्रकारमाह प्रत्येकमिति त्रिभिः । आदौ मूलेन चतुर्वारं प्रतर्पयेत् । प्रत्येकमित्यस्यायमर्थः । या या देवता तर्पणीया तत्र तत्रादौ मूलेन चतुर्वारं चतुर्वारं तर्पणं कर्त्तव्यम् । स्वबीजाद्या इति । स्वस्वबीजाद्याः प्रियान्विताः प्रत्येकं तर्पयेदिति सम्बन्धः ॥ ५९ ॥

स्वबीजाद्यानिति गणपतिबीजाद्यान् । यथा चतुर्वारं स्वप्रियान्वितानिति वसुधारावसुमतीसहितौ । तद्यथा । मूलमन्त्रेण महागणपतिं तर्पयामीति चतुर्वारं सन्तर्प्य श्रीं श्रीश्रीपती तर्पयामीति चतुर्वारं सन्तर्पयेत् । अत्र लक्ष्मी-शब्देन पञ्चमक्रममिथुनं संगृहीतम् पूजाक्रमविवक्षया । तदुक्तमाचार्यैः स्तवे—

पञ्चकारणभेदेन यस्मान्मिथुनपञ्चकम् ।
करोति पञ्च कृत्यानि तदाद्यं मिथुनं भजेत् ॥ इति ।

अन्यत्रापि—प्रथमं पूजयेद्देवं ततो मिथुनपञ्चकम् ॥ इति ।

अन्यत्रापि न्यासावसरे—

शिरोवक्त्रहृदम्भोजगुह्यपत्स्वपि पञ्चकम् ।
मिथुनानां न्यसेत् स्वीयैर्बीजैः स्वैर्नामभिः पृथक् ॥ इति ॥

एवं त्रयोदश देवतानां तर्पणानि भवन्ति । त्रयोदशवारं मूलतर्पणानि । सर्वान्ते मूलेन चतुर्वारं तर्पणम् । एवमष्टोत्तरशतं तर्पणानि भवन्ति । अयं कनिष्ठः प्रकारः । पद्मपादाचार्यैः कनिष्ठप्रकारे चतुर्विंशत्यधिकैकशततर्पणान्युक्तानि । तद्यथा । मूलं ४ महागणपं ४ मूलं ४ पुष्टिं ४ पञ्चमिथुनानि ४० आमोदादि ६४ मूलं ४ एवमिति । मध्यमप्रकारस्तु प्रियान्विता इति व्यस्ततर्पणेन । तत्र व्यस्तत्वं मूले प्रियान्विताः शक्तियुक्तानित्युक्तेर्लभ्यते । तद्यथा । मूलं चतुर्वारं सन्तर्प्य श्रीं श्रीपतिसहितां श्रियं तर्पयामीति चतुर्वारं पुनः श्रीं श्रीसहितं श्रीपतिं तर्पयामीति चतुर्वारं तर्पयेत् । एवं षड्विंशतिदेवतातर्पणानि षड्विंशतिवारं

नामादिबीजसहितौ तर्पयेत् स्वप्रियान्वितौ ।
तर्पणेनाऽमुना स्तोयमिष्टमाप्नोति मण्डलात् ॥ ६१

मूलतर्पणानि च अन्ते मूलेन चतुर्वारं तर्पणं सर्व्वादौ च मूलेन स्वतन्त्रतया चतुर्वारं तर्पणम् । एवं षोड़शोत्तरा द्विशती तर्पणानां भवति । उत्तमप्रकारस्तु प्रत्येकमादौ वक्ष्यमाणतर्पणानामिति शेषः । चतुर्वारं तर्पयेदादावन्ते चेत्यर्थः । मूलेन प्रत्यर्णमित्यर्थः । मूलमन्त्रस्याक्षराणि प्रत्येकं तर्पयेत् । तद्यथा । आदौ मूलम् ४ प्रथमाक्षरम् ४ पुनर्मूलम् ४ एवमष्टाविंशति वर्णतर्पणानि अष्टाविंशतिवारं मूलतर्पणानि च अन्ते चतुर्वारं मूलेन । एवं द्विशती अष्टाविंशत्यधिका तर्पणानाम् । ततो मध्यमप्रकारवदेव द्विशती षोड़शोत्तरा । एवं चतुश्चत्वारिंशदधिकं चतुःशतं तर्पणानि भवन्ति । तदुक्तं गणेश्वरविमर्शिन्याम्—

सर्व्वाभीष्टप्रदं वक्ष्ये चतुरावृत्तितर्पणम् ।
एकान्ते विजने रम्ये सर्व्वोपद्रववर्जिते ॥
कृतस्नानादिको मन्त्री पूर्व्ववन्न्याससंयुतः ।
तड़ागमध्ये सञ्चिन्त्य पुष्पितं नलिनीवनम् ॥
तस्य मध्ये महापद्मं तरुणादित्यसन्निभम् ।
समुन्नतं सुगन्धाढ्यं रमणीयं मनोहरम् ॥
सद्योविकसितं ध्यायेन्मन्त्री पूर्व्वोक्तमन्त्रवित् ।
शुद्धरजतसोपानपङ्क्त्याभरविमण्डलात् ॥
विनिर्गत्याऽवरुह्याऽथ कर्णिकामध्यसंस्थितम् ।
इति ध्यात्वा सावरणं महागणपतिं सुधीः ॥
प्रवरैर्गन्धकुसुमैः समभ्यर्च्याऽथ पूर्व्ववत् ।
निधाय पुष्करमुखं साधकेन्द्रस्य मूर्द्धनि ॥
वर्षन्तं रत्नधाराभिर्ध्यात्वा देवस्य मूर्द्धनि ।
चन्द्रचन्दनकाश्मीरकस्तूरीलोलितैर्जलैः ॥
प्रथमं मूलमन्त्रेण चतुर्वारं प्रतर्प्य च ।
मिथुनानि च षड्विघ्नान् शङ्खपद्मनिधी अपि ॥
स्वस्वबीजादिकैर्मन्त्री स्वाहान्तैश्च चतुश्चतुः ।
मूलमन्त्रं चतुर्वारपूर्व्वकं तर्पयेत् पृथक् ॥
सम्भूयाऽष्टोत्तरशतं कनिष्ठः स्यादयं क्रमः ।

अथवा मूलमन्त्राद्यैर्व्यस्तैरेतैश्च पूर्व्ववत् ॥
मन्त्रैर्वा तर्पयेद्विद्वानचनोक्तप्रकारतः ।
सध्यक्रमोऽयं सम्भूय द्विशतं षोड़शोत्तरम् ॥
अथवा मूलमन्त्रेण चतुर्वारं प्रतर्प्य च ।
पूर्व्वमन्त्राक्षरैर्मन्त्रैः स्वाहान्तैश्च चतुश्चतुः ॥
मूलमन्त्रं चतुर्वारपूर्व्वकं सन्तर्प्य च ।
मिथुनादींस्ततः पश्चात् पूर्व्ववत्सम्प्रतर्पयेत् ॥
भवेत् सम्भूय स चतुश्चत्वारिंशच्चतुःशतम् ।
एवं ज्येष्ठक्रमः प्रोक्तो बुधैरागमपारगैः ॥
एवं सन्तोष्य तत्पश्चात् पूर्व्ववत् सोपचारकैः ।
सर्व्वाभीष्टं च सम्प्रार्थ्य प्रणम्योद्वासयेत् सुधीः ॥
य एवं तर्पयेन्नित्यं मण्डलात् सकलं लभेत् ।
अनावृष्ट्यां भये घोरे राजचौराद्युपद्रवे ॥
महाज्वरे विवादे च महादारिद्र्यसङ्कटे ।
विवाहादिषु कार्य्येषु सर्व्वेषु च विशेषतः ॥
एवं वै तर्पणं कुर्य्यान् मानवेन्द्रः प्रसन्नधीः ।
महागणेश्वरः प्रीतो महासम्पत्करो भवेत् ॥ इति ॥

अन्ये तु लक्ष्मीशब्देन शक्तिमत्प्राधान्यमिति वदन्ति । मन्त्रोऽयं क्रमो विवक्षितः । तथाहि प्रथमं विंशतिवारं ततोऽष्टाविंशतिमन्त्राक्षरैः तावत्कृत्वो मूलेन एतदन्तं चतुर्वारं मूलेन ततश्चतुर्विंशतिदेवतातर्पणानि । तावत्कृत्वो मूलतर्पणानि तदन्ते मूलेन चतुर्वारम् । एवं चतुःशतचतुश्चत्वारिंशत्तर्पणानि भवन्ति । तदुक्तं रहस्यपटले मूलनारायणीये—

विंशत्संख्यं तर्पयित्वा तु पूर्व्वं सान्त्वैर्वर्णैर्वेदवारं द्विठान्तैः ।
मध्ये मध्ये तर्पयेद्विघ्नराजं लक्ष्म्यादीनां तर्पणं चैवमेव ॥ इति ॥

अन्यत्रापि—प्रथमं विंशतिवारं मिथुनानां विघ्नषट्शक्तीनाम् ।
प्रत्येकं निधिशक्त्योश्चतुरावृत्त्या च मूलेन ॥
मूलात्मकवर्णानामेवं सन्तर्पिते च निश्चितधिया ।
स चतुश्चत्वारिंशच्चतुःशतं संख्यया भवेदेवम् ॥ इति ॥

ये तु महागणपतिशब्दं सम्बुद्ध्यन्तमाहुः त एकोनत्रिंशदक्षरतर्पणं तावत्कृत्वो मूलेन षड्विंशतिमिथुनतर्पणं तावत्कृत्वो मूलान्ते मूलेन चतुर्वारमिति

स्मृतिस्थं मांसमौबिन्दुयुक्तं भूबीजमीरितम् ॥ ६२

संख्यापूर्त्तिमाहुः । ये तु गणपतिपदं सम्बुध्यन्तमाहुः ते मूलं ४ महागणपतिं ४ मूलं ४ पुष्टिं ४ ततोऽक्षरतर्पणं तावन्मूलेन पूर्ववन्मिथुनादितर्पणम् अन्ते मूलेनेति संख्यापूर्त्तिमाहुः । त्रिंशदक्षरे तु अक्षरमूलतर्पणानि अन्ते ४ मूले ४ मूलेनेति २४४ ततो मिथुनाष्टकेनाऽन्ते मूलेनेति ६८ तत आमोदादीनामन्ते मूलेनेति १३२ । एवं संख्यापूर्त्तिर्ज्ञेया । ये तु श्रीमहागणपतिशब्दं सम्बुध्यन्तं वशंशब्दस्य च द्वित्वमाहुः ते द्वात्रिंशदक्षरं तर्पणं तावत्कृत्वो मूलेन बीजपूराद्येकादशभिः ८८ मिथुनचतुष्टयषड्विघ्ननिधिद्वयेन कनिष्ठोक्तप्रकारेण तावत्कृत्वो मूलेनाऽन्ते च चतुर्वारं मूलेनेत्याहुः । बीजापूरादिमन्त्रास्तु—

बीजापूरं गदा चेक्षुकार्मुकं च त्रिशूलयुक् ।
चक्राब्जपाशोत्पलानि कलमाग्रं विषाणयुक् ॥
डेन्ताश्च रत्नकलशो ह्यन्ताः प्रणवादिकाः ।
गंबीजाद्यादिकाः पञ्च श्रीबीजाद्यादिकाः पुनः ॥
षड्बीजाद्योऽन्तिमश्चैते वक्ष्यमाणपदादिकाः ।
यथाक्रमं महाविघ्नायुधानां मनवः स्मृताः ॥

बीजपूरादयः पञ्च विलोमेन गंबीजाद्यानि गं ग्लौं क्लीं ह्रीं श्रींबीजानि आदौ येषां तथा । पुनः रत्यादयः पञ्च क्रमेण श्रीबीजाद्याः श्रीमित्यादि पञ्चबीजादिकाः । अन्तिमो रत्नकलशः प्रणवादिषड्बीजाद्य इत्यर्थः ।

मन्त्रकला शक्तिमप्राणत्रिगुणः कालचक्रत्रयचयौ च ।
व्याप्तिरतिभूस्वरूपं विद्यात्रैलोक्यमात्मने युक्तम् ॥ इति ॥

पद्मपादाचार्यास्त्वन्यथा चतुरावृत्तितर्पणमाहुः । तद्यथा । दशधा भिन्नेन मूलमन्त्रेण बीजपूराद्येकादशभिर्महागणपतिविघ्नप्रसादनतदुक्तविघ्नाद्यष्टनामयुतेन गणपतय इत्यस्मात् पूर्वं मूलमन्त्रेण चतुर्विंशतिदेवताश्च एवं पञ्चपञ्चाशद्देवतातर्पणानि तावन्ति मूलेन अन्ते चतुर्वारं मूलेनेति चतुःशतं चतुश्चत्वारिंशत् ।

प्रयोगसारे तु—अष्टाविंशतिरक्षराणि दशभिर्युक्तं चतुर्भिः पदैः

पश्चात् पञ्चरमादिकांश्च गणपान् षट् द्वौ निधी तर्पयेत् ॥
प्रत्येकं मनुनाऽमुना च चतुरावृत्त्या विभोर्मस्तके
ध्यात्वा रत्नमयं महागणपतिं भक्तप्रसन्नं सुधीः ॥ इति ॥६०॥६१॥

भूबीजमुद्धरति स्मृतीति । मांसं लकारः स्मृतिस्थं गकारस्थं औ स्वरूपं बिन्दुश्च एतद्युक्तः । तेन ग्लौं इति ॥ ६२ ॥

बीजं षट्कोणमध्ये स्फुरदनलपुरे तारगं दिक्षु लक्ष्मीं
मायाकन्दर्पभूमीस्तदनु रसपुटेष्वालिखेद्बीजषट्कम् ।
तत्सन्धिष्वङ्गमन्त्रान् वसुदलकमले मूलमन्त्रस्य वर्णान्
श्लिष्टान् पत्रेषु विद्वान् विलिखतु गुणशस्त्वाऽन्त्यमन्त्ये पलाशे ॥ ६३

आवीतं लिपिभिः क्रमोत्क्रमवशात् पाशाङ्कुशाभ्यामपि
भूगेहद्वितयेन वेष्टितमिदं यन्त्रं गणाधीशितुः ।
लाक्षाकुङ्कुमरोचनामृगमदैर्भूर्जे वरे हेम्नि वा
संलिख्याऽभिवहन् लभेत सकलैः संप्रार्थनीयां श्रियम् ॥ ६४

उक्तं महागणपतेर्विधानं सुरपूजितम् ।
सर्व्वसिद्धिकरं पुंसां समस्तपुरुषार्थदम् ॥ ६५
माया विरिपदद्वन्द्वं ततो गणपतिं वदेत् ।
खड्गीशपावकौ मस्वाहरदान्ते वदेत् पुनः ॥ ६६
सर्व्वलोकं मे पदान्ते वशमानय ठद्वयम् ।
षड्विंशत्यक्षरो मन्त्रो भजतां सुरपादपः ॥ ६७
गणकः स्यादृषिश्छन्दो गायत्रं देवता मनोः ।
विरिविघ्नेश्वरः प्रोक्तो भजतां सर्व्वकामदः ॥ ६८

यन्त्रमाह बीजमिति । वसुदलकमले अष्टदलपद्मे षट्कोणमध्ये स्फुरदनलपुरे लसत्त्रिकोणे तारगं प्रणवस्थं बीजं गणपतिबीजं गमिति लिखेदित्यन्वयः । दिक्षु त्रिकोणाद्बहिः श्रमादीति ज्ञेयम् । रसपुटेषु । षट्सु कोणेषु । बीजषट्कं मन्त्राद्यम् । तस्य अग्रादि षट्कोणस्य सन्धिषु अङ्गमन्त्रान् महागणपतेः षडङ्गमन्त्रान् । पत्रेषु मन्त्रस्य द्वाविंशतिवर्णान् श्लिष्टान् गुणशस्त्रिशः अन्त्यं वर्णमष्टमे दल एकमेव लिखेत् । ततः क्रमोत्क्रमलिपिभिर्वेष्टयेत् । ततः पाशाङ्कुशाभ्यां वेष्टयेत् । पद्मपादाचार्य्यैस्तु "अष्टपदान्यष्टपत्रे विलिख्य तद्बहिर्वृत्तत्रये मातृकापाशाङ्कुशार्णान् विलिख्य तद्बहिर्भूपुरद्वये पाशमायाबीजे लिखेत्" इत्युक्तम् । लाक्षा अलक्तकरसः । कुङ्कुमं काश्मीरजम् । रोचना गोरोचना । मृगमदः कस्तूरी ॥ ६३ ॥ ६४ ॥ ६५ ॥

विरिगणपतिमन्त्रमाह मायेति । खड्गीशो वः पावको रेफः । हृल्लेखा बीजं स्वाहा शक्तिः । के मन वरेत्यादिपञ्चाक्षराणि लोकमिति च हित्वा एकोन-

अन्तःकरणवेदेषुभूतपञ्चविलोचनैः।
एवं विभक्तैर्मन्त्रार्णैर्मायाद्यैरङ्गकल्पना।
महागणपतेः प्रोक्ते स्थाने मन्त्री विचिन्तयेत्॥ ६९

सिन्दूराभमिभाननं त्रिनयनं हस्तेषु पाशाङ्कुशौ
बिभ्राणं मधुमत्कपालमनिशं साद्वेन्दुमौलिं भजे।
पुष्ट्याश्लिष्टतनुं ध्वजाग्रकरया पद्मोल्लसद्धस्तया
तद्योन्याहितपाणिमात्तवसुमत्पात्रोल्लसत्पुष्करम्॥ ७०

चतुर्लक्षं जपेन्मन्त्रं तद्दशांशं हुतक्रिया।
प्राक्प्रोक्तैरष्टभिर्द्रव्यैस्त्रिमध्वक्तैः समीरिता॥ ७१
पूर्वोक्ते पूजयेत् पीठे तीव्रादिनवशक्तिके।
मूलेन मूर्त्तिं संकल्प्य तत्रावाह्याऽर्चयेद्विभुम्॥ ७२

विंशत्यक्षरमाहुः। अस्य निचृच्छन्दः। अन्यत् पूर्ववत्। केचन लोकपदे जनपदं पठन्ति। अन्ये विरीत्यादौ महागणपतिबीजषट्कं प्रयोजयन्ति॥ ६६॥६७॥६८॥

षडङ्गमाहान्तरिति। अन्तःकरणानि चत्वारि वेदाश्चत्वार इषवः पञ्च भूतानि पञ्च लोचने द्वे। द्वितीयस्य षट्पदैः षडङ्गम्। तृतीयस्य महागणपति-मन्त्रवत्॥ ६९॥

पुष्करं करिहस्ताग्रम्। ध्याने तु दक्षे पाशः वामे अङ्कुशः अधोदक्षे मधु-मत्कपालम् अधोवामः प्रियायोन्याहितः। तद्वत् पुष्टिरपि चतुर्भुजा। तत्र दक्षवामयोः पद्मे। पद्मोल्लसद्धस्तयेत्यत्र पद्माभ्यां उल्लसन्तौ हस्तौ यस्याः सा तथेति विग्रहः। अधोदक्षिणेन प्रियस्याश्लेषः अधोवामेन तद्ध्वजाग्रस्पृगिति सम्प्रदाय-विदः। कश्चित्तु पुष्टिं द्विहस्तामेवाह। एकहस्ते पद्मं द्वितीयहस्तो ध्वजा-ग्रस्पृगिति। तन्मते आश्लेषो नाम निकटत्वं न तु हस्तेनालिङ्गनमिति। द्वितीयमन्त्रेऽपि इदमेव ध्यानम्। तृतीयमन्त्रे तु—

बीजापूरगदे शरासनमरिं मालां च दक्षैः करै-
र्वामैर्बाणसपाशकोत्पलरदान् रत्नाढ्यकुम्भं दधत्।
सिन्दूरारुणविग्रहस्त्रिनयनो योन्यस्तशुण्डो गणः
सश्लिष्टाहितपाणिमम्बुजकरां पुष्टिं वहन् वोऽवतात्॥

पूजादिकं त्रयाणां समानम्॥ ७०॥ ७१॥

पूर्वोक्त इति महागणपतिपूजायाम्। तीव्रादिनवशक्तिक इत्यनेन

मिथुनाद्यत्विराद्या स्यादामोदाद्यैर्दिगम्बरैः ।
द्वितीयाऽङ्गैस्तृतीया स्याच्चतुर्थी मातृभिः स्मृता ॥ ७३
पञ्चमी लोकपालैः स्यात् षष्ठी वज्रादिभिः स्मृता ।
इति सिद्धमनुर्मन्त्री प्रफुल्लैः सरसीरुहैः ॥ ७४
जुहुयादष्टभगाः सर्वे तण्डुलैस्तिलमिश्रितैः ।
हुत्वा श्रियमवाप्नोति मोदकैराज्यलोलितैः ।
हुत्वा विजयमाप्नोति पार्थिवो युद्धभूमिषु ॥ ७५
मधुत्रयेण हवनं वशं नयति पार्थिवान् ।
भक्ष्यभोज्यादिकं सर्वं हुत्वाऽभीष्टानि साधयेत् ॥ ७६

पीठमन्त्रस्य मायादित्वमुक्तम् ॥ ७३ ॥ ७४ ॥ ७५ ॥

मधुत्रयेण पयोमधुघृतेन । भक्ष्यभोज्यादिकमिति । भक्ष्यं लड्डुकादि । भोज्यमन्नादि । आदिशब्देन लेह्यचोष्यादिकं गृह्यते । तत्र लेह्यं रसालादि ।

तल्लक्षणं सूपशास्त्रे—

अर्द्धाढकं सुचिरपर्युषितस्य दध्नः खण्डस्य षोडश पलानि शशिप्रभस्य ।
सर्पिः पलं मधु पलं मरिचं द्विकर्षं शुण्ठीपलार्द्धमपि चार्द्धपलं चतुर्णाम् ॥
शुक्लोपले ललनया मृदुपाणिघृष्टा कर्पूरपूरसुरभीकृतभाण्डसंस्था ।
एषा वृकोदरकृता सरसा रसाला या स्वादिता भगवता मधुसूदनेन ॥ इति ।

चतुर्णां त्वगेलापत्रकेसराणाम् अर्द्धपलमिति मिलित्वा ।

तन्त्रान्तरोक्तमस्य यन्त्रं लिख्यते ।

वक्ष्ये महासिद्धिकरं हि यन्त्रं भूर्जस्य पत्रे पशुरोचनाक्तैः ।
दूर्वाङ्कुरैर्भूपृहयुग्मशक्तौ संलिख्य साध्यं विरिसंपुटं च ॥
कोणेषु मन्त्रं श्रुतिशोऽवशिष्टं तेनापि नाम्नाऽप्यथ वेष्टयित्वा ।
संलिख्य यन्त्रं च गणाधिराजमावाह्य चाभ्यर्च्य च गन्धपुष्पैः ॥
संजप्य तद्धारणतश्च नित्यं वशं प्रयात्यस्य जगत् समस्तम् ॥ इति ।

प्रथममन्त्रे श्रुतिश इति विशः । अन्त्यकोणे द्वयम् । द्वितीयमन्त्रे श्रुतिः कर्णस्तेन द्विश इत्यर्थः । तदुक्तम्—

वकाररेफावपि लोचनाढ्यौ पुनस्तथोद्धृत्य गणात्पतीति ।
सर्वं समुच्चार्य च मे वशः स्यात् मकारमायुक्तमतो नयेति ॥
शब्दाद्धिरः स्यात् । इति ।

शक्तिरुद्धं निजं बीजं महागणपतिं वदेत् ।
ङेऽन्तमग्निवधूः प्रोक्तो मन्त्रोऽयं द्वादशाक्षरः ॥ ७७

गणकः स्यादृषिश्छन्दो गायत्री निचृदादिका ।
उदिता देवता तन्त्रे नाम्ना शक्तिगणाधिपः ।
व्यस्तैः समस्तैर्मन्त्रस्य पदैरङ्गानि कल्पयेत् ॥ ७८

मुक्तागौरं मदगजमुखं चन्द्रचूडं त्रिनेत्रं
हस्तैः स्वीयैर्दधतमरविन्दाङ्कुशौ रत्नकुम्भम् ।
अङ्कस्थायाः सरसिजरुचः स्वध्वजालम्बिपाणे-
र्देव्या योनौ विनिहितकरं रत्नमौलिं भजामः ॥ ७९

लक्षमेकं जपेन्मन्त्रमपूपैस्तद्दशांशतः ।
जुहुयादर्चिते वह्नौ दिनशो देवमर्चयेत् ॥ ८०

प्राक्प्रोक्ते पूजयेत्पीठे प्रागुक्तेनैव वर्त्मना ।
हुत्वेक्षुखण्डैर्मतिमान् राज्यश्रियमवाप्नुयात् ॥ ८१

नारिकेलफलैस्तद्वद्रम्भापक्वफलैस्ततः ।
वशयत्यखिलं लोकं पृथुकैः शर्करान्वितैः ॥ ८२

वशं नयति राजानं सक्तुभिर्ब्राह्मणान् शुभैः ।
घृतहोमेन धनवान् जायते नात्र संशयः ॥ ८३

शक्त्या रुद्धं निजं बीजं वशमानय ठद्वयम् ।
ताराद्यो मनुराख्यातो रुद्रसंख्याक्षरान्वितः ॥ ८४

तृतीयमन्त्रे शुलिशस्तुर्थो। अत्र मध्यगतशक्तिस्तु मन्त्रबाह्या। अन्त्ये दले एकमक्षरं लिखेत् ॥ ७६ ॥

शक्तिगणपतिमन्त्रमाह शक्तीति। निजं बीजं गं। ङेऽन्तमित्यस्य पश्चात्तनेन सम्बन्धः। ह्रीं गं ह्रीं महागणपतये स्वाहा। गं बीजं स्वाहा शक्तिः। व्यस्तैरिति। मन्त्रस्य पञ्चभिः पदैः पञ्चाङ्गानि सर्वेण षष्ठम् ॥ ७८ ॥

ध्याने तु ऊर्द्ध्वयोर्दक्षवामयोराद्ये। अधोदक्षे रत्नकुम्भः अधोवामो देवीयोनिस्थः। शुण्डादण्डस्तु रत्नकुम्भोपरीति सम्प्रदायः। सरसिजेन दक्षहस्तस्थितेन रुक् यस्याः सा तथा। तद्वामो ध्वजाग्रस्थक्। प्रागुक्तेनेत्यव्यवहितेन ॥ ७९—८३ ॥

मन्त्रान्तरमाह शक्त्येति। रुद्रेत्येकादश। ॐ ह्रीं गं ह्रीं वशमानय स्वाहा।

ऋष्याद्याः पूर्व्वमुक्ताः स्युरङ्गं मन्त्रपदैर्भवेत् ।
एकेनादौ त्रिभिर्द्वाभ्यां त्रिभिर्द्वाभ्यामनन्तरम् ।
समस्तेनाऽस्त्रमाख्यातं अङ्गक्लृप्तिरियं मता ॥ ८५

हस्तैर्बिभ्रतमिक्षुदण्डवरदौ पाशाङ्कुशौ पुष्कर-
स्पृष्टस्वप्रमदावराङ्गमनयाऽऽश्लिष्टं ध्वजाग्रस्पृशा ।
श्यामाढ्या विधृताब्जया त्रिनयनं चन्द्रार्द्धचूडं जवा-
रक्तं हस्तिमुखं स्मरामि सततं भोगातिलोलं विभुम् ॥ ८६

लक्षत्रयं जपेन्मन्त्रमिक्षुखण्डैर्दशांशतः ।
अपूपैराज्ययुक्तैर्वा जुहुयान्मन्त्रसिद्धये ॥ ८७
स्वगुरुं धनधान्याद्यैः प्रीणयेत् प्रीतमानसः ।
पूजा पूर्व्ववदादिष्टा ततः काम्यानि साधयेत् ॥ ८८
हुत्वाऽपूपैस्त्रिमध्वक्तैर्वशयेद् भुवि पार्थिवान् ।
चतुर्थ्यां नारिकेलेन महतीं श्रियमश्नुते ॥ ८९
लवणैर्मधुसंयुक्तैर्वशयेद्वनिताजनम् ।
संवर्त्तको नेत्रयुतः पार्श्वो वज्रासनस्थितः ॥ ९०
प्रसादनाय हृन्मन्त्रः स्वबीजाद्यो दशाक्षरः ।
गणको मुनिरस्य स्याद्विराट् छन्द उदाहृतम् ॥ ९१
क्षिप्रप्रसादनो विघ्नो देवताऽस्य समीरिता ।
दीर्घयुक्तेन बीजेन षडङ्गानि प्रकल्पयेत् ॥ ९२

गं बीजं स्वाहा शक्तिः ॥ ८४ ॥

पूर्व्वमित्यव्यवहितम् । पदान्येवाह । एकेनेति ॥ ८५ ॥

ध्याने तु वामाधस्ताद्वामोर्ध्वपर्य्यन्तम् । देवीध्यानं त्रिरिगणपतिध्यानोक्तं ज्ञेयम् । पूर्व्ववदिति त्रिरिगणपतिवदित्यर्थः ॥ ८६॥८७॥८८॥८९॥९० ॥

क्षिप्रप्रसादमन्त्रमाह संवर्त्तक इति । संवर्त्तः क्षः नेत्रमिकारः तद्युतः । पार्श्वः पकारो वज्रासनो रेफासनः । स्वबीजाद्यो गमिति बीजाद्यः । गं क्षिप्रप्रसादनाय नमः । श्रीबीजाद्य इति केचित् । गं बीजं आयेति शक्तिः । दीर्घयुक्तेन बीजेनेति आदिबीजेन ॥ ९०॥९१॥९२ ॥

पाशाङ्कुशौ कल्पलतां विषाणं दधत् स्वशुण्डाहितबीजपूरः ।
रक्तस्त्रिनेत्रस्तरुणेन्दुमौलिर्हारोज्ज्वलो हस्तिमुखोऽवताद्वः ॥ ९३

लक्षं जपेज्जपस्यान्ते जुहुयादयुतं तिलैः ।
समधुत्रितयैर्द्रव्यैरथवाऽष्टाभिरीरितैः ॥ ९४
एकाक्षरोदिते पीठे वक्ष्यमाणेन वर्त्मना ।
पूजयेद्गन्धपुष्पाद्यैर्धूपदीपैर्गजाननम् ॥ ९५
अङ्गानि पूर्व्वमभ्यर्च्य विघ्नानष्टौ यजेत्ततः ।
विघ्नं विनायकं वीरं शूरं वरदसंज्ञकम् ॥ ९६
इभवक्त्रं चैकदन्तं लम्बोदरमनन्तरम् ।
पत्राग्रेष्वर्चयेत्पश्चाद् ब्राह्म्याद्यास्तदनन्तरम् ॥ ९७
लोकपालांस्तदस्त्राणि विघ्नपूजा समीरिता ।
आज्यान्नैर्जुहुयान्नित्यमन्नवान् वत्सराद्भवेत् ॥ ९८
पायसान्नेन महतीं श्रियमाप्नोति मानवः ।
आज्यहोमेन वशयेत्प्राणिनः सकलान् सुधीः ॥ ९९
नारिकेलफलं पक्वं लोष्टचर्मसमन्वितम् ।
जुहुयात्प्रत्यहं मन्त्री मण्डलात् सिद्धिमाप्नुयात् ॥ १००
जुहुयादष्टभिर्द्रव्यैर्मधुरत्रयसंयुतैः ।
वशयेत्पार्थिवान् सर्व्वान् तत्पत्नीर्विधिनाऽमुना ॥ १०१
दिनादिषु चतुश्चत्वारिंशद्वारैः शुभोदकैः ।
तर्पयेद्विघ्नराजस्य मस्तके श्रीप्रसिद्धये ॥ १०२

पाशेति । विषाणं दन्तम् । आयुधध्यानं दक्षाद्यूर्द्ध्वयोराद्ये तदधस्थयोरन्त्ये वामोर्द्ध्वादि वामाधस्तनं यावत् । इत्येके ॥ ९३ ॥

समधुत्रितयैः पयोमधुघृतसहितैरिति तिलविशेषणम् । तदुक्तमाचार्य्यैः—अथ तिलैरयुतं त्रिमधुरसिक्तैर्जुहुयात् । इति । मधुरत्रितयैरिति पाठे मधुरस्य त्रितयं येष्विति बहुव्रीहिणा नेयम् ॥ ९४-९९ ॥

लोष्टशब्देन अन्तर्वर्त्तिनारिकेलोपरिभागः तदुपरिभागः त्वग्लक्षणः चर्मशब्द-वाच्यः । अष्टधा नारिकेलमित्यस्यापवादः । विधिनाऽमुनेत्यष्टद्रव्यहोमेन ॥१००॥

शुभोदकैरिति अमृतरूपैर्जलैरित्यर्थः ॥ १०१ ॥ १०२ ॥

पाशाङ्कुशौ कल्पलतां स्वदन्तं करैर्वहन्तं कनकाद्रिकान्तम् ।
सोपानपङ्क्त्या दिननाथबिम्बादायान्तमम्भोजगतं विचिन्त्य ॥ १०३

प्रागुक्तमन्त्रसम्प्रोक्तान् प्रयोगान्मनुनाऽमुना ।
तैरस्मिन्नथवा प्रोक्तान् कुर्य्यान्मन्त्री विधानवित् ॥ १०४

तर्पणे तु ध्यानविशेषमाह पाशेति। सोपानपङ्क्त्या राजतया। दिननाथबिम्बात् सूर्य्यमण्डलात्। आयान्तं आगतं इति शेषः। अम्भोजगतं जलस्थकल्पिताम्भोजगतं गणपतिं साध्यमूर्ध्नि पुष्करं दत्वा स्थितं विचिन्त्य। एवं ध्यानं कृत्वेत्यर्थः। विघ्नराजस्य मस्तके क्षिप्रसिद्धये शुभोदकैस्तर्पयेदिति सम्बन्धः।

तदुक्तम्—बिम्बादम्बुदवत् समेत्य सवितुः सोपानकै राजतै-
स्तोये तोयजविष्टरैर्धृतलतादन्तं सपाशाङ्कुशम्।
नासां साध्यनृके निधाय सुधया तद्रन्ध्रनिर्यातया
सिञ्चन्तं पुनरन्वहं गणपतिं स्मृत्वाऽम्भतैस्तर्पयेत् ॥ इति ॥

अथ यन्त्रद्वयम्—

नामषट्कोणके बीजमध्ये लिखेद्वेष्टयित्वाऽमुनाऽथाङ्गमन्त्रैस्ततः।
अष्टपत्रे स्वरान् केसरे युग्मशः च्यादिवर्णान्विहीनान् लिखायादिकैः ॥
अग्रतो लिख्य गायत्रिवर्णांस्त्रिशो बाह्यतः कादिभिर्वेष्टयित्वा बहिः।
भूपुरद्वन्द्वके भूमिबीजं लिखेद्यन्त्रमेतन्मतं सिद्धिसंपत्प्रदम् ॥ इति ॥
अथातो महायन्त्रराजं प्रवच्मि पशोः रोचनासिक्तदूर्व्वाङ्कुरेण।
लिखेत् पञ्चपत्रे दशारं सरोजं गणेशस्य बीजं तु तारोदरे तु ॥
ततस्तस्य मध्ये तु रत्नेति नाम्ना दशैतेषु मन्त्रांश मन्त्रे लिखेच्च।
ततो बाह्यतः पाशवर्णाङ्कुशार्णौ लिखित्वा बहिः शक्तिबिम्बद्वयं तत्।
लिखित्वा तथा तं गणेशानमस्मिन् समभ्यर्च्य गन्धादिभिः पुष्पजातैः ॥
भुजे कण्ठदेशे वहेत् सर्व्वरक्षा ततो मङ्गलं नाऽन्यदस्तीह किञ्चित् ॥ इति।

उक्तञ्च—क्षिप्रप्रसादनः पूर्व्वो महागणपतिः परम्।
विघ्नो विनायको वीरः शूरो वरद एव च ॥
इभवक्त्रैकदन्तस्तथा हस्तिमुखः स्मृतः।
ङेऽन्ता नमोऽन्ता मन्त्राः स्युरेतैस्तर्पणहोमतः ॥
साधवेदोष्पितं मन्त्रो। इति।

तत्कल्पान्मन्त्रमिति मूलं युग्मशः पञ्चपत्रे ॥ १०३॥१०४

पञ्चान्तको बिन्दुयुतो वामकर्णविभूषितः ।
तारादिर्हृदयान्तोऽयं हेरम्बमनुरीरितः ॥ १०५

चतुर्वर्णात्मको नॄणां चतुर्वर्गफलप्रदः ।
षड्दीर्घभाजा बीजेन षडङ्गानि समाचरेत् ॥ १०६

मुक्ताकाञ्चननीलकुन्दघुसृणच्छायैस्त्रिनेत्रान्वितै-
र्नागास्यैर्हरिवाहनं शशिधरं हेरम्बमर्कप्रभम् ।
हस्तं दानमभीतिमोदकरदान् टङ्कं शिरोऽक्षात्मिकां
मालां मुद्गरमङ्कुशं त्रिशिखकं दोर्भिर्दधानं भजे ॥ १०७

लक्षत्रयं जपेन्मन्त्रं दशांशं जुहुयात्तिलैः ।
तीव्रादिपूजिते पीठे देवं हेरम्बमर्चयेत् ॥ १०८

प्रणवः कवचद्वन्द्वं महासिंहाय गां ततः ।
हेरम्बेति पदं पश्चादासनाय हृदन्वितः ॥ १०९

हेरम्बमनुमाह पञ्चान्तक इति। पञ्चान्तको गः वामकर्ण ऊकारः। ॐ गूं नमः। गणक ऋषिर्गायत्री छन्दः हेरम्बगणपतिर्देवता। गकारो बीजं बिन्दुः शक्तिः। बीजेनेति। एतन्मन्त्रोक्तेन ॥ १०५॥१०६ ॥

मुक्तेति। घुसृणं कुङ्कुमम्। ऊर्ध्वादिमुक्तादिवर्णाः। नागास्यैर्हस्तिमुखैरुपलक्षितम्। हरिः सिंहः। टङ्कं परशुम्। त्रिशिखं त्रिशूलम्। क्वचिदङ्कुशं च त्रिशिखमिति पाठः। तत्र क्षेत्राष्टासंयुता व्यस्तेत्यनेन चकारस्य लघुता। अतोऽप्रयत्नोच्चारणेन। तेन न छन्दोभङ्गः। आयुधध्यानं दक्षवामयोरधस्थयोः वराभये तदूर्ध्वोर्ध्वस्थयोरन्यानि एवमन्तम्। क्वचिद् हस्तमित्यत्र कुम्भमिति पाठः। तदा कुम्भः शुण्डाग्रे। हस्तमिति पाठे तु मोदकोपरि शुण्डादण्ड इति ज्ञेयम्। केचित् मुद्गरमित्यत्र पन्नगमिति पठन्ति। तदुक्तम्—

वन्दे दोर्भिर्दधानं जपवलयभुजे साङ्कुशे मोदकाभी-
टङ्कानुद्यत्कपालं भुजगवररदान् स्वर्णकुम्भाढ्यशुण्डम् ।
सिंहस्थं पञ्चवक्त्रं त्रिनयनमरुणं दिव्यवस्त्रोरुभूषं
हेरम्बाख्यं महान्तं गणपतिमखिलस्वार्थदं प्रार्थयेऽहम् ॥ इति ॥१०७॥

तीव्रादिपूजित इत्यनेन पीठमन्त्रस्याऽन्यत्वं सूचयति ॥ १०८ ॥

तमेवाह प्रणव इति। कवचद्वन्द्वं हुं हुं। गामिति स्वरूपम् ॥ १०९ ॥

अयमासनमन्त्रः स्यात्प्रदद्यादमुनाऽऽसनम् ।
तारादिविघ्नबीजेन मूर्त्तिं तस्य प्रकल्पयेत् ।
आवाह्य पूजयेत् तस्यामङ्गावरणसंयुतम् ॥ ११०
बाह्ये लोकेश्वराः पूज्या वज्रादीनि ततः परम् ।
एवमभ्यर्चयेन्नित्यं साधयेत् स्वमनीषितान् ॥ १११
मोदकैर्जुहुयात् षष्ठ्यामष्टम्यां कृशरैस्तथा ।
चतुर्दशीदिनेऽपूपैर्जुहुयाद्वाञ्छिताप्तये ॥ ११२
एभिर्द्रव्यैः प्रजुहुयान्मन्त्री पर्वदिनेष्वपि ।
साधयेत्सकलान् कामान् प्रयत्नेनैव साधकः ॥ ११३

अम्भोजं प्रथमं लिखेद्वसुदलं मध्ये स्वबीजान्तरे
साध्याख्यां बहिरङ्गमन्त्रविलसत्किञ्जल्कसंशोभितम् ।
पत्राणामुदरे विभज्य मुनिशो मालामनुं शेषितान्
षड्वर्णांश्चरमे दले परिवृतं शक्त्या शकारेण च ॥ ११४

रोचनामदकाश्मीरैर्भूर्जपत्रे विलिख्य तत् ।
वेष्टितं श्वेतसूत्रेण लोहैस्त्रिभिरपि क्रमात्
धारयेद्बाहुना यन्त्रं सर्व्वान् कामानवाप्नुयात् ॥ ११५
शक्त्यङ्कुशं ध्रुवान्ते स्यात् स्वबीजं हृदयं ततः ।
सर्व्वविघ्नाधिपायाऽन्ते ङेऽन्तं सर्व्वार्थसिद्धिदम् ॥ ११६

तारादीति। नमो रहितेन मूलमन्त्रेणेत्यर्थः ॥ ११०॥१११ ॥

षष्ठ्यामित्युभयत्र पक्षे। एवमग्रेऽपि। कृशरैर्मिश्रैस्तिलतण्डुलैः। एभिर्मोदककृशरापूपैः। पर्वदिने पूर्णिमामावस्ययोः ॥ ११२॥११३ ॥

धारणयन्त्रमाह अम्भोजमिति। मध्ये अष्टदलकर्णिकायाम्। स्वबीजान्तरे एतन्मन्त्रबीजमध्ये। साध्याख्यां साधककर्मसहितामिति ज्ञेयम्। बहिरिति कर्णिकायाः। अङ्गमन्त्रेति। पूजावदग्रे नेत्रम्। मुनिशः सप्तधा। मालामनुं वक्ष्यमाणम्। चरमे अष्टमे। शक्त्या शकारेण चेत्यावृत्तिद्वयम् ॥ ११४ ॥

मदो गजमदः। त्रिभिर्लौहैः। षष्ठपटलोक्तैः। क्रमादिति। ताम्ररजतसुवर्णैः ॥ ११५ ॥

मालामन्त्रमाह शक्तीति। स्वबीजं मन्त्रस्यबीजम्। भुवनेशीस्वबीजं

प्रवदेत् सर्व्वदुःखप्रशमनायपदं ततः।
एह्येहि भगवन् सर्व्वा आपदः स्तम्भयद्वयम् ॥ ११७

भुवनेशीं स्वबीजं गां नतिः पावकवल्लभा।
पुनरङ्कुशमायान्तं पञ्चपञ्चाशदक्षरः ॥ ११८

मालामन्त्रोऽयममुना प्रयोगान् साधयेत् सुधीः।
तारं खड्गीश्वरः कूर्म्मो निःस्वरो णान्त ईरितः ॥ ११९

भुवे नतिः सप्तवर्णः सुब्रह्मण्यात्मको मनुः।
वह्निबीजेन षड्दीर्घयुक्तेनाऽङ्गक्रिया मता ॥ १२०

सिन्दूरारुणकान्तिमिन्दुवदनं केयूरहारादिभि-
र्दिव्यैराभरणैर्विभूषिततनुं स्वर्गस्य सौख्यप्रदम्।
अम्भोजाभयशक्तिकुक्कुटधरं रक्ताङ्गरागांशुकं
सुब्रह्मण्यमुपास्महे प्रणमतां भीतिप्रणाशोद्यतम् ॥ १२१

भुवनेश्वाः स्वस्य च बीजं क्रीं गूम्। गामिति स्वरूपम्। पञ्चपञ्चाशदक्षर इत्युक्तेः शमनाय एह्येहीति न सन्धिः। ॐ क्रीं क्रों गूं नमः सर्व्वविघ्नाधिपाय सर्व्वार्थसिद्धिदाय सर्व्वदुःखप्रशमनाय एह्येहि भगवन् सर्व्वा आपदः स्तम्भय स्तम्भय क्रीं गूं गां नमः स्वाहा क्रों क्रीं। अमुना प्रयोगान् साधयेदित्यनेनास्य स्वातन्त्र्येण मन्त्रत्वमप्युक्तम्। तद्विधानं यथा। अस्य अमितं छन्दः हेरम्बगणतिवत् सर्व्वं ज्ञेयम् ॥ ११६॥११७॥११८॥११९ ॥

सुब्रह्मण्यमन्त्रमाह तारमिति। खड्गीशो वः कूर्म्मश्चकारः। निस्वरः स्वरहीनो व्यञ्जनमिति यावत्। णान्तः तः। भुवे स्वरूपम्। अत्र सन्धौ तकारे दकार इति ज्ञेयम्। तदुक्तं प्रयोगसारे—

वचद्भुवे नमो मन्त्रः सुब्रह्मण्याधिदैवतः। इति।

नारायणीये तु—तारं वचनाभिजले शिवयोनियुते नमः। इति।

अग्निगायत्री ऋषिश्छन्दसी। प्रणवो बीजं वकारः शक्तिः। केचन प्रणव-पुटितमाहुः। अन्ये तु मायाद्यमाहुः।

तदुक्तं प्रयोगसारे—प्रशस्तः प्रणवाद्यन्तःशक्तिपूर्व्वं परे जगुः। इति।

वह्निबीजेनेति रेफेण ॥ ११९॥१२० ॥

ध्यानं तु दक्षयूर्ध्वयोराद्ये तदधस्थयोरन्त्ये। सुब्रह्मण्य इति कार्त्तिकेयनाम।

लक्षमेकं जपेन्मन्त्रं साज्येन हविषा ततः ।
दशांशं जुहुयादन्ते ब्राह्मणानपि भोजयेत् ॥ १२२

धर्म्मादिकल्पिते पीठे वह्निमण्डलपश्चिमे ।
पूजयेद्विधिना देवमुपचारैर्यथोदितैः ॥ १२३

केसरेष्वङ्गपूजा स्यात्पत्रमध्यगतानिमान् ।
जयन्ताख्यमग्निवेश्यं कृत्तिकापुत्रसंज्ञकम् ॥ १२४

अनन्तरं भूतपतिं सेनान्यं गुहसंज्ञकम् ।
इभशूलं विशालाक्षं शक्तिवज्र[शूल]करान् यजेत् ॥ १२५

दिग्दलाग्रेषु पूर्व्वादि देवसेनापतिं पुनः ।
विद्यां मेधां ततो वज्रं कोणस्थान् शक्तिकुक्कुटौ ॥ १२६

मयूरं हौममभ्यर्चेदाद्ये लोकेश्वरान् पुनः ।
अस्त्राणि तेषामन्ते स्युः सुब्रह्मण्यार्च्चनेरिता ॥ १२७

स्वादुभिर्भक्ष्यभोज्याद्यैः षष्ठ्यां संप्रीणयेद्विभुम् ।
पूजयेद्देवताबुद्ध्या कुमारान् ब्रह्मचारिणः ॥ १२८

सन्तानं विजयं वीर्य्यं रक्षामायुः श्रियं यशः ।
प्रदद्यात् साधकस्याशु सुब्रह्मण्यः सुरार्चितः ॥ १२९

जपतर्पणपूजादौ विशेषं सर्व्वसिद्धिदम् ।
प्रीणयेदनया स्तुत्या प्रार्थये सर्व्वसम्पदाम् ॥ १३०

तदुक्तं हयशीर्षपञ्चरात्रे—

अभयं वामहस्ते स्याद्वज्रं दक्षिणे करे ।
कुक्कुटं वामहस्ते तु शक्तिं दक्षिणतो न्यसेत् ॥
चतुर्भुजः समाख्यात एकवक्त्रोऽग्निजस्त्वयम् । इति ॥१२१॥१२२॥

वह्निमण्डलपश्चिम इति । अनेन चतुर्थपटलोक्तवह्निमण्डलान्तरेव पूजा । पीठशक्तिपीठपूजा नास्ति । अन्यथा वह्निमण्डलपश्चिम इति न वदेत् । चतुर्थपटल एवोक्तत्वात् ॥ १२३ ॥

विधिनेत्युक्तं विधिमाह केसरेष्विति । तत्र नैवेद्यांशदानं धूर्त्तसेनाय ॥१२४॥ १२५॥१२६॥१२७॥१२८॥१२९॥

ॐकारमाद्यं प्रवदन्ति सन्तो वाचः श्रुतीनामपि यं गृणन्ति ।
गजाननं देवगणानताङ्घ्रिं भजेऽहमर्द्धेन्दुकृतावतंसम् ॥ १३१
पादारविन्दार्चनतत्पराणां संसारदावानलभङ्गदक्षम् ।
निरन्तरं निर्गतदानतोयैस्तं नौमि विघ्नेश्वरमम्बुदाभम् ॥ १३२
कृताङ्गरागं नवकुङ्कुमेन मत्तालिमालां मदपङ्कलग्नाम् ।
निवारयन्तं निजकर्णतालैः को विस्मरेत् पुत्रमनङ्गशत्रोः ॥ १३३
शम्भोर्जटाजूटनिवासिगङ्गाजलं समादाय कराम्बुजेन ।
लीलाभिराराच्छिवमर्चयन्तं गजाननं भक्तियुता भजन्ति ॥ १३४
कुमारभुक्तौ पुनरात्महेतोः पयोधरौ पर्व्वतराजपुत्र्याः ।
प्रक्षालयन्तं करशीकरेण मौग्ध्येन तं नागमुखं भजामि ॥ १३५
त्वया समुद्धृत्य गजास्य हस्तं ये शीकराः पुष्कररन्ध्रमुक्ताः ।
व्योमाङ्गणे ते विचरन्ति ताराः कालात्मना मौक्तिकतुल्यभासः ॥ १३६
क्रीडारते वारिनिधौ गजास्ये वेलामतिक्रामति वारिपूरे ।
कल्पावसानं परिचिन्त्य देवाः कैलासनाथं स्तुतिभिः स्तुवन्ति ॥ १३७
नागानने नागकृतोत्तरीये क्रीडारते देवकुमारसङ्घैः ।
त्वयि क्षणं कालगतिं विहाय तौ प्रापतुः कन्दुकतामिनेन्दू ॥ १३८

गणेशस्तुतिमारभते ॐकारमिति । अपिर्भिन्नक्रमः । सन्तः यं श्रुतीनामाद्यं ॐकारं वाचोऽप्याद्यं गृणन्ति । शब्दब्रह्मस्वरूपमिति यावत् ॥ १३०॥१३१ ॥

कराम्बुजेन शुण्डाग्रेण । आरात् समीपे । भक्तियुता भजन्ति इत्यत्र तं शरणं भजामि इत्यपि क्वचित् पाठः ॥ १३४ ॥

मौग्ध्येनेति । देवीस्तनौ सदानुच्छिष्टाविति भावः ॥ १३५ ॥

भो गजास्य कालात्मना त्वया हस्तमुद्धृत्य ये शीकराः पुष्कररन्ध्रमुक्ताः । पुष्करं करिहस्ताग्र इति नामलिङ्गानुशासने । ते ताराः विचरन्तीति गम्योत्प्रेक्षा शीकरा न भवन्ति । ताराः इत्युत्प्रेक्षा इत्यर्थः ॥ १३६ ॥

स्तुवन्तीति अन्यकृतः कल्पावसाने न्यस्य स्तुत्यसङ्गतिरित्यलङ्कारः । वस्तुतस्तु अनन्यनिवारणीयत्वेन तत्स्तुतिः ॥ १३७ ॥

नागकृतोत्तरीये सर्पोत्तरीये त्वयि क्रीडारत इति सम्बन्धः । कालगतिं

मदोल्लसत्पञ्चमुखैरजस्रमध्यापयन्तं सकलागमार्थान् ।
देवानृषीन् भक्तजनैकमित्रं हेरम्बमर्कारुणमाश्रयामि ॥ १३९

पादाम्बुजाभ्यामतिवामनाभ्यां कृतार्थयन्तं कृपया धरित्रीम् ।
अकारणं कारणमाप्तवाचां तं नागवक्त्रं न जहाति चेतः ॥ १४०

येनाऽर्पितं सत्यवतीसुताय पुराणमालिख्य विषाणकोट्या ।
तं चन्द्रमौलेस्तनयं तपोभिरवाप्यमानन्दघनं भजामि ॥ १४१

पदं स्तुतीनामपदं श्रुतीनां लीलावतारं परमात्ममूर्त्तेः ।
नागात्मको वा पुरुषात्मको वेत्यभेद्यमाद्यं भज विघ्नराजम् ॥ १४२

पाशाङ्कुशौ भग्नरदं त्वभीष्टं करैर्दधानं कररन्ध्रमुक्तैः ।
मुक्ताफलाभैः पृथुसीकरौघैः सिञ्चन्तमङ्गं शिवयोर्भजामि ॥ १४३

अनेकमेकं गजमेकदन्तं चैतन्यरूपं जगदादिबीजम् ।
ब्रह्मेति यं ब्रह्मविदो वदन्ति तं शम्भुसूनुं शरणं भजामि ॥ १४४

स्वाङ्कस्थिताया निजवल्लभाया मुखाम्बुजालोकनलोलनेत्रम् ।
स्मेराननाब्जं मदवैभवेन रुद्धं भजे विश्वविमोहनं तम् ॥ १४५

ये पूर्व्वमाराध्य गजानन त्वां शास्त्राणि सर्व्वाणि पठन्ति तेषाम् ।
त्वत्तो न चाऽन्यत् प्रतिपाद्यमेतैस्तदस्ति चेत् सर्व्वमसत्यकल्पम् ॥ १४६

कालपारवश्यं त्यक्त्वा ॥ १३८ ॥

वामनाभ्यां सुखकन्दाद्यपेक्षया कृशता। एतेनास्य कृशावेवाङ्घ्री ध्येयाविति सूचितम्। आप्तवाचां वेदानां कारणं प्रवर्त्तयितारम् ॥ १३९॥१४० ॥

पुराणं भारताख्यम्। पदं स्थानम्। अपदमगोचरम्। क्वचित् स्तुतिश्रुतिपदयोः व्यत्ययः। परमात्ममूर्त्तेरित्यत्र परमेष्टेवि केचित् पठन्ति ॥ १४१॥१४२ ॥

शिवयोः पित्रोः ॥ १४३ ॥

अनेकमिच्छया। एकं तत्त्वतो ॥ १४४॥१४५ ॥

ये पठन्ति तेषां पुरुषाणां त्वत्तोऽन्यत् प्रतिपाद्यं ज्ञेयं नास्ति। चकारात्तेषां शास्त्राणामपि त्वत्तोऽन्यत् प्रतिपाद्यं नास्तीत्यर्थः। यतः सर्व्वेषु शास्त्रेष्वात्मनः प्रतिपादितत्वात् एतैः शास्त्रैस्त्वदन्यत्प्रतिपाद्यते चेत् तत् सर्व्वमसत्यकल्पम्। तानि शास्त्राण्येव न भवन्तीत्यर्थः। बौद्धशास्त्रादिवत् ॥ १४६ ॥

हिरण्यगर्भं जगदीशितारं कविं पुराणं रविमण्डलस्थम् ।
गजाननं यं प्रविशन्ति सन्तस्तत्काल योगैस्तमहं प्रपद्ये ॥ १४७

वेदान्तगीतं पुरुषं भजेऽहमात्मानमानन्दघनं हृदिस्थम् ।
गजाननं यन्महसा जनानां विघ्नान्धकारो विलयं प्रयाति ॥ १४८

शम्भोः समालोक्य जटाकलापे शशाङ्कखण्डं निजपुष्करेण ।
स्वभग्नदन्तं प्रविचिन्त्य मौग्ध्यादाक्रष्टुकामः श्रियमातनोतु ॥ १४९

विघ्नार्गलानां विनिपातनार्थं यं नारिकेलैः कदलीफलाद्यैः ।
प्रतारयन्तो मदवारणास्यं प्रापुर्नरोऽभीष्टमहं भजे तम् ॥ १५०

यज्ञैरनेकैर्बहुभिस्तपोभिराराध्यमाद्यं गजराजवक्त्रम् ।
स्तुत्याऽनया ये विधिना स्तुवन्ति ते सर्व्वलक्ष्मीनिधयो भवन्ति ॥ १५१

इति श्रीशारदातिलके त्रयोदशः पटलः ।

तत्कालयोगैरिति हिरण्यगर्भाद्यवतारो गणेश एवैको लीलया भवति। परमात्मरूपत्वादित्यर्थः ॥ १४७ ॥

तदेव रूपमाह वेदान्तगीतमिति ॥ १४८ ॥

मौग्ध्यादिति लीलया। तस्य कदाचिदपि ज्ञानभ्रंशाभावात् ॥ १४९ ॥

विघ्नेत्यादिना भक्तवात्सल्यमुक्तम्। नर इति बहुवचनम् ॥ १५०॥१५१ ॥

इति श्रीशारदातिलकटीकायां सम्प्रदायकृतव्याख्यायां
पदार्थादर्शाभिख्यायां त्रयोदशः पटलः ।

चतुर्दशः पटलः ।

अथोच्यते चन्द्रमसो मनुः सर्व्वसमृद्धिदः ।
खड्गीशस्थो भृगुर्बिन्दुर्मनुस्वरसमन्वितः ॥ १
सोमाय हृदयान्तोऽयं मन्त्रः प्रोक्तः षडक्षरः ।
ऋषिरुक्तो भृगुः छन्दः पङ्क्तिः सोमोऽस्य देवता ॥ २
दीर्घभाजा स्वबीजेन मनोरङ्गक्रिया मता ॥ ३

कर्पूरस्फटिकावदातमनिशं पूर्णेन्दुबिम्बाननं
मुक्तादामविभूषितेन वपुषा निर्मूलयन्तं तमः ।
हस्ताभ्यां कुमुदं वरं च दधतं नीलालकोद्भासितं
स्वस्याऽङ्कस्थमृगाङ्कोदिताश्रयगुणं सोमं सुधाब्धिं भजे ॥ ४

अथ क्रमप्राप्तान् सौरमन्त्रान् वक्तुकामस्तस्य तेजस्त्रयात्मकत्वादाद्यन्तयोः सोमाग्न्योर्मन्त्रान् वदन् तन्मन्त्रान् वक्तुमुपक्रमते अथेति। सर्व्वसमृद्धिद इति विनियोगोक्तिः। मन्त्रमुद्धरति खड्गीशेति। खड्गीशो वः तत्स्थो भृगुः सः मनुस्वरः चतुर्दशस्वर औ बिन्दुश्च तद्युक्तः तेन स्वौं। प्रयोगसारे तु—

सवौबिन्द्वादिसोमाय नमो मन्त्रः प्रकीर्त्तितः। इति।

क्वचिद्बिन्दुमानो स्वर इति पाठः। नारायणीये च आचार्य्यैश्च स्वौमित्युद्धृतम्। अन्ये तु इदं मृत्युञ्जयबीजम्। एतदाद्यो ग्रन्थकृताऽनुद्धत इति वदन्ति। स्वौं बीजं। आयेति शक्तिः। पद्मपादाचार्य्यैर्मेति शक्तिरुद्धृता। अन्यत्र तु—

ऋषिरत्रिर्विराट्छन्दो बीजमाद्यमुदाहृतम्।

नमः शक्तिः। इति।

प्रणवप्रासादसंपुट इति केचन। श्रीकामैः श्रीपुटः कार्य्य इत्यपरे। स्वबीजेनेति। मन्त्राद्यबीजेन स्व इति बीजेन वा ॥ १॥२॥३॥

ध्यानमाह कर्पूरेति। दक्षिणवामाभ्यां कुमुदवरे। क्वचिद्धनमिति पाठः। धनं निधिपात्रम्। अङ्कस्थमृगात् उदित उत्पन्नः आश्रयगुणो नीलिमा यत्र। तेनाङ्कोऽपि ध्येय इत्यर्थः।

तदुक्तम्—भवतु भवदभीष्टद्योतिताङ्कः शशाङ्कः। इति।

अथवा स्वस्याङ्कस्थमृगेणोदित आश्रयगुणः सेवनीयगुणो येन कलङ्कित्वापवादे सत्यप्यत्यागात्। सुधाब्धिं अमृतस्वरूपम् ॥ ४ ॥

रसलक्षं जपेन्मन्त्रं साधको विजितेन्द्रियः।
षट्सहस्रं प्रजुहुयात्पायसेन ससर्पिषा ॥ ५
सोमान्तं पूजिते पीठे पूजयेद्रोहिणीपतिम्।
अङ्गानि केसरेषु स्युस्तद्बह्यः पत्रमध्यगाः ॥ ६
रोहिणी कृत्तिका भूयो रेवती भरणी पुनः।
रात्रिदार्द्रा ततो ज्योतिः कला हारसमप्रभाः ॥ ७
सितमाल्याम्बरधरा मुक्ताहारविभूषणाः।
पयोधरभराक्रान्ता रचिताञ्जलयः शुभाः ॥ ८
वल्लभासक्तमनसो मदविभ्रममन्थराः।
समभ्यर्च्याः सरोजाढ्यश्चन्द्रबिम्बनिभाननाः ॥ ९

रसलक्षं षड्लक्षम्। साधकसत्तम इत्यनेन विद्यामन्त्रस्य दशांशजप उक्तः। प्रयोगेऽपि तज्जपः। तत्र धनलाभे श्रीयोगः कवित्वे वाग्भवयोगः सुखादौ प्रणवयोग इति पद्मपादाचार्य्याः ॥ ५ ॥

सोमान्तमिति। चतुर्थपटले तस्मिन् सूर्य्येन्दुपावकानिति अनेन अग्निमण्डलान्ता पूजोक्ता। अत्र तु सूर्य्याग्निमण्डले सम्पूज्य अन्ते सोममण्डलं पूजनीयम्। कश्चित् सोमान्तमिति वह्निमण्डले पूजा न कर्त्तव्येत्याह। तन्न। असाम्प्रदायिकत्वात्। मन्त्रदेवप्रकाशिकादिबहुग्रन्थविरोधाच्च। पीठक्रमो तु सोमान्तमिति। प्रपञ्चसारपद्यव्याख्याने पद्मपादाचार्य्यैः पीठार्च्चने सूर्य्यवह्निमण्डलार्च्चनं कृत्वा ततः सोममण्डलमभ्यर्च्य तत्र भगवन्तमावाहयेदित्युक्तम्। पूजिते पीठ इति। पीठनवशक्तिपूजापूर्वकं पीठमन्त्रेणेति शेषः। तास्त्र पीठमन्त्रा अपि तन्त्रान्तरोक्ता ज्ञेयाः। तद्यथा—

अमृता तारका ज्योत्स्ना विमला व्यापिनी तथा।
चित्रा च कृत्तिका कान्तिः श्रवणा नव शक्तयः ॥
अमृतान्ते कलात्मने संवित्पीठाय ते नमः। इति।

पद्मपादाचार्य्यैरन्याः पीठशक्तय उक्ताः ॥

राका कुमुद्वती नन्दा सुधा सञ्जीवनी क्षमा।
आप्यायनी चन्द्रिका च ह्लादिनी नव शक्तयः ॥
पूर्व्वादिक्रमतो मन्त्री नत्यन्ताः पूजयेदिमाः ॥ इति।

आदित्यमङ्गलबुधमन्दवाक्पतिराहवः ।
शुक्रकेतुयुताः पूज्या दलाग्रेषु ग्रहा इमे ॥ १०

स्वस्ववर्णाम्बरोपेताः स्वनामाद्यर्णबीजकाः ।
रक्तारुणश्वेतनीलपीतधूम्रसितासिताः ॥ ११

वामोरुन्यस्तहस्ता दक्षिणेन धृताभयाः ।
अम्बुजाढ्यकरो भानुर्दंष्ट्राभीममुखः शनिः ॥ १२

राहुर्विकृतवक्त्रः स्यात्केतुः स्याद्विहिताञ्जलिः ।
लोकपालास्ततः पूज्या वज्राद्यस्त्रैः सह क्रमात् ॥ १३

एवं सिद्धमनुर्मन्त्री सम्पदां वसतिर्भवेत् ।
हृत्पुण्डरीकमध्यस्थं तारहारविभूषितम् ॥ १४

तारापतिं स्मरन्मन्त्री त्रिसहस्रं मनुं जपेत् ।
राज्यैश्वर्य्यं दरिद्रोऽपि प्राप्नुयाद्वत्सरान्तरे ॥ १५

कलेति शक्तिनाम । "कलामीशदलेषु" इत्युक्तेः । कश्चित्करालीति शक्तिनाम । "कराली च क्रमादिमाः" इत्युक्तेः । हारसमप्रभाः श्वेता इत्यर्थः ॥ ६॥७॥८॥९ ॥

आदित्येति । मङ्गलः अङ्गारकः । मन्दः शनैश्चरः । वाक्पतिर्बृहस्पतिः । तत्र चतुर्दिक्षु आदित्यादयः अग्निकोणादिषु भौमादयः पूज्या इति ज्ञेयम् । यदाहुः—

पूर्व्वदक्षिणपाश्चात्यसौम्यपत्राग्रके क्रमात् ।
रविश्चान्द्रिर्गुरुः शुक्रः सम्पूज्याः साधकैरमी ॥
आग्नेयादिषु कोणेषु भौममन्दाहिकेतवः । इति ।

स्वनाम्नाम् आद्यर्णाः आद्यक्षराणि सबिन्दूनि बीजानि येषां ते । एतेन ग्रहाणां मन्त्राः सूचिताः । ग्रहयन्त्राङ्गत्वेन तत्र सूर्य्यमन्त्रं वक्ष्यति । अन्येषां ससानाम् अं अङ्गारकाय नम इत्यादयो ज्ञेयाः । ग्रहाग्रे च पूजायामपि अयमेव प्रयोगोऽनुसन्धेयः ॥ १०॥११ ॥

वामोर्विति सूर्य्यकेतू हित्वा अन्येषां ध्यानम् । सूर्य्यस्तु पद्मकरः केतुस्तु विहिताञ्जलिरित्युक्तेः । तदुक्तं महाकपिलपञ्चरात्रे—

आदित्यो द्विभुजः प्रोक्तो युवा लक्षणलक्षितः ।
हस्तयोः पङ्कजे तस्य कार्य्ये स्कन्धमिते शुभे ॥
केतोस्तु—खड्गदीपधरं कार्य्यमथवा विहिताञ्जलिम् । इति ।

पूर्व्वोक्तसंख्यं प्रजपेत् शशिनं मूर्ध्नि चिन्तयन् ।
रोगापमृत्युदुःखानि जित्वा वर्षशतं वसेत् ॥ १६

ब्रह्मचर्य्यरतः शुद्धश्चतुर्लक्षमिमं जपेत् ।
निधानं भूगतं सद्यः प्राप्नुयाद्यत्नवर्जितः ॥ १७

जितेन्द्रियो जपेन्मन्त्रं पौर्णमास्यां विशेषतः ।
भवेत्सौभाग्यनिलयः सम्पदामपरो निधिः ॥ १८

घोरान् ज्वरान् शिरोरोगानभिचारानुपद्रवान् ।
विषाणामपि संघातं नाशयेन्मनुनाऽमुना ॥ १९

पौर्णमास्यां निराहारो दद्यादर्घं विधूदये ।
प्राक्प्रत्यगायतं कुर्य्याद् भूतले मण्डलत्रयम् ॥ २०
निषण्णः पश्चिमे मन्त्री मण्डले विहितासने ।
मध्यस्थे स्थापयेत्तस्मात् पूजाद्रव्याण्यशेषतः ॥ २१
अन्यस्मिन्मण्डले सोममर्चयित्वाऽम्बुजान्विते ।
राजतं चषकं तत्र स्थापयेत् पुरतः सुधीः ॥ २२

प्रयोगसारेऽपि—पूर्व्वार्द्धकायः पिङ्गभ्रू रक्तनेत्रः कृताञ्जलिः । इति । तार उज्ज्वलो हारो मुक्ताहारः । तारापतिमिति नायिकासहितम् ॥ १२॥१३॥ ॥ १४॥१५ ॥

पूर्व्वोक्तसंख्यमिति त्रिसहस्रम् । शुद्ध इत्यनेन त्रिषवणस्नायी पयआहारश्चेत्युक्तम् । यत्प्रयोगसारे—

कृत्वा त्रिषवणं स्नानं क्षीराहारो निरन्तरः ।
जपेच्चत्वारि लक्षाणि निधानं लभते ध्रुवम् ॥ इति ॥

मण्डलत्रयमिति । गोमयादिना ॥ १६॥१७॥१८॥१९॥२०॥२१ ॥

अन्यस्मिन् पौरस्त्ये । सोममर्चयित्वेति पीठादिन्यासं विधाय आत्मयागं कृत्वा बहिः पीठे पङ्कजान्विते अर्चयित्वेत्यर्थः । उक्तञ्च—

आसीनः पश्चिमे मध्यसंस्थे द्रव्याणि विन्यसेत् ।
आत्मानं सकलीकृत्याऽभ्यर्च्याचान्तः सुरेश्वरः ॥
पूर्व्वस्मिन् पङ्कजोपेते मण्डले सोममर्चयेत् ॥ इति ।

सुधीरित्यनेनैतदुक्तं भवति । विलोममन्त्रं जपन् पूरणं कर्पूरादीनां कुमुदादीनां

गोदुग्धेन समापूर्य्य स्पृष्ट्वा तं प्रजपेन्मनुम् ।
अष्टोत्तरशतं पश्चाद्विद्यामन्त्रेण देशिकः ॥ २३

दद्यादर्घं शशाङ्काय सर्व्वकार्य्यार्थसिद्धये ।
अनेन विधिना कुर्य्यात्प्रतिमासमतन्द्रितः ॥ २४

षण्मासाभ्यन्तरे सिद्धिं साधकेन्द्रः समश्नुते ।
श्रियमभ्युर्जितान् पुत्रान् सौभाग्यं पुष्कलं यशः ॥ २५

कन्यामिष्टामवाप्नोति कन्याऽपि वरमाप्नुयात् ।
बहुना किमिहोक्तेन सर्व्वं दद्यान्निशापतिः ॥ २६

विद्ये विद्यामालिनि स्याच्चन्द्रिच्चन्द्रमुखि ततो भवेत् ।
पुनश्चन्द्रमुखि स्वाहा विद्यामन्त्र उदाहृतः ॥ २७

च पुष्पाणां तत्र निक्षेप इति । यदाहुः—

संस्थाप्य राजतं तत्र चषकं परिपूरयेत् ।
विलोमं प्रजपन् मन्त्रं गव्येन पयसा सुधीः ॥
क्षिपेच्च तत्र कर्पूरशीतकाश्मीरकाक्षतान् ।
कुशग्रन्थियवांश्चैव पुष्पाख्येतानि चादरात् ॥
कुमुदेन्दीवरस्वर्णकेतकीनवमल्लिकाः ।
चम्पकानि यथालाभं शतपत्राणि च क्षिपेत् ॥
आवाहयेच्चन्द्रबिम्बान्निजाद्वा हृदयाद्विभुम् ।
एवं समावाह्य गन्धपुष्पाद्यैरर्चयेद्विभुम् ॥ इति ॥

निराहारोऽर्घ्यं दद्यादित्युक्तत्वादर्घ्यदानादनन्तरं रात्रौ भोजनमनिषिद्धम् । कन्याऽपीत्यनेनैवमादिषु स्त्रियां अप्यधिकार इत्युक्तं भवति ॥ २२॥२३॥२४॥२५॥२६ ॥

विद्यामन्त्र उदाहृत इत्यनेनैतदुक्तम् । नवाक्षराद्य एष एव कन्याप्रदानसमर्थ इति । नवाक्षराणि तु ।

रक्षयुग्मं गजौ प्रोक्ता कर्णिनि स्यान्नवाक्षरम् । इति ।

नारायणीये नवाक्षरादिविद्यामन्त्रमुद्धृतम् ।

विलोमान्तरितं मन्त्रं पत्रे लिख्य तदासनः ।
जपेद्द्वादशसाहस्रमेतदेकादिनेन यः ॥
ज्येष्ठामाराध्य शुक्रार्चे कन्या तस्याशु दीयते । इति ।

अथ तन्त्रान्तरोक्तं यन्त्रमुच्यते—

तारो घृणिर्भृगुः पश्चाद्वामकर्णविभूषितः ।
वह्न्यासनो मरुच्छेषः सनेत्रोऽवित्यपश्चिमः ॥ २८

अष्टाक्षरो मनुः प्रोक्तो भानोरभिमतप्रदः ।
देवभागो मुनिः प्रोक्तो गायत्री छन्द ईरितम् ॥ २९

आदित्यो देवता प्रोक्तो दृष्टादृष्टफलप्रदः ।
सत्याय हृदयं प्रोक्तं ब्रह्मणे ठिठ ईरितः ॥ ३०

विष्णवे स्याच्छिखा वर्म रुद्राय परिकीर्त्तितम् ।
अग्नये नेत्रमाख्यातं शर्वायाऽस्त्रमुदीरितम् ॥ ३१

चक्रं चन्द्रकलाभिरन्विते शशाङ्के नामतारोदरे ।
षट्पत्रे परितो विलिख्य च भृगुर्दन्तेन बिन्द्वन्वितः ॥
सोमायेति पदं नमः पदयुतं चालिख्य तद्वाह्यतः ।
कादिक्षान्तगतं समर्च्य विधिना कण्ठ्यां गले मस्तके ॥
जप्तं यन्त्रमिदं क्षणेन गरलप्रध्वंसि तत्पुष्टिदम् । इति ॥ २६॥२७ ॥

सूर्य्यमन्त्रमाह तार इति । घृणिरिति स्वरूपम् । भृगुः सः वामकर्णः ऊ तेन विभूषितस्तेन सू । मरुद्यकारो वह्निः रेफस्तदासनः तेन र्यः । शेषः अमन्त्र आ अविदः सनेत्र इकारयुक्तस्तेन दि । त्यपश्चिम इति मन्त्रविशेषणं त्य इत्यन्तमक्षर-मित्यर्थः । पश्चिम इत्यनेन श्रीमन्तोऽपि भवतीति सूचितम् । अभिमतप्रद इत्यनेन विनियोगोक्तिः । अयं मन्त्रः साक्षाच्छ्रुतिपठित इति शूद्रादेरत्र नाधिकारः ।

तदुक्तं तैत्तिरीयशाखायां । नारायणीयोपनिषदि—घृणिरिति द्वे अक्षरे सूर्य्य इति त्रीणि आदित्य इति । त्रीणि एतद्वै सावित्रस्याष्टाक्षरं पदं श्रियाभिषिक्तं य एवं वेद श्रिया हैवाभिषिच्यत इति ।

के चन श्रीमन्त्रमाहुः । अन्ये श्रीकामकलारेखापुटितं मन्त्रं लक्ष्मीं प्रयच्छेत्यनेन पल्लवितमाहुः । रं बीजं यं शक्तिः । के चन शक्तिबीजाद्यं श्रीमन्त्रमाहुः । तन्मते प्रणवो बीजं माया शक्तिः । तदुक्तम्—

श्रीबीजान्तः सम्प्रदाये मूलमन्त्रस्तु याजुषः [मानुषः] ।
अयं श्रीकामकलारेखासंपुटोऽन्ते प्रयच्छ मे ॥
लक्ष्मीमित्थं पल्लवितः शङ्कराचार्य्यसम्मतः ।
कलारेखापूर्व्वकोऽन्त श्रीबिन्दुरूपमते स्थितः ॥ इति ।

तेजोज्वालामणि हुंफट्स्वाहान्ताः पृथगीरिताः ।
अङ्गमन्त्रान् पुनर्न्यस्येत् पञ्च मूर्त्तीर्यथाक्रमम् ॥ ३२

आदित्यं विन्यसेन्मूर्ध्नि रविं मुखगतं न्यसेत् ।
हृदये भानुनामानं भास्करं गुह्यदेशतः ॥ ३३

सूर्य्यं चरणयोर्न्यस्येत् ह्रस्वैः सद्यादिपञ्चभिः ।
प्रधानमूर्त्तिप्रतिमाः सर्व्वाभरणभूषिताः ॥ ३४

मूर्द्धास्यकण्ठहृदयं कुक्षिनाभिध्वजाङ्घ्रिषु ।
मन्त्रवर्णान् न्यसेदष्टौ प्रत्येकं प्रणवादिकान् ।
एवं न्यस्तशरीरोऽसौ चिन्तयेत्तेजसां निधिम् ॥ ३५

रक्ताब्जयुग्माभयदानहस्तं केयूरहाराङ्गदभूषणाढ्यम् ।
माणिक्यमौलिं दिननाथमीडे बन्धूककान्तिं विलसत्त्रिनेत्रम् ॥ ३६

द्विठः स्वाहा । ईरिता उक्ताः । सत्यायेत्यादयोऽङ्गमन्त्राः पृथक् प्रत्येकमेतदन्ता ज्ञेयाः । तत्र प्रयोगः । सत्याय तेजो ज्वालामणि हुं फट् स्वाहा । हृदयाय नम इत्यादि । अन्ये तु सत्यायेत्यादिचतुर्थी अविवक्षितेत्याहुः । तेन सत्यतेजोज्वालामणि हुं फट् स्वाहा हृदयाय नम इत्यादि प्रयोगः । एष एव साम्प्रदायिकः । अपेक्षितार्थद्योतनिकाकारादिभिस्तथा लिखितत्वात् । अत एव प्रपञ्चसारटीकाकारैः अङ्गेत्यत्राकारश्रुतिश्चतुर्थीनिवारणायेति व्याख्यातम् । पुनरित्यनेनाऽष्टाङ्गोऽपि सूचितः । सूत्रमन्त्रषड्वर्णानि षडङ्गस्थानेषु षडङ्गवद्विन्यस्य उदरपृष्ठयोर्नमोऽन्तयोर्वर्णद्वयं न्यसेदित्यष्टाङ्गम् । सद्यादीति । ओकारादिविपरीतनपुंसकवर्जितपारिभाषिक पञ्चह्रस्वैः सह यथाक्रमं पञ्चमूर्त्तीर्न्यसेदिति सम्बन्धः । ॐ आदित्याय नमः एं रवये नमः उं भानवे नमः इं भास्कराय नमः अं भ सूर्य्याय नम इति प्रयोगः । यथाक्रमम् इत्यनेन ऊर्द्धादिमुखेष्वपि न्यसेदित्युक्तम् । प्रत्येकमिति । तेन ॐ ॐनमो मूर्ध्नीति प्रयोगः । एवं न्यस्तेत्यनेन नवग्रहन्यासोऽपि सूचितः । स उक्तो मया प्राक् ॥ २८॥२९॥३०॥३१॥३२॥३३॥३४॥३५ ॥

दानं वरम् । आयुधध्यानं वामाद्युर्द्धयो रक्ताब्जे तदधस्तनयोरन्ये । अत्र ध्यानानन्तरं कमलबिम्बमुद्रे प्रदर्शनीये ।

कमलाकृतिमुद्रा तु सौरमुद्रेयमीरिता । इत्युक्तेः ।

वसुलक्षं जपेन्मन्त्रं समिद्भिः क्षीरशाखिनाम् ।
तत्सहस्रं प्रजुहुयात् क्षीराक्ताभिर्जितेन्द्रियः ॥ ३७
पीठस्य क्लृप्तेः प्रथमं दिक्षु मध्ये च संयजेत् ।
प्रभूतं विमलं सारं समाराध्यमनन्तरम् ॥ ३८

प्रयोगसारेऽपि—दर्शयेदथतत्त्वज्ञबिम्बमुद्रे यथोदिते । इति ।

तत्रावाजमुद्रालक्षणं यथा—

करौ तु संमुखौ कृत्वा संहतावुन्नताङ्गुली ।
तलान्तमिलिताङ्गुष्ठौ कुर्यादेषाऽब्जमुद्रिका ॥ इति ॥

नारायणीये बिम्बमुद्रालक्षणम्—

पद्माकारौ करौ कृत्वा अविश्लिष्टे तु मध्यमे ।
अङ्गुल्यौ धारयेत्तस्मिन् बिम्बमुद्रेति मोच्यते ॥ इति ।

एते सर्व्वसौरमन्त्रसाधारणी इति ज्ञेयम् ॥ ३६ ॥

वसुलक्षमष्टलक्षम् । अत्र विशेषः प्रयोगसारे—

रक्ताम्बरधरो रक्तगन्धमाल्यविभूषितः ।
घृतक्षीरसमायुक्तगुड़भक्ताशनो निशि ॥
भैक्षाहारोऽथवा वीतसङ्गः सन्तोषवान् सदा ।
मन्त्रमावर्त्तयेन्नित्यमाराधनपरायणः ॥ इति ।

अन्यः पुरश्चरणसामान्यविधिर्वक्ष्यमाण एवानुसन्धेयः । तत्सहस्रमष्टसहस्रम् ॥३७॥

पीठस्य क्लृप्तेः प्रथममिति । मण्डूकादिवेदिकान्तं सम्पूज्य धर्म्मादेः प्राक् परमसुखान्तान् पश्च सम्पूज्य पश्चाद्धर्म्मादिपूजेति केचन । अन्ये तु धर्म्मादिस्थाने प्रभूतादिकान् सम्पूज्य मध्ये फलकरूपेण परमसुखं पूजयेत् । धर्म्माधर्म्मादिपूजा नास्तीत्याहुः । एतदेव साम्प्रदायिकम् । उक्तञ्च नारायणीये—

पीठाङ्गानि कल्पयेदेतान् हृदा मध्ये विदिक्षु च । इति ।

एतत् सर्व्वसूर्य्यमन्त्रसाधारणम् । दिक्ष्विति सामान्यत उक्तेराग्नेयादिकोणा एव गृह्यन्ते । विदिक् मध्येषु संयजेदिति पाठः । यदाहुराचार्य्याः—

प्रयजेदथ प्रभूतां विमलां साराह्वयां समाराध्याम् ।
परमसुखामग्न्यादिष्वस्त्रिषु मध्ये च पीठक्लृप्तेः प्राक् ॥ इति ॥

प्रयोगसारेऽपि—ईशानान्तं च विदिक्ष्वेतान् प्रपूजयेत् । इति ॥ ३८ ॥

परमादिसुखं पीठं खबिम्बान्तं प्रकल्पयेत्।
दीप्ता सूक्ष्मा जया भद्रा विभूतिर्विमला पुनः॥ ३९
अमोघा विद्युता सर्व्वतोमुखी पीठशक्तयः।
दीप्तदीपशिखाकारा बीजान्यासां विदुः क्रमात्॥ ४०
अक्लीवह्रस्वत्रितयस्वरान् बिन्द्वग्निसंयुतान्।
वदेत्पदं चतुर्थ्यन्तं ब्रह्मविष्णुशिवात्मकम्॥ ४१
सौराय योगपीठाय नमः पदमनन्तरम्।
पीठमन्त्रोऽयमाख्यातो दिनेशस्य जगत्पतेः॥ ४२
तारादि खं खखोल्काय मनुना मूर्त्तिकल्पना।
साक्षिणं सर्व्वलोकानां तस्यामावाह्य पूजयेत्॥ ४३

खबिम्बान्तमिति। सोमाग्निमण्डले सम्पूज्य सूर्य्यमण्डलं पूजनीयमित्यर्थः। दीप्तेत्यासां ध्यानम्। तदुक्तं प्रयोगसारे—

दीप्तदीपशिखाकारा ध्येयाः स्युर्नव शक्तयः। इति॥ ३९॥ ४०॥

अक्लीवेति। ह्रस्वत्रितयं अइउ। अत्र क्लीबह्रस्वत्रितयपदाभ्यां नञा सह सम्बन्धः। अग्नी रेफः। रां रीं रूं रैं इत्यादि नव बीजानि। अन्ये तु ह्रस्वत्रयम् अइऋ इत्याहुः। तदुक्तं महाकपिलपञ्चरात्रे—

आद्यापान्त्यं तृतीयं च त्यक्त्वा चैवं नपुंसकम्।
भेदयेन्नवधा यान्तं स्वरैरेभिर्यथाक्रमम्।
बिन्दुयुक्तानि बीजानि शक्तीनामुद्धृतानि वै॥ इति।

अन्यत्राकारैकारविसर्गान् हित्वा नव बीजानीति।
तदुक्तं प्रयोगसारनारायणीययोः—

आद्यमन्त्यं तृतीयं च त्यक्त्वाऽपि च नपुंसकान्। इति।

पीठमन्त्र इति। सर्व्वसूर्य्यमन्त्रसाधारण इति ज्ञेयम्॥ ४१॥ ४२॥

तारादीति। खखोल्कायेति स्वरूपम्। तदुक्तं महाकपिलपञ्चरात्रे—

यान्तमं बिन्दुना युक्तं कद्वितीयं तथैव च।
तदेव केवलं भूय ओभिन्नं सविलोमकम्॥
सविलोमाच्चतुर्थं तु यत्तृतीयोपरि स्थितम्।
अक्षरं तद्द्वितीयेन स्वरेणैव प्रभेदितम्॥

अङ्गानि पूजयेदादौ दिक्पत्रेष्वर्कमूर्त्तयः ।

तानुलोमाच्चतुर्थं तु केवलं तदनन्तरम् ।

समासादुद्धृतो वत्स मूर्त्तिमन्त्रः षडक्षरः ॥ इति ।

अयमन्येषामपि सूर्य्यमन्त्राणां मूर्त्तिमन्त्र इति ज्ञेयम् । तत्राकाशबीजादिरुद्धृत इति विशेषः । अथवात्रैवं व्याख्येयम् । तारस्य आदिशब्देन प्रथमोत्पन्नत्वात् आकाशस्तस्य बिन्दुः सम्प्रदायादिति । अथवा खमिति तन्त्रेण द्वयमुपात्तम् एकेनाकाशबीजमन्येन स्वरूपम् ।

प्रयोगसारेऽपि—सूर्य्यकान्ताक्षरे प्रोक्ता बिन्दुभूषितमस्तके । इति ।

नारायणीये च—खकान्तौ दण्डिनौ दण्डो मज्जा दशनसंयुता ।

मांसं दीर्घी जवदायुरन्ते तस्यापि कुण्डिदुः ॥

एतस्य साधयेत्कामानभिषेकजपादिना । इति ।

निर्बीजोऽपि तत्रैवोद्धृतः । अत्र लकारतकारौ वेदिकापीठभेदेनेति उभावपि साम्प्रदायिकौ । निर्बीजो मूर्त्तिकल्पनायां सबीजो जपादाविति ज्ञेयम् । अयं स्वतन्त्रोऽपि मन्त्रः । अस्यर्ष्यादि यथा—

ऋषिः सूत्रक आख्यातो जगती छन्द ईरितम् ।

देवः सूर्य्यो बीजशक्ती कान्तमज्जास्थिद्वतुस्मृते ॥

सूक्ष्मरूपायाग्निवधूः स्वाहान्तः सूक्ष्मतेजसे ।

सूक्ष्मकरा[रूपा]याग्निवधूः सूक्ष्मबलाय ठद्वयम् ॥

सूक्ष्मकायाय सहुंफट्जातियुक्ताः समीरिताः ।

पञ्चाङ्गमन्त्रा मन्त्रार्णैः षडङ्गं वा प्रकल्पयेत् ॥

रक्तपद्मद्वयं हस्ते बिभ्राणं वरदाभये ।

बन्धूकाभं त्रिनेत्रं च रविं ध्यायेत् सुभूषितम् ॥

लक्षमेकं जपेन्मन्त्रं क्षीराहारी जितेन्द्रियः ।

जुहुयात्तद्दशांशेन बिल्वाश्वत्थसमिद्वरैः ॥

सूर्य्यपीठेऽष्टाक्षरवत्पूजा । वक्ष्यमाणार्घ्यदानं च । खेचरीसिद्धिश्च फलं ज्ञेयम् । उक्तञ्च नारायणीये—एतेन बहुभिः प्राप्ताः खेचरत्वादिसिद्धयः । इति ।

मूर्त्तिकल्पनेति । मूलमन्त्रमुच्चार्य्य पश्चादिममुच्चार्य्य मूर्त्तिकल्पनेति पद्मपादाचार्य्याः ॥ ४३ ॥

अङ्गानि पूजयेदिति कर्णिकायाम् । तदुक्तं नारायणीये—

वह्निरक्षोमारुतेशदिक्षु पूज्या हृदादयः ।

आदित्याद्याश्चतस्रोऽर्च्याः शक्तयः कोणपत्रगाः ॥ ४४

स्वस्वनामादिवर्णाः स्युस्तासां बीजान्यनुक्रमात्।
उषा प्रज्ञा प्रभा सन्ध्या शक्तयः परिकीर्त्तिताः ॥ ४५

पत्राग्रसंस्था ब्राह्म्याद्याः पुरतोऽरुणमर्चयेत्।
चन्द्रादीनर्चयेत् पश्चाद् ग्रहानष्टौ ततो बहिः ॥ ४६

इन्द्रादींश्च तदस्त्राणि यथापूर्व्वं समर्चयेत्।
एवं सम्पूज्य विधिवद्भास्करं भक्तवत्सलम् ॥ ४७

दद्यादर्घ्यं प्रतिदिनं वारे वा तस्य चोदिते।
प्रभाते मण्डलं कृत्वा पूर्व्ववत्पीठमर्चयेत् ॥ ४८

स्वमन्त्रैः कर्णिकान्तस्था दिक्स्थत्वं पुरतश्च दिक् ॥ इति ।

आदावित्यनेन केसरेष्वष्टाङ्गपूजा सूचिता। आदित्याद्या इति न्यासोक्त-बीजसहिताः। अत्र केचनादित्यादिमूर्त्तयश्चतस्र इति सामानाधिकरण्यं कृत्वा सूर्य्यं न पूजयन्ति। तदसत्। उद्दिष्टपञ्चकमध्ये एकत्यागे कारणाभावात्। मुख्यतया कर्णिकायां स पूजित इति चेत्। पञ्चसु कः पूजितः को नेति नियामकाभावात्। पूर्व्वत्र परत्र च यत्र यत्र पञ्चकमुक्तम् तत्र त्यागस्याऽदृष्टचरत्वाच्च। तेन पद्मपादा-चार्य्योक्तरीत्या आदित्यं मध्ये सम्पूज्य रव्यादयो दिक्चतुष्के पूज्याः। चतस्र इति शक्तिविशेषणत्वेन योज्यम्। पुरतोऽरुणमर्चयेदित्युक्तेः। कल्पितदिगपेक्षया तदीशदलमपि संमुखदलमिति। तेन महालक्ष्मीस्थाने अरुणः पूज्यः। "मातृ-भिररुणान्ताभिः" इत्याचार्य्योक्तेः। पद्मपादाचार्य्यास्तु मातॄः सम्पूज्य पुरतोऽरुण-मर्चयेदित्यूचुः। अतएव नारायणीये पूर्व्वपत्रे अरुणस्तथेत्युक्तम् ॥ ४४॥४५॥४६॥

चन्द्रादीनिति स्वबीजाद्यान्। चन्द्रः सोमः। तत्र पूर्व्वादिषु चन्द्रबुध-गुरुशुक्रान् आग्नेयादिषु भौममन्दराहुकेतूनिति ज्ञेयम्। प्रयोगस्तु पूर्वोक्तोऽनु-सन्धेयः। अतएव नारायणीये—

पूर्व्वादिदिक्षु सम्पूज्याश्चन्द्रज्ञगुरुभार्गवाः।
आग्नेयादिषु कोणेषु कुजमन्दाहिकेतवः ॥ इति ।

विधिवदित्यनेन सूर्य्यपरिषद्भ्यो नम इति बहिः पारिषदान् पूजयेदित्युक्तम्। "ग्रहैः सुरैश्चापि सूर्य्यपरिषद्भिः" इत्युक्तेः ॥ ४६ ॥ ४७ ॥

प्रभाते अर्चयेदिति सम्बन्धः। मण्डलमिति वृत्तम्। कृत्वेति रक्तचन्दनेन।

पात्रं ताम्रमयं प्रस्थतोयग्राहि मनोहरम् ।
निधाय तत्र मनुना पूरयेत्तच्छुभोदकैः ॥ ४९

कुङ्कुमं रोचनाराजीरक्तचन्दनवैणवान् ।
करवीरजवाशालिकुशश्यामाकतण्डुलान् ॥ ५०

निक्षिपेत्सलिले तस्मिन्नैक्यं सञ्चिन्त्य भानुना ।
साङ्गमभ्यर्चयेत्तस्मिन् भास्करं प्रोक्तलक्षणम् ॥ ५१

गन्धपुष्पादिनैवेद्यैर्यथाविधि विधानवित् ।
तत् पिधाय जपेन्मन्त्रं सम्यगष्टोत्तरं शतम् ॥ ५२

तदुक्तं प्रयोगसारे—

रक्तचन्दनगन्धेन कृत्वा वृत्तं सुशोभनम् । मण्डलम् । इति ॥४८॥

प्रस्थतोयग्राहीति । प्रस्थप्रमाणमुक्तं श्रीधराचार्यैः—

कुडवश्चतुःपलः स्यात्प्रस्थः कुडवैश्चतुर्भिः स्यात् । इति ।

मनुना विलोमपठितेनेति विशेषः । यदाहुः—

प्रजपन्मनुं प्रतिगतक्रमतः परिपूरयेत् सुविमलैः सलिलैः । इति ।

शुभोदकैरिति । आदित्यमण्डलान्निस्सरदमृतधारारूपत्वेन ध्यातैरित्यर्थः ॥ ४९ ॥

राजी आसुरी । रक्तं रक्तचन्दनम् । चन्दनं श्वेतचन्दनम् । वैणवं वेणुबीजानि । करवीरं रक्तकरवीरपुष्पमिति परमगुरवः । जवा रक्तजवा । कुशं कुशाग्रं तण्डुला अक्षताः ॥ ५० ॥

निक्षिपेदिति । यथालाभं क्वचित्तिला अपि । तदुक्तमाचार्यैः—

गोरोचनास्त्रतिलवैणवराजिरक्त-
शीताख्यशालिकरवीरजपाकुशाग्रान् ।
श्यामाकतण्डुलयुतांश्च यथाप्रलाभान्
संयोज्य भक्तिभरतोऽर्घविधिर्विधेयः ॥ इति ।

ऐक्यं सञ्चिन्त्येति स्वात्मन इति शेषः । “स्वैक्यं सम्भावयन् समाहितधीः दृष्ट्वा दिनेशम्” इत्युक्तेः । तस्मिन् पात्रे । साङ्गमिति षडङ्गाष्टाङ्गसहितम् । अष्टाङ्गेनाऽभिसम्पूज्येति प्रयोगसारे उक्तेः । तत्र मन्त्रषड्वर्णानि षडङ्गस्थानेषु षडङ्गवद्विन्यस्य उदरपृष्ठयोर्वर्णद्वयं विन्यसेदिति । प्रोक्तलक्षणं पूर्वोक्तध्यानम् ॥ ५१ ॥

आदिशब्दात् धूपदीपौ । यथाविधीत्यनेनैतदुक्तं भवति । सावरणमिति ।

पुनः सम्पूज्य गन्धाद्यैर्जानुभ्यामवनिं गतः ।
आमस्तकं तदुद्धृत्य व्योम्नि सावरणे रवौ ॥ ५३
दृष्टिं निधाय स्वैक्येन मूलमन्त्रं धिया जपन् ।
दद्यादर्घ्यं दिनेशाय प्रसन्नेनाऽन्तरात्मना ॥ ५४
कृत्वा पुष्पाञ्जलिं भूयो जपेदष्टोत्तरं शतम् ।
यावदर्घ्यामृतं भानुः समादत्ते निजैः करैः ॥ ५५
तेन तृप्तो दिनमणिर्दद्यादखिलं मनोरथान् ।
अर्घ्यदानमिदं पुंसामायुरारोग्यवर्द्धनम् ॥ ५६
धनधान्यपशुक्षेत्रपुत्रमित्रकलत्रदम् ।
तेजोवीर्य्ययशःकान्तिविद्याविभवभाग्यदम् ॥ ५७
आकाशमग्निदीर्घेन्दु संयुक्तं भुवनेश्वरी ।
सर्गान्वितो भृगुर्भानोस्त्र्यक्षरो मनुरीरितः ॥ ५८
आधारादि पदाग्रान्तं कण्ठादाधारकावधि ।
मूर्द्धादि कण्ठपर्य्यन्तं क्रमाद्बीजत्रयं न्यसेत् ॥ ५९

व्योम्नि सूर्य्यमण्डलेऽपि स्थितमावरणसहितं देवं विलोक्य मनसा सम्पूज्येति च ।
उक्तञ्च— दृष्ट्वा दिनेशमथ पीठगतं तथैव
व्योमस्थितं परिवृतावरणं विलोक्य । इति ।

विधानवित् तत् पिधायेति सम्बन्धः । विधानविदित्यनेनैतदुक्तं भवति । सोमात्मना भावितामृतबीजयुतेन वामोपष्टब्धेन स्वदक्षिणहस्तेनेति । सम्यगिति प्राणायामत्रयं षडङ्गन्यासं विधायेत्युक्तम् । पुनः सम्पूज्य । जलमिति शेषः । अर्घ्यं दद्यादिति । तत्र प्रकारः । मूलान्ते भगवते रवये अर्घ्यं कल्पयामि नम इत्युच्चार्येति । प्रसन्नेनान्तरात्मनेति भक्त्या दद्यादित्युक्तम् ॥ ५२—५७ ॥

प्रयोजनतिलकमन्त्रमाह आकाशेति । आकाशो ह: अग्नो रेफः दीर्घं आ इन्दुर्बिन्दुः एतद्युतः तेन ह्रामिति । भुवनेश्वरी ह्रीँ । विसर्गान्वितो विसर्गयुक्तः । भृगुः सः । ह्रां ह्रीँ सः ।

ऋष्यादि यथा—मनोरस्य भवेद् ब्रह्मा मुनिरुक्तोऽथवा भृगुः ।
छन्दोऽपि खलु गायत्री देवता तीव्रदीधितिः ॥ इति ।

आद्यं बीजं द्वितीयं शक्तिः । प्रणवादिरिति केचित् । प्रयोगविशेषे

षड्दीर्घस्वरयुक्तेन मध्येनाऽङ्गानि कल्पयेत् ॥ ६०

रक्ताम्बुजासनमशेषगुणैकसिन्धुं
भानुं समस्तजगतामधिपं भजामि ।
पद्मद्वयाभयवरान् दधतं कराब्जै-
र्माणिक्यमौलिमरुणाङ्गरुचिं त्रिनेत्रम् ॥ ६१

भानुलक्षं जपेन्मन्त्रमन्नाज्येन दशांशतः ।
तिलैर्वा मधुरासिक्तैर्जुहुयाद्विजितेन्द्रियः ॥ ६२

परमात्मादिरजपादिर्वेति पद्मपादाचार्य्याः ॥ ५८ ॥ ५९ ॥

अङ्गानीति नेत्रान्तानीति ज्ञेयम् । अग्रे वक्ष्यमाणत्वादत्र नोक्तम् । तदुक्तं प्रयोगसारे— अङ्गुष्ठादिकनिष्ठान्तमङ्गुलीषु यथाक्रमात् ।

न्यस्त्वा विनेत्रमङ्गानि नेत्रं हस्ततले न्यसेत् ॥ इति ।

नारायणीयेऽपि—न्यस्याङ्गुलीषु पञ्चाङ्गं लोचनं तलयोर्न्यसेत् । इति ।

तथा—न्यस्त्वा नेत्रान्तमङ्गानि तथैवात्मनि संयतः ॥ इति ।

प्रयोगसारे नारायणीये चान्यान्यङ्गान्युक्तानि—

कद्वतीयं विलोमेन बीजं हृदयमुच्यते ।
अर्कः शिरश्चतुर्थ्यन्तः कथ्यते भूर्भुवः स्वरोँ ॥
ज्वालिनीति शिखा गीता हुं वर्म समुदाहृतम् ।
द्वितीयस्वरसंभिन्नं शचतुर्थं सबिन्दुकम् ॥
नेत्रं स्वरान्तमारूढं यान्तमस्त्रमिति क्रमात् । इति ।

नारायणीये तु—प्रयोजनादितिलकः साच्यङ्गान्तः स्मृतो मनुः । इति ।

न्यासे क्रमसंग्रहे विशेषः—

हस्तयोस्तलपृष्ठे च न्यस्य मन्त्राक्षरत्रयम् ।
पदान्तराधिवक्त्रेषु तथा सप्तग्रहानपि ॥
मुखे बाहौ च पदयोरुदरे वक्षसि क्रमात् ।
मूर्द्धादिपञ्चस्थानेषु हृल्लेखायाश्च विन्यसेत् ॥ इति ।

मूर्त्तिपञ्चकमिति नवग्रहन्यासे इति पद्मपादाचार्य्याश्च ॥ ६० ॥

आयुधध्यानं पूर्व्ववत् ॥ ६१ ॥

भानुलक्षं द्वादशलक्षम् ॥ ६२ ॥

पूर्वोक्ते पूजयेत्पीठे विधानेनाऽमुना रविम् ।
प्रथमावृत्तिरङ्गैः स्यात् परा चन्द्रादिभिर्ग्रहैः ॥ ६३

तृतीया लोकपालैः स्याच्चतुर्थी स्यात्तदायुधैः ।
इति सम्पूज्य निर्माल्यं तेजश्चण्डाय दीयताम् ॥ ६४

अर्घ्यं प्रागीरितं दद्याद्भानवे संयतेन्द्रियः ।
सोऽपि रत्नं धनं धान्यं पुत्रपौत्रान् पशून् यशः ।
वस्त्राणि भूषणादीनि दद्यादस्मै न संशयः ॥ ६५

अङ्गैरिति । तत्राङ्गध्यानं यथा—

भास्वत्सरोजहस्तानि शान्तानि वरदान्यपि ।
अङ्गानि दिव्यरूपाणि ध्येयानि बलवन्ति च ॥
दंष्ट्राकरालमस्त्रं तु विद्युत्पुञ्जसमप्रभम् । इति ।

प्रयोगसारे नारायणीयेऽपि—

रक्ता हृदादयः सौम्या वरदाः पद्मधारिणः ।
विद्युत्पुञ्जनिभं त्वस्त्रमुग्रदंष्ट्रंभयावहम् ॥ इति ॥

परा चन्द्रादिभिर्ग्रहैरिति । अत्र स्वस्वनामादिवर्णादित्वमनुसन्धेयम् । "स्वनामाद्य-क्षरैर्बिन्दुभूषितैरन्वितं यजेत्" इति प्रयोगसारे उक्तेः । तत्रायं विशेषः । प्रागादिस्थितैः चन्द्रबुधगुरुशुक्रैः आग्नेयादिस्थितैर्भौममन्दराहुकेतुभिः । तदुक्तमाचार्यैः—प्रागादि दिशासंस्थाः शशिबुधगुरुभार्गवाः क्रमेण स्युः ।

आग्नेयादिष्वस्त्रिषु धरणिजमन्दाहिकेतवः पूज्याः ॥ इति ।

प्रयोगसारेऽपि—सोममैन्द्रे बुधं याम्ये पश्चिमे तु बृहस्पतिम् ।
सौम्ये शुक्रं तथाग्नेय्यामङ्गारकमथाऽऽसुरे ॥
शनैश्चरं ततो राहुं वायव्यां केतुमीश्वरे । इति ।

तेजश्चण्डोऽर्कगणः । प्रयोगसारे प्रयोगविशेष उक्तः—

स्वजन्मदिननक्षत्रे ग्रहणे वा स्वजन्मभे ।
ग्रहाणामपि वैषम्ये भये वा प्रत्युपस्थिते ॥
इष्ट्वा दिवाकरं देवं ग्रहैः सार्द्धं यथोदितम् ।
मूलेन सवितुर्बीजैरन्येषां च पुरोदितैः ॥
प्रत्येकं जुहुयात्तेषां ग्रहाणां तद्दिशि क्रमात् ।
एकत्र वाऽथवा वह्निकार्यं कृत्वा विधानतः ॥

आकाशमग्निपवन सद्यान्त्यार्घीशबिन्दुमत् ।
मार्त्तण्डभैरवं नाम बीजमेतदुदाहृतम् ॥ ६६

पुटितं विश्वबीजेन सर्व्वकामफलप्रदम् ।
टान्तं दहननेत्रेन्दुसहितं तदुदीरितम् ॥ ६७

पञ्चह्रस्वाद्यबीजेन पञ्चमूर्त्तीः प्रविन्यसेत् ।
मध्यमादिकनिष्ठान्तमङ्गुलीषु क्रमादिमाः ॥ ६८

सूर्य्याख्यो भास्करो भानुस्ततो रविर्दिवाकरौ ।
शिरोवदनहृद्गुह्यपाददेशे तु ताः पुनः ॥ ६९

दीर्घयुक्तेन बीजेन नेत्रान्ताङ्गानि विन्यसेत् ।
व्यापकं मूलबीजेन कुर्वीत तदनन्तरम् ॥ ७०

समित्सर्पिश्चरुव्रीहैः क्रमादष्टोत्तरं शतम् ।
प्रतिव्याहृतिसंयुक्तं प्रत्येकं शरणान्वितम् ॥
अर्कः पलाशापामार्गाश्वत्थोदुम्बरौ तथा ।
खदिरश्च शमी दूर्वा दर्भाश्च समिधः क्रमात् ॥
पूर्णाहुतिं ततो दद्यात्तेषां प्रत्येकमन्ततः ।
कृतेनाऽनेन यज्ञेन ग्रहास्तुष्यन्ति भाविताः ॥
सर्वे रोगाः प्रणश्यन्ति संग्रामेषु जयं लभेत् ।
अभिचारादयो दोषाः शान्तिं यान्ति न संशयः ॥ इति॥६३॥६४॥६५॥

मार्त्तण्डभैरवबीजमाह आकाशमिति । आकाशो ह: अग्नी रेफः पवनो यः सद्यान्त औ अर्घीश उ बिन्दुः एतद्युक्तः । अत्र स्वरद्वयमपि गुरूपदेशतो यथा सम्प्रदायमुखारणीयम् । ब्रह्मा ऋषिर्निवृच्छन्दः । हं बीजं बिन्दुः शक्तिः । विश्वबीजमाह टान्तमिति । टान्तं ठः दहनो रेफः नेत्रमिः इन्दुर्बिन्दुः एतद्युक्तेन ठ्रिमिति । सर्व्वकामफलप्रदमित्यनेनैतत् संदृष्टीतम् । यदुक्तं नारायणीये—

अरोग्यमायुः श्रीर्विद्या कान्तिः पुष्टिर्धनं यशः ।
सौभाग्यं शक्तिरैश्वर्य्यं रक्षा मेधा वचो द्युतिः ।
सिध्यन्त्येवंविधाः कामा मन्त्रस्यास्य प्रभावतः ॥ इति ॥ ६६॥६७॥

पञ्चेति । सद्यान्तपञ्चह्रस्वाद्यमित्यर्थः । "मूर्त्तीः षड्यावसानिकाः" इति नारायणीय उक्तेः । मध्यमादीति । मध्यमातर्जन्यङ्गुष्ठानामाकनिष्ठास्वित्यर्थः ।

हैमाम्भोजप्रवालप्रतिमनिजरुचिं चारुखट्वाङ्गपद्मौ
चक्रं शक्तिं सपाशं सृणिमतिरुचिरामक्षमालां कपालम् ।
हस्ताम्भोजैर्दधानं त्रिनयनविलसद्वेदवक्त्राभिरामं
मार्त्तण्डं वल्लभार्द्धं मणिमयमुकुटं हारदीप्तं भजामः ॥ ७१

"मध्यमादिभुजान्ततः" इति नारायणीय उक्तेः । बीजेनेति मार्त्तण्डभैरवेण । पूर्व्वेणापि दीर्घयुक्तेन षड्दीर्घयुक्तेन । नेत्रान्ताङ्गानीति । हृदयशिरःशिखाकवचानि विन्यस्याऽस्त्रमपि विन्यस्य पश्चान्नेत्रं विन्यसनीयमिति सम्प्रदायविदः । केचित्तु नेत्रान्तानीति पञ्चाङ्गान्येव नेत्रान्तानि न्यसनीयानि "पञ्चाङ्गानि मनोर्यस्य नेत्रं तस्य न विद्यते" इति श्रुत्याऽपवादमाहुः । तदसाम्प्रदायिकम्—

अङ्गानि कुर्य्याद्दीर्घाच्चस्नाबीजेन मन्त्रवित् । इति श्रीपटले ।
मध्येन दीर्घयुक्तेन प्राक्पुटेन प्रकल्पयेत् ।
अङ्गानि जातियुक्तानि क्रमेण मनुवित्तमः ॥

इति भुवनेशीपटले । एवमन्यत्रापि यत्र यत्र दीर्घवचनं तत्र तत्र षण्णां दीर्घाणां ग्रहणात् अत्र सङ्कोचे कारणाभावात् नेत्रान्ताङ्गानीति वचनेन सङ्कोच इति चेत् तत्तदपि न । साम्प्रदायिकव्याख्यानुसारेणाऽप्युपपत्तेः । किञ्च नेत्रं तस्य विवर्जयेदिति साक्षान्निषिद्धस्य नेत्राङ्गस्य सामान्यभूतेनाऽन्यथाऽप्युपपद्यमानेन नेत्रान्ताङ्गानीति वचनेन बाधोऽपि न कर्त्तुं शक्यते । अन्यथाग्रे अङ्गपूजा यथा पूर्वमिति वचनात् दिग्दलस्थपूजोक्तैव । नेत्रमात्रे विशेष उक्तः । अग्रे पुरुषोत्तम-मन्त्रेऽपि नेत्रान्ताङ्गान्युक्तानि । तत्र च षडङ्गमन्त्रा नेत्रान्ता एवोद्धृताः ।

षडङ्गमन्त्राः सन्दिष्टा नेत्रान्तास्तन्त्रवेदिभिः ।

इत्यनेन । पूर्वोक्तमन्त्रे लिखितप्रयोगसारवचनाच्च । अस्मिन् मन्त्रे नारायणीये च प्रायशोऽङ्गानि षडिति तेन साम्प्रदायिकव्याख्यैव गरीयसीत्यलम् । अत्र नेत्राङ्गोत्कर्षे तदपकर्षोऽपि ज्ञेयः । न्यायसिद्धत्वात् ॥ ६८॥६९॥७० ॥

ध्यानमाह हैमेति । प्रवालश्च तेन रक्तम् । तदुक्तं नारायणीये—

सिन्दूरारुणमीशानं वामार्द्धदयितं रविम् । इति ।

सृणिरङ्कुशः । वेदवक्त्रश्चतुर्वक्त्रम् । तदुक्तं नारायणीये—

पाशाङ्कुशधरं देवं साक्षमालं कपालिनम् ।
खट्वाङ्गाब्जारिशक्तीश्च दधानं चतुराननम् ॥ इति ॥

दक्षाधूर्ध्वयोराद्ये वामान्तमायुधानि ध्येयानि । त्रिनयनेत्यनेन द्वादशनेत्रत्वमुक्तम् ।

तल्लक्षं जपेन्मन्त्री बीजं बिम्बपुटीकृतम् ।
दशांशं कमलैः फुल्लैर्जुहुयान्मधुरोक्षितैः ॥ ७२

पीठे दीप्तादिभिर्युक्ते कर्णिकायामुषादिकाः ।
पूर्व्वादिदिक्षु सम्पूज्य मूर्त्तिं मूलेन कल्पयेत् ॥ ७३

आवाह्य पूजयेद्देवं वक्ष्यमाणविधानतः ।
सूर्य्यादींश्चतुरो दिक्षु विदिक्ष्वन्यं समर्च्चयेत् ॥ ७४

अङ्गपूजा यथापूर्व्वं नेत्रमीशानदिग्गतम् ।
ग्रहानष्टौ ततो बाह्ये लोकपालांस्ततः परम् ॥ ७५

अर्घ्यप्रदानं प्रयजेन्मन्त्री मार्त्तण्डभैरवम् ।
इति सिद्धमनुर्मन्त्री साधयेदिष्टमात्मनः ॥ ७६

शाल्याज्यतिलबिल्वानां लक्षहोमाद्भवेन्निधिः ।
राजवृक्षसमुद्भूतैः पुष्पैर्होमो रमाकरः ॥ ७७

जवाकुसुमहोमेन वशयत्यचिरान्नृपान् ।
मातुलिङ्गफलैर्हुत्वा धनमिष्टं लभेत सः ॥ ७८

अष्टबाहुं द्विषट्काक्षमिति नारायणीय उक्तः । वल्लभार्द्धमिति वामे ॥ ७१ ॥ ७२ ॥

दीप्तादिभिर्युक्ते पीठे सौर इत्यर्थः । उषादिकाः सम्पूज्येति पीठमन्त्रात् पूर्व्वगतकर्णिकायामिति ज्ञेयम् । आसां बीजेऽपि विशेषो नारायणीये उक्तः ।

यदाहुः—न्यसेदुषां प्रभां सन्ध्यां प्रज्ञां दिक्षु च कर्णिके ।
दक्षिणे दीर्घस्वनामादि वर्णैरावाहयेत्ततः ॥ इति ।

न्यसेदित्यनेन पीठन्यासेऽप्ययं क्रम इत्युक्तम् । पूजयेद्देवमिति । बिम्बबीजपुटीकृतेन नमोऽन्तेन बीजेन । "यजेद्यथोपचारान्ते बिम्बेन हृदयेन च" इत्युक्तेः । सूर्य्यादीनिति आदिपदेन भास्करभानुरवयः संगृहीताः । विदिक्ष्वन्यमिति पञ्चमं दिवाकरम् । यथापूर्व्वमिति । चतुर्थोक्तरीत्या । नेत्रमिति । तेन ईशानदिशि अङ्गद्वयपूजनम् । ग्रहानिति पूर्व्वमन्त्रोक्तक्रमेण । ततः परमिति वज्रादिभिः । अर्घ्यप्रदानमिति । पूर्व्वोक्तमर्घ्यविधानमत्रापि कुर्य्यादित्यर्थः ॥ ७३ ॥ ७४ ॥ ७५ ॥ ७६ ॥

साधयेदिष्टमित्युक्त्वा तदेवाह शालीति । बिल्वेति बिल्वफलानि ।
तदुक्तम्—सर्पिर्व्रीहितिलैर्बैल्वैः फलैर्लक्षं हुतेर्निधिः । इति ।

इमं मन्त्रं जपन्मर्त्यः कीर्त्तिं पुत्रान् बलं द्युतिम् ।
वाक्सिद्धिममितां लक्ष्मीं सौभाग्यमपि साधयेत् ॥ ७९

वियदर्द्धेन्दुसहितं तदादिः सर्गसंयुतः ।
अजपाख्यो मनुः प्रोक्तो द्व्यक्षरः सुरपादपः ॥ ८०

ऋषिर्ब्रह्मा स्मृतो देवी गायत्री छन्द ईरितम् ।
देवता जगतामादिः संप्रोक्तो गिरिजापतिः ॥ ८१

हसा षड्दीर्घयुक्तेन कुर्य्यादङ्गक्रियां मनोः ॥ ८२

उद्यद्भानुस्फुरिततडिदाकारमर्द्धाम्बिकेशं
पाशाभीती वरदपरशू संदधानं कराग्रैः ।
दिव्याकल्पैर्नवमणिमयैः शोभितं विश्वमूलं
सौम्याग्नेयं वपुरवतु वश्चन्द्रचूडं त्रिनेत्रम् ॥ ८३

लक्षहोमादिति । पञ्चविंशतिसहस्रमित्या प्रत्येकम् । भवेन्निधिरिति । मन्त्रिण इति शेषः । मतुलिङ्गो बीजपूरः । लभेन्निधिमिति वा पाठः ॥ ७७ ॥ ७८ ॥ ७९ ॥

अजपामन्त्रमाह वियदिति । अग्नीषोमात्मकत्वादस्याऽत्र पटले उक्तिः । तयोराद्यन्तयोरुक्तेः । वियत् हः अर्द्धेन्दुः बिन्दुः तदादिः सः सर्गो विसर्गः । द्व्यक्षरः सुरपादप इत्यनेनैतदुक्तं भवति । जपकाले एवं ध्यायेदिति । तदुच्यते । मन्त्रोच्चारणकाले मन्त्रं सुषुम्नारन्ध्रपूर्णं विश्वरूपं सदानन्दात्मकं सप्तविंशकं ब्रह्म ध्यात्वा तत्प्रभया विहसर्व्वाङ्गमात्मानम् अर्द्धनारीश्वररूपं षड्विंशकमीश्वरं चिन्तयेत् । पिङ्गलारन्ध्रस्थमादिबीजपञ्चविंशकं पुरुषबीजरूपं प्राणात्मना ध्यात्वा द्वितीयबीजमिडारन्ध्रमध्यस्थचतुर्विंशकप्रकृतिरूपम् अपानात्मना चिन्तयेत् । विश्वरूपान् मन्त्रान् दीपाद्दीपान्तमिव निर्गच्छन्तौ वामदक्षिणभागौ इडापिङ्गले परिपूर्णसुषुम्णायाः स्त्रीपुरुषचिह्नितौ कृतौ ध्यायेत् । हं बीजं सः शक्तिः ॥८०॥८१॥

हसेति संयुक्तेन । साम्प्रदायिका अन्यथा षडङ्गमाहुः । सूर्य्यात्मने हृत् । सोमात्मने शिरः । निरञ्जनात्मने शिखा । निराभासात्मने कवचम् । अव्यक्तात्मने नेत्रम् । अतनु सूक्ष्मः प्रचोदयात्मने अस्त्रम् । हसा[क्रा]मित्याद्यैरेभिरिति केचित् ॥ ८२ ॥

वामोर्ध्वादि दक्षिणोर्ध्वान्तमायुधध्यानम् ॥ ८३ ॥

भानुलक्षं जपेन्मन्त्रं पायसेन ससर्पिषा ।
दशांशं जुहुयात्सम्यक् ततः सिद्धो भवेन्मनुः ॥ ८४
दीप्तादिपूजिते पीठे प्रागुक्ते प्रयजेद्विभुम् ।
मूर्त्तिं मूलेन सङ्कल्प्य यजेदङ्गादिभिः सह ॥ ८५
ऋतं वसुं नरवरौ दिग्दलेषु विदिक्ष्वथ ।
अर्चयेद्दृतजां गोजासत्याख्यामद्रिजां पुनः ॥ ८६
लोकेश्वरांस्तदस्त्राणि पूजयेत् देवमन्वहम् ।
अर्घ्यं च विधिवद्दद्यात् प्राक् प्रोक्तेनैव वर्त्मना ॥ ८७
मन्त्राढ्यमातृकाम्भोजे पूर्णकुम्भं निधाय तम् ।
पिधाय वामहस्तेन न्यस्तमन्त्रेण संयतः ॥ ८८
अष्टोत्तरशतं मन्त्रं जपेत्तोयं सुधामयम् ।
स्मृत्वा तेनाऽभिषिञ्चेद् यं स भवेद्विगतामयः ॥ ८९
आयुरारोग्यविभवानमितान् लभते नरः ।
अनेनैव विधानेन विषार्त्तो निर्विषो भवेत् ॥ ९०

इन्दुभ्यां विगलत्सुधाविप्लुतं मन्त्रान्त्यबीजं ततः
प्रच्योतत्परमामृतार्द्रशशिना संसिक्तमाद्यं स्मरन् ।

भानुलक्षं द्वादशलक्षम् ॥ ८४ ॥

प्रागुक्ते पीठे मूर्त्तिं मूलेन सङ्कल्प्य विभुं अङ्गादिभिः सह प्रयजेदिति अन्वयः । आदिशब्दार्थमाह ऋतमित्यादि । यजेदङ्गैः सह क्रमादित्यपि पाठः । अङ्गैः सह ऋतादीन् दिग्दलेषु अर्चयेदित्यन्वयः ॥ ८५ ॥ ८६ ॥ ८७ ॥

मन्त्रेति अजपाख्यकर्णिके मातृकोक्ताचार्यपद्मे । संयत इत्येनेनैतदुक्तं भवति । वामहस्ततले चन्द्रमण्डलं ध्यात्वा तन्मध्ये मन्त्रं सञ्चिन्त्य तेन हस्तेन तन्मुखं पिधायेति । स्मृत्वेति पूर्वेण सम्बध्यते । यमिति लिङ्गमविवक्षितम् । "नारी नरो वा विधिनाऽभिषिक्तः" इत्युक्तेः ॥ ८८ ॥ ८९ ॥ ९० ॥

इन्दुभ्यामित्यन्त्यबीजगाभ्यां विसर्गावयवबिन्दुभ्याम् । तत इत्यन्त्यबीजात् । तत्र प्रकारः । मनोरमप्रदेशे पद्मासने उपविश्य सुषुम्णाग्रन्थिताधोमुखसहस्रदल-पद्मकर्णिकामध्ये विसर्गं चन्द्रमण्डलद्वयरूपेण ध्यात्वा तस्मात् चन्द्रमण्डलद्वयात् विगलितबहुलसुधाधारया संसिच्यमानमनाहतकमलकर्णिकागतं सकारं सञ्चिन्त्य

मन्त्री मन्त्रमिमं जपेद्विषगदोन्मादापमृत्युज्वरान्
जित्वा वर्षशतं विशिष्टविभवो जीवेत् सुखं बन्धुभिः ॥ ८१

सुषुम्णारन्ध्रेण सकारनिर्गतसुधारसेनाऽभिषिच्यमानं परिपूर्णसुधामयं मणिपूरस्थं बिन्दुं ध्यात्वा ततः स्रवदमृतधारापरिपूर्णं मूलाधारस्थितं हकारं चिन्तयित्वा ततोऽमृतरसपरिपूर्णं मन्त्राक्षरामृतसंसिक्तमात्मानं परमानन्दसन्दोहनिमग्नमिव ध्यायेदिति । अस्य जीवमन्त्रस्य तन्त्रान्तरोक्तो विशेष उच्यते—

ईश्वर उवाच—अजपाराधनं देवि कथयामि तवाऽनघे ।
यस्य विज्ञानमात्रेण परंब्रह्माऽधिगच्छति ॥
हंसःपदं परेशानि प्रत्यहं जपते नरः ।
मोहान्धो यो न जानाति मोक्षस्तस्य न विद्यते ॥
श्रीगुरोः कृपया देवि ज्ञायते जप्यते ततः ।
तस्योच्छ्वासैस्तु निश्वासैस्तदा बन्धक्षयो भवेत् ॥
उच्छ्वासे चैव निश्वासे हंस इत्यक्षरद्वयम् ।
तस्मात्प्राणस्तु हंसाख्य आत्माकारेण संस्थितः ॥
नाभेरुच्छ्वासनिश्वासा हृदयाग्रे व्यवस्थिताः ।
षष्टिश्वासैर्भवेत् प्राणः षट् प्राणा घटिका मता ॥
षष्टिर्नाड्या अहोरात्रं जपसंख्याऽजपामनोः ।
एकविंशतिसाहस्रं षट्शताधिकमीश्वरि ॥
प्रत्यहं जपते प्राणः स्वन्दा[सदा]नन्दमयीं पराम् ।
उत्पत्तिर्जप आरम्भो मृतिरस्य निवेदनम् ॥
विना जपेन देवेशि जपो भवति मन्त्रिणः ।
अजपेयं ततः प्रोक्ता भवपाशनिकृन्तनी ॥
एवं जपं महेशानि प्रत्यहं विनिवेदयेत् ।
गणेशब्रह्मविष्णुभ्यो हराय परमेश्वरि ॥
जीवात्मने क्रमेणैव तथा च परमात्मने ।
षट् शतानि सहस्राणि षडेव च तथा पुनः ॥
षट्सहस्राणि च पुनः सहस्रं च सहस्रकम् ।
पुनः सहस्रं गुरवे क्रमेण तु निवेदयेत् ॥
आधारे स्वर्णवर्णाभे वादिसान्तानि संस्मरेत् ।
द्रुतसौवर्णवर्णानि दलानि परमेश्वरि ॥

व्याहृतित्रयमग्निः स्याज्जातवेद इहावह ।
सर्व्वकर्म्माणि संभाष्य साधयाऽग्निप्रिया ततः ॥ ९२
ताराद्योऽयं मनुः प्रोक्तः पञ्चविंशतिवर्णवान् ।
ऋषिर्भृगुर्भवेच्छन्दो गायत्रं देवताऽनलः ॥ ९३

स्वाधिष्ठाने विद्रुमाभे वादिलान्तानि च स्मरेत् ।
विद्युत्पुञ्जप्रभाभानि सुनीलमणिपूरके ॥
डफान्तानि महानीलप्रभाणि च विचिन्तयेत् ।
पिङ्गवर्णे महावह्नि कर्णिकाभानि चिन्तयेत् ॥
कादिठान्तानि पत्राणि चतुर्थेऽनाहते प्रिये ।
विशुद्धौ धूम्रवर्णे तु रक्तवर्णान् स्वरान् स्मरेत् ॥
आज्ञायां विद्युदाभायां शुभ्रौ हक्षौ विचिन्तयेत् ।
कर्पूरद्युतिसंराजत्सहस्रदलनीरजे ॥
नादात्मकं ब्रह्मरन्ध्रं जानीहि परमेश्वरि ।
एतेषु सप्तचक्रेषु स्थितेभ्यः परमेश्वरि ॥
जपं निवेदयेदेनमहोरात्रभवं प्रिये ।
अजपा नाम गायत्री त्रिषु लोकेषु दुर्लभा ॥
अजपां जपतो नित्यं पुनर्जन्म न विद्यते ।
अजपा नाम गायत्री योगिनां मोक्षदायिनी ॥
अस्याः सङ्कल्पमात्रेण नरः पापैः प्रमुच्यते ।
अनया सदृशी विद्या अनया सदृशो जपः ॥
अनया सदृशं पुण्यं न भूतं न भविष्यति ॥ इति ॥ ९१ ॥

अग्निमन्त्रमाह व्याहृतीति । अग्निरिति स्वरूपम् । विसर्गस्य सन्धौ रेफः । अग्निप्रिया स्वाहा । प्रणवशक्तिपुटित इति केचित् । श्रीकामैः श्रीबीजादिर्जप्तव्यः । प्रणवो बीजं स्वाहा शक्तिः । व्याहृतित्रयं ततोऽग्निप्रिया ताराद्योऽयं मनुरित्यनेन सप्ताक्षरः सप्तदशाग्निमन्त्रोऽपि सूचितः । तदुक्तमाचार्य्यैः—

वियतो दशमोऽर्घिसर्गयुक्तो भुवसर्गौ भृगुलान्तषोडशाचः ।
हुतभुग्दयिता ध्रुवादिकोऽयं मनुरुक्तः सुसमृद्धिदः कृशानोः ॥ इति ।

अस्य प्रणवो बीजं स्वाहा शक्तिः । एतन्मन्त्रोक्तमेवर्ष्यादि । द्विरुक्ताभिर्व्याहृतिभिः षडङ्गम् । ध्यानं तु—

विभक्तैः पञ्चभिः षड्भिश्चतुर्भिः पञ्चभिस्त्रिभिः ।
द्वाभ्यामङ्गक्रिया प्रोक्ता वर्णैर्मूलमनोः क्रमात् ॥ ९४

अंसासक्तसुवर्णमाल्यमरुणास्रक्चन्दनालङ्कृतं
ज्वालापुञ्जजटाकलापविलसन्मौलिं सुशुक्लांशुकम् ।
शक्तिस्वस्तिकदर्भमुष्टिकजपस्रक्स्रुक्स्रुवाभीवरान्
दोर्भिर्बिभ्रतमञ्चितत्रिनयनं रक्ताभमग्निं भजे ॥ ९५

गुरोर्लब्धमनुर्मन्त्री चतुर्दश्यामुपोषितः ।
जपेद्भानुसहस्राणि शुद्धाचारो जितेन्द्रियः ॥ ९६

शक्तिस्वस्तिकपाशान् साङ्कुशवरदाभयान् दधत् त्रिमुखः ।
मुकुटादिविविधभूषोऽवताच्चिरं पावकः प्रसन्नो वः ॥
जपेदिमं मनुमतुलक्षमादराद्दशांशतः प्रतिजुहुयात् पयोऽन्धसा ।
ससर्पिषा सुसिततरैश्च षाष्टिकैः । इति ।

पूजा तु वक्ष्यमाणक्रमेणैवेति । अग्निरित्यादि स्वाहान्तोऽपि पृथक् मन्त्र इत्यपि सूचितम् । तदुक्तं प्रयोगसारे—

मन्त्रोऽप्यग्निर्जातवेद इहावहसमन्वितः ।
सर्वकर्माण्यतः साधय स्वाहेति क्रमोदितः ॥ इति ।

अपेक्षितार्थद्योतनिकायामप्येतादृश उक्तः । "द्विवेदवेदेषुवह्निद्विवर्णैरङ्गकल्पना" इति । ऋष्यादि ध्यानपूजादिकं समानमेव ॥ ९२॥९३॥९४ ॥

आयुधध्यानं वामादूर्ध्वयोराद्ये तदधस्थयोरन्ये । एवमान्तम् । ध्यानानन्तरं सप्तजिह्वाख्यमुद्रां प्रदर्शयेत् । तल्लक्षणं यथा—

मणिबन्धस्थितौ कृत्वा प्रसृताङ्गुलिकौ करौ ।
कनिष्ठाङ्गुष्ठयुगले मिलित्वाऽन्याः प्रसारयेत् ।
सप्तजिह्वाख्यमुद्रेयं वैश्वानरवशङ्करी ॥ इति ।

इयं सर्वाग्निमन्त्रसाधारणीति ज्ञेयम् ॥ ९५ ॥

गुरोर्लब्धमनुर्मन्त्री चतुर्दश्यामुपोषितो जपेदित्यन्वयः । चतुर्दश्यामिति चैत्रकृष्णचतुर्दश्याम् । तदुक्तम्—

वत्सरादेश्चतुर्दश्यां दिनादावेव दीक्षितः ।
मन्त्रं द्वादशसाहस्रं जपेत्तस्यामुपोषितः ॥ इति ॥ ९६ ॥

अमावस्यादिने विप्रान् भोजयेन्मधुरोत्तरैः ।
भक्ष्यभोज्यैर्यथाशक्ति दद्यात्तेभ्योऽथ दक्षिणाम् ॥ ९७
भुक्त्वा[दृष्ट्वा] स्वयं समानीय होमद्रव्याणि शोधयेत् ।
अपरं दिनमारभ्य होमं कुर्य्यादतन्द्रितः ॥ ९८
क्रमाद्वटसमिद्व्रीहि तिलराजी हविर्घृतैः ।
प्रत्येकमष्टोत्तरशतं जुहुयाद् दिनशः सुधीः ॥ ९९
दशाहमेवं निर्वर्त्य विधानेन विधानवित् ।
दत्त्वा पूर्णाहुतिं सम्यगेकादश्यां द्विजोत्तमान् ॥ १००
सम्पूज्य तर्पयेद्वित्तैर्यथाविभवमादरात् ।
गुरवे दक्षिणां दद्यादरुणां गां पयस्विनीम् ॥ १०१
वासांसि धनधान्यानि दत्त्वा सम्प्रीणयेत् पुनः ।
स्वमण्डलान्तं प्रयजेत्पीठं सनवशक्तिकम् ॥ १०२
पीता श्वेताऽरुणा कृष्णा धूम्रा तीव्रा स्फुलिङ्गिनी ।
रुचिरा ज्वालिनी प्रोक्ता कृशानोर्नव शक्तयः ॥ १०३
स्वबीजेनासनं दद्यान्मूर्त्तिं मूलेन कल्पयेत् ।
तत्र संपूजयेद्वह्निं विधिना प्रोक्तलक्षणम् ॥ १०४

मधुरोत्तरैः शर्करादि मधुरद्रव्याधिकैः । अपरं दिनमिति शुक्लप्रतिपदम् । तदुक्तम्—परेऽह्नि प्रतिपद्येतैर्जुहुयादर्चितेऽनले । इति । नारायणीये च—अग्न्यादिषु दिगन्तेषु तिथिष्वष्टोत्तरं शतम् । इति ॥ ९७ ॥ ९८ ॥

क्रमात् वटेति षड्द्रव्याणि । नारायणीये तु सप्तद्रव्याण्युक्तानि—न्यग्रोधसमिधो व्रीहितिलराजीघृतान्विताः । सपायसघृत नित्यम् । इति । तथा—तैर्द्रव्यैः सप्तभिः पृथक् । इति ॥ ९९ ॥

दशाहमिति । एवं विधानेन दशाहं निर्वर्त्य विधानविदेकादश्यां पूर्णाहुतिं हुत्वा द्विजोत्तमान् सम्यक् सम्पूज्येत्यन्वयः । तत्र विधानविदित्यनेन महाव्याहृतिहोमं कृत्वा अङ्गमूर्त्तिलोकपालास्त्राणामेकैकामाहुतिं दत्त्वा पूर्णाहुतिरित्युक्तम् । सम्यक् तर्पयेदित्यनेन अर्घ्यादिभिरुपचारैरित्युक्तम् । स्वमण्डलान्तं वह्निमण्डलान्तम् ॥ १०० ॥ ॥ १०१ ॥ १०२ ॥ १०३ ॥

स्वबीजेनेति रमित्यनेन । रं वह्नियोगपीठाय नमः इति आसनमन्त्रः ।

अङ्गपूजां पुरा कृत्वा मूर्त्तीरष्टौ दलेष्विमाः ।
जातवेदाः सप्तजिह्वो हव्यवाहनसंज्ञकः ॥ १०५

अश्वोदरजसंज्ञोऽन्यः पुनर्वैश्वानराह्वयः ।
कौमारतेजाः स्याद्विश्वमुखो देवमुखः परः ॥ १०६

अर्च्याः स्वस्तिकशक्तिभ्यां विराजितकराम्बुजाः ।
लोकेशानर्चयेद्बाह्ये वज्राद्यायुधसंयुतान् ॥ १०७

इति संपूजयेन्नित्यं जपेत् सायं सहस्रकम् ।
जायते वत्सरादर्वाग्धनधान्यसमृद्धिमान् ॥ १०८

साज्यमन्नं प्रजुहुयाद्वत्सराल्लभते श्रियम् ।
कुसुमैर्नन्द्यवृक्षस्य दधिक्षौद्रघृतप्लुतैः ॥ १०९

करवीरप्रसूनैर्वा सवत्सरात् स्यात्समृद्धिमान् ।
षण्मासं कपिलाज्येन जुहुयाद्वत्सरान्तरे ॥ ११०

तस्य सञ्जायते लक्ष्मीः कीर्त्तिस्त्रैलोक्यवन्दिता ।
शालिभिर्जुहुयान्नित्यं विधिनाऽष्टोत्तरं शतम् ॥ १११

व्रीहिगोमहिषाश्वाद्यैर्भवनं तस्य पूर्य्यते ।
तिलहोमेन महतीं लक्ष्मीमाप्नोति मानवः ॥ ११२

पलाशबिल्वखदिरशमीदुग्धमहीरुहाम् ।
विकङ्कतारग्वधयोः समिद्भिः करवीरजैः ॥ ११३

विधिनेति षोडशोपचारैः । प्रोक्तलक्षणमुक्तध्यानम् । मूर्त्तीनां कथनमन्यमूर्त्ति-निवृत्त्यर्थम् । प्रयोगसार नारायणीययोरन्या मूर्त्तय उक्ताः—

अग्निर्वैश्वानरः पश्चात्परः प्रोक्तो हुताशनः ।
हुतवर्त्मा जातवेदास्ततश्चापि हुतावहः ।
भूयो देवमुखः सप्तजिह्वश्चेत्यग्निमूर्त्तयः ॥ इति ।

एता व्याहृतित्रयरहिते मन्त्रे ज्ञेयाः ॥ १०४ ॥ १०५ ॥ १०६ ॥ १०७ ॥

जपेत् सायं सहस्रकमिति नित्यजपसंख्योक्ता । इयं सर्व्वत्रापि ज्ञेया ॥ १०८ ॥

जुहुयादिति षण्मासम् । विधिनाऽष्टोत्तरं शतमिति । विधिनेति प्रति प्रतिपदं चेत्यक्तम् । नित्यं जुहुयात् प्रति प्रतिपदं चेति विकल्पः । एकेन नित्यमष्टोतरं शतमिति । दुग्धमहीरुह एकस्य यस्य कस्य चिद्ग्रहणात् ।

प्रसूनैः कुमुदैः पद्मैः कह्लारैररुणोत्पलैः।
जातीप्रसूनैर्दूर्वाभिर्नित्यमष्टोत्तरं शतम्॥ ११४
एकैकेन जुहुयान्मन्त्री प्रतिपत्स्वथवा सुधीः।
साधयेदखिलान् कामान् षण्मासान्नाऽत्र संशयः॥ ११५
उत्तिष्ठपुरुष ब्रूयाद्धरिपिङ्गल तत्परम्।
लोहिताक्षपदं देहि मे ददापय ठद्वयम्॥ ११६
चतुर्विंशत्यक्षरात्मा सप्तर्द्धिमनुरीरितः।
ऋष्याद्यः पुरा प्रोक्ताः षड्भूतकरणैस्त्रिभिः॥ ११७
चतुर्भिर्युगलैनाऽर्णैर्मूलमन्त्रसमुद्भवैः।
विदधीत षडङ्गानि जातियुक्तानि मन्त्रवित्॥ ११८

स्वर्णाश्वत्थविनिर्गतं हुतवहं सिन्दूरपुञ्जप्रभं
ज्वालाभिर्निचिलाङ्गरोमनिचयं कान्त्या जगन्मोहनम्।
अश्वाकारमनर्घरत्नविलसद्भूषालसत्कन्धरं
रत्नैरिन्द्रियनिर्गतैर्वसुमतीमाच्छादयन्तं स्मरेत्॥ ११९

अरुणोत्पलैः रक्तकमलैः रक्तकुवलयैरित्यपि। यत्कोशश्च—"रक्तोत्पलं कोकनदं रक्ताब्जे रक्तसन्ध्यके" इति। अतः सप्त समिधः सप्त पुष्पाणि एका दूर्वेति पञ्चदश द्रव्याणि। तत्र प्रतिपदादि पर्वपर्यन्तं प्रत्यहमेकैकेनोक्तसंख्यया जुहुयात्। एवं प्रतिपक्षं यावत् षण्मासपूर्त्तिः। अथवा प्रतिपत्स्विति पक्षे एकेन एकैकेन तेन तस्मिन् दिवसे पञ्चदशभिर्द्रव्यैः प्रत्येकमष्टोत्तरशतसंख्यया जुहुयात्॥१०९—११५॥

तुरगाग्निमन्त्रमाह उत्तिष्ठेति। ठद्वयं स्वाहा। सप्तर्द्धिमनुरित्यनेन विनियोगोक्तिः। मन्त्रस्य हलो बीजानि। स्वराः शक्तयः। प्रणवो बीजं स्वाहा शक्तिरिति पद्मपादाचार्याः। प्रणवाद्य इति केचित्। नृसिंहबीजाद्य इत्यन्ये। लक्ष्मीबीजाद्य इत्यपरे। मृत्युञ्जयाद्य इत्यपि केचन। प्रयोगे देहि मे एतत्पूर्वं साध्ययोगोऽपि ज्ञेयः। भूतैरिति पञ्चभिः। करणैश्चतुर्भिः। प्रयोगसारनारायणीययोः लोहिताक्षेपदद्वयातिरिक्तः प्रणवादिविंशत्यक्षर एवोद्धृतः।

तदुक्तम्—उत्तिष्ठपुरुषेत्युक्त्वा हरिपिङ्गल देह्यथ।
ददापयेति तारादिः स्वाहान्तो मन्त्र ईरितः॥ इति।
चतुस्त्रोषुद्वयब्धियुगैर्वर्णैर्ह्याऽङ्गं पुरोदितम्। इति॥११६॥११७॥११८॥

तुरगाग्निध्यानमाह स्वर्णेति॥ ११९॥

लक्षं मनुं जपेदेनं पयोऽन्नेन ससर्पिषा ।
दशांशं जुहुयादग्नौ तुरगारिमनुं स्मरन् ॥ १२०

पीठे प्रागीरितेऽभ्यर्च्य तदङ्गैर्मूर्त्तिभिः सह ।
आशापालैस्तदीयास्त्रैरर्चयेद्धव्यवाहनम् ॥ १२१

प्रातःस्नानरतो मन्त्री सहस्रं यो जपेन्मनुम् ।
जित्वा रोगान् सुखं जीवेत् श्रिया वर्षशतं नरः ॥ १२२

हृत्प्रमाणे जले स्थित्वा भानुमालोक्य संयतः ।
चतुःसहस्रं प्रजपेन्नित्यं संवत्सरावधि ॥ १२३

अपमृत्युभयं रोगकृत्यादाविद्रासम्भवान् ।
क्लेशान्निर्जित्य तेजस्वी जीवेद्वर्षशतं सुधीः ॥ १२४

कृत्तिकायां प्रतिपदि शालिहोमो धनप्रदः ।
दध्ना शमीसमिद्भिर्वा प्रतिपत्सु भवेद्धनम् ॥ १२५

इष्टावाप्तिर्भवेदाज्यैः पद्मैः ग्राममवाप्नुयात् ।
ते[ति]लैर्ज्योतिष्मतीभूते रिपुराज्यं जयेन्नृपः ॥ १२६

अश्वत्थसमिधो मेषीघृताक्ता जुहुयान्नरः ।
कन्यामिष्टामवाप्नोति स्त्रापि तं प्राप्नुयात् पतिम् ॥ १२७

शुद्धाज्येन कृतो होमो ज्वरनाशकरः स्मृतः ।
सप्ताहं जुहुयान्मन्त्री बन्धूककुसुमैः शुभैः ॥ १२८

साग्रं सहस्रमचिरान्महतीं श्रियमश्नुते ।
मासं क्षीरेण गव्येन क्षीराहारो जितेन्द्रियः ॥ १२९

लक्षं मनुं जपेदिति । तत्र प्रकारोऽपेक्षितार्थद्योतनिकायाम् । कृत्तिकाविशाखयोर्मध्ये अष्टमी चतुर्दशी वा यदि भवति तदाऽत्र अभिजित्काले पुरश्चरणमारभ्य शमीरक्तचन्दनकरवीरकाणाम् अन्यतमेनाऽग्निप्रतिमाम् आपाद्य मूलेनावाहनादि विसर्गान्तं कर्म कुर्वन् त्रिषवणस्नायी त्रिसहस्रं त्रिशतं चतुस्त्रिंशदधिकं नित्यं जप्त्वा घृताभिघारितशमीसमिद्भिः तादृक्पायसेन वा तदर्द्धं जुहुयात् मासं गुरोश्च गामपि दद्यात् सिद्धो भवति । उभयोः सन्ध्ययोर्मध्याह्ने वा करवीरपुष्पैरर्चयेदिति । प्रागीरित इत्यव्यवहिते । तत्र कल्पतरुस्थाने स्वर्णाश्वत्थः पूजनीयः । स्थाने

सहस्रं जुहुयान्मन्त्री सम्पदामधिपो भवेत् ।
आज्याक्तदूर्वाहोमेन जीवेद्वर्षशतं नरः ॥ १३०

अष्टोत्तरशतं नित्यं हविषा मृगमुद्रया ।
जुह्वतो जायते लक्ष्मीर्धनधान्यसमृद्धिदा ॥ १३१

प्रतिमासं प्रतिपदि जुहुयादयुतं घृतैः ।
श्रीर्भवेन्महती तस्य षण्मासादनपायिनी ॥ १३२

अरुणैरुत्पलैः फुल्लैर्मधुरत्रयसंयुतैः ।
जुहुयाद्वत्सराद् यः स भवेदिन्दिरापतिः ॥ १३३

अमृताज्यैस्त्रिमध्वक्तैर्जुहुयादन्वहं सुधीः ।
सहस्रं वत्सरार्द्धेन भवेद् भूमिपुरन्दरः ॥ १३४

वत्सरं जुह्वतस्तस्य लक्ष्मीरिन्द्रेण वाञ्छिता ।
जुहुयादमृताखण्डैः पयोऽक्तैः सप्तवासरम् ॥ १३५

त्रिसहस्रं प्रतिदिनं मन्त्रविद्विजितेन्द्रियः ।
कृत्याद्रोहज्वरोन्मादरोगान् जित्वा निरन्तरम् ॥ १३६
जीवेद्वर्षशतं भूत्वा तेजसा भास्करप्रभः ।
करवीरजवाबिल्वपलाशनृपभूरुहाम् ॥ १३७
प्रसूनैः कुमुदैः फुल्लैः कुरण्टैर्जातिसम्भवैः ।
पुष्पैर्हुत्वा त्रिमध्वक्तैर्मन्त्री प्रतिपदं प्रति ॥ १३८
प्राप्नुयान्महतीं लक्ष्मीं वत्सराद्वाञ्छिताधिकाम् ।
आदाय तण्डुलप्रस्थं निर्मलं साधुशोधितम् ॥ १३९
गोदुग्धेन हविः कृत्वा कवलं तेन कल्पयेत् ।
आज्याक्तं तत् समादाय पूजिते हव्यवाहने ॥ १४०

तयोक्तः । मृगमुद्रयेति । मृगमुद्रालक्षणं तु—

मिलित्वाऽनामिकाङ्गुष्ठमध्यमाग्राणि योजयेत् ।
शिष्टाङ्गुल्युच्छ्रिते कुर्यान्मृगमुद्रेयमीरिता ॥ इति ॥ १३०—१३४ ॥

अमृता गुडूची । नृपभूरुट् राजवृक्षः । हुत्वेति प्रत्येकम् । एकैकशः शतमिति आचार्योक्तः । गोदुग्धेनेति रक्तवर्णगोदुग्धेन । तदुक्तं प्रयोगसारे—

गन्धपुष्पादिभिः सम्यग् जपित्वाऽष्टोत्तरं शतम् ।
जुहुयात् प्रतिपद्यग्निं ध्यात्वा तुरगविग्रहम् ॥ १४१

जायते वत्सरादर्वाग्लक्ष्मीस्त्रैलोक्यमोहिनी ।
मन्त्रेणाऽनेन सञ्जप्तां वचां खादेद्दिनागमे ।
भारती निवसेत्तस्य मुखाम्भोजे विनिश्चला ॥ १४२

अष्टोत्तरशतं जप्तं जलं प्रातः पिबेन्नरः ।
जठराग्निर्ज्वलेत्तस्य हविषेव हुताशनः ॥ १४३

कृत्वा नवपदात्मानं मण्डलं प्रागुदीरितम् ।
कलशान्नव कल्याणान् स्थापयेत् प्रोक्तवर्त्मना ॥ १४४

क्षीरवृक्षत्वगुद्भूतैः क्वाथैस्तान् पूरयेत् क्रमात् ।
वस्त्रादिभिरलङ्कृत्य नव रत्नानि निक्षिपेत् ॥ १४५

मध्ये सम्पूजयेदग्निं मूर्तीरष्टौ दिशां क्रमात् ।
कुम्भेषु गन्धपुष्पाद्यैर्धूपदीपैर्मनोहरैः ॥ १४६

स्पृष्ट्वा जपेत्ततः कुम्भान् मन्त्रमष्टोत्तरं शतम् ।
अभिषिञ्चेत्ततः साध्यं विनीतं दत्तदक्षिणम् ॥ १४७

ज्वरग्रहमहारोगदारिद्र्यादीन् विजित्य सः ।
जीवेद्वर्षशतं सम्यगभिषिक्तः श्रिया सह ॥ १४८

इति श्रीशारदातिलके चतुर्दशः पटलः ।

शालेयैस्तन्दुलैः प्रस्थैः शोणगोक्षीरसाधितम् ।
हविः पिष्टं घृताक्तं तु जुहुयादाज्यमिश्रितम् ॥ इति ॥ १३५—१४०॥

सम्यक् जपित्वेति लक्ष्मीबीजाद्यमित्युक्तम् । केवलहोमानन्तरमष्टोत्तरं सहस्रं शतं वा घृतेन जुहुयादिति अपेक्षितार्थद्योतनिकाकार आह स्म ॥१४१॥१४२॥१४३॥ नवपदात्मानं नवनाभम् । प्रागिति तृतीये । प्रोक्तवर्त्मना अष्टपटलोक्तरीत्या । ॥ १४४॥१४५॥१४६॥१४७॥१४८ ॥

इति श्रीशारदातिलकटीकायां सत्सम्प्रदायकृतव्याख्यायां
पदार्थादर्शाभिख्यायां चतुर्दशः पटलः ।

पञ्चदश पटलः ।

अथ वक्ष्ये महामन्त्रान् विष्णोः सर्व्वार्थसाधकान् ।
यस्य संस्मरणात् सन्तो भवाब्धेः पारमाश्रिताः ॥ १
तारं नमःपदं पश्चान्नरौ दीर्घसमन्वितौ ।
पवनो णाय मन्त्रोऽयं प्रोक्तो वस्वक्षरान्वितः ॥ २
साध्यनारायणः प्रोक्तो मुनिश्छन्द उदाहृतम् ।
मन्त्रस्य देवी गायत्री देवता विष्णुरव्ययः ॥ ३

क्रमप्राप्तान् विष्णुमन्त्रानाह अथेति । सर्व्वार्थेति सकामं प्रति विनियोगोक्तिः । मुमुक्षुं प्रत्याह यस्येति ॥ १ ॥

मन्त्रमुद्धरति तारमिति । नरौ नकाररेफौ दीर्घ आ तेन समन्वितौ तेन नारा इति । अत्र नमः शब्दस्य रोरुत्वे गुणे च ओङ्कार इति ज्ञेयम् । पवनो यः । णायेति स्वरूपम् । वस्वक्षरः अष्टाक्षरः । तदुक्तं मन्त्रतन्त्रप्रकाशे—

नाभसं पञ्चमे षष्ठे स्थितं वर्णद्वयं क्रमात् ।
द्वितीयो मिश्रसंयुक्तस्तृतीयः स्यात्तु पञ्चमः ॥
वह्निर्वायुस्ततः प्रोक्तौ सानन्तौ त्रिचतुर्थकौ ।
चतुर्थं पञ्चमस्तद्वन्मन्त्रान्ते वायुवर्णकम् ॥ इति ।

अत्र नाभसमित्यनुषज्यते । तेन पञ्चमे तवर्गे यन्नाभसं नकाररूपाक्षरं तत् तृतीयं मन्त्रे तृतीयमक्षरमित्यर्थः । अत्र तृतीयमिति प्रणवं विना । सानन्तौ आकारयुक्तौ । त्रिचतुर्थकौ नकाररेफौ । चतुर्थे टवर्गे यत् पञ्चममक्षरं णकारमित्यर्थः । पञ्चमे तवर्गे षष्ठे पवर्गे यन्नाभसमक्षरं नकारमकाररूपं क्रमेणोद्धरणीयम् । तत्र द्वितीयो मकारः मिश्रेण ओकारेण संयुक्तः । प्रणवो बीजं आयेति शक्तिः । तदुक्तं मन्त्रतन्त्रप्रकाशे—

ज्वलत्प्रभः श्रुतेरादिर्बिन्दुमान् विष्णुरव्ययः ।
बीजमष्टाक्षरस्य स्यात्तेनाऽष्टाक्षरता भवेत् ॥
अथ पञ्चदशाद्वर्णात् केवलं व्यजनीकृतात् ।
उत्तरो मन्त्रशेषस्तु शक्तिरित्यस्य कथ्यते ॥ इति ।

क्रुद्धोल्काय हृदाख्यातं महोल्काय शिरः स्मृतम् ।
वीरोल्काय शिखा प्रोक्ता द्यूल्काय कवचं स्मृतम् ॥ ४

सहस्रोल्कायाऽस्त्रमुक्तमङ्गक्लृप्तिरियं मता ।
भूयो वर्णैर्मनोः षड्भिः षडङ्गानि समाचरेत् ॥ ५

साध्यनारायणो नामाऽन्तर्यामीति देशिकाः । तदुक्तं मन्त्रतन्त्रप्रकाशे—

अन्तर्यामी ऋषिः छन्दो गायत्री । इति ।

प्रत्यर्णमृष्यादि यथा—गौतमश्च भरद्वाजो विश्वामित्र ऋषिस्तथा ।
जमदग्निर्वशिष्ठश्च कश्यपोऽत्रिश्च कुम्भजः ॥
गायत्र्युष्णिगनुष्टुप् च बृहती पङ्क्तिरेव च ।
त्रिष्टुब्जगत्यौ च विराट् वसवोऽष्टौ च देवता ॥ इति ॥२॥३॥

पञ्चाङ्गमन्त्रोद्धारमाह क्रुद्धोल्कायेत्यादि । चतुर्थ्यन्तोद्धारेण सर्वेषां स्वाहान्तता जातिः पूर्वमुक्ता । उक्तं च मन्त्रतन्त्रप्रकाशे—

उल्कैः क्रुद्धमहावीरद्युसहस्रेति पूर्वकैः ।
एषां विभक्तियुक्तानां भवेदन्तेऽग्निवल्लभा ॥ इति ॥

अन्यत्रापि—क्रुद्धोल्कादिपदैर्वह्निजायान्तैर्जातिसंयुतैः । इति ।

अङ्गक्लृप्तिरियं मतेत्यनेन पूर्वं करन्यासः सूचितः । स यथा—

कुर्यात्करयोर्विधिवत् सृष्ट्यादिन्यासमष्टमन्त्रार्णैः ।
दक्षिणतर्जन्याद्या सृष्टिः स्याद्वामतर्जनीं यावत् ॥
तर्जन्युभयाद्येह स्थितिः कनिष्ठाद्वयान्तिका क्रमतः ।
सृष्टेर्विपरीतः स्यात् संहारोऽयं करे प्रोक्तः ॥
अष्टाङ्गं विन्यस्य स्थितिक्रमादङ्गपञ्चकं न्यसेत् ॥ इति ।

तत्र विशेषो नारायणीये—

कनिष्ठादि तदन्तानामङ्गुलीनां विपर्ययः ।
ज्येष्ठाग्रेण क्रमात्तारुद्धानष्टाक्षरान् न्यसेत् ॥ इति ॥ ४॥५ ॥

पञ्चाङ्गमुक्त्वाऽष्टाङ्गमाह भूय इति । तत्र षडङ्गवदेव षडक्षराणि विन्यस्य णां उदराय नमः यं पृष्ठाय नमः इति कुक्षिपृष्ठयोर्न्यसेत् । तदुक्तम्—

अष्टाक्षरेण व्यस्तेन कुर्याच्चाऽष्टाङ्गकं सुधीः ।
सहृच्छिरःशिखावर्मनेत्रास्त्रोदरपृष्ठके ॥ इति ।

ईशानशिवेनाप्युक्तम्—

अवशिष्टौ पुनर्वर्णौ विन्यसेत् कुक्षिपृष्ठयोः ।
बद्धदिक् चक्रमन्त्रेण मन्त्रवर्णांस्ततो न्यसेत् ॥ ६

आधारे हृदये वक्त्रे दोःपन्मूलेषु नासिके ।
कण्ठे नाभौ हृदि कुचे पार्श्वपृष्ठेषु तत्परम् ॥ ७

अस्य स्याद्धृदयं तारः शिरो नार्णः शिखा च मो ।
नार्णः कवचं श[चा]स्त्रं रावर्णौ नयनं परः ॥
उदरं पृष्ठमन्त्यौ च वर्णौ हि नमसा युतौ ॥ इति ।

अन्यत्रापि—हृदयशिरः पूर्वशिखा कवचास्त्राच्युदरपृष्ठसञ्ज्ञिते: । इति ॥
इदमेव साम्प्रदायिकम् ।

बद्धदिगिति छोटिकां वादयन् । चक्रमन्त्रेणेति अष्टिमपटले वज्रनाभेन ऐन्द्रीचक्रेण बध्नामि इत्यादिना । चतुर्थपटले सामान्यास्त्रमन्त्रेण दिग्बन्ध उक्तः । अत्र मन्त्रविशेषकथनाय पुनर्वचनम् । मन्त्रवर्णांस्ततो न्यसेदित्यनेन सृष्टिस्थिति-संहारन्यासः सूचितः । यदाहुः—

मूर्धन्यस्योरास्ये हृदि नाभौ गुह्यजानुपादेषु ।
सृष्टिरियं निर्दिष्टा नाभ्यादि हृदन्तिका स्थितिस्तद्वत् ॥
संहारः पादाद्यो मूर्धान्तः कथित एष सृष्ट्यादिः ॥ इति ।

मन्त्रतन्त्रप्रकाशे तु—

नाभावारभ्यते यस्तु हृदये च समाप्यते ।
स्थितिन्यासः स विज्ञेयो दृष्टादृष्टफलप्रदः ॥ इति ।

इदमेव साम्प्रदायिकम् । तत्रैव विशेषः—

विन्यसेद्वर्णमेकैकं बिन्द्वन्तं भुववेष्टितम् ।
तत्राङ्गुलीभिर्न्यासः स्याच्छिरस्येकैव मध्यमा ॥
तर्जनीमध्यमाभ्यां तु चक्षुषोर्न्यास इष्यते ।
अङ्गुष्ठानामिकाभ्यां तु मुखे न्यासः प्रकीर्त्तितः ॥
हृदये ज्ञानमुद्रा स्यादङ्गुष्ठस्य कनिष्ठिका ॥
नाभौ प्रकीर्त्तिता गुह्ये अनङ्गुष्ठाः प्रकीर्त्तिताः ।
सर्व्वा जानौ च पादे च पञ्चापि परिकीर्त्तिताः ॥ इति ॥ ५॥६ ॥

एवं पञ्चाङ्गाष्टाङ्गाक्षरन्यासानुक्त्वा दशाष्टत्रिमयं विभूतिपञ्जरन्यासमाह आधारेति । अत्र प्रत्येकमक्षरं प्रणवपुटितं कृत्वा न्यसेत् । मन्त्रतन्त्रप्रकाशे तथोक्तेः । प्रत्या-

मूर्द्धास्यनेत्रश्रवणघ्राणेषु तदनन्तरम् ।
दोःपादसन्ध्यङ्गुलिषु धातुप्राणेषु हृत्स्थले ॥ ८
मूर्द्धवणास्यहृत्कुक्षिसोरुजङ्घपदद्वये
एकैकशो न्यसेद्वर्णान् गरुडांसोरुपदेषु च ॥ ६
चक्रशङ्खगदाम्भोजं पदेष्ववहितो न्यसेत् ।
अष्टार्णोऽष्टप्रकृत्यात्मा न्येयोऽसौ चतुरात्मनाम् ॥ १०

वृत्तिसंपूर्णेन व्यापकं च। तथाच पद्मपादाचार्याः—"मन्त्री मन्त्रवर्णेति न्यासमन्त्राणां प्रणवपुटितत्वं प्रतिपर्यायं व्यापकन्यासश्चोक्तः" इति। पूर्वार्द्धेनैकावृत्तिः। तत्र कः समासः। द्वितीयार्द्धेन द्वितीया। तृतीयार्द्धेन तृतीया। चतुर्थार्द्धेन तुर्याद्यष्टमान्तं पञ्च। तत्र दक्षकरसन्धिचतुष्टयाङ्गुष्ठवर्जं चतुरङ्गुलिष्वेका। अन्ये तु दक्षहस्तसन्धित्रयपञ्चाङ्गुलिष्वित्यूचुः। एवं वामकरे द्वितीया। दक्षपादे तृतीया। वामपादे चतुर्थी। अन्ये तु करद्वयसन्धिष्वेका। पादद्वयसन्धिष्वन्या। अङ्गुष्ठद्वयवर्जकराङ्गुलिषु तृतीया। एवं पादाङ्गुलिषु चतुर्थीत्याहुः। हृदय एव त्वगादिषु पञ्चमी। पञ्चमार्द्धेन नवमी। श्लोकेन दशमी। तत्र गरुडांसोरुचरणेषु चतुरो वर्णान् विन्यस्य चक्रशङ्खगदापद्मप्रस्थानेषु शिष्टांश्चतुरो वर्णान् तदायुधमुद्रासहितान् विन्यसेत् इत्यवहितपदेन सूचितमिति सम्प्रदायविदः।

तन्मुद्रालक्षणं तु—वाममुष्ट्यन्तरेऽङ्गुष्ठे दक्षिणे सरलाङ्गुली: ।
वामाङ्गुष्ठः स्पृशेदग्रे योजितः सरलोदरः ॥
अन्योन्याभिमुखौ हस्तौ कृत्वा तु ग्रथिताङ्गुली: ।
अङ्गुष्ठौ मध्यमे भूयः संलग्ने सुप्रसारिते ॥
गदामुद्रेयमाख्याता भुक्तिमुक्तिकरी तथा । इति ॥

चक्रपद्ममुद्रालक्षणे प्रागुक्ते ॥ ७ ॥ ८ ॥ ६ ॥ १० ॥

मूर्त्तिपञ्जरं वक्तुं तदुपोद्घातत्वेन द्वादशाष्टाक्षरयोरैक्यमाह अष्टेति। अष्ट प्रकृतयः प्रथमपटलोक्ताः। अष्टप्रकृतय इत्यनेनाऽष्टतत्त्वन्यासः सूचितः। स द्विविधः संहारसृष्टिरूपः। तत्र संहारे मन्त्रः अनुलोमः। सृष्टौ मन्त्र प्रतिलोमः। तत्त्वानि पृथिव्यप्तेजोवाय्वाकाशाहङ्कारमहत्प्रकृतिरूपाणि। स्थानानि तु पादलिङ्गहृदयमुखमूर्द्धहृदयहृदयानि सप्त। सर्वतनौ चैकम्। सृष्टौ तत्त्वानुलोम्यञ्च विज्ञेयम्। तत्र प्रयोगः। ॐ नमः पराय पृथिव्यात्मने नमः पादयोः नं नमः पराय

संयोगात् सूरिभिः प्रोक्तो विशिष्टो द्वादशाक्षरः ।
अतस्तन्मन्त्रवर्णाद्या द्वादशस्वरसंयुताः ॥ ११
द्वादशादित्यसहिता मूर्तीर्द्वादश विन्यसेत् ।
केशवाद्याः क्रमाद्देहे वक्ष्यमाणविधानतः ॥ १२
ललाटे केशवं धात्रा कुक्षौ नारायणं पुनः ।
अर्यम्णा हृदि मित्रेण माधवं कण्ठदेशतः ॥ १३
वरुणेन च गोविन्दं पुनर्दक्षिणपार्श्वके ।
अंशुना विष्णुमंसस्थं भगेन मधुसूदनम् ॥ १४

जलात्मने नमः लिङ्ग इत्यादि संहारे। ततः सृष्टौ प्रयोगः। यं नमः पराय प्रकृत्यात्मने नमः सर्वशरीरे। णां नमः पराय महदात्मने नमो हृदीत्यादि। तदुक्तम्—

> क्षितिसलिलानलपवनव्योमाहङ्कृतिमहत्प्रकृत्याख्यैः ।
> व्युत्क्रमगदितैरेतैः क्रमगतमन्त्रार्णसंयुतैर्मन्त्री ॥
> चरणान्धुहृदयवक्त्रकहृदयव्यापकेषु विन्यसेत् ।
> संहारोऽयं गदितो विपरीता सृष्टिरस्य निर्दिष्टा ॥ इति ॥

चतुरात्मनां तुर्यान्तानाम्। अनेन बिन्दुनादशक्तिशान्तरूपाणाम् आत्मादिचतुष्टयानां शरीरे व्यापकत्वेन न्यासः सूचितः। प्रयोगश्च। ॐ बिन्दुरूपात्मने नमः ॐ नादरूपान्तरात्मने नमः ॐ शक्तिरूपपरमात्मने नमः ॐ शान्तिरूपज्ञानात्मने नम इति ॥ १० ॥ ११ ॥

न्यासमेवाह अत इति। तन्मन्त्रवर्णाद्याः द्वादशाक्षरमन्त्रवर्णाद्याः। द्वादशस्वराः नपुंसकचतुष्टयव्यतिरिक्ताः तैः संयुताः। द्वादशादित्यसहिताः केशवाद्या द्वादश मूर्तीः देहे वक्ष्यमाणविधानतः क्रमात् विन्यसेदिति सम्बन्धः। तत्र प्रयोगः। ॐ अं केशवधातृभ्यां नमः ललाट इत्यादि। केचन धातृसहिताय केशवाय नमः इति। अन्ये तु केशवाय धात्रे नमः इत्याहुः। कुक्षाविति नैकव्याख्याभिभागो लक्ष्यते। अर्यम्णेति। पश्चात्तनेन सम्बध्यते। कण्ठदेशत इत्यस्याऽग्रिमेण सम्बन्धः। अंशुना विष्णुमिति पश्चात्तनेन सम्बध्यते।

अंसस्थमिति दक्षिणांसस्थम्। गले ग्रीवादक्षिणभागे। दक्षिणपार्श्वक इत्यतो दक्षिणपदानुषङ्गस्तूभयत्र। अथांसक इत्यस्याग्रिमेण सम्बन्धः। तत्रांसके वामांसके।

गले विवस्वता युक्तं त्रिविक्रममनन्तरम् ।
वामपार्श्वस्थमिन्द्रेण वामनाख्यमथांसके ॥ १५

पुषा श्रीधरनामानं गले पर्जन्यसंयुतम् ।
हृषीकेशाह्वयं पृष्ठे पद्मनाभं ततः परम् ॥ १६

त्वष्ट्रा दामोदरं पश्चाद्विष्णुना ककुदि न्यसेत् ।
द्वादशार्णं महामन्त्रं ततो मूर्ध्नि प्रविन्यसेत् ॥ १७

गले ग्रीवावामभागे। वामपार्श्वस्थमित्यतो वामपदानुवृत्तेरुभयत्र। तदुक्तं दक्षिणपार्श्वांसतद्गले तथा वामत्रय इति। अन्यत्तोभयत्र गलस्थाने कर्णमाहुः।

हृषीकेशाह्वयमिति पूर्वेण सम्बध्यते। त्वष्ट्रेत्यस्यापि पूर्वेणाऽन्वयः। ककुदीति पृष्ठगतग्रीवाभागे। तदुक्तं स्वायम्भुवे नारसिंहे—

केशवं विन्यसेल्लार्श्वमूर्द्धदेशेऽथ विष्णुना ।
नाभौ नारायणं देवं विष्णुं तेन समन्वितम् ॥
माधवं हृदि विन्यस्येत् मन्मथेन च संयुतम् ।
मन्मथान्तेन संयुक्तं गले गोविन्दसंज्ञकम् ॥
विष्णुं भूतस्वरेणाऽथ दक्षपार्श्वे विनायकम् ।
तदंशे आद्यबीजेन सूदनं मधुपूर्वकम् ॥
बिन्दुना शिवयुक्तेन दक्षकर्णे त्रिविक्रमम् ।
वामनं श्रीधरं चैव हृषीकेशमतः परम् ॥
वामे चैकारमोकारमौकारं बिन्दुना सह ।
बिन्दुना पद्मनाभं च पृष्ठदेशे तदङ्गयुक् ॥
अन्त्यं ककुदि दामेन द्वादशाङ्गमिति स्मृतम् ।
द्वादशेमानि बीजानि नादबिन्दुयुतानि च ॥
आदित्या द्वादश प्रोक्ता द्वादशाक्षरसंयुताः । इति ।

अन्यत्रापि—केशवादि युगषट्कमूर्त्तिभिर्धातृपूर्वमिहिरादमोऽन्तगान् ।
द्वादशाक्षरभवाक्षरैः स्वरैः क्लीबवर्णरहितैः पृथग् न्यसेत् ॥ इति ।

केशवादि मूर्त्तीनां मन्त्रोद्देशाच्च क्लीबरहितत्वं गम्यते। महामन्त्रमष्टाक्षरम्। तदुक्तं मन्त्रतन्त्रप्रकाशे—अष्टाक्षरेण सहितं विन्यसेद् द्वादशाक्षरम्। इति। "मन्त्रविन्मूर्ध्नीत्यष्टाक्षरेण सार्द्धमित्यर्थः" इति पद्मपादाचार्याः ॥ ११-१७ ॥

पुनः किरीटमन्त्रेण व्यापकं विन्यसेत्ततः ।
ब्रूयात्किरीटकेयूरहारं मकरकुण्डलम् ॥ १८
शङ्खचक्रगदाम्भोजहस्तं पीताम्बरं धरम् ॥
श्रीवत्साङ्कितवक्षोऽन्ते स्थलशब्दमुदीरयेत् ॥ १९
श्रीभूमिसहितस्वात्मज्योतिर्द्वयमुदाहृतम् ॥
पश्चाद्दीप्तिकरायेति सहस्रादित्यतेजसे ॥ २०
नमोऽन्तः प्रणवाद्योऽयं किरीटमनुरीरितः ।
एवं न्यासं तनौ कृत्वा ध्यायेन्नारायणं परम् ॥ २१

उद्यत्कोटिदिवाकराभमनिशं शङ्खं गदां पङ्कजं
चक्रं बिभ्रतमिन्दिरावसुमतीसंशोभिपार्श्वद्वयम् ।
कोटीराङ्गदहारकुण्डलधरं पीताम्बरं कौस्तुभो-
द्दीप्तं विश्वधरं स्ववक्षसि लसच्छ्रीवत्सचिह्नं भजे ॥ २२

किरीटमन्त्रमुद्धरति ब्रूयादिति । हारमित्यादौ शब्दकर्मणि द्वितीया । मन्त्रे तु सम्बुध्यन्तानि सर्वाणि । कुण्डलमिति कुण्डलालङ्कृतेति मन्त्रभागः । तथापि पद्मपादाचार्याः—"मन्त्रविन् मकारान्ते कुण्डलमिति मकरकुण्डलालङ्कृत इति पदाध्याहारः सूचितः" इति । मन्त्रतत्त्वप्रकाशेऽपि—

तारः किरीटकेयूरहारान्ते मकरं पदम् ।
कुण्डलालङ्कृतेत्यन्ते चक्रशङ्खगदापद्मम् ॥ इति

श्रीभूमिसहितस्वात्मज्योतिर्द्वयमिति स्वरूपम् । न तु ज्योतिः पदस्य द्विरुक्तिः । तथा चाचार्याः—श्रीभूमिसहितस्वात्मज्योतिर्द्वयपदं वदेत् । इति ॥ १८॥१९ ॥ ॥ २०॥२१ ॥

आयुधध्यानं तु दक्षाधोवामोर्ध्वदक्षोर्ध्ववामाधःक्रमेण । तदुक्तं हयशीर्ष-पञ्चरात्रे—पङ्कजं दक्षिणे यस्य पाञ्चजन्यं तथोपरि ।

वामाधस्तु गदा यस्य चक्रं चोर्ध्वं व्यवस्थितम् ॥
आदिमूर्त्तेस्तु भेदोऽयं केशवेन प्रकीर्त्त्यते ।

इति केशवलक्षणमुक्ता—

अथवोत्तरभावेन कृतमेतत्तु यत्र वै ।
नारायणाख्या विज्ञेया स्थापिता भुक्तिमुक्तिदा ॥ इति ।

मन्त्रतन्त्रप्रकाशेऽपि—

सव्यान्यपाणौ प्रथमे तु पद्मं बिभ्राणमब्जं तदनन्तरे च ।
आद्ये गदां वामकरेऽथ चक्रं विराजयन्तं भुवनानि भासा ॥ इति ।

ध्यानविशेषाश्च तत्रैव—

वामे विचिन्त्या कमलायताक्षी हेमाभवर्णा कमला च देवी ।
विभूतिकामैन सुवर्णहारा प्रेम्णा सृजन्ती नयने हरौ या ॥

तदा देवं सुवर्णाभं चिन्तयेद्रत्नभूषितम् ।
तेनधान्यसुवर्णानां प्राप्तये धरणीं स्मरेत् ॥
देवीं दूर्वादलश्यामां दधानां शालिमञ्जरीम् ।
चिन्तयेद् भारतीं देवीं वीणापुस्तकधारिणीम् ॥
दक्षिणे देवदेवस्य पूर्णचन्द्रनिभाननाम् ।
क्षीराब्धिफेनपुञ्जाभे वसानां श्वेतवाससी ॥
भारत्या सहितं विष्णुं ध्यायेदेवं परात्परम् ।
वेदवेदार्थसंवेदी जायते सर्ववित्तमः ॥ इति ।

नारायणीये तु—

प्रणवद्वयमध्यस्थो नमोऽन्तश्च सबीजकः ।
निर्बीजो मोक्षकृन् मन्त्रो यथोक्तप्रणवादिकः ॥ इति ।

अत्र ध्यानानन्तरं श्रीवत्सकौस्तुभवनमालायुधमुद्राः प्रदर्शयेत् । तल्लक्षणानि तु—

अन्योन्यपृष्ठकरयोर्मध्यमानामिकाङ्गुली ।
अङ्गुष्ठेन तु बध्नीयात्कनिष्ठा मूलसंश्रिते ॥
तर्जन्यौ कारयेदेषा मुद्रा श्रीवत्ससंज्ञिका ।
अनामापृष्ठसंलग्ना दक्षिणस्य कनिष्ठिका ॥
कनिष्ठिकान्या बध्नीयादनामादक्षतर्जनीम् ।
गृहीत्वा दक्षिणाङ्गुष्ठमध्यमानामिकात्रयम् ॥
उच्छ्रयित्वा तत्र वामे तर्जनीमध्यमे न्यसेत् ।
दक्षिणे मणिबन्धे च वामाङ्गुष्ठं तु योजयेत् ॥
मुद्रेयं कौस्तुभस्योक्ता दर्शनीया प्रयत्नतः ।
स्पृशेत्कण्ठादि पादान्तं तर्जन्याङ्गुष्ठनिष्ठया ॥
करद्वयेन मालावन् मुद्रेयं वनमालिका । इति ।

आयुधमुद्रालक्षणं तत्र तत्र पूर्वमेवोक्तम् ॥ २२ ॥

विकाराल्यं प्रजपेन्मन्त्रमेनं समाहितः ।
तद्दशांशं सरसिजैर्जुहुयान्मधुराप्लुतैः ॥ २३

पीठे सम्पूजयेद्देवं विमलादिसमन्विते ।
विमलोत्कर्षिणी ज्ञाना क्रिया योगा ततः परम् ॥ २४

प्रह्वी सत्या तथेशानाऽनुग्रहा नवमी तथा ।
नमो भगवते ब्रूयाद्विष्णवे च पदं वदेत् ॥ २५

सर्वभूतात्मने वासुदेवायेति वदेत्ततः ।
सर्वात्मसंयोगपदाद्योगपद्मपदं पुनः ॥ २६

पीठात्मने हृदन्तोऽयं मन्त्रस्ताराद्युदीरितः ।
दत्वाऽनेनासनं मन्त्री मूर्त्तिं मूलेन कल्पयेत् ॥ २७

आवाह्य पूजयेद्देवं सुगन्धिकुसुमादिभिः ।
अङ्गान्यभ्यर्च्य मन्त्रार्णान् केसरेषु समर्चयेत् ॥ २८

विकारलक्षं षोड़शलक्षम् ॥ २३॥२४॥२५ ॥

दत्वाऽनेनासनं मन्त्रीत्यनेनैतदुक्तम् । आत्मपूजायामासनं दत्त्वा आसनादि गन्धान्तं कृत्वा किरीटमन्त्रेण पुष्पाञ्जलिपञ्चकं दद्यादिति ।

तदुक्तमाचार्य्यैः—विधिवत्किरीटमन्त्रेण कुर्य्यात् पुष्पाञ्जलिमपि । इति ।
॥ २५॥२६॥२७ ॥

आदिशब्देन धूपदीपनैवेद्यानि । अङ्गानीति कर्णिकान्तश्चतुर्थपटलोक्तप्रकारेणाऽङ्गानि सम्पूज्याऽग्न्यादिकेसरेषु क्रमादष्टाङ्गभूतान् मन्त्रार्णानर्चयेत् । ॐ नमः नं नम इत्यादि प्रयोगः । "बीजैः पूजा स्यादिभक्त्या वियुक्तैः" इत्युक्तेः । अत्राङ्गपूजावत् पूजा न कार्य्या । "अष्टाङ्गकं सुधीरिति न्यास एवाऽष्टाङ्गविनियोगः नतु पूजायामिति विशेषज्ञ इत्यर्थः" इति पद्मपादाचार्य्यैरुक्तत्वात् । अत एवात्र मन्त्रार्णानित्युक्तं नाष्टाङ्गमिति । मन्त्रार्णध्यानमुक्तं महाकपिलपञ्चरात्रे—

ॐकारं तु सदा ध्येयं ज्योतिर्मालासमाकुलम् ।
नकारं मेघवर्णाभं मोकारं चिन्तयेत्ततः ॥
भिन्नाञ्जनसमाकारं तृतीयं बीजमुत्तमम् ।
नाकारं श्यामवर्णाभं सौम्यरूपं सुशोभनम् ॥
राकारं जलवर्णाभं सम्यक् सन्दीप्ततेजसम् ।
धूम्रवर्णं सदा ध्येयं यकारं परमुत्तमम् ॥

दलेषु वासुदेवाद्या मूर्त्तीः शक्तिसमन्विताः ।
वासुदेवं संकर्षणं प्रद्युम्नमनिरुद्धकम् ॥ २९

हिमपीततमालेन्द्रनीलाभाः पीतवाससः ।
शङ्खचक्रगदाम्भोजधरा एते चतुर्भुजाः ॥ ३०

शान्तिं श्रियं सरस्वत्या रतिं कोणदलेषु ताः ।
श्वेतकाञ्चनगोदुग्धदूर्वावर्णाः सुभूषिताः ॥ ३१

हेतीनर्चेद्दलाग्रेषु शङ्खं चक्रं गदाम्बुजे ।
कौस्तुभं मुसलं खड्गं वनमालां यथाक्रमम् ॥ ३२

रक्ताच्छपीतकनकश्यामकृष्णासितपाण्डुरान् ।
बहिरग्रे समभ्यर्चेत् गरुडं कुङ्कुमप्रभम् ॥ ३३

मुक्तामाणिक्यसंकाशौ दक्षिणोत्तरतो निधी ।
ध्वजं वरुणदिग्भागे श्यामलं पूजयेत्ततः ॥ ३४

अरुणं विघ्नमाग्नेये श्याममार्यं निशाचरे ।
श्यामां दुर्गां वायुकोणे सेनान्यं पीतमीश्वरे ॥ ३५

इन्द्रादीन् पूजयेत्पश्चाद्वज्राद्यायुधसंयुतान् ।
इति संपूजयेद्विष्णुं प्रोक्तैरावरणैः सह ।
धर्मार्थकामान् लब्ध्वाऽन्ते विष्णोः सायुज्यमाप्नुयात् ॥ ३६

अनौपम्यगुणाकारं णाकारं च विचिन्तयेत् ।
यकारं तु ततो ध्येयं पद्मरागसमप्रभम् ॥ इति ॥ २८ ॥

दलेष्विति दलमध्येषु इदं सामान्यवचनम् । अग्रे कोणदलेषु ता इत्युक्तेः मूर्त्तीनामग्न्यादिचतुर्दिग्दलमध्ये पूजेति ज्ञेयम् । आसां ध्यानं मूलमन्त्रदेवतावत् ज्ञेयम् । एवमग्रिममन्त्रेऽपि । कोणदलेष्विति । आग्नेयादि कोणदलमध्ये । "तथा वज्रादयः कोणा विदिक् वाचकयोगतः" इत्युक्तेः ॥ २९॥३०॥३१ ॥

हेतीनिति वक्ष्यमाणान्यायुधानि । हेतिशब्दः पुंलिङ्गोऽप्यस्ति । यथाक्रममित्युत्तरत्र सम्बध्यते । बहिरिति । अष्टदलाद्बहिः चतुरस्रान्त इत्यर्थः । निधी शङ्खपद्मौ वरुणदिग्भागे । देवतापृष्ठदेशे ।

नारायणीये तु—आद्यावृत्तेर्बहिस्तार्क्ष्यं देवस्य पुरतोऽर्चयेत् । इति ।

धर्मार्थकामेति । अर्थे श्रीबीजादित्वं ज्ञेयम् । तदुक्तं मन्त्रतन्त्रप्रकाशे—

श्रीबीजेन युतं मन्त्रं तत्कामस्तन्मना जपेत् । इति ।

कामनायामपि विशेषः —

नारसिंहमिवात्मानं देवं ध्यात्वाऽतिभैरवम् ।
मन्त्रेण स्पर्शयेच्छस्त्रं नाऽविजित्य निवर्त्तते ॥
नारसिंहेन बीजेन मन्त्रं योज्य तदा जपेत् ।
शतमष्टोत्तरं जप्त्वा वामहस्ताभिमन्त्रिताः ॥
पुनः पुनरपः सिञ्चेत् सर्पदष्टोऽपि जीवति ।
गारुडेन तदा युक्तं पञ्चार्णेन तदा जपेत् ॥
निर्विषीकरणे ध्यायेद्विष्णुं गरुडवाहनम् ।
अशोकफलके यक्षीमालिख्याऽशोकसंहतौ ॥
अशोकपुष्पैराराध्य भगवन्तं तदग्रतः ।
जुहुयात्तानि पुष्पाणि त्रिसन्ध्यं सप्तरात्रकम् ॥
प्रत्यक्षा जायते यक्षी वरमिष्टं प्रयच्छति ।
गाणपत्यसमायुक्तं जपेन्मन्त्रं पयोव्रतः ॥
महागणपतिं देवं प्रत्यक्षमिह पश्यति ।
भारतीबीजसंयुक्तं षाण्मासिकजपाच्च ताम् ॥ इति ॥

तथा—यो जपेत्प्रणवं पूर्वं मन्त्रे त्रैवर्णिकः पुमान् ।
योषितश्च तथा शूद्रा जपेयुः प्रणवं विना ॥
आदावष्टाक्षरस्य स्यात्प्रणवः सार्वकामिकः ।
आदावन्ते यदा ह्येष ज्ञानवृद्धिस्तदा भवेत् ॥
आदितः सहितां कुर्य्यादन्ततस्तु न संहिताम् ॥ इति ।

कल्पोक्तं यन्त्रमुच्यते—

अष्टपत्रं च षट्कोणं रविसंख्यदलाम्बुजम् ।
दन्तपत्रं च तद्बाह्ये वृत्तं भूमिपुरं शुभम् ॥
ससाध्यं कर्णिकायां तु लिखेदाद्यक्षरं सुधीः ।
अष्टपत्रेषु मूलार्णान् पत्राग्रे श्रीकारं लिखेत् ॥
षट्कोणे चक्रमन्त्रार्णान् सूर्य्यारे द्वादशार्णकम् ।
दन्तपत्रे मन्त्रराजं वृत्ते नृहरिबीजकम् ॥
षण्मन्त्रे रविसंयुक्तं साक्षाद्विष्णोश्च मन्दिरम् ।
आवाह्य मन्त्रैराराध्य स्तवैर्बद्ध्वा दृढं वहन् ॥

प्रणवो हृद्भगवते वासुदेवाय कीर्त्तितः ।
प्रधानो वैष्णवे तन्त्रे मन्त्रोऽयं द्वादशाक्षरः ॥ ३७
ऋषिः प्रजापतिश्छन्दो गायत्री परिकीर्त्तितम् ।
देवताऽस्य मनोः प्रोक्ता वासुदेवो मनीषिभिः ॥ ३८
तारेण हृदयं प्रोक्तं नमसा शिर ईरितम् ।
चतुर्वर्णैः शिखा प्रोक्ता पञ्चार्णैः कवचं मतम् ।
समस्तेन भवेदस्त्रमङ्गकल्पनमीरितम् ॥ ३९

सर्वदा यस्य वर्द्धन्ते धनारोग्यार्थसम्पदः ।
सायुज्यं सार्ष्टिं सालोक्यं सारूप्यं वाथ वाञ्छितम् ॥ इति ॥३२-३६॥

द्वादशाक्षरवासुदेवमन्त्रमाह प्रणव इति । हृन्नमः । अत्रापि भगवते परतः पूर्व्ववत् सन्धिः । तदुक्तं मन्त्रतन्त्रप्रकाशे—

अन्त्यौ यौ पञ्चमे षष्ठे वर्गाव्यौ क्रमतस्तु तौ ।
द्वितीयो मिश्रसंयुक्तास्तस्माद्भगवते पदम् ॥
सानन्तं वारुणं बीजं जीवः स्याच्छिवसंयुतः ।
पञ्चमस्थो भगी रामो वा यान्ते द्वादशार्णकः ॥
स्त्रीशूद्रयोर्वितारोऽयं सतारोऽयं द्विजन्मनाम् ॥ इति ।

अन्त्यौ पञ्चमे वर्गे अन्त्यो नः । षष्ठे वर्गे अन्तो मः । स मिश्रसंयुक्तः ओयुक्तः । वारुणं बीजं वः । सानन्तं आयुतं तेन वा । जीवः सः शिवः उ तेन युतः । पञ्चमवर्गस्तस्य रामस्तृतीयो दः स भगी एकारयुतः । स्पष्टमन्यत् । ॐ बीजं नमः शक्तिः । तदुक्तं बीजं तारः शक्तिर्नम इति । अङ्गकॢप्तिरुदीरितेत्यनेन द्वादशाङ्गमपि कर्त्तव्यमित्युक्तम् । तद्यथा । ॐ हृदयाय नम इत्यादि । पञ्चाङ्गन्यासस्थानेषु पञ्चाङ्गवदेव विन्यस्य नेत्रयोर्नैत्राभ्यां वौषडिति विन्यस्य ते जठराय नम इत्यादि षट्सु स्थानेषु न्यसेत् । तदुक्तम्—

हृदादि नेत्रजठरपृष्ठबाहूरुजानुषु ।
सपादेषु मनोर्वर्णैः सोन्तैर्द्वादशाङ्गकम् ॥ इति ॥

पद्मपादाचार्य्यास्तु पुरुषसत्याच्युतवासुदेवसंकर्षणप्रद्युम्नानिरुद्धनारायणब्रह्मविष्णुनरसिंहवाराहमूर्त्तीनां द्वादशाङ्गे योगमाहुः । अन्यत्रापि—

आदौ पुरुषः सत्याच्युतौ पुनर्वासुदेवपूर्वाः स्युः ।
नारायणयुग्ब्रह्मा विष्णुनृसिंहौ तथा वराहश्च ॥ इति ॥ ३७॥३८॥३९ ॥

मूर्ध्नि भाले दृशोरास्ये गले दोर्हृदयाम्बुजे ।
कुक्षौ नाभौ ध्वजे जानुद्वये पादद्वये न्यसेत् ॥ ४०

विष्णुं शारदचन्द्रकोटिसदृशं शङ्खं रथाङ्गं गदा-
मम्भोजं दधतं सिताब्जनिलयं कान्त्या जगन्मोहनम् ।
आबद्धाङ्गदहारकुण्डलमहामौलिं स्फुरत्कङ्कणं
श्रीवत्साङ्कमुदारकौस्तुभधरं वन्दे मुनीन्द्रैः स्तुतम् ॥ ४१

मूर्ध्नीति । मूर्ध्नि न्यसेन्मन्त्रवर्णानिति शेषः । अयं सृष्टिन्यासः । अत्र स्थितिसंहारावपि ज्ञेयौ । यदाहुः—

हृदादिकान्तावधीमं स्थितिन्यासं प्रचक्षते ।
पादादारभ्य शीर्षान्तं न्यासं संहारमूचिरे ॥
संहृतेर्दोषसंहारः सृष्टेश्च सुतपुष्टयः ।
स्थितेस्तु शान्तिविन्यासस्तस्मात् कार्यस्त्रिधा च सः ॥ इति ।

अन्यत्र व्यवस्थाऽप्युक्ता । यदाहुः—

स्थितिन्यासो गृहस्थानामुद्दिष्टः सर्वसिद्धिदः ।
प्रथमाश्रमिणां न्यास उत्पत्तिः समुदाहृतः ॥
यतीनां च वनस्थानां संहारः समुदाहृतः ।
विरक्तस्य गृहस्थस्य संहारोऽपि विधीयते ॥
सपत्नीकवनस्थानां स्थितिन्यासो विधीयते ।
विद्यार्थिनामथैतेषां सृष्ट्यन्तोऽपि विशिष्यते ॥ इति ।

अत्र सामान्यतो न्यसेदित्युक्तत्वादेषु द्वादशतत्त्वान्यपि न्यसेत् । तद्यथा । ॐ नमः पराय जीवात्मने नमः मूर्ध्नीत्यादि । तत्त्वानि तु—

जीवप्राणधियश्चित्तं हृत्पद्मं सूर्यमण्डलम् ।
चन्द्रमण्डलमग्नेश्च मण्डलं स्वकलान्वितम् ॥
वासुदेवादयश्चेति तत्त्वानि द्वादशाऽवदन् । इति ॥ ४० ॥

आयुधध्यानं तूर्ध्वादिदक्षयोश्चक्रपद्मे । एवं वामयोर्गदाशङ्खौ । तदुक्तं हयशीर्षपञ्चरात्रे—

वासुदेवं तु कुर्वीत चतुर्बाहुं सुरेश्वरम् ।
दक्षिणोपरि चक्रं तु पद्मञ्चाऽधः प्रकल्पयेत् ॥

वर्णलक्षं जपेन्मन्त्रं दीक्षितो विजितेन्द्रियः ।
तत्सहस्रं प्रजुहुयात्तिलैराज्यपरिप्लुतैः ॥ ४२

पीठे प्रागीरिते मूर्त्तिं मूलमन्त्रेण कल्पयेत् ।
पूजयेद्विधिनाऽनेन वासुदेवं विधानवित् ॥ ४३

प्रथमावृतिरङ्गैः स्यात् वासुदेवादिभिः परा ।
शान्त्यादिशक्तिसहितैः परा द्वादशमूर्त्तिभिः ॥ ४४

चतुर्थी सुरनाथाद्यैर्वज्राद्यैः पञ्चमी मता ।
एवं सम्पूजितो विष्णुः प्रदद्यादिष्टमात्मनः ॥ ४५

पायसेन घृताक्तेन मन्त्रवर्णसहस्रकम् ।
जुहुयान्मनसः शुद्ध्यै समिद्भिः क्षीरभूरुहाम् ।
तत्संख्यया पयोऽक्ताभिः सर्वपापविमुक्तये ॥ ४६

हृल्लेखाबीजयुगलं रमाबीजयुगं पुनः ।
लक्ष्म्यन्ते वासुदेवाय हृदन्तः प्रणवादिकः ॥ ४७

चतुर्दशाक्षरो मन्त्रः प्रोक्तोऽयं सुरपादपः ।
हृदयं शक्तिबीजाभ्यां रमाभ्यां शिर ईरितम् ॥ ४८

लक्ष्म्या प्रोक्ता शिखा वर्म वासुदेवाय कीर्त्तितम् ।
नमसाऽस्त्रं समुद्दिष्टं सर्व्वं तारादि कल्पयेत् ॥ ४९

वामोपरि गदा कार्य्या शङ्खश्चाऽधः सुशोभनम् । इति ।
अत्र ध्यानानन्तरं श्रीवत्सकौस्तुभवनमालाञ्जलिमुद्राः प्रदर्शयेत् । "अञ्जल्याऽञ्जलिमुद्रा स्याद्वासुदेवाभिधा च सा" इत्युक्तेः । एता अग्रिममन्त्रेऽपि दर्शनीयाः ॥४१॥

वर्णलक्षं द्वादशलक्षम् । दीक्षितो वैष्णवमार्गेणेत्यर्थः । सा च दीक्षा वैष्णवतन्त्रनारदपञ्चरात्रादितो ज्ञेया । तत्सहस्रं द्वादशसहस्रम् । विधानविदित्यनेनोपचारोक्तागमश्लोकानामत्राऽवश्यकत्वं सूचितम् ॥ ४२ ॥ ४३ ॥

द्वादशमूर्त्तिभिरिति केशवाद्यैः । एषां ध्यानं मूलदेवतावत् ॥ ४४॥४५॥४६ ॥

लक्ष्मीवासुदेवमन्त्रमाह हृल्लेखेति । हृल्लेखा भुवनेशीबीजम् । यथा हृल्लेखाशब्देन भुवनेशी उच्यते तथा प्रागेव दर्शितम् । रमा श्रीबीजम् । लक्ष्म्यन्ते लक्ष्मीपदान्ते इत्यर्थः । हृदन्तो नमोऽन्तः । ॐ ह्रीँ ह्रीँ श्रीँ श्रीँ लक्ष्मीवासुदेवाय नमः । प्रणवो बीजं माया शक्तिः ॥ ४७॥४८॥४९ ॥

विद्युच्चन्द्रनिभं वपुः कमलजावैकुण्ठयोरेकतां
प्राप्तं स्नेहवशेन रत्नविलसद्भूषाभरालङ्कृतम् ।
विद्या पङ्कजदर्पणं मणिमयं कुम्भं सरोजं गदा
शङ्खं चक्रममूनि बिभ्रदमितां दिश्याच्छ्रियं वः सदा ॥ ५०

वर्णलक्षं जपेदेनं तत्सहस्रं सरोरुहैः ।
होमं कुर्य्याद्विकसितैर्मधुरत्रयसंयुतैः ।
पूजा स्याद्वैष्णवे पीठे द्वादशाक्षरवर्त्मना ॥ ५१
पायसेन कृतो होमो लक्ष्मीवश्यप्रदायकः ।
मधुराक्तैस्तिलैर्हुत्वा सर्व्वकार्य्याणि साधयेत् ॥ ५२
तारो हृद्विष्णवे पश्चात् ङेऽन्तः सुरपतिर्भवेत् ।
महाबलाय ठद्वन्द्वं मनुरष्टादशाक्षरः ॥ ५३
ऋषिरिन्दुर्विराट् छन्दो देवता दधिवामनः ।
हृदेकेन शिरो द्वाभ्यां शिखा त्रिभिरुदीरिता ॥ ५४
कवचं पञ्चभिः प्रोक्तं नेत्रं तावद्भिरक्षरैः ।
द्वाभ्यामस्त्रमिति प्रोक्तः प्रकारोऽङ्गस्य सूरिभिः ॥ ५५

विद्युदिति । एकतामिति देहार्धविभागेन । विद्यादीनि प्रथमानिर्दिष्टानि । पश्चादमूनि बिभ्रदित्यन्वयः । वामेष्वाद्यचतुष्टयमूर्ध्वादि दक्षेष्वन्त्यचतुष्टयमित्यायुधध्यानम् ॥ ५० ॥

वर्णलक्षं चतुर्दशलक्षम् । तत्सहस्रं चतुर्दशसहस्रम् । विकसितैरिति । पूजायां कुड्मलानामपि ग्रहणादत्र विकसितैरिति विशेषोक्तिः । स्वयं विकसितस्य तु निषिद्धत्वादेव निवृत्तिः ॥ ५१ ॥ ५२ ॥

दधिवामनमन्त्रमाह तार इति । हृत् नमःपदम् । अत्रापि पूर्ववद्विसर्गेण सह सन्धिर्ज्ञेयः । ङेऽन्तः सुरपतिः सुरपतये । ठद्वन्द्वं स्वाहा । प्रणव श्रीबीजसम्पुटः इति केचित् । प्रणवो बीजं स्वाहा शक्तिः । तावद्भिरिति पञ्चभिः । प्रकारोऽङ्गस्य सूरिभिरित्यनेन साम्प्रदायिकाः अन्यथा षडङ्गमाहुरिति सूचितम् । तद्यथा । प्रणवादिपञ्चभिः पदैः पञ्चाङ्गानि कृत्वा सर्वेण षष्ठमिति ॥ ५३॥५४॥५५ ॥

मूर्ध्नि भाले दृशोर्युग्मे कर्णनासौष्ठतालुषु ।
कण्ठे बाहुद्वये पृष्ठे हृदयोदरनाभिषु ॥ ५६

गुह्योरुजानुयुग्मेषु जङ्घयोः पादयोर्न्यसेत् ।
अष्टादश मनोर्वर्णान् पश्चादेवं विचिन्तयेत् ॥ ५७

मुक्तागौरं नवमणिलसद्भूषणं चन्द्रसंस्थं
भृङ्गाकारैरलकनिकरैः शोभि वक्त्रारविन्दम् ।
हस्ताब्जाभ्यां कनककलशं शुद्धतोयाभिपूर्णं
दध्यन्नाढ्यं कनकचषकं धारयन्तं भजामः ॥ ५८

गुणलक्षं जपेन्मन्त्रं तद्दशांशं घृतप्लुतैः ।
पायसान्नैः प्रजुहुयाद्दध्यन्नैर्वा यथाविधि ॥ ५९

चन्द्रान्तं कल्पिते पीठे प्रागुक्ते तं समर्चयेत् ।
मूर्त्तिं मूलेन सङ्कल्प्य वक्ष्यमाणविधानतः ॥ ६०

मूर्ध्नीत्यादिषु सर्वत्र एकैकवर्णन्यासः । कर्णयुग्मौष्ठतालुष्वित्यपपाठः । कर्णनासौष्ठतालुष्विति पाठः । पश्चादिति पृष्ठे । मन्त्रतन्त्रप्रकाशे तु—

मूर्ध्नि दृक्श्रवणद्वन्द्वे नासायां मुखमध्यतः ।
कण्ठहृद्बाहुयुग्मे च नाभौ पृष्ठे च गुह्यके ॥
जान्वोश्च पादयोरर्णान् ।

इति स्थानान्युक्तानि । पश्चादित्यनेन पदन्यासोऽपि सूचितः ।

यदाहुः—भ्रूमध्यगलहृन्नाभिलिङ्गाधारेषु विन्यसेत् । इति ॥ ५६॥५७ ॥

ध्यानमाह मुक्तेति ॥ ५८ ॥

गुणलक्षं त्रिलक्षम् । यथाविधीत्यग्रे सम्बध्यते । चन्द्रान्तमिति । रविवह्निमण्डले सम्पूज्य अन्ते चन्द्रमण्डलं पूजयेदित्यर्थः । अत्र चन्द्रमण्डलान्ता पूजा । तस्य तदासनत्वात् । तदुक्तं मन्त्रतन्त्रप्रकाशे—

धर्मज्ञानमये पीठे पूजयेच्चन्द्रमण्डलम् । इति ।

चन्द्रमण्डलमन्त्रोऽप्युद्धृतः ।

विष्णवे सह सोमाय त्रैलोक्याप्यायनाय च ।
स्वाहान्तस्तारहृत्पूर्वो मन्त्रेणैवाऽर्चयेच्च तत् ॥ इति ॥

एतद्यथाविधिपदेन सूचितम् । प्रागुक्ते नारायणाष्टाक्षरोक्ते पीठे वक्ष्यमाण-

षडङ्गानि समभ्यर्च्य केसरेषु यथा पुरा ।
अभ्यर्च्य वासुदेवादीन् ध्वजादीनर्चयेत्ततः ॥ ६१

केशवाद्या दलाग्रेषु सुरेन्द्रादीननन्तरम् ।
वज्रादीनि गजानष्टौ सप्तावरणमीरितम् ।
विधानमेतद्देवस्य कीर्त्तितं सुरपूजितम् ॥ ६२

पायसाज्येन जुहुयात्सहस्रं श्रियमाप्नुयात् ।
धान्यहोमेन धान्याप्तिः शतपुष्पीसमुद्भवैः ॥ ६३

बीजैः सहस्रसंख्यातो होमो भयविनाशनः ।
दध्योदनेन शुद्धेन हुत्वा मुच्येत दुर्गतेः ॥ ६४

स्मृत्वा त्रैविक्रमं रूपं जपेन्मन्त्रमनन्यधीः ।
मुक्तो बन्धाद्भवेत्सद्यो नात्र कार्या विचारणा ॥ ६५

पट्टे संपाद्य देवेशं भित्तौ वा पूजयेत् सुधीः ।
सुगन्धिकुसुमैर्नित्यं महतीं श्रियमाप्नुयात् ॥ ६६

ससाध्यतारोज्ज्वलकर्णिकाब्जमष्टाक्षरैरुज्ज्वलकेशराढ्यम् ।
मन्त्राक्षरद्वन्द्वयुताष्टपत्रं शिष्टार्णयुग्मोल्लसितान्त्यपत्रम् ॥ ६७

विधानतः तं समर्चयेदिति सम्बन्धः । यथा पुरेति चतुर्थोक्तरीत्या । वासुदेवादीन् सशक्तिकान् पूर्ववत् । ध्वजादीनित्यष्टौ प्रसिद्धदिक्क्रमेण । तदुक्तम्—

ध्वजश्च वैनतेयश्च शङ्खपद्मौ दिशो गताः ।
विघ्नार्यकौ तथा दुर्गा विष्वक्सेनौ विदिग्गताः ॥ इति ।

तत्र ग्रन्थकृता नारायणाष्टाक्षरे अग्रदक्षिणोत्तरपश्चिमादिपूजाकथनार्थम् एते एव वैनतेयाद्या उपदिष्टाः । केशवाद्या द्वादश दलाग्रेषु अष्टदलाद्बहिरित्यर्थः । गजानित्यष्टसोमान् स्वस्वदिक्षु ॥ ५८॥६०॥६१॥६२ ॥

शतपुष्पी कान्यकुब्जभाषायां सौंफ इति प्रसिद्धा । दुर्गतेः दारिद्र्यात् ॥६३॥६४॥ ॥ ६५॥६६ ॥

यन्त्रमाह ससाध्येति । कर्णिकायां साध्यसाधककर्मसहितं प्रणवं लिखेत् । अष्टाक्षरैरिति नारायणाष्टाक्षरैः । शिष्टार्णेत्यनेनाऽन्त्यपत्रे वर्णचतुष्टयं लिखेदित्युक्तम् । तद्बहिर्मातृकाक्षरैर्वेष्टितं विदध्यादिति सम्बन्धः । अस्य तन्त्रान्तरोक्तं विधानमभिधीयते—

द्वादशाक्षरसंवीतं तद्बहिर्मातृकाक्षरैः ।
विदध्याद्वैष्णवं यन्त्रं सर्व्वसम्पत्प्रदायकम् ॥ ६८

अस्य तैलो मुनिश्छन्दो जगत्यन्नप्रदो हरिः ।
देवता प्रणवाद्यैश्च पदैः सर्वेण चाऽङ्गकम् ॥
कर्पूरधवलं देवं निविष्टं सरसीरुहे ।
सुप्रसन्नं सुनेत्रं च चारुस्मितमनोहरम् ॥
दण्डं चाऽमृतकुण्डं च शरच्चन्द्रसमप्रभम् ।
दधिभक्तं सोपदंशं वसुपात्रं च बिभ्रतम् ॥
चिन्तयेज्जगदीशानं जगदार्त्तिहरं हरिम् ।
दीक्षां प्राप्य शुचिर्भूत्वा जपेद् द्वादशलक्षकम् ॥
तदन्ते जुहुयाद्विद्वान् पायसेन दशांशकम् ।
पूजा तु वैष्णवे पीठे कर्त्तव्या साधकोत्तमैः ॥
लिखेत्पद्मं सप्तदशदलं प्रणवमालिखेत् ।
कर्णिकायां ससाध्यं तं स्वरैरावेष्टयेत् क्रमात् ॥
चतुस्त्रिंशत्केसरेषु कादिक्षान्तान् लवर्जितान् ।
दलेषु मन्त्रवर्णांश्च ताराभ्यां वेष्टयेद्बहिः ॥
श्री[स]बीजाभ्यां तद्बहिश्च यन्त्रं सर्वफलप्रदम् ।
अस्मिन् यन्त्रे समावाह्य देवमङ्गानि पूर्ववत् ॥
इष्ट्वा शक्तीश्च पत्रेषु लोकेशास्त्राणि पूजयेत् ।
पूषा सुमनसा प्रीतिर्ज्योतिः सौम्या मरीचिका ॥
अंशुमालिन्यङ्गिरा च शशिनी चन्द्रिका तथा ।
अमोघा करुणा चैव छाया सम्पूर्णमण्डला ॥
पुष्टिस्तथाऽमृता सिद्धिः शक्तयः समुदीरिताः । इति ।

अथ ब्रह्मयामलोक्तं यन्त्रमुच्यते—

वृत्ताकारमथो कृत्वा चन्द्रमण्डलमध्यतः ।
सम्यक् च विलिखेत्तारं साध्यनामसमन्वितम् ॥
वारुणार्णान् लिखित्वा च साग्निमायासबिन्दुकम् ।
दलैश्च सप्तदशभिः कृत्वा पद्मं सकर्णिकम् ॥
नादिव्योमान्तमन्त्रं वै पद्मस्यैव दलेषु च ।
कृत्वा यन्त्रं महाभाग समालभ्य जपेन्मनुम् ॥

उद्गिरत्पदमाभाष्य प्रणवोद्गीथशब्दतः ।
सर्व्ववागीश्वरेत्यन्ते प्रवदेद्वीश्वरेत्यथ ॥ ६९
सर्व्ववेदमयाचिन्त्यपदान्ते सर्व्वमुच्चरेत् ।
बोधयद्वितयान्तोऽयं मन्त्रस्तारादिरीरितः ॥ ७०
ऋषिर्ब्रह्माऽस्य सन्दिष्टश्छन्दोऽनुष्टुबुदाहृतम् ।
देवता स्याद्धयग्रीवो वागैश्वर्य्यप्रदो विभुः ।
तारेण पादैर्मन्त्रस्य पञ्चाऽङ्गानि प्रकल्पयेत् ॥ ७१

महारक्षा समाख्याता धारणाच्च श्रियावहम् ॥ इति ।

नारदकल्पोक्तं यन्त्रान्तरम्—

दलैः षोडशभिर्युक्तं सतारं कर्णिकोज्ज्वलम् ।
कलारूढदलं बाह्ये पद्ममष्टदलं लिखेत् ॥
तेष्वष्टाक्षरमालिख्य तदग्रे वृत्तमालिखेत् ।
अष्टादशदलं बाह्ये तेष्वप्यष्टादशाक्षरम् ॥
आलिख्यान्ते च भूगेहमष्टशूलसमन्वितम् ।
कोणेष्वक्षरमालिख्य वज्रादिषु यथाक्रमम् ॥
शूलाक्षिरोगगुल्मादिगर्भस्फोटादिकानपि ।
विषादिकाज्वरः सम्यक् मन्त्री यन्त्रेण नाशयेद् ॥ इति ॥

अक्षरं ठकारम् । तन्त्रान्तरोक्तमेतदुपासककर्त्तव्यमुच्यते—

नाऽश्नीयात्तण्डुलीशाकं तथा चोदुम्बरं फलम् ॥
श्राद्धानां नवकं चैव भक्षयेन्न कदाचन ।
पद्मपत्रे न भुञ्जीत तथा चार्कदलेष्वपि ॥
तुषकार्पासबीजानि न स्पृशेच्च कदाचन ।
वल्मीकं गोमयं विप्रच्छायामपि न लङ्घयेत् ॥
देवाग्निगुरुपूजां च कुर्याद्भक्तिसमन्वितः । इति ॥ ६७ ॥ ६८ ॥

हयग्रीवमन्त्रमाह उद्गिरदिति । प्रणवोद्गीथेति स्वरूपम् । **सर्वमुच्चरेदिति मन्त्रेऽपि** द्वितीयान्तमेव । श्लोकरूपो महामन्त्रः । श्लोकादौ तारः । **मन्त्रस्य हलो बीजानि** स्वराः शक्तयः । वागैश्वर्य्यप्रद इति विनियोगोक्तिः ॥ ६९॥७०॥७१ ॥

शरच्छशाङ्कप्रभमश्ववक्त्रं मुक्तामयैराभरणैरुपेतम्।

रथाङ्गशङ्खाङ्कितबाहुयुग्मं जानुद्वयन्यस्तकरं भजामः॥ ७२

वर्णलक्षं जपेन्मन्त्रं कुन्दपुष्पैर्मधुप्लुतैः।

दशांशं वैष्णवे वह्नौ जुहुयान्मन्त्रसिद्धये॥ ७३

अष्टाक्षरोदिते पीठे हयग्रीवं प्रपूजयेत्।

बीजेन मूर्त्तिं सङ्कल्प्य बीजमुद्ध्रियते यथा॥ ७४

वियद्भृगुस्थमर्घीशबिन्दुमद्बीजमीरितम्।

केसरेषु चतुर्वेदांश्चतुर्दिक्षु समर्चयेत्॥ ७५

ध्यानमाह शरदिति। अत्र ध्यानानन्तरमियं मुद्रा दर्शनीया।

वामहस्ततले दत्त्वा अङ्गुलीस्तास्त्वधोमुखीः।

संरोप्य मध्यमां तासामुन्नम्याऽधो विकुञ्चयेत्॥

हयग्रीवप्रिया मुद्रा तन्मूर्त्तेरनुकारिणी॥ इति॥ ७२॥

वर्णलक्षं द्वात्रिंशल्लक्षम्। वैष्णवे वह्नाविति। तत्र वैष्णवपीठमभ्यर्च्येत्यर्थः॥७३॥७४॥

हयग्रीवबीजमुद्धरति वियदिति। वियत् हः। भृगुस्थं सकारस्थम्। अर्घीशः

आकारः बिन्दुश्च तद्वत्। कल्पान्तरे चतुर्दशस्वरयुक्तमुदाहृतम्। तदुक्तं

शाङ्करकल्पे—

शून्यं शून्यसमायुक्तं जीवस्योपरि संस्थितम्।

अनुग्रहयुतं कृत्वा वागीशं सर्वकामदम्॥ इति॥

केचिद्रुद्रेण भूषितं कृत्वेति पठन्ति। एतद्बीजाद्यो ङेऽन्त हयग्रीवशब्दनत्यन्तोऽष्टा-

क्षरो मन्त्रः। हं बीजम्। सौ शक्तिः। देवीगायत्री छन्दः। अन्यद्वक्ष्यमाणैकाक्षर-

विधानवत् सर्व्वं ज्ञेयम्। एतावपि स्वतन्त्रौ मन्त्रौ। विद्याकामेन वाक्पुटौ जप्यौ

बालातार्त्तीयसंपुटौ वा वश्यकामेन कामराजसंपुटौ वा। हं बीजं सं शक्तिः।

तदृष्यादिकं यथा—

ब्रह्मत्रिष्टुप्हयग्रीवा ऋष्याद्याः परिकीर्त्तिताः।

षड्दीर्घयुक्तमूलेन षडङ्गविधिरीरितः॥

धवलनलिननिष्ठं क्षीरगौरं कराग्रैर्जपवलयसरोजे पुस्तकाभीष्टदाने।

दधतममलवक्त्राकल्पजालाभिरामं तुरगवदनविष्णुं नौमि देवारिजिष्णुम्॥

वेदलक्षं जापित्वाऽन्ते तद्दशांशं हुनेद्घृतैः।

पुरोक्ते प्रयजेत् पीठे गायत्र्यावाह्य पूजयेत् ॥
ङेऽन्तं वागीश्वरपदं विद्महे पदमुच्चरेत् ।
हयग्रीवं च ङेऽन्तं स्याद्धीमहीति ततो वदेत् ॥
तन्नोहंसःपदान्ते च प्रवदेच्च प्रचोदयात् ।
प्रथमावृतिरङ्गैः स्यात् द्वितीया चाष्टभिर्हयैः ॥
प्रज्ञाहयस्तथा मेधाहयः स्मृतिहयस्तथा ।
विद्याहयः श्रीहयश्च वागीशोहय एव च ॥
विद्याविलासस्तुहयो हयान्तो नादमर्दनः ।
मेधादिभिस्तृतीया स्यात्ताश्च मेधा सरस्वती ॥
प्रज्ञा तृतीया विजया पञ्चमी चाऽपराजिता ।
तुष्टिः पुष्टिः सप्तमी स्याच्छ्रद्धा चैवाऽष्टमी मता ॥
कल्पान्तरे तु लक्ष्म्याद्यास्ताश्च लक्ष्मीः सरस्वती ।
रतिप्रीती कीर्त्तिकान्ती तुष्टिः पुष्टिस्तथाऽष्टमी ॥
चतुर्थी कुमुदाद्यैस्ते कुमुदः कुमुदाक्षकः ।
पुण्डरीकः सर्वनेत्रो वामनः शङ्कुकर्णकः ॥
सुमुखः सुप्रतिष्ठः स्याल्लोकपालैस्तु पञ्चमी ।
तदायुधैश्च षष्ठी स्यादेवं पूजा समीरिता ॥ इति ॥
बीजं रेफसमायुक्तं हुङ्कारद्वयमध्यगम् ।
यस्य नाम्ना जपेन्मन्त्रं मारयेत्तं न संशयः ॥
हुङ्कारद्वयमध्यस्थं बीजराजं सुरेश्वरि ।
विद्वेषयेज्जगत् सर्वं मासं जप्त्वा न संशयः ॥
लिखेद्रोचनया भूर्जे मन्त्रं बाहौ विधारयेत् ।
महारक्षा भवेदेषा सर्वदोषविनाशिनी ॥ इति ॥

शाङ्करकल्पोक्तं यन्त्रमुच्यते—

प्रणवद्वयसंयुक्तसकारद्वयमध्यगम् ।
वादिनाम लिखेद्बीजे भूर्जपत्रे हरिद्रया ॥
पत्राष्टके हयग्रीवाष्टाक्षरं स्वरकेसरे ।
कादि क्षान्तवृतं बाह्ये तद्बहिर्भूपुरं लिखेत् ॥
वाक्स्तम्भनमिदं प्रोक्तं शरावद्वयसंपुटे ।
वेष्टितं पीतसूत्रेण मूकत्वं कुरुतेऽचिरात् ॥ इति ॥ ७५ ॥

विदिक्ष्वङ्गस्मृतिन्यायसर्व्वशास्त्राणि पूजयेत्।
अर्चयेत् पत्रमध्येषु विधानेनाऽङ्गदेवता:॥ ७६

बाह्ये लोकेश्वरांस्तेषां वज्राद्यस्त्राणि संयजेत्।
एवं यो भजते देवं साक्षाद्वागीश्वरो भवेत्॥ ७७

बैल्वै: फलै: कृतो होम: श्रीकर: परिगीयते।
कुन्दपुष्पाणि जुहुयादिच्छन् वाक्श्रियमव्ययम्॥ ७८

मनुनाऽनेन सञ्जप्तं घृतं ब्राह्मीरसै: सृतम्।
कवितामावहेत्पुंसामनर्गलविजृम्भणाम्॥ ७९

वचामनेन सञ्जप्तां भक्षयेत् प्रातरन्वहम्।
सर्व्ववेदागमादीनां व्याख्याता जायतेऽचिरात्।
मनोरस्य समो नास्ति ज्ञानैश्वर्य्यप्रदोऽपर:॥ ८०

अनन्तोऽग्न्यासन: सेन्दुर्बीजं रामाय हृन्मनु:।
षड़क्षरोऽयमादिष्टो भजतां कामदो मणि:॥ ८१

विदिक्ष्विति। शिक्षाकल्पव्याकरणनिरुक्तज्योतिषछन्दोरूपेभ्य: षड़ङ्गेभ्यो नम: स्मृतिभ्यो नम: न्यायशास्त्रेभ्यो नम: सर्वशास्त्रेभ्यो नम: इत्यादि प्रयोग:। विधानेनेति चतुर्थ्यन्ताग्नेयादिस्थानेषु पत्रमध्येष्विति चतुर्थ्यन्तकेसराङ्ग पूजापवाद: ॥ ७६ ॥ ७७ ॥ ७८ ॥

मनुनेति। "अकल्कोऽपि भवेत् स्नेहो य: साध्य: केवले द्रवे" इत्युक्तत्वात्। घृताच्चतुर्गुणे ब्राह्मीरसे घृतं पचेत्। घृतावशेषमुत्तार्य्याऽनेन संजप्तं पिबेत्॥७९॥८०॥

राममन्त्रमाह अनन्त इति। अनन्त आकार: अग्न्यासनो रेफासन: सेन्दु: सबिन्दु:। बीजमित्यनेनैकाक्षरोऽप्ययं मन्त्र इति सूचितम्।

तदुक्तम्—वह्निस्थं शयनं विष्णोरर्धचन्द्रविभूषितम्।
एकाक्षरो मनु: प्रोक्तो मन्त्रराज: सुरद्रुम:॥ इति।

अस्यर्थ्यादिकं सर्वं वक्ष्यमाणमेव। एतदर्थं उक्त: स्कान्दयामले निर्वाणखण्डे—

रेफोऽग्निरहमेवोक्तो विष्णु: सोमो म उच्यते।
मध्यगस्त्वावयोर्ब्रह्मा रविराकार उच्यते॥
ज्योतींषि कवलीकृत्य त्रीण्याकाशो विभु: स्वयम्।
नादोऽभिधत्ते सम्यातं त्वमेव परमेश्वरम्॥ इति॥

ब्रह्मा प्रोक्तो मुनिश्छन्दो गायत्रं देवता मनोः।
देशिकेन्द्रैः समाख्यातो रामो राक्षसमर्दनः॥ ८२

रामाय हृदित्यनेनाऽयं पञ्चाक्षरोऽपि मन्त्र इत्युक्तम्। यदाहुः—

सप्रतिष्ठो रमो वायुर्हृत् पञ्चार्णो मनुः स्मृतः।
विश्वामित्रो मुनिः प्रोक्तः पङ्क्तिश्छन्दोऽस्य देवता॥
रामभद्रो बीजशक्ती प्रथमार्णनतो क्रमात्।
भ्रूमध्ये हृदि नाभ्यन्धुपादयोर्विन्यसेन् मनुम्॥
षडङ्गं पूर्ववद्यद्वा पञ्चार्णैर्मनुनाऽखिलकम्।
मध्ये वनं कल्पतरोर्मूले पुष्पलताकुलम्॥
लक्ष्मणेन प्रगुणितमक्ष्णः कोणेन सायकम्।
अवेक्षमाणं जानक्या धृतव्यजनयेश्वरम्॥
जटाभारलसच्छीर्षं श्यामं मुनिगणावृतम्।
लक्ष्मणेन धृतच्छत्रमथवा पुष्पकोपरि॥
दशास्यमथनं प्राग्वत् ससुग्रीवविभीषणम्।
विजयार्थी विशेषेण वर्णलक्षं जपेन्मनुम्॥ इति।

मनुरिति। एवं मिलित्वा मन्त्रः षडक्षर इत्यर्थः। कामदो मणिश्चिन्तामणिरित्यनेनास्य विनियोगं वदता स्वबीजं विनापि बहुप्रकारं षड्वर्णत्वं बहुप्रकारं च सप्तवर्णत्वं सूचितम्। तदुक्तं स्कान्दयामले निर्वाणखण्डे—

विश्वरूपस्य ते नाम विश्वे शब्दादि वाचकाः।
तथापि मूलमन्त्रस्ते विश्वेषां बीजमव्ययम्॥
मुक्तये प्रणवाद्योऽयं रमादिरपि भुक्तये।
वाग्भवादिस्तु वाक्सिद्ध्यै मायादिरखिलेष्टदः॥
अखिलोऽयं महाशक्तिर्मन्त्रचिन्तामणिर्विभो। इति।

अन्यत्र—स्वकामशक्तिवाग्लक्ष्मी ताराद्यः पञ्चवर्णकः।
षडक्षरः षड्विधः स्याच्चतुर्वर्गफलप्रदः॥
पञ्चाशन्मातृकामन्त्रवर्णप्रत्येकपूर्वकः।
लक्ष्मीवागमन्मथादिश्च तारादिः स्यादनेकधा॥
श्रीमायामन्मथैकैक बीजाद्यन्तगतो मनुः।
चतुर्वर्णः स एव स्यात् षड्वर्णो वाञ्छितप्रदः॥
स्वाहान्तो हुंफडन्तो वा नत्यन्तो वा भवेदयम्।

दीर्घभाजा स्वबीजेन कुर्य्यादङ्गानि षट् क्रमात्
ब्रह्मरन्ध्रे भ्रुवोर्मध्ये हृन्नाभ्यन्धुषु पादयोः।
षडक्षराणि विन्यस्येन्मन्त्रस्य मनुवित्तमः॥ ८३

कालाम्भोधरकान्तिकान्तमनिशं वीरासनाध्यासितं
मुद्रां ज्ञानमयीं दधानमपरं हस्ताम्बुजं जानुनि।
सीतां पार्श्वगतां सरोरुहकरां विद्युन्निभां राघवं
पश्यन्तीं मुकुटाङ्गदादिविविधाकल्पोज्ज्वलाङ्गं भजे॥ ८४

ब्रह्मा सम्मोहनः शक्तिर्दक्षिणामूर्त्तिरेव च॥
अगस्त्यः श्रीशिवः प्रोक्ता मुनयोऽत्र क्रमादिमे।
छन्दो गायत्रसंज्ञं च श्रीरामश्चैव देवता॥
अथवा कामबीजादेर्विश्वामित्रो मुनिर्मनोः।
छन्दो देव्यादि गायत्री रामभद्रोऽस्य देवता॥
बीजशक्ती यथा पूर्व्वम्। इति।

राक्षसमर्दनः इति विशेषणं विधेयम्। रां बीजं नमः शक्तिः। तदुक्तं शौनककल्पे—जानीयात्प्रथमं वर्णं बीजं शक्तिं नतिं तथा। इति। केचन आयेति शक्तिमाहुः। दीर्घभाजा षड्दीर्घभाजा। स्वबीजेन मन्त्राद्य-बीजेन। क्रमादित्यनेन षड्वर्णैर्वा षडङ्गमित्युक्तम्। यदाहुः—

बीजैः षड्दीर्घयुक्तैर्वा मन्त्रार्णैर्वा षडङ्गकम्। इति।

अन्धु गुह्यम्। मनुवित्तम इत्यनेनैतदुक्तं भवति। पञ्चाक्षरे पादन्यासः। सप्ताक्षरे ब्रह्मरन्ध्रभ्रूमध्यकण्ठहृन्नाभिगुह्यपादेषु न्यासः। द्व्यक्षरे ब्रह्मरन्ध्रहृदोः। त्र्यक्षरे गुह्यान्तयोः। चतुरक्षरे गुह्यपादान्तयोरिति॥ ८१॥ ८२॥ ८३॥

ध्यानमाह कालेति। वीरासनमग्रे वक्ष्यति। ज्ञानमुद्रालक्षणं प्राक्। अपरं वामम्। राघवं पश्यन्तीं पार्श्वगतां सीताञ्च भजे इति सम्बन्धः। अस्मिन् पाठे वक्ष्यमाणसीतामन्त्रस्यापि ध्यानमुक्तं भवति। क्वचित्पश्यन्तमिति पाठः। तदा सीतां पश्यन्तं राघवं भजे इति सम्बन्धः। उक्तञ्च—

वामाङ्कारूढसीतामुखकमलमिलल्लोचनं नीरदाभम्। इति।

आकल्पो भूषा। अत्र ध्यानानन्तरं नारायणाष्टाक्षरोक्तां गरुडमुद्रां च दर्शयेत्॥८४॥

वर्णलक्षं जपेन्मन्त्रं दशांशं कमलैः शुभैः ।
जुहुयादर्चिते वह्नौ ब्राह्मणान् भोजयेत्ततः ॥ ८५
पूजयेद्वैष्णवे पीठे मूर्त्तिं मूलेन कल्पयेत् ।
श्रीं सीतायै द्विठान्तेन सीतां पार्श्वगतां यजेत् ॥ ८६
अग्रे पार्श्वद्वये शार्ङ्गं शरानङ्गानि तद्बहिः ।
हनूमन्तं ससुग्रीवं भरतं सविभीषणम् ॥ ८७

वर्णलक्षं षट्लक्षम् । अर्चिते वह्नाविति रामपीठं वह्नावावाह्येत्यर्थः ॥८५॥
श्रीं सीतायै स्वाहा इति । अयं स्वतन्त्रोऽपि मन्त्रः । तदुक्तम्—

सीतामन्त्रोऽपि कथितः स्वतन्त्रोऽङ्गपरोऽपि च । इति ।

रुद्रयामले निर्वाणखण्डेऽपि—

ब्रह्मा स्तौति त्वत्कुक्षिं देवीं वाचं त्वदास्यये ।
विष्णुर्ध्यायति त्वामेव सुषुम्णां पारमेश्वरीम् ॥
सीतामुपास्ते व्योमान्तरीश्वरी बिन्दुरूपिणीम् ।
सदाशिवो नादमयीं स्वातीतामुन्मनीं शिवः ॥ इति ।

अस्यर्ष्यादिकमगस्त्यसंहितोक्तं यथा—

जनकोऽस्य ऋषिश्छन्दो गायत्रं देवता मनोः ।
सीता भगवती प्रोक्ता श्रीबीजं शक्तिरन्तजो ॥
दीर्घस्वरयुजाद्येन षडङ्गानि प्रकल्पयेत् ।
पूजयेद्वैष्णवे पीठे ध्यायेद्राघवसंयुताम् ॥
सुवर्णाभाम्बुजकरां रामालोकनतत्पराम् ।
वर्णलक्षं जपेन्मन्त्रमिष्टार्थान् साधयेत्ततः ॥ इति ॥ ८६ ॥

अग्रे पार्श्वद्वय इति व्यधिकरणे सप्तम्यौ । तेनाग्रे पुरतः पार्श्वद्वये वामदक्षिण-
पार्श्वयोः शार्ङ्गं शरानिति सम्बन्धः । अनेनैतावत्पर्यन्तं मुख्यपूजेत्युक्तम् । उक्तञ्च—

वामपार्श्वे त्रिकोणस्य शार्ङ्गं दक्षिणके शरान् ।
शं शार्ङ्गाय नमोऽस्त्वेवं शं शरेभ्यो नमोऽस्त्विति ॥
पूजानुज्ञां ततो लब्ध्वा रश्मीनङ्गान्ययो यजेत् । इति ।

पूजायन्त्रं तु तन्त्रान्तरोक्तं यथा—

भूगृहाष्टकपत्रान्तः षट्कोणमतिसुन्दरम् । इति ।

अत्रैव वक्ष्यमाणं धारणयन्त्रं वा । तदुक्तमगस्त्यसंहितायाम्—

लक्ष्मणाङ्गदशत्रुघ्नान् जाम्बवन्तं दधीच्छिमान्।
वाचयन्तं हनूमन्तमग्रतो धृतपुस्तकम्॥ ८८
यजेद्भरतशत्रुघ्नौ पार्श्वयोर्धृतचामरौ।
धृतातपत्रं हस्ताभ्यां लक्ष्मणं पश्चिमे यजेत्॥ ८९

षट्कोणादि धरण्यन्तं पूर्ववद्विलिखेदथ।
तस्य मध्ये लिखेत्तारं षट्सु कोणेष्वपि क्रमात्॥
मूलमन्त्राक्षराण्येव सन्धिष्वङ्गं च मान्मथम्।
मायां गण्डेषु किञ्जल्के स्वराणां लेखनं मतम्॥
पत्रेषु पूर्ववन् मालामन्त्रो लेख्यः क्रमेण हि।
दशाक्षरेण संवेष्ट्य काद्यानि व्यञ्जनानि च॥
दिग्विदिक्षु लिखेद्बीजे नरसिंहवराहयोः।
एतद्यन्त्रान्तरं चात्र साङ्गावरणमर्चयेत्॥
सौवर्णे राजते भूर्जे लिखित्वाऽर्चनमारभेत्। इति।

अङ्गानि तत्रस्थैरिति आग्नेयादि षट्सु कोणेषु॥

तदुक्तम्—इष्टाङ्गदेवताः षट्कोणेष्वग्निकोणादि। इति।

अन्यत्रापि—षट्कोणे प्रथमावृत्तिः स्यादङ्गैरन्वितः क्रमात्। इति।

पश्चिमे देवपृष्ठभागे। अत्र हनूमन्तमित्यादि प्रथममुद्दिश्य पश्चाद्वाचयन्तमित्यादिना यत्प्राधान्येन चतुर्णां सध्यानं पूजनमाह। तेनैषां चतुर्णां मन्त्रा अपि प्रधानभूता इत्यपि सूचितम्। यदगस्त्यसंहितायाम्—

आञ्जनेयमनुं वक्ष्ये भुक्तिमुक्त्येकसाधनम्।
प्रकाशितं शङ्करेण लोकानां हितकाम्यया॥
भूतप्रेतपिशाचादिडाकिनीब्रह्मराक्षसाः।
दृष्ट्वाऽथ प्रपलायन्ते मन्त्रानुष्ठानतत्परम्॥
प्रधानस्याऽङ्गभूतोऽयं मन्त्रराजो ह्यनुत्तमः।
पूर्वं नमः पदश्चोक्त्वा ततो भगवते पदम्॥
आञ्जनेयपदं ङेऽन्तं महाबलपदं तथा।
वह्निजायान्त एव स्यात् मन्त्रो हनूमतः परः॥
सर्वसिद्धिकरः प्रोक्तो मन्त्रस्याऽष्टादशाक्षरः।
ऋषिरीश्वर एव स्यादनुष्टुप् छन्द उच्यते॥

सृष्टिं जयन्तं विजयं सुराष्ट्रं राष्ट्रवर्द्धनम्।
अकोपं धर्मपालाख्यं सुमन्त्रं च दलाग्रतः॥ ६०
सर्वाभरणसम्पन्नान् लोकेशानर्चयेत्ततः।
तदस्त्राणि ततो बाह्ये वज्रादीनि प्रपूजयेत्॥ ६१

हनूमान् देवता प्रोक्तो ह्रं बीजं शक्तिरन्तगौ।
हनूमत्प्रीणनं चैव फलमाद्यमुदाहृतम्॥
नमो भगवते चाञ्जनेयायाऽङ्गुष्ठयोर्न्यसेत्।
रुद्रमूर्त्तये इत्येवं तर्जनीभ्यामनन्तरम्॥
वायुसुतायाऽपि तथा मध्यमाभ्यामपि स्फुटम्।
अग्निगर्भाय च तथाऽनामिकाभ्यां प्रविन्यसेत्॥
रामदूताय च पुनः कनिष्ठाभ्यां विचक्षणः।
ब्रह्मास्त्रवारणार्थाय चाऽस्त्रमन्त्रः समीरितः॥
एवं षडङ्गं च मुने कृत्वा ध्यायेदनन्यधीः।
स्फटिकाभं स्वर्णकान्तिं द्विभुजं च कृताञ्जलिम्॥
कुण्डलद्वयसंशोभिमुखाम्भोजं मुहुर्मुहुः।
अयुतं तु पुरश्चर्या रामस्याग्रे शिवस्य वा॥
पूजां तु वैष्णवे पीठे शैवे वा विदधीत वै।
आहुतिभिर्विना नित्यं नक्ताशी विजितेन्द्रियः॥ इति।
रेफपूर्वं समुद्धृत्य बिन्दुलक्ष्मणसंयुतम्।
ङेऽन्तोऽयं लक्ष्मणमनुर्नमसा च समन्वितः॥
अगस्त्य ऋषिरस्याऽथ गायत्रं छन्द उच्यते।
लक्ष्मणो देवता प्रोक्तो लं बीजं शक्तिरस्य हि॥
नमस्तु विनियोगो हि पुरुषार्थचतुष्टये।
दीर्घभाजा स्वबीजेन षडङ्गानि प्रकल्पयेत्॥
द्विभुजं स्वर्णरुचिरं तनुं पद्मनिभेक्षणम्।
धनुर्वाणकरं रामसेवासंसक्तमानसम्॥
पूजापि वैष्णवे पीठे साङ्गावरणवर्जिते।
सप्तलक्षं पुरश्चर्या ततः सिद्धस्तु साधयेत्॥
भरतस्यैवमेव स्याच्छत्रुघ्नस्याऽप्ययं विधिः।

एवं पूजादिभिः सिद्धे मन्त्रौ कर्म्माणि साधयेत् ।
जातीप्रसूनैर्जुहुयाच्चन्दनाम्भःसमुक्षितैः ॥ ९२

राजवश्याय कमलैर्धनधान्यादिसम्पदे ।
नीलोत्पलानां होमेन वशयेदखिलं जगत् ॥ ९३

अङ्गत्वेनोदिता ह्येते प्राधान्येनापि संमताः ॥
आदौ वाऽप्यन्ततो वापि पूजायां राघवस्य तु ।
एतेषामपि कर्त्तव्या पूजा भुक्तिफलेप्सुभिः ॥
प्राधान्येन पृथक्त्वेन अङ्गत्वे रामपीठके ।
लक्ष्मणस्तु सदा पूज्यः प्राधान्येनैव नित्यशः ॥
यथा रामस्य पूजा स्यात्तथा तस्यापि नित्यशः ।
साफल्यं रामपूजाया यदीच्छेन्नियतव्रतः ॥
तेन यत्नेन कर्त्तव्या लक्ष्मणस्यापि विस्तरात् ।
श्रीराममन्त्रभेदास्तु बहवः सन्ति वै मुने ॥
तत्साधकैः सदा कार्य्या सौमित्रेरपि नित्यशः ।
अष्टोत्तरसहस्रं वा शतं वा सुसमाहितः ॥
लक्ष्मणस्य मनुर्जप्यो मुमुक्षुभिरतन्द्रितम् ।
अजप्त्वा लक्ष्मणमनुं राममन्त्रं जपन्ति ये ॥
तज्जपस्य फलं नैव प्रयान्ति कुशला अपि ।
अरिमित्रविधिः कोऽपि नैव कार्यो भवेदिह ॥
यो जपेल्लक्ष्मणमनुं नित्यमेकान्तमास्थितः ।
मुच्यते सर्वपापेभ्यः स कामानप्नुतेऽखिलान् ॥
प्रयोगायैव मन्त्रोऽयमुपदिष्टो हि शार्ङ्गिणा ।
सन्ध्यामुपास्य विधिवन् मूलमन्त्रेण मन्त्रवित् ॥
त्रिकालं नियतो भूत्वा कृतनित्यविधिः स्वयम् ।
दीक्षायुतो यथान्यायं गुर्वनुज्ञापुरःसरम् ॥
मुच्यते सर्वपापेभ्यो याति विष्णोः परं पदम् ।
ऐहिकाननपेक्ष्यैवं निष्कामो योऽर्चयेद्विभुम् ॥
दीक्षां प्राप्य विधानेन गुरोर्विगतकल्मषात् ।
आचारादिरताच्छान्ताद् गृहस्थाद्विजितेन्द्रियात् ॥

बिल्वप्रसूनैर्जुहुयादिन्दिरावाप्तये नरः ।
दूर्वाहोमेन दीर्घायुर्भवेन्मन्त्री निरामयः ॥ ९४

रक्तोत्पलहुतान्मन्त्री धनमाप्नोति वाञ्छितम् ।
मेधाकामेन होतव्यं पलाशकुसुमैर्नवैः ॥ ९५

तज्जप्तमम्भः प्रपिबेत्कविर्भवति वत्सरात् ।
तन्मन्त्रितान्नं भुञ्जीत महदारोग्यमाप्नुयात् ॥ ९६

तारं मध्ये विलिखतु मनुं षट्सु कोणेषु सन्धि-
ष्वङ्गं मायां स्मरमपि लिखेत्कोणगण्डेषु पश्चात् ।
किञ्जल्केषु स्वरगणमथो पत्रमध्येषु माला-
मन्त्रोत्थार्णान् गुहमुखमितानष्टमे पञ्च वर्णान् ॥ ९७

दशाक्षरेण संवेष्ट्य कादिवर्णैश्च भूपुरे ।
दिग्विदिक्षु लिखेद्बीजे नरसिंहवराहयोः ॥ ९८

तदनुज्ञानुसारेण पुरश्चर्या यथाविधि ।
स सर्वान् पुण्यपापौघान् दग्ध्वा निर्मलमानसः ॥
पुनरावृत्तिरहितं शाश्वतं पदमाप्नुयात् ।
सकामो वाञ्छितान् लब्ध्वा भुक्त्वा भोगान् यथेप्सितान् ॥
जातिस्मरश्चिरं भूत्वा याति विष्णोः परं पदम् ।
यथा श्रीराममन्त्राणां प्रयोक्तुः पापसम्भवः ॥
तथा नो लक्ष्मणमनोः किन्तु याति परां गतिम् ।
केचिन् मुक्त्यर्थमेव स्युः केचिदैहिकसाधनाः ॥
भुक्तिमुक्तिप्रदश्चाऽयमेको विज्ञायते परम् ॥ इति ॥ ८७-९६ ॥

धारणयन्त्रमाह तारमिति । मध्ये कर्णिकायां साध्यसाधककर्मसहितं प्रणवं लिखेत् । मनुं रामषडक्षरम् । सन्धिषु षट्सन्धिषु । अङ्गं षडङ्गमन्त्राः । कोणगण्डेषु कोणकपोलेषु । एकत्र मायाम् अपरत्र कामं लिखेत् । ततोऽष्टदल-केसरस्थाने षोडशस्वरान् लिखेत् । मालामन्त्रो वक्ष्यमाणः सप्तचत्वारिंशदक्षरः । गुहमुखमितान् षट्परिमितान् । दशाक्षरेण वक्ष्यमाणेन । कादिवर्णैः सं-वेष्ट्येति सम्बन्धः । भूपुरे दिग्विदिक्षु बीजे लिखेदिति सम्बन्धः । नरसिंह-बीजमग्रिमपटले वक्ष्यमाणम् । वराहबीजं वाराहमन्त्रे वक्ष्यमाणम् ॥ ९७॥९८ ॥

नमो भगवते ब्रूयाच्चतुर्थ्यां रघुनन्दनम् ।
रक्षोघ्नविषदायाऽन्ते मधुरादि समीरयेत् ॥ ९९
प्रसन्नवदनायेति पश्चादमिततेजसे ।
बलाय पश्चाद्रामाय विष्णवे तदनन्तरम् ।
प्रणवादि नमोऽन्तोऽयं मालामनुरुदीरितः ॥ १००

मालामन्त्रमाह नम इति । रघुनन्दनाच्चतुर्थीं रघुनन्दनाय । प्रसन्नवदनाय अमिततेजसे इत्यत्र न सन्धिः । सप्तचत्वारिंशदक्षराणि यन्त्रे नियमितत्वात् अयं मालामन्त्रोऽपि स्वतन्त्रः । तदृष्यादिकं यथा—

मुनिः पितामहश्छन्दः सात्यनुष्टुप च देवता ।
राज्याभिषिक्तो रामस्य बीजशक्ती तथा पुरा ॥
तारवाक्कामबीजैस्त सम्पुटं प्रजपेदमुम् ।
शिरस्याननवृत्ते च भ्रूमध्येऽक्षिद्वयेऽपि च ॥
श्रोत्रयोर्घ्राणयोश्चैव गण्डयोरोष्ठयोरपि ।
दन्तयोरास्यदेशे च दोःपत्सन्ध्यग्रकेषु च ॥
कण्ठे स्तने हृदि द्वन्द्वे पार्श्वयोः पृष्ठदेशतः ।
जठरे नाभ्यधिष्ठाने गुह्ये वर्णान् प्रविन्यसेत् ।
समस्तैस्सप्तदशषड्रुद्रसंख्यैः षडङ्गकम् ॥

उद्भिन्ननीलशकलामलकान्तिमन्तचापासिबाणकरमम्बुजपत्रनेत्रम् ।
पीताम्बरं स्मितसुधामधुरं मुरारिं सञ्चिन्तयेन् मिथिलराजसुतासहायम् ॥

जपेद्द्वादशलक्षं च ध्यात्वैवं विजितेन्द्रियः ।
बैल्वैः फलैः प्रसूनैश्च पत्रैस्त्रिमधुसंयुतैः ॥
मधुरत्रययुक्तेन पयोऽन्नेन सिताम्बुजैः ।
होमं दशांशतः कुर्यात्तथा सर्वत्र तर्पणम् ॥
प्राक्प्रोक्ते पूजयेत् पीठे मूर्त्तावावाह्य देवताम् ।
प्रथमाङ्गावृतिः प्रोक्ता द्वितीया लक्ष्मणादिभिः ॥
नारदाद्यैस्तृतीया स्याल्लक्ष्म्याद्याभिस्तुरीयका ।
चतुर्दिक्स्थैश्च सुग्रीवाद्यैः पञ्चमी लोकनायकैः ॥
षष्ठी वज्रादिभिः प्रोक्ता सप्तमीज्या प्रकीर्त्तिता ।
लक्ष्मणो भरतश्चैव शत्रुघ्नश्च हनूमता ॥

जानकीवल्लभायाऽथ भवेत् पावकवल्लभा ।

हुमादिरेषः कथितो राममन्त्रो दशाक्षरः ॥ १०१

सुग्रीवः पञ्चमः प्रोक्तः षष्ठ उक्तो विभीषणः ।
अङ्गदः सप्तमः प्रोक्तो नीलोऽष्टम उदाहृतः ॥
नारदश्च वसिष्ठश्च वामदेवस्तृतीयकः ।
जाबालो गौतमश्चापि भरद्वाजोऽथ कश्यपः ॥
वाल्मीकिश्चाष्टमः प्रोक्तो लक्ष्मीश्चापि सरस्वती ।
रतिप्रीती कीर्तिकान्ती तुष्टिपुष्टी इमाः क्रमात् ॥
दृष्टिर्जयन्तविजयौ सिद्धार्थः कार्यसाधकः ।
अशोकश्चैव पूर्वस्यां श्रीवत्सश्च गदा तथा ॥
पाञ्चजन्यः कौस्तुभाख्यो वनमाला च दक्षिणे ।
उत्तरे चक्रपद्मे च शार्ङ्गबाणाश्च खड्गकाम् ॥
पश्चिमे धर्मगरुडधर्मपालसुमन्तकान् ॥ इति ॥ ९८॥१०० ॥

दशाक्षरोऽपि स्वतन्त्रो मन्त्रः । तदृष्यादिकं यथा --

दशाक्षरोऽयं मन्त्रोऽस्य वसिष्ठः स्यादृषिर्विराट् ।
छन्दस्तु देवता रामः सीतापाणिपरिग्रही ॥
आद्यं बीजं द्विठः शक्तिः कामेनाङ्गानि पूर्ववत् ।
शिरोललाटभ्रूमध्य तालुकण्ठेषु हृद्यपि ॥
नाभ्यरुजानुपादेषु दशार्णान् विन्यसेन्मनोः ।
अयोध्यानगरे चित्रसर्वसौवर्णमण्डपे ॥
मन्दारपुष्पैराबद्धविताने तोरणाञ्चिते ।
सिंहासने समारूढं पुष्पकोपरि राघवम् ॥
रक्षोभिर्हरिभिर्मौलैर्दिव्ययानगतैः शुभैः ।
संस्तूयमानं मुनिभिः भक्तैश्च परिसेवितम् ॥
सीतालङ्कृतवामाङ्गं लक्ष्मणेनोपसेवितम् ।
श्यामं प्रसन्नवदनं सर्वाभरणभूषितम् ॥
ध्यानान्ते च जपेन्मन्त्रं वर्णलक्षं विचक्षणः ।
दशांशं जुहुयाद्बिल्वैः फलैर्मधुरसंयुतैः ॥ इति ॥

अस्य पूजा षडक्षरवदेव ज्ञेया ॥ १०१ ॥

जपादिसाधितं यन्त्रं स्वर्णपट्टादिकल्पितम् ।
बाहुना विधृतं दद्याद्विजयश्रीपराक्रमान् ॥ १०२

गदितं राममन्त्रस्य विधानं सुरपूजितम् ।
तारं नमो भगवते वराहपदमीरयेत् ॥ १०३

रूपाय भूर्भुवःस्वः स्यात् पतये तदनन्तरम् ।
भूपतित्वं मे पदान्ते देह्यन्ते च ददापय ॥ १०४

वह्निजायावधिर्मन्त्रः स्यात् त्रयस्त्रिंशदक्षरः ।
भार्गवो मुनिराख्यातश्छन्दोऽनुष्टुबुदाहृतम् ॥ १०५

देवतादिवराहोऽस्य मन्त्रस्य कथितो बुधैः ।
एकदंष्ट्राय हृदयं व्योमोल्काय शिरः स्मृतम् ॥ १०६

शिखा तेजोऽधिपतये विश्वरूपाय वर्म च ।
महादंष्ट्राय शस्त्रं स्यात् पञ्चाङ्गमिति कल्पयेत् ॥ १०७

जपादीति आदिशब्देन पूजासम्पातौ । स्वर्णपट्टादिकल्पितमित्यादिशब्देन रजतताम्रभूर्जपत्राणि । तत्तल्लेख्यविशेषे कालविशेषोऽपि । यदगस्त्यसंहितायाम्—

यावज्जीवं तु सौवर्णे रौप्ये विंशतिवार्षिकम् ।
भूर्जे द्वादशवर्षाणि तदर्धं ताम्रपत्रके ॥
एवं लेख्यविशेषेण यन्त्रसिद्धिः प्रतिष्ठिता ॥ इति ।

इदं गदितं विधानं राममन्त्रस्य राम इति द्व्यक्षरस्य मन्त्रस्य ज्ञेयमिति शेषः ।

वह्निर्नारायणेनाढ्यो जठरः केवलोऽपि च ।
द्व्यक्षरो मन्त्रराजोऽयं भुक्तिमुक्तिफलप्रदः ॥
एकाक्षरोक्तमृष्यादि स्यादाद्येन षडङ्गकम् ।
तारमायारमानङ्गवाक्स्वबीजैस्तु षड्विधः ॥
द्व्यक्षरो मन्त्रराजः स्यात् सर्वाभीष्टफलप्रदः ।
द्व्यक्षरश्चन्द्रभद्रान्तो द्विविधश्चतुरक्षरः ॥
इत्यादि पूर्ववत् ज्ञेयमेतेषां तु विचक्षणैः ॥ इति ॥ १०२॥१०३ ॥

एवं महाकपिलनारदहयशीर्षपञ्चरात्रस्कन्दयामलवैष्णवतन्त्रप्रोक्तमन्त्रचतुष्टयमुक्त्वा राममन्त्रयन्त्रे नरसिंहवराहयोरुद्दिष्टत्वात् तत्र नरसिंहे बहुवक्तव्यत्वादादौ वाराहमन्त्रमुद्धरति तारमिति । वह्निजाया स्वाहा । हुं बीजं स्वाहा शक्तिः ।

आपादं जानुदेशाद्वरकनकनिभं नाभिदेशादधस्ता-
न्मुक्ताभं कण्ठदेशात्तरुणरविनिभं मस्तकान्नीलभासम् ।
ईडे हस्तैर्दधानं रथचरणदरौ खड्गखेटौ गदाख्यां
शक्तिं दानाभये च क्षितिचरणलसद्दंष्ट्रमाद्यं वराहम् ॥ १०८

लक्षमेकं जपेन्मन्त्रं मधुराक्तैः सरोरुहैः ।
जुहुयात्तद्दशांशेन पीठे विष्णोः प्रपूजयेत् ॥ १०९
मूर्त्तिं मूलेन सङ्कल्प्य वक्ष्यमाणविधानतः ।
पूर्वादिषु चतुर्दिक्षु हृदाद्यङ्गानि पूजयेत् ॥ ११०
अस्त्रं कोणेष्वधश्चोर्ध्वं चक्राद्यस्त्राणि तद्बहिः ।
चक्रं शङ्खमसिं खेटं गदां शक्तिं वराभये ॥ १११
संपूज्य बाह्ये लोकेशान् बहिरस्त्राणि संयजेत् ।
ध्यानाद्देवो धनं दद्याज्जपात् दद्याद्वसुन्धराम् ।
प्रयच्छेज्जपूजाद्यैर्धनधान्यमहीश्रियः ॥ ११२
रवौ सिंहगतेऽष्टम्यां शुक्लपक्षे सितां शिलाम् ।
पञ्चगव्येषु निक्षिप्य स्पृष्ट्वा तमयुतं जपेत् ॥ ११३

तत्र मन्त्रार्थेन विनियोगोक्तिः ॥ १०३॥१०४॥१०५॥१०६॥१०७ ॥

ध्यानमाह आपादमिति । रथचरणं चक्रम् । दरः शङ्खः । गदाख्यां गदाम् । क्षितिः पृथिवी तस्याश्चरणो मूलं तत्र लसन्ती दंष्ट्रा यस्य तम् । दंष्ट्रालग्नभूमिमित्यर्थः । दक्षाद्यूर्ध्वयोराद्ये तदधोधस्थयोरन्योन्य इत्यायुधध्यानम् । अथ ध्यानानन्तरमिदं मुद्राद्वयं दर्शनीयम् । तल्लक्षणं यथा—

वामहस्तमधोत्तानं कृत्वा देवस्य चोपरि ।
नामयेदिति संप्रोक्ता मुद्रा वाराहसंज्ञिता ॥ इति ॥
दक्षहस्तं चोर्ध्वमुखं वामहस्तमधोमुखम् ।
अङ्गुल्यग्रन्तु संयुक्तं मुद्रा वाराहसंज्ञिता ॥ इति ॥ १०८ ॥

विष्णोः पीठे वक्ष्यमाणविधानतः पूजयेद्वराहमिति शेषः । पूर्वादीति चतुर्थी-माग्नेयादिस्थानापवादः । तद्बहिरिति पत्रमध्येषु ॥ १०९ ॥ ११० ॥ १११ ॥ ११२ ॥

सिंहेति मेषचापयोरप्युपलक्षणम् । उक्तञ्च नारायणीये—

शुक्लाष्टम्यां रवौ मेषसिंहचापगते खनेत् । इति ।

उत्तराभिमुखो भूत्वा तां शिलां निखनेद्भुवि ।
शत्रुचौरमहाभूतैः कृतां बाधां प्रणाशयेत् ॥ ११४
भानूदये भौमवारे साध्यक्षेत्रात्समाहरेत् ।
मृत्तिकां सञ्जपन्मन्त्री तां पुनर्विभजेत् त्रिधा ॥ ११५
चुल्ल्यामेकां समारोप्य पाकपात्रे तथापरम् ।
गोदुग्धे परमालोड्य शोधितांस्तण्डुलान् क्षिपेत् ॥ ११६
संस्कृतेऽग्नौ पचेत्सम्यक् चरुं मन्त्री जपन्मनुम् ।
अवतार्य चरुं पश्चादग्नौ देवं यथाविधि ॥ ११७
धूपदीपादिकैरिष्ट्वा पुनराज्यप्लुतं चरुम् ।
जुहुयादेधिते वह्नौ यावदष्टोत्तरं शतम् ॥ ११८
एवं सप्तारवारेषु जुहुयात् क्षेत्रसिद्धये ।
प्रातःकाले भृगोर्वारे मृदं साध्यमहीतलात् ॥ ११९
आदाय हविरापाद्य पूर्ववज्जुहुयात् सुधीः ।
विरोधो नश्यति क्षेत्रे सह चौराद्युपद्रवैः ॥ १२०
राजवृक्षसमुत्थाभिः समिद्भिर्मनुनाऽमुना ।
त्रिसहस्रं प्रजुहुयात्तस्य स्युः सर्वसम्पदः ॥ १२१
शालिभिर्जुहुयान्मन्त्री नित्यमष्टोत्तरं शतम् ।
समृद्धैर्धान्यसङ्घातैः शोभते तस्य मन्दिरम् ॥ १२२
तावदाज्येन जुहुयात् मण्डलात् स्वर्णमाप्नुयात् ।
लाजैः कन्यामवाप्नोति मध्वक्तैर्निजवाञ्छितम् ॥ १२३

सितां शिलामिति । कलाधिकाम् । दशपलमिताम् बिल्वपात्रादिस्थामिति पद्मपादाचार्याः ॥ ११३ ॥

निखनेदिति । भूबीजसहितं वराहमन्त्रं जपन्निति ज्ञेयम् । तदुक्तमाचार्यैः—उदग्वक्त्रो मन्त्री मनुजपरतः स्थापयतु ताम् । इति ॥ ११४ ॥

मन्त्रीत्यनेन भूबीजसाहित्यमुक्तमिति पद्मपादाचार्याः । निखननमभिजित्येव । "क्षेत्रमध्येऽभिजित्काले" इत्युक्तः । साध्यक्षेत्राज्जिष्टसितात् । सञ्जपन्निति सर्वत्र सम्बध्यते । सभा [संजपेदित्यत्र संपदेन] भूबीजयोग उक्तः । सम्यक् संस्कृतेऽग्नौ

मधुरत्रयसंयुक्तैर्जुहुयादुत्पलैर्नवैः ।
महतीं श्रियमाप्नोति मण्डलात्पूर्वसंख्यया ॥ १२४

मध्ये बीजं सतारं दहनपुरयुगे चक्रवर्णान् षडस्रे-
ष्वालिख्याङ्गानि सन्धिष्वथ करणदलैरम्बुजं केसरेषु ।
अष्टार्णान् मन्त्रमध्ये लिखतु वसुमितान्मन्त्रवर्णांश्चतुर्थे
शिष्टं पत्रे पुरस्ताद्वसुदलकमले केसरस्थस्वराढ्ये ॥ १२५

मन्त्रार्णान् देवसंख्यान् दलमनु विलिखेदन्त्यमन्त्रोऽथ बाह्ये
किञ्जल्कैः कादिवर्णैर्विकसितकमले षोडशारे यथावत् ।
मन्त्रार्णान् युग्मशस्तच्चरमदलगतं शिष्टवर्णं लिखित्वा
तारक्ष्माकोलबीजैस्तदनु परिवृतं साध्यनामार्णमध्यैः ॥ १२६

चरुं पचेदिति सम्बन्धः । तत्र सन्ध्यागतत्वेन अष्टादशसंस्कारादि महागणपतिमन्त्रहोमान्तमित्युक्तं भवति । मन्त्रीत्यनेन भूबीजयोगः । होमेऽपि तद्बीजयोगो ज्ञेयः । यथा विधीत्यनेनाग्नौ मण्डूकादि पुष्पान्तं समभ्यर्च्येत्युक्तम् । आदिशब्देन नैवेद्यग्रहणम् । पुनरनन्तरम् । आरो भौमः । हविरापाद्येति चरुं कृत्वा । पूर्ववद्धविरापाद्य पूर्ववत् जुहुयादित्यनेन भौमवारप्रयोगोक्तक्रमेणाष्टोत्तरशतमित्युक्तम् । नवैरित्यनेनान्यत्र पर्युषितग्रहणमपि । अत्र तु न तथेत्युक्तम् । पूर्वसंख्यया त्रिसहस्रमित्यादि ॥ ११५—१२४ ॥

यन्त्रमाह मध्य इति । दहनपुरयुगे परस्परव्यतिभिन्ने षट्कोणे मध्ये व्यधिकरणे सप्तम्यौ । तत्र सतारं सप्रणवं साध्यसाधकनामकर्मसहितं बीजं वक्ष्यमाणं वाराहं लिखेत् । अत्र तारः चक्रमन्त्रस्य इति ज्ञेयम् । षडस्रेषु षट्कोणेषु । चक्रवर्णान् वक्ष्यमाणप्रणवव्यतिरिक्तचक्रमन्त्रार्णान् । अङ्गानि सन्धिषु चक्रमन्त्रषडङ्गानीति सम्प्रदायविदः । यन्त्रेष्वङ्गमनूनपीत्यस्य प्रपञ्चसारपद्यस्य व्याख्याने पद्मपादाचार्यैः चक्रमन्त्रषडङ्गानीति व्याख्यातम् । करणदलैश्चतुर्दशैः । अष्टार्णान् नारायणाष्टार्णान् । एकैकस्मिन् केसरे वर्णद्वयक्रमेण मन्त्रवर्णान् वाराहमन्त्रार्णान् । वसुमितानष्टमितान् । चतुर्थपत्रे नव वर्णाः । यथावदिति । अत्र पत्रादीति सर्वत्र सम्बध्यते । तारः प्रणवः । क्ष्मा भूबीजं महागणपतिपटले उद्धृतम् । कोलबीजं वक्ष्यमाणं वाराहबीजम् । एतैः किंविशिष्टैः साध्यनाम्नोऽक्षराणि मध्ये येषां तैर्वेष्टयेत् । एतेन साध्यनामाक्षरपरिपुटितत्वं बीजानामुक्तं

दर्भितैः साध्यनामार्णैर्मन्त्रवर्णैर्वृतं बहिः।
भूबिम्बेनाऽस्य कोणेषु भूबीजं साध्यसंयुतम्
अष्टशूलेषु वाराहं भूबीजसहितं लिखेत् ॥ १२७

सार्वीशबिन्दुगगनं बीजं वाराहमीरितम्।
रोचनागुरुकर्पूरलाक्षाकुङ्कुमचन्दनैः ॥ १२८

गोमयाम्भसि सम्पिष्टैर्लिखेद्यन्त्रं शुभे दिने।
लेखन्या हेममय्या च सर्वकामप्रसिद्धये ॥ १२९

स्वर्णपट्टे लिखेद्यन्त्रं राज्यश्रीसमवाप्तये।
ग्रामसिद्धै च रजते ताम्रपट्टे धनाप्तये ॥ १३०

भूर्जपत्रे निजेष्टाप्त्यै बोमे भूसिद्धये लिखेत्।
जपपूजादिभिः सिद्धं यन्त्रं कुर्यान्निजेप्सितम् ॥ १३१

ग्रामपत्तनराष्ट्रेषु यन्त्रमेतत् सुसाधितम्।
निखनेच्छुभवारादौ साङ्गं दिक्षु समर्चयेत् ॥ १३२

क्षुद्रापमृत्युचौरादि भूतव्यालमृगाभयैः।
न शक्यते परं द्रष्टुं तं देशं देवताबलात् ॥ १३३

भवति। तदुक्तमाचार्य्यैः—

तारलक्ष्मीकोलार्णैः प्रवेष्टयेत् साध्यपरिपुटितैः। इति।

मन्त्रवर्णैर्दर्भितैः साध्यनामार्णैः वृतमिति सम्बन्धः। दर्भितलक्षणं क्रोधेविधौ वक्ष्यति। "तद्वाह्ये मनुवर्णैर्विदर्भिताभिश्च साध्यपदलिपिभिः" इत्याचार्य्योक्तेः बहिर्भूबिम्बेन वृतमिति सम्बन्धः। अष्टशूलेष्विति वह्निसाष्टरेखाग्रकृतेषु। तत्र मध्यरेखाया दक्षे वाराहं वामे भूबीजं लिखेदिति सम्प्रदायः ॥ १२५॥१२६॥१२७॥

वाराहबीजमुद्धरति सार्वीशेति। गगनं हः अर्वीशः ऊकारः बिन्दुरेतद्युतम्। अयमपि स्वतन्त्रो मन्त्रः। अस्यर्ष्यादिकं यथा।

हयग्रीव ऋषिः प्रोक्तश्छन्दस्त्रिष्टुप् च देवता।
वराहो दीर्घयुक्तेन षडङ्गानि च कल्पयेत्।
ध्यानपूजादिकं सर्वमस्य वाराहमन्त्रवत् ॥ इति।

कल्पान्तरे तु भूरित्युद्धृतम्। तदुक्तम्—

नाभिर्वीमध्रवाः सर्गी तस्य बीजमिहोच्यते । इति ।

जपपूजादिभिरित्यादिशब्देन सम्पातः । तदुक्तम्—

मन्त्रं सञ्जप्तमेतद्धुतशतसम्पातपातं करोतीति ।

सुसाधितमिति जपपूजासम्पातैः । शुभवारादावित्यादिशब्देन स्थिरराश्यादावि इति ज्ञेयम् । शाङ्गं दिक्षु समर्चयेत् इत्यस्य अयमभिप्रायः । आत्मानं वाराहरूपं ध्यात्वा तत्र यन्त्रे वाराहमावाह्य सम्पूज्य पूजोक्तक्रमेण हृदयादीनि पूर्वादि चतुर्दिक्षु सम्पूज्य अस्त्रं दिक्षु ऊर्ध्वाधश्च पूजयेदिति । तदुक्तम्—

मन्त्री समास्थाय वराहरूपं साध्यप्रदेशे निखनेच्च यन्त्रम् ।

स्थिराख्यराशावभिवाह्य कोलमङ्गानि दिक्षु क्षिपतां यथावत् ॥ इति ।

परमत्वर्थम् । अस्याऽष्टाक्षरोऽपि मन्त्रः प्रसङ्गेन प्रकाश्यते—

अष्टाक्षरे महामन्त्रे प्राग्वादिः प्रथमाक्षरम् ।

द्वितीयं व्याहृतिस्तस्माद्वाराहाय हृदं ततः ॥ इति ।

अस्य ब्रह्मा ऋषिः जगती छन्दः श्रीवाराहो देवता । भं बीजम् । ॐ शक्तिः ।

ध्यानम्—कृष्णाङ्गं त्वतिनीलवक्त्रनलिनं पद्मस्थितं स्वाङ्क्ग-

क्षोणीमतिसुदारबाहुभिरथो शङ्खं गदामम्बुजम् ।

चक्रं बिभ्रतमुग्रकान्तिमनिशं देवं वराहं भजे

भूलक्ष्मीरतिकान्तिभिः परिहृतं चर्मासिसन्दीप्तिभिः ॥ इति ।

शेषं समानम् । अस्य यन्त्रद्वयमुच्यते—

चतुर्दले मध्यबीजे केसरेऽष्टाक्षरं मनुम् ।

दलेष्वस्त्रमस्त्राय समस्ता व्याहृतीर्लिखेत् ॥

केसरेषु स्वरानष्ट पत्रे नारायणं मनुम् ।

दन्तसंख्यदले कादीन् पत्रेष्वानुष्टुभं मनुम् ॥

क्ष्मेतिनाम्ना परितस्ततः पाशाङ्कुशावृतम् ।

अस्य धारणात्तस्य सर्वमिष्टफलं लभेत् ॥ इति ।

तथा—मध्ये बीजे तथाऽष्टारे तदीयाष्टाक्षरं लिखेत् ।

बहिर्द्वदंष्टारपङ्क्तौ तु मन्त्रानुष्टुभमालिखेत् ॥

इन्द्ररूपेण तद्यन्त्रं वाराहमिति विश्रुतम् ।

यद्यत्कामयते मन्त्री सर्वमेतेन साधयेत् ॥ इति ।

मन्त्रस्तु—परजात महाराज वराहाङ्काऽवनेर्धव ।

वर्धते योऽन्वहं देवं वन्देऽहं वालिजाधवम् ॥ इति ॥ १२२ ॥

हृदयं भगवत्यै स्याद्धरण्यै तदनन्तरम् ।
धरण्यन्ते धरेद्वन्द्वं द्विठान्तोऽयं ध्रुवादिकः ॥ १३४

एकोनविंशत्यर्णाढ्यं धराहृदयमीरितम् ।
वराहोऽस्य मुनिः प्रोक्तश्छन्दो निचृदुदाहृतम् ॥ १३५

देवता सर्वभूतानां प्रकृतिर्वसुधा मता ।
हृदयं त्रिभिराख्यातं चतुर्भिः शिर ईरितम् ॥ १३६

त्रिभिः शिखा समुद्दिष्टा कवचं पञ्चभिर्मतम् ।
द्वाभ्यां नेत्रं समाख्यातं द्वाभ्यामस्त्रं पुनर्भवेत् ।
मन्त्रवर्णैः षडङ्गानि कुर्यादेवं विधानवित् ॥ १३७

श्यामां विचित्रांशुकरत्नभूषां पद्मासनां तुङ्गपयोधरान्ताम् ।
इन्दीवरे द्वे नवशालिमञ्जरीं शुकं दधानां वसुधां भजामहे ॥ १३८

लक्षमेकं जपेन्मन्त्री धराहृदयमादरात् ।
ससर्पिषा पायसेन जुहुयात्तद्दशांशतः ॥ १३९

तां विष्णोः पूजयेत्पीठे वक्ष्यमाणविधानतः ।
अङ्गानि पूजयेदादौ भुवह्निजलमारुतान् ॥ १४०

दिक्पत्रेषु समभ्यर्च्य कोणपत्रेषु तत्क्रमात् ।
आशापालाः पुनः पूज्या वज्राद्यस्त्रसमन्विताः ॥ १४१

एवं सिद्धमनुर्मन्त्री साधयेत् स्वमनोरथान् ।
मधुरत्रयसंयुक्तैर्जुहुयादरुणोत्पलैः ॥ १४२

सहस्रं भूसमृद्धिः स्यात्तथा नीलोत्पलैः शुभैः ।
प्रियङ्गुपुष्पैर्मध्वक्तैर्धनधान्यसमृद्धिश्रियः ॥ १४३

वराहमन्त्रप्रसङ्गात् धरणीमन्त्रमाह हृदयमिति । हृदयं नमःपदम् । अत्रापि पूर्ववद्विसर्गेण सह सन्धिर्ज्ञेयः । प्रणवो बीजं स्वाहा शक्तिः । विधानवित् इत्यनेन शाक्तषडङ्गमुद्राभिरित्युक्तम् ॥ १३४॥१३५॥१३६॥१३७ ॥

दक्षादूर्ध्वयोराद्ये तदधस्थयोरन्त्ये इत्यायुधध्यानम् ॥ १३८॥१३९ ॥

विष्णोरिति । ग्लौं वसुन्धरायोगपीठाय नम इति पीठमन्त्रः । अनेनैव बीजेन मूर्तिकल्पनं ज्ञेयम् । दिक्पत्रेषु अग्रपृष्ठदक्षोत्तरेषु । कोणपत्रेषु इत्य-

मञ्जरीं शालिसम्भूतां मधुरत्रयलोलिताम् ।
जुहुयात्साधिते वह्नौ मण्डलात् स्याद्धरापतिः ॥ १४४

शुक्रवारे दिनमुखे गृहीत्वा साध्यभूमृदम् ।
तामम्भसि विनिक्षिप्य शोधितेऽत्र चरुं पचेत् ॥ १४५

पयोघृताभ्यां सहितं जुहुयात्तं हुताशने ।
सप्तमासं शुक्रवारेषु हुत्वैवं प्राप्नुयान्महीम् ॥ १४६

धरामेवं भजन्मन्त्री पशुरत्नधनादिभिः ।
धरायाः वल्लभः स स्यान्नात्र कार्या विचारणा ॥ १४७

इति श्रीशारदातिलके पञ्चदशः पटलः ।

त्वाऽऽग्नेयादिषु । तत्कलाः इति निवृत्तिप्रतिष्ठाविद्याशान्तयः । स्वमनोरथान्नित्यनेन पृथ्वीप्राप्तौ स्वबीजयोगः । धनधान्यलाभे श्रीयोगः । कीर्त्तौ शक्तियोगोऽन्यत्र वराहबीजयोगोऽपि सूचितः ॥ १४०॥१४१॥१४२॥१४३॥१४४ ॥

शुक्रवार इति । तामम्भसीति तृतीयांशम् । दुग्धे वा । तत्रैकमंशं चुल्लामेकं पात्रे इति ज्ञेयम् ॥ १४५॥१४६॥१४७ ॥

इति श्रीशारदातिलकटीकायां सत्सम्प्रदायकृतव्याख्यायां
पदार्थादर्शाभिख्यायां पञ्चदशः पटलः ॥ ॐ ॥

षोडशः पटलः ।

अथाऽभिधास्ये विधिवन्नारसिंहं महामनुम् ।
उग्रं वीरं वदेत्पूर्वं महाविष्णुमनन्तरम् ॥ १
ज्वलन्तं पदमाभाष्य सर्वतोमुखमीरयेत् ।
नृसिंहं भीषणं भद्रं मृत्युमृत्युं वदेत्ततः
नमाम्यहमयं प्रोक्तो मन्त्रराजः सुरद्रुमः ॥ २
ऋषिर्ब्रह्मा समुद्दिष्टश्छन्दोऽनुष्टुबुदाहृतम्
देवता नरसिंहोऽस्य सुरासुरनमस्कृतः ॥ ३
चतुर्भिर्हृदयं वर्णैः शिरस्तावद्भिरीरितम् ।
शिखाऽष्टाभिः समुद्दिष्टा षड्भिः कवचमीरितम् ॥ ४

नृसिंहमन्त्रराजमुद्धरति उग्रमिति । मन्त्रे सर्वाणि द्वितीयान्तानि । श्लोकरूपो द्वात्रिंशदक्षरो मन्त्रः । वैदिकत्वादस्य प्रणवादित्वं ज्ञेयम् । तापनीये तथोक्तत्वात् । साम्प्रदायिकास्तु सुरद्रुम इत्यनेन शक्तिबीजपुटितमेनमाहुः । अस्य हं बीजं ईं शक्तिः । तथा च तापनीये—

ॐ देवा ह वै प्रजापतिमब्रुवन् आनुष्टुभस्य मन्त्रराजस्य नारसिंहस्य शक्तिं बीजं नो ब्रूहि भगव इति । स होवाच प्रजापतिः । माया वा एषा नारसिंही सर्वमिदं सृजति सर्वमिदं रक्षति सर्वमिदं संहरति तस्मान्मायामेतां शक्तिं विद्यात् । य एतां मायां शक्तिं वेद स पाप्मानं तरति स मृत्युं जयति सोऽमृतत्वं च गच्छति महतीं श्रियमश्नुते मीमांसन्ति ब्रह्मवादिनः । ह्रस्वा वा दीर्घा वा प्लुता वेति । यदि ह्रस्वा भवति सर्वं पाप्मानं तरति अमृतत्वं च गच्छति । यदि दीर्घा भवति महतीं श्रियमाप्नोति अमृतत्वं च गच्छति । यदि प्लुता भवति ज्ञानवान् भवति अमृतत्वं च गच्छति ।

सर्वेषां वा एतद्भूतानामाकाशः परायणम् । सर्वाणि ह वा इमानि भूतानि आकाशादेव जायन्ते आकाशादेव जातानि जीवन्ति । आकाशं प्रयन्त्यभिसंविशन्ति । तस्मादाकाशं बीजं विद्यादिति ॥ १॥२॥३ ॥

तावद्भिरिति चतुर्भिः । तावद्भिः षड्भिः । करणाक्षरैरिति चतुर्भिः ।

तावद्भिर्नयनं प्रोक्तमस्त्रं स्यात्करखाक्षरैः ।
शिरोललाटनेत्रेषु मुखबाह्वङ्घ्रिसन्धिषु ॥ ५
साग्रेषु कुक्षौ हृदये गले पार्श्वद्वये पुनः ।
अपराङ्गे ककुदि च न्यसेद्वर्णान् यथाक्रमम् ॥ ६

साम्प्रदायिकास्त्वन्यथा षडङ्गमाहुः । तद्यथा । छामाद्यैश्चतुर्भिः पादैरर्द्धद्वयसहितै-रानन्दात्मने प्रियात्मने ज्योतिरात्मने मायात्मने ज्वालात्मने ध्यानात्मने क्षमा-देतदन्तैः षडङ्गानि । तापनीये तु पञ्चाङ्गमेवोक्तम्—

तस्य ह्रि पञ्चाङ्गानि भवन्ति । चत्वारः पादाः चत्वार्यङ्गानि भवन्ति । सप्रणवं सर्वं पञ्चमं भवतीति ।

अक्षरन्यासमाह शिर इति । तत्र प्रणवयोर्मध्ये एकैकमक्षरं सबिन्दुकमुच्चार्य न्यसनीयम् । यत्तापनीये—

ओमित्येतदक्षरमिदं सर्वम् । तस्मात् प्रत्यक्षरमुभयत ओङ्कारो भवति । अक्षराणां न्यासमुपदिशन्ति ब्रह्मवादिनः इति ।

अपराङ्गे पृष्ठे । ककुदि अपरगले । अथ तन्त्रान्तरोक्तो नृसिंहसान्निध्यकारकः सर्वरक्षाकरो दशविधन्यास उच्यते । यदाहुः—

नृसिंहसान्निध्यकरो न्यासो दशविधस्त्विह ।
प्रोच्यते तत्र पूर्वोऽयमङ्गुलीन्यास उच्यते ॥
कराङ्गुष्ठाद्यङ्गुलीषु पृथगाद्यन्तपर्वणोः ।
सर्वाङ्गुली न्यसेच्छिष्टं तलयोरक्षरद्वयम् ॥
ब्रह्मरन्ध्रललाटभ्रूमध्यदृक्षु दृशोप्यधः ।
कपोले कर्णमूले च चिबुकोर्ध्वाधरोष्ठके ॥
कण्ठोरोदक्षदोर्वामदोर्हृत्तनुषु नाभिके ।
दक्षान्यदोस्तले कट्यां मेढ्रोर्वोर्जानुजङ्घयोः ॥
गुल्फे पादकराङ्गुल्योः सर्वसन्धिषु रोमसु ।
रक्तास्थिमज्जासु मनोवर्णान्न्यसेद्विचक्षणः ॥
द्व्यर्णान् पदे गुल्फजानुकटिनाभिषु हृत्स्थले ।
बाह्वोः कण्ठे तु चिबुके ओष्ठे गण्डे प्रविन्यसेत् ॥
कर्णयोर्वदने नासापुटे नेत्रे च मूर्धनि ।
पदानि तु मुखे केशे चक्षुःश्रोत्रेषु विन्यसेत् ॥

माणिक्याद्रिसमप्रभं निजरुचा संत्रस्तरक्षोगणं
जानुन्यस्तकराम्बुजं त्रिनयनं रत्नोल्लसद्भूषणम् ।
बाहुभ्यां धृतचक्रशङ्खमनिशं दंष्ट्रोग्रवक्त्रोल्लस-
ज्ज्वालाजिह्वमुदग्रकेशनिचयं वन्दे नृसिंहं विभुम् ॥ ७

मूर्ध्नि च हृदये नाभौ कटिजानुपदेष्वपि ।
नासाद्वन्द्वकर्णनाभीहृत्कटोःपत्सु प्रविन्यसेत् ॥
चतुर्वर्णान् मनोः पादान् ककुब्बाशिषु सर्वतः ।
अर्धद्वयं न्यसेन्मूर्ध्नि आद्यन्त्यादास्यदङ्गकम् ॥
उग्राद्युग्रादीनि नव पदानीह नमाम्यहम् ।
इत्यन्तान्याद्यकप्राणद्वन्द्वयोः च पत्सु ॥
हृदि नाभौ च कव्यादिपादान्तं नवसु न्यसेत् ।
वीरा[तारा]द्यान्यपि तान्येव यथा पूर्वं प्रविन्यसेत् ॥
नृसिंहाद्यानि तान्येव पूर्ववद्विन्यसेत् सुधीः ॥ इति ॥ ४॥५॥६ ॥

ध्यानमाह माणिक्येति । अत्र ध्यानानन्तरमेता मुद्राः प्रदर्शयेत् ॥

जानुमध्यगतौ कृत्वा चिबुकोष्ठौ समावुभौ ।
हस्तौ च भूमिसंलग्नौ कम्पमानः पुनः पुनः ॥
मुखं विजृम्भितं कृत्वा लेलिहानां च जिह्विकाम् ।
एषा मुद्रा नारसिंही प्रधानेति प्रकीर्त्तिता ॥
वामस्याङ्गुष्ठतो बद्धा कनिष्ठामङ्गुलीत्रयम् ।
त्रिशूलवत् सम्मुखोर्ध्वं कुर्यान् मुद्रां नृसिंहगाम् ॥
अङ्गुष्ठाभ्यां च करयोस्तथाक्रम्य कनिष्ठिके ।
अधोमुखाभिः श्लिष्टाभिः शेषाभिर्नृहरेर्मता ॥
हस्तावधोमुखौ कृत्वा नाभिदेशे प्रसार्य च ।
तर्जनीभ्यां नयेत् स्कन्धौ प्रोक्तैषाऽन्त्राख्यमुद्रिका ॥
हस्तावूर्ध्वमुखौ कृत्वा तले संयोज्य मध्यमे ।
अनामायां तु वामायां दक्षिणां तु विनिक्षिपेत् ॥
तर्जन्यौ पृष्ठतो लग्ने अङ्गुष्ठौ तर्जनीश्रितौ ।
चक्रमुद्रा भवेदेषा नृहरेः सन्निधौ मता ॥
चक्रमुद्रां तथा कृत्वा तर्जनीभ्यां तु मध्यमे ।

वर्णलक्षं जपेन्मन्त्रं तत्सहस्रं घृतप्लुतैः।
पायसान्नैः प्रजुहुयाद्विधिवत् पूजितेऽनले ॥ ८
एवं कृते भवेन्मन्त्री सिद्धमन्त्रः प्रतापवान्।
पूजा प्रागीरिते पीठे मूर्त्तिं मूलेन कल्पयेत् ॥ ९
पूजयेद्विधिवत्तस्यां दैत्यशत्रुमनन्यधीः।
अङ्गान्यादौ समाराध्य दिग्दलेषु यजेत् पुनः ॥ १०
पक्षीन्द्रं शङ्करं शेषमब्जयोनिं यथाक्रमम्।
श्रियं ह्रियं धृतिं पुष्टिमग्न्यादिषु यजेत् पुनः ॥ ११
लोकपालाः समभ्यर्च्यास्तदस्त्राणि ततः परम्।
इत्थं जपादिभिः सिद्धे मनौ काम्यानि साधयेत् ॥ १२

उद्यत्कोटिरविप्रभं नरहरिं कोटीरहारोज्ज्वलं
दंष्ट्राभीममुखं लसन्नखमुखैर्दीर्घैरनेकैर्भुजैः।
निर्भिन्नासुरनाथमग्निशशभृत्सूर्य्यात्मनेत्रत्रयं
विद्युत्पुञ्जसटाकलापभयदं वह्निं वमन्तं भजे ॥ १३

सौम्ये सौम्यं स्मरेत्कार्य्ये क्रूरे क्रूरमिमं भजेत्।
श्रीपुष्पैर्जुहुयान्मन्त्री बिल्वकाष्ठैर्धृतेऽनले ॥ १४

पीड़येद् दंष्ट्रमुद्रैषा सर्वपापप्रणाशिनी ॥ इति ॥

एताः सर्वनृसिंहमन्त्रसाधारण्य इति ज्ञेयम् ॥ ७ ॥

वर्णलक्षमिति द्वात्रिंशल्लक्षम्। तत्सहस्रं द्वात्रिंशत्सहस्रम्। विधिवदिति देवतापीठं सम्प्राभ्यर्च्येत्यर्थः। प्रागीरिते इति नारायणाष्टाक्षरोक्ते। विधिवदिति वक्ष्यमाणविधानेन। किञ्च विधिवदित्यनेन तापनीयोक्तयन्त्रे दशावरणानि पूजयेदित्युक्तम्। समाराध्येति तूर्य्योक्तरीत्या ॥ ८॥९॥१०॥११॥१२ ॥

ध्यानमाह उद्यदिति ॥ १३ ॥

सौम्य इति। एतदुपासनाविषये। सौम्यं पूर्वोक्तध्यानम्। क्रूरे प्रयोगविषय इत्यर्थः। क्रूरमनन्तरोक्तम्। तदुक्तमाचार्य्यैः—

प्रतिपत्तिरस्य चोक्ता प्रसन्नता क्रूरता विशेषेण।
द्विविधा प्रसन्नया स्यात् साधनपूजाऽन्यया प्रयोगविधिः ॥ इति ॥

सहस्रं श्रियमाप्नोति पत्रैर्वा बिल्वसम्भवैः ।
प्रसूनैर्वा फलैस्तद्वद्दूर्वाहोमादरोगताम् ॥ १५

अन्तरजप्तां वचां श्वेतां भक्षयेत् प्रातरन्वहम् ।
वाक्सिद्धिं लभते मन्त्री वाचस्पतिरिवापरः ॥ १६

सलिले देवमभ्यर्च्य गन्धपुष्पादिभिः शुभैः ।
दूर्वाभिस्तत्र जुहुयान्नित्यमष्टोत्तरं शतम् ॥ १७

उपसर्गा विनश्यन्ति क्षुद्रभूतज्वरादिभिः ।
दुःस्वप्ने निशि सञ्जाते स्नात्वा मन्त्रममुं जपेत् ॥ १८

अनिद्रो मन्त्रवित् पश्चात् सुस्वप्नस्तस्य जायते ।
व्याघ्रचौरमृगादिभ्यो महारण्ये भयाकुले ॥ १९

रक्षेन्मनुरयं जप्तो भयेष्वन्येषु मन्त्रिणम् ।
अनेन मन्त्रितं भस्म विषग्रहमहामयान् ॥ २०

नाशयेदचिरादेव मन्त्रस्याऽस्य प्रभावतः ।
घोरेऽभिचारे सोन्मादे महोत्पाते महाभये ॥ २१

जपेन्मन्त्रं स्मरेद्देवं दुःखान्मुक्तो भवेन्नरः ।
सिंहरूपं महाभीमं नखदंष्ट्रातिभीषणम् ॥ २२

श्रीरिति लक्ष्मीलता । तद्वदिति श्रियमाप्नोतीत्यर्थः । अरोगतामित्यत्राप्नोतीत्यनुवर्त्यते । तत्रेति जले । उपसर्गा उपद्रवाः । तदुक्तमाचार्यैः—

दूर्वात्रिकैरष्टसहस्रसंख्यैराराध्य मन्त्री जुहुयादथाप्सु ।
शान्तिं प्रयान्त्येव तदोपसर्गा आपो हि शान्ता इति च श्रुतिः स्यात् ॥
उत्पाते सति महति ह्युपद्रवाणां होमोऽयं भवति स शान्तिदो नराणाम् ।
यद्यान्यद्विजमनसेप्सितं च कामं तत्प्राप्नोत्यखिलनृणां प्रियश्च भूयात् ॥ इति ॥

॥ १४॥१५॥१६॥१७॥१८ ॥

दुःस्वप्नानन्तरं तदैव । जपेदित्यष्टोत्तरशतम् । सुस्वप्न इति । स एव दुःस्वप्न एवं सुस्वप्नफलदो भवति । मृगाः सिंहाद्याः । विषेत्यनेन सर्पादीनां विषम् । ग्रहा अष्टादश । महामयानित्यनेन ज्वरादयः संगृहीताः । यदाहुः—

मूषिकालूतावृश्चिकवड्डुपादाद्युत्थितं विषं शमयेत् ।
अष्टोत्तरशतजापान् मनुरयमभिमन्त्रितं च भस्मादयम् ॥

स्मृत्वाऽऽत्मानं रिपुं पश्चाद्ध्यायेन्मृगशिशुं पुरा।
गृहीत्वा गलदेशे तं पुनर्दंष्ट्रु क्षिपेद् द्रुतम्।
पुत्रमित्रकलत्राद्यैर्नाशो जायते रिपोः॥ २३

पूर्वमृत्युपदे साध्यनाम कृत्वा स्वयं हरिः।
निशितैर्नखदंष्ट्राग्रैः खण्डयमानं रिपुं स्मरेत्॥ २४

नित्यमष्टोत्तरशतं जपेन्मन्त्रमतन्द्रितः।
जायते मण्डलादर्वाक् मनुर्वैवस्वतः प्रियः॥ २५

यत्नं कुर्वीत विधिवच्छत्रुसेनानिवारणे।
बिभीतकाष्ठैर्ज्वलिते पावके रिपुमर्दनम्॥ २६

विचिन्त्य देवं नृहरिं सम्पूज्य कुसुमादिभिः।
समूलतूलैर्जुहुयात्क्रूरैर्दशशतं पृथक्।
रिपुं खादन्निव जपेन्निर्भिन्दन्निव तान् क्षिपेत्॥ २७

हुत्वा सप्तदिनं मन्त्री सेनामिष्टां महीपतेः।
प्रस्थापयेच्छुभे लग्ने परराज्यजयेच्छया॥ २८

शिरोऽक्षिकर्णशूलकुक्षिरुजाज्वरविसर्पवमिहिक्काः।
मन्त्रौषधाभिचारिककृतान् विकारानयं मनुः शमयेत्॥ इति॥

रिपुमित्यग्रिमेण सम्बध्यते। तं रिपुं क्षिपेदित्यन्वयः। पुरेति पाठे आत्मानं पुरा स्मृत्वेत्यन्वयः। पुरः इति पाठे आत्मनः अग्रे इत्यर्थः॥ १८-२३॥

पूर्वमृत्युपदे इति। मन्त्रे मृत्युमृत्युमिति मृत्युपदद्वयमस्ति। तत्र पूर्वमृत्युपदं त्यक्त्वा तत्स्थाने साध्यनामप्रयोग इत्यर्थः। स्वयं हरिरिति। आत्मानं नृसिंहरूपं ध्यात्वेत्यर्थः॥ २४॥२५॥

यत्नं कुर्वीतेत्यादि अनर्थः स्यान् महीपतेरित्यन्तमेक एव प्रयोगः। विधि-वत्प्रकारमेवाह बिभीतेति। रिपुमर्दनमित्यनेन क्रूरध्यानं कर्त्तव्यमिति सूचितम्। पृथगिति प्रत्यहम्। रिपुं खादन्निव जपेदित्यस्यायमर्थः। होमसमये रिपुं खादन्निव नृसिंहोऽहमित्यात्मानं ध्यात्वा जपेत् मन्त्रमुच्चरेत्। ततोऽरीन् भिन्दन्निव नृसिं-होऽहमिति आत्मानं ध्यात्वा तान् शरान्मन्त्री क्षिपेदिति। तदुक्तम्—

खादन्निवोच्चरेन् मनुमरीन् भिन्दन्निव क्षिपेत् समिधः। इति॥२६॥२७॥

हुत्वा महीपतेरिष्टां सेनां शुभे लग्ने प्रस्थापयेदिति सम्बन्धः॥ २८॥

तस्याः पुरस्तान्नृहरिं निघ्नन्तं रिपुमण्डलम् ।
स्मृत्वा प्रयोगं कुर्वीत यावदायाति सा पुनः ॥ २९
विजित्य निखिलाञ्छत्रून् सह वीरश्रिया सुखम् ।
आगत्य विजयी राजा ग्रामच्छेवधनादिभिः ॥ ३०
प्रीणयेन्मन्त्रिणं सम्यग्विभवैः प्रीतमानसः ।
मन्त्री यदि न सन्तुष्येदनर्थः स्यान्महीपतेः ॥ ३१

स्मृत्वा प्रयोगमिति । यावदायाति तावज्जपं पूर्वोक्तध्यानं च कुर्यादित्यर्थः ।

तदुक्तम्—यावज्जितारिरेष्यति नृपतिस्तावज्जपेत् स्मरन् देवम् । इति ॥

तन्त्रान्तरोक्ता ध्यानभेदा लिख्यन्ते—

नरसिंहं महाभीमं कालानलसमप्रभम् ।
अक्षमालाधरं रौद्रं कण्ठहारेण शोभितम् ॥
नागयज्ञोपवीतं च पञ्चाननसुशोभितम् ।
चन्द्रमौलिं नीलकण्ठं प्रतिवक्त्रं त्रिनेत्रकम् ॥
भुजैः परिघसङ्काशैर्दशभिश्चोपशोभितम् ।
अक्षसूत्रं गदां पद्मं शङ्खं गोक्षीरसन्निभम् ॥
धनुश्च मुषलं चैव बिभ्राणं चक्रमुत्तमम् ।
खड्गं शूलं च बाणं च नृहरिं रुद्ररूपिणम् ॥
इन्द्रगोपाभनीलाभं चन्द्राभं स्वर्णसन्निभम् ।
पूर्वादि चोत्तरं यावदूर्ध्वास्यं सर्ववर्णकम् ॥
एवमुग्रं हरिं ध्यायेत् सर्वव्याधिविमुक्तये ।
सर्वमृत्युहरं दिव्यं स्मरणात् सर्वसिद्धिदम् ॥
ध्येयो यदा महत्कर्म तदा षोडशहस्तवान् ।
नृसिंहः सर्वलोकेशः सर्वाभरणभूषितः ॥
द्वौ विदारणकर्माढ्यौ द्वौ चान्त्रोद्धरणान्वितौ ।
चक्रशङ्खधरौ द्वौ तु द्वौ च बाणधनुर्धरौ ॥
खड्गखेटधरौ द्वौ च द्वौ गदापद्मधारिणौ ।
पाशाङ्कुशधरौ द्वौ तु द्वौ रिपोर्मुकुटार्पितौ ॥
इति षोडशदोर्दण्डमण्डितं नृहरिं विभुम् ।
ध्यायेन्नीरदनीलाभमुग्रकर्मण्यनन्यधीः ॥

बीजं साध्यसमन्वितं प्रविलिखेन्मध्येऽष्टपत्रेष्वथो
मन्त्रार्णान् श्रुतिशो विभज्य विलिखेत् लिप्या बहिर्वेष्टयेत् ।
बाह्ये कोणगबीजवद्वसुधा गेहद्वयेनावृतं
यन्त्रं क्षुद्रविषग्रहामयरिपुप्रध्वंसनं श्रीपदम् ॥ ३२

कृत्वा नवपदात्मानं मण्डलं यन्त्रसंयुतम् ।
अस्मिन् संस्थापयेन्मन्त्री कलशान्नव शोभनान् ॥ ३३

ध्येयो महत्तमे कार्ये दशहाविंशहस्तवान् ।
नृहरिः सर्वभूताढ्यः सर्वसिद्धिकरः प्रभुः ॥
दक्षिणे चक्रपद्मे च परशुं पाशमेव च ।
हलं च मुषलं चैवमभयं चाङ्कुशं तथा ॥
पट्टिशं भिन्दिपालं च खड्गमुद्गरतोमरान् ।
वामभागे करैः शङ्खं खेटं पाशं च शूलकम् ॥
अग्निं च वरदं शक्तिं कुण्डिकां च ततः परम् ।
कार्मुकं तर्जनीमुद्रां गदां डमरुसर्पकौ ॥
द्वाभ्यां कराभ्यां च रिपोर्जानुमस्तकपीडनम् ।
ऊर्ध्वीकृताभ्यां बाहुभ्यामन्त्रमालाधरं हरिम् ॥
अधःस्थिताभ्यां बाहुभ्यां हिरण्यकविदारणम् ।
प्रियङ्करं च भक्तानां दैत्यानां च भयङ्करम् ॥
नृसिंहं संस्मरेदित्थं महामृत्युभयापहम् ।
अथोच्यते ध्यानमन्यत् सुखरोगहरं शुभम् ॥

स्वर्णाद्यामे सुपर्णे स्थितमभिमुखं कोटिपूर्णेन्दुवर्णं
विद्युज्ज्वालासटाभिर्ज्वलितशिखमयष्टदृशं पीतवस्त्रोरुभूषम् ।
हस्तोद्यच्चक्रशङ्खाभयवरमखिलक्ष्वेलरोगादिमृत्युं
सैध्यानैर्ध्वंसयन्तं सुरनुतमनिशं संस्मरेच्छ्रीनृसिंहम् ॥ इति ॥ २९-३१ ॥

यन्त्रमाह बीजमिति । बीजं वक्ष्यमाणम् नारसिंहम् । श्रुतिशश्चत्वारि चत्वारि । लिप्या मातृकया । कोणगं बीजं नृसिंहबीजम् । यन्त्रं एवंभूतम् । वर्णं अतिभिर्व यद्वसुधागेहद्वयं तेन वृतम् ॥ ३२ ॥

यन्त्रसंयुतमिति नवनाभमध्यपद्मकर्णिकायाम् । अस्मिन् नवनाभमण्डले । कषायः क्षीरद्रुमत्वचां रस एव तोयम् । वस्त्ररत्नादीत्यादिशब्देन हेम ।

कषायतोयसम्पूर्णान् वस्त्ररत्नादिसंयुतान्।
मध्ये सम्पूजयेद्देवं नृसिंहं शान्तविग्रहम्॥ ३४
तार्क्ष्यादीन् पूजयेन्मन्त्री पूर्वादिषु यथाक्रमम्।
इति संसाधितैस्तोयैरभिषिञ्चेत् प्रियं नरम्॥ ३५
अभिचारग्रहोन्मादा विनश्यन्त्यरिभिः सह।
अभिषिक्तस्तदा विप्रान् भोजयेद्देवताधिया॥ ३६
यथावत् पूजयेत्पश्चाद्भक्त्या गुरुमवञ्चयन्।
राजा विजयमाप्नोति युद्धेषु विधिनाऽमुना॥ ३७

बीजाढ्यं फणपञ्चकं प्रविलिखेच्छेषस्य भोगे पुन-
र्नागैर्नवपदसंयुते परिलिखेन्मन्त्राक्षराणि क्रमात्।
पुच्छे नाम जपादिसाधितमिदं होमेन सम्पातितं
भूतापस्मृतिदुःखरोगशमनं यन्त्रं रिपुध्वंसनम्॥ ३८

शान्तविग्रहमिति। भाषितेति प्रोक्तध्यानम्। तार्क्ष्यादीनिति पूर्वोक्तपक्षीन्द्रादीन्। पूर्वादिषु अग्रादिषु। देवताधिया यथावद् गुरुं पूजयेदिति सम्बन्धः। यथावदित्यनेन पाद्याद्युपचारोक्तिः॥ ३३॥३४॥३५॥३६॥३७॥

यन्त्रान्तरमाह बीजाढ्यमिति। पूर्वापरायताः पञ्च रेखाः कुर्यात्। दक्षिणोदग्गता नव रेखाः कुर्यात्। प्रागग्रेषु पञ्चसु फणाकारता कार्या। पश्चिमाग्रेषु पञ्चसु पुच्छाकारता कार्या। तत्र प्रतिफणमेकैकं बीजं लिखेत्। जपादीत्यादिशब्देन प्राणप्रतिष्ठापूजे। तन्त्रान्तरस्थं यन्त्रमुच्यते—

षोडशारं महाचक्रं लिखेद् भूर्जे प्रयत्नतः।
दलेषु मन्त्रवर्णानि युग्मयुग्मक्रमाल्लिखेत्॥
त्रैलोक्यमोहनं बीजं कर्णिकायां लिखेद्बुधः।
श्रीबीजेन संवेष्ट्य क्रौंकारेणाऽवरुध्य च॥
विवादे कलहे न्याये तथा राजकुले जयी।
मेधाकरी वश्यकरी नरनारीवशङ्करी॥
शिखायां धारयेद्बाहौ कण्ठे वा कटिसूत्रके।
सर्वत्र सुभगो लोके सर्वत्राऽप्रतिमो भवेत्॥

थकारो वह्निमारूढो मनुस्वरसमन्वितः ।

बिन्दुनादलसन्मूर्धा बीजं नारहरैकम् ॥ ३७ ॥

चिन्तामणिर्नाम रक्षा स्वयं विष्णुविनिर्मिता ।
पुनरन्यां प्रवक्ष्यामि रक्षां त्रैलोक्यमोहिनीम् ॥
यस्याः सन्धारणादेव भवेयुः सर्वसम्पदः ।
श्वेतभूर्जे लिखेत्पद्मं द्वात्रिंशत्सिंहसंयुतम् ॥
मध्ये सिंहेश्वरं बीजं लिखेत् पूर्ववदेव तु ।
श्रीबीजेन तु संवेष्ट्य वलयत्रयसंयुतम् ॥
पाशाङ्कुशैश्च संवेष्ट्य पूजयेत्कुसुमादिकम् ।
त्रैलोक्यमोहनं नाम सर्वकामार्थसाधनम् ॥
चक्रराजं महाराजं सर्वचक्रेश्वरेश्वरम् ।
धारणात्सर्वमाप्नोति सत्यं सत्यं न संशयः ॥ इति ॥
कृष्णं रुद्रं महाघोरं भीमं भीषणमुज्ज्वलम् ।
करालं विकरालं च दैत्यान्तं मधुसूदनम् ॥
रक्ताक्षं पिङ्गलाक्षं च अञ्जनं दीप्ततेजसम् ।
सुघोरं सुहनुं चैव विश्वाक्षं राक्षसान्तकम् ॥
विशालं धूम्रकेशं च हयग्रीवं घनस्वनम् ।
मेघनादं मेघवर्णं कुम्भकर्णं कृतान्तकम् ॥
तीव्रतेजमग्निवर्णं महोग्रं विश्वभूषणम् ।
विघ्नक्षमं महासेनं सिंहा द्वात्रिंशदीरिताः ॥ इति ॥ ३८ ॥

नृसिंहबीजमुद्धरति थकार इति । वह्नी रेफः मनुस्वर औ । अयमपि स्वतन्त्रो मन्त्रः । अस्यर्ष्यादिकं यथा—

ऋषिरत्रिश्च गायत्री छन्दः श्रीनृहरिः प्रभुः ।
देवता दीर्घयुग्बीजेनैवाऽङ्गं परिकल्पयेत् ॥
ध्यानं पूर्ववदेव स्याद्दशलक्षं जपेन्मनुम् ।
तद्दशांशं हुनेत्सम्यक् घृताक्तैः पायसैः शुभैः ॥
अर्चा होमादिकं सर्वमस्य पूर्ववदाचरेत् ।
मन्त्रराजवदेवाऽस्य प्रयोगानपि साधयेत् ॥
हृल्लेखासम्पुटं केचित् सङ्गिरन्ते मनुं त्वमुम् ॥ इति ।

बीजं नमो भगवते नरसिंहाय तत्परम् ।
ज्वालाज्वालामालिने पश्चाद्दीप्तदंष्ट्राय तत्परम् ॥ ४०
अग्निनेत्राय सर्वादि रक्षोघ्नाय पदं वदेत् ।
सर्वभूतविनाशान्तं नकारो दीर्घवान् मरुत् ॥ ४१
सर्वज्वरविनाशान्ते नायार्थी दहयुग्मकम् ।
पचद्वयं रक्षयुग्मं हुं फट् स्वाहा भुजादिकः ॥ ४२

तथा—अष्टारं विलिखेत्पद्मं कृत्वा [कुर्यात्] कर्णिकया युतम् ॥
मूलमन्त्रं लिखेत्तत्र प्रणवेन समन्वितम् ।
पत्राक्षरं नारसिंहं नाम्ना चैव ससाधकम् ॥
अपिदष्टसहस्रं तु सूत्रेणावेष्ट्य तद्बहिः ।
सुवर्णेन तु संवेष्ट्य रौप्येणावेष्टयेत्ततः ॥
ताम्रेणावेष्टयेत् पश्चादाज्ञया च प्रयत्नतः ।
पुनर्मन्त्रेण संमन्त्र्य शक्तिमुत्तारयेत् प्रिये ॥
कण्ठे भुजे शिखायां वा धारयेद्यन्त्रमुत्तमम् ।
नरनारीनरेन्द्राश्च सर्वे स्युर्वशगा भुवि ॥
दुष्टास्तं नैव बाधन्ते पिशाचोरगराक्षसाः ।
यन्त्रराजप्रसादेन सर्वत्र जयमाप्नुयात् ॥
द्वादशारं महाचक्रं पूर्ववद्विलिखेत् सुधीः ।
मालाद्वादशसम्भिन्नं दले तल्लेखयेद्बुधः ॥
मध्ये मन्त्रं शक्तियुतं श्रीबीजेन तु वेष्टयेत् ।
कालान्तकं नाम चक्रं सुरासुरभयङ्करम् ॥
चक्रमुल्लेखयेत् भूर्जे सर्वशत्रुनिवारणम् ।
यस्य धारणमात्रेण सर्वत्र विजयी भवेत् ॥
स शक्योऽथ भवेल्लोके यथा देवो नृकेसरी ॥ इति ॥ ३९ ॥

ज्वालानृसिंहमन्त्रमाह बीजमिति । बीजं नारसिंहम् । नकारो दीर्घवान् ना । मरुत् यकारः । ब्रह्मा ऋषिः अति छन्दः ज्वालामाली नृसिंहो देवता । क्षौं बीजं स्वाहा शक्तिः । करणाक्षरैश्चतुरस्रैः । ननु मन्त्रस्य समपञ्चाशदक्षरत्वमुक्तम् । कृत् क्षयोदशभिरित्यादिनाऽत्रोक्तौ अष्टपञ्चाशदक्षराणि लभ्यन्ते इति पूर्वापरविरोध इति

सप्तषष्ट्यक्षरैः प्रोक्तो ज्वालामाली महामनुः ।
हृत् त्रयोदशभिः प्रोक्तं शिरो दशभिरीरितम् ॥ ४३
शिखैकादशभिः प्रोक्ता वर्माऽष्टादशभिर्मतम् ।
वर्णैर्द्वादशभिर्नेत्रमस्त्रं स्यात्करणाक्षरैः ।
एवमङ्गानि विन्यस्य चिन्तयेन्मन्त्रदेवताम् ॥ ४४

उज्ज्वलत्प्रलयानलाभसयुग्मनेत्रमनारतं
भासुरं शिखिनः शिखाभिरुदग्रदंष्ट्रमुखाम्बुजम् ।
रक्षसां भयदं विकीर्णसटाकलापविभीषणं
शङ्खचक्रकृपाणखेटकधारिणं नृहरिं भजे ॥ ४५

लक्षमेकं जपेन्मन्त्रं तद्दशांशं समाहितः ।
कपिलाज्येन जुहुयात् समिद्धे हव्यवाहने ॥ ४६
प्रागुक्ते पूजयेत्पीठे देवं संप्रोक्तवर्त्मना ।
कुर्वीत मन्त्रराजोक्तान् प्रयोगान्मनुनाऽमुना ।
विशेषात् क्षुद्रभूतादिनाशनोऽयं मनुः स्मृतः ॥ ४७
पाशः शक्तिर्नरहरिरङ्कुशो वर्म फट् मनुः
षडक्षरो नरहरेः कथितः सर्वकामदः ॥ ४८
ऋषिर्ब्रह्मा समुद्दिष्टः पङ्क्तिश्छन्द उदाहृतम् ।
देवता नरसिंहोऽस्य षड्बीजैरङ्गकल्पना ॥ ४९

चेत् सत्यम् । तत्राङ्गकरणे पदविभेदेनैव अङ्गकरणाद् दंष्ट्राय तत्रैव शिरोऽन्तस्य समाप्तिः । शिखा तु अग्निनेत्रायेत्याद्येकादशभिः । मन्त्रे तु दंष्ट्रायाऽग्नीति सन्धिरेवेति न दोषः ॥ ४०॥४१॥४२॥४३॥४४ ॥

रक्षसां भयदमिति विनियोगोक्तिर्ज्ञेया । सटाकलापं स्कन्धकेशरसमूहम् । "सटा जटाकेसरयोः" इति कोशः । वासावृध्वोद्दामाधस्तनं यावदायुधध्यानम् । ॥ ४६॥४७ ॥

लक्ष्मीनृसिंहमन्त्रमाह पाश इति । पाशः आं । शक्तिर्मायाबीजम् । नरहरिर्नृसिंह-बीजम् । अङ्कुशः क्रों । वर्म हुं । फट् स्वरूपम् । क्षौं बीजं माया शक्तिः । सर्वकामद इत्यनेन विनियोग उक्तः ॥ ४८॥४९ ॥

कोपाद्दोलोलजिह्वं विवृतनिजमुखं सोमसूर्य्याग्निनेत्रं
पादादानाभि रक्तप्रभमुपरि सितं भिन्नदैत्येन्द्रगात्रम् ।
चक्रं शङ्खं सपाशाङ्कुशकुलिशगदादारणान्युद्वहन्तम्
भीमं तीक्ष्णोग्रदंष्ट्रं मणिमयविविधाकल्पमीडे नृसिंहम् ॥ ५०

ऋतुलक्षं जपेदेनं घृतेन जुहुयात्ततः ।
तत्सहस्रं समिद्धेऽग्नौ तोषयेद्द्रविणैर्गुरुम् ॥ ५१

अर्चाप्रागीरिते पीठे मूर्त्तिं मूलेन कल्पयेत् ।
अङ्गावृतेर्बहिश्चक्रं शङ्खं पाशाङ्कुशौ पुनः ॥ ५२

वज्रं कौमोदकीं खड्गखेटौ पत्त्रेषु पूजयेत् ।
इन्द्राद्यानेतदस्त्राणि पूजयेदात्मवान् सुधीः ॥ ५३

एवं कृत्वा पुरश्चर्यां मन्त्रेणाऽनेन मन्त्रवित् ।
प्रयोगान् कल्पनिर्दिष्टान् कुर्य्यात् स्वस्य परस्य च ॥ ५४

आयुधध्यानं तु दक्षाधूर्ध्वयोराद्ये तदधोऽधस्थयोरन्योन्ये इति । एवं क्रमेण चतुर्थाभ्यां दक्षवामाभ्यां दारणमुद्रा । तल्लक्षणं तु ।

मिथः संसृष्टसंमुख्योऽङ्गुलयो ऋज्वधोऽग्रकाः ।
सव्यानपरलाङ्गुष्ठौ मुद्रेयं दारणा मता ॥ इति ।

ईडे स्तुवे । ईड् स्तुताविति धातुः ॥ ५० ॥

ऋतुलक्षं षड्लक्षम् । तत्सहस्रं षट्सहस्रम् ॥ ५१ ॥ ५२ ॥ ५३ ॥

एवं कृत्वा पुरश्चर्यामिति । अत्र सर्वमन्त्राणां साधारणपुरश्चरणविधानमुच्यते । तत्र पुरश्चरणशब्दार्थो वायवीयसंहितायाम्—

साधनं मूलमन्त्रस्य पुरश्चरणमुच्यते ।
पुरतश्चरणीयत्वाद्विनियोगाख्यकर्मणाम् ॥
पुरतो विनियोगस्य चरणाद्वा तथोदितम् ॥ इति ।

अगस्त्यसंहितायामपि—

अथ वक्ष्ये विधानानि पौरश्चरणिके विधौ ।
विना न येन सिद्धः स्यान्मन्त्रो वर्षशतैरपि ॥
तत् पुरश्चरणं नाम मन्त्रसिद्ध्यर्थमात्मनः ।
यथोक्तं नियमं कृत्वा स्वकल्पोक्तजपस्य हि ॥

करणं द्विजयागान्तं प्रोक्तं देशिकसत्तमैः ॥ इति ॥

मन्त्रतन्त्रप्रकाशेऽपि—

धर्मार्थकाममोक्षेषु शास्त्रमार्गेण योजनम् ।
सिद्धमन्त्रस्य संप्रोक्तो विनियोगो विचक्षणैः ॥
पुरश्चरणपूर्वोऽसौ विनियोगो मनोर्मतः ।
फलाय मन्त्रसेवाया राजसेवा यथा तथा ॥
चरणात्पूर्वसेवाऽसौ पुरश्चरणमुच्यते ॥ इति ।

तथा—सितैकविधहैमन्तशाल्यन्नं स्त्रीयसञ्चितम् ॥
अशूद्रावहतं पद्‌भ्यामनुत्तोल्य च यद्धृतम् ।
दधि क्षीरं घृतं गव्यं ऐक्षवं गुडवर्जितम् ॥
तिलाश्चैव सिता मुद्गाः कन्दः केमुकवर्जितः ।
नारिकेलफलं चैव कदलं लवली तथा ॥
आम्रमामलकं चैव पनसं च हरीतकी ।
व्रतान्तरे प्रशस्तं च हविष्यं मन्यते बुधः ॥
अवैष्णवमसत्यं च यदशस्तं व्रतान्तरे ।
त्याज्यमेवात्र तत्सर्वं यदीच्छेत् सिद्धिमात्मनः ॥
क्षारं च लवणं मांसं गृञ्जनं कांस्यभोजनम् ।
माषाढकीमसूरांश्च कोद्रवांश्चणकानपि ॥
ताम्बूलं च द्विभुक्तं च दुःसंवासं [भाषं] प्रमत्तताम् ।
श्रुतिस्मृतिविरुद्धं च जपं रात्रौ च वर्जयेत् ॥ इति ॥

तथा—मनःसंहरणं शौचं मौनं मन्त्रार्थचिन्तनम् ।
अव्यग्रत्वमनिर्वेदो जपसम्पत्तिहेतवः ॥ इति ॥

तथा—भूशय्या ब्रह्मचारित्वं मौनं चर्य्यानसूयिता ।
नित्यं त्रिषवणस्नानं क्षुद्रकर्मविवर्जनम् ॥
नित्यपूजा नित्यदानं देवतास्तुतिकीर्त्तनम् ।
नैमित्तिकार्चनं चैव विश्वासो गुरुदेवयोः ॥
जपनिष्ठा द्वादशैते धर्माः स्युर्मन्त्रसिद्धिदाः । इति ॥

तथा—स्त्रीशूद्रपतितव्रात्यनास्तिकोच्छिष्टभाषणम् ।
असत्यभाषणं जिह्मभाषणं दरिवर्जयेत् ॥
सत्यैरपि न भाषेत जपहोमार्चनादिषु ।

अपवित्रकरो नग्नः शिरसि प्रावृतोऽपि वा ॥

वाङ्मनःकर्मभिर्नित्यं निस्पृहो वनितादिषु ।
वर्जयेद् गीतवाद्यादिश्रवणं नृत्यदर्शनम् ॥
ताम्बूलं गन्धलेपं च पुष्पधारणमेव च ।
मैथुनं तत्कथालापं तद्गोष्ठीः परिवर्जयेत् ॥
कौटिल्यं क्षौरमभ्यङ्गमनिवेदितभोजनम् ।
असङ्कल्पितकृत्यं च वर्जयेन् मर्दनादिकम् ॥
त्यजेदुष्णोदकस्नानं सुगन्धामलकादिकम् ।
शिरोऽङ्गं पञ्चगव्येन पावयेद्वहिरन्तरम् ॥
स्नायाच्च पञ्चगव्येन केवलामलकेन वा ।
शक्तौ त्रिषवणस्नानमन्यथा सकृदाचरेत् ॥ इति ॥

तथा—अपवित्रकरो नग्नः शिरसि प्रावृतोऽपि वा ।
प्रलपन् वा जपेद्यावत् तावन्निष्फलमुच्यते ॥
सकृदुच्चरिते शब्दे प्रणवं समुदीरयेत् ।
प्रोक्ते पामरशब्देऽपि प्राणायामं सकृच्चरेत् ॥
बहुप्रलापे चावश्यं न्यस्याऽङ्गानि ततो जपेत् ।
क्षुतेऽप्येवं तथाऽस्पृश्यस्थानानां स्पर्शने तथा ॥ इति ।

वायवीयसंहितायामपि—
उष्णीषी कञ्चुकी नग्नो मुक्तकेशोऽङ्गनावृतः ।
अपवित्रकरोऽशुद्धः प्रलपन्न जपेत् क्वचित् ॥
असंवृतौ करौ कृत्वा शिरसा प्रावृतोऽपि वा ।
चिन्ताव्याकुलचित्तो वा क्रुद्धो भ्रान्तः क्षुधान्वितः ॥
अनासनः शयानो वा गच्छन्नुत्थित एव वा ।
रथ्यायामशिवस्थाने न जपेत्तिमिरान्तरे ॥
उपानद्गूढपादो वा यानशय्यागतस्तथा ।
प्रसार्य न जपेत् पादावुत्कटासन एव वा ॥
पतितानामन्त्यजानां दर्शने भाषिते श्रुते ।
क्षुतेऽधोवायुगमने जृम्भणे जपमुत्सृजेत् ॥
प्राप्तावाचम्य चैतेषां प्राणायामं षडङ्गकम् ।
कृत्वा सम्यग् जपेच्छेषं यद्वा सूर्यादिदर्शनम् ॥

मार्जारं कुक्कुटं क्रौञ्चं श्वानं गृध्रं खरं कपिम्।
दृष्ट्वाऽऽचम्य चरेत्कर्म स्पृष्ट्वा स्नानं विधीयते॥
एवमादींश्च नियमान् पुरश्चरणकृच्चरेत्॥ इति॥
क्रोधं मदं क्षुतं त्रीणि निष्ठीवनविजृम्भणे।
दर्शनं श्वस्य नीचानां वर्जयेज्जपकर्मणि॥
आचामेत् सम्भवे त्वेषां स्मरेद्वा मां त्वया सह।
ज्योतींषि च प्रपश्येद्वा कुर्याद्वा प्राणसंयमम्॥ इति॥
एवमुक्तविधानेन विलम्बत्वरितं विना।
उक्तसंख्याजपं कुर्य्यात् पुरश्चरणसिद्धये॥
देवतागुरुमन्त्राणामैक्यं सम्भावयन्धिया।
जपेदेकमनाः प्रातःकालान्मध्यन्दिनावधि॥
जपाङ्गानां दशांशेन विधेयः सिद्धिमिच्छता।
यत्संख्यायां समारब्धं तत्कर्त्तव्यमहर्निशम्॥
यदि न्यूनाधिकं कुर्य्याद् व्रतभ्रष्टो भवेन्नरः।
प्रजपेदुक्तसंख्यायाश्चतुर्गुणजपं कलौ॥ इति॥

अन्यत्रापि—कृते जपस्तु कल्पोक्तस्त्रेतायां द्विगुणो जपः।
द्वापरे त्रिगुणः प्रोक्तश्चतुर्गुणजपः कलौ॥ इति॥

मन्त्रतन्त्रप्रकाशे नारायणाष्टाक्षरे—
जपेन्निरन्तरं विद्वानष्टलक्षाण्यतन्द्रितः।
मन्त्रसिद्धिरियं प्रोक्ता युगे त्वाद्ये मनीषिभिः॥
द्वितीये द्विगुणा तस्मात्तृतीये त्रिगुणा तु सा।
कलौ चतुर्गुणा प्रोक्ता मुनिभिर्नारदादिभिः॥ इति॥
संख्यापूर्त्तौ निजैर्द्रव्यैर्जपसंख्यादशांशतः।
यथोक्तकुण्डे जुहुयाद्यथाविधि समाहितः॥
अथवा प्रत्यहं जप्त्वा जुहुयात्तद्दशांशतः।
ततो होमदशांशं तु जले सम्पूज्य देवताम्॥
तर्पयामीति मन्त्रान्ते प्रोक्ताऽद्भिर्मूर्ध्नि तर्पयेत्।
स्वाभिषेकावमर्षौ च सूर्य्यार्घ्यं जलपानकम्॥
प्रणामं मन्त्रतः कुर्यात् पूर्वपूर्वदशांशतः।
तदन्ते महतीं पूजां कुर्याद् ब्राह्मणभोजनम्॥

गुरुं सन्तोषयेदेवं मन्त्राः सिध्यन्ति मन्त्रिणः ।
इत्थं पुरश्चरणतः प्रसन्ना देवता भवेत् ॥
दशाङ्गोपासनं भक्त्या पुरश्चरणमुच्यते ।
जपो होमस्तर्पणं च पूजा ब्राह्मणभोजनम् ॥
पूर्वपूर्वदशांशेन कुर्यात्पञ्चाङ्गसंयुतम् ।
यद्यदङ्गं विहीयेत तत्संख्याद्विगुणो जपः ॥
कर्त्तव्यश्चाऽङ्गसिद्ध्यर्थं तदशक्तेन भक्तितः । इति ॥

मन्त्रतन्त्रप्रकाशेऽपि—

असम्भवे तु होमस्य होमात् स्याद् द्विगुणो जपः । इति ॥

अन्यत्रापि—होमकर्मण्यशक्तानां विप्राणां द्विगुणो जपः ।
इतरेषां तु वर्णानां त्रिगुणादिः समीरितः ॥ इति ॥
एकमङ्गं विहीयेत ततो नेष्टमवाप्नुयात् ।
अङ्गहीनं भवेद्यद्यत्तत्तन्नेष्टार्थसाधकम् ॥
सर्वथा भोजयेद्विप्रान् कृतसाङ्गत्वसिद्धये ।
विप्राराधनमात्रेण व्यङ्गं साङ्गं भवेत् सदा ॥
न्यूनातिरिक्तकर्माणि न फलन्ति मनोरथान् ।
तान्येव पूर्णतां यान्ति समस्तानि कृतानि च ॥
अतो यत्नेन विदुषो भोजयेत् सर्वकर्मसु ।
यानि यान्यपि कर्माणि हीयन्ते द्विजभोजनैः ।
निरर्थकानि तानि स्युर्बीजान्यूषरगाणि च ॥ इति ॥

कुलप्रकाशतन्त्रेऽपि—

संसारे दुःखभूयिष्ठे यदीच्छेत् सिद्धिमात्मनः ।
पञ्चाङ्गोपासनेनैव मन्त्रजापी सुखं व्रजेत् ॥
पूजा त्रैकालिकी नित्यं जपस्तर्पणमेव च ।
होमो ब्राह्मणभुक्तिश्च पुरश्चरणमुच्यते ॥
यद्यदङ्गं विहीयेत तत्संख्याद्विगुणं जपम् ।
कुर्वीत त्रिचतुःपञ्चसंख्यया साधकः प्रिये ॥
कुर्वीत साङ्गसिद्ध्यर्थं तदशक्तेन भक्तितः ।
एकमङ्गं विहीयेत मन्त्रान्नेष्टमवाप्नुयात् ॥
अन्नैश्चतुर्विधैर्देवि पदार्थैः षड्रसान्वितैः ।

सुभोजितेषु विप्रेषु सर्वं हि सफलं भवेत् ॥
सम्यक्सिद्धैकमन्त्रस्य पञ्चाङ्गोपासनेन हि।
सर्वे मन्त्राश्च सिध्यन्ति तत्प्रभावात् कुलेश्वरि ॥ इति ॥

अन्यत्र विशेषः—

अशक्तानां होमे निगमरसनागेन्द्रगुणितो
जपः कार्य्यश्चेति द्विजनृपविशामाहुरपरे।
स होमस्तेदेषां सम इह जपो होमरहितो
य उक्तो वर्णानां स खलु विहितस्तच्चलदृशाम् ॥
यं वर्णमाश्रितो यः शूद्रः स च तत्तत्तभ्रुवां विहितम्।
विदधीत जपं विधिवच्छ्रद्धावान् भक्तिभारनम्रतनुः ॥ इति ॥
अथवाऽन्यप्रकारेण पुरश्चरणमुच्यते।
ग्रहणेऽर्कस्य चेन्दोर्वा शुचिः पूर्वमुपोषितः ॥
नद्यां समुद्रगामिन्यां नाभिमात्रेऽम्भसि स्थितः।
ग्रहणादि तु मोक्षान्तं जपेन्मन्त्रं समाहितः ॥
अनन्तरं तद्दशांशक्रमाद्धोमादिकं चरेत्।
तदन्ते मन्त्रसिद्ध्यर्थं गुरुं सम्पूज्य तोषयेत् ॥
ततश्च मन्त्रसिद्धिः स्याद् देवता च प्रसीदति।
अथवा देवतारूपं गुरुं भक्त्या प्रतोषयेत् ॥
पुरश्चरणहीनोऽपि मन्त्रः सिद्धेन्न संशयः।
एवं साधितमन्त्रस्तु काम्यकर्माण्यथाचरेत् ॥ इति ॥

अन्यत्रापि—उपदेशस्य सामर्थ्याच्छ्रीगुरोश्च प्रसादतः।
मन्त्रप्रभावाद्भक्त्या च मन्त्रसिद्धिः प्रजायते ॥
सिद्धमन्त्राद् गुरोर्लब्ध्वा मन्त्रसिद्धिं च भावयेत्।
पूर्वजन्मकृताभ्यासान् मन्त्रः शीघ्रेण सिद्धिदः ॥ इति ॥

अन्यत्र तु—त्रिकालं गन्धपुष्पाद्यैर्याऽर्च्यते देवता निशि।
पुरश्चरणकृत्येन विनैवाऽसौ प्रसीदति ॥ इति ॥

तथा वैशम्पायनसंहितायाम्—

पुरश्चरणसम्पन्नो मन्त्रो हि फलदायकः।
किं होमैः किं जपैश्चैव किं मन्त्रन्यासविस्तरैः ॥
रहस्यानां च मन्त्राणां यदि न स्यात् पुरस्क्रिया।

पुरश्क्रिया तु मन्त्राणां प्रधानं बीजमुच्यते ॥
व्याधिग्रस्तो यथा देही सर्वकर्मसु न क्षमः ।
पुरश्चरणहीनोऽयं तथा मन्त्रोऽपि कीर्त्तितः ॥
येषां जपे च होमे च संख्या नोक्ता मनीषिभिः ।
तेषामष्टसहस्राणि संख्योक्ता जपहोमयोः ॥
यस्मिंश्च निगदेनैव मन्त्रे संख्याऽभिधीयते ।
तत्र सर्वंत्र मन्त्राणां संख्यावृद्धिर्युगक्रमात् ॥
कल्पोक्ता च कृते संख्या त्रेतायां द्विगुणा भवेत् ।
द्वापरे त्रिगुणा प्रोक्ता कलौ संख्या चतुर्गुणा ॥
अनुक्ते तु हविर्द्रव्ये तिलाज्यं हविरुच्यते ।
शाकं मूलं फलं भैक्ष्यं हविष्यं सक्तवोऽथवा ॥
अथवा क्षीरमात्रं स्यात् पुरश्चर्त्तुश्च वृत्तये ।
न सेवेत स्त्रियं मांसं मधु वा मन्त्रसाधकः ॥
एतानि सेवमानस्य न सिध्यति पुरस्क्रिया ।
स्त्रियं शूद्रं न भाषेत पुरश्चरणकृत्वरः ॥
जपं च प्रातरारभ्य कुर्यान् मध्यन्दिनावधि ।
असत्यं नाभिभाषेत नेन्द्रियाणि प्रलोभयेत् ॥
नैरन्तर्यविधिः प्रोक्तो न दिनं व्यतिलङ्घयेत् ।
दिवसातिक्रमात् पुंसो मन्त्रसिद्धिर्भवेन् न हि ॥
शक्तिहीनश्च यो मन्त्रो न सिध्यति कदाचन ।
यावत्संख्यं जपेदह्नि पूर्वस्मिंस्तावदेव तु ॥
दिनान्तरेऽपि प्रजपेदन्यथा सिद्धिरोधकृत् ।
शिवस्य सन्निधाने च सूर्याग्न्योश्च गुरोरपि ॥
दीपस्य ज्वलितस्यापि जपकर्म प्रशस्यते ।
शयनं कुशशय्यायां विन्यसेच्छुचिवस्त्रधृक् ॥
तद्वासः क्षालयेन् नित्यमन्यथा विघ्नभाग्भवेत् ।
स्नानं त्रिषवणं प्रोक्तमशक्त्या द्विः सकृत्तु वा ॥
अस्नातस्य फलं नास्ति न चाऽतर्पयतः पितॄन् ।
नाऽप्यतर्पयतो देवान् नाऽसत्यमपि जल्पतः ॥
नैकवासा जपेन् मन्त्रं बहुवस्त्रावृतोऽपि वा ।

विपर्यासं न कुर्याच्च कदाचिदपि मोहतः ॥
उपर्यधो बहिर्वस्त्रे पुरश्चरणकृद्बुधः ।
विनियोगविधाने तु भवेदनियमः क्वचित् ॥
पुरश्चरणकार्येषु वर्जयेत्तं प्रयत्नतः ।
कृत्वा मन्त्रजपं मन्त्री पुरस्काराय संयतः ॥
दशांशं जुहुयादग्नौ यथोक्तविधिना बुधः ।
यद्वा जपचतुर्थांशं स्वाहान्तं मन्त्रमुच्चरन् ॥
ततो होमदशांशं तु स्वाहान्तं तर्पयेज्जलैः ।
तर्पणस्य दशांशेन नमोऽन्तं मन्त्रमुद्धरेत् ॥
अभिषिञ्चेत् स्वमूर्द्धानं जलैः कुम्भाख्यमुद्रया ।
एवंविधविधानेन कृतमन्त्रपुरस्क्रियः ॥
विनियोगसमारम्भं यथायथमथाचरेत् । इति ।

गोपालमन्त्रे विशेषस्तर्पणे तत्रैवोक्तः—

इह गोपालमन्त्राणां तर्पणं होमसंख्यया ।
समं ज्ञेयं तु सर्वेषामित्यागमविदो विदुः ॥ इति ॥

अन्यत्रापि—तर्पयेत्तावदन्येषां मनूनां हुतसंख्यया ।
तर्पणं विहितं नित्यम् । इति ॥

अथारब्धपुरश्चरणमध्ये सूतकादिकं चेत् निपतति तथापि सङ्कल्पितस्य पुरश्चरणस्य समाप्तिरेव कर्त्तव्या । तथाच विष्णुः—

व्रतयज्ञविवाहेषु श्राद्धे होमेऽर्चने जपे ।
प्रारब्धे सूतकं न स्यादनारब्धे तु सूतकम् ॥ इति ।

सूतकमित्युभयं प्रारम्भश्च तत्रैवोक्तः—

प्रारम्भो वरणं यज्ञे सङ्कल्पो व्रतजापयोः ।
नान्दीमुखं विवाहादौ श्राद्धे पाकपरिक्रिया ॥ इति ॥

मन्त्रतन्त्रप्रकाशे पुरश्चरणे सर्वनियमानुक्ता—

शक्तश्चेत्सर्वमेवैतदशक्तः शक्तितो जपेत् ।
न दोषो मानसे जाप्ये सर्वदेशेऽपि सर्वदा ॥
जपनिष्ठो द्विजः श्रेष्ठः सर्वयज्ञफलं लभेत् ।
सर्वेषामेव यज्ञानां जपयज्ञः प्रशस्यते ॥
अहिंसया हि भूतानां जायतेऽसौ महाफलः ।

यज्ञानां जपयज्ञोऽहमित्याह भगवान् हरिः ॥
जपेनैव तु संसिध्येद् ब्राह्मणो नात्र संशयः ।
कुर्यादन्यन्न वा कुर्यान् मैत्रो ब्राह्मण उच्यते ॥
इत्याहुर्मुनयः शान्ता जपसिद्धा अकिञ्चनाः । इति ।

पद्मनाभीयेऽपि—यावन्तः कर्मयज्ञाः स्युः प्रदिष्टानि तपांसि च ।
सर्वे ते जपयज्ञस्य कलां नार्हन्ति षोडशीम् ॥
जपेन देवता नित्यं स्तूयमाना प्रसीदति ।
प्रसन्ना विपुलान् भोगान् दद्यान् मुक्तिं च शाश्वतीम् ॥ इति ॥

भृगुसंहितायामपि—

ये पाकयज्ञाश्चत्वारो विधियज्ञसमन्विताः ।
सर्वे ते जपयज्ञस्य कलां नार्हन्ति षोडशीम् ॥ इति ॥

नारायणीये तु— जपाशक्तस्य सर्वतः ।
मूलमन्त्राद्दशांशं स्यादङ्गादीनां जपादिकम् ।
जपात् सशक्तिर्मन्त्रः स्यात्कामदा मन्त्रदेवता ॥ इति ॥

जपलक्षणमुक्तं वायवीयसंहितायाम्—

जपः स्यादक्षरावृत्तिः स उच्चोपांशुमानसः ।
य उच्चनीचस्वरितैः शब्दैः स्पष्टपदाक्षरैः ॥
मन्त्रमुच्चारयेद्वाचा जपयज्ञः स वाचिकः ।
शनैरुच्चारयेन् मन्त्रमीषदोष्ठौ प्रचालयेत् ॥
किञ्चिच्छ्रवणयोग्यः स्यादुपांशुः स जपः स्मृतः ।
धिया यदक्षरश्रेणीं वर्णस्वरपदात्मिकाम् ॥
उच्चरेदर्थसंस्मृत्या स उक्तो मानसो जपः ।
उच्चैर्जपो विशिष्टः स्याद्यज्ञादेर्दशभिर्गुणैः ॥
उपांशुः स्याच्छतगुणः सहस्रो मानसः स्मृतः । इति ।

भृगुसंहितायामपि—

विधियज्ञाज्जपयज्ञो विशिष्टो दशभिर्गुणैः ।
उपांशुः स्याच्छतगुणः सहस्रो मानसः स्मृतः ॥ इति ।

अन्यत्र तु—न कम्पयेच्छिरो ग्रीवां जिह्वामोष्ठं न चालयेत् ।
मनसा चिन्तितं बीजं दन्तघातं न कारयेत् ॥ इति ॥

आचार्या अपि—नातिद्रुतं नातिविलम्बितं च । इति ।

रक्तोत्पलैस्त्रिमध्वक्तैः सहस्रं जुहुयान्नवैः ।

नित्यं मासाद्भवेदिष्टं वत्सराद्धनधान्यवान् ॥ ५५

रक्तैस्त्रिमधुरोपेतैः पद्मैर्भानुसहस्रकम् ।

जुहुयान्महतीं लक्ष्मीमायुर्वश्यमवाप्नुयात् ॥ ५६

मन्त्रतन्त्रप्रकाशे तु विशेषः—

अपि चान्यं प्रवक्ष्यामि मन्त्रसिद्धिकरं परम् ।

मन्त्रसाधकयोरैक्यं दुर्लभं भुवि मानवैः ॥

उक्तं साङ्कर्षणे तन्त्रे शिवेनाऽखिलवेदिना ।

आनन्दाख्ये पञ्चरात्रे शुक्राय कवये पुरा ॥

संस्कृतं पूजितं मन्त्रं दत्त्वा शिष्याय देशिकः ।

कुर्यादथ तयोरैक्यं शास्त्रदृष्टेन वर्त्मना ॥

मन्त्रं विदर्भयित्वा तु नामवर्णैर्यथाक्रमम् ।

आद्यन्ते सकलं नाम ततः प्रणवमालिखेत् ॥

स्वराः पत्रेषु संलेख्या ध्यायेत्तानमृतात्मकान् ।

भूर्जे रोचनगन्धाद्यैः पद्ममध्ये सुशोभने ॥

मृदा पवित्रयाऽऽवेष्ट्य तत् पुनः सिक्थकेन च ।

निक्षिपेन्मधुरे तत् तु मृन्मये लघुभाजने ॥

क्षीरपूर्णे नवे कुम्भे तत् क्षिपेल्लघुभाजनम् ।

धारयेद् देशिकः कुम्भमग्निकुण्डसमीपतः ॥

मन्त्रसाधकयोरैक्यसिद्ध्यर्थं जुहुयात्ततः ।

मूलमन्त्रेण मन्त्रज्ञः सहस्रं शतमेव वा ॥

कुम्भे सम्पातयेच्चैव मधुराणां त्रयं शुभम् ।

निधाय निक्षिपेत् कुम्भं शनैस्तं महदम्भसि ॥

मन्त्रसाधकयोरैक्यं भवेदेव फलप्रदम् ।

एतद्यो न विजानाति नासौ देशिक उच्यते ॥

रहस्यं कथितं चैतन् न वदेद्यस्य कस्य चित् ।

उत्तमाय तु शिष्याय प्रियपुत्राय वा वदेत् ॥ इति ॥ ५४ ॥

रक्तोत्पलैः रक्तकुवलयैः । नवैरपर्युषितैः । रक्तैः पद्मैः कोकनदैः ॥ ५५ ॥

॥ ५६ ॥

लाजांस्त्रिमधुरोपेतान् प्रातःकालेषु जुह्वतः ।
कन्यासिद्धिर्भवेत्पश्चात् कन्यायाः सदृशो भवेत् ॥ ५७

दूर्वाः पयोघृताभ्यक्ता दशोत्तरशतं सुधीः ।
अन्वहं जुहुयात्सम्यग्दीर्घमायुरवाप्नुयात् ॥ ५८

तस्य रोगाः प्रणश्यन्ति कृत्याद्रोहादिभिः सह ।
सपञ्चगव्यं जुहुयादपामार्गस्य मञ्जरीम् ॥ ५९

नित्यं सहस्रमानेन सप्ताहं विजितेन्द्रियः ।
होमोऽयं सर्वथा भूतकृत्यारोगान् प्रणाशयेत् ॥ ६०

सतिलै राज्यपामार्गहविराज्यैर्यथाक्रमम् ।
द्विसहस्रं प्रजुहुयात् क्षुद्ररोगग्रहान् जयेत् ॥ ६१

पयोऽक्तैरमृताखण्डैस्त्रिसहस्रं चतुर्दिनम् ।
अनेन विहितो होमो ग्रहज्वरविनाशनः ॥ ६२

नृसिंहशक्तिबीजे द्वे शूलि तारगते लिखेत् ।
तत्र ग्रहार्त्तं संस्थाप्य जपेन्मन्त्रं षडक्षरम् ।
आविश्य सद्यस्तं मुञ्चेद् ग्रहः क्रन्दन् भयाकुलः ॥ ६३

आलिख्याऽग्निपुरद्वयं तदुदरे शक्तिं ससाध्यां लिखेत्
षट्कोणेषु षडक्षराण्यथ मनोः किञ्जल्कसंस्थान् स्वरान् ।
पत्रेष्वष्टसु मन्त्रराजविहितान्वर्णान् क्रमाद्वेदशः
काद्यर्णैः पुनरावृतं क्षितिपुरे कोणेषु चिन्तामणिम् ॥ ६४

अमृता गुडूची । तारगते शूले इति प्रणवस्यादौ यच्छूलाकारं तत्र । जपेन्मन्त्र-मिति तदुपर्यपवेशितं ग्रहार्त्तं स्पृशन्नित्यर्थः ॥ ५७॥५८॥५९॥६०॥६१॥६२॥६३ ॥

यन्त्रमाह आलिख्येति । अग्निपुरद्वयं परस्परव्यतिभिन्नम् । मनोः षडक्षर-नृसिंहमन्त्रस्य । चिन्तामणिं नारसिंहमिति सामानाधिकरण्यम् । तेन नृसिंह-स्यैकाक्षरं भूर्जपत्रके लिखितमिदं यन्त्रं हरेदिति सम्बन्धः ।

तदुक्तं नृसिंहकल्पे—

षट्कोणबीजेन विशिष्टकर्णिकं शक्तयर्णयुक्शूलचतुष्कलाष्टकम् ।
वृतं जनन्या जगतीगृहात्मके यन्त्रं सचिन्तामणिकं विचिन्तयेत् ॥

नारसिंहमिदं यन्त्रं लिखितं भूर्जपत्रके ।
विधृतं शिरसा शीर्षरोगभूतज्वरान् हरेत् ॥ ६५
बहुनाऽत्र किमुक्तेन मन्त्रैरेतैरुदीरितैः ।
समो नास्ति मनुः कश्चिच्छापानुग्रहकारकः ॥ ६६
तारो भृगुर्वियद्भूयस्तदाद्यं वह्निदीर्घयुक् ।
पावकः कवचास्त्रान्तो मनुः सप्ताक्षरः स्मृतः ॥ ६७
अहिर्बुध्न्यो मुनिः प्रोक्तश्छन्दोऽनुष्टुबुदाहृतम् ।
देवता मुनिभिः प्रोक्ता चक्ररूपो हरिः स्वयम् ॥ ६८
आचक्राय हृदाख्यातं विचक्राय शिरः स्मृतम् ।
सुचक्राय शिखा प्रोक्ता धीचक्राय तनुच्छदम् ॥ ६९
संचक्राय स्मृतं नेत्रं ज्वालाचक्राय तत्परम् ।
षडङ्गमन्त्राः प्रत्येकं द्विठान्ता जातिसंयुताः ॥ ७०
ऐन्द्रीचक्रेण बध्नामि नमश्चक्राय ठद्वयम् ।
मन्त्रेणाऽनेन कुर्वीत दिशां प्रागादि बन्धनम् ॥ ७१
त्रैलोक्यान्ते रक्षयुगं हुं फट् स्वाहा भुवादिकः ।
अग्निप्राकारमन्त्रोऽयं रक्षार्थं पुनरात्मनः ॥ ७२

आं क्रीं च्रौं क्रों च हुं फट् च शक्तिमन्त्रः कलाष्टकम् ।
अचां युग्मानि चिन्तामणौ नृसिंहैकाक्षरो मनुः ॥ इति ॥ ६४॥६५॥६६ ॥

वाराहयन्त्रे सुदर्शनमन्त्रस्योद्दिष्टत्वात्तमाह तार इति । तारः प्रणवः । भृगुः स । वियत् ह । तदाद्यं सः । वह्नी रेफः । दीर्घ आकारः तद्युक् तेन स्रा । पावको रेफः । कवचं च हुं । अस्त्रं फट् । सं बीजम् । हुं शक्तिः । तत् परमस्त्रम् । द्विठान्ताः स्वाहान्ताः ॥ ६७॥६८॥६९॥७० ॥

प्रागादिदिशामित्यनेन ऐन्द्रीचक्रेण बध्नामीत्यस्मिन् मन्त्रे ऐन्द्रीपदस्थाने आग्नेयीत्यादीनां पदानामूहः कार्य इत्युक्तं भवति । एवं दशस्वपि दिक्षु । तदुक्तम्—ऐन्द्रीं समारभ्य दिशस्त्वधस्तादन्तं समुक्त्वा क्रमशो दशानाम् ।
चक्रेण बध्नामि नमस्तथोक्त्वा चक्राय शीर्षं च दिशां प्रबन्धः ॥ इति ॥ ७१ ॥
त्रैलोक्यान्त इत्यत्र मन्त्रे त्रैलोक्यपदं द्वितीयान्तं ज्ञेयम् । रक्षेति क्रिया श्रवणात् ।

प्राकारं तेन कुर्वीत मन्त्रेण मनुवित्तमः ।
सितरक्ताञ्जनप्रख्यं तारं मूर्धनि विन्यसेत् ॥ ७३

अन्यानग्निनिभान्वर्णान् भ्रुवोर्मध्ये मुखे हृदि ।
गुह्यजानुपदद्वन्द्वसन्धिषु क्रमशो न्यसेत् ॥ ७४

कल्पान्तार्कप्रकाशं त्रिभुवनमखिलं तेजसा पूरयन्तं
रक्ताक्षं पिङ्गकेशं रिपुकुलभयदं भीमदंष्ट्राट्टहासम् ।
चक्रं शङ्खं गदाब्जे पृथुतरमुषलं चापपाशाङ्कुशान् स्वैः
बिभ्राणं दोर्भिराद्यं मनसि मुररिपुं भावयेच्चक्रसंज्ञम् ॥ ७५

अर्कलक्षं जपेन्मन्त्रं जुहुयात्तत्सहस्रकम् ।
तिलैः समर्षपैः पद्मैर्बिल्वैर्दुग्धौदनैः क्रमात् ॥ ७६

विष्णोः सम्पूजयेत्पीठे मूर्त्तिं मूलेन कल्पयेत् ।
अङ्गानि पूर्वमभ्यर्च्य चक्राद्यस्त्राणि तद्बहिः ॥ ७७

तदुक्तम्-- त्रैलोक्यं रक्षरक्षेति हुं फट्स्वाहेति चोदितः ।
तारादिकोऽयं मन्त्रः स्यादग्निप्राकारसंज्ञकः ॥ इति ॥ ७२ ॥

कुर्वीतेति । मनसा अग्निप्राकारं चिन्तयन् आत्मनः प्रदक्षिणं परिभ्रमदुदकं क्षिपेदिति परमगुरवः । उक्तञ्च--

आत्मनः परितो वह्निप्राकारं त्राणनाय च ।
भूतप्रेतपिशाचेभ्यो विधाय तदनन्तरम् ॥
अद्भिः पुष्पाक्षतैश्चैव वह्निबीजास्त्रसन्वितैः ।
प्रक्षिपेत् परितो मन्त्री भयविघ्ननिवृत्तये ॥ इति ।

सितेति । अकारोकारमकाराणां क्रमेण ध्यानम् । पदद्वन्द्वसन्धिषु अन्त्यवर्णन्यासः ॥ ७३॥७४ ॥

कल्पान्तेति । चापं सशरं ज्ञेयम् । तदुक्तम्--

दोर्भिश्चक्रदरौ गदाब्जकुलिशांश्चास्त्रं च पाशाङ्कुशौ ॥ इति ।

अतएव पूजायां सशरं धनुरिति वक्ष्यति । आयुधध्यानं दक्षोर्ध्वाभ्यामाद्ये तदधराधराभ्यामन्य इति । अत्र ध्यानानन्तरं चक्रमुद्रां प्रदर्शयेत् ॥ ७५ ॥

अर्कलक्षं द्वादशलक्षम् । क्रमात् तत्सहस्रं द्वादशसहस्रं न तु प्रत्येकम् । तिलैरिति प्रत्येकं चतुर्विंशतिशतानि । विष्णोः पीठे नारायणाष्टाक्षरोक्ते ।

चक्रं शङ्खं गदां पद्मं मुषलं सशरं धनुः ।
पाशाङ्कुशौ दलाग्रेषु लक्ष्म्याद्याः पूजयेत्ततः ॥ ७८

लक्ष्मीं सरस्वतीं पश्चाद्रतिं प्रीतिं ततः परम् ।
कीर्त्तिकान्ती तुष्टिपुष्टी सर्वा एताः स्मृता द्विशः ॥ ७९

पीतरक्तासितश्यामा इन्द्राद्यस्त्राणि तद्बहिः ।
इति सिद्धे मनौ प्रोक्तप्रयोगान् कर्त्तुमर्हति ॥ ८०

आत्मनो वा परार्थं वा दृष्टादृष्टफलप्रदान् ।
दूर्वाहोमो विधातव्यो दीर्घमायुरभीप्सता ॥ ८१

श्रीकामो जुहुयात्पद्मैः फुल्लैराज्यपरिप्लुतैः ।
मेधाकामेन होतव्यं प्रसूनैर्ब्रह्मवृक्षजैः ॥ ८२

दिनत्रयं यो जुहोति गुलिकाः पुरुनिर्मिताः ।
अष्टोत्तरसहस्रेण स जयेन्निखिलापदः ॥ ८३

गव्येनाज्येन गोसिद्ध्यै जुहुयाद्दिवसत्रयम् ।
उदुम्बरसमिद्धोमः पुत्रदायी भवेन्नृणाम् ॥ ८४

प्रलयाग्निसमं चक्रं यस्य मूर्धनि चिन्तयेत् ।
सप्ताहाज्ज्वरमूर्च्छार्त्तो मण्डलान्मृतिमेति सः ॥ ८५

अभ्यर्च्येति केसरेष्विति शेषः । तद्बहिरिति पत्रमध्ये । सशरं धनुरित्येकम् । दलाग्रेष्विति उत्तरेण सम्बध्यते । लक्ष्म्याद्या इत्युत्तरपटलोक्तबीजाद्याः । द्विश इति । आद्ये द्वे पीते । रतिप्रीती रक्ते । उपान्त्ये सिते । अन्त्ये श्यामे । प्रयोगान् कर्त्तुमर्हतीत्यनेनैतदुक्तं भवति । ॐ सुदर्शनाय विद्महे चक्रराजाय धीमहि तन्नश्चक्रः प्रचोदयात् । अस्य प्रयोगेषु मूलमन्त्रदशांशजप इति । केचिन् महाचक्राय धीमहीति पठन्ति । अपेक्षितार्थद्योतनिकायां तु नमश्चक्राय विद्महे सहस्रज्वालाय धीमहि तन्नो निवारितः प्रचोदयादिति गायत्री पठिता । पक्षत्रयमपि साम्प्रदायिकमेव । यथागुरूपदेशं च निर्णयः । दीर्घमायुरिति मृत्युञ्जयादित्वम् ॥ ७६॥७७॥७८॥७९॥८०॥८१ ॥

श्रीकाम इति श्रीबीजादित्वम् । मेधाकामेनेति वाग्भवादित्वं ज्ञेयम् । जुहोतीति । त्रिदिनमिति । चतुर्दिनं वा ।
"जुहुयात्त्रिदिनं गुग्गुलगुलिकासहस्रकं चाष्टकं च सन्त्रितमः त्रिदिनं चतुर्दिनं वा"

अकारादिस्वरावीतं याहियाहिपदावृतम् ।
सकारं चिन्तयेच्छत्रोर्मूर्धन्युच्चाटमावहेत् ॥ ८६

अनेन विधिना शत्रुर्मण्डलान्मृत्युभाग्भवेत् ।
शरच्चन्द्रनिभं सार्णं सुधाधाराभिवर्षिणम् ॥ ८७

स्मरेन्मूर्धनि यस्याऽसौ स जीवेद्विगतामयः ।
आत्मानं चक्रनाभिस्थं ध्यात्वा मन्त्रममुं जपेत् ॥ ८८

एकोऽपि रणभूमिस्थो जयेत् प्रत्यर्थिनो बहून् ।
अपामार्गस्य समिधो जुहुयादयुतावधि ॥ ८९

रक्षोभूतपिशाचादिपीड़ा तस्य न जायते ।
निर्गुण्डीसर्जकनकश्वेतकिंशुकसम्भवैः ॥ ९०

समिद्वरैः कृतो होमः क्षुद्ररोगग्रहापहः ।
अपामार्गस्य समिधः सर्पिर्मध्ये शृतश्चरुः ॥ ९१

साज्यमेतानि जुहुयादष्टोत्तरशतं पृथक् ।
साधकाय पुनर्दद्याच्चरुं सम्पातसाधितम् ॥ ९२

अभिचारकृता द्रोहास्तस्य नश्यन्ति सर्वथा ।
अपामार्गस्य समिधः पञ्चगव्यपरिप्लुताः ॥ ९३

इत्युक्तेः । पुरुर्गुग्गुलः । निखिलापद इति । नृसिंहबीजादित्वम् । मूर्च्छाभी भवेदिति शेषः ॥ ८२॥८३॥८४॥८५ ॥

अकारादीति । अकारादीनां वायुबीजयोगो ज्ञेयः । तेन यंयामित्यादि उच्चाटमावहेदिति दशाहत इति ज्ञेयम् । तदुक्तमाचार्यैः —

दशाहतोऽसौ प्रतिबाध्यते रिपुः । इति ॥ ८६ ॥

अनेन विधिनेत्यनेन प्रयोगान्तरमपि तादृशं सूचितम् । यदाहुराचार्याः—

सान्तं वायसवर्णं शत्रोः शिरसि स्मरेच्च सप्ताहम् ।

उच्चाटयति चिप्रं मारयते वा धियोऽस्य नैश्चिल्यात् ॥ इति ॥

शरच्चन्द्रनिभमित्यनेन सितं वं वामित्यादिवीतमिति ज्ञेयम् । सार्णं सकाराक्षरं जपेदिति । सह नमो स्वार नाश हुं फट् पक्षेति पादत्रयान्तम् ॐ इति चतुःपादान्तगीतामन्त्रादित्वं ज्ञेयम् ॥ ८७॥८८॥८९ ॥

अपामार्गस्येति । फट्स्थाने वषट्कारो ज्ञेयः । सर्जः शालः । कनको

जुहुयादयुतं मन्त्री दिशासु बलिमाहरेत् ।
दध्योदनेन मनुना क्षुद्ररोगादिशान्तये ॥ ९४

क्षीरवृक्षसमित्क्षीरहविराज्यैः पृथक् पृथक् ।
चतुःसहस्रं होतव्यं शान्तिः स्यात्सर्वतोमुखी ॥ ९५

दक्षिणोत्तरगं मन्त्री चक्रयुग्मं समालिखेत् ।
षडादि विलिखेन्मध्ये मन्त्रवर्णान् षडक्षिषु ॥ ९६

मध्यं पीतं कोणषट्कं रक्तं श्यामलमन्तरम् ।
नेमिं श्वेतां लसद्वह्निशिखाभिरुपशोभिताम् ॥ ९७

पार्थिवं मण्डलं बाह्ये कुर्यादेवं यथाविधि ।
रक्ततोयेन सम्पूर्णं कुम्भं सौम्ये प्रविन्यसेत् ॥ ९८

आवाह्य पूजयेत्तस्मिंश्चक्रात्मानं जनार्दनम् ।
दक्षिणे मण्डले कुर्याद्धोमकर्म विधानवित् ॥ ९९

धत्तूरः । क्षुद्राः स्तम्भाद्याः षड्रोगाः प्रसिद्धाः । ग्रहाः अष्टादश महाग्रहाः सप्त व्यन्तराः । पृथगिति प्रत्येकम् । चरुं दद्यादिति होमचरुशेषं मन्त्रजप्तञ्च । सम्पातसाधितमिति प्रतिद्रव्यसम्पातसाधितम् ।

हुत्वा संपातितं शेषं तज्जप्तं प्राशयेच्चरोः । इति नारायणीये उक्तेः ।

सर्वघेत्यनेन तद्भस्मानुलेपः ।

क्षुद्रग्रहामयध्वंसि तद्भूत्या चानुलेपनम् । इति तत्रैवोक्तेः ।

मनुना वक्ष्यमाणबलिमन्त्रेण ॥ ८९॥९०॥९१॥९२॥९३॥९४ ॥

क्षीरेति समिद्द्रव्यैः । पृथक् पृथगिति प्रत्येकम् ॥ ९५ ॥

दक्षिणोत्तरगमित्यारभ्य न संशय इत्यन्तमेकः प्रयोगः । चक्रयुग्ममिति । षडारं परिधिनेमिसहितम् । मन्त्रवर्णानिति सुदर्शनमन्त्रवर्णान् । अन्तरमिति षडारमध्यः । नेमिमिति चक्रपरिधिरेखाम् । वह्निशिखाभिरिति । अग्निज्वालाकारैव वक्ररेखा कार्या इत्यर्थः । तदुक्तम्—

विरचितशिखिरेखाकुलम् । इति ॥ ९६॥९७ ॥

पार्थिवमिति । कृष्णवर्णं । तदुक्तं नारायणीये—

बहिः कृष्णवर्णरेखा च पार्थिवो । इति ।

कुर्यादेवं यथाविधीत्यनेनैतत् पञ्चम्यादि पूर्णान्ततिथिषु कर्त्तव्यमिति सूचितम् ।

क्रमात् सर्पिरपामार्गैस्तण्डुलैः सर्षपैस्तिलैः ।
पायसैर्गव्यसर्पिर्भ्यां षड्विंशत्यधिकं शतम् ॥ १००
जुहुयादेधिते वह्नौ प्रतिद्रव्यं विधानवित् ।
सम्पातयेत् कुम्भतोये पूजिते सौम्यमण्डले ॥ १०१
प्रस्थार्धं चरुणा पिण्डं कृत्वा तस्मिन्विनिक्षिपेत् ।
बाह्ये बलिप्रदानार्थं तदर्धमवशेषयेत् ॥ १०२
स्नातं विशुद्धवस्त्राद्यैः साध्यमानीय तं पुनः ।
दक्षिणे स्थापयेन्मन्त्री कुम्भाग्निभ्यामनन्तरम् ॥ १०३

तदुक्तम्—पूर्वाह्णे माङ्गल्यविवाहयात्रासपौष्टिकशान्तिकर्म कार्यम् । इति

तथा—हस्तादि पञ्चनक्षत्रे रेवत्याश्विनमुत्तरम् ।
श्रविष्ठा रोहिणी पुष्या शान्तिकार्येषु पूजितम् ॥ इति ॥

रक्ततोयेनेति लाक्षादिरसेन रक्ततोयं कृत्वेत्यर्थः । सौम्ये उत्तरदिक्स्थचक्र इत्यर्थः । तस्मिन्निति कुम्भे । दक्षिणे मण्डले दक्षिणदिक्स्थचक्रे । विधानविदित्यनेन सपदां इमन्तिकां संस्थाप्य तत्राग्निं प्रतिष्ठाप्य होमकर्म कुर्यादिति सूचितम् ॥ ९८॥९९ ॥

अपामार्गैरपामार्गसमिद्भिः । उक्तं च नारायणीये "साज्यापामार्गसमिधैः" इति । गव्यं पञ्चगव्यम् । "सकलैर्गव्यैः" इत्युक्तेः । प्रतिद्रव्यमित्यष्टोत्तरसहस्रं मिलित्वा भवति । तदुक्तं नारायणीये "सहस्राष्टकसंख्यया" इति । घृतस्य वारद्वयमुक्तिः क्रमार्था । विधानवित् संपातयेदित्यनेनाष्टद्रव्यहोमेऽपि संपात इति सूचितम् । प्रतिद्रव्यमिति काकाक्षिगोलकन्यायेनोभयत्र सम्बध्यते । तदुक्तम्—

हुत्वा तद्धुतशिष्टमत्र विधिवत् क्षिप्त्वा प्रतिद्रव्यकम् । इति ।

नारायणीयेऽपि—हुतशेषं क्षिपेत् कुम्भे प्रतिद्रव्यं विधानवित् । इति ।

विधानविदित्यनेन समिधादि होमे आहुत्यग्रे कलशे हस्तमात्रस्पर्शा एव संपाता इति सूचितम् । पूजिते सौम्यमण्डले इति व्यधिकरणे सप्तम्यौ ।

तस्मिन्निति कुम्भमुखे । विनिक्षिपेदिति वषडन्तमूलान्वितसुदर्शनगायत्र्या । सा पूर्वोक्ताऽनुसन्धेया । तदर्धशेषं होमार्थकृतपायसार्धम् । दक्षिण इति चक्रे । तत्रत्यां हसन्तीमन्यत्र संस्थाप्येत्यर्थः । मन्त्रीत्यनेन सह नमो इति स्वार नारा इति हुं फडिति पादत्रयान्तेन ओमिति चतुर्थपादान्तेन गीतामन्त्रेण विशिष्टं साध्यस्य सकलीकरणं सूचितम् ॥ १००॥१०१॥१०२॥१०३ ॥

नीराज्य तौ नयेद्राश्रो ग्रामादष्टमराशिषि।
स्थापयेत्तौ यथापूर्वं सपरिस्तरणौ क्रमात् ॥ १०४
हुत्वा वह्नौ यथापूर्वं शिष्टान्नेन बलिं हरेत्।
मनुना वक्ष्यमाणेन दशदिक्षु यथाविधि ॥ १०५
सद्वद्विष्णुगणेभ्योऽन्ते सर्वशान्तिकरे पुनः।
भ्यो बलिं प्रतिगृह्णन्तु शान्तये हृदयं ततः ॥ १०६
ब्राह्मणान् भोजयेत् सम्यङ्मधुरोत्तरमादरात्।
गुरवे दक्षिणां दद्याद्वस्त्रभूषणसंयुताम् ॥ १०७
हन्त्यादयं विधिः पुंसां कृत्यारोगग्रहज्वरान्।
रक्षःपिशाचमार्यादिक्लेशान् शीघ्रं न संशयः ॥ १०८
विधाय पञ्जरं मन्त्री फलकैः क्षीरशाखिनाम्।

नीराज्येति। नीराजनं गोतामन्त्रेण। एकदैव कुम्भाग्निभ्यां नीराजनं यत् तत् पुरुषान्तरसाहाय्येनेति ज्ञेयम्। ताविति कुम्भाग्नी अष्टमराशिके स्थापयेदिति। राशिस्थानान्युक्तानि कादिमते—

प्राच्यां मेषवृषौ वह्नौ मिथुनं दक्षिणे तथा।
कुलीरसिंहस्तथ तवैर्ऋत्यां कन्यका स्थिता॥
तुलाकोटी पश्चिमतो धनुर्वायौ तु संस्थितम्।
नक्रकुम्भावुत्तरतो मीनमैशे तु संस्थितम्॥ इति॥

एतद्राशिस्थानं ज्ञात्वा साध्यस्य योऽष्टमराशिस्तत्र स्थापयेदित्यर्थः। यथापूर्वमिति। तद्दक्षिणभागेऽग्निं स्थापयेत्। तदुक्तम्—

अग्न्यादिकमपि सर्वं क्षिपेदथ घटस्य पश्चिमे भागे। इति ॥ १०४ ॥

यथापूर्वमित्यष्टभिर्द्रव्यैः उक्तप्रमाणेन च। शिष्टान्नेनेति हुतशिष्टान्नेन। तदुक्तं नारायणीये—दद्यादनेन मन्त्रेण हुतशेषान्नतो बलिम्। इति। आचार्या अपि—हुतशेषान्नेन बलिम्। इति। यथाविधीति। लोकपालबलिरपि सूचितः ॥ १०५ ॥

बलिमन्त्रमाह सद्वदिति। द्रव्यमःपदम्। हृदयं नमःपदम् एतदन्तो मन्त्रः। अस्य प्रणवशक्त्यादित्वं ज्ञेयम्। मारी कृत्याविशेषः। आदिशब्देनेत्यादिकापदादि ॥ १०६॥१०७॥१०८ ॥

क्षीरशाखिनामिति पलाशस्याप्युपलक्षणम्। तदुक्तं नारायणीये—

पञ्चगव्येन संपूर्य तस्मिन् साध्यं निवेशयेत् ॥ १०९
धौतवस्त्रं विशुद्धाङ्गं स्पृष्ट्वा सम्यग्जपेत्तनुम् ।
पूर्वादिदिक्षु संस्थाप्य वह्निं ब्राह्मणसत्तमैः ॥ ११०
कारयेत्पूर्वसन्दिष्टैर्द्रव्यैर्होमं विधानवित् ।
तोषयेद्दक्षिणाभिस्तान् यजमानः स्वशक्तितः ॥ १११
गुरुं च धनधान्याद्यैर्नत्वा सम्प्रीणयेत्सदा ।
सर्वरोगहरः प्रोक्तः कृत्याद्रोहादिनाशनः ॥ ११२
अपमृत्युहरः पुंसां विधिरेष प्रकीर्तितः ।
पञ्चगव्यैः कषायैर्वा क्षीरभूरुहकल्कजैः ॥ ११३
पूरितैः कलशैर्जप्तैः कृतसम्पातसंयुतैः ।
अभिषिञ्चेद् ग्रहाविष्टमभिचारातुरं नरम् ॥ ११४
सुस्थो भवति शीघ्रेण विधानेनाऽमुना नरः ।
भानुवारेऽभिषेकस्य विधानेन सुसाधितैः ॥ ११५
सलिलैः स्नापयेन्नारीं सुखप्रसवकाङ्क्षिणीम् ।
सप्तवाराभिषेकेण सर्वे नश्यन्त्युपद्रवाः ॥ ११६

कल्कैः कल्किते पात्रे क्वाथः क्षीरशाखिनाम् । इति ।

आचार्याश्च—पल्लवैर्वा स्तनजद्रुमजैर्वा पङ्कवे कृते कल्कैः । इति ॥

अनेन क्षीरद्रुमेष्वपि विकल्पो ज्ञेयः । सम्यक् जपेदिति चतुर्दिक्षु क्रियमाणहोमसमाप्तिपर्यन्तमित्युक्तम् । पूर्वसन्दिष्टैः घृतादिभिरष्टद्रव्यैः । विधानविदित्यनेन प्रतिद्रव्यं षड्विंशत्यधिकशतं होम इत्युक्तम् । पञ्चगव्यैः पूरितैरिति व्यधिकरणे तृतीये । कलशैरिति नवभिः । सम्पातेन होमशेषः । होमोऽपि पूर्वोक्ताष्टद्रव्यैः पूर्वोक्तसंख्यः । अमुना विधानेन नरः शीघ्रेण सुस्थो भवतीति सम्बन्धः । तद्विधानप्रकारो यथा । पूर्वोक्तं नवनाभं मण्डलं कृत्वा पूर्ववत् कलशान्नव संस्थाप्य उक्तद्रव्यैरापूर्य मध्ये मन्त्रोक्तदेवतां संपूज्य परितोऽष्टकलशेषु आयुधाष्टकं संपूज्य कार्यानुरूपं होमं कृत्वा तत्सम्पातयुक्तैर्घटैरभिषिञ्चेदिति । पञ्चकलशपक्षे पद्माङ्कं मण्डलं कृत्वा दिक्षु चक्रगदामुसलपाशा अर्चनीयाः । शेषं पूर्ववत् । अभिषेकस्य विधानेनेति । एककलशस्थापनप्रकारेण उक्तरूपेण चेत्यर्थः । सुसाधितैरित्यनेन पूर्ववद्धोमः सम्पातश्च । सप्तसु वारेषु भानुवारेषु योऽभिषेकस्तेन ॥ १०९—११६ ॥

पञ्चगव्ये भृतं सर्पिर्मन्त्रितं मनुनाऽमुना ।
गर्भिणीनां ग्रहार्तानां सेवितं तच्छुभावहम् ॥ ११७

उच्चस्थानगते शुक्रे मनुना साधुसाधिता ।
त्रिलोहीमुद्रिका हन्यात् क्षुद्रभूतग्रहान् ज्वरान् ॥ ११८

तद्वर्णसंख्यया सूत्रे ग्रन्थीन् कृत्वा जपादिभिः ।
साधितं कल्पयेद्धस्ते कण्ठे वा दुःखशान्तये ॥ ११९

पञ्चगव्यं जपेत् स्पृष्ट्वा मन्त्रं दशशतावधि ।
न्यस्तं तत् पद्मपत्रादौ पत्रे वा ब्रह्मवृक्षजे ॥ १२०

फले बिल्वस्य वा मन्त्री गृहे स्वस्य परस्य च ।
निखनेत् सर्वरक्षा स्याद्वर्धते सर्वसम्पदः ॥ १२१

पलाशक्षीरवृक्षाणां त्वचो मलयजं पुरम् ।
कुङ्कुमं यामिनीं कुष्ठं विल्वापामार्गसर्षपान् ॥ १२२

पञ्चगव्य इति । "अकल्कोऽपि भवेत् स्नेहो यः साध्यः केवले द्रवे" इति परिभाषणात् कल्कं विनैव तद्धृतं साध्यम् । तत्र

पञ्चप्रभृति यत्र स्युर्द्रव्याणि स्नेहसंविधौ । तत्र स्नेहसमान्याहुः । इत्युक्तेः । घृतसमान्येव पञ्चगव्यानि दत्त्वा घृतं पचेत् । क्षीरदध्यारनालैः वचनात् प्रायमपि जलं न देयम् । गोमूत्रस्य सत्त्वादिति ॥ ११७ ॥

शुक्रे उच्चस्थानगते मीनगते । साधुसाधितेति षष्ठोक्तरीत्या ॥ ११८ ॥

तद्वर्णसंख्यया मन्त्रवर्णसंख्यया । इदमुभयत्र सम्बध्यते । तेन सप्त सूत्राणि कृत्वा तत्र सप्त ग्रन्थयो देयाः । अस्य प्रयोगस्य विशेषो नारायणीये—

इनेदु गव्याक्तापामार्गसमिदाज्यं चरुं घृतम् ।
परिस्तीर्णसितातान्तसूत्रसन्धिक्षिलान् घटान् ॥
क्षीरवृक्षक्वाथपूर्णान् होमकालेऽभिमन्त्रयेत् ।
तत्संख्यपातैः स्नापयेत् गव्यशेषपुरःसरम् ॥
कल्पयेत्तस्य हस्तादौ तत् सूत्रं ग्रन्थितं जपात् । इति ।

जपादिभिरित्यादिशब्देन पूजासम्पातौ हस्ते कण्ठे चेति । पुमान् दक्षिणे स्त्री वाम इति ज्ञेयम् ॥ ११९ ॥

पद्मपत्रादावित्यादिशब्देन ब्रह्मपत्रादिपात्र इत्यादि । मन्त्री नरः स्वस्य परस्य वा गृहे निखनेदिति सम्बन्धः । पुरं गुग्गुलम् । यामिनी हरिद्रा । कुष्ठं कूडम् ।

तिलदूर्वायवान् देवीं तुलसीयुगलं कुशम् ।
लक्ष्मीं गोरोचनां पद्मं वचां गोमयसंयुताम् ॥ १२३
विष्णुक्रान्तामर्कयुतां जपन्मन्त्रं विनिक्षिपेत् ।
पञ्चगव्येन सम्पूर्णे पात्रे तत् संस्कृतेऽनले ॥ १२४
संस्थाप्य क्वाथयेत् सम्यग्यावद्भस्म भविष्यति ।
तदादाय जपेद् भूयः प्रयुतं देवता धिया ॥ १२५
लिपेत्सर्वाङ्गमेतेन किञ्चिच्छिरसि निक्षिपेत् ।
कृत्याद्रोहग्रहोन्माद्व्याधिदुःखनिवारणम् ॥ १२६
सर्वशत्रुप्रशमनं सर्वपापहरं परम् ।
शुभदं वश्यदं पुंसां समस्तापन्निवारणम् ॥ १२७
गर्भिणीबालरुग्नानां विशेषेण प्रशस्यते ।
अस्मात्परतरा रक्षा नास्ति लोके प्रकीर्त्तिता ॥ १२८
मुस्ता शुण्ठी निशा वह्निरेला यष्टिर्वचा वृषा ।
पाठा विड़ङ्गं मञ्जिष्ठा द्राक्षा दार्वी सरोहिणी ॥ १२९
फलत्रयं च तैः कल्कैः पञ्चगव्येषु सर्पिषाम् ।
प्रस्थं पचेद्यथान्यायं मन्त्रेणाऽनेन साधितम् ॥ १३०
कान्तिदं सुतदं स्त्रीणां भूतप्रेतभयापहम् ।
गर्भरक्षाकरं शुद्धं पञ्चगव्यघृतं विदुः ॥ १३१

बिल्वेति बिल्वपञ्चाङ्गम् । देवी सहदेवी । पद्मेति । पद्मपञ्चाङ्गम् । पद्म-दलादिकमित्यस्य व्याख्याने अपेक्षितार्थद्योतनिकायां बिल्वपञ्चाङ्गं पद्मपञ्चाङ्ग-मित्युक्तम् । अर्केति अर्कत्वक् । तदिति पात्रम् । सम्यक् क्वाथयेदिति । मन्त्रं जपन्नित्युक्तम् । प्रयुतमिति दशलक्षम् । क्वचिदयुतमिति पाठः ॥ १२०॥१२१॥ ॥ १२२॥१२३॥१२४॥१२५॥१२६॥१२७॥१२८ ॥

मुस्तेति । मुस्ता मोच्छ्रय [मुथा] । निशा हरिद्रा । वह्निश्चित्रकः । यष्टिः यष्टिमधु । वृषा आटरूषः । वासक इति यावत् । दार्वी दारुहरिद्रा । रोहिणी कटकी । फलत्रयं हरितकीबिभीतकामलकानि । यथान्यायं वैद्यकशास्त्रोक्तप्रकारेण । तत्र सर्पिःप्रमाणमुक्तमेव । कल्कश्च स्नेहपादिकमित्युक्तत्वात् कुडवमात्रं कल्को ग्राह्यः । पञ्चप्रभृतीति वचनात् प्रत्येकं पञ्चगव्यानि स्नेहसमानि । आज्यावशेषमुत्तार्य शीतलं ज्ञात्वाऽनेन मन्त्रेण साधितं संजप्तम् ॥ १२९॥१३०॥१३१ ॥

टान्तान् सप्त लिखेन्मध्ये षट्सु कोणेषु तेष्वथ।
मन्त्रवर्णान् लिखेदेतच्चक्रमापन्निवारणम् ॥ १३२

षट्कोणमध्ये विलिखेत् ससाध्यं तारं षड़स्त्रिष्ववशिष्टवर्णान्।
अङ्गानि तत्सन्धिषु यन्त्रमेतत्करोति रक्षां विधिवत् प्रजप्तम् ॥ १३३

तारं लिखेत् ठान्तगतं ससाध्यं कोणेषु शिष्टं मनुवर्णषट्कम्।
अङ्गानि सन्धिष्वथ षोड़शारं सषोड़शार्णं वसुधापुरस्थम् ॥ १३४

जपित्वा कृतसम्पातं गर्भिणीनां हितं पुरम्।
अभिचारग्रहोन्मादान् यन्त्रमेतद्विनाशयेत् ॥ १३५

यन्त्रमाह टान्तानिति। मध्यादिषट्कोणेषु सप्त ठकारान् विलिख्य तेषु ठकारेषु क्रमेण मन्त्राक्षराणि लिखेत्। मध्ये साध्यसाधककर्मलिखनं च ज्ञेयम्। आपदिति महाज्वरी। "चक्रं श्वासज्वरापहम्" इति नारायणीये उक्तः ॥ १३२ ॥

यन्त्रान्तरमाह षडिति। षड़स्त्रिष्वित्यस्त्र्यादि। विधिवदित्यनेनाऽष्टोत्तरसहस्रं जप उक्तः। रक्षां करोति तत्र स्थापितमिति शेषः। तदुक्तम्—

मध्ये तारं तदनु च मनुं वर्णशः कोणषट्के
बाह्ये चाऽङ्गं लिखतु कनके ताम्रके वाऽथ रौप्ये॥
पाषाणे वा विधिवदभिजप्याऽथ संस्थापितं तत्
चक्रं चोरग्रहरिपुभयध्वंसि रक्षाकरं च॥ इति ॥ १३३ ॥

यन्त्रान्तरमाह तारमिति। ठान्तगतमिति तारविशेषणम्। षोड़शारमिति।

षोड़शाङ्के समे वृत्ते पञ्चमे पञ्चमे लिखेत्।
रेखा अङ्के षोड़शाद्यं षोड़शारमिदं मतम्॥

इति षोड़शारलेखनप्रकारः। षोड़शार्णं वक्ष्यमाणषोड़शाक्षरं चक्रमन्त्रम्। अन्येषां षोड़शाक्षरशब्देन षोड़शदलं तदुपरि च वृत्तं तदुपरि पार्थिवमण्डलम्। मन्त्रश्च। ॐ नमो भगवते वासुदेवाय हुं फट् स्वाहा। तदुक्तं नारायणीये—

सांख्यादिन्दोर्बहिः कोणषट्के मन्त्राक्षरान् लिखेत्।
सन्धिष्वङ्गाद्बहिर्वृत्तात्पत्रषोड़शके मनुम्।
पुनर्वृत्तं च भूगेहे लिखेदेतद्यथाविधि॥ इति।

क्वचित् षोड़शार्णं तत्संख्यपत्रे इति पाठः। जपित्वेत्यतो हुत्वेति शेषः ॥१३४॥१३५॥

मध्ये तारं ससाध्यं मनुमथ विलिखेत् षट्सु कोणेषु सम्भि-
ष्वङ्गान्यन्ते कलानां युगयुगविलसत्केशराष्टार्णपद्मम्।
किञ्जल्कान् आदिवर्णैर्द्विवसुदललसत्षोडशार्णं स्वनाम्ना
ह्वाभ्यां त्रिःप्रवीतं लिखतु परिवृतं तत् त्रिपाशाङ्कुशाभ्याम् ॥ १३६

तारं नमो भगवते महासुदर्शनाय च।
वर्मास्त्रान्तश्चक्रमन्त्रः षोडशाक्षर ईरितः ॥ १३७

चक्रयन्त्रमिदं प्रोक्तं सर्वभीतिनिवारणम्।
क्षुद्राभिचारशमनं राज्ञां विजयवर्धनम् ॥ १३८

यन्त्रान्तरमाह मध्ये इति। मनुं तारव्यतिरिक्तचक्रमन्त्रम्। अङ्गे षट्-कोणवाह्ये। कलानां स्वराणाम्। अष्टार्णो नारायणाष्टाक्षरः। द्विवसुदलं षोडश-दलम्। स्वनाम्ना साध्यनाम्ना सह ह्वाभ्यां त्रिःप्रवीतं ह्वयोर्मध्ये साध्यना-मित्यर्थः। तत् त्रिपाशाङ्कुशाभ्यामित्यावृत्तित्रयम्। यत्तु त्रिःप्रवीतमित्यावृत्तित्रयं प्रथमावृत्तित्रयमिति लिपेत्यायां स्वनाम्ना ह्वाभ्यामेका द्वितीया पाशेन तृतीयाऽ-ङ्कुशेन। द्वितीयं त्रिःपदं सस्वरजस्तमोरूपतया आवृत्तिध्यानमिति व्याख्यानात्। स नमस्य एव। केचन तारं पाशाङ्कुशाभ्यामिति पाठं पठित्वा बीजत्रित्रि। त्रिःप्रवीतं तत्रैका ह्वाभ्यां स्वनाम्ना अपरा तारेण तृतीया पाशाङ्कुशाभ्यामिति। अयमेव पक्षः साम्प्रदायिकः। केचन द्वितीयत्रिपदस्यैव अकारोकारमकारा-त्मकत्वात् प्रणव एवार्थ इति व्याचक्षते। द्विवचनमात्रत्वपेक्षया। तदुक्तम्—

त्रिवीतं व्योमास्यार्णं स्वनाम्ना विरचितगुणपाशाङ्कुशं चक्रयन्त्रम्। इति। एतद्व्याख्याने पद्मपादाचार्याः। गुणः प्रणवः। केवलह्वाभ्यामावृत्तित्रयम्। अपरायामाहुस्तौ तारमुक्त्वा साध्यनाम्नोऽक्षरद्वयमुच्चार्य पुनः पाशमुच्चार्य साध्यनाम्नो-ऽक्षरद्वयमुच्चार्य पुनरङ्कुशबीजमुच्चार्य पुनः साध्यनाम्नोऽक्षरद्वयमुच्चारयेत्। एवं रूपैर्वर्णैर्वेष्टयेदित्याहुः। पाशाङ्कुशवेष्टितमित्यस्य व्याख्याने अपेक्षितार्थद्योत-निकायां पाशेन त्रिवारं अङ्कुशेनापि त्रिवारमित्युक्तम् ॥ १३६ ॥

षोडशाक्षरं मन्त्रमुद्धरति तारमिति। अयमपि स्वतन्त्रो मन्त्रः। अस्यर्ष्यादि सर्वं पूर्वमन्त्रोक्तम्। अथास्य तन्त्रान्तरस्थं यन्त्रमुच्यते—

षट्कोणं चक्रमालिख्य तस्यारेषु सुदर्शनम्।
अष्टारं पङ्कजं बाह्ये दलेष्वष्टाक्षरं परम् ॥

रेखा विलिख्याऽष्ट शिरांसि तासामाबध्य बाह्ये श्रुतिशः क्रमेण ।
स्थानेहृषीकेशमनुं विभज्य पादान् लिखेत् कोष्ठचतुष्टयस्थान् ॥ १३९
अष्टाक्षरार्णैः प्रविदर्भितांस्तान् कोष्ठद्वये चक्रमनुं यथावत् ।
मध्यस्थकोष्ठे विलिखेत्ससाध्यं स्यात्सप्तकोष्ठाह्वययन्त्रमेतत् ॥ १४०
स्थाने हृषीकेश तव प्रकीर्त्या जगत् प्रहृष्यत्यनुरज्यते च ।
रक्षांसि भीतानि दिशो द्रवन्ति सर्वे नमस्यन्ति च सिद्धसङ्घाः ॥ १४१

तद्बाह्ये द्वादशारं स्यात्तिखेच्च द्वादशाक्षरम् ।
षोड़शारं ततः पद्मं मूलमन्त्रं समालिखेत् ॥
कामबीजेन परितो वेष्टयेद्यन्त्रमुत्तमम् ।
महासुदर्शनं बाह्ये विलिखेद्देशिकोत्तमः ॥
तारं नमो भगवते महासुदर्शनाय च ।
महाचक्राय च महाज्वालाङे दीप्तरूपङे ॥
सर्वतो रक्षयुग्मं च महावलसङे द्विठः ।
मध्ये साध्यं समालिख्य प्रणवस्योदरे मुने ॥
सर्वसिद्धिप्रदं यन्त्रमिति देवोऽब्रवीत् स्वयम् । इति ॥ १३७ ॥

सप्तकोष्ठयन्त्रमाह रेखा इति । पूर्वापरायता रेखा लिखेत् । तासां शिरांसि बाह्ये क्रमेण श्रुतिश आबध्येति सम्बन्धः । प्रथमादिरेखाग्रं स्वतुर्याग्रेण मेलयेत् । तेन हरीतकीवद्भवतीति केचित् । पद्मपादाचार्यप्रभृतिभिः श्रुतिशश्चिश्च इति व्याख्यातम् । तेषां मते प्रथमादिरेखाग्रं स्वस्वतृतीयादिरेखाग्रेण सह मेलये-दित्यर्थः । अन्ये तु पूज्यपादा एवं व्याचक्षते । प्रथमरेखाग्रं स्वतुर्यरेखाग्रेणाबध्य पुनस्तृतीयरेखाग्रात् षष्ठरेखाग्रमाबध्य पुनः पञ्चमरेखाग्रादष्टमरेखाग्रं बन्धयेत् । एवं द्वितीयपार्श्वेऽपि । तदा द्वितीयरेखा सप्तमी च केवलं मध्येऽवशिष्यते । ततो द्वितीयरेखायाः पूर्वाग्रमारभ्योत्तरतो नीत्वा तत्पश्चिमाग्रेण बन्धयेत् । एवं सप्तमरेखापूर्वाग्रमारभ्य दक्षिणतो नीत्वा तत्पश्चिमाग्रेण बन्धयेत् । एवं बाह्ये इत्युक्तिश्च सार्थका भवति । एवं मध्यकोष्ठत्रयमेकरेखाबद्धं च भवतीति । एवमेतद्यन्त्रलिखनं स्वगुरुसम्प्रदायानुसारेण बोद्धव्यमिति संक्षेपः । अष्टाक्षर प्रविदर्भिताम् पादान् कोष्ठचतुष्टयस्थान् प्रथमद्वितीयषष्ठसप्तमस्थान् लिखेत् । विदर्भितलक्षणं त्रयोविंशे वक्ष्यते । कोष्ठद्वये तृतीयपञ्चमरूपे । यथावदिति

धारितं सप्तकोष्ठं तत् त्रायते महतो भयात् ।
दुःस्वप्नदुर्निमित्तादिशमनं कीर्त्तितं बुधैः ॥ १४२

इति श्रीशारदातिलके षोड़शः पटलः ।

ससाध्यम् । मध्यस्थकोष्ठे चतुर्थकोष्ठे । ससाध्यं चक्रमनुमित्यनुषज्यते ।
तदुक्तमाचार्यैः—कोष्ठत्रयलिखितसाध्य सुदर्शनं च । इति ॥ १३९॥१४०॥१४१ ॥

धारितमिति । धारणप्रकार उक्त आचार्यैः—

भूर्जे वा क्षौमपट्टे तनुमहृणतरे कर्पटे वाऽस्य यन्त्रं
मन्त्री सम्यग् लिखित्वा पुनरपि गुलिकीकृत्य लाक्षाभिवीतम् ॥
कृत्वा भक्त्यादिहोमप्रविहितहुतसम्पातपातात्तशक्ति
जप्तं सम्यक् प्रबध्नात्प्रतिशमनुपयान्त्येव सर्वे विकाराः ॥ इति ॥

तन्मन्त्रमित्यर्थः । नपुंसकलिङ्गेऽपि मन्त्रशब्दस्य बहुषु स्थलेषु प्रयोगात् ।
तेनायमर्थः । गीतास्थमन्त्रविदर्भितः साष्टाक्षरचक्रमन्त्रोऽपि जप्त एतत्फलद इति ।
तदुक्तमाचार्यैः—

स्थाने हृषीकेशविदर्भितं च साष्टाक्षरं चाप्यभिजप्तमेतत् ।
रक्षां ग्रहादेः सततं विधत्ते यन्त्रं सुकृतं च मनुष्ययोग ॥ इति ॥

स्थाने हृषीकेशेति मन्त्रस्य चतुर्भिश्चरणैः सर्वेण पञ्चाङ्गं कृत्वा

अग्निर्मूर्धा चक्षुषी चन्द्रसूर्यौ दिशः श्रोत्रे वाग्विवृत्ताश्च वेदाः ।
वायुः प्राणो हृदयं विश्वमस्य पद्भ्यां पृथिवी ह्येष सर्वभूतान्तरात्मा ॥

इति ध्यात्वा कर्णिकायां देवं पत्रेष्वङ्गानि तद्बहिर्लोकपालानर्चयेत् । दशलक्षजपः पुरश्चरणम् । दशांशं घृतेन होमः । सर्वपापक्षयसर्वशान्तिसर्वग्रहनिवारण-सर्वरक्षोघ्नमिति फलम् ॥ १४२ ॥

इति श्रीशारदातिलकटीकायां सत्सम्प्रदायकृतव्याख्यायां
पदार्थादर्शाभिख्यायां षोड़शः पटलः ॥ ॐ ॥

अथ वक्ष्ये जगन्मूलं मन्त्रं श्रीपुरुषोत्तमम् ।
गोपितं वैष्णवे तन्त्रे भुक्तिमुक्तिफलप्रदम् ॥ १

तारमाररमाबीजं नत्यन्ते पुरुषोत्तमम् ।
पुनरप्रतिरूपान्ते ततो लक्ष्मीनिवास च ॥ २

सकलान्ते जगत्पूर्वं क्षोभणेतिपदं पुनः ।
सर्वस्त्रीहृदयोपेतं विदारणपदं पुनः ॥ ३

ततः परं त्रिभुवनमदोन्मादकरं ततः ।
सुरासुरान्ते मनुजसुन्दरीजनशब्दतः ॥ ४

मनांसि तापयद्वन्द्वं दीपयद्वितयं पुनः ।
शोषयद्वितयं भूयो मारयद्वितयं पुनः ॥ ५

स्तम्भयद्वितयं पश्चान्मोहयद्वितयं पुनः ।
द्रावयद्वितयं पश्चादाकर्षययुगं ततः ॥ ६

वैष्णवतन्त्रगोपितत्वादन्ते स्मरणारूढत्वात् पुरुषोत्तमादिमन्त्रान् वक्तुमुपक्रमते अथेति । उक्तं च मन्त्रतन्त्रप्रकाशे—

पुरुषोत्तमसंज्ञस्य विष्णोर्भेदचतुष्टयम् ।
त्रैलोक्यमोहनस्तेषां प्रथमः प्रकृतिर्मतः ॥
श्रीकरस्य हृषीकेशः कृष्णस्तत्र चतुर्थकः ।
श्रीधरो वा चतुर्थः स्यात्प्रद्युम्नो वेति केचन ॥ इति ॥

मन्त्रदेवतयोरभेदेन पुरुषोत्तममित्युक्तिः । अतिरहस्यत्वाद् गोपितम् । अत एवाऽऽचार्यैः गुप्तपटले उद्धारः कृतः । भुक्तिमुक्तीत्यनेन विनियोग उक्तः ॥ १ ॥

मन्त्रमुद्धरति तारेति । तारो देवीप्रणवः । ओङ्कारस्य सामान्येन सर्वमन्त्रादित्वेनोक्तेः अत्रापि तथा सम्प्रदायाद्वा प्रणवादित्वम् । यद्वा तारश्च तारश्चेत्येकशेषे तारौ पश्चाद्‌मादिपदैः सह समासः । तत्र प्रथमतारपदेन प्रणवः द्वितीयतारपदेन देवीप्रणवः । इदं व्याख्यानं पद्मपादाचार्याणां सम्मतम् । मारः कामबीजम् । रमा श्रीबीजम् । नतिर्नमःपदम् । सर्वस्त्रीहृदयेति स्वरूपम् ।

समस्तपरमोपेतसुभगेन च संयुतम् ।
सर्वसौभाग्यशब्दान्ते करेतिपदसंयुतम् ॥ ७

सर्वकामप्रदपदममुकं हनयुग्मकम् ।
चक्रेण गदया पश्चात् खड्गेन तदनन्तरम् ॥ ८

सर्वबाणैर्भिन्द्युगं पाशेनेतिपदं ततः ।
कटुद्वयान्तेऽङ्कुशेन ताडयद्वितयं पुनः ॥ ९

कुरुशब्दद्वयमथो किं तिष्ठसि पदं पुनः ।
तावद्यावत्पदस्यान्ते समीहितमनन्तरम् ॥ १०

ततो मे सिद्धमाभाष्य भवत्यन्ते सवर्म फट् ।
नमोऽन्तोऽयं मनुः प्रोक्तो द्विशताक्षरसंयुतः ॥ ११

जैमिनिर्मुनिराख्यातश्छन्दोऽस्याऽमितमीरितम् ।
समस्तजगतामादिर्देवता पुरुषोत्तमः ॥ १२

पुरुषोत्तमशब्दान्ते वदेत् त्रिभुवनं ततः ।
मदोन्मादकरान्ते हुं हृदयं सकलं ततः ॥ १३

जगत्क्षोभणशब्दान्ते लक्ष्मीदयित हुं शिरः ।
मन्मथोत्तमसंयुक्तमङ्गजे कामदायिनि ॥ १४

हुं शिखा परमोपेत सुभगाक्षरसंयुतम् ।
सर्वसौभाग्यकर हुं कवचं परिकीर्त्तितम् ॥ १५

ततः सुरासुरोपेतमनुजान्वितसुन्दरी ।
ततः परस्ताद्धृदयविदारणपदं वदेत् ॥ १६

अत्र क्वापि न सन्धिः। द्वितीयान्तानि सर्वाणि आभाष्येत्यस्य कर्माणि मन्त्रे तु सम्बुद्धयः। समीहितं सिद्धमिति च मन्त्रेऽपि द्वितीयान्तम्। द्विशताक्षर इत्युक्तिस्तु अमुकेति साध्यनामपरमित्येतत्केति केचन। अन्ये तु अमुकपदस्थाने दुरितादिपद-प्रक्षेपाद् द्विशताक्षरसंयुत इत्युक्तेः अधिकाक्षरत्वमपि न दोषायेत्यूचुः।

केचिदेवमाहुः—शक्तिश्रीमारैभिः पुटितः स्मरणाच्च लोकमोहनकृत्। इति। प्रणवो बीजं हुं शक्तिः ॥ २ ॥ ३ ॥ ४ ॥ ५ ॥ ६ ॥ ७ ॥ ८ ॥ ९ ॥ १० ॥ ११ ॥ १२ ॥

षडङ्गमन्त्रानुद्धरति पुरुषोत्तमेति। शिखामन्त्रे अङ्गजे इत्यस्य पूर्वेण सह सन्धिः।

सर्वग्रहरणाधर सर्वकामिक तत्परम् ।
हनद्वयं च हृदयं बन्धनानि ततः परम् ॥ १७
आकर्षयद्वन्द्वं महाबल हुमस्त्रकम् ।
त्रिभुवनेश्वरपदं ततः सर्वजनान्ततः ॥ १८
मनांसि हनयुग्मान्ते दारयद्वितयं च मे ।
वशमानय हुं नेत्रं ताराद्याः फट् नमोऽन्तिकाः ।
षडङ्गमन्त्राः सन्दिष्टा नेत्रान्तास्तत्त्ववेदिभिः ॥ १९
त्रैलोक्यमोहनार्णान्ते हृषीकेशपदं पुनः ।
पश्चादप्रतिरूपादि मन्मथानन्तरं वदेत् ॥ २०
सर्वादि स्त्रीपदं पश्चाद्धृदयाकर्षणं ततः ।
आगच्छाऽऽगच्छ मन्त्रोऽयं ताराद्यो नमसाऽन्वितः ॥ २१
अनेन मनुना कृत्वा व्यापकं न्यस्य बाहुषु ।
अष्टायुधानि मुद्राभिर्मन्त्रैः सार्धं विचिन्तयेत् ॥ २२

तदुक्तम्—मन्मथवर्णानुक्त्वा तदनु वदेदुत्तमाङ्गजेवर्णान् । इति ।

अस्त्रमन्त्रे हृदयेतिद्वयमपि स्वरूपम् । ताराद्या इति । उक्ता नेत्रान्ताः षडङ्गमन्त्राः । ताराद्याः प्रणवाद्याः फट् नमोऽन्तिकाः सन्दिष्टा इति सम्बन्धः । तत्त्ववेदिभिरित्यनेनैतदुक्तं भवति । यदाहुः—

करयोर्व्यापकं मन्त्रं न्यस्याऽङ्गान्यङ्गुलीषु तलयोश्च ।
न्यस्य बाणाननङ्गसहितान् व्यापकमन्त्रं ततो न्यसेद्वपुषि ॥
मातृकया विन्यसेत् प्रत्यगं मारबीजसंपुटया ।
न्यसेच्च मारमालामन्त्रार्णान् मातृकावदङ्गानि [दानाभि] ॥
चत्वारिंशद्वर्णान् पश्चोदरमुहृद्गलास्यनासासु ।
संव्यापयेच्च देहे त्रीनर्णान् सकृत् सकृत् समस्तेन ॥
क्लींमातृकार्णपूर्वा मूर्तीर्न्यस्येच्च कामरतिपूर्वाः । इति ।

पीठमन्त्रात् पूर्वं गरुडमुद्रया गरुडमन्त्रं हृदि न्यसेत् । यदाहुः—

इतिरीत्या देहे पीठन्यासान्तिकं विधाय हृदि ।
गरुडस्य मुद्रया तन्मन्त्रं न्यस्य न्यसेत् तु पीठमनुम् ॥ इति ॥

व्यापकमन्त्रे अप्रतिरूपेत्यस्य पूर्वेण सह सन्धिर्नाऽन्यस्येति । बाहुषु तत्तन्-

क्षीराम्भोनिधिमध्यस्थं निरन्तरसुरद्रुमम् ।
उद्यदर्केन्दुकिरणदूरीकृततमोभरम् ॥ २३

कालमेघसमालोकनृत्यद्बर्हिकदम्बकम् ।
उत्फुल्लकुसुमामोदप्रहृष्यद्भृङ्गसंकुलम् ॥ २४

कूजत्कोकिलसंघेन वाचालितदिगन्तरम् ।
नानाकुसुमसौरभ्यवाहिगन्धवहान्वितम् ॥ २५

कल्पवल्लीनिकुञ्जेषु क्रीडत्सिद्धकदम्बकम् ।
देवगन्धर्वकन्याभिर्गायन्तीभिरलङ्कृतम् ॥ २६

अनेकदीर्घिकायुक्तमुद्यानं महदद्भुतम् ।
तस्य मध्ये मणिमये मण्डपे तोरणान्विते ॥ २७

मुद्राभिः तत्तन्मन्त्रैः सार्धमष्टायुधानि विन्यस्य चिन्तयेत् देवमिति शेषः । अष्टायुधानि ध्यानोक्तानि । न्यासक्रमोऽपि तत्रैव वक्ष्यते । मुद्रालक्षणानि तु । पूर्वोक्ता पाशमुद्रा ज्ञेया । अथवेयं पाशमुद्रा । यदाहुः—

तर्जन्यङ्गुष्ठकौ कृत्वा सक्ताग्रौ कुञ्चिताः पराः ।
पाशमुद्रा समाख्याता । इति ।
वामस्य मध्यमाग्रं तु तर्जन्यग्रे नियोजयेत् ।
अनामिकां कनिष्ठां च तस्याङ्गुष्ठेन पीडयेत् ॥
दर्शयेद्दक्षिणस्कन्धे धनुर्मुद्रेयमीरिता ॥ इति ।

अथवेयं धनुर्मुद्रा ज्ञेया । यदाहुः—

बाहुमूलं स्पृशेत्तेन बाह्वग्रेणैव साधकः ।
धनुर्मुद्रा यशःकीर्त्तिबलवीर्यविवर्धिनी ॥ इति ॥
कनिष्ठानामिके बद्ध्वा स्वाङ्गुष्ठेनैव वामतः ।
शिष्टाङ्गुली तु प्रसृते संश्लिष्टे खड्गमुद्रिका ॥ इति ॥

शङ्खमुशलचक्रगदाङ्कुशमुद्रा मया पूर्वमुक्ताः । एतदनन्तरं देहे श्रीवत्सकौस्तुभवनमाला यथास्थानं स्वमन्त्रमुद्राभिर्न्यसेत् । तदुक्तम्—

अथ भूषणानि विद्वान् विन्यसेन्निजतनौ यथास्थानम् । इति ।

एतेषां मुद्राः प्रागुक्ताः । मन्त्रास्तु वक्ष्यन्ते ॥ १३-२२ ॥

क्षीरेत्यनेन पृथिव्यनन्तरं क्षीरसमुद्ररत्नद्वीपाद्भुतोद्यानमणिमण्डपकल्पतरु-

ऋतुभिः षड्भिरनिशं सेवितस्य महीयसः ।
सुरद्रुमस्य मूलस्थे महासिंहासने शुभे ॥ २८

रक्तारविन्दमध्यस्थगरुडोपरि संस्थितम् ।
ध्यायेद्वल्लभया सार्धं जगन्नाथं जगन्मयम् ॥ २९

देवं श्रीपुरुषोत्तमं कमलया स्वाङ्कस्थया पङ्कजं
बिभ्रत्या परिरब्धमम्बुजरुचा तस्यां निबद्धेक्षणम् ।
ध्यायेच्चेतसि शङ्खपाशमुशलांश्चापेषुखड्गान् गदां
हस्तैरङ्कुशमुद्वहन्तमरुणं स्मेरारविन्दाननम् ॥ ३०

एवं ध्यात्वा श्रियः कान्तं मनुं लक्षचतुष्टयम् ।
जपेद्वशी विधायाऽथ कुण्डमर्धेन्दुसन्निभम् ॥ ३१

महासिंहासनगरुडान् पीठन्यासादौ योजयेदित्युक्तम् ॥ २३॥२४॥२५॥२६॥२७ ॥ ॥ २८॥२९ ॥

ध्यानमाह देवमिति । अम्बुजरुचेति पीतवर्णया । तत्र कमला द्विभुजा । वामे पद्मं दक्षेणालिङ्गनम् । तदुक्तम्—

साब्जवामकरां पीतां श्लिष्यन्तीं पाणिना पतिम् ॥ इति ।

अन्यत्रापि—वामकरस्थाम्बुजया प्रतप्तकनकाभयाऽतिसुन्दर्या । इति ।

आयुधध्यानं तु वामेषु ऊर्ध्वादि बाणशङ्खधनुर्गदाः दक्षेषु ऊर्ध्वादि अङ्कुशमुशल-खड्गचक्राणि । तदुक्तं मन्त्रतन्त्रप्रकाशे—

दक्षिणाधःकरे चक्रं चिन्तयेदर्कभास्वरम् ।
खड्गं तथोपरितने मुशलं च तदुत्तरे ॥
सव्योर्ध्वदक्षिणे हस्ते चिन्तयेद्रुचिराङ्कुशम् ।
वामोर्ध्वे चिन्तयेत् पाशं तदधः शङ्खमेव च ।
सशरं च धनुर्वामे गदां ध्यायेदधःकरे ॥ इति ।

पूर्वोक्तायुधन्यासो देहेऽनेन क्रमेण ज्ञेयः । अत्र ध्यानानन्तरमेता मुद्रा दर्शनीयाः ।

यदाहुः—श्रीवत्सकौस्तुभौ वनमालाख्या च मारबीजेन ।
ऊर्ध्वाङ्गुष्ठौ मुष्टी नियोजितौ मस्तके मिथः श्लिष्टौ ॥
त्रैलोक्यमोहनाख्या मुद्रा तां मूर्ध्नि योजयेत्तदनु । इति ॥ ३० ॥

वशीत्यनेनाचार्योक्ता पूर्वमेव सूचिता । यदाहुः—

जुहुयाद्वैष्णवे वह्नौ पद्मैर्जातिसमुद्भवैः ।
पुष्पैर्यवैः क्रमात्पश्चाद् ब्राह्मणानपि भोजयेत् ॥ २१

अर्चयिष्यन् जगन्नाथं गायत्र्या परिशोधयेत् ।
आत्मानं यागवस्तूनि यागभूमिं च देशिकः ॥ २२

त्रैलोक्यमोहनायेति विद्महे पदमीरयेत् ।
स्मराय धीमहि पश्चात्तन्नो विष्णुः प्रचोदयात् ॥ २४

गायत्र्येषा समाख्याता वैष्णवी सर्वसिद्धिदा ।
प्राक्प्रोक्ते वैष्णवे पीठे कल्पयेदासनं ततः ॥ २५

पक्षिराजाय ठद्वन्द्वमस्य मन्त्रः प्रकीर्त्तितः ।
सङ्कल्पितायां मूलेन मूर्त्तौ देवमनन्यधीः ॥ २६

ध्यात्वा यथार्थसंख्यं जपतु मनुमिमं प्राप्तमन्त्राभिषेको
द्रव्यैरेभिश्च जुह्वद्भवति मनुवरस्याऽधिकारी क्रियासु ॥

शतं दधिघृतं पयः पृथगथाऽयुतं साज्यहविषा
घृतेन पयसा कुनेन्द्रविलसितं तथा साक्षततिलैः ।
तथा दशदशोन्मितं त्रिमधुभिर्वरैस्तार्क्ष्यफलैः
पलाशसमिधां शतं समभितोषयेत् स्वगुरुवरम् ॥ इति ॥

जुहुयादिति । दशांशमिति शेषः । तदुक्तं "दशांशं वैष्णवे वह्नौ" इति । क्रमात् पश्चादित्यनेन तर्पणाद्युक्तम् ॥ २१॥२२ ॥

देशिक इत्यनेन कामाद्यर्थयेत्युक्तम् ॥ २३॥२४ ॥

सर्वसिद्धिदेति स्वातन्त्र्येण जपेत् । तदृष्यादिकं यथा—

संकर्षणो मुनिश्छन्दो गायत्रं पुरुषोत्तमः ।
देवता मूर्ध्नि भालाक्षिदोःपत्सन्ध्यग्रकेषु च ॥
अक्षराणि प्रविन्यस्य षडङ्गानि समाचरेत् ।
पञ्चभिश्च त्रिभिश्चैव पञ्चभिश्च त्रिभिः पुनः ॥
चतुर्भिश्च चतुर्भिश्च कुर्यादङ्गानि वर्णकैः ।
त्रिंशताक्षरवत्याऽस्याः पूजाद्यन्यत् समीरितम् ॥ इति ॥

प्राक्प्रोक्ते पञ्चदशोक्ते पीठे । अनेन विमलाद्याः शक्तीः पूजयेदित्यर्थः । पूजायन्त्रं तु मन्त्रतन्त्रप्रकाशोक्तम् । यथा—

आवाह्य मनुना विद्वान् व्यापकेन समर्चयेत् ।
भृगुर्लान्तयुत: सेन्दुर्बीजं देव्या: प्रकीर्त्तितम् ॥ ३७
कर्णिकायां यजेदादौ विधानेनाऽङ्गदेवता: ।
दलेषु पूजयेत् पश्चाल्लक्ष्म्याद्या धृतचामरा: ॥ ३८
मुक्ताहारलसच्चारुपयोधरभरानता: ।
जवाकुसुमसङ्काशा मदविभ्रममन्थरा: ॥ ३९
क्ष्लब्लयक्षौबसर्गैरहितस्वरशोभितम् ।
देवीबीजं क्रमादासां मन्त्रमाहुर्मनीषिण: ॥ ४०

लिखेदष्टदलं पद्मं चन्दनेन सुगन्धिना ।
युगद्वारं सुशोभाढ्यं कामं तन्मध्यतो लिखेत् ॥ इति ।

पद्मेत्यासनस्य ॥ ३५ ॥ ३६ ॥

अवधानं विना आवाहनमेव कर्त्तुमशक्यमित्यनन्यधीरित्युक्ति: ।

आवाह्येति । व्यापकेन मनुना देवमावाह्य कर्णिकायां समर्चयेदिति सम्बन्ध: । व्यापकेनेति पूर्वोक्तेनैव व्यापकमन्त्रेण । विद्वानिति । षोडशोपचारा व्यापकमन्त्रेणैवेत्युक्तम् । तदुक्तम्—आवाहनविसर्गान्तेपूक्तोऽयं पूर्वसूरिभि: । इति ।

देवीबीजमुद्धरति भृगुरिति । भृगु: स: । लान्तयुतो वयुक् । सेन्दु: सबिन्दु: । इदं देव्या बीजम् । अनेनाऽङ्गपूजाया: पूर्वम् भङ्गस्थाया देव्या: पूजां कुर्यादिति शेष: । तदुक्तम्—

दक्षेतरोरौ कमलामथेष्ट्वा समर्चयेदावरणानि भूय: । इति ।

अन्यत्रापि—वामोरौ संस्थितामिष्ट्वा श्रियमङ्गानि पूजयेत् । इति ।

अत्र भूषणानि पूजयित्वाऽङ्गानि पूजयेत् । तदुक्तं नारायणीये—

श्रीवत्सकौस्तुभौ विद्वान् स्तनस्योपरि वक्षसि ।
वनमालां गले चान्यत् पीतवस्त्रादि पूजयेत् ॥ इति ॥ ३६॥३७ ॥

विधानेनेति । केसरेष्वग्न्यादिचतुर्दिक्षु वर्मान्तानि सम्पूज्य विदिक्षु अस्त्रं पुरतो नेत्रमित्यर्थ: । तदुक्तं मन्त्रतन्त्रप्रकाशे—

पूर्वादि दिक्षु चाऽभ्यर्च्य हृदाद्यङ्गचतुष्टयम् ।
कोणेष्वस्त्रं प्रपूज्याऽथ पुरतो नेत्रमर्चयेत् ॥ इति ॥

अन्यत्रापि—अङ्गानि वर्मावधिकानि दिक्षु विदिक्षु चास्त्रं पुरतश्च नेत्रम् । इति । दलेषु दलमूलेषु । लक्ष्म्याद्या इति पूर्वमन्त्रोक्ता: । सर्गो विसर्ग: । एभिरष्टभी

दलाग्रेषु यजेच्छङ्खं शार्ङ्गं चक्रमसिं गदाम् ।
अङ्कुशं मुशलं पाशमेतान्यस्त्राणि शार्ङ्गिणः ॥ ४१
स्वमुद्राभिः स्वमनुभिः कथ्यन्ते मनवः क्रमात् ।
आद्यो जलचरायाऽन्ते ठद्वयं मनुरीरितः ॥ ४२
शार्ङ्गाय सशरायाऽन्ते स्वाहान्तोऽनन्तरो मनुः ।
सुदर्शनमहाचक्रराजाऽन्ते स्याद्हृद्वयम् ॥ ४३
सर्वदुष्टभयं पश्चात् कुरु छिन्दिद्वयं पृथक् ।
विदारयपदद्वयं परमन्त्रान् ग्रस ग्रस ॥ ४४
भक्षयत्रासयद्वन्द्वं प्रत्येकं वर्म फट् द्वयम् ।
चक्राय नम इत्येष तृतीयो मन्त्र ईरितः ॥ ४५

रक्षिताः स्वराः । आ ई ऊ ए ऐ ओ औ अं एतद्युक्तं देवीबीजमासां मन्त्रमाहुरिति सम्बन्धः ॥ ३८ ॥ ३९ ॥ ४० ॥

स्वमुद्राभिरिति । दलाग्रेषु शार्ङ्गिण एतान्यस्त्राणि स्वमुद्राभिः सह स्वमनुभिर्यजेदिति सम्बन्धः । तत्र मुद्रालक्षणं मयोक्तं प्राक् । आद्यः शङ्खमन्त्रः । जलचरायेति महाजलचरायेति ज्ञेयम् । अन्ते ठद्वयमिति च कवचास्त्रयोः पूर्वमुच्चारणं सूचितम् । मनुरीरित इत्यनेन पाञ्चजन्याय नम इत्यस्यान्ते प्रयोगः सूचितः । आचार्यैः प्रथमं चक्रमन्त्रोद्धारे महासुदर्शनायेति हुं फट् स्वाहेत्यन्तः सुदर्शनाय नम इत्युद्धृतम् । तदनन्तरं शङ्खादिमन्त्रा उद्धृताः । तत्र पद्मपादाचार्यैर्व्याख्यातं शङ्खादिमन्त्रेष्वपि महाशब्दः अन्ते च पाञ्चजन्याय नम इत्यादि प्रयोक्तव्यम् इति । मन्त्रतन्त्रप्रकाशे अपेक्षितार्थद्योतनिकायामपि एवमेव मन्त्रा उद्धृताः । मूलकारेणापि चक्रमन्त्रे चक्राय नम इति । कौमोदकीमन्त्रे च कौमोदकीपर इति वदता स्पष्टमेवोक्तम् । तेनायं मन्त्रः ॐ महाजलचराय हुं फट् स्वाहा पाञ्चजन्याय नमः[१ । अन्ते महाशब्दान्ते शार्ङ्गाय सशराय । स्वाहान्त इत्यनेन हुं फट् स्वाहान्त इत्युक्तम् । अन्यथा स्वाहेत्येव वदेत् । तदुक्तम्—

धनुषः शार्ङ्गायाऽथ सशराय हुं फट् युक्तको मन्त्रः । इति ।

आचार्यैरपि "हुं फट् स्वाहा मुशलस्य" इत्युद्धृत्य "शार्ङ्गाय सशराय च" इत्युक्तम् । तत्र चकारेण हुं फट स्वाहेत्यस्य समुच्चय इति । एवं तदग्रिमयोरपि खड्गाङ्कुशयोः तट्टीकाकारैर्व्याख्यातम् । मनुरित्यनेन शार्ङ्गाय नम इत्युक्तम् । अनन्तरः शार्ङ्गमन्त्रः । मन्त्रस्तु महाशार्ङ्गाय सशराय हुं फट् स्वाहा शार्ङ्गाय नमः[२ ।

खड्गतीक्ष्णपदान्ते स्याच्छिन्दयुग्मं हुमादि च ।
चतुर्थोऽयं मनुः प्रोक्तः कौमोदकि महाबले ॥ ४६
सर्वासुरान्तकिपदं प्रसीदयुगवर्मफट् ।
स्वाहान्तोऽयं मनुः प्रोक्तः सद्भिः कौमोदकीपरः ॥ ४७
अङ्कुशान्ते कद्वयुगं षष्ठोऽयं मनुरीरितः ।
संवर्त्तकान्ते मुशल पोथयद्वितयं पुनः ॥ ४८

सुदर्शनेति । पृथगिति । कुरुकुरु छिन्दिछिन्दीति । प्रत्येकमिति । भक्षय भक्षय त्रासय त्रासयेति । अनयोर्मध्ये भूतानीत्यपि ज्ञेयम् ।
तदुक्तमाचार्यैः—भक्षयद्वयभूतानि त्रासयद्वयवर्मफट् । इति ।
अन्यत्रापि—भूतानि त्रासयद्वयम् । हुं फडिति द्वयं । ठद्वयं स्वाहेत्यर्थः ।
चक्रायेति सुदर्शनायेति ज्ञेयम् । तदुक्तम्—

स्वाहा सुदर्शनायेत्यथ नतिरिति चक्रमन्त्र उपदिष्टः । इति ।

तृतीय इति चक्रमन्त्रः । मन्त्रो यथा । सुदर्शन महाचक्रराज दह दह सर्वदुष्टभयं कुरु कुरु छिन्दि छिन्दि विदारय विदारय परमन्त्रान् ग्रस ग्रस भक्षय भक्षय भूतानि त्रासय त्रासय हुं फट् स्वाहा सुदर्शनाय नमः[३ ॥ ४१॥४२॥४३॥४४॥४५ ॥

खड्गेति । महाखड्गेति ज्ञेयम् । छिन्दिकद्वयुगं पृथगित्यपपाठः । बहुग्रन्थ-विरोधात् । अपेक्षितपदानुद्धाराच्च । तदुक्तमाचार्यैः—

खड्गतीक्ष्णान्ते छिन्दयुक् खड्गमन्त्रकः । इति ।

"खड्गतीक्ष्णछिन्दयुगं हुं फडाद्ययं मन्त्रः" इति

अपेक्षितार्थद्योतनिकायां मन्त्रतन्त्रप्रकाशेऽपि एतादृशस्यैव दृष्टत्वात् । तेनायं पाठः छिन्दयुग्मं हुमादि चेति । आदिशब्दात् फट् स्वाहेति च । खड्गाय नम इति । चतुर्थः खड्गमन्त्रः । मन्त्रो यथा । महाखड्ग तीक्ष्ण छिन्द छिन्द हुं फट् स्वाहा खड्गाय नमः[४ ।

कौमोदकीति महाकौमोदकीपरः । कौमोदक्यै नम इत्यन्तः । मन्त्रस्तु । महाकौमोदकि महाबले सर्वासुरान्तकि प्रसीद प्रसीद हुं फट् स्वाहा कौमोदक्यै नमः[५ ॥ ४६ ॥ ४७ ॥

अङ्कुशेति महाङ्कुशेति । अयमिति हुं फट् स्वाहा समुदायः । तदुक्तम् "अङ्कुशकद्वयुगोपरि हुमादि" इति । मनुरित्यङ्कुशाय नम इति । षष्ठ इत्यङ्कुशस्य । मन्त्रस्तु । महाङ्कुश कट्ट कट्ट हुं फट् स्वाहा अङ्कुशाय नमः[६ ।

हुं फट् द्विठान्तो मन्त्रोऽयं सप्तमः परिकीर्त्तितः ।
पाशैर्बन्धद्वयं पश्चादाकर्षय पदद्वयम् ॥ ४९

वह्निजायावधिः सद्भिरष्टमो मन्त्र ईरितः ।
लोकेशान् पूजयेत् पश्चाद्वज्राद्यैरायुधैः सह ॥ ५०

इत्थमभ्यर्चयन्नित्यं यथावत् पुरुषोत्तमम् ।
प्राप्नोति महतीं लक्ष्मीं सौभाग्यमतुलं यशः ।
आयुरारोग्यमैश्वर्य्यं मनोऽभीष्टानि विन्दति ॥ ५१

मुशलेति महामुशल । मन्त्र इति मुशलाय नम इति । सप्तम इति मुशलस्य । मन्त्रस्तु । संवर्त्तक महामुशल पोथय पोथय हुं फट् स्वाहा मुशलाय नमः[७ ।

पाशैति महापाश । वह्निजायावधिरिति हुं फट् स्वाहान्त इत्यर्थः । तदुक्तम्—महापाशपदोपरि बन्धद्वयं तथा कर्षयद्वयं हुं फट् स्वाहा । इति । पाशमन्त्र इति । पाशाय नम इति । अष्टम इति पाशस्य । मन्त्रस्तु । महापाश बन्ध बन्ध आकर्षय आकर्षय हुं फट् स्वाहा पाशाय नमः[८ ।

मन्त्रेषां प्रणवकामादित्वमुक्तम् । आयुधमन्त्राः क्रमतो वच्मस्ते । तारमारबीजाद्या इति । एषां पूजायां विशेषः । यदाहुराचार्याः—

दरचक्रगदामुशलाः पूर्वाद्याशासु चाथ कोणेषु ।
वह्न्यादिषु शार्ङ्गखड्गाङ्कुशपाशाः । इति ॥

आयुधानां वर्णा उक्ता मन्त्रतन्त्रप्रकाशेऽपि—

चक्रं भास्करसङ्काशं खड्गमाकाशसन्निभम् ।
मुशलं श्यामलं ज्ञेयमङ्कुशः कृष्णवर्णकः ॥
पीतं पाशं विजानीयाच्छङ्खं चन्द्रप्रभं स्मरेत् ।
धनुः स्याद्धेमपिङ्गाभं गदा पावकसन्निभा ॥ इति ॥

पश्चादित्यनेन श्रीवत्सकौस्तुभवनमाला अपि स्वस्वस्थाने स्वमुद्रास्वमन्त्रैः पूजनीया इत्युक्तम् । अपेक्षितार्थद्योतनिकामन्त्रतन्त्रप्रकाशादिषु उक्तत्वात् । केचन प्रधानपूजायामेव पूजयन्ति । तथोक्तं मया प्राक् । तत्र मुद्रालक्षणानि मयोक्तानि प्राक् । मन्त्रास्तु । ॐ महाश्रीवत्साय हुं फट् स्वाहा श्रीवत्साय नमः । ॐ महामृतसम्भवाय हुं फट् स्वाहा कौस्तुभाय नमः । ॐ महावनमाले हुं फट् स्वाहा वनमालायै नमः ॥ ४८॥४९॥५० ॥

यथावदिति । पूर्वोक्तप्रकारेण ॥ ५१ ॥

हयारिकुसुमैर्देवमर्चयित्वा यथाविधि ।
शशिप्रसूनैर्जुहुयादष्टोत्तरसहस्रकम् ॥ ५२
मासमात्रेण वशगास्तस्य स्युः सकला नृपाः ।
हुत्वा बिल्वफलैः पक्वैः श्रियं विन्देदनिन्दिताम् ॥ ५३
प्रफुल्लैररुणाम्भोजैस्तामेव लभते पुनः ।
हुत्वा ज्योतिष्मतीतैलं सहस्रं वसुसंख्यकम् ॥ ५४
सुभगो जायते सम्यक् सर्वेषां नात्र संशयः ।
विधानेनाऽमुना मन्त्री महारोगात् प्रमुच्यते ॥ ५५
अश्वत्थसमिधां होमः पराहृतधनप्रदः ।
आज्याक्तदूर्वाहोमेन मुच्यते महतो भयात् ॥ ५६
यस्य नामयुतं मन्त्रं जपेदयुतसंख्यया ।
स भवेद्दासवत् तस्य नात्र कार्या विचारणा ॥ ५७
बहुना किमिहोक्तेन मनुना साधकोत्तमः ।
साधयेत्सकलान् कामान् साक्षाद्विष्णुरिवापरः ॥ ५८
उत्तिष्ठपदमाभाष्य श्री क्रोधीशहुताशनौ ।
वह्निजायावधिर्मन्त्रो वस्वक्षरसमन्वितः ॥ ५९
ऋषिरस्य भवेद्वामः पङ्क्तिश्छन्द उदाहृतम् ।
श्रीकराख्यो हरिः प्रोक्तो देवताऽस्य मनीषिभिः ॥ ६०

हयारिः करवीरः । यथाविधीत्यस्मिन् पीठपूजापूर्वकमित्यर्थः । शशिप्रसूनैः कुमुदैः । वसुसंख्यकं सहस्रम् अष्टसहस्रम् । यस्य नामयुतमिति अमुकपदस्थाने ॥ ५२ ॥ ५३ ॥ ५४ ॥ ५५ ॥ ५६ ॥ ५७ ॥ ५८ ॥

श्रीकरमन्त्रमाह उत्तिष्ठेति । श्री स्वरूपम् । क्रोधीशः कः । हुताशो रेफः । वस्वक्षरः अष्टाक्षरः । केचन श्रीबीजपूर्वकम् अपरे तारपूर्वकमेनमाहुः । तदुक्तम्—केचिच्छ्रीबीजाद्यं केचित्ताराद्यमेनमिच्छन्ति । इति । प्रणवमारश्रीबीजैः सम्पुट इति पद्मपादाचार्याः । अतएव समन्वित इत्युक्तिः ॥५९॥

वामो वामदेव इत्यर्थः । तदुक्तम् "ऋषिरस्य वामदेवः" इति । ॐ बीजं

हृदयं भीषयद्वन्द्वं त्रासयद्वितयं शिरः ।
शिखा प्रमर्दययुगं वर्म प्रध्वंसयद्वयम् ॥ ६१
अस्त्रं रक्षयुगं सर्वे हुमन्ताः समुदीरिताः ।
मूर्ध्नि नेत्रद्वये कण्ठे हृदयोदरयोः पुनः ॥ ६२
ऊरुजङ्घापदद्वन्द्वे मन्त्रवर्णान् प्रविन्यसेत् ।
मुखे न्यसेद् ब्राह्मणोऽस्य मुखमासीदिमं मनुम् ॥ ६३
बाहू राजन्यः कृतोऽयं न्यस्तव्यो बाहुयुग्मके ।
ऊरू तदस्य यद्वैश्य इममूरुद्वये न्यसेत् ॥ ६४
पादद्वये न्यसेन्मन्त्रं पद्भ्यां शूद्रो अजायत ।
चक्रं शङ्खं गदां पद्मं हस्ताग्रेष्वथ विन्यसेत् ॥ ६५
इत्थं न्यासं तनौ कृत्वा देवं पूर्वोक्तमण्डपे ।
रक्तपद्मासनस्थस्य गरुड़स्योपरि स्थितम् ॥ ६६

काञ्चनाद्रिसमप्रभं कमलाननं कमलेक्षणं
चक्रशङ्खगदासरोजधरं मनोहरदर्शनम् ।
कौस्तुभाङ्कितवक्षसं मुकुटाङ्गदादिविभूषणं
तार्क्ष्यवाहनमच्युतं हृदि भावयामि जगत्पतिम् ॥ ६७

स्वाहा शक्तिः । तदुक्तम्—

विष्णुः सबिन्दुरुदितो बीजं शक्तिः शिरोऽस्य विज्ञेयम् । इति ।

मनीषिभिर्हुमन्ताः समुदीरिता इति सम्बन्धः । मनीषिभिरित्यनेन पञ्चाङ्गा-न्तरमष्टाङ्गं कर्त्तव्यमित्युक्तम् । यदाहुः—

अष्टाङ्गानि च कुर्यान् मन्त्रार्णैरुदितवर्त्मना क्रमतः ।
हृदयशिरःपूर्वशिखाकवचास्त्राक्ष्युदरपृष्ठसंभिन्नैः ॥ इति ॥

मूर्ध्नीति । अयं सृष्टिन्यासः । यदाहुः—

सृष्टिरियं निर्दिष्टा तुन्दादिहृदन्तिका स्थितिस्तद्वत् ।
पादाद्यो मूर्धान्तः कथित एष सृष्ट्यादिः ॥ इति ॥

विन्यसेदिति स्वस्वमन्त्रैः स्वस्वमुद्राभिः ॥ ६०॥६१॥६२॥६३॥६४॥६५॥६६ ॥

न्यासस्थानमायुधध्यानेन ज्ञेयम् । आयुधध्यानं तु दक्षोर्ध्वयोराद्ये तदध-स्थयोरन्ये । अत्र ध्यानानन्तरं श्रीवत्सकौस्तुभवनमालामुद्राः प्रदर्शयेत् ॥ ६७ ॥

अष्टलक्षं जपेन्मन्त्री मन्त्रसेनं दशांशतः ।
बिल्वक्षीरद्रुमोत्थाभिः समिद्भिररुणाम्बुजैः ॥ ६८

पयोऽन्नैः सर्पिषा हुत्वा गुरुं सन्तोषयेद्धनैः ।
मूर्त्तौ मूलेन क्लृप्तायां पूजयेद् देवमन्वहम् ॥ ६९

अङ्गान्यादौ केसरेषु दिक्पत्रेषु समर्चयेत् ।
श्रियं रतिं धृतिं कान्तिं लीलापङ्कजधारिणीः ॥ ७०

पीतारुणाश्यामनीला विदिक्पत्रेषु पूजयेत् ।
वासुदेवादिकाः मूर्त्तीः पार्श्वयोर्निधियुग्मकम् ॥ ७१

विष्वक्सेनं यजेदीशे लोकपालाननन्तरम् ।
एवं सम्पूजयेद् देवं साधयेदिष्टमात्मनः ॥ ७२

दूर्वाचरुभ्यां साज्याभ्यां जुहुयादयुतं बुधः ।
सम्पातितं चरुं पश्चात्साध्यो भुञ्जीत साधितम् ॥ ७३

ब्राह्मणान् भोजयेत् सम्यङ्मधुरैर्होमवासरे ।
तोषयेद् गुरुमर्थेन वस्त्रैर्धान्यैर्विभूषणैः ॥ ७४

जित्वाऽपमृत्युरोगादीन् दीर्घमायुः स विन्दति ।
आज्यसिक्तैः सरसिजैर्जुहुयादयुतत्रयम् ॥ ७५

निवसेत् कमला तस्मिन् न त्यजेत् तत्सुतानपि ।
बिल्ववृक्षसमिद्धोमात् साक्षाद्धनपतिर्भवेत् ॥ ७६

पूगपुष्पसमायुक्तैस्तन्दुलैर्मधुरोक्षितैः ।
जुहुयादचिरादेव सम्पदां जायते निधिः ॥ ७७

क्षीरद्रुमेति अश्वत्थोदुम्बरप्लक्षवटाः । तेनाष्टभिर्द्रव्यैः प्रत्येकमयुतरीत्या दशांशसिद्धिः । मूलेन क्लृप्तायामिति । पूर्वोक्ते वैष्णवे पीठे इति शेषः । अङ्गानि समाराध्येति शेषः । समाराध्येति केसरेष्विति शेषः । अन्ये कर्णिकायां पूजयन्ति । पार्श्वयोरित्यष्टदलबाह्ये ॥ ६८॥६९॥७०॥७१ ॥

विष्वक्सेनं यजेदिति । अत्र विष्वक्सेनमुद्रा प्रदर्शनीया । यदाहुः—

नासिकाग्रसमीपस्थां कृत्वा वामस्य तर्जनीम् ।
दण्डवद्दक्षिणे कुर्याद्दक्षिणस्य प्रदेशिनीम् ॥

आज्येन जुहुयाच्छत्रं परान् जयति पार्थिवः ।
अक्षसूत्रं भुजे बद्धं मनुनाऽनेन साधितम् ॥ ७८

रोगापमृत्युदुःखानि नाशयेन्नाऽत्र संशयः ।
जलाञ्जलिभिरात्मानमभिषिञ्चेत् दिने दिने ॥ ७९

स्नानकालेषु स भवेत् सौभाग्यश्रीसमृद्धिमान् ।
ऊर्ध्वबाहुद्वयो मन्त्री पश्यन्नादित्यमण्डलम् ॥ ८०

सहस्रमानं प्रजपेन्नित्यं निश्चितधीर्मनुम् ।
सर्वे मनोरथास्तस्य सिद्ध्येयुर्नाऽत्र संशयः ॥ ८१

विष्वक्सेनस्य मुद्रेयं तत्पूजायां प्रदर्शयेत् ॥ इति ।

ईश इति पश्चाद्भागे । अन्ये अग्रे पूजयन्ति । एतदन्तं द्वितीयावरणम् । अनन्तरमिति अग्न्यादीन् । चरुमिति होमशेषम् । सुसाधितमिति जपादिना ॥ ७२ ॥ ॥ ७३ ॥ ७४ ॥ ७५ ॥ ७६ ॥ ७७ ॥

अक्षसूत्रमिति मन्त्रवर्णसंख्यान्यक्षसूत्राण्यानीय मन्त्रेणाऽष्टौ ग्रन्थयो देयाः । तदुक्तफलदम् ॥ ७८ ॥ ७९ ॥ ८० ॥

निश्चितधीरित्यनेन तत्र देवतां ध्यायन्नित्युक्तम् । गौतमकल्पोक्तं यन्त्रमुच्यते—

तारं समाध्यमष्टारे कोणे मूलाक्षराणि तु ।
प्रत्येकं शक्तिश्रीपुञ्जिकोणाग्रेषु षडङ्गकम् ॥
बहिरष्टदले पद्मे लिखेदष्टाक्षरं मनुम् ।
पश्चाद्वेष्टयेद्बाह्ये द्वादशाक्षरसंयुतम् ॥
पद्मं द्वादशपत्रं तु वृत्तात् षट्कोणकं बहिः ।
कोणेष्वनङ्गबीजं तु बहिरष्टदलाम्बुजम् ॥
केसरेषु कलाः पत्रे द्वन्द्वशः श्रीकरं मनुम् ।
तारः श्रीकरकृष्णौ च ङेन्तौ गोपीकुचान्ततः ॥
भूषणायेति मन्त्रोऽयं तत्पाशाङ्कुशवेष्टितम् ।
संवीतं च सदृत्तेन ब्योमैतद्यन्त्रमुत्तमम् ॥
भूतप्रेतपिशाचाश्च यक्षगन्धर्वराक्षसाः ।
लयं यान्ति तथा सर्वे केवलं यन्त्रधारणात् ॥
संसाधितं महायन्त्रमपस्मारहरं परम् ।

कृष्णाय पदमाभाष्य गोविन्दाय ततः परम् ।
गोपीजनपदस्याऽन्ते वल्लभाय द्विठावधिः ॥ ८२

कामबीजादिराख्यातो मनुरष्टादशाक्षरः ।
नारदोऽस्य मुनिः प्रोक्तो गायत्रं छन्द उच्यते ॥ ८३

देवता कथितः कृष्णः सर्वकामफलप्रदः ।
चतुःकरणवेदाब्धिनेत्रसंख्याक्षरैः क्रमात् ।
पञ्चाङ्गानि मनोः कुर्यान्मन्त्रविज्जातिसंयुतैः ॥ ८४

स्मरेद् वृन्दावने रम्ये मोहयन्तं मनोरमम् ।
गोविन्दं पुण्डरीकाक्षं गोपकन्याः सहस्रशः ॥ ८५

आत्मनो वदनाम्भोजप्रेषिताक्षिमधुव्रताः ।
पीड़िताः कामबाणेन चिरमाश्लेषणोत्सुकाः ॥ ८६

मुक्ताहारलसत्पीततुङ्गस्तनभरानताः ।
स्रस्तधम्मिल्लवसना मदस्खलितभाषणाः ॥ ८७

दन्तपङ्क्तिप्रभोद्भासि स्पन्दमानाधराञ्चिताः ।
विलोभयन्तीर्विविधैर्विभ्रमैर्भावगर्भितैः ॥ ८८

साध्यनामाङ्कितं यन्त्रं धारयित्वा वशङ्करम् ॥
यद्यत्कामयते वत्स तत् प्राप्नोति समाहितः ॥ इति ॥ ८०॥८१ ॥

गोपालमन्त्रमाह कृष्णायेति । द्विठेति स्वाहा । क्लीं बीजं स्वाहा शक्तिः । तदुक्तम्—

वक्ष्ये मन्त्रस्याऽस्य बीजं सशक्ति चक्री शक्रो वामनेत्रप्रदीप्तः ।
सप्रद्युम्नो बीजमेतत्प्रदिष्टं मन्त्रः प्राद्युम्नो जगन्मोहनोऽयम् ॥
हंसो भेदो वह्निवृत्ताभ्युपेतः पोत्रीनेत्राद्यन्वितोऽसौ युगार्णा ।
प्रोक्ता शक्तिः सर्वगीर्वाणवृन्दैर्वन्द्यस्याम्भेर्वल्लभा कामदेयम् ॥ इति ॥

करणेति चत्वारि ॥ ८२ ॥ ८३ ॥ ८४ ॥

गोपकन्या मोहयन्तमिति सम्बन्धः । आत्मनो जगदात्मनः । तासां वात्मरूपस्य कृष्णस्येत्यर्थः । स्पन्दमानाः सस्फुरणा ये अधराः तैरञ्चिताः पुष्पिताः ॥ ८५ ॥ ८६ ॥ ८७ ॥ ८८ ॥

फुल्लेन्दीवरकान्तिमिन्दुवदनं बर्हावतंसप्रियं
श्रीवत्साङ्कमुदारकौस्तुभधरं पीताम्बरं सुन्दरम् ।
गोपीनां नयनोत्पलार्चिततनुं गोपालसङ्घावृतं
गोविन्दं कलवेणुवादनपरं दिव्याङ्गभूषं भजे ॥ ८९

मन्त्रमेनं यथान्यायमयुतद्वितयं जपेत् ।
जुहुयादरुणाम्भोजैस्तद्दशांशं समाहितः ॥ ९०

फुल्लेति। इन्दीवरं नीलोत्पलम्। बर्हावतंसं मयूरपिच्छकर्णाभरणम्। कलवेणुवादनपरम्। अनेन द्विभुजं ध्यानमुक्तम्। अत्र ध्यानानन्तरं वेणुश्रीवत्सकौस्तुभवनमालाबिल्वमुद्राः प्रदर्शयेत्। तत्र वेणुबिल्वमुद्रालक्षणं यथा—

ओष्ठे वामकराङ्गुष्ठो लग्नस्तस्य कनिष्ठिका ।
दक्षिणाङ्गुष्ठसंसक्ता तत्कनिष्ठा प्रसारिता ॥
तर्जनीमध्यमानामाः किञ्चित् सङ्कुच्य चालिताः ।
वेणुमुद्रेह कथिता सुगुप्ता प्रेयसी हरेः ॥
उच्यतेऽच्युतमुद्राणां भद्रा बिल्वफलाकृतिः ।

अङ्गुष्ठं वाममुद्दण्डितमितरकराङ्गुष्ठकेनाऽथ बद्धा
तस्याऽग्रं पीडयित्वाऽङ्गुलिभिरपि च ता वामहस्ताङ्गुलीभिः ।
बद्धा गाढं हृदि स्थापयतु विमलधीर्व्याहरन् मारबीजं
बिल्वाख्या मुद्रिकैषा स्फुटमिह गदिता गोपनीया विधिज्ञैः ॥

मनो वाणी देहैर्यदिह च पुरा वापि विहितं
त्वमत्वा मत्वा वा तदखिलमसौ दुष्कृतचयम् ।
इमां मुद्रां जानन् क्षपयति नरस्तं सुरगणा
नमस्यस्याऽधीना भवति सततं सर्वजनता ॥ इति ॥ ८९ ॥

यथान्यायमित्यनेनैतदुक्तं भवति। यदाहुः—

अद्रेः शृङ्गे नद्यास्तटे बिल्वमूले तोये हृद्ये गोकुले विष्णुगेहे ।
अश्वत्थाधस्तादम्बुधेश्चापि तीरे स्थानेष्वेतेष्वासीन एकैकशस्तु ॥
अजपेदयुतचतुष्कं दशाक्षरं मनुवरं पृथक् क्रमशः ।
अष्टादशाक्षरं वेदयुतद्वयमित्युदीरिता संख्या ॥
शाकं मूलं फलं गोस्तनभवदधिनी भैक्ष्यमन्नं च सक्तुम् ।
दोग्धान्नं चेत्याददानः क्षितिधरशिखरादौ क्रमात् स्थानभेदे ॥

वैष्णवे पूजयेत् पीठे यथावत् देवकीसुतम् ।
अङ्गावरणमाराध्य पत्रेषु प्रयजेत् प्रियाः ॥ ९१
कालिन्दी नाग्नजित्याख्या मित्रविन्दा ततः परम् ।
चारुहासिन्यथ परा रोहिणी जाम्बवत्यथ ॥ ९२
रुक्मिणी सत्यभामेति कथिताश्चारुभूषणाः ।
पीताम्बरधराः सौम्याः कराम्बुजधृताम्बुजाः ॥ ९३
ऐरावतादीनभ्यर्च्येत् गजानष्टौ ततो बहिः ।
लोकपालान् यजेन्मन्त्री वज्राद्यस्त्राणि तद्बहिः ॥ ९४
इति सम्पूजयेत् देवं गोविन्दं जगतां पतिम् ।
कुर्वीत कल्पनिर्दिष्टान् प्रयोगान्निजवाञ्छितान् ॥ ९५
लक्ष्मीप्रसूनैर्जुहुयाच्छ्रियमिच्छन्ननिन्दिताम् ।
साज्येनाऽन्नेन जुहुयादाज्यान्नस्य समृद्धये ॥ ९६

एकं चैषामशक्तौ गदितमिह मया पूर्वसेवाविधानम् ।
निर्वृत्तेऽस्मिन् पुनश्च प्रजपतु विधिवत् सिद्धये साधकेशः ॥
दशलक्षमक्षयफलप्रदं मनुं प्रतिजप्य शिक्षितमतिर्दशाक्षरम् ।
सुषिरयुगलवर्णं चेन्मनुं पञ्चलक्षम् । इति ॥

तद्दशांशं पञ्चलक्षदशांशम् । समाहित इत्यनेनैतदुक्तं भवति । यदाहुः—
अमलमतिरलाभे पायसैरम्बुजानां ससितघृतसुसिक्तैरारभेद्धोमकर्म । इति ॥ ९० ॥

वैष्णव इति नारायणाष्टाक्षरोक्ते । यथावदित्यनेनैतदुक्तं भवति । दामादि-
वज्रास्त्रान्तैः सप्तभिरावरणैर्देवमर्चयेत् । अन्योक्ताङ्गादिवज्रास्त्रान्तं पञ्चावरणं वा ।
अङ्गलोकपालतदस्त्राणीत्यावरणत्रयं वा । कृष्णाष्टकेनैकावरणं वेति ।
तदुक्तम्—कथितमावृतिसप्तकमच्युतार्चनविधाविति सर्वसुखावहम् ।
प्रयजतादथवाऽङ्गपुरन्दराशनिमुखैस्त्रितयावरणं त्विदम् ॥

श्रीकृष्णो वासुदेवश्च नारायणसमाह्वयः ।
देवकीनन्दनो यदुश्रेष्ठो वार्ष्णेय इत्यपि ॥
असुराक्रान्तशब्दान्ते भारहारीति सप्तमः ।
धर्मसंस्थापकश्चाऽष्टौ चतुर्थ्यन्ताः क्रमादिमे ॥

आरण्यैः कुसुमैर्विप्रान् जातिभिः पृथिवीपतीन्।
प्रसूनैरसितैर्वैश्यान् शूद्रान्नीलोत्पलैर्नवैः॥ ९७

वशयेन्नवकैः सर्वान् पङ्कजैर्वनिताजनान्।
गोशालासु कृतो होमः पायसेन ससर्पिषा॥ ९८

गवां शान्तिं करोत्याशु गोविन्दो गोकुलप्रियः।
शिशुवेशधरं देवं किङ्किणीदामशोभितम्॥ ९९

स्मृत्वा प्रतर्पयेन्मन्त्री दुग्धबुध्या शुभैर्जलैः।
धनधान्यांशुकादीनि प्रीतस्तस्मै ददाति सः॥ १००

पिण्डं मूलेन वीतं दहनपुरयुगे कोणराजद्रसार्णं
कुर्यात् पद्मं दशार्णस्फुरितदशदलं कामबीजेन वीतम्।
पद्मं किञ्जल्कसंस्थं स्वरविकृतिदलं प्रोल्लसत्षोड़शार्णं
किञ्जल्कं व्यञ्जनाढ्यं विकृतियुगदलेष्वर्पितानुष्टुबर्णम्॥ १०१

पाशाङ्कुशाभ्यामावीतं क्षौणीपुरयुगस्त्रिषु।
अष्टाक्षरेण लसितं यन्त्रं गोविन्ददैवतम्।
धर्मार्थकामफलदं सर्वरक्षाकरं स्मृतम्॥ १०२

पञ्चान्तको धरेरस्थो मनुबिन्दुविभूषितः।
पिण्डबीजमिदं प्रोक्तं सर्वसिद्धिकरं परम्॥ १०३

एभिरेवाऽथवा पूजा कर्त्तव्या कंसवैरिणः॥ इति।

एते चत्वारोऽपि पद्मा मुख्या एव। कल्पभेदाद्भेदः। आराध्येति केसरेष्विति। ऐरावतादीनष्टमोक्तान्॥ ९१—१००॥

यन्त्रमाह पिण्डमिति। वक्ष्यमाणं पिण्डबीजम्। परस्परव्यतिभिन्ने दहनपुरयुगे षट्कोणे। रसार्णं षड्वर्णम्। षड्वर्णदशार्णषोड़शार्णानुष्टुबष्टार्णान् वक्ष्यति। विकृतिदलं षोड़शदलम्। विकृतियुगदलं द्वात्रिंशद्दलम्। अत्रोभयत्र केसरस्थानेषु एकैकार्णलेखः। पाशाङ्कुशाभ्यामित्येकावृत्तिः॥ १०१॥१०२॥

पिण्डबीजमाह पञ्चान्तक इति। पञ्चान्तको गः धरा लः इरो यः तत्संस्थः ग्ल्यः। मनुरौ बिन्दुश्च एतद्युक्तस्तेन ग्लौं। सर्वसिद्धिकरं परमित्यनेनाऽस्य स्वातन्त्र्यं नमोऽन्तत्वेन त्र्यक्षरत्वम्। प्रणवमायादित्वेन वा त्र्यक्षरत्वमुक्तम्।

अस्यर्ष्यादिकमुच्यते—

मुनिर्नारद आख्यातश्छन्दो गायत्रमीरितम् ।
देवता बालकृष्णोऽङ्गं षड्दीर्घाक्रान्तबीजतः ॥

अव्यात् व्याकोशनीलाम्बुजरुचिररुणाम्भोजनेत्रोऽम्बुजस्थो
बालो जङ्घाकटीरस्थलकलितरणत्किङ्किणीको मुकुन्दः ।
दोर्भ्यां हैयङ्गवीनं दधदतिविमलं पायसं विश्ववन्द्यो
गोगोपीगोपवीतो रुरुनखविलसत्कण्ठभूषश्चिरं वः ॥

जपेल्लक्षं मनुवरं पायसैरयुतं हुनेत् ।
पूजा तु वैष्णवे पीठे अङ्गदिक्पालवज्रकैः ॥ इति ॥

यद्दृषिर्नारदः प्रोक्तो जगती छन्द ईरितम् ।
श्रीकृष्णो देवता बीजं ग्लौं य शक्तिः प्रकीर्त्तिता ॥
षडङ्गं मूलमन्त्रेण कुर्यात् देवं विचिन्तयेत् ।
कदम्बमूले तिष्ठन्तं देवदेवं जनार्दनम् ॥
इन्दीवरदलश्यामं पूर्णचन्द्रनिभाननम् ।
देवगन्धर्वयक्षौघकिन्नरोरगसेवितम् ॥
मोहनं गोपगोपीनां वल्लभं देवकीसुतम् ।
मयूरपिच्छसंयुक्तं वनमालाविभूषितम् ॥
पूर्णचन्द्रनिभं कान्तं वृन्दावननिवासिनम् ।
वेणुं गायन्तममलं सर्वभूतमनोहरम् ॥
लेलिह्यमानं वत्सैश्च मृगैः सिंहैस्तथा द्विजैः ।
सर्वाभरणसंयुक्तं सर्वाभरणशोभितम् ॥
कौस्तुभोद्भासितोरस्कं दामपिच्छसमावृतम् ।
अप्रमेयमचिन्त्यं च गोपालं शिशुरूपिणम् ॥
ध्यायेत्तं देवदेवेशं सर्वलोकैकनायकम् ।
अङ्गैश्च वासुदेवाद्यैरुक्मिण्याद्यैस्ततीयकम् ॥
कुमुदेन्द्रायुधैश्चापि षडावरणमीरितम् ।
जपोऽयुतचतुष्कः स्याद्दशांशं जुहुयात्ततः ॥
पायसेन सिताक्तेन तर्पयेत्तावदेव तु ।
मन्त्रसिद्धस्य लोकोऽयं सद्यो वश्यो भविष्यति ॥ इति ॥ १०३ ॥

स्मरः कृष्णाय ठद्वन्द्वं षड्‌र्णो मनुरीरितः ॥ १०४

गोपीजनान्ते प्रवदेद्‌ वल्लभायाऽग्निसुन्दरी ।

अयं दशाक्षरो मन्त्रो दृष्टादृष्टफलप्रदः ॥ १०५

प्रणवं हृदयं कृष्णं ङेऽन्तमुक्त्वा ततः परम् ।

तादृशं देवकीपुत्रं हुंफट्स्वाहासमन्वितम् ॥ १०६

षोड़शाक्षरमन्त्रोऽयं गोविन्दस्य समीरितः ।

पिण्डं रतिपतेर्बीजं नमो भगवते ततः ॥ १०७

नन्दपुत्राय बालादिवपुषे श्यामलाय च ।

गोपीजनपदस्याऽन्ते वल्लभाय द्विठावधिः ॥ १०८

अनुष्टुब्मन्त्र आख्यातो गोपालस्य जगत्पतेः ।

अनङ्गः कृष्णगोविन्दौ ङेऽन्तावष्टाक्षरो मनुः ॥ १०९

षड्‌र्णमाह स्मर इति। स्मरः कामबीजम्। मनुरीरित इत्यनेनाऽयमपि स्वतन्त्रो मन्त्र इत्युक्तम्। अस्य मुन्यादि पूजान्तं अष्टादशार्णवत्। षड्लक्षं जपः। दशांशं होमोऽष्टादशार्णोक्तद्रव्येणेति ज्ञेयम्। पञ्चाङ्गानि तु—

ङेस्वाहान्तैश्चक्रपदैः पञ्चाङ्गान्यावितुस्थितैः ।

त्रैलोक्यरक्षणयुतैरसुरान्तकसंयुतैः । इति ॥ १०४ ॥

दशार्णमाह गोपीति। अग्निसुन्दरी स्वाहा। दृष्टादृष्टफलप्रद इत्यनेनाऽस्य स्वातन्त्र्यमुक्तम्। अस्य सर्वं षडक्षरवत् ज्ञेयम् ॥ १०५ ॥

षोड़शार्णमाह प्रणवमिति। हृदयं नमः पदम्। ङेऽन्तं कृष्णं कृष्णाय। तादृशञ्च ङेऽन्तं तेन देवकीपुत्रायेति। गोविन्दस्येत्यनेनाऽयमपि स्वतन्त्रो मन्त्र इत्युक्तम्। अस्य सर्वं दशाक्षरवत् ज्ञेयम् ॥ १०६ ॥ १०७ ॥

द्वात्रिंशदर्णमाह पिण्डमिति। पूर्वोक्तं पिण्डबीजम्। रतिपतेर्बीजं कामबीजम्। गोपालस्य जगत्पतेरित्यनेनाऽयमपि स्वतन्त्रो मन्त्र इत्युक्तम्। अस्यर्ष्यादिकं यथा—

अस्य नारद ऋषिश्छन्दोऽनुष्टुप् समीरितम् ।

देवता हरिराख्यात आचक्राद्यैरथाऽङ्गकम् ॥

दक्षिणे रत्नचषकं वामे सौवर्णवेत्रकम् ।

करे दधानं देवीभ्यामाश्लिष्टं चिन्तयेद्धरिम् ॥

जपेल्लक्षं मनुवरं पायसैरयुतं हुनेत् ।

पूजा तु वैष्णवे पीठे ह्यङ्गदिक्पालवज्रकैः ॥

प्राक्प्रत्यगुदक्षिणोदग्विधिवदभिलिखेत् स्पष्टरेखाचतुष्कं
कोणोद्यच्छूलयुक्तं वलययुगयुतं मध्यपूर्वं तदन्तम्।
श्लोकस्याऽर्णान् परस्ताद्वसुपदविवरेष्वष्टवर्णान् लिखित्वा
तद्बाह्ये द्वादशार्णैस्तदनु परिवृतं देवकीपुत्रयन्त्रम्॥ ११०

तं सुकीदेवदेवे तं तं देवे वरतो रतम्।
तं रतो रुटतो ख्यातं तं ख्यातं देवकीसुतम्॥ १११

एवं सिद्धमनुर्मन्त्री त्रैलोक्यैश्वर्यभाग्भवेत्॥ इति।

अष्टार्णमाह अनङ्गेति। अनङ्गः कामबीजम्। ॐऽक्लीं कृष्णगोविन्दौ कृष्णाय गोविन्दाय। अयमपि स्वतन्त्रो मन्त्रः। अस्य मुन्यादि सर्वं पूर्वोक्तषडक्षरवत् ज्ञेयम्॥ १०७॥१०८॥१०९॥

कामलिङ्गयन्त्रमाह प्रागिति। प्राक्प्रत्यग्रेखाद्वयं दक्षिणोदग्रेखाद्वयं लिखेत्। एवमुभयं मिलित्वा रेखाचतुष्कं भवति। इदमेव विधिवत्पदेनोक्तम्। कोणोद्यच्छूलयुक्तम्। मध्यकोष्ठकोणेभ्यो बहिः कर्णसूत्रचतुष्टयं दद्यात् तेन शूलाकारता भवत्येव। वलययुगयुतम्। तत्रैकं वृत्तं रेखाग्रस्पर्शि द्वितीयं मध्यकोष्ठे तद्वृत्तान्तराले। मध्यपूर्वमिति। मध्यकोष्टमारभ्य लेखनारम्भः। तदन्तम्। मध्यकोष्ठ एव समाप्तिरित्यर्थः। तत्राऽक्षरलेखनक्रमः। प्राक्संस्थतया मध्यादि कोष्ठत्रये आद्यवर्णत्रयमालिख्य आग्नेय्यां वृत्तद्वयान्तराले कोणरेखामभितः कोष्ठद्वये देवेत्यक्षरं लिखेत्। ततो दक्षिणे ऊर्ध्वादि कोष्ठद्वये देवे इत्यक्षरद्वयं लिखेत्। तकारस्तु मध्यकोष्ठस्थ एव वाचनीयः। ततो मध्यकोष्ठाद्दक्षिणस्थमेवाक्षरद्वयं संवाच्य नैर्ऋत्यकोणे मध्यरेखोभयतः कोष्ठद्वये वरेत्यक्षरद्वयं लिखेत्। पश्चिमे तु दक्षिणवदेव। ततो वायव्यकोणे मध्यरेखोभयतः कोष्ठद्वये रुटेत्यक्षरद्वयं लिखेत्। ततः उत्तरे तु दक्षिणवदेव। ईशकोणे मध्यरेखोभयतः कोष्ठद्वये देवेत्यक्षरद्वयं लिखेत्। ततः प्राच्यां लिखितान्यक्षराणि ऊर्ध्वतो वाचयेत्। एवं श्लोकमन्त्राक्षरलेखनक्रमः। परस्तादिति मध्यकोष्ठाद्बहिः प्रथमवृत्तान्तः एकैकस्मिन् कोणे कर्णसूत्रोभयतः कोष्ठद्वन्द्वमवशिष्यते। तत्र प्रादक्षिण्यक्रमेण ईशानादि पूर्वोक्तमष्टवर्णं लिखेत्। तदनु तदनन्तरम्। तद्बाह्ये द्वितीयवृत्तबाह्ये। द्वादशार्णैः पञ्चदशोक्तवासुदेवमन्त्रार्णैः परिवृतम्। शूलोत्पन्नद्वादशसु कोष्ठेषु द्वादशवर्णलिखनेनार्थात् वृत्तं भवति इति वृत्तमित्युक्तिः। एवंभूतं यन्त्रमुक्तफलदम्। एष साम्प्रदायिकः पक्षः। केचन प्रागपरायताश्वतस्रः उदग्दक्षिणायताश्चतस्रो

लिखितं भूर्जपत्रादौ यन्त्रमेतद्यथाविधि।
विधृतं बाहुना नित्यं सर्वकामफलप्रदम् ॥ ११२

पलाशवृक्षफलके लिखितं साधुसाधितम्।
गोस्थाने निखनेदेतद् गवां वृद्धिर्भवेत् सदा ॥ ११३

श्लोकं चतुःषष्टिपदेषु भूर्जे शिवादि दैत्यादि लिखेत् क्रमेण।
तत् सर्वतोभद्रमिति प्रसिद्धं यन्त्रं यशःश्रीविजयप्रदायि ॥ ११४

फलके खादिरे क्लृप्तं गवां गोष्ठे निवेशितम्।
रक्षाकृच्चौरमारिघ्नं सवत्सानां गवां हितम् ॥ ११५

चौरगोपयगोरक्षीरक्षमाक्षक्षमाक्षर।
गोमानोगगनोमागोपक्षगक्षक्षगक्षप ॥ ११६

ब्रह्मा भूम्यां समासीनः शान्तिबिन्दुसमन्वितः।
बीजं मनोभुवः प्रोक्तं जगत्त्रितयमोहनम् ॥ ११७

रेखाः कुर्यात्। एवं नवकोष्ठानि संपद्यन्ते। तत्र मध्यकोष्ठे वलययुगयुतं कार्यमित्याहुः। ते मध्यपूर्वं तदन्तमित्यस्य व्याख्यानं प्रष्टव्या भवन्ति। भूर्जपत्रादावित्यादिशब्देन ताम्ररजतकाञ्चनादीनां ग्रहणम्। तत्तल्लेख्यविशेषेण कालविशेषोऽपि पूर्वोक्तोऽनुसन्धेयः। यथाविधीति विधिर्दर्शितः। एवं लिखनप्रस्तावे ॥ ११०॥१११॥११२॥११३ ॥

यन्त्रान्तरमाह श्लोकमिति। श्लोकं वक्ष्यमाणम्। चतुःषष्टिपदेष्विति। सर्वतः सशूलेष्विति ज्ञेयम्। तदुक्तमपेक्षितार्थद्योतनिकायाम्—

चतुःषष्टिपदोपेतं शूलमालाभिभूषितम्। इति।

शिवादि ईशानादि। दैत्यादि नैर्ऋत्यादि। कोष्ठोत्पादनसाध्यादि लेखनप्रकारो दशमे सदुक्तोऽनुसन्धेय। एतावपि द्वौ सिद्धमन्त्रौ। आभ्यां क्रमेण आर्त्तबालगोरक्षां कुर्यात् ॥ ११४॥११५॥११६ ॥

एकाक्षरं काममन्त्रमाह ब्रह्मेति। ब्रह्मा कः। भूमिर्लः। एतदासीनः। शान्तिरी बिन्दुस्तेन क्लीं। ककारो बीजम् ईकारः शक्तिः। तदुक्तं दक्षिणामूर्त्तिसंहितायां "कतुर्यं बीजशक्तिके" इति। जगत्त्रितयमोहनमित्यनेन हकारसकारादित्वं सूचितम्। केवलहकारादित्वं महावश्यदम्। केवलसकारादित्वं दीर्घायुष्यदमिति। तदुक्तं—

ऋषिः सम्मोहनः प्रोक्तो गायत्रं छन्द ईरितम् ।

सर्वसम्मोहनः साक्षाद्देवता मकरध्वजः ॥ ११८

हंसारूढो मदनस्त्रैलोक्यक्षोभको भवेदाशु ।

लघुतो रञ्जनकृत् स्याज्जीवेन युतस्तथाऽऽयुषे मन्त्रः ॥ इति ॥११७॥

"सर्वसम्मोहनकृष्ण एतयोः स्याद्देवता" इत्युक्तेः साक्षादित्यनेन केवलः कृष्णोऽपि ।

तत्र सम्मोहनकृष्णदेवतापक्षे अष्टभुजध्यानम् । यदाहुः—

विश्वत्राणस्यायतप्रोतनद्युतिः सुपर्णस्थ ।

आसीनस्तुङ्गतांसे वैकुण्ठस्तङ्काङ्कमङ्कजोर्भाधितम् ॥

चक्रदराङ्कुशपाशान् सुमनोबाणेक्षुचापमुसलगदाः ।

दधतं स्वदोर्भिररुणायतविपुलविघूर्णिताक्षियुगनलिनम् ॥

स्वाभासिदतयेत्थं ध्यात्वैकादशसहस्राऽष्टवर्णं वा ।

प्रजपेद्दिनकरलक्षं त्रिमधुरसिक्तैश्च किंशुकप्रसवैः ॥

जुहुयात्तरणिसहस्रं विमलैः सलिलैश्च तर्पयेत्तावत् । इति ।

एवमष्टभुजो वा ध्येयः । तदुक्तं मन्त्रतन्त्रप्रकाशे—

नित्यमष्टभुजं ध्यायेत्कृष्णं पुरुषोत्तमम् ।

रमयाऽऽलिङ्गितं वामे लोकत्रितयमोहनम् ॥

चक्रं खड्गं च मुसलं दधे बिभ्राणमङ्कुशम् ।

वामे पाशं तथा शङ्खं सशरं चापमेव च ॥

कौमोदकीं च बिभ्राणं सर्वभूषणभूषितम् ।

दशलक्षजपादेष सिद्धमन्त्रः प्रजायते ॥ इति ॥

अस्य मन्त्रद्वयस्य पूजादिकं सर्वं पुरुषोत्तममन्त्रवदेव । यदाहुः—

प्रायः पुरुषोत्तमविधिरत्रमतोऽन्यत्ततोऽवगन्तव्यम् । इति ।

केवलकृष्णदेवतापक्षे तु अष्टादशाक्षरोक्तमार्गेण ध्यानपूजादिकं सर्वमस्य विज्ञेयम् ।

विधानान्तरं च—एतदेव रमाबीजपुटितं चाखिलार्थदम् ।

लक्ष्मीनारायणौ हेमरूपौ चिन्तयेच्छुभौ ॥

तदेव मायापुटितं विद्यावश्यं प्रयच्छति ।

स्वभावादश्वदं ह्येतद् धनदं भोगदं तथा ॥

यद्यस्मात्कामयेद्विद्यां द्विजेन्द्रो मन्त्रतत्त्ववित् ।

भारत्या सहितं विष्णुं तत्र ध्यायेच्छशिप्रभम् ॥

गद्यपद्यैस्तथा शास्त्रैः पूरयन्तौ जगत्त्रयम् ।

बीजेन दीर्घयुक्तेन षडङ्गविधिरीरितः ॥ ११९

ध्यातव्या तु तदा दत्ते विश्वोर्वाणी सुभूषणा । इति ॥

तारेण वेष्टितं कामं प्रजपेद्दर्भमोजयोः ।

सिद्धये योऽहरिं ध्यायेत् श्वेतं मुनिगणाहृतम् । इति ॥

अन्यच तु—कमलासनखो नकुली वामनेत्रार्धचन्द्रवान् । इति ।

अनेन कामबीजानन्तरं भुवनेशीबीजमित्युक्तम् । ध्यानं च—

नाभिमध्ये समुद्भूतां भ्रूमध्ये च विनिःसृताम् ।

प्रणवांबुजमध्यस्थां मुक्तालङ्कारभूषिताम् ।

लिखन्तीं पुस्तकं हस्ते धारयन्तीं समभ्यसेत् ॥ इति ।

तत्रैव विशेषः—लिपिभिर्वा मनुर्जप्तो लोककामकरो भवेत् । इति ।

अन्यत्रापि—वरपाशाङ्कुशधरां मद्यपूर्णकपालभृत् ।

नित्यां ध्यात्वा जपेत् कामबीजमिष्टार्थसिद्धये ॥ इति ।

अन्यत्रापि—सकृज्जप्तेन बीजेन ब्रह्महत्यां व्यपोहति ।

द्विजप्तेन तथा ब्रह्मचतुर्भिरितरैरपि ॥

सर्वयज्ञफलं चापि त्रिजप्तेन तु लभ्यते ।

चतुर्जप्तेन तृप्यन्ते सर्वदेवगणास्तथा ॥

पञ्चजप्तेन देवेन्द्रं षड्जप्तेन तथा पितॄन् ।

सप्तजप्तेन योगीन्द्रान् सर्वान् प्रीणाति साधकः ॥

अष्टजप्तेन प्रीणाति स्वयमेव पितामहः ।

नवजप्तेन वै विष्णुर्दशजप्तेन शङ्करः ॥

कारणं यत्प्रधानाख्यं प्रकृतिः सगुणात्मकम् ।

प्रीणाति साधकेन्द्रस्तु नासैकादशभिर्मुने ॥

तथा द्वादशजप्तेन सर्वगं पुरुषं हितम् ।

मोक्षं च साधकेन्द्राणां नित्यं जप्तं प्रयच्छति ॥

विधानेन गृहीतं स्यान्मोक्षदं सवतो मुने ।

अन्यथा भोगदं तत्र स्त्रीणामाकर्षणे मुने ॥

यथा यथा हि जपति व्याप्तिं गत्वा तु साधकः ।

तथा तथा हि सिध्यन्ति सिद्धविद्याधरस्त्रियः ॥ इति ॥ ११८ ॥

दीर्घयुक्तेन षड्दीर्घयुक्तेन । एतदनन्तरं आत्मास्यकण्ठहृन्मूलाधारेषु पञ्चबाणान् विन्यसेत् । अग्रे पूजायामप्रतिलेनोक्तेः । तदुक्तमाचार्यैः—"**न्यस्तशरबीजदेह**:"

जवारुणं रत्नविभूषणाढ्यं मीनध्वजं चारुकृताङ्गरागम् ।
कराम्बुजैरङ्कुशमिक्षुचापं पुष्पास्त्रपाशौ दधतं भजामि ॥ १२०

लक्षत्रयं जपेन्मन्त्रं मधुरत्रयसंयुतैः ।
पुष्पैः किंशुकजैः कुर्याज्जुहुयात्तद्दशांशतः ॥ १२१

वक्ष्यमाणे यजेत् पीठे विधिना मकरध्वजम् ।
मोहिनी क्षोभिणी त्रासा स्तम्भिन्याकर्षिणी पुनः ॥ १२२

द्राविण्युन्मादिनी ख्यातिस्ताश्चेति कथिताः पीठशक्तयः ।
बीजाद्यमासनं दत्त्वा मूर्तिं मूलेन कल्पयेत् ॥ १२३

अस्यां सम्यग्यजेद् देवं वक्ष्यमाणेन वर्त्मना ।
इष्ट्वाऽङ्गावरणं पूर्वं मध्ये दिक्षु यजेच्छरान् ॥ १२४

द्रामाद्यं शोषणं पूर्वं द्रीमाद्यं मोहनं ततः ।
संदीपनाख्यं क्लीमाद्यं ब्लूमाद्यं तापनं ततः ॥ १२५

सर्गान्तभृगुणा भूयो मादनं पञ्चमं ततः ।
प्रणामबाणहस्ताश्च ध्येयास्ता बाणदेवताः ॥ १२६

इति ॥ ११८ ॥

आयुधध्यानं वामोर्ध्वादिदक्षोर्ध्वं यावत् । अत्र ध्यानानन्तरमेते मुद्रे दर्शनीये ।

हस्तौ तु संपुटौ कृत्वा प्रसृताङ्गुलिकौ तथा ।
तर्जन्यौ मध्यमापृष्ठे अङ्गुष्ठौ मध्यमान्वितौ ॥
काममुद्रेयमाख्याता सर्वसत्त्ववशङ्करी ।
मूर्धन्यङ्गुष्ठमुष्टी द्वे मुद्रा त्रैलोक्यमोहिनी ॥ इति ॥ १२० ॥

वक्ष्यमाणे पीठे विधिना वक्ष्यमाणेन यजेदिति । मण्डूकादिपरतत्त्वान्तं संपूज्य वक्ष्यमाणाः पीठशक्तीः पूजयेदित्यर्थः । बीजाद्यमिति । क्लीं कामयोगपीठाय नमः इति आसनं पूजयेदित्यर्थः ॥ १२१॥१२२॥१२३ ॥

वक्ष्यमाणेनेत्युक्तं वर्त्माऽऽह इष्ट्वेति । कर्णिकायामिति शेषः । तदुक्तम्—"इष्ट्वा कर्णिकायामङ्गानि" इति । मध्य इति पञ्चमम् । "दिक्षु शरान् मध्ये च पञ्चमं पुनः" इत्युक्तेः । द्रामित्यादौ अनुस्वारे आचार्याणां ङकारव्यवहार इति ज्ञेयम् । सर्गान्तभृगुरिति सः । प्रणामेति । एकहस्ते प्रणामः अपरहस्ते बाणः ॥ १२४ ॥ १२५ ॥ १२६ ॥

सम्पूज्यास्तत्र मध्येषु शक्तयोऽष्टौ यथाक्रमम् ।
अनङ्गरूपाऽऽद्याऽनङ्गमदनाऽनङ्गमन्मथा ॥ १२७
अनङ्गकुसुमा पश्चादनङ्गमदनातुरा ।
अनङ्गशिशिराऽनङ्गमेखलाऽनङ्गदीपिका ॥ १२८
लीलाकमलधारिण्यः स्मेरवक्त्राः सुशोभिताः ।
बहिःषोडशपत्रेषु पूज्याः षोडश शक्तयः ॥ १२९
युवतिर्विप्रलब्धाऽन्या ज्योत्स्ना सुभ्रूर्मदद्रवा ।
सुरता वारुणी लोला कान्तिः सौदामिनी पुनः ॥ १३०
कामच्छत्रा चन्द्ररेखा शुक्री स्यान्मदना पुनः ।
ज्योतिर्मायावती ताः स्युः कह्लारविलसत्कराः ॥ १३१
स्मेरवक्त्रा युवतयो मदविभ्रमसन्थराः ।
दलाग्रेषु पुनः पूज्याः स्मरस्य परिचारकाः ॥ १३२
शोकमोही विलासोऽन्यो विभ्रमो मदनातुरः ।
अपचयो युवा कामी चूतपुष्पो रतिप्रियः ॥ १३३
ग्रीष्मस्तपान्त ऊर्जोऽन्यो हेमन्तः शिशिरो मदः ।
इक्षुकार्मुकपुष्पेषुधरा रक्ताः सुभूषिताः ॥ १३४
अपराङ्गनिषङ्गाढ्या वनितासक्तमानसाः ।
रतिप्रियानष्टदिक्षु यजेदष्टौ विशिष्टधीः ॥ १३५
परभृत्सारसौ पश्चाच्छुकमेधाह्वयौ पुनः ।
अपाङ्गभ्रूविलासौ द्वौ हावभावौ प्रकीर्त्तिताः ॥ १३६

यथाक्रममित्यनेन कामबीजादित्वम् । युवत्यादीनां सर्वासां मायाबीजादित्वं ज्ञेयम् । यदाहुः—

हृल्लेखया स्वनाम्ना च शक्त्यादीनां समर्चनम् । इति ॥

विशिष्टधीरित्यनेन सर्वत्र सम्बध्यमानेनेदमेव सूचितम् । युवतयस्तरुण्य इत्यर्थः ॥ १२७ ॥१२८॥१२९॥१३०॥१३१॥१३२॥१३३॥१३४॥१३५॥१३६ ॥

चतुरस्रस्य कोणेषु पूज्यास्तत्परिचारिकाः ।
माधवी मालती पश्चाद्वनिताश्री मदोत्कटा ॥ १३७
सितचामरधारिण्यः सर्वाभरणभूषिताः ।
बाह्ये लोकेश्वरान् पश्चात्तदस्त्राण्यर्चयेत् क्रमात् ॥ १३८
इत्थं यो भजते देवं सुगन्धिकुसुमादिभिः ।
स भवेल्लब्धसौभाग्यो लक्ष्म्या जितधनेश्वरः ॥ १३९
अशोकपुष्पैर्दध्यक्तैर्जुहुयाद्दिवसत्रयम् ।
अष्टोत्तरसहस्रं यो स भवेज्जगतां प्रियः ॥ १४०
गव्येनाज्येन जुहुयान्मन्त्रेणाऽष्टोत्तरं शतम् ।
साधकेन्द्रः ससम्पातमर्चिते हव्यवाहने ॥ १४१
सम्पाताज्येन वनिता भोजयेदात्मनः पतिम् ।
अनया यद्यदादिष्टं तत्तत् स कुरुते सदा ॥ १४२
कन्यार्थी जुहुयाल्लाजैर्दध्यक्तैर्मण्डलान्तरे ।
कन्यामिष्टामवाप्नोति साऽपि सत्पतिमाप्नुयात् ॥ १४३
कामोल्लासितमध्यमङ्गविलसत्षट्कोणमेतद्बहि-
र्गायत्रीगुणवर्णवद्वसुदलं मालामनोरक्षरैः ।
षट्संख्यैः सहिताष्टपत्रसहितं क्षौणीपुरेणावृतं
कोणन्यस्तमनोभवेन कथितं यन्त्रं जगन्मोहनम् ॥ १४४

अर्चिते हव्यवाहने जुहुयादिति सम्बन्धः । ससम्पातमिति । पात्रान्तरे सम्पातं कुर्वन् । साधकेन्द्र इत्यनेन सम्पातस्याऽष्टोत्तरशतवारं जप उक्तः ॥ १३७ ॥ ॥ १३८ ॥ १३९ ॥ १४० ॥ १४१ ॥

सम्पाताज्यस्य विनियोगमाह सम्पातेति । मण्डलान्तरे कन्यामाप्नोतीति सम्बन्धः । तेन एकोनपञ्चाशद्दिनं होम उक्तः ॥ १४२ ॥ १४३ ॥

यन्त्रमाह कामेति । षट्कोणमध्ये कामबीजान्तः साध्यसाधककर्मनाम लिखनीयम् । कामषडङ्गान्याग्नेयादिषट्कोणेषु लिखेत् । तदुक्तम्—

षडङ्गान्यग्निकोणादिकोणेष्वेव क्रमाल्लिखेत् । इति ।

एतद्बहिरष्टदलमध्ये वक्ष्यमाणगायत्र्यर्णांस्त्रिशस्त्रिशो लिखित्वा मालामनोर्वक्ष्यमाणस्य षट् षडक्षराणि दलाग्रेषु लिखेत् । मूले वसुदलाष्टपत्रशब्दौ तत्रैकत्र दलमध्यमन्यत्र दलाग्रमिति ज्ञेयम् । कोणन्यस्तमनोभवेन क्षौणीपुरेणावृतमिति

कामदेवायशब्दान्ते विद्महे ङेऽन्तमीरयेत् ।
पुष्पबाणं धीमहि स्यात् तन्नोऽनङ्गः प्रचोदयात् ॥ १४५

नमोऽन्ते कामदेवाय वदेत् सर्वजनं ततः ।
प्रियाय सर्ववर्णान्ते जनसम्मोहनाय च ॥ १४६

ज्वलद्वयं प्रज्वलार्णान् वदेत् सर्वजनस्य च ।
हृदयं मम शब्दान्ते वशं कुरुद्वयं गिरः ।
मालामनुरयं साष्टचत्वारिंशद्भिरक्षरैः ॥ १४७

सम्बन्धः । तदुक्तमाचार्यैः—

आलिख्याकर्णिकायामनलपुरयुगे मारबीजं ससाध्यं
तद्रन्ध्रेष्वङ्गषट्कं बहिरपि गुणशो मारगायत्रिवर्णान् ।
मालामन्त्रं दलाग्रेष्वपि गुरुभुवनः पार्थिवाश्रिष्वनङ्गम् ॥ इति ॥ १४४ ॥

कामगायत्रीमुद्धरति कामदेवायेति । ङेऽन्तं पुष्पबाणं पुष्पबाणाय ॥ १४५ ॥

मालामन्त्रमाह नमोऽन्ते इति । सर्व इति यद्वर्णद्वयं तदन्ते । हृदयमिति स्वरूपम् । गिरः स्वाहा । अयं स्वतन्त्रो मन्त्रः । अस्यर्ष्यादिकं यथा—

नारदो जगती कामो मुन्याद्याः परिकीर्त्तिताः ।
सप्तसप्तनवमुनिदशाष्टार्णैः षडङ्गकम् ॥
यद्वाऽमृतोद्भवश्चैव परो मकरकेतनः ।
सङ्कल्पजन्मान्यश्चाऽनन्तरूपेक्षुधनुर्धरौ ॥
पुष्पबाणश्च कामाद्यैर्ङेस्वाहान्तैः षडङ्गकम् ।
बाणान् भालास्यगलहृदाधारेषु प्रविन्यसेत् ॥
शेषमन्यत्तु पूजादिकामबीजवदीरितम् ।
जपादौ मारबीजाद्यो जपस्तत्रवशीकरः ॥
विलिप्य गन्धपङ्केन लिखेदष्टदलाम्बुजम् ।
कर्णिकायां लिखेद्वह्निपुटितं मण्डलद्वयम् ॥
तस्य मध्ये लिखेत्कामं साध्याख्याकर्मसंयुतम् ।
साध्याख्यापुटितैः कामैस्तं कामं वेष्टयेद् बुधः ॥
श्रियं च षट्सु कोणेषु ऐन्द्रनिर्ऋतिवायुषु ।
आलिखेच्च तथा मायां वह्निवारुणशूलिषु ॥
अक्षरैः कामगायत्र्या वेष्टयेत् केसरं सुधीः ।

साध्याख्यापुटितैः स्वरैः परिवृतं कामं लिखेन्मध्यतः
पश्चात्तारविकारपञ्चकमराज्ञासार्घिभ्रिस्टीग्रघान् ।
मूलाब्याष्टदलेषु साधु विलिखेत्ताम्बुलमध्योदरे
यन्त्रं यां निशि खादयेत् क्षतजपं वश्या भवेत्तस्य सा ॥ १४८

कथितं पुष्पबाणस्य साङ्गोपाङ्गसमर्चनम् ।
सौभाग्यकान्तिविभवदारपुत्रसन्ततिप्रदम् ॥ १४९

मारमालामनोर्वर्णैर्दलेष्वष्टसु मन्त्रवित् ॥
लिखेद् गुहाननसंख्यैर्मातृकां तु विलेखयेत् ।
भूबिम्बं च लिखेद्बाह्ये श्रीमाये दिग्विदिक्ष्वपि ॥
यन्त्रमेवं समालिख्य जातरूपमये पटे ।
राजते ताम्रपट्टे वा भूर्जे क्षौममयेऽपि वा ॥
सूक्ष्मतन्तुमये वापि प्रतिष्ठाप्य समीरणम् ।
हुत्वा सहस्रमाज्येन यन्त्रसम्पातपूर्वकम् ॥
अर्चयित्वाऽयुतं जप्त्वा धारयेत्तदनुत्तमम् ।
त्रैलोक्यैश्वर्यमाप्नोति देवैरपि सुपूजितम् ॥
आकर्षणं सुरस्त्रीणां नागलोकनिवासिनाम् ।
पिशाचयक्षरक्षांसि गन्धर्वाप्सरकिन्नराः ॥
दुष्टसत्त्वाश्च ये सत्त्वाः प्रसर्पन्त्येव दूरतः ।
यन्त्रराजमिमं दृष्ट्वा विद्रवन्त्यतिमोहिताः ॥
बहुना किमिहोक्तेन सर्वलोकसुखावहम् ।
स्त्रीणामाकर्षकं सद्यो राज्ञो वश्यकरं भुवि ॥
योगसिद्धिकरं पुंसां भवसागरतारकम् ।
भुक्तिमुक्तिप्रदं पुंसामिति प्रोक्तं स्वयम्भुवा ॥ इति ॥ १४६॥१४७ ॥

यन्त्रान्तरमाह साध्येति। मध्यतः अष्टदलकर्णिकायाम् साध्यसाधककर्मनामपुटितैः स्वरैः कामबीजैः परिवृतं कामं साध्यसाधककर्मसहितं लिखेत्। अष्टसु दलेषु लिखनीयमाह तार इति। तारेण त्रिलसंख्यातेन इकारः। अन्ये प्रणवमाहुस्तदसत्। पद्मपादाचार्यादिबहुग्रन्थविरोधात्। विकारोऽन्त्यः स्वरः। पञ्चो द्वितीयः स्वर इति। केचन साम्प्रदायिकास्तु पञ्चदश स्वरमाहुः। पद्मपादाचार्यस्य सम्मतिः। को वायुस्तेन यः स परो यस्य तेन मकारः। तदुक्तं

आदाय वेदाः सकलाः समुद्रान्निहत्य शङ्खासुरमत्युदग्रम् ।
दत्ताः पुरा येन पितामहाय विष्णुं तमाद्यं भज मत्स्यरूपम् ॥ १५०
दिव्यामृतार्थं मथिते महाब्धौ देवासुराभ्यां वासुकिमन्दराभ्याम् ।
भूमेर्महावेगविघूर्णितायास्तं कूर्ममाधारगतं स्मरामि ॥ १५१
समुद्रकाञ्ची सरिदुत्तरीया वसुन्धरा मेरुकिरीटभारा ।
दंष्ट्राग्रतो येन समुद्धृता भूस्तमादिकोलं शरणं प्रपद्ये ॥ १५२
भक्तार्त्तिभञ्जनमया धिया यः स्तम्भान्तरालादुदितो नृसिंहः ।
रिपुं सुराणां निशितैर्नखाग्रैर्विदारयन्तं न च विस्मरामि ॥ १५३
चतुःसमुद्राभरणा धरित्री न्यासाय नाऽलं चरणस्य यस्य ।
एकस्य नाऽन्यस्य पदं सुराणां त्रिविक्रमं सर्वगतं स्मरामि ॥ १५४

गौतमेन मन्त्रव्याकरणं—

ब्रह्मणो वाचकः कः स्यात् कशब्दो सूर्यवाचकः ।
सूर्यस्य वाचकः कः स्यात् कशब्दो वायुवाचकः ॥ इति ॥

अन्ये कपरः ख इत्याहुस्तदसत् । पद्मपादाचार्यग्रन्थविरोधात् । नामाशब्देन तदुच्चारणीयः अनुनासिकः । तस्यार्थेऽपि प्रथमातिक्रमे कारणाभावात् ङकारः । केचन नामा ञकार इत्यूचुस्तदसत् । तद्ग्रन्थादिविरोधादेव । अग्निरग्नीशः ऊ । भिंटीश ए । व इति स्वरूपम् । क्वचित् भिण्टीशकानिति पाठः । स प्रामादिकः । तदुक्तमाचार्यैः—तारर्त्विक्प्रसजाष्टादशसमिद्वतुगण्डान्तगान्ताचराख्यम् । इति । एतद्व्याख्याने पद्मपादाचार्यैर्व्याख्यातम् । तार ॐ । ऋत्विक् ॠ । पद्मः ॐ । जाष्टादशो म । समित् ङः ऋतुः ऊ । गण्डान्तः ए । आन्तो व इति । शूलाब्जेति दलाग्रेषु शूलानि कुर्यात् ॥ १४८ ॥ १४९ ॥

एवं सप्रपञ्चं विष्णुमन्त्रान्निरूप्य शिष्यचेतसि दृढभक्तेरुत्पादनाय दशावतारक्रमेण विष्णुं स्तौति आदायेत्यादिना ।

येन शङ्खासुरं निहत्य समुद्रादादाय तेनेत्यर्थात् पितामहाय ब्रह्मणे सकला वेदा दत्ता इत्यन्वयः । वेदानिति पाठे ते इत्यर्थः ॥ १५० ॥

भूमेराधारगतमिति सम्बन्धः ॥ १५१ ॥

येनैवंभूता भूर्दंष्ट्राग्रतो दंष्ट्राग्रेण उद्धृतेति सम्बन्धः ॥ १५२ ॥ १५३ ॥

अन्यस्य द्वितीयस्य चरणस्य न्यासाय सुराणां पदं नालमिति सम्बन्धः ॥१५४॥

त्रिःसप्तवारं नृपतीन् निहत्य यस्तर्पणं रक्तमयं पितृभ्यः ।

चकार दोर्दण्डबलेन सम्यक् तमादिशूरं प्रणमामि भक्त्या ॥ १५५

कुले रघूणां समवाप्य जन्म विधाय सेतुं जलधेर्जलान्तः ।

लङ्केश्वरं यः शमयाञ्चकार सीतापतिं तं प्रणमामि भक्त्या ॥ १५६

हलेन सर्वानसुरान् विकृष्य चकार चूर्णं मुशलप्रहारैः ।

यः कृष्णमासाद्य बलं बलीयान् भक्त्या भजे तं बलभद्ररामम् ॥ १५७

पुरा पुराणामसुरान् विजेतुं सम्भावयन् चीवरचिह्नवेशम् ।

चकार यः शास्त्रममोघकल्पं तं मूलभूतं प्रणतोऽस्मि बुद्धम् ॥ १५८

कल्पावसाने निखिलैः खुरैः स्वैः सङ्कट्टयामास निमित्तमात्रात् ।

यस्तेजसा निर्दहतीलि भीमो विश्वात्मको तं तुरगं भजामः ॥ १५९

शाङ्गं सुचक्रं सुगदां सरोजं दोर्भिर्दधानं गरुड़ाधिरूढ़म् ।

श्रीवत्सचिह्नं जगदादिमूलं तमालनीलं हृदि विष्णुमीडे ॥ १६०

क्षीराम्बुधौ शेषविशेषतल्पे शयानमन्तःस्मितशोभिवक्त्रम् ।

उत्फुल्लनेत्राम्बुजमम्बुजाभमाद्यं श्रुतीनामसकृत् स्मरामि ॥ १६१

प्रीणयेदनया स्तुत्या जगन्नाथं जगन्मयम् ।

धर्मार्थकाममोक्षाणामाप्तये पुरुषोत्तमम् ॥ १६२

इति श्रीशारदातिलके सप्तदशः पटलः ।

चूर्णं चूर्णीभूतान् चकारेत्यन्वयः । यः कृष्णं बलं सहायमासाद्य ॥ १५५ ॥

॥ १५६ ॥ १५७ ॥

चीवरचिह्नवेशं सम्भावयन् धारयन्नित्यन्वयः ॥ १५८॥१५९॥१६० ॥

शेष एव विशेषः असाधारणात् ॥ १६१॥१६२ ॥

इति श्रीशारदातिलकटीकायां सत्सम्प्रदायकृतव्याख्यायां

पदार्थादर्शाभिख्यायां सप्तदशः पटलः ॥ ॐ ॥

अथ वक्ष्ये महेशस्य मन्त्रान् सर्वसमृद्धिदान् ।
यैः पूर्वमृषयः प्राप्ताः शिवसायुज्यमञ्जसा ॥ १

हृदयं वपरं साक्षि लान्तोऽनन्तान्वितो मरुत् ।
पञ्चाक्षरो मनुः प्रोक्तस्तारााद्योऽयं षडक्षरः ॥ २

वामदेवो मुनिश्छन्दः पङ्क्तिरीशोऽस्य देवता ।
षड्भिर्वर्णैः षडङ्गानि कुर्यान्मन्त्रस्य देशिकः ॥ ३

मन्त्रवर्णादिका न्यस्येत् पञ्चमूर्त्तीर्यथाक्रमम् ।
तर्जनीमध्ययोरन्त्यानामिकाङ्गुष्ठके पुनः ॥ ४

ताः स्युस्तत्पुरुषाघोरसद्योवामेशसंज्ञकाः ।
वक्त्रहृत्पादगुह्येषु निजमूर्धनि ताः पुनः ॥ ५

क्रमप्राप्तान् शैवमन्त्रानाह अथेति । सर्वसमृद्धिदान् यैरित्यादिना च तत्तदधिकारिणं प्रति विनियोग उक्तः ॥ १ ॥

मन्त्रमुद्धरति हृदयमिति । हृदयं नमःपदम् । वपरं शः साक्षि इकारयुक् तेन शि । लान्तो वः अनन्त आ तदन्वितस्तेन वा । मरुत् यः । षडक्षर इत्यनेन वाग्भवादिरित्युक्तम् । आद्यं बीजम् उमेति शक्तिः । केचित्प्रणवादनन्तरं प्रासादबीजप्रक्षेपात् सप्ताक्षरमिति वदन्ति । तन्त्रान्तरे—

आद्यन्ते सम्पुटीकृत्य हंसवागीश्वरं मनुम् ।
शिवमन्त्रं जपेद्धीमान् सद्यः प्रत्ययमेष्यति ॥
सम्पुटं शिवमन्त्रस्य जपेन् मासमतन्द्रितः ।
एकाकी यतचित्तात्मा वश्यमर्थं स विन्दति ॥ इति ॥

अत्र वागीश्वरशब्देन वाग्भवं केवलं रेफरहितं तार्त्तीयं चेति परमगुरवः । षड्भिरिति षडङ्गमन्त्रोद्धारमात्रमुक्तम् । न्यासमग्रे वक्ष्यतीति न पुनरुक्तिः । देशिको यथाक्रममिति । प्रत्यक्षरमादौ प्रणव इत्युक्तम् । अन्त्या कनिष्ठा ॥ २॥३॥४ ॥

ता मूर्त्तयः । सद्यः सद्योजातः । वामो वामदेवः । ईश ईशानः । ताः पुनर्मूर्धनीत्यन्तेषु स्थानेषु न्यसेदिति पश्चात्तनेन सम्बन्धः । चतुर्थीनमोऽन्ताश्च

प्राग्याम्यवारुणोदीच्यमध्यवक्त्रेषु पञ्चसु।
मन्त्राङ्गानि न्यसेत् पश्चाज्जातियुक्तानि षट् क्रमात्॥ ६
कुर्वीत गोलकन्यासं रक्षार्थं तदनन्तरम्।
हृदि वक्त्रेंऽसयोरूर्वोः कण्ठे नाभौ द्विपार्श्वयोः॥ ७
पृष्ठे हृदि ततो मूर्ध्नि वदने नेत्रयोर्नसोः।
दोःपत्सन्धिषु साग्रेषु विन्यसेत्तदनन्तरम्॥ ८

मूर्ध्नय इति सम्प्रदायविदः। मूर्धनीति काकाक्षिगोलकन्यायेन उभयत्र सम्बध्यते। ताः पुनर्निजमूर्धनि पञ्चसु वक्त्रेषु न्यसेदिति पश्चात्तनेन सम्बन्धः। तदुक्तमाचार्यैः—वक्त्रहृत्पादगुह्याख्यामूर्धस्वपि च नामभिः।

प्राग्याम्यवारुणोदीच्यवक्त्रेष्वपि च मूर्धनि॥ इति॥

मन्त्राङ्गानीति। तत्र प्रयोगः। ॐ हृत् नं शिर इत्यादि। सम्प्रदायविदस्तु। ॐ ॐ सर्वज्ञधाम्ने हृत्। ॐ नं तृप्तिधाम्ने शिरः। ॐ मः अनादिबोधधाम्ने शिखा। ॐ शिं अलुप्तशक्तिधाम्ने वर्म। ॐ वां स्वतन्त्रशक्तिधाम्ने नेत्रम्। ॐ यं अनन्तशक्तिधाम्ने अस्त्रम्। एवं षडङ्गमिच्छन्ति। तदुक्तं वायवीयसंहितायाम्—

तथैव तु षडङ्गानि पुनरस्योपपादयेत्।
सर्वज्ञतां तथा तृप्तिं बोधं चाद्यन्तवर्जितम्॥
अलुप्तशक्तिं स्वातन्त्र्यमनन्तां शक्तिमेव च॥ इति।

क्वचित्तु वर्मनेत्रयोर्व्यत्ययः। तदुक्तम्—

सर्वज्ञता तृप्तिरनादिबोधः स्वतन्त्रता नित्यमलुप्तशक्तिः।
अनन्तशक्तिश्च विभोर्विधिज्ञाः प्राहुः षडङ्गानि महेश्वरस्य॥ इति॥

यथागुरुसम्प्रदायमूहनीयम्॥ ५॥ ६॥

दशाहुतिमयं गोलकन्यासमाह कुर्वीतेति। तदनन्तरं तत्त्वन्यासानन्तरमित्यर्थः। तत्त्वन्यासो यथा—

वक्ष्यतेऽथो शैवतत्त्वन्यासः प्रसादतः परम्।
पञ्चाक्षरी परार्थेति तत्त्वनामात्मने नमः॥
आवृत्त्या शिवपञ्चाक्षर्यर्णयुक्तं पृथक् सह।
द्वितीयादि त्वादिवर्णैरान्तैराद्यं ध्रुवादिकैः [कम]॥
शिवः शक्तिः सदापूर्वः शिव ईश्वर एव च।
शुद्धविद्या च माया च कालश्च नियतिः कला॥

शिरोवदनहृत्कुक्षिसोरुपादद्वये पुनः ।
हृदि वक्त्राम्बुजे टङ्के मृगाभयवरेष्वथ ॥ ९
वक्त्रांसहृत्स्वपार्श्वोरुजठरेषु क्रमान्न्यसेत् ।
मूलमन्त्रस्य षड्वर्णान् यथावद्देशिकोत्तमः ॥ १०
मूर्ध्नि भालोदरांसेषु हृदये ताः पुनर्न्यसेत् ।
पश्चादनेन मन्त्रेण कुर्वीत व्यापकं सुधीः ॥ ११
नमोऽस्तु स्थाणुरूपाय ज्योतिर्लिङ्गामृतात्मने ।
चतुर्मूर्तिवपुश्छायाभासिताङ्गाय शम्भवे ।
एवं न्यस्तशरीरोऽसौ चिन्तयेत्पार्वतीपतिम् ॥ १२

स्मर्तापरागः पुरुषः प्रकृतिर्बुद्ध्यहङ्कृती ।
मन एतान् हृदि न्यस्येत् श्रोत्रादिषु स्थले तथा ।
वागाद्यप्ययशब्दादि मूर्धास्योरो गुदे पदे ॥
आकाशादीन्न्यसेदेषु वक्ष्यमाणं च पञ्चकम् ।
सदाशिवाद्या आकाशाद्याधिपत्यन्तकाः सङेः ॥
शान्त्यतीताकलाद्यन्ता निवृत्त्याद्याः स्वबीजतः ।
न्यसेत् पादादिशीर्षान्ते मूर्धादिचरणान्तिके ॥
शान्त्यात्मेशानमूर्धा च ङेयुतश्च सदाशिवः ।
सत्यात्मा तत्पुरुषवक्त्रो ङेसंयुत ईश्वरः ॥
नादात्माऽघोरहृदयो ङेयुतश्च महेश्वरः ।
बिन्द्वात्माऽथो वामदेवगुह्यो विष्णुश्च ङेयुतः ॥
बीजात्मा च सद्योजातपादो ब्रह्मा च ङेयुतः ।
ईशानाद्यानूर्ध्ववक्त्राद्यान् सदाशिवपूर्वकान् ॥
ऊर्ध्वादिपञ्चवक्त्रेषु ङेन्तानक्षरपूर्वकान् ॥ इति ।

स्वबीजत इति । ह्रां ह्रीं ह्रूं ह्रैं ह्रौं । ईशानाद्यान् ईशानतत्पुरुषाघोरवामसद्यान् । ऊर्ध्ववक्त्राद्यान् ऊर्ध्वपूर्वदक्षोत्तरपश्चिमान् । प्रयोगस्तु । ॐ ह्रौं नमः शिवाय पराय शिवात्मने नमः । नं चं ह्रीं नमः शिवाय पराय शक्त्यात्मने नमः । मं लं ह्रौं नमः शिवाय पराय सदाशिवात्मने नमः इत्यादि । प्रथमचरणैकाऽऽवृत्तिः । कण्ठादिहृदन्तं द्वितीया । मूर्धादिनासिकान्तं तृतीया ।

ध्यायेन्नित्यं महेशं रजतगिरिनिभं चारुचन्द्रावतंसं
रत्नाकल्पोज्ज्वलाङ्गं परशुमृगवराभीतिहस्तं प्रसन्नम् ।
पद्मासीनं समन्तात् स्तुतममरगणैर्व्याघ्रकृत्तिं वसानं
विश्वाद्यं विश्वरूपं निखिलभयहरं पञ्चवक्त्रं त्रिनेत्रम् ॥ १३

ततोऽर्धेनाहुतिचतुष्टयम् । अत्र सर्वत्र दोःपत्सन्धयश्चत्वार एव गृहीताः । अत्राऽङ्गुलिमध्यसन्धिमपि गृहीत्वा पञ्च सन्धयः । पञ्चमग्रमिति । एकैकस्मिन्नेकैकावृत्तिः । साग्रमित्यत्राऽङ्गुलीनामन्त्यसन्धियोगात् अग्रत्वमपि ज्ञेयम् । अत्र सर्वत्र केचन पञ्चाक्षरन्यासमाहुः । तन्मते मूलमन्त्रस्य षड्वर्णानित्यनेन । अन्यत्रापि "हृन्मुखांसोरुयुग्मेषु षड्वर्णान् क्रमशो न्यसेत्" इत्यनेन च विरोधः स्यात् । तत्परिहाराय प्रत्यगमादौ प्रणवमाहुः । एवमपि अष्टमनवमदशमेषु पृथक् षष्ठस्थाननिर्देशो वृथा स्यात् । अन्यत्रापि दशमावृत्तौ "मुखांसहृदयेषु तान् परान् पादोरुकुक्षिषु" इति अनेन विरोधात् तदसङ्गतम् । कश्चित्तु दोःसन्धिद्वयं तृतीयमग्रम् एवं दोर्द्वन्द्वे एका पद्द्वन्द्वे एका इत्यष्टौ न्यासानिवाह । स भ्रान्त एव । यतः सर्वत्र गोलकन्यासे ग्रन्थान्तरे च दशाङ्गुलीनामेवोक्तत्वात् । सन्धिशब्दार्थस्य सङ्कोचे कारणाभावाच्च । ततोऽर्धेनाऽष्टमी । पुनरर्धेन नवमी । तत्र टङ्कादिषु तत्तन्मुद्रया न्यासो विधेय इति साम्प्रदायिकाः । टङ्कः परशुः । मुद्रालक्षणानि तु—

करे करं तु करयोस्तिर्यक् संयोज्य चाऽङ्गुलीः ।
संहताः प्रसृताः कुर्यात् मुद्रेयं परशोर्मता ॥
मिलित्वाऽनामिकाङ्गुष्ठमध्यमाग्राणि योजयेत् ।
शिष्टाङ्गुल्युच्छ्रिति कुर्यात् मृगमुद्रेयमीरिता ॥ इति ॥
ऊर्ध्वीकृतो वामहस्तः प्रसृतोऽभयमुद्रिका ।
अधोमुखो दक्षहस्तः प्रसृतो वरमुद्रिका ॥ इति ॥

अर्धेन दशमी । यथावदिति । देशिकोत्तमः ता मूर्तीर्यथावत् पुनर्न्यसेदिति सम्बन्धः । यथावदित्यनेन प्रणवादि मन्त्रवर्णा इत्युक्तम् । देशिकोत्तम इत्यनेन तत्तदङ्गुल्येति ज्ञेयम् । इदं पूर्वन्यासयोरप्युक्तम् । अंसेति अंसद्वयम् ॥ ७ ॥ ८ ॥
॥ ९ ॥ १० ॥ ११ ॥ १२ ॥

ध्यायेदिति । पद्मासीनमिति श्वेतपद्मं चिन्तनीयम् । आयुधध्यानं दक्षोर्ध्वयोराद्ये तदधस्तनयोरन्त्ये । अनेनैव क्रमेण स्वशरीरे पूर्वोक्तो न्यासः । अत्र ध्यानानन्तरं पद्मलिङ्गमुद्रे दर्शनीये । आयुधमुद्राश्च ।

तत्त्वलक्षं जपेन्मन्त्रं दीक्षितः शैववर्त्मना।
तावत्संख्यासहस्राणि जुहुयात् पायसैः शुभैः।
ततः सिद्धो भवेन्मन्त्रः साधकाभीष्टसिद्धिदः॥ १४

देवं सम्पूजयेत्पीठे वामादिनवशक्तिके।
वामा ज्येष्ठा ततो रौद्री काली कलपदादिका॥ १५

विकरिण्याह्वया प्रोक्ता बलाद्या विकरिण्यथ।
बलप्रमथनी पश्चात्सर्वभूतदमन्यथ॥ १६

मनोन्मनीति संप्रोक्ताः शैवपीठस्य शक्तयः।
नमो भगवते पश्चात्सकलादि वदेत् पुनः॥ १७

गुणात्मशक्तियुक्ताय ततोऽनन्ताय तत्परम्।
योगपीठात्मने भूयो नमस्तारादिको मनुः॥ १८

तदुक्तं प्रयोगसारे—दर्शयित्वा ततः पद्मलिङ्गमुद्रे तदग्रतः। इति।
तत्र पद्ममुद्रालक्षणमुक्तं प्राक्। लिङ्गमुद्रालक्षणं तु—

उच्छ्रितं दक्षिणाङ्गुष्ठं वामाङ्गुष्ठेन बन्धयेत्।
वामाङ्गुलीर्दक्षिणाभिरङ्गुलीभिश्च वेष्टयेत्।
लिङ्गमुद्रेयमाख्याता शिवसान्निध्यकारिणी॥ इति॥

इयं सर्वशैवमन्त्रसाधारणीति ज्ञेयम्॥ १३॥

शैववर्त्मना दीक्षितः कृतदीक्षः। सा च शैवतन्त्रात् कामिकादितो ज्ञेया। तत्त्वलक्षं चतुर्विंशतिलक्षं मन्त्रं जपेदित्यन्वयः।

उक्तञ्च—अक्षरलक्षचतुष्कं जप्यात्। इति।

तावत्संख्यासहस्राणि चतुर्विंशतिसहस्राणि। अत्र द्रव्यप्रोक्षणे मूलमन्त्रो हुं-फडन्तो ज्ञेयः। तदुक्तं नारायणीयप्रयोगसारयोः—

वर्मास्त्रान्तेन मूलेन सम्प्रोक्ष्यैवं प्रकल्पितम्। इति॥ १४॥

देवमिति। वामादिनवशक्तिके पीठे देवं पूजयेदिति सम्बन्धः। तत्र मण्डूकादि परतत्त्वान्तं पीठं सम्पूज्य नव शक्तीः पूजयेदित्यर्थः। कलपदादिका इति अग्रिमाया विशेषणम्। आसां ध्यानमुक्तं प्रयोगसार नारायणीययोः—

श्वेता रक्तासिता पीता श्यामाऽरुणा सिताऽसिता।
गौणा च ताः स्मरेच्छक्तीः पीठरूपा यथाक्रमम्॥ इति॥१५॥१६॥१७॥

अमुना मनुना दद्यादासनं गिरिजापतेः ।
मूर्त्तिं मूलेन सङ्कल्प्य तत्राऽऽवाह्य यजेच्छिवम् ॥ १९
कर्णिकायां यजेन्मूर्त्तीरीशमीशानदिग्गतम् ।
शुद्धस्फटिकसंकाशं दिक्षु तत्पुरुषादिकाः ॥ २०
पीताञ्जनश्वेतरक्ताः प्रधानसदृशायुधाः ।
चतुर्वक्त्रसमायुक्ता यथावत् संप्रपूजयेत् ॥ २१
कोणेष्वर्च्याः निवृत्त्याद्यास्तेजोरूपाः कलाः क्रमात् ।
अङ्गानि केसरस्थानि विघ्नेशान् परगान् यजेत् ॥ २२
अनन्तं सूक्ष्मनामानं शिवोत्तममनन्तरम् ।
एकनेत्रमेकरुद्रं त्रिनेत्रं तदनन्तरम् ॥ २३
पश्चाच्छ्रीकण्ठनामानं शिखण्डिनमनन्तरम् ।
रक्तपीतसितारक्तकृष्णारक्ताञ्जनासितान् ॥ २४
किरीटार्पितबालेन्दून् पद्मस्थान् भूषणान्वितान् ।
त्रिनेत्रान् शूलवज्रास्त्रचापहस्तान् मनोहरान् ॥ २५
उत्तरादि यजेत्पश्चादुमां चण्डेश्वरं पुनः ।
ततो नन्दिमहाकालौ गणेशवृषभौ पुनः ॥ २६

गिरिजापतेरित्यनेनैतदुक्तम् । आत्मयागे आसनं सम्पूज्य स्वागतादिगन्धान्तं दत्त्वा नमोऽस्तु स्थाणुभूतायेति मन्त्रेण पञ्च पुष्पाञ्जलीर्दद्यादिति । तदुक्तमाचार्यैः—

कुर्यादनेन मन्त्रेण निजदेहे समाहितः ।
मन्त्री पुष्पाञ्जलिं सम्यक् त्रिशः पञ्चश एव च ॥ इति ॥१८॥१९॥

कर्णिकायां दिक्षु तत्पुरुषादिका मूर्त्तीस्तत्रो यथावत् संपूजयेदित्यन्वयः । यथावदित्यनेन प्रणवादि मन्त्रवर्णाद्या इत्युक्तम् । ईशानदिग्गतं शुद्धस्फटिकसङ्काशमीशं पञ्चमं यजेदित्यन्वयः ॥ २० ॥ २१ ॥

कोणेषु आग्नेयादिषु । द्वितीयोक्ता निवृत्त्याद्याश्चतस्रः । तेजोरूपा इति ध्यानम् । प्रथमपटलोक्ता पञ्चीकृतभूतबीजाद्या इति ज्ञेयम् । शान्त्यतीतामपि ईशे यजेदिति क्रमादित्यनेनोक्तमित्यन्ये ॥ २२ ॥

विद्येशानेवाह अनन्तमिति । अस्त्रं बाणः । पश्चादेतानुत्तरादि यजेदिति सम्बन्धः । शतलक्षमिति कोटिम् । तन्त्रान्तरादिदं यन्त्रं लिख्यते—

अथ भृङ्गीरिटिं स्कन्दमेतान् पद्मासनस्थितान् ।
स्वर्णतोयारुणश्यामरुक्मेन्दुसितपाटलान् ॥ २७

इन्द्रादयस्ततः पूज्या वज्राद्यायुधसंयुताः ।
इत्थं संपूजयेद्देवं सहस्रं नित्यशो जपेत् ॥ २८

सर्वपापविनिर्मुक्तः प्राप्नुयाद्वाञ्छितां श्रियम् ।
द्विसहस्रं जपेद्रोगान्मुच्यते नात्र संशयः ॥ २९

त्रिसहस्रं जपेन्मन्त्रं दीर्घमायुरवाप्नुयात् ।
सहस्रवृद्ध्या प्रजपन् सर्वान् कामानवाप्नुयात् ॥ ३०

आज्यान्वितैस्तिलैः शुद्धैर्जुहुयाल्लक्षमादरात् ।
उत्पातजनितान् क्लेशान्नाशयेन्नात्र संशयः ।
शतलक्षं जपेत्साक्षाच्छिवो भवति मानवः ॥ ३१

रेखाषट्कं न्यसेदूर्ध्वं तथा तिर्यक्प्रमाणकम् ।
अथाथसंहताकारं कृत्वाग्रं च सरेखकम् ॥
वसुपत्रस्वराङ्कं च मातृकार्णसमन्वितम् ।
चतुरस्रं द्विधा कृत्वा यन्त्रं पञ्चाक्षराख्यकम् ॥
पञ्चाक्षरीं न्यसेन्मध्ये द्वादशार्णैस्ततः परम् ।
विद्येश्वरांस्तथा न्यस्य द्वादशार्कैस्ततः परम् ॥
वृत्तत्रयं ततो न्यस्य कलाशक्तीस्ततः परम् ।
गायत्रीमष्टमातॄश्च स्वरांश्चैव ततः परम् ॥
मातृका लोकपालांश्च यन्त्रं पञ्चाक्षराख्यकम् ॥ इति ।
हृदयं ङेणभगवन्नादित्यस्य सङ्के सह ॥
आद्यं च किरणं सद्योत मानिङे च ठद्वयम् ।

अयं महासौरः कलाशक्तीरस्ततायाः । तत्पुरुषायेति गायत्री । मातृका ककाराद्या सान्ता । शैवागमोक्तं यन्त्रान्तरमुच्यते—

षट्कोणान्तः साध्ययुक्तं प्रासादं मूलमस्त्रिषु ।
मूर्त्यष्टाङ्गानि तद्बाह्ये पद्मं पञ्चदलं त्विह ॥
ईशानाद्याः पञ्चमूर्तीर्ह्रदन्ता लिखेत्ततः ।
अष्टपत्रं मातृकाष्टवर्गयुक्तं लिखेद्बहिः ॥

षड़क्षरः शक्तिरुद्धः कथितोऽष्टाक्षरो मनुः ।
ऋषिश्छन्दः पुरा प्रोक्तो देवता स्यादुमापतिः ॥ ३२
अङ्गानि पूर्वमुक्तानि सोममीशं विचिन्तयेत् ॥ ३३

बन्धूकाभं त्रिनेत्रं शशिशकलधरं स्मेरवक्त्रं वहन्तं
हस्तैः शूलं कपालं वरदमभयदं चारुहासं नमामि ।
वामोरुस्तम्भगायाः करतलविलसच्चारुरक्तोत्पलाया
हस्तेनाऽऽश्लिष्टदेहं मणिमयविलसद्भूषणायाः प्रियायाः ॥ ३४

मनुलक्षं जपेन्मन्त्रं तत्सहस्रं यथाविधि ।
जुहुयान्मधुरासिक्तैरारग्वधसमिद्वरैः ॥ ३५
प्राक्प्रोक्ते पूजयेत् पीठे गन्धपुष्पैरुमापतिम् ।
अङ्गावृतीर्बहिः पूज्या हृल्लेखाद्या यथा पुरा ॥ ३६
मध्यप्राग्दक्षिणोदीच्यपश्चिमेषु विधानतः ।
हृल्लेखा गगना रक्ता चतुर्थी तु करालिका ।
महोच्छुष्मा क्रमादेताः पञ्चभूतसमप्रभाः ॥ ३७

संवेष्ट्याऽनुष्टुभा यन्त्रं जपहोमादिसाधितम् ।
आरोग्यायुःसुतैश्वर्यचतुर्वर्गफलप्रदम् ॥ इति ॥ २३—३१ ॥

मन्त्रान्तरमाह षड़िति । रुद्धः सम्पुटितः । प्रणवो बीजं माया शक्तिः । पुरा प्रोक्त इति । वामदेव ऋषिः पङ्क्तिश्छन्दः ॥ ३२ ॥

अङ्गानीति । तत्र षड्दीर्घयुक्तबीजाद्यैः षड़र्णैः षड़ङ्गविधिरिति सम्प्रदायविदः । प्रयोगस्तु ह्रां ॐ हृत् । ह्रीं नं शिरः । ह्रूं मः शिखा । ह्रैं शिं वर्म । ह्रौं वां नेत्रम् । ह्रः यं अस्त्रम् । सोममित्युमया सहितम् ॥ ३३ ॥

आयुधध्यानं दक्षाद्यूर्ध्वयोराद्ये तदधस्तनयोरन्त्ये । करतलेति वामे । तदुक्तम्—
वामोरुपीठगतया निजवामहस्तन्यस्तारुणोत्पलयुजा परिरब्धदेहम् । इति ।
हस्तेनेति दक्षिणेन ॥ ३४ ॥

मनुलक्षं चतुर्दशलक्षम् । तत्सहस्रं चतुर्दशसहस्रम् । यथाविधीति तान्त्रिकाग्निमुखविधानेनेत्यर्थः । यथा पुरेति नवमपटलोक्तस्वस्वबीजाद्या इत्युक्तम् । विधानतः पूज्या इति सम्बन्धः ॥ ३५ ॥ ३६ ॥

विधानमेवाह मध्येति । मध्यं कर्णिकामध्यम् । पश्चिमेषु दिग्भागेष्विति

पाशाङ्कुशवराभीतिधारिण्योऽमितभूषणाः।
यजेत् पूर्वादिपत्रेषु वृषभाद्याननुक्रमात्॥ ३८
हिमालयाभं वृषभं तीक्ष्णशृङ्गं त्रिलोचनम्।
सर्वाभरणसन्दीप्तं साक्षाच्छन्दःस्वरूपिणम्॥ ३९
कपालशूलविलसत्करं कालघनप्रभम्।
क्षेत्रपालं त्रिनयनं दिगम्बरमथाऽर्चयेत्॥ ४०
शूलटङ्काक्षवलयं कमण्डलुलसत्करम्।
रक्ताकारं त्रिनयनं चण्डेशमथ पूजयेत्॥ ४१
चक्रशङ्खाभयाभीष्टकरां मरकतप्रभाम्।
दुर्गां प्रपूजयेत् सौम्यां त्रिनेत्रां चारुभूषणाम्॥ ४२
कल्पशाखां रत्नघण्टां दधानं द्वादशेक्षणम्।
बालार्काभं शिशुं कान्तं षण्मुखं पूजयेत् ततः॥ ४३
नन्दिनं पूजयेत्सौम्यं रत्नभूषणमण्डितम्।
मरश्रेणवराभीतिधारिणं श्यामविग्रहम्॥ ४४
पाशाङ्कुशवराभीष्टधारिणं कुङ्कुमप्रभम्।
विघ्ननायकमभ्यर्चेच्चन्द्रार्धकृतशेखरम्॥ ४५
श्यामं रक्तोत्पलकरं वामाङ्कन्यस्ततत्करम्।
त्रिनेत्रं रक्तवस्त्राढ्यं सेनापतिमथाऽर्चयेत्॥ ४६
ततोऽष्टमातरः पूज्या ब्राह्म्याद्याः प्रोक्तलक्षणाः।
इन्द्रादिकान् लोकपालान् स्वस्वदिक्षु समर्चयेत्॥ ४७

शेषः। पञ्चभूतेति पृथिव्यादि॥ ३७॥ ३८॥

ध्यानपूर्वकमनुक्रममेवाह हिमालयेति। प्रतिश्लोकमेकैकध्यानसमाप्तिः। एणो मृगः। अयुधध्यानक्रमस्तु तत्तत्प्रकरणेऽनुसन्धेयः।

तत इति पत्राग्रेषु॥ ३९॥ ४०॥ ४१॥ ४२॥ ४३॥ ४४॥ ४५॥ ४६॥

प्रोक्तलक्षणा यथोक्तस्वरूपाः॥ ४७॥ ४८॥

वज्रादीनि तदस्त्राणि तद्बहिः क्रमशोऽर्चयेत्।
एवं यो भजते मन्त्री देवेशं तमुमापतिम्।
स भवेत् सर्वलोकानां प्रियः सौभाग्यसम्पदाम्॥ ४८
सान्तः सद्यान्तसंयुक्तो बिन्दुभूषितमस्तकः।
प्रासादाख्यो मनुः प्रोक्तो भजतां सर्वसिद्धिदः॥ ४९
षड्दीर्घयुक्तबीजेन षडङ्गविधिरीरितः।
वामदेवो मुनिश्छन्दः पङ्क्तिर्देवः सदाशिवः॥ ५०
ईशानादीन्न्यसेन् मूर्त्तीरङ्गुष्ठादिषु देशिकः।
ईशानाख्यं तत्पुरुषमघोरं तदनन्तरम्।
वामदेवाह्वयं सद्य आसां बीजं क्रमाद्विदुः॥ ५१
ओकाराद्यैः पञ्चह्रस्वैर्विलोमात् संयुतं वियत्।
तत्तदङ्गुलिभिर्भूयस्तत्तद्बीजादिका न्यसेत्॥ ५२
शिरोवदनहृद्गुह्यपाददेशे तथा क्रमात्।
ऊर्ध्वप्राग्दक्षिणोदीच्यपश्चिमेषु मुखेषु ताः॥ ५३

प्रासादमन्त्रमाह सान्त इति। सान्तो हः सद्यान्त औ तेन हौं। अस्य नामव्युत्पत्तिरुक्ताऽऽचार्यैः—

प्रसादनत्वान् मनसो यथावत् प्रासादसंज्ञाऽस्य मनोः प्रदिष्टा। इति।

हृल्लेखासम्पुटम् इति केचित्। हकारो बीजम् औमिति शक्तिः।

तदुक्तम्—सान्तोऽनुग्रहसंयुक्तो बिन्दुभूषितमस्तकः।

प्रासादाख्यो मनुः प्रोक्तो बीजं हं शक्तिरौं स्मृता॥ इति॥

सर्वसिद्धिद इत्यनेन विनियोगोक्तिः। बीजेनेति मूलमन्त्रेण। वामदेव इत्यर्धं पठित्वा षड्दीर्घेत्यर्धं पठनीयम्। लेखकदोषवशात् व्यत्ययः॥ ४९॥ ५०॥ ५१॥

ओकाराद्यैरिति। ओ ए उ इ अ एतैः। तत्तदिति। यस्यां यस्यां यो यो न्यस्तस्तया तया। तेन समुच्चाङ्गुष्ठेन शिरसि। साङ्गुष्ठतर्जन्या वदने। साङ्गुष्ठमध्यमया हृदि। साङ्गुष्ठानामया गुह्ये। साङ्गुष्ठकनिष्ठिकया पादयोः। एवं पञ्चस्वपि मुखेष्विति साम्प्रदायिकाः। तथेति। ऊर्ध्वमुखादीनां समुच्चयः। ता इति मूर्त्तीः। तत्तद्बीजादिकाः तत्तदङ्गुलीभिर्न्यसेदिति सम्बन्धः॥ ५२॥ ५३॥

ततः प्रविन्यसेद्विद्वानष्टत्रिंशत्कलास्तनौ ।
ईशानाद्या ऋचः सम्यगङ्गुलीषु यथाक्रमम् ॥ ५४

अङ्गुष्ठादिकनिष्ठान्तं न्यसेद्देशिकसत्तमः ।
मूर्धास्यहृदयाम्भोजगुह्यपादेषु ताः पुनः ॥ ५५

अष्टत्रिंशत्कलान्यासं वक्तुमारभते तत इति । अयं न्यासो ग्रन्थकृता यद्यपि प्रासादमन्त्राङ्गत्वेनोक्तः तथापीदं पञ्चब्रह्मविधानं स्वतन्त्रं सर्वशैवमन्त्रसाधारणं चेति ज्ञेयम् । आचार्यैः स्वतन्त्रतयैवोक्तम् । अङ्गानि प्रकल्पयेदिति वदता तेनापि सूचितमेव स्वातन्त्र्यम् । तानि षडङ्गानि पञ्चर्चानामेव न तु प्रासाद-मन्त्रस्य । तदुक्तम्—

वक्ष्यामि शैवागमसारमष्टत्रिंशत्कलान्यासविधिं यथावत् ।
सपञ्चभिर्ब्रह्मभिरीशपूर्वैः सद्यादिकैः साङ्गविशेषकैश्च ॥ इति ॥

अतस्तन्त्रान्तरोक्तस्तथादि लिख्यते ।

ईशोऽनुष्टुप्भूरिक्शिवास्तत्पुरुषसंज्ञे गायत्र्यापः ।
पुनरघ्न्यनुष्टुबापो वामकृतिभगाहरस्त्वनुष्टुप्भगयुक् ॥ इति ॥

न्यासक्रममेवाह ईशानाद्या इति । ता ऋचो यथा—

ईशानः सर्वविद्यानामीश्वरः सर्वभूतानां ब्रह्माधिपतिर्ब्रह्मणोऽधिपतिर्ब्रह्मा शिवो मे अस्तु सदाशिवोम् ।

तत्पुरुषाय विद्महे महादेवाय धीमहि तन्नो रुद्रः प्रचोदयात् ।

अघोरेभ्योऽथ घोरेभ्यो घोरघोरतरेभ्यः सर्वतः सर्वशर्वेभ्यो नमस्ते अस्तु रुद्ररूपेभ्यः ।

वामदेवाय नमो ज्येष्ठाय नमः श्रेष्ठाय नमो रुद्राय नमः कालाय नमः कलविकरणाय नमो बलविकरणाय नमो बलाय नमो बलप्रमथनाय नमः सर्वभूतदमनाय नमो मनोन्मनाय नमः ।

सद्योजातं प्रपद्यामि सद्योजाताय वै नमः भवेऽभवे नातिभवे भज[व]स्व मां भवोद्भवाय नमः ।

सम्यगित्यनेनैतदुक्तं भवति । एतास्तैत्तिरीयशाखायां नारायणीयोपनिषदि द्राविडपाठानुसारा ज्ञेयाः । आम्नायास्त्वन्यथा पठन्तीति । तत्पाठो नात्राऽभिप्रेत इति । देशिकसत्तम इत्यनेन अङ्गुष्ठाभ्यां नम इत्यादि योग उक्तः ॥ ५४॥५५ ॥

वक्त्रेषूर्ध्वादि विन्यसेद्भूयोऽङ्गानि प्रकल्पयेत्।
तारपञ्चकमुच्चार्य सर्वज्ञाय हृदीरितम्॥ ५६
अमृततेजोमालिनितृप्तायेति पदं पुनः।
तदन्ते ब्रह्म शिरसे शिरोऽङ्गं ज्वलितं ततः॥ ५७
शिखिशिखाय परतोऽनादिबोधाय तच्छिखा।
वज्रिणे वज्रहस्ताय स्वतन्त्राय तनुच्छदम्॥ ५८
सौं वौं हौमिति संभाष्य पुरतो लुप्तशक्तये।
नेत्रमुक्तं श्लौं पशुं हुं फडन्तेऽनन्तशक्तये।
अस्त्रमुक्तषडङ्गानि कुर्याद्देशिकसत्तमः॥ ५९
पूर्वदक्षिणपाश्चात्यसौम्यमध्येषु पञ्चसु।
वक्त्रेषु पञ्च विन्यस्येदीशानस्य कलाः क्रमात्॥ ६०
ईशानः सर्वविद्यानां शशिनी प्रथमा कला।
ईश्वरः सर्वभूतानामङ्गदा तदनन्तरम्॥ ६१
ब्रह्माधिपतिशब्दान्ते ब्रह्मणोऽधिपतिः पुनः।
ब्रह्मेष्टदा तृतीया स्याच्छिवो मेऽस्तु ततः परा॥ ६२
मरीची कथिता तन्ते चतुर्थी च सदाशिवोम्।
अंशुमालिन्यथ परा प्रणवाद्या नमोऽन्विताः॥ ६३

अङ्गानि प्रकल्पयेदित्युक्तम्। तान्येवाह तारेति। तारपञ्चकमिति द्वादशे मूर्त्तिकल्पनायामुक्तम्। शिरोऽङ्गं शिर इत्यर्थः। ज्वलितमित्यग्रिमेण सम्बध्यते। तनुच्छदं कवचम्। एवमुक्तानि षडङ्गानि देशिकसत्तमः कुर्यादिति सम्बन्धः। अत्र देशिकसत्तम इत्यनेनैतदुक्तं भवति। शिरोऽङ्गे तृप्तायेत्यस्य पूर्वं नित्यपदप्रयोगः। अस्त्रे श्लौमित्यस्याऽनन्तरं शक्तिबीजप्रयोग इति॥ ५६॥५७॥५८॥५९॥

ईशमन्त्रकलान्यासक्रममाह पूर्वेति। इष्टदेति कलानाम। सदाशिवोमित्यग्रिमेण सम्बध्यते। परा पञ्चमी। प्रणवाद्या इति। प्रणवशक्तिप्रासादाद्या इत्यर्थः। पद्मपादाचार्याः पञ्चाक्षरीयोगमप्याहुः। नमोऽन्विता इति। पञ्चापि चतुर्थ्यन्ता इत्यपि। चतुर्थ्यन्ताः कलाः सर्वा इति वक्ष्यमाणत्वात्। तेन ॐ ह्रीं हौं नमः शिवाय। ईशानः सर्वविद्यानां शशिन्यै नम इत्यादि प्रयोगः॥ ६०॥ ॥ ६१॥ ६२॥ ६३॥

पूर्वपश्चिमयाम्योदग्वक्त्रेषु तदनन्तरम् ।
चतस्रो विन्यसेन् मन्त्री पुरुषस्य कलाः क्रमात् ६४

आद्या तत्पुरुषायेति विद्महे शान्तिरीरिता ।
महादेवाय शब्दान्ते धीमहि स्यात् ततः परम् ॥ ६५

विद्या द्वितीया कथिता तन्नो रुद्रः पदं ततः ।
प्रतिष्ठा कथिता पश्चात् तृतीया स्यात् प्रचोदयात् ।
निवृत्तिस्तत्परा सर्वाः प्रणवाद्या नमोऽन्विताः ॥ ६६

हृद्ग्रीवांसद्वये नाभौ कुक्षौ पृष्ठे च वक्षसि ।
अघोरस्य कला न्यस्येदष्टौ मन्त्री यथाविधि ॥ ६७

अघोरेभ्यस्तथा पूर्वमीरिता प्रथमा कला ।
अथ घोरेभ्य इत्यन्ते मोहा स्यात्तदनन्तरम् ॥ ६८

घोरान्ते स्यात् क्षमा पश्चात् तृतीया परिकीर्त्तिता ।
घोरतरेभ्यो निद्रा स्यात् सर्वतः सर्वतत्परा ॥ ६९

व्याधिस्तु पञ्चमी प्रोक्ता शर्वेभ्यस्तदनन्तरम् ।
मृत्युर्निगदिता षष्ठी नमस्ते अस्तु तत्परम् ॥ ७०

क्षुधा स्यात्सप्तमी रुद्ररूपेभ्यः कथिता तृषा ।
अष्टमी कथिता एता ध्रुवाद्या नमसाऽन्विताः ॥ ७१

गुह्यमुष्कोरुयुग्मेषु जानुजङ्घायुगे स्फिचोः ।
कट्यां पार्श्वद्वये वामकला न्यस्येत् त्रयोदश ॥ ७२

प्रथमा वामदेवाय नमोऽन्ते स्याद्रजा कला ।
स्याज्ज्येष्ठाय नमो रक्षा द्वितीया परिकीर्त्तिता ॥ ७३

पुरुषस्य तत्पुरुषस्य । प्रचोदयादित्यग्रिमेण सम्बध्यते । तत्परा चतुर्थी । सर्वा इति चतुर्थ्यन्ता इत्यपि ॥ ६४ ॥ ६५ ॥ ६६ ॥

यथाविधीति । वक्ष्यमाणोऽङ्गुलीभिर्न्यासः सूचितः । अथ घोरेभ्य एतावान्मन्त्रांशः । एता इति । चतुर्थ्यन्ता इत्यपि ॥ ६७ ॥ ६८ ॥ ६९ ॥ ७० ॥ ७१ ॥

मुष्कोऽण्डकोशः । वामकला वामदेवकलाः । कलकामित्यत्र कलेति मन्त्रांशः

स्याद्रुद्राय नमः पश्चात् तृतीया रतिरीरिता ।
कालाय नम इत्यन्ते पालिनी परिकीर्त्तिता ॥ ७४

कलकामा पञ्चमी स्यात्ततो विकरणाय च ।
नमः संयमनी षष्ठी कथिता तदनन्तरम् ॥ ७५

बलक्रिया समादिष्टा बलविकरणाय च ।
नमो वृद्धिरष्टमी स्याद्बलान्ते च स्थिरा कला ॥ ७६

पश्चात् प्रमथनायाऽन्ते नमो रात्रिरुदीरिता ।
सर्वभूतदमनाय नमोऽन्ते भ्रामणी कला ॥ ७७

नमोऽन्ते मोहिनी प्रोक्ता मन्त्रज्ञैर्द्वादशी कला ।
उन्मनाय नमः पश्चाज्जरा प्रोक्ता त्रयोदशी ।
प्रणवाद्यास्तुर्थ्यन्ता नमोऽन्तास्ताः प्रकीर्तिताः ॥ ७८

पादद्वोस्तलनासासु मूर्ध्नि बाहुयुगे न्यसेत् ।
सद्योजातोद्भवाः सम्यगष्टौ मन्त्री कलाः क्रमात् ॥ ७९

सद्योजातं प्रपद्यामि सिद्धिः स्यात्प्रथमा कला ।
सद्योजाताय वै भूयो नमः स्याद्वृद्धिरीरिता ॥ ८०

भवे द्युतिस्तृतीया स्याद्भवे तदनन्तरम् ।
लक्ष्मीश्चतुर्थी कथिता ततो नातिभवे पदम् ॥ ८१

मेधा स्यात् पञ्चमी प्रोक्ता कला भूयो भज[व]स्व माम् ।
प्रज्ञा समीरिता षष्ठी भवान्ते स्यात् प्रभा कला ।
उद्भवाय नमः पश्चात् स्वधा स्यादष्टमी कला ॥ ८२

प्रणवाद्यास्तुर्थ्यन्ताः कलाः सर्वा नमोऽन्विताः ।
अष्टत्रिंशत्कलाः प्रोक्ताः पञ्चब्रह्मपदान्तिकाः ॥ ८३

कामेति कला। विकरणाय नम इति ऋगंशः।
बलेति ऋगंशः। क्रियेति कला। अत्रापि विकरणाय नम इति ऋगंशः।
॥ ७२॥७३॥७४॥७५॥७६॥७७॥७८ ॥

भूय इति पादपूरणे। भव इति ऋगंशः। पञ्चब्रह्मपदानि पञ्चानां

इति विन्यस्तदेहोऽसौ भवेद्गङ्गाधरः स्वयम् ।
ततः समाहितो भूत्वा ध्यायेदेवं सदाशिवम् ॥ ८४

मुक्तापीतपयोदमौक्तिकजवावर्णैर्मुखैः पञ्चभि-
स्त्र्यक्षैरञ्चितमीशमिन्दुमुकुटं पूर्णेन्दुकोटिप्रभम् ।
शूलं टङ्कृपाणवज्रदहनान्नागेन्द्रघण्टाङ्कुशान्
पाशं भीतिहरं दधानममिताकल्पोज्ज्वलं चिन्तयेत् ॥ ८५

ऋचां पदानि । अत्र पञ्चानामृचां पदानि कलासहितानि क्रमेण उक्ताऽङ्गुष्ठाद्य-ङ्गुलिभिर्विन्यसेत् । तत्र प्रथमऋक्कलाः साङ्गुष्ठमुष्टिना द्वितीयऋक्कला-स्तर्जन्यङ्गुष्ठाभ्यां तृतीयऋक्कला मध्यमाङ्गुष्ठाभ्यां चतुर्थऋक्कला अनामाङ्गु-ष्ठाभ्यां पञ्चमऋक्कलाः कनिष्ठाङ्गुष्ठाभ्यामिति ।

तदुक्तम्—इति विशदधीर्विन्यसेदङ्गुलीभिः । इति ।

अन्यत्रापि—कनिष्ठाद्यङ्गुलीभिस्तु न्यसेत् सद्यादिकाः क्रमात् ।

साङ्गुष्ठाभिस्तथेशानं समुष्ट्यङ्गुष्ठकेन तु ॥ इति ॥

अस्य स्वतन्त्रत्वात् ध्यानावरणपूजादि वक्तव्यम् । तत्र ध्यानं प्रासादावरणपूजावसरे ग्रन्थकृदुक्तं ज्ञेयम् । आवरणपूजा तु आचार्योक्ता यथा—

न्यस्यैवं पञ्चभिर्ब्रह्मभिरथ शिवमाराधयेद्दृग्भिराभि-
र्मध्यप्राग्याम्यसौम्यापरदिशि पुनरङ्गैरनन्तादिभिश्च ।
अन्योमाद्यैर्दिशापैः पुनरपि कुलिशाद्यैर्यजेदेवमुक्तं
पाञ्चब्राह्मं विधानं सकलसुखयशोभुक्तिमुक्तिप्रदञ्च ॥ इति ॥ ७९ ॥

॥ ८० ॥ ८१ ॥ ८२ ॥ ८३ ॥ ८४ ॥

मुक्तेति । मुक्तावर्णमूर्ध्वमुखं पीतवर्णं पूर्वमुखं नीलवर्णं दक्षिणमुखं मुक्तावर्णं पश्चिममुखं विद्रुमवर्णमुत्तरमुखम् । पयो ददातीति व्युत्पत्त्या नीलमेघ एव विवक्षितः । तदुक्तं वायवीयसंहितायाम्—

अस्य पूर्वमुखं सौम्यं बालार्कसदृशप्रभम् ।
त्रिलोचनारविन्दाढ्यं बालेन्दुकृतशेखरम् ॥
दक्षिणं नीलजीमूतसमानं चन्द्रभूषितम् ।
वक्रभ्रुकुटिलं घोरं रक्तवृत्तविलोचनम् ॥
उत्तरं विद्रुमप्रख्यं नीलालकविभूषितम् ।
सविलासं त्रिनयनं चन्द्राभरणशेखरम् ॥

एवं ध्यात्वा जपेन्मन्त्रं पञ्चलक्षं मधुप्लुतैः।
प्रसूनैः करवीरोत्थैर्जुहुयात्तद्दशांशकम्॥ ८६
पूर्वोक्ते प्रयजेत्पीठे मूर्त्तिं मूलेन कल्पयेत्।
आवाह्य पूजयेत्तस्यां मूर्त्याद्यावरणैः सह॥ ८७

पश्चिमं पूर्णचन्द्राभं लोचनत्रितयोज्ज्वलम्।
चन्द्ररेखाधरं सौम्यं मन्दस्मितमनोहरम्॥
पञ्चमं स्फटिकप्रख्यं चन्द्ररेखासमुज्ज्वलम्।
अतीवसौम्यमुत्फुल्ललोचनत्रितयोज्ज्वलम्॥ इति॥

इन्दुमुकुटमिति प्रतिवक्त्रं ज्ञेयम्। टङ्कः परशुः। नागेशः सर्पेशः। भीतिहरम् अभयम्। आयुधध्यानं तु ऊर्ध्वादि दक्षे शूलाद्यग्न्यन्तानि वामे अन्यानि। तदुक्तं वायवीयसंहितायाम्—

दक्षिणे शूलपरशुवज्रखड्गानलोज्ज्वलम्।
सव्ये च नागेशाभीतिघण्टापाशाङ्कुशोज्ज्वलम्॥ इति॥

अन्यत्र ऊर्ध्वदक्षवामयोराद्यम् एवमान्तमिति क्रमेणोक्तम्—

शूलाही टङ्कघण्टासिसृणिकुलिशपाशाग्न्यभीतीर्दधानं दोर्भिः। इति।

अन्यत्र व्यत्ययोऽप्युक्तः। यदाहुः—

भुजङ्गघण्टाभयदाङ्कुशांश्च पाशं भुजैर्दक्षिणतो दधानम्।
तथा त्रिशूलं परशुं च खड्गं वज्रं च वह्निं क्रमशो परैश्च॥ इति॥

अन्यत्र एकवक्त्रं चतुर्भुजं च ध्यानमुक्तम्। अथवैकवक्त्रम्।

दोर्भिश्चतुर्भिर्युतमिन्दुमौलिं धृताक्षमालात्रिशिखं क्रमात् तम्।
यजेत् सखट्वाङ्गकपालहस्तम्। इति॥

अन्यत्र तु—देवं नमामि शिरसा परशुत्रिशूल-
विद्याकपालपरिघमण्डितबाहुखण्डम्॥ इति॥ ८५॥ ८६॥

मूर्त्तीति। आदिशब्देनाऽङ्गावृतिरुक्ता। मूर्त्त्यावरणं च अङ्गावरणं च आवरणानि अनन्तोमिन्द्रवज्रादीनि च तैः मूर्त्याद्यावरणैरित्येकशेषेण समासः कार्यः। तेन मूर्त्तिपञ्चकनिवृत्त्यादिपञ्चकेन प्रथमावरणं सम्पूज्य द्वितीयाङ्गैस्तृतीया विद्येश्वरादिभिरित्यर्थः। तदुक्तं प्रयोगसारे "मूर्त्यङ्गावरणोपेतम्" इति। अन्यत्रापि मूर्त्तिपूजामुक्त्वा उक्तम्—

आग्नेयेशाननैर्ऋत्यवायुपत्रेष्वथो परः।

शक्तिं डमरुकाभीतिवरान् सन्दधतं करैः ।
ईशानं लोक्षणं शुभ्रमैशान्यां दिशि पूजयेत् ॥ ८८
परश्वेणवराभीतीर्दधानं विद्युदुज्ज्वलम् ।
चतुर्मुखं तत्पुरुषं त्रिनेत्रं पूर्वतोऽर्चयेत् ॥ ८९
अक्षस्रजं मृगपाशौ खर्विं डमरुकं ततः ।
खट्वाङ्गं निशितं शूलं कपालं बिभ्रतं करैः ॥ ९०
अञ्जनाभं चतुर्वक्त्रं भीमदंष्ट्रं भयावहम् ।
अघोरं चोक्षणं याम्ये पूजयेन्मन्त्रवित्तमः ॥ ९१
कुङ्कुमाभं चतुर्वक्त्रं वामदेवं त्रिलोचनम् ।
वराभयाक्षवलयकुठारं दधतं करैः ॥ ९२
विलासिनं स्मेरवक्त्रं सौम्ये सम्यक् समर्चयेत् ।
कर्पूरेन्दुनिभं सौम्यं सद्योजातं त्रिलोचनम् ॥ ९३
हरिणाक्षगुणाभीतिवरहस्तं चतुर्मुखम् ।
बालेन्दुशेखरोल्लासिमुकुटं पश्चिमे यजेत् ॥ ९४
निवृत्त्याद्यास्ततः कोणे तेजोरूपाः कलाः क्रमात् ।
केसरेषु षडङ्गानि पूर्ववत् पूजयेत् सुधीः ॥ ९५

संपूज्याऽङ्गानि चोक्तानि दिक्षस्त्रमपि पूजयेत् ॥
स्वनामकलितैर्मन्त्रैरनन्तं सूक्ष्ममेव च । इत्यादिना ।

वायवीयसंहितायामपि—पूजयेत्परमेश्वरम् । ब्रह्मभिश्च षडङ्गैश्च । इति । पद्मपादाचार्यैरपि मूर्त्यावरणाद्बहिरङ्गावरणं द्रष्टव्यमित्युक्तम् । तेन यत् केचन मूर्त्यावरणात् पूर्वम् अङ्गावरणं वदन्ति तदयुक्तम् ।

नारायणीयेऽपि—मूर्त्यङ्गानि यजेद्यथाविधि । इति ।
पूर्वत इत्यादि दिग्ग्रहणं व्यक्तता प्रसिद्धदिशामेव कृतमिति ज्ञेयम् । मन्त्रवित्तमः सम्यक् समर्चयेदित्यनेनेशादीनां न्यासोक्तबीजादित्वेन पूजयेदित्युक्तं भवति ॥ ८७ ॥ ॥ ८८ ॥ ८९ ॥ ९० ॥ ९१ ॥ ९२ ॥ ९३ ॥ ९४ ॥

तेजोरूपा इति । एषां शरीराद्याकाराभावे कारणमुक्तमाचार्यैः—

भूतानां शक्तित्वाद्व्याप्तत्वाज्जगति वा निवृत्त्याद्याः ।
तेजोरूपाः करपदवर्णविहीना मनीषिभिः प्रोक्ताः ॥ इति ॥

विद्येश्वराननन्ताद्यान् पत्रेषु परितो यजेत् ।
उमादिकास्ततो बाह्ये शक्राद्यानायुधैः सह ॥ ९६

इति सम्पूज्य देवेशं भक्त्या परमया युतः ।
प्रीणयेन्नृत्यगीताद्यैः स्तोत्रैर्मन्त्री मनोहरैः ॥ ९७

तन्त्रान्तरे आकारोऽप्युक्तः ।

वज्राक्षमालामभयमम्बुजं बिभ्रती करैः ।
हेमाभा चारुसर्वाङ्गा निवृत्तिः सितभूषणा ॥
श्वेताकल्पाऽक्षमालाब्जपाशाभयकरा सिता ।
सर्वाभरणसन्दीप्ता प्रतिष्ठाऽतिमनोहरा ॥
शक्त्यक्षमालाब्जाभीतिहस्ता गुञ्जारुणोज्ज्वला ।
कपर्देन्दुस्त्रिकमुखी ध्येया विद्या कला त्रिदृक् ॥
चतुर्वक्त्रभुजा कृष्णा नीलवस्त्रा कपर्दिनी ।
ध्वजाक्षमालाब्जाभीतिहस्ता शान्तिकला त्रिदृक् ॥
स्फटिकाभा पञ्चवक्त्रा वेदाक्षस्त्रग्वराभयान् ।
दधती सकपर्देन्दुः शान्त्यतीताऽच्छभूषणा ॥ इति ।

कला इत्यनेन प्रथमपटलोक्तापञ्चीकृतभूतभोजाद्या इत्युक्तम् । क्रमादित्यनेनै-तदुक्तम् । आग्नेयादिषु निवृत्त्यादि चतुष्कं संपूज्य ईशस्थाने शान्त्यतीतां पूर्वमेव पूजयेदिति । अन्ये तु ईशानशान्त्यतीतं मध्ये पूजयेदित्याहुः । प्रपञ्चसार-सम्मतमेतत् । पूर्वमूर्ध्वप्रागित्युक्त्वा पश्चात् पूर्वोक्तादिक्षु मूर्त्तीरित्युक्तेः । अन्ये त्वेवं तयोः पूजामाहुः । उमादिका इति पूर्ववदुत्तरादि यजेत् । अस्य तन्त्रान्तरस्थं यन्त्रद्वयमुच्यते—

षट्कोणमण्डलं बाह्ये रोचनाचन्दनाक्तया ।
दूर्वया विलिखेन्मन्त्री प्रासादं नामसंयुतम् ॥
बहिः षट्सु च कोणेषु प्रणवाद्यं षडक्षरम् ।
त्रयस्त्रिंशद्दलं बाह्ये त्रिंशद्वर्णमालिखेत् ॥
ईशानवर्णषट्कं च तत्पुरुषं तु सप्तकम् ।
अघोरवर्णषट्कं च वामदेवस्य सप्तकम् ॥
सद्योजातं तथा सप्त नमोऽन्तं वर्णमालिखेत् ।
मृत्युञ्जयेन संवेष्ट्य धारयेद्यन्त्रमुत्तमम् ॥ इति ।

तारो माया वियद्‌ बिन्दुमनुस्वरसमन्वितम् ।
पञ्चाक्षरसमायुक्तो वसुवर्णो मनुर्मतः ॥ ९८

पञ्चाक्षरोक्तवत् कुर्यादङ्गन्यासादिकं बुधः ॥ ९९

वन्दे सिन्दूरवर्णं मणिमुकुटलसच्चारुचन्द्रावतंसं
भालोद्यन्नेत्रमीशं स्मितमुखकमलं दिव्यभूषाङ्गरागम् ।
वामोरुन्यस्तपाणेररुणकुवलयं सन्दधत्याः प्रियाया
वृत्तोत्तुङ्गस्तनाग्रे निहितकरतलं वेदटङ्केष्टहस्तम् ॥ १००

अष्टलक्षं जपेदेनं मन्त्रं मनुविदां वरः ।
तत्सहस्रं प्रजुहुयात् पायसान्नैर्घृतप्लुतैः ॥ १०१

प्राक्पीठे मूलमन्त्रेण मूर्त्तिं सङ्कल्प्य पूजयेत् ।
अङ्गैरावरणं पूर्वमनन्ताद्यैरनन्तरम् ॥ १०२

उमादिभिः समुद्दिष्टं तृतीयं लोकनायकैः ।
चतुर्थं पञ्चमं तेषामायुधैः परिकीर्त्तितम् ॥ १०३

एवं प्रतिदिनं देवं पूजयेत्साधकोत्तमः ।
पुत्रमित्रादिसहितां श्रियं प्राप्य प्रमोदते ॥ १०४

षट्कोणान्तः साध्ययुक्तं प्रासादं मूलमस्त्रिषु ।
सन्धिष्वङ्गानि तद्बाह्ये पद्मं पञ्चदलं लिख ॥
ईशानाद्याः पञ्चमूर्त्तीर्डेऽन्तदन्त्वा लिखेत्ततः ।
अष्टपत्रं मातृकाष्टवर्गयुक्तं लिखेद्बहिः ॥
संवेष्ट्याऽनुष्टुभा यन्त्रं जपहोमादिसाधितम् ।
आरोग्यायुःसुतैश्वर्यचतुर्वर्गफलप्रदम् ॥ इति ॥ ९५॥९६॥९७ ॥

अष्टाक्षरं प्रासादमन्त्रमाह तार इति । तारः प्रणवः । माया शक्तिबीजम् । वियत् हः बिन्दुमनुस्वरौ औं तद्युक् तेन हौं । पञ्चाक्षर इति शैवपञ्चाक्षरः । वसुवर्णोऽष्टाक्षरः । पूर्वोक्तौ ऋषिच्छन्दसी । उमापतिर्देवता ॥ ९८ ॥

पञ्चाक्षरोक्तवदिति । मायाषड्दीर्घाद्यबीजषडक्षरैः षडङ्गमिति संप्रदायविदः । आदिशब्देन मूर्त्तिपञ्चकन्यासः ॥ ९९ ॥

वन्दे इति । वेदः पुस्तकं टङ्कः परशुः । वामोरुन्यस्तपाणेरिति दक्षपाणेः । अरुणकुवलयमिति । वामपाणौ । निहितकरतलमिति । वामाधस्तनम् ।

तारं स्थिरा सकर्णेन्दुः भृगुः सर्गविभूषितः ।
त्र्यक्षरात्मा निगदितो मनुर्मृत्युञ्जयादिकः ॥ १०५
ऋषिः कहोलो देव्यादिगायत्री छन्द ईरितम् ।
मृत्युञ्जयो महादेवो देवताऽस्य समीरितः ॥ १०६
भृगुणा दीर्घयुक्तेन षडङ्गानि समाचरेत् ॥ १०७

तदुक्तम्—वामाङ्कन्यस्तवामेतरकरकमलायास्तथा वामबाहु-
न्यस्तरक्तोत्पलायाः स्तनविधृतलसद्वामबाहुः प्रियायाः । इति ।
ऊर्ध्ववामे इष्टं वरमित्यर्थः । वेदटङ्के दक्षस्थे ।
उमादिभिरिति पूर्वोक्तिः ॥ १०० ॥ १०१ ॥ १०२ ॥ १०३ ॥ १०४ ॥

एवं पञ्चवक्त्रशिवस्य मन्त्रानभिधाय ऊर्ध्ववक्त्रप्रधानं मृत्युञ्जयमन्त्रमाह तारमिति । तारं प्रणवम् । स्थिरा जः । कर्णो वामकर्णः ऊ । अथवा कर्णशब्देन षट्संख्या तेन ऊ इन्दुर्बिन्दुः तेन जूं । भृगुः सकारः सर्गो विसर्गः तद्युक्तः ।

द्वन्द्वावयवसम्पाते पूर्वस्यादौ परिग्रहः ।

इति यद्यपि सामान्यपरिभाषा तथाप्यत्र विशेषवचनात्तद्बाधः पूर्वव्याख्याने । तदुक्तं प्रयोगसारे—

वेदादिः काष्टमः षष्ठस्वरार्धेन्द्वन्वितश्च सः ।
स्वरश्चतुर्थो बिन्द्वन्तो जलौ[जसौ] बिन्द्वन्वितः शशी ॥
पञ्चाक्षरस्य मन्त्रस्य बीजान्युक्तानि यत्नतः ।
तस्यादितः क्रमाद्बीजैस्त्र्यक्षरः प्रोच्यते त्रिभिः ॥
बीजेनाऽन्त्येन तस्यैव स्यादेकाक्षर ईरितः ।
एते मृत्युञ्जया मन्त्राः क्रमात्प्रोक्ताः फलोत्तराः ॥ इति ॥

नारायणीयेऽपि—सशिवं वामदोर्मध्यं बिन्दुमत्सकलो भृगुः । इति ।
तट्टीकायां सशिवं षष्ठस्वरयुक्तम् । शिवशब्देन षष्ठस्वरोऽत्र विवक्षितः इत्युक्तम् ।
प्रणवो बीजं स इति शक्तिः । जूं बीजमिति पद्मपादाचार्याः ॥ १०५ ॥ १०६ ॥

भृगुणा सकारेण । दीर्घयुक्तेन षड्दीर्घयुक्तेन समाचरेदिति । नाभिहृद्-भ्रूमध्येऽप्यक्षरन्यासानन्तरमित्यर्थः ॥ १०७ ॥

चन्द्रार्काग्निविलोचनं स्मितमुखं पद्मद्वयान्तःस्थितं
मुद्रापाशमृगाक्षसूत्रविलसत्पाणिं हिमांशुप्रभम्।
कोटीरेन्दुगलत्सुधाप्लुततनुं हारादिभूषोज्ज्वलं
कान्त्या विश्वविमोहनं पशुपतिं मृत्युञ्जयं भावयेत्॥ १०८

गुणलक्षं जपेन्मन्त्रं तद्दशांशं विशालधीः।
जुहुयादमृताखण्डैः शुद्धदुग्धाज्यलोलितैः॥ १०९
शैवे संपूजयेत्पीठे मूर्त्तिं मूलेन कल्पयेत्।
अङ्गावरणमाराध्य पश्चाल्लोकेश्वरान् यजेत्॥ ११०
तदस्त्राणि ततो बाह्ये पूजयेत् साधकोत्तमः।
जपपूजादिभिः सिद्धे मन्त्रेऽस्मिन्मनुना क्रमात्॥ १११
कुर्यात् प्रयोगान् कल्पोक्तानभीष्टफलसिद्धये।
दुग्धयुक्तैः सुधाखण्डैर्मन्त्री मासं सहस्रकम्॥ ११२
आराधितेऽग्नौ जुहुयाद्विधिवद्विजितेन्द्रियः।
सन्तुष्टः शङ्करस्तेन सुधाप्लावितविग्रहः॥ ११३
आयुरारोग्यसम्पत्तियशःपुत्रान् विवर्धयेत्।
सुधावटी तिलो दूर्वा पयः सर्पिः पयोहविः॥ ११४
इत्युक्तैः सप्तभिर्द्रव्यैर्जुहुयात्सप्तवासरम्।
क्रमाद्दशांशतो नित्यमष्टोत्तरमतन्द्रितः॥ ११५
सप्ताधिकान् द्विजान्नित्यं भोजयेन्मधुरान्वितम्।
विकारानुगुणं मन्त्री वर्धयेद्धोमवासरान्॥ ११६

पद्मद्वयान्तःस्थितमिति। एकमूर्ध्वमुखं तदुपर्युपविष्टं द्वितीयमधोमुखं शिरसि। मुद्रा ज्ञानमुद्रा। दक्षोर्ध्वात् दक्षाधस्तनं यावदायुधध्यानम्॥ १०८॥

गुणलक्षं त्रिलक्षम्। विशालधीरित्यनेन शैवं पीठमभ्यर्च्येत्युक्तम्। अमृता गुडूची। शुद्धेति वस्त्रादिना गालितैः। सुधा गुडूची। मन्त्रीति। एकाक्षरबीजादित्वमुक्तम्। मासं जुहुयादिति सम्बन्धः। सहस्रकमिति प्रत्येकम्। विधिवदाराधित इत्यग्नौ शैवं पीठं सम्पूज्येत्यर्थः। पयोहविरिति पायसम्। विकारमिति। रोगानुसाराच्चतुर्दशैकविंशेत्यादि दिनवृद्धिः॥ १०९—११६॥

होतृभ्यो दक्षिणां दद्यादरुणा गाः पयस्विनीः ।
गुरुं संप्रीणयेत्पश्चाद्धनाद्यैर्देवताधिया ॥ ११७

अनेन विधिना साध्यः कृत्याद्रोहज्वरादिभिः ।
विमुक्तः सुचिरं जीवेच्छरदां शतमञ्जसा ॥ ११८

अभिचारे ज्वरे तीव्रे घोरोन्मादे शिरोगदे ।
असाध्यरोगक्ष्वेडादौ महादाहे महाभये ॥ ११९

होमोऽयं शान्तिदः प्रोक्तः सर्वसम्पत्प्रदायकः ।
द्रव्यैरेतैः प्रजुहुयात् त्रिजन्मसु यथाविधि ॥ १२०

भोजयेन्मधुरैर्भोज्यैर्ब्राह्मणान् वेदपारगान् ।
दीर्घमायुरवाप्नोति वाञ्छितां विन्दति श्रियम् ॥ १२१

एकादशाहुतीर्नित्यं दूर्वाभिर्जुहुयाद् बुधः ।
अपमृत्युजिदेषः स्यादायुरारोग्यवर्धनः ॥ १२२

त्रिजन्मसु सुधावल्लीकाश्मरीबकुलोद्भवैः ।
समिद्वरैः कृतो होमः सर्वमृत्युगदापहः ॥ १२३

सिद्धान्नैर्विहितो होमो महाज्वरविनाशनः ।
अपामार्गसमिद्धोमः सर्वामयविषूदनः ॥ १२४

प्रणवरचितनालं मन्त्रमध्यार्णपत्रं
भृगुविलसितमध्यं पद्मयुग्मं तदन्तः ।
कृतवसतिमुमेशं वर्णनिर्यत्सुधार्द्रं
कलयतु हृदि नित्यं सर्वदुःखप्रशान्त्यै ॥ १२५

द्रव्यैरेतैरिति । पूर्वोक्तैः सप्तभिः । त्रिजन्मस्विति प्रथमदशमएकोनविंशतिसंख्येषु नक्षत्रेषु । यथाविधीति । पूर्वोक्तप्रकारेण ॥ ११७॥११८॥११९॥१२० ॥
॥ १२१॥१२२॥१२३॥१२४ ॥

प्रणवेति । मन्त्रमध्यार्णौ जूं स चाष्टावृत्त्या अष्टसु पत्रेषु । भृगुविलसितेति । सविसर्गसकारेण । पद्मयुग्मं कलयतु तदन्तः कृतवसतिमुमेशं कलयत्विति सम्बन्धः । एवं पद्मद्वयसम्पुटमध्ये उमेशं ध्यायेत् । वर्णः कर्णिकास्थः सकारः तस्मान्निर्यती या सुधा तया आर्द्रम् ॥ १२५ ॥

यन्त्राढ्ये कमले सौम्ये कलशं प्रोक्तवर्त्मना ।
नवरत्नसमायुक्तं दुकूलाभ्यामलङ्कृतम् ॥ १२६

आपूर्य सलिलैः शुद्धैस्तस्मिन् देवं प्रपूजयेत् ।
उपचारैः षोडशभिर्विधानेन विधानवित् ।
अभिषिञ्चेत् प्रियं साध्यं विनीतं दत्तदक्षिणम् ॥ १२७

आधिव्याधिमहारोगकृत्याद्रोहनिवारणः ।
अभिषेकोऽयमाख्यातः कीर्त्तिलक्ष्मीजयप्रदः ॥ १२८

मध्ये साध्याक्षराढ्यं ध्रुवमभिविलिखेन्मध्यगं दिग्दलस्थं
कोणेष्वन्त्यं मनोस्तत्क्षितिभुवनमथो दिक्षु चन्द्रान्विदिक्षु ।
टान्तं यन्त्रं तदुक्तं सकलभयहरं क्ष्वेड़भूतापमृत्यु-
व्याधिव्यामोहदुःखप्रशमनमुदितं श्रीप्रदं कीर्त्तिदायि ॥ १२९

इति श्रीशारदातिलके अष्टादशः पटलः ॥

अभिषेकमाह यन्त्रेति । यन्त्राढ्य इति वक्ष्यमाणयन्त्रयुक्ते । कमल इति भद्रकमण्डलस्थले । सौम्यं मनोहरम् । प्रोक्तवर्त्मेति । षष्ठपटलोक्तरीत्या । विधानविद्विधानेनेत्यनेनैतदुक्तम् । तुर्यौक्तागमश्लोकैरुपचारेषु तत्तद्द्रव्यविशेषैस्तत्तन्मुद्राभिरिति ॥ १२६ ॥ १२७ ॥ १२८ ॥

यन्त्रमाह मध्य इति । मध्ये कर्णिकायाम् । मध्यगं जूंकारम् । अन्त्यं सः । चन्द्रं ठकारम् । तदुक्तम्—

खड्गौघलाङ्गलिभ्यां तु दिग्विदिक्ष्वङ्कितं बहिः ।
भूपुरं विनिवेश्याऽस्मिन् कलशं समलङ्कृतम् ॥ इति ॥ १२९ ॥

इति श्रीशारदातिलटीकायां सम्प्रदायकृतव्याख्यायां
पदार्थादर्शाभिख्यायाम् अष्टादशः पटलः ॥ ॐ ॥

ऊनविंशः पटलः ।

अथ वक्ष्ये मन्त्ररत्नं समस्तपुरुषार्थदम् ।
अवाप्नुर्येन जप्तेन दिव्यं ज्ञानं मुनीश्वराः ॥ १
दक्षिणामूर्त्तये पूर्वं तुभ्यं पदमनन्तरम् ।
वटमूलपदस्याऽन्ते पदं पश्चान्निवासिने ॥ २
ध्यानैकनिरताङ्गाय पश्चाद् ब्रूयान्नमःपदम् ।
रुद्राय शम्भवे तारशक्तिरुद्धोऽयमीरितः ॥ ३
षट्त्रिंशदक्षरो मन्त्रः सर्वकामफलप्रदः ।
मुनिः शुकः समुद्दिष्टश्छन्दोऽनुष्टुप्समीरितम् ॥ ४
दक्षिणामूर्त्तिनामाऽस्य देवता शम्भुरीरितः ।
षड्भिर्वर्णैर्हृदाख्यातं द्वाभ्यां शिर उदीरितम् ॥ ५
शिखाऽष्टभिः समुद्दिष्टा वस्वर्णैः कवचं मतम् ।
पञ्चभिर्नेत्रमाख्यातं त्रिभिरस्त्रमुदाहृतम् ॥ ६
षडेते तारशक्त्याद्या क्षाङाद्यन्ताः सजातयः ।
अङ्गमन्त्राः समुद्दिष्टा यथावद्देशिकोत्तमैः ॥ ७
मूर्ध्नि भाले दृशोः श्रोत्रे गण्डयुग्मेऽथ नासिके ।
आस्ये दोःसन्धिषु गले स्तनहृन्नाभिमण्डले ॥ ८

एवमूर्ध्ववक्त्रप्रधानमन्त्रनिरूपणानन्तरं दक्षिणवक्त्रप्रधानं सौम्य[शैव]मन्त्रमाह । अथेति । समस्तपुरुषार्थदमित्यनेन विनियोग उक्तः ॥ १ ॥

मन्त्रमुद्धरति दक्षिणेति । श्लोकरूपो मन्त्रः । तारशक्तिरुद्धोऽयमित्युभाभ्यां रुद्धः पुटितः तेनान्ते व्युत्क्रमः । प्रणवो बीजं माया शक्तिः ।

क्षाङादीति मकारे ङकारः । प्रयोगस्तु ॐ ह्रीं दक्षिणामूर्त्तये ह्रां हृदयाय नमः ॐ ह्रीं शिरसे स्वाहा इत्यादि । यथावद्देशिकोत्तमैरित्यनेन शैवषडङ्ग-मुद्राभिः सह कर्त्तव्यतोक्ता ॥ २ ॥ ३ ॥ ४ ॥ ५ ॥ ६ ॥ ७ ॥

मूर्ध्नीत्यादि चतुस्त्रिंशत्स्थानेषु चतुस्त्रिंशद्वर्णान् विन्यस्य शिष्टाभ्यां व्यापकं कुर्यादित्यर्थः ।

तदुक्तम्—एवं प्रणवहृल्लेखापूर्वाक्षरन्यासादिकं कृत्वा । इति ।

कर्ण्यां गुह्ये पुनः पादसन्धिष्वर्णान्न्यसेत् क्रमात्।
व्यापकं तारशक्तिभ्यां कुर्याद्देहे ततः परम्॥ ९

हेमाचलतटे रम्ये सिद्धकिन्नरसेविते।
विविधद्रुमशाखाभिः सर्वतो वारितातपे॥ १०

सुपुष्पितैर्लताजालैराश्लिष्टकुसुमद्रुमैः।
शिलाविवरनिर्गच्छन्निर्भरानिलसेविते॥ ११

गायद्भृङ्गाङ्गनासङ्घे नृत्यद्बर्हिकदम्बके।
कूजत्कोकिलसङ्घेन मुखरीकृतदिङ्मुखे॥ १२

परस्परविनिर्मुक्तमात्सर्यैर्मृगसेविते।
आद्यैः शुकाद्यैर्मुनिभिरजस्रं समुपस्थिते॥ १३

पुरन्दरमुखैर्देवैः सेवायातैर्विलोकितम्।
वटवृक्षं महोच्छ्रायं पद्मरागफलोज्ज्वलम्॥ १४

गारुत्मतमयैः पत्रैर्निविडैरुपशोभितम्।
नवरत्नमयाकल्पैर्लम्बमानैरलङ्कृतम्॥ १५

जलजैः स्थलजैः पुष्पैरामोदिभिरलङ्कृतम्।
शृण्वद्भिर्वेदशास्त्राणि शुकवृन्दैर्निषेवितम्॥ १६

आचार्या अपि—पुनर्द्वाभ्यां मन्त्रविद्व्यापकं न्यसेत्। इति।

केचित् तु नसोस्तनयोरेकैकमक्षरं न्यसनीयमिति द्वात्रिंशदक्षरन्यासमेवाहुः। एष एव सांप्रदायिकः पक्षः।

तदुक्तमाचार्यैः—कालिकश्रुतिदृग्गण्डद्वयनासास्यके दश। इत्यादिना।

पूर्वलिखिताचार्यपद्यव्याख्याने पद्मपादाचार्यैर्द्वाभ्यां मन्त्रविदित्यनेन आद्यन्तप्रणवशक्त्योरेकत्वं जानन्नित्यर्थं इति व्याख्यातम्। व्यापकं तारशक्तिभ्यामिति वदता मूलकारेणापि सूचितमेव। तेन ॐ ह्रीं दं नम इत्यादि प्रयोगः। "कृतसंदोषो मन्त्रो" इत्यनेन न्यासमन्त्रादौ प्रणवशक्तियोग उक्त इत्यादि पद्मपादाचार्याः॥ ८॥ ९॥

ध्यानमाह हेमेति। हेमाचलतटे वटवृक्षं सञ्चिन्त्येति सम्बन्धः। लम्बमानैरिति वटप्ररोहैः। लोबणी इति गौडभाषायाम्। अनेनैतदुक्तं भवति। मणिमण्डपानन्तरं हेमाचलतटे वटवृक्षं तदधो रत्नसिंहासनमिति पीठन्यासे विशेषः

संसारतापविच्छेदकुशलच्छायमद्भुतम् ।
विचिन्त्य तस्य मूलस्थे रत्नसिंहासने शुभे ॥ १७
आसीनममिताकल्पं शरच्चन्द्रनिभाननम् ।
स्तूयमानं मुनिगणैर्दिव्यज्ञानाभिलाषिभिः ।
संस्मरेज्जगतामाद्यं दक्षिणामूर्त्तिमव्ययम् ॥ १८

कैलासाद्रिनिभं शशाङ्कशकलस्फूर्जज्जटामण्डितं
नासालोकनतत्परं त्रिनयनं वीरासनाध्यासितम् ।
मुद्राटङ्ककुरङ्गजानुविलसत्पाणिं प्रसन्नाननं
कक्षाबद्धभुजङ्गमं मुनिवृतं वन्दे महेशं परम् ॥ १९

अयुतद्वयसंयुक्तं गुणलक्षं जपेन्मनुम् ।
तद्दशांशं तिलैः शुद्धैर्जुहुयात् क्षीरसंयुतैः ॥ २०
पश्चाच्चरोदिते पीठे विधानेन प्रपूजयेत् ।
उपचारैः समुत्पन्नैः पाद्याद्यैः परमेश्वरम् ॥ २१
एवं कृतपुरश्चर्यः सिद्धमन्त्रो भवेत् सुधीः ।
भिक्षाहारो जपेन्मासं मनुमेनं जितेन्द्रियः ॥ २२
नित्यं सहस्रमष्टार्धं परं विन्दति वाङ्मयम् ।
त्रिवारं जप्तमेतेन मनुना सलिलं पिबेत् ॥ २३
नित्यशो दक्षिणामूर्त्तिं ध्यायन् साधकसत्तमः ।
शास्त्रव्याख्यानसामर्थ्यं लभते वत्सरान्तरे ॥ २४

शेषं समानमिति ॥ १०॥११॥१२॥१३॥१४॥१५॥१६॥१७॥१८ ॥

ध्यानमाह कैलासेति। वीरासनमन्यपटले वक्ष्यति। मुद्रा ज्ञानमुद्रा।

तदुक्तमाचार्यैः—मुद्रां भद्रार्थदात्रीम्। इति।

टङ्कः परशुः। दक्षयोराद्ये वामयोरन्ये आयुधे ॥ १९ ॥

गुणलक्षं त्रिलक्षम्। समुत्पन्नैः समुत्तैः समुत्पादितैरिति वार्थः। तेनोक्तप्रकारेणैवोपचारान् कुर्यात् न जलादिनेत्युक्तं भवति ॥ २०॥२१॥२२॥२३॥२४ ॥

ब्राह्मीसैन्धवसिद्धार्थवचाकुष्ठकणोत्पलैः।

सुगन्धिसंयुतैः कल्कैः शृतं ब्राह्मीरसे घृतम् ॥ २५

मनुनाऽनेन सञ्जप्तमयुतं साधुसाधितम्।

निपीतं कविताकान्तिरक्षायुःश्रीधृतिप्रदम् ॥ २६

सिद्धार्थो गौरसर्षपः। कणा पिप्पली। उत्पलं मुस्ता। सुगन्धिशब्देन त्वक्पत्रैलाकेसराणि। तदुक्तं वैद्यकनिघण्टौ—

त्वक्पत्रैलाकेसराणि चातुर्जातं सुगन्धिकम् ॥ इति।

एतेषां कल्केन ब्राह्मीरसे घृतपाकः। तत्र—

स्नेहः सिध्यति शुद्धाम्बुनि क्वाथस्वरसैः क्रमात्।

कल्कस्य योजयेदंशं चतुर्थं षष्ठमष्टमम् ॥

इति विशेषपरिभाषावचनात् पलमितेन कल्केन षट्पलं घृतं पचेत्।

पञ्चप्रभृति यत्र स्युर्द्रव्याणि स्नेहसंविधौ।

तत्र स्नेहसमान्याहुरर्वाक् च स्याच्चतुर्गुणम् ॥

इत्युक्तत्वात् चतुर्विंशतिपलानि ब्राह्मीरसः। घृतावशेषमुत्तारितमुक्तफलदम्। शृतं पक्वम् ॥ २५ ॥

साधु साधितमिति। अयमर्थः। घृते उक्तप्रकारेण देवतापीठमभ्यर्च्य तत्र सावरणं देवमिष्ट्वा वह्निरग्निं प्रतिष्ठाप्य तत्रापि ब्राह्मीरसेन देवपीठमभ्यर्च्य हुत्वा तत्सम्पाताज्येनाऽऽप्लुतं कुर्यादिति। निपीतमिति। शुचिना प्रातरिति शेषः। तन्त्रान्तरोक्तं यन्त्रमुच्यते—

अथ मेधाकरं ज्ञानवाक्सिद्धिकविताकरम्।

वक्ष्येऽहं दक्षिणामूर्त्तियन्त्रं सर्वार्थसाधकम् ॥

दन्तपत्रदलोपेतं पङ्कजं भूर्जचर्मणि।

दूर्वाग्रैः पशुपित्ताद्यैर्लिखेच्च कर्णिकोदरे ॥

साध्याख्यां प्रविलिख्याऽथ पत्रेष्वानुष्टुभं लिखेत्।

तद्बहिः पृथिवीगेहं तत्कोणे नकुलीश्वरम् ॥

तस्मिन्नावाह्य संपूज्य देवं सन्तर्प्य धारयेत्।

तस्य हस्तगतं सद्यो ब्रह्मज्ञानादिकं भवेत् ॥ इति ॥ २६ ॥

प्रणवो हृदयं पश्चात्ततो भगवते पदम्।
ङेयुतं दक्षिणामूर्त्तिं मह्यं मेधामुदीरयेत्॥ २७

प्रयच्छ ठद्वयान्तोऽयं द्वाविंशत्यक्षरो मनुः।
मुनिश्चतुर्मुखश्छन्दो गायत्री देवता मनोः॥ २८

दक्षिणामूर्त्तिराख्यातो वेदव्याख्यानतत्परः।
तारुद्धैः स्वरैर्दीर्घैः षड्भिरङ्गानि कल्पयेत्॥ २९

अथवा मनुसम्भूतैः पदैर्वा कल्पयेत् क्रमात्।
पूर्वोक्तवटमूलस्थं चिन्तयेन्मन्त्रनायकम्॥ ३०

स्फटिकरजतवर्णं मौक्तिकीमक्षमाला-
ममृतकलशविद्याज्ञानमुद्राः कराग्रैः।
दधतमुरगकक्षं चन्द्रचूडं त्रिनेत्रं
विधृतविविधभूषं दक्षिणामूर्त्तिमीडे॥ ३१

मन्त्रान्तरमाह प्रणव इति। हृदयं नमःपदम्। अत्रापि पूर्ववद्विसर्गेण सन्धिः। ङेयुतो दक्षिणामूर्त्तिः दक्षिणामूर्त्तये। मह्यं मेधामित्यत्र हसमेधामित्येके। प्रज्ञामेधामित्यन्ये। केचन मेधापदस्थाने प्रज्ञाशब्दमाहुः। इदं तु स्वस्वगुरुसम्प्रदायानुसारेण बोद्धव्यम्। प्रणवान्तो नादो बीजं स्वाहा शक्तिः। नारदीये तु शक्तिरहस्येह वाग्भव इत्युक्तम्। तारुद्धैरिति प्रणवसंपुटितैः। षड्भिर्दीर्घैः स्वरैः। आईऊऐऔअः एभिरित्यर्थः॥ २७॥ २८॥ २९॥

अथवेति। अत्र प्रणवाद्यैर्नमोऽन्तैः षड्भिः पदैः षडङ्गमिति परमगुरवः। अक्षरन्यासस्तु नारदीये—

शिरोललाटहृदयनासागण्डरदद्वये।
जिह्वानेत्रे गले बाह्वोर्हृन्नाभ्यन्धुगुदोरुषु।
जानुजङ्घापार्ष्णिपादे सर्वसन्धिषु चान्तिमम्॥ इति।

वटमूलस्थमित्यत्र विशेषः।

व्याख्यापीठे समासीनमाकाल्लापस्मृतिं पदे। इति॥ ३०॥

उरगकक्षं विलम्बबद्धसर्पम्। दक्षोर्ध्वात् दक्षाधस्तनं यावत् आयुधध्यानम्।

तदुक्तम्—दक्षिणे चाऽक्षमालां च ज्ञानमुद्रां च पावनीम्।
वामे पुस्तकमापूर्णपीयूषकलशं तथा॥ इति॥ ३१॥

लक्षमेकं जपेन्मन्त्रं ब्रह्मचारिव्रते स्थितः ।
जुहुयात् सघृतैः पद्मैर्दशांशं संस्कृतेऽनले ॥ ३२
पूर्वोदिते यजेत्पीठे वक्ष्यमाणेन वर्त्मना ।
अङ्गानभ्यर्चयेदाद्ये पत्रेष्वष्टसु पूजयेत् ॥ ३३
सरस्वतीं वाचयन्तीं पुस्तकं सस्मिताननाम् ।
ब्रह्माणं सनकं पश्चात् सनन्दनमतःपरम् ॥ ३४
सनत्कुमारनामानं शुकं व्यासं गणेश्वरम् ।
सिद्धगन्धर्वयोगीन्द्रविद्याधरगणान् बहिः ॥ ३५
बाह्ये लोकेश्वरानर्चेद्वज्राद्यायुधसंयुतान् ।
इत्थं पूजादिभिः सिद्धे मन्त्रेऽस्मिन् साधकोत्तमः ॥ ३६
वल्लभो जायते वाचां वाचस्पतिरिवाऽपरः ।
मन्त्रेणाऽनेन सञ्जप्तैर्विशुद्धैः सलिलैः सुधीः ॥ ३७
अभिषिञ्चेत् स्वशिरसि श्रियमारोग्यमाप्नुयात् ।
कण्ठमात्रे जले स्थित्वा जपेन्मन्त्रं सहस्रकम् ।
प्रत्यहं मण्डलादर्वाक्कवीनामग्रणीर्भवेत् ॥ ३८
गौर्या पार्श्वस्थया सार्द्धं श्रीकामी चिन्तयन् विभुम् ।
अयुतं प्रजपेन्मन्त्रं भूयसीं श्रियमाप्नुयात् ॥ ३९
भुञ्जानः प्रयतो मन्त्री गोमूत्रे श्रृतमोदनम् ।
भिक्षान्नमथवा मन्त्रमयुतद्वितयं जपेत् ।

बहिरिति चतुरस्रान्तर्दिक्षु ॥ ३२॥३३॥३४॥३५॥३६॥३७॥३८ ॥

गौर्येति । तद्ध्यानं यथा—

ऐश्वर्यकामो देवेशं देव्या सार्धं यजेत् सुधीः ।
उदयार्कसमप्रख्यां बन्धूकसदृशप्रभाम् ॥
आपीनतुङ्गकठिनकुचद्वयविराजिताम् ।
त्रिनेत्रां द्विभुजां पद्महस्तां च जनमोहिनीम् ॥
देवस्य वामपार्श्वस्थां सञ्चिन्त्याऽऽराधयेन्नरः ।
तदा मन्त्रे विशेषोऽस्ति मेधास्थाने श्रियं न्यसेत् । इति ॥

श्रीकामी इत्यत्र श्रीपुटितत्वं ज्ञेयम् ॥ ३६ ॥ ३७ ॥ ३८ ॥

अश्रुतान् वेदशास्त्रादीन् व्याचष्टे नात्र संशयः॥ ४०
सिद्धगन्धर्वमुनिभिर्योगीन्द्रैरपि सेवितौ।
ज्ञानवागर्थिनां प्रीत्यै कथितौ मन्त्रनायकौ॥ ४१
लोहितोऽग्न्यासनः सद्योविन्दुमान् प्रथमं ततः।
द्वितीयं वह्निबीजस्था दीर्घा शान्तीन्दुभूषितः॥ ४२
तृतीयं लाङ्गली सर्गी मन्त्रो बीजत्रयान्वितः।
नीलकण्ठात्मकः प्रोक्तो विषद्वयहरः परः॥ ४३
हरद्वयं वह्निजाया हृदयं परिकीर्त्तितम्।
कपर्दिने ठयुगलं शिरोमन्त्र उदाहृतः॥ ४४

भुञ्जान इत्यत्र प्रयोगे ध्यानविशेषो यथा—

वामपाणिगतद्योतज्जातवेदसपुस्तकम्।
व्याख्यामुद्राक्षमालाभ्यां विराजितकरद्वयम्॥ इति॥

भिक्षान्नमथवेति भुञ्जान इति सम्बन्धः। अश्रुतानित्यत्र बालापुटितत्वं ज्ञेयम्॥४०॥
सिद्धेत्यनेन वश्यादिप्रयोगा अपि सूचिताः।

वश्यकामो महादेवं रक्तवर्णं विचिन्तयेत्।
वामोरुसंस्थितां देवीं चिन्तयेन् मदविह्वलाम्।
प्रजासृष्टिनिमित्तं च चिन्तयन्तौ स्मरेच्छिवौ॥ इति॥

कल्पोक्तं यन्त्रं लिख्यते—

भूर्जे रोचनया दशारसहितं पद्मं लिखेत्कर्णिका-
मध्ये तारलिपौ ससाधकनराभिख्यं मनुं द्वन्द्वशः।
पत्रेष्वन्यदलेपि मन्त्रलिपिभिः संवेष्टयेद्बाह्यतः
सम्पूज्याऽथ जपेन तस्य फलितं कर्णेन सर्वज्ञताम्॥
यात्येतेन च साधयेदनुदिनं स्तम्भादिकं वश्यकृ-
द्यद्वाञ्छितमन्यदत्र सुधियः कामानिहाऽमुत्र च। इति॥४१॥

नीलकण्ठमन्त्रमाह लोहित इति। लोहितः पः अग्नौ रेफः तदासनः तेन प्र। सद्य ओ बिन्दुश्च तेन प्रों। दीर्घा नकारः वह्निबीजं रेफः तत्स्था तेन न्र्। शान्तिरी इन्दुर्बिन्दुः तद्युक्ता तेन न्रीं। लाङ्गली ठकारः। सर्गी विसर्गः

नीलकण्ठाय ठद्वन्द्वं शिखामन्त्र उदाहृतः।
कालकूटपदस्याऽन्ते विषभक्षणङेयुतम्॥ ४५

हुं फट् कवचमादिष्टं विद्वद्भिर्नीलकण्ठिने।
स्वाहान्तमस्त्रमेतानि पञ्चाङ्गानि मनोर्विदुः॥ ४६

मूर्ध्नि कण्ठे हृदम्भोजे क्रमाद्बीजत्रयं न्यसेत्।
ततः समाहितो भूत्वा नीलकण्ठं विचिन्तयेत्॥ ४७

बालार्कायुततेजसं धृतजटाजूटेन्दुखण्डोज्ज्वलं
नागेन्द्रैः कृतभूषणं जपवटीं शूलं कपालं करैः।
खट्वाङ्गं दधतं त्रिनेत्रविलसत्पञ्चाननं सुन्दरं
व्याघ्रत्वक्परिधानमब्जनिलयं श्रीनीलकण्ठं भजे॥ ४८

लक्षत्रयं जपेन्मन्त्रं तद्दशांशं ससर्पिषा।
हविषा जुहुयात् सम्यक् संस्कृते हव्यवाहने॥ ४९

शैवे पीठे यजेदेनं मृत्युञ्जयविधानतः।
एवं पूजादिभिः सिद्धे मनौ मन्त्री विषद्वयम्॥ ५०

नाशयेदचिरादेव नीलकण्ठ इवाऽपरः।
मनुनाऽनेन सञ्जप्तैः कुम्भस्थैः सलिलैः शुभैः॥ ५१

अभिषिञ्चेद्विषाक्रान्तं स विषान्मुच्यते ध्रुवम्।
स्पृष्ट्वा जपेद्विषाक्रान्तं तत्क्षणं निर्विषो भवेत्॥ ५२

बीजाभ्यां प्रथमान्ताभ्यां पार्श्वयोर्विषमाहरेत्।
मध्येन मध्यगं सर्वं मनुनाऽनेन संहरेत्॥ ५३

बहुना किमिहोक्तेन मन्त्रेणाऽनेन मन्त्रवित्।
कालकूटविषं साक्षाद् भुक्तं स्यात्परमामृतम्॥ ५४

तदुक्तः। अरुणा ऋषिः त्रिष्टुप् छन्दः। आद्यं बीजम् अन्त्यः शक्तिः। विषद्वयं स्थावरजङ्गमम्। तद्धरमेतदिति विनियोग उक्तः। ङेयुतमिति चतुर्थ्येकवचनान्तम्॥ ४२॥४३॥४४॥४५॥४६॥४७॥

ध्यानमाह बालेति। आयुधध्यानं पूर्ववत्॥ ४८॥४९॥५०॥५१॥५२॥५३॥५४॥

अग्निः संवर्त्तकादित्यरानिलौषष्ठबिन्दुमत् ।
चिन्तामणिरिति ख्यातं बीजं सर्वसमृद्धिदम् ॥ ५५
काश्यपो मुनिराख्यातश्छन्दोऽनुष्टबुदाहृतम् ।
अर्द्धनारीश्वरः प्रोक्तो देवता जगतां पतिः ॥ ५६
रेफादिव्यञ्जनैः षड्भिः कुर्यादङ्गानि षट् क्रमात् ॥ ५७

नीलप्रवालरुचिरं विलसत्त्रिनेत्रं
पाशारुणोत्पलकपालत्रिशूलहस्तम् ।
अर्धाम्बिकेशमनिशं प्रविभक्तभूषं
बालेन्दुबद्धमुकुटं प्रणमामि रूपम् ॥ ५८

दक्षिणवक्त्रप्रधानमन्त्रानन्तरं उत्तरवक्त्रप्रधानं चिन्तामणिमन्त्रमाह अग्निरिति । अग्नी रेफः संवर्तः क्षः आदित्यो मः रः स्वरूपम् । अनिलो यः औ स्वरूपम् षष्ठ ऊ बिन्दुः एतद्युक्तं बीजम् । अत्र स्वरद्वयोच्चारणमपि गुरूपदेशतो ज्ञेयम् । रेफो बीजम् । ऊकारः शक्तिः । सर्वसमृद्धिदमित्यनेन पौष्टिके सकारादिः शुक्लः । आकर्षणवश्ययोर्यथोद्धृतो यथाख्यानं च ।

क्षोभे हकारादौ रक्तः ध्वंसादिरपि यथोक्त उच्चाटने यकारादिर्धूम्रः ।

स्तम्भने लकारादिः पीतः मोक्षार्थं क्षादिः रेफरहितो वासितः ॥

इति सूचयता विनियोगः उक्तः । एषां संयोग ऊर्ध्वाग्निस्थानेमित्युक्तेः । जगतां पतिरित्यनेनोमेशोऽपि देवतेत्युक्तम् । यदाहुराचार्याः—

छन्दोऽनुष्टुप् देवतोमेशः । यान्तैः षड्भिर्वर्णैरङ्गं वा देवताऽर्धनारीशः । इति ।

रेफादीति । क्षयोगे च इति चकारस्य व्यञ्जनद्वयम् । एवं रेफादि यान्तैः षड्भिः सबिन्दुकैः षडङ्गानीति सम्प्रदायविदः ॥ ५५॥५६॥५७ ॥

अर्धनारीश्वरपक्षे ध्यानमाह नीलेति । अर्धाम्बिकेशं महेशार्धं नीलं पार्वत्यर्धं प्रवालरुक् । पाशोत्पले देव्यर्धहस्ताग्रे । अन्ये महेशार्धहस्तजे । प्रविभक्तभूषमिति । महेशांशे सर्पाद्यलङ्कृतं पार्वत्यंशे रत्नताटङ्काद्यलङ्कृतमिति । उमेशपक्षे ध्यानमाचार्योक्तं यथा—

अहिशशधरगङ्गाबद्धतुङ्गात्ममौलिस्त्रिदशगणनताङ्घ्रिस्त्रीक्षणः स्त्रीविलासः ।

भुजगपरशुशूलान् खड्गवह्नी कपालं शरमपि धनुरीशो बिभ्रदव्याच्चिरं वः ।

इदं ध्यानं प्रयोगविषये । पुरश्चरणनित्यजपादौ तु अर्धनारीश्वरध्यानमेव ।

एकलक्षं जपेद्बीजमित्थं मन्त्री विचिन्तयेत् ।
अयुतं मधुना सिक्तैर्जुहुयात्तिलतण्डुलैः ॥ ५९

शैवोदिते यजेत्पीठे प्रागङ्गैः षड्भिरीरितैः ।
वृषाद्यैर्मातृभिः पश्चाल्लोकपालैस्तदायुधैः ॥ ६०

एवमभ्यर्चयेद् देवमर्धनारीश्वरं परम् ।
तेजःकान्तियशोलक्ष्मीवाचां भवति वल्लभः ॥ ६१

प्रासादाद्यं जपेन्मन्त्रमयुतं रोगशान्तये ।
स्वरावृतमिदं बीजं विगलत्परमामृतम् ॥ ६२

चन्द्रबिम्बस्थितं मूर्ध्नि ध्यातं क्ष्वेडगदापहम् ।
प्रतिलोमात्स्वरावीतं बीजं वह्निगृहे स्थितम् ॥ ६३

रेफादिव्यञ्जनोल्लासि षट्कोणाभिवृतं बहिः ।
भूतार्त्तस्य स्मृतं मूर्ध्नि भूतमाशु विनाशयेत् ॥ ६४

बीजं चन्द्रगतं वीतं स्वरैः षोडशभिः क्रमात् ।
गलत्परसुधापूरं नेत्रे ध्यातं रुजं हरेत् ॥ ६५

एवमेव स्मृतं बीजं कुक्षौ शूलादिरोगहृत् ।
स्फोटे विषज्वरे दाहे मोहे शीर्षगदे भ्रमे ॥ ६६

यदाहुराचार्याः—हावभावललितार्धनारिकं भीषणार्धमथवा महेश्वरम् ।
पाशसोत्पलकपालशूलिनं चिन्तयेज्जपविधौ विभूतये ॥ इति ॥५८॥

यजेत्पीठे। उमेशमित्यर्थः। परमर्धनारीश्वरम् एवमभ्यर्चयेदित्यन्वयः। एवमुपदेशमार्गेणेत्यर्थः। तत्र शैवं पीठं सम्पूज्यार्धनारीश्वरमावाह्याऽभ्यर्च्याऽङ्गैः प्रथमावरणं राद्यष्टवर्णैर्द्वितीयं मातृभिः तृतीयं तदनु लोकपालैर्वज्राद्यैश्च। तदुक्तमाचार्यैः—आरभ्यादिज्वलनमथ दिक्संस्थैरष्टभिर्मनोर्वर्णैः।
आराधयेच्च मातृभिरिति संप्रोक्तः प्रयोगविधिरपरः॥ इति॥

चन्द्रबिम्बस्थितं ठकारस्थं मूर्ध्नि ध्यातं विषार्त्तस्येति शेषः। वह्निगृह इति। ऊर्ध्वाग्रे त्रिकोणे। रेफादीति रकषमरयानि ॥ ५९॥६०॥६१॥६२॥६३॥६४ ॥ चन्द्रगतं ठकारगम्। एवमेवेति ठकारगं स्वरावृतं गलत्परसुधारूपमिति ॥६५॥६६॥

बीजमेतत्तथा ध्यातं तत्तत्क्लेशान् विनाशयेत् ।
कुङ्कुमाभमिदं बीजं त्रिकोणगतमुज्ज्वलम् ॥ ६७
यस्य मूर्ध्नि स्मरेन्मन्त्री स वश्यो जायतेऽचिरात् ।
ऊर्ध्वरेफस्थसाध्याख्यं बीजं वह्निगृहे स्थितम् ॥ ६८
वह्निगेहद्वयेनाऽग्नियुक्तकोणेन संवृतम् ।
प्रतिलोमस्वरावीतं चुल्लीस्थाने निवेशितम् ॥ ६९
वशीकरोत्यामरणादचिरेणैव दासवत् ।
मधुरत्रययुक्तेन शालिपिष्टेन पुत्तलीम् ॥ ७०
कृत्वा प्रतिष्ठितप्राणां विभज्य जुहुयाद्वशी ।
दिवासरमनेनैव साध्यस्तस्य वशीभवेत् ॥ ७१
मकारगतसाध्याख्यमनलस्थगदाह्वयम् ।
चन्द्रगं चतुरस्रेण टान्तकोणेन वेष्टितम् ॥ ७२
बीजं ताम्बूलपत्रस्थं प्रजप्तं मनुनाऽमुना ।
भक्षितं नाशयेत्सम्यक् शिरोरोगं न संशयः ॥ ७३
लिखित्वा बन्धुजीवेन त्रिकोणं बीजगर्भितम् ।
अत्र वह्निं समाधाय सम्यगाराध्य देवताम् ॥ ७४
जुहुयात् कृतसम्पातं सर्पिषाऽष्टोत्तरं शतम् ।
सम्पाताज्येन संसिक्ता त्रिलोहकृतमुद्रिका ।
विधृता भूतवेतालकृत्यारोगविनाशिनी ॥ ७५

तथेति । ठकारगं स्वरावृतं गलत्परसुधापूरमिति । ध्यातं विनाशयेदिति । तत्तत्स्थाने । अग्नौ रेफः । भूर्जपत्रादौ यन्त्रं कृत्वा चुल्ल्यां निखनेदित्यर्थः ।

पुत्तलीमिति । द्वादशाङ्गुलाम् । प्रतिष्ठितप्राणामिति । त्रयोविंशे वक्ष्यमाणप्रकारेण ॥ ६६॥६७॥६८॥६९॥७०॥७१ ॥

मकार इति मन्त्रस्थे । अनलस्थेति ऊर्ध्वरेफगतरोगनामयुक्तम् । "विषपावकोद्यत्" इत्यस्य व्याख्याने विषसम्बन्धिरेफ इति पद्मपादाचार्यैर्व्याख्यातम् । चन्द्रगं ठकारस्थम् । टान्तकोणेन चतुरस्रेण वेष्टितं बीजमिति सम्बन्धः ॥ ७२॥७३ ॥

बन्धुजीवपुष्परसेन । अन्यत्र बन्धुजीवपदेन जवापुष्पं पठ्यते । उक्तञ्च— "जपात्रिकोणगो वह्नौ" इति । प्रपञ्चसारटीकाकारेण विज्ञानचन्द्रिकाकृता

ऊर्ध्ववह्निरहितं मनुमेनं वह्निगेहयुगले परिलिख्य।
अग्निमस्त्रिषु महीपुरवीतं यन्त्रमेतदुदितं ग्रहवैरि॥ ७६

अग्निबीजलसत्कोणद्विकोणालिखिते ध्रुवे।
शरावे कपिलाज्याक्तसूत्रदीपं प्रविन्यसेत्॥ ७७

घटेनैनं पिधायाऽस्य पृष्ठे यन्त्रमिदं लिखेत्।
भूतार्त्तमत्र संस्थाप्य चिन्तामणिमनुं जपेत्।
तमाविश्य क्षणान् मुञ्चेद् ग्रहः क्रूरोऽपि सर्वथा॥ ७८

कृशानुभवनद्वये मनुमिमं लिखित्वा पुन-
स्तदस्त्रिषु हलो लिखेत्स्वरयुगं ततः सन्धिषु।
ध्रुवेण परिवेष्टितं धरणिगेहमध्यस्थितं
मनोरथफलप्रदं भवति यन्त्रमेतन्नृणाम्॥ ७९

व्याख्यातम्—"बन्धुजीवं बन्धूकं जपा वा" इति। त्रिलोहकृतेति। पञ्चोक्तरीत्या। पद्मपादाचार्यैर्मन्त्राक्षरसंख्यं लोहत्रयं ग्राह्यमित्युक्तम्॥ ७४॥ ७५॥

अग्निं रं। अस्त्रिषु षट्सु कोणेषु॥ ७६॥

लिखिते इति। रक्तरजसेति ज्ञेयम्। उक्तञ्च नारायणीये—

तारे बीजाङ्ककोणाग्निगेहस्थे रजसाऽर्पिते। इति।

अपेक्षितार्थद्योतनिकायां व्याख्यातं रक्तेन रजसाऽग्निगेहं संश्लिष्य तत्कोणेष्वग्नि-बीजं लिखित्वा तन्मध्ये प्रणवं लिखेदिति। एनं शरावम्। अस्य घटस्य। इदमित्युक्तम्। लिखेदिति जपया। अत्रेति। लिखितयन्त्रपृष्ठे। जपेदिति। ग्रस्तं संस्पृश्येति शेषः। मुञ्चेदिति। मन्त्राभिषेकेण। तदुक्तं नारायणीये—

तत् पिधाय घटेनाऽन्यत् स्वयन्त्रे जपया कृते।
घटपृष्ठगते ग्रस्तं न्यस्य चिन्तामणिं जपेत्॥
ग्रहावेशविनाशार्थं ग्रस्तं तेनाऽभिषेचयेत्॥ इति।

स्वेति चिन्तामणियन्त्रे। तेनेति चिन्तामणिमन्त्रेणेति लघुटीकायां व्याख्यातम्॥ ७७॥ ७८॥

तदस्त्रिषु तत्कोणेषु। हलो व्यञ्जनानि बीजस्थानि रकषमरयाः। स्वरयुगं बीजस्थं ऋी ऊ। ध्रुवेण प्रणवेन एकावृत्तिः। धरणिगेहास्त्रिषु नृसिंहबीज-लिखितं ज्ञेयम्॥ ७९॥

षट्कोणान्तस्त्रिकोणे लिखतु मनुमिमं साध्यनामाक्षराढ्यं
षट्कोणेष्वङ्गमन्त्रान् वसुदलविवरेष्वष्टमन्त्राक्षराणि ।
वीतं बाह्ये कलाभिस्तदनु परिवृतं कादिभिर्यादिभिस्तत्
क्षौणीबिम्बेन युक्तं नृहरिमनुयुतं यन्त्रमापद्ग्रहघ्नम् ॥ ८०

अस्मिन्यन्त्रे प्रतिष्ठाप्य कलशं प्रोक्तवर्त्मना ।
कृतोऽभिषिक्तः स्यात् कृत्याभूतद्रोहादिशान्तिदः ॥ ८१

स्वरावृतममुं मनुं लिखतु टान्तमध्ये ततः
षडस्रिषु हुताशनं तदनु कादिवर्गैर्वृतम् ।
धरापुरयुगेन तन्नृहरिबीजयुक्तास्रिणा
प्रवेष्टितमुदाहृतं दुरितरोगकृत्यापहम् ॥ ८२

क्षकारो साग्निपवनवामकर्णार्धचन्द्रवान् ।
उक्तं तुम्बुरुबीजं तु येन सिध्यन्ति साधकाः ॥ ८३
षड्दीर्घभाजा बीजेन षडङ्गानि प्रकल्पयेत् ।
क्षकाररहितं बीजं क्रमाज्जभसहान्वितम् ॥ ८४
चत्वारि देवीबीजानि देव्यो ज्ञेया इमाः क्रमात् ।
जयाख्या विजया पश्चादजिता चाऽपराजिता ॥ ८५

अष्टमन्त्राक्षराणीति । षट् हलः द्वौ स्वरौ एकैकवर्णरीत्या । कलाभिः षोडशस्वरैः । कादिभिर्यादिभिरित्यनेन मातृकया आवृत्तित्रयमुक्तम् । नृहरिमन्विति । नृसिंहबीजं भूगृहकोणेषु । तदुक्तम्—"कुगेहास्रके नारसिंहम्" इति ॥ ८० ॥

प्रोक्तवर्त्मनेति । षष्ठोक्तरीत्या ॥ ८१ ॥

टान्तमध्ये ठकारमध्ये । षडस्रिषु षट्कोणेषु । हुताशनं रेफम् ॥ ८२ ॥

तुम्बुरुबीजमाह क्षकार इति । क्षकारः म स्वरूपम् । अग्नौ रेफः पवनो यः वामकर्ण ऊकारः अर्धचन्द्रो बिन्दुः तद्युक्तः । बीजशक्ती पूर्ववत् ॥ ८३ ॥

षड्दीर्घेति षडङ्गमन्त्रोद्धारः । न्यासं त्वग्रे वक्ष्यति । जभसह इति स्वरूपम् । एतानि क्रमेण क्षकारस्थाने योजितानि चत्वारि देवीबीजानि ।
तदुक्तं प्रयोगसारे—बीजं जभसहोपेतं क्षेत्रस्थाने यथाक्रमात् । इति ।
नारायणीयेऽपि—मूलं जभसहोपेतं देवीबीजान्यमन्दिरम् । इति ॥

अपेक्षितार्थद्योतनिकायामेव बीजान्युद्धृतानि । क्वचित्तु लेखकदोषवशात्

बीजमङ्गुलिषु न्यस्य करयोर्व्यापकं ततः ।
कनिष्ठादिषु विन्यस्येत् षड़ङ्गानि तलावधि ॥ ८६
देवं देवीः स्वबीजादि कनिष्ठादिषु विन्यसेत् ।
पादान् मूर्धावधि न्यस्येन् मुष्टिनाऽवयवेषु तत् ॥ ८७
तलाभ्यां व्यापकं कुर्यान् मूर्धादिचरणावधि ।
षड़ङ्गानि ततो न्यस्येद्यथास्थानं विशालधीः ॥ ८८
देवं देवीर्यथापूर्वं मूर्धास्यहृदयाम्बुजे ।
नाभौ गुह्ये क्रमान् न्यस्येत् पश्चाद्देवं विचिन्तयेत् ॥ ८९

रक्ताभमिन्दुशकलाभरणं त्रिनेत्रं
खट्वाङ्गपाशसृणिशुभ्रकपालहस्तम् ।
वेदाननं चिपिटनासमनर्घभूषं
रक्ताङ्गरागकुसुमांशुकमीशमीडे ॥ ९०

लक्षमानं जपेन्मन्त्रं जुहुयात्सर्पिषाऽन्वितम् ।
वक्ष्यमाणे यजेत्पीठे देवमावरणैः सह ॥ ९१

क्वचित् दृश्यते ॥ ८४ ॥ ८५ ॥

बीजमिति मूलबीजम् । करयोर्व्यापकमिति । हस्ततलयोरत्रोपरि च मूलबीजेनेति शेषः । तदुक्तं नारायणीये—

न्यस्याऽङ्गुलिषु मूलं तद्धस्तयोर्व्यापकं न्यसेत् । इति ।

अङ्गुष्ठादिष्वङ्गुलीषु न्यसेद्बीजमित्यनेनैव करन्यासस्य प्राप्तत्वात् । कनिष्ठादिष्विति । विशेषविधानार्थं पुनरुक्तिः ॥ ८६ ॥

स्वबीजादीति । देवस्य मूलं देवीनां तूक्तानि चत्वारि जभसहान्वितमूलम् । मुष्टिना दक्षिणेन । अवयवेषु पादजानुगुह्यनाभिहृदयकण्ठमुखशिरःसु । एवमपेक्षितार्थद्योतनिकाकारोक्ततत्रमूलम् । उक्तञ्च नारायणीये—

मुष्टिनाऽवयवेषु च पादादि न्यस्य मूर्धादि हस्ताभ्यां व्यापकं न्यसेत् । इति । व्यापकं कुर्यादिति । मूलेनेति शेषः । विशालधीरित्यनेन शैवमुद्राभिः सहेत्युक्तम् । यथापूर्वमिति । स्वस्वबीजादि ॥ ८७ ॥ ८८ ॥ ८९ ॥

ध्यानमाह रक्ताभमिति । सृणिरङ्कुशः । दक्षाधस्ताद्वामाधःपर्यन्तमायुधध्यानम् ॥ ९० ॥ ९१ ॥

नपुंसकस्वरैर्विद्वान् स्वराद्यन्तद्वयेन च ।
धर्मादिकानधर्माद्यान् पादान् गात्राणि विन्यसेत् ॥ ८२

हूंकारेण न्यसेत्पश्चात्तनुरूपान् गुणानथ ।
शान्त्या तत्परवर्णेन मायाविद्यामये क्रमात् ॥ ८३

अथऊर्ध्वच्छदे न्यस्येदर्घीशेन ततोऽम्बुजम् ।
सन्ध्यक्षरैर्यजेन्मन्त्री शक्तीर्वामादिकाः क्रमात् ॥ ८४

वामां ज्येष्ठां तथा रौद्रीमिच्छां ज्वालास्वरूपिणीः ।
एवं प्रकल्पिते पीठे मूर्त्तिं मूलेन कल्पयेत् ॥ ८५

आवाह्य पूजयेद्देवं तस्यामावरणैः सह ।
अङ्गावृतेर्बहिर्देवीर्दिक्पत्रेषु समर्चयेत् ॥ ८६

जयाद्याः स्वस्वबीजेन रक्ता रक्तानुलेपनाः ।
अरुणांशुकपुष्पाढ्यास्ताम्बूलापूरिताननाः ॥ ८७

स्वदेहे पीठकल्पनमाह नपुंसकेति । अनुलोमविलोमगैरिति लेखकदोषवशात्प्रामादिकः । स्वराद्यन्तद्वयेन चेति पाठः । तदुक्तं नारायणीये—

नासादिभिः स्वराद्यन्त्यैश्चतुर्भिश्च क्रमाद् बुधः । इति ।

प्रयोगसारेऽपि—क्लीवैराभ्याममोभ्यां च क्रमाद्धर्मादिपूजनम् । इति ।
एवं षोडशापि स्वरा उपयुक्ता भवन्ति । अपेक्षितार्थद्योतनिकाकारेण एवमेव प्रयोगो लिखितः । तेन क्लीबाद्यान् धर्मादीन् । अन्त्या अंअः एतदाद्यानधर्मादीन् । विन्यसेदिति चतुर्थीस्थानेषु ॥ ८२ ॥

गुणानिति । सत्त्वादीन् त्रिवर्णान् । शान्त्या ईकारेण । तत्परवर्णेन उकारेण । अर्घीशेन ऊकारेण । सन्ध्यक्षरैरिति । ए ऐ ओ औ एभिः । एषां यथा सन्निसम्भवत्वं तथा द्वितीयपटले प्रतिपादितम् ॥ ८३ ॥ ८४ ॥

ज्वालास्वरूपिणीरिति पीठशक्तिध्यानम् । तदुक्तं नारायणीये—

ज्वलदनलशिखाभा भास्वराः शक्तयः स्युः । इति ।

मूलबीजमुच्चार्य तुम्बुरुयोगपीठाय नम इति पीठमन्त्रोऽपि सूचितः । एवं प्रकल्पिते पीठे इत्यनेन एवमिति येन प्रकारेण देहे पीठं प्रकल्पितं तेनैव क्रमेण मण्डलेऽपि पीठे परिकल्पित इत्यर्थः । तस्यामिति । मूर्त्तौ ॥ ८५ ॥ ८६ ॥
॥ ८७ ॥ ८८ ॥

वल्लकीवादनपरा मदमन्मथपीडिताः।
ईशादिकोणेष्वभ्यर्चेद् दूतीर्बीजादिकाः क्रमात् ॥ ९८

दुर्भगां सुभगां भूयः करालीं मोहिनीमिमाः।
बद्धाञ्जलिपुटाः किञ्चिदानम्रवदनाम्बुजाः ॥ ९९

देवीसदृशभूषाढ्या दूतीमन्त्रान् विदुः क्रमात्।
चतुरः शादिकान् वर्णानर्धेन्दुकृतशेखरान् ॥ १००

लोकपालान् यजेद् बाह्ये वज्राद्यायुधसंयुतान्।
एवं यो भजते भक्त्या देवमुक्तेन वर्त्मना।
न तस्य दुर्लभं किञ्चित् त्रिषु लोकेषु विद्यते ॥ १०१

वायुवह्निपुरान्तस्थं बीजं स्मृत्वा जपेत् सुधीः।
ज्वरभूतमहारोगा नश्यन्ति तेन तत्क्षणात् ॥ १०२

क्रुद्धस्य हृदये ध्यात्वा जपेद् बीजमनन्यधीः।
स वश्यो जायते शीघ्रं मन्त्रस्याऽस्य प्रभावतः ॥१०३

हृद्रोगे कामलारोगे विष्टम्भे श्वासकासयोः।
एतज्जप्तं जलं प्रातः पिबेत्तद्रोगशान्तये ॥ १०४

ईशादिकोणेष्विति। ईशकोणमारभ्याप्रदक्षिणम् आग्नेयपर्यन्तमित्यर्थः। बीजादिकाः वक्ष्यमाणबीजादिकाः। देव्यो जयाद्यास्तत्सदृशभूषणाः। तदुक्तं नारायणीये—

ताट्टग्रूपाश्च दूत्यो रचितकरपुटाः किञ्चिदानम्रवक्त्राः।
शर्वाद्यन्त्यन्तसंस्थाः। इति ॥ ९८॥९९॥१०० ॥

शादिकानिति। शषसहान्। अर्धेन्दुर्बिन्दुः। तदुक्तं प्रयोगसारे—

जशाणौ बिन्दुशेखरा दूतीनामिति तद्बीजम्। इति।

नारायणीयेऽपि—बीजानि दूतीनामूष्माणो बिन्दुशेखराः। इति ॥ १००॥१०१ ॥

वायुरिति। प्रथमपटलोक्तवायुमण्डलं तत्राग्निपुरं तदन्तस्थं बीजमित्यर्थः। स्मृत्वा मूर्ध्नीति शेषः ॥ १०२ ॥

वश्यो जायत इत्यत्र कामबीजादित्वम्। रोगशान्तये इत्यत्र नृसिंहबीजादित्वम् ॥ १०३॥१०४ ॥

कृत्वा नवपदात्मानं मण्डलं तत्र शोभनान् ।
कलशान् स्थापयेन्मन्त्री नव पूर्वोक्तलक्षणान् ॥ १०५

मध्ये देवं यजेत्सम्यक् देवीः पूर्वोक्तकुम्भगाः ।
दृष्ट्वा कोणस्थिता दूतीरभिषिञ्चेत् पतिव्रताम् ॥ १०६

नारी सा लभते पुत्रं बन्ध्याऽपि किमुताऽपरा ।
भूतकृत्याग्रहद्रोहशान्तिदः सम्पदावहः ॥ १०७

अभिषेकोऽयमाख्यातो राज्ञां विजयवर्द्धनः ॥ १०८

अन्तर्बीजं स्वरगणलसत्केसरं तस्य बाह्ये
देवीदूतीमनुयुतदलं दिग्विदिक्षु क्रमेण ।
काद्यैर्वर्णैर्वृतमथ बहिर्भूमिगेहेन वीतं
यन्त्रं प्रोक्तं सकलसुखदं रोगकृत्याग्रहघ्नम् ॥ १०९

प्रणवो हृदयं पश्चात् ङेऽन्तं पशुपतिं पुनः ।
तारो नमो भूतपदं ततोऽधिपतये ध्रुवम् ॥ ११०

नमो रुद्राय युगलं खड्गरावणशब्दतः ।
विहरद्वितयं पश्चात्सरन्नृत्ययुगं पृथक् ॥ १११

श्मशानभस्मार्चितान्ते शरीराय ततः परम् ।
घण्टाकपालमालादिधरायेति पदं पुनः ॥ ११२

व्याघ्रचर्मपदस्याऽन्ते परिधानाय तत्परम् ।
शशाङ्ककृतशब्दान्ते शेखराय ततः परम् ॥ ११३

नवपदान्वितं नवनाभं तृतीयोक्तम् । पूर्वोक्तेति । षष्ठोक्तम् । कोणस्थिता ईशादि । लभते पुत्रमित्यत्र मायाबीजादित्वम् । विजयवर्द्धन दुर्गाबीजादित्वं ज्ञेयम् ॥ १०५ ॥ १०६ ॥ १०७ ॥ १०८ ॥

यन्त्रमाह अन्तरिति । अष्टदलं कमलं कृत्वा तत्कर्णिकायां मूलमालिख्य दिग्दलेषु देवीबीजानि विदिक्षु दूतीबीजानि क्रमेणेति पूर्ववल्लिखेत् ॥ १०९ ॥

खड्गरावणमन्त्रमाह । प्रणव इति । ङेऽन्तं पशुपतिं पशुपतये । तारः प्रणवः । ततः अधिपतये । अत्र प्राक्तनेन सह सन्धिः । ध्रुवं प्रणवम् । पृथगिति सरसर नृत्यनृत्य । रुद्रो इति स्वरूपम् । अथाऽनन्तरमग्निसुन्दरी स्वाहा । अस्यत्र कुत्रापि न सन्धिः । प्रणवो बीजं स्वाहा शक्तिः । कान्तः खः ॥११०—११८॥

कृष्णासर्पपदं पश्चात्ततो यज्ञोपवीतिने ।
चलयुग्मं चलयुगलं जितयुगलं त्रिवत्तकापालिने ॥ ११४

हनयुग्मं ततो भूतान् त्रासयद्वितयं पुनः ।
भूयो मण्डलमध्ये स्यात् कटयुग्मं ततः परम् ॥ ११५

रुद्राङ्कुशेन शमय प्रवेशययुगं ततः ।
आवेशययुगं पश्चाच्चण्डासिपदमीरयेत् ॥ ११६

धराधिपतिरुद्रोऽय ज्ञापयेत्त्रिनसुन्दरी ।
खड्गरावणमन्त्रोऽयं सप्तत्यूर्ध्वशताक्षरः ॥ ११७

भूताधिपतये स्वाहा पूजामन्त्रोऽयमीरितः ।
सद्यादिपञ्चहृस्वाद्यकान्तबीजादिकान् न्यसेत् ॥ ११८

ईशानाद्याः पञ्चमूर्तीर्देहे वक्त्रेषु च क्रमात् ।
षड्दीर्घबिन्दुयुक्तेन कान्तेनाऽङ्गक्रिया मता ॥ ११९

घण्टाकपालकृतिमुण्डकृपाणखेट-
खट्वाङ्गशूलडमरूनभयं दधानम् ।
रक्ताङ्गमिन्दुशकलाभरणं त्रिनेत्रं
पञ्चाननाञ्जमरुणांशुकमीशमीडे ॥ १२०

अयुतद्वितयं मन्त्रं जपित्वा तद्दशांशतः ।
पायसेन घृताक्तेन जुहुयात्तस्य सिद्धये ॥ १२१

पञ्चाक्षरोदिते पीठे पूजयेत् खड्गरावणम् ।
बीजेन मूर्तिक्लृप्तिः स्यात् तत् कान्तं मनुबिन्दुमत् ॥ १२२

ईशानाद्या इति पूर्वपटलोक्ताः। देह इति शिरोवदनहृद्गुह्यपादेषु। वक्त्रेष्विति। ऊर्ध्वादिपञ्चसु। कान्तेनेति। खकारेण ॥ ११९ ॥

आयुधध्यानं दक्षवामोर्ध्वयोराद्ये तदधस्तनयोरन्त्ये एवमन्तम् ॥ १२०॥१२१ ॥

पञ्चाक्षरोदिते शैवपञ्चाक्षरपीठे पूजा। बीजेनेति। अनन्तरं वक्ष्यमाणेन। तदिति बीजम्। मनुः औः। दूतीरिति। वक्ष्यमाणाः। चन्द्राङ्कितजटामित्यष्टमीम्। सव्येनेत्यप्रादक्षिण्यतः। उदीच्यामित्युत्तरेण सम्बध्यते। कोण-

अङ्गानि दलमूलेषु दूतीः पत्रेषु संयजेत् ।
चुलुकुण्डां प्रज्वलिनीं तृतीयां कृष्णपिङ्गलाम् ॥ १२३
फल्गुनीं टिरिटिल्लीं च पञ्चमीं मन्त्रमालिकाम् ।
सप्तमीं शङ्खिनीं पश्चाच्चन्द्राङ्कितजटाभिधाः ॥ १२४
पूर्वपत्रादि सव्येन खङ्गरावणवल्लभाः ।
ऐन्द्रीं कौमारिकीं ब्राह्मीं वाराहीं वैष्णवीं पुनः ॥ १२५
वैनायकीं च चामुण्डां माहेशीं दिक्षु पूजयेत् ।
द्वारपालान् यजेद्दिक्षु द्वौ द्वौ प्रागादि देशिकः ॥ १२६
रौद्रपिङ्गलनामानौ द्वौ श्मशानविभीषणौ ।
हढकर्णं भृङ्गिरीटिमुदीच्यामर्चयेत् पुनः ॥ १२७
आमर्दकमहाकालौ कोणपालान् यजेत् पुनः ।
कुम्भकर्णमशोकाख्यं भल्लाट जातहारकम् ॥ १२८
इन्द्रादिकान् लोकपालान् सायुधान् पूजयेत् ततः ।
धूपदीपादिभिर्देवं प्रीणयित्वा महेश्वरम् ॥ १२९
पञ्चक्रूरान्धसा बाह्ये ततो भूतबलिं हरेत् ।
एवं पूजादिभिः सिद्धे मन्त्रे मन्त्रविदां वरः ॥ १३०
नाशयेत्सकलान् भूतान् कृत्याग्रहमहाभयान् ।
आदेशं तस्य कुर्वन्ति भूता भीता महात्मनः ॥ १३१
बहुना किमिहोक्तेन मन्त्रेणाऽनेन भूतले ।
सदृशो नास्ति मन्त्रोऽन्यो भूतनिग्रहसाधने ॥ १३२

इति श्रीशारदातिलके ऊनविंशः पटलः ।

पालानिति । आग्नेयादि । केशरेष्वङ्गपूजा ॥ १२२—१२९ ॥

पञ्चक्रूरान्धसेति । अन्नदधिसक्तुहरिद्रालाजातिलरूपेण । तदुक्तमाचार्यैः—लाजतिलनक्तरजोदधिसक्तन्नानि भूतक्रूराख्यम् । इति ॥ १३० ॥ ॥ १३१ ॥ १३२ ॥

इति श्रीशारदातिलकटीकायां सत्सम्प्रदायकृतव्याख्यायां
पदार्थादर्शाभिख्यायामेकोनविंशतिः पटलः ॥ ॐ ॥

विंशः पटलः ।

अथाऽभिधास्ये विधिवदघोरास्त्रमनुत्तमम् ।
यस्य संस्मरणादेव सर्वे नश्यन्त्युपद्रवाः ॥ १

माया स्फुरद्वयं भूयः प्रस्फुरद्वितयं ततः ।
घोरघोरतरेत्यन्ते तनुरूपपदं पुनः ॥ २

चटयुग्मं तदन्ते स्यात् प्रचटद्वितयं ततः ।
कहयुग्मं वमद्वन्द्वं ततो बन्धयुगं पुनः ॥ ३

घातयद्वितयं वर्म फडन्तः समुदाहृतः ।
एकपञ्चाशदर्णोऽयमघोरास्त्रमहामनुः ॥ ४

अघोरोऽस्य मुनिः प्रोक्तश्छन्दस्त्रिष्टुबुदाहृतम् ।
अघोररुद्रः सन्दिष्टो देवता मन्त्रवित्तमैः ॥ ५

हृदयं पञ्चभिः प्रोक्तं शिरः षड्भिरुदाहृतम् ।
शिखा दशभिराख्याता तावद्भिः कवचं मतम् ॥ ६

मन्त्रमुद्धरति मायेति । माया शक्तिबीजम् । तनुरूपेति स्वरूपम् । वर्म हुं । महामनुरित्यनेन कामनाविशेषे तत्तद्बीजान्तत्वमुक्तम् । यदाहुः—

इमन्तः स्तम्भने मन्त्रः क्रोमाकृष्टौ समापने ।
वषडन्तः संवनने नमोऽन्तो विषनाशने ॥
ग्रहचौररिपुध्वंसे हुं क्रोमन्तो विधीयते ।
शम्यन्तस्त्वाऽखिलेष्टाप्त्यै चौमन्तो मारणे भवेत् ॥
फडन्तो भूतसंहारे मन्त्रोऽयं कल्पपादपः ॥ इति ।

ईश्वरकल्पे तु प्रस्फुरद्द्वयबन्धद्वयवर्जितः एकचत्वारिंशदक्षर उद्धृतः । मन्त्रस्य हलो बीजानि । स्वराः शक्तयः । हुं बीजं क्रों शक्तिरिति पद्मपादाचार्याः । मन्त्रवित्तमैरित्युत्तरत्र सम्बध्यते । तेनाऽङ्गमन्त्रेषु एकादशभागेष्वपि प्रत्येकं प्रणवमायाबीजयोगः सूचितः । पद्मपादाचार्यसम्मतेः । तावद्भिर्दशभिः । वसुवर्णैरष्टार्णैः । सामार्णैर्द्वादशभिः । क्वचिदन्त्यार्णैरिति पाठः । तदा

वसुवर्णैः स्मृतं नेत्रं मासार्णैरस्त्रमीरितम् ।
मूर्धमेचास्यकण्ठेषु हृन्नाभ्यन्धूरुषु क्रमात् ॥ ७
जानुजङ्घापदद्वन्द्वे रुद्रभिन्नाक्षरैर्न्यसेत् ।
पञ्चभिश्च पुनः षड्भिर्द्वाभ्यामष्टभिरक्षरैः ॥ ८
चतुर्वर्णैः षड्वर्णैश्च करणैः करणैः पुनः ।
चतुर्भिः षड्भिरक्षिभ्यां वर्णभेदोऽयमीरितः ॥ ९

सजलघनसमाभं भीमदंष्ट्रं त्रिनेत्रं
भुजगधरमघोरं रक्तवस्त्राङ्गरागम् ।
परशुडमरुखड्गान् खेटकं बाणचापौ
त्रिशिखिनरकपाले बिभ्रतं भावयामि ॥ १०

अभिचारे ग्रहध्वंसे कृष्णवर्णो भवेद्विभुः ।
वश्ये कुसुम्भसङ्काशो मुक्तौ चन्द्रसमप्रभः ॥ ११

अवशिष्टाक्षरैरित्यर्थः । रुद्रभिन्नेति एकादशधा भिन्नैः । तमेव भेदमाह । पञ्चभिरिति । करणैः चतुर्भिः ॥ १॥२॥३॥४॥५॥६॥७॥८ ॥

ध्यानमाह सजलेति । दक्षैर्भुजैः परशुखड्गबाणशूलानि वामैरन्यान्येवमायुधध्यानम् ॥ १० ॥

ग्रहध्वंसे ग्रहवैकृते । यदाहुः—"कृष्णोऽभिचारग्रहवैकृते च" इति । अभिचार इत्याद्युपलक्षणम् । तेन कामनाविशेषे ध्यानविशेषा अपि ज्ञेयाः । यदाहुः—

सहस्राब्धिरवं हस्तैर्धनुः पञ्चशतैरपि ।
सन्धायाकृष्य च शरान् विमुञ्चन्तमनारतम् ॥
धावन्तं रिपुसेनायां वमहिद्युत्घनोपमम् ।
ज्वलत्पिङ्गोर्ध्वकेशं च गजचर्मावगुण्ठितम् ॥
ध्यायेन्नाशाय सैन्यानामरातीनां महास्त्रनम् ।
त्रिपादहस्तनयनं नीलाञ्जनचयोपमम् ॥
शूलासिशूचीहस्तं च घोरदंष्ट्राट्टहासिनम् ।
घोरापस्मृतिनाशाय ग्रहशान्त्यै विचिन्तयेत् ॥
धावन्तं वैरिणं पश्चादत्युग्रं सधनुःशरम् ।
ध्यायेदुच्चाटनायाऽरेः स तु देशान्तरं व्रजेत् ॥

लक्षमेकं जपेन्मन्त्रं घृतसिक्तैस्तिलैः शुभैः ।
तद्दशांशं प्रजुहुयान्मन्त्री मन्त्रस्य सिद्धये ॥ १२

शैवे संपूजयेत्पीठे षट्कोणान्तस्थपङ्कजे ।
अङ्गपूजां केसरेषु कृत्वा पत्रेषु तत्परम् ॥ १३

परशुं डमरुं खड्गं खेटं बाणं च कार्मुकम् ।
शूलं कपालं प्रयजेदष्टास्त्राण्यस्य देशिकः ॥ १४

दलाग्रेषु ततः पूज्या ब्राह्म्याद्याः प्रोक्तलक्षणाः ।
लोकेशान् पूजयेत्पश्चादायुधैः स्वैः समन्वितान् ॥ १५

इति पूजादिभिः सिद्धे मन्त्रेणाऽनेन साधकः ।
इष्टान् प्रयोगान् कुर्वीत सिध्यन्ते नात्र संशयः ॥ १६

क्रमात् सर्पिरपामार्गतिलसर्षपपायसैः ।
साज्यैः सहस्रं प्रत्येकं यामिन्यां जुहुयात् सुधीः ॥ १७

खड्गं खेटं तथा घण्टां वेतालं शूलमेव च ।
कपालं चापि बिभ्राणं पिङ्गोर्ध्वकचभीषणम् ॥
भूतप्रेतादिनाशाय ध्यायेद्घोराट्टहासिनम् ।
सीताब्जशीतांशुपुटमिन्दुकान्तेन्दुवर्चसम् ॥
आशाम्बरं व्याघ्रनखप्रमुखैर्बालभूषणैः ।
अलङ्कृताङ्गं द्विभुजं त्रिवर्षार्धकरूपिणम् ॥
कम्राङ्गं सुमुखं सौम्यं नीलकुञ्चितकुन्तलम् ।
स्मरन्नेवमघोरं यः स मृत्युविजयी भवेत् ॥
तप्तजाम्बूनदनिभं शूलखड्गवराभयम् ।
रक्तारविन्दवसतिं स्मरन्नुच्चैः श्रियं लभेत् ॥ इति ॥ ११ ॥

शुभैरित्यनेनाऽवकरं दूरीकृत्य प्रक्षाल्य शोषितैरित्युक्तम् ॥ १२ ॥

सम्पूजयेदेवमिति शेषः । षट्कोणेति । अष्टदलं पद्मं कृत्वा तदुपरि षट्कोणं विधाय चतुरस्रं चतुर्द्वारं कुर्यात् । प्रोक्तलक्षणाः षष्ठपटलोक्तस्वरूपाः ॥ १३ ॥ ॥ १४ ॥ १५ ॥

अपामार्गेति अपामार्गसमिधः । साज्यैरिति । षष्ठं द्रव्यमाज्यमित्यर्थः । हेम धत्तूरः । पूर्ववदिति । यामिन्यां प्रत्येकं सहस्रम् । पञ्चगव्यस्त्विति ।

होमोऽयं नाशयेत् सद्यो भूतकृत्याद्युपद्रवान् ।
सितकिंशुकनिर्गुण्डीहिंस्रापामार्गसम्भवैः ॥ १८
समिद्वरैः कृतो होमः पूर्ववद्भूतशान्तिदः ।
अपामार्गादिजसमिधः पञ्चगव्यसमुक्षिताः ॥ १९
समिधो जुहुयात् कृष्णपञ्चम्यां निशि संयतः ।
पृथक् सहस्रहोमेन भूतानां निग्रहो भवेत् ॥ २०
क्रमात् सर्पिरपामार्गपञ्चगव्यहविर्घृतैः ।
हुत्वा सहस्रं प्रत्येकं पात्रे सम्पातयेत् सुधीः ।
सम्पातसर्पिषा साध्यं भोजयेद् भूतशान्तये ॥ २१

मध्ये शक्तिं ससाध्यां स्वरगणसहितां केसरेष्वष्ट वर्गान्
पत्रान्तर्मन्त्रवर्णान् लिखतु गुणमितानग्रदेशेषु तद्वत् ।
वर्मास्त्रोल्लासिकोणे दहनपुरयुगे कल्पिते भूपुरस्थे
यन्त्रेऽस्मिन् प्राग्विधानात् कृतकलशविधिः सर्वदुःखापहारी ॥ २२

पञ्चगव्यसिद्धपायसमित्यर्थः । तदुक्तं क्रियाकालगुणोत्तरे तन्त्रे—

पञ्चगव्योद्भवं शुद्धं चरुं तद्वत् घृतं नवम् । इति ।

हुत्वा निशीति शेषम् ॥ १६॥१७॥१८॥१९॥२०॥२१ ॥

यन्त्रमाह मध्य इति । साध्येति । साधकादीनामुपलक्षणम् । **अथवा** साध्यते यत्तत् साध्यं तत्सहितम् । तेनाऽमुकस्याऽमुकं वशं कुरु कुरु । **अयमर्थः** साध्यशब्दसंगृहीतो भवति । अष्टदलं पद्मं कृत्वा तत्कर्णिकायां साध्यसाधककर्म-सहितं शक्तिबीजं स्वरावीतमालिखेत् । तदुक्तम्—

हृल्लेखास्थितसाध्याक्षरविलसत्कर्णिकं कलावीतम् । इति ।

अष्ट वर्गानिति । कचटतपयशलान् । गुणमितान् त्रिशः । **मन्त्रवर्णान्** स्फुराद्यान् चटचटान्तान् । अग्रदेशेषु पत्राग्रेषु । तद्वदिति त्रिशः । **मन्त्रवर्णान्** प्रचटाद्यान् घातयान्तान् । तद्बाह्ये परस्परव्यतिभिन्नं त्रिकोणद्वयं कृत्वा **तत्कोणेषु** **वर्मास्त्रे लिखेत् ।** प्राग्विधानादिति वक्ष्यमाणरीत्या । तदुक्तम्—

मन्त्राक्षरत्रयोद्यदुदलमध्यदलाग्रकं च तद्बाह्ये ।
वह्निपुटास्त्रिसमाश्रितकवचास्त्रम् ॥ इति ॥

केचित्तु वर्मास्त्रोल्लासिकोणे दहनपुरयुगे मध्ये शक्तिमिति विप्रकृष्टान्वयेनाऽष्टदल-कर्णिकायां षट्कोणमाहुः । तदसम्बद्धम् । लिखिताचार्यवचनविरोधात् ॥ २२ ॥

षट्कोणे शक्तिरन्तः स्फुरयुगलवृता प्रस्फुरद्वन्द्वकोणे
शिष्टैर्मन्त्रस्य वर्णैः रसकरणचतुःषट्चतुर्वेदवेदैः ।
षड्भिः क्लृप्ताष्टपत्रं दहनपुरयुगेनावृतं वर्मफड्भ्यां
राजत्कोणेन वीतं धरणिपुरयुगं यन्त्रमाघोरमेतत् ॥ २३

क्षुद्रचौरग्रहव्यालभूतापस्मारनाशनम् ।
यन्त्रमेतत् समाख्यातं सर्वसम्पत्प्रदायकम् ॥ २४

यन्त्रान्तरमाह षडिति । एकान्तरक्रमेण प्रस्फुरद्वन्द्वकोणे षट्कोणे अन्तर्मध्ये स्फुरयुगलवृता यथावत् साध्यसाधककर्मसहिता शक्तिर्लेख्या । शिष्टैरिति । घोराद्यैर्वर्णैतयान्तैः । दहनपुरयुगेनावृतमिति । बाह्ये । सर्वसिद्धिप्रदायकमित्यनेनैतदुक्तं भवति । यदाहुः—

अथ शत्रुजयं वाञ्छन् घातयप्रपुटं रिपोः ।
नाम कृत्वा चिताभूमौ नियुतं प्रजपेन्मनुम् ॥
लवणोषणधूमाग्निसूरणोन्मत्तवारिभिः ।
सिक्तैः कारस्करफलैर्जुहुयादयुतं सुधीः ॥
उच्चाटे प्रस्फुरपुटं मोहने कहसंयुतम् ।
मंस्तम्भने चटपुटं वियोगे प्रचटेन तु ॥
वमेत्युत्सादने भूयो बन्धयुग्मेन बन्धने ॥ इति ॥

अथ चतुस्त्रिंशदक्षराघोरस्य यन्त्रमुच्यते—

अथो सप्तपङ्क्त्यारयुक्तं सरोजं ततः कर्णिकामध्यतारस्य मध्ये ।
× × × चयोसार संभिन्नसाध्याह्वयं स्यात् ॥
मनुं द्वन्द्वशः पत्रमध्येषु लिप्या वृतं यन्त्रराजं समाबध्य सूत्रैः ।
करे वा गले मस्तके वाथ कट्यां वहन्यः समग्रश्रियो भाजनं स्यात् ॥
तथैवाणिमाद्यैरलं विस्तरेण । इति ।

सप्तपङ्क्त्यारयुतं सप्तदशदलम् । मन्त्रः प्रथमपटले मदुक्तोऽनुसन्धेयः । द्विषड्वसुचरद्भिः (?) षडक्षरैर्वर्मास्त्रद्विठान्तैरङ्गम् । अस्याऽन्यत् सर्वं पूर्वमन्त्रवत् ज्ञेयम् । एकचत्वारिंशदक्षरस्य तु—

वेदषड्वेददिङ्नागषड्वर्णैः शक्तिपूर्वकैः ।
हुं फडन्तैः षडङ्गं स्यात् अन्यत् पूर्ववदीरितम् ॥ इति ॥ २३ ॥ २४ ॥

तारो वान्तो धरासंस्थो वामनेत्रेन्दुभूषित: ।
पार्श्वो वक्र: कर्णयुतो वर्मास्त्रान्त: षडक्षर: ॥ २५
मनु: पाशुपतास्त्राख्यो ग्रहक्षुद्रनिवारण: ।
षड्भिर्वर्णै: षडङ्गानि हुं फडन्तै: सजातिभि: ॥ २६
मध्याह्नार्कसमप्रभं शशिधरं भीमाट्टहासोज्ज्वलं
त्र्यक्षं पन्नगभूषणं शिखिशिखाश्मश्रुस्फुरन्मूर्धजम् ।
हस्ताब्जैस्त्रिशिखं समुद्गरमसिं शक्तिं दधानं विभुं
दंष्ट्राभीमचतुर्मुखं पशुपतिं दिव्यास्त्ररूपं स्मरेत् ॥ २७
वर्णलक्षं जपेन्मन्त्रं जुहुयात् तद्दशांशत: ।
गव्येन सर्पिषा मन्त्री संस्कृते हव्यवाहने ॥ २८
शैवे पीठे यजेद्देवं प्रागङ्गैरष्टमातृभि: ।
इन्द्रादिभिर्लोकपालैर्वज्राद्यैरायुधैस्तत: ॥ २९
अनेन मन्त्रितं तोयं ग्रस्तस्य वदने क्षिपेत् ।
सद्यस्तं मुञ्चति क्रन्दन् ग्रहो मन्त्रप्रभावत: ॥ ३०
अमुना मन्त्रितान् बाणान् विसृजेद् युधि भूपति: ।
जयेत् क्षणेन निखिलान् शत्रून् पार्थ इवापर: ॥ ३१
वर्णान्त्यमौबिन्दुयुतं क्षेत्रपालाय हृन्मनु: ।
तारादो वसुवर्णोऽयं क्षेत्रपालस्य कीर्त्तित: ॥ ३२

पाशुपतास्त्रमाह । तार इति । तार: प्रणव: । वान्त: श: धरा ल: तत्संस्थ: तेन श्ल । वामनेत्रम् ई इन्दु: बिन्दु: तेन श्लीं । पार्श्व: प: वक्र: श: कर्णयुत उकारयुत: तेन शु । ब्रह्मा ऋषि: गायत्री छन्द: । श्लीं बीजं हुं शक्ति: । ग्रहेत्यादि विनियोगोक्ति: । षड्भिर्वर्णैर्मन्त्रस्थै: । हुं फडन्तैरिति । प्रत्येकम् । हृदयाय नम: इत्यादि जातिसहितै: ॥ २५॥२६ ॥

आयुधध्यानं तु दक्षाद्यूर्ध्वयोराद्ये तदधस्थयोरन्त्ये ॥ २७ ॥

वर्णलक्षं षड्लक्षम् । मुञ्चतीत्यत्र नृसिंहबीजादित्वम् । जपेदित्यत्र दुर्गा-बीजादित्वमित्यादि ज्ञेयम् ॥ २८॥२९॥३०॥३१ ॥

क्षेत्रपालमन्त्रमाह वर्णेति । वर्णान्त्य: क्ष: । क्षौ स्वरूपम् । हृन्नम:पदम् । वसुवर्णोऽयमिति । वसुवर्णत्वमनुद्य तारादत्वं विधीयत इति ज्ञेयम् । ब्रह्मा

षड्दीर्घभाजा बीजेन षडङ्गान्यस्य योजयेत् ।
ऋषिर्ब्रह्मा भवेदस्य गायत्रं छन्द ईरितम् ।
क्षेत्रपालो देवता च लायेति शक्तिरीरिता ॥ ३२

ऋषि: गायत्री छन्द: । क्षौं बीजं आयेति शक्ति: । क्वचिदेकाक्षर एवोद्धृत: ।
तदुक्तं प्रयोगसारे—औबिन्दुसंयुतं बीजं वर्णान्त्यं सर्वसिद्धिदम् । इति ।
अत्र विशेष: प्रयोगसारे—

भेदा एकोनपञ्चाशत् क्षेत्रपालस्य कीर्त्तिता: ।
मातृकाबीजभेदेन संभिन्ना नामभेदत: ॥
अजरश्चापकुम्भश्च इन्द्रमू[मु]तिस्तत: पर: ।
ईड़ाचारश्चोल्कसंज्ञ ऊष्माद ऋषिसूदन: ॥
ऋमुक्तो लृप्तकेशश्च लृपकश्चैकदंष्ट्रक: ।
ऐरावतश्चौघबन्धुरौषधिघ्न[धीश]स्तथैव च ॥
अञ्जनश्चाऽस्त्रबाहु[वार]श्च कवल: खरश्चानल: ।
गोमुखश्चैव घण्टादो ङणारश्चक्षचारण: ॥
छटाटोपो जटालाख्यो झङ्कारोऽथ ञठश्वर: ।
टङ्कपाणिस्तथा चान्यष्ठाणबन्धुश्च डामर: ॥
ढक्कारवो णकर्णश्च तडिद्देहस्थिरस्तथा ।
दन्तुरो धनदश्चाऽथ नतिक्रान्त: प्रचण्डक: ॥
फट्कारो वीरसम्ब[ङ्ग]श्च भङ्गाख्यो मेघभासुर: ।
युगान्तो रौरवश्चाऽथ लम्बोष्ठो वसवस्तथा ॥
शुकनन्द: षड़ालाख्य: सुनामा हंभ्र[श्र]कस्तथा ।
एते भेदा: समाख्याता मातृकाक्षरयोनिजा: ॥
नाम यद्यस्य वर्णानां यो वर्णो मातृकान्तरे ।
दृश्यते प्रथमं तत्र तत्रायं क्षेत्रपालक: ॥
तत्र तत्र विशिष्टाग्रामेदैरेतैर्व्यवस्थित: ।
ततो विशिष्टो यष्टव्य: क्षेत्रपालस्तु सर्वत: ॥
क्षेत्रपालमसंपूज्य य: कर्म कुरुते क्वचित् ।
तस्य कर्मफलं हन्ति क्षेत्रपालो न संशय: ॥ इति ॥ ३२ ॥

बीजेनेति । मन्त्रद्वितीयेन ॥ ३३ ॥

नीलाञ्जनाद्रिनिभमूर्ध्वपिशङ्गकेशं
वृत्तोग्रलोचनमुपात्तगदाकपालम् ।
आशाम्बरं भुजगभूषणमुग्रदंष्ट्रं
क्षेत्रेशमद्भुततनुं प्रणमामि देवम् ॥ ३४

लक्षमेकं जपेन्मन्त्रं जुहुयात्तद्दशांशतः ।
चरुणा घृतसिक्तेन ततः क्षेत्रेशमर्चयेत् ॥ ३५
धर्मादिकल्पिते पीठे पूर्वमङ्गानि पूजयेत् ।
अनलाख्यमग्निकेशं करालं तदनन्तरम् ॥ ३६
घण्टारवं महाकोपं पिशिताशनसंज्ञकम् ।
पिङ्गलाक्षमूर्ध्वकेशं दलेषु परितो यजेत् ॥ ३७
प्रधानमूर्त्तिप्रतिमाञ्ज्ञानालङ्कारबन्धुरान् ।
लोकपालांस्तदस्त्राणि यथापूर्वं प्रपूजयेत् ॥ ३८
तस्मै सपरिवाराय बलिमेतेन निर्हरेत् ।
पूर्वमेहिद्वयं पश्चाद्विदुषि स्यात् पुरुद्वयम् ॥ ३९
भञ्जयद्वितयं भूयो नर्त्तयद्वितयं पुनः ।
ततो विघ्नपदद्वन्द्वं महाभैरव तत्परम् ॥ ४०
क्षेत्रपाल बलिं गृह्णद्वयं पावकसुन्दरी ।
बलिमन्त्रोऽयमाख्यातः सर्वकामफलप्रदः ॥ ४१

नीलेति । नीलः अत एवाञ्जनाद्रिनिभः तम् । उपात्ते गृहीते हस्ताभ्यामिति शेषः । गदाकपाले । दक्षे गदा वामे कपालमित्यायुधध्यानम् । आशाम्बरं नग्नम् । "कपालिनं गदापाणिम्" इति नारायणीये । "करधृतोग्रगदाकपालम्" इति प्रयोगसारे । क्वचित् जटाकलापमिति पाठः ॥ ३४॥३५ ॥

धर्मादिकल्पित इति चतुर्थोक्तप्रकारेण । न तु शक्तिपीठपूजा । महाकोपमिति महाक्रोधमिति ज्ञेयम् । प्रयोगसारनारायणीययोः तथोक्तेः । प्रधानमूर्त्तीत्यनलादीनां ध्यानम् ॥ ३५॥३६॥३७॥३८ ॥

सपरिवारायेत्यङ्गादिसहिताय । सर्वकामफलप्रद इति सिद्धः सन् । सिद्धिश्च सहस्रवारजपादित्यपेक्षितार्थद्योतनिकाकारः ॥ ३९॥४०॥४१ ॥

सोपदंशं बृहत् पिण्डं कृत्वा रात्रिषु साधकः ।
स्मृत्वा यथोक्तं चेत्रेशं तस्य हस्ते बलिं हरेत् ॥ ४२
बलिनाऽनेन सन्तुष्टः क्षेत्रपालः प्रयच्छति ।
कान्तिं मेधां बलारोग्यतेजःपुष्टियशःश्रियः ॥ ४३
उद्धरेद् वटुकं ङेऽन्तं आपदुद्धारणं तथा ।
कुरुद्वयं पुनर्ङेऽन्तं वटुकं तं समुद्धरेत् ॥ ४४
एकविंशत्यक्षरात्मा शक्तिरुद्धो महामनुः ।
अभीष्टफलसंसिध्यै कीर्त्तितः सुरपादपः ॥ ४५
[बृहदारण्यक ऋषिश्छन्दोऽनुष्टुबुदाहृतम् ।
आपदुद्धारणो देवो भैरवो देवता बुधैः ॥ ४६]
अङ्गुलीदेहवक्त्रेषु मूर्त्तीर्न्यस्येद्यथा पुरा ।
सद्यादिपञ्चकस्वाद्यशक्तिबीजपुरःसरम् ॥ ४७

उपदंशं व्यञ्जनम् । रात्रिषु । प्रहरादूर्ध्वम् । यथोक्तं पूर्वोक्तध्यानम् । नील-सारमेयारूढम् । हस्ते इति वामहस्तगतकपाले इत्यर्थः । तदुक्तं नारायणीये—

सिद्धेनाऽनेन मन्त्रेण तत्कपाले बलिं हरेत् ।
वामदोष्णाऽष्टदिक्स्थानामन्येषां चानलादिभिः ॥ इति ॥

प्रयोगसारेऽपि—अथवा प्राङ्गणे ध्यात्वा क्षेत्रेशं प्रोक्तलक्षणम् ।
शितिश्वानसमारूढं तत्कपाले बलिं हरेत् ॥ इति ॥

तत्र प्रयोगः । रात्रौ प्रहरादूर्ध्वं प्राङ्गणे गोचर्ममात्रं विलिप्य रक्तगन्धपुष्पाक्षतादीन् तत्र संस्थाप्य कराङ्गन्यासं कृत्वा मूलं दशधा जप्त्वा पीठं संपूज्य तत्र क्षेत्रपाल-मावाह्य उपचारान् कृत्वा सावरणमभ्यर्च्य विजनो भूत्वा बलिमन्त्रेण वामहस्तेन तत्कपाले त्रिर्बलिमुदकं च दत्त्वा अनलाय स्वाहेत्यादि मूर्त्तिभ्योऽङ्गेभ्यश्च सकृद्दत्वा हस्तं प्रक्षाल्य स्वयं देवः सन्नष्टोत्तरशतं मूलमावर्त्तयेदिति ॥ ४२॥४३ ॥

आपदुद्धरणमन्त्रमाह उद्धरेदिति । वटुकं ङेऽन्तं वटुकाय । तथेति ङेऽन्तम् । तेन आपदुद्धारणाय । शक्तिरुद्धः शक्तिबीजपुटितः । सुरपादपः साधकानां वाञ्छितप्रदत्वात्कल्पतरुरित्यर्थः । भैरव ऋषिः गायत्री छन्दः । वं बीजं माया शक्तिः । वेष्टनेस्थोंऽशः क्वचिदधिकः ॥ ४४॥४५॥४६ ॥

अङ्गुलीति । अङ्गुष्ठाद्यङ्गुलीषु । देहेति । शिरोवदनहृद्गुह्यपादेषु ।

वकारं पञ्चवक्त्राख्यमीशानादिषु योजयेत् ।
षड्दीर्घयुक्तया शक्त्या वकारेण च तद्वता ॥ ४८
अङ्गानि जातियुक्तानि प्रणवाद्यानि कल्पयेत् ।
तस्य ध्यानं त्रिधा प्रोक्तं सात्त्विकादिविभेदतः ॥ ४९

वन्दे बालं स्फटिकसदृशं कुन्तलोल्लासिवक्त्रं
दिव्याकल्पैर्नवमणिमयैः किङ्किणीनूपुराद्यैः ।
दीप्ताकारं विशदवसनं सुप्रसन्नं त्रिनेत्रं
हस्ताब्जाभ्यां वटुकमनिशं शूलदण्डौ दधानम् ॥ ५०

सात्त्विकं ध्यानमाख्यातमपमृत्युनिवारणम् ।
आयुरारोग्यजननमपवर्गफलप्रदम् ॥ ५१

उद्यद्भास्करसन्निभं त्रिनयनं रक्ताङ्गरागस्रजं
स्मेरास्यं वरदं कपालमभयं शूलं दधानं करैः ।
नीलग्रीवमुदारभूषणशतं शीतांशुचूडोज्ज्वलं
बन्धूकारुणवाससं भयहरं देवं सदा भावये ॥ ५२

ध्यायेन्नीलाद्रिकान्तं शशिशकलधरं मुण्डमालं महेशं
दिग्वस्त्रं पिङ्गकेशं डमरुमथ सृणिं खड्गपाशाभयानि ।
नागं घण्टां कपालं करसरसिरुहैर्बिभ्रतं भीमदंष्ट्रं
सर्पाकल्पं त्रिनेत्रं मणिमयविलसत्किङ्किणीनूपुराढ्यम् ॥ ५३

वक्त्रेष्विति । ऊर्ध्वप्राग्दक्षिणोदीच्यपश्चिमेषु । यथा पुरेति । ईशानाद्यानां देहे वक्त्रेषु च न्यासे तत्तदङ्गुलीभिर्न्यास इत्युक्तम् । सद्यादय औकाराद्याः क्लीबवर्जिताः । ईशानादिष्विति । आदिशब्देन तत्पुरुषाघोरवामसद्याः । ह्रौं वौं ईशानाय नमः अङ्गुष्ठे इत्यादिप्रयोगः । तद्वता षड्दीर्घयुक्तेनेत्यर्थः । ॐ ह्रां वां हृदयाय नमः इत्यादि प्रयोगः ॥ ४७॥४८॥४९ ॥

सात्त्विकध्याने शूलदण्डौ वामदक्षाभ्याम् । तदुक्तं विश्वसारोद्धारे—

वामहस्ते त्रिशूलं च सूक्ष्मदण्डं तु दक्षिणे । इति ॥ ५०॥५१ ॥

राजसध्याने वामयोराद्ये दक्षयोरन्त्ये । तदुक्तं विश्वसारोद्धारे—

दक्षे शूलाभयं वामे कपालं वरदं तथा । इति ॥ ५२ ॥

तामसध्याने तु दक्षाद्यूर्ध्वयोराद्ये तदधस्थयोर्द्वितीये तदधस्थयोरुपान्त्ये तदध-

राजसं ध्यानमाख्यातं धर्मकामार्थसिद्धिदम् ।
तामसं शत्रुशमनं कृत्याभूतग्रहापहम् ॥ ५४

वर्णलक्षं जपेन्मन्त्रं हविष्याशी जितेन्द्रियः ।
तद्दशांशं प्रजुहुयात्तिलैर्मधुरसंयुतैः ॥ ५५

धर्माधर्मादिभिः क्लृप्ते पीठे पङ्कजशोभिते ।
षट्कोणान्तस्त्रिकोणस्थव्योमपङ्कजसंयुते ॥ ५६

वटुकं पूजयेद्देवं मूर्त्तिं मूलेन कल्पयेत् ।
मूलादिसद्योजातेन देवमावाहयेत्ततः ॥ ५७

वामदेवेन मन्त्रेण स्थापयेत्परमेश्वरम् ।
मूलमन्त्रेण कर्त्तव्यं सान्निध्यं तदनन्तरम् ॥ ५८

अघोरेण सुधीः कुर्यात् सन्निरोधमनन्तरम् ।
पुरुषाख्येन मनुना योनिमुद्रां प्रदर्शयेत् ॥ ५९

देवाय वन्दनं कुर्यादीशानेन समाहितः ।
एतत्सर्वं विधातव्यं तत्तन्मुद्राभिरादरात् ॥ ६०

स्वयोरन्ते । अत्र ध्यानानन्तरं डमरुकमुद्रां दर्शयेत् । तल्लक्षणं तु—

मुष्टिं सुशिथिलां बध्वा ईषदुत्क्षिप्तमध्यमाम् ।
दक्षिणादूर्ध्वमुन्नम्य कर्णदेशे प्रचालयेत् ।
एषा मुद्रा डमरुका सर्वविघ्नविनाशिनी ॥ इति ॥ ५३॥५४ ॥

वर्णलक्षं एकविंशतिलक्षम् ॥ ५५ ॥

क्लृप्ते पीठे इति । चतुर्थोक्तप्रकारेण । नलव पीठशक्तयः । कोष्टस्थे पीठे । षट्कोणान्तस्त्रिकोणस्थव्योमपङ्कजसंयुते । पुनः कोष्टस्थे । पङ्कजशोभिते । तेन मातृकापद्मं कृत्वा तदुपरि त्रिकोणं तदुपरि षट्कोणं तदुपरि अष्टदलं पद्मं तदुपरि चतुरस्रं चतुर्द्वारमिति पूजायन्त्रम् । तदुक्तं विश्वसारोद्धारे—

चतुरस्रासने पद्ममष्टपत्रं सकर्णिकम् ।
तस्य मध्ये च षट्कोणं मण्डलं तु विधीयते ॥
तन्मध्ये च त्रिकोणं च तन्मध्ये व्योमपङ्कजम् ।
मध्ये वटुकमावाह्य । इति ।

व्योमपङ्कजन्तु मातृपटलोक्तवर्णाब्जम् । मूलादिसद्योजातेनेति । एवं पञ्चसु

ईशानादीन् यजेद्देवाद्यासमार्गेण देशिक: ।
सकलीकरणं कृत्वा यजेन्मूर्त्तीर्यथा पुरा ॥ ६१
व्योमपद्मदलेष्वर्चेदसिताङ्गादिभैरवान् ।
असिताङ्गं रुरुं चण्डं क्रोधमुन्मत्तभैरवम् ॥ ६२
कपालिनं भीषणाख्यं संहारं च क्रमादमून् ।
षट्कोणेषु षडङ्गानि क्रमेणाऽभ्यर्चयेत् सुधी: ॥ ६३
पूर्वादीशानपर्यन्तं तद्बहि: पूजयेदिमान् ।
डाकिनीपुत्रकान् पूर्वं राकिणीपुत्रकांस्तत: ॥ ६४
लाकिनीपुत्रकान् पश्चात्काकिनीपुत्रकांस्तत: ।
शाकिनीपुत्रकान् भूयो हाकिनीपुत्रकान् पुन: ॥ ६५
मालिनीपुत्रकान् पश्चाद्देवीपुत्रांस्तत: परम् ।
अथोमारुद्रमातृणां पुत्रान्दक्षिणतो यजेत् ॥ ६६
ऊर्ध्वमुख्या: सुतानूर्ध्वमधोमुख्या: सुतानध: ।
इति संपूजयेन्मन्त्री पुत्रवर्गांस्त्रयोदश ॥ ६७
तद्बहि: पद्मपत्रेषु लोकेशवटुकान् यजेत् ।
ब्रह्माणीपुत्रकं पूर्वं माहेशीपुत्रमैश्वरे ॥ ६८

सम्बध्यते। तत्तन्मुद्राभिरिति। मुद्रास्त्रयोविंशे वक्ष्यन्ते। ललाटस्थोऽञ्जलिर्वन्दनमुद्रा ॥ ५६॥५७॥५८॥५९॥६० ॥

न्यासमार्गेणेति। देवदेहे तत्तदङ्गुलीभिर्मूर्धादिषु पञ्चवक्त्रेष्वपि नत्वङ्गुलीषु। तदुक्तं नारायणीये—यथात्मनि तथा देवे न्यास: कार्य: करं विना। इति।

क्रौं वौं ईशानाय नम: इत्यादि पूजयेत्। तत्र देवदेहे प्रथमं विन्यस्य पश्चात् पूजनमिति ज्ञेयम्। सकलीकरणं कृत्वा यजेद्देवमिति शेष:। मूर्त्तीर्यथा पुरा यजेदिति अनुषज्यते। यथा पुरेत्यनेनावरणपूजायां पूर्वदक्षिणसौम्यपश्चिमे ईशे च मूर्त्तिपूजेत्युक्तम्। विश्वसारोद्धारे तु विशेष:। इन्द्राग्नियमसोमाप्सु पञ्च ब्रह्मण: अर्चयेत् इति। अइउऋऌएओअं एतद्बीजपूर्वानित्युक्तम्। प्रयोगस्तु। अं असिताङ्गभैरवाय नम: इत्यादि। भैरवपदं सर्वेषु योज्यम्। पुनर्भैरवोद्देशो मात्रनिवृत्त्यर्थ:। क्रमात् सुधीरित्यनेनाग्नेयादि पूजनमित्युक्तम् ॥ ६१॥६२॥६३ ॥

तद्बहिरिति। षट्कोणबाह्ये। अष्टपत्रान्त: पूर्वादीशानपर्यन्तमिमान्

वैष्णवीपुत्रकं सौम्ये कौमारीपुत्रमानिले ।
इन्द्राणीपुत्रकं भूयः पूजयेत्पश्चिमे ततः ॥ ६९
महालक्ष्मीसुतं पश्चाद्वारुणीदिशि समर्चयेत् ।
वाराहीपुत्रकं याम्ये चामुण्डासुतमानले ॥ ७०
वटुकान् दशदिक्ष्वर्चेद्धेतुकं त्रिपुरान्तकम् ।
वेतालं वह्निजिह्वाख्यं कालान्तकाख्यं करालकम् ॥ ७१
एकपादं भीमदंष्ट्रमचलं हाटकेश्वरम् ।
दिग्विदिक्ष्वन्तरालेषु श्रीकण्ठादीन् यजेत् पुनः ॥ ७२
क्रोधीश्वरादिस्त्र्यक्षान्तांस्तद्बाह्ये समर्चयेत् ।
ततस्त्रीन्नकुलीशाद्यान्दक्षिणे पूजयेत् सुधीः ॥ ७३
दिव्यान्तरिक्षभूमिष्ठान् योगीशान् शक्तिसंयुतान् ।
योगिनीभिः सहाऽभ्यर्चेदीशाग्निनिर्ऋतिस्थितान् ॥ ७४
इति संपूजयेद्देवं वटुकं प्रोक्तवर्त्मना ।
धर्मार्थकाममोक्षाणां पतिर्भवति मानवः ॥ ७५
विघ्नं दुर्गां समाराध्य बलिं दत्त्वा विधानतः ।
काम्यानि साधयेन्मन्त्री यथोक्तां सिद्धिमाप्नुयात् ॥ ७६
शाल्यन्नं पललं सर्पिर्लाजाचूर्णानि शर्करा ।
गुडमिक्षुरसापूपैर्मध्वक्तैः परिमिश्रितैः ॥ ७७

वक्ष्यमाणान् पूजयेदिति सम्बन्धः ॥ ६४॥६५॥६६॥६७॥६८॥६९॥७० ॥

दिग्विदिक्ष्विति । दिशश्चतस्रः विदिशश्चतस्रस्तदन्तरालान्यष्टौ एवं षोडश । पुनस्तद्वदिति । दिग्विदिक्ष्वन्तरालेषु । तत्र दिशोऽष्टौ विदिशोऽष्टौ तदन्तरालानि षोडशेति द्वात्रिंशत् स्थानानि ज्ञेयानि ॥ ७१॥७२॥७३ ॥

शक्तिसंयुतानिति सामान्येन विशेषणमात्रम् । ताः शक्तयः का इत्यपेक्षायां योगिनीभिः सहेति पदम् । तदुक्तं विश्वसारोद्धारे—

दिव्यान्तरिक्षभूमिष्ठान्योगीशान् पूजयेत्ततः ।
ईशाग्नेय्याश्च नैर्ऋत्यां योगिनीभिः समन्वितान् ॥ इति ॥७४॥७५॥

काम्यमात्रे परिभाषामाह विघ्नमिति ॥ ७६ ॥

तदेव बलिविधानमाह शाल्यन्नमिति । पललं मांसम् । एकीकृतं

कृत्वा कवलमाराध्य देवं प्रागुक्तवर्त्मना।
रक्तचन्दनपुष्पाद्यैर्निशि तस्मै बलिं हरेत्॥ ७८
ततः सिध्यन्ति कार्याणि बलिनाऽनेन मन्त्रिणः।
जुहुयात्सर्पिषा मन्त्री यथोक्तां सिद्धिमाप्नुयात्॥ ७९
वश्याय जुहुयाद्दिक्षु शकलैर्वशयेज्जनान्।
जुहुयात् पुत्रलाभाय प्रफुल्लैः कैरवैः सुधीः॥ ८०
धनधान्यादिसम्पत्त्यै जुहुयात्तिलतण्डुलैः।
बिल्वप्रसूनैर्जुहुयान्महतीं विन्दति श्रियम्॥ ८१
लोणैर्मधुरसंमिश्रैर्वशयेद्वनिताजनान्।
वृष्टिकामेन होतव्यं वेतसानां समिद्वरैः॥ ८२
अन्नेन जुहुयान्नित्यं धनधान्यादिसम्पदे।
वश्याय जुहुयाल्लक्ष्मी मधुना दिवसत्रयम्॥ ८३
रोगोक्तौषधहोमेन रोगा नश्यन्ति तत्क्षणात्।
कृत्याद्रोहे ग्रहद्रोहे भूतापस्मारसम्भवे॥ ८४
व्याघ्राजिने समासीनो जुहुयादयुतं तिलैः।
भूतादयः पलायन्ते नेक्षन्ते तां दिशं भयात्॥ ८५
कृष्णाष्टमीं समारभ्य यावत् स्याच्चतुर्दशी।
तिलैस्तण्डुलसंमिश्रैर्मधुरत्रयलोलितैः॥ ८६
त्रिसहस्रं प्रतिदिनं जुहुयात् संस्कृतेऽनले।
वटुकेश्वरमभ्यर्च्य भक्ष्यभोज्यफलान्वितम्॥ ८७

पिण्डरूपं कवलं ग्रासम्। रक्तचन्दनपुष्पाद्यैर्निशि देवमाराध्य प्रागुक्तवर्त्मना निशि बलिं हरेदिति सम्बन्धः। आद्यशब्देन धूपदीपनैवेद्यानि। प्रागुक्तेत्यनेन क्षेत्रपालोक्तबलिमन्त्रे क्षेत्रपालशब्दे वटुकेति पदं दत्त्वा देयमस्त इत्युक्तम्। यथोक्तामिति। स्वमनसि स्थिताम्॥ ७६॥७७॥७८॥७९॥८०॥८१॥८२॥८३॥

रोगोक्तेति वैद्यकशास्त्रे यस्मिन् रोगे यदौषधमुक्तं तस्य होमादित्यर्थः॥ ८४॥८५॥

कृष्णेत्यादि भूपतेरित्यन्तमेकः प्रयोगः। अवग्रहो वृष्ट्यभावः। विषवे

नित्यं निवेद्य नैवेद्यं मध्यरात्रे बलिं हरेत्।
एवं जपित्वा प्रयतः सहस्राण्येकविंशति ॥ ८८

समाप्तिदिवसे रात्रावजं हत्वा बलिं हरेत्।
ततः कारयिता राजा तोषयेत्साधकं धनैः ॥ ८९
विधिनाऽनेन सन्तुष्टो वटुकेशः प्रयच्छति।
तेजो बलं यशः पुत्रान् कान्तिं लक्ष्मीमरोगताम् ॥ ९०
नश्यन्ति शत्रवः सर्वे वर्धन्ते बन्धुबान्धवाः।
अवग्रहो न जायेत विषये तस्य भूपतेः ॥ ९१
जुहुयात् केवलैर्लोणैरयुतं स्तम्भनेच्छया।
निगडादिविमोक्षाय प्रयोगोऽयमुदाहृतः ॥ ९२
वचाचूर्णपलं जप्तं गव्येनाज्येन लोलितम्।
विभज्य भक्षयेद्वन्ध्या मण्डलात् पुत्रकाङ्क्षिणी ॥ ९३
विनीतं पुत्रमाप्नोति मेधारोग्यबलान्वितम्।
आदावन्ते प्रयोगस्य वटुकाय बलिं हरेत् ॥ ९४
द्विविधो बलिराख्यातो राजसः सात्त्विको बुधैः।
राजसो मांसरक्ताढ्यः पलत्रयसमन्वितः ॥ ९५

देशी ॥ ८६॥८७॥८८॥८९॥९०॥९१॥९२ ॥

विभज्येति किञ्चिन्न्यूनसप्तसप्तगुञ्जामितम्। मण्डलमेकोनपञ्चाशद्दिनानि। विश्वसारोद्धारे तु विशेषः—

वचाचूर्णपलं देवि कुडवं पलसंयुतम्।
पद्मपत्रे विनिक्षिप्य स्थापयेद्देवसन्निधौ ॥
सिद्धान् संपूज्य विधिवज्जपेत् स्पृष्ट्वा तदौषधम्।
मन्त्रं सहस्रमावर्त्य सिद्धानभ्यर्च्य बुद्धिमान् ॥
ध्यात्वा देवीसुतस्तातां प्राशयेत्तन्महौषधम् ॥ इति ॥९३॥९४॥

राजसो मांसरक्ताढ्य इति। तत्र किं मांसमित्यपेक्षायां पलत्रयसमन्वित इति। तत्र पलत्रयं भूचरखेचरजलचरजम्। तदुक्तं विश्वसारोद्धारे—

मेषकुक्कुटयोर्मांसं शाल्यन्नं घृतसंयुतम्।
लाजाचूर्णमपूपं च गुडमिक्षुरसान्वितम्।

मुद्गपायससंयुक्तो मधुत्रयविलोलित: ।
सात्त्विको मांसरहित: शेषमन्यत् पुरोक्तवत् ॥ ९६
ब्राह्मणो नियत: शुद्ध: सात्त्विकं बलिमाहरेत् ।
साधयेन्मनुनाऽनेन भस्म सर्वार्थसिद्धिदम् ॥ ९७
उशीरं चन्दनं कुष्ठं घनसारं सकुङ्कुमम् ।
श्वेतार्कमूलं वाराहीं लक्ष्मीं चौरमहीरुहाम् ॥ ९८
त्वचो बिल्वतरोर्मूलं शोषयित्वा सुचूर्णयेत् ।
चूर्णं व्योम्नि गृहीतेन गोमयेन विमिश्रितम् ॥ ९९
कृत्वा पिण्डानि संशोष्य संस्कृते हव्यवाहने ।
मूलेन दग्ध्वा तद्भस्म शुद्धपात्रे विनि:क्षिपेत् ॥ १००
केतकीमालतीपुष्पैर्वासयेद् भस्म शोधितम् ।
अयुतं प्रजपेन्मन्त्रं स्पृष्ट्वा भस्म सुपूजितम् ॥ १०१
एतदादाय दिवश: प्रात: पुण्ड्रं करोति य: ।
तस्य रोगा: प्रणश्यन्ति कृत्याद्रोहग्रहादय: ॥ १०२
रिपुचौरमृगादिभ्यो भयमस्य न जायते ।
वर्धन्ते सम्पद: सर्वा: पूज्यते सकलैर्जनै: ॥ १०३

मधुमत्स्यकपित्थादि बलिद्रव्यं समीरितम् ॥ इति ।
मरीचैर्जीरकैश्चैव गुडखण्डैस्तथैव च ।
शालितण्डुलसम्भक्तगोक्षीरेण समन्वितम् ।
सैन्धवं दग्धमीनेन पलत्रयसमन्वितम् ॥ इति ॥

तथाऽन्यत्रापि—पलत्रयं माषचूर्णं दधि क्षीरं घृतं तथा ।
गुडौदनेन संयुक्तं मिश्रीकृत्य विचक्षण: ॥ इति ॥

केचित् फलत्रयमिति पाठमपठन् । तच्चिन्त्यम् ॥ ९५ ॥ ९६ ॥ ९७ ॥

भस्मसाधनमेवाह उशीरमित्यादि । घनसार: कर्पूर: ।

वाराही शूकरी क्रान्ता मागधी गृष्टि कारिका ।

इति कैयटदेवनिघण्टौ वाराहीनाम्नी ओषधी प्रसिद्धा ॥

शमी लक्ष्मी: शिवा शीता माङ्गल्या केशहृत्फला ॥

इति कैयटदेवनिघण्टौ लक्ष्मीशब्देन शमी उक्ता । व्योम्नि गृहीतेनेति भूतला-

राजा वश्यो भवेत्तस्य सामात्यः सपरिच्छदः ।
अभिषेकं प्रकुर्वीत राज्ञो विजयकाङ्क्षया ॥ १०४

पूर्वोक्तमण्डपे कृप्ते वितानध्वजशोभिते ।
सर्वतोभद्रमालिख्य कर्णिकां तस्य पूरयेत् ॥ १०५

अष्टद्रोणप्रमाणेन शालिभिः शोधितैः शुभैः ।
तदर्धांस्तण्डुलांस्तस्मिन् न्यस्य दूर्वाक्षतान्वितान् ॥ १०६

हेमादिविहितं कुम्भं नवरत्नसमन्वितम् ।
संस्थाप्य विमलैस्तोयैरापूर्यास्मिन्विनिःक्षिपेत् ॥ १०७

क्षीरद्रुमप्रवालानि लक्ष्मीं दूर्वां सहां पुनः ।
कर्पूरं चन्दनं विल्वमुशीरं कुङ्कुमं पुनः ॥ १०८

कक्कोलमगुरुं जातिं मल्लिकां चम्पकोत्पलैः ।
गोमेदं दाडिमं पश्चात्पट्टयुग्मेन वेष्टयेत् ॥ १०९

तस्मिन्नावाह्य वटुकं राजसं सम्प्रपूजयेत् ।
वहिरष्टसु कुम्भेषु भैरवानष्ट पूजयेत् ॥ ११०

त्रयोदशसु कुम्भेषु त्रयोदशगणान् यजेत् ।
बाह्ये दशसु कुम्भेषु लोकेशानर्चयेत् सुधीः ॥ १११

तद्बहिर्द्व्यष्टकुम्भेषु श्रीकण्ठादीन् सुरेश्वरान् ।
पञ्चत्रिंशद्घटेष्वर्चेत् कादिवर्णेश्वरान् क्रमात् ॥ ११२

स्पृष्टेन । पुण्ड्रं त्रिपुण्ड्रस्तिर्यक्तिलकः । मृगो व्याघ्रः ।

अभिषेकं प्रकुर्वीतेति । सप्तभिः पञ्चभिर्वाऽहोभिरित्यर्थः । "सप्ताहं वापि पञ्चाहम्" इत्युक्तेः । तत्र पूर्वमेव सप्तमं पञ्चमं वा शुभदिनमालोच्य प्रथमारम्भः कार्यः ॥ ९८॥९९॥१००॥१०१॥१०२॥१०३॥१०४ ॥

अभिषेकप्रकारमाह पूर्वोक्तेति । तृतीयोक्ते इत्यर्थः । अष्टद्रोणेति । अर्धखारी । तदर्धमिति । खारीचतुर्थांशः । नवरत्नानि पञ्चोक्तानि । प्रवालानि पल्लवाः । सहा सहदेवी । गोमेदं पत्रजम् । "गोमेदकं पीतमणौ कक्कोले पत्रकेऽपि च" इति विश्वः ॥ १०५॥१०६॥१०७॥१०८॥१०९ ॥

राजसमिति राजसध्यानोक्तमूर्त्तिम् । लोकेशान् लोकेशवटुकान् । क्रमादि-

इति गन्धादिभि: सम्यक् पञ्चावरणमर्चयेत् ।
अयुतं प्रजपेत्स्पृष्ट्वा तान् घटान् देशिकोत्तम: ॥ ११३

पायसै: सर्पिषा शुद्धैस्तिलैर्दशशतं पृथक् ।
जुहुयात्तान् घटान् स्पृष्ट्वा प्रत्यहं बलिमाहरेत् ॥ ११४

राजसोक्तप्रकारेण रात्रौ देशिकसत्तम: ।
सुदिने शोभने लग्ने वाचयित्वा द्विजन्मभि: ॥ ११५

स्वस्तिमङ्गलवाक्यानि विशुद्धैर्वेदपारगै: ।
नदत्सु पञ्चवाद्येषु प्रणम्य वटुकेश्वरम् ॥ ११६

जितेन्द्रियं शुद्धकायं राजानं ब्राह्मणप्रियम् ।
आस्तिकं सत्यवचनमभिषिञ्चेत् प्रसन्नधी: ॥ ११७

अभिषिक्तो नरपति: प्रणिपत्य गुरुं परम् ।
भूयसीं दक्षिणां दद्यात् प्रसीदति तया गुरु: ॥ ११८

राजाऽभिषिक्तो भवति साक्षाद्भूमिपुरन्दर: ।
परान् विजयते भूपान् स्तूयते सकलैर्जनै: ॥ ११९

कृताभिषेक: षण्मासं प्रतिमासं महीपति: ।
चतुरम्भोधिवलयां शास्ति सर्वां वसुन्धराम् ॥ १२०

गजाश्वशान्तिविषये तेषां शालासु साधक: ।
कुण्डं कृत्वा विधानेन होमं कुर्याद्यथाविधि ॥ १२१

पायसाज्यतिलैर्विद्वानयुतत्रितयावधि ।
ब्राह्मणान् भोजयेन्नित्यं भक्ष्यभोज्यफलादिभि: ॥ १२२

त्र्यंशेन परितो भ्रामयेत् दक्षिणे शोणित्युक्तम् । स्पृष्ट्वेत्यभयत्र । कूर्चादिना । पृथगिति । प्रत्येकम् । तेन सहस्रत्रयं होम: प्रत्यहं समाहं पञ्चाहं वा ॥ ११० ॥

॥ १११॥११२॥११३॥११४॥११५॥११६॥११७॥११८॥११९ ॥

पश्चैवाह्य। फलविशेषमाह कृतेति। षण्मासं प्रतिमासमिति पञ्चाहत्तय: ॥ १२० ॥

गजेति। प्राक्प्रोक्तविधिना कुम्भान् स्थापयित्वा गन्धानुलेपै: पुष्पाद्यैरभ्यर्च्य विधानेन कुण्डं कृत्वा यथाविधि होमं कुर्यादिति सम्बन्ध: । तत्र विधानेनेति ।

प्राक्प्रोक्तविधिना कुम्भान् स्थापयित्वाऽत्र देशिकः ।
अभ्यर्च्य गन्धपुष्पाद्यैस्तज्जलैः प्रोक्षयेद्गजान् ॥ १२३

अश्वशालासमेतेनैव वर्धन्ते ते दिने दिने ।
युद्धेषु महती शक्तिर्जायते पूर्वतोऽधिका ॥ १२४

सर्वरोगाः प्रणश्यन्ति कृत्याद्रोहाः परैः कृताः ।
अस्मात्परतरा रक्षा नास्ति तेषां महीतले ॥ १२५

अभिषिच्य महीपालं परेषां विजयोद्यतम् ।
उक्तेन विधिना मन्त्री याम्यिन्यां बलिमाहरेत् ॥ १२६

अन्यूनाङ्गमजं हत्वा राजसं प्रागुदाहृतम् ।
बलिप्रदानसमये रिपूणां सर्वसैन्यकम् ॥ १२७
निवेदयेद्बलित्वेन वटुकाय विशिष्टधीः ।
विदर्भयेच्छत्रुनाम्ना बलिमन्त्रं तथा सुधीः ॥ १२८

त्रिकोणम् । यथाविधीति । वटुकमन्त्रादभ्यर्च्य वटुकं च तत्र पूजयित्वेत्यर्थः ॥ १२१ ॥ १२२ ॥

प्राक्प्रोक्तविधिना । चतुर्थोक्तविधिना । कुम्भानिति पञ्च । अत्र । पञ्चसु कुम्भेषु । अभ्यर्च्येति । मध्ये वटुकम् ईशानं चतुर्ष्वन्या मूर्तीरिति शेषः ।

उक्तञ्च—पश्चात्मानं पदं कृत्वा स्वालिप्ते शुद्धभूतले ।
कोष्ठेषु स्थापयेत् सद्भ्यो कलशान् पञ्च शोभनान् ॥
धूपादिवासितान् भूयो जलैरापूरयेत् पृथक् ।
माणिक्यं मौक्तिकं वज्रं नीलं मरकतं तथा ॥
प्रोक्तानि पञ्च रत्नानि निक्षिप्य तेषु पञ्चसु ।
तत्र देवं च मूर्तीश्च समभ्यर्च्य यथाविधि ॥ इति ॥

अन्यत्र तु—सुवर्णं रजतं मुक्ता राजावर्त्तं प्रवालकम् ।
रत्नपञ्चकमाख्यातम् । इति ।

गजान् अश्वान् शालाश्च गजाश्वशालां प्रोक्षयेदिति सम्बन्धः । ते गजा अश्वाः । शक्तिर्जायत इति । तेषामित्यनुषज्यते । रोगाः प्रणश्यन्तीत्यत्रापि । अभिषिच्येति हरेदित्यन्तं पूर्वोक्ताभिषेकबल्योरनुवादः ॥ १२३ ॥ १२४ ॥ १२५ ॥ १२६ ॥

तत्रैव विशेषमाह । अन्यूनेत्यादिना ॥ १२७॥१२८॥१२९॥१३०॥१३१ ॥

शत्रुपक्षस्य रुधिरं पिशितं च दिने दिने ।
भक्षय खगणै: साद्धं सारमेयसमन्वित: ॥ १२९
बलिमन्त्रोऽयमाख्यात: सर्वेषां विजयप्रद: ।
अनेन बलिना हृष्टो वटुक: परसैन्यकम् ॥ १३०
सर्वं गणेभ्यो विसृजेदामिषं क्रुद्धमानस: ।
एवं कृते परबलं क्षीयते नाऽत्र संशय: ।
विजयश्रियमेतेन राजा प्राप्नोत्ययत्नत: ॥ १३१
श्रीमायास्मरकूटमत्र विलिखेन्मध्ये दलेष्वष्टसु
द्वि:प्रोक्तं वटुकायशब्दमपरान् मन्त्रस्य वर्णान् बहि: ।
अष्टद्वन्द्वदलेषु तद्बहिरतस्तत्संख्यपत्रेष्वथ
द्वात्रिंशद्दलकादिसान्तसहितं यन्त्रं लिखेद् भूमरे ॥ १३२
आपदुद्धरणं यन्त्रमपमृत्युभयापहम् ।
सर्वसम्पत्प्रदं नित्यं सर्वसौभाग्यदायकम् ॥ १३३
रक्षाकरं ग्रहार्त्तानां राज्ञां विजयवर्धनम् ।
आपदुद्धरणादस्मादापदुद्धरणाक्षम: ॥ १३४
तन्त्रेषु नास्ति मन्त्रोऽन्य इत्याहुर्मन्त्रवेदिन: ।
अर्घीशो वह्निशिखरो लान्तस्थो दान्त ईरित: ॥ १३५

यन्त्रमाह श्रीमायेति । श्री श्रीबीजम् । माया शक्तिबीजम् । स्मर: कामबीजं क्लीं । कूटं क्ष्रौं । मध्ये कर्णिकाया: । तदुक्तं विश्वसारोद्धारे—

तत्रादौ कर्णिकामध्ये लक्ष्मीबीजं न्यसेद् बुध: ।
मायाबीजं ततो न्यस्य कामबीजं तत: परम् ॥
कूटाक्षरं तत: पश्चादग्निमायासमन्वितम् ।
चतुर्बीजसमायुक्तं कर्णिकामन्त्रमुद्धरेत् ॥ इति ॥

एतेन केषाञ्चन स्मररूपमेव कूटं लिखेदिति व्याख्यानं निरस्तम् । अष्टदलेषु वटुकाय इत्येकाक्षरक्रमेण लिखनीयम् । मन्त्रस्य वर्णानिति । आपदित्यादिमायान्तान् । प्रथमषोड़शदले । तद्बहि: प्रथमषोड़शदलाद्बहि: । तत्संख्यपत्रेषु षोड़शसु । तदुपरि द्वितीयषोड़शदले षोड़शस्वरान् लिखेत् ॥ १३२॥१३३॥१३४ ॥

चण्डमन्त्रमाह अर्घीश इति । अर्घीश ऊ: । दान्तो ध: लान्तस्थो

फडन्तश्चण्डमन्त्रोऽयं त्रिवर्णात्मा समीरितः ।
अस्य त्रिको मुनिः प्रोक्तश्छन्दोऽनुष्टुबुदाहृतम् ॥ १३६
चण्डेशो देवता प्रोक्ता कुर्यादङ्गविधिं पुनः ।
हृदयं दीप्त फट् प्रोक्तं ज्वल फट् शिर ईरितम् ॥ १३७
शिखा ज्वालामालिनी फट् ज्ञेया फट् कवचं मतम् ।
हन फट् नेत्रमाख्यातं सर्वज्वालिनि फट् परम् ।
विन्यस्यैवं षडङ्गानि ततो देवं विचिन्तयेत् ॥ १३८
चण्डेश्वरं रक्ततनुं त्रिनेत्रं रक्तांशुकाढ्यं हृदि भावयामि ।
टङ्कं त्रिशूलं स्फटिकाक्षमालां कमण्डलुं बिभ्रतमिन्दुचूडम् ॥ १३९
वर्णलक्षं जपेन्मन्त्रं होमं कुर्याद्दशांशतः ।
मधुरत्रयसंयुक्तैर्विशुद्धैस्तिलतण्डुलैः ॥ १४०
पश्चाज्जरोदिते पीठे चण्डेशं साधु पूजयेत् ।
मूर्तौ बीजेन क्लृप्तायां तत् कूर्मो बिन्दुसंयुतः ॥ १४१
चण्डेश्वराय हृद् बीजपूर्वः पूजामनुर्मतः ।
अङ्गैर्मातृभिराशेशैर्वज्राद्यैरायुधैर्यजेत् ॥ १४२
चतुरावरणं प्रोक्तं चण्डेशस्य समर्चने ।
इति सिद्धे मनौ मन्त्री धनवान् जायतेऽचिरात् ॥ १४३

वह्निशिखरः तेन र्घ्वं। जकारो बीजं फट् शक्तिः। त्रिक इति ऋषिनाम ॥१३५॥
॥ १३६॥१३७॥१३८ ॥

ध्यानमाह चण्डेश्वरमिति। टङ्कं परशुम्। तदुक्तं नारायणीये—

शूली परशुकमण्डल्वक्षमाली त्रिलोचनः। इति।

वामोर्ध्वात् वामाधःपर्यन्तमायुधध्यानम् ॥ १३९ ॥

तदिति बीजम्। कूर्मः चकारः ॥ १४० ॥ १४१ ॥

पूजामन्त्रमाह चण्डेति। चण्डेश्वराय स्वरूपम्। हृन्नमः। बीजपूर्वः स्वस्य बीजपूर्व इत्यर्थः। आचार्यैस्तु गायत्रीं जपेदित्युक्तम्। यदाहुः—

चण्ड चण्डायेत्युक्त्वा प्राग्वदेतद्विद्महे पदम्।
चण्डेश्वराय च प्रोक्त्वा धीमहीति पदं वदेत् ॥
तन्नश्चण्ड इति प्रोक्त्वा ब्रूयाद् भूयः प्रचोदयात्।

तर्पयेन्मनुनाऽनेन नित्यमष्टोत्तरं शतम् ।
श्रियमाप्नोति महतीं पुत्रमित्रसमन्वितः ॥ १४४
प्रियङ्गुकुसुमैः फुल्लैस्तत्काष्ठज्वलितेऽनले ।
जुहुयादयुतं मन्त्री पुरः क्षोभो प्रजायते ॥ १४५
साध्यवृक्षत्वचो लोणं पिष्ट्वा पिष्टसमन्वितम् ॥
पुत्तलीं रुचिरां कृत्वा प्रतिष्ठाप्य समीरणम् ॥ १४६
छित्त्वा छित्त्वा प्रजुहुयादष्टोत्तरशतं निशि ।
सप्ताहमेवं कुर्वीत साध्यो दासो भवेत् स्वयम् ॥ १४७
शैवमन्त्रेषु निष्णातश्चण्डेश्वरमनुं भजेत् ।
सर्वान् कामानवाप्नोति परत्रेह च नन्दति ॥ १४८

एषा तु चण्डगायत्री जपात् सान्निध्यकारिणी ॥ इति ॥१४२॥१४३॥

श्रियमाप्नोतीति । श्रीबीजादित्वम् ॥ १४४ ॥

मन्त्रीत्यनेन दुर्गाबीजादित्वं सूचितम् ॥ १४५ ॥

साध्यवृक्षेति । साध्यस्य यन्नक्षत्रं तन्नक्षत्रवृक्षत्वचः । तान् द्वाविंशे वक्ष्यति । पिष्टं तण्डुलपिष्टम् । तदुक्तमाचार्यैः—

साध्यर्क्षाङ्घ्रिपचर्मणां सुसकृणां पिष्टैश्च लोणैः समं
कृत्वा पुत्तलिकां प्रतिष्ठितचलां जप्त्वा च रात्रौ हुनेत् । इति ।

पुत्तलीम् । षष्णवत्यङ्गुलाम् । समीरणं प्राणं प्रतिष्ठाप्येति त्रयोविंशप्रकारेण । छित्त्वा छित्त्वेति । द्वाविंशे वक्ष्यमाणरीत्या । साध्य इति । लिङ्गमविवक्षितम् । पुरुषं स्त्रियमपि वशयेत् । तदुक्तम्—

सप्ताहं पुरुषोऽङ्गना यदि चिरं वश्यस्त्ववश्यं भवे-
दस्मिन् जन्मनि नात्र चोद्यविषयो देहान्तरे संशयः ॥ इति ॥

अथ च साध्यमिति सामान्यत उक्तेर्द्विजादिः । तत्र विशेषो नारायणीये—

प्रज्वाल्याऽग्निमपामार्गैरेवं वश्यो भवेद् द्विजः ।
दीप्ते वह्नौ चिताकाष्ठैः प्रतिकृत्या तथा हुनेत् ।
राजा वशीभवेदेवं वश्यः स्याद्वैश्यशूद्रयोः ॥ इति ।

दासो भवेदत्र कामादित्वं ज्ञेयम् ॥ १४६ ॥ १४७ ॥

शैवमन्त्रेष्वित्यनेनेतदुक्तं भवति । यावान् चण्डेश्वरजपस्तावान् शैवषडक्षर-

धरापोऽग्निमरुद्व्योममखेशेन्दुर्कमूर्त्तये ।
सर्वभूतान्तरस्थाय शङ्कराय नमो नमः ॥ १४९

श्रुत्यन्तकृतवासाय श्रुतये श्रुतिजन्मने ।
अतीन्द्रियाय महसे शाश्वताय नमो नमः ॥ १५०

स्थूलसूक्ष्मविभागाभ्यामनिर्देश्याय शम्भवे ।
भवाय भवसम्भूतदुःखहन्त्रे नमोऽस्तु ते ॥ १५१

तर्कमार्गातिदूराय तपसां फलदायिने ।
चतुर्वर्गवदान्याय सर्वज्ञाय नमोनमः ॥ १५२

आदिमध्यान्तशून्याय निरस्ताशेषभीतये ।
योगिध्येयाय महते निर्गुणाय नमो नमः ॥ १५३

विश्वात्मनेऽविचिन्त्याय विलसच्चन्द्रमौलिने ।
कन्दर्पदर्पकालाय कालहन्त्रे नमो नमः ॥ १५४

मन्त्रजपः । यदाहुः—

त्र्यक्षरस्य जपो यावत्तावज्जप्यः षडक्षरः ।
ऐहिकामुष्मिकीं सिद्धिं तथा हि लभते नरः ॥ इति ॥

सर्वान् कामानिति ।

सतिलैस्तन्दुलैर्हेमकाष्ठाग्नौ जुहुयाद्दरैः ।
उन्मादाय पयोहोमस्तत्कान्तिः खादिरानले ॥ इति ॥
यद्यद्वर्णैः प्रसूनैस्तु मन्त्री सप्तदिनं हुनेत् ।
लभेत्तद्रूपवासोऽयम्भणहा कामदो मनुः ॥ इत्यादि ज्ञेयम् ॥१४८॥

धरेत्यादि शैवमन्त्रान्ते शिवस्तुतिः । धरेति श्लोकेनाऽष्टमूर्त्तित्वमुक्तम् । मखेशो यजमानः ॥ १४९ ॥

श्रुत्यन्तेति । उपनिषत्प्रतिपाद्यत्वात्तत्र कृतावासायेत्युपचारतः प्रयोगः । श्रुतये श्रुतिरूपाय । श्रुतीनां जन्म यस्मात् । तेनाऽनादिवेदप्रवक्त्रे । अतीन्द्रियायेति । "यतो वाचो निवर्त्तन्ते अप्राप्य मनसा सह" इति श्रुतेः ॥ १५० ॥

भवाय भवनाश्ने । भवो जन्म तद्दुःखहन्त्रे ॥ १५१ ॥

तर्कः दुस्तर्कः । चतुर्वर्गप्रदात्रे ॥ १५२ ॥

आदिः सर्गः मध्यः पालनं अन्तः संहारः तत्र शून्याय । फलानुपगमात् ।

विषाशनाय विहरद्वृषस्कन्धमुपेयुषे ।
सरिद्दामसमाबद्धकपर्दाय नमो नमः ॥ १५५

शुद्धाय शुद्धभावाय शुद्धानामन्तरात्मने ।
पुरान्तकाय पूर्णाय पुण्यनाम्ने नमो नमः ॥ १५६

भक्ताय निजभक्तानां भुक्तिमुक्तिप्रदायिने ।
विवाससे विवासाय विश्वेशाय नमो नमः ॥ १५७

त्रिमूर्त्तिमूलभूताय त्रिनेत्राय नमो नमः ।
त्रिधाम्नां धामरूपाय जन्मघ्नाय नमो नमः ॥ १५८

देवासुरशिरोरत्नकिरणारुणिताङ्घ्रये ।
कान्ताय निजकान्तायै दत्तार्धाय नमो नमः ॥ १५९

स्तोत्रेणाऽनेन पूजायां प्रीणयेज्जगतः पतिम् ।
भुक्तिमुक्तिप्रदं भक्त्या सर्वज्ञं परमेश्वरम् ॥ १६०

इति श्रीशारदातिलके विंशः पटलः ।

अविचिन्त्याय । इयत्ताभावात् । कालायाऽन्तकाय ॥ १५३ ॥ १५४ ॥

सरिद् गङ्गा सैव दाम तेन प्रबद्धः कपर्दो जटाजूटो येन तस्मै । "कपर्दोऽस्य जटाजूटः" इति कोषः ॥ १५५ ॥ १५६ ॥ १५७ ॥

त्रिमूर्त्तेः ब्रह्मविष्णुरुद्रमूर्त्तेः । त्रिधाम्नामिति सूर्याग्निचन्द्रमसाम् ॥ १५८ ॥ ॥ १५९ ॥ १६० ॥

इति श्रीशारदातिलकटीकायां सत्सम्प्रदायकृतव्याख्यायां
पदार्थादर्शाभिख्यायां विंशतिः पटलः ॥ ॐ ॥

एकविंशः पटलः ।

अथो वक्ष्यामि गायत्रीं तत्त्वरूपां त्रयीमयीम् ।
यया प्रकाश्यते ब्रह्म सच्चिदानन्दलक्षणम् ॥ १

एवं तान्त्रिकान् पञ्च देवतामन्त्रानुक्त्वा कतिचिद्गायत्र्यादिवैदिकाद्यन्त्राण्युपक्रमते अथो इति। तत्त्वरूपां चतुर्विंशतिवर्णानां चतुर्विंशतितत्त्वात्मत्वात्तद्रूपता। तान्यक्षरन्यासे वक्ष्यन्ते। अनेन गायत्र्यक्षरैः सार्द्धं तत्त्वन्यासोऽपि सूचितः। त्रयीमयीमित्यनेन एतया सम्यग्यथाविधि पठितया त्रयीपाठफलप्राप्तिरुक्ता। यया गायत्र्या सच्चिदानन्दलक्षणं ब्रह्म प्रकाश्यते। ततः प्रणवस्य तत्प्रतिपादकत्वमन्ते वक्ष्यति। व्याहृत्यादीनां तत्प्रतिपादकत्वमाहुराचार्याः—

भूःपदाद्या व्याहृतयो भूशब्दस्सदि[ः सति] वर्त्तते ।
तत्पदं सदिति प्रोक्तं तद्यात्मत्वाच्च भूरतः ॥
भूतत्वात् कारणत्वाच्च भुवः शब्दस्य सङ्गतिः ।
सर्वस्वीकरणात् स्वात्मतया च स्वरितीरितम् ॥
महत्त्वाच्च महस्त्वाच्च महःशब्दस्य सङ्गतिः ।
तदेव सर्वजनता तस्मात् तु व्याहृतिर्जनः ॥
तपोज्ञानतया चैव तथा तापतया स्मृतम् ।
सत्यं परत्वादात्मत्वादनन्तज्ञानतः स्मृतम् ॥
प्रणवस्य व्याहृतीनामतः सम्बन्ध उच्यते ।
अकारो भूरुकारस्तु भुवो मार्णः स्वरीरितः ॥
बिन्दुर्महस्तथा नादो जनः शक्तिस्तपः स्मृतम् ।
शान्तिः सत्यमिति प्रोक्तं यत्तत्परतरं पदम् ॥
अत्रापि तत्पदं पूर्वं प्रोक्तं तदनुवक्ष्यते ।
प्रणवस्य व्याहृतीनां गायत्र्यैक्यमथोच्यते ॥
तदृद्वितीयैकवचनमनेनाऽखिलवस्तुनः ।
सृष्ट्यादिकारणं तेजोरूपमादित्यमण्डले ॥
अभिध्येयं परानन्दं परं ब्रह्माऽभिधीयते ।
यत्तत्सवितुरित्युक्तं षष्ठ्येकवचनात्मकम् ॥
धातोरिह विनिष्पन्नं प्राणिप्रसववाचकात् ।
सर्वासां प्राणिजातीनामिति प्रसवितुः सदा ॥

वरेण्यं वरणीयत्वात् सेवनीयतया तथा।
भजनीयतया सर्वैः प्रार्थनीयतया स्मृतम्॥
पूर्वस्याऽष्टाक्षरस्यैवं व्याहृतिर्भूरितीरिता।
पापस्य भर्जनाद्भर्गो भक्तस्निग्धतया तथा॥
देवस्य वृष्टिदानादिगुणयुक्तस्य नित्यशः।
प्रभूतेन प्रकाशेन दीप्यमानस्य वै तथा॥
ध्यै चिन्तायामतो धातोर्निष्पन्नं धीमहीत्यतः।
निगमाद्येन दिव्येन विद्यारूपेण चक्षुषा॥
दृश्यो हिरण्मयो देव आदित्यो नित्यसंस्थितः।
हीनतारहितं तेजो यस्य स्यात् स हिरण्मयः॥
यः सूक्ष्मः सोऽहमित्येवं चिन्तयामः सदैव तु।
द्वितीयाष्टाक्षरस्यैवं व्याहृतिर्भुव ईरिता॥
धियो बुद्धेर्मनोरस्य छान्दसत्वाद् य ईरितः।
अतश्च लिङ्गव्यत्यासः सूत्रात् सुप्तिङुपग्रहात्॥
यत्तत्तेजो निरुपमं सर्वदेवमयात्मकम्।
भजतां पापनाशस्य हेतुभूतमिहोच्यते॥
न इति प्रोक्त आदेशः षष्ठ्या बहिति चास्मदः।
तस्मादस्माकमित्यर्थः प्रार्थनायां प्रचोदयात्॥
तृतीयाष्टाक्षरस्यापि व्याहृतिः स्वरितीरिता।
एवं दशपदान्यस्यास्त्रयश्चाऽष्टाक्षराः स्मृताः॥
षडक्षराश्च चत्वारः स्युश्चतुर्विंशदक्षराः।
इत्यंभूतं यदेतस्य देवस्य सवितुर्विभोः॥
वरेण्यं भजतां पापविनाशनकरं परम्।
भर्गोऽस्माभिरभिध्यातं धियस्तन्नः प्रचोदयात्॥
उक्तैवमत्र गायत्री पुनस्तच्छिर उच्यते।
आपो ज्योती रस इति सोमाग्न्योस्तेज उच्यते॥
तदात्मकं जगत् सर्वं रसस्तेजोद्वयं स्मृतम्।
अमृतं तदनाशित्वाद् बृहत्त्वाद् ब्रह्म गद्यते॥
यदानन्दात्मकं ब्रह्म सत्यज्ञानादिलक्षणम्।
तद् भूर्भुवःस्वरित्युक्तं सोऽहमित्यो[म]मुदाहृतम्॥

प्रणवाद्या व्याहृतयः सप्त स्युस्तत्पदादिका ।
चतुर्विंशत्यक्षरात्मा गायत्री शिरसाऽन्विता ॥ २
सर्ववेदोद्धृतः सारो मन्त्रोऽयं समुदाहृतः ।
ब्रह्मा देव्यादिगायत्री परमात्मा समीरिताः ॥ ३
ऋष्याद्याः प्रणवस्यैते मुनिभिः परिकीर्त्तिताः ।
जमदग्निभरद्वाजभृगुगौतमकश्यपान् ॥ ४
विश्वामित्रवसिष्ठाख्यौ व्याहृतीनामृषीन्विदुः ।
गायत्र्युष्णिगथाऽनुष्टुब्बृहतीपङ्क्तयः पुनः ॥ ५
त्रिष्टुब्जगत्यौ च्छन्दांसि कथितानि मनीषिभिः ।
सप्तार्चिरनिलः सूर्यो वाक्पतिर्वरुणो वृषः ॥ ६
विश्वेदेवाः क्रमादासां देवताः परिकीर्त्तिताः ।
गायत्र्या मुनिराख्यातो विश्वामित्रो महाद्युतिः ॥ ७
गायत्री छन्द इत्युक्तं देवता सविता स्मृता ।
शिरसोऽस्य मुनिर्ब्रह्मा छन्दो देव्यादिका स्मृता ॥ ८
गायत्री परमात्माऽस्य देवता कथिता बुधैः ।
व्याहृतीः सप्त भूराद्या हृन्मुखांसोरुयुग्मके ॥ ९
जठरे न्यस्य मन्त्रज्ञो गायत्र्यार्णांस्ततो न्यसेत् ।
पत्सन्धिषु ध्वजे नाभौ हृत्कण्ठभुजसन्धिषु ॥ १०

एतत्तु वेदसारस्य शिरस्त्वाच्छिर ईरितम् । इति ॥ १ ॥

प्रणवाद्या इति प्रतिव्याहृति सम्बध्यते । तत्पदादिकेत्यस्याऽग्रिमेण सम्बन्धः । शिरसेति । ॐ आपो ज्योती रसोऽमृतं ब्रह्म भूर्भुवः स्वरोमिति । मुनिभिः परिकीर्त्तिता ऋष्याद्याः प्रणवस्य समीरिता इति सम्बन्धः ।

अस्याः कल्पोक्तं बीजादिप्रोक्तम्—

रे इत्येतत् तु बीजं स्यादावर्णं शक्तिरुच्यते ।
णित्येतत्कीलकं प्रोक्तं गायत्र्यास्त्रिपदात्मनः ॥ इति ॥

कल्पान्तरे—यं तु बीजं स्यादो शक्तिर्णं च कीलकम् । इति ॥२॥३॥४॥५॥६॥७॥८॥

मन्त्रज्ञो न्यसेदित्यनेन प्रणवं विन्यस्य सप्तव्याहृतीर्विन्यस्तव्या इत्युक्तं भवति ।

यदाहुः—ॐ नमो ब्रह्मणे नाभौ हृदये ॐ च विष्णवे ।

आस्यनासाकपोलाक्षिकर्णभ्रूमस्तके पुनः ।
पाश्चात्योत्तरयाम्यप्रागूर्ध्ववक्त्रेषु साधकः ॥ ११

मं शिवाय नमो मूर्ध्नि तत्तद्रूपं स्मरन् न्यसेत् ॥ इति ॥

पत्सन्धिष्विति । पादद्वयसन्धिचतुष्के अक्षरचतुष्कम् । तदुक्तम्—"पदद्वयसन्धिचतुष्के" इति । अयं न्यासः अङ्गुलिमारभ्य कर्त्तव्यः । अत्र यद्यपि सन्धिशब्दग्रहणमस्ति तथापि तदवध्यङ्ग एव न्यासो विधेय इति ज्ञेयम् । एवं भुजद्वयसन्धिचतुष्के अक्षरचतुष्कम् । न्यासादिष्वेकैकमक्षरम् । शिरेत्यस्य पृथग्भावेन चतुर्विंशत्यक्षरात्मकत्वम् । साधक इत्यनेन प्रत्यक्षरमादौ प्रणवः अन्ते च नमःशब्द इत्युक्तम् । कल्पान्तरे तु—

वर्णन्यासमथो वक्ष्ये आर्षं छन्दश्च दैवतम् ।
तत्त्वशक्ती वर्णमुद्रे स्मृत्वा वर्णान् क्रमान् न्यसेत् ॥
भितोक्ताग्न्यचलाह्लादि पीतो वक्राङ्गुली करौ ।
सम्मुखं मोहपापघ्नं चरणाङ्गुष्ठयोस्तु तत् ॥
मधुच्छन्दो निवाद्यम्बु प्रभा श्यामोऽब्जकोशवत् ।
सम्मुखौ सम्पुटं चोपपापघ्नं गुल्फयोस्तु सं ॥
गर्गमध्यार्कतेजोजा कपिलो विततं करौ ।
प्रसारितोत्तानशाखौ पापघ्नं जङ्घयोस्तु विं ॥
उपमन्युः प्रतिष्ठा च विद्युद्वायुश्च विश्वसृत् ।
विस्तीर्णं संहतोत्तानतर्जनीमुक्तहस्तकम् ॥
इन्द्रनीलनिभं रोगग्रहघ्नं जानुनोस्तु तुं ।
काश्यपः सुप्रतिष्ठा च यमः खं च विलासिनी ॥
वज्राभं सम्मुखासक्तपार्श्वोर्ध्वक्तकनिष्ठयोः ।
अन्यत्र विरलाङ्गुल्योरङ्गुष्ठद्वययोगतः ॥
द्विमुखं भ्रूणहत्याघ्नमूर्वोर्वं विन्यसेत् सुधीः ।
भृगुर्देवो जलं गन्धः प्रभाच्छः पूर्वरूपयोः ॥
त्रिमुखं तर्जनीयोगाद् गुह्योऽगम्यावधकृत् तु रें ।
वसुर्वह्निशिखायसी लोला विद्युत्तद्वच्चतुर्मुखम् ॥
मध्यायोगादभक्ष्याघहरं वृषणयोस्तु णिं ।
विष्णवनुष्टुब्विष्णु[धरा]रूपं शान्ताच्छः पञ्चवक्त्रकम् ॥

अनामयोगतो ह्रत्वाहरं कण्ठ्यां तु यं तथा ।
हारोतो ह्रहतोन्द्रस्त्वक् कान्ति[कीर्त्ति]र्नीलस्तथा तयोः ॥
तिर्यग्युक्ताग्राङ्गुलिकयोः कनिष्ठा मोचयेत् सति ।
षण्मुखं नरहत्याघ्नं नाभौ भं याज्ञवल्क्यकः ॥
पङ्क्तिर्विद्याधरः शब्दो दुर्गा रक्तमधोमुखम् ।
वक्राग्रावाक्तलकरं जठरे गौं गवां हितम् ॥
कविश्छिष्टुब्रविर्वार्गौ रक्तरुग्व्यापकाञ्जलिः ।
उत्तानौ पूर्ववद्धस्तौ स्वाघभुत् स्तनयोश्च दें ॥
अङ्गिरा जगती शर्वो हस्तौ विद्यास्कुरुखाधः ।
मुक्ताग्राङ्गुष्ठकौ मुष्टौ शकटं हृदि वं गुरोः ॥
स्यं ब्र[य ?]मो जगतो त्वष्टोपरुक्षेशाः काञ्चनच्छविः ।
यमपाशं बद्धमुष्ट्योरुत्ताना वामतर्जनी ॥
वक्राग्रा न्युब्जया युक्ताऽन्यया कण्ठे मनोऽघहृत् ।
आपस्तुच्छः शङ्करो च पायुराप्यायिनो वसुः ॥
शङ्खो मिथः सन्धिलीनाङ्गुलिकौ सम्मुखौ करौ ।
दीर्घाङ्गुष्ठौ ग्रथितकं धीं मुखे पितृ[नृप]पापनुत् ॥
संवर्त्तोऽर्त्तिर्मकल्पादौ विमला पद्मरागभः ।
सन्धिश्रोर्ध्वाङ्गुलिर्वामस्ताद्दृशोऽधोमुखः परः ॥
सुसम्मुखोन्मुखं तालुमध्ये मं पूर्वपापहम् ।
कात्यायनस्त्रिवृत् सोमः शोलं मात्स्यं विपापहम् ॥
उत्तानोन्नतकोटी द्वौ लम्बं हिं नासिकागतम् ।
वसिष्ठोत्यङ्गिरा त्वग्धिरण्या पाण्डु परिक्रमात् ॥
अन्योन्यसंहतोत्तानौ मुष्टिकं नेत्रयोस्तु धिं ।
व्यासो धृतिः सुराशत्रुः सूक्ष्मा रक्तश्च संमुखौ ॥
युक्तानामाकनिष्ठौ संयुक्तवक्राग्रयोमकौ ।
मत्स्यप्राणिवधाघघ्नं भ्रूमध्ये यों न्यसेद् द्विजः ॥
पराशरो धृतिर्दस्रो जिह्वा योनिश्च रक्तरुक् ।
कूर्मः पृष्ठे समाक्रान्तो दक्षिणेन त्वधोमुखः ॥
यों ललाटेऽखिलाघघ्नं शङ्कुः क्षतिः प्रजापतिः ।
प्राशं जया बलाकाभः कनिष्ठाभ्यां सम्प्रयौ करौ ॥

पदानि दश विन्यस्येदेषु स्थानेषु मन्त्रवित् ।
शिरोभ्रूमध्यदृग्वक्त्रकण्ठहृन्नाभिगुह्यके ।
जानुनोः पादयोर्युग्मे तच्छिरः शिरसि न्यसेत् ॥ १२
ब्रह्मणे हृदयं प्रोक्तं विष्णवे शिर ईरितम् ।
शिखा रुद्राय कवचमीश्वराय समीरितम् ॥ १३
नेत्रं सदाशिवायोक्तमस्त्रं सर्वात्मने स्मृतम् ।
षडङ्गान्येवमुक्तानि यथास्थानं प्रविन्यसेत् ॥ १४

वामोर्ध्वमध्यो वाराहः पूर्वास्ये नं सुखार्थदम् ।
शङ्खप्रकृतिदेवा हृत् पद्मा नीलः श्रुतिस्थितौ ॥
प्रसारिताङ्गुली सिंहो दक्षास्ये प्रं शिवप्रदम् ।
दक्षाकृती शिवाऽहं मा हरित् पूर्वीदितौ करौ ॥
कुञ्चिताग्रौ महाक्रान्तसुन्दरे चौ हरिप्रदम् ।
गौतमाकृतिकाच्छाया मुद्रः किञ्चिदूर्ध्वयोः ॥
करयोर्वामहस्तस्य तर्जनीदक्षमुष्टिना ।
गृहीता ब्रह्मसौख्यस्य प्रदं दं पश्चिमानने ॥
शातातपः कृतिर्विष्णुर्गुणो भद्रेशरूपधृक् ।
दक्षिणोऽधोमुखो मूर्ध्नि पल्लवः के यवर्गि यात् ॥ इति ॥८॥१०॥११॥

पदन्यासमाह पदानीति । एषु वक्ष्यमाणेषु । पदानि तु—एकशरश्मिद्वयग्निवह्निद्वेदकैकाब्ध्यक्षरैः क्रमात् । कल्पान्तरे शिरःपदन्यासोऽप्युक्तः—

ॐ आपस्तनयोर्ज्योतिर्नसि नेत्रे रसो मुखे ।
अमृतं शिरसि ब्रह्म शिखायां भूर्भुवः स्वरोम् ॥ इति ॥ १२ ॥

षडङ्गमाह ब्रह्मण इति । अस्त्रं सर्वात्मने स्मृतमित्यात्मनेपदोच्चारो ग्रन्थकृतः सर्वत्राऽभिप्रेतः । ब्रह्मात्मने हृदयाय नम इत्यादि प्रयोगः । साम्प्रदायिकास्तु ॐ भूर्भुवः स्वस्तत्सवितुर्ब्रह्मात्मने हृत् । वरेण्यं विष्ण्वात्मने शिरः । भर्गो देवस्य रुद्रात्मने शिखा । धीमहि ईश्वरात्मने कवचम् । धियो यो नः सदाशिवात्मने नेत्रम् । प्रचोदयात् सर्वात्मने अस्त्रमिति षडङ्गक्रमं वदन्ति । कल्पान्तरे तु—

ब्रह्मा विष्णुः क्रमाद्रुद्र ईश्वरश्च सदाशिवः ।
सर्वात्मतेजसोऽन्तस्य व्याहृत्यादिषडङ्गके ॥ इति ।

आदिशब्देन व्याहृतित्रयं पदत्रयं च । ॐ भूर्ब्रह्मतेजस इत्यादि प्रयोगः ॥१३॥१४॥

मुक्ताविद्रुमहेमनीलधवलच्छायैर्मुखैस्त्रीक्षणै-
र्युक्तामिन्दुनिबद्धरत्नमुकुटां तत्त्वात्मवर्णात्मिकाम् ।
सावित्रीं वरदाभयाङ्कुशकशाः शुभ्रं कपालं गुणं
शङ्खं चक्रमथाऽरविन्दयुगलं हस्तैर्वहन्तीं भजे ॥ १५

प्राणायामान् पुरा कृत्वा गायत्रीं सन्ध्ययोर्जपेत् ।
सप्तव्याहृतिसंयुक्तां गायत्रीं शिरसाऽन्विताम् ॥ १६

ध्यानमाह मुक्तेति । कशा अश्वादेस्ताडनीरज्जुः । शुभ्रमिति कपालविशेषणम् । गुणः पाशः । आयुधध्यानं तु । दक्षाद्यूर्ध्वयोरन्त्ये तदधस्तनयोश्चक्रशङ्खौ । तदधस्थयोः पाशकपाले । तदधस्थयोः कशाङ्कुशौ । तदधस्तनयोरभयवरौ । अत्र ध्यानानन्तरं वरादिमुद्रा प्रदर्शयेत् । यदाहुः—

वराभयाब्जपद्मेन्द्रशक्तिमुद्राः प्रदर्शयेत् । इति ।

त्रिसन्ध्यं ध्यानम् । यथा—

हंसारूढां सिताङ्गे त्वरुणमणिलसद्भूषणां भालनेत्रां
वेदाख्या[स्या]मक्षमालां स्रुवमथ कमलं दण्डमप्यादधानाम् ।
ध्यायेद्दोर्भिश्चतुर्भिस्त्रिभुवनजननीं पूर्वसन्ध्यादिवन्द्यां
गायत्रीमर्कसवित्रीमभिनववयसं मण्डले चण्डरश्मेः ॥

विश्वमातः सुराभ्यर्च्ये पुण्ये गायत्रि वैधसि ।
आवाहयाम्युपास्त्यर्थं एह्येनोघ्नि पुनीहि माम् ॥
वृषेन्द्रवाहना देवी ज्वलत्त्रिशिखधारिणी ।
श्वेताम्बरधरा श्वेतनागाभरणभूषणा ॥
श्वेतस्रगक्षमालालङ्कृता रक्ता च शङ्करा ।
जटाधारा धरा धात्री धरेन्द्राङ्गभवा भवा ॥
मातर्भवानि विश्वेशि आहूतेहि पुनीहि माम् ।
सन्ध्या सायन्तनी कृष्णा विष्णुदेवा सरस्वती ॥
खगगा कृष्णवर्णा तु शङ्खचक्रधरा परा ।
कृष्णस्रग्भूषणैर्युक्ता सर्वज्ञानमयी वरा ॥
वीणाक्षमालिकाचारुहस्ता स्मितवरानना ।
मातर्वाग्देवते स्तुत्ये आहूतेहि पुनीहि माम् ॥ इति ॥ १५ ॥

प्राणायामानिति बहुवचनं कपिञ्जलाधिकरणन्यायेन त्रित्वे पर्यवस्यति ।

विरुचरन् धिया प्राणान् धारयेदात्मानसः ।
प्राणायामोऽयमाख्यातः समस्तदुरितापहः ॥ १७

व्याहृतित्रयसंयुक्तां गायत्रीं दीक्षितो जपेत् ।
तत्त्वलक्षं विधानेन भिक्षाशी विजितेन्द्रियः ॥ १८

क्षीरौदनतिलान् दूर्वाक्षीरद्रुमसमिद्वरान् ।
पृथक् सहस्रत्रितयं जुहुयान्मन्त्रसिद्धये ॥ १९

विधाय मण्डलं विद्वान् त्रिकोणोज्ज्वलकर्णिकम् ।
सौरं पीठं यजेत्तत्र दीप्तादिनवशक्तिभिः ॥ २०

मूलमन्त्रेण क्लृप्तायां मूर्त्तौ देवीं प्रपूजयेत् ।
कोणेषु त्रिषु सम्पूज्या ब्रह्माद्याः शक्तयो बहिः ॥ २१

आदित्याद्यास्ततः पूज्या उषादिसहिताः क्रमात् ।
ततः षडङ्गान्यभ्यर्चेत् केसरेषु यथाविधि ॥ २२

तत्स्वरूपमेवाह । समेति । धिया विरुच्चरन्निति सम्बन्धः ॥ १६॥१७ ॥

व्याहृतीति । व्याहृतित्रयमाद्यम् । सोचार्यो तु "परोरजसे सावदोम्" इति चतुर्थपादसहितां जपेदिति ज्ञेयम् । अस्य विमल ऋषिः गायत्री छन्दः परमात्मा देवतेति । तत्त्वलक्षमिति । चतुर्विंशतिलक्षम् । विधानेनेति पुरश्चरणोक्तेन ॥१८॥

क्षीरौदनेति । क्षीरमोदनस्तिला दूर्वा इति द्रव्यचतुष्टयम् । क्षीरद्रुमा अश्वत्थोदुम्बरप्लक्षवटाः ॥ १९ ॥

मण्डलमिति । सर्वतोभद्रम् । त्रिकोणोज्ज्वलकर्णिकम् । तत्कर्णिकायां त्रिगुणितं यन्त्रं लिखेदित्यर्थः । त्रिकोणशब्दस्य त्रिगुणितोपलक्षकत्वात् । तदुक्तमाचार्यैः—अथ त्रिगुणिते प्रोक्ते विचित्रे मण्डलोत्तमे । इति । तत्र पूर्वोक्ते । दीप्तादीति । चतुर्दशपटलोक्ताः ॥ २० ॥ २१ ॥

कोणेष्विति । अग्निवरुणेशानेषु । ब्रह्माद्या ब्रह्मविष्ण्वीशाः । शक्तयो गायत्रीसावित्रीसरस्वत्याख्याः । कोणेषु त्रिष्वित्येव । ऐन्द्रनैर्ऋत्यवायव्यभागेष्वित्यर्थः । एभिः प्रथमावरणम् । अत्र यद्यपि ब्रह्माद्या इत्युक्तं तथापि शक्तिपूजा पूर्वं ज्ञेया । "त्रिशक्तिमूर्त्तीः प्रथमं समर्च्य" इत्याचार्योक्तेः । अन्यत्रापि—

गायत्रीं शतमखजे निशाचरोत्थे सावित्रीं पवनगते सरस्वतीं च ।
ब्रह्माणं हुतभुजि वारुणे च विष्णुं षष्ठेऽस्त्रे समभियजेत्तथेशमैशे ॥ इति ॥

प्रह्लादिनीं प्रभां पश्चान्नित्यां विश्वम्भरां पुनः।
विलासिनीप्रभावत्यौ जयां शान्तिं यजेत् पुनः॥ २३
कान्तिं दुर्गासरस्वत्यौ विश्वरूपां ततः परम्।
विशालसंज्ञितामीशां व्यापिनीं विमलां यजेत्॥ २४
तमोऽपहारिणीं सूक्ष्मां विश्वयोनिं जयावहाम्।
पद्मालयां परां शोभां पद्मरूपां ततोऽर्चयेत्॥ २५
ब्राह्म्याद्याः सारुणा बाह्ये पूजयेत् प्रोक्तलक्षणाः।
ततोऽर्चयेद् ग्रहान् बाह्ये शक्रादीनायुधैः सह॥ २६
इत्थमावरणैर्देवीं दशभिः परिपूजयेत्।
धर्मार्थकाममोक्षाणां भोक्ता स्याद् द्विजसत्तमः॥ २७

अन्यत्रापि—रक्ता रक्ताकल्पा चतुर्मुखी कुण्डिकाक्षमालेऽब्जे।
दधती प्राक्कोणस्था गायत्री तादृशोऽग्निगो ब्रह्मा॥
अरिदरगदाब्जहस्ता किरीटकेयूरसंभिन्ना।
निशिचरकोणसमुत्था सावित्री वरुणगस्तथा विष्णुः॥
टङ्काक्षाभयवरदान् दधती च त्रीक्षणेन्दुकलितजटा।
वाणी वायव्यस्था विशदाकल्पा तथेश्वरस्त्वैशे॥ इति।

कल्पान्तरे तु—षट्कोणाग्निषु सावित्र्यै प्राग् गायत्र्यै च नैर्ऋते।
वायुकोणे सरस्वत्यै आग्नेये ब्रह्मणे नमः।
पश्चिमे विष्णवेऽथैशे रुद्राय प्रथमावृतिः॥ इति॥

तत्र आदित्याद्याश्चतुर्दशपटलोक्ताः। उषादयश्च तत्पटलोक्तप्रकारेणैवात्र पूज्याः। एतेन द्वितीयावरणम्। तत इति तृतीयावरणम्। यथाविधीति। चतुर्थपटलोक्तरीत्या॥ २१॥ २२॥

प्रह्लादिनीमिति। आसां ध्यानमुक्तमन्यत्र—
कुन्देन्दुधवलाकारा मणिमुक्ताद्यलङ्कृताः।
गुणाङ्कुशवराभोजकराः प्रह्लादिनीमुखाः॥ इति॥

आभिरष्टाभिरष्टाभिरावरणत्रयम्। अतएव दशभिरावरणैरिति वक्ष्यति॥ २३॥ ॥ २४॥ २५॥

ब्राह्म्याद्याः सारुणा इति अरुणान्ताः। महालक्ष्मीस्थाने अरुणः पूज्य इत्यर्थः। पद्मपादाचार्यास्तु अरुणपूजामधिकामाहुः। प्रोक्तलक्षणा इति। षष्ठपटलोक्त-

तत्त्वसंख्यासहस्राणि मन्त्रविज्जुहुयात्तिलैः ।
सर्वपापविनिर्मुक्तो दीर्घमायुः स विन्दति ॥ २८

आयुषे साज्यहविषा केवलेनाऽथ सर्पिषा ।
दूर्वात्रिकैस्तिलैर्मन्त्री जुहुयात् त्रिसहस्रकम् ॥ २९

अरुणाब्जैस्त्रिमध्वक्तैर्जुहुयादयुतं ततः ।
महालक्ष्मीर्भवेत्तस्य षण्मासान्नाऽत्र संशयः ॥ ३०

ब्रह्मश्रियै प्रजुहुयात् प्रसूनैर्ब्रह्मवृक्षजैः ।
बहुना किमिहोक्तेन यथावत् साधुसाधिता ।
द्विजन्मनामियं विद्या सिद्धा कामदुघा मता ॥ ३१

आग्नेयमभिधास्यामि मन्त्रं सर्वार्थसाधकम् ।
मारीचः काश्यपः प्रोक्तो मुनिरस्य महामनोः ॥ ३२

ध्यानाः । आभिः सप्तमम् । ग्रहानिति । सूर्यमन्त्रोक्तान् । एभिरष्टमम् । कल्पान्तरे तु—अष्टमो ग्रहैरादित्यपरिषदान्तैस्तैः । इति । इन्द्राद्यैर्नवमम् । तदायुधैर्दशमम् ॥ २६॥२७॥२८ ॥

आयुष इति । साज्यहविषेत्येकम् । केवलेनेति । पायसेन । सर्पिषेति च सम्बन्धः । त्रिसहस्रमिति । पञ्चानामपि संख्या । तदुक्तम्—

आयुष्कामो जुहुयात् पायसहविराज्यकेवलाज्यैश्च ।
दूर्वाभिः सतिलाभिः सर्वैस्त्रिसहस्रसंख्यकं मन्त्री ॥ इति ॥

तन्त्रान्तरस्थं धारणयन्त्रमुच्यते—

शक्तेर्बाह्यक्रशानुकोणविलसद्भूरादिसत्कर्णिकं
वस्वब्जं स्वरयुग्मकेसरदलैर्वर्गैस्त्रिवर्णैर्मनोः ।
गायत्र्याः कथितं महःप्रभृतिभिर्यन्त्रं तु दिक्ष्वङ्कितं
चूडामन्त्रतुरीयवेष्टितमिदं क्ष्माकोणताराङ्कितम् ॥ इति ॥

रामवल्लभे तु द्वादशगुणितं यन्त्रं गायत्रीयन्त्रत्वेनोक्तम् ॥ २९॥३०॥३१ ॥

त्रिष्टुप्मन्त्रमाह आग्नेयमिति । स मन्त्रो यथा—

ॐ जातवेदसे सुनवाम सोममरातीयतो नि दहाति वेदः । स नः पर्षदति दुर्गाणि विश्वा नावेव सिन्धुं दुरितात्यग्निः । इति ।

अयं मन्त्र ऋग्वेदे प्रसिद्धः तेनात्र नोक्तः ।

त्रिष्टुप् छन्दो देवताऽत्र जातवेदोऽग्निरीरितः।
नवभिः सप्तभिः षड्भिः सप्तभिः पुनरष्टभिः॥ ३३
सप्तभिर्मूलमन्त्रार्णैः षडङ्गविधिरीरितः।
अङ्गुष्ठगुल्फजङ्घासु जानुनोरुयुग्मके॥ ३४
कट्यन्धुनाभिषु हृदि स्तनयोः पार्श्वयोर्द्वयोः।
पृष्ठतः स्कन्धयोर्मध्ये बाहुमूलोपबाहुषु॥ ३५
प्रकूर्परप्रकोष्ठेषु मणिबन्धतलेषु च।
मुखनासाक्षिकर्णेषु मस्तमस्तिष्कमूर्धसु॥ ३६
क्रमेण विन्यसेद्वर्णान्मन्त्री मन्त्रसमुद्भवान्।
शिखाललाटनयनकर्णाधररसनास्वथ॥ ३७
सकण्ठबाहुहृत्कुक्षिकटिगुह्योरुजानुषु।
जङ्घयोः पादयोर्न्यस्येत्पदान्यस्य मनोः सुधीः॥ ३८

हृल्लेखासंपुटो जप्तव्यः। मारीचः। काश्यप इति विशेषणं विधेयम्। हलंशो बीजं स्वरांशः शक्तिः॥ ३२॥ ३३॥ ३४॥

अङ्गुष्ठेति। पादाङ्गुष्ठद्वयम्। स्कन्धयोरिति भिन्नम्। मध्य इति। कन्धरायाम्। उपबाहुष्विति। बाहुमूलप्रकूर्परमध्यभागः। मस्तं ललाटकेशसन्धिः। मस्तिष्कं तदूर्ध्वदेशः। मूर्धा ब्रह्मरन्ध्रम्। वर्णानिति। चतुश्चत्वारिंशत्। परिषदित्यस्य पृथक् पाठात्। अत्राङ्गुष्ठादिस्थानद्वये वर्णद्वयन्यासः॥ ३४॥ ३५॥ ३६॥ ३७॥

पदन्यासमाह शिखेति। शिखा मूर्धा। गुह्यं लिङ्गम्। अत्र पदन्यासे नयनयोः पदद्वयं कर्णद्वये पदद्वयं अन्यत्रैकैकं पदम्। तदुक्तमीशानशिवेन—

> स्मृतमिह तु पदानां कं ललाटाक्षिकर्णौ
> त्वधररसनकण्ठं बाहुहृन्नाभिदेशाः।
> कटिरपि मदनोरू जानुजङ्घाङ्घ्रयोऽमी
> श्रवणनयनयोर्द्वे स्थानमेकैकमन्यत्॥ इति।

पदान्यष्टादश। तानि यथा—

> शराब्धिद्वीष्वेकवह्निद्वेरकेकद्विद्विपावकैः।
> द्वग्निद्वग्निद्विद्विवर्णैरष्टादश पदानि हि॥ इति॥ ३७॥ ३८॥

विद्युद्दामसमप्रभां मृगपतिस्कन्धस्थितां भीषणां
कन्याभिः करवालखेटविलसद्धस्ताभिरासेविताम्।
हस्तैश्चक्रदरासिखेटविशिखं चापं गुणं तर्जनीं
बिभ्राणामनलात्मिकां शशिधरां दुर्गां त्रिनेत्रां स्मरेत्॥ ३९

मन्त्रवर्णसहस्राणि जपेन्मन्त्रं विशालधीः।
तदन्ते तिलसिद्धार्थबिल्वमूलैः समिद्वरैः॥ ४०

विद्युदिति। दरः शङ्खः। गुणस्त्रिशूलम्। "इष्वासाख्यत्रिशूलान्" इत्याचार्योक्तेः। आयुधध्यानं तु। दक्षाद्यूर्ध्वयोराद्ये। तदधस्थयोरसिमे। तदधस्थयोश्चापविशिखौ। तदधस्थयोः शूलतर्जन्यौ। तदुक्तम्—

हेमाचलतटे रम्ये कल्पवृक्षोपशोभिते।
दिव्योद्यानं चिन्तयेच्च विशालं हेमभूतलम्॥
कृशानुरूपवप्रेण करालेन समावृतम्।
तन्मध्ये चिन्तयेद् दिव्यं विचित्रमणिमण्डपम्।
तस्मिन् सिंहासनेऽम्भोजकर्णिकायां विचिन्तयेत्।
दंष्ट्राकरालाट्टहासं कृष्णवर्णं भयानकम्॥
अतितीव्रमुखं सिंहं वमदग्निशिखोज्ज्वलम्।
तस्योपरिष्टात्तां देवीं चिन्तयेज्ज्वालरूपिणीम्॥
तडित्कोटिनिभां देवीं कोटिबालार्कसन्निभाम्।
चक्रासिबाणशूलाख्यान् दधतीं दक्षिणैर्भुजैः॥
शङ्खं चक्रधनुर्बाणतर्जनीर्वामबाहुभिः।
चन्द्रखण्डसमायुक्तामतिभीमत्रिलोचनाम्॥
ऊर्ध्वज्वलत्केशपाशामशेषाहरणोन्मुखीम्।
अङ्गाद्यावृतिसंयुक्तामस्त्रशस्त्रपरीवृताम्।
इन्द्रादिलोकपालैश्च सेवितां विन्ध्यवासिनीम्॥ इति॥ ३९॥

विशालधीरित्यनेन दीक्षाप्रकारेणाऽयं मन्त्रो ग्राह्य इत्युक्तम्। तदुक्तमाचार्यैः—

दीक्षा प्रवर्त्यते पूर्वं यथावद्देशिकोत्तमैः।
ततोऽस्य कल्पितः सम्प्रोक्ता स्यात् प्रयोगविधिस्ततः॥ इति।

अन्यत्रापि—मन्त्राणि दीक्षितस्यैव कथयेत् स तु साधयेत्। इति।
बिल्वमूलैर्बिल्वकमूलैः। हविषा पायसेन। घृताक्तैर्घृतसिक्तैः।

क्षीरद्रुमाणामाज्येन हविषाऽन्नैर्घृतान्वितैः।
चतुश्चत्वारिंशदाढ्यं चतुःशतसमन्वितम्॥ ४१

चतुःसहस्रं जुहुयादर्चिते हव्यवाहने।
मण्डले सर्वतोभद्रे षट्कोणाङ्कितकर्णिके॥ ४२

विधिना वक्ष्यमाणेन पीठं देव्याः प्रपूजयेत्।
जयाख्यां विजयां भद्रां भद्रकालीमनन्तरम्॥ ४३

सुमुखीं दुर्मुखीसंज्ञां पश्चाद् व्याघ्रमुखीं पुनः।
अथ सिंहमुखीं दुर्गां नव शक्तीः प्रपूजयेत्॥ ४४

आसनं सिंहमन्त्रेण दद्यादुक्तेन देशिकः।
मूर्त्तिं सङ्कल्प्य मूलेन तस्यामावाह्य पूजयेत्॥ ४५

षडङ्गानि यथापूर्वं केसरेष्वर्चयेत् सुधीः।
वह्न्यादिपादाष्टकोत्पन्ना मूर्त्तयोऽर्च्या बहिः पुनः॥ ४६

जातवेदाः सप्तजिह्वो हव्यवाहनसंज्ञकः।
अश्वोदरजसंज्ञोऽन्यः पुनर्वैश्वानराह्वयः॥ ४७

तिलराज्यनलक्षीरद्रुमेध्महविराज्यकैः।

सर्पिःसिक्तैः क्रमाद्धोमः साधयेत् समुदायतः॥ इति आचार्योक्तेः।
तेन नव द्रव्याणि। तेनैकैकद्रव्येण चतुःशतीचतुर्नवतिराहुतयः॥ ४०॥४१॥४२॥

मण्डल इति। तृतीयोक्ते। षट्कोणाङ्कितेति। तत्पद्मकर्णिकायां षड्गुणितं यन्त्रं लिखेदित्यर्थः। षट्कोणशब्देन षड्गुणितस्योपलक्षितत्वात्।
तदुक्तमाचार्यैः—दीक्षकाख्याक्षराख्यादौ शक्त्यावेष्ट्य ततो बहिः।

यन्त्रं षड्गुणितं कृत्वा दुर्वर्णलसितास्रकम्॥

बहिरष्टदलं पद्मम्। इत्यादिना॥

शक्तीः प्रपूजयेदिति। आसां ध्यानमुक्तमन्यत्र—

ज्वलज्ज्वलनसङ्काशाः सर्पा[र्वा]लङ्कारशोभिताः।

शूलं कुठारडमरुदहनान् करपङ्कजैः।

दधत्यश्चिन्तनीयाः स्युर्जयाद्या नव शक्तयः॥ इति॥४२॥४३॥४४॥

उक्तेनेति। एकादशेऽग्न्यादौ त्वनेन मूर्तीनां तदादित्वमुक्तं पूजायां न्यासे च।
तत्र वह्न्यादिपादाष्टकमग्रे वक्ष्यति॥ ४५॥ ४६॥

कौमारतेजाः स्वाहिष्वमुखो देवमुखः स्मृतः ।
ततो भूसलिलाग्नीशानात्मनेऽन्तान्नमोऽन्वितान् ॥ ४८
चतुर्दिक्षु समभ्यर्चेत्कोणेष्वेतत्कलाः पुनः ।
पूर्वादिदिक्षु सम्पूज्या जार्णाद्या वर्णशक्तयः ॥ ४९
जाग्रता तपनी वेदगर्भा दहनरूपिणी ।
सेन्दुखण्डा शुम्भहन्त्री नभश्चारिण्यनन्तरम् ॥ ५०
वागीश्वरी मदवहा सोमरूपा मनोजवा ।
मरुद्वेगा रात्रिसंज्ञा तीव्रकोपा यशोवती ॥ ५१
तोयात्मिका पुनर्नित्या दयावत्यपि हारिणी ।
तिरस्क्रिया वेदमाता तत्परा दमनप्रिया ॥ ५२
समाराध्या नन्दिनी च परा रिपुविमर्दिनी ।
षष्ठी च दण्डिनी तिग्मा दुर्गा गायत्र्यनन्तरम् ॥ ५३
निरवद्या विशालाक्षी श्वासोद्वाहा च नादिनी ।
वेदना वह्निगर्भाख्या सिंहवाहाह्वया तथा ॥ ५४
धुर्या दुर्विषहा पश्चात् रिरंसा तापहारिणी ।
त्यक्तदोषा निःसपत्ना चत्वारिंशच्चतुर्युताः ॥ ५५

मूर्त्तयोऽर्च्या इति उक्तम्। ताः का इत्यपेक्षायामाह जातवेदा इति। मूर्त्तीनां पुनरुक्तिरन्यमूर्त्तिनिवृत्त्यर्था। आसां ध्यानमुक्तमन्यत्र—

तडित्कोटिसमप्रख्याः सर्वभूषणभूषिताः ।
शूलं शरं कार्मुकं च कपालं स्वैर्महाभुजैः ॥
दधत्यो रक्तवसनाः क्रूरेक्षणभयानकाः ।
ज्वलज्ज्वलनवक्त्राः स्युर्जातवेदादिमूर्त्तयः ॥ इति ॥ ४७ ॥ ४८ ॥

आत्मनेऽन्तानिति। स्वा[भूतस्वा]त्मने नम इत्यादि। एषां ध्यानं स्वस्वस्थले प्रोक्तमनुसन्धेयम्। जलस्य वक्ष्यमाणं वरुणध्यानं ज्ञेयम्। एतत्कला निवृत्तिप्रतिष्ठा-विद्याशान्तिरूपाः। आसां ध्यानं प्रासादमन्त्रोक्तमनुसन्धेयम् ॥ ४८॥४९ ॥

पूर्वादिदिक्ष्विति। एकैकस्यां दिशि एकादशैकादश शक्तीः पूजयेत्।

तदुक्तम्—मन्त्रविधानविच्च दिशि दिश्येकादशैकादश। इति।

जार्णाद्या इति। जाप्रभृतिमन्त्राक्षराद्याः। तत्परेति। दमनप्रियाविशेषणम्।

लोकपालांस्ततोऽभ्यर्चेद्वज्राद्यायुधसंयुतान्।
इत्थं जपादिभिः सिद्धे मन्त्रेऽस्मिन् साधकोत्तमः॥ ५६
आग्नेयास्त्राधिकारी स्यात्तद्विधानमुदीर्यते।
आग्नेयास्त्रमिति प्रोक्तं विलोमपठितो मनुः॥ ५७
पूर्वोक्ता एव ऋष्याद्या मन्त्रस्याऽस्य प्रकीर्त्तिताः।
प्रतिलोमक्रमादस्य षडङ्गानि प्रकल्पयेत्॥ ५८
वर्णन्यासपदन्यासौ विदध्यात् प्रतिलोमतः।
ध्यानभेदान् विजानीयाद्गुर्वादेशान्न चाऽन्यथा॥ ५९
पूर्ववज्जपक्लृप्तिः स्याज्जुहुयात् पूर्वसंख्यया।
पञ्चगव्यसुपक्केन चरुणा तस्य सिद्धये॥ ६०

परेति कलानाम। षष्ठीत्यपि नाम॥ ४८॥५०॥५१॥५२॥५३॥५४॥५५॥५६॥५७॥

प्रतिलोमेति। संख्यायाः प्रातिलोम्यम्। वर्णप्रातिलोम्यम्। वर्णप्रातिलोम्यस्योक्तत्वात्। प्रकल्पयेदिति। पूर्वोक्तसंख्याक्षरैः सम्प्रदायात् तारमायादुर्गाद्यैः जातवेदसे मां रक्षरक्षाग्नयेऽस्त्रायफडन्तैः। तदुक्तम्—

शिलाद्रि लोकाङ्गसंख्यैर्धातुनन्दप्रसंख्यकैः।
विलोमभूतैस्ताराादि बीजत्रयशिरोगतैः॥
आद्यं पदं मां रक्षाऽग्नयेऽस्त्राय फट्युतैः।
जातियुक्तैः षडङ्गानि दहनास्त्रस्य कल्पयेत्॥ इति॥५७॥५८॥

ध्यानभेदानिति। तत्राग्नेयास्त्रदेवताध्यानं यथा—

मध्ये तालवनस्याऽग्निर्वप्राढ्ये वह्निभूतले।
महतस्तालवृक्षस्य मूलाभ्यासविराजिते॥
सिंहस्कन्धाग्निकोणे वा चलच्चरणसंस्थिताम्।
तडित्कोटिसमप्रख्यां कल्पान्तदहनोज्ज्वलाम्॥
अक्षत्रिमोग्रदंष्ट्रास्यां घण्टामालास्फुरत्कटिम्।
शूलभोगीन्द्रडमरुविद्युदङ्गीन् ज्वलत्प्रभान्॥
दधानां करदण्डैः स्वैर्भूषामदबलाकुलैः।
भूषितां भूषणैरुग्रैः फणीन्द्रपरिकल्पितैः॥
क्ष्म्यादिवर्णमयीं देवीं संविद्रूपां विचिन्तयेत्॥ इति॥ ५९॥

पूर्ववदिति। पूर्वोक्तसंख्यया। विशेषस्तन्त्रान्तरे—

अर्चनं पूर्ववत् कुर्याच्छक्तीस्तु प्रतिलोमतः ।
सर्वत्र देशिकः कुर्याद्गायत्र्या द्विगुणं जपम् ॥ ६१
क्रूरकर्माणि कुर्वीत प्रतिलोमविधानतः ।
शान्तिकं पौष्टिकं कर्म कर्त्तव्यमनुलोमतः ॥ ६२
प्रयोगकाले प्रजपेदष्टौ पादान् विलोमतः ।
शोधितो जायते पश्चान्मन्त्रोऽयं विधिनाऽमुना ॥ ६३

मौनी व्रतपरो मन्त्री शुद्धाचारो जितेन्द्रियः ।
पूर्वोक्तासनमध्यस्थः प्राङ्मुखः स्वस्तिकासनः ।
आग्नेयास्त्रं जपेद्विद्वान् सिद्धयर्थं पूर्वसंख्यया ॥ इति ॥

तस्य निश्चय इति । उभयासिद्धत्वे प्रयोगानर्हत्वात् । तदुक्तम्—

यो हि सम्यगसाध्यैतत् क्रियाः कर्त्तुमभीप्सति ।
दिव्यास्त्रदेवतास्तं वै नाशयन्त्येव दारुणाः ॥
तस्मात् सर्वप्रयत्नेन पक्षकालादिभिर्व्रतैः ।
देहं विशोध्य शस्त्राणि साधयित्वा चरेत् क्रियाः ॥ इति ॥

अन्यत्रापि—प्रतिलोमानुलोमान्तां विद्यां संसाध्य देशिकः ।
प्रयोगमारभेदेषामस्त्राणामुक्तमार्गतः ॥ इति ॥ ६० ॥

अर्चनमिति । तत्र विशेषस्तन्त्रान्तरे—

पीठे पूर्वोदिते देवीमावाह्योक्तेन वर्त्मना ।
प्रवरैर्गन्धकुसुमैः साङ्गां मूलेन पूजयेत् ॥
अङ्गान्यग्न्यादिकोणेषु वह्निमूर्त्तीर्दिशास्वपि ।
दुर्गा नारायणी चैव दुर्मना शमनप्रिया ॥
नित्यानन्दोत्करा चैव सुवेशा जागरप्रिया ।
पदशक्तीरिमास्त्वष्टौ तृतीयावरणेऽर्चयेत् ।
मन्त्रार्णशक्तीस्तद्बाह्ये लोकपालांश्च पूजयेत् ॥ इति ॥

सर्वत्रेति । प्रयोगेषु गायत्र्या द्विगुणं जपम् । प्रयोगोक्तजपाद् द्विगुणं जपं कुर्यादित्यर्थः ॥ ६१ ॥

प्रतिलोमविधानतः । आग्नेयास्त्रेण । अनुलोमत इति जातवेदसे इत्यनेन ॥ ६२ ॥

प्रजपेदिति पृथक् पृथक् । शोधित इति । तदुक्तम्—

मन्त्रोः स्थिरादिदोषाणां सर्वेषामुपशान्तये ।

न्याद्यः पञ्चाक्षरः पादो ज्ञेयो ज्ञानेन्द्रियात्मकः ।
धुमाद्योऽन्यः पञ्चवर्णः स्मृतः कर्मेन्द्रियात्मकः ॥ ६४
प्वाद्यस्तृतीयः पञ्चार्णः पञ्चभूतमयः स्मृतः ।
त्याद्यः सप्ताक्षरः पादश्चतुर्थो धातुरूपकः ॥ ६५
दःपूर्वः पञ्चमः पाद ऊर्मिरूपः षडक्षरः ।
तोवर्णादिः षड्वर्णोऽन्यः षाट्कौशिकमयो मतः ॥ ६६
सोपूर्वः पञ्चवर्णोऽन्यः शब्दादिमय ईरितः ।
सिवर्णाद्योऽष्टमो ज्ञेयः पञ्चार्णो वचनादिकः ॥ ६७
एवं तत्त्वसमायोगात् पादक्लृप्तिरुदीरिता ।
तत्तत्पदाक्षरोत्पन्नास्तावत्यो वह्निदेवताः ॥ ६८
प्रधानमूर्त्तिप्रतिमाः स्वस्ववर्णोदितप्रभाः ।
प्रज्वलत्केशवदना भीमदंष्ट्रा भयानकाः ॥ ६९
देवता इन्द्रियोत्पन्ना ऊर्ध्वदृष्टय ईरिताः ।
देवता भूतपादोत्थास्तिर्यग्वक्त्राः प्रकीर्त्तिताः ॥ ७०
धातुरूपाक्षरोद्भूता उभयाननशोभिताः ।
ऊर्मिजा ऊर्ध्ववदना कोशोत्थास्तिर्यगाननाः ॥ ७१
एताः सर्वाः स्मृताः क्लीबा इन्द्रियार्थोद्भवाः स्त्रियः ।
अधस्तिर्यङ्मुखोपेता ईरिता वर्णदेवताः ॥ ७२

अभिचारकृतानां च मनुपादाष्टकं जपेत् ॥ इति ॥ ६२ ॥

ज्ञानेन्द्रियात्मक इति । घ्राणरसनचक्षुःश्रोत्रत्वग्रूपाणि ज्ञानेन्द्रियाणि । तदात्मकत्वं वर्णक्रमेण । एवमग्रेऽपि । कर्मेति । वाक्पाणिपादपायूपस्थानि ॥६४॥

पञ्च भूतानि । पृथिव्यप्तेजोवाय्वाकाशानि । धात्विति । त्वगसृङ्मांसमेदोऽस्थिमज्जाशुक्राणि॥ ६५ ॥

ऊर्मीति । बुभुक्षापिपासाशोकमोहजरामृत्युरूपाः । षाट्कौशिकेति । स्नाय्वस्थिमज्जात्वङ्मांसासृञ्जि । शब्दादीति । शब्दस्पर्शरूपरसगन्धाः । वचनेति । वचनादानगतिविसर्गानन्दाः ॥ ६६ ॥ ६७ ॥

एवं तत्त्वसमायोगादित्यनेन एतदक्षरैस्तत्त्वन्यासः सूचितः ॥ ६८ ॥

इन्द्रियोत्पन्ना इति । आद्यपदद्वयोत्थाः । इन्द्रियार्थोद्भवाः स्त्रियः अधस्ति-

अभिमुख्यः स्मृताः सौम्ये पराङ्मुख्योऽन्यकर्मणि ।
आम्योऽसंख्याः समुत्पन्ना देवता ज्वलिताननाः ॥ ७३
याभिर्मन्त्री दहेच्छत्रो राज्यं सगिरिकाननम् ।
अस्त्रं मनुष्यनक्षत्रेष्वारभेत विचक्षणः ॥ ७४
आसुरेषु प्रयुञ्जीत देवतारासु संहरेत् ।
पूर्वोत्तरत्रयं पश्चाद्भरण्यार्द्राऽथ रोहिणी ।
इमानि मानुषाण्याहुर्नक्षत्राणि मनीषिणः ॥ ७५
ज्येष्ठा शतभिषा मूलधनिष्ठाश्लेषकृत्तिकाः ।
चित्रामघाविशाखाः स्युस्तारा राक्षसदेवताः ॥ ७६
अश्विनी रेवती पुष्यः स्वाती हस्ता पुनर्वसुः ।
अनुराधामृगशिरःश्रवणा देवतारकाः ॥ ७७
उपक्रमेत नन्दासु रिक्तास्वस्त्रं विसर्जयेत् ।
भद्रास्वाहरणं कुर्याज्जयास्वत्यन्तमुत्तमम् ॥ ७८
उपक्रमो भौमवारे शनिवारे विसर्जनम् ।
प्रतिसंहरणं वारे गुरोः शुक्रस्य वा भवेत् ॥ ७९
स्थिरेषु राशिष्वारम्भश्चरेषु स्याद्विसर्जनम् ।
अस्त्रसंहरणं कुर्यादुभयेषु विचक्षणः ॥ ८०
कृष्णपक्षेऽनलेनाऽस्त्रं विसृजेच्छशिना पुनः ।
शुक्लपक्षे क्रमादस्त्रं पुनरात्मनि संहरेत् ॥ ८१

येङ्मुखोपेता इति सम्बन्धः । इन्द्रियार्थोद्भवा इति । अन्त्यपादद्वयोत्थाः । सर्वासामुपसंहारः । ईरिता वर्णदेवता इति ॥ ६८॥७०॥७१॥७२॥७३ ॥

नन्दास्विति । प्रतिपत्षष्ठेकादशीषु । रिक्तास्विति । चतुर्थीनवमीचतुर्दशीषु । भद्रास्विति । द्वितीयासप्तमीद्वादशीषु । जयास्विति । तृतीयाष्टमीत्रयोदशीषु । अत्यन्तमुत्तममाहरणमित्यनुषज्यते । "भद्रासु संग्रहं कुर्याज्जयासु तु विशेषतः" इत्युक्तेः ॥ ७४॥७५॥७६॥७७॥७८॥७९ ॥

स्थिरेष्विति । वृषसिंहवृश्चिककुम्भेषु । चरेष्विति । मेषकर्कटतुलामकरेषु । उभयेष्विति । द्विस्वभावेषु । मिथुनकन्याधनुर्मीनेषु ॥ ८० ॥

अनलेन तु दक्षिणनासापुटसञ्चरन्मरुता । साम्प्रदायिकास्त्वेवं मन्यन्ते ।

भानुना मोक्षसंहारौ कुर्यात्पक्षद्वये सुधीः।
पश्चिमाभिमुखो भूत्वा कर्म सर्वत्र साधयेत्॥ ८२

नक्षत्रवृक्षशकलान् साध्याख्याकर्मसंयुतान्।
तत्तन्मन्त्राक्षरोपेतान्मन्त्री मन्त्रार्णसंख्यया॥ ८३

जुहुयादेधिते वह्नौ मारयेद्रिपुमात्मनः।
कृष्णाष्टमीं समारभ्य यावत् कृष्णचतुर्दशी॥ ८४

धत्तूरविषवृक्षाक्षभूरुहोत्थान् समिद्वरान्।
राजीतैलेन संलिप्तान् पृथक् सप्तसहस्रकम्॥ ८५

जुहुयात् संयतो भूत्वा रिपुर्यमपुरं व्रजेत्।
सप्तरात्रं प्रजुहुयात् सिद्धार्थस्नेहलोलितैः॥ ८६

अत्राऽनलशब्देनाऽग्निमण्डलम्। रमिति बीजम्। कृत्तिकादिनक्षत्रमप्युच्यते। तद्वच्छशिशब्देन चन्द्रमण्डलं चन्द्रबीजं सौम्यास्तिथयश्चोच्यन्ते। तेनायमर्थः। अग्निमण्डलं स्वबीजसंयुक्तं ध्यात्वा नक्षत्रप्रधानमेव विसर्जनकर्म कुर्यात्॥ ८१॥

भानुनेति। आत्मनो भास्कररूपध्यानेन। एवमात्मनो भास्कररूपं विचिन्त्य पूर्वोक्तप्रकारेण पक्षद्वये मोक्षसंहारौ सुधीः कुर्यादित्यनुवादः। आत्मनो भास्कररूपत्वध्यानमात्रं विशेषः। तदुक्तमाचार्यैः—

नक्षत्रात्मा हुताशः स्यात्तिथ्यात्मेन्दुरुदाहृतः।
ताभ्यां करोति दिनकृद्विसर्गादानकर्मणी॥ इति॥

सर्वत्रेति। आरम्भे प्रयोगे उपसंहारे च। सामग्रीसम्पादनपूर्वकं कर्मसङ्कल्प आरम्भः। हुतक्रियाऽस्त्रविमोचनम्। दृष्टफलानन्तरमुद्वासनं संहृतिः। अन्यत्र कालनियमं विना प्रारम्भोऽप्युक्तः—

परचक्रभयादौ च तीव्ररूपे महाभये।
न कालनियमो गम्यः प्रयोगाणां कदाचन॥ इति॥ ८२॥

नक्षत्रवृक्षा द्वात्रिंशे वक्ष्यमाणाः। शकलानिति। प्रादेशमितान्। साध्याख्याकर्मसंयुतान् तत्तन्मन्त्राक्षरोपेतानि। अनेन क्रमेण

"अन्ते नाम्नो भवेन्मन्त्रः पल्लवो मारणे मतः" इति पल्लव उक्तः॥ ८३॥८४॥

विषवृक्षः कारस्करः। अक्षो विभीतकः। सिद्धार्थस्नेहं सर्षपतैलम्। ॥ ८५॥८६॥

आर्द्रवस्त्रो विष्टिकाले मरीचैर्मनुनाऽमुना ।
निगृह्यते ज्वरेणाऽरिः प्रलयाग्निसमेन सः ॥ ८७
तालपत्रे समालिख्य शत्रुनाम यथाविधि ।
आग्नेयास्त्रेण संवेष्ट्य कुण्डमध्ये निधापयेत् ॥ ८८
जुहुयान्मरिचैः क्रुद्धो ज्वराक्रान्तः स जायते ।
तदादाय क्षिपेत्तोये शीतले स वशो भवेत् ॥ ८९
पिष्ट्वाऽपामार्गबीजानि मरीचं मधुसंयुतम् ।
अत्युष्णे लवणे तोये निःक्षिप्य क्वाथयेत्ततः ॥ ९०
रुद्धतत्प्रतिकृतेर्हृदये वदने नमि ।
किञ्चित् किञ्चित् क्षिपेत्तोयं दर्व्या कारस्करोत्थया ॥ ९१
आग्नेयमुच्चरन्मन्त्री सोऽचिराज्ज्वरितो भवेत् ।
क्वथितेऽम्भसि तां क्षिप्त्वा हन्याच्छत्रुमयत्नतः ॥ ९२
तीक्ष्णस्नेहेन संलिप्तां शत्रुप्रतिकृतिं निशि ।
तापयेदेधिते वह्नौ प्रतिलोममनुं जपन् ॥ ९३
ज्वरेण बाध्यते सद्यो होमादस्य मृतिर्भवेत् ।
सामुद्रे सलिले हिङ्गुविषजीरकलोलिते ॥ ९४
क्वथिते पुत्तलिं साध्यनक्षत्रतरुनिर्मिताम् ।
अधोवक्त्रां विनिक्षिप्य यष्ट्या विषतरूत्थया ॥ ९५
तच्छिरस्ताड़नं कुर्वन् जपेदस्त्रं विलोमतः ।
सप्ताहान्मरणं याति शत्रुर्ज्वरविमोहितः ॥ ९६

विष्टिकाल इति विष्टौ करणे । विषारिघातादि च तत्र सिध्येदित्युक्तेः ॥ यथाविधीति । कर्मसहितम् । संवेष्ट्येति । परितो लेखनम् । धत्तूररसेनेति परमगुरवः ॥ ८६॥८७॥८८॥८९ ॥

कारस्करेति । कुचिला ॥ ९०॥९१॥९२ ॥

तीक्ष्णस्नेहेन सर्षपतैलेन । प्रतिलोममित्याग्नेयमस्त्रम् । होमादित्यर्थात् प्रतिकृतेः । अस्येति रिपोः ॥ ९३॥९४ ॥

सामुद्रे सलिले । लवणोदके । विलोमत इति । जातभेदोऽभिप्रायेण । तेनाग्नेयास्त्रमित्यर्थः ॥ ९४॥९५॥९६ ॥

आदित्यरथनागेन्द्रग्रस्ताङ्घ्रिं तद्विषाहतम्।
नग्नं तैलेन लिप्ताङ्गं दग्धं भानुमरीचिभिः॥ ९७

अधोमुखं निजरिपुं ध्यात्वा क्वथितवारिणा।
तर्पयेद्भानुमालोक्य शत्रुर्मृत्युप्रियो भवेत्॥ ९८

बिभ्रतीं मुशलं शूलं ध्यायन् कालघनप्रभाम्।
कार्पासबीजैर्निम्बस्य पत्रैर्मेषीघृतप्लुतैः॥ ९९

हुत्वा विद्वेषयेच्छत्रूनस्त्रेणाऽनेन देशिकः।
बिभ्राणां तर्जनीं शूलं ध्यात्वा दुर्गां भयङ्करीम्॥ १००

महिषीघृतसंसिक्तैः पल्लवैर्विषवृक्षजैः।
हुत्वा रिपोः क्षणात् सेनामुच्चाटयति मन्त्रवित्॥ १०१

ध्यात्वा देवीं पुरा प्रोक्तां चतुर्भिर्मरिचान्वितैः।
अजारुधिरसंसिक्तैर्जुहुयाद्दिवसत्रयम्॥ १०२

रिपोरुच्चाटनं कुर्यात् सेनाया नाऽत्र संशयः।
अग्निशूलकरां दुर्गां ज्वलन्तीं प्रलयाग्निवत्॥ १०३

ध्यात्वा सर्षपतैलाक्तैर्बीजैर्धत्तूरसम्भवैः।
हुत्वा विमोहयेच्छत्रून्मरिचैर्वा ससर्षपैः॥ १०४

कालाञ्जननिभां दुर्गां शूलखड्गधरां स्मरन्।
नक्तवृक्षसम्भूतैर्व्रणवृक्षस्नेहसंयुतैः॥ १०५

समिद्वरैः प्रजुहुयाद्धन्यान्मासेन वैरिणम्।
सिंहाधिरूढां धावन्तीं धावमानं रिपुं प्रति॥ १०६

शरान् कार्मुकनिर्मुक्तान् वह्निज्वालामुखाकुलान्।
मुञ्चन्तीं संस्मरन्दुर्गां तर्पयेदुष्णवारिणा।
भानुबिम्बं समालोक्य रिपोरुच्चाटनं भवेत्॥ १०७

नागेन्द्रः सर्पः। तर्पयेदिति दुर्गाम्॥ ९७॥ ९८॥

तर्जनीमिति। तर्जनीमुद्राम्। तल्लक्षणमुक्तं दुर्गापटले॥ ९९॥१००॥१०१॥

सर्षपतैलाक्तैरित्युत्तरत्राप्यन्वेति॥ १०२॥ १०३॥ १०४॥

व्रणवृक्षो भल्लातः॥ १०५॥ १०६॥ १०७॥

अतिदुर्गामयोन्मुष्टिगदाहस्तां विचिन्तयेत् ।
विद्युद्दामसमानाभां महिषीघृतसंप्लुतैः ॥ १०८

पुलाकैर्जुहुयान्निम्बविभीतकसमिद्वरैः ।
कोद्रवैरथ शत्रोश्च सेनायाः स्तम्भनं भवेत् ॥ १०९

आत्तपाशाङ्कुशां रक्तां गणिदुर्गामनु स्मरेत् ।
लोणैः समधुरैः साध्यवृक्षकाष्ठैर्धितेऽनले ॥ ११०

जुहुयान्निशि सप्ताहान्मन्त्रविद्दशयेन्नृपान् ।
पाशाङ्कुशधरां रक्तां विश्वदुर्गां विचिन्तयेत् ॥ १११

फलिनीकुसुमैः फुल्लैश्चन्दनाम्भःसमुक्षितैः ।
जुहुयान्निशि यो मन्त्री तस्य विश्वं वशं भवेत् ॥ ११२

शरच्चन्द्रनिभां देवीं विगलत्परमामृताम् ।
पाशाङ्कुशधरां ध्यायन् सिन्धुदुर्गां समिद्वरैः ॥ ११३

वैतसैर्मधुरासिक्तैर्जुहुयात् वृष्टिसिद्धये ।
कपालं त्रिशिखं पाशमङ्कुशं बिभ्रतीं करैः ॥ ११४

जवाकुसुमसंकाशामग्निदुर्गां विचिन्तयन् ।
हुत्वा लवणपुत्तल्या मधुरत्रययुक्तया ॥ ११५

आकर्षेद्वाञ्छितान् साध्यान्मन्त्रविन्नाऽत्र संशयः ।
अतिदुर्गयमल्याद्या षडन्ता त्रिष्टुबीरिता ॥ ११६

दुर्वर्णान्ताऽथ गणाद्या गणिदुर्गा समीरिता ।
विश्वाद्या ग्यन्तवर्णान्ता सा विश्वदुर्गा समीरिता ॥ ११७

सिन्ध्वाद्या सा वकारान्ता सिन्धुदुर्गा निगद्यते ।
त्यन्तामग्न्यादिकामेनामग्निदुर्गां विदुर्बुधाः ॥ ११८

अतिदुर्गादयः पञ्च जातवेदोमन्त्रभेदा एव वक्ष्यमाणाः। पुलाकैस्तुच्छधान्यैः। अतीति। अतिदुर्गाणि विश्वा इत्यारभ्य परिषदन्ता सर्वा ऋक्। एवमग्रेऽपि। गूढार्थदीपिकाकारस्तु। अतिषदिति। त्रिवर्णं मन्त्रं वदन् भ्रान्तमेव ॥१०८॥१०९॥११०॥१११॥११२॥११३॥११४॥११५॥११६॥११७॥११८॥

अङ्गणे स्थण्डिलं कृत्वा सुगन्धिकुसुमादिभिः ।
देवीमभ्यर्चयेन्नित्यं प्रागुक्तेनैव वर्त्मना ॥ ११९
आहरेद्द्वारदिक्षु बलिं चरुणा सर्वसिद्धिदम् ।
कृत्यारोगभयद्रोहभूतादीन्नाऽत्र संशयः ॥ १२०
यथावदग्निमाराध्य गन्धैः पुष्पैर्मनोरमैः ।
स्थित्वा तस्याऽग्रतो मन्त्री जपेन्मन्त्रमनन्यधीः ॥ १२१
जपोऽयं सर्वसिद्ध्यै स्यान्नाऽत्र कार्या विचारणा ।
लवणैर्मधुरासिक्तैर्जुहुयात्पश्चिमामुखः ॥ १२२
मन्त्रार्णसंख्यया मन्त्री रिपुमात्मवशं नयेत् ।
शालीन् प्रक्षाल्य संशोष्य शुभ्रान् कुर्वीत तण्डुलान् ॥ १२३
जपित्वा पञ्चगव्येषु संस्कृते हव्यवाहने ।
चरुं पचेज्जपन्मन्त्रमवतार्य पुनः सुधीः ॥ १२४
अर्चयित्वा विशदधीर्देवीमग्नौ यथा पुरा ।
जुहुयाच्चरुणाऽनेन साज्येनाऽष्टसहस्रकम् ॥ १२५
पात्रे सम्पातनं कुर्वन् साध्यं तत् प्राशयेत् सुधीः ।
शेषं तं निखनेद् वारिसम्पातं प्राङ्गणान्तरे ॥ १२६
कृत्या रोगा विनश्यन्ति सह भूतग्रहामयैः ।
परैकृत्यादिता कृत्या पुनस्तानेव भक्षयेत् ॥ १२७
व्रीहिभिर्हविषा क्षीरैः पयोवृक्षसमिद्वरैः ।
आज्यैर्मधुवयोपेतैरेतैर्दशशतं पृथक् ॥ १२८
जुहुयात् सम्पदां भूमिः साधको भवति ध्रुवम् ।
भास्करे मेषराशिस्थे मन्त्रज्ञोऽनुगुणे दिने ॥ १२९
नद्यां सागरगामिन्यां सततं पुष्कलाम्भसि ।
उद्धृत्यादाय सिकताः संशोष्य परिशोधयेत् ॥ १३०

तस्येत्यग्ने: ॥ ११९—१२९ ॥

सिकताप्रयोगमाह भास्कर इति। सागरगामिन्यामिति साक्षात्। पञ्च-गव्येष्विति। आलोडनपर्याप्तेषु। गृहग्रामादीत्यादि शब्देन नगरम्। प्रक्षेति।

न्यस्य ताः पञ्चगव्येषु संस्कृते हव्यवाहने ।
भर्जयेन्मनुना सिद्ध्यै दर्व्या ब्रह्मकहोत्यया ॥ १३१
सिंहमेषधनुस्थेऽर्के कृष्णपक्षेऽष्टमीतिथौ ।
विशाखाकृत्तिकामूलहस्तोत्तरमघास्वथ ॥ १३२
रोहिण्यां श्रवणे वारौ मन्दवाक्पतिदैवतौ ।
विहायाऽन्येषु कुर्वीत सिकतास्थापनं सुधीः ॥ १३३
गृहग्रामादिराष्ट्राणां रक्षार्थं सिकताः शुभाः ।
प्रस्थाढकघटोन्माना मध्यादिष्ववटेष्विमाः ॥ १३४
नवसु प्रक्षिपेज्जप्तास्तेषु सम्पूजयेत् क्रमात् ।
मध्यादि देवीशस्त्राणि कपालान्तानि देशिकः ॥ १३५
चक्रं शङ्खमसिं खेटं बाणश्चापं त्रिशूलकम् ।
कपालं स्वस्वमन्त्रेण सम्पूज्याऽन्ते बलिं हरेत् ॥ १३६
नक्षत्रग्रहराशीनां लोकेशानां बलिं हरेत् ।
विहिता यत्र रक्षेयं वर्धन्ते तत्र सम्पदः ॥ १३७
क्षुद्रग्रहमहारोगसौरभूतसरीसृपाः ।
अमुना विलयं यान्ति विधिना नाऽत्र संशयः ॥ १३८

गृहे प्रस्थमिताः । ग्रामे नगरे आढकमिताः । राष्ट्रे घटोन्मिताः । अशीतिगुञ्जः कर्षः । चतुर्गुणः पलम् । चतुष्पलः कुडवः । चतुःकुडवः प्रस्थः । प्रस्थचतुष्कमाढकः । आढकचतुष्कं द्रोणः । द्रोणचतुष्कं घटः । दशाङ्गुलाधिकं चतुर्विंशत्यङ्गुलं केचिदाहुः ॥ १२८॥१३०॥१३१॥१३२॥१३३॥१३४॥१३५ ॥

स्वस्वमन्त्रेणेति । सप्तदशोक्तेन । अन्ते बलिमिति । देव्याः चक्राद्यस्त्राणां च । ॥ १३५ ॥ १३६ ॥

नक्षत्रेत्यधिपतीनामप्युपलक्षकम् । एषां बलिमन्त्राः । अश्विनीदेवताभ्यो दिवानक्तञ्चारिभ्यः सर्वेभ्यो भूतेभ्यो नमः । एवं भरणीकृत्तिकापाददेवताभ्यः कृत्तिकापादत्रयदेवताभ्य इत्याद्यूह्यम् । ततस्तदधिपतिभ्यः अश्विन्यधिपत्यश्विदेवताभ्यः । एवं यमादिषूह्यम् । ततो राशिबलिः । अश्विनीभरणीकृत्तिकापादे मेषदेवताभ्यस्तदधिपतिभ्यः । एवं वृषादिषूह्यम् । ततो ग्रहबलिः । अश्विनीभरणीकृत्तिकापादमेषराश्यधिपत्यङ्गारकदेवताभ्यः । एवमन्येषामप्यूह्यम् ।

सिकतानां विशुद्धानां विकारकुडवं सुधीः ।
पञ्चगव्ययुते पात्रे ब्रह्मवृक्षेण निर्मिते ॥ १३९

निक्षिप्य विधिना यत्र स्थापयेत्तत्र सम्पदः ।
दिने दिने प्रवर्धन्ते कालवृष्ट्यादिभिः सह ॥ १४०

महोत्पाता विनश्यन्ति कृत्याद्रोहमहाग्रहाः ।
चरुगव्याश्मनां कुर्यात् स्थापनं विधिनाऽमुना ॥ १४१
गोमूत्रं प्रस्थमानं स्याद्गोमयात्स्यात्तदर्द्धकम् ।
आज्यात् सप्तगुणं क्षीरं गोमूत्रात् त्रिगुणं दधि ॥ १४२

गोमूत्रेण समं सर्पिः सर्वं वा सममुच्यते ।
गावः स्युः कपिलाश्वेतहिमधूम्रारुणप्रभाः ।
अभावे गदिताः सर्वाः सर्वथा कपिलोद्भवम् ॥ १४३

लोकेशबलिर्बास्तौ मदुक्तोऽनुसन्धेयः । बलिं हरेदिति परितः ॥ १३७॥१३८ ॥

विशुद्धानामिति । नद्यामित्याद्युक्तप्रकारेण । विकारकुडवं षोडशकुडवम् । प्रस्थं गोमूत्रादीनाम् ॥ १३९॥१४०॥१४१ ॥

विधिनेति । पूर्वोक्तस्थापनप्रकारेण । चर्वश्मनोः । गव्ये तु विशेषो नारायणीये—

गव्येषु शालीन् यवमुद्गमाषगोधूमबिल्वास्थितिलाब्जबीजम् ।
पञ्चच्छदस्थं विनिधाय पात्रे क्षुद्रा निखन्याद्भुवि नागयोगे ॥

नागयोगमाहात्म्यः—

सार्पे मुहूर्ते सर्पर्क्षकरणे सर्पसंज्ञिते ।
संयोगो नागयोगोऽयमथवा करणर्क्षयोः ॥ इति ॥

पृथक् शिरः पञ्च सरोजपत्रं छिद्रमेकीकृतवद्धनालम् ।
गव्ये प्रपूर्णे निखनेदधूनां[नन्न] स्मृत्वा तदा क्षुद्रविनाशि गेहे ॥ इति ॥

तत्स्थापननक्षत्रादिकमपि तत्रैव—

पूषा पुष्यपुनर्वसू वसुहरी चित्रा भगो[तथा] रोहिणी
तारास्तास्तिथयोऽश्रमतफणियमा दिक्पञ्चदशी हरिः ।
वारास्त्विन्दुसुतेन्दुशुक्रगुरवो युग्मं कुलीरो धनुः
कुम्भान्त्यावपि राशयो निगदिता गव्यप्रयोगाय ते ॥ इति ॥

समं वेति । वाशब्देनान्यत् प्रकारद्वयमुपक्षिप्तम् । योजने तत्तक्रमेण

एकोनपञ्चाशत्कोष्ठे फलके ब्रह्मशाखिनः ।
विहाय कोणकोष्ठानि शक्त्याद्यं जातवेदसम् ॥ १४४

लिखित्वा मध्यकोष्ठादि पूजयेत्तत्र देवताम् ।
कृत्वा होमं समस्यान्ते निखनेत्तद्यथा पुरा ।
दद्याद् बलिं यथा पूर्वमस्य पूर्वोदितं फलम् ॥ १४५

मध्ये मायामष्टकोष्ठेषु पादानष्टौ कृत्वा मातृकार्णैः प्रवीतम् ।
भूबिम्बस्थं सर्वभूतामयघ्नं रक्षायुःश्रीकीर्त्तिदं यन्त्रमेतत् ॥ १४६

आग्नेयास्त्रस्य स्थानानि विसर्गादानकर्मणो ।
यः पुमान् गुरुणा शिष्टस्तस्याऽधीनं जगत्त्रयम् ॥ १४७

इति श्रीशारदातिलके एकविंशः पटलः ।

योजनमित्यपि ज्ञेयम् । तदुक्तम्—

मूत्रं प्रस्थं गोमयं स्यात्पलार्द्धं क्षीरं प्रस्थं दध्यपि क्षीरतोऽर्द्धम् ।
आज्यं दध्नोऽप्यर्द्धमेवं प्रमाणं स्वीयैर्मन्त्रैर्योजयेत् पञ्चगव्यम् ॥
मूत्रं द्विभागं शकृदेकभागं पयोऽष्टभागं दधि तत्समानम् ।
क्षीरार्द्धकं वा चतुरंशमाज्यम् । इति ।

मन्त्रास्त्वाचार्यैरुक्ताः । तद्यथा—

तारभवाभिरथगर्भिः क्रमेण संयोजयेच्च गव्यानि ।
आम्नाष्टाक्षरमन्त्रैरथवा योज्यानि पञ्चभिः पञ्च ॥ इति ॥

॥ १४१॥१४२॥१४३ ॥

एकोनपञ्चाशदिति । पूर्वापरायतदक्षिणोत्तरायताष्टाष्ट रेखाक्रमेण । तत्र मध्यकोष्ठे शक्तिबीजं लिखित्वा पूर्वाद्यावृत्तित्रयेण जातवेदोमन्त्रं लिखेत् । तत्र तृतीयावृत्तौ । आद्ये कोणचतुष्टयपरित्यागः ॥ १४४॥१४५ ॥

यन्त्रमाह मध्य इति । पूर्वापरायता दक्षिणोत्तरायताश्चतस्रो रेखाः कुर्यात् । तदा नवकोष्ठं भवति । मध्य इति । मध्यकोष्ठे ॥ १४६ ॥

विसर्गादानकर्म्मणोति । विसर्गः संहारः । आदानं प्रयोगानन्तरं पुनर्मन्त्रस्वाकारः । यदाहुः—

विधिवन्मारणं कृत्वा सिद्धमन्त्रेण मन्त्रवित् ।
कर्मान्ते देवतापूजां सविशेषं प्रकल्पयेत् ॥

शक्त्या सन्तर्प्य विप्रांश्च मन्त्रमूर्तिं विसृज्य च ।
समुद्रगायां नद्यां तु कण्ठमात्रे जले स्थितः ॥
अहोरात्रं जपेन्मन्त्रमष्टाधिकसहस्रकम् ।
शुद्धं मनुं तं स्वीकुर्यात् । इति ॥ १४७ ॥

इति श्रीशारदातिलकटीकायां सत्सम्प्रदायकृतव्याख्यायां
पदार्थादर्शाभिख्यायामेकविंशः पटलः ॥ ॐ ॥

द्वाविंशः पटलः ।

अथो दिनास्त्रं कृत्यास्त्रं वक्ष्ये शत्रुविमर्दनम् ।
अतिदुर्गामनुं प्राहुर्दिनास्त्रं मन्त्रवित्तमाः ॥ १

प्रतिलोममिमं मन्त्रं कृत्यास्त्रं परिचक्ष्यते ।
दिनास्त्रस्य षडङ्गादीन् प्रतिलोमोदितान् विदुः ॥ २

भानुबिम्बगतं शत्रुमधोवक्त्रं विषाहतम् ।
मूलादुत्थितया ग्रस्तं कुण्डल्या भावयेत् सुधीः ॥ ३

अथो इति । अतिदुर्गामनुः पूर्वोक्तः ॥ १ ॥

इममतिदुर्गामनुम् । षडङ्गादीनित्यादिशब्देनाऽक्षरपदन्यासावुभयत्र । अनुलोमोदितान् जातवेदसे इत्यत्रोक्तान् । जातवेदसे ह्यङ्गाद्यन्तैरिति सम्प्रदायात् ।

तदुक्तम्—मनोराद्यपदेनैव षट्पदानि च पूर्ववत् ।
ह्यङ्गाद्यन्तेन तानि स्युरतिदुर्गामनोरपि ॥ इति ॥

आचार्या अपि—अनुलोमजपेऽङ्गानामपि पाठोऽनुलोमकः । इति ।
पद्मपादाचार्यैर्व्याख्यातम् अपिशब्दात् पदाक्षरयोरपीति ।
प्रतिलोमोदितानित्याग्नेयास्त्रोक्तान् ।

तदुक्तम्—शैलाब्धिलोकाङ्गमुनिरससंख्याक्षरैः क्रमात् ।
मनोरस्त्रविलोमस्य षडङ्गान्यपि कल्पयेत् ॥ इति ॥

आचार्याश्च—प्रतिलोमानि तानि स्युः प्रतिलोमविधौ तथा । इति ।
अत्रापि तथेति पूर्ववत् पद्मपादाचार्यैर्व्याख्यातम् । अनयोर्ध्यानं यथा—

उद्यानमध्ये पूर्वोक्तसिंहस्कन्धोपरिस्थिताम् ।
कालमेघनिभामुग्रां सर्पभूषणभूषिताम् ॥
शूलं खड्गं कुठारं च खर्परखेटकतर्जनीः ।
दधानां दक्षिणान्यैः स्वैः करदण्डैरितस्ततः ।
अतिदुर्गामनोर्मूर्त्तिं धावमानां विचिन्तयेत् ॥ इति ॥
वरदारिदराभीति पाणिपद्मैर्विराजिताम् ।
तामन्त्यप्रतिलोमाख्यां सिंहस्थां चिन्तयेत् समाम् ॥ इति ।

पुरश्चरणं तु जातवेदोमन्त्रपुरश्चरणेनैव ज्ञेयम् ॥ २ ॥

विषाहतमिति । भानुरथगत-सर्पविषैराहतमित्यर्थः ॥ ३ ॥

मूलाधारे क्षिपेत्तस्य: प्रस्फुरत्कालपावके ।
दिनत्रयात् ज्वराक्रान्तो रिपु: प्राणान् विमुञ्चति ॥ ४

दिनास्त्रेण प्रविद्धाङ्गं स्वाधिष्ठानगतं रिपुम् ।
पञ्चवायुसमिद्धेन वह्निना दग्धविग्रहम् ॥ ५

ध्यायन्मनुं जपेत् सद्य: स भवेद्यमवल्लभ: ।
मणिपूरगतं शत्रुमग्निना दीप्तविग्रहम् ॥ ६
ध्यायन् दिनास्त्रं प्रजपेत् स मृत्युवशतां व्रजेत् ।
अनाहताहित: शत्रुर्निर्दग्धो मन्त्रवह्निना ॥ ७
पाशेन बद्ध्वा शीघ्रेण नीयते यमकिङ्करै: ।
विशुद्धस्थानगो वैरी दिनबाणेन पीड़ित: ॥ ८
अधोमुख: मृतस्तूर्णं निरायु: स्याद्दिनत्रयात् ।
आज्ञायां निहितं शत्रुं दहेत् ज्ञानाग्निना धिया ॥ ९

पुत्रमित्रकलत्रादीन् हित्वा मृत्युमुपाश्रयेत् ।
नाभिमात्रोदके स्थित्वा ध्यायन् विम्बे दिनेशितु: ॥ १०
वैरिणं दग्धसर्वाङ्गं मन्त्रमष्टोत्तरं शतम् ।
जपेत् सप्तदिनादर्वाग्यमलोकं स गच्छति ॥ ११
आरवारं समारभ्य सप्ताहं प्रजपेन्मनुम् ।
सूर्योदयं समारभ्य यावदस्तमयो भवेत् ॥ १२
सन्निपातज्वराविष्टो यमग्रस्तो भवेदरि: ।
स्थित्वा दुर्गालये मन्त्री त्रिरात्रं वर्जिताशन: ॥ १३
दिनबाणेन विद्धाङ्गं वैरिणं प्रविचिन्तयेत् ।
जपेन्मनुमिमं शत्रुर्ज्वरितो मरणं व्रजेत् ॥ १४

मूलाधारे गुदमेढ्रान्तरालदेशे । प्रस्फुरत्कालपावक इति ध्यानम् ॥ ४ ॥

स्वाधिष्ठानं लिङ्गोपरिदेश: । मणिपूरकं नाभिस्थानम् । अनाहतं हृदयम् । विशुद्धि: कण्ठ: । दिनबाणेन दिनास्त्रेण । आज्ञा भ्रूमध्यम् । मन्त्रमिति । जपेदित्यनेन सम्बध्यते ॥ ५ ॥ ६ ॥ ७ ॥ ८ ॥ ९ ॥ १० ॥ ११ ॥

आरो भौम: । प्रजपेदिति । पूर्ववदरिं ध्यायन् ॥ १२॥१३॥१४ ॥

स्पृष्ट्वा [स्मृत्वा] दुर्गां जपेन्मन्त्रमनग्नस्त्रिदिनं स्मरन् ।
शूलप्रोतं निजरिपुं दिनास्त्रेण प्रदीपितम् ॥ १५
ज्वरेण महताऽऽविष्टो जायतेऽसौ यमातिथिः ।
रविमण्डलगं शत्रुं दष्टं तद्रथपन्नगैः ॥ १६
विषाग्निदग्धसर्वाङ्गं ध्यायन्नुष्णेन वारिणा ।
तर्पयेद्दिनवाणेन स्यादसौ यमवल्लभः ॥ १७
रविबिम्बादागतया ज्वालया ग्रस्तविग्रहम् ।
रिपुं ध्यात्वा जपेन्मन्त्रं स क्रीडति यमान्तिके ॥ १८
ग्रहयुक्तार्कबिम्बस्थं विद्धं मन्त्रमयैः शरैः ।
प्रतिबध्य निजं शत्रुं जपेदयुतमस्त्रवित् ॥ १९
रिपुं नयति शीघ्रेण यमदूतो यमालयम् ।
प्रलयानलसङ्काशां कालरात्रिमिवाऽपराम् ॥ २०
शूलपाशधरां घोरां सिंहस्कन्धनिषेदुषीम् ।
सवितुर्मण्डलान्तःस्थां रक्तनेत्रत्रयोद्गतैः ॥ २१
विस्फुलिङ्गैर्निर्दहन्तीं रिपुमाकुलविग्रहम् ।
स्पष्टदंष्ट्राधरां नृत्यद्भ्रुकुटीभीषणाननाम् ॥ २२
तर्जयन्तीं निजं शत्रुं तर्जन्या भीमरूपया ।
दंष्ट्रामयूखजालेन द्योतयन्तीं दिगन्त[म्ब]रम् ॥ २३
शूलेन वैरिणो वक्षो दारयन्तीं भयङ्करीम् ।
जपेद्दिनत्रयं मन्त्री मारयेद्रिपुमात्मनः ॥ २४
अस्त्रमन्त्रकृतन्यासः प्रलयाग्निसमप्रभाम् ।
रक्तवस्त्रधरां क्रुद्धां रक्तनेत्रत्रयान्विताम् ॥ २५
सिंहाधिरूढां धावन्तीं धावमानं रिपुं प्रति ।
खड्गेन तच्छिरश्छित्वा क्षणाद्व्योमस्थलीं गताम् ॥ २६

विषाग्नीति । विषं तद्रथपन्नगसम्भूतमेव १५॥१६॥१७॥१८ ॥

ग्रहयुक्तो राहुग्रस्तः । प्रतिबध्य ध्यात्वेत्यर्थः ॥ १९ ॥ २० ॥

प्रलयानलेत्यादि भयङ्करीमित्यन्तस्य ध्यात्वेति शेषः ॥ २०—२७ ॥

ध्यात्वा दुर्गां जपेन्मन्त्रं त्रिदिनं वर्जिताशनः।
अनेनैव विधानेन रिपुर्मृत्युप्रियो भवेत्॥ २७

कर्माण्येतानि कुर्वीत दिवसे न तु रात्रिषु।
पश्चिमामुखलिङ्गस्य सजीवं महिषं पुरः॥ २८

निखा[धा]य तस्य शिरसि कुण्डं कृत्वा त्रिकोणकम्।
तस्मिन् समेधिते वह्नौ यथावद्देशिकोत्तमः॥ २९

सत्रिकोणान् समन्त्वार्णान् साध्यनामसमन्वितान्।
अजारक्तेन संसिक्तान् कारस्करसमिद्वरान्॥ ३०

सहस्रं जुहुयाद्देवीं ध्यात्वा सत्रिह्मण्डले।
प्रलयाग्निसमां घोरां द्वात्रिंशद्भुजशोभिताम्॥ ३१

उद्यदायुधसन्दीप्तां नृत्यन्तीं सिंहमस्तके।
महादंष्ट्रां महाभीमां ज्वलत्केशीं नदन्मुखीम्॥ ३२

रक्तान्त्र[द्र]मांसवदनां घूर्णितोग्रविलोचनाम्।
अनेन विधिना शत्रुर्महाज्वरनिपीड़ितः॥ ३३

विमुञ्चति निजं देहं पुत्रमित्रादिभिः सह।
ऊर्ध्वमुखान्नसौ मन्त्री लम्बयित्वा भुजङ्गमम्॥ ३४

भानुविम्बगतां दुर्गां सहस्रादित्यसन्निभाम्।
सहस्रपाणिचरणां सहस्राक्षिशिरोमुखीम्॥ ३५

सहस्रनागवद्धाङ्गीं त्रासयन्तीं जगत्त्रयम्।
ध्यायन्ननेन सर्पास्ये तर्पयेदुष्णवारिणा॥ ३६

संयतः कालपाशेन वैरी मुञ्चेत् स्वजीवितम्।
मध्याह्नार्कायुतप्रख्यां नदन्तीं नरसिंहवत्॥ ३७

पश्चिमामुखेति। शिवालयद्वारस्य पश्चिममुखता। केचित् स्थावरलिङ्गस्य पश्चिमामुखतामाहुः। एष एव साम्प्रदायिकः पक्षः। सत्रिकोणानिति। लिखितत्रिकोणान्। समन्त्वार्णानिति। पल्लवरीत्या॥२८॥२९॥३०॥३१॥३२॥३३॥

भुजङ्गममिति। जीवन्तं कृष्णम्। अधोमुखम्। अनेनास्त्रमन्त्रेण। तर्पये-

घोरसिंहसमासीनां महाभीषणदर्शनाम् ।
शूलप्रोताहितां ध्यायन् जपन्मन्त्रमनन्यधीः ॥ ३८

तर्पयेदुष्णतोयेन सर्पवक्त्रो दिनत्रयम् ।
यमस्य भवनं गच्छेदरातिर्नात्र संशयः ॥ ३९

रुद्रवृक्षप्रतिकृतिं प्रतिष्ठितसमीरणाम् ।
उष्णोदके विनिक्षिप्य विषाक्ते विधिना ततः ॥ ४०

अर्केन्द्वनलसङ्काशां खड्गखेटकधारिणीम् ।
नयनत्रयनिर्गच्छद्विस्फुलिङ्गशताकुलाम् ॥ ४१

सिंहस्थां सर्पभूषाढ्यां त्रैलोक्यभयदायिनीम् ।
खड्गकृत्ताहितां ध्यायन् प्रजपेदयुतं मनुम् ॥ ४२

विधानेनाऽमुना शत्रुर्यन्त्रो भवति मृत्युना ।
प्रकल्प्य दुर्गायतने त्रिकोणं कुण्डमुत्तमम् ॥ ४३

तत्र संज्वलिते वह्नौ महिषीमकृता कृताम् ।
पुत्तलीमजरक्ताक्तां प्रतिष्ठितसमीरणाम् ॥ ४४

छित्वा छित्वा प्रजुहुयादजरक्तान्वितां निशि ।
ध्यात्वा दुर्गां प्रनृत्यन्तीं महिषोरःस्थलान्तरे ॥ ४५

शूलेन महिषस्याऽङ्गं भिन्दन्तीं घोरदर्शनाम् ।
अट्टहासैरजस्त्रोत्थैर्भीषितासुरसैनिकाम् ॥ ४६

प्रलयानलसङ्काशां भ्रमन्नेत्रत्रयान्विताम् ।
सन्दष्टाधरसंभिन्नां दंष्ट्राभीममुखाम्बुजाम् ॥ ४७

खड्गखेटकयुक्ताभिः कन्यकाभिः समावृताम् ।
अनेन विधिना शत्रुः प्रयाति यमसन्निधिम् ॥ ४८

दिनास्त्वमेवं कथितं शत्रुनिग्रहकारकम् ।
कृत्यास्त्वदेशितान् कुर्यात् प्रयोगान् मन्त्रवित्तमः ॥ ४९

दिति । कारस्करदर्व्या । अनन्यधीरित्यनेन तथैव तर्पणमित्युक्तम् ॥ ३४—३९ ॥

विधिना मनुं प्रजपेदित्यन्वयः । विधिः पल्लवेन नामयोगः । खड्गेन कृत्तः छिन्नः भक्षितः शत्रुर्येति ॥ ४०—४९ ॥

आधाराद्गतां देवीं कुण्डलीं सर्प[वं]रूपिणीम् ।
तां ब्रह्मरन्ध्रमार्गेण यातां व्योमस्थलीं ततः ॥ ५०
मुखेन शत्रुमादाय निवृत्तां स्वगृहं प्रति ।
ज्वलत्कालानलोद्दीप्तां विचिन्त्य प्रजपेन्मनुम् ॥ ५१
सप्तभिर्वासरैः शत्रुर्मृत्युं प्राप्नोति मोहितः ।
अङ्गारवारे चित्यग्नौ सर्षपस्नेहलोलितम् ॥ ५२
सिद्धार्थकुडवं जप्तं जुहुयात्पञ्चमालतः ।
कृत्यास्त्रज्वालया दग्धो रिपुर्यमपुरं व्रजेत् ॥ ५३
चतुर्दश्यामर्द्धरात्रे चितास्थीन्यस्त्रसाधकः ।
व्रणतैलविलिप्तानि चिताग्नौ जुहुयात्ततः ॥ ५४
अनेन विधिना शत्रुर्मृत्युमेष्यति कातरः ।
तुषास्थिनिर्मितां शत्रोर्व्रणतैलपरिप्लुताम् ॥ ५५
प्रतिमां स्थापितप्राणां जुहुयान्निशि साधकः ।
छित्वा छित्वाऽजरक्तेन सप्ताहान् म्रियते रिपुः ॥ ५६
श्मशानबालुकाः स्पृष्ट्वा सात्तता नियुतं जपेत् ।
विकिरेत्तास्तडागादौ कृत्यास्त्रकथितं जलम् ॥ ५७
तदीयं पीतमचिरान्निहन्ति सकलान् जनान् ।
कृष्णाङ्गारचतुर्दश्यां प्रजप्तैः प्रेतभस्मभिः ॥ ५८
महिष्याज्येन लुलितास्तन्मन्त्राक्षरसंख्यया ।
निर्माय गुटिका एताः सम्यग्जप्तसमीरणाः ॥ ५९
चितिकाष्ठैर्धिते वह्नौ जुहुयाद्दृढमानसः ।
चतुर्दशीवयादर्वाक् शत्रुर्मृत्युवशो भवेत् ॥ ६०

चित्यग्नाविति । कुण्डस्थापिते यथोक्तसंस्कारसंस्कृते । व्रणतैलं भल्लाततैलम् ॥ ५०॥५१॥५२॥५३॥५४॥५५ ॥

तुषा धान्यस्य । अस्थीति मनुष्यास्थीनि । एतदुभयमेकीकृत्य प्रतिमां कुर्यात् ॥ ५५॥५६ ॥

कृत्यास्त्रकथितमिति । तड़ागादौ सिकताप्रक्षेपेण ॥ ५७॥५८॥५९॥६० ॥

श्मशानभस्मसिद्धार्थान् पञ्चगव्ये विनिक्षिपेत् ।
माहिषे संस्मरेद्देवीं कालाग्निसदृशप्रभाम् ॥ ६१
भर्जयेत् प्रजपन्मन्त्रं विषकाष्ठेधितानले ।
दुर्गागारं प्रजुहुयाद्दनेनाऽयुतमन्त्रवित् ॥ ६२
पुनरादाय तद्भस्म सेनायां वैरिणः क्षिपेत् ।
सा सेना बहुधा भिन्ना ज्वररोगविमोहिता ॥ ६३
आयुधानि परित्यज्य युद्धकाले पलायते ।
गेहग्रामादिषु क्षिप्तं कुर्यादुच्चाटनं क्षणात् ॥ ६४
सप्तवारेषु कुलिके दुर्गाविश्वासु शर्कराः ।
सप्त माहेन्द्रदिग्वर्जं गृहीत्वा प्रजपेन्मनुम् ॥ ६५
माहिषीपञ्चगव्येन भर्जयेत्ता यथा पुरा ।
भूयो जपित्वा विकिरेद्द् गेहग्रामपुरेष्विमाः ॥ ६६
स देशो नश्यति क्षिप्रं दग्धो मन्त्रसवाग्निना ।
ब्रह्मदण्डीं मर्कटिकां करक्रोशनिकां त्रयम् ॥ ६७
भौमवारस्य कुलिके गृहीत्वा प्रजपेन्मनुम् ।
चतुर्दश्यां रिपोर्गेहे निखनेत् प्रजपन्मनुम् ॥ ६८
साद्धं पुत्रकलत्राद्यैरुत्सादो जायते रिपोः ।
एकैकं वा खनेन्मन्त्री मण्डलात् तत्फलं भवेत् ॥ ६९
षड्बिन्दुषट्कं पुत्तल्यां निखनेदोदनान्वितम् ।
स्पृष्ट्वा तां प्रजपेदस्त्रं कृष्णाष्टम्यां निशार्द्धतः ॥ ७०

माहिषे पञ्चगव्ये प्रयोग उपचारात् ॥ ६१॥६२॥६३॥६४ ॥

सप्तवारेष्विति। सप्तवाराणामपि कुलिका मया एकादशी उक्ताः। तत्र प्राचीवर्जं दुर्गालयाग्नेयादिसप्तस्थानशर्करासु एकैकां शर्करां क्रमात् प्रत्यहं रव्यादेः कुलिके गृहीत्वा सप्तमेऽहनि सर्वा एकीकृत्य स्पृष्ट्वा प्रजपेत्। यथा पुरेति। विषकाष्ठाग्नौ विषकाष्ठदर्व्या भर्जयेत् ॥ ६५॥६६॥६७ ॥

मर्कटी कपिकच्छुः। करक्रोशनिका वज्रदण्डः। उत्सादः पुनरप्यागमनं यथा न भवति तथा उच्चाटनम् ॥ ६७॥६८॥६९ ॥

षड्बिन्दुषट्कमिति। षड्बिन्दुः कीटविशेषः। स च प्रथमजलपाते उत्पद्यते।

शत्रुनामसमायुक्तं श्मशाने निखनेदिमाम्।
प्रणश्येत् स रिपुः शीघ्रं सकुटुम्बः सबान्धवः॥ ७१

कपालशकलान्मन्त्री कृत्वाऽस्त्राक्षरसंख्यकान्।
स्पृष्ट्वा तान् प्रजपेदस्त्रं प्राणस्थापनपूर्वकम्॥ ७२

कृष्णाङ्गारचतुर्दश्यां श्मशाने विषवृक्षजे।
जुहुयादजरक्ताक्तान् कृत्यास्त्रज्वालया ततः॥ ७३

रिपुर्यमपुरं गच्छेन्महाज्वरविमोहितः।
अजरक्तेन संपूर्णे कलशे निक्षिपेदहिम्॥ ७४

कपालेन पिधायैनं छादयेद्रक्तवाससा।
पूजयेद्रक्तपुष्पाद्यैः स्पृष्ट्वा तमयुतं जपेत्॥ ७५

भौमवारे निशामध्ये कारस्करसमेधिते।
श्मशानवह्नौ जुहुयाद् गच्छेद्यमपुरं रिपुः॥ ७६

साव्यनचलवृक्षेण कृत्वा कुम्भं प्रपूरयेत्।
माहिषैः पञ्चगव्यैस्तं विड़ालं तत्र निक्षिपेत्॥ ७७

जपपूजादिकं सर्वं यथापूर्वं समाचरेत्।
कारस्करभवे वह्नौ कृत्यास्त्रेण समेधिते॥ ७८

तस्य पञ्चकुष्ठ इति नामान्तरम्। तस्य पञ्च बिन्दवः श्वेता भवन्ति। एकबिन्दुः भिन्नवर्णः। तदुक्तं नीतिनिर्णीतादौपनिषदोः—

पञ्चकुष्ठस्य कीटस्य पञ्च स्युः श्वेतबिन्दवः।
भिन्नवर्णस्तथा चैकः सुस्निग्धश्चैव वर्णतः।
भवेत् स जलदारम्भे षड्बिन्दुरिति कीर्त्तितः॥ इति।

पुत्तल्यामिति। तज्जन्मर्क्षवृक्षोद्भवायाम्। शत्रोर्नामसंयुक्तम् अस्त्रमस्त्रमन्त्रं प्रजपेदित्यन्वयः। तत्र योगः पल्लवरीत्या। क्वचित् समायुक्तामिति पाठः। तदा पुत्तलीविशेषणम्॥ ७०॥७१॥

कपालशकलान् अजरक्ताक्तान् श्मशाने जुहुयादिति सम्बन्धः। संस्पृश्येति। तानेव। विषवृक्षज इति। विषकाष्ठेधिते अग्नाविति शेषः॥ ७२॥७३॥७४॥

अहिमिति। जीवन्तं कृष्णम्। एनं घटम्। तं घटं शत्रुरूपम्॥७४॥७५॥७६॥

विड़ालं कृष्णम्। जपपूजादिकमिति आदिशब्देन कपालेन पिधानं रक्त-

अयुतं व्रणतैलेन हुत्वाऽग्नौ तं घटं पुनः।
आमस्तकं समुद्धृत्य जपेन्मन्त्रमनन्यधीः।
जुहुयाद्विधिनाऽनेन त्रिदिनैर्म्रियते रिपुः॥ ७९
सुन्दरं महिषीवत्समेकरात्रमुपोषितम्।
पाययन् महिषीसर्पिःप्रस्थं मन्त्रेण मन्त्रितम्॥ ८०
कुशैरावद्धसर्वाङ्गं स्थापितप्राणमञ्जसा।
कारस्करैधिते वह्नौ व्रणतैलेन मन्त्रवित्॥ ८१
होमं कृत्वाऽयुतं वत्सं जुहुयाद्यतमानसः।
एकेन दिवसेनाऽरिर्गच्छेद्यमपुरं प्रति॥ ८२
त्रिकोणकुण्डनिहिते वह्नौ मन्त्रेण दीपिते।
अर्चिते गन्धपुष्पाद्यैरयुतं जुहुयात् क्रमात्॥ ८३
राजिभल्लातकतिलतैलैः सप्तदिनं ततः।
प्रसूतिसमयप्राप्तां महिषीं स्थापितानिलाम्॥ ८४
पूजितां गन्धपुष्पाद्यैः स्पृशन् कूर्चेन तां जपेत्।
मस्तकाद्योनिपर्यन्तं धिया वत्समनुस्मरन्॥ ८५
आकृष्य हस्ते पतितं जुहुयादेधितेऽनले।
एवं कृते समुत्पन्ना कृत्या दीप्ता हुताशनात्॥ ८६
भक्षयेदचिराच्छत्रुमीश्वरेणाऽपि रक्षितम्।
पुनरग्नौ विशत्येषा कर्तारमपि काङ्क्षिणी॥ ८७
एवंविधानि कर्माणि यः कुर्यान्मन्त्रवित्तमः।
स जपेदात्मरक्षार्थं मन्त्रान् मृत्युञ्जयादिकान्॥ ८८

वस्त्राच्छादनं च। कारस्करभवे कारस्करकाष्ठैधिते। वह्नौ श्मशानाग्नौ। व्रणतैलेन भल्लाततैलेन। अनन्यधीरित्यनेन पूर्ववटहोमेऽपि अयं होम इत्युक्तम्। ॥ ७७॥७८॥७९॥८०॥८१॥८२॥

क्रमादिति प्रत्येकमयुतहोमः। तैलशब्दः प्रत्येकमभिसम्बध्यते। स्थापितानिलां प्रतिष्ठितप्राणाम्। हस्ते पतितमिति। भुवमस्पृष्टम्। जुहुयादिति। शस्त्रबुद्ध्या। कर्तारमपि काङ्क्षिणीत्युक्तेस्तद्रक्षामाह स जपेदिति॥ ८३॥ ॥ ८४॥८५॥८६॥८७॥८८॥

अथो लवणमन्त्रस्य विधानमभिधीयते ।
ऋगाद्या कथिता पूर्वं लवणाक्षसिपूर्विका ॥ ८९
लवणाक्षसि तीक्ष्णोऽसि उग्रोऽसि हृदयं तव ।
लवणमन्त्रस्य पृथिवी माता लवणस्य वरुणः पिता ॥ ९०
लवणे हूयमाने तु कुतो निद्रा कुतो रतिः ।
लवणं दहति पचति माचयति लवणं छिन्दति भिन्दति ॥ ९१
अमुकस्य दह गात्राणि दह मांसं दह त्वचम् ।
दह त्वगस्थिमज्जानि अस्थिभ्यो मज्जिकां दह ॥ ९२
यदि वसति योजनशते नदीनां वा शतान्तरे ।
नगरे लोहप्राकारे कृष्णसर्पशतार्गले ॥ ९३
तं दग्ध्वा नय मे शीघ्रमग्रे लोणस्य तेजसा ।
तत्रैवं वशमायातु लवणमन्त्रपराक्रमः ॥ ९४
या ते रात्रिः शल्यविद्धस्य शूलाग्रारोपितस्य च ।
या ते रात्रिर्महारात्रिः सा ते रात्रिर्महानिशा ॥ ९५
लवणादि द्वितीयाऽन्या दहाद्या परिकीर्त्तिता ।
तं दग्ध्वाऽन्या चतुर्थी स्याद्यातिपूर्वाऽथ पञ्चमी ॥ ९६
अङ्गिरा मुनिराख्यातश्छन्दोऽनुष्टुबुदाहृतम् ।
अग्नी रात्रिः पुनर्दुर्गा भद्रकाली च देवताः ॥ ९७

लवणमन्त्रविधानमाह अथो इति। लवणादिद्वितीयेत्यत्र आकारे परे एचोयवायाव इति अयिकृते यकारलोपे च छान्दसत्वात् सन्धिः कृतः। प्रातिपदिकमात्रस्य लवणशब्दस्य वा ग्रहणम्। तेन लवणे इत्याद्या द्वितीया। तदुक्तमाचार्यैः—"द्वितीया लवणे" इति। अन्या तृतीया। एवमृक्पञ्चकं चिटिमन्त्रसहितमेका विद्या। प्रणवपाशादि त्र्यक्षरादित्वम्। वायुिन्द्रामृतबीजादित्वं च सम्प्रदायात् ज्ञेयम्। पद्मपादाचार्योक्तो मन्त्रोद्धारो यथा—

पृथिवीमुदकं चोक्त्वा (लव)णाक्षसीति ततः परम् ।
तीक्ष्णोऽस्युग्रोऽसि हृदयं तवेति लवणस्य गोः ॥
पृथिवीति च माता लवणस्य वरुणः पिता ।
प्रथमेयं द्वितीयाया लवणे इत्युपक्रमः ॥

क्षयमाने त्विति क्रुतो निद्रेति च कुतो रतिः ।
लवणं पचतीत्युक्त्वा तथा पाचयतीति च ॥
लवणं छिन्दतीत्युक्त्वा भिन्दतीति च भाष्यताम् ।
अमुकस्य दह गात्राणि दह मांसं दह त्वचम् ॥
दहेति च तृतीयाया भवेद्‌च उपक्रमः ।
त्वगस्थिमज्जानीत्यस्थिभ्योशब्दं मज्जिकां दह ॥
[क्वचित्पुस्तके त्वगसृङ्मांसमेदोऽस्थिभ्यो शब्दमिति पाठः ।]
ततो यदीति सम्भाष्य वसतीति पदं वदेत् ।
योजनेति शते वर्णाद्रदीनां वा शतान्तरे ॥
तं दग्ध्वेति चतुर्थ्यादौ नय मे शीघ्रमित्यतः ।
अग्ने इत्येतदन्ते स्याल्लवणस्येति तेजसा ॥
नगरे लोहवर्णाः स्युः प्राकारे कृष्णवर्णकाः ।
सर्पैरन्ते कृतार्गेति ते अतीव वशाचराः ॥
माया त्विति स्याल्लवणमन्त्रवर्णाः पुरस्कृताः ।
या ते रात्रिः शल्यविद्धस्य शूलायारोपितस्य च ॥
या ते रात्रिरिति प्रोक्ता महारात्रिरितीरयेत् ।
सा ते रात्रिर्मम्रेत्युक्त्वा निशेत्येवं तु पञ्चमी ॥ इति ॥

टीकान्तरेऽपि—माता स्याल्लवणस्येति वरुणः स्यात्पिता तथा ।
द्वितीया लवणे प्रोक्ता । इति ।

तथा—प्रवदेदमुकस्याऽन्ते दह गात्राणि पञ्चकम् ।
दह मांसं दहेत्युक्त्वा त्वचमुक्त्वा समापयेत् ॥
तृतीयाऽथ दह प्रोक्ता त्वगिति प्रवदेदतः ।
स्थिमज्जानीत्यतोऽस्थिभ्यो मज्जिकां स्वाहहेति च ॥ इति ॥

तथा—या ते रात्रिः सशूलान्ते भिन्नस्येत्यक्षरत्रयम् ।
शूलायारोपितस्येति[स्यापि] चान्ते या ते इतीरयेत् ॥
रात्रिः स्याच्च महारात्रिर्या रात्रिरमुकं विना ।
इत्येवं पञ्चमी ऋक् स्यात् मन्त्रोऽयं प्रणवादिकः ॥ इति ॥

तथाऽत्राऽऽचार्यैः छन्दःकथनावसरे उक्तम्—
अङ्गिराः स्यादृषिश्छन्दोऽनुष्टुप्त्रिष्टुप् । इति ॥

मन्त्रमुक्तावलीमन्त्रदेवप्रकाशिकाकारादीनामिदमेव सम्मतम् । पद्मपादाचार्यैः

चिटिमन्त्राक्षरैः कुर्यात् षडङ्गानि समाहितः।
पञ्चभिर्हृदयं प्रोक्तं त्रिभिर्वर्णैः शिरः स्मृतम्॥ ९८
पञ्चवर्णैः शिखा प्रोक्ता कवचं करणाक्षरैः।
पञ्चभिर्नेत्रमुदितं युगलेनाऽस्त्रमीरितम्॥ ९९
तारः चिटिद्वयं पश्चाच्चण्डालि तदनन्तरम्।
महत्पदाद्यां तां ब्रूयादमुकं मे ततः परम्॥ १००
वशमानय ठद्वन्द्वं चिटिमन्त्र उदाहृतः।
चतुर्विंशत्यक्षरात्मा सर्वकामफलप्रदः॥ १०१

नवकुङ्कुमसंभिन्नं त्रिनेत्रं रुचिराकल्पशतं भजामि वह्निम्।
स्रुवशक्तिवराभयानि दोर्भिर्दधतं रक्तसरोरुहे निषण्णम्॥ १०२
कालाम्बुवाहद्युतिमिन्दुवक्त्रां हारावलीशोभिपयाधराढ्याम्।
कपालपाशाङ्कुशशूलहस्तां नीलाम्बरां यामवतीं नमामि॥ १०३
कालाम्बुदाभामरिशङ्खशूलखड्गाढ्यहस्तां तरुणेन्दुचूडाम्।
भीमां त्रिनेत्रां जितशत्रुवर्गां देवीं स्मरेत् दुर्गतिभङ्गहस्ताम्॥ १०४

बीजशक्ती उक्ते—क्रीं बीजं शक्तिरीरिता क्रोमित्येव च बीजं स्यादिति।

तैरेव एतत्समफलं मन्त्रान्तरमुक्तम्—

चिटीति शब्दं संवीप्स्य चित्कालिपदमीरयेत्।
महाचित्कालिशब्दान्ते क्रीं सवौषट् हिठान्तिकः॥
मन्त्रान्तरमिति ज्ञेयं मतं तुल्यफलं शिवे॥ इति॥ ८९॥ ९०॥
॥ ९१॥ ९२॥ ९३॥ ९४॥ ९५॥ ९६॥ ९७॥

षडङ्गमाह चिटीति। समाहित इत्यनेन पञ्चभिः पञ्चाङ्गं वा कुर्यादित्युक्तम्। यदाहुराचार्याः—

ऋग्भिराभिस्तु पञ्चाङ्गं पञ्चभिर्वा समीरितम्।
विद्याक्षरैः षडङ्गं वा प्रणवाद्यैर्निगद्यते॥ इति॥ ९८॥ ९९॥

चिटिमन्त्रमुद्धरति तार इति। महत्पदाद्यां तामिति महाचाण्डालि। अत्र मानुमहत इत्यनेनाऽऽत्वम्। क्वचित्तु महापदाद्यामिति पाठः। तदुक्तम्—

चाण्डालीति महेत्युक्त्वा चाण्डालीत्यभिमन्त्रयेत्। इति॥ १००॥१०१॥

दक्षाद्यूर्ध्वयोराद्ये तदधस्तनयोरन्त्ये इत्यायुधध्यानम् अग्निध्याने। तदुत्तरं तु

टङ्कं कपालं डमरुं त्रिशूलं सम्बिभ्रती चन्द्रकलावतंसा।
पिङ्गोर्ध्वकेशी सितभीमदंष्ट्रा भूयाद्विभूत्यै मम भद्रकाली ॥ १०५

स्रक्पञ्चकं जपेत्सम्यगयुतं तद्दशांशतः।
हविषा घृतसिक्तेन जुहुयादर्चितेऽनले ॥ १०६

एवं कृतपुरश्चर्यः प्रयोगे कुशलो भवेत्।
अग्निर्यामवतो ध्येयौ वश्याकर्षणकर्मणोः ॥ १०७

स्मरेद् दुर्गां भद्रकालीं मन्त्री मारणकर्मणि।
जानुप्रमाणे सलिले स्थित्वा निशि जपेन्मनुम् ॥ १०८

अनेन वाञ्छितः साध्यः किङ्करो जायते क्षणात्।
नाभिमात्रोदके स्थित्वा जपेन्मन्त्रमिमं सुधीः ॥ १०९

अष्टोत्तरसहस्रं यस्तस्य साध्यो वशो भवेत्।
स्रक्पञ्चकं जपेत्सम्यक्कण्ठमात्राम्भसि स्थितः ॥ ११०

वामाधस्ताद्दक्षाधस्तनं यावत्। दुर्गाध्याने दक्षोर्ध्वाद्दक्षाधस्तनं यावदायुधध्यानम्। टङ्कः परशुः। अन्ये दक्षाधस्ताद्दक्षोर्ध्वं यावत् ॥ १०२ ॥ १०३ ॥ १०४ ॥ १०५ ॥

सम्यगयुतमिति। त्रिटिमन्त्रसहितस्रक्पञ्चकम् अयुतं जपेदित्यर्थः। तदुक्तमाचार्यैः—अयुतं नियतो मन्त्री मन्त्रस्रक्पञ्चकान्वितम्।
प्रजपेत् त्रिसहस्रं वा सम्यगेनं समाहितः॥ इति ॥

तन्त्रान्तरे तु विशेषः—
गङ्गादिमुख्यसरितां तीरदेशे समाश्रिते।
स्वयमेव समुद्भूते दुर्गानिलयने वशी ॥
त्रिसहस्रं जपेदेतदथवाऽयुतसंख्यया।
पूर्वोक्तं त्रिटिमन्त्रं तु जपेत्तस्य चतुर्गुणम् ॥ इति ॥ १०६ ॥

एवं कृतपुरश्चर्य इत्यनेन नित्यपूजापि सूचिता। तया विना तस्याऽसम्पादनात्। सीता रामकण्ठेन—
भीषणी बहुरूपा च तीक्ष्णदंष्ट्रा मदोत्कटा।
मारणी मोहनी कान्ता कमण्डलुधरा अपि।
अभिचारकरी चेति लोणमन्त्रस्य शक्तयः।
पाशाङ्कुशपुटा शक्तिः सर्वशक्तिपदंकमो ॥

सप्तभिर्दिवसैर्भूपान् वशयेद्विधिनाऽमुना ।
विलिख्य तालपत्रे तं साध्यनाम्ना विदर्भितम् ॥ १११

निःक्षिप्य क्षीरसंमिश्रे जले तत् क्राथयेन्निशि ।
वश्यो भवति साध्योऽस्य नात्र कार्या विचारणा ॥ ११२

तालपत्रे लिखित्वैवं भद्रकाली गृहे खनेत् ।
वश्याय सर्वजन्तूनां प्रयोगोऽयमुदाहृतः ॥ ११३
तालपत्रे लिख्य मन्त्रं साध्यनामविदर्भितम् ।
तापयेत् खादिरे वह्नौ मासं वश्यो भवेन्नरः ॥ ११४
त्रिकोणं कुण्डमापाद्य सम्यक् शास्त्रोक्तलक्षणम् ।
तस्मिन् होमं प्रकुर्वीत संस्कृते हव्यवाहने ॥ ११५
प्रक्षाल्य गव्यदुग्धेन संशोष्य लवणं सुधीः ।
सुचूर्णितं प्रजुहुयात् सप्ताहाद्वशयेज्जनान् ॥ ११६
दधिमध्वाज्यसंसिक्तैः सैन्धवैर्जुहुयात्तथा ।
वशयेदखिलान्देवानचिरात् किमु पार्थिवान् ॥ ११७
विशुद्धं लवणप्रस्थं विभक्तं पञ्चधा पृथक् ।
एकैकया प्रजुहुयाहृचा पञ्चाहमादरात् ॥ ११८

लासनाय नमोऽन्तः स्यात्पीठमन्त्रो भ्रुवादिकः ।
मूर्त्तावावाह्य गन्धाद्यैर्देवताः सम्प्रपूजयेत् ॥
अङ्गैरावरणं पूर्वं द्वितीयं वह्निमूर्त्तिभिः ।
तद्बहिः शूलहस्तादिशक्तिभिश्च समीरिता ॥
उत्कटाद्यैश्चतुर्थी तु पञ्चमाष्टतिरीरिता ।
लोकेशैर्लौणमन्त्रस्य विधानमिति कीर्त्तितम् ॥
शूलहस्ता विकेशी च दारुणा लवणप्रिया ।
वरा कराली चात्युग्रा तामस्यस्याऽष्टशक्तयः ॥
उत्कटो विकटाक्षश्च शूलहस्तो महाबलः ।
अग्निजिह्वः खड्गधरः कपाली तारणप्रियः ॥ इति ॥ १०७॥१०८ ॥

॥ १०८॥११०॥१११॥११२॥११३ ॥

एवमिति साध्यनाम्ना विदर्भितमित्यर्थः ॥ ११४॥११५॥११६॥११७ ॥

यस्य नाम्ना स वश्यः स्यादनेन विधिनाऽचिरात् ।
शुद्धं लवणमादाय जुहुयान्मधुरान्वितम् ॥ ११९
ऊनपञ्चाशदाहुत्या वशं नयति वाञ्छितम् ।
नित्यं शुद्धेन लोणेन हुत्वा शत्रून् वशं नयेत् ॥ १२०
मधुरत्रयसंयुक्तैर्लवणैः साधु चूर्णितैः ।
जुहुयाद्वशयेन्नारीर्नरान् नरपतीनपि ॥ १२१
मन्त्रं कृष्णतृतीयादि प्रजपेद्यावदष्टमी ।
पुत्तलीः पञ्च कुर्वीत साङ्गोपाङ्गाः समाः शुभाः ॥ १२२
एका साध्यद्रुमेण स्यादन्या पिष्टमयी मता ।
चक्रिहस्तमृदाऽन्या स्यादन्या सिक्थमयी स्मृता ॥ १२३
लवणं पोतसम्भूतं चूर्णितं परिशोधितम् ।
कुडवं प्रोच्चयेत् क्षीरदध्याज्यमधुभिः क्रमात् ॥ १२४
गुडाज्यमधुभिः सम्यङ्मिश्रितेनाऽमुना ततः ।
कुर्वीत पुत्तलीं सौम्यां सर्वावयवशोभिताम् ॥ १२५

विशुद्धमिति । प्रक्षालितं पूर्ववत् । लवणेति सैन्धवम् । एवमग्रेऽपि ॥ ११८ ॥ ॥ ११९॥१२०॥१२१ ॥

प्रयोगान्तरमाह मन्त्रमित्यादिना । यावदष्टमीति कृष्णा । कुर्वीतेत्यष्टम्याम् । साङ्गोपाङ्गा इति । अङ्गानि तु—

कहस्तद्वत्पार्श्वकटी पत्स्कन्धौ कन्धराभुजौ ।
पृष्ठं तथोदरं तूरू जङ्घे इत्यङ्गसंग्रहः ॥
उपाङ्गानि भ्रूपुटौ च तारागण्डौ च नासिका ।
ओष्ठौ तु दशना जिह्वा चिबुकास्यं सनाभि च ॥
जघनं योनिगुह्ये च जानुनी मणिबन्धकौ ।
पार्ष्णीगुल्फौ तथाऽङ्गुल्यः करयोः पादयोस्तले ॥ इति ।

साध्यद्रुमेणेति । साध्यनक्षत्रवृक्षेण । साध्यनक्षत्रवृक्षमग्रिमेऽपि वक्ष्यति । पिष्टमयीति । तण्डुलपिष्टमयी । चक्री कुलालः । सिक्थं मधूच्छिष्टम् । पोतसम्भूतमिति सामुद्रम् । अमुना लवणेन । सौम्यां सुन्दरीम् । पञ्चाऽपि द्वादशाङ्गुलाः ॥ १२२॥१२३॥१२४॥१२५ ॥

प्राणमन्त्रकृतं यन्त्रमासां हृदि विनिःक्षिपेत्।
आसु प्राणान् प्रतिष्ठाप्य पूजयेत् कुसुमादिभिः॥ १२६

पश्चात् कृष्णाष्टमीरात्रौ याममात्रे गते सति।
विधाय मातृकान्यासं मन्त्रन्यासमनन्तरम्॥ १२७

चिटिमन्त्रसमुद्भूतान् चतुर्विंशतिसंख्यकान्।
ताराद्यान्विन्यसेद्वर्णान् स्थानेष्वेषु समाहितः॥ १२८

मूर्ध्नि भाले दृशोः श्रुत्योर्नासास्यचिबुकेष्वथ।
कण्ठहृत्स्तनयुग्मेषु कुक्षौ नाभौ कटिद्वये॥ १२९

मेढ्रे पायौ प्रविन्यस्य शिष्टवर्णचतुष्टयम्।
ऊरुद्वये जानुयुगे जङ्घायुग्मे पदद्वये॥ १३०

एवं विन्यस्तसर्वाङ्गो रक्तमाल्यानुलेपनः।
रक्तवस्त्रधरः शुद्धः पुत्तलीं दारुणा कृताम्॥ १३१

अधोमुखीं खनेत् कुण्डे पिष्टजामासनादधः।
मृन्मयीं प्रतिमां पाददेशे न्यसेत्तथात्मनः॥ १३२
मधूच्छिष्टमयीं व्योम्नि कुण्डस्योर्ध्वं प्रलम्बयेत्।
लवणेन कृतां पश्चात् पुत्तलीं संस्पृशन् जपेत्॥ १३३

यन्त्रमित्यग्रिमपटले वक्ष्यमाणम्। प्राणानित्यग्रिमपटले वक्ष्यमाणेन प्रकारेण। आचार्यास्तु—तस्यां तु स्थापयेत् प्राणान् गुर्वादेशविधानतः। इति। अत्र साम्प्रदायिका विशेषमाहुः। पुत्तलिकाया हृदयं स्पृशन् प्राणा इह प्राणा जीव इह स्थित इति इन्द्रियाणि स्पृशन् सर्वेन्द्रियाणि वाङ्मनश्चक्षुःश्रोत्रघ्राणेति सर्वाङ्गं स्पृशन् प्राणा इहायान्तु सुखं चिरं तिष्ठन्तु इति शिरः स्पृशन् स्वाहेति जपेत्। मन्त्रन्यासमिति। पञ्चभिः पञ्चाङ्गमित्यर्थः॥ १२६॥१२७॥

अथवान्यमेवाह चिटीति। दारुणेति। साध्यनक्षत्रवृक्षकाष्ठेन कृतां कुण्डे खनेन्निखनेदित्यर्थः। तत्र द्वयङ्गुलाधोनिखननं ज्ञेयम्। अधोमुखीमिति मारणकर्मविषयम्। वशीकरणकर्मणि उत्तानेति ज्ञेयम्। यदाहुः—

कुण्डान्तर्द्वयङ्गुलाधो निखनतु तरुजां मूर्तिमुत्तानरूपाम्। इति।
आचार्यास्त—उत्तानां दारवीं कुण्डे खनेन् मन्त्राभिमन्त्रिताम्। इति।

ऋक्पञ्चकं यथान्यायमष्टोत्तरसहस्रकम् ।
संहृत्य चिटिमन्त्रार्णान् पुनस्तस्यास्तनौ न्यसेत् ॥ १३४
अङ्गुष्ठसन्धिप्रपदजानुजङ्घोरुपायुषु ।
लिङ्गदेशे पुनर्नाभौ जठरे हृदयाम्बुजे ॥ १३५
स्तनद्वये कन्धरायां चिबुके वदने पुनः ।
घ्राणयोः कर्णयोरक्ष्णोर्ललाटे मूर्ध्नि विन्यसेत् ॥ १३६
अग्निमादाय सन्दीप्य साध्यनक्षत्रदारुभिः ।
तस्मिन्नभ्यर्च्य मन्त्रोक्तां देवतां कृत्यपावके ॥ १३७

तथा न्यसेदिति । अधोमुखीं न्यसेदित्यर्थः । विषयव्यवस्था तु पूर्वोक्तैव ज्ञेया । एतयोरपि द्व्यङ्गुलाधोनिखननमेव । प्रलम्बयेदित्यधोमुखीमित्येव ।

यदाहुः—धूमेन स्पृश्यमानामुपरि मदनजां लम्बयेदूर्ध्वपादाम् । इति ।

आचार्याश्च—लम्बयेदम्बरे सिक्थमयीमूर्ध्वामधोमुखीम् । इति ।

यथान्यायमिति । षडङ्गन्यासं स्वतनौ पुत्तल्यां च कृत्वा चिटिमन्त्रग्रथितम् ऋक्पञ्चकं जपेदित्यर्थः ।

तदुक्तम्—अङ्गानि विन्यसेत् स्वाङ्गे तथा प्रतिकृतावपि । इति ।

संहृत्येति विपरीतान् स्वाङ्गे प्रतिकृतावपि ।

तदुक्तम्—न्यस्याऽङ्गान्यनुमन्त्र्याथ प्रतिकृतौ संहारयुक्त्या न्यसेत् । इति । पुनरनन्तरमित्यनेनैवदुक्तम् । स्वदेहे न्यासं विधायान्तर्यागान्तं कृत्वा पश्चात् पुत्तल्यां न्यास इति । अतएव पश्चादासने देवतापूजा । तस्याः पुत्तलिकायाः ॥ १२८॥१२९॥१३०॥१३१॥१३२॥१३३॥१३४ ॥

अङ्गुष्ठेति । जङ्घान्तेषु षट्सु एकैकाक्षरन्यासः । अन्यत्र स्थानद्वये सर्वत्राऽक्षरद्वयम् । यदुक्तमाचार्यैः—

अधो गुह्यादभेदः स्यादूर्ध्वं भेदो द्विके सति । इति ॥१३५॥१३६॥

तस्मिन्निति । तन्त्रान्तरोक्त आसन इत्यर्थः । अग्नौ देवतापूजा चतुर्थपटल एवोक्ता । तस्योक्तावत्र प्रयोजनाभावादग्रेऽर्घ्यदानमपि वक्ष्यति । यदाहुः—

कुण्डस्य पूर्वदिग्भागे चतुरस्रं समुन्नतम् ।
हस्तमात्रायतं लाक्षारक्तपादादिकं नवम् ॥
चित्राङ्गं रुचिराकारं कुण्डोत्सेधसमुन्नतम् ।
चतुरङ्गुलमानं वा अष्टाङ्गुलमथापि वा ॥

कुशीतराजिपुष्पाद्भिर्दत्वाऽर्घ्यं प्रणमेत् सुधीः ।
मन्त्रैरेतैः प्रयोगादावन्ते संयतमानसः ॥ १३८

त्वमाननममिवश्न निशाया हव्यवाहन ।
हविषा मन्त्रजप्तेन तृप्तो भव तया सह ॥ १३९

जातवेदो महादेव तप्तजाम्बूनदप्रभ ।
स्वाहापते विश्वभक्ष लवणं दह शत्रुहन् ॥ १४०

ॐ ईशि शर्वरि शर्वाणि यस्तं मुक्तं त्वया जगत् ।
महादेवि नमस्तुभ्यं वरदे कामदा भव ॥ १४१

तमोमयि महादेवि महादेवस्य सुव्रते ।
त्रियामे पुरुषं हुत्वा वशमानय देवि[व्यु]मे ॥ १४२

ॐ दुर्गे स[दु]र्गादिरक्षिते दुर्गसंरोधनार्गले ।
चक्रशङ्खधरे देवि दुष्टशत्रु[सत्व]भयङ्करि ॥ १४३

नमस्ते दह शत्रून् मे वशमानय चण्डिके ।
शाकम्भरि महादेवि शरणं मे भवाऽनघे ॥ १४४

ॐ भद्रकालि भवाभीष्टे भद्रसिद्धिप्रदायिनि ।
सपत्नान्मे हन हन दह शोषय तापय ॥ १४५

शूलासिशक्तिवज्राद्यैरुत्कृत्योत्कृत्य मारय ।
महादेवि महाकालि रक्षाऽस्मानक्षतात्मिके ॥ १४६

द्वादशाङ्गुलकं वापि कुण्डादुन्नतमासनम् ।
तस्मिन् सुविमलं वस्त्रं आस्तीर्य्यादौ सुशोभनम् ॥
सूक्ष्मं चतुर्गुणीकृत्य सप्तहस्तायतं नवम् ।
तस्योपरि परिस्तीर्य रक्तवस्त्रद्वयं पुनः ॥
विशालमतिसूक्ष्मं च पूर्ववद्द्विगुणितं नवम् ॥ इति ॥

तन्त्रान्तरोक्तप्रकारेणासनं परिकल्प्य तत्र पूर्वोक्तं पीठं परिपूज्य देवतामावाह्य पूर्ववत् सावरणं सम्पूज्य रक्तचन्दनादिना वक्ष्यमाणद्रव्ययुक्तेन शुद्धजलेन कृष्णं चषकमापूर्य तेनार्घ्यं दद्यात् । ततो वक्ष्यमाणमन्त्रैर्देवतामुपतिष्ठेत् ।

कुशीतं रक्तचन्दनम् । राजिः राजिका । प्रयोगादाविति । एतन्मन्त्र-प्रयोगादावन्ते च । अत्र वशीकृतौ यद्यपि एते एव देवते तथापि नतिप्रकरण-

साध्यं संस्मृत्य निर्भिद्य पुत्तलीं सप्तधा ततः ।
स्वकपञ्चकं समुच्चार्य जुहुयादेधितेऽनले ॥ १४७

प्रथमो दक्षिणः पादस्तत्करस्तदनन्तरम् ।
शिरस्तृतीयमाख्यातं वामहस्तं ततः परम् ॥ १४८

मध्यादूर्ध्वं पञ्चमः स्यादधोंऽशः षष्ठ ईरितः ।
सप्तमो वामपादः स्यादेवं भागक्रमः स्मृतः ॥ १४९

सप्तसप्तविभागो वा प्रोक्तेष्वेषु यथाविधि ।
हुत्वैवमर्चयित्वाऽग्निं प्रणमेद्दण्डवत्ततः ॥ १५०

यजमानो धनैर्धान्यैः प्रीणयेद्गुरुमात्मनः ।
अनेन विधिना मन्त्री वशयेदसुरान् सुरान् ॥ १५१

किं पुनर्मनुजान् भूपानमात्यान् नृप[वर]योषितः ।
मारणे पूर्वसप्रोक्तं पुत्तलीनां चतुष्टयम् ॥ १५२

प्रसङ्गादितरयोरपि मन्त्रावुक्तौ । तत्प्रयोजनमग्रे मारणकर्मणि भविष्यति ॥ १३७ ॥ ॥ १३८ ॥ १३९ ॥ १४० ॥ १४१ ॥ १४२ ॥ १४३ ॥ १४४ ॥ १४५ ॥ १४६ ॥

पुत्तलीमिति । लवणमयीम् । निर्भिद्येत्युक्तम् । तमेव भेदमाह प्रथम इति । आचार्यैः प्रकारान्तरमप्युक्तम्—

दक्षिणं चरणं पूर्वं दक्षार्द्धन्तु द्वितीयकम् ।
दक्षहस्तं तृतीयं स्याद्गलादूर्ध्वं चतुर्थकम् ॥
पञ्चमं वामहस्तः स्यात् षष्ठं वामार्द्धमेव च ।
सप्तमं वामपादः स्यादन्यापि स्याद्धुतक्रिया ॥ इति ॥१४७॥१४८॥१४९॥

प्रोक्तेष्विति । सप्तावदानेषु प्रत्येकं सप्तसप्तविभागाः तैरेकोनपञ्चाशदाहुतयः । उक्तपुत्तलीषु सर्वत्रावदानक्रमोऽयमेव ज्ञेयः । अन्यत्र विशेषः—

सप्तसप्तविभागो वा क्रमादङ्गेषु सप्तसु ।
एकादशांशभिन्नैर्वा तदङ्गैः सप्तभिर्हुनेत् ॥ इति ॥

अन्यत्रापि—सप्तानामङ्गानामेकैकं सप्तभागान्वा ।
रुद्रांशान्वा कृत्वा होतव्यं मन्त्रिवर्येण ॥ इति ॥

स्त्रीवशीकरणे वामपादादि ज्ञेयम् । "योषितो वामपूर्वाम्" इत्युक्तेः । एवं स्त्रीमारणे दक्षपादाद्यवदानक्रमो ज्ञेयः । प्रणमेदिति । पूर्वोक्तमन्त्रैः । साधकेन्द्रो

निवेशयेद्यथापूर्वं साधकेन्द्रो विधानवित्।
अपरां वक्ष्यमाणेन विधानेन प्रकल्पयेत्॥ १५३

वराहपारावतविट्तिलत्र्यूषणरामठैः।
व्रणकृन्निम्बसिद्धार्थसाध्यवामाङ्घ्रिरेणुभिः॥ १५४

महिषीमूत्रसंपिष्टैः पूर्वोक्तलवणान्वितैः।
विधाय पुत्तलीं सम्यक् प्राणस्थापनमाचरेत्॥ १५५

जपपूजादिकं सर्वं कुर्यात् प्रागुक्तवर्त्मना।
ततः पूर्वोदिते कुण्डे रात्रौ प्रज्वलितेऽनले॥ १५६

दुर्गां वा भद्रकालीं वा समाराध्य यथाविधि।
धारयन्निशितं शस्त्रं सव्यहस्तेन साधकः॥ १५७

वामपादं समारभ्य दक्षिणाङ्घ्र्यवसानकम्।
छित्त्वा छित्त्वा प्रजुहुयान्निराहारो जितेन्द्रियः॥ १५८

विधानविदित्यनेन पुत्तलीनां द्व्यङ्गुलाधःखननमुक्तम्॥१५०॥१५१॥१५२॥१५३॥

त्र्यूषणं शुण्ठी पिप्पलि मरीचानि। रामठं हिङ्गुः। व्रणकृद्भल्लातः। निम्बं निम्बबीजम्। अत्र तिलभल्लातनिम्बबीजसिद्धार्थानां तैलं ग्राह्यम्।

तदुक्तमाचार्यैः—सनिम्बतिलसिद्धार्थव्रणकृत्तैलसंयुतैः। इति।

पूर्वोक्तलवणं सामुद्रम्। सम्यक् पुत्तलीं विधायेत्यनेन तन्त्रान्तरोक्तो विशेषः सूचितः—

आयामः पादयोस्तस्या आकट्याश्चतुरङ्गुलः।
पादोनद्व्यङ्गुला कुक्षिस्तावदेवाऽङ्गुलोदरम्।
अङ्गुलद्वयमावक्त्रात् कण्ठदेशस्य मानकम्॥
शिरसो वक्त्रमानं स्यात् सार्द्धद्वयमिहाऽङ्गुलैः।
द्वादशाङ्गुलयः सर्वाः साध्यपुत्तलिकाः स्मृताः॥ इति॥

तन्त्रान्तरे तु विशेषः—

पञ्चांशेन मुखं कृत्वा तदर्द्धेन गलं पुनः।
शिष्टेन सर्वाण्यङ्गानि पुत्तलीनां प्रकल्पयेत्॥
मारणे दारुरूपां तां द्वादशाङ्गुलसम्मिताम्।
षष्ठवत्यङ्गुलां वापि कुर्यान्मात्राङ्गुलैः क्रमात्॥

कृष्णाष्टमीं समारभ्य यावत् कृष्णचतुर्द्दशी ।
अनेनैव विधानेन होमं कुर्याद्विचक्षणः ॥ १५९
विसप्ताहप्रयोगेन मारयेद्रिपुमात्मनः ।
कारस्करोऽथ धात्री स्यादुदुम्बरतरुः पुनः ॥ १६०
जम्बुः खदिरकृष्णाख्यौ वंशपिप्पलसंज्ञिकौ ।
नागरोहिणनामानौ पलाशप्लक्षसंज्ञकौ ॥ १६१
अम्बष्ठबिल्वार्जुनाख्या विकङ्कतमहीरुहः ।
बकुलः सरलः सर्जो वञ्जुलः पनसार्ककौ ॥ १६२

होमार्थं कल्पितायास्तु तस्याः प्रोक्तो विधिस्त्वयम् ।
वश्याकर्षणयोः प्रोक्तां तां कुर्याद् द्वादशाङ्गुलैः ॥ इति ॥

यथाविधीति । पूर्वोक्तप्रकारेण । कुर्याद्धोममिति प्रत्यहम् ॥

त्रिसप्ताहेति । एभिरेव सप्तभिः । तेन मासत्रयेण प्रयोगसिद्धिः । मारणकर्मणि दक्षिणाविशेष उक्तस्तन्त्रान्तरे—

सस्वर्णां च समुक्तां गां क्षीणां दद्यात् सतर्णकाम् ।
दक्षिणां सप्तकर्षं तु दद्यात् मारणकर्मणि ॥ इति ॥

अन्यो विशेषः—श्मशाने निर्जने देशे विदध्यादाभिचारिकम् ।
यत्राऽभिचारहोमं तु करोति भुवि साधकः ॥
तत्राऽभितो भटै रक्षां कारयेदात्मसिद्धये ।
नचेदन्यः क्षितिपतिश्चारैर्ज्ञात्वा निहन्त्यमुम् ॥
स्वराष्ट्रसन्धौ कुर्वीत न कुर्वीत स्वमण्डले ।
यदि कुर्यात्प्रमादेन मान्त्रिकोऽज्ञानमोहितः ।
तद्राष्ट्रं पीडयत्येव शनकैर्वैरिभूभृतः ॥ इति ॥

अन्योऽपि विशेषस्तन्त्रान्तरे—

तस्यां रात्रामुपोष्याऽथ परेऽहनि तु साधकः ।
प्राणायामादिभिरपि गायत्रीजपहोमकैः ।
विमुक्तपातको भूत्वा स पुनर्विहरेद्वशी ॥ इति ॥ १५४—१६० ॥

नववृक्षानाह कारस्कर इति । कारस्करः कुचिला । धात्री आमलकी । मृगशिरसस्तु श्वेतसार एव खदिरः । आर्द्रायास्तु कृष्णसारः खदिरः । नागो

शमीकदम्बनिम्बाम्रमधूका क्षत्त्रशाखिनः।

आत्मरक्षादिकं सर्वं कुर्यान्मन्त्री यथा पुरा॥ १६३

अमुना मनुना सम्यगभीष्टफलसाधने।

सदृशो नास्ति मन्त्रोऽन्यः सत्यमेतन् न चान्यथा॥ १६४

इति श्रीशारदातिलके द्वाविंशः पटलः।

नागकेसरः। रोहिणो वटः। प्लक्षः पर्कटी। अम्बष्ठः आम्रातः। अर्जुनः ककुभः। विकङ्कतः स्रुचां वृक्षः। सर्जः शालः। वञ्जुलोऽशोकः। एषां सामान्यतः फलमुक्तम्—

आयुष्कामः स्वर्चंवृक्षं छेदयेन्न कदाचन। इति॥ १६०॥१६१॥१६२॥१६३॥

यथा पुरेति। आग्नेयास्त्रप्रोक्तमार्गेण। एतच्चात्मरक्षणं मारणकर्मस्वेवेति ज्ञेयम्॥ १६३॥ १६४॥

इति श्रीशारदातिलकटीकायां सत्सम्प्रदायकृतव्याख्यायां

पदार्थादर्शाभिख्यायां द्वाविंशः पटलः॥ ॐ॥

त्रयोविंशः पटलः ।

अथ त्रैयम्बकं मन्त्रमभिधास्याम्यनुष्टुभम् ।
यं भजन्तं नरं कालः स्वयं वीक्षितुमक्षमः ॥ १

वशिष्ठोऽस्य मुनिः प्रोक्तश्छन्दोऽनुष्टुबुदाहृतम् ।
देवताऽस्य समुद्दिष्टस्त्र्यम्बकः पार्वतीपतिः ॥ २

विभक्तैर्मन्त्रवर्णैः स्यात् षडङ्गानां प्रकल्पना ।
हृदयं त्रिभिराख्यातं चतुर्भिः शिर ईरितम् ॥ ३

शिखाऽष्टभिः समुद्दिष्टा नवभिः कवचं मतम् ।
पञ्चभिर्नेत्रमाख्यातमस्त्रं त्रिभिरुदाहृतम् ॥ ४

पूर्वपश्चिमयाम्येन्दुवक्त्रेषु तदनन्तरम् ।
उरोगलास्येषु पुनर्नाभिहृत्पृष्ठकुक्षिषु ॥ ५

अथेति । मन्त्रो यथा । त्र्यम्बकं यजामहे सुगन्धिं पुष्टिवर्द्धनम् । उर्वारुकमिव बन्धनान् मृत्योर्मुक्षीय मामृतात् । इति । मृत्युञ्जयपुटित इति केचित् । साम्प्रदायिकास्तु प्रणवप्रासादमृत्युञ्जयव्याहृतिभिः सम्पुटमिच्छन्ति । श्रीं बीजं माया शक्तिः । तदुक्तम्—

श्रीदेव्यौ प्रणवौ बीजशक्ती योगः शिवार्चने । इति ॥ १ ॥ २ ॥

विभागमेवाह हृदयमिति । येषां मते प्रणवादि सम्पुटः तन्मते तदादिभिरेभिर्वर्णैः षडङ्गम् । तदुक्तम्—

प्रासादमृत्युञ्जयभूर्भुवःस्वस्तदङ्गमन्त्रैः क्रमशः समेतम् । इति ।

साम्प्रदायिकास्तु । प्रणवप्रासादमृत्युञ्जयव्याहृति मन्त्रान्तरनमो भगवते रुद्रायेत्युक्त्वा शूलपाणये स्वाहा हृत् । अमृतमूर्त्तये मां जीवय शिरः । चन्द्रशिरसे जटिले स्वाहा शिखा । त्रिपुरान्तकाय ह्रां ह्रीं कवचम् । त्रिलोचनाय ऋग्यजुःसाममन्त्राय नेत्रम् । अग्नित्रयाय ज्वल ज्वल मां रक्ष अघोरास्त्राय अस्त्रम् इति षडङ्गमाहुः ॥ ३ ॥ ४ ॥

वर्णन्यासमेवाह पूर्वेति । उरःशब्देन हृदूर्ध्वभागो विस्तीर्ण इह गृह्यते । अंसमूलयोर्द्वौ । ऊर्वन्तयोर्द्वौ । तदधस्तयुग्मे जानूपरिस्थवृत्तयोः । सर्वस्थानद्वये वर्णद्वयन्यासः । साम्प्रदायिकाः प्रणवादिपुटितवर्णन्यासमाहुः ।

लिङ्गपायूरुमूलान्तजानुयुग्मेषु तत्परम् ।
तद्वृत्तयुग्मे स्तनयोः पार्श्वयोः पादयोः पुनः ॥ ६
पाण्योर्नासिकयोः शीर्षे मन्त्रवर्णान् न्यसेत् क्रमात् ।
पदान्येकादश न्यस्येच्छिरोभ्रूयुगलाक्षिषु ॥ ७
वक्त्रे गण्डयुगे भूयो हृदये जठरे पुनः ।
गुह्योरुजानुपादेषु न्यासमेवं समाचरेत् ॥ ८
हस्ताभ्यां कलशद्वयामृतरसैराप्लावयन्तं शिरो
द्वाभ्यां तौ दधतं मृगाक्षवलये द्वाभ्यां वहन्तं परम् ।
अङ्कन्यस्तकरद्वयामृतघटं कैलासकान्तं शिवं
स्वच्छाम्भोजगतं नवेन्दुमुकुटं देवं त्रिनेत्रं भजे ॥ ९
जपेन्मन्त्रमिमं लक्षमेवं ध्यायन् जितेन्द्रियः ।
जुहुयाद्दशभिर्द्रव्यैरयुतं घृतसंप्लुतैः ॥ १०
बिल्वं पलाशं खदिरं वटं च तिलसर्षपौ ।
दौग्धं दुग्धं दधि पुनर्दूर्वान्तानि विदुर्बुधाः ॥ ११
पश्चाच्चरोदिते पीठे पूजयेद् वृषभध्वजम् ।
मूर्त्तिं मूलेन संकल्प्य वक्ष्यमाणेन वर्त्मना ॥ १२
पूर्वमङ्गानि संपूज्य पश्चान्मूर्त्तीः प्रपूजयेत् ।
अर्केन्दुवसुधातोयवह्नीरवियदात्मनः ॥ १३

तन्त्रान्तरे स्थानान्तराण्युक्तानि—

चरणाग्रसन्धिगुह्याधारोदरहृदयकन्धरासु पुनः ।
बाह्वोः सन्ध्यग्रास्यौष्ठघ्राणदृक्श्रुतिभ्रूशीर्षेषु ॥ इति ॥

पदानीति । वक्त्ररब्धरग्नीषुवेदद्विलिद्विलेरकत्रिवर्णकैः ॥ ५॥६॥७॥८ ॥

ताविति । घटौ । अत्र ध्यानानन्तरमेता मुद्राः प्रदर्शयेत् ।
यदाहुः—लिङ्गपञ्चास्यमुख्याम्बुजशक्तिमुद्राः प्रदर्शयेत् । इति ॥ ९॥१० ॥

बिल्वं फलम् । ततस्त्रयाणां समिधः । दौग्धमिति । पायसम् ॥ ११ ॥

वक्ष्यमाणेन वर्त्मना पीठे वृषभध्वजं पूजयेदित्यन्वयः ॥ १२ ॥

संपूज्येति । कर्णिकायाम् । मूर्त्तीः पश्चात् द्वितीयावरणे पूजयेदित्यन्वयः ।
ता एवाह अर्केति । ईरो वायुः । आत्मा यजमानः । तथा च श्रुतिः—

द्वितीयावरणे पूज्या मूर्त्तयोऽष्टौ क्रमादथ ।
रामा राका प्रभा ज्योत्स्ना पूर्णोषा पूरणी सुधा ॥ १४
अष्टाविमाः क्रमात् पूज्यास्तृतीयावरणे ततः ।
विश्वा विद्या सिता प्रह्वा सारा सन्ध्या शिवा निशा ॥ १५
चतुर्थावरणे पूज्याः शक्तयोऽष्टौ क्रमादिमाः ।
आर्या प्रज्ञा प्रभा मेधा शान्तिः कान्तिर्धृतिर्मतिः ॥ १६
पञ्चमावरणे पूज्याः क्रमादेतास्ततः परम् ।
धरा मायाऽवनी पद्मा शान्ताऽमोघा जयाऽमला ॥ १७
षष्ठावरणगाः पूज्या लोकपालास्ततः परम् ।
एवं कृते प्रयोगार्हो जायतेऽयं महामनुः ॥ १८
अयुतं जुहुयाद्बिल्वसमिद्भिः सम्पदे सुधीः ।
जुहुयाद्ब्रह्मवृक्षस्य समिद्भिर्ब्रह्मतेजसे ॥ १९
खादिरैरयुतं हुत्वा कान्तिपुष्टिमवाप्नुयात् ।
वटवृक्षस्य समिधो जुहुयादयुतावधि ॥ २०
धनधान्यसमृद्धः स्यादचिरेणैव साधकः ।
तिलैस्तत्संख्यया हुत्वा सर्वपापैः प्रमुच्यते ॥ २१
सिद्धार्थैरयुतं हुत्वा शत्रून्विजयते नृपः ।
अनेनैव विधानेन नश्येन् मृत्युरकालजः ॥ २२
पायसेन कृतो होमो रक्षाश्रीकीर्त्तिकान्तिदः ।
पशुदुग्धेन सि[शु]द्धान्नं हुत्वा कृत्यां विनाशयेत् ॥ २३

आत्मा वै यज्ञस्य यजमानोऽङ्गानि ऋत्विजः । इति ॥ १३ ॥

अष्टमूर्त्यादिपञ्चावरणानि पत्रेषु दलमूल उत्तरोत्तरत्र पूजनीयानि । धरोमा पावनीत्यपि पाठः । ततः परमिति । वज्रादिपूजेत्युक्तम् ।

यदाहुः—आनुष्टुभमित्यष्टावरणं प्रोक्तं विधानवरमेवम् । इति ।

कल्पान्तरे तु "सप्तमी लोकपालैः स्यादष्टम्यर्कादिभिर्ग्रहैः" इत्युक्तेरेतदेव सूचयितुं लोकपालान्ता पूजा ग्रन्थकारेणोक्ता ॥ १४॥१५॥१६॥१७॥१८ ॥

खादिरैरिति । सप्तसमिद्वरैरिति शेषः । पशुदुग्धेन गोदुग्धेन । पृथगिति । प्रत्येकम् । अनामयमारोग्यम् । "अनामयं स्यादारोग्यम्" इत्यमरः ॥ १९—३० ॥

अयमेव मतो होमः शान्तिश्रीसम्पदावहः ।
दधिहोमेन संवादं[प्रातं] कुर्याद्विद्वेषिणोर्मिथः ॥ २४
प्रत्यहं जुहुयान्मन्त्री दूर्वामष्टोत्तरं शतम् ।
आमयान्निखिलान् जित्वा दीर्घमायुरवाप्नुयात् ॥ २५
जुहुयाज्जन्मदिवसे पायसान्नैर्घृतान्वितैः ।
दूत्त्वान्ननिन्दितां लक्ष्मीमारोग्यमतुलं यशः ॥ २६
गव्यदुग्धघृताक्ताभिर्दूर्वाभिर्जुहुयाद्वशी ।
सविंशतिशतं सम्यक् स्वजन्मदिवसे सुधीः ॥ २७
आमयैः सकलैर्मुक्तो जीवेद्वर्षशतं सुधीः ।
काश्मरीसमिधस्तिलाः पयोऽन्नं विशतं पृथक् ॥ २८
जुहुयाद् ब्राह्मणानन्ते भोजयेन्मधुरान्वितम् ।
प्रीणयेद्धनधान्याद्यैरात्मनो गुरुमादरात् ॥ २९
अनामयमवाप्नोति दीर्घमायुः श्रिया सह ।
सघृतेन पयोऽन्नेन हुत्वा पर्वणि पर्वणि ॥ ३०
राज्यश्रियमवाप्नोति षण्मासान्नाऽत्र संशयः ।
लाजैर्विशुद्धैर्जुहुयात्कन्याप्तैः सा वराप्तये ॥ ३१
क्षीरद्रुमसमिद्धोमाद्ब्राह्मणादीन्वशं नयेत् ।
स्नात्वा सहस्रं प्रजपेदादित्याभिमुखो मनुम् ॥ ३२
आधिव्याधिविनिर्मुक्तो दीर्घमायुरवाप्नुयात् ।
अनेन मनुना सर्वं साधयेदिष्टमात्मनः ॥ ३३

सा कन्या वराप्तये जुहुयादित्यन्वयः । क्षीरद्रुमाः । अश्वत्थोदुम्बरप्लक्षवटाः । यथासंख्यं विप्रादिवशकारकाः । ब्राह्मणादिषु यथासंख्यं मधुरत्रययुक्तत्वमपि ज्ञेयम् । "स्वादुत्रयस्तनजं तु होमविधिना" इत्याचार्योक्तेः ।

तन्त्रान्तरादन्यमुच्यते—

विम्बद्वन्द्वे कृशानोर्विलिखतु मनुमैशं[मिनं] समायं तदस्त्रि-
ष्वग्न्यादिव्यञ्जनाख्यान् स्मृतिहरणमथो सन्धिषट्के सतारम् ।
अष्टारं तारयुग्व्याहृतिकुपरिवृतं नारसिंहास्त्रि चानु
द्वात्रिंशत्पत्रगवरम्बकमनु च जगज्जम्भूम्याभिवीतम् ॥ इति ॥३१॥३२॥३३॥

गायत्रीत्रिष्टुबनुष्टुब्वर्णैः प्रोक्तः शताक्षरः ।
पूर्वोक्ता एव मुन्याद्याः परं तेजोऽस्य देवता ॥ २४

हृत् त्रयोदशभिः प्रोक्तं रुद्रार्णैः शिर ईरितम् ।
द्वाविंशत्या शिखा प्रोक्ता तावद्भिः कवचं मतम् ॥ २५

स्यात् पञ्चदशभिर्नेत्रमस्त्रं सप्तदशाक्षरैः ।
वर्णन्यासादिकं सर्वं कुर्यात् पूर्वोक्तवर्त्मना ॥ २६

सत्यं मानविवर्जितं श्रुतिगिरामाद्यं जगत्कारणं
व्याप्तं स्थावरजङ्गमं मुनिवरैर्ध्यातं निरुद्धेन्द्रियैः ।
अर्काग्नीन्दुमयं शताक्षरवपुस्तारात्मकं सन्ततं
नित्यानन्दगुणालयं गुणपरं वन्दामहे तन्महः ॥ २७

शताक्षरमन्त्रमाह गायत्रीति । शताक्षर इति गायत्र्याश्चतुर्विंशतिवर्णत्वम् । त्रिष्टुभश्चतुश्चत्वारिंशद्वर्णत्वम् । अनुष्टुभो द्वात्रिंशद्वर्णत्वं चाभिप्रेत्योक्तम् । कश्चित्तु वैदिकत्वादस्य मन्त्रस्याद्यन्तयोः प्रणवदानात् शताक्षरतामाह स्म । तदसम्बद्धम् । यतः षडङ्गोक्तौ "द्वाविंशत्या शिखा प्रोक्ता तावद्भिः कवचं मतम्" इत्यङ्गद्वयमुक्तम् । तदवक्तृतं स्यात् । पूर्वोक्ता इति मन्त्रत्रयस्यापि । तदुक्तम्—

ऋष्याद्याः पूर्वोक्तास्त्रिविधाः स्युः । इति ॥ २४ ॥

रुद्रार्णैरित्येकादशाक्षरैः । तावद्भिरिति । द्वाविंशत्यक्षरैः ॥ २५॥२६ ॥

ध्यानमाह सत्यमिति । अरूपस्य ब्रह्मणो भावनरूपं ध्यानमेतत् । सत्यम् । असत्यव्यावृत्तिरूपम् । "सत्यं ज्ञानमनन्तं ब्रह्म" इति श्रुतेः । मानविवर्जितम् । प्रमाणागोचरीकृतम् । "यतो वाचो निवर्त्तन्ते" इति श्रुतेः । श्रुतिगिरामाद्यम् । वेदप्रवक्तृ । "शास्त्रयोनित्वात्" इति बादरायणिसूत्रणात् । जगत्कारणम् । "जन्माद्यस्य" इति सूत्रणात् । व्याप्तस्थावरजङ्गमम् । "सहस्रशीर्षा" इत्यादि श्रुतेः । मुनिवरैर्नारदादिभिः । अर्काग्नीन्दुमयमिति गायत्र्यादिदेवताक्रमेण । यद्वा अर्को विष्णुः अग्नी रुद्र इन्दुर्ब्रह्मा तन्मयम् । तत्र तत्प्रवृत्तत्वात् । यद्वा ॐकाररूपत्वं वक्ष्यति । एतेनाऽकारोकारमकारात्मकत्वेनाऽग्नीन्द्वर्करूपत्वम् । शताक्षरवपुरिति । शताक्षरैः परं महः प्रतिपाद्यते । प्रतिपाद्यप्रतिपादकयोरभेदात् शास्त्रयोनित्वेन कार्यकारणाभेदाद्वा शब्दब्रह्मरूपत्वाद्वा तथोक्तिः । यद्वा यतः अर्काग्नीन्दुरूपत्वम् अतएव शताक्षरवपुरिति हेतुहेतुमद्भावेन योजना ।

लक्षमानं जपेदेनमयुतं पायसान्धसा।
जुहुयात् घृतसिक्तेन मन्त्रविद्विजितेन्द्रियः॥ ३८
सौरे पीठे यजेत्सम्यक् वक्ष्यमाणविधानतः।
आद्यामावृतिमभ्यर्चेत् षडङ्गैर्देशिकोत्तमः॥ ३९
गायत्रीशक्तिभिस्तिस्रः पूजयेदावृतीः क्रमात्।
आवृतिः पञ्चमी प्रोक्ता त्रिष्टुबुद्भूतशक्तिभिः॥ ४०
अनुष्टुप्शक्तिभिः प्रोक्तमावृतीनां चतुष्टयम्।
इन्द्राद्यैर्दशमी प्रोक्ता वज्राद्यैस्तत्परा मता॥ ४१
एवं सिद्धे मनौ मन्त्री भवेद्भास्करसन्निभः।

ॐकाररूपत्वमस्य ग्रन्थकृदेवाऽन्ये पटले वक्ष्यति। नित्यानन्दचित्त्वं तत्स्वरूपमेव। तदालयत्वं च भगवत उपचारात्। गुणेभ्यः सत्वरजस्तमोभ्यः परं तद्रूपितम्। तद्वेदशिरसि प्रसिद्धम्। महः। नित्यं प्रकाशकत्वान् मह इव। एते च सर्वे शब्दास्तस्य वस्तुनो लक्षका एव न वाचकाः। एतेषां शब्दानामेकार्थत्वमपर्यायत्वेऽपि अतद्व्यावृत्त्यर्थतया न पौनरुक्त्यम्।

यद्वा महस्तेजोरूपा कुण्डलिनी उच्यते। सत्यं नित्यत्वात्तस्याः। "नित्या शक्तिः परा देवी" इत्युक्तेः। मानमियत्ता तद्वर्जिता। "सूक्ष्मात् सूक्ष्मतरा विभुः" इत्युक्तेः। व्याप्तस्थावरजङ्गमा। "सर्वगा विश्वरूपिणी दिक्कालाद्यनवच्छिन्ना" इत्युक्तेः। निरुद्धेन्द्रियैर्मुनिवरैर्ध्याता। "योगिध्येया च सर्वदा" इत्युक्तेः। "योगिनां हृदयाम्भोजे नृत्यन्ती नित्यमञ्जसा" इत्यपि। अर्काग्नीन्दुरूपा। "त्रिधामजननी देवी" इत्युक्तेः। "सोमसूर्याग्निरूपा च" इत्यपि। शताक्षरवपुः। "विश्वात्मना प्रबुद्धा सा सूते मन्त्रमयं जगत्" इत्युक्तेः। तारात्मकम्।

तन्मध्ये चिन्तयेद्देवीमृज्वाकारां तडित्प्रभाम्।
ॐकाररूपिणीं ज्योत्स्नामात्मरूपां शुभोदयाम्। इत्युक्तेः॥

नित्यानन्दगुणालया। "नित्यानन्दगुणोदया" इत्युक्तेः। गुणपरा। गुणरूपा परा च। "शक्तिः कुण्डलिनी गुणत्रयवपुर्विद्युल्लतासन्निभा" इत्युक्तेः। "परापरविभागेन परशक्तिरियं मता" इत्युक्तेश्च॥ ३७॥

पायसान्धसा पायसेन॥ ३८॥

अभ्यर्चेदिति। कर्णिकायाम्। देशिकोत्तमः क्रमादित्यनेन दलमूलमध्याग्रेष्वित्युक्तम्। तिस्र इति। अष्टाष्टदेवतात्मिकाः। त्रिष्टुबिति।

सुधालतोद्भवैः खण्डैर्जुहुयात्क्षीरसंयुतैः ॥ ४२
दीर्घमायुरवाप्नोति निराधिर्व्याधिवर्जितः।
दूर्वाभिर्घृतसिक्ताभिस्तदेव फलमाप्नुयात् ॥ ४३
मधुरत्रयसंसिक्तैर्जुहुयादरुणाम्बुजैः।
महालक्ष्मीमवाप्नोति षड्भिर्मासैर्विधानवित् ॥ ४४
रक्तोत्पलैस्त्रिमध्वक्तैर्जुहुयात्सर्वसम्पदे।
श्रीप्रसूनैः प्रजुहुयाद्रमाया वसतिर्भवेत् ॥ ४५
सहस्रं जुहुयान्नित्यं मासमेकं तिलैः शुभैः।
भानुसंख्यान् द्विजान्नित्यं भोजयेन्मधुरान्वितैः ॥ ४६
सर्वपापैर्विनिर्मुक्तः सर्वरोगविवर्जितः।
कृत्याद्रोहग्रहद्रोहान् जित्वा दीर्घं स जीवति ॥ ४७
प्रातःस्नानरतो मन्त्री जपेन्नित्यं शतं शतम्।
भानुमालोकयन् सम्यक् स जीवेच्छरदां शतम् ॥ ४८
तारव्याहृतिसंरुद्धं जपेन्मन्त्रं शताक्षरम्।
नित्यमष्टोत्तरशतं निःश्रेयसफलाप्तये ॥ ४९
गायत्र्याद्यं जपेन्मन्त्रं सर्वपापविमुक्तये।
सर्वशत्रुविनाशाय त्रिष्टुबाद्यमिमं जपेत् ॥ ५०
अनुष्टुबाद्यं प्रजपेदायुरारोग्यसिद्धये।
शताक्षरो मनुः प्रोक्तः समस्तपुरुषार्थदः ॥ ५१

जागताद्याभिः दिशि दिशि एकादशैकादशभिः। चतुष्टयमिति। अष्टाष्टशक्तिरूपत्वेन। अष्टदिक्षु पुनरिति ज्ञेयम् ॥ ३८॥३९॥४०॥४१॥४२॥

सुधालता गुडची। भानुसंख्यानिति द्वादश ॥ ४२—४८ ॥

रुद्धमिति सम्पुटितम्। तदुक्तमाचार्यैः—

प्रणवव्याहृत्याद्या व्याहृतितारान्तिका च मन्त्रिवरैः। इति।

केचित्तु संरुद्धशब्देन संरोधनमाहुः। तच्च "नाम्न आद्यन्तमध्येषु मन्त्रः स्याद्रोधनं स्मृतम्" इति प्रकारेण प्रतिमन्त्रादौ तारव्याहृतीरिच्छन्ति। तदसाम्प्रदायिकम्। लिखितवचनविरोधात् ॥ ४९ ॥

गायत्र्याद्यमिति। यथा त्रिष्टुबाद्यम्। त्रिष्टुबनुष्टुब्गायत्र्यः।

ऋचो विधानं वारुण्या यथावदभिधीयते ।
ऋग्वेदे सा समुद्दिष्टा ध्रुवाखाद्या मनीषिभिः ॥ ५२

वशिष्ठो मुनिराख्यातश्छन्दस्त्रिष्टुबुदाहृतम् ।
वरुणो देवता प्रोक्तस्तद्वर्णैरङ्गकल्पना ॥ ५३

अष्टभिर्हृदयं प्रोक्तं सप्तभिः शिर ईरितम् ।
शिखा षड्वर्णैराख्याता वस्ववर्णैः कवचं मतम् ।

सप्तभिर्नेत्रमाख्यातमस्त्रं षड्भिरुदीरितम् ॥ ५४
साग्रेषु सन्धिषु पदोर्गुदाम्बुधारनाभिषु ।

कुक्षौ पृष्ठे हृदि कुचे गले बाह्वग्रसन्धिषु ॥ ५५
वक्त्रे कपोलनासाक्षिकर्णभ्रूमध्यमस्तके ।
शिरःसर्वाङ्गयोर्न्यस्येन्मन्त्रवर्णान् यथाविधि ॥ ५६

चन्द्रप्रभं पङ्कजसन्निषण्णं पाशाङ्कुशाभीतिवरं दधानम् ।
मुक्ताविभूषाञ्चितसर्वगात्रं ध्यायेत् प्रसन्नं वरुणं विभूत्यै ॥ ५७

लक्षमेकं जपेन्मन्त्रं पायसेन दशांशतः ।
सर्पिःसिक्तेन जुहुयान्मन्त्री मन्त्रस्य सिद्धये ॥ ५८
धर्मादिकल्पिते पीठे वरुणं सम्यगर्चयेत् ।
कृत्वाऽङ्गपूजनं शेषं वासुकिं तक्षकं पुनः ॥ ५९

अनुष्टुबाद्यमिति । अनुष्टुप् गायत्री त्रिष्टुप् ॥ ५०॥५१ ॥

ध्रुवासाद्येति । मन्त्रो यथा । ध्रुवासु त्वासु क्षितिषु क्षियन्तो व्यस्मत्पाशं वरुणो मुमोचत् । अवो वन्वाना अदितेरुपस्थाद्यूयं पात स्वस्तिभिः सदा नः । इति ॥ ५२ ॥ ५३ ॥ ५४ ॥

वर्णन्यासमेवाह साग्रेष्विति । पदोः साग्रेषु सन्धिषु दशवर्णाः । गलान्तेषु नववर्णाः । बाह्वग्रसन्धिषु दशवर्णाः । शिष्टेषु त्रयोदश । मस्तकं केश-ललाटसन्धिः । शिरो ब्रह्मरन्ध्रम् ॥ ५५ ॥ ५६ ॥

ध्यानमाह चन्द्रेति । आयुधध्यानं दक्षाधूर्ध्वयोराद्यो तदधस्तनयोरन्त्ये ॥ ५७ ॥

धर्मादीति । पीठशक्तिपूजा रहिते । सम्यगित्यनेन पीठशक्तयस्तन्त्रान्तरोक्ताः पूजनीया इत्युक्तम् । ता यथा—

कर्कोटकं ततः पद्मं महापद्ममनन्तरम् ।
शङ्खपालाख्यकुलिकौ सम्यक् पत्रेषु पूजयेत् ॥ ६०
इन्द्राद्यानायुधान्येषामर्चयेत्तदनन्तरम् ।
ऋणमुक्त्यै जपेन्मन्त्रं प्रत्यहं साष्टकं शतम् ॥ ६१
जपेनाऽनेन लभते महतीमव्ययां श्रियम् ।
सितेक्षुशकलैर्मन्त्री जुहुयाद् घृतसंप्लुतैः ॥ ६२
चतुर्दिनं दशशतमृणमुक्त्यै महाश्रिये ।
समिद्भिर्वेतसोत्थाभिः चीराक्ताभिर्दिनत्रयम् ॥ ६३
जुहुयाद् वृष्टिसंसिद्ध्यै मन्त्रविद्विजितेन्द्रियः ।
अनेन विधिना मन्त्री सूर्ये शतभिषं गते ॥ ६४
चतुःशतं घृतयुतं पायसं जुहुयाद्वशी ।
ऋणनाशाय सम्पत्त्यै वश्यारोग्याभिवृद्धये ॥ ६५
भृगुवारे कृतो होमः पायसेन ससर्पिषा ।
महतीं सम्पदं कुर्यान्नाशयेत् सकलापदः ॥ ६६
शालिभिर्घृतसंसिक्तैः सरिदन्तरितः सुधीः ।
त्र्यहं चतुःशतं हुत्वा स्तम्भयेत्परसैन्यकम् ॥ ६७
सायं प्रत्यङ्मुखो वह्निमाराध्य प्रजपेन्मनुम् ।
चतुःशतं विमुच्येत मन्त्री सर्वैरुपद्रवैः ॥ ६८
मन्त्री प्रत्यङ्मुखो भूत्वा तर्पयेद्विमलैर्जलैः ।
सर्वोपद्रवनाशाय समस्ताभ्युदयाप्तये ॥ ६९
बहुना किमिहोक्तेन मन्त्रेणाऽनेन साधकः ।
साधयेत् सकलान् कामान् जपहोमादितत्परः ॥ ७०

सुधा कुमुदिनी पूर्णा वारुणी विश्वतोमुखी ।
तरङ्गिणी च सुरसा सुशीताप्यायनी तथा ॥ इति ॥

कृत्वाऽङ्गपूजनमिति । केसरेष्वित्यर्थः । सम्यक् पत्रेषु पूजयेदिति । सम्यगित्यनेन शेषादीनां ध्यानं कर्त्तव्यमित्युक्तम् । तत् त्वरितापटले मदुक्तमनुसन्धेयम् ॥ ५८॥५९॥६०॥६१ ॥

ऋणमुक्त्यै इति । अत्र पाशमित्यस्य पूर्वं ऋणशब्दमधिकमुच्चार्य जपेदित्यर्थः ।

प्राणप्रतिष्ठामन्त्रस्य विधानमभिधीयते ।
येन प्राणेरिता मन्त्राः प्राणवन्तो भवन्ति ते ॥ ७१

पाशाङ्कुशपुटा शक्तिर्वालो बिन्दुविभूषितः ।
याद्याः सप्त सकारान्ता व्योमसद्येन्दुसंयुतम् ॥ ७२

तदन्ते हंसमन्त्रः स्यात् ततोऽमुष्यपदं वदेत् ।
प्राणा इति वदेत्पश्चादिह प्राणास्ततः परम् ॥ ७३

अमुष्य जीव इह च स्थितोऽमुष्यपदं वदेत् ।
सर्वेन्द्रियाण्यमुष्यान्ते वाङ्मनश्चक्षुरन्ततः ॥ ७४

श्रोत्रघ्राणमादप्राणा इहागत्य सुखं चिरम् ।
तिष्ठन्त्वग्निवधूरन्ते प्राणमन्त्रोऽयमीरितः ॥ ७५

सितेक्षुशकलैः पवखण्डा इति प्रसिद्धैः । सरिदन्तरितः द्वीपस्थः ॥ ६१—७० ॥

येनेति । मन्त्राणां यद्यपि प्राणप्रतिष्ठा नास्ति तेषां स्वत एव समर्थत्वात् तथापि यन्त्रादौ लिखितानां प्रतिष्ठा क्रियत इति तद्द्वारा प्राणवन्त इत्युक्तिः । प्राणप्रतिष्ठया पूर्वोक्तसमस्तमन्त्रविहितयन्त्रप्रयोगपुत्तल्यादि सर्वं प्रतिष्ठितप्राणं क्रियत इति । अवश्यं ज्ञेयोऽयं सर्वसारभूतो मन्त्र इति तत्स्तुतिः । तदुक्तम्—

तस्मादृतेऽमी कथिताः प्रयोगा व्यर्था भवेयुर्गतजीवकल्पाः । इति ॥ ७१ ॥

मन्त्रोद्धारमाह पाशेति । प्रथमं पाशबीजं ततः शक्तिबीजं ततोऽङ्कुशबीजम् । वालो यः बिन्दुभूषितः यं । याद्या इति उद्धृतयकारानुवादेन । अतद्गुणसंविज्ञानबहुव्रीहिणा वा सप्त न तु तद्यमिति बीजं भिन्नम् । पूर्वं पृथगुद्धारस्तु समानामपि सबिन्दुताख्यापनाय अग्रे न्यासावसरे अन्यक्तताऽस्य बीजस्य न्यासो नोक्तः । तेनास्य पृथगुद्धारः । तदुक्तमाचार्यैः—

पाशाङ्कुशान्तरितशक्तिमनोः परस्ता-
दुच्चार्य यादिवसुवर्णगणं सहंसम् । इति ॥

अन्यथापि—अङ्कुशवायुनलावनिवरुणबीजानि । इति ।

व्योम हः सद्य औ इन्दुः बिन्दुः तेन हौं । प्रपञ्चसारपद्येऽपि गण औ तेन हौमित्येव पद्मपादाचार्यैर्व्याख्यातम् । समन्ते हंसमन्त्र इत्यपपाठः । इह चेति । चकारो न मन्त्रमध्ये । क्वचिदिहत इति पाठः । तदा इहशब्दादित्यर्थः । स्थितोऽमुष्येति । छन्दोऽनुरोधात् सन्धिः । मन्त्रे तु न सन्धिः । सर्वेन्द्रियाणि

प्रत्यमुष्यपदं पूर्वं पाशादीनि प्रयोजयेत् ।
प्रयोगेषु समाख्यातः प्राणमन्त्रो मनीषिभिः ॥ ७६

ब्रह्मविष्णुशिवाः प्रोक्ता मुनयस्तत्त्ववेदिभिः ।
उक्तामृग्यजुषोः साम्नश्छन्दश्छन्दोविशारदैः ॥ ७७

चैतन्यरूपा प्राणात्मा देवता शक्तिरीरिता ।
कवर्गेण वियत्पूर्वभूतैर्हृदयमीरितम् ॥ ७८

शिरश्चवर्गशब्दाद्यैरीरितं तदनन्तरम् ।
घ्राणेन्द्रियैष्टवर्गाद्यैस्तच्छिखा परिकीर्त्तिता ॥ ७९

अमुष्येत्यत्रापि तथैव । षडधिकषष्ट्यक्षरो मन्त्रः । अमुष्यपदार्थश्चतुर्थ उक्तः । अत्र मन्त्रे इहागत्येत्यत्र इहैवागत्येति एव शब्दो ज्ञेयः ।
तथा चाचार्यः—सैवेहागमथो त्वयुक् सुखं चिरं तिष्ठन्तु ठद्वन्द्वयुक् । इति ।
पद्मपादाचार्यैरप्येवमेव पठितम् । आं बीजं क्रों शक्तिः ॥ ७२॥७३॥७४॥७५ ॥

प्रयोगकाले विशेषमाह प्रतीति । पद्मपादाचार्यास्तु । एवं सति प्रयोगमन्त्रो भवतीति यादीनां त्रिरावृत्तिरभिहिता । प्राणजीवसर्वेन्द्रियाकर्षणार्थम् । केचिद्यादीनां चतुरावृत्तिं वर्णयन्ति । प्राणजीवेन्द्रियसामान्यतद्विशेषाणामाकर्षणार्थम् । केचित् पञ्चावृत्तिं । प्राणसामान्यजीवसामान्येन्द्रियसामान्येन्द्रियविशेषप्राणविशेषाणामाकर्षणार्थम् । केचिन् नवावृत्तिं । मन्त्रोक्तानां सर्वेषां प्रत्येकमाकर्षणार्थमित्याहुः । मनीषिभिरित्यनेन हंसमन्त्रादौ ॐ यं सं हं सः क्रों ॐ स्वाहान्ते च ॐ यं सं हं सः क्रों ॐ इत्युच्चारणीयमिति सूचितम् । पद्मपादाचार्यैः "मन्त्रोऽयमित्थमुदितो ग्रहसंख्ययैव" इत्यस्य व्याख्याने ग्रहाः सप्त तत्संख्याक्षरैः युक्तमिति व्याख्यातम् । तेनात्मनि यन्त्रे पुत्तल्यादावपि प्राणप्रतिष्ठासमये प्रत्यमुष्यपदं पाशाद्यानि प्रयोज्याऽमुष्यपदस्थाने षष्ठ्यन्तं साध्यनाम प्रयुज्य मन्त्रमुच्चरेदिति ज्ञेयम् ॥ ७६॥७७॥७८ ॥

षडङ्गमाह कवर्गेणेति । अत्र वियत्पूर्वभूतैरित्युक्तेः प्रथमपटलोक्तसृष्टिक्रमो विवक्षितः । तेनाऽक्षराणां तथा व्यत्यास इति ज्ञेयम् । तदुक्तम्—

प्रत्येकं कादिवर्गैः प्रतिगतलिपिभिः बिन्दुयुक्तैः । इति ।

अत्र चात्मनेऽन्ताः सजातय इत्युक्तत्वात् प्रयोगो यथा । ङं कं खं घं गं आकाशवायुवह्निसलिलभूम्यात्मने हृत् । ञं चं छं झं जं शब्दस्पर्शरूपरसगन्धात्मने

कर्मेन्द्रियैस्तवर्गाद्यैः कवचं परिकीर्त्तितम् ।
वचनाद्यैः पवर्गाद्यैर्विलोचनमुदीरितम् ॥ ८०

बुद्ध्याद्यैर्यादिसंयुक्तैरस्त्रमस्य समीरितम् ।
आत्मनेऽन्ताः समाख्याता अङ्गमन्त्राः सजातयः ॥ ८१

नाभेश्चरणपर्यन्तं पाशबीजं प्रविन्यसेत् ।
हृदयान्नाभिपर्यन्तं शक्तिबीजं ततः परम् ॥ ८२

मूर्धादि हृदयं यावदङ्कुशं विन्यसेत्ततः ।
हृदये धातुषु न्यसेद्यादीन् सप्त यथाक्रमम् ॥ ८३

प्राणे जीवे ततो न्यस्येद्धंसवर्णद्वयं पृथक् ।
कुर्याद्व्यापकमेतेन समस्तेन विधानवित् ।
ततो विचिन्तयेद्देवीं जीवभूतां जगन्मयीम् ॥ ८४

रक्ताब्धिपोतारुणमध्यसंस्थां पाशाङ्कुशाविक्षुशरासबाणान् ।
शूलं कपालं दधतीं कराब्जै रक्तां त्रिनेत्रां प्रणमामि देवीम् ॥ ८५

एवं ध्यात्वा जगद्धात्रीं लक्षमेनं जपेन्मनुम् ।
जुहुयात्तद्दशांशेन चरुभिर्घृतसंयुतैः ॥ ८६

शिरः। णं टं ठं ढं डं श्रोत्रत्वक्चक्षुर्जिह्वाघ्राणात्मने शिखा। नं तं थं धं दं वाक्पाणिपादपायूपस्थात्मने वर्म। मं पं फं भं बं वचनादानविहरणविसर्गानन्दात्मने नेत्रम्। शं यं रं वं लं हं षं क्षं सं लं बुद्धिमनोऽहङ्कारचित्तज्ञानात्मने अस्त्रम्। पद्मपादाचार्यैर्वर्णानां स्वरपुटितत्वं विपरीतत्वमप्युक्तम्। यथाक्रममिति। ह्रोमित्यस्य ओजसि न्यास इत्युक्तम् ॥ ७८॥७९॥८०॥८१॥८२॥८३॥

प्राण इति। हृदय इत्यनुषज्यते। तेन प्राणजीवयोरपि हृदय एव न्यासः। पृथगिति। प्रत्येकम्। एतेन समस्तेनेति। मूलेनेत्यर्थः। विधानविदित्यनेन मूर्धादिपादान्तमित्युक्तम्। तदुक्तम्। "न्यसेन्मूलं व्यापकं मस्तकादि" इति ॥८४॥

रक्ताब्धीति। रक्तेति पोतविशेषणम्। आयुधध्यानं तु वामाद्यूर्ध्वयोराद्ये। तदधस्तनयोर्मध्ये। तदधस्तनयोः कपालशूले इति ॥ ८५ ॥

तद्दशांशेनेत्यस्यायमर्थः। ॐ आं स्वाहा ॐ ह्रीं स्वाहा ॐ क्रों स्वाहा ॐ यं स्तताये स्वाहा। एवं राद्यक्षरयुताभिः वैवस्वताद्याभिः सकृत् सकृत् हुत्वा ॐ यं सं हं सः ह्रीं ॐ इत्यक्षरैरपि तथा हुत्वा मूलेनोक्तसंख्यां जुहुयादिति। अयमर्थः

षट्कोणाढ्ये शक्तिपीठे विधिनाऽनेन पूजयेत् ।
अर्चयेत् षट्सु कोणेषु ब्रह्माणं विष्णुमीश्वरम् ॥ ८७
वाणीं लक्ष्मीमुमां पश्चात् षडङ्गानि प्रपूजयेत् ।
दलेषु मातरः पूज्यास्तद्बाह्ये लोकपालकाः ॥ ८८
एवं प्रपूजयेद्देवीं सुगन्धिकुसुमादिभिः ।
इति संसाधितो मन्त्रः षट्कर्मफलदो भवेत् ॥ ८९
स्थापयेन्मनुनाऽनेन प्राणान् सर्वत्र देशिकः ।
बीजान्तेऽमुष्यशब्दानामादौ दूतीः प्रयोजयेत् ॥ ९०
मृता वैवस्वता भूयो जीवहा प्राणहा ततः ।
आकृष्या मथनी पश्चात् प्रमादा विस्फुलिङ्गिनी ॥ ९१

पद्मपादाचार्याणां सम्मतः ॥ ८६ ॥

शक्तिपीठ इत्यनेन नवशक्तिः पीठशक्तयोऽत्र पूज्या इत्युक्तम् । पूजयेदिति । जगद्धात्रीमिति पश्चात्तनेन सम्बध्यते । अनेन वक्ष्यमाणेन । तमेव विधिमाह अर्चयेदिति । तत्र प्रकारः । प्राङ्निर्ऋतिवायुकोणस्थाः ब्रह्मविष्णवीशाः आग्नेयवारुणैशेषु वाण्याद्या इति परमगुरवः । प्रागुक्तं ब्रह्मादीनां शक्तीनां च बीजमनुसन्धेयम् । प्रपूजयेदिति केसरेषु ॥ ८७॥८८॥८९ ॥

सर्वत्रेति आत्मयन्त्रपुत्तल्यादौ । दूतीमन्त्रानुद्धरति बीजेति । बीजान्ते पाशादिहंसमन्त्रान्ते । केचन बीजान्त इति बीजत्रयान्त इत्याहुः । तदसम्बद्धम् । आचार्यवचनविरोधात् । अमुष्यशब्दानामादाविति चासम्बद्धं स्यात् । अमुष्य-शब्दानामादाविति । साध्यनाम्न आदौ । तदुक्तम्—

अथ यादीन् दूतीशोक्ता साध्यनामाऽथ मन्त्री । इति ।

आं ह्रीं क्रों यं रं लं वं शं षं सं हों ॐ क्षं सं हं सः ह्रीं ॐ यं मृते अमुष्य मृतात्मकान् प्राणानिहाहर प्राणा इह प्राणा इति वा इहैवेत्याद्योमन्तमुक्त्वा पुनरामादि ओमन्तमुक्त्वा यं मृते अमुष्य मृतात्मकं जीवमिहाहर जीव इह स्थित इति वा इहैवेत्याद्योमन्तमुक्त्वा पुनरामादि ओमन्तमुक्त्वा यं मृते अमुष्य मृतात्मकानि सर्वेन्द्रियाणि इहाहर सर्वेन्द्रियाणि इह वा पुनरिहैवेत्यादि ओमन्तमुक्त्वा पुनरामादि ओमन्तमुक्त्वा यं मृते अमुष्य मृतात्मकान् वाङ्मनश्चक्षुः-श्रोत्रघ्राणप्राणान् इहाहर वाङ्मनश्चक्षुःश्रोत्रघ्राणप्राणा इह वा । इहैवेत्यादि

क्षेत्रज्ञप्रतिहार्येता: प्राणदूत्यो नव स्मृता: ।
पाशेन बद्धचेष्टस्य शक्त्या स्वीकृतचेतस: ॥ ९२

अङ्कुशेनाहृतस्याभि: साध्यस्याऽसून् समाहरेत् ।
द्वादशाङ्गुलमानेन कृत्वा साध्यस्य पुत्तलीम् ॥ ९३

तस्यां प्राणात्मकं यन्त्रं सकीटं हृदये न्यसेत् ।
निशीथसमये साध्ये सुप्ते तस्य हृदम्बुजे ॥ ९४

दलेषु वायुवह्नीन्द्रवरुणानामत:परम् ।
ईशराक्षसशीतांशुयमानां कर्णिकान्तरे ॥ ९५

यादीन् हंससमायुक्तान् भृङ्गाकाराननुस्मरेत् ।
शिरोबिन्दुसमुद्भूततन्तुसम्बद्धविग्रहान् ॥ ९६

एवमात्महृदम्भोजे भृङ्गीरूपान् धिया स्मरेत् ।
आत्महृत्पद्मगा भृङ्गी: प्रस्थाप्य श्वासवर्त्मना ॥ ९७

एकैकात् साध्यहृत्पद्माद्भृङ्गमेकैकमानयेत् ।
पुत्तल्यां स्थापयेन्मन्त्री स्वचित्ते वा विधानवित् ॥ ९८

श्रोमन्त्रं वदेत्। एवं वैवस्वतादिमन्त्रा ऊहनीया: ॥ ८०॥८१॥८२ ॥

युगपद्वा प्राणप्रतिष्ठाप्रकारमाह पाशेनेत्यादिना सर्वेषु कर्मस्वित्यन्तेन। आभिर्दूतीभि:। प्राणात्मकं यन्त्रं वक्ष्यमाणं सकीटम्। तत्र प्राणप्रतिष्ठारम्भात् प्रागेव साध्यप्रतिकृते: हृदये यन्त्रं सजीवं कीटं च निक्षिप्याक्राम्य प्रयोगमारभेतेत्यर्थ:। प्राणप्रतिष्ठायां कर्त्तव्यमाह निशीथेति। पद्मपादाचार्यास्तु कालदण्डेन सन्ताड्य बोधनमाहु:। अन्यथा प्राणप्रतिष्ठायोगादिति।

बद्ध्वा तं च निपीडमेव सहसा कालस्य यष्ट्या शिर-

स्याताड्य क्षुभिताखिलेन्द्रियगणं साध्यं स्मरेत् साधक:। इत्युक्ते: ॥८२॥८३॥८४॥

स्वहृदये साध्यहृदये पुत्तलीहृदये च श्वतादिदूतीनां स्थानमाह दलेष्विति। भृङ्गाकाराननुस्मरेदिति। याद्यक्षररूपश्वतादीन् साध्यहृत्पद्मपत्रेषु कर्णिकायां भृङ्गरूपान् स्वहृदयपद्मे भृङ्गीरूपान् ध्यायेदित्यर्थ:। शिर इति। यकारादिबीजानां शिरसि ये बिन्दव: तत्समुद्भूता ये तन्तव: तै: सम्बद्धविग्रहानिति। तदुक्तमाचार्यै:—"स्वीयबिन्दुप्रबद्धान्" इति। पुत्तल्यामिति। क्रूरकर्मणि। स्वचित्ते इति वश्यादौ। विधानविदिति। स्ववहन्नाड्या प्रवेशनिर्गमनकुशल

तन्तुच्छेदं प्रकुर्वीत वह्निबीजेन संयतः ।
आकृष्टान् साध्यहृद्भृङ्गान् भुवा संस्तम्भयेत्ततः ॥ ९९
एवमेकादशावृत्तीः कुर्यात् सर्वेषु कर्मसु ।
वश्याकर्षणयोर्यादीनरुणान् संस्मरेत् सुधीः ॥ १००
मोहविद्वेषयोर्धूम्रान् कृष्णान्मारणकर्मणि ।
पीतां संस्तम्भने ध्यायेत् प्राणाकर्षणकर्मणि ॥ १०१
आकृष्टान् साध्यहृत्प्राणान् स्थापयेदात्मनो हृदि ।
क्रूरकर्मसु पुत्तल्यां तेषां स्थापनमीरितम् ॥ १०२

इत्युक्तम्। वह्निबीजेन रमित्यनेन। संयतः अस्मिन्नस्मिन् दले स्वतादिस्थानमिति सावधान इत्यर्थः। भुवा ग्लौमिति बीजेन। तत्र प्रकारः। साध्यस्य शक्तिं पाशशक्तितेजोऽङ्कुशमहाभ्रमरकालदण्डरूपेण पञ्चधा निःसार्य पाशबीजमुच्चरन् साध्यं पाशेन गले बद्धा शक्तिबीजतेजसा तं स्ववशे कृत्वाऽङ्कुशेनाकृष्याऽग्रतः संस्थाप्य याद्यष्टकमुच्चरन् साध्यस्य त्वगादीन् व्याप्यापकृष्य महाभृङ्गेण साध्यं कवलीकृत्य कालदण्डताडनेन सुप्तं तं सम्बोध्य त्वमिति सपरिवारमुन्मूलीकृत्य समिति स्वप्राणशक्तिरूपमहाभ्रमरेण मेलयित्वा हंस इति स्वैक्यं सम्भाव्य क्रोमोमिति वश्यादौ जीवनाय प्लावनं कृत्वा यं स्वते इत्यादिना स्वस्वतां सम्बोध्य अमुष्य स्वतात्मकाः इह प्राणा इत्यादिना स्वस्वताप्राणानितरप्राणैः संयोज्य रमिति साध्यस्वतातन्तुच्छेदं विधाय सकोटहृदयायां पुत्तल्यामात्मनि वा साध्यस्वताप्राणान् संस्थाप्य ग्लौमिति संस्तभ्य तस्य स्वताजीवादिकमप्येवमानयेत्। युगपदेव वा स्वताप्राणादीन् स्थापयेत्। ततः स्वहृदि चेत्। आं क्रोमित्यादि मयि प्राणा इह प्राणा मयि जीव इह स्थित इत्यादिरूपम्। पुत्तल्यां चेत्। पुत्तल्यां प्राणा इह प्राणा पुत्तल्यां जीव इह स्थित इति जपेत्। इत्थं स्वताप्रतिष्ठाक्रमः। एवं वैवस्वतादिप्राणा अपि स्थापनीयाः। ततो यादीन् होमन्तानुक्त्वा साध्यस्य धातून् जीवं च सपरिकरं पुनः स्वमण्डले सङ्कोचितं कवलीकृत्य यादीन् दूतीश्च स्वस्य सम्मुखरत्नान् साध्यस्य चामुष्य प्राणानिहाहर अमुष्य प्राणा इह प्राणा इति चोक्त्वा पुनरपि अमुष्य धातूनिहाहरेत्यादि वदेत्। एवं जीवेऽपि। अयमेव प्रकारः पुत्तल्यामपि। तदुक्तम्—

आकृष्टानां साध्यदेशादसूनां पुत्तल्यादावप्ययं स्यात् प्रकारः। इति ॥

एवमिति। पूर्वोक्तं कर्म एकादशावृत्तिं कुर्यात्। अयं च पूर्वविधिः। इत

प्राणान् साध्यस्य मण्डूकानात्मनस्तु भुजङ्गमान् ।
संस्मरेत्तत्र निपुणः सदा क्रूरेषु कर्मसु ॥ १०३

वाय्वग्निशक्रवरुणेश्वरराक्षसेन्दु-
प्रेतेशपत्रलिखितैरथ यादिवर्णैः ।
बिन्द्वन्तिकैः स्वगतहंससमेतसाध्यं
प्राणात्मयन्त्रमथ वर्णवृतं धरास्थम् ॥ १०४

इत्थं प्रयोगकुशलो मनुनाऽनेन मन्त्रवित् ।
वशयेत्सकलान्देवान् किं पुनः पार्थिवान् जनान् ॥ १०५

आवाहन्यादिका मुद्राः प्रवक्ष्यामि यथाक्रमम् ।
याभिर्विरचिताभिस्तु मोदन्ते सर्वदेवताः ॥ १०६

ऊर्ध्वं यदृच्छया कुर्यात् । तदुक्तम् —

प्राणप्रतिष्ठाकर्मेदं विधायैकादशावरम् । इति ॥ ९५॥९६॥९७ ॥
॥ ९८॥९९॥१००॥१०१॥१०२॥१०३ ॥

यन्त्रमाह वाय्विति । यादिवर्णैरिति होमन्तैः । धरास्थमिति । बाह्ये भूगृहावृतमित्यर्थः । पद्मपादाचार्यास्त्वन्यथा यन्त्रमाहुः । तद्यथा । अष्टदल-मध्यगतशक्तौ साध्यादिकमालिख्य पाशाङ्कुशाभ्यां तां संवेष्ट्य याद्यष्टकमष्टदलेषु लिखित्वा अवशिष्टेन बहिः संवेष्ट्य भूपुरद्वये पाशाङ्कुशौ लिखेदिति यन्त्र-विधिरिति ॥ १०४॥१०५ ॥

मुद्रा आह आवाहनीति । रा दाने । मुदं राति ददाति मुद्रेति निर्वचनम् । इदमेव मोदन्ते सर्वदेवता इत्यनेन सूचितम् । अतएव तद्दर्शनेन देवताहर्षो-त्पत्तिः । स्वाङ्गुल्यो हि पञ्चभूतात्मिकाऽङ्गुष्ठाद्याः आकाशवाय्वग्निसलिलभू-रूपाः । तासां मिथः संयोगरूपसङ्केतात् कोपि देवताप्रगुणीभावपूर्वको मोदः सान्निध्यकरो भवति । तदुक्तम्—

पृथिव्यादीनि भूतानि कनिष्ठाद्याः क्रमान् मताः ।
तेषामन्योन्यसंभेदप्रकारैस्तत्प्रपञ्चता ॥
अर्चने जपकाले तु ध्याने काम्ये च कर्मणि ।
तत्तन्मुद्राः प्रयोक्तव्या देवतासन्निधापिकाः ॥ इति ॥

अन्यत्रापि—मुदं रातीति मुद्रा स्यादेनैका मुष्टिरेव तु ।

सम्यक् संपूरितः पुष्पैः कराभ्यां कल्पितोऽञ्जलिः ।
आवाहनी समाख्याता मुद्रा देशिकसत्तमैः ॥ १०७

अधोमुखी कृता सैव प्रोक्ता स्थापनकर्मणि ।
आश्लिष्टमुष्टियुगला प्रोन्नताङ्गुष्ठयुग्मका ॥ १०८

सन्निधाने समुद्दिष्टा मुद्रेयं तन्त्रवेदिभिः ।
अङ्गुष्ठगर्भिणी सैव सन्निरोधे समीरिता ॥ १०९

उत्तानौ द्वौ कृतौ मुष्टी सम्मुखीकरणी स्मृता ।
देवताङ्गे षडङ्गानां न्यासः स्यात् सकलीकृतिः ॥ ११०

सव्यहस्तकृता मुष्टिर्दीर्घाधोमुखतर्जनी ।
अवगुण्ठनमुद्रेयमभितो भ्रामिता सती ॥ १११

अन्योन्याभिमुखाश्लिष्टा कनिष्ठानामिका पुनः ।
तथा च तर्जनीमध्या धेनुमुद्रा समीरिता ॥ ११२

स्वल्पभेदात् कोपहर्षौ प्राणिनां जनयत्यतः ॥
तेनैव सर्वदेवानां मुद्रा हर्षप्रदा मता ।
पूजाकाले दर्शनीया मुद्रास्ताः सर्वदा शिवे ॥ इति ॥

तथा—खादिमार्गक्रमाद् भूतान्यङ्गुष्ठाद्यङ्गुलिक्रमात् ।
क्वापि मुक्तन्मिथोयोगात् सान्निध्यप्रकृताकरी ॥ इति ॥

अनयाहूतो भवेदिति प्रार्थनपूर्वकमावाहनी कार्या । तन्त्रान्तरे तु विशेषः—

हस्ताभ्यामञ्जलिं कृत्वाऽनामिकामूलपर्वणोः ।
अङ्गुष्ठौ निक्षिपेत् सेयं मुद्रा त्वावाहनी स्मृता ॥ इति ॥

एष एव साम्प्रदायिकः पक्षः ॥ १०६॥१०७॥१०८॥१०९॥११० ॥

भ्रामितेति वामावर्तक्रमेण । साम्प्रदायिका हस्तद्वयेनैतां मुद्रामाहुः ।
तदुक्तम्—वर्मणा समवगुण्ठय दोर्युजा । इति ॥ १११ ॥

धेनुमुद्रामाह अन्योन्येति । कनिष्ठाऽनामिका अन्योन्याभिमुखाश्लिष्टा तर्जनी मध्या तथैवान्योन्याभिमुखाश्लिष्टेत्यर्थः । हस्तद्वयाङ्गुल्यः अन्योन्यान्तरालप्रदेशेन पूर्वमधःकृतदक्षकनिष्ठाव्यतिषक्ताः कार्याः । तत्र दक्षकनिष्ठा दक्षानामापृष्ठमुल्लङ्घ्य तद्वामभागमागता वामानामिकया योज्या । वामा कनिष्ठिका तु यथास्थितैव दक्षानामया । एवं वामतर्जनी वाममध्यमापृष्ठमुल्लङ्घ्य तद्दक्ष-

अमृतीकरणं कुर्यात्तया देशिकसत्तमः।
अन्योन्यग्रथिताङ्गुष्ठा प्रसारितकराङ्गुली॥ ११३
महामुद्रेयमुदिता परमीकरणे बुधैः।
प्रयोजयेदिमां मुद्रां देवतायागकर्मणि॥ ११४
आदिक्षान्तार्णयोगित्वादक्षमालेति कीर्त्तिता।
तद्वर्णसंख्यैर्मणिभिर्जपमालां प्रकल्पयेत्॥ ११५

भागागतदक्षमध्यमया योज्या। दक्षतर्जनी यथास्थितैव वाममध्यमया योज्या।
तदुक्तम्—वामाङ्गुलीर्दक्षिणानामङ्गुलीनां च सन्धिषु।
प्रवेश्य मध्यमाभ्यां तु तर्ज्जन्यौ द्वौ प्रयोजयेत्।
कनिष्ठे ऽनामिकाभ्यां युञ्ज्यात् सा धेनुमुद्रिका॥ इति॥ ११२॥ ११३॥

महामुद्रामाह अन्योन्येति। पाण्योरङ्गुष्ठौ परस्परग्रन्थनेन ग्रन्थिरूपौ शेषाः सरलाः। एता मुद्रास्तत्तन्मन्त्रे च मदुक्तविशेषमुद्राश्च न कस्यचिद्दर्शयेत्।
तदुक्तं महासंहितायाम्—
न जातु दर्शयेन् मुद्रा महाजनसमागमे।
गुह्यमेतन् मुनिश्रेष्ठ तस्माद्रहसि योजयेत्॥
नाऽदीक्षितस्य मुद्राणां लक्षणानि प्रकाशयेत्।
क्षुभ्यन्ति देवतास्तस्य विफलं च भवेदिति॥
अन्यत्राऽपि—अक्षमालां च मुद्रां च गुरोरपि न दर्शयेत्। इति॥
अथ चैताः सर्वा रहस्येव कुर्यात्। मोक्षार्थिना मनसैव दर्शयितव्याः।
तदाहुः—मानसरूपसंकल्पा मुद्रा मोक्षार्थिनां विदुः।
इतरेषां तु सर्वेषां हस्ताभ्यां शस्यते बुधैः॥ इति॥ ११३॥ ११४॥

अक्षमालामाह आदीति। अकारादिक्षकारान्तानां वर्णानां माला अक्षमालेत्यर्थः। अत्रैकोऽधिकः क्षः स एव मेरुः। एतेन पञ्चाशद्गुलिकाभिरक्षमाला कार्येत्यपि सूचितम्।
तदुक्तम्—ब्रह्मनाडीगतानादिक्षान्तवर्णान् विभाव्य च।
अर्णं बिन्दुयुतं कृत्वा श्रेष्ठं मन्त्रं जपेत् पुनः॥
अकारादिषु संयोज्य तथा कादिषु च क्रमात्।
क्षार्णं मेरुमथो तत्र कल्पयेज्जगदीश्वरि॥

रुद्राक्षमालिका सूते जपेन स्वमनोरथान्।
पद्माक्षैर्विहिता माला शत्रूणां नाशिनी मता ॥ ११६

कुशग्रन्थिमयी माला सर्वपापविनाशिनी।
पुत्रजीवफलैः क्लृप्ता कुरुते पुत्रसम्पदम् ॥ ११७

तदा लिपिर्भवेदक्षमालाऽष्टशतसंख्यया।
अनया सर्वमन्त्राणां जपः सर्वार्थसाधकः ॥ इति ॥

अत्राऽक्षमालापदप्रयोगो गौण इति ज्ञेयम्। अनेनैतादृश्यक्षमाला पुरश्चरणविषयेऽप्युक्तम्। किञ्चाऽनेनाऽष्टोत्तरशतसंख्याकमणिभिर्नित्यजपेऽपि माला कार्या इत्यपि उक्तं भवति। अकारादि लकारान्तं सञ्जप्य विलोमेन लकारादि अकारान्तं च सञ्जप्य अष्टवर्गैरष्टवारं जप्त्वा क्षकारं मेरुं कुर्यादिति।

यदाहुः—अकारादि लकारान्तं पञ्चाशन्मणिस्तबकम्।
क्षकारं मेरुसंस्थाने लकारादि विलोमतः ॥
वर्गाष्टकविभेदेन शतमष्टोत्तरं भवेत्।
एकैकान्तरितं मन्त्रं जपादेवं फलप्रदम् ॥ इति ॥

तन्त्रान्तरे तु विशेषः—

पञ्चविंशतिभिर्मोक्षस्त्रिंशद्भिर्धनसिद्धयः।
सर्वार्थाः सप्तविंशत्या पञ्चदश्याभिचारिकम् ॥
पञ्चाशद्भिः काम्यकर्मसिद्धिः स्याच्चतुरुत्तरैः।
अष्टोत्तरशतैः सर्वसिद्धिरक्षैः कृतस्रजा ॥ इति ॥

तेन सप्तविंशत्या चतुःपञ्चाशता अष्टोत्तरशतेन च सर्वेषां सर्वकार्यसिद्ध्यर्थं नित्यजपार्थं च मालां कुर्यादित्युक्तम्। यदाहुः—

अष्टोत्तरशतैर्माला पञ्चाशच्चतुरन्वितैः।
सप्तविंशतिभिश्चाऽक्षैः सर्वसाधारणो जपः ॥ इति ॥ ११५ ॥

मणिविशेषे फलविशेषमाह रुद्राक्षेति। सर्वैरेतैरित्येकैकस्य पञ्च पञ्च मणयः।

पिङ्गलामते तु विशेषः—

स्फटिकप्रवालमुक्ताचामीकरपुत्रजीवकृतमणिभिः।
अष्टोत्तरशतसंख्यैः कुर्याज्जपमालिकां मन्त्री ॥
मोक्षाभिचारशान्तिकवश्याकर्षेषु योजयेत् क्रमशः।
अङ्गुष्ठाद्यङ्गुलिकामणयोऽङ्गुष्ठेन चाल्यन्ते ॥ इति ॥

निर्मिता रौप्यमणिभिर्जपमालेप्सितप्रदा ।
हिरण्मयैर्विरचिता माला कामान् प्रयच्छति ॥ ११८

अक्षमालाकरणप्रकारस्तु तन्त्रान्तरोक्तो यथा—

समासेनाऽक्षसूत्रस्य विधानमभिधीयते ।
यथालाभं यथाबुद्धि अक्षाण्यानीय यत्नतः ॥
अन्योन्यसमरूपाणि नातिस्थूलकृशानि च ।
जन्तुभिर्न विशीर्णानि न जीर्णानि नवानि च ॥
गव्यैस्तु पञ्चभिस्तानि सम्प्रक्षाल्य पृथक् पृथक् ।
ततो द्विजेन्द्रपुत्रस्त्रीनिर्मितं ग्रन्थिवर्जितम् ॥
त्रिगुणं त्रिगुणीकृत्य सूत्रं प्रक्षाल्य पूर्ववत् ।
अश्वत्थपत्रनवकैः पद्माकारेण कल्पयेत् ॥
सूत्रं मणींश्च गन्धाद्भिः क्षालितांस्तत्र निक्षिपेत् ।
तारं शक्तिं मातृकां च सूत्रे चैव मणिष्वथ ॥
विन्यस्य पूजयेदाज्यैर्जुहुयाच्चैव शक्तितः ।
मणिमेकैकमादाय सूत्रे तत्र तु योजयेत् ॥
मुखे मुखं तु संयोज्य पृष्ठे पृष्ठं तु योजयेत् ।
प्रोक्तसंख्यातमेवाऽक्षं मेरुत्वेनाऽग्रतो न्यसेत् ॥
एकैकमालामध्ये तु ग्रन्थिबन्धं प्रकल्पयेत् ।
सम्यक् प्रतिष्ठितप्राणामुपचारैः प्रपूजयेत् ॥
एवं कृताक्षमालायां जपेन् मातृकया ततः ।
गुरुं संपूज्य तद्धस्तात् गृह्णीयात् सर्वसिद्धये ॥ इति ॥

अन्यत्रापि—समानवर्णवनितानिर्मितं सूत्रमानयेत् ।
सूत्रं मणींश्च त्रिदिनं पञ्चगव्ये विनिक्षिपेत् ॥
सम्यक् चतुर्थदिवसे जलेन क्षालयेत्ततः ।
दृढां तां ग्रन्थयेन्मन्त्री गोपुच्छाकारसन्निभाम् ॥
मणिमध्ये नागपाशं ब्रह्मग्रन्थिमथाऽर्पयेत् ।
हुं मन्त्रेण ततो मेरुं प्रणवेनैव बन्धयेत् ॥
पूर्वोक्तं मण्डलं कृत्वा सम्पूज्याऽत्रेष्टदेवताम् ।
मनुं त्वष्टसहस्रं तु सञ्जपेन्नियतः सुधीः ॥
तद्दशांशं हुनेदाज्यैस्तन्मन्त्रोक्तैर्यथा पुरा ॥ इति ।

प्रवालैर्विहिता माला प्रयच्छेत् पुष्कलं धनम्।
सौभाग्यं स्फाटिकी माला मौक्तिकैर्विहिता श्रियम्॥ ११९

निर्मिता शङ्खमणिभिः कुरुते कीर्त्तिमव्ययाम्।
सर्वैरेतैर्विरचिता माला स्यान्मुक्तये नृणाम्॥ १२०

शैवागमे तु—गोपुच्छसदृशी कार्या एकास्या वा [सर्पाकारा] समेरुका।
प्रोतव्या सितवर्णाद्यैस्तत्तत्कर्मप्रसिद्धये॥
जपमालां विधायेत्थं ततः संस्कारमारभेत्।
क्षालयेत् पञ्चगव्यैस्तां सद्योजातेन सज्जलैः॥
चन्दनागुरुगन्धाद्यैर्वामदेवेन घर्षयेत्।
धूपयेत्तामघोरेण लिम्पेत् तत्पुरुषेण तु॥
मन्त्रयेत् पञ्चमेनैव प्रत्येकन्तु शतं शतम्।
मेरुञ्च पञ्चमेनैव यथा मन्त्रेण मन्त्रयेत्॥ इति॥

अक्षमालायां जपप्रकारोऽपि तत्रैवोक्तः—
मध्यमायां न्यसेन् मालां ज्येष्ठेनावर्त्तयेत् क्रमात्।
भुक्तिमुक्तिप्रदः सोऽयं मातृकागणनक्रमः॥
अङ्गुष्ठानामिकाभ्यां तु कुर्यादुत्तमकर्मणि।
अङ्गुष्ठमध्यमाभ्यां तु जपेदाकृष्टिकर्मणि॥
तर्जन्यङ्गुष्ठयोगाद्धि विद्वेषोच्चाटने जपः।
कनिष्ठाङ्गुष्ठकाभ्यां तु जपेन्मारणकर्मणि।
जपान्यकाले तां मालां पूजयित्वा च गोपयेत्।
जीर्णे सूत्रे पुनः सूत्रं ग्रन्थयित्वा शतं जपेत्॥
जपेन्निषिद्धसंस्पर्शे क्षालयित्वा यथोचितम्॥
कासे क्षुते च जृम्भायामेकमावर्त्तकं त्यजेत्॥
प्रमादात्तर्ज्जनीस्पर्शे भवेदावर्त्तकं त्यजेत्।
यदा सन्त्रुट्यते माला ग्रन्थयित्वाऽथ पूर्ववत्॥
प्रतिष्ठितायां तस्यां तु मन्त्रं जप्यादनन्यधीः।
एवं प्रतिष्ठितायां तु अन्यं नैव जपेन्मनुम्॥ इति॥

अन्यत्रापि—येन प्रतिष्ठिता माला तमेव तु मनुं जपेत्।
अन्यमन्त्रजपा विद्या न कार्या कर्हिचिद्बुधैः॥

तर्जन्या न स्पृशेत् सूत्रं कम्पयेन्नो विधूनयेत् ।
न स्पृशेद्वामहस्तेन करभ्रष्टां न कारयेत् ॥
अक्षाणां चालनेऽङ्गुष्ठेनाऽन्यमक्षं न संस्पृशेत् ।
जपकाले सदा विद्वान् मेरुं नैव विलङ्घयेत् ॥
परिवर्त्तनकाले च सङ्घट्टं नैव कारयेत् ।
एवं सर्वं परिज्ञाय मालायां जपमारभेत् ॥ इति ॥

आचार्या अपि—तस्मानसस्तर्जनिवर्जिताभिः अक्षस्रजा वाऽङ्गुलिभिर्जपेत । इति ।

अन्यत्रापि—अङ्गुल्यग्रेण यज्जप्तं यज्जप्तं मेरुलङ्घने ।
असंख्यातेन यज्जप्तं तज्जप्तं निष्फलं भवेत् ॥ इति ॥

अन्यत्र विशेषः—

अक्षमालां गुरोर्लब्ध्वां तदभावे स्वनिर्मिताम् ।
गोपयेत् सर्वकर्मान्तं यदीच्छेत् सिद्धिमुत्तमाम् ॥
स्वमन्त्रमक्षसूत्रं च गुरोरपि न दर्शयेत् ।
जपकाले च गोप्तव्यमक्षसूत्रं च षण्मुख ॥
परदृष्टिगतं सूत्रं सर्वथा निष्फलं भवेत् ।
तस्मात् सर्वत्र यत्नेन गोपनीयं सदा बुधैः ॥ इति ॥

मन्त्रतन्त्रप्रकाशे अङ्गुलिभिरङ्गुलिपर्वभिरपि जप उक्तः । तद्यथा—

अङ्गुलीजपसंख्यानं फलमेकगुणं स्मृतम् ।
रेखास्वष्टगुणं विद्यादक्षैश्च शतसंगुणम् ॥
तत्राङ्गुलिजपं कुर्वन् साङ्गुष्ठाङ्गुलिभिर्जपेत् ।
अङ्गुष्ठेन विना कर्म कृतं तदफलं भवेत् ॥
अङ्गुलीपर्वभिर्मन्त्रजपं नित्यं प्रकल्पयेत् ।
मध्यमानामिकामध्यपर्वद्वितयकल्पितम् ॥
मेरुं प्रदक्षिणीकुर्वन्ननामामूलपर्वणि ।
आरभ्य मध्यमामूलपर्वान्तं गणयेत् क्रमात् ॥
मध्यापर्वयुगेन प्रकल्प्य मेरुं त्वनामिकामध्यात् ।
तर्जनिकामूलान्तं गणयेदेतत् प्र[प्र]कारतो वाथ ॥
अगुलीर्न वियुञ्जीत किञ्चिदाकुञ्चिते तले ।
अङ्गुलीनां वियोगे तु छिद्रेषु स्रवते जपः ॥
गणनाविधिमुल्लङ्घ्य यो जपेत्तं जपं यतः ।

अथाऽभिधास्ये तन्त्रेऽस्मिन् सम्यक् षट्कर्मलक्षणम्।
सर्वतन्त्रानुसारेण प्रयोगफलसिद्धिदम्॥ १२१

शान्तिवश्यस्तम्भनानि विद्वेषोच्चाटने ततः।
मारणान्तानि शंसन्ति षट्कर्माणि मनीषिणः॥ १२२

रोगकृत्याग्रहादीनां निरासः शान्तिरीरिता।
वश्यं जनानां सर्वेषां विधेयत्वमुदीरितम्॥ १२३

प्रवृत्तिरोधः सर्वेषां स्तम्भनं समुदाहृतम्।
स्निग्धानां द्वेषजननं मिथो विद्वेषणं मतम्॥ १२४

उच्चाटनं स्वदेशादेर्भ्रंशनं परिकीर्त्तितम्।
प्राणिनां प्राणहरणं मारणं समुदाहृतम्॥ १२५

स्वदेवतादिकालादीन् ज्ञात्वा कर्माणि साधयेत्।
रतिर्वाणी रमा ज्येष्ठा दुर्गा काली यथाक्रमम्॥ १२६

षट्कर्मदेवताः प्रोक्ताः कर्मादौ ताः प्रपूजयेत्।
ईशचन्द्रेन्द्रनिर्ऋतिवाय्वग्नीनां दिशो मताः॥ १२७

गृह्णन्ति राक्षसास्तेन गणयेत् सर्वथा बुधः॥ इति ॥११६॥११७॥११८॥११९॥१२०॥

षट्कर्माण्याह अथेति। विधेयत्वं वचनकारित्वम्। सर्वेषां स्तम्भनमिति। जनजलशक्रखड्गधारासैन्यप्रतिवादिवचनमरुदादीनाम्। स्वदेशादेरित्यादिशब्देन गृहग्रामनगरादयो गृह्यन्ते॥ १२१॥१२२॥१२३॥१२४॥१२५ ॥

स्वदेवतेति। अत्रादिशब्देन आसनमुद्राभूतोदयमण्डलाक्षरग्रथनादिप्रकारवर्णलेखनद्रव्यलेखनीकुण्डस्रुक्स्रुवसमिज्जपमालिकादीनि। प्रपूजयेदिति। तत्र पुष्पविशेषः पिङ्गलामते—

स्तम्भाकृष्टिवशोच्चाटशान्तिमारे यथाक्रमम्।
पीतनीलारुणं धूम्रं श्वेतं कृष्णं प्रसूनकम्॥ इति॥

दिश आह ईशेति। अन्यत्र विशेषः—

पूर्वामुखे भवेद्वश्यं दक्षिणे त्वाभिचारिकम्।
पश्चिमे बन्धनं विद्यादुत्तरे शान्तिकं स्मृतम्॥
आकर्षणमथाग्नेये नैर्ऋते मारणं तथा।
उच्चाटनं च वायव्ये ऐशाने मोक्षदायकम्॥ इति॥ १२६॥१२७॥

सूर्योदयं समारभ्य घटिकादशकं क्रमात् ।
ऋतवः स्युर्वसन्ताद्या अहोरात्रं दिने दिने ॥ १२८
वसन्तग्रीष्मवर्षाख्यशरद्धेमन्तशैशिराः ।
हेमन्तः शान्तिके प्रोक्तो वसन्तो वश्यकर्मणि ॥ १२९
शिशिरः स्तम्भने ज्ञेयो विद्वेषे ग्रीष्म ईरितः ।
प्रावृडुच्चाटने ज्ञेयो शरन् मारणकर्मणि ॥ १३०

सूर्येति । दिने दिने प्रतिदिनम् । अहोरात्रमध्ये सूर्योदयमारभ्य घटिकादशकं क्रमात् वसन्ताद्या ऋतवः स्युरित्यन्वयः । अत्र मुख्यो ऋतुर्मासद्वयात्मक एव । शीघ्रकार्यापेक्षस्त्वयमिति ज्ञेयम् । तदभिप्रायेणाऽन्यत्राऽप्युक्तम्—

शुक्लपक्षे द्वितीया च तृतीया पञ्चमी तथा ।
बुधदेवगुरूपेता शान्तिके वाऽथ सप्तमी ॥
षष्ठी त्रयोदशी चैव चतुर्थी नवमी तथा ।
सोमदेवगुरूपेता पौष्टिके शंसिता बुधैः ॥
अष्टमी नवमी चैव दशम्येकादशी तथा ।
शुक्रभानुसुतोपेता शस्ता विद्वेषकर्मणि ॥
अथो चतुर्दशी कृष्णा शनिवारे तथाऽष्टमी ।
उच्चाटनेऽथ शस्तोऽत्र जपः शङ्करभाषितः ॥
अमावस्याऽष्टमी कृष्णा तादृगेव चतुर्दशी ।
भानुना तत्सुतपेता भूसुतेनाऽपि संयुता ।
मारणे स्तम्भने चैव मोहे द्रोहे प्रशस्यते ॥ इति ॥

तथा वशिष्ठसंहितायामपि—

प्रसिद्धा ऋतवो ग्राह्याः षट्कर्मादिकसाधने ।
यस्मिन् कस्मिन्नृतौ कार्यं मन्त्राणां वाथ साधनम् ॥
पूर्वाह्णे वश्यपुष्ट्यर्थम् । इत्यादिना ।

पिङ्गलामते—पुष्ट्याकृष्टिशुभोच्चाटशान्तिस्तम्भनरोधनम् ।
गुरौ कुजे रवौ शुक्रे सोमे मन्दे बुधे क्रमात् ॥ इति ॥

अन्यो विशेषः पिङ्गलामते—

हेमन्तो धवलो वृद्धो वसन्तो लोहितो युवा ।
आरक्तधवलो बालः शिशिरः संप्रकीर्त्तितः ॥

पद्माख्यं स्वस्तिकं भूयो विकटं कुक्कुटं पुनः ।
वज्रं भद्रकमित्याहुरासनानि मनीषिणः ॥ १३१

षण्मुद्राः क्रमतो ज्ञेयाः पद्मपाशगदाह्वयाः ।
मुसलाशनिखड्गाख्याः शान्तिकादिषु कर्मसु ॥ १३२

जलं शान्तिविधौ शस्तं वश्ये वह्निरुदाहृतः ।
स्तम्भने पृथिवी शस्ता विद्वेषे व्योम कीर्त्तितम् ।
उच्चाटने स्मृतो वायुर्भूयोऽग्निर्मारणे मतः ॥ १३३
तत्तद्भूतोदये सम्यक् तत्तन्मण्डलसंयुतम् ।

ग्रीष्मो धूम्रशरीरस्तु श्यामाङ्गो जलदागमः ।
शरत्कालः कृष्णवर्णः शान्त्यादावृतवस्त्विमे ॥ इति ॥

विशेषान्तरं महाकपिलपञ्चरात्रे—

शान्तिके मानसो जाप उपांशुः पौष्टिके स्मृतः ।
सशब्दस्त्वाभिचारे स्यात् प्रागुदग्दक्षिणामुखः ॥ इति ॥

यत् तु दिनास्त्रादिप्रयोगे अर्द्धरात्रग्रहणं मारणे कृतं स तत्कृतो विशेषविधिरिति ज्ञेयम् । अत्र तु ऋतुशब्दोपादानान्न तथा ॥ १२८॥१२९॥१३० ॥

पद्मेति । तत्राद्ययोरन्त्ययोश्च लक्षणमन्त्ये वक्ष्यति । विकटकुक्कुटासनयोर्लक्षणे यथा—जानुजङ्घान्तराले तु भुजयुग्मं प्रकाशयेत् ।

विकटासनमेतत् स्यादुपविश्योत्कटासने ॥
कृत्वोत्कटासनं पूर्वं समपादद्वयं ततः ।
अन्तर्जानुकरद्वन्द्वं कुक्कुटासनमीरितम् ॥ इति ॥

अन्यत्रासनविशेषा उक्ताः—

स्तम्भने गजचर्म स्यात् मारणे माहिषं तथा ।
मेषचर्म तथोच्चाटे खड्गजं वश्यकर्मणि ॥
विद्वेषे जम्बुकस्योक्तं गोचर्म शान्तिके तथा ।
व्याघ्रचर्मासनं प्रोक्तं सर्वसिद्धिप्रवर्त्तकम् ॥ इति ॥ १३१ ॥

षण्मुद्रा इति । "कनिष्ठाङ्गुष्ठयुग्मुद्रा त्रिकोणा त्वशनेर्मता" इति अशनिमुद्रालक्षणम् । अन्यासां मुद्राणां लक्षणं पुरुषोत्तममन्त्रव्यासावसरे मयोक्तम् ॥१३२॥

तत्तद्भूतोदय इति । भूतोदयमन्त्यपटले वक्ष्यति । विशेषस्त्वीशानशिवेनोक्तः—

तत्तत्कर्म विधातव्यं मन्त्रिणा निश्चितात्मना ॥ १३४

शीतांशुसलिलक्षोणीव्योमवायुहविर्भुजाम् ।

वर्णाः स्युर्मन्त्रबीजानि षट्कर्मसु यथाक्रमम् ॥ १३५

उभयधरणिरिष्टं साधयेद्दीर्घकाले
उभयमरुति किञ्चित्कालपाकेन सिध्येत् ।
उभयगगनवक्त्रेणैव सिद्धिर्न हानि-
स्तत उभयजलस्थः क्षिप्रमेवेष्टदः स्यात् ॥
शशिजलधरयोस्थे शान्तिकं पौष्टिकं वा
शशिमरुदनलाभ्यां वश्यमाकर्षणं च ।
दिनकरभुवि कुर्यात् स्तम्भनं त्वर्कतोये
वशमिनमरुदाविभ्रामणोच्चाटने च ॥
दिनकरवियति स्यान् मोहनं त्वर्कवह्नौ
द्रुततरमरिवर्गान् साध[द]येन् मारयेच्च ॥ इति ।

तत्तन्मण्डलैः प्रथमपटलोक्तैः संयुतम् । मन्त्रिणा निश्चितात्मनेत्यनेनोर्ध्वाधोभेदेनाऽहोरात्रं ज्ञात्वा तत्तत्कर्म कुर्यादित्युक्तम् । तदुक्तं गौतमेन—

देहवायोर्विभोरूर्ध्वं वृत्तिः प्राणो भवेद्दिवा ।
अधोवृत्तिमयोऽपानो रात्रिर्वा देहसंस्थिता ॥
परचक्रभयादौ तत्कालोक्तं कर्म मन्त्रवित् ।
तत्र कुर्याद्विभागेन सम्यगुच्चाटनादिकम् ॥ इति ॥ १३३॥१३४ ॥

शीतांश्विति । षोडशस्वराः सठौ शीतांशुवर्णाः । एतद्वर्णव्यतिरिक्ता द्वितीयपटलोक्ता भूतवर्णा ज्ञेयाः । तदुक्तम्—

रक्षास्तम्भनकर्माणि वर्णैः कुर्यात् धरामयैः ।
शान्तिकं पौष्टिकं कर्म कर्षणं सलिलात्मकैः ॥
दाहमोहाङ्गभङ्गानि चाकृष्टिं दहनात्मकैः ।
सेनाभङ्गभ्रमोच्चाटद्वेषकर्माणि वायुजैः ॥
कालभस्मादि चूर्णानि विविधान्यपि मारणम् ।
क्षुद्राणां स्थापने वर्णैर्नाभसैः पङ्क्तिसंख्यकैः ॥ इति ॥

आचार्या अपि—वर्णदशकैः स्युः स्तम्भनाद्याः क्रियाः । इति ।
केचित्तु सवलहयरेफानाहुः । तदुक्तं महाकपिलपञ्चरात्रे—

लं पीता पृथिवी ज्ञेया वं शुक्लं कीर्त्तितं पयः।
रं रक्तोऽग्निर्मरुत् कृष्णो यं हं शुक्लतरं वियत्॥ इति॥

अन्यान्तरे तु विशेषः—

हेमरूप्यशिलामृत्स्ना[सूक्ष्म]पात्रं शान्त्यादिषु स्मृतम्।
बिल्वाद्यशिवघटितं मारणोच्चाटनादिषु॥ इति॥

अन्यत्राऽपि—सौवर्णान्यपि राजतान्यपि तथा पात्राणि शैल्वानि वा
मृत्पात्राण्यपि शान्तिकादिषु परं शस्तानि कर्मस्विह।
शैल्वद्रुमशिग्रुभूरुहकृतान्येतानि विद्वेषणो-
च्चाटोत्सादनमारणादिषु भृशं शस्तानि पात्राण्यपि॥ इति।

कुलप्रकाशतन्त्रे तु—

तिस्रो मुद्राः स्मृता होमे मृगी हंसी च शूकरी।
शूकरी करसङ्कोचो हंसी मुक्तकनिष्ठिका॥
मृगी कनिष्ठातर्जन्यौ मुक्ता मुद्रात्रयं मतम्।
यत्र शान्तिककार्येषु मृगी हंसी प्रकीर्त्तिता॥
आभिचारिककार्येषु शूकरी तु प्रकीर्त्तिता॥ इति॥

पिङ्गलामते तु मुद्रान्तराण्यपि उक्तानि—

ततो द्रव्यस्य होमे तु तर्जन्यङ्गुष्ठयोगतः।
ज्वरनाशारिसन्तापावुच्चाटो मोहनं क्रमात्॥ इति॥

अन्यत्र जातिविशेषोऽपि उक्तः। यदाहुः—

नमः स्वाहा स्वधा वौषट् हुंफडन्ताश्च जातयः।
शान्तौ वश्ये तथा स्तम्भे विद्वेषोच्चाटमारणे॥ इति॥

अन्यत्राऽपि—अर्चने क्रोधशान्त्यादौ नमःशब्दं प्रयोजयेत्।
अग्निकार्ये च वश्यादौ स्वाहाशब्दं प्रयोजयेत्॥
मारणादिषु फट्कारं विद्वेषादौ च हुंपदम्।
वौषडाप्यायनादौ स्याद् द्वेषोत्सादे वषट् स्मृतम्॥ इति॥

तथान्यत्र तु—वश्याकर्षणसन्तापे होमे स्वाहा प्रयोजयेत्।
क्रोधोपशमने शान्तौ पूजने च नमो वदेत्॥
वौषट् सम्मोहनोद्दीपपुष्टिमृत्युञ्जयेषु च।
हुंकारं प्रीतिनाशे च छेदने मारणे तथा॥
उच्चाटने च विद्वेषे तथा धीविकृतौ तु फट्।

विघ्नग्रहविनाशे च हुंफट्कारं प्रयोजयेत् ॥
मन्त्रोद्दीपनकार्ये च लाभालाभे वषट् स्मृतम् ॥ इति ।

पिङ्गलामते तु—स जपः स्तम्भने लक्ष्यैर्विद्वेषे हुंसमन्वितैः ।
उच्चाटे वायुबीजस्थैः सविसर्गैश्च सिद्धये ॥
मारणे फट्कृतैर्दीप्तैरूर्ध्वाधोरेफसंयुतैः ।
छेदने क्लिव[त्य]दीपितैः पुष्टावाप्यायने गवैः ॥
अमृताक्षरगैर्मृत्युनिवृत्तौ देशिकोत्तमैः ।
स्वकल्पसिद्धजात्या वा कृतोपपदलक्षणैः ॥
एवं यत् क्रियते कर्म तदिष्टफलसाधकम् ॥ इति ।

द्रव्यविशेषोऽपि मोहशूरोत्तरे—
दूर्वा भव्याश्च समिधो गोघृतेन समन्विताः ।
होतव्याः शान्तिके देवि शान्तिर्येन भवेत् स्फुटम् ॥
समिधो राजवृक्षोत्था होतव्याः स्तम्भकर्मणि ।
मेषीघृतेन संयुक्ताः स्तम्भसिद्धिर्भवेद् ध्रुवम् ॥
खादिरा मारणे प्रोक्ताः कटुतैलेन संयुताः ।
होतव्याः साधकेन्द्रेण मारणं येन सिध्यति ॥
उच्चाटने चूतजाताः कटुतैलेन संयुताः ।
उच्चाटयेन्महीं सर्वां सशैलवनकाननाम् ॥
वश्ये चैव सदा होमः कुसुमैर्दाडिमोद्भवैः ।
अजाघृतेन देवेशि वशयेत् सचराचरम् ॥
विद्वेषे चैव होतव्या उन्मत्तसमिधो मताः ।
अतसीतैलसंयुक्ता विद्वेषणकरं परम् ॥ इति ॥

वायवीयसंहितायां स्रुक्स्रुवयोरपि विशेष उक्तः—
आयसौ स्रुक्स्रुवौ कार्यौ मारणादिषु कर्मसु ।
तदन्यत्र तु सौवर्णौ शान्तिकाद्येषु कृत्स्नशः ॥ इति ॥

अन्यत्र तत्तत्कर्मणि जिह्वा अप्युक्ताः—
जिह्वां तु हिरण्याख्यां शान्तिकर्मणि तथा च गगना[कनका]ख्याम् ।
रक्तां कर्षण[कार्मण]कर्मणि कृष्णां क्षुद्रक्रियासु बुधाः ॥
या सुप्रभेति गदिता तामाहुर्मोक्षकारिणीं जिह्वाम् ।
अतिरक्तामाकृष्टौ बहुरूपामखिलसिद्धिदां जिह्वाम् ॥ इति ।

तथाऽन्यत्र—स्तम्भनादिषु मता कनकाख्या द्वेषणादिषु मता खलु रक्ता ।

मारणे निगदिता खलु कृष्णा सुप्रभा बुधवरैरिह शान्त्याम् ॥

उच्चाटनेऽतिरक्ता या बहुरूपोत्तरे सिद्धिम् ।

ऋद्धिं दक्षिणतः सा तनुते सर्वे शुभानि सदा ॥ इति ॥

अन्यत्राऽग्निविशेषोऽपि उक्तः—

लौकिकेऽग्नौ शान्तिकं स्यात् पौष्टिकं च शुभं तथा ।

वटजे स्तम्भनं मोहः श्मशानस्थेऽपि मारणम् ।

बिभीतकाग्नौ विद्वेषः षट्कर्मस्वग्नयो मताः ॥ इति ॥

अन्यत्र तु—बिल्वार्कविप्रनृपदग्धतरुप्रदीप्ते

सौम्यं चिकीर्षुरथ कर्म जुहोतु ताश्चे ।

रौद्रं विषद्रुमकलिद्रुमशैलुनिम्ब-

धत्तूरकाष्ठचयसन्निचितेऽथ सन्धौ ॥ इति ॥

सोमशम्भौ तु अग्निमुखानामपि नियम उक्तः—

कुण्डं भानुमुखं ध्यात्वा सदाहुतिभिरोप्सितम् ।

पश्चिमे शिष्यसंस्कारनित्यहोमौ समाचरेत् ॥

वश्याकर्षणसौभाग्यपुष्टिभाग्याधिरोपणे ।

शान्तिके पापे[श]शुद्धौ च वामे होमः प्रशस्यते ॥

गुटिकाञ्जननिस्त्रिंशपादलेपजिगीषया ।

शोषसञ्जननार्थं च प्राचीनवदने यजेत् ॥

मारणोच्चाटनद्वेषस्तम्भनार्थं च दक्षिणे ।

प्रायश्चित्तं तु तत्रैव पश्चिमे तु विमुक्तये ॥ इति ।

आकर्षणाद्यपि उक्तकाले विधेयम् । तदुक्तम् "आकर्षणं वसन्ते स्यात्" इति ।

कामिके तु होमादिसंख्याविशेषः—

शान्तिके पौष्टिके वापि वशीकरणकर्मणि ।

हुतसंख्यादशांशं स्यादुत्तमं द्विजभोजनम् ॥

तत्त्वसंख्यं मतं मध्यं शतांशमधमं मतम् ।

उक्तद्विगुणमानं स्यात् स्तम्भने विप्रभोजनम् ॥

त्रिगुणं सादनोच्चाटे द्वेषणे तु प्रकीर्त्तितम् ।

हुतसंख्यासमानं स्यादपि मारणकर्मणि ॥

हुतावसाने विप्रेन्द्रानतिशुद्धकुलोद्भवान् ।

ग्रथनं च विदर्भश्च संपुटो रोधनं तथा।
योगः पल्लव इत्येते विन्यासाः षट्सु कर्मसु॥ १३६
मन्त्रार्णान्तरितान् कुर्यान्नामवर्णान् यथाविधि।
ग्रथनं तद्विजानीयात् प्रशस्तं शान्तिकर्मणि॥ १३७
मन्त्रार्णद्वन्द्वमध्यस्थं साध्यनामाक्षरं लिखेत्।
विदर्भ एष विज्ञेयो मन्त्रिभिर्वश्यकर्मणि॥ १३८
आद्यावन्ते च मन्त्रः स्यान्नाम्नोऽसौ संपुटं मतम्।
एषः संस्तम्भने शस्त इत्युक्तो मन्त्रवेदिभिः॥ १३९
नाम्न आद्यन्तमध्येषु मन्त्रः स्याद्रोधनं मतम्।
विद्वेषणविधानेषु प्रशस्तमिदमीरितम्॥ १४०

भोजयेत् साङ्गवेदज्ञान् स्वादुभिर्भोज्यवस्तुभिः॥
देवताप्रतिपत्त्या तान्नमस्कृत्य यथाविधि।
वित्तं च यथाशीर्भिरभीष्टफलदं भवेत्॥ इति॥

प्रयोगस्य दक्षिणामाह—

पञ्चविंशं सुवर्णानि दद्याद् वश्ये विचक्षणः।
स्तम्भे त्रिंशन्मानं स्यादुच्चाटे षष्टिहाटकम्॥
विद्वेषे पञ्चपञ्चाशन्मारणे तु शताधिकम्।
अष्टौ दद्याद् द्विजेन्द्राणां चेलादीनां विशेषतः॥ इति॥

विशेषत इति सन्तोषं यथा भवति तथा कुर्यादिति॥ १३५॥

मन्त्रेति। अन्तरितान् व्यवहितान्। तदुक्तम्—
एकं मन्त्राक्षरं पूर्वं ततो नामाक्षरं पुनः। मन्त्राक्षरमिति ग्रन्थः। इति।
मन्त्रार्णेति। मन्त्रार्णद्वन्द्वयोर्मध्यस्थं साध्यनामाक्षरमिति समासः। तदुक्तम्—
द्वौ द्वौ मन्त्राक्षरौ यत्र एकैकं साध्यवर्णकम्। विदर्भितं तु तत्प्रोक्तम्। इति।
असौ विन्यासः सम्पुटं मतमिति। अत्र केचन नामान्ते विपरीतं मन्त्रपाठमाहुः।
एष एव साम्प्रदायिकः पक्षः। तदुक्तम्—

मन्त्रमादौ वदेत् सर्वं साध्यसंज्ञामनन्तरम्।
विपरीतं पुनश्चाऽन्ते मन्त्रं तत् सम्पुटं स्मृतम्॥ इति॥

अन्यत्रताऽप्युक्तम्—भूतलिप्या पुटीकृत्य यो मन्त्रं भजते नरः।
क्रमोत्क्रमाच्छताव्रत्त्या॥ इति॥

मन्त्रस्याऽन्ते भवेन्नाम योगः प्रोच्चाटने मतः ।
अन्ते नाम्नो भवेन्मन्त्रः पल्लवो मारणे मतः ॥ १४१

अनेकाक्षरमन्त्रादौ तदेवावर्त्तनीयम् । अन्ये अन्यथा वदन्ति । एकाक्षरस्यैवा-वयवं कर्त्तव्यमिति । तदसत् । अनेकाक्षरेऽपि तन्न्यायात् साध्येऽपि तथात्वा-पत्तिः । विषमाक्षरे पुनरावर्त्तनीयमिति पद्मपादाचार्याः ॥ १३६—१४० ॥

मन्त्रस्याऽन्त इत्यस्य पद्यस्य प्रामादिकचरणव्यत्ययः—

अन्ते नाम्नो भवेन् मन्त्रो योगः प्रोच्चाटने मतः ।
मन्त्रस्याऽन्ते भवेन्नाम पल्लवो मारणे मतः ॥

इति तु पाठः पठनीयः । तथाच पद्मपादाचार्याः । नामान्ते मन्त्रयोजनं योगः । स्तम्भोच्चाटनविद्वेषेषु समस्तमन्त्रान्ते समस्तनामयोजनं पल्लवः । मारणेऽस्य विनियोग इति । अन्यत्राऽपि—"पल्लवे साध्यनामादौ भवेन् मन्त्रपदक्रमः" इति । "मन्त्रान्ते जपकर्माणि" इति मारणे गौतमेनाप्युक्तम् । भैरवस्तोत्रस्यापि "मन्त्रार्ध-गेऽग्रतः साध्यं पल्लवं तद्विपर्ययात्" इति । योगपल्लवयोरन्यत्रापि विनियोग उक्तः ।

यदाहुः—शान्तिके पौष्टिके दिव्ये प्रायश्चित्तविशोधने ।
मोहने दीपने योगं प्रयुञ्जन्ति मनीषिणः ॥
मारणे विषनाशे च ग्रहभूतविनिग्रहे ।
उच्चाटने च विद्वेषे पल्लवः सम्प्रचक्षते ॥ इति ॥

अन्यत्र विशेषः—अर्द्धार्द्धनादितोऽन्ते च मन्त्रं कुर्याद्विचक्षणः ।
मध्ये चाऽस्य भवेत् संज्ञा ग्रस्तं तत् समुदाहृतम् ॥
अभिचारादिसर्वेषु योजयेन् मारणादिषु ।
अभिधानं लिखेत् पूर्वं मध्ये वापि महामते ॥
मन्त्रमेवं द्विधा कृत्वा समस्तमभिधीयते ।
द्वेषोच्चाटनकार्येषु योजयेदविशङ्कितः ॥
अर्द्धार्द्धेनादितोऽन्ते च मन्त्रं कुर्याद्विचक्षणः ।
मध्ये चान्ते च साध्याख्या मन्त्रिणा क्रियते यदा ॥
आक्रान्तं तद्भवेन् मन्त्रं सदा सर्वार्थसिद्धिदम् ।

अत्रार्द्धार्द्धीकरणे विषमाक्षरे पूर्वमधिकमन्ते न्यूनञ्चेति साम्प्रदायिकाः ।
स्तम्भस्तोभसमावेशवश्योच्चाटनकर्मणि ॥
सकृत् पूर्वं लिखेन् मन्त्रमन्ते चैव त्रिधा पुनः ।
मध्ये चैव भवेत् संज्ञा आद्यन्तमिति तद्विदुः ॥

सितरक्तपीतमिश्रकृष्णाधूम्राः प्रकीर्त्तिताः ।
वर्णतो मन्त्रसंप्रोक्ता देवताः षट्सु कर्मसु ॥ १४२

य[म]न्त्राणां लेखनद्रव्यं चन्दनं रोचना निशा ।
गृहधूमचिताङ्गारौ मारणेऽष्ट विषाणि च ॥ १४३

श्येनाग्निलोणपिण्डानि धत्तूरकरसं ततः ।
गृहधूमस्त्रिकटुकं विषाष्टकमुदाहृतम् ॥ १४४

परस्परप्रीतियुजोर्विद्वेषजननं परम् ।
आद्यन्तं च तथा चार्द्धं विधा मन्त्रं समालिखेत् ॥
साध्यनाम सकृन् मध्ये तं विदुः सर्वतोमुखम् ।
सर्वोपद्रवशमनं महामृत्युविनाशनम् ॥
सर्वसौभाग्यजननं मृतानाममृतप्रदम् ॥ इति ।

पिङ्गलामते अन्यान्यप्युक्तानि—

ततश्च शृङ्खला सूची नाराचः क्रकचोऽशनिः ।
भुशुण्डी मुद्गरश्चक्रं कर्त्तरी मुशलाम्बुजे ॥
टङ्कशूलासिशक्तीश्च मन्त्रकर्मणि चादिशेत् ।
षड़ादौ षट् पुनश्चान्ते मन्त्रवर्णास्तदन्तरे ॥
साध्यनामेति संप्रोक्ता शृङ्खलान्येष्वयं क्रमः ।
रसा ६ ग्नो ३ न्द्रा १४ श्व ७ कामा १३ हो १५
वेदा ४ र्का १२ चौ २ षु ५ राजभिः १६ ।
रुद्रा ११ ष्टा ८ ङ्क ९ ककुब् १० वर्णः शृङ्खलादीन्यनुक्रमात् ॥
बन्धभेदरिपुध्वंसच्छेदसन्धिविभेदने ।
सैन्यभञ्जनविद्वेषमन्त्रच्छेदनचालने ॥
मारणे सर्वकार्येषु घातस्तम्भनकर्षण[कारणे] ।
शृङ्खलादीनि वेद्यानि साध्यमन्त्रार्णयोगतः ॥ इति ॥१४१॥१४२॥

चन्दनमित्यादिक्रमेण शान्त्यादौ अयं विशेषः । वक्ष्यमाणं सामान्यमपि ज्ञेयम् मारणव्यतिरेकेण । श्येनेति । श्येनः श्येनविष्ठा । अग्निश्चित्रकः । लोणपिण्डं लोणमलम् । त्रिकटुकं शुण्ठीपिप्पलीमरीचानि । पिङ्गलामते लेखनीविशेषोऽप्युक्तः ।

दूर्वामयूरपिच्छाग्निबिभीतकनरास्थिजा ।
विषाङ्गारत्रिलोहोत्था हेमरूप्यार्कसम्भवा ॥

देवताकालमुद्रादीन् सम्यक् ज्ञात्वा विचक्षणः ।
षट् कर्माणि प्रयुञ्जीत यथोक्तफलसिद्धये ॥ १४५

इति श्रीशारदातिलके त्रयोविंशः पटलः ।

लेखनी वश्य आकृष्टौ सन्तापे स्तम्भमारणे ।
सर्वोपद्रवनाशाय शान्तौ पुष्टौ च जातिजा ॥ इति ॥

अन्यत्रापि—लेखन्या विलिखेद्यन्त्रं वश्ये दूर्वाङ्कुरोत्थया ।
आकर्षे शिखिपिच्छोत्था सङ्कोचे मुनिसम्भवा ॥
हैमजा रौप्यजा वान्या सर्वरक्षाऽपि सा प्रिये ।
करञ्जाख्यमयी वाथ मारणेऽपि नरास्थिजा ॥
स्तम्भकर्मणि विज्ञेया राजवृक्षसमुद्भवा ।
शान्तिके पौष्टिके चैव आयुःकर्मविधौ तथा ॥
सर्वोपसर्गशमने कर्त्तव्या जातिसम्भवा ।
अपामार्गोद्भवा वापि शुभकर्मसु सिद्धिदा ॥
आसुरेषु च सर्वेषु शस्यते तीक्ष्णलोहजा ।
विष्ट्यङ्गारदिने घोरे यदि चोत्पादिता च सा ॥
ज्वालखड्गसमा ज्ञेया सर्वभूतनिकृन्तनी ॥ इति ।

आधारविशेषोऽपि—

नारजे द्वीपिकृत्तौ वा लिखितं स्तम्भकृद्भवेत् ।
खरचर्मणि विद्वेषं तथैवोच्चाटनं ध्वजे ॥
वश्याकर्षणसिद्ध्यर्थं भूर्जपत्रे नियोजयेत् ॥ इति ।

कुण्डजपमालिके पूर्वोक्ते अनुसन्धेये ॥ १४२॥१४३॥१४४ ॥

उपसंहरति देवतेति । आदिशब्दः पूर्वमेव व्याख्यातः । इदं च काम्यकर्मन्यासादिकं कृत्वा आत्मरक्षां च कृत्वा अन्यत् सर्वं कुर्यात् । यतः काम्यकर्मरतस्य देवाद्यैरभिभवसम्भवात् । यदाहुः—

काम्यकर्मप्रसक्तस्य शुभस्याऽप्यशुभस्य च ।
अरित्वं भजते मन्त्रः सिद्धत्वं तद्विपर्ययात् ॥ इति ॥ १४५ ॥

इति श्रीशारदातिलकटीकायां सत्सम्प्रदायकृतव्याख्यायां
पदार्थादर्शाभिख्यायां त्रयोविंशः पटलः ॥ ॐ ॥

चतुर्विंशः पटलः ।

अथ वक्ष्यामि यन्त्राणां भेदांस्तन्त्रेषु गोपितान् ।
यैः साधयन्ति सततं मन्त्रिणो निजवाञ्छितम् ॥ १

मार्णे लिखेत् सार्णयुतं स्वसाध्यं वर्गाख्यपत्रे स्वरकेशरेऽब्जे ।
बहिः सदीर्घैर्गगनैः प्रवीतं रक्षाकरं यन्त्रमिदं प्रशस्तम् ॥ २

अथेति । यन्त्रशब्दव्युत्पत्तिरुक्ता संहितायाम्—

मनोरथाचराण्यत्र नियन्त्रयन्ते तपोधन ।
कामक्रोधादिदोषोत्थदोर्षदुःखनियन्त्रणात् ॥
यन्त्रमित्याहुः । इति ।

यथा मन्त्रो देवतारूपः तद्वद्यन्त्रमपि देवतारूपम् । अतएव इष्टसाधनक्षमं भवतीति यैः साधयन्तीत्युक्तम् ॥ १ ॥

रक्षायन्त्रमाह मार्णे इति । अब्जे मार्णे इति व्यधिकरणे सप्तम्यौ । कर्णिकास्थमकारमध्ये सार्णयुतं सबिन्दुमकारयुतं स्वसाध्यं लिखेदित्यन्वयः । साध्यसाधककर्मसहितमिति सर्वत्र बोद्धव्यम् । तत्र स्वनामपदं षष्ठ्यन्तं साध्यस्य द्वितीयान्तम् । ततः फलवाचकं पदं द्वितीयान्तम् । ततः कुरु इति द्विरभ्यसे-दिति साम्प्रदायिकाः । वर्गाख्यपत्रे कचटतपयशलैर्वर्गैराख्यानि युक्तानि पत्राणि दलानि यस्य तस्मिन् । स्वराः द्विद्विक्रमेण केसरेषु यस्य तस्मिन् । सदीर्घैर्गगनैर्ह्रा-मिति बीजैः । अत्र मातृका देवता । तां सम्पूज्य प्राणप्रतिष्ठापनं कृत्वा धारयेत् । अत्र सर्वत्रापि यन्त्रे सामान्यप्रक्रियोच्यते । तत्रोच्चाटनादौ यन्त्रे लेख्ये वायुचराणि द्वन्द्वशः अं आं नमः एं कं नमः इत्यादिक्रमेण पञ्च मन्त्राः । तत्र त्रिकोणं सञ्चिन्त्य तन्मध्ये प्रथममन्त्रं द्वितीयतृतीयचतुर्थमन्त्रानग्न्यादिकोणेषु पञ्चमं मध्ये सञ्चिन्त्य पूजयेत् । पूर्वोक्तरक्षादिस्थानेष्वेवमुक्तो विनियोगोऽनुसन्धेयः ।

दशभिर्दशभिरर्णैर्भिर्नमोऽन्तिकैर्द्वन्द्वशश्च बिन्दुयुतैः ।
योनेर्मध्ये कोणत्रितये मध्ये च संयजेन् मन्त्री ॥

इत्याचार्योक्तेः । अन्यत्राप्याचार्याः—

प्राक् प्रोक्तान् भूतवर्णान् दश दश युगशो बिन्दुयुक्तान्नमोऽन्ता
न्योनेर्मध्यान्तमध्येष्वपि पुनरथ संस्थाप्य भूताभवर्णान् । इति ॥

पुटीकृते भूमिपुरस्य युग्मे मायां लिखेत् मध्यगसाध्ययुक्ताम् ।
वकारकोणेन महीपुरेण संवेष्टितं वश्यकरं तदुच्चैः ॥ ३

ह्रां ह्रीं ह्रूं ह्रैं ह्रौं एतानि अपञ्चीकृतानि बीजानि । एतन्मध्ये तत्तत्कार्ये एकं बीजं विलिख्य तद्बिन्दूर्ध्वाधोभागादिषु साध्यसाधककर्मयोगान् विलिख्य ल्ह्रीं [ह्सौः] इति यन्त्रजीवं मध्यबीजाधोभागे विलिख्य मध्यबीजचतुर्विदिक्षु ऐशान्यादिक्रमेण हंसः सोऽहमिति यन्त्रप्राणं मध्याभिमुखं विलिख्य मध्यबीजपार्श्वद्वये इं ईं विलिख्य उं ऊं इत्यप्यालिख्य तत्तद्यन्त्रविशेषमुक्तमालिख्य यन्त्रगायत्रीं त्रिवर्णक्रमेणाऽष्टदले विलिख्य तद्बहिर्दशदिक्षु लं रं मं चं वं यं सं हं क्रौं आं इति यन्त्रहृदयं विलिख्य तद्बहिः प्राणप्रतिष्ठामन्त्रमपि विलिखेत् । तद्बहिस्तन्मण्डलेन वेष्टयेत् । इदं पूर्वोक्तयन्त्रेष्वपि ज्ञेयम् । तदुक्तं कामिके—

> ल्ह्रीं[ह्सौः] यन्त्रस्य जीवः स्यान्मध्यबीजादधो न्यसेत् ।
> हंसः सोऽहमिति प्राणं ऐशान्यादिक्रमाल्लिखेत् ॥
> इं ईं नेत्रे न्यसेत् पार्श्वे उं ऊं श्रोत्रे तथैव च ।
> विशेषोऽष्टदलादौ तु गायत्रीलेखनं स्मृतम् ॥
> इत्यर्णान् यन्त्रगायत्र्याः प्रतिपत्रं त्रिशो लिखेत् ।
> अग्रे रेखावकाशेषु प्रतिष्ठां प्राणदां लिखेत् ॥ इति ॥

तन्त्रान्तरेऽपि — लरमचान्वयौ सहौ क्रौं आं ।

> यन्त्रस्य हृदयं बिन्दुयुतं लेख्यं समन्ततः ॥
> हंसः सोऽहं प्राणजीवौ यन्त्रे लेख्यौ प्रयत्नतः ।
> हंसादौ सर्गसंयुक्तौ यन्त्रान्तर्विलिखेद्बुधः ॥ इति ।

यन्त्रगायत्री यथा —

यन्त्रराजाय विद्महे वरप्रदाय धीमहि तन्नो यन्त्रः प्रचोदयात् । इति ।

अन्योऽपि विशेषोऽपेक्षितार्थद्योतनिकाकारोक्तः । यत्राधारो नोक्तस्तत्रोक्तशान्त्यादिकर्माधारेषु भूर्जपत्रे नेत्रपट्टे तालपत्रे वा विलिख्य गुलिकां बद्ध्वा सूत्रजतुच्छन्नं क्रमेण कृत्वा रजतताम्रसुवर्णहिङ्गुलकाद्यन्यतमेन संवेष्ट्य बीजेन मन्त्रेण वा मातृकया वाऽधिदैवतं ध्यात्वाऽभ्यर्च्य संजप्य हुत्वा गलादिषु योजयेदिति ॥ २ ॥

वश्यकृदाह पुटीकृत इति । महीपुरेण सह पुटीकृते भूमिपुरस्य युग्मे इति सम्बन्धः । पुटीकृते पुटीकृतवदन्तरं तत्र्य इत्यर्थः । लिखेदिति । तत्र प्रथमं चतुष्कोणं कृत्वा तदन्तस्तद्रेखालग्नदिकोणाग्रं द्वितीयं तदन्तस्तद्रेखालग्न-

मध्ये सार्णविदर्भितं प्रपुटितं मृत्युञ्जयं चाक्षरैः
चान्तःस्थं निजसाध्यनाम विलिखेत् किञ्जल्कसंस्थान् स्वरान्।
पत्रेष्वष्टसु नाम मन्त्रपुटितं वर्गांस्तदग्रेष्वथो
यन्त्रं पद्मपुटीकृतं निगदितं मृत्युञ्जयाख्यं परम्॥ ४

विषज्वरशिरोरोगनाशनं श्रीजयप्रदम्।
कान्तिपुष्टिप्रदं वश्यं सर्वकामार्थसाधकम्॥ ५

साध्याढ्यचिन्तामणिमग्निगेहे विलिख्य बाह्येऽनलगेहवीतम्।
प्रवेष्टयेत् तत् बहिरष्टवर्णमन्त्रेण यन्त्रं ज्वरशान्तिदं स्यात्॥ ६

संप्लवसः प्लावयसो मन्त्रोऽष्टाक्षर ईरितः।
एष एव भवेद्दन्त्रो ग्रहज्वरविनाशने॥ ७

विदिक्कोणाग्रं तृतीयं लिखित्वा तन्मध्ये मायांससाध्यां लिखेत्। तत्र साध्यकर्मलेखनप्रकारस्तु त्रिगुणितादावुक्तोऽनुसन्धेयः। ततो वकारकोणेन संवेष्टितम् उच्चैर्वश्यकरमिति सम्बन्धः। उक्तञ्च नारायणीये—

बाह्यस्य रेखामध्यस्थामान्तरस्यास्त्रमीदृशे।
शक्रवेश्मत्रये शक्तिवश्यं स्यात् कुम्भवेष्टितम्॥ इति॥

व्याख्यातं चापेक्षितार्थद्योतनिकायाम्। पार्थिवमण्डलं लिखित्वा तस्य पूर्वदक्षिणपश्चिमोत्तरदिग्भागे दिक्षु अस्रं कोणं यथा भवति तथा तदन्तः पार्थिवमण्डलं लिखित्वा पुनरपि तदन्तस्तथा लिखित्वा तन्मध्ये ससाध्यां शक्तिं लिखित्वा कुम्भेन चतुर्थेन वेष्टयेदिति। अथवा नागरलिपौ नकारतकारयोर्लिपिसाम्यात् वकारकोणितमहीपुरेणेति पठनीयम्। तत उक्तवदन्तरन्तर्भूपुरद्वयं विधाय तत्र शक्तिं विलिख्य वकारस्य कोणे इतं सम्बद्धं यन्महीपुरं ताभ्यां संवेष्टितमिति व्याख्येयम्। अत्र शक्तिर्देवता॥ ३॥

मृत्युञ्जययन्त्रमाह मध्य इति। मध्ये अष्टदलकर्णिकायाम्। विशेषणद्वयविशिष्टं साध्यनाम सकारमध्ये लिखेत्। अष्टसु पत्रेषु मन्त्रपुटितं मृत्युञ्जयमन्त्रपुटितं नाम साध्यनाम लिखेदित्यर्थः। वर्गान् कादीन्। तदग्रेषु पत्राग्रेषु। पद्मपुटीकृतमिति। अधऊर्ध्वमुखेन उपर्यधोमुखेन पद्मेनेत्यर्थः। अत्र मृत्युञ्जयो देवता॥ ४॥ ५॥

ज्वरघ्नमाह साध्येति। चिन्तामणिं ग्लौम्। अनलगेहेनेति द्वितीयेन।

तारठद्वयपुटं कुरुकुल्ले मन्त्रमत्र हुतभुग्गृहद्वयुग्मे ।
मध्यकोणविवरेषु लिखेत् तद्यन्त्रमाशु विनिहन्ति भुजङ्गान् ॥ ८
ॐकारमायादिकमेखलेऽग्निवधूमनं वह्निगृहस्य युग्मे ।
मध्यादिकोणेषु विलिख्य भूर्जे यन्त्रं विदध्यात् रिपुनागहारि ॥ ९
शूलाङ्किते वह्निगृहस्य युग्मे धूमावतीमन्त्रं लिखेत् क्रमेण ।
मध्यादिकोणेषु मरुद्गृहस्थं यन्त्रं हुताशानिलवर्णवीतम् ॥ १०

दान्तौ सार्घीशबिन्द्वन्तौ बीजे धूमावति द्विठः ।
धूमावतीमनुः प्रोक्तः शत्रुनिग्रहकारकः ॥ ११

अत्र चिन्तामणिर्देवता । एष एवेति । केवलमन्त्रोऽप्याराधितो ज्वरघ्नः । उक्तञ्च नारायणीये—दष्टमुत्थापयेदेष स्वजप्ता[जात्या]म्भोऽभिषेकतः ।

तज्जप्तशङ्खभेर्यादिनिस्वनश्रवणेन च ॥ इति ॥ ६ ॥ ७ ॥

सर्पघ्नमाह तारेति । तारठद्वयपुटमिति मन्त्रविशेषणम् । तेनादौ तारः अन्ते स्वाहा मध्ये कुरुकुल्ले इति स्वरूपम् । तेनास्य मन्त्रस्य सप्ताक्षरता । हुतभुग्गृहयुग्मे परस्परव्यतिभिन्ने । लिखेदिति रोचनया । उक्तञ्च तत्रैव—"भूर्जे रोचनया षडस्रिलिखिते" इति । विनिहन्ति गृहाद्बिलाच्चोच्चाटयतीत्यर्थः ॥ तथा च नारायणीये—सर्पोन्निर्गमयेद्बिलेषु निहितो गेहात्तथोच्चाटयेत् । इति ।

अत्र कुरुकुल्ला देवता ॥ ८ ॥

अन्यत् सर्पघ्नयन्त्रमाह ओमिति । मेखले स्वरूपम् । ॐकारमायाद्यः सप्ताक्षरो मन्त्रः । विलिख्येति गोरोचनया । तथैव तन्त्रोक्तेः । रिपवो नागाः तद्धारि । नारायणीये "पूर्वोक्ततुल्यक्रिये" इत्युक्तेः । अत्र मेखला देवता ॥ ९ ॥

उच्चाटनकृदाह शूलेति । शूलाङ्कित इति बहिःकोणाग्रेषु । मध्यादीति । मध्ये बीजद्वयं शिष्टाक्षराणि कोणेषु । मरुद्गृहं प्रथमपटलोक्तम् । हुताशो रेफः अनिलो यः अनेनावृत्तिद्वयम् । तेन पूर्वमावृत्तिद्वयं पश्चात् मरुद्गृहवेष्टनमिति ज्ञेयम् । अत्र धूमावती देवता ॥ १० ॥

धूमावतीमन्त्रमाह दान्ताविति । दान्तौ धकारौ । अर्घीश ऊ बिन्दुश्च प्रत्येकं तदन्तौ तेन धूं धूमिति । अष्टाक्षरो मन्त्रः । शत्रुनिग्रहकारक इत्यनेन पृथगाराधनाऽप्यस्योक्ता । अस्यर्ष्यादि यथा । पिप्पलादो नाम ऋषिः निवृच्छन्दो ज्येष्ठा देवता शत्रुनिग्रहे विनियोगः । बीजद्वयरहितषड्वर्णैः षडङ्गानि ।

विशेषा कनकाम्भोभिः प्रेतकर्पटकल्पितम्।
श्मशाने निखनेदेतत् शत्रूनुच्चाटयेद्द्रुतम्॥ १२

हुताशगेहद्वितयं लिखित्वा वैवस्वताय द्विठवर्णमन्त्रम्।
मध्यान्तमाकल्पितमिन्दुबिम्बे यन्त्रं महाभूतपिशाचवैरि॥ १३

सर्वजनोद्वेगकारिक्षतिविषमचेता दीर्घा मलिनाम्बरा विमुक्तपरुषकेशा रूक्षा विधवा विरलदशना काकध्वजा काकरवा शूर्पोदरी क्षुत्पिपासया कलहातुरक्तेति ध्यानम्। कृष्णचतुर्दश्यामुपोष्य ध्यात्वा दिगम्बरः स्वयं मुक्तशिरोरुहः सन् चितिस्थाने शून्यागारे शैले विपिने वा नक्तभोजी लक्षं जपेत्। कृतपुरश्चरणो भवति। उक्तञ्च धूमावतीकल्पे—

अथातः संप्रवक्ष्यामि विद्यां धूमावतीं पराम्।
तस्या धूमावति स्वाहा विद्या वेद्या षडक्षरी॥
षडङ्गान्यत्र योज्यानि विद्याबीजैः षडक्षरैः[सबिन्दुकैः]।
पूर्वसेवा जपेत् पूर्वं ज्येष्ठागारे दिगम्बरः॥
रात्रौ कृष्णचतुर्दश्यामनाशी मुक्तमूर्द्धजः।
ततः शून्यालये शैले श्मशाने विपिनेऽपि वा॥
पुरो धूमावतीं ध्यायन् जपेल्लक्षं चपाशनः।
काकारूढाऽतिकृष्णा प्रविरलदशना मुक्तकेशी विरक्ता
धूम्राक्षी क्षुत्तृषार्त्ता प्रतिभटचकिता चञ्चला कामलोला।
क्लिष्टा पुष्टालसाङ्गी श्रमजलमलिना व्यक्तदर्पा विरूपा
भूतिं धूमावती वः प्रदिशतु विपुलां धूतसूर्पाग्रहस्ता॥
एषा धूमावती नाम्ना ज्येष्ठा देवी वरप्रदा॥ इति॥

दाम्ब इति प्रामादिकः पाठः। तदुक्तं नारायणीये—

धृगुणं मावति शिरो नाम्ना धूमावतीमनुः। इति।

अग्रे धूमावतीं पत्रगामिति च वक्ष्यति। कनकाम्भोभिरिति। धत्तूरपत्ररसमृष्टेन विशेषा कारस्करेण लिखेदित्यर्थः। प्रेतकर्पटे प्रेतवस्त्रे॥ ११॥१२॥

भूतघ्नमाह हुताशेति। द्विठः स्वाहा। सप्ताक्षरो मन्त्रः। मध्यान्तमिति क्रियाविशेषणम्। मध्यादि अन्तपर्यन्तमित्यर्थः। तेन मध्ये षट्सु कोणेषु शेषवर्णानालिखेदित्यर्थः। मध्याद्यमिति क्वचित्पाठः। इन्दुबिम्बे इति वृत्ते। अत्र यमो देवता॥ १३॥

नामालिख्य मकारकोष्ठयुगले कोणेषु तस्यालिखेत्
मन्त्रज्ञो ङञणान्मकारसहितान् धूमावतीयन्त्रगान् ।
पीतं घुर्मुटिकादिना परमिदं वायुर्विगेहावृतं
यन्त्रं प्राणपरेतभूमिनिहितं विद्वेषणं स्याद् द्विषाम् ॥ १४

पूर्वं घुर्मुटिकीयुग्मं ततो मर्कटिकीयुगम् ।
घोरे विद्वेषकारिणि विद्वेषोद्वेगकारिणि ॥ १५

अथ घोराघोरयोः स्यादमुकामुकयोस्ततः ।
विद्वेषयद्वयं हुं फट् विद्या घुर्मुटिकीरिता ॥ १६

प्राक्प्रत्यग्दक्षिणोदग्विधिवदभिलिखेत् स्पष्टरेखाचतुष्कं
कोणोद्यच्छूलयुक्तं वलययुगयुतं मध्यपूर्वं तदन्तम् ।
मन्त्रस्याऽर्णान् परस्तात् वसुपदविवरेष्वष्टवर्णान् लिखित्वा
शूलोद्यद्द्वादशार्णं विधिवदभिहितं प्रेतराजस्य यन्त्रम् ॥ १७

विद्वेषणकृदाह नामेति । नाम साध्यसाधककर्मरूपम् । मकारकोष्ठयुगल इति वृत्तचतुरस्रे एकत्र साध्यनामाऽपरत्र साधकनाम । तस्य मकारचतुरस्रस्य कोणेषु ईशादि लेखनीयम् । मन्त्रज्ञ इत्यनेन ङञणानां सबिन्दुत्वमुक्तम् । अष्टदलं कमलं विलिख्य तत्कर्णिकायां मकारं तत्पत्रेषु धूमावत्यक्षराणि तदुपरि घुर्मुटिकादिनाऽऽवृत्तिः । बहिस्त्रोणि वायुग्रहाणि । अत्र धूमावतीघुर्मुटिके देवते । अमुकामुकयोरित्यत्र साध्यनामप्रक्षेपः । नारायणीयेऽयं विशेषः—

चक्रं ताडयेत कार्पासयष्ट्या विद्वेषणं द्वयोः । इति ॥ १४॥१५॥१६ ॥

मारणयन्त्रमाह प्रागिति । व्याख्यातमिदं सप्तदशे । अत्र शूलेषु शूलोत्पन्न-द्वादशकोष्ठेषु द्वादशार्णलिखनम् । तदुक्तम्—

यमान्तकं दलाग्रेषु नेमिबाह्यगतेषु । इति ।

अनेन द्वादशरेखाप्रान्तेषु द्वादश शूलानि कर्त्तव्यानीत्युक्तम् । नारायणीये तथोक्तेः । मन्त्रान्तरत्वेन भेदः । विधिवदभिहितमिति । विधिस्त्वयम् । आदौ पार्श्वद्वये महिषाश्वशिरसौ विलिख्य तन्मध्ये यन्त्रं सम्पादयेदिति ।

तदुक्तं नारायणीये—चिताङ्गारारचनिम्बाङ्घ्रिर्महिषाश्वशिरोऽन्तरा । इति ।

यमो देवता । तदुक्तम्—

मारणे मोहने स्तम्भे विद्वेषोच्चाटने वशे ।

यमराजसदोमेय यमेदोरुणयोदय ।
यदियोनिरपक्षेय यक्षेयवनिरामय ॥ १८

उक्तो धूमान्धकाराय स्वाहेत्यष्टाक्षरो मनुः ॥ १९

प्रणवः ष्ट्रीं ततो दंष्ट्रा तत्परं विकृतान्ततः ।
आननाय बधूर्वह्निर्मन्त्रोऽयं द्वादशाक्षरः ॥ २०

विषवृक्षस्य फलकी नृचर्मणि पटेऽथवा ।
आलिख्याऽष्टविषैरेतत् श्मशाने निखनेत् निशि ॥ २१

ज्वरेण महताऽऽविष्टो मूर्च्छाकुलितमानसः ।
रिपुर्गच्छति पक्षेण यमलोकं न संशयः ॥ २२

एवं यमार्गलं वृत्तं बहुधा तु व्यवस्थितम् ॥
द्वादशारं लिखेच्चक्रं वृत्तत्रयसमन्वितम् ॥ इति ।

नारायणीयेऽपि—चतुःकुल्याशलाके त्रिवर्त्तुले च चतुर्गुणे ।
बहिरष्टगुणे वस्त्रे विधिना तं मनुं लिखेत् ॥ इति ॥

इदं व्याख्यातमपेक्षितार्थद्योतन्याम् । त्रिवर्त्तुलं लिखित्वा तन्मध्ये दक्षिणोत्तररूपेण रेखाद्वयं पूर्वपश्चिमरूपेण रेखाद्वयं च लिखित्वा आग्नेयादिकोणेषु रेखाचतुष्टयं लिखित्वा दिग्गतरेखाग्रेषु अष्टौ शूलान् कोणरेखाग्रेषु शूलचतुष्टयमेतत् लिखित्वा तत्र शास्त्रोक्तप्रकारेण मन्त्राक्षराणि लिखेदिति । [तदन्तमिति । मध्यादारभ्य यमराजश्लोकं वलयद्वयं यथा भवति तथा लिखेत् । अवशिष्टकोष्ठेषु अग्रतः प्रदक्षिणं वक्ष्यमाणं धूमान्धकाराविष्ठनं शूलस्थानेषु वक्ष्यमाणद्वादशाक्षरेण वेष्टयेत् । धूमान्धकारमन्त्रमाह उक्तेति । इति गूढार्थदीपिन्याम्] ॥१७॥१८॥१९॥

यमान्तकमन्त्रमाह प्रणव इति । ततो मायेति पठित्वा केचित् प्रणवमायाष्ट्रींपूर्वं विकृतानन हुं फट् स्वाहेत्या हुः । मन्त्रद्वयस्य षडङ्गं यथा । ॐ क्रां कृष्णवर्णाय हृत् । मन्त्रग्रीवेण शिरः । ॐ नववक्त्रपिङ्गलजटामुकुटधारिणे शिखा । ॐ हुं सहस्रादित्योदयप्रभाय वर्म । ॐ क्रीं त्रिनेत्राय त्रिनेत्रम् । ॐ श्रीं भ्रूविकृताननाय इत्यस्त्रम् । ध्यानं गुरुमुखाद् ज्ञेयम् ॥ २० ॥

विषवृक्षस्य कारस्करस्य । पटे प्रेतपटे । अष्टविषैरिति । पूर्वपटलान्तोक्तैः । आलिख्येति । काकपक्षलेखन्या । श्मशाने निखनेदिति । शरावसम्पुटस्थं कृत्वा स्निग्धयोरन्तरा नीत्वेति शेषः ।

एकाशीतिपदेषु मध्यदहने साध्यं लिखेत् क्रूं पुनः
घ्रूं श्रूं वलूमिति दिग्गतासु विलिखेत् बीजानि पङ्क्तिष्वथ ।
शिष्टेष्वीशनिशाचरादि विलिखेत् कालीमनुं पङ्क्तिश-
स्तद्बाह्ये यमवीतमग्निपवनावीतञ्च यन्त्रं लिखेत् ॥ २३

ओदनो रजनीचूर्णं घृतं दधि पयो मधु ।
पललं मुद्गमाषौ च सक्तुलाजाश्च मोदकम् ॥

इत्येतैर्द्रव्यैश्चक्रस्य दक्षिणदिशि यमराजकालधर्ममनुवैवस्वतशान्तप्रेतराजमृत्युकृतान्तनामभिश्चतुर्थ्यन्तैर्नमोऽन्तैरष्टाक्षरायैरष्टभिर्बलिर्देयः । ततो मातृभ्यः लोकपालेभ्योऽपि स्वस्वनामभिः स्वस्वदिक्षु बलिं दत्त्वा उत्तरस्मिन् यक्षेभ्यो नैर्ऋते राक्षसेभ्यः सर्वासु दिक्षु भूतेभ्यो बलिं हरेत् । पूर्वमीशाने द्वादशाक्षरेण त्वष्टाक्षरेण वा यममुखे बलिं विधाय पश्चादयं बलिः । तदुक्तं नारायणीये—

शरस्वसम्पुटस्थं तत् स्निग्धयोर्नीतमन्तरा ।
यमराजचक्रमेतत् श्मशाने द्वेषकृत् खनेत् ॥ इति ॥

बलिस्तु अपेक्षितार्थद्योतनिकायामुक्तोऽत्र यन्त्रे त्रिषु कर्मसु ज्ञेयः । तत्र विद्वेषे प्रेतवस्त्रे नारायणीयप्रोक्तमार्गेण लिखनं श्मशाने खननं च । मारणे ग्रन्थकारोक्तरीत्या विषवृक्षफलके नरचर्मणि वा लिखनं श्मशाने खननं च । स्तम्भने तु अस्यैव यन्त्रस्य विशेषो नारायणीये—

मेरुस्थं स्तम्भकृत् यन्त्रं तत्तु पेषण्यधः क्षिपेत् । इति ।

अस्य व्याख्याने अपेक्षितार्थद्योतन्यामुक्तम् । बिभीतकफलके शिलायामिष्टकायां वा पीतद्रव्येण ताम्रसूच्या चक्रमालिख्य मेरुगं कृत्वाऽभ्यर्च्य जप्त्वा बलिं निर्हृत्य शत्रुमार्गारिगृहश्मशाननिर्माल्यपेषण्यधोगतस्थलेषु स्थिरनक्षत्रराशिषु निखनेदिति ।

तदुक्तम्—ताम्रलेखन्या पीतेन लिखितं स्तम्भने खनेत् ।
अपि भारतसङ्ग्रामे समरे रिपुवारणम् ॥ इति ॥ २१॥२२ ॥

मारणयन्त्रान्तरमाह एकेति । इदं त्वरितापटले व्याख्यातम् । मध्यदहने मध्यकोष्ठरेफ इति पद्मपादाचार्याः । मन्त्रान्तरत्वेन भेदः । तद्बाह्य इत्यनेन षषडन्तया त्वरितया संवेष्टयेदित्युक्तम् । यमवीतमिति । ईशानादि निर्ऋतान्तमेकवारं विलिख्य पुनश्च निर्ऋत्यादि ईशान्तं लिखेत् । आचार्यैः—
"शैवादि नैर्ऋत्यादि कालीमनुं लिखेत्" इत्युक्त्वा "तथाक्रमायमवृतम्" इत्युक्तम् ।

केचित्तु चतुर्दिक्षु चतुर्भिरक्षरैरिति वदन्ति । अग्नी रेफः पवनो यः

कालीमारमालीका लीनमोच्चमोनली ।

मामोदेततदेमोमा रच्चतत्वत्वतच्चर ।

कालीमनुरयं प्रोक्तः कालरात्रिः स्ववैरिणाम् ॥ २४

यमापाटटपामाय माटमोटटमोटमा ।

वामोभूरिरिभूमोवा टटरीस्वस्वरीटट ॥ २५

यमात्मकोऽयमाख्यातः श्लोको वैरिविनाशकः ।

लिखेदष्टविषाङ्गारनिम्बनिर्यासकज्जलैः ॥ २६

निग्रहाख्यमिदं यन्त्रं काकपत्त्रेण कर्पटे ।

विभीतवृक्षे वल्मीके श्मशाने वा चतुष्पथे ॥ २७

ताभ्यामावृतिद्वयम् । एष साम्प्रदायिकः पक्षः । कश्चित्तु अग्निपवनशब्देन तद्दृष्टे गृह्णीते इत्याह स्म । तदसाम्प्रदायिकम् । मन्त्रमुक्तावल्यादिबहुग्रन्थविरोधात् । तदुक्तम्—

वषडन्तां लिखेद्विद्यां त्वरितां पूर्ववद्बहिः ।

यममन्त्रगतान् वर्णान् वह्निबीजं समन्ततः ॥

प्रभञ्जनमयं बीजं तद्बाह्ये चाऽभितो लिखेत् ।

पटे शोसोद्भवे शावे वसने भूर्जकेऽपि वा ॥ इति ॥

अग्निमयन्त्रे ग्रन्थकृदेव वक्ष्यति । कृशानुवायुबीजावृतमिति । त्वरिताविद्यया माहिषाज्येनाऽष्टोत्तरसहस्रं हुत्वा यन्त्रे सम्पातं सम्पात्य पश्चाद्यन्त्रं खनेदिति ज्ञेयम् । तदुक्तम्—

माहिषेण घृतेनाऽष्ट सहस्रसहितेन च ।

हुतेन सिद्धं सम्पातं योजयेन् मूलविद्यया ॥ इति ॥

अयं मन्त्रविलेखनप्रकारस्तु पुरुषमुद्दिश्य । स्त्रियमुद्दिश्य तु भद्रकालीश्लोकस्थाने यमश्लोकमालिख्य यमश्लोकस्थाने भद्रकालीश्लोकेन वेष्टयेत् । अन्यत् समानमिति सम्प्रदायविदः । अत्र कालरात्रिः स्ववैरिणां वैरिविनाशक इत्यनेन चानयोः स्वतन्त्रताऽपि उक्ता ॥ २३॥२४॥२५॥२६ ॥

अङ्गारश्चिताङ्गारः । एतेषां कज्जलैः । तत्र कज्जलकरणप्रकारः । मनुष्यकपाले नरादिस्नेहेन शूलारूढप्रेतकर्पटवर्त्या अष्टविषादिमय्या कुर्यात् ।

कर्पटे शूलाधिरूढप्रेतकर्पटे । तदुक्तम् । "शोसपट्टेऽथवा शावे" इति । विभीतकवृक्ष इति । तत्कोटरे । तदुक्तम्—

दक्षिणस्थेऽनिले मन्त्री निखनेदर्द्धरात्रके।
सर्वथा शत्रुरेतेन समाहान् मरणं व्रजेत् ॥ २८
निगृह्यते महारोगैः पतितो वा भवेदसौ।
शिलायामिष्टकायां वा चक्रमेतत् प्रकल्पितम् ॥ २९
मर्कटीविषदण्डीभिः समालिप्तमधोमुखम्।
यत्र रात्रौ खनेत्तत्र भूयो भूयोऽशुभं भवेत् ॥ ३०
लिखेच्चतुःषष्टिपदेषु कालीमीशादिकन्यादि यमात्मकेन।
श्लोकेन संवेष्ट्य कृशानुवायुबीजावृतं यन्त्रमिदं विदध्यात् ॥ ३१
लिप्तं विषमसीदण्डीमर्कटीभिरधोमुखम्।
निखनेद्यत्र तत्र स्यात् नृणामुच्चाटनं सदा।
शस्यहानिमनावृष्टिं गवां नाशं करोति तत् ॥ ३२
वल्मीके चत्वरे वाऽन्तरविवरे वा निदध्यात्। इति॥

दक्षिणस्थेऽनिले सूर्यगवायावित्यर्थः। मरणमिति विभीतव्ये। महारोगैरिति चतुष्पथे। पतित इति श्मशाने। वाशब्दः समुच्चये। तेन वल्मीके अवयववैकल्यमिति पद्मपादाचार्याः। शिलायामिति। रजकशिलायाम्। इष्टकायामिति। शिवालयस्थायाम्। दण्डो ब्रह्मदण्डो। यत्र ग्रामनगरादौ। मन्त्री देशेषु निक्षिपेद्यत्युक्तः। अत्र साध्यनामस्थाने ग्रामनगरनामनी लेखनीये ॥ २६॥२७॥२८॥२९॥३०॥

उच्चाटनकृदाह लिखेदिति। त्वरिताचतुःषष्टिपदवदिदमपि। कालीमित्यनन्तरोक्तश्लोकरूपकालीमन्त्रम्। यमात्मकेनेत्युत्तरेण सम्बध्यते। वेष्टनं पूर्ववच्छोक्तवत्। अत्र यमवेष्टनात् प्राक् वषडन्तत्वरितावेष्टनमपि। अत्र सम्प्रदायात् रेफवेष्टने साध्यसाधककर्मयुक्तरेफेण वेष्टयेदिति। क्रियाशुद्धिस्तु पूर्वोक्तामनुसन्धेयम्। तन्त्रान्तरे तु—

चतुःषष्टिपदे कालीमीशदोषाचरादिकम्।
विन्यस्य मध्ये चतुर्षु हुङ्काराद्यक्षराणि च॥
अन्तराले तु तेषां च साध्यानां नाम कर्म च।
शिखान्तविद्यया याम्यमनुना दहनेन च॥
वायुना च समावेष्ट्य कृतमेतत् सुसाधितम्।
मारणोन्मादनादीनि कर्माण्याशु प्रसाधयेत्॥ इति॥

आख्यां तुम्बुरुमध्यतः स्मरगतामालिख्य जम्भादिकां
विद्यां दिग्गतपत्रकेष्वथ लिखेत् देवीर्दलेषु स्मरम् ।
कोणस्थेषु सनामकं बहिरतः पाशाङ्कुशाभ्यां वृतं
यन्त्रं वश्यकरं ग्रहादिभयहृत् क्षुद्राभिचारापहम् ॥ ३३

जम्भे जम्भिनि ठद्वन्द्वं मोहे मोहिनि ठद्वयम् ।
अन्धे अन्धिनि ठद्वन्द्वं रुन्धे रुन्धिनि ठद्वयम् ॥ ३४
हित्वा कामं लिखेत् शान्तिं यन्त्रेऽस्मिन् न्नृकपालके ।
सन्ध्यासु तापयेदेतदुच्चैः साध्यं वशं नयेत् ॥ ३५
हित्वा शान्तिं लिखेद्वर्मं पटे वा नरचर्मणि ।
वह्निवायुगृहावीतं श्मशानस्थं रिपून् हरेत् ॥ ३६
हित्वा वर्म लिखेदस्त्रं फलकेऽक्षतरूद्भवे ।
वह्निवायुयुतं नाम विषाढ्यरुधिरेण तत् ॥ ३७
चत्वरे निखनेत् जप्तं विद्वेषं कुरुते मिथः ।
हित्वा रेफयकारौ द्वौ लकारं मध्यतो लिखेत् ॥ ३८
धरापुरेण वीतं तद्दिष्टकान्तर्निवेशितम् ।
सर्वेषां स्तम्भनं कुर्यान्नात्र कार्या विचारणा ॥ ३९

मसी पूर्वोक्तं कज्जलम् । दण्डो ब्रह्मदण्डो । मर्कटो कपिकच्छु । उभयोस्त्वरिता देवता ॥ ३१॥३२ ॥

वश्यकृदाह आख्यामिति । आख्यां कर्मसहितं साध्यसाधकनाम । तुम्बुरुमध्यतः कर्णिकास्थतुम्बुरौ । अथ देवीरिति तुम्बुरुमन्त्रोक्तदेवीबीजचतुष्टयं सनामकं स्मरञ्च विदिग्दलेषु लिखेत् । तेनायमर्थः सम्पन्नः । देवीबीजमध्ये कामबीजं तन्मध्ये नाम एवं कोणचतुर्दलेष्विति । तुम्बरुः देवता ॥ ३३॥३४॥

हित्वा काममिति । कामबीजपञ्चकं हित्वा त्यक्त्वा शान्तिं दीर्घमोकारं सबिन्दुकं लिखेत् । अन्यत् पूर्ववत् । उच्चैरित्यतिशयेन । लिखेदिति शान्तिस्थाने । वर्म हुं । पटे प्रेतपटे । वह्निवायुगृहावीतमिति शेषः । अन्यत् पूर्ववत् । अक्षतरुर्विभीतकः । चत्वरे अङ्गणे । अत्रापि वह्निवायुगृहावीतमिति ज्ञेयम् । जप्तमिति तुम्बुरुबीजेन । हित्वेति तुम्बुरुबीजमालिख्य तत्र लकारं लिखेत् । धरापुरेणेति । वह्निवायुनिवृत्तिः । शेषं

हित्वा लकारं तन्मध्ये वायुबीजं समालिखेत्।
विषरक्तमसीकाकपुरीषैर्ध्वजवाससि ॥ ४०

श्मशाने निहितं कुर्यात् कुलोच्छेदं स्ववैरिणाम्।
मुक्त्वा वायुमयं बीजं तत्र फट्कारमालिखेत् ॥ ४१

प्रेतवस्त्रे काकस्य रुधिरेण यथाविधि।
इप्सिते निखनेत् स्थाने विद्वेषं कुरुते नृणाम् ॥ ४२

अस्त्रबीजमपास्याऽस्मिन् लकारं सोर्णसंयुतम्।
विलिखेत् यन्त्रमेतत् स्यात् लोहत्रयसमावृतम् ॥ ४३

सर्वरोगप्रशमनं कृत्याद्रोहादिशान्तिदम्।
विहाय बीजं लङ्कारं ग्लौंकारं तत्र संलिखेत् ॥ ४४

चकारेणावृतं बाह्ये पाशाङ्कुशवृतं पुनः।
टपरेण वृतं भूयो भूमिमण्डलमध्यगम् ॥ ४५

लकारैर्बिन्दुसंयुक्तैर्वेष्टितं तद्बहिः क्रमात्।
सर्गान्तमातृकाबीजं सर्वं वृत्तेन वेष्टितम् ॥ ४६

कौशेयकर्पटे कृप्तमिष्टकाद्वयमध्यगम्।
सेनाग्रे निखनेद्यन्त्रं स्तम्भनं कुरुते ध्रुवम् ॥ ४७

मध्ये श्रीनरसिंहबीजमथ तद्बाह्ये स्वरान् केसरे
वारीट्चन्द्रयमेन्द्रदिक्षु विलिखेन् मध्ये मनुं गारुड़म्।
अन्तस्थान् मरुदग्निनिर्ऋतिशिवेष्वालिख्य वर्णावृतं
यन्त्रं सर्गिभिरष्टभिः परिवृतं संवर्त्तकैर्गारुड़म् ॥ ४८

पूर्ववत्। इष्टकान्तः इष्टकाद्वयान्तः। अग्निमभेदत्वये धरापुरमेव कार्यम्। तन्मध्ये तुम्बुरुमध्ये वायुबीजं यं लिखेत्। अन्यत् समानम्। रक्तमजारक्तम्। मसी पूर्वोक्तकज्जलम्। ध्वजवाससि। प्रेतपताकावस्त्रे। यथाविधीति। काकपक्षलेखन्येत्युक्तम्। ईप्सित इति। ययोर्विद्वेषणं क्रियते ताभ्यां यस्योल्लङ्घ्यते तत्र देश इत्यर्थः। बाह्ये इति। पश्चाद्बहिः। टपरेण ठकारेण। सर्गान्तेति। विसर्गान्ता ॥ ३५—४७ ॥

गारुडयन्त्रमाह मध्य इति। मध्ये कर्णिकायां श्रीयुक्तं नरसिंहबीजं

संवर्त्तको नेत्रयुतः पार्श्वस्तारोऽग्निसुन्दरी ।
गारुडो मनुराख्यातो विषद्वयविनाशनः ॥ ४९

स्मरन् गरुडमात्मानं मन्त्रमेनं जपेन्नरः ।
विषमालोकनेनैव हन्यात् नागकुलोद्भवम् ॥ ५०

षोडशपटलोक्तम् । श्रीशब्देन चैकदेशो रेफो गृहीतः । स जहं इति ज्ञेयम् । तदुक्तं नारायणीये—बिन्दुमदग्निरूर्ध्वान्त्यकर्णिकायाम् । इति ।

वारीडिति पश्चिमदिक् । चन्द्रेति उत्तरदिक् । यमेति दक्षिणदिक् । इन्द्रेति पूर्वदिक् । विलिखेत् मध्य इति । गारुडमन्त्रान्त्यं कर्णिकायां लिखेदित्यर्थः । अन्तस्थान् यरलवान् सबिन्दून् । वर्गावृतमिति ग्रामादिकः पाठः । वर्णावृतमिति पाठान्तरपाठः साम्प्रदायिकः । सर्गिभिर्विसर्गयुक्तैः । संवर्त्तकैः क्षकारैः । परिवृतमित्यष्टदिक्षु । तदुक्तं नारायणीये—

वृतं लिप्या सर्गि कषाष्टकावृतमिदं यन्त्रं फणिभ्योऽवति । इति ।

अपेक्षितार्थद्योतनिकायां व्याख्यायते । लिप्यक्षरैर्मालेव वेष्टयित्वा सविसर्गमन्त्रमष्टदिक्षु लिखेदित्यर्थः इति । गरुडो देवता ॥ ४८ ॥

गारुडमन्त्रमाह संवर्त्तक इति । संवर्त्तकः क्षः नेत्रमिकारस्तद्युतः तेन क्षि । पार्श्वः पकारः तारः प्रणवः अग्निसुन्दरी स्वाहा । विषद्वयविनाशन इत्यनेन केवलमन्त्रस्यापि स्वतन्त्रतोक्ता । इदमेव यन्त्रफलम् । विषद्वयं स्थावरजङ्गमम् । मन्त्रस्य ऋष्यादिकं तन्त्रान्तराद्यथा—

ऋष्यादिका रुद्रपङ्क्तिगरुडाः परिकीर्त्तिताः ।
हृदयं ज्वलयुग्मान्ते महामतिपदं शिरः ॥
गरुडं चूडाननं स्यादगरुडान्ते शिखि शिखा ।
कवचं प्रोच्य गरुडान् प्रभञ्जनयुगं ततः ॥
प्रभेदनयुगं वित्रासयद्युक् युग्विमर्दय ।
नेत्रमन्त्रस्तूग्ररूपधर सर्व[र्व]विषं हर ॥
भीषयद्वयसर्वं स्याद्दहभस्मीकुरुद्वयम् ।
अस्त्रमन्त्रोऽप्रतिहतबलाप्रतिहतेति च ॥
शासनान्ते हुं फडन्तः स्वाहान्तैरेभिरङ्गकम् ।
नेत्रान्तमर्णकान् पादकटिहृद्वक्त्रमूर्धसु ।
अङ्गुष्ठादिष्वङ्गुलीषु न्यस्य देवं विचिन्तयेत् ॥

मध्ये वार्णं भृगुस्थं विलिखतु विधिवत्साध्यनाम्ना समेतं
किञ्जल्केषु स्वरा: स्युर्वसुदलविवरेष्वालिखेन्मध्यबीजम् ।
काद्यर्णान् केसरेषु द्विगुणवसुदलेष्वर्पयेत् मध्यबीजं
यन्त्रं सञ्जीवनाख्यं सलिलपुरगतं क्षुद्ररोगापहारि ॥ ५१

मध्ये पिण्डमचो दलादिषु लिखेद्वारीशताराधिप-
प्रेताधीश्वरशक्रदिक्षु वियतैर्मध्ये च वर्णान् लिखेत् ।

वर्गा[र्मा]न्तर्वह्नियुग्मान्तरकमलगतं पञ्चभूताद्यवर्णं
कृत्वाकल्पं फणीन्द्रैरभयवरकरं पद्मनेत्रं सुवक्त्रम् ।
दुष्टाहिच्छेदतुण्डं स[स्म]रदखिलविषप्रोषणं प्राणभूतं
प्राणिभ्रेष्ठास्त्रिवेदीतनुसमृतमयं पक्षिराजं भजेऽहम् ॥ इति ॥

एतदनन्तरं गरुडमुद्रा दर्शनीया । तल्लक्षणं चतुर्थपटले मदुक्तमनुसन्धेयम् ।

वर्णलक्षं जपेन्मन्त्रं जुहुयात्तद्दशांशत: ।
घृताक्तै: कृष्णकुसुमैर्मालकाले यजेदमुम् ॥
अङ्गाष्टनागदिक्पालतदस्त्राणि च पूजयेत् ॥ इति ।

बीजस्याऽपीदमेव । नारायणीये तु—

एवमुक्तानि नेत्रान्तान्यङ्गानि वियतैश्च षट् ।
आजानुत: सुवर्णाभमानाभेस्तुहिनप्रभम् ॥
कुङ्कुमारुणमाकण्ठादाकेशान्तात् सितेतरम् ।
ब्रह्माण्डव्यापिनं तार्क्ष्यं रक्ताक्षं नागभूषणम् ॥
नीलाग्रनासमात्मानं हेमपक्षं स्मरेद् बुध: ।
कृष्णं विषस्य संग्रामे रक्ताभं क्षोभकर्मणि ॥
पीतं स्तम्भे शशिप्रख्यं नाशे तार्क्ष्यं विचिन्तयेत् ॥ इति ॥४८॥५०॥

सञ्जीवनयन्त्रमाह मध्य इति । मध्ये इति कर्णिकायाम् । भृगुस्थं सकारस्थम् वार्णं वकारम् । तेन स्वमिति बीजं लिखेत् । साध्यनाम्ना विधिवत्समन्वितमिति । विदर्भितमित्यर्थ: । उक्तञ्च नारायणीये—

जीवं[बीजं] नामविदर्भितं कलशगं मध्ये लिखेत् । इति ।

मध्यबीजं स्वं । काद्यर्णान् सान्तान् । द्विगुणवसुदले षोडशदले । मध्यबीजं स्वं । सलिलपुरं प्रथमपटलोक्तम् । अत्र मृत्युञ्जयो देवता ॥ ५१ ॥

पिण्डयन्त्रमाह मध्य इति । मध्ये अष्टदलकर्णिकायाम् । पिण्डं वक्ष्यमाणं

याद्दीन्मारुतवह्निराचसशिवेष्वर्णान् बहिर्वेष्टयेत्
काद्यैर्वामविलोचनेन कलितं पिण्डाख्ययन्त्रं परम् ॥ ५२

मनुस्वरेन्द्वजेशाग्निसंयुतश्चतुराननः ।
पिण्डबीजमिदं प्रोक्तं पुंसां सर्वार्थसाधकम् ॥ ५३

बीजेनाऽनेन सम्प्रमं यन्त्रं रक्षाकरं परम् ।
आयुरारोग्यजननं लक्ष्मीसौभाग्यवर्धनम् ॥ ५४

विलिख्य तन्मध्ये तत्तद्बीजाक्यं विदर्भितं नाम लिखेत्। वश्ये पाशबीजं शान्तौ वरुणबीजम् उच्चाटने क्रोधाग्निबीजमिति नारायणीय उक्तः। दलादिषु केसरेषु। अचः स्वरान्। दिग्दिक्क्रमेण। वारीशेति पश्चिमदिक्। ताराधिपेति उत्तरदिक्। प्रेताधीश्वरेति दक्षिणदिक्। शक्रेति पूर्वदिक्। वियतेगंवङ्मन्त्रस्य मध्ये कर्णिकान्तरन्त्यमक्षरम्। यादीन् यरलवान्। वामविलोचनेन दीर्घेकारेण। सबिन्दुना चिरिति ज्ञेयम्। "त्रिर्बहिर्मायया पश्चा वेष्टयेद्बिन्दुयुक्तया" इति नारायणीय उक्तः। अत्र पिण्डात्मा देवता ॥ ५२ ॥

पिण्डबीजमुद्धरति मन्विति। मनुस्वर औ इन्दुर्बिन्दुः अजेशो झकारः अग्नी रेफ एतद्युतश्चतुराननः जकारः। सर्वार्थसाधकमिति। तत्र प्रकारो नारायणीयेऽपि—पिण्डं चन्द्रेन्द्रगेहस्थं कुलिशाकारमुज्ज्वलम् ।

पीतं चिन्तितमश्वादौ सैन्यस्तम्भकरं भवेत् ॥
सोमेन्द्रवह्निपुरगं मूर्ध्नि ध्यातं तथाकृति ।
विद्विषत्सर्वमत्तेभमहिषादिनिवारणम् ॥
तदेवाऽग्निसमप्रख्यं परसैन्ये विचिन्तयेत् ।
यायात् पराङ्मुखा पिण्डज्वालादग्धाऽरिवाहिनी ॥
भेदं परकृते स्तम्भे करोत्येव विचिन्तिते ।
अनिलानलसंयुक्तं ध्यानात् क्षोभं करोति तत् ॥
प्रयान्ति हित्वा स्वग्रस्तमात्तनादा ग्रहादयः ।
एतद्रोचनया लिख्य पटादौ यत्र पूज्यते ॥
त्यजन्ति गेहं तच्चौरक्षुद्रभूतोरगादयः ।
उद्यत्सं स्तम्भयत्यस्त्रमैन्द्रस्थं तदन्नीनपि ॥
वारुणान्तर्गतं पिण्डं तेजोऽनुग्रहवर्जितम्[वर्धनम्] ।
दष्टोत्तमाङ्गे विन्यस्तं विषनाशं करोति तत् ॥ इति ।

चौरसर्पमृगव्यालभूतामयनिकृन्तनम् ।
गर्भरक्षाकरं स्त्रीणां पुत्रदं क्षुद्रनाशनम् ।
धृतं मूर्ध्नि करोत्येतत् लोकवश्यमनुत्तमम् ॥ ५५

मध्ये तोयगृहे लकारविवरे सार्णाढ्यसाध्यं लिखेत्
पत्रेष्वष्टसु हंसमन्त्रमभितो हंसार्णसंवेष्टितम् ।
यन्त्रं भूमिगृहेण वेष्टितमिदं मूर्ध्ना सदा धारितं
हन्यात् क्षुद्रमहाज्वरामयरिपून् दद्यात् यशः सम्पदः ॥ ५६

मृगो व्याघ्रः । व्यालो दुष्टगजः । क्षुद्राः सप्त । लोकवश्यमिति । तत्र विशेषः—पद्ममध्ये लिखेदिन्दौ पिण्डान्तर्नामबीजयुक् ।
वियतिस्ताश्चयन्त्रोक्ता लेख्या यरलवास्तथा ॥
त्रिर्महामायया पद्मं वेष्टयेदिन्दुयुक्तया ।
गोमयाम्बुयुजा यन्त्रमेतद्रोचनया लिखेत् ॥
भूर्जे सुवर्णलेखन्या जतुरौप्येण वेष्टयेत् ।
हेम्ना च जपपूजाभ्यां हवनेन च साधयेत् ॥
आयुष्यं पावनं पुष्टिलक्ष्मीसौभाग्यवश्यकृत् ।
चौरव्यालमृगारण्यसलिलादिभयापहम् ॥
पुत्रदं गर्भरक्षाकृद् ग्रहसर्पभ[वीम]यादिहृत् ।
क्षुद्रोपशमनं यन्त्रं विद्यात् सर्वार्थसाधकम् ॥
उत्तमाङ्गस्थितं तत् स्याल्लोकवश्यमनुत्तमम् ।
शिखान्तं पाशपुटितं पिण्डं वश्ये सदा जपेत् ॥
वातानीतापतत्पत्रे काकपक्षेण कल्पितम् ।
बिम्बान्तस्थेन्दुरहितं यन्त्रमुच्चाटनं रिपोः ॥
क्रोधाग्निपुटितं मन्त्री पिण्डमुच्चाटने जपेत् ।
आकाशः साग्निकर्णार्द्धचन्द्रः क्रोधाग्निरुच्यते ॥ इति ॥ ५३॥५४॥
॥ ५५ ॥

यन्त्रान्तरमाह मध्य इति । मध्ये तोयगृह इति व्यधिकरणे सप्तम्यौ । मध्ये कर्णिकायाम् । तोयगृहं च प्रथमपटलोक्तम् । लकारविवरे लकारान्तः सार्णाढ्यसाध्यं सकारसहितसाध्यसाधककर्मनाम लिखेत् । हंसो देवता ॥ ५६ ॥

ईकारमध्ये विलिखेत् स्वसाध्यं तमष्टपत्रेषु पुनर्विलिख्य।
संवेष्टयेत् तेन धरापुरस्थं यन्त्रं भवेत् वश्यकरं नराणाम्॥ ५७

तान्नपत्रे समालिख्य यन्त्रमेतत् प्रपूजयेत्।
वशयेत् सकलान्मर्त्यान् नात्र कार्या विचारणा॥ ५८

मध्ये भान्तं भृगुविनिहितं नामवर्णैः प्रवीतं
टान्तं लान्तान्वितमथ विलिखेदष्टपत्रेषु भूयः।
भूबिम्बस्थं निगदितमिदं साधु सञ्जीवनाख्यं
शस्त्रो[त्रू]द्‌भूतं भयमपहरेत् धार्यमाणं भुजेन॥ ५९

वार्णावृतं साध्ययुतं सकारं टान्ते लिखेदष्टदलेषु हंसम्।
आवेष्टयेदम्बुगृहेण बाह्ये लान्तावृतं यन्त्रमिदं ज्वरघ्नम्॥ ६०

टान्ते नाम लिखेत् चकारविवरे मृत्युञ्जयत्र्यक्षरी-
रुद्धं तद्बहिरष्टपत्रविवरे साध्यान्वयं पूर्ववत्।
अच्‌किञ्जल्कयुते वसुद्वयदले पद्मे तथैवान्वयं
द्वात्रिंशद्दलपङ्कजेऽपि च तथा काद्यर्णयुक्केसरे॥ ६१

ईकारेण समावीतं यन्त्रं मृत्युञ्जयान्वयम्।
सर्वरोगाभिचारघ्नं सर्वसौभाग्यसिद्धिदम्॥ ६२

वश्यकृदाह ईकारेति। तम् ईकारम्। तेनेकारेण। माया देवता॥५७॥५८॥

अस्त्रभयघ्नदाह मध्य इति। मध्ये अष्टदलकर्णिकायाम्। नामवर्णैः साध्यसाधककर्मनामाक्षरैः प्रवीतं भृगुविनिहितं सकारस्थं भान्तं मकारं लिखेदित्यर्थः। टान्तं ठकारं लान्तान्वितं च। मृत्युञ्जयो देवता॥ ५९॥

ज्वरघ्नमाह वार्णेति। वार्णावृतं वकारेण वृतम्। टान्ते ठकारे। लान्तावृतं बाह्ये अम्बुगृहेण वेष्टयेदिति सम्बन्धः। अम्बुगृहेण प्रथमपटलोक्तेन। हंसो देवता॥ ६०॥

रोगाभिचारघ्नमाह टान्त इति। टान्ते चकारविवर इति व्यधिकरणे सप्तम्यौ। मृत्युञ्जयत्र्यक्षरीरुद्धं नाम लिखेदिति अन्वयः। पूर्ववन्मृत्युञ्जयपुटितं नामेत्यर्थः। अच्‌किञ्जल्कयुते वसुद्वयदले षोडशदले। तथैवेति। पूर्ववन्नामेत्यर्थः। काद्यर्णयुक्केसरे द्वात्रिंशद्दलपङ्कजे तथा पूर्ववन्नामेत्यर्थः। मृत्युञ्जयो देवता॥ ६१॥ ६२॥

ग्लौं रुद्धं प्रणवद्वयं प्रविलिखेत् साध्यस्य नामान्वितं
बाह्ये भूपुरमष्टवज्रविलसत्तारं लिखित्वा पुनः।
तत्कोणेषु दिशासु लं प्रविलिखेत् पाशाङ्कुशतारचरी-
वीतं स्तम्भनयन्त्रमावृतिलसज्जम्भादिविद्याष्टकम् ॥ ६३

जम्भे वह्निवधूः पूर्वं पश्चाज्जम्भिनि ठद्वयम्।
मोहे पावकजाया स्यात्ततो मोहिनि ठद्वयम् ॥ ६४
अन्धे हुतभुजो जाया ततोऽन्धिनि ठयुग्मकम्।
रुन्धे कृशानुपत्नी स्यात् रुन्धिनि द्विठसंयुतम् ॥ ६५

लान्ते नाम विलिख्य दिक्षु विलिखेत् भूयस्तमेवाऽष्टसु
कोणेष्वेवमथो नरेन्द्रभुजगावन्योन्यबद्धौ लिखेत्।
शाख्यां तन्मुखयोर्बिभीतफलके यन्त्रं समापादितं
निर्माल्ये निहितं सदा वितनुते वाचां द्विषां स्तम्भनम् ॥ ६६

स्तम्भनकृदाह ग्लौमिति। प्रविलिखेदिति। वृत्तान्तरित्यर्थः। अष्टवज्र-
विलसत्तारं बाह्ये भूपुरं लिखित्वेत्यन्वयः। तदुक्तमाचार्यैः—

प्रणवयुगलं भूयुग्मान्तस्थितं ठगतश्च
तदनुकुलिशगं तेषां मध्ये ध्रुवं भुवमन्तरा।
अमरपतिदिक्कोणे ग्लौं पाशाङ्कुशान्तरमायया
वलयितमथो जम्भाद्यष्टौ लिखेत् कुरुते जयम् ॥ इति।

कोणेष्विति भूपुरस्य। पाशाङ्कुशतारचरीति। पाशमायाङ्कुशतारचरीत्यर्थः।
भूमिर्देवता ॥ ६३॥६४॥६५ ॥

वाक्स्तम्भनकृदाह लान्त इति। लान्ते वकारे नाम विलिखेत्। सम्प्रदायात्
लकारविदर्भितमिति ज्ञेयम्। तमिति। लकारम्। अथवा लान्ते नाम
लकारदर्भमभितो भूयस्तमिति पठनीयम्। अभित इति। कर्णिकायामेवा-
ष्टकलिखनम्। मूलपाठे दिक्ष्वित्यस्याप्ययमेवार्थः। अष्टसु दिक्ष्वित्येव। तत्र
वक्ष्यमाणभूरष्टहान्तः। नरेन्द्रभुजगाविति। वासुकि शङ्खपालौ। स्वचिह्नयुतौ।
लिखेदिति गैरिकेण। निर्माल्ये इति। शिवनिर्माल्ये। अपेक्षितार्थद्योतनिकोक्तेः।
द्विषां वाचां स्तम्भनं वितनुते शिलाक्रान्तमिति ज्ञेयम्। तदुक्तं नारायणीये—

मांसाष्टकवृतेर्णान्ते नाम मांसविदर्भितम्।
माष्टाशावथमैन्द्रं च पार्थिवाह्वितं लिखेत् ॥

साध्याढ्यं कवचं लिखेत् बहिरथो दिक्पत्रमध्येषु तत्
ग्लौमन्येषु महीपुरस्य विलिखेत् कोणेषु गं लान्वितम् ।
वज्रेष्वष्टसु वर्म तोयपुरगं भूबिम्बमध्ये स्थितं
यन्त्रं रात्रिविनायकान्तरगतं न्यस्येत्करावद्वये ॥ ६७

रहस्यस्थाननिक्षिप्तं पूजितं प्रतिवासरम् ।
स्तम्भनं कुरुते वाचां सेनादीनां च वैरिणाम् ॥ ६८

कृत्वा रेखाष्टकमृजु पुनस्तिर्यगालिख्य षट्कं
बाह्यावृत्त्या लिखतु विधिवत् बिन्दुयुक्तं चकारम् ।
अन्तःपङ्क्तौ लिखतु धरणीं शिष्टकोष्ठत्रयान्तः
कृत्वा नाम प्रथितमुदितं यन्त्रमेतज् ज्वरघ्नम् ॥ ६९

यन्त्रमेतत्समभ्यर्च्य दत्त्वा भूतबलिं ततः ।
साध्यस्य मूर्ध्नि बध्नीयात् सर्वज्वरविमुक्तये ॥ ७०

आस्ये च फणिनोराख्यां बिभीतफलकेऽर्पितम् ।
गैरिकेण शिलाक्रान्तं निर्माल्ये स्तम्भकृत् खनेत् ॥ इति ॥ ६६ ॥

अन्यच्च वाक्स्तम्भनकृदाह साध्येति । लिखेदित्यष्टदलकर्णिकायाम् । तदिति ठुम् । अन्येषु विदिक्पत्रेषु । गं लान्वितमिति ग्लं महीपुरस्य कोणेषु लिखेदिति । वज्रे निशारसैरिति ज्ञेयम् । रात्रिविनायकान्तरगतं हरिद्रागणपतिमूर्त्तिं कृत्वा तदुदरे यन्त्रं स्थापनीयमिति सम्प्रदायविदः । केचित् तु हरिद्रागणपतिमन्त्रेण संवेष्टितमिति वदन्ति । तदसाम्प्रदायिकम् । मन्त्रस्याऽनुदधृतत्वादत्र । पूजितमिति । पीतपुष्पैः । विनायको देवता । वैरिणां वाचामिति व्यधिकरणे षष्ठ्यौ । वैरिणां सेनादीनामित्यपि । आदिशब्देन विवादगत्यादि । तदुक्तं नारायणीये—

लिखेद्यन्त्रं निशारसैः ।
विघ्नस्य कुक्षौ निक्षिप्य निशापिष्टमयस्य तत् ॥
शरावसंपुटे स्थाप्य पीतपुष्पैश्च पूजयेत् ।
स्तम्भः स्याद्दुष्टसेनावाग्विवादागमनादिषु ॥ इति ॥ ६७॥६८ ॥

ज्वरघ्नमाह कृत्वेति । बाह्यावृत्त्येति । विंशतिकोष्ठेषु । विधिवदिति । प्रादक्षिण्येन । अन्तःपङ्क्तौ द्वादशसु कोष्ठेषु धरा लं बिन्दुयुक्तमिति सम्बध्यते । कोष्ठत्रयान्तः कोष्ठत्रयमेकीकृत्य तत्र नाम लिखेत् । दत्त्वा भूतबलिमिति ।

तारं लिखेद्वह्निपुरस्य युग्मे तत्पार्श्वयोर्लार्णमथाऽग्निबीजम् ।
कोणेषु पूर्वापरयोश्च यन्त्रं पाशाङ्कुशावीतमिदं ज्वरघ्नम् ॥ ७१

यन्त्रमभ्यर्च्य मन्त्रेण तारपाशाङ्कुशात्मना ।
निबध्नीयाज्ज्वरार्त्तस्य हस्तादौ ज्वरशान्तये ॥ ७२

पिण्डे लिखेन्नाम ससर्गटान्तविदर्भितं सस्वरकेसराढ्यम् ।
टान्ताष्टपत्रं वसुधापुरस्थं कान्तिप्रदं यन्त्रमिदं ज्वरघ्नम् ॥ ७३

ताराद्दि लुद्वयजलद्विठवर्णवीता
टान्तान्तरे विलिखिता विधिनैव माया ।
साध्यावृता बहिरधोवदनार्द्धचन्द्रै-
र्यन्त्रं शिशौ कुरुदिषां विनिहन्ति सद्यः ॥ ७४

पञ्चवर्णौदनेनेति शेयम् । तदुक्तं नारायणीये—

ऋजुरेखा लिखित्वाऽष्टौ षट्तिर्यक् चावृतिद्वये ।
मारीबाह्यपुटे सेन्द्रौ लेख्यौ नाम पदत्रये ॥
पञ्चवर्णं बलिं दत्त्वा कलयेच्च क्रमार्चितम् ।
आ[त्रा]ह्निकं ज्वरदेवादि ज्वराभासप्रशान्तये ॥ इति ॥

अपेक्षितार्थद्योतनिकायां पञ्चवर्णौदनबलिं दत्त्वेति व्याख्यातम् । भूर्देवता ॥६८॥७०॥

अन्यज्ज्वरघ्नमाह तारमिति । वह्निपुरस्य युग्मे दक्षिणोत्तररूपेण लिखिते । तत्पार्श्वयोस्तारपार्श्वयोः लार्णम् अथ कोणेष्वग्निबीजं सर्वेषु कोणेष्वित्यर्थः पूर्वापरयोश्च दिशोर्बहिर्भागस्थयोः । पाशाङ्कुशेति । अन्ये तु गुणाङ्कुशावीतमिति पाठमपठन् । गुणशब्देन त्रिसंख्या तेन पूर्वापरभागयोः प्रत्येकमङ्कुशत्रयं लिखेदित्यर्थः । तदुक्तं नारायणीये—

सौम्ययाम्यमुखे तारं लिखेद्वह्निगृहद्वये ।
तारस्य पार्श्वयोरिन्द्रं कोणकोष्ठेषु चाऽनलम् ।
प्राक्प्रतीच्योर्बहिस्त्रक्रमङ्कुशत्रयभूषितम् ॥ इति ॥

अत्र प्रणवपाशाङ्कुशात्मैव देवता ॥ ७१॥७२ ॥

अन्यज्ज्वरघ्नमाह पिण्ड इति । पिण्डे पूर्वोक्ते । ससर्गटान्तं सविसर्गठकारम् । तद्विदर्भितं नामित्यन्वयः । अत्र पिण्डात्मा देवता ॥ ७३ ॥

शिशुरोदनघ्नमाह तारेति । लुद्वयं लुलु । जलं वं । द्विठः स्वाहा । विधिनैव साध्या साध्योऽस्यामस्तीति साध्या । अर्श आदित्वादच् । मध्यकृत्ते साध्यनाम-

व्योमार्णमालिख्य सबिन्दुमाख्याविदर्भितं लुत्रययुक्तकोणे ।
वसुन्धरागेहयुगे निबद्धं यन्त्रं समस्तज्वरनाशनं स्यात् ॥ ७५

सार्णं नाम विदर्भितं परिलिखेत् बाह्येऽष्टपत्रे भृगुं
पद्मं स्यादथ कादिशान्तलिपिमत्त्रिंशद्दलं बाह्यतः ।
वीतं तोयपुरेण यन्त्रमुदितं भूर्जोदरे कल्पितं
भूतव्याधिमहाज्वरप्रशमनं कृत्यापहं श्रीप्रदम् ॥ ७६

चक्रे चतुःषष्टिपदे सबिन्दूनन्तस्थवर्णान् क्रमशो विलिख्य ।
रेखाशिरःकल्पितशूलयुक्तं यन्त्रेऽथ शीतज्वरशान्तिहेतोः ॥ ७७

युक्तां एतन्मन्त्रावृतां च मायां विलिख्य बहिर्वृत्तद्वयं कृत्वा तत्राऽधोमुखैरर्द्धचन्द्रैः संवेष्ट्य बध्नीयात् । अधोवदनैरधोमुखैरर्द्धचन्द्रैर्वृतं हिरिति शेषः । द्वेधा शिशो स्तदिषां विनिहन्ति यन्त्रमिति वा पठनीयम् । उक्तञ्च नारायणीये—

तारं लुयुग्ममुदकं शिर एभिरर्णैः शक्तिर्वृता च शिशुनामवती शशाङ्कैः ।
अर्द्धेन्दुकैर्बहिरधोवदनैः परीतौ यन्त्रं तदाशु शिशुरोदनमुत्छिनोति ॥ इति ।

व्याख्यातञ्चाऽपेक्षितार्थद्योतनिकायाम् । देवीं लिखित्वा तन्मध्ये शिशुनाम लिखित्वा ॐ लुलु वं स्वाहेति मन्त्रेण तां मालेव वेष्टयित्वा तद्बहिश्चन्द्रमण्डलद्वयं विलिख्य एकैकमधोमुखार्द्धेन्दुभिः सम्भूष्य बध्नीयादिति । शक्तिर्देवता ॥ ७४ ॥

ज्वरघ्नमाह व्योमिति । व्योमार्णं हकारम् । कीदृशम् । बिन्दुश्च मश्च बिन्दुमौ ताभ्यां सहितं सबिन्दुमं तच्च तदाख्याविदर्भितं च सबिन्दुमाख्याविदर्भितमालिख्य मध्य इति शेषः । तेन लं साध्यसाधकनामाक्षरविदर्भितं मध्ये लिखेदित्यर्थः । एकैकस्मिन् कोणे लुत्रयं लिखेत् । निबद्धं हस्तादाविति शेषः । तदुक्तं नारायणीये—लुत्रयं तस्य कोणेषु मध्ये च सविषं वियत् ।

आख्याविदर्भितं यन्त्रमेतत् सर्वज्वरापहम् ॥ इति ॥

व्योम देवता ॥ ७५ ॥

यन्त्रान्तरमाह सार्णमिति । परिलिखेदित्यष्टदलकर्णिकायाम् । अष्टपत्रेष्विति वक्तव्ये बाह्य इति वदति । तेन व्यधिकरणे सप्तम्यौ । तेनाऽष्टपत्रेषु बहिर्भागे भृगुं सकारं लिखेत् । पत्रमूले केसरस्थाने द्विद्विक्रमेण स्वरा लेख्या इत्यभिप्रायः । तदत्र केचिद्वर्णाष्टपत्र इति पठन्ति । अन्ये ह्यष्टपत्र इति पठन्ति । अत्र मातृका देवता ॥ ७६ ॥

ज्वरघ्नमाह चक्र इति । अन्तस्थवर्णान् यरलवान् विलिख्य । क्रमश

पुटितभूमिपुरद्वयमध्यतः प्रविलिखेत् वनितां गिरिजापतेः।
प्रणवमस्य लिखेत् वसुकोणगं ज्वरहरं परमेतदुदीरितम्॥ ७८
वार्णे लिखेन् नाम शशाङ्कमध्ये टान्तं बहिर्भूमिपुरं पुरस्तात्।
वृत्तावृतं यन्त्रमिदं समुक्तं वश्याय नृणां सकलार्त्तिशान्त्यै॥ ७९

सस्वस्तिके दहनगेहयुगे ससाध्यां
मायां लिखेत् ललितनागलतादलान्तः।
पाशाङ्कुशावृतमिदं निशि तापयेत् यो
मन्त्रं जपन् व्रजति तं स्वयमेव साध्या॥ ८०

इत्यनेनैतदुक्तम्। प्रथमावृत्तौ अष्टाविंशतिकोष्ठेषु सबिन्दुं यं द्वितीयावृत्तौ विंशतिकोष्ठेषु सबिन्दुं रं तृतीयावृत्तौ द्वादशसु कोष्ठेषु सबिन्दुं लं अन्तः कोष्ठचतुष्टये सबिन्दुं वं इति। लिखनं च तत्तद्गतवर्णद्रव्येण भूमाविति ज्ञेयम्। तदुक्तं नारायणीये—

चतुःषष्टिपुटे क्षेत्रे षट्त्रिंशच्छूलदीपिते।
ज्वरनाशत्रयीभानुकोष्ठेषु वृत्तिषु क्रमात्॥
लिखेत् सबिन्दूनन्तस्थान् चक्रं तद्भूस्थमर्चयेत्।
नश्यन्त्यस्य शयानस्य ज्वराः सर्वे विधानतः॥ इति॥

अपेक्षितार्थद्योतनिकायां तत्तद्वर्णद्रव्येण भूमौ लिखित्वा तत्र शय्यायामापाद्येति व्याख्यातम्। वाय्वग्निभूजलानि देवताः॥ ७७॥

अन्यदप्याह पुटितेति। गिरिजापतेर्वनितां मायाम्। शक्तिर्देवता॥ ७८॥

वश्यकृदाह वार्णे इति। शशाङ्कमध्ये ठकारमध्ये वार्णे इति व्यधिकरणे सप्तम्यौ। टान्तं बहिरिति। ठकारेण वेष्टयेत्। चन्द्रो देवता॥ ७९॥

स्त्रीवश्यकृदाह सेति। पाशाङ्कुशावृतमिति षट्कोणाग्रः। ललितेति। सखण्डताम्बूलपत्रे। मन्त्रमिति पाशाङ्कुशपुटा शक्तिः। एष पन्थाः साम्प्रदायिकः। तापयेदिति। दीपशिखायाम्। तदुक्तमाचार्यैः—

हृल्लेखाग्निस्थसाध्याह्वयमथ बहिरांक्रोवृतं वह्निगेह-
द्वन्द्वाश्रिस्वस्तिकाढ्यं प्रविलिखतु दले यन्त्रकं नागवल्ल्याः।
जप्त्वा शक्तिं तु पाशाङ्कुशलिपिसहितां तापयेद्दीपवह्नौ
नक्तं भक्त्या नताङ्गी स्मरशरविवशा प्रेमलोलाऽभियाति॥ इति॥

शक्तिर्देवता॥ ८०॥

षट्कोणे निजसाध्यनामसहितां मायां लिखेन्मध्यत-
स्तत्कोणेषु विदर्भितामभिलिखेत् शक्तिं स्वसाध्याख्यया ।
बाह्ये भूमिपुरं सकोणसदनं ताम्बुलपत्रे कृतं
जप्तं खादयतु प्रियां निशि भवेत् सा तस्य वश्या चिरम् ॥ ८१

अन्यदप्याह षडिति। अत्रापि शक्तिर्देवता। ताम्बूलपत्रे कृतमिति। कोकिलाक्षकण्टकैरिति शेषः। जप्तं माययेति शेषः। अन्यत्र तु विशेषः। कामस्य षट्कोणेषु लेखनं साध्याविदर्भिशक्त्या बहिर्वेष्टनमिति। मूले वा लिखेच्च स्मरमिति पाठः साम्प्रदायिकः। तदुक्तमाचार्यैः—

शक्तिस्थं निजनाम वह्निभवनद्वन्द्वोदरे स्मारथं
बीजं साध्यविदर्भया परिवृतं शक्त्या बहिः पार्थिवम् ।
तत्कोणस्मरमन्त्रपुष्टनयनप्रोत्थैः पुनः कण्टकै-
स्ताम्बूले लिखिताभिजप्तमदयेद् योषिन्मनोमोहनम् ॥ इति ।

खादयत्वित्यज्ञातमेव। स्त्रिया विदितं भक्षितं न वशयत्येव। एवमन्यथा प्रयोगेष्वपि साध्यामज्ञाप्यैव देयमिति रहस्यम्। तन्त्रान्तरे—

वायोरष्टममग्निबिन्दुसहितं संरुद्धमायाक्षरं
मध्ये संस्थितसाध्यनामवलयद्वन्द्वावृतं बाह्यतः ।
तद्बाह्ये दलषोडशस्वरयुतं पश्चात् महीमण्डलं
कोणे कल्पितकामबीजकमिदं यन्त्रं जगद्वश्यकम् ॥ इति ॥

अन्यत्र तु—हृल्लेखामध्यसाध्यवलययुगयुतं चाऽष्टपत्रं सरोजं
यन्त्रे तद्बीजसंस्थं बहिरपि च दलैः षोडशैराढ्यमब्जम् ।
अब्जस्यालिख्य पत्रे स्वरगणनमितं मण्डलं पार्थिवाख्यं
कोणे क्लिंकारयुक्तं सकलजनमनोहारि कूष्माण्डयन्त्रम् ॥ इति ॥

अन्यत्र तु—शक्तिस्थं निजनाम वह्निभवने षट्कोणयुक्ते लिखेत्
क्लींकारं परितो विदर्भ्य मतिमान् साध्येन नाम्नाऽङ्कुशम् ।
एतत्कण्टकसूचितं सुविपुले नागस्य पृष्ठे लिखेत्
पश्चान्मारुतवेश्मना परिवृतं योषिन्मनोमोहनम् ॥ इति ॥
कृत्वा षट्कोणमध्ये वियदनलयुतं बिन्दुमायाविचित्रं
तत्कोणेष्वङ्कुशास्त्रं पुनरपि कमलं शक्तिगर्भाष्टपत्रम् ।
पश्चात्तद्युग्मपत्रं रजनिकरकलालङ्कृतं गोपुरस्थं
भूर्जे गोरोचनासृग्जमदरचितं वश्यमाहुर्मुनीन्द्राः ॥ इति ॥

शक्तौ नाम लिखेत् चतुर्भिरभितो बीजैः समावेष्टयेत्
वीतं शक्तिमनोभवाङ्कुशमनुप्रोंबीजकैः पिष्टजे।
रूपे साध्यनरस्य जप्तपवने लिखादुना भर्ज्य तत्
खादेत् तस्य वशं प्रयाति नियतं साध्यः सदा दासवत्॥ ८२
कामं लिखेत्साध्ययुतं सरोजे स्वरोल्लसत्केसरगंवपत्रे।
उदीरितं मन्मथमन्त्रमेतत्सौभाग्यलक्ष्मीविजयप्रदायि॥ ८३

तन्त्रान्तरे आचार्याश्च—

सान्तं शिखोल्लवयुतं दहनांशसाध्यं
मायांशसाधकमथाऽभिहतं कलाभिः।
सव्योल्लसद्द्विमुखशूलमिदं तु भर्तु-
र्यन्त्राह्वयं नरनताङ्घ्रिवशीकरं स्यात्॥

मृत्कारङ्गुलिकात्तया सकृत्कलासान्तर्वसायुक्तया
साध्यस्याऽङ्घ्रिरजोयुजा मृदुमृदा कृतस्य शक्तिं हृदि।
रूपस्याऽभिविलिख्य तद्विवरके साध्यं तदीरान् प्रति-
ष्ठाप्याजप्य निखन्य तत्र दिनशो मेहेच्चिरं वश्यकृत्॥ इति॥८१॥

वश्यकृदाह शक्ताविति। साध्यनरस्य पिष्टजे रूपे प्रतिकृतिहृदय इत्यर्थः। शक्तिं विलिख्य तत्र कर्मसहितं साध्यनामाऽऽलिख्य तां शक्तिं चतुर्भिर्बीजैर्वेष्टयेत्। तत्र केचनोपदेशान् नृसिंहचिन्तामणिशक्तिदुर्गाबीजानीत्याहुः। अन्ये तु चतुर्भिर्बीजैः समावेष्टयेदित्युक्तम्। तदेव विशदयति वीतं शक्तीत्यादिना। पुनः श्लोकोक्तैश्चतुर्भिर्बीजैर्वीतं कुर्यात्। अत्र केचन मरुत्प्रोंबीजकैरिति पठित्वा यमिति पञ्चमं वदन्ति। तदसङ्गतम्। तन्त्रान्तरविरोधात्। यदाहुराचार्याः—

शक्त्यन्तःस्थितसाध्यनामपरितो बीजैश्चतुर्भिः समा-
बद्धं शक्तिमनोभवाङ्कुशलिपिप्रोंभिः समावेष्टितम्। इति।

अत्र पद्मपादाचार्यैर्व्याख्यातं समावेष्टितमिति समाबद्धमित्यस्य व्याख्येति। केचिच्चतुर्भिः शक्तिबीजैरित्याहुः। जप्तपवनं प्रतिष्ठितप्राणम्। शक्तिर्देवता॥ ८२॥

यन्त्रान्तरमाह काममिति। अत्र कामो देवता।

कानिचित् सिद्धयन्त्राणि सिद्धयोगेश्वरीमतात्।
सर्वलोकानुग्रहाय लिख्यन्तेऽत्र मया स्फुटम्॥
कर्णिकायां लिखेन्नाम पुटितं मायया बहिः।

अष्टपत्रेषु विन्यस्य नाऽघ रेखरीवृतम् ॥
अघोरेखरि हुं फट् मन्त्रः प्रोक्तोऽथ वैदिकः ।
द्वात्रिंशदक्षराघोरं ह्यष्टपत्रेषु बाह्यतः ॥
त्रि[द्वि]गुणं मायया वेष्ट्य रेखान्ते क्रों नियोजयेत् ।
भूतप्रेतपिशाचानां शाकिनीग्रहरक्षसाम् ।
दोषं बाहुस्थिता हन्ति रक्षेयं विधिना कृता ॥ १ ॥
कर्णिकायां लिखेन्नाम तदधस्त्र्यक्षरं मनुम् ।
अष्टपत्रेषु मायां च कांस्यपात्रे सुनिर्मले ॥
रोचनालिखिते यन्त्रे क्षीरमध्ये निवेशिते ।
स वशो जायते तस्य माया तारपुटा मनुः ॥ २ ॥
क्ष्माबीजपुटितं नाम लिखेत्पत्रचतुष्टये ।
तस्मिन्नाज्ये विनिक्षिप्ते गृहान्तर्वा विलम्बिते ॥
शान्तिर्लक्ष्मीर्यशः पुष्टिः सततं तस्य जायते ।
न व्याधिर्न भयं शत्रु[त्रो]र्यन्त्रसामर्थ्ययोगतः ॥ ३ ॥
ज्वालावृतं त्रिकोणेषु हुंयुतं वह्निमण्डलम् ।
रेफेण पुटितं नाम मध्ये शक्त्या बहिर्वृतम् ॥
श्मशानकर्पटे किंवा कपाले लिखितं द्रुतम् ।
तापितं[नं] वैरिणः कुर्याज्ज्वरं रौद्रं न संशयः ॥ ४ ॥
पद्ममष्टदलं मध्ये नाम संलिख्य दिक्ष्वधः ।
हुं विदिक्षु स्थिता चौरे रक्षा द्यूते जयावहा ॥ ५ ॥
नभोमण्डलमध्यस्थं नाम बाह्येऽथ षोडश ।
स्वरास्तद्वाह्यतो ज्वालाजटिलं वह्निमण्डलम् ॥
श्मशानकर्पटे लेख्यं धत्तूरस्य रसेन च ।
प्रेतभूनिहितं यन्त्रमिदं सौभाग्यनाशनम् ॥ ६ ॥
कर्णिकायां लिखेन्नाम चतुःपत्रे तु क्लीं कजे ।
गोचनाहस्तिदानाभ्यां कुङ्कुमेन शुभे दिने ॥
वेष्टयित्वाऽथ सिक्थेन धृते यन्त्रे धृते सति ।
सौभाग्यमतुलं स्त्रीणां जायते जीवितावधि ॥ ७ ॥
अष्टपत्राम्बुजे मध्ये सविसर्गमवेष्टितम् ।
नाम तद्बाह्यपत्रेषु सपरः सविसर्गकः ॥

रोचनाकुङ्कुमेनेदं यन्त्रं संलिख्य दापयेत् ।
कारागृहगतो यस्तु तस्य मोक्षः प्रजायते ॥ ८ ॥
अष्टपत्राम्बुजे मध्ये नाम क्रीं दिग्दलेषु च ।
क्रोमन्यतो लिखित्वा तु यन्त्रं देवकुले धृते ।
व्याधिना मुच्यते प्राणी बलं चाप्नोति दुर्बलः ॥ ८ ॥
चतुरस्त्रे शिरोहीनह्[ह्]ङ्कारोदरसंस्थितम् ।
नाम तद्वाह्यतो लेख्यं[भूयो] भूपुरं कोणशक्तिगम् ॥
काकपिच्छस्य लेखन्या लिखित्वेदं शरावके ।
संपूर्याऽधोमुखं भूमौ मूर्छिते तस्य चोपरि ॥
विवादे दुष्टचित्तानां विपरीतार्थभाषिणाम् ।
मुखस्तम्भो भवेत् पुंसां सभायां वा जयो ध्रुवम् ॥ १० ॥
लकारपुटितं नाम तस्योर्ध्वाधश्च लद्वयम् ।
चतुरस्रद्वयं बाह्ये वृतं सर्वत्र शक्तिभिः ॥
भूर्जे रोचनया लिख्य गुप्तदेशे धृते सति ।
शतयोजनमध्वानं गच्छतो न भयं भवेत् ॥ ११ ॥
अष्टपत्राम्बुजे मध्ये नाम ह्रीं दलसञ्चये ।
बहिर्वृत्तद्वयं भूर्जे लिखेत् कुङ्कुमगोमृदा ॥
अजितानाम विद्येयं संग्रामे विषमेऽध्वनि ।
भूपालादिभये रक्षां कुरुते बाहुसंस्थिता ॥ १२ ॥
प्रणवद्वयमध्यस्थं नाम मध्ये चतुर्दले ।
त्रयः पश्चिमदिक्पत्रे प्रणवाः पूर्वतस्त्रयः ॥
एकैकमुत्तरे दक्षे भूर्जे रोचनया लिखेत् ।
जीवरक्षेयमाख्याता व्याधौ जातेऽतिदुःसहे ॥ १३ ॥
ठं [वं] चतुष्टयमध्यस्थं नाम मध्ये ततो बहिः ।
अष्टपत्रेषु रं लेख्यं रोचनाचन्द्रकुङ्कुमैः ॥
इयं वैश्वानरो रक्षा बालानां कण्ठसंस्थिता ॥ १४ ॥
वृत्तमध्यस्थितं नाम तद्बहिश्चतुरस्रकम् ।
तद्बाह्ये स्युः स्वराः सर्वे तद्बहिर्वृत्तमालिखेत् ॥
तत्र द्वादश पत्राणि कल्पयेदेतदन्तरे ।
यंचोवंचोति रक्षेयं पक्षदिग्ध्वनिरोधिनी ॥ १५ ॥

काश्मीररोचनालाक्षामृगेभमदचन्दनैः ।

विलिखेत् हेमलेखन्या यन्त्राण्येतानि देशिकः ॥ ८४

ज्वालावृतत्रिकोणान्तर्नाम जूँ पुटितं बहिः ।

वेष्टितं सविसर्गैर्वैस्तद्बहिर्वह्निमण्डलम् ॥

ज्वालाकुलमिदं भूर्जे गोमूदा कुङ्कुमेन च ।

लिखित्वा स्वकरे बद्धं ज्वरं चातुर्थिकं हरेत् ॥ १६ ॥

वृत्तान्तःसंस्थितं नाम बहि[वह्नि]रोंक्रींनमोऽक्षरैः ।

वेष्टितं त्वथ तद्बाह्ये कोणे लं वह्निमण्डले ॥

तद्बाह्ये क्ष्मापुरं वीतं चतुःकोणेषु शक्तिभिः ।

एकान्तरं ज्वरं हन्ति रक्षेयं बाहुसंस्थिता ॥ १७ ॥

कर्णिकायां लिखेन्नाम रूं[वूं] बीजानि दलाष्टके ।

रोचनाचन्दनेनेदं द्व्याहिकज्वरनाशनम् ॥ १८ ॥

षट्कोणमध्यतो नाम रूं कोणेषु समालिखेत् ।

भित्तौ खटिकया दृष्टं सततज्वरनाशनम् ॥ १९ ॥

वसमेतिपदं वायुदीर्घान्त्य[न्त्याप्त]मनिलं शिरः ।

एतत् स्तम्भनमन्त्रमैन्द्रस्याब्जदलार्पितम् ॥ २० ॥

तालेनेन्दौ लिखेद्धस्ते वैरिनामेन्दुदर्शितम् ।

सेनामार्गे खनेदेतत् सैन्यस्तम्भनमुत्तमम् ॥ २१ ॥ इति ॥ ८३ ॥

नारायणीययन्त्रलिखनद्रव्याण्याह काश्मीरेति । काश्मीरं कुङ्कुमम् । रोचना गोरोचना । लाक्षा यावकः । अनेनैव सर्वेषां घर्षणम् । मृगमदः कस्तूरी । इभमदो गजमदः । एभिर्मिलितैरेव लेखनम् । यदाहुः—

गजमृगमदकाश्मीरैर्मन्त्रितमः सुरभिरोचनायुक्तैः ।

विलिखेदलक्तकरसालुलितैर्यन्त्राणि सकलकार्यार्थी ॥ इति ॥

अन्यत्र द्रव्यविशेषोऽपि उक्तः—

नागेन्द्रमदयुक्ता वै तथा वश्ये च रोचना ।

विषधत्तूरयुक्तेन चिताङ्गारेण सप्रुषा ॥

ताडनोच्चाटनादीनि क्षुद्रकर्माणि साधयेत् ।

विषार्कचीरगुञ्जायाः संयोगे मारणं स्मृतम् ॥ इति ॥

हेमलेखन्येति शुभकर्मादौ । अन्यकर्मणि तु षट्कर्मोक्ता लेखन्यो द्रष्टव्याः । लिखनं च साक्षादुपात्ताधारस्थलं विना अन्यत्र काञ्चनरजतताम्रपत्रभूर्जादिषु

भूमिस्पृष्टं शवस्पृष्टं दग्धं निर्माल्यसंगतम् ।
विशीर्णं लङ्घितं मन्त्री यन्त्रं जातु न धारयेत् ॥ ८५

अथानन्दमयीं देवीं शब्दब्रह्मस्वरूपिणीम् ।
ईडे सकलसम्पत्त्यै जगत्कारणमम्बिकाम् ॥ ८६

ज्ञेयम् । तत्र कालविशेषोऽपि पूर्वोक्तोऽनुसन्धेयः । अन्यत्राधारविशेषा अप्युक्ताः—

शान्तिके पौष्टिके चैव आयुःकामविधौ तथा ।
सर्पोपशमने चैव जल्पसंस्तम्भने तथा ॥
विभ्रमोत्पादने चैव शिलायान्तु प्रशस्यते ।
खर[ङ्ग]चर्मणि विद्वेषे महदुच्चाटनं ध्वजे ॥
ज्वरसन्तापशोकञ्च शत्रूणां मारणं तथा ।
लिखित्वा साधयेत् सर्वं पीतवस्त्रे तु नान्यथा ॥ इति ॥

तथा मुहूर्त्तादि विशेषोऽपि तन्त्रान्तरोक्तो लिख्यते—

सुदिने शुभनक्षत्रे सुदेशे शल्यवर्जिते ॥
सन्निधस्तत्र आचार्यः शिष्यो वा तदभावतः ।
उदङ्मुखः प्राङ्मुखो वा उपविश्य प्रणम्य च ॥
गुरुं विश्वेश्वरं देवं ततो यन्त्रं समालिखेत् ॥ इति ।

कामनाविशेषे नक्षत्रविशेषोऽपि तत्रैवोक्तः—

वश्याकृष्टौ लिखेत् पुष्येऽहिभे विद्वेषणं स्मृतम् ।
आर्द्रायां मारणं प्रोक्तं मघासूच्चाटनं भवेत् ॥ इति ॥

अहिभे अश्लेषायाम् । तत्रैव धारणे स्थानविशेषोऽपि—

करे कण्ठे शिखायां च यथा सन्निहितं भवेत् । इति ॥

इमानि पूर्वोक्तान्यपि यन्त्राणि यस्मै कस्मै यथाकथंचिन्न देयानि । तदुक्तं हिरण्यगर्भसंहितायां—

त्वया पुत्र न दातव्यं यन्त्रमेतन्महोदयम् ।
नाऽशिष्याय न पापाय नाऽशान्तायाऽप्रियाय च ॥
शिष्याय मन्त्रनिष्ठाय शुभभक्तियुताय च ।
वसुप्रदाय दातव्यमन्यथा नरकं व्रजेत् ॥ इति ॥ ८४ ॥

भूमिस्पृष्टमिति साक्षात् ॥ ८५ ॥

ईडे स्तौमि ॥ ८६ ॥

आद्यामशेषजननीमरविन्दयोने-
र्विष्णोः शिवस्य च वपुः प्रतिपादयन्तीम् ।
सृष्टिस्थितिक्षयकरीं जगतां त्रयाणां
स्तुत्वा गिरं विमलयाम्यहमम्बिके त्वाम् ॥ ८७

पृथ्व्या जलेन शिखिना मरुताऽम्बरेण
होत्रेन्दुना दिनकरेण च मूर्त्तिभाजः ।
देवस्य मन्मथरिपोरपि शक्तिमत्ता-
हेतुस्त्वमेव खलु पर्वतराजपुत्रि ॥ ८८

त्रिस्रोतसः सकललोकसमर्चितायाः
वैशिष्ट्यकारणमवैमि तदेव मातः ।
त्वत्पादपङ्कजपरागविचित्रितासु
शम्भोर्जटासु सततं परिवर्त्तनं यत् ॥ ८९

आनन्दयेत् कुमुदिनीमधिपः कलानां
नाऽन्यामिनः कमलिनीमथ नेतरां वा ।
एकस्य मोदनविधौ परमेक इष्टे
त्वन्तु प्रपञ्चमभिनन्दयसि स्वदृष्ट्या ॥ ९०

आद्याऽप्यशेषजगतां नवयौवनाऽसि
शैलाधिराजतनयाऽप्यतिकोमलाऽसि ।
त्रय्याः प्रसूरपि तया न समीक्षिताऽसि
ध्येयाऽसि गौरि मनसो न पथि स्थिताऽसि ॥ ९१

वपुः प्रतिपादयन्तीमिति । एषां विग्रहत्वे कारणम् । अतएवाग्रिमे विशेषणम् । अहं त्वां स्तुत्वा गिरं विमलयामीति सम्बन्धः ॥ ८७ ॥

पृथ्व्येत्यष्टमूर्त्त्युपन्यासः । शक्तिमत्तेति । अन्यथाऽसङ्गस्योदासीनत्वात् ॥८८॥८९॥

नान्यां कमलिनीम् । नेतरां कुमुदिनीम् ॥ ९० ॥

आद्येत्यादि विरोधाभासचतुष्टयम् । न समीक्षिता इयत्तया न ज्ञातेति परिहारः । मनसो न पथि स्थितेति । अचिन्त्यरूपेति परिहारः ॥ ९१ ॥

आसाद्य जन्म मनुजेषु चिराद् दुरापं
तत्रापि पाटवमवाप्य निजेन्द्रियाणाम् ।
नाऽभ्यर्चयन्ति जगतां जनयित्रि ये त्वां
निःश्रेणिकाग्रमधिरुह्य पुनः पतन्ति ॥ ९२

कर्पूरचूर्णहिमवारिविलोलितेन
ये चन्दनेन कुसुमैश्च सुजातगन्धैः ।
आराधयन्ति हि भवानि समुत्सुकास्त्वां
ते खल्वशेषभुवनाधिभुवः प्रथन्ते ॥ ९३

आविश्य मध्यपदवीं प्रथमे सरोजे
सुप्ताहिराजसदृशी विरचय्य विश्वम् ।
विद्युल्लतावलयविभ्रममुद्वहन्ती
पद्मानि पञ्च विदलय्य खमश्नुवाना ॥ ९४

तन्निर्गतामृतरसैरभिषिक्तगात्री
मार्गेण तेन निलयं पुनरप्यवाप्ता ।
येषां हृदि स्फुरसि जातु न ते भवेयु-
र्मातर्महेश्वरकुटुम्बिनि गर्भभाजः ॥ ९५

आलम्बिकुन्तलभरामभिरामवक्त्रा-
मापीवरस्तनतटीं तनुवृत्तमध्याम् ।
चिन्ताक्षसूत्रकलशालिखिताढ्यहस्ता-
मावर्त्तयामि मनसा तव गौरि मूर्त्तिम् ॥ ९६

मनुजेष्विति । मनुष्याधिकारत्वाच्छास्त्रस्य ॥ ९२ ॥

अधिभुवो नायकाः । "अधिभूर्नायको नेता" इति कोशः ॥ ९३ ॥

आविश्येति युग्मम् । मध्यपदवीं सुषुम्णामध्यमार्गम् । विद्युल्लतेति कुण्डलीरूपाम् । प्रथमे सरोजे आधारे । अत्र प्रथम इत्याद्युद्वहन्तीत्यन्तमनूद्य मध्यपदवीमाविश्य पञ्च पद्मानि विदलय्येत्यन्वयः । पञ्च पद्मानि । स्वाधिष्ठान-मणिपूरकानाहतविशुद्धाज्ञाख्यानि । खं ब्रह्मरन्ध्रम् ॥ ९४॥९५ ॥

चिन्ता ज्ञानमुद्रा । आलिखितं पुस्तकम् । इदं सरस्वतीरूपध्यानम् ॥ ९६ ॥

आस्थाय योगमवजित्य च वैरिषट्क-
मावद्ध्य चेन्द्रियगणं मनसि प्रसन्ने ।
पाशाङ्कुशाभयवराढ्यकरां सुरक्ता-
मालोकयन्ति भुवनेश्वरि योगिनस्त्वाम् ॥ ९७

उत्तप्तहाटकनिभा करिभिश्चतुर्भि-
रावर्त्तितामृतघटैरभिषिच्यमाना ।
हस्तद्वयेन रुचिरे नलिने वहन्ती
पद्मापि साभयवरा भवसि त्वमेव ॥ ९८

अष्टाभिरुग्रविविधायुधवाहिनीभि-
र्दोर्वल्लरीभिरधिरुह्य मृगाधिराजम् ।
दूर्वादलद्युतिरमर्त्यविपक्षपक्षान्
न्यक्कुर्वती त्वमसि देवि भवानि दुर्गा ॥ ९९

आविर्निदाघजलशीकरशोभिवक्त्रां
गुञ्जागुणेन परिकल्पितहारयष्टिम् ।
पत्रांशुकामसितकान्तिमनङ्गतन्त्वा-
माद्यां पुलिन्दतरुणीमसकृत् स्मरामि ॥ १००

हंसैर्गतिक्वणितनूपुरदूरकृष्टै-
र्मूर्त्तैरिवाप्तवचनैरनुगम्यमानौ ।
पद्माविवोर्ध्वमुखरूढसुजातनालौ
श्रीकण्ठपत्नि शिरसैव दधे तवाऽङ्घ्री ॥ १०१

द्वाभ्यां समीक्षितुमतृप्तिमतेव दृग्भ्या-
मुत्पाद्य भालनयनं वृषकेतनेन ।
सान्द्रानुरागतरलेन निरीक्षमाणे
जङ्घे उभे अपि भवानि तवानतोऽस्मि ॥ १०२

योगादीनां लक्षणमरिषड्वर्गमनन्तरमेव वक्ष्यति ॥ ९७॥९८॥९९ ॥

अनङ्गतन्वां कामप्रधानाम् ॥ १०० ॥

हंसैरित्यादिना चरणादिमूर्धान्तवर्णना । वचनं शब्दः ॥ १०१॥१०२ ॥

ऊरू स्मरामि जितहस्तिकरावलेपौ
स्थौल्येन पाण्डुरतया परिभूतरम्भौ ।
श्रोणीभरस्य सहनौ परिकल्प्य दत्तौ
स्तम्भाविवाऽङ्ग वयसा तव मध्यमेन ॥ १०३

श्रोण्यौ स्तनौ च युगपत् प्रथयिष्यतोच्चै-
र्बाल्यात्परेण वयसा परिकृष्टसारः ।
रोमावलीविलसितेन विभाव्यमूर्त्ति-
र्मध्यस्तव स्फुरतु मे हृदयस्य मध्ये ॥ १०४

सख्युः स्मरस्य हरनेत्रहुताशभीरो-
र्लावण्यवारिभरितं नवयौवनेन ।
आपाद्य दत्तमिव पल्वलमप्रधृष्यं
नाभिं कदापि तव देवि न विस्मरेयम् ॥१०५

ईशोपगूहपिशुनं भसितं दधाने
काश्मीरकर्दममनु स्तनपङ्कजे ते ।
स्नानोत्थितस्य करिणः क्षणलब्धफेनौ
सिन्दूरितौ स्मरयतः समदस्य कुम्भौ ॥ १०६

कण्ठातिरिक्तगलदुज्ज्वलकान्तिधारा-
शोभौ भुजौ निजरिपोर्मकरध्वजेन ।
कण्ठग्रहाय रचितौ किल दीर्घपाशौ
मातर्मम स्मृतिपथं न विलङ्घयेथाः ॥ १०७

अवलेपो गर्वः । मध्यमेन वयसा यौवनेन ॥ १०३॥१०४ ॥

पल्वलमल्पसरः ॥ १०५ ॥

पिशुनं सूचकम् । भसितं भस्म ॥ १०६ ॥

कण्ठातिरिक्तेति । हरकण्ठादतिरिक्तौ अधिकौ । बन्धनीयादधिकेनैव पाशेन बन्धनं घटते । यद्वा कण्ठात्पार्वतीकण्ठात् अतिरिक्ते अधिके अतएव गलन्त्यौ उज्ज्वले ये कान्तिधारे तद्वच्छोभा ययोस्तौ ॥ १०७ ॥

नि[ना]त्यायतं रुचिरकम्बुविलासचौर्यं
भूषाभरेण विविधेन विराजमानम् ।
कण्ठं मनोहरगुणं गिरिराजकन्ये
सञ्चिन्त्य तृप्तिमुपयामि कदापि नाऽहम् ॥ १०८

अत्यायताक्षमभिजातललाटपट्टं
मन्दस्मितेन दरफुल्लकपोलरेखम् ।
बिम्बाधरं वदनमुन्नतदीर्घनासं
यस्ते स्मरत्यसकृदेव स एव जातः ॥ १०९

आविस्तुषारकरलेखमनल्पगन्धं
पुष्पोपरि भ्रमदलिव्रजनिर्विशेषम् ।
यश्चेतसा कलयते तव केशपाशं
तस्य स्वयं गलति देवि पुराणपाशः ॥ ११०

श्रुतिसुचरितपाकं धीमतां स्तोत्रमेतत्
पठति य इह मर्त्यो नित्यमार्द्रान्तरात्मा ।
स भवति पदमुच्चैः सम्पदां पादनम्र-
क्षितिपमुकुटलक्ष्मीलक्षणानां चिराय ॥ १११

इति श्रीशारदातिलके चतुर्विंशतितमः पटलः ।

कम्बुः शङ्खः ॥ १०८ ॥

अभिजातं सुन्दरम् । दरमीषत् । स एव जातस्तस्यैव सार्थकं जन्मेत्यर्थः ॥१०९॥

पुराणपाशः अविद्यारूपः ॥ ११० ॥

धीमतां श्रुत्योः कर्णयोः सुचरितपाकम् ॥ १११ ॥

इति श्रीशारदातिलकटीकायां सत्सम्प्रदायकृतव्याख्यायां
पदार्थादर्शाभिख्यायां चतुर्विंशः पटलः ॥ ॐ ॥

पञ्चविंशः पटलः ।

अथ योगं प्रवक्ष्यामि साङ्गं संवित्प्रदायकम् ।
ऐक्यं जीवात्मनोराहुर्योगं योगविशारदाः ॥ १

शिवात्मनोरभेदेन प्रतिपत्तिः परे विदुः ।
शिवशक्त्यात्मकं ज्ञानं जगुरागमवेदिनः ॥ २

लैङ्गीक्रियामन्त्रवतीस्त्रिविधज्ञानाख्याः पञ्च भवन्ति दीक्षाः ।
चतुर्विधास्ताः समयाभिधानसामान्यनिर्वाणविशेषदीक्षाः ॥

एवं दीक्षासु सर्व्वासु गुरुः शिष्यं प्रबोधयेत् ।
बोधितोऽबोधितश्चेत् स्यान्नाऽन्यथा दीक्षितो भवेत् ॥

इत्युक्तेः योगं विना दीक्षाया अनिर्वाहात् सूर्यमन्त्रादौ च प्रयोगविषये अनेके योगप्रकारा उक्ताः । तेषां च ज्ञानाय योगं वक्तुं प्रतिजानीते अथेति । साङ्गं यमनियमादियुक्तम् । संवित्प्रदायकं नित्यानन्दानुभवरूपमोक्षदायकमित्यर्थः । एतेन आत्मविशेषगुणोच्छेदो मोक्ष एतन्मतम् निरस्तम् । सुखाभावस्य पुरुषार्थत्वाभावात् ।

वेदान्तपक्षमाश्रित्याह ऐक्यमिति । तच्च "तत्त्वमसि" इत्यादि श्रुतिसिद्धम् । यत् प्रयोगसारे—निष्कलस्याऽप्रमेयस्य देवस्य परमात्मनः ।

सन्धानं योगमित्याहुः संसारोच्छित्तिसाधनम् ॥ इति ॥ १ ॥

शिवप्रोक्तसूत्रमतप्रवृत्तप्रत्यभिज्ञादिग्रन्थमतमाह शिवेति । प्रतिपत्तिर्ज्ञानम् । परे शैवाः । तदुक्तं शिवसूत्रवृत्तौ—

धीः स्वात्त्विकी विमर्शेन जायते नियतात्मनः ।
संक्रमन्ती शिवं प्राप्य लीयते चेन्द्रियैः सह ॥ इति ॥

त्रिकभेदेऽपि—सत्त्वस्थश्च रजःस्थश्च तमःस्थो गुणभेदकः ।
एवं पर्यटते देही स्थानात् स्थानान्तरं व्रजन् ॥
तन्मात्रोदयरूपेण मनोऽहंबुद्धिवर्त्मना ।
पूर्यष्टकेन संरुद्धो दुःखं तत्प्रत्ययोद्भवम् ॥
भुङ्क्ते परवशो भोगं तत्रस्थं संहरेच्छिवः ॥ इति ॥

पुराणपुरुषस्याऽन्ये ज्ञानमाहुर्विशारदाः ।
जित्वाऽऽदावात्मनः शत्रून् कामादीन् योगमभ्यसेत् ॥ ३
कामक्रोधौ लोभमोहौ तत्परं मदमत्सरौ ।
वदन्ति दुःखदानेतानरिषड्वर्गमात्मनः ॥ ४
योगाष्टाङ्गैरिमान् जित्वा योगिनो योगमाप्नुयुः ।
यमनियमावासनप्राणायामौ ततः परम् ॥ ५
प्रत्याहारं धारणाख्यं ध्यानं सार्द्धं समाधिना ।
अष्टाङ्गान्याहुरेतानि योगिनो योगसाधने ॥ ६

स्वच्छन्दभैरवेऽपि—अणुमात्रं शिवानन्दस्फुरणं सर्वदोषहृत् ।
मलत्रयविनाशाच्च माया गच्छेत् समूलतः ॥ इति ॥

आनन्दभैरवेऽपि—
प्राणादिभावनं त्यक्त्वा तथा तद्दृश्यसम्पदः ।
स्वात्मभावेन चित्तेन विशेच्छिवपदं शनैः ॥ इति ॥

उत्तराम्नायमतमाह शिवेति । शिवशक्त्यात्मकं ज्ञानं शिवशक्त्योरभेदज्ञानमित्यर्थः । यदाहुः—
एषा बोधमयी शक्तिः परमानन्दरूपिणी ।
सत्त्वादिगुणसंबद्धा स्वमायान्तर्गता विभुः ॥
समस्ततत्त्वजातानामिह सृष्टेरनन्तरम् ।
सर्वैः शरीरैस्तत्संस्थैरपि मर्त्यैः परस्परम् ॥
अनाद्यध्याससम्बद्धं विस्मृत्यात्मस्वरूपिणी ।
शिवा[विश्वा]त्मिका भवेदेषा देवी सर्वात्मन शिवे ॥ इति ॥२॥

भेदवादिवैष्णवादिमतमाह पुराणेति । पुरुषोत्तमः । पुरुषः सांख्यमते । ईश्वरो न्यायमते । नारायणो वैष्णवमते । तत्परिचयो योगः । तत्र पूज्यत्वात् प्रथमोपन्यस्तत्वाच्च प्रथमं मतं ग्रन्थकृत्सम्मतमिति गम्यते ॥ ३ ॥

कामेति । स्त्रीभोगाद्यभिलाषः कामः । सत्वादिजिघांसा क्रोधः । धनादितृष्णा लोभः । तत्त्वाज्ञानं मोहः । अहं सुखी धनी विद्यावानिति गर्वः मदः । अन्यशुभद्वेषो मत्सरः इति । दुःखदानेतान् आत्मनः अरिषड्वर्गमाहुरित्यन्वयः । आत्मस्वरूपचिन्तन व्यापार तिरोधानेन तेषां शत्रुत्वम् ॥ ४ ॥

एतज्जयोपायमाह योगेति । तान्याह यमेति ॥ ५ ॥ ६ ॥

अहिंसा सत्यमस्तेयं ब्रह्मचर्यं कृपार्जवम् ।
क्षमा धृतिर्मिताहारः शौचं चेति यमा दश ॥ ७

क्रमादेषां स्वरूपमाह अहिंसेति। न कञ्चन हन्मि इत्यभ्यासप्रवणता अहिंसा। असत्यं न वच्मि इत्यभ्यासप्रवणचित्तता सत्यम्। चौर्यनिवृत्तिः अस्तेयम्। स्त्रीभोगेच्छानिवृत्तिः ब्रह्मचर्यम्। प्राणिषु क्रूरबुद्धिनिवृत्तिः कृपा। चित्तकौटिल्यनिवृत्तिः आर्जवम्। अभिभावकं प्रति अक्रोधप्रवणचित्तता क्षमा। इष्टवस्त्वाद्यलाभतश्चिन्ताभावो धृतिः। क्रमेण आहारापकर्षणात् यावच्छरीरस्थितिमात्रभोजनं मिताहारः। चित्तनैर्मल्यार्थं यथोक्तशौचशीलता शौचम्। यमा इति 'यमु' उपरमे कामादेर्निवृत्तिरूपा इत्यर्थः। तत्र धृतिः सर्वत्राऽनुगता। अहिंसाब्रह्मचर्याभ्यां कामस्य जयः। कृपाक्षमाभ्यां क्रोधस्य। अस्तेयसत्यार्जवेभ्यो लोभस्य। मिताहारशौचाभ्यां मोहस्य। क्षमार्जवाभ्यां मदस्य। अहिंसाकृपार्जवक्षमाभ्यो मत्सरस्य। इत्यन्यदपि यथायथमूह्यम्। तदुक्तं संहितायाम्:—

सर्वेषामपि जन्तूनामक्लेशजननं मुने।
वाङ्मनःकर्मभिर्नूनमहिंसेत्यभिधीयते॥
यथादृष्टश्रुतार्थानां स्वरूपकथनं पुनः।
सत्यमित्युच्यते॥ इति॥
तृणादेरप्यनादानं परस्वस्य तपोधन॥
अस्तेयम्॥ इति॥
अवस्थास्वपि सर्वासु कर्मणा मनसा गिरा।
स्त्रीसङ्गतिपरित्यागो ब्रह्मचर्यं प्रचक्षते॥
परेषां दुःखमालोक्य स्वस्यैवालोक्य तस्य तु।
उत्पादनानुसन्धानं दया॥ इति॥
व्यवहारेषु सर्वेषु मनोवाक्कायकर्मभिः।
सर्वेषामपि कौटिल्यराहित्यमार्जवं भवेत्॥ इति॥
सर्वात्मना सर्वदाऽपि सर्वत्राऽप्यपकारिषु।
बन्धुष्विव समाचारः क्षमा स्यात्॥ इति॥
इच्छाप्रयत्नराहित्यं जातेषु विषयेष्वपि।
लोभवत्सु धृतिः॥ इति॥
भोज्यस्यैव चतुर्थांशभोजनं स्वच्छचेतसः।

तपः सन्तोष आस्तिक्यं दानं देवस्य पूजनम् ।
सिद्धान्तश्रवणं चैव ह्रीर्मतिश्च जपो हुतम् ॥ ८
दशैते नियमाः प्रोक्ताः योगशास्त्रविशारदैः ।

हितं मध्यं सुतीक्ष्णेन मिताहारं प्रचक्षते ॥
निर्गतं रोमकूपेभ्यो नवरन्ध्रेभ्य एव च ।
मलं वदन्ति द्वाराणां [तोयैस्तत्]क्षालनं शौचमुच्यते ॥
मृज्जलाभ्यां बहिः सम्यगान्तरं त्वथवा पुनः ।
पूर्वोक्तभूतशुद्ध्यन्तं शौचमाचक्षते बुधाः ॥ इति ॥ ७ ॥

तप इति । कृच्छ्रादिव्रतचर्या तपः । बहिष्टतरानभिलाषः सन्तोषः । अस्ति परलोक इति मतिर्यस्य स आस्तिकः । तस्य भाव आस्तिक्यम् । परलोकबुद्ध्या धर्माद्याचरणमिति यावत् । यथाविभवं देवपितृमनुष्योद्देशेन वितरणं दानम् । देवस्य पूजनम् उक्तरीत्याऽनुष्ठानादेव मोक्षोपायप्रवृत्तस्य विघ्ना-भावाय भवति । सिद्धान्त उपनिषन्मोक्षोपायोपदेशपरिमलादिशास्त्रम् तस्य श्रवणम् । कुत्सिताचारात् स्वत उद्वेगो ह्रीः । तथा सति चित्तमालिन्येन ज्ञानानुदयात् । मतिर्मननम् । तथा च स्मृतिः—

श्रोतव्यः श्रुतिवाक्येभ्यो मन्तव्यश्चोपपत्तिभिः । इति ।

जप इत्युक्तप्रकारेण । "जपतो नास्ति पातकम्" इत्युक्तेः । चित्तशुद्धावुप-योगात् । हुतमग्निहोत्रादिहोमः । यदकरणे प्रत्यवायात् चित्तमालिन्येन ज्ञानानुदयात् । यद्वा हुतं मन्त्रजपस्य दशांशहोमः । तथा चोक्तम्—

नाऽजपात् सिध्यते मन्त्रो नाऽहुताच्च फलप्रदः ।
अनर्चितो हरेत् कामान् तस्मात् त्रितयमाचरेत् ॥ इति ॥

नियमा इति । अवश्यकर्त्तव्यतया नियमत्वमेषाम् । अतः कदाचिदालस्यादिना त्यागो न कार्यः । तदुक्तं संहितायाम्—

तपस्त्वनशनं नाम विधिपूर्वकमिष्यते ।
अनायासोपवासेन त्वशनं भैक्ष्यसेवनम् ॥
तुष्टिरेषा । इति ॥
श्रुत्याद्युक्तेषु विश्वास आस्तिक्यं संप्रचक्षते ।
यदिष्टदेवतां ध्यात्वा तदर्पणधियाऽन्वहम् ॥
सत्पात्रे दीयतेऽन्नादि तद्दानमभिधीयते ।
इष्टदेवार्चनं सम्यक् विधिपूर्वकमन्वहम् ॥

पद्मासनं स्वस्तिकाख्यं वज्रं भद्रासनं तथा ॥ ९

वीरासनमिति प्रोक्तं क्रमादासनपञ्चकम् ।

ऊर्वोरुपरि विन्यस्य सम्यक् पादतले उभे ॥ १०

अङ्गुष्ठौ च निबध्नीयाद्धस्ताभ्यां व्युत्क्रमात्ततः ।

पद्मासनमिति प्रोक्तं योगिनां हृदयङ्गमम् ॥ ११

जानूर्वोरन्तरे सम्यक् कृत्वा पादतले उभे ।

ऋजुकायो विशेद्योगी स्वस्तिकं तत् प्रचक्षते ॥ १२

> त्रिसन्ध्यमेकदा वा तु भवत्येव तदर्चनम् ।
> वैष्णवागमसिद्धान्तश्रवणं श्रावणं [स्मरणं] तथा ॥
> श्रुत्यादिभिर्लौकिकैश्च यदत्यन्तविनिन्दितम् ।
> तत्राऽप्रवर्त्तनं लज्जा । इति ॥
> तर्कैर्यदनुसन्धानं सम्यक् शब्दस्थितेरपि ।
> शास्त्रोक्तयोर्मतिरियम् ॥ इति ॥
> गुरोर्लब्धस्य मन्त्रस्य शश्वदावर्त्तनं जपः ।
> द्रव्यैः कल्पोदितैर्होमो हुतम् ॥ इति ॥ ८॥८ ॥

आसनपञ्चकमिति । स्थितं श्रमः तल्पादौ दण्डवत् पतितं तु निद्राऽभिभवति इति उपविष्टस्यैव ध्यानाभ्यासाधिकारः । तत्र यथाकथञ्चिदुपवेशने रोगः कुष्ठस्यानुगुण्याभावश्च । तस्मात् पद्मासनाद्युक्तिः ।

तदुक्तं वशिष्ठसंहितायाम्—

> आसनेन रुजो हन्ति प्राणायामेन पातकम् ।
> विकारं मानसं योगी प्रत्याहारेण सर्वदा ॥
> धारणाभिर्मनोधैर्यं ध्यानादैश्वर्यमुत्तमम् ।
> समाधौ मोक्षमाप्नोति त्यक्तकर्मशुभाशुभः ॥ इति ॥

ऊर्वोरिति । ऊर्वोरुपरि परस्परस्योर्वोरुपरि । व्युत्क्रमात् इत्यस्य अत्रापि सम्बन्धात् । निबध्नीयादित्यत्र व्युत्क्रमादिति पृष्ठभागे हस्तमात्रव्युत्क्रमः । अङ्गुष्ठबन्धने तु तत्तद्धस्तेनैव तत्तदङ्गुष्ठबन्धनम् ॥ ९॥१०॥११ ॥

जान्विति । अन्तरे इति दक्षिणे वामपादं वामे दक्षिणम् । पूर्वासने अङ्गुष्ठबन्धेनैव ऋजुकायता सिद्धा । अत्र तु तथाऽभावात् ऋजुकाय इति उक्तम् ॥ १२ ॥

सीवन्याः पार्श्वयोर्न्यस्येद् गुल्फयुग्मं सुनिश्चलम् ।
वृषणाधः पार्ष्णिपादौ पाणिभ्यां परिबन्धयेत् ॥ १३

भद्रासनं समुद्दिष्टं योगिभिः पूजितं परम् ।
ऊर्वोः पादौ क्रमान्न्यस्येज्जान्वोः प्रत्यङ्मुखाङ्गुली ॥ १४

करौ निदध्यादाख्यातं वज्रासनमनुत्तमम् ।
एकं पादमधः कृत्वा विन्यस्योरौ तथेतरम् ॥ १५

ऋजुकायो विशेद्योगी वीरासनमितीरितम् ।
इडयाऽऽकर्षयेद्वायुं बाह्यं षोडशमात्रया ॥ १६

सीवन्या इति। गुदमेढ्रान्तरालोर्ध्वरेखा सीवनी। तस्याः पार्श्वयोः। वामपार्श्वे दक्षिणपादगुल्फम्। अन्यस्मिन् अन्यम्। वृषणाधः अण्डकोषाधः पादपार्ष्णी व्यत्यासेन भवत इति शेषः। "तद्ग्रन्थी घुटिके गुल्फौ पुमान् पार्ष्णिस्तयोरधः" इति कोशः। पाणिभ्यां परिबन्धयेत् पूर्ववत् अङ्गुष्ठाविति शेषः। अङ्गुष्ठबन्धनेन ऋजुकायत्वं सिद्धम्। तदुक्तं योगसारे—

सीवन्या आत्मनः पार्श्वे गुल्फौ निक्षिप्य पादयोः ।
सव्ये दक्षिणगुल्फञ्च दक्षिणे दक्षिणेतरम् ॥
दक्षे सव्यकरं न्यस्य सव्ये न्यस्येतरं करम् ।
अङ्गुष्ठौ च निबध्नीयाद्धस्ताभ्यां व्युत्क्रमेण तु ॥ इति ॥

ऊर्वोरिति। स्वस्योरुमूले क्रमात् पादद्वयं कुर्यात्। प्रत्यङ्मुखाङ्गुली स्वसम्मुखाङ्गुली। प्रत्यङ्मुखाङ्गुली करौ जान्वोरुपरि निदध्यादित्यन्वयः। अत्र ऋजुकायत्वं जानुहस्तदानादेव सिद्धम्।

एकमिति। अध इति अपरस्फिचः ॥ १३॥१४॥१५॥१६ ॥

षोडशमात्रयेति। मात्रालक्षणमुक्तं तन्त्रान्तरे—

कालेन यावता स्वीयो हस्तः स्वं जानुमण्डलम् ।
पर्येति मात्रा सा तुल्या स्वीयैकश्वासमात्रया ॥ इति ॥

अन्ये अन्यथा मात्रालक्षणमाहुः—

स्वजानुमण्डलं पूर्वं त्रिः परामृश्य पाणिना ।
प्रपद्य छोटिकामेकां मात्रा सा स्याल्लघीयसी ॥ इति ॥

अन्यत्र तु—सोऽङ्गुलिस्फोटतुल्यश्च मात्राष्टाभिश्च तैः स्मृता ॥ इति ॥
वायवीयसंहितायां तु—

धारयेत् पूरितं योगी चतुःषष्ट्या तु मात्रया ।
सुषुम्णामध्यगं सम्यक् द्वात्रिंशन्मात्रया शनैः ॥ १७

नाड्या पिङ्गलया चैनं रेचयेद्योगवित्तमः ।
प्राणायाममिमं प्राहुर्योगशास्त्रविशारदाः ॥ १८

भूयो भूयः क्रमात्तस्य व्यत्यासेन समाचरेत् ।
मात्रावृद्धिक्रमेणैव सम्यग्द्वादश षोडश ॥ १९

प्राणायामो हि द्विविधः सगर्भोऽगर्भ एव च ।
जपध्यानादिभिर्युक्तं सगर्भं तं विदुर्बुधाः ॥ २०

तदपेतं विगर्भं च प्राणायामं परे विदुः ।
क्रमादभ्यसतः पुंसो देहे स्वेदोद्गमोऽधमः ॥ २१

मध्यमः कम्पसंयुक्तो भूमित्यागः परो मतः ।
उत्तमस्य गुणावाप्तिर्यावच्छीलनमिष्यते ॥ २२

जानु प्रदक्षिणीकृत्य न द्रुतं न विलम्बितम् ।
अङ्गुलिस्फोटनं कुर्यात् सा मात्रेति प्रकीर्त्तिता ॥ इति ॥

आकर्षयेदिति पूरकः । पूरितं धारयेदिति कुम्भकः । सुषुम्णामध्यगं सम्यगिति पूर्वेण सम्बध्यते । रेचयेदिति रेचकः । केचन रेचकादिकुम्भकान्तं मन्यन्ते । एवं क्रमाद् भूयोभूयः पौनःपुन्येन क्रमेण एकैकवृद्ध्या द्विविवृद्ध्यादिक्रमेण तस्य व्यत्यासेन उक्तवैपरीत्येन द्वादश षोडश वा प्राणायामान् समाचरेदित्यन्वयः ।

तदुक्तम्—शुचिः प्राणायामान् प्रणवसहितान् षोडश वशी
प्रभाते सायं च प्रतिदिवसमेवं वितनुते ।
द्विजो यस्तु भ्रूणग्रहणनकृतांहोऽभिकलितं
पुनस्थेते मासादपि दुरिततूलौघदहनाः ॥ इति ॥

परमतमाह श्लोकेन जपेति । परे बुधा विदुरित्यन्वयः । अयं च प्राणायामः पूजाविषय इति ज्ञेयम् । तदुक्तम्—

अयं प्राणायामः सकलदुरितध्वंसनकरो
विगर्भः प्रोक्तोऽसौ शतगुणफलो गर्भकलितः ।
जपध्यानापेतः स तु निगदितो गर्भरहितः
सगर्भस्तद्युक्तो मुनिपरिवृढैर्योगनिरतैः ॥ इति ॥

शीलनं प्राणायामस्येति शेषः ॥ १६॥१७॥१८॥१९॥२०॥२१॥२२ ॥

इन्द्रियाणां विचरतां विषयेषु निरर्गलम् ।
बलादाहरणं तेभ्यः प्रत्याहारोऽभिधीयते ॥ २३

अङ्गुष्ठगुल्फजानूरुसीवनीलिङ्गनाभिषु ।
हृद्ग्रीवाकण्ठदेशेषु लम्बिकायां ततो नसि ॥ २४

भ्रूमध्ये मस्तके मूर्ध्नि द्वादशान्ते यथाविधि ।
धारणं प्राणमरुतो धारणेति निगद्यते ॥ २५

इन्द्रियाणामित्यादिना मनस एव एकत्र स्थितिः कार्येत्युक्तं भवति। यतो मनःसहायानामेव एतेषां स्वस्वविषयग्रहणशक्तिः अतस्तन्निरोधेनैव निरोधादिति भावः। लम्बिका तालुमूलम्। मस्तकं ललाटकेशसन्धिः। मूर्ध्नीति तदुपरिभागः। द्वादशान्ते ब्रह्मरन्ध्रे। यथाविधि इति गुरूक्तक्रमेण। वशिष्ठ-संहितायां पञ्च धारणा उक्ता—

भूतानां मानसञ्चैकं धारणा च पृथक् पृथक् ।
मनसो निश्चलत्वे तु धारणा च विधीयते ॥
या पृथ्वी हरितालहेमरुचिरा तत्त्वं कलालान्वितं
संयुक्ता कमलासनेन च चतुष्कोणा हृदि स्थायिनी ।
प्राणांस्तत्र विलीय पञ्चघटिका चित्तान्वितं धारये-
देषा स्तम्भकरी सदा क्षितिपरा ख्याता क्षमाधारणा ॥ १ ॥
अर्द्धेन्दुप्रतिमं च कुन्दधवलं कण्ठे च तत्त्वान्वितं
तत् पीयूषवकारबीजसहितं युक्तं सदा विष्णुना ।
प्राणांस्तत्र विलीय पञ्चघटिका चित्तान्वितं धारये-
देषा दुःसहकालकूटजरणा स्याद् वारुणी धारणा ॥ २
तत्त्वस्थं शिवमिन्द्रगोपसदृशं तत्र त्रिकोणेऽनलं
तेजोऽनेकमयं प्रवालरुचिरं रुद्रेण तत् सङ्गतम् ।
प्राणांस्तत्र विलीय पञ्चघटिका चित्तान्वितं धारये-
देषा वह्निसमं वपुर्विदधती वैश्वानरी धारणा ॥ ३
यन्मूलं कमलं प्रपञ्चसहितं दृष्टं भ्रुवोरन्तरे
तद्वत् सत्त्वमयं यकारसहितं तत्रेश्वरो देवता ।
प्राणांस्तत्र विलीय पञ्चघटिका चित्तान्वितं धारये-
देषा खे गमनं करोति नियतं वायोः सदा धारणा ॥ ४

समाहितेन मनसा चैतन्यान्तरवर्तिना ।
आत्मन्य[नोऽ]भीष्टदेवानां ध्यानं ध्यानमिहोच्यते ॥ २६

समत्वभावना नित्यं जीवात्मपरमात्मनोः ।
समाधिमाहुर्मुनयः प्रोक्तमष्टाङ्गलक्षणम् ॥ २७

षण्णवत्यङ्गुलायामं शरीरमुभयात्मकम् ।
गुदध्वजान्तरे कन्दमुत्सेधाद्द्व्यङ्गुलं विदुः ॥ २८

तस्मात् द्विगुणविस्तारं वृत्तरूपेण शोभितम् ।
नाड्यस्तत्र समुद्भूता मुख्यास्तिस्रः प्रकीर्त्तिताः ॥ २९

आकाशं सुविशुद्धवारिसदृशं यद्ब्रह्मरन्ध्रस्थितं
तन्नाथेन सदाशिवेन सहितं युक्तं हकाराक्षरैः ।
प्राणांस्तत्र विलीय पञ्चघटिका चित्तान्वितं धारये-
देषा मोक्षकपाटभेदनपटुः प्रोक्ता नभोधारणा ॥
कर्मणां साधकाः सर्वा धारणाः पञ्च दुर्लभाः ।
तासां विज्ञानतो योगी सर्वपापैः प्रमुच्यते ॥ इति ॥ २१—२५ ॥

अभीष्टदेवानामिति सगर्भं ध्यानमुक्तम् । विगर्भमपि ध्यानमुक्तं तन्त्रान्तरे ।
यदाहुः—यत्तत्त्वे निश्चलं चित्तं तद्ध्यानं परमं मतम् ।
द्विधा भवति तद्ध्यानं सगुणं निर्गुणं तथा ॥
सगुणं वर्णभेदेन निर्गुणं केवलं तथा ।
अश्वमेधसहस्राणि वाजपेयशतानि च ॥
एकस्य ध्यानयोगस्य कलां नार्हन्ति षोडशीम् ।
अन्तश्चेतो बहिश्चक्षुरधः स्थाप्य सुखासनः ॥
समत्वञ्च शरीराणां ध्यानमाहुश्च सिद्धिदम् ।
नासाग्रे दृष्टिमादाय ध्यात्वा मुच्यति बन्धनात् ॥ इत्यादिना ॥
गुदे मेढ्रे च नाभौ च हृदये कण्ठदेशके ।
घण्टिकालम्बिकास्थाने भ्रूमध्ये परमेश्वरम् ॥
निर्गुणं गगनाकारं मरीचिजलसन्निभम् ।
शून्ये सर्वमयं ध्यात्वा योगी योगमवाप्नुयात् ॥ इत्यन्तेन ॥२६॥२७॥

योगसिद्ध्यर्थं शरीराभ्यन्तरे मूलाधारमारभ्य तत्तन्नाडीस्थाने वायुसञ्चारं वक्तुं शरीरप्रमाणमाह षडिति । उभयात्मकं शिवशक्त्यात्मकम् । अग्नीषोमा-

इडा वामे स्थिता नाडी पिङ्गला दक्षिणे मता ।
तयोर्मध्यगता नाडी सुषुम्णा वंशमाश्रिता ॥ ३०

पादाङ्गुष्ठद्वये याता शिफाभ्यां शिरसा पुनः ।
ब्रह्मस्थानं समापन्ना सोमसूर्याग्निरूपिणी ॥ ३१

तस्या मध्यगता नाडी चित्राख्या योगिवल्लभा ।
ब्रह्मरन्ध्रं विदुस्तस्यां पद्मसूत्रनिभं परम् ॥ ३२

आधारांश्च विदुस्तत्र मतभेदादनेकधा ।
दिव्यमार्गमिदं प्राहुरमृतानन्दकारणम् ॥ ३३

त्मकं वा शुक्रशोणितात्मकं वा इति प्रथमपटलोक्तानुवादः । तस्मादित्युत्सेधात् ।
वंशं पृष्ठवंशम् आश्रिता तदन्तर्गता । यदाहुः—

या सुषुम्णाधारदण्डान्तरविवरगता । इति ।

शिफाभ्यां मूलाभ्याम् ॥ २८॥२९॥३०॥३१॥३२ ॥

आधारान् इति केचन द्वादश अन्ये षोडश आहुः । परे बहूनि च ।

यदाहुः—ततस्तु ब्रह्मकङ्काले ध्यायेच्चक्रक्रमं सुधीः ।

आधारचक्रं प्रथमं कुलदीपमनन्तरम् ॥
वज्र[यन्त्र]चक्रं ततः प्रोक्तं स्वाधिष्ठानात्मकं परम् ।
रौद्रं करालचक्रं च गह्वरात्मकमेव च ॥
विद्याप[प्र]दं च त्रिमुखं त्रिपदं कालदण्डकम् ।
सा[उ]कारचक्रं च ततः कालोदारं करङ्क[बन्ध]कम् ॥
दीपकं क्षोभजनकमानन्दकलिला[ललिता]त्मकम् ।
मणिपूरकसंज्ञञ्च लाङ्गलं का[कु]लभेदनम् ॥
महोत्साहञ्च परमं माद[र्ग]कं पदमुच्यते ।
कल्पजालं ततश्चिन्त्यं घोषकल्लोलनं ततः ॥
नादावर्त्तपदं प्रोक्तं त्रिपुटञ्च तदुत्तरम् ।
कङ्कालकं तम[मन]श्चक्रं विख्यातं पुटभेदनम् ॥
महाग्रन्थिविकाशं च बन्धोज्ज्वलनसंश्रितम् ।
अनाहतं पद्मपुटं व्योमचक्रं तथा भवेत् ॥
बोधनं ध्रुवसंज्ञञ्च काल[कला]कन्दलकं ततः ।
क्रौञ्चं भेरण्डविभवं डामरं कुलपीठकम् ॥

इड़ायां सञ्चरेच्चन्द्रः पिङ्गलायां दिवाकरः ।
ज्ञातौ योगनिदानज्ञैः सुषुम्णायां तु तावुभौ ॥ ३४

आधारकन्दमध्यस्थं त्रिकोणमतिसुन्दरम् ।
ज्योतिषां निलयं दिव्यं प्राहुरागमवेदिनः ॥ ३५

तत्र विद्युल्लताकारा कुण्डली परदेवता ।
परिस्फुरति सर्वात्मा सुप्ताहिसदृशाकृतिः ॥ ३६

बिभर्ति कुण्डलीशक्तिरात्मानं हंसमाश्रिता ।
हंसः प्राणाश्रयो नित्यं प्राणो नाड़ीसमाश्रयः ॥ ३७

आधारादुद्गतो वायुर्यथावत् सर्वदेहिनाम् ।
देहं व्याप्य स्वनाड़ीभिः प्रयाणं कुरुते बहिः ॥ ३८

द्वादशाङ्गुलमानेन तस्मात् प्राण इतीरितः ।

कुलकोलाहलं हालाहलावर्त्तं महद्द्वयम् [द्वयम्] ।
वीरभैरवसंज्ञञ्च विशुद्धिः कण्ठमुत्तमम् ॥
घूर्णकंपदमाख्यातमाज्ञाकाकपुटं तथा ।
शृङ्गाटं कामरूपाख्यं पूर्णगिर्यात्मकं परम् ।
महाव्योमात्मकं चक्रं शक्तिरूपमनुस्मरेत् ॥ इति ॥ ३३॥३४ ॥

कुण्डलीस्थानमाह आधारेति । कुण्डलीशक्तिः आत्मानं परमात्मानं बिभर्त्ति तद्योगभागिनी भवतीत्यर्थः । कीदृक् । हंसं जीवात्मानम् आश्रिता जीवाधिष्ठाना सतीत्यर्थः । हंसः प्राणाश्रयः प्राणवायुसमाश्रय इत्यर्थः । प्राणो नाड़ीसमाश्रयः ।
॥ ३५॥३६॥३७ ॥

कथं तस्य नाड़ीसमाश्रयत्वमित्यत आह आधारादिति । प्रयाणं कुरुते अतएव प्राण इति प्राणशब्दव्युत्पत्तिः दर्शिता । द्वादशाङ्गुलमानेनेति वाम-दक्षिणयोरिति शेयम् । एतत्फलमुक्तं तन्त्रान्तरे—

भोजनं मैथुनं युद्धं फलपुष्पग्रहं तथा ।
कुर्यात् क्रूराणि कर्माणि वायौ दक्षिणसंस्थिते ॥
यात्राविवाहकर्माणि शुभकर्माणि यानि च ।
तानि सर्वाणि कुर्वीत वामे वायौ तु संस्थिते ॥

तथा—व्यायामं शयनं क्रूरं षट्कर्मादिकसाधनम् ।
तानि सिध्यन्ति सूर्येण नात्र कार्या विचारणा ॥ इति ॥

रम्ये मृद्वासने शुद्धे पटाजिनकुशोत्तरे ॥ ३९

बद्ध्वैकमासनं योगी योगमार्गपरो भवेत् ।

ज्ञात्वा भूतोदयं देहे विधिवत् प्राणवायुना ॥ ४०

तत्तद्भूतं जपेद्देहदृढत्वावाप्तये सुधीः ।

दण्डाकारा गतिर्भूमेः पुटयोरुभयोरधः ॥ ४१

तोयस्य पावकस्योर्द्ध्वङ्गतिस्तिर्यङ्नभस्वतः ।

गतिर्व्योम्नो भवेन्मध्ये भूतानामुदयः स्मृतः ॥ ४२

धरणेरुदये कुर्यात् स्तम्भनं वश्यमात्मवित् ।

शान्तिकं पौष्टिकं कर्म तोयस्य समये वसोः ॥ ४३

मारणादीनि मरुतो विपच्चोच्चाटनादिकम् ।

क्षुद्रा[क्ष्वेड़ा]दिनाशनं शस्तमुदये च विहायसः ॥ ४४

अन्यत्र—देवदक्षिणभागगेऽथ पुरुषे रोगातुरे दक्षिणे

स्थित्वा पृच्छति पृच्छकः स पुरुषो जीवत्यरोगश्चिरम् ।

वामायां तु रुजाऽऽकुलीकृततनौ वामाश्रिते चेश्वरे

वामे पृच्छति चेत् स्थिता गतगदा वामा चिरं जीवति ॥ इति ॥

देवे गते पृच्छति वामभागं

स्थित्वा नरो दक्षिणतो यदीह ।

व्यत्यासतोऽस्मादपि कृच्छ्रसाध्यं

वदन्ति सन्तः खलु रोगजातम् ॥ इति ॥

अथवा आधारात् उद्गतः बहिः प्रयाणं कुरुत इत्यनेन उत्पत्तिलये सन्ध्ये अहोरात्रमित्यादि सर्वमुक्तम् । यदाहुः—

जानीयादुदयं बुधः स्वजठरे देवस्य कन्दे नृणां

प्राणास्तिग्मकराङ्गुले खलु लयं सन्ध्ये च पूर्वापरे ।

उत्पत्तिं च लयं च सन्ततमधोवृत्तिं निशां वासरं

ऊर्ध्वां वृत्तिमधस्तथा हिमकरं चोर्ध्वां दिनेशं गतिम् ॥ इति ॥३८॥३९॥

योगप्रकारमाह रम्य इति । रम्य एकान्ते इत्यर्थः । अन्यथा चित्तविक्षेपः स्यादिति । काठिन्ये सति देहपीड़या तत्रैव मनो गमिष्यतीति मृद्वासन इत्युक्तम् । भूतपरिचर्यार्थमाह दण्डेति ॥ ३९॥४०॥४१॥४२ ॥

प्रसङ्गतस्तत्तद्भूतोदयमाह धरणेरिति । वसोरग्नेः ॥ ४३॥४४ ॥

अङ्गुलीभिर्दृढं बद्ध्वा करणानि समाहितः।
अङ्गुष्ठाभ्यामुभे श्रोत्रे तर्जनीभ्यां विलोचने॥ ४५

नासारन्ध्रे मध्यमाभ्यामन्याभिर्वदनं दृढम्।
बद्ध्वात्मप्राणमनसामैकत्वं समनुस्मरन्॥ ४६

धारयेन्मरुतं सम्यग्योगोऽयं योगिवल्लभः।
नादः सञ्जायते तस्य क्रमादभ्यसतः शनैः॥ ४७

मत्तभृङ्गाङ्गनागीतसदृशः प्रथमो ध्वनिः।
वंशिकस्याऽनिलापूर्णवंशध्वनिनिभोऽपरः॥ ४८

घण्टारवसमः पश्चात् घनमेघस्वनोपमः।
एवमभ्यसतः पुंसः संसारध्वान्तनाशनम्॥ ४९

बद्ध्वेति। अन्यथा यदि इन्द्रियमार्गेण हठात् वायुः निर्गच्छेत् तदुपघातः स्यात्। करणानि इन्द्रियाणि। उभे इति त्रिषु अन्वेति। घनो निविडो मेघस्वनवत् स्वनो यस्य इति मध्यपदलोपी समासः। एवमित्यनेनाऽन्वेति। ध्वनिदशकमाहुः—चिणीति प्रथमः शब्दश्चिञ्चिणीति द्वितीयकः।

चिञ्चिचाकी तृतीयस्तु चतुर्थो घर्घरः स्वरः॥
पञ्चमस्तु मनागुच्चः षष्ठो मदकलध्वनिः।
सप्तमः सूक्ष्मनादः स्यादष्टमो वेणुवर्द्धनः॥
नवमो मधुरध्वानो दशमो दुन्दुभिस्वनः॥ इति॥

हंसोपनिषद्यपि—अथ दशकोषो नादमनुभवति। हंसवशात् नादो दशविधो जायते। चिणीति प्रथमः। चिणिचिणीति द्वितीयकः। घण्टानादस्तृतीयकः। शङ्खनादस्तुर्यः। पञ्चमस्तन्त्रीनादः। षष्ठस्तालनादः। सप्तमो वेणुनादः। अष्टमो भेरीनादः। नवमो मृदङ्गनादः। दशमो मेघनादः। नवमं परित्यज्य दशममभ्यसेत्। अस्मात् मनो विलीयते। विलीने मनसि गते सङ्कल्पविकल्पे दग्धे पुण्यपापे सदाशिवोमिति। सदाशिवः शक्त्यात्मा सर्वत्रावस्थित स्वयं ज्योतिः शुद्धो बुद्धो नित्यो निरञ्जनः शान्तः प्रकाशत इति।

हंसलक्षणं शिवशक्त्यात्मकं जीवात्मकं वा।

प्रयोगसारे तु—कम्परोमोद्गमानन्दं वैमल्यस्थैर्यलाघवम्।
प्रकाशज्ञानवैदूर्यं भावोऽद्वैतात्मसञ्चयः॥
सम्भवन्ति दशाऽवस्था योगिनः सिद्धिसूचकाः।

ज्ञानमुत्पद्यते पूर्वं हंसलक्षणमव्ययम् ।
पुंप्रकृत्यात्मकौ प्रोक्तौ बिन्दुसर्गौ मनीषिभिः ॥ ५०

ताभ्यां क्रमात्समुद्भूतौ बिन्दुसर्गावसानकौ ।
हंसौ तौ पुंप्रकृत्याख्यौ हं पुमान् प्रकृतिस्तु सः ॥ ५१

अजपा कथिता ताभ्यां जीवोऽयमुपतिष्ठति ।
पुरुषं स्वाश्रयं मत्वा प्रकृतिर्नित्यमास्थिता ॥ ५२

यदा तद्भावमाप्नोति तदा सोऽहमयं भवेत् ।
सकारार्णं हकारार्णं लोपयित्वा ततः परम् ।
सन्धिं कुर्यात् पूर्वरूपस्तदाऽसौ प्रणवो भवेत् ॥ ५३

परानन्दमयं नित्यञ्चैतन्यैकगुणात्मकम् ।
आत्माभेदस्थितं योगी प्रणवं भावयेत्सदा ॥ ५४

ततस्त्रैकाल्यविज्ञानं महाप्रज्ञा मनोज्ञता ॥
छन्दतः प्राणसंरोधो नाडीनां क्रमणं तथा ।
वाचां सिद्धिश्चिरायुष्यमिन्द्रजालानुवर्त्तनम् ॥
देहाद्देहान्तरप्राप्तिरात्मज्योतिःप्रकाशनम् ।
प्रत्यया दश दृश्यन्ते प्राप्तयोगस्य योगिनः ॥ इति ॥ ४५—५० ॥

प्रणवोत्पत्तिमाह पुमिति। क्रमादिति बिन्दोः हं विसर्गात् सः। पुंप्रकृत्याख्यौ इति नाम काल्पनिकम्। तत्त्वतः बिन्दुविसर्गावेव। हं पुमानिति। अतएव अत आदौ अकारे निपाते योजिते अहमिति लोकप्रसिद्ध आत्माभिनयः। उपतिष्ठति आराधयति। पुरुषं स्वाश्रयं मत्वा नित्यं तमेव आस्थिता प्रकृतिरिति सम्बन्धः। यदा तु प्रकृतेर्नित्यमात्मन इति पाठः तदा आत्मनः प्रकृतेरिति समानाधिकरणे षष्ठी। प्रकृतिरविद्या सा ब्रह्माभिन्नत्वेन जीवकल्पकत्वात् तदभिन्नैव स्वाश्रयं सदाश्रयं गत्वा इयं यदा तद्भावमाप्नोतीति सम्बन्धः। तद्भावमिति। प्रकृतिपुरुषयोरभेदात् परमात्मैवाऽहम् इति जीवब्रह्मणोरैक्यम्। अस्यार्थः। अजपाभ्यासाच्चैवमैक्यमुदेतीति व्यञ्जितम्। लोपयित्वेति। व्यञ्जनयोः कल्पितत्वादेव लोपः। पूर्वरूपं "एङः पदान्तादति" इत्यनेन ॥ ५०॥५१॥५२॥५३ ॥

परानन्दमयमिति। "आनन्दं ब्रह्मणो रूपं तच्च मोक्षे प्रतिष्ठितम्" इति श्रुतेः।

आम्नायवाचामतिदूरमाद्यं वेद्यं स्वसंवेद्यगुणेन सन्तः ।
आत्मानमानन्दरसैकसिन्धुं पश्यन्ति तारात्मकमात्मनिष्ठाः ॥ ५५

सत्यं हेतुविवर्जितं श्रुतिगिरामाद्यं जगत्कारणं
व्याप्तस्थावरजङ्गमं निरुपमं चैतन्यमन्तर्गतम् ।
आत्मानं रविवह्निचन्द्रवपुषं तारात्मकं सन्ततं
नित्यानन्दगुणालयं सुकृतिनः पश्यन्ति रुद्धेन्द्रियाः ॥ ५६

तारस्य सप्तविभवैः परिचीयमानं
मानैरगम्यमनिशं श्रुतिमौलिमृग्यम् ।
संवित्समस्तगमनश्वरमच्युतं तत्
तेजः परं भजत सान्द्रसुधाम्बुराशिम् ॥ ५७

नित्यं वक्ष्यमाणश्रुतेरेव। चैतन्यं ज्ञानं स चासावेको गुणश्च तदात्मकम्। "सत्यं ज्ञानमनन्तं ब्रह्म" इति श्रुतेः। यद्वा चैतन्यं ज्ञानरूपमेकम्। "एकमेवाद्वितीयं ब्रह्म" इति श्रुतेः। संसारोत्पत्तिकर्तृत्वात् कल्पितसत्त्वरजस्तमोगुणरूपम्। आत्माभेदस्थितं सोऽहंशब्दोत्थतया तस्य च तदर्थकत्वात् ॥ ५४ ॥

आम्नायेति। "यतो वाचो निवर्त्तन्ते" इति श्रुतेः। आद्यम्। शास्त्रयोनित्वात्। स्वसंवेद्यगुणेन वेद्यं स्वप्रकाशमित्यर्थः। आनन्दमिति। "आनन्दं ब्रह्मणो रूपम्" इति श्रुतेः। तारात्मकमुक्तरीत्या। आत्मनिष्ठा आदरनैरन्तर्यदीर्घकालाभ्यासैस्तच्चिन्तनपरा योगिनः ॥ ५५ ॥

सत्यम्। "सत्यं ज्ञानम्" इति श्रुतेः। हेतुविवर्जितम्। नित्यत्वात् अनुत्पाद्यम्। यद्वा ये हेतवो दुस्तर्कास्तद्विवर्जितम्। श्रुतिगिरामाद्यम्। "शास्त्रयोनित्वात्" इति सूत्रे वेदकर्तृत्वोक्तेः। प्रणवात्मकत्वाद्वा। जगत्कारणम्। "आनन्दाद्धेव खल्विमानि भूतानि जायन्ते" इति श्रुतेः। व्याप्तेति। तद्विवर्त्तरूपत्वात् जगतः। निरुपममिति। अद्वितीयत्वेन। चैतन्यमन्तर्गतम्। प्रत्यक्चैतन्यम् आत्मरूपचैतन्यमित्यर्थः। रविचन्द्रवह्निवपुरिव वपुर्यस्य। प्रकाशरूपमित्यर्थः। न तु तत्तदाकारग्राहित्वे अयं दृष्टान्तः। तस्य निराकारत्वात् प्रणवरूपत्वात् वा तदुक्तिः ॥ ५६ ॥

तारस्येति। अकारोकारमकारबिन्दुनादशक्तिशान्ताख्यैः परिचीयमानं तद्रुच्यमानम्। तदेवाह मानैरगम्यमिति। श्रुतिमौलिरुपनिषत् तन्मृग्यम्। सत्तात्मकमस्ति इति भानात्। संवित् प्रकाशम्। "सद्धीदं सर्वं सत् सत्" इति "चिद्धीदं

हिरण्मयं दीप्तमनेकवर्णं त्रिमूर्त्तिमूलं निगमादिबीजम् ।
अङ्गुष्ठमात्रं पुरुषं भजन्ते चैतन्यमात्रं रविमण्डलस्थम् ॥ ५८
ध्यायन्ति दुग्धाब्धिभुजङ्गभोगे शयानमाद्यं कमलासहायम् ।
प्रफुल्लनेत्राम्बुजमञ्जनाभं चतुर्मुखेनाश्रि[श्चि]तनाभिपद्मम् ॥ ५९

आम्नायगं त्रिचरणं घननीलमुद्य-
च्छ्रीवत्सकौस्तुभगदाम्बुजशङ्खचक्रम् ।
हृत्पुण्डरीकनिलयं जगदेकमूल-
मालोकयन्ति कृतिनः पुरुषं पुराणम् ॥ ६०

सर्वं प्रकाशते" इति श्रुतेः। समस्तगं व्यापकम्। अनश्वरम् अविध्वंसि। अच्युतमेकरूपत्वात्। वाक्यान्तरोपदेशात् श्लोकत्रयस्थानां पदानां परस्परं न पौनरुक्त्यम् ॥ ५७ ॥

सगुणब्रह्मोपास्तिरपि सगुणब्रह्म[हिरण्यगर्भ]लोकप्राप्तिद्वारा मुक्तेः क्रमात् कारणमिति शास्त्रोक्तेः निर्गुणब्रह्मोपास्तौ असमर्थानां सगुणब्रह्मोपास्तिमाह हिरण्मयमिति। त्रिमूर्त्तिमूलमित्यनेन अस्याऽभ्यसनीयानि नामानि सूचितानि। यदाहुः—ब्रह्मा विष्णुश्च रुद्रश्च ॐकारः प्रलयस्तथा ।
सर्वव्यापी ह्यनन्तश्च तारः सूक्ष्मश्च शुक्लकः ॥
वैद्युतश्च परं ब्रह्म एकश्चाऽप्येकरुद्रकः ।
ईशानो भगवांश्चैव ततः स्यात्तु महेश्वरः ॥
महादेवः सदापूर्वः शिवः सर्वादयस्त्रयः ।
रचितावगतश्चैव तथा प्रियतमः स्मृतः ॥
नित्यत्वमश्च सर्वाद्या षोडशान्तः प्रकीर्त्तिताः ।
आद्यश्चावगमः कान्तः प्रदिष्टश्चोत्वस्वामिनी ॥
समर्थो यावकश्चैव क्रियेच्छादीप्त एव च ।
अवाप्तालिङ्गितो चैव हिंसको दाहकस्तथा ॥
भावग्रह्णो गुणं बीजं ध्रुवो वेदादिरादियुक् ।
उभयो मपरश्चैव त्रिमात्रो योनिरेव च ॥
देहाश्रयश्च संवादात्मानो सर्वादिकास्त्रयः । इति ॥ ५८ ॥

क्रममुक्त्यर्थमन्यां साकारोपास्तिमाह ध्यायन्तीति श्लोकद्वयेन । आम्नाया वेदास्तदग्रथितस्त्रष्टं[सुष्ठु ?] वचनं यस्य ॥ ५९ ॥ ६० ॥

बिन्दोर्नादसमुद्भवः समुदिते नादे जगत्कारणं
तारं तत्त्वमुखाम्बुजं परिवृतं वर्णात्मकैर्भूतजैः।
आम्नायाङ्घ्रिचतुष्टयं [मुखं]पुररियोरानन्दमूलं वपुः
पायाद्वो मुकुटेन्दुखण्डविगलद्दिव्यामृतौघप्लुतम् ॥ ६१

पिण्डं भवेत् कुण्डलिनी शिवात्मा पदं तु हंसः सकलान्तरात्मा।
रूपं भवेद्बिन्दुरनन्त[मन्द]कान्तिरतीतरूपं शिवसामरस्यम् ॥ ६२

पिण्डादियोगं शिवसामरस्यात् सबीजयोगं प्रवदन्ति सन्तः।
शिवे लयं नित्यगुणाभियुक्ते निर्बीजयोगं फलनिर्व्यपेक्षम् ॥ ६३

मूलोन्निद्रभुजङ्गराजमहिषीं यान्तीं सुषुम्णान्तरं
भित्वाऽऽधारसमूहमाशु विलसत्सौदामिनीसन्निभाम्।
व्योमाम्भोजगतेन्दुमण्डलगलद्दिव्यामृतौघप्लुतं[घैः पतिं]
सम्भाव्य स्वगृहं गतां पुनरिमां सञ्चिन्तयेत् कुण्डलीम् ॥ ६४

क्रममुक्त्यर्थमन्यसाकारध्यानयोगमाह बिन्दोरिति। बिन्दुः शिवात्मा ॐकारस्य शिरोरूपः। तत्त्वमुखाम्बुजं चतुर्विंशतितत्त्वमयमुखकमलम् ॥ ६१ ॥

सबीजयोगमाह पिण्डमिति। अकारोकारमकारात्मकत्वात् पिण्डं प्रणवः। कुण्डलिनी तद्रूपा सैव शिवात्मा सकलान्तरात्मा हंसः। तस्याः पदं स्थानम्। अनयोरनन्तकान्तिः बिन्दुरूपम्। परमार्थतस्तु शिवयोः सामरस्यमतीतरूपं नीरूपमेव। यद्वा अतीतेति अतिपूर्वस्येणो लोट्मध्यमपुरुषबहुवचनम्। हे लोकाः यूयं सर्वं जगदतिक्रम्यैवं ध्यानात् शिवसामरस्यरूपमतीत अतियात गच्छतेत्यर्थः ॥ ६२ ॥

अनेन सायुज्यमुक्तिर्भवतीत्याह पिण्डादीति। सारूप्यमुक्तिमाह शिव इति ॥ ६३ ॥

सम्प्रति आत्मानुभवैकगम्यकुण्डलिनीचिन्तनरूपं राजयोगादिप्रकारमाह मूलेति। मूलात् मूलाधारात्। उन्निद्रा जाग्रद्रूपा। कुण्डल्या सर्पाकारत्वात् भुजङ्गराजमहिषीव्यपदेशः। सुषुम्णान्तरमाशु यान्तीम्। आधारसमूहं स्वाधिष्ठान मणिपूरकानाहत विशुद्धाज्ञारूपम्। व्योमाम्भोजेति। सहस्रदलपतिं शिवम्। स्वगृहं मूलाधारम् ॥ ६४ ॥

हंसं नित्यमनन्तमव्ययगुणं स्वाधारतो निर्गता
शक्तिः कुण्डलिनी समस्तजननी हस्ते गृहीत्वा च तम्।
याता शम्भुनिकेतनं परसुखं तेनाऽनुभूय स्वयं
यान्ती स्वाश्रयमर्ककोटिरुचिरा ध्येया जगन्मोहिनी ॥ ६५

अव्यक्तं परबिन्दुमञ्चितरुचिं नीत्वा शिवस्यालयं
शक्तिः कुण्डलिनी गुणत्रयवपुर्विद्युल्लतासन्निभा।
आनन्दामृतमध्यगं पुरमिदं चन्द्रार्ककोटिप्रभं
संवीक्ष्य स्वपुरं गता भगवती ध्येया न वेद्या गुणैः ॥ ६६

मध्ये वर्त्म समीरणद्वयमिथःसङ्घट्टसंक्षोभजं
शब्दस्तोममतीत्य तेजसि तडित्कोटिप्रभाभासुरे।
उद्यन्तीं समुपास्महे नवजवासिन्दूरसन्ध्यारुणां
सान्द्रानन्दसुधामयीं परशिवं प्राप्तां परां देवताम् ॥ ६७

गमनागमनेषु जा[ला]ङ्गिकी सा तनुयाद्योगफलानि कुण्डली।
मुदिता कुलकामधेनुरेषा भजतां काङ्क्षितकल्पवल्लरी ॥ ६८

आधारस्थितशक्तिबिन्दुनिलयां नीवारशूकोपमां
नित्यानन्दमयीं गलत्परसुधावर्षैः प्रबोधप्रदैः।

तं जीवं जप्यमानं हंसं हस्ते गृहीत्वेति सम्बन्धः। यथा च जीवो जपति तथा हंसमन्त्रप्रस्ताव एव उक्तम्। स्वाश्रयं मूलाधारम्। पूर्वश्लोकाद्धंसं गृहीत्वा यातेति विशेषः ॥ ६५ ॥

अव्यक्तं परबिन्दुं नीत्वेति। पूर्वतो विशेषः। स्वपुरं मूलाधारम् ॥ ६६ ॥

समीरणद्वयेति। अपानवायुनिरोधात् प्राणवायुनिरोधाच्चोर्ध्वाधोगतयोस्तयो मिथः संघट्ट इत्यर्थः। अत्र प्राणापानसंघट्टजशब्दातिक्रमणमेव विशेषः आरक्तध्यानञ्च।

तदुक्तम्—श्वेतध्याने वाग्विलास आरक्ते वश्यता भवेत्। इति।
अन्यत्रापि—ध्यायेदृश्याकर्षणे तां जपाभां श्वेतां शान्तौ स्तम्भने पीतवर्णाम्।
श्यामां मुक्तौ मारणे कृष्णवर्णां धूम्राभासां द्वेषणोच्चाटने च ॥
इत्याद्यानुषङ्गिकं फलमपि ज्ञेयम् ॥ ६७ ॥

गमनेति। अत्र गमनागमनेषु जाङ्गिकीति विशेषः ॥ ६८ ॥

सित्त्वा षट् सरसीरुहाणि विधिवत् कोदण्डमध्योदितां
ध्यायेद्भास्वरबन्धुजीवरुचिरां संचि[वि]न्मयीं देवताम् ॥ ६९

हृत्पङ्केरुहभानुबिम्बनिलयां विद्युल्लतामत्सरां
बालार्कारुणतेजसा भगवतीं निर्भर्त्सयन्तीं तमः।
नादाख्यं पदमर्द्धचन्द्रकुटिलं संविन्मयं शाश्वतं
यान्तीमक्षररूपिणीं विमलधीर्ध्यायेद्विभुं तेजसाम् ॥ ७०

भाले पूर्णनिशापतिप्रतिजटां नीहारहारत्विषा
सिञ्चन्तीममृतेन देवममितैनानन्दयन्तीं तनुम्।
वर्णानां जननीं तदीयवपुषा संप्राप्य विश्वं स्थितां
ध्यायेत् सम्यगनाकुलेन मनसा संवि[चि]न्मयीमम्बिकाम् ॥ ७१

मूले भाले हृदि च विलसद्वर्णरूपा सवित्री
पीनोत्तुङ्गस्तनभरनम[लस]न्मध्यदेशा महेशी।

आधारेति। आधारो मूलाधारचक्रम्। तत्र स्थिता या शक्तिः त्रिकोणं तस्या मध्यस्थानं बिन्दुः तन्निलयाम्। यद्वा आधारस्थिता या शक्तिः त्रिकोणं यच्च तत्रस्थं कामबीजं तदपि शक्तिबीजमेव। तस्य शिरसि यो बिन्दुः तन्निलयामित्यर्थः। यदाहुः—

तडित्कोटिप्रख्यं स्वरुचिजितकालानलरुचिं
सहस्रादित्यांशुप्रकरसदृशोद्योतकलितम्।
स्फुरन्तं योन्यन्तः स्फुटदरुणबन्धूककुसुम-
प्रभं कामं ध्यायेद्रुचिरशशभृत्कोटिशिरसम् ॥
तस्योर्ध्वेऽग्निशिखा चिरद्युतिलतापुञ्जप्रभाभास्वरा
सूक्ष्मा ब्रह्मपथान्तराम्बरगता चैतन्यमात्रा कला ॥ इति ॥

कोदण्डमध्यं भ्रूमध्यम् आज्ञाचक्रम्। तत्रोदिता। अत्रायमेव विशेषः ॥ ६९ ॥

मत्सरशब्दः सदृशार्थः। बालार्कारुणतेजसा तमो निर्भर्त्सयन्तीमिति सम्बन्धः। अत्र हृदयादेव नादं प्रति गमनं वर्णमयध्यानमिति विशेषः। एतच्च प्रतिचक्रं भिन्नाः कुण्डस्य इति मते तैः कुण्डलिनीषट्कस्य स्वीकृतत्वात् ॥ ७० ॥

भाल इति। अत्राज्ञायां शिवेन सङ्गः वर्णोत्पादकत्वञ्च विशेषः। तदुक्तम्—

स्वयम्भुलिङ्गं निजयोनिमध्यरन्ध्रान्तरे हृत्सरसीरुहान्तः।
बाणाह्वयं चेतरमन्तराले वदन्ति सन्तो गगनाम्बुजेऽन्यः ॥ इति ॥ ७१ ॥

चक्रे चक्रे गलितसुधया सिक्तगात्रा प्रकामं
दद्यादाद्या श्रियमविकलां वाङ्मयी देवता वः ॥ ७२

निजभवननिवासादुच्चरन्ती विलासैः
पथि पथि कमलानां चारुहासं विधाय।
तरुणतरणिकान्तिः कुण्डली देवता सा
शिवसदनसुधाभिर्दीपयेदात्मतेजः ॥ ७३

आधारबन्धप्रमुखक्रियाभिः समुत्थिता कुण्डलिनी सुधाभिः।
त्रिधामबीजं शिवमर्चयन्ती शिवाङ्गना वः शिवमातनोतु ॥ ७४

सिन्दूरपुञ्जनिभमिन्दुकलावतंस-
मानन्दपूर्णनयनत्रयशोभिवक्त्रम्।
आपीनतुङ्गकुचनम्रमनङ्गतन्त्रं
शम्भोः कलत्रममितां श्रियमातनोतु ॥ ७५

नयनकमलैर्दीर्घादीर्घैरलङ्कृतदिङ्मुखं
विनतमरुतां कोटीराग्रैर्निघृष्टपदाम्बुजम्।
तरुणशकलं चान्द्रं बिभ्रद् घटस्तनमण्डलं
स्फुरतु हृदये बन्धूकाभं कलत्रमुमापतेः ॥ ७६

वर्णैरर्णवषड्दिशारविकलाचत्वर्विभक्तैः क्रमा-
दाद्यैः सादिभिरावृतान् चहयुतैः षट्चक्रमध्यानिमान्।

स्थानत्रयेऽपि शिवसङ्गमाह मूल इति। मूलाधारादाज्ञापर्यन्तं गत्वा ततो निवृत्तिर्विशेषः ॥ ७२ ॥

इतः परं वासनादाढ्याय कुण्डलिनीध्यानविशेषान् वदन् स्तुतिमाह निजभवनेत्यादिना। अपानवायुसङ्कोचादाधारबन्धः। एवं प्राणवायुनिरोधेऽपि प्रमुखशब्दवाच्यः। अनङ्गतन्त्रम् अनङ्गप्रधानम् ॥ ७३॥७४॥७५ ॥

दीर्घादीर्घैरिति। कटाक्षेण दीर्घत्वं तत्संकोचेनाऽदीर्घत्वञ्च। विनतमरुतां विनतदेवानाम्। कोटीराग्रैः मुकुटाग्रभागैः ॥ ७६ ॥

अन्तर्मातृकाक्रमेण कुण्डलिनीध्यानमाह वर्णैरिति। अर्णवाश्चत्वारः दिशा दश रवयो द्वादश कलाः षोडश चत्वर्द्वयम्। सादिभिरित्यनेन व्युत्क्रमो दर्शितः। आद्यैरिति मूलाधारस्थितत्वेन आद्यत्वम्। यद्वा साद्यैः सकारादिककारान्तैः।

डाकिन्यादिभिराश्रितान् परिचितान् ब्रह्मादिभिर्दैवतै-
र्भिन्दाना परदेवता त्रिजगतां चित्ते विधत्तां मुदम् ॥ ७७

आद्यैः षोडशस्वरैः इत्यसंयुतैरिति योजना। तत्र विशुद्धचक्रे अकारादीनां क्रमेण स्थितैराद्यैरिति पृथक्ग्रहणमिति केचित्। अथवाऽन्यत्राकारस्याद्यत्वम्। अत्र वैपरीत्यक्रमेण सकारस्य आद्यत्वमिति आद्यैरित्युक्तम्।

द्विदले वह्नौ प्रतिलोमार्थमेव वह्नेतिग्रहणम्। डाकिन्यादिभिराश्रितान्। डाकिनी राकिणी लाकिनी काकिनी शाकिनी हाकिनीभिः। ब्रह्मादिभिर्दैवतैः परीतान्। ब्रह्मादिस्थितिः दीक्षापटले उक्ता। एवम्भूतान् षट्चक्रमध्यान् भिन्दानेति सम्बन्धः। तदुक्तम्—

आधारस्तु चतुर्दलोऽरुणरुचिर्वासान्तवर्णाश्रयः
स्वाधिष्ठानमनल्पविद्युतनिभं बालान्तषट्पत्रकम्।
रक्ताभं मणिपूरकं दशदलं डाद्यं फकारान्तकं
पत्रैर्द्वादशभिस्त्वनाहतपुरं हैमं कठान्तान्वितम् ॥
मात्राषोडशपत्रकं विशदरुग्युक्तं विशुद्धाम्बुजं
हक्षेत्यक्षरयुग्दलद्वययुतं रक्ताभमाज्ञापुरम्।
तस्मादूर्ध्वमधोमुखं विकसितं पद्मं सहस्रच्छदं
नित्यानन्दमयं भजे शिवपदं शश्वर्णमच्छारुणम् ॥ इति ॥

अन्यत्र तु—मूलाधारं ब्रह्मणः स्थानमेतत् सौवर्णाभं डाकिनी देवताऽत्र।
स्वाधिष्ठानं विष्णुगेहं प्रदिष्टं बालार्काभं राकिणी देवताऽत्र ॥
मणिपूरकं तु नीलं रुद्रस्थानं लाकिनी देवताऽत्र।
रक्तमनाहतमीश्वरगेहं तु शाकिन्यपीहोक्ता ॥
सदाशिवस्थानमिदं विशुद्धं काकिन्यथेहाऽपि च धूम्रवर्णम्।
आज्ञापुरं शारदचन्द्रकान्तं हाकिन्यथोक्ता शिवगेहमेतत् ॥ इति ॥

अध्यात्मविवेके एषां प्रतिदलं जीवसञ्चारे फलमुक्तम्—

गुदलिङ्गान्तरे चक्रमाधारं तु चतुर्दलम्।
परमः सहजस्तद्वदानन्दो वीरपूर्वकः ॥
योगानन्दश्च तस्य स्यादीशानादिदले फलम्।
स्वाधिष्ठानं लिङ्गमूले षट्पत्रञ्च क्रमस्य तु ॥
पूर्वादिषु दलेष्वाहुः फलान्येतान्यनुक्रमात्।
प्रश्रयः क्रूरता गर्वो नाशो मूर्च्छा ततः परम् ॥

आधाराद्गुणवृत्तशोभिततनुं लिङ्गत्रयं सत्वरं
भिन्दन्तीं कमलानि चिन्मयघनानन्दप्रबोधोत्तराम् ।
संक्षुब्धध्रुवमण्डलामृतकरप्रस्यन्दमानामृत-
स्रोतःकन्दलिता[निभा]ममन्दतडिदाकारां शिवां भावयेत् ॥ ७८

आनन्दमौलिमनिशं श्रुतिमौलिमृग्य-
मर्द्धेन्दुभूषणमधिष्ठितसर्वलोकम् ।
भक्तार्त्तिभञ्जनपरं परमीश्वरस्य
दद्याच्छुभानि नियतं वपुरम्बिकायाः ॥ ७९

मञ्जुसिञ्जितमञ्जीरं वाममर्द्धं महेशितुः ।
आश्रयामि जगन्मूलं यन्मूलं वचसामपि ॥ ८०

स्थूलेन्द्रनीलरुचिरं कुचभारनम्रं
भास्वत्सुभूषणगणैः प्रविभक्तशोभम् ।
विश्वैकमूलमनिशं श्रुतिमौलिमृग्य-
मर्द्धं महेशितुरखण्डितमाश्रयामः ॥ ८१

अवज्ञा स्यादविश्वासो जीवस्य चरतो ध्रुवम् ।
नाभौ दशदलं चक्रं मणिपूरकसंज्ञकम् ॥
सुषुप्तिरत्र तृष्णा स्यादीर्ष्या पिशुनता तथा ।
लज्जा भयं घृणा मोहः कषायोऽथ विषादिता ॥
हृदयेऽनाहतं चक्रं दलैर्द्वादशभिर्युतम् ।
लौल्यं प्रनाशः कपटं वितर्कोऽप्यनुतापिता ॥
आशा प्रकाशश्चिन्ता च समीहा ममता ततः ।
क्रमेण दम्भो वैकल्यं विवेकोऽहंकृतिस्तथा ॥
फलान्येतानि पूर्वादिदलस्थस्यात्मनो जगुः ।
कण्ठेऽस्ति भारतीस्थानं विशुद्धिः षोडशच्छदम् ॥
तत्र प्रणव उद्गीथो हुं फट् वषट् स्वधा तथा ।
स्वाहा नमोऽमृतं सप्त स्वराः षड्जादयो विषम् ॥
इति पूर्वादिपत्रस्थे फलान्यात्मनि षोडश ॥ इति ॥ ७७ ॥

आधारादिति । त्रिकोणकर्णिकं वृत्तं वर्त्तुलमाधारस्वरूपं तस्माद्गुणवृत्तं

दिक्कालादिविवर्जिते परशिवे चैतन्यमात्रात्मके
शून्ये कारणपञ्चकस्य विलयं नीते निरालम्बने ।
आत्मानं विनिवेश्य निश्चलधिया निर्लीनसर्वेन्द्रियो
योगी योगफलं प्रयाति सुलभं नित्योदितं निष्क्रियम् ॥ ८२

महाबलाय प्रणतोऽस्मि तस्मै
संविज्ञतालिङ्गनशीतलाय ।
येनाऽर्पितं मुक्तिफलं विपक्व-
माम्नायशाखाभिरुपाश्रितेभ्यः ॥ ८३

तस्मादभूदखिलदेशिकवारणेन्द्रः
षट्कर्मसागरविहारविनोदशीलः ।
यस्य त्रिलोकविततं विजयाभिधान-
माचार्यपण्डित इति प्रथयन्ति सन्तः ॥ ८४

तन्नन्दनो देशिकदेशिकोऽभूच्छ्रीकण्ठ इत्यभ्युदितप्रभावः ।
यत्पादकारुण्यसुधाभिषिक्ताल्लक्ष्मीं परामश्नुवते कृतार्थाः ८५

आचार्यविद्याविभवस्य तस्य जातः प्रभोर्लक्ष्मणदेशिकेन्द्रः ।
विद्यास्वशेषासु कलासु सर्वास्वपि प्रथां यो महतीं प्रपेदे ॥ ८६

सत्त्वरजस्तमोगुणात्मकम् । [लिङ्गत्रयमित्यत्र निर्गच्छन्तीमिति निर्गलरीमिति च क्वचित्पाठौ दृश्येते] ॥ ७८ ॥ ७९ ॥ ८० ॥ ८१ ॥

दिगिति देशतः कालतः । आदिशब्दात् स्वरूपतश्चाऽनवच्छिन्ने । कारणपञ्चकस्य उपादानसमवायिनिमित्तप्रयोजकसहकारिकारणपञ्चकस्य । यद्यपि प्रयोजकसहकारिकारणे निमित्तकारणान्तर्गते एवेति तार्किकाः कारणत्रयमेवाहुः । तथापीषद्भेदमाश्रित्य कारणपञ्चकोपन्यासः । यद्वा पञ्चभूतानां पञ्चतन्मात्ररूपाणि कारणानि । तदुक्तं महाकपिलपञ्चरात्रे—

मात्राः पञ्च परित्यज्य ततः कारणपञ्चकम् ।
दिव्यन्तु कारणं कृत्वा योजयेत् परमं पदम् ॥ इति ॥

अतएव शून्ये अरूपे । निरालम्बने आधाररहिते । आत्मानं जीवात्मानम् । निश्चलधिया विनिवेश्य योगफलं प्रयाति ॥ ८२ ॥

ग्रन्थकर्त्ता स्ववंशमाख्याति महाबलायेति । महाबलनाम ग्रन्थकर्तुः पूर्वजः । तत्पुत्र आचार्यपण्डितः तत्पुत्रः श्रीकण्ठः ॥ ८३ ॥ ८४ ॥ ८५ ॥ ८६ ॥

आदाय सारमखिलं निखिलागमेभ्यः
श्रीशारदातिलकनाम चकार तन्त्रम् ।
प्राज्ञः स एष पटलैरिह तत्त्वसंख्यैः
प्रीतिप्रदानविषये विदुषां चिराय ॥ ८७

अनाद्यन्तात् शम्भोर्वपुषि कलितार्द्धेन वपुषा
जगद्रूपं शश्वत् सृजति महनीयामपि गिरम् ।
सदर्था शब्दार्थस्तनभरनता शङ्करवधू-
र्भवद्भूत्यै भूयाद्भवजनितदुःखौघशमनी ॥ ८८

सुखदा दात्हसुभगा शङ्करार्द्धशरीरिणी ।
ग्रन्थपुष्पोपहारेण प्रीता नः पार्वती सदा ॥ ८९

इति श्रीशारदातिलके पञ्चविंशः पटलः ॥

समाप्तोऽयं ग्रन्थः ॥

तत्त्वसंख्यैः पञ्चविंशतिसंख्यैः । अत्र आद्यपटलः सृष्टिप्रतिपादकत्वेन मूलप्रकृतिप्रतिपादनपरः । मध्ये त्रयोविंशतिपटलास्तु प्रकृतिविकृतिप्रतिपादनपराः । अन्त्यपटलस्तु प्रकृतिविकृतिव्यतिरिक्तपुरुषप्रतिपादनपरः । एवं पञ्चविंशतितत्त्वात्मकत्वम् अस्य ग्रन्थस्योक्तं भवति ॥ ८७ ॥

परदेवतैव ध्येयेति सकलतन्त्रार्थमुपसंहरन् आशिषा मङ्गलं करोति अनादीति ।

मङ्गलादीनि मङ्गलमध्यानि मङ्गलान्तानि च शास्त्राणि प्रथन्ते ।
वीरपुरुषकाणि भवन्ति आयुष्मपुरुषकाणि च ।

इति भगवत्पतञ्जलिवचनादिति । शिवम् ॥ ८८ ॥ ८९ ॥

पुरं गोदावर्या विलसदुपकण्ठे जनततं
जनस्थानं नाम प्रथितमभवद्दक्षिणदिशि ।
महाराष्ट्रे देशे जनकतनयालक्ष्मणवृतः
पुरा रामो यस्मिन्नवसदतितुष्टेन मनसा ॥

तस्मिन् पुरे ब्राह्मणसत्तमानां कुले विशुद्धे महति प्रसिद्धे ।
श्रीभट्टरामेश्वर इत्युदारो गुणैरभूद्वादिमहेभसिंहः ॥
तस्मादभूत् तीक्ष्णकुशाग्रबुद्धिः श्रीभट्टपृथ्वीधरनामधेयः ।
अनेकधाऽध्यापयदेष भाट्टो वेदान्तशास्त्रं फणिभाषितादि ॥

गीर्वाणाचार्यवर्यौ दिविकृतवसतिर्यद्भयादेव शङ्के
शेषः पातालमूलं स च सपदि पराभूतिभीत्या विवेश ।
अन्येषां कैव वार्त्ता कृतकृतकवचश्चापलानां कृतं तैः
सम्यक् शक्योऽस्य वक्तुं नहि वदनशतैरप्यशेषप्रभावः ॥

कैश्चिद्दिनैरतिपवित्रचरित्र एष
वाराणसीमभिगमय्य विवराजधानीम् ।
तत्रैव वासमकरोत् तदनुप्रतीकः
कायावसानमवधिं परिचिन्त्य धीरः ॥

तस्माद् राघवभट्ट एष समभूत् वेदान्तसन्न्यायवित्
ख्यातो भट्टनये समस्तगणिते साहित्यरत्नाकरः ।
आयुर्वेदनिधिः कलासु कुशलः कामार्थशास्त्रे गुरुः
सङ्गीते निपुणः सदागमनिधेः पारं प्रयातः परम् ॥

श्रीदुर्गे गणनायक ग्रह गुरो गोविन्द गौरीपते
युष्मानर्थयते नतेन शिरसा सोऽयं प्रबद्धाञ्जलिः ।
मन्त्रार्चादिविवेचने यदि भवेत् स्खालित्यमत्र भ्रमात्
क्वाचित्कं मम भक्तिभावितहृदो दासस्य तत् क्षम्यताम् ॥

अत्युष्णातीक्ष्णधीभिर्जगदुपकृतये राघवो यद्विवव्रे
गूढार्थं मन्त्रशास्त्रं निधिमिव परमं सम्प्रदायाञ्जनेन ।
सन्तः सन्तोषमस्मिन् वितरत तरसा स्वादितस्वस्वकामा
दुष्टादौष्ट्यं स्वकीयं जहित हितधिया नान्यथाऽर्थागमो वः ॥

पिशुनजनोऽन्तर्मलिनः परगुणसन्तोषविमुखमतिः ।
तव मनो न विषीदति दूषणमात्रात्तु यत्न विरतोऽयम् ॥

कायस्था इव वाचकाः कतिचन प्रायेण मूका इव
श्रोतारस्त्वपरे शुका इव परे साधुप्रलापाः पुनः ।
ग्रन्थग्रन्थिविवेचनैकचतुरा ये कोविदाः केवलं
छिन्नास्ते तदुदीरितावगतये विज्ञाः पुनः पञ्चषाः ॥

आकाशेषुशरक्षमापरिमिते रौद्राभिधे वत्सरे
पौषे मासि सिते दले रवितिथौ पक्षे च सिद्धान्विते ।
तन्त्रेऽस्मिन् सुधिया व्यधायि रुचिरा श्रीराघवेन स्फुटा
टीका सद्गुरुसम्प्रदायविमला विश्वेशपुर्यामियम् ॥

इति श्रीशारदातिलकटीकायां सत्सम्प्रदायकृतव्याख्यायां
पदार्थादर्शाभिख्यायां पञ्चविंशः पटलः ॥ ॐ ॥

समाप्तोऽयं पदार्थादर्शः ।

॥ ॐ तत् सत् ॐ ॥

शुद्धिपत्रम्

पृष्ठाङ्कः	पङ्क्तिः	अशुद्धम्	शुद्धम्	पृष्ठाङ्कः	पङ्क्तिः	अशुद्धम्	शुद्धम्
७	२६	मन्के	मते	२९१	१	धापायेत्	धापयेत्
८	१२	त्रिवर्गा	त्रिवर्णा	३१८	२३	उकार:	ऊकार:
१०	५	ग्रन्ध	ग्रन्थ	३२६	७	शिवात्तान्	शिवात्मान्
१०	७	भूलोत्	मूलोत्	३३७	१०	भंवना	भुवना
१८	७	एते	अत एते	३४९	४	इवि	दृभुवि
१८	१२	स्थल:	स्थूल:	३७०	७	एभि	आख्यायन्ते एभि
२१	२२	बन्धक	बन्धूक	३७३	१५	गिपि	गिरिपि
२२	१	मुल	मूल	३७५	१४	क्रूरी	क्रूरी
२२	८	पृष्ठः	पृष्टः	३७६	२	मनुभि:	मनुभि:
२२	१०	पृष्ठः	पृष्टः	३९१	६	मणिग्रं	मनिग्रं
२३	२	श्रिर्वङ्क्षौ	श्रिवङ्क्षौ	३९१	११	जर्ह्व दित:	जर्ह्वादित:
२५	२०	भूत	भूत	४०३	१३	लाक	लोक
२८	२१	भूवङ्क्षा	भूवङ्क्षा	४०८	२	सुकुटा	मुकुटा
३२	१२	बुहुदम्	बुद्बुदम्	४१४	१८	प्रमार्थ्ये	प्रसार्थ्ये
३७	२	मंध्ये	संध्ये	४२९	१५	रभ्यै	रम्यै
३८	२	भूला	मूला	४४६	१५	वेदनाङ्ग	वेदनाऽनङ्ग
४२	२१	श्यामतत्	श्यामतत्	४७०	३	प्राप्तितान्	प्रापितान्
५६	२६	सृष्टे	सृष्टि	४७०	५	ह्लच्छिर	ह्लच्छिर
७३	१५	षोडेशी	षोडशी	४८२	१५	यजेद्वेदौ	यजेद्देवौ
७६	१५	भूर्त्तय:	मूर्त्तय:	४८७	१	जेपेदेनं	जपेदेनं
७८	१५	भूर्त्तय:	मूर्त्तय:	४९२	२३	१२७	१२०-१२३
८०	१८	भूलौ	मूलौ	४९५	१९	कामंक	कार्मुक
१२७	३	दीक्षा	दीचा	४९९	७	श्याकढ़ां	श्याधिरूढ़ा
१२७	८	वंक्षि:	वृंक्षि:	५०३	१	दायुघ	दायुध
१९९	२५	साम्यत	साम्यत्वम	५०३	१९	भूर्ध्नि	मूर्ध्नि
२२९	१	मन्त्राणां	मन्त्रिणां	५०५	२	विश्वेषं	विद्वेषं
२६८	५	भूर्ध्नि	मूर्ध्नि	५०६	२३	मुज	भुज
२७९	६	मूर्त्तिमिष्टा	मूर्त्तिं सृष्टा	५१०	८	स्त्रिंग	स्त्रिंश

पृष्ठाङ्कः	पङ्क्तिः	अशुद्धम्	शुद्धम्
५११	१६	उद्धास्य	उद्वास्य
५१४	२	कान्तो	क्रान्तो
५१४	११	घ्यात्वा	ध्यात्वा
५१८	१	र्णियां	र्णिकायां
५१९	८	ह्विष्ट	द्विष्ट
५२०	२१	साङ्काशां	सङ्काशां
५२१	२६	नरतिपति	नरपति
५२२	२९	नामेद	नामेदं
५२३	२	रध्वृज	रध्वज
५२३	९	किया	क्रिया
५२६	१०	मध्यक्तैः	मध्वक्तैः
५२८	२०	योन्यन्तरि	योन्यन्तरे
५३०	१८	माक्	भाक्
५३३	१९	त्वत	त्रिक
५३३	२९	धात्वा	ध्यात्वा
५३४	७	ब्रह्मादय	ब्रह्मादयः
५४५	१९	माघ्वी	माध्वी
५४७	१५	रुद्रतः	रुद्रष्टतः
५५०	२३	क्रोड़न्	क्रोड़न्
५५३	१२	विधिवद्दो	विधिर्द्दो
५७१	१७	गणाति	गणपति
५७४	८	पुरषा	पुरुषा
५८२	३	मूर्ध्नि	मूर्ध्नि
५९२	१५	ततदपि	तदपि
६०४	१५	षिञ्चेततः	षिञ्चेत्ततः

पृष्ठाङ्कः	पङ्क्तिः	अशुद्धम्	शुद्धम्
६३७	१३	ज्जपूजा	ज्जपपूजा
६४७	११	रोज्वलं	रोज्ज्वलं
६४९	७	स्वतःप्रिय	स्वतप्रिय
६५०	९	तन्मातरो	तन्मान्तरो
६५१	१६	वाहुस्यां	बाहुभ्यां
६५४	१२	वष्टयेत्	वेष्टयेत्
६५५	२४	॥ ४६	॥ ४५ ॥ ४६
६६४	२६	र्गणैः	र्गुणैः
६६९	८	परिपप्लुतैः	परिप्लुतैः
६६९	२०	तोध्यने	तोत्थने
६७२	७	वस्त्राद्यै	वस्त्राद्यं
७०३	२२	गतव्यं	गन्तव्यं
७०९	१	मध्यतः	मध्यस्तः
७२२	१०	गसार	गमसार
७३९	१४	ह्सभेधा	हंसमेधा
७४३	१३	शुम्त्रः	शुभ्रः
७४३	१७	स्थानेमि	स्थाने कात्पूर्व्वमि
७९६	२५	ताति	तामिति
७९७	४	स्त्रण	स्त्रेण
८०२	२२	[नन्त्र]	[मन्त्र]
८१६	२५	मन्त्र	मन्त्र
८७९	२८	भ्रिम्यु	भ्रिष्यु
८९४	२१	सर्वात्मन	सर्वात्मना
९०४	२३	प्राणास्ति	प्राणास्ति

वधयोस्तथा मभयोरन्ययोश्च लिपिसाम्यात् दृग्दोषात् मतिमान्द्याच्च क्वचित् क्वचित् यत् स्खलितं तत् स्खलितजातं हंसक्षीरन्यायेन शोधनीयं विदुषा सारग्राहिणा दयावता पाठकेन।

श्लोकानुक्रमणिका

अ

ष

स